EUROPE
1450 TO 1789
ENCYCLOPEDIA OF THE EARLY MODERN WORLD

EDITORIAL BOARD

EUROPE
1450 TO 1789
ENCYCLOPEDIA OF THE EARLY MODERN WORLD

Volume 5
Popular Culture to Switzerland

Jonathan Dewald, Editor in Chief

CHARLES SCRIBNER'S SONS®

New York • Detroit • San Diego • San Francisco • Cleveland • New Haven, Conn. • Waterville, Maine • London • Munich

THOMSON

GALE

Europe 1450 to 1789:
Encyclopedia of the Early Modern World

Jonathan Dewald, Editor in Chief

For permission to use material from this product,
submit your request via Web at http://www.gale-
edit.com/permissions, or you may download our
Permissions Request form and submit your request
by fax or mail to:

Permissions Department
The Gale Group, Inc.
27500 Drake Rd.
Farmington Hills, MI 48331-3535

Permissions Hotline:
248-699-8006 or 800-877-4253, ext. 8006
Fax: 248-699-8074 or 800-762-4058

LIBRARY OF CONGRESS CATALOGING-IN-PUBLICATION DATA

Europe 1450 to 1789 : encyclopedia of the early modern world / Jonathan Dewald, editor in
chief.
    p. cm.
Includes bibliographical references and index.
    ISBN 0-684-31200-X (set : hardcover) — ISBN 0-684-31201-8 (v. 1) —
ISBN 0-684-31202-6 (v. 2) — ISBN 0-684-31203-4 (v. 3) — ISBN 0-684-31204-2 (v. 4) —
ISBN 0-684-31205-0 (v. 5) — ISBN 0-684-31206-9 (v. 6)
    1. Europe—History—15th century—Encyclopedias. 2. Europe—History—1492–1648—
Encyclopedias. 3. Europe—History—1648–1789—Encyclopedias. 4. Europe—Intellectual
life—Encyclopedias. 5. Europe—Civilization—Encyclopedias. I. Title: Encyclopedia of the early
modern world. II. Dewald, Jonathan.
    D209.E97 2004
    940.2—dc22
                                                                    2003015680

This title is also available as an e-book.
ISBN 0-684-31423-1 (set)
Contact your Gale sales representative for ordering information.
Printed in United States of America
10 9 8 7 6 5 4 3 2 1

CONTENTS OF THIS VOLUME

CONTENTS OF OTHER VOLUMES

VOLUME 1

A

Absolutism
Academies, Learned
Academies of Art
Accounting and Bookkeeping
Acoustics
Addison, Joseph
Advice and Etiquette Books
Africa
    North
    Sub-Saharan
Agriculture
Alba, Fernando Álvarez de Toledo, duke of
Alchemy
Aldrovandi, Ulisse
Alembert, Jean Le Rond d'
Alexis I (Russia)
American Independence, War of (1775–1783)
Amsterdam

Anabaptism
Anatomy and Physiology
Ancien Régime
Ancient World
Ancients and Moderns
Andrusovo, Truce of (1667)
Anglo-Dutch Naval Wars
Anguissola, Sofonisba
Anna (Russia)
Anne (England)
Anne of Austria
Anne of Brittany
Anticlericalism
Antwerp
Apocalypticism
Apothecaries
Archaeology
Architecture
Arctic and Antarctic
Aristocracy and Gentry
Aristotelianism
Armada, Spanish
Arnauld Family
Art
    Art Exhibitions
    The Art Market and Collecting
    Art Theory, Criticism, and Historiography
    Artistic Patronage
    The Conception and Status of the Artist
Artisans
Asam Family
Asia
Assassination
Astrology

VOLUME 2

C (CONTINUED)

D

E

VOLUME 3

VOLUME 4

M

VOLUME 6

USING THE ENCYCLOPEDIA

Tables of contents. Each volume contains a table of contents for the entire *Encyclopedia*. Volume 1 has a single listing of all volumes' contents. Volumes 2 through 6 contain "Contents of This Volume" followed by "Contents of Other Volumes."

Maps of Europe. The front of each volume contains a set of maps showing Europe's political divisions at six important stages from 1453 to 1795.

Alphabetical arrangement. Entries are arranged in alphabetical order. Biographical articles are generally listed by the subject's last name (with some exceptions, e.g., Leonardo da Vinci).

Royalty and foreign names. In most cases, the names of rulers of French, German, and Spanish rulers have been anglicized. Thus, Francis, not François; Charles, not Carlos. Monarchs of the same name are listed first by their country, and then numerically. Thus, Henry VII and Henry VIII of England precede Henry II of France.

Measurements appear in the English system according to United States usage, though they are often followed by metric equivalents in parentheses. Following are approximate metric equivalents for the most common units:

1 foot = 30 centimeters
1 mile = 1.6 kilometers
1 acre = 0.4 hectares
1 square mile = 2.6 square kilometers
1 pound = 0.45 kilograms
1 gallon = 3.8 liters

Cross-references. At the end of each article is a list of related articles for further study. Readers may also consult the table of contents and the index for titles and keywords of interest.

Bibliography. Each article contains a list of sources for further reading, usually divided into Primary Sources and Secondary Sources.

Systematic outline of contents. After the last article in volume 6 is an outline that provides a general overview of the conceptual scheme of the *Encyclopedia*, listing the title of each entry.

Directory of contributors. Following the systematic outline of contents is a listing, in alphabetical order, of all contributors to the *Encyclopedia*, with affiliation and the titles of his or her article(s).

Index. Volume 6 concludes with a comprehensive, alphabetically arranged index covering all articles, as well as prominent figures, geographical names, events, institutions, publications, works of art, and all major concepts that are discussed in volumes 1 through 6.

MAPS OF EUROPE,
1453 TO 1795

The maps on the pages that follow show political boundaries within Europe at six important stages in the roughly three hundred and fifty years covered by this *Encyclopedia:* 1453, 1520, 1648, 1715, 1763, and 1795.

Europe, 1453

— International border

• City

0 100 200 mi.

0 100 200 km

Norwegian Sea

N

RUSSIAN STATES

• Moscow

NORWAY

SWEDEN

Gulf of Bothnia

• Stockholm

Gulf of Finland

Baltic Sea

TEUTONIC KNIGHTS

POLAND-LITHUANIA

SCOTLAND

• Edinburgh

North Sea

DENMARK
Copenhagen •

• Danzig

IRELAND

ENGLAND

• Dublin

Brandenburg

• Warsaw

• London

• Cologne

Bohemia
• Prague
Moravia

Silesia

ATLANTIC OCEAN

HOLY ROMAN EMPIRE

MOLDAVIA

• Brittany

• Paris

Vienna •
Austria

Buda •
• Pest

FRANCE

HUNGARY

WALLACHIA

Black Sea

• Milan

Venice •

VENICE

Bay of Biscay

NAVARRE

• Genoa

BOSNIA

Bulgaria

Florence •
PAPAL STATES

Adriatic Sea

SERBIA
VENICE

• Constantinople

PORTUGAL

ARAGÓN

Corsica
(Holy Roman Empire)

• Rome

NAPLES

OTTOMAN EMPIRE

Madrid •

Barcelona •

VENICE

Lisbon •

CASTILE

Minorca
(Aragón)

Sardinia
(Aragón)

Tyrrhenian Sea

• Athens

Iviza
(Aragón)

Majorca
(Aragón)

VENICE

GRANADA

Sicily
(Aragón)

Ionian Sea

VENICE

VENICE

Crete
(Venice)

Mediterranean Sea

1453. In the years around 1450, Europe settled into relative political stability, following the crises of the late Middle Ages. France and England concluded the Hundred Years' War in 1453; the Ottoman Turks conquered Constantinople in the same year and established it as the capital of their empire; and in 1454 the Treaty of Lodi normalized relations among the principal Italian states, establishing a peaceful balance of power among Venice, Florence, the duchy of Milan, the Papal States, and the Kingdom of Naples.

Europe, 1520

International border
• City

0   100   200 mi.
0   100 200 km

1520. In 1520, the Habsburg prince Charles V was elected Holy Roman emperor, uniting in his person lordship over central Europe, Spain, the Low Countries, parts of Italy, and the newly conquered Spanish territories in the Americas. For the next century, this overwhelming accumulation of territories in the hands of a single dynasty would remain the most important fact in European international politics. But in 1520 Habsburg power already faced one of its most troublesome challenges: Martin Luther's Reformation, first attracting widespread notice in 1517, would repeatedly disrupt Habsburg efforts to unify their territories.

Europe, 1648

International border
• City

0   100   200 mi.
0   100 200 km

1648. The 1648 Peace of Westphalia ended the Thirty Years' War, one of the most destructive wars in European history. The peace treaty formally acknowledged the independence of the Dutch Republic and the Swiss Confederation, and it established the practical autonomy of the German principalities—including the right to establish their own religious policies. Conversely, the Holy Roman Empire lost much of its direct power; although its institutions continued to play some role in German affairs through the eighteenth century, the emperors' power now rested overwhelmingly on the Habsburg domain lands in Austria, Bohemia, and eastern Europe.

Europe, 1715

— International border
• City

0 100 200 mi.
0 100 200 km

1715. The Peace of Utrecht (1713) ended the War of the Spanish Succession, the last and most destructive of the wars of the French king Louis XIV. The treaty ended Spain's control over present-day Belgium and over parts of Italy, and it marked the end of French hegemony within Europe. In the eighteenth century, France would be only one of five leading powers.

Europe, 1763

——— International border
- - - - Internal border
• City

N

0   100   200 mi.
0   100 200 km

Norwegian Sea

DENMARK AND NORWAY

S W E D E N

Finland

Gulf of Bothnia

• Helsingfors

Gulf of Finland

• St. Petersburg

• Christiania

• Stockholm

Baltic Sea

• Moscow

RUSSIAN EMPIRE

North Sea

Scotland

• Edinburgh

GREAT BRITAIN AND IRELAND

Ireland

• Dublin

England

• Copenhagen

• Königsberg

PRUSSIA

POLAND

UNITED NETHERLANDS

• Amsterdam

• London

• Brussels

Austrian Netherlands

Prussia

• Berlin

Saxony

• Hanover

HOLY ROMAN EMPIRE

• Warsaw

ATLANTIC OCEAN

• Paris

FRANCE

Bavaria

• Munich

• Vienna

Austria

• Buda
• Pest

HUNGARY

Moldavia

SWITZERLAND

Bay of Biscay

Milan •

• Turin

SAVOY

• Genoa

• Monaco

• Venice

V E N I C E

Walachia

Black Sea

• Modena

Lucca •

• Florence

TUSCANY

Bosnia

Adriatic Sea

MONTENEGRO

RAGUSA

Albania

• Constantinople

O T T O M A N   E M P I R E

PORTUGAL

• Madrid

SPAIN

• Lisbon

Corsica (Genoa)

PAPAL STATES

• Rome

KINGDOM OF THE TWO SICILIES

• Naples

Corfu (Venice)

Tyrrhenian Sea

Minorca (Great Britain)

SARDINIA

Majorca (Spain)

Iviza (Spain)

Cephalonia (Venice)

• Athens

Ionian Sea

Zante (Venice)

Sicily

• Gibraltar (Great Britain)
• Ceuta (Spain)

• Algiers

• Tunis

• Melilla (Spain)

FEZ

ALGERIA

TUNIS

Mediterranean Sea

Crete (Ottoman Empire)

1763. The 1763 Treaty of Paris ended the Seven Years' War, a war that involved all the major European powers and included significant campaigns in North America and southern Asia, as well as in Europe. The war made clear the arrival of Prussia as a great power, at least the equal of Austria in central and eastern Europe.

Europe, 1795

International border
Internal border
• City

0   100   200 mi.
0   100 200 km

N

Norwegian Sea

Finland

SWEDEN

Helsingfors
• St. Petersburg
Gulf of Finland

Christiania
Stockholm

• Moscow

North Sea

DENMARK AND NORWAY

RUSSIA

Scotland
Edinburgh

Copenhagen
Königsberg

PRUSSIA

Ireland
GREAT BRITAIN
Dublin

UNITED NETHERLANDS

Warsaw

England
Amsterdam
Hanover
Berlin

GALICIA

London
Prussia
Saxony

Brussels
Austrian
Netherlands

HOLY
ROMAN
EMPIRE

Bohemia

HUNGARY

TRANSYLVANIA

ATLANTIC
OCEAN

Paris

Munich
Vienna
Buda
Pest

Bavaria
Austria

SWISS
CONFED.

Bay of Biscay

FRANCE

Milan
Venice

Black Sea

Genoa
Florence

TUSCANY

Adriatic Sea

Constantinople

OTTOMAN EMPIRE

Corsica
(France)

Rome

PORTUGAL

• Madrid

Minorca
(Great Britain)

SARDINIA

Naples
SICILY-
NAPLES

Albania

Corfu
(Venice)

Athens

Lisbon

SPAIN

Tyrrhenian Sea

Cephalonia
(Venice)

Majorca
(Spain)

Iviza
(Spain)

Sicily

Ionian Sea

Zante
(Venice)

• Algiers

Tunis

Crete
(Ottoman Empire)

FEZ

ALGIERS

TUNIS

Mediterranean Sea

1795. By 1795, French armies had repelled an attempted invasion by Prussia, Austria, and England, and France had begun annexing territories in Belgium and western Germany. These military successes ensured the continuation of the French Revolution, but they also meant that European warfare would continue until 1815, when the modern borders of France were largely established. Warfare with France did not prevent the other European powers from conducting business as usual elsewhere: with agreements in 1793 and 1795, Prussia, Austria, and Russia completed their absorption of Poland.

COMMON ABBREVIATIONS
USED IN THIS WORK

A.D.   *Anno Domini,* in the year of the Lord

A.H.   *Anno Hegirae,* in the year of the
         Hegira

b.   born

B.C.   before Christ

B.C.E.   before the common era (= B.C.)

c.   *circa,* about, approximately

C.E.   common era (= A.D.)

ch.   chapter

d.   died

ed.   editor (pl., eds.), edition

e.g.   *exempli gratia,* for example

et al.   *et alii,* and others

etc.   *et cetera,* and so forth

exh. cat. exhibition catalogue

fl.   *floruit,* flourished

i.e.   *id est,* that is

MS.   manuscript (pl. MSS.)

n.d.   no date

no.   number (pl., nos.)

n.s.   new series

N.S.   new style, according to the Gregorian
         calendar

O.S.   old style, according to the Julian
         calendar

p.   page (pl., pp.)

rev.   revised

S.   *san, sanctus, santo,* male saint

SS.   saints

Sta.   *sancta, santa,* female saint

supp.   supplement

vol.   volume

?   uncertain, possibly, perhaps

EUROPE
1450 TO 1789
ENCYCLOPEDIA OF THE EARLY MODERN WORLD

POPULAR CULTURE.

POPULAR CULTURE. Few theoretical concepts are as value-laden as popular culture, and defining it can be likened to entering a minefield. And yet, it has proved a resilient and useful tool for assessing the attitudes and beliefs of the nonliterate masses in early modern society. From the onset, however, one should be aware of the limitations and theoretical problems associated with its use and misuse in the past.

THEORETICAL PROBLEMS

The term "popular culture" was not in contemporary use during the early modern period, when political and social structure was understood in reference to three orders or estates. The closest contemporary equivalent of "the people" would have been the Third Estate or the commoners, a social conglomeration of urban burghers and rural peasants, as well as any other persons belonging neither to the nobility nor the clergy. Reference was made to the common man or the community, and the elite/intellectual perception of their customs and practices ranged from the paternal curiosity of Michel de Montaigne (1533–1592) to the satire of artists like Peter Bruegel the Elder (c. 1525–1569) and the disdain of the moralist Sebastian Brant (1458?–1521), who presented a mirror of immoral behavior in a world gone mad in his *Das Narrenschiff* (1494; The ship of fools). One common allegory of contemporary social structure is the famous *Leviathan* of Thomas Hobbes (1588–1679), which depicted society as the torso of the king, itself composed of thousands of people, his subjects. In this allegory, the rulers and clergy made up the head, the noble warriors the arms, and the masses the visceral lower body parts. After experiencing the horrors perpetrated during the wars of religion in the sixteenth century, the Neostoic author on statecraft, Justus Lipsius (1547–1606), wrote to compare the undisciplined mob to a headless body and popular protest to mass insanity.

The discovery (or "invention") of the people as a group worthy of study is attributed to a group of German intellectuals at the end of the eighteenth and beginning of the nineteenth centuries (Burke). One of the earliest philosophical justifications for a scholarly interest in the culture of the common people *(Kultur des Volkes)* was offered by Johann Gottfried Herder (1744–1803), who consciously juxtaposed it with learned culture *(Kultur der Gelehrten)*. Widespread interest followed as European folklorists flocked to the countryside to save the oral tradition of the preindustrial peasantry from oblivion. In the process, Romantic scholars embellished the occasionally unsavory content of folk tales and songs. At the time, scholars also tended to conflate the early modern period with the Middle Ages, and traditional customs and rituals were dubbed "medieval."

The ambivalent nature of the term "popular," sometimes casually equated with populism, is highly controversial, and popular culture studies have regularly been hijacked for partisan political purposes. The long-standing identification of the popular will with national identity since Jean-Jacques Rousseau (1712–1778) has led to the exploitation of popular

1

culture studies by nationalists, racists, populists, and communists alike. The association of folk studies (*Volkskunde*) with the National Socialist dictatorship marginalized cultural anthropology and ethnography in post-war Germany. The Marxist Antonio Gramsci expressed faith in the culture of the people as a means to exercise discontent and protest against a hegemonic ruling elite. However, not until "pop" culture in art and music began to symbolize grass roots protest during the 1960s did popular culture studies succeed in entering into the mainstream of scholarly debate. Detractors have subsequently labeled radical research on popular culture "PC" in pejorative association with "political correctness," originally a prejudicial policy to weed out the middle classes under Stalinism.

One crass example of the abuse of early modern popular culture studies is the case of nine million witch burnings. Briefly, in an attack on medieval barbarism, an enlightened archivist fancifully concocted a mythical figure of nine million people burned during the European witch craze. Anti-Catholic authors revived this fantastic claim during the nineteenth-century *Kulturkampf* in Germany. Later, credulous Nazi propagandists proclaimed that the statistic evidenced a racist persecution perpetrated on Nordic Aryan people by evil Mediterraneans through the office of the Holy Inquisition. During the 1970s, several authors and journalists uncritically cited the very same Nazi authors to denounce the slaughter of nine million innocent women at the hands of misogynist theologians. Today, scholars of popular culture have successfully revealed these claims for the groundless exaggerations they are (Behringer). In fact, we now know beyond a reasonable doubt that: (1) The vast majority of witch trials took place not in the Middle Ages but from 1560 to 1650, with legal executions continuing into the late eighteenth century; (2) Most trials were conducted by secular state officials, and persecutions were remarkably low in those few areas where an inquisition was present, like Spain and Italy, as it appears that the institution had a mitigating effect; (3) Trials were often instigated by popular pressure rather than official initiative, and most of the trials took place in central Europe; (4) Local women often accused other local women of witchcraft as the result of petty neighborhood disputes. The case of nine million witches demon-

strates the continuing importance of popular culture studies not only to correct the glorification of history from the top down, but also to avoid the pitfalls of hackneyed eulogizing of "the people" and romanticized history from the bottom up.

A further theoretical complication is that the term "culture" is also ambivalent. The original ideal of a collective group consciousness put forward by the French sociologist Émile Durkheim stresses the unifying aspects of culture, but it lacks an explanatory dynamic for historical change. A dialectic or conflict model is the most common method to overcome this inadequacy. As a representative of this dialectical tradition, Robert Redfield (1897–1958) emphasized the divisive nature of the "great tradition" (elite or official culture) and the "little tradition" (plebian or unofficial culture), echoing Herder's distinction between popular and learned culture. The Jesuit Michel De Certeau (1925–1986) juxtaposed the relevant advantages and disadvantages facing the ruling elite and the ruled in a class-struggle model, employing the blatantly militant terms "strategy" (extensive application of great resources for long-term effect) and "tactics" (intensive maximization of limited resources with limited permanency). Modernist ethnographers tend to define culture in relational terms as a communicative system for the transmission of ideas, rather than enduring institutions or structures. In this sense, popular culture is viewed as one form of expressive culture that plays a crucial role in power struggles to negotiate meaning in everyday life (Little).

There are also many contradictory claims regarding the mechanisms of popular culture. Clearly, the view of early folklorists that popular culture is unchanging, not artificial and unadulterated by exogenous influence, is romantic and no longer tenable (Greenblatt). Proponents of dialectical materialism as well as supporters of the Annales paradigm (a historical movement in twentieth-century France) generally view even supernatural aspects of popular culture as contingent upon material circumstances (Scribner). Contrarily, Michel Foucault has reflected on the marginalization of folly and its transformation into madness as a product of discourses. He depicts the development of a system of social discipline, the "Great Confinement" of undesirables, as a power struggle played out in largely arbitrary and individualized discourses to gain control over cultural meanings. The Italian historian Carlo Ginzburg seeks the origins of early modern popular culture as an egalitarian tradition in the pre-Christian heritage of Indo-European languages, while the German historian Peter Blickle points to the late medieval origins of communalism. Again, popular culture studies serve to remind us that traditions evolve and culture is always changing in relationship to historical contexts.

Ultimately, the exact nature of popular culture is so difficult to pin down because it is applied in broad terms, to include ritual, art, literature, and cosmology. Many popular beliefs, rituals, and customs of the ordinary people were also shared by members of the social elite, clouding the boundaries between the two traditions. Tentatively, we can summarize popular culture as an expressive and shared system for the production, transmission, and consumption of cohesive yet simple values readily accessible to and accepted by most members of a given society at any given time, simultaneously fulfilling both normative and practical social interests. In the end, however, popular culture continues to elude precise definition. Perhaps the very ambivalence of the term renders it so theoretically flexible and at the same time dangerously seductive.

HISTORIOGRAPHIC HIGHLIGHTS

Without doubt, historians of the early modern period have paid more attention to popular culture than have any other historians. There are sound practical and methodological reasons for this. In comparison to the overwhelming documentary evidence available to historians of the nineteenth and twentieth centuries, early modernists face source limitations that require them to approach their subject in a more circumspect manner. Because of this, they have proven particularly open to the interdisciplinary methods of cultural anthropology used to study comparable forms of culture in "traditional" societies. Nevertheless, the advent of printing and nascent bureaucracy coupled with a higher rate of documentary and artistic survivals offers early modernists a more satisfactory pool of evidence than is regularly available for the study of popular culture in earlier periods. Another major impetus has been the modernity thesis. In the nineteenth century, culture was generally equated with civilization and ranked according to a teleological (and Eurocentric) scale

of development. Following the rise of academic sociology and anthropology, the question of modernity also informed historical consensus on the pivotal status of the early modern period as an age of transition from feudalism to capitalism in which the power of the church waned and early modern states were formed. Hence, there has been an intense search for signs of modernity in early modern popular culture.

Since the birth of the academic disciplines of sociology and anthropology in the late nineteenth century, there have been many successful attempts to recover the mental processes whereby the European identity evolved from the later Middle Ages to the late eighteenth and early nineteenth centuries. The interdisciplinary study of popular culture has provided vital access to mentality of Europeans before industrialization and secularization. Through the encouragement of the early annalists, such as Marc Bloch and Lucien Febvre, historians' attention began to focus on Durkheim's concept of the collective consciousness and modify it to explain slow changes over time *(la longue durée)*. Bloch's account of popular perceptions of the magic touch of the king in the Middle Ages and Febvre's study of disbelief in the Renaissance concurred that the mental equipment *(outillage mentale)* of our ancestors was radically different from our own. Historians often miss that point by commencing their research with "a poorly posed question" *(une question mal posée)*. Developmentally, the Soviet literary critic Mikhail Bakhtin thought he had found the key to a lost golden age prior to modern social polarization in a his study of Rabelais. Bakhtin's significant impact lies in his historical interpretation of the carnivalesque. For him, the spontaneity and laughter/ridicule of popular culture can be juxtaposed with the elite puritanical culture of Lent, the forerunner of modern bourgeois sentimentality. Similarly, the Dutch sociologist Norbert Elias charted the evolution of household manners as a "civilizing process," a form of modern psychogenesis, literally a change in our patterns of thought through behavior modification. Elias focused his research on court society, which he viewed as the source of our modern social code of etiquette.

Since the 1960s, the trend has been less toward progressive and linear interpretations in favor of examining events, material circumstances, and ideological explanations of popular culture. One of the pioneering figures has been Natalie Zemon Davis. In 1975, she published a seminal collection of essays on a variety of topics from sixteenth-century France, such as rituals of violence and the *charivari*. *Charivaris* were a virtually ubiquitous and ritualized form of autonomous popular justice. In one form of *charivari,* youth abbeys—literally gangs of unmarried journeymen or peasants—staged public mockeries to punish local persons of ill repute and reinforce communal norms. Young artisans employed the *charivari* to regulate access to limited marriage prospects, targeting cuckolded husbands, widowed masters who married younger women, or widows of masters who refused to remarry. Peasants sometimes used the *charivari* to harass outsiders, protest perceived injustice at the hands of a local official, or punish an immoral village priest. *Charivaris* might begin during a festivity or a bout of drinking at a local tavern, when it was decided to punish a local "deviate." The masked or costumed gang adjourned to the house of the person in question, harassing them with vulgar or obscene songs. When the target of abuse appeared, he or she was apprehended and humiliated—forced to ride backward on an ass, burned in effigy, or ducked in a pond. Ultimately, *charivaris* functioned as a method of resolving social conflicts through rough and ready communal consensus on propriety. In this and subsequent works, Davis dispenses with standard clichés and characterizes the human experiences in terms of identity formation. She has demonstrated the self-fashioning of pardon tales and the creation of identity in *The Return of Martin Guerre,* the subject of a French motion picture (1983) and a Hollywood spin-off, *Sommersby* (1993). Her historical actors are simultaneously faced with limitless individual possibilities and fettered by social constraints. Her work continues to influence an entire generation of scholarship.

In 1978, Peter Burke published what has become the standard text on early modern popular culture. Burke takes his cue from the dialectic models of the elite/popular traditions promoted by Redfield and Bakhtin. His developmental conception of popular culture is graphically illustrated by Bruegel's famous painting of *Combat of Carnival and Lent,* a mock joust between a fat man astride a barrel and a thin woman seated on a chair (Burke, p. 208). The Carnival season prior to Lent set the stage for a ritual inversion of normative values. In this "world turned upside down," people cross-dressed, ate and drank excessively, engaged in blatant sexual innuendo, openly mocked the clergy, and elected a prince of fools who held court in the town square. During the period between 1500 and 1650, Europe entered into the first phase of the reform of popular culture by the culture of the godly, as the arbiters of morality set a more somber tone during the catastrophic years of the Protestant Reformation, Catholic Renewal, and wars of religion. Popular performances and carnivals were banned in many areas as the elite gradually withdrew from participation in the plebian culture of mockery and grass roots protest. From 1650 to 1800, popular culture was politicized, denigrated, and completely abandoned by the ruling elite until its rediscovery by nineteenth-century folklorists.

Since the publication of Burke's text, there has been an explosion of interest in popular culture studies, many of which have introduced us to new and innovative ways of approaching the topic. Much attention has also been paid to the role of the print revolution as an innovative force during the early modern period. Roger Chartier and Robert Scribner have examined chapbooks and broadsheets and found evidence of a vibrant print culture with meanings influenced by popular consumption and appropriation. They also note how shifting demand acts as a driving force behind historical change. Individual case studies and village reconstitutions have also explored the contributions of popular culture to political and social change in early modern Europe. Chief among these has been the work of David Warren Sabean, who conducted nearly two decades of research studying the inhabitants of the small Swabian village of Neckarhausen. Sabean subtly employed a conflict model to interpret apparently minor incidents of ritualized tensions between rulers and subjects as another engine for historical change from below. Here again, historians have begun to pay more attention to negotiations and the fundamental role of transmission through cultural interlocutors.

SOURCES AND METHOD

Since early modern popular culture was primarily oral or performance-oriented, the paucity of documentary evidence of practices and beliefs has proven a difficult obstacle. The so-called superstitions and fleeting theatrics of everyday custom and ritual were seldom regarded as worthy of attention. Initially, much of the pioneering work in early modern popular culture involved the identification of useful sources to document a largely undocumented historical phenomenon. Gradually, however, certain types of evidence have been exploited with great success, and a standard repertoire of sources and methods has evolved. Current scholarship still benefits greatly from the work of folklorists and anthropologists. National and regional folklore collections and dictionaries of dialect from the early nineteenth century regularly provide valuable insights. Many folktales and folk practices have since been catalogued in standard guides to folkloric motifs and ethnographic encyclopedias, like Bächtold-Stäubli's *Handwörterbuch des deutschen Aberglaubens* (Handbook of German superstition). These works allow the historian to critically cross-reference customs and practices that were glossed over in primary source documents, as their original meaning was largely self-evident to contemporaries but has since become lost. Early thesauruses and encyclopedias, themselves primary sources, continue to prove their worth. Some of these are now easily accessible online, such as Zedler's early-eighteenth-century *Universal Lexikon,* a virtual treasure trove of early modern thought. Nevertheless, one of the major attractions of popular culture studies remains the necessity to work eclectically and creatively, and historians still regularly locate hitherto unsuspected finds in the archives as the field continues to expand.

Scholars now regularly access a wide and sometimes unexpected variety of sources in their search for manifestations of popular culture. The role of cultural interlocutors, responsible for the recording and transmission of customs and traditions, is central in most of these transmissions. Standard sources include civic chronicles and diaries depicting events both everyday and unusual, such as carnivals or the elaborate Corpus Christi processions popular in Catholic urban areas. Illustrated broadsheets—the newspapers of the illiterate—depicted occurrences both mundane (the effects of drunkenness on the humors) and wondrous (monstrous births, comets, Marian apparitions, etc.). Broadsheets were the subjects of public readings by literate members of the

community, both in the privacy of the home and in taverns. The hub of the local communications network, the tavern was where people from every walk of life congregated to exchange news, conduct business, and, not infrequently, foment protest and revolt. Grievances, such as songs of protest or the famous Twelve Articles of the Peasantry issued during the German Peasants' War of 1525 by an artisan named Sebastian Lotzer and a pastor named Christoph Schappeler, both of Memmingen, also inform us of popular complaints against the ruling classes as well as utopian and communal aspirations and popular rituals of justice. In one popular ritual during the revolt of the Poor Conrad in 1514, for example, community members of Schorndorf put the devalued weights and measures introduced by Duke Ulrich the Mad of Württemberg (1498–1550) to the water test in a nearby river, claiming that if the weights floated, then they had passed the judgment of God.

However, official recorders of popular culture did not always play a positive or even a neutral role in its transmission and were prominently involved in elite attempts to suppress unofficial practices. Legal records—edicts, law codes, and criminal interrogatories—are another rich genre of documentation. In their attempts to enforce elite norms, early modern rulers released a plethora of edicts reviling impious deviations from religious orthodoxy and breaches of sumptuary and moral legislation—the wearing of prohibited clothing styles, lewd dancing, and excessive consumption at weddings. They attest to the rude nature of early modern sexuality, complaining of clerical concubinage, fornication between serving men and women, and clandestine marriages. One courtship ritual in particular, the nocturnal visit, was highly suspect. Reminiscent of the balcony scenes from *Romeo and Juliet* or *Cyrano de Bergerac* and practiced throughout Europe, nocturnal visits of suitors to unmarried women took the form of a non-coerced entry, generally through the window, whereupon the couple might sit and chat until the morning hours or, not uncommonly, sleep together chastely in the same bed, at times with the full consent of parents; naturally, accidents did occur, as the edicts take pains to remind us. All-too-frequent repetitions of prescriptive legislation suggest the nature, extent, and tenacity of popular practices throughout Europe despite well-intentioned moral campaigns to eradicate them.

Inquisitorial sources provide important if somewhat less appealing information, especially in the realm of witchcraft studies. This is also the area where anthropological field research among traditional peoples, such as E. Evans-Prichard's 1937 study of witchcraft among the Azande in central Africa, has had its greatest impact. Records of interrogations are perhaps as close as we can hope to come to hearing the actual voices of ordinary individuals. They reveal a cleft between elite and popular perceptions of witchcraft. For example, the attempt to superimpose a cumulative or learned concept of demonology on the masses, replete with devil's pacts, copulations with paramours, and attendance at the Sabbath, proved alien to the popular consciousness. However, the records of criminal interrogations reveal much about the real and widespread practice of white magic—love potions, rituals to enhance fertility, talismans and charms to ward off illness in humans and animals, treasure-finding spells, counter-magic to relieve the enchanted, and so on—that persisted well into the age of the Enlightenment. Of course, it would be wrong to presume that even firsthand testimonies offered by illiterate peasants represent the unadulterated voice of the people without considering the actual circumstances of their production. Judicial confessions were exacted under duress or torture in answer to the leading questions of inquisitors and judges, only to be recorded by court scribes, who sometimes inserted their own confessions of bewilderment at certain popular beliefs and practices.

Public trials and executions were themselves a form of popular entertainment, as thousands of onlookers, hawkers, pickpockets, and prostitutes gathered in a festive mood to witness the spectacular brutality of contemporary justice. Audience participation, though not officially encouraged, regularly manifested itself as onlookers threw rotting vegetable matter at the delinquent as he or she was carted from the jail to mount the terrible stage of retribution. Of course, the presence of an audience at the official execution meant that events could take unexpected turns from the official script. Audience pressure and the threat of or actual recourse to violence effected a release if the verdict was vehemently in question or if the criminal was a local folk

hero. If the executioner gave a sloppy performance and failed to carry out sentencing in one blow, crowds were known to mob the scaffold, threatening to pummel or rend the headsman, who was forced to flee for his life. Naturally, for those unable to attend the execution of infamous villains in person, details were recorded and distributed in illustrated woodcuts and broadsheets. Nor was the death sentence necessarily the end of the criminal in the popular understanding of ritual justice. After the rotting corpse was put on display and ultimately removed for dishonorable burial, executioners, who operated thriving medical practices on the side, sold decomposed body parts (so-called mummy) for use as popular remedies.

In another type of method similar to the anthropological "thick-description" used by Clifford Geertz to document Balinese customs, practitioners of microhistory have descended to the level of ordinary individuals to rescue nonprominent persons from the dustbin of history, giving a voice back to them. By far the most successful example of microhistory is Carlo Ginzburg's study of the heresiarch (the creator of his own heresy) and Friulian miller Mennochio. Ginzburg began his career as a professor in Bologna, were he was closely associated with the author Umberto Eco and the historian Piero Camporesi. Ginzburg documents Mennochio's trial and execution for, among other things, maintaining that the Virgin Mary was a whore and that the universe arose as a waste product of a cheese-eating worm. Ginzburg concludes that Mennochio's fantastic cosmological theories were in fact the product of an unconscious filter of pre-Christian notions, part of a subculture shared by peasants from Italy to Lithuania. His continued detective work in search of clues of this common antihierarchical heritage has spawned a large following, and microhistory has since found a home in the Italian journal *Quaderni Storici*. There are those who argue that Ginzburg's net is cast far too broadly and that his claims about the common pagan origins of European popular culture are overgeneralized. Critics have focused on particular regional or local contexts, as in Wolfgang Behringer's microhistory of the Alpine herdsman Chonrad Stoeckhlin (1549–1587) or Richard Kagan's analysis of the political content of the dreams of Lucretia de Leon of Madrid, which at once empowered and endangered her. Whether one agrees with Ginzburg's conclusions or not, the fact remains that his method of accessing contemporary cosmology through the experiences of one ordinary person has reached a large audience, reawakening interest in popular culture and generating lively and productive debate.

SOCIAL EXPERIENCES OF POPULAR CULTURE

The story of popular culture in early modern Europe is one of mounting social stratification and a concerted effort at repression by the political and religious elite. An interesting example of this is found in a series of questionnaires on communal religious practices distributed by Spanish officials under Philip II (ruled 1552–1598) in the sixteenth century. Communities had long associated themselves with local patron saints, who served as symbols of both internal unity and external competition. Communities entered into sacred contractual agreements with their saints, promising to honor them with lavish shrines, feast days, and votive offerings in return for agrarian fertility, economic prosperity, and protection from internal factionalism or natural catastrophes. Many of the saints operated as specialists, and localities often received outside pilgrims seeking types of assistance particular to their patron saint; some saints cured specific illnesses, others ensured good harvests, and so on. Spanish authorities in turn considered the plethora of local feast days and specialized saints as an obstacle to their campaign of centralization. Gradually, particularistic interests were countered through crown sponsorship of multipurpose cults associated with the ruling dynasty, especially the cult of the Virgin and the Bleeding Heart. Furthermore, the crown fought against popular disrespect for saints who failed to fulfill their local obligations. One such ritual included the ducking of a saint's image in a river or lake as an expression of communal displeasure. Analogous struggles occurred in other areas of Europe, as in seventeenth-century Bavaria under Duke Maximilian I, where ducking of saints' images was legally prohibited and local revolts over access to communal cemeteries were put down under threat of force. With the help of the Jesuits, the ruling dynasty gradually subordinated local saints in a regimented hierarchy to the Virgin Mary, a policy manifest in artistic representations as well as an offi-

cial sacred geography, the *Bavaria Sancta et Pia* (1615–1628) authored by the Tyrolian Jesuit Matthaeus Rader (1561–1634).

Hierarchical subordination had gender implications as well, the most prominent example being the rise and fall in the popularity of apparitions, sainthood, exorcism, and demonic possession. Once again in Spain, women initially availed of apparitions as a means of empowerment during the fifteenth century, but church authorities ultimately discouraged this practice. With this avenue closed to them, women like Teresa of Ávila and the Italian Angela Merici, founder of the Ursulines, sought recognition as holy women, and after their deaths their followers petitioned for their beatification and canonization. Church officials generally discouraged female incursions into the male-dominated realm of Catholic spirituality, though many succeeded through almost irrepressible popular support. Dynastic support for the cult of the Virgin had an ambivalent effect on the role of women in society, enabling empowerment only for exceptional figures while popularizing the image of merciful women as powerful and personal intercessors for those in need or seeking justice. At the end of the sixteenth and beginning of the seventeenth century, cases of demonic possession were clearly on the rise and opened another window of opportunity for women to enter the public domain. However, this means of access was fraught with danger, and it was not unusual for demoniacs to end their lives at the stake as accused witches. In one rare case, a peasant woman even achieved official recognition as an exorcist; during the Thirty Years' War (1618–1648), Rosina Huber survived sixteen weeks of severe torture, but was subsequently allowed to exorcise ghosts from prominent households in southern Germany.

Youth culture also found itself increasingly on the defensive as the representatives of established authority channeled youthful exuberance into officially sanctioned activities. The so-called youth abbeys and other such unofficial organizations of apprentices and journeymen were integrated into religious confraternities sanctioned by urban masters. This was part of a broader trend in political culture to limit guild participation in civic government in cities of the Holy Roman Empire after the Schmalkaldic War (1546–1547) and regulate cooption into the ruling elite. Cooption into the large council in Venice or in German towns with a Venetian-style constitution, primarily a ceremonial body, provided a testing ground for the political reliability of up-and-coming town councillors and created a pool of future recruits for the small council, where true political authority lay. In the eighteenth century, male vagrants became the target of persecutions for witchcraft in Austria, as the gender stereotype of the witch shifted from the traditional image of the witch as an old hag to incorporate unruly gangs of young men.

The fight against superstitions and popular magic is one of the best-documented examples of the attempt of the mixed success of the ruling elite in limiting popular access to the supernatural. Initially, the ruling elite reviled superstitions as real and diabolical magic. In 1585, the papal bull *Coeli et Terri* condemned all forms of popular superstitions, including incantations, treasure finding, and necromancy, as covenants with Satan, "the Father of Lies." The Flemish jurist and demonologist Martin Del Rio attacked magic and the veneration of evil spirits as vile superstitions—as dangerous and efficacious magic. Still, in the sixteenth and seventeenth centuries, it was often difficult to differentiate between popular and elite superstitions since many attitudes remained shared. During the witch craze in Augsburg during the 1560s, the Jesuit Peter Canisius and the wealthy Fugger family supported a series of exorcisms that ended with accusations that Johann Fugger shared in an "old and damnable heresy" about demoniacs, which held that they were possessed by repentant souls from purgatory rather than by the devil.

Another common belief involved the fear that the interment of suicides in hallowed ground resulted in celestial displeasure, manifesting itself in the form of hailstorms that destroyed crops and livestock. In fact, this belief reveals that many popular superstitions had a sound empirical basis. For example, waves of suicides sometimes followed famine and plague, but the popular consciousness held the former responsible for natural catastrophes, in an inversion of cause and effect. In the sixteenth century, elites also shared similar fears about ghosts, but by the eighteenth century, the Enlightenment adopted a new method of combating them—derision. By then, superstitions were no longer viewed as dangerous practices, rather as backward peasant ignorance and nonsense. Ironically, however, the victory of the Enlightenment over popular culture was short-lived. As folklorists reacted against pure reason, popular culture became the rallying point of nationalists and Romantics, who sought originality, purity, and the source of common aspirations in the simple culture of the common people of early modern Europe.

See also **Brant, Sebastian; Catholic Spirituality and Mysticism; Enlightenment; Festivals; Hobbes, Thomas; Magic; Montaigne, Michel de; Romanticism; Songs, Popular; Witchcraft.**

BIBLIOGRAPHY

Bakhtin, Mikhail. *Rabelais and His World.* Translated by Helene Iswolsky. Cambridge, Mass., 1968.

Behringer, Wolfgang. "Neun Millionen Hexen. Entstehung, Tradition und Kritik eines populären Mythos." In *Geschichte in Wissenschaft und Unterricht* 11 (1998): 664–685.

———. *Shaman of Oberstdorf: Chonrad Stoeckhlin and the Phantoms of the Night.* Translated by H. C. Erik Midelfort. Charlottesville, Va., 1998.

Blickle, Peter. *From the Communal Reformation to the Revolution of the Common Man.* Leiden and Boston, 1998. Translated by Beat Kümin.

Bloc, Marc. *The Royal Touch: Sacred Monarchy and Miracles in England and France.* Translated by J. E. Anderson. London, 1973. Translation of *Les rois thaumaturges: étude sur le caractère surnaturel attribué à la puissance royale, particulièrement en France et en Angleterre.* Strasbourg, 1924.

Burke, Peter. *Popular Culture in Early Modern Europe.* London, 1978.

Chartier, Roger. *Cultural History: Between Practices and Representations.* Ithaca, N.Y., 1988. Translated by Lydia G. Cochrane.

Christian, William B. *Apparitions in Late-Medieval and Renaissance Spain.* Princeton, 1981.

———. *Local Religion in 16th Century Spain.* Princeton, 1981.

Davis, Natalie Zemon. *Fiction in the Archives: Pardon Tales and Their Tellers in Sixteenth-Century France.* Stanford, 1987.

———. *The Return of Martin Guerre.* Cambridge, Mass., 1983.

———. *Society and Culture in Early Modern France: Eight Essays.* Stanford, 1975.

De Certeau, Michel. *The Practice of Everyday Life.* Translated by Steven Rendall. Berkeley, 2002.

Durkheim, Emile. *The Elementary Forms of Religious Life.* Translated by Karen E. Fields. New York, 1995.

Elias, Norbert. *The Civilizing Process: Sociogenic and Psychogenic Investigations.* Translated by Edmund Jephcott. Rev. ed. Oxford, 2000.

Febvre, Lucien. *Au coeur religieux du XVI siècle.* Paris, 1957.

Foucault, Michel. *Madness and Civilization: A History of Insanity in the Age of Reason.* Translated by Richard Howard. New York, 1965.

Ginzburg, Carlo. *The Cheese and the Worms: The Cosmos of a Sixteenth-Century Miller.* Translated by John and Anne Tedeschi. Baltimore, 1980.

Greenblatt, Stephen. *Marvelous Possessions: The Wonder of the New World.* Chicago, 1991.

Hsia, R. Po-Chia. *The World of the Catholic Renewal: 1540–1777.* Cambridge, U.K., and New York, 1998.

Kagan, Richard. *Lucrecia's Dreams: Politics and Prophecy in Sixteenth-Century Spain.* Berkeley, 1990.

Klapisch-Zuber, Christiane. *Women, Family and Ritual in Renaissance Italy.* Chicago, 1985. Translated by Lydia Cochrane.

Lederer, David. *A Bavarian Beacon: Madness and its Treatment in Early Modern Germany.* Forthcoming.

———. "Living with the Dead: Ghosts in Early Modern Bavaria." In *Werewolves, Witches and Wandering Spirits: Traditional Belief & Folklore in Early Modern Europe,* edited by Kathryn A. Edwards, pp. 25–53. Kirksville, Mo. 2002.

Little, W. Kenneth. "Popular Culture." In *Encyclopedia of Cultural Anthropology,* edited by David Levinson and Melvin Ember, vol. 3, pp. 984–988. New York, 1996.

Sabean, David Warren. *Power in the Blood: Popular Culture and Village Discourse in Early Modern Germany.* Cambridge, U.K., and New York, 1988.

Scribner, Robert W. "Elements of Popular Belief." In *Handbook of European History, 1400–1600: Late Middle Ages, Renaissance, and Reformation,* edited by Thomas A. Brady, Heiko A. Obermann, and James D. Tracy, pp. 231–262. Leiden and New York, 1995.

———. *Popular Culture and Popular Movements in Reformation Germany.* London, 1987.

Wolfart, Johannes C. *Religion, Government and Political Culture in Early Modern Germany: Lindau, 1520–1628.* Basingstoke, U.K., 2002.

Zedler, Johann Heinrich. *Grosses vollständiges Universal-Lexicon aller Wissenschafften und Künste, welche bisshero durch menschlichen Verstand und Witz erfunden und verbessert worden.* 68 vols. Leipzig, 1732–1754.

DAVID LEDERER

POPULAR PROTEST AND REBELLIONS.

In the early modern period, the vast majority of Europeans lacked a formal voice in the major governmental decisions that affected their lives. Kings ruled without much contact with their subjects, towns were governed by oligarchies of well-to-do families, and rural villages were run by a few of the richest landowners, who were often in league with the village lord. Ordinary people did have many opportunities for everyday sociability, such as parish committees, citizen militia forces, guild procedures, occasional convocations of all the heads of household, and festive celebrations. On rare occasions they might even see the monarch processing through their streets or attending a ceremonial Mass. But when taxes were raised, war was declared, property laws were modified, or food prices became exorbitant, most people had no formal channel for complaint.

Nevertheless, people did have opinions about how things ought to be done, and they were perfectly capable of taking matters into their own hands if justice was not carried out to their satisfaction. Lacking official input in the decision making process, people adopted a language of protest that mixed tradition and initiative, violence and restraint. This popular protest was a significant phenomenon all over early modern Europe.

Forming a precise definition of "popular" involvement is not easy. Ideally this concept should encompass movements in which everyday men and women expressed their own points of view. These would be instances when the commoners agitated on their own behalf, expressing moral indignation at the violation of community-held values or intervening through direct action to change the course of events. Such activity should be distinguished from upper-class rebellions, in which popular crowds played a subordinate role. Even genuine popular movements often had assistance from elite leaders. Thus there was no hard line between elite-inspired and autonomous popular protests; instead there was a spectrum of possible combinations. "Popular protest and rebellions" should be defined as attempts by ordinary people to influence, or comment upon, issues decided by governments.

DIFFERENT APPROACHES

Before the 1960s historians paid little attention to popular uprisings, with the exception of a few inescapable episodes such as the 1525–1526 German Peasants' War or the *Comuneros* Revolt of 1520–1521 in Spain. In their books, historians devoted a paragraph or two to such events, describing them as unfortunate excesses arising from desperation. The rebels were presented as ignorant, crude, and impulsive, or at the very least misguided, and history focused on the rich, the powerful, and the successful.

This picture has changed dramatically. A generation of historians has come to realize the importance of focusing on the history of the common people, not only because these people did most of society's hard labor, but also because the story of the past would be superficial without considering the impact of events on the largest segment of the population. The tide began to turn in the 1960s when a first wave of historians reexamined well-known historical episodes and learned more about people fighting back against their oppressors. As the historians looked deeper for new evidence, they found many instances of popular protest. Such uprisings were everywhere they looked, especially in England and France, where most of the early research took place. René Pillorget found 532 incidents of protest in the single French province of Provence between 1596 and 1715. Buchanan Sharp found more than 40 food riots in the west of England between 1586 and 1631. Pieter Bierbrauer identified 125 German peasant revolts between 1336 and 1789, more than half of which took place after 1525. Jean Nicolas and a team of French researchers located 8,528 incidents of protest in France from 1660 to 1789. The majority of these incidents were relatively minor in scope, but the everyday events were arguably just as influential as the major outbursts.

Historians first attempted to fit these episodes into the story of the developing bourgeois revolution. While virtually all of the protesters had succumbed to superior forces of repression, these "primitive rebels," historians argued, had made a difference by establishing traditions of resistance and by striking fear into the hearts of those in power. Their failure to prevail could be explained by a poorly developed class consciousness, by precocious timing, or by the rebels' inability to develop a viable blueprint for bringing about social change. Conservative historians responded that this analysis was pure romanticism. Most revolts were openly led or encouraged by leaders from elite groups. Thus popular rebels were just pawns in their larger power games. Furthermore, the conservative historians argued that focusing on uprisings gave undue attention to exceptional cases and obscured the fact that, most of the time, people accepted the system and lived by it.

The grandfather of the analysis of popular revolt was Friedrich Engels (1820–1895), who wrote the classic Marxist account of the German Peasants' War. Writing in the wake of the failed revolutions of 1848, Engels argued that the Peasants' War had been a premature revolt against feudalism, which had failed because the German bourgeoisie was not prepared to lead the struggle. The issue was published in a major study by Günther Franz in 1933. But the real pioneers in the study of the rebellious crowd were Georges Lefebvre, who attributed a positive collective purpose to the crowds in the French Revolution, and Georges Rudé, who made a science out of crowd study by analyzing the social identity of those arrested. Rudé showed that eighteenth-century crowds were composed of respectable individuals from the urban lower classes: minor officials, artisans and their journeymen and apprentices, wives and children, laborers, and market women. Connected by local networks of sociability, crowds acted like an impromptu community and exercised rudimentary politics by focusing their attention on specific targets. This important insight was a reaction against the old theory that crowds were an irrational mob with a single mind bent on destruction. The studies of the crowd were an important step, but they had limitations. The sociology of the crowd is dependent on the occupational categories used in arrest records, and it fails to address the question of the actors' motivation and to explain the forms of action they chose to use.

In France in the 1960s the discussion of popular protest was the subject of a great debate about the nature of early modern social structure. A Soviet scholar, Boris Porchnev, who had access to a large collection of detailed letters written by the French king's provincial agents in the period 1620–1660, found in them evidence of widespread riots against tax collectors and other authorities. Porchnev used this rich source to argue that these uprisings were an expression of class conflict in which a heterogeneous plebeian population was transferring its resistance from the local nobility to the representatives of the state because the state had taken over the nobility's role of extracting value from the peasants. Like Engels, Porchnev concluded that the essence of absolutist France was class struggle, and that the Revolution was only held off because of the cooption of the bourgeoisie by the absolute monarchy.

Roland Mousnier, a French expert on the seventeenth century, took up this challenge. Using similar documents, he attempted to demonstrate that there were in fact no classes at all in seventeenth-century France. Society was organized into "orders" and "estates," which were groups based on common levels of esteem. Whereas Porchnev said revolts were expressions of class difference, Mousnier argued that they were conflicts between the modernizing state and vertical alliances of nobles, commoners, and laborers defending traditional privileges. Porchnev saw the crowds as protesting spontaneously. Mousnier said that crowds were incapable of spontaneous revolt. Faced with a standoff between these contradictory interpretations, scholars did more research and concluded that the answer was not one or the other position, but rather a combination of both. This analysis of revolts as indicators of social structure produced much valuable research, but it drew attention away from the culture of the rioters themselves.

To avoid the classification of crowds by their occupational composition or their adherence to a certain kind of social relations, one must look at their behavior anthropologically, that is, as a language expressing a specific set of values and objectives, often in terms of symbolic meanings. Two practitioners of this approach stand out: E. P. Thompson, who analyzed the culture of the preindustrial British working class of the eighteenth and nineteenth centuries in terms of the level of class consciousness it had reached; and Natalie Zemon Davis, who pioneered the study of popular rituals and their meaning. While Thompson saw grain riots, enclosure riots, and poaching in royal forests as forms of resistance to the rise of capitalism, Davis understood ritual behavior like *charivari* or Carnival as an expression of community values related to fertility, adolescence, and the purification of the community.

Another way of approaching the study of crowd actions is to use quantitative methods to find patterns in the location, time of day, type of complaint, size of group, or methods used by a succession of protest movements. To develop causal connections, these patterns can then be correlated with variables such as harvest yields, the incidence of warfare, or level of taxation. Many such studies have been conducted, and they generally confirm that popular protest was connected to hard times, and that its incidence was higher in some regions than in others. But without including other dimensions of the problem, such studies only illuminate the context of the protest and not its substance or why it took place where and when it did. A more promising approach is that of historical sociologist Charles Tilly. He was interested in linking the changing nature of crowd protest to what he called "large processes," namely the rise of capitalism and the rise of the modern state. By this interpretation, the "repertoires" of popular action, that is, the ways in which people protested, changed in response to the nature of the forces they were contesting.

A new wave of scholarship has abandoned symbolic meaning in favor of political expression, or "popular politics." This approach was pioneered in the German-speaking world and was heavily influenced by Jürgen Habermas's theory of the public sphere. Attempting to escape the rigid dichotomy of ruler versus ruled, these scholars, led by Swiss historian Peter Blickle, focused their attention on the ways ordinary people could become involved in the political process. This approach is particularly well suited to early modern Germany, where many small states had a variety of systems of consultation and representation. Blickle focused on the local and regional demands drawn up by the peasants in 1525. He asserted that they were inventing alternative political forms, which were derived from their experiences with existing representative bodies. Blickle also organized a program of international conferences, at which experts assessed the potential strength of popular politics under three related categories: communities, the strength of which provided the backbone for protest; representation, which took many forms and was often indirect; and rebellion, which could also be an effective resource.

Thus, recent scholarship has reacted against the idea of the people being powerless through its emphasis on multiple forms of interaction between rulers and people.

PEASANT REVOLTS

Popular protest was endemic throughout Europe, as Table 1 indicates. But lists cannot convey the wide range of styles, forms, and sizes of popular disturbances. It is useful to distinguish between peasant uprisings and urban revolts. Peasant uprisings involved thousands of angry men in military formations who ultimately would have to be put down by military force. Because peasants lived in dispersed villages, their uprisings were planned in advance. At the same time, their objectives had to be stated in writing and publicized for them to have any impact, since there was no immediately accessible individual on whom they could blame their grievances. So a set of demands would be drawn up at some kind of general assembly, often with the aid of literate allies. Examples are the Twelve Articles of the Upper Swabian Peasants in 1525 or the Manifesto of the Peasants of Angoumois in 1637.

The history of Hungary is filled with peasant revolts. In that country, resistance to the Turks and opposition to the Habsburgs was sometimes initiated by the peasants and sometimes led by the ferocious Magyar nobility. There were also recurring conflicts between lords and serfs. In 1514 peasants, artisans, and students were eagerly enlisting in a planned crusade against the Turks when the nobles, fearing a liberated peasantry, canceled the campaign. The peasants turned on their masters and raised an army of thousands that swept across the country capturing castles until it was stopped by a superior noble army. Their leader, Dosza, was burned alive, thousands of peasants were hanged, and the Hungarian diet passed a law binding the peasants perpetually to the soil. In 1672–1685 and in 1697 an army of warrior peasants rose again. In 1703 they initiated the uprising that became the unsuccessful war of liberation from the Habsburgs after its leadership was assumed by Ferenc Rákóczi.

An English example of a peasant insurrection was the Pilgrimage of Grace of 1536. Protesting the dissolution of the monasteries, high taxes, and general misgovernment by Thomas Cromwell (c. 1485–1540) and the ministers of Henry VIII (ruled 1509–1547), the gentry of Lincolnshire and York began a rebellion that was joined by thousands of people from all walks of life who swore an oath to God and king and marched under the banner of the Five Wounds of Christ. The city of York was occupied by 30,000 disciplined soldiers who set up a dissident government of the north. They negotiated a truce with the king, then disbanded and went home. None of the royal promises were kept. Of note are the incredible orderliness of this movement, its elite leadership, and the participants' strong belief in the right of their cause.

Some peasant revolts took the form of waves of separate but related attacks on local objectives. The German peasants in 1525 and the French peasants in the Great Fear of 1789 attacked the castles of their lords. Letters from Brittany in 1675 convey the nature of the fear that swept the upper classes during such a movement: "These people are still very stirred up in Lower Brittany. They have killed a gentleman and burned the houses of others on pretext that they were extortionists. My lord, there is no safety in the countryside for anyone. The parishes are murmuring on all sides . . ." wrote an agent of the king. A priest sympathetic to the peasants reported that in one of "a thousand inhuman acts," they had dragged a noble out of a church by his hair and thrown him half dead into a ditch.

URBAN REVOLTS

Urban riots were shorter and more focused than peasant revolts. Because walled cities had crowded, narrow streets, urban rioters tended to go after specific targets that symbolized their grievances. Crowds would storm through the streets shouting slogans, attack persons or property, form armed companies, take hostages, occupy the city hall, or seize strategic towers. Along with the major urban uprisings came a host of lesser disturbances, and many signs of simmering discontent: the appearance of anonymous manifestos on doorways and public walls, muttering heard in the streets, sabotage of the work of detested officials, and passive resistance through noncompliance.

Urban crowds could form spontaneously, provided the participants shared a common set of values that they felt had been violated, and provided there was a specific incident or experience to set people off. Such an event would require considerable prep-

TABLE 1

Selected Instances of Popular Protest and Revolt in Early Modern Europe 1500–1780

Date	Location	Event
1502	Speyer, Germany	Bundshuhe revolt
1513–14	Berne, Lucerne	First war of Swiss peasants
1514	Hungary	Peasant army led by Dosza sweeps the country
1515	Carniola, Carinthia, Stryria	Peasant War in Inner Austria
1517	Baden, Alsace	Bundshuhe revolt
1520	Castile	Comuneros revolt (league of towns)
1523–30	Denmark	Peasants revolt against their new status
1525	Southern Germany	German Peasants' War: Peasants unite to overthrow government representatives
1525	Laveriham, England	Crowd of 4,000 demands tax relief
1526	Salzburg, Austria	German Peasants' War: Peasants revive their war
1529	Lyon, France	La Grande Rebeine: Attack on grain stores and houses of the rich
1536	North of England	Pilgrimage of Grace against Protestant religious reform
1548	Saintonge, Angoumois, France	Revolt of the Pitauds
1549	Midlands, East Anglia, England	Kett's Rebellion against enclosures
1566	Netherlands	Iconoclastic riots against Catholic images
1569–70	Hungary	led by George Karacsonyi
1573	Croatia	General revolt in Croatia and parts of Styria; 60,000 peasants demand rights, end of tithe, 4,000 executed
1573	Carniola, Carinthia, Styria, Austria	Peasant Uprising
1573–75	Norway	Peasants in revolt; uprisings in Trondheim province
1579–80	Romans, France	Carnival of Romans, peasant risings in region
1579	Normandy	Revolt of the Gautiers
1585	Naples	Urban bread riots crushed by Philip II
1586, 1596	Troyes, France	Two urban revolts against taxes
1588	Paris	Day of Barricades: Crowds support duke of Guise over King Henry III
1588	Steyer, Austria	Lower classes; spreads to countryside against lords
1591–93	Ukraine	Kosinsky leads rebellion around Kiev, Bratslav
1593–95	Limousin, Périgord, France	Revolt of Tard-Avisés (peasants)
1594–95	Upper and Lower Austria	Peasant Uprisings
1594–97	Reichstenstein, Austria	Lutherans against war tax; 4,000 peasants
1596	Midlands, England	Laborers rise
1597	Hungary	Peasants rise against demands of nobles, very orderly.
1605–07	Rettenberg, Augsburg	Peasant uprisings
1607	Midlands, England	Revolt against enclosures
1607	Hungary	20,000 Haiduks (bandits) and serfs; against lords as part of rebellion against Habsburgs
1626–27	Upper Austria	"War" led by nobles against Catholic repression, death taxes; 12,000 peasants killed
1627	Troyes, France	Urban riot against the "gabelle"
1628–32	England	Skimmington revolts: 3,000 tear down forest enclosures
1630	Lyon, France	Urban riot of weavers
1630	Aix-en-Provence, France	Urban riot (Cascaveoux)
1630	Dijon, France	Urban riot by vinegrowers (Lanturelu)
1632	Lyon, France	Urban riot against taxes
1632–36	Machland, Austria	Martin Limbauer revolt; executions in Linz 1636
1633–34	Benediktbeuren region, Upper Bavaria	10,000 peasants put down by Swedish and Imperial troops
1635	Bordeaux, France	Urban riot against "gabelle"
1635	Agen, France	Violent urban revolt against tax farmers
1636	Saintonge, Angoumois, France	Assemblies of peasants
1637	Périgord, Quercy, France	Revolt of Croquants (peasants)
1639	Lower Normandy, France	Nu-pieds revolt
1640	Catalonia	Villages revolt against Castille
1641	Troyes, France	Urban riot against taxes on merchandise
1642	Stour Valley, Colchester, England	Crowd attacks houses of gentry
1645	Montpellier, France	Urban revolt: women and men riot against new taxes
1645	Wiltshire and Dorset, England	4000 Clubmen and Levellers against royalist troops
1647–48	Naples, Palermo, and Sicily	Masaniello Revolt in Naples over bread, taxes, spreads to Palermo and Sicily
1648	Moscow	Crowds encouraged by Boyars sack government buildings, result is a new code of feudalism
1652	Granada, Cordoba, Seville	Crowds attack officials, establish a sort of commune
1653	Swiss Cantons	Conspirators hold meetings, then 3,000 march on Lucern; they swear a general oath, 250,000 men

(continued)

TABLE 1—*CONTINUED*

Selected Instances of Popular Protest and Revolt in Early Modern Europe 1500–1780

Date	Location	Event
1657	Châlons-sur-Marne, France	Urban riot against tax on serge
1658	Sologne, France	Revolt of Sabotiers
1659	Aix-en-Provence, France	Urban revolt, St. Valentine's Day Revolt
1662	Boulogne, France	Revolt of Lustucru
1670	Vivarais, France	Rural revolt led by Roure
1675	Bordeaux, France	Large urban uprising against new excise taxes
1675	Rennes, Brittany, France	Urban protest against excise taxes, peasant revolt against lords (Bonnets Rouges)
1685	England	Popular support for Monmouth to usurp throne
1697	Hungary	Peasant revolt in Tokaj region
1703	Hungary	Peasant war against serfdom becomes national liberation movement
1710	London	Sacherevell riots
1736	London	Rioting against hiring of cheap Irish workers
1750	Paris	Rioting over rumors that police were abducting children and deporting them to the colonies
1766	Spain	Uprising causes king to flee the capital for several months
1766	West of England	Waves of food riots
1768	London	Biggest of a series of Wilkite riots in favor of liberty and John Wilkes
1775	France, region around Paris	"Flour War," a wave of grain riots
1780	London	Gordon Riots against toleration act for Catholics

SOURCE: Hughes Neveux, *Les Révoltes paysannes en Europe XIVe-XVIIe siècles* Paris, 1997, 292–98; Henry Kamen, *The Iron Century: Social Change in Europe 1550–1660,* New York, 1972, 331–385; William Beik, *Urban Protest in Seventeenth-Century France: The Culture of Retribution,* London, 1997; and diverse mentions.

aration, not in the form of conspiratorial planning, although this sometimes occurred, but in the form of talk: people complaining about the injustice of a current abuse until a consensus emerged regarding who was to blame and what should be done about it. The classic case is the British grain riot analyzed by E. P. Thompson, who inaugurated the concept of the "moral economy" of the crowd. When emerging capitalist market forces caused the traditional rules of the marketplace to break down, the crowd took matters into its own hands by confiscating the grain and selling it at a traditional price, then turning the proceeds over to the owner. The crucial elements here are belief in an accepted, traditional norm; intervention by the crowd to regulate the system, not to damage it; and attacks focused only on violators of the accepted norm, with no general, indiscriminate violence. Grain riots took place all over Europe.

This concept of moral economy has been extended to include any crowd motivated by moral indignation and measured objectives. In France this concept can be applied to the many revolts against tax collectors, who were often private contractors *(traitants)* collecting the king's special taxes for their own profit. Here the moral economy turns into what can be called the "culture of retribution." Rather than regulating an abuse, like a new tax, over which they had no control, crowds went after a person or object that symbolized the abuse, with the aim of inflicting punishment. If the movement continued to develop, the crowd's targets expanded to include the authorities responsible for the abuse or the rich citizens who backed it financially.

The violence of these riots was strictly measured, and its purpose was to humiliate the offender. In many cases he escaped with minor bruises, duly chastened. In some cases, if he were actually caught, he might be beaten or killed. Torture of a living person was rare, but a dead body was fair game for ritual mutilation, dragging through the streets, or dismemberment. All of these seemingly cruel measures mimicked official justice; thus they may not have seemed particularly brutal in the eyes of the perpetrators. Such acts were essentially attempts to humiliate and insult. In the largest revolts, an initial wave of attacks was followed by a strong counterreaction by the authorities. This, in turn, caused larger riots enveloping whole sections of the city, along with threats uttered against the city's elites or attacks on the jail to release the prisoners.

In Bordeaux in 1675, popular crowds angered at a tax on pewter attacked and destroyed the houses of two pewter merchants who were reported to have paid the new tax. They then accosted and beat to death a man who was said to be the assistant to the royal intendant in Bordeaux, and who may have provoked them. There followed a ritual parade, in which the rebels dragged the body up and down more prosperous streets of Bordeaux, knocking on the doors of royal officials, and culminating at the house of the man's supposed boss. There they placed the body in the boss's carriage and set fire to it while the entire building was pillaged.

In 1750 the people of Paris sent the same sort of symbolic message during riots sparked by rumors that the police were rounding up children of the poor and transporting them to the West Indies. A crowd murdered a man known to be a police spy and, after parading him through the streets, deposited his bloody body at the door of the police commissioner.

Actions like these were part of an international language of gestures, at least in southern Europe. In Naples in 1585 at a time of high bread prices, a crowd seized a man named Starace, who was supposed to represent them in the city council, and paraded him through the streets seated backward in a chair while crowds jeered. They then killed him, dragged his body through the streets by the feet, mutilated it, castrated it, sold off the body parts to the highest bidder, and pillaged his house.

English protests followed a similar pattern, although the English, who seemed to have more of a national orientation and more constitutional options for participation than the French, focused less on retribution and more on petitioning authorities. The Gordon Riots of 1780 in London are an example of this. These demonstrations were initiated by Lord Gordon, head of the Protestant Association, as part of a lobbying effort to get Parliament to repeal the 1778 Catholic Relief Act. On 2 June 1780, fifty thousand persons turned up in St. George's fields and marched peacefully to the Houses of Parliament to petition for repeal. When Parliament turned a deaf ear, the crowd became unmanageable and began acting on its own. Five days of rioting followed, in which hundreds of buildings were pillaged and major monuments, such as Downing Street,

Lambeth Palace, and the Bank of England, were threatened. Catholic chapels and schools were torn down, the houses of members of Parliament who were on the wrong side of the issue were targeted, and eventually the protesters besieged the prisons and released the prisoners. When troops were finally brought in to restore order, over two hundred people, including women and children, were shot in the streets. Despite the destructiveness of the riot, the crowd's behavior, as analyzed by Nicholas Rogers, corresponds closely to the expected model. The members of the crowd acted on their own. Except for some deterioration in the last phase, their actions were deliberate and focused. They limited themselves to targeting prominent Catholics and Catholic institutions, and they were well informed about which these were. The motive of the rioters was essentially political: to bring about a change in the law, not to attack all Catholics.

RELIGIOUS RIOTS

In addition to values relating to subsistence, survival, and tax extortion, crowds also protested troop disorders, arrests of criminals for whom the crowd felt sympathy, legal actions, and occasionally labor grievances. In England a very important objective was tearing down the hedges and filling in the ditches to stop enclosures.

Another source of conflict was religion. During the German Reformation, Protestant minorities frequently bore witness to their faith by gathering publicly to worship, occupying a church, or attacking symbols of idolatry, like statues of saints. The wave of iconoclasm that hit the Netherlands and the north of France in the summer of 1566 is a famous example. For months people had been flocking to incendiary sermons by Calvinist preachers in woods and fields outside the walls of cities. On 10 August in a tiny town called Steenvoorde, the audience stormed out of the church after a fiery sermon and broke into the nearby Abbey of Saint Lawrence, where they smashed pictures and statues. This first blow set off a wave of vandalism that swept across the region. On 20 August the cathedral in Antwerp was occupied by an enormous crowd of excited believers. Men started climbing up the pillars and making their way across the vaulted ceiling with hammers, smashing every image and dumping the broken pieces down into the nave.

The next day all the other churches in Antwerp were attacked. In two weeks almost two hundred churches and monasteries were attacked over the whole region.

Such movements might have enjoyed the support of sympathizers within the city council, or they might have represented a challenge to the constituted authorities. In France, where the Huguenots and the Catholics were forced by circumstance to live side by side, there were frequent confrontations over rituals and symbols. Quarrels arose over the deference shown to a statue of the Virgin Mary, the location of burials, and jurisdiction over the last rites of the dying. Each faith claimed to be purifying the community in the name of God by persecuting the other party. It is interesting to note that the punishments meted out by religious crowds were remarkably similar to the treatment of tax agents. When the duke of Guise, leader of the Catholic party in the French Religious Wars, assassinated Admiral Coligny and his followers on the night of Saint Bartholomew in 1572, the victims' bodies were seized by celebrating Parisians who triumphantly dragged them through the streets.

THE ROLE OF WOMEN

Women played a prominent role in most riots. They were closely associated with bread riots and other protests involving family and subsistence. But they also turned up everywhere except in formal military operations. Women served as the conscience and moral repository of the community. They were often the first to cry out publicly when an abuse surfaced, and many a riot was set off by just such a cry. Their boldness was partly predicated on the knowledge that as "weak and helpless" women, they could not be held responsible for their actions before the law. They could be seen encouraging the men wherever roofs were being stripped and rocks were being thrown. Women were active in every country, but they were especially strong in the Dutch Republic. When reminded that they had no vote, women demonstrating before the town hall in Rotterdam in 1747 snarled "Here we do!" In Oudewater in 1628, when a crowd chased a tax farmer into the city hall, women cried out "Let us sound the drum and send our husbands home. We will catch the villain and beat him, as we cannot be tried for fighting." At a demonstration in Rotter-

dam in 1690, women formed a female military contingent in front of the *stathuis* (city hall). They carried sticks and clubs on their shoulders and appeared "ready to storm the gates of Hell."

THE CLASSIC RIOT

All of these instances, rural and urban, admirably fit a classic definition of collective action. The participants had opinions about politics and they challenged authority in a logical, informed way. Their action was legitimized by widely held values that might even have been tacitly shared by local elites. The crowd always went after specific targets that were perceived as being either the real culprit or someone or something associated with him. The action was designed to correct the abuse or to punish the abuser. Their frame of reference was local. They did not generally question the king or the system in general. In fact, the demonstrators usually believed that the king would agree with them if only he knew their plight. Their punishments, though sometimes brutal, were extremely selective. They knew their enemy and they left other people alone.

COMPLICATING THE PICTURE

In recent years there have been a number of critiques of the kind of analysis outlined above. Critics argue that it is too simplistic to speak of the crowd as having a single voice and to attribute honorable motives to all its actions when different participants may have had different intentions. New studies are punching holes in the old generalizations by finding exceptions and by demonstrating the ambiguity and complexity of the participation and the motivation behind popular revolts. Some have cited cases that do not fit this mold, often using the intense scrutiny of a microhistorical approach. Others are looking critically at the nature of the discourses from which we get our information on popular rebellion.

For example, a study by Hughes Neveux questions the very concept of a peasant uprising, charging that it is a cultural construction imposed on a set of diverse episodes that have no common denominator. Another example is John Walter's intensive study of the well-known series of attacks by crowds on the houses of the English gentry in the Stour Valley in 1642. These attacks are usually cited as prime examples of class conflict. A crowd of poor, angry commoners took the opportunity to attack the homes of the rich. In fact, this description, repeated by historians since the event itself, expresses the Royalist view of the Parliamentary opposition. Lucas was a Catholic and a Royalist who was rumored to be raising support for the king. His attackers came from nearby Colchester and may have been supported by the town corporation itself. In fact, the riots were the culmination of years of conflicts between the Lucas family and the town of Colchester. There were elements of anti-Catholicism and class hatred in these attacks, but there was a host of other reasons why the sides lined up as they did. Like many confrontations, this one had a long history that is not captured by studying the actions of the crowd alone.

Another example is David Martin Luebke's study of the peasant wars in Upper Austria between 1725 and 1745, called the Saltpeter Wars. The villages of the county of Hauenstein were struggling against the exactions of the powerful monastery of St. Blasien, which dominated the area. One might expect that this was a classic conflict of lord versus villagers, with the solidarity of the collective peasantry being a major source of strength in its struggles for independence. Instead, the community was split into two warring factions named the *salpeterisch* faction and the *müllerisch* faction. There was no identifiable economic or social difference between the two groups, but they attributed to each other completely different personalities and reputations derived from their different interpretations of the relationship of law and custom in their struggle with the monastery. Luebke's study thus calls into question the concept of community that is central to early modern social history.

These studies do not negate the fundamental insights of the previous analyses, but they do suggest pitfalls and avenues for further exploration. Whatever the approach, there is one central point on which there is now general agreement: that ordinary people were intelligent critics of the world around them. They were involved, they made themselves heard, and they did make a difference.

See also **Class, Status, and Order; *Comuneros* Revolt (1520–1521); Food Riots; Naples, Revolt of (1647); Peasants' War, German; Popular Culture; Pugachev Revolt (1773–1775); Rákóczi Revolt; Revolutions, Age of.**

BIBLIOGRAPHY

Beik, William. *Urban Protest in Seventeenth-Century France: The Culture of Retribution.* Cambridge, U.K., 1997.

Bercé, Yves-Marie. *History of Peasant Revolts: The Social Origins of Rebellion in Early Modern France.* Translated by Amanda Whitmore. Ithaca, N.Y., 1990.

Blickle, Peter, ed. *Resistance, Representation, and Community.* Oxford, 1997.

———. *The Revolution of 1525: The German Peasants' War from a New Perspective.* Translated by Thomas A. Brady, Jr., and H. C. Erik Midelfort. Baltimore, 1981.

Bouton, Cynthia A. *The Flour War: Gender, Class and Community in Late Ancien Régime French Society.* University Park, Pa., 1993.

Davis, Natalie Zemon. *Society and Culture in Early Modern France: Eight Essays.* Stanford, 1975.

Farge, Arlette, and Jacques Revel. *The Vanishing Children of Paris: Rumor and Politics before the French Revolution.* Translated by Claudia Miéville. Cambridge, Mass., 1991.

Franz, Günther. *Der Deutsche Bauernkrieg.* 4th ed. Darmstadt, 1956.

Harris, Tim. *London Crowds in the Reign of Charles II: Propaganda and Politics from the Restoration until the Exclusion Crisis.* Cambridge, U.K., 1987.

Lefebvre, Georges. *The Great Fear of 1789: Rural Panic in Revolutionary France.* Translated by Joan White. Princeton, 1973.

Luebke, David Martin. *His Majesty's Rebels: Communities, Factions, and Rural Revolt in the Black Forest, 1725–1745.* Ithaca, N.Y., 1997.

Manning, Roger B. *Village Revolts: Social Protest and Popular Disturbances in England, 1509–1640.* Oxford, 1988.

Mousnier, Roland. *Peasant Uprisings in Seventeenth-Century France, Russia, and China.* Translated by Brian Pearce. New York, 1970.

Neveux, Hugues. *Les révoltes paysannes en Europe XVIe–XVIIe siécle.* Paris, 1997.

Nicolas, Jean. *La rébellion française: mouvements populaires et conscience sociale 1661–1789.* Paris, 2002.

Rogers, Nicholas. *Crowds, Culture, and Politics in Georgian Britain.* Oxford, 1998.

Rudé, Georges. *Paris and London in the Eighteenth Century: Studies in Popular Protest.* New York, 1973.

Sharp, Buchanan. *In Contempt of All Authority: Rural Artisans and Riot in the West of England, 1586–1660.* Berkeley, 1980.

Thompson, E. P. *Customs in Common: Studies in Traditional Popular Culture.* New York, 1993.

Tilly, Charles. *The Contentious French.* Cambridge, Mass., 1986.

Walter, John. *Understanding Popular Violence in the English Revolution: The Colchester Plunderers.* Cambridge, U.K., 1999.

Würgler, Andreas. *Unruhen und Öffentlichkeit: Städtische und ländliche Protestbewegungen im 18. Jahrhundert.* Tübingen, 1995.

WILLIAM BEIK

POPULAR RELIGION. *See* Religious Piety.

POPULAR REVOLT. *See* Popular Protest and Rebellions.

POPULAR SONGS. *See* Songs, Popular.

PORCELAIN. *See* Ceramics, Pottery, and Porcelain.

PORNOGRAPHY. By the time the Marquis de Sade (1740–1814) penned his infamous *Philosopher in the Bedroom* (1795), there was little doubt that obscene, erotic, sexually explicit writing had become a well-established and profitable genre. Books, pamphlets, and prints were sold in the capital cities of Europe, and authors and publishers were occasionally prosecuted for the production of such lascivious material. Readers recorded their responses to such works and even joked about them, as the French philosophe Jean-Jacques Rousseau (1712–1778) would do in his *Confessions,* as books designed to be read with only one hand. The term *pornography,* however, had yet to be invented to describe this sort of material, though only a decade later the French bibliographer Étienne-Gabriel Peignot (1767–1849) would talk about "sotadic or pornographic" books when describing works that had been censured due to their moral impropriety in his *Dictionnaire critique, littéraire et bibliographique des principaux livres, condamnés au feu, supprimés ou censurés* (1806). The English equivalent of this work did not appear until the mid-nineteenth century. The crystallization of a terminology for this kind of erotic and obscene literature and imagery at the beginning of the early modern era reflected the importance of the period in bringing such material into being.

The origins of pornography are highly debated, in part because determining such origins depends on our ability to find people in the past reacting negatively to the circulation of sexually explicit material. The erotic statuary and poetry of Greco-Roman culture, with its celebration of the god Priapus (identified by his large, erect penis) and its explicit depictions of male and female sodomy, became "pornographic" to a later age that saw them as the embodiment of a kind of sexual libertinism condemned by Christianity. Antonio Beccadelli's *Hermaphroditus* (1425), for example, was burned in several Italian cities because its poetic dialogue between a penis and a vagina, dedicated to Cosimo de' Medici, future ruler of Florence, was considered morally offensive. Renaissance humanists delighted in writing priapic poems in imitation of ancient erotic poetry; the twenty-two editions of the ancient *Carmina Priapea* in circulation by 1517 suggest how popular these writings were in the early days of printing. Yet the fact that such works were published in Latin generally made them socially acceptable because they were intended for an educated audience. By contrast, eighteenth-century invocations of priapic cults seem far more "pornographic" because they were written in more accessible prose accompanied by engravings that recreated vividly the ancient rituals of erotic worship.

In the early decades of the sixteenth century, two works composed by Pietro Aretino (1492–1556) challenged the humanist approach to ancient sexuality by bringing the discussion of sex and society into the marketplace. Aretino's *Sonnetti lussuriosi* (Lecherous sonnets, 1527), written to accompany the engraver Marc'Antonio Raimondi's sixteen images depicting different sexual positions, became the quintessential image of "Renaissance pornography" as a reinvention of ancient Greco-Roman paintings of whores coupling with their clients. Today only one copy of this text survives, although dozens of imitations of the "Aretine postures" competed with each other during the next two centuries, increasing the number of sexual positions to well over forty. More powerfully, Aretino's

Ragionamenti (Dialogues, 1534–1536) invented the idea of erotic initiation as a conversation between an old whore and a young girl. Later works such as Ferrante Pallavicino's *La retorica delle puttane* (The whore's rhetoric, 1642) and John Cleland's *Memoirs of a Woman of Pleasure* (1748–1749), more popularly known as *Fanny Hill,* elaborated on the theme that whores, as society's sexual experts, were best able to converse about this subject. Aretino's reputation as a pornographer grew steadily across the centuries. Eighteenth-century readers delighted in works such as *Aretinus Redivivus*—a book listed in a 1745 London indictment against a bookseller known for his stock of lewd books—*L'Arétin français, par un member de l'académie des dames* (The French Aretine, by a member of the ladies' academy, 1787), and *Le petit-neveu de l'Arétin* (Aretino's grandnephew, 1800).

The themes of early modern pornographic writing are, like most pornography, highly repetitive. The sodomitical rituals of the schoolroom, the sexual antics of convents, the amours of rulers, and, of course, whorish conversation defined the terrain. What changed primarily were the availability of this material to a reading public and the willingness of readers to talk about it. Renaissance pornography was defined by a handful of works, primarily associated with Aretino and his Venetian associates, and it was only retrospectively described as pornography. We need to contrast this situation with the dramatic increase in erotic publications in the late seventeenth and eighteenth centuries. Consider the famous case of the English diarist Samuel Pepys (1633–1703) who first saw *L'escole des filles* (1655), a popular French erotic work that chastely presented itself as a "school for girls," at his bookseller's on 13 January 1668. He thought it was lewder than the popular *La puttana errante* (Wandering whore), often attributed to Aretino, and finally gave in to the temptation of buying it on 8 February. The next morning he read it at home, recorded its ability to arouse him, and then burned it. Pepys, in other words, was a connoisseur of erotic writing, even as he sought to present himself as a reader who ultimately did the right thing by refusing to keep such works at home. He knew where to find such works, he knew what to do with them, and he recorded his excitement and his shame.

By the late seventeenth century the publication of pornography shifted decisively from Italy to northern Europe. The English, Dutch, and French increasingly played a greater role in its production and dissemination. Early works were reprinted and translated, and new works reached a much wider audience. Pornographic writings did not remain entirely static in their content; they began to reflect new social issues. Popular French works such as Jean Barrin's *Venus dans le cloître* (Venus in the cloister, 1683) and the *Histoire de Dom Bougre, portier des Chartreux* (The history of Don Bougre, the gatekeeper of Chartreux, 1741), which recounted the lesbianism of the convent and the voracious sexual appetites of male clergy, respectively, took up the old theme of anticlericalism with new vigor in the post-Reformation era. Other works reflected the fascination with new philosophies, such as materialism, that allowed people to think about the human body as an anatomical machine, as was the case with the popular *Thérèse philosophe* (1748) and Cleland's controversial *Fanny Hill.* At the same time, pornography increasingly became a means of attacking political authority. The culmination of this final development can be found in the numerous pornographic satires of the sexual life of Marie Antoinette (1755–1793), wife of the French King Louis XVI (ruled 1774–1792) in the 1790s. The French queen was dead by the time Sade wrote his violent apotheosis of sexuality in the mid-1790s, thus he was left to imagine an impersonal world of sex and violence that sought to dissect virtually every pretension of earlier erotic works to offer a message beyond pure materialism. These were the books that Peignot had in mind when he talked about "sotadic or pornographic" works that had been condemned over the centuries.

See also **Sexuality and Sexual Behavior.**

BIBLIOGRAPHY

Barkan, Leonard. *Transuming Passion: Ganymede and the Erotics of Humanism.* Stanford, 1991.

DeJean, Joan. *The Reinvention of Obscenity: Sex, Lies, and Tabloids in Early Modern France.* Chicago, 2002.

Foxon, David. *Libertine Literature in England, 1660–1745.* New Hyde Park, N.Y., 1965.

Frantz, David O. *Festum Voluptatis: A Study of Renaissance Erotica.* Columbus, Ohio, 1989.

Ginzburg, Carlo. "Titian, Ovid and Sixteenth-Century Codes for Erotic Illustration." In his *Myth, Emblems,*

Clues, translated by John Tedeschi and Anne C. Tedeschi, pp. 77–95. London, 1990.

Goulemot, Jean Marie. *Forbidden Texts: Erotic Literature and Its Readers in Eighteenth-Century France.* Translated by James Simpson. Philadelphia, 1994.

Hunt, Lynn, ed. *The Invention of Pornography: Obscenity and the Origins of Modernity, 1500–1800.* New York, 1993.

Kendrick, Walter. *The Secret Museum: Pornography in Modern Culture.* New York, 1987.

Moulton, Ian Frederick. *Before Pornography: Erotic Writing in Early Modern England.* Oxford, 2000.

Naumann, Peter. *Keyhole und Candle: John Cleland's* Memoirs of a Woman of Pleasure *und die Entstehung des pornographischen Romans in England.* Heidelberg, 1976.

Talvacchia, Bette. *Taking Positions: On the Erotic in Renaissance Culture.* Princeton, 1999.

Thompson, Roger. *Unfit for Modest Ears: A Study of Pornographic, Obscene and Bawdy Works Written or Published in England in the Second Half of the Seventeenth Century.* Totowa, N.J., 1979.

Turner, James Grantham. *Schooling Sex: Libertine Literature and Erotic Education in Italy, France, and England 1534–1685.* Oxford, 2003.

Wagner, Peter. *Eros Revived: Erotica of the Enlightenment in England and America.* London, 1988.

PAULA FINDLEN

PORTE. *Porte* or, more precisely, *the Sublime Porte (bab-i âli)* is a term used for certain Ottoman institutions connected with the imperial palace and the offices of the grand vizier and the state secretary, later foreign minister *(reisülküttab)*. *Porte* has also been used as a synonym for Istanbul, the capital of the Ottoman Empire. The term entered the English language sometime about 1600, via the French *(la Porte Sublime)* and, ultimately, the Italian *(la Porta Sublima)*. The literal meaning of the term is "elevated gate" or "lofty gate," and "gate" here has deep symbolic and ideological meaning, mirroring the patrimonial character of the Ottoman state. It stands for household, sultanic or grand vizierial, and is the symbolic point of (non)acceptance, dividing the inner and outer worlds of particular households. To cross the threshold *(der)* of the house and to be allowed to enter the gate *(bab, kapi)* of the house were symbolic acts of someone's acceptance into Ottoman society. The same symbolism of the gate and threshold as terms for the ruler's palace and the main administrative office of the state is encountered in the Pharaonic Egypt, ancient Israel, Sasanian Iran, Mamluk Egypt, and medieval Japan.

FROM PALACE TO GRAND VIZIERIAL OFFICE

From the mid-fifteenth to the mid-seventeenth century, especially in the earlier part of that period, the Sublime Porte predominantly meant the imperial palace, and particularly its official section *(divan-i hümayûn, bab-i hümayûn)*. Gradually, the sultan's role at meetings of the imperial council had changed. From being an active participant, the sultan became a spectator, and even later, his "spectator's booth," a small window overlooking the council chamber, was covered so that council members could never be sure whether or not the sultan was monitoring their deliberations.

In 1654, during the vizierate of Dervish Mehmed Pasha, a special building was assigned as a residence in which the grand vizier was to live and convene meetings of the imperial council. When Köprülü Mehmed Pasha, the founder of the mighty Köprülü vizierial family, was appointed vizier, this residence was given to him. By the beginning of the eighteenth century, the Ottomans had a clear notion of the office of the grand vizier as a space and institution independent of both the grand vizier's private household and the imperial residence. This institutional independence came into being due to the spatial separation of the private residence of the Grand Vizier from the High Porte offices which took place before 1700. The building was destroyed twice by fire, in 1755 and 1808, and was a victim of subsequent fires during the nineteenth and the early twentieth centuries.

THE RISE OF THE OTTOMAN BUREAUCRACY

The rise of the Ottoman bureaucracy is a phenomenon unprecedented in the history of the preindustrial world, from Scandinavia to Japan. The number of documents the Ottoman scribes produced is truly impressive, even if one counts only those still extant, leaving out all that has perished through the ages. Thousands of archival records, for instance, carefully noted the consumption of chewing gum in the harem, to cite only one of the more bizarre cases of scribal diligence. Still, in the time of Bayezid II (ruled 1481–1512), the state and palace bureaucracies did not have a strong sense of forming a distinct social and intellectual stratum, nor were they numerically strong. In that era, there were not more than two dozen palace scribes, although there were, of course, additional ad hoc bureaucrats who came mostly from the ranks of religious scholars *(ulema)*. However, by the end of the reign of Suleiman the Lawgiver (d. 1566), the court bureaucrats had become a large and defined body known as the "people of pen" *(kalemiyye),* who distinguished themselves from the military elites *(seyfiyye)* and religious intellectuals *(ilmiyye).* To become a bureaucrat, a boy needed to enter an apprenticeship between the ages of twelve and fourteen with one of the palace scribes and to work diligently on mastering Islamic calligraphy and the rules of a complicated Ottoman epistolography influenced by the Arab and Persian literary styles; he also needed to acquire specific clinical knowledge of certain subspecializations. Each scribal branch had its own trade secrets and peculiarities, including distinctive calligraphic codes. Some of the greatest Ottoman intellectuals before the Tanzimat reforms of the nineteenth century, such as polymaths Katib Çelebi (d. 1657) and Huseyn Hezarfenn Efendi (d. 1699), came from the scribal estate and not from that of the religious intellectuals.

The grand vizier would have under his auspices various chancelleries headed by high-ranking bureaucrats directly responsible to him. After the peace treaty of Karlowitz in 1699, the office of one of them, *Reisülküttab,* grew in prominence, with many eighteenth-century grand viziers rising to their post from that office. Two of the most famous were Rami Mehmed Pasha and Koca Ragib Pasha, both of whom showed exceptional diplomatic gifts in days that were precarious for the empire. Rami Mehmed, together with the Ottoman Phanariote Grand Dragoman Alessandro Mavrocordato, brokered the treaty of Karlowitz, and Ragib succeeded in keeping the Ottoman Empire out of the Seven Years' War despite pressures from various European powers.

CONTACT WITH EUROPE AND EUROPEAN VIEWS OF THE SUBLIME PORTE

European attitudes toward the Sublime Porte as an institution began with an excessive admiration and ended in uncontrolled and ungrounded contempt.

While Niccolò Machiavelli, the Italian political philosopher, and the humanist Guillaume Postel had only admiration for the government of the Grand Turk, contempt was evident in the works of Charles-Louis de Secondat de Montesquieu and Edward Gibbon. The Sublime Porte considered all peaceful contacts with the European powers until 1699 as acts of Ottoman unilateral grace and saw war or truce—not peace or a diplomatic exchange based on equality—as a normal state of relations. This was mirrored in Ottoman ceremonies vis-à-vis European envoys. The Ottoman rulers' title had been considered an expression of world order, and the Ottomans were therefore determined to preserve the notion of the exclusivity of the sultan's title—Kayser-i Rum, or Caesar of the Roman (Byzantine) Empire—consistently denying the Habsburgs' right to the same title.

The situation began to change after 1699, when the Ottomans had to accept the European powers as equals, at least in diplomatic exchanges. Still, there were many subtle games in which the Ottomans tried to win at least the ceremonial upper hand. This gave rise to what were, in their time, serious diplomatic incidents. For example, the sultan would not communicate directly with foreign envoys; he would instead give instructions via sign language to the grand vizier, who would speak to the envoy. In 1700 Charles de Ferriol, the envoy of the Ottomans' long-time ally France, instigated a grave diplomatic and ceremonial incident when he refused to put aside his sword while in audience with Sultan Mustafa II. He finally had to leave the palace without completing the audience. The Ottoman chronicler Raşid called de Ferriol a "crazy envoy" *(deli elci).*

See also **Austro-Ottoman Wars; Gibbon, Edward; Machiavelli, Niccolò; Montesquieu, Charles-Louis de Secondat de; Ottoman Dynasty; Ottoman Empire.**

BIBLIOGRAPHY

Abou-El-Haj, Rifa'at Ali. *The Reisulkuttab and the Ottoman Diplomacy at Karlowitz.* Ph.D. diss. Princeton University, 1963.

———. *The 1703 Rebellion and the Structure of Ottoman Politics.* Leiden, 1984.

Aksan, Virginia H. *An Ottoman Statesman in War and Peace: Ahmed Resmi Efendi, 1700–1783.* Leiden, 1995.

Efendi, Yirmisekiz Mehmed Çelebi. *Le paradis des infidels, relation de Yirmisekiz elebi Mehmed Efendi, ambassa-*

deur Ottoman en France sous le régence. Translated and edited by J. C. Galland and G. Veinstein. Paris, 1981.

Galland, Antoine. *Journal d'Antoine Galland pendant son séjour à Constantinople. (1672–1673).* Edited by C. H. Schefer, vols. 1–2. Paris, 1881.

Hammer-Purgstall, Josef von. *Des Osmanischen Reichs Staatsverfassung und Staatsverwaltung.* Vols. 1–2. Vienna, 1815.

Itzkowitz, Norman. *Mehmed Raghib Pasha: The Making of an Ottoman Grand Vezir.* Ph.D. diss. Princeton University, 1959.

————. *Mubadele: An Ottoman-Russian Exchange of Ambassadors.* Annotated and translated by Norman Itzkowitz and Max Mote, Chicago 1970.

Mouradgea d'Ohsson, Ignatius. *Tableau général de l'empire Othoman, 7.* Paris, 1824.

Teply, Karl. *Kaiserliche Gesandschaften aus Goldene Horn.* Stuttgart, 1968.

Unat, Faik Reşit. *Osmanli Sefirleri and Sefaretnameleri.* Ankara, 1968.

Uzunçarili, Ismail Hakki. *Osmanli Devletinin Merkez ve Bahriye Teşkilati.* Ankara, 1948.

Valensi, Lucette. *Venise et la Sublime Porte: La naissance du despote.* Paris, 1987.

NENAD FILIPOVIC

PORTRAIT MINIATURES.

The portrait miniature was an art form that flourished from the sixteenth to the mid-nineteenth century. These small-scale portraits derived from the tradition of manuscript illumination, in which vellum pages with text decorated with images in watercolor were bound together to form a book. In the sixteenth century, these marginal images were adapted into a separate art form, usually a half-length or bust-length portrait, painted in watercolor on vellum. Ranging in size from an inch to five or six inches in height, the portrait would then be either housed in a metal locket, sometimes decorated with pearls or diamonds, which could be worn or carried on the person, or placed in a frame and displayed in the home. Hans Holbein (1497?–1543), a German painter working in England at the court of Henry VIII, and François Clouet (c. 1516–1572), a French painter at the French court, were the first prominent miniaturists, although their careers were not exclusively devoted to the form. Both artists produced striking likenesses set against solid jewel-tone backgrounds, usually blue. The art form became most popular in England and developed into a distinct specialty for English artists, but was also practiced throughout continental Europe.

ENGLAND

Nicholas Hilliard (1547?–1619) became the first specialized practitioner in England. His career was tied to the Elizabethan court, where miniatures played a prominent role in court life, and he trained a number of prominent pupils, including Isaac Oliver, Peter Oliver, John Hoskins, and his own son, Lawrence Hilliard. Throughout the seventeenth century, miniaturists such as Samuel Cooper and his brother Alexander Cooper continued to serve the monarchy and aristocracy, and, during the Interregnum in England, Oliver Cromwell. Cooper's style departed from Hilliard's careful handling of watercolor with his freer use of brushstrokes. In the eighteenth century, the watercolor on vellum miniature was eclipsed by the new technique of painting in watercolor on ivory. Bernard III Lens (1681–1740) was the first miniature painter in England to adopt this technique, which had been invented in Italy by Venetian pastelist Rosalba Carriera. Watercolor on ivory soon replaced watercolor on vellum as the signature medium of the portrait miniature. The portrait would be painted on a thin slice of ivory, usually shaped in an oval but sometimes rectangular. The ivory was sanded down to make a rough texture that would catch the paint more easily. The watercolor, mixed with gum arabic, was then applied either in short, controlled brushstrokes or in dots of paint, called stippling. Enamel miniatures also enjoyed popularity in England, particularly in the first half of the eighteenth century, alongside watercolor on vellum, until eclipsed by watercolor on ivory. The most prominent practitioner in England was Christian Friedrich Zincke (c. 1683–1767) from Dresden, another enameler trained as a goldsmith.

With the new significance placed in the eighteenth century on affective relationships and emotions, demand for portrait miniatures expanded from the court circles of the sixteenth and seventeenth centuries to the middle and upper classes. The heyday of the miniature spanned the mid-eighteenth to the early nineteenth century. Miniatures played an important role in personal relations. They were exchanged as tokens of affection and love, and

Portrait Miniatures. Self-portrait by Nicholas Hilliard (right) and portrait of Richard Hilliard, the artist's father. THE ART ARCHIVE/ VICTORIA AND ALBERT MUSEUM LONDON/SALLY CHAPPELL

as stand-ins for absent loved ones, or served as commemorations of the dead. The housing for the ivory portrait was often decorated with other elements that reinforced these functions, such as initials, woven hair, or symbols of love or mourning. Many portraits were painted posthumously to commemorate a lost loved one. They often included mourning imagery on the reverse, painted in grisaille with chopped hair dissolved into the watercolor, which might depict mourners at tombs inscribed with the loved one's name. Among the most prominent eighteenth-century English miniaturists were Jeremiah Meyer (1735–1789), John Smart (1743–1811), George Engleheart (1753–1829), and Richard Cosway (1742–1821). Although each miniaturist developed an individual style, eighteenth-century miniatures generally have in common a light palette of colors, monochromatic backgrounds, and brushwork that exploited the translucency of the ivory support.

CONTINENTAL EUROPE

The miniature tradition in continental Europe followed a trajectory similar to that in England but was never quite as popular. After Clouet's work in France, the miniature did not really have a resurgence there until the eighteenth century, and the watercolor-on-vellum and watercolor-on-ivory techniques were not as common as in England. Instead, the medium of choice tended to be enamel. This choice ensured a different quality to the continental miniature because of the saturated, opaque colors and the techniques for painting enamels, resembling oil painting, in contrast to the light, translucent quality of watercolor on ivory. Enamels are produced by painting with metallic oxide paints on a metal plaque, usually made of copper, although other metals were used as well. The metal was prepared by being covered with a white enamel paste, made from ground glass. Each color was applied separately and then fired in a kiln or oven. Jean Petitot (1607–1691), one of the first masters of enamel painting in the seventeenth century, was trained as a goldsmith, as were most of the early enamelers, and most of his portraits were of royalty and court in both England and France. In the eighteenth century, several more enamelers rose to prominence by painting royalty and aristocracy. As in England the small-scale likeness became an important part of the everyday life of the middle classes, and the number of artists who specialized in the art form increased. Many artists, however, practiced both enamel and watercolor painting or other forms, such as pastel or drawing in ink or graphite.

Portrait Miniatures. Sir Frederick Augustus D'Este, by Richard Cosway. ©Victoria & Albert Museum, London/Art Resource, N.Y.

Enamelers, moreover, also supplied enamels for watchcases and snuffboxes as well as separate miniature portraits. Although enamel miniatures were sometimes painted from life, they were often small-scale copies after oil paintings.

The portrait miniature continued to play an important role in the life of the middle and upper classes into the nineteenth century. But with the advent of photography, which made small-scale portraits available quickly, more cheaply, and on a much wider scale than before, the demand for painted miniatures gradually ceased, although it continued to be practiced as a polite accomplishment by amateur artists.

See also **Britain, Art in; Carriera, Rosalba; Clouet, François; Holbein, Hans, the Younger; Painting.**

BIBLIOGRAPHY

Caffrey, Paul. *Treasures to Hold: Irish and English Miniatures 1650–1850 from the National Gallery of Ireland Collection.* Exh. cat. Dublin, 2000.

Coffin, Sarah, and Bodo Hofstetter. *The Gilbert Collection: Portrait Miniatures in Enamel.* London, 2000.

Coombs, Katherine. *The Portrait Miniature in England.* London, 1998.

Foskett, Daphne. *Miniatures: Dictionary and Guide.* Woodbridge, U.K., 1987.

Diane Waggoner

PORT-ROYAL. *See* **Jansenism.**

PORTUGAL. In 1385 a new dynasty came to power in Portugal under John I (João of Avis; 1357–1433; ruled 1385–1433). With the capture of the last Muslim stronghold in 1249, Portugal, located on the southwest corner of Europe and bordered by Castile to the east, had achieved roughly its modern boundaries. Though hit hard by the Black Death in 1348–1349, its population a century later had recovered to about one million inhabitants.

But the year 1450 marked a critical time in Portuguese history. Eighteen-year-old Afonso V (ruled 1438–1481), grandson of the founder of the Avis dynasty, was on the throne. The previous year (1449) his uncle, father-in-law, and former regent, Prince Pedro (1392–1449), had been killed at the battle of Alfarrobeira, the victims of civil war. Afonso V's reign might be described as the last hurrah for Portuguese royal chivalry. It clearly was the high-water mark for Portugal's upper nobility and higher clergy, who were lavishly rewarded by the monarch. Afonso V was greatly interested in campaigning in North Africa, personally leading Portuguese forces there in 1458, 1463–1464, and 1471. With the death of Henry (Enrique) IV of Castile in 1474, Afonso V took his kingdom down a dangerous path as he tried to take advantage of Castile's many civil wars. He attempted to marry his niece and Henry IV's young daughter and heiress Joan (Juana) and eventually join the thrones of Castile and Portugal. The plan had both immediate and long-term disastrous results, leading to a destructive Portuguese-Castilian war in the first place and in the second a series of Castilian-Portuguese marriages that eventually resulted in Philip II of Spain becoming king of Portugal.

In the aftermath of his father's lax reign, John (João) II (ruled 1481–1495) asserted strong royal authority. In this he was backed by the Cortes (meeting of the Three Estates) in Evora in 1481–1482. He cowed the titled nobility by having Dom Fernando, third duke of Bragança and head of Portugal's most powerful noble family (1430–1484), executed for treason in 1483 and by personally stabbing to death his own first cousin and brother-in-law, Dom Diogo, duke of Viseu and master of the Order of Christ (1462/63–1484), the following year. John II strongly promoted Portuguese expansion and discovery down the west coast of Africa. During the last years of his reign, tens of thousands of Jews expelled from Spain in 1492 sought refuge in Portugal, doubling the number already there. In the meantime, beginning in the 1440s, increasing numbers of black slaves were brought to Portugal from sub-Saharan Africa. Though a large number of the slaves were sold to Castile and other European kingdoms, many remained in the southern part of Portugal. It is estimated that by 1550 African slaves made up 10 percent of Lisbon's population.

John II was succeeded by Manuel I (ruled 1495–1521), the duke of Viseu's younger brother. Manuel brought the Bragança family back into favor. To appease his future wife Isabella and his Spanish in-laws Ferdinand of Aragón and Isabella of Castile, Manuel in late 1496 and 1497 forced Jews in Portugal to convert to Christianity. When Isabella died after childbirth in 1498, Manuel married her younger sister Maria that year. Two of their sons, John (João) (1502–1557) and Henry (Henrique) (1512–1580), later succeeded to the throne. Toward the end of his life, Manuel in 1518 married Leonor, sister of Emperor Charles V (ruled 1519–1558). Manuel usually receives high marks for administration, and he seems to have healed some of the wounds opened by his predecessor. He undertook major legal reforms, issuing new town charters *(forais)* and updating the earlier crown legislation of the Ordenações Afonsinas with the Ordenações Manuelinas (Manueline Ordinances). Manuel presided over a Portugal making important and often prosperous overseas contacts in East Africa, India, Southeast Asia, and Brazil.

John III's lengthy reign of thirty-six years (1521–1557) has long been the subject of controversy. Son of Manuel, he has been strongly criticized for establishing the Inquisition in Portugal beginning in 1536 and for inviting the newly founded Jesuits to Portugal in 1540. On the other hand, humanism reached its apogee in Portugal during his reign. The University of Coimbra was reformed, and the College of Arts was founded. However, John III was faced with a number of serious problems left behind by his father. Portugal, with a population of between 1 and 1.5 million inhabitants, was overextended and in serious financial difficulties, many caused by its rapid and widespread overseas expansion. The effects of the Council of Trent, 1545–1563, were also beginning to be felt.

John III was succeeded by his three-year-old grandson Sebastian (ruled 1557–1578), who required a double regency, that of his grandmother Catherine from 1557 to 1562 followed by that of his great-uncle Cardinal Henry (Henrique) from 1562 to 1568. Sebastian invaded Morocco twice, in 1574 and 1578. In August of the latter year he and more than seven thousand Portuguese nobility and soldiers died in battle. The childless Sebastian was succeeded by the aging Cardinal Henry, who died in January 1580. Though Dom António (1531–1595), prior of Crato, illegitimate son of Henry's brother Dom Luís (1506–1555), was acclaimed king of Portugal, the troops of Philip II of Spain (ruled 1556–1598) invaded Portugal, and the kingdom was acquired by conquest, inheritance, and bribery. Between 1580 and 1640 Portugal was under Spanish Habsburg rule, part of a dual monarchy. In 1581 at Tomar, Philip II swore to respect Portuguese sovereignty. Philip II spent less than two years in Portugal, and his son Philip III (ruled 1598–1621) visited briefly in 1619. Though most Portuguese seemed to accept Habsburg rule during its first few decades, economic crises and efforts at centralization by Gaspar de Guzmán y Pimental, count-duke of Olivares and chief minister of Philip IV (ruled 1621–1665), set the stage for Portuguese rebellion.

On 1 December 1640 John (João) (1604–1656), eighth duke of Bragança, was proclaimed King John IV (ruled 1640–1656). He married Luisa de Gusmão, daughter of Spain's eighth duke of Medina Sidonia. Generally well received as monarch, John IV encountered difficult times for Portugal and its overseas empire, but he managed to thwart Spanish efforts to restore Portugal to Habsburg rule. There was a period of twenty-eight years of warfare before peace was signed in 1668. When John IV died in 1656, he left behind a sickly and disturbed heir, Afonso VI (ruled 1656–1683). Queen Luisa held the regency until 1662, when a palace coup headed by Luis de Vasconcelos e Sousa (1636–1720), third count of Castelo Melhor, brought the eighteen-year-old Afonso to the throne. Vasconcelos e Sousa became Afonso's key adviser and the dominant figure in Portugal. Afonso VI married the French Marie-Françoise of Nemours in 1666.

A second palace coup ousted Afonso VI in November of 1667 and replaced him with his younger brother Peter (Pedro) (1648–1706), who, in turn, married his sister-in-law (after she had received an annulment) the following year. Peter held the title of regent until his imprisoned brother's death in 1683, after which he became known as Peter (Pedro) II until his own death in 1706. The unorthodox removal of his brother from power placed Peter in a difficult position for his almost thirty-nine years of rule, forcing him into playing the "politics of the possible" and sharing power with the titled nobility. After the death of Maria-Francisca in 1683, Pedro in 1687 married Maria Sophia of Neuburg, daughter of the elector palatine. In this marriage was born John (João) V (ruled 1706–1750), who married Maria Anna of Austria, daughter of the Holy Roman Emperor Leopold I (ruled 1658–1705).

Though Portugal managed to stay out of the international conflicts of the late seventeenth century, the kingdom did become involved in the War of the Spanish Succession (1701–1714). Initially allied with Bourbon France and Spain, Portugal soon sided with England and the Grand Alliance and backed the cause of Archduke Charles of Austria (future Holy Roman emperor Charles VI, ruled 1711–1740). Though Portuguese troops briefly captured Madrid, parts of Portugal were devastated by the war. The war's end ushered in more than half a century of relative peace for Portugal, though the Portuguese, in league with the papacy and Venice, were credited with the victorious sea battle against the Turks off Cape Matapan along the Greek coast in 1717. John V's reign saw a flood of wealth from the Brazilian gold rush, and with this newfound wealth he attempted to imitate Louis XIV (ruled 1643–1715) and the French court. There was an important building and artistic boom, and Portugal's prestige rose at the courts of Europe, especially Rome, Paris, and Vienna. John V created a patriarchate in Lisbon and was granted the title of "Most Faithful" Majesty by Pope Benedict XIV (reigned 1740–1758). Voltaire remarked that when John wanted a building, he built a monastery, and when he wanted a mistress, he took a nun. John's son, Joseph (José) I (ruled 1750–1777), married Mariana Victoria, daughter of Philip V (ruled 1700–1724, 1724–1746) of Spain. Joseph's reign saw significant reforms, especially through the efforts of his chief minister, Sebastião José de Carvalho e Melo (1699–1782), better known as the marquês of Pombal. In the aftermath of the catastrophic earthquake that hit Lisbon on 1 November 1755 and killed between five thousand and ten thousand people, Pombal consolidated his power. The controversial statesman is best understood as an economic nationalist who was also determined to subordinate the titled nobility and the higher clergy to crown control. He greatly reduced the power of the Inquisition, making it little more than a state tribunal. In 1759 he expelled the Jesuits from Portugal and the entire Portuguese world.

Joseph I was succeeded by his daughter Maria I (ruled 1777–1816). Her royal consort was her husband and uncle Pedro, known as Peter (Pedro) III (ruled 1777–1786), who died in 1786. Shortly after the French Revolution, Maria showed evidence of mental instability. In 1792 her son Prince John (João) (1767–1826) was named regent. After her death in 1816, he became John (João) VI of Portugal.

See also **Lisbon; Olivares, Gaspar de Guzmán y Pimentel, Count of; Philip II (Spain); Portuguese Colonies; Portuguese Literature and Language.**

BIBLIOGRAPHY

Boxer, C. R. *Salvador de Sá and the Struggle for Brazil and Angola, 1602–1686.* London, 1952.

Hanson, Carl A. *Economy and Society in Baroque Portugal, 1668–1703.* Minneapolis, 1981.

Livermore, H. V. *A History of Portugal.* Cambridge, U.K., 1947.

Maxwell, Kenneth. *Pombal: Paradox of the Enlightenment.* Cambridge, U.K., 1995.

Oliveira Marques, A. H. de. *History of Portugal.* 2nd ed. New York, 1976.

Saunders, A. C. de C. M. *A Social History of Black Slaves and Freedmen in Portugal, 1441–1555.* Cambridge, U.K., 1982.

FRANCIS A. DUTRA

PORTUGUESE COLONIES

This entry includes four subentries:

AFRICA
BRAZIL
THE INDIAN OCEAN AND ASIA
MADEIRA AND THE AZORES

AFRICA

Portuguese colonial and trading ventures in Africa, whose beginning is conventionally dated from the conquest of Ceuta in 1415, continued with the gradual exploration of the Saharan and then West African Atlantic coastline from the mid-1430s to the mid-1480s. Having reached an early peak in the first three decades of the sixteenth century, the colonial enterprise stalled for the time being, as a result of defeats in Morocco and settlement setbacks in West Africa and Angola. The latter were partially offset, however, by the prosperity of the Cape Verde Islands and of São Tomé Island, as well as by commercial breakthroughs in West and East Africa. Subsequent economic stagnation, foreign competition, and the Dutch assaults and occupation of 1620–1648 helped to erode Portugal's African interests. New vigorous expansion followed, however, above all in Angola and Mozambique, from 1650 onward. Portuguese adventurers, entrepreneurs, and chartered companies maintained an important role in the trans-Atlantic slave trade and in Indian Ocean commerce throughout the eighteenth century, and swings in the prosperity of Brazil and in the attendant demand for slaves visibly shaped the economic fortunes of the African colonies.

MOROCCO

Between 1415 and 1521, Portugal occupied six Moroccan coastal towns (Ceuta, 1415; Ksar as-Saghir, 1458; Arzilla and Tangier, 1471; Safi and Azemmur, 1507–1513), and built six new strategic forts along Morocco's Atlantic shore. Failing to tap into the trans-Saharan caravan trade, the outposts remained largely isolated, and maintaining them quickly became a serious burden. Following an era of neglect in the 1520s and 1530s, the outposts were repaired and new fortifications built by the early 1540s (particularly at Mazagan). A spirit of retrenchment nonetheless prevailed, and heavy losses between 1541 and 1550 reduced the Portuguese holdings to Ceuta, Tangier, and Mazagan. When Portugal reclaimed its independence from Spain in 1640, Ceuta pledged allegiance to Spain; Catherine of Bragança's marriage to Charles II gave Tangier to England in 1661; and Mazagan (modern El Jadida), a textbook early modern fortress town, surrendered to Morocco in 1769.

CAPE VERDE AND WEST AFRICA

Discovered around 1460, three of the Cape Verde Islands (Santiago, Fogo, and Maio) were quickly colonized and developed an economy buttressed by trade in slaves, cattle, salt, and dyestuffs. On the African mainland, a small fort was built at Arguim (Mauritania; c. 1450), but the key Portuguese footholds were the fort of São Jorge da Mina (Ghana; 1482), nearby Axim (1490s), and another outpost near Cabo das Redes (1500). A short-lived trading post was maintained at Ughoton (Benin) (1487–1507). An important seasonal station sprang up at the site of the native merchant fairs held at Kantor, on the upper Gambia River. Elsewhere, in Senegal, in Gambia, in the "Guinea Rivers" region, and farther on to Sierra Leone, Liberia, and Ivory Coast, as well as in the Bight of Benin, the Portuguese traded intermittently, often from shipboard. African gold, slaves, ivory, civet, wax, and spices—malaguetta (also known as "grains of paradise," the subtly pungent seeds of the West African plant *Aframomum melegueta,* belonging to the ginger family [Zingiberaceae]) and tailed pepper (the slightly bitter pungent seeds of so-called false cubeb pepper [*Piper guinense* or *Piper clusii*])—were exchanged for horses, European cloth, North African fabrics, Indian cottons, salt, hats, iron, brass, copper, and tin articles, beads, and cowrie shells.

Mismanagement, foreign interlopers (Spanish, French, English, and then the Dutch), policy failures, and African politics eroded trade profits after 1525. By the 1530s Arguim was in decline, and

Mina's gold exports tapered off after 1550. Military penetration into the hinterland of Mina failed, as did projects to establish a full-scale colony in the 1570s and 1590s. Cape Verde experienced some prosperity, but viable local export production was limited to horses, the violet dyestuff orchil (obtained from local lichens), salt, maize, and cotton. In the 1600s, mainland trading posts between Mauritania and Sierra Leone came to depend more heavily on Cape Verde, and the Portuguese asserted themselves between the Casamance and Geba rivers. The Mina gold trade recovered in the early 1600s, but after 1618–1619 its decline was precipitous. In 1620–1641, the Portuguese forts in West Africa fell to the Dutch, Mina capitulating in 1637 and Arguim in 1638. The losses were never recovered.

In 1680–1706, trade between Cape Verde and the African mainland was controlled by the Company of Cape Verde and Cachéu, a privileged exporter of slaves to Spanish America. The English, however, established a stake in the island trade after 1706. From 1757 to 1786, chartered companies, notably the Company of Grão-Pará and Maranhão, once again dominated Cape Verde and the Guinea coast. Reforms brought the demise of the last donatory privileges and the creation of a new Captaincy General of Cape Verde. The authority of the captains, however, was curtailed by the power of the companies, and new trading stations replaced only partially those lost by 1641. The most conspicuous addition was the fort of São João Baptista de Ajudá (1677–1680) in Dahomey, which became a hub of the slave and ivory trade. Subordinate to the Captaincy of São Tomé, Ajudá was controlled by the Company of Cape Verde and Cachéu until 1706. Subsequently, exports of slaves to Brazil secured maintenance subsidies from Bahia for the Ajudá fort.

SÃO TOMÉ AND PRÍNCIPE

Following the discovery of the islands of São Tomé, Ano Bom, and Príncipe (originally Santo Antão) in 1470–1471, effective settlement was undertaken in 1486–1510. The already inhabited island of Fernão do Pó, by contrast, resisted colonization. São Tomé, populated by Portuguese, free Africans, and baptized Jews sent out by the crown, quickly became a slaveholding society geared toward sugar production and the reexport of African slaves. By 1529, there were some sixty sugar mills on the island, but the heyday of sugar production was over by 1600, and internal unrest, Brazilian competition, sugarcane blight, and the emigration of planters to Brazil reduced São Tomé to dire straits by 1615. The island's role as a transit point for slaves also declined, and Dutch raids (from 1612 onward) culminated in the occupation of the island's strategic port in 1641–1644. Although sugar continued to be produced and the cultivation of ginger was attempted, by the 1670s São Tomé was only a modest hub of regional trade. Administrative reforms in 1753–1770 helped to improve conditions, but maintaining Portuguese control over all four islands was a burden. The treaties of San Ildefonso and El Pardo (1777–1778) ceded Fernão do Pó (now Fernando Póo) and Ano Bom (now Annobón) to Spain.

ANGOLA

Following a haphazard expansion of trade in the 1540s–1560s, a *doação*, 'crown donation', of land south of the Kwanza River was made in 1571 to Paulo Dias de Novais. The first settlement was organized in Luanda Bay in 1575, and the colony quickly became involved in slaving (exporting c. 10,000 slaves in the 1570s). The failure to extract concessions from the kingdom of Ndongo led to a series of wars (1579–1590), which the colonists at first fought in alliance with King António I of Kongo. Demographic losses to disease and warfare were severe, however, and by 1590 exhaustion and defeats stalled the inland expansion. The crown assumed direct control of the colony.

In the 1600s, commerce replaced raids and warfare as a source of captives in the Luanda hinterland. As Portuguese military influence revived, permanent slave market networks stretched eastward (to the Kwango and the middle Kwanza rivers) and, in 1617, fresh conquests were launched from the new coastal outpost of Benguela in central Angola. Raids yielded cattle, sheep, and cheaper slaves than those exported through Luanda. The Dutch occupation of Luanda (1641–1648) partly isolated the colony from the remaining Portuguese Atlantic networks, but slaving continued, based on the (Portuguese) loyalist refuge of Massangano. The liberation of Luanda by the Brazilian fleet of Salvador Correia de

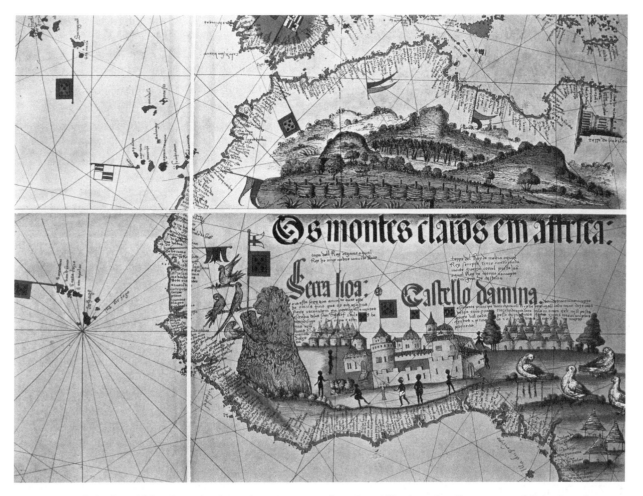

Portuguese Colonies: Africa An early-sixteenth-century map of western Africa based on the voyages of Columbus shows the colony of São Jorge da Mina. BRITISH MUSEUM, LONDON, U.K./BRIDGEMAN ART LIBRARY

Sá reaffirmed the ties between Angola and its main outlet for slaves, Brazil.

Thrusting from Benguela into central Angola's highlands, dominated by the recently formed Ovimbundu kingdoms of Imbangala warlords, the Portuguese reached the upper Katumbela River by the 1650s, and the Kunene River by c. 1720. Here too, raiding gradually yielded to organized trade in slaves, and in the 1770s many of the Ovimbundu warlords were replaced with merchant rulers. In the north, campaigns were fought in 1744 against the kingdom of Matamba. The liberalization of trade in 1755–1758 could not halt a relative decline during the Brazilian depression of the 1760s–1770s, and attempts to stimulate settlement, agriculture, and manufacturing failed. The revival of Brazilian plantations in the 1780s and 1790s, however, brought the trade in slaves to a new high, and fresh sources of slaves were tapped by Portuguese, Luso-African, and Ovimbundu traders as far east as the sources of the Zambezi River.

MOZAMBIQUE

Initial cautious contacts with the Muslim seaside towns of Sofala (Mozambique), Mozambique, and Malindi (Kenya), were followed in 1505 by conquest, in spite of the hostility of Mombasa (Kenya) and Kilwa (Tanzania). The Portuguese then penetrated up the Zambezi River, establishing a trading post at Sena in 1531, and reaching Tete shortly thereafter. The magnet that drew them was the gold and imaginary silver of the Karanga empire of Mwene Matapa (south of the middle and upper Zambezi River) and of its southern outliers (Manica and Butua), as well as the ivory traded in these areas and in the Malawian realm of Kalonga. The military expeditions up the Zambezi and into Manica in the 1570s secured only mixed results, but by then tiny, yet tenacious, groups of Portuguese, Luso-African, and East Indian merchants had already scattered inland. Commerce shifted from Arab networks to Portuguese-dominated ones, with Portuguese India as the focal point and Goa as the administrative pivot.

At first hampered by ill-suited policies, the crown trade failed to prosper. Subsequently, corruption, smuggling, and lack of control over private traders made the Portuguese crown oscillate between direct administration and farming out all commerce to the entrepreneur Captains of Mozambique. Monopoly companies asserted themselves later on. By the 1650s, the inability of Mwene Matapa and Malawi to control dissident regions enticed Portuguese and other adventurers to become overlords or local protectors of large territories (*prazos*). At the same time, however, Arab resurgence in the north led to the loss of Mombasa and its dependencies, Pate (Kenya) and Zanzibar (lost in 1698, and then briefly recaptured and definitively lost in 1728–1729).

The heyday of the large *prazos* was over by c. 1730. Internecine warfare, the twists of African politics, and low production levels spelled their doom. Trade, tribute, and surface mining of gold, iron, and copper were by far the most lucrative activities. Despite state inducements and liberal reforms in 1755–1761, the much smaller, successor *prazo* estates of 1750–1800 never became effective producers of cash crops. The growth of the trade in slaves during the last decades of the eighteenth century, fueled by economic pressures, resurgent Brazilian demand, and the famines of 1792–1796 led to abuses that undermined the legitimacy and political stability of the *prazos,* initiating their decline.

See also **Slavery and the Slave Trade.**

BIBLIOGRAPHY

Birmingham, David. *Central Africa to 1870: Zambezia, Zaire and the South Atlantic.* Cambridge, U.K., 1981.

Cook, Weston F. *The Hundred Years War for Morocco: Gunpowder and the Military Revolution in the Early Modern Muslim World.* Boulder, Colo., 1994.

Garfield, Robert. *A History of São Tomé Island, 1470–1655: The Key to Guinea.* San Francisco, 1992.

Isaacman, Allen F. *Mozambique: The Africanization of a European Institution: The Zambezi Prazos, 1750–1902.* Madison, Wis., 1972.

Newitt, Malyn. *A History of Mozambique.* London, 1995.

Parreira, Adriano T. *The Kingdom of Angola and Iberian Interference, 1483–1643.* Uppsala, 1985.

Vogt, John. *Portuguese Rule on the Gold Coast, 1469–1682.* Athens, Ga., 1979.

MARTIN MALCOLM ELBL

BRAZIL

On 22 April 1500 Pedro Álvares Cabral (1467 or 1468–1520), commander of the thirteen-ship fleet that was following up Vasco da Gama's (c. 1460–1524) epoch-making voyage to India (1497–1498), sighted Brazil or, more accurately, Portuguese America. In 1501 Gonçalo Coelho led an expedition that explored almost two thousand miles of Brazil's coastline. The following year Brazil was leased to brazilwood interests, and over the next few decades several trading posts (*feitorias*) were established. By 1516 King Manuel (1469–1521; ruled 1495–1521) was sending small coast guard fleets to patrol against French and Spanish interlopers in the region. On 3 December 1530 Martim Afonso de Sousa and his brother Pero Lopes de Sousa, with a fleet of five ships carrying almost four hundred settlers, sailed from Portugal to explore and colonize Portuguese America. They set up a colony at São Vicente in 1532. In 1534 King John (João) III (1502–1557; ruled 1521–1557) divided Brazil into fifteen captaincies stretching from the Amazon in the north to Sant'Ana in the south and granted them to twelve lord proprietors (*donatários*). The two most successful of these captaincies were Pernambuco in the northeast and São Vicente in the south.

In 1548 the administration of Portuguese America was placed in the hands of a governor-general. The first governor-general arrived the following year and made Salvador in Bahia his capital shortly after that captaincy came under royal control. As time went by an increasing number of other captaincies also became royal colonies. By 1540 there were an estimated two thousand Portuguese settlers in Brazil. By 1600 the number had risen to twenty-five thousand. By the middle of the seventeenth century the Portuguese population had probably reached fifty thousand.

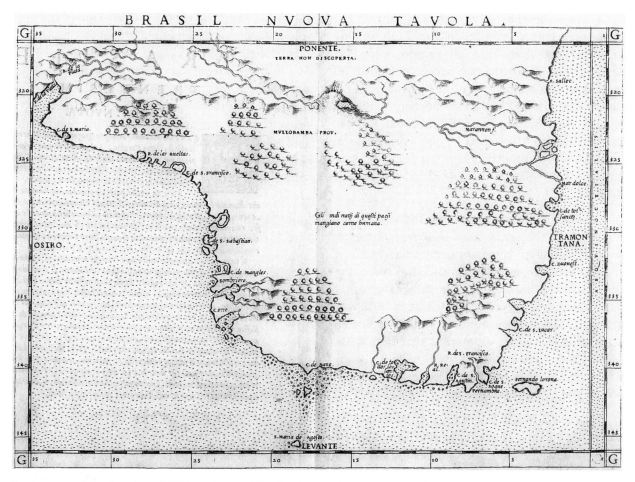

Portuguese Colonies: Brazil. This small map of Brazil, oriented with north to the right, first appeared in Girolamo Ruscelli's edition of Ptolemy's *Geographia,* published in Venice in 1561. The map shows the area not long after its discovery by the Portuguese navigator Pedro Cabral, who was blown off course while on a voyage around Africa to India in 1500. Since Brazil lay within the area allocated to Portugal by the Treaty of Tordesillas, it was promptly claimed by the crown. MAP COLLECTION, STERLING MEMORIAL LIBRARY, YALE UNIVERSITY

In 1551 Portuguese America's first bishopric also was established in Bahia. It remained Portuguese America's only diocese until 1676–1677, when three new dioceses—Rio de Janeiro, Olinda, and Maranhão—were created and Bahia was raised to the status of an archdiocese. In the eighteenth century another three dioceses were created: Pará (1719), Mariana (1745), and São Paulo (1745). Though these dioceses had parish priests under their jurisdictions, members of the regular orders probably played a more important role in Brazil's religious life. The Jesuits, who began arriving in 1549, were the most important order until their expulsion in 1759. Franciscans, Benedictines, and Carmelites also played important roles beginning in the late sixteenth century. In the seventeenth cen-

tury they were joined by the Capuchins, Mercedarians, and Oratorians. Because of crown prohibitions, Brazil was slow in establishing convents for women, the first one not being founded until 1677. A tribunal of the Inquisition was never established in Brazil, though there were visitations in 1591–1595 (Bahia and Pernambuco), 1618 (Bahia), and 1763–1769 (Pará).

In 1549 a chief justice official—the *ouvidor-geral*—was appointed for all of Portuguese America (there were also justice officials for each of the captaincies). It was not until 1609 that judges of Brazil's first High Court *(Relação)* arrived in Brazil's capital. The High Court was disbanded in 1626 but was revived in 1652.

Toward the end of the sixteenth century the most important captaincies in Brazil, ranked by wealth, mostly from sugar production, were Pernambuco and Bahia (the two having more than 80 percent of the wealth). The other captaincies included Itamaracá, Ilhéus, Espírito Santo, Rio de Janeiro, São Vicente, Porto Seguro, and Paraíba. Paraíba had been occupied by the Portuguese in 1584 as they expanded northward from Pernambuco. In 1599 Natal was founded in what became Rio Grande do Norte.

The late sixteenth century and the seventeenth century were the age of sugar in Brazil. The sugar industry required large amounts of capital and credit. One of its greatest demands was labor. Initially American Indians made up the workforce, but they were soon replaced by African slaves, who quickly became the most numerous part of Brazil's population. The best estimate is that during the years 1500–1800 more than 2.5 million African slaves arrived in Portuguese America, 1.7 million during the eighteenth century.

By the middle of the seventeenth century tobacco had become another important crop for local consumption, for export to Europe, and for use in the African slave trade. Cattle raising for food, transportation, and hides was another important part of the colonial Brazilian economy, especially on the various frontier regions.

In 1612 a fort was established in Ceará. By 1615 the French were ousted from Maranhão, and the following year the town of Belém do Pará was founded. In 1621 the state of Maranhão was created. Including Maranhão, Pará, and Ceará, this state was separated from the jurisdiction of the governor general in Bahia, and it remained separate for more than a century and a half. However, the European population remained sparse even into the eighteenth century. The economy depended heavily on Indian labor, and there were frequent clashes between missionaries (especially the Jesuits) and the colonists for such labor. Cacao, which grew wild, became an important product in Pará. Other extractive forest products contributed to the region's economy.

In the meantime, in the south São Paulo, founded in 1554 by the Jesuit Manuel da Nóbrega (1517–1570), became an important center for expansion into land on the Spanish side of the line of the Treaty of Tordesillas (1494). By the seventeenth century *bandeirantes* were radiating from São Paulo, looking for precious minerals or for Amerindians to enslave or both. These *bandeirantes,* or *Paulistas,* pushed southward, reaching the province of Guairá and raiding Spanish Jesuit mission villages. They also pushed westward and northward, following the many tributaries of the Paraná-Paraguay and Amazon River systems.

In 1624 the Dutch captured the city of Bahia and held it for a year before being ousted by a joint Spanish-Portuguese armada. In 1630 the Dutch attacked and captured Recife and Olinda in Pernambuco and gradually expanded southward to Sergipe and northward to Maranhão. However, Brazilian and Portuguese resistance foiled Dutch efforts to establish themselves permanently in Portuguese America. In 1654, with the surrender of Recife, the Dutch presence in Brazil came to an end. Zumbi, head of the runaway slave community of Palmares, south of Pernambuco, was defeated and killed in 1695, bringing an end to almost a century of efforts to destroy the largest refuge of runaway slaves in the Americas.

Though some alluvial gold had been found in the sixteenth and seventeenth centuries, it was not until the early 1690s that major gold discoveries began to be made in what became the captaincy of Minas Gerais. In 1709 the captaincy of São Paulo and Minas Gerais was established in an attempt to bring order to that region and to better collect the crown's share of mining revenues. In 1722 gold was discovered further west in Goiás and Cuiabá. In 1729 diamonds were discovered in Serro do Frio in Minas Gerais, about 150 miles north of the first gold discoveries. The precious stones soon became a royal monopoly. Large numbers of slaves were imported into the mining regions from Africa, and by 1750 Minas Gerais was the most heavily populated captaincy in Portuguese America.

In 1680 Colônia do Sacramento on the east bank of the Río de la Plata was founded. An important center for contraband, it was frequently captured and later returned by Spaniards until it was ceded to them by the Treaty of San Ildefonso in 1777. In 1737 colonization of Rio Grande do Sul was begun. In 1748 the captaincy of Mato Grosso

Portuguese Colonies: Brazil. Panoramic view in Brazil by Jansz Post (1612–1680). NOORTMAN, MAASTRICHT, THE NETHERLANDS/ BRIDGEMAN ART LIBRARY

was created as the Portuguese sought to consolidate territory on what had originally been designated as being on the Spanish side of the line drawn by the Treaty of Tordesillas.

During the years (1750–1777) that the marquês of Pombal, Sebastião José de Carvalho e Mello (1699–1782), was in power as Portugal's chief minister, the remaining captaincies under private control were royalized and absorbed by nearby crown captaincies. Brazil's second High Court (*Relação*) was established in Rio de Janeiro (1751). In 1763 the capital of Portuguese America was moved to Rio de Janeiro, and Brazil was raised to the status of a viceroyalty. The captaincy of São José do Rio Negro was founded in 1755. In the early 1770s the state of Grão Pará and Maranhão was incorporated into the state of Brazil, and in 1772 Brazil was divided into nine captaincy generals, some of them with subordinate captaincies.

Estimates of Brazil's population by the end of the eighteenth century vary greatly. An oft-cited statistic points to approximately 1 million whites,

1.5 million slaves, 400,000 free persons of African heritage, and several hundred thousand Brazilian Indians. Subsequent studies, however, suggest lower figures. What is clear, however, is that Brazil's population increased significantly during the last half of the eighteenth century.

See also **Portugal.**

BIBLIOGRAPHY

Alden, Dauril. *Royal Government in Colonial Brazil, with Special Reference to the Administration of the Marquis of Lavradio, Viceroy, 1769–1779.* Berkeley, Los Angeles, and London, 1968.

Bethell, Leslie, ed. *Colonial Brazil.* Cambridge, U.K., 1987.

Boxer, C. R. *The Golden Age of Brazil, 1695–1750: Growing Pains of a Colonial Society.* Berkeley, Los Angeles, and London, 1962.

———. *Salvador de Sá and the Struggle for Brazil and Angola, 1602–1686.* London, 1952.

Diffie, Bailey W. *History of Colonial Brazil, 1500–1792.* Malabar, Fla., 1987.

Schwartz, Stuart B. *Sovereignty and Society in Colonial Brazil: The High Court of Bahia and Its Judges, 1609–1751.* Berkeley, Los Angeles, and London, 1973.

———. *Sugar Plantations in the Formation of Brazilian Society: Bahia, 1550–1835.* Cambridge, U.K., 1985.

FRANCIS A. DUTRA

THE INDIAN OCEAN AND ASIA

The Portuguese Asian Empire, known as the Estado da India, extended over the entire Indian Ocean littoral and well beyond it into the South China Sea. The Portuguese arrived in Asian waters in 1498 and established a series of islands and enclaves connected by maritime links to each other and to Goa, its administrative and religious center and largest city. This string of outposts and cities stretched from Mozambique Island, north along the African coast to Mombasa, farther north to Hormuz and Muscat, east to Diu and Daman in modern Gujarat, south to Bombay Island, Goa, Cochin, most of coastal Sri Lanka, across the Indian Ocean to Malacca, and beyond to Timor and Macau. Macau was the second city in this system.

FUNCTION AND INTERACTION

These critical outposts were positioned to maximize Portuguese control of Indian Ocean trade and direct it to areas for taxation. The idea was to tax the ancient and well-established Indian Ocean trade in goods such as rice, cotton textiles, horses, silks, and spices via a system of Portuguese-issued passes, called *cartazes.* Because the system depended on maritime strength to enforce it, it was only partially successful at best and only during its first century, from around 1520 to 1620.

Because of the tremendous distances and the loosely structured and fragmented nature of this empire, each area under Portuguese control developed local economic and social strategies to survive, if not prosper. These, in turn, shaped Portuguese activities in each region of the Estado da India, making it difficult to generalize about the empire as a whole. On Mozambique Island, the Portuguese developed a dense urban area trading in slaves, ivory, and gold. On the African mainland nearby, in the Zambezi River Valley, the Portuguese crown established land grants (known as *prazos*) based on matrilineal inheritance. In Mombasa, the Portu-

guese built the massive Fort Jesus and attempted to dominate the maritime trade along the Swahili coast. In Ethiopia, the Portuguese first made contact in 1541 and attempted to forge an alliance with this Christian kingdom, but were expelled in 1634. Muscat and Hormuz were fortified outposts intended to control the entrance to the Persian Gulf. Diu and Daman were on opposite sides of the Gulf of Cambay and were intended to direct the maritime trade with northern India. Bombay Island and the lands immediately around it were rich farmland, some of the most productive lands in the empire. Goa was a large urban area surrounded by farmlands, and Cochin and Macau were important urban centers. Sri Lanka, especially its coastal areas, was occupied, and revenues from its villages were awarded to a variety of Portuguese in a largely futile effort to colonize the island. Macau directed trade among southern China, Japan, and Southeast Asia and developed into a major city. A couple of smaller islands in what is now Indonesia (Flores, Timor) were reminders of the spices (nutmeg, cloves) that had originally attracted the Portuguese, and later the Dutch, to the region. Some outposts were abandoned or handed over to the Spanish once the demarcation line laid out in the treaty of Tordesillas (1494–1495) was established in Asian waters.

ADMINISTRATION

At the top of the system was the governor or viceroy in Goa. He was advised by councils of finance and state, as well as by justices of the Goan High Court and the powerful town council. Each of the outposts had a captain, and the towns were governed by their councils. Positions in this imperial administration were normally awarded for three years. The church had a parallel administration, with Goa being the seat of the archbishop primate of Asia. Bishops were present in the larger cities such as Cochin and Macau. Priests, both Jesuit and Franciscan, were active throughout the region, although the Jesuits were better known and active in both China and Japan (among other areas). In China they had limited success at conversion, but their scientific knowledge attracted the attention of the emperors. In Japan, they were more successful in converting larger numbers, but their efforts were viewed with alarm and suspicion, leading to their expulsion (as well as that of all Portuguese) from Japan in 1617. The most famous of these early

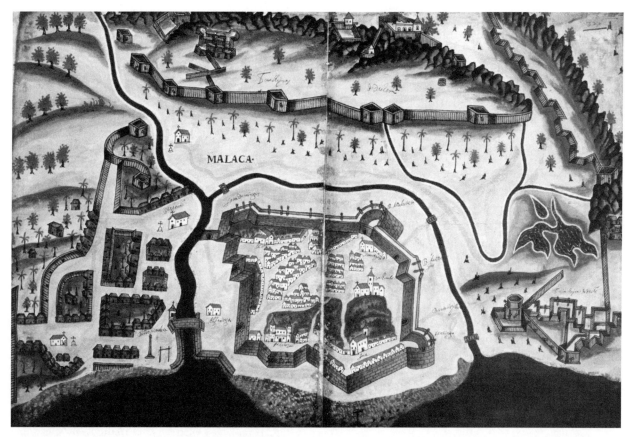

Portuguese Colonies: The Indian Ocean and Asia. Plan of the city of Malacca, c.1511, illustrated by Pedro Barretti de Resende. Strategically located on the Strait of Malacca, the city was a thriving seaport throughout the fifteenth and sixteenth centuries. It was seized by the Portuguese in 1511 but lost to the Dutch in 1641. BRITISH LIBRARY, LONDON, U.K./BRIDGEMAN ART LIBRARY

Jesuits was St. Francis Xavier, who died in Portuguese Asia and was later adopted as the patron saint of Goa, where he was buried.

INFORMAL COMMUNITIES

In addition to the formal regions under their political control, the Portuguese were notable for their ability to establish unofficial communities during this period, especially in South Asia. São Tomé of Meliapor (near modern Madras) and Hughly (near Calcutta) were two such places, but the Portuguese were scattered throughout the area and lived in Agra, Burma, Thailand, Yemen, and elsewhere. In South Asia, many of them were fugitives from Portuguese justice or soldiers seeking better pay or new careers. Elsewhere, many were freelance merchants. Thus, the Portuguese Asian Empire spread beyond simple political control to encompass these communities.

POPULATION

One often-cited figure for the Portuguese population in the Estado da India at its height in the late sixteenth century is 10,000. Because large sections of the archives in Lisbon were damaged in the earthquake and fire of 1755, the exact figure will never be known with certainty. Whatever the figure was, the Portuguese presence was a small fraction of the overall totals. In Goa itself, the Portuguese were rarely more than 2 percent of the population. Women, Portuguese as well as Asian, were a critical component in maintaining this empire around the Indian Ocean. Some Portuguese women, very limited in number, arrived in Asia, but much more common were marriages between Portuguese men and local women. The crown also went to great effort and expense to encourage two major convents for women in Portuguese Asia: Santa Mónica in Goa and Santa Clara in Macau. In addition, there were a number of shelters established with assistance from the crown and local charities (known as the *misericórdia*) to assist orphaned girls and single women, and to reform prostitutes.

LONG-TERM PORTUGUESE INFLUENCES

The survival of these widely scattered outposts throughout the region depended on accommodating local interests through intermarriage and trade. That accommodation, in turn, explains much of the longevity of the Portuguese presence in Asia well after the decline of political or economic power. The missionary activities of the Catholic church in Asia further supported and helped to define the Portuguese in Asia.

Portuguese-speaking Christian African and Asian communities emerged in many of these towns and would act as cultural intermediaries for the Dutch and English who would follow. This was especially true in India, where Luso-Indian communities living near the future cities of Bombay and Madras would be a critical asset for the British administration.

DECLINE

By 1610, Portuguese control was slipping. By the 1640s and 1650s, many of their outposts had been lost to the Dutch (Malacca in 1641, Sri Lanka in 1658, and Cochin in 1662), the English (Hormuz in 1622), the Omanis (Muscat, Mombasa), or other rivals. A parallel struggle with the Dutch in Brazil and Africa drained Portuguese resources and forced the crown in Lisbon to sacrifice much of Portuguese Asia to save Brazil. The recapture of Brazil and the simultaneous loss of Sri Lanka to the Dutch in the years from 1654 to 1658 marked a critical turning point in the history of Portuguese Asia. In 1661, Bombay Island was given to the British as part of Catherine of Braganza's dowry for her marriage to King Charles II. By the late 1600s only Mozambique Island, scattered holdings in the Zambezi River Valley, Diu, Daman, Goa, Macau, and Timor were left of what had been a wealthy and powerful presence throughout the Indian Ocean region.

Portuguese continued to be a language of commerce in Asia well after the decline of Portuguese power, and pockets of Portuguese speakers continued in Sri Lanka and Southeast Asia until the twentieth century. The impact of the Catholic Church was (and remains) widespread in many parts of India and elsewhere in Asia.

See also **Dutch Colonies: East Indies; Goa; Macau.**

BIBLIOGRAPHY

Primary Sources

Lobo, Jerónimo. *The Itinerário of Jerónimo Lobo.* Translated by Donald M. Lockhart. London, 1984.

Pinto, Fernão Mendes. *The Travels of Mendes Pinto.* Translated and edited by Rebecca Katz. Chicago, 1989.

Pires, Tomé. *The Suma Oriental of Tomé Pires, an Account of the East, from the Red Sea to Japan, Written in Malacca and India, 1512–1515.* Edited by Armando Cortesão. London, 1946.

Secondary Sources

Boxer, Charles R. *The Portuguese Seaborne Empire, 1415–1825.* London, 1969. The best single work on the Portuguese Empire, written by the outstanding authority on the subject.

Chaudhuri, K. N. *Trade and Civilisation in the Indian Ocean: An Economic History from the Rise of Islam to 1750.* Cambridge, U.K., 1985. Provides an important overview of the Indian Ocean region, placing Portuguese activities in the broader context.

Coates, Timothy J. *Convicts and Orphans: Forced and State-Sponsored Colonizers in the Portuguese Empire, 1550–1755.* Stanford, 2001.

Silva, Daya da, ed. *The Portuguese in Asia.* Zug, Switzerland, 1987. The indispensable annotated bibliography for study of this region.

Subrahmanyam, Sanjay. *The Portuguese Empire in Asia, 1500–1700: A Political and Economic History.* London and New York, 1993. A solid, modern history of Portuguese Asia.

Winius, George D. *The Fatal History of Portuguese Ceylon: Transition to Dutch Rule.* Cambridge, Mass., 1971.

TIMOTHY J. COATES

MADEIRA AND THE AZORES

The Madeira archipelago, located about 350 miles from the northwest coast of Africa and 520 miles southwest of Portugal itself, consists of the main island of Madeira and a smaller one, Porto Santo, twenty-five miles to the northeast. Though previously known, the islands were uninhabited when claimed by the Portuguese around 1419. The Portuguese began to settle them about 1425. Wood, especially cedar and yew, became important exports, along with such dyes as dragon's blood, orchil, and woad. The rich volcanic soil was made even more fertile by burning much of the tree-covered island. Because Madeira was very mountainous, terraces had to be built. Wheat became an important earlier product. It is estimated that from 1450 to 1470 Madeira was producing 3,000 to 3,500 tons a year. Grapevines were planted, sugar was introduced, and by about 1452 Madeira had its first sugar mill. Soon sugar became the archipelago's main product and was sold throughout Europe. However, by the mid-sixteenth century the sugar boom was beginning to end, and wine gradually replaced it as the island's main export.

Sugar, of course, required a workforce. At first Guanches from the Canaries and Muslim slaves from North Africa were used, followed by black slaves in the aftermath of voyages sponsored by Prince Henry (1394–1460). While sugar was king, the slave portion of the archipelago's population was approximately 10 percent. By the 1460s it was estimated that the Madeiras had two thousand inhabitants. By the early sixteenth century there were twenty thousand people living there, including about two thousand slaves. In the meantime, to encourage colonization, the main island of Madeira was divided into two hereditary lord proprietorships, Funchal and Machico, with extensive administrative, fiscal, and judicial privileges. The island of Porto Santo, with much less water and vegetation, was granted to a third lord proprietor. This lord proprietorship system was introduced to Brazil in the 1530s.

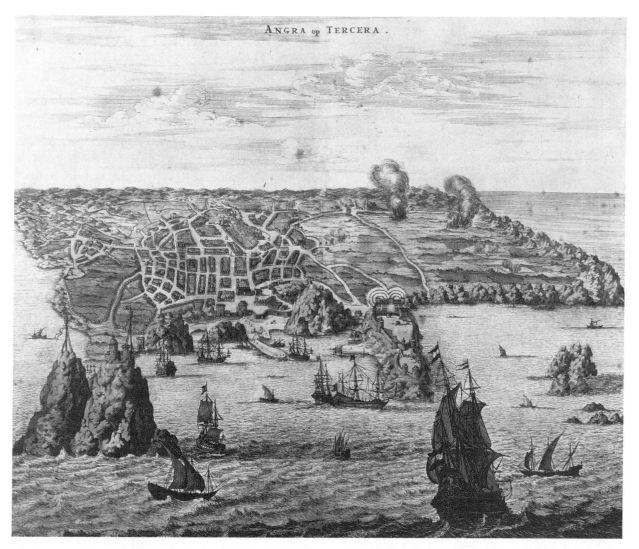

Portuguese Colonies: Madeira and the Azores. View of Angra, also called Tercera, an island in the Azores, seventeenth century. THE ART ARCHIVE/MARINE MUSEUM LISBON/DAGLI ORTI

By the early sixteenth century Funchal, the capital of Madeira, was large enough with five thousand inhabitants to be raised to the dignity of a city (1508). Six years later it became the seat of a diocese (1514) with jurisdiction over all the Portuguese Overseas. During this time the Madeira archipelago continued to be an important way station for ships sailing to and from the Canaries and along the west coast of Africa. By 1676 the population of Madeira reached fifty thousand, with ten thousand residing in Funchal.

The Azores seem to have been discovered in 1427 and were uninhabited. The two most easterly islands (Santa Maria and São Miguel) of the Azorean archipelago are about 840 miles away from Portugal and 420 miles from Madeira. At first animals (especially sheep and goats) were left on the unpopulated islands so that lost or shipwrecked sailors would have food. By 1439 seven islands were known, including the middle group of Terceira, Faial, São Jorge, Pico, and Graciosa, with Terceira seventy-five nautical miles from São Miguel. Finally the two most western islands (Flores and Corvo), located about 1,000 miles from Newfoundland and 375 miles west of Santa Maria, were discovered about 1450 by Diogo de Teive. The lord proprietor approach was also used in the Azores and may have been even more important than in Madeira. Wood and woad were early exports, then wheat became important, though woad and other dyestuffs were major exports until the late seventeenth century. Initial settlement was a slow process, but by the end of the fifteenth century all nine islands in the Azores were populated with settlers from Portugal, Flanders, and the Madeiras. By 1500 there were five towns. By 1550 there were two cities—Angra in Terceira and Ponta Delgada in São Miguel—and twelve towns. In 1534 Angra became the seat of a diocese with jurisdiction over all the Azores.

In 1582 (on São Miguel) and 1583 (on Terceira) the forces of Dom António (1531–1595), prior of Crato and pretender to the Portuguese throne, backed by the French, were defeated by Spain's Alvaro de Bazán (1526–1588), marquis of Santa Cruz. During the Spanish Habsburg period (especially the early years), the Azores were frequently attacked by English, French, and Dutch pirates and corsairs. By 1587 the archipelago had a population of thirty-three thousand, and by 1695

the number of inhabitants was estimated at eighty-five thousand. Throughout the sixteenth, seventeenth, and eighteenth centuries, large numbers of the surplus population of the Azores and the Madeiras migrated to the Portuguese overseas colonies, especially Brazil.

See also **Portugal.**

BIBLIOGRAPHY

Duncan, T. Bentley. *Atlantic Islands: Madeira, the Azores, and the Cape Verdes in Seventeenth-Century Commerce and Navigation.* Chicago and London, 1972.

Oliveira Marques, Antonio Henrique de. *History of Portugal.* 2nd ed. New York, 1976.

FRANCIS A. DUTRA

PORTUGUESE LITERATURE AND LANGUAGE

OCEANIC PERSPECTIVES OF THE PORTUGUESE "SEABORNE EMPIRE"

Portugal contributed to the shaping of early modern Europe through voyages along the West African coast beginning in the mid-fifteenth century and by fulfilling oceanic perspectives implicit in Renaissance maps that depicted the Iberian Peninsula as the "head" of Europe and Portugal as its "face." Under Prince Henry the Navigator (1394–1460) during the late 1400s, African voyages initiated almost two centuries of overseas discoveries and maritime routes that built what historian Charles R. Boxer has termed the "seaborne empire." This vast network of outposts and enclaves, extending from Brazil to Japan, mythologized in the Western imagination by Vasco da Gama's voyage to India (1497–1499) and the voyage of Fernão de Magalhães (more commonly known as Ferdinand Magellan), who in 1519–1521 was the first explorer to circumnavigate the globe, shaped subsequent European literature. What particularly influenced those early writers were encounters with other regions and peoples, the linguistic contacts between Portuguese and indigenous languages, and the very materials and vocabulary of maritime travel and reporting. Portuguese travel literature became a principal source of knowledge, and the nature of that literature in its broadest dimensions would largely determine the form and content of knowledge itself well into the seventeenth century. Oceanic perspectives enlarged the European imagination, transformed the meaning of distance and ideas about the sea, and for the first time placed Europe both in dialogue with and in opposition to other peoples, lands, and cultures. Echoing the title of a book by the historian A. J. R. Russell-Wood, Portuguese was "a language on the move" in Brazil, Africa, and Asia from 1450 to 1640.

Historiographical writings followed models of medieval prose. Chivalric and bucolic prose works evolved into moral and doctrinal allegories or long, sentimental monologues, such as *Diana* (c. 1559), a pastoral fiction by Jorge de Montemor (c. 1520–1561) incorporating intrigue, devices of classical comedy, and bucolic poetry, and *História da Menina e Moça* (1554; Story of the maiden and lass) by Bernardim Ribeiro (1482–1552), a sentimental novel of love and feminine psychology, which relates the tragic love of Binmarder for Aónia and of Avalor for Arima. The narrative cycle *Amadis de Gaula* (1508) and a cycle by Francisco de Morais (c. 1500–1572) called the *Cronica do famoso e muito esforçado cavalleiro palmerim dinglaterra, filho del rey dõ Duardos, Évora,* (1564–1567) continued the vogue of chivalric novels and ideals of gallantry, service to the monarchy, and crusades against Islam.

The variety of literary and dramatic genres increased rapidly as a result of the voyages, encompassing maps, letters, verses, essays, travel diaries, shipwreck accounts, religious theater, ballads, legends, vocabularies, grammars, routes, descriptions, itineraries, documents, designs, blueprints of forts, and portraits of viceroys and governors. Navigational and natural science were represented in travel routes and charts, such as the *Primeiro roteiro da costa da Índia desde Goa até Diu* by D. João de Castro (1538–1539; pub. 1843) and the log of Vasco da Gama's voyage in 1497–1499 (pub. 1838). Garcia da Orta's horticultural treatise, the *Coloquios dos simples, e drogas he cousas mediçinais de India* . . . (pub. 1563; Colloquies on the simples and drugs of India), was the third book printed in Goa. The great mass of religious literature included letters from the religious orders and biographies (for example, *História da vida do Padre Francisco de Xavier* by João de Lucena, 1600).

The oral tradition, consisting of ballads, folk tales, popular and religious verses, aphorisms, riddles, and so forth, spread throughout the empire, at times becoming creolized with the contact languages. The *Cancioneiro geral* (1516; General songbook) compiled by Garcia de Resende (c. 1470–1536) is a collection of poetry by three hundred poets in regional Iberian forms, including *redondilhas, vilancetes,* and *cantigas.* Francisco de Sá de Miranda (1481–1558), who contributed to the *Cancioneiro,* later brought the Italian forms of the *dolce stil nuovo* to Portugal after a prolonged visit to Italy (1521–1526). His poetry—in Spanish and in Portuguese—treats Petrarchan love themes, applying a classical erudition critical of the court and praising the values of rural life. The lyrical works of poet Luís Vaz de Camões (c. 1525–1580) include traditional Iberian forms while perfecting the Italianate forms, particularly his sonnets, which remain among the best-known poems in the Portuguese language.

LINGUISTIC CHANGES: A LANGUAGE ON THE MOVE

The early development of Portuguese historiographical prose, beginning with the vivid chronicles of Fernão Lopes (c. 1380–c. 1460), was decisive in the evolution of the modern Portuguese language, which reached its modern form well before English did. Renaissance grammarians emphasized the close relationship between Portuguese and classical Latin. João de Barros (c. 1496–1570), for example, composed poetry that could be read as either language. During the sixteenth century, Latin dictionaries and grammars were compiled by Estêvão Cavaleiro (1516) and Jerónimo Cardoso (1570), and Portuguese literary language underwent a lexical and syntactical Latinization. The first Portuguese grammars, by Fernão de Oliveira (1536) and Barros (1539), as well as the orthographies by Magalhães de Gândavo (1562) and Duarte Nunes do Leão (1576), demonstrate that the Portuguese language was fully developed by the mid-1500s.

The dissemination of the Portuguese language in Asia and its contact with African and Asian languages has constituted one of the principal topics of research in linguistics. The Portuguese language contributed extensive vocabulary to contact languages in Africa and Asia, also making possible the development of creoles based on Portuguese. Portuguese-related works printed in Asia include grammars, vocabularies, dictionaries, etymologies, glossaries, phrase books, and dialogues. The production of Portuguese grammars and vocabularies in various foreign lands from Brazil to Japan resulted in the creation of comparative linguistics, placing Portuguese alongside indigenous or local languages such as Konkani and Malay, or major languages of Asian cultures such as Tamil, Chinese, or Japanese. Important early works include the *Arte da grammatica da lingoa, mais vsada na costa do Brasil* by José de Anchieta (Coimbra, 1595); *Arte da lingoa canarim* by Tomás Estevão (Rachol, Goa, 1640); *Cartilha . . . em lingoa Tamul e Portugues* by Vicente Nazareth, Jorge Carvalho, and Thomé Cruz (Lisbon, 1554); and the *Arte da lingoa de Iapam* by João Rodrígues, S. J. (Nagasaki, 1604). A trilingual Portuguese-Latin-Japanese dictionary was published at the Jesuit press in Nagasaki before 1600.

The first comprehensive study of the vocabulary that passed from Portuguese to other languages is the *Vocabulário* (1913) by priest and Goan linguist Sebastião Dalgado (1855–1922). In 1919 Dalgado published the *Glossário Luso-Asiático*, in two volumes, in which he registered the terms in Asiatic languages that were absorbed into Portuguese and/or into other European languages. Derived from the study of more than fifty Asiatic languages, Dalgado's work was characterized as a monument of erudition. The bibliography includes more than five hundred works that he consulted on Asia, from sixteenth-century historiographical works to contemporary linguistic studies. The vocables and Anglo-Indian etymologies studied in the glossary of Anglo-Indian expressions by Henry Yule and A. C. Burnell, popularly known as the *Hobson-Jobson* (1886), reveal the extensive and extraordinary penetration of Asiatic Portuguese. The Portuguese language in Brazil quickly incorporated vocabulary from African languages—particularly Yoruba—and Brazil's indigenous Tupi language.

REPORTING TO LISBON: TRAVEL KNOWLEDGE

The celebration in Portugal of the five-hundredth anniversary of the overseas discoveries of Vasco da Gama, which included the publication of a substantial library of primary and secondary texts by the National Commission for the Commemoration of the Portuguese Discoveries, has brought the histori-

cal, literary, and intercultural perspectives of the Portuguese voyages to the forefront of Portuguese society. Sixteenth- and seventeenth-century Portuguese ships and overseas outposts were manned by writers—whether scribes, priests, soldiers, or administrators—who reported to Lisbon or left valuable manuscripts about different areas of knowledge. Travel and knowledge were interrelated, just as writing, languages, cultures, historiography, religion, and early cultural anthropology coexisted in texts, experience, and the imagination of voyagers. Through Portuguese, Europe encountered its "other," exemplified by such "exotic" visitors to Lisbon as indigenous Brazilians, Africans, South Asians, and Japanese, many of whom stayed. Emigration and settlement throughout the far-flung maritime routes created diverse racial, cultural, and linguistic communities; those that have survived in Sri Lanka, Malacca, and Korlai (the Kolaba District in India) are the recent subjects of ethnographic, ethnomusicological, and linguistic studies (by Jackson, Sarkissian, Clements). Contacts with previously unknown geographies, peoples, and cultures brought about by the maritime discoveries had a profound impact on literature, linguistics, and learning. A substantial literary tradition developed in Portuguese India.

Historiography drew on early chronicles of the nation's historical past and its literary traditions to compose epic relations of the voyages, writing characterized by a renewed assimilation and influence of Greco-Latin culture. The voyages to India and the Far East marked the life and works of many of the most prominent intellectuals, clerics, writers, and soldiers of the sixteenth century—Afonso de Albuquerque, Diogo do Couto, Gaspar Correa, Garcia da Orta, Fernão Mendes Pinto, St. Francis Xavier—culminating in the epic poem *Os Lusíadas* (1572; The Lusiads) by Luís Vaz de Camões, who spent seventeen years in Portuguese Asia, as well as Camões's lyrical poetry (including the meditation on exile, "Babel e Sião") and his letters. All incorporated a vision of the Orient and a dimension of personal experience in their works, preserving the impact of the voyages on European writing and anticipating modern currents of orientalism and exoticism in Western literature.

João de Barros, reflecting the range of a Renaissance man of letters, and perhaps influenced by his post in the Casa da India in charge of all commerce arriving from the overseas possessions, planned a monumental project: a geographical, economical, and historical account of Portugal's overseas expansion, to be called the *Décadas da Ásia* (Decades of Asia). He first wrote a chivalric novel, *Crónica do Imperador Clarimundo* (1522), celebrating the genealogy and aristocratic virtues of the heroes of the Portuguese monarchy, then a grammar, *Gramática da língua Portuguesa* (1539) and several moral dialogues, such as the colloquy *Ropica pnefma* (1532; Spiritual merchandise), which are comparable to works by Spanish humanist Juan Luis Vives (1493–1540). In *Ropica pnefma*, Reason defends orthodox doctrine amid the questioning of heretical voices and the calming reflections of Time, Understanding, and Will. Barros is most widely known as the chronicler of Portuguese expansion in Asia in the early sixteenth century. In the four volumes of the *Décadas da Ásia* that he completed (1552–1563), Barros refined the historiographical style that was established by Fernão Lopes in the first half of the fifteenth century and continued by Gomes Eanes de Zurara (c. 1420–c. 1474) and Rui de Pina, by placing this tradition in a broader perspective of regions and continents, linking history to geography, using the heroic and epic frames of classical rhetoric.

Humanist, scholar, and chronicler Damião de Góis (1502–1574) spent twenty-two years outside of Portugal, first as the representative of commercial interests in Antwerp and later as a student in Italy and France, a humanist and friend of Erasmus, and the author of Latin essays on topics including rituals of the faith. On his return to Portugal in 1545 as chief archivist of the Torre do Tombo, Portugal's national archive, Góis was denounced by the Inquisition, before which he defended humanist orthodoxy.

Francisco de Holanda (1517–1584), the son of a Dutch painter in Portugal, studied in Italy, as did Damião de Góis. Trained by his father as an illuminator, Holanda went to Rome in 1538 and became a friend and disciple of Michaelangelo. Holanda wrote a series of essays, *Da pintura Antiga* (1548), the first treatise on painting in the Iberian Peninsula, in which he considered the painter as an original creator, guided by divine inspiration.

Portuguese literature treated the history of the dramatic voyages and documented maritime, commercial, and military life in the empire. India became the center of attention, in the four volumes of *Décadas da Ásia* by Barros and the nine additional volumes by Diogo do Couto (the last one written in 1616); the *História do descobrimento & conquista da Índia pelos Portugueses* (1540) by Fernão Lopes de Castanheda (c. 1500–1559); and the *Chronica do felicissimo Rei Dom Emanuel* (1566–1567) by Damião de Góis, the *Commentarios* (1557) of Afonso de Albuquerque (1453–1515), and numerous works on the conquests of Diu and Goa. The description of lands, peoples, and cultures encountered by the Portuguese produced a literature of its own, including the *Livro das coisas da India* (1510, pub. 1889; an account of the countries bordering on the Indian Ocean) by Duarte Barbosa (1480–1521); the *Lendas da Índia* (1518, pub. 1858; Indian memoranda) by Gaspar Correia (1495–1561), with ink engravings by the author. The Portuguese wrote early descriptions of China (*Tratado das cousas da China* by Gaspar da Cruz, 1569) and were the first Westerners to enter Japan, producing a significant body of historical and descriptive literature (*Relação . . . de Iapam, 1590*), by Father Luís Fróis; writings of João Rodrigues Tçuzzu, S.J.).

Voyage literature included dramatic narratives of shipwrecks, documenting the tragic fate of one-third of the India fleets between 1552 and 1604, which were later collected in the *História trágico-marítima* (pub. 1735). The major prose work of the discoveries is Fernão Mendes Pinto's *Peregrinação* (pub. 1614; The travels of Mendes Pinto), a fantastic first-person account of his travels and adventures throughout Portuguese Asia and one of the most widely read books of the seventeenth century. The constant encounter between the Portuguese narrator and Asians, amounting to an early form of anthropology, enabled the narrator to objectify himself and the Portuguese from the other's critical point of view. Long considered to contain fabrications and intentional exaggerations, the *Peregrinação* has proved to be substantially accurate in the light of recent investigations. The novel contributed to the development of the picaresque or self-conscious hero and to narrative style.

THE MANUELINE STYLE: MANNERISM AND THE "DISCONCERT OF THE WORLD"

Tensions and conflicting perceptions in the Portuguese world, heightened by the establishment of the Inquisition in 1536, promoted the early development of mannerist and baroque qualities in art and literature there, as manifested in the Manueline style, named for Portugal's king Manuel I (ruled 1495–1521). Humanistic and commercial perspectives made possible by the voyages conflicted with an ecclesiastical and orthodox social and religious background. "The Old Man of the Restelo" by Camões (*The Lusiads,* IV, 94–104) and the *Diálogo do soldado prático* (written 1590, published 1790; The experienced soldier) by Diogo do Couto (1542–1616) defended a humanistic outlook, questioning the ethics and the philosophy of a militant mercantile colonial system. In shipwreck narratives, Couto criticized the hubris of officials who threw their slaves and servants into the sea in a vain attempt to save themselves. The contrasts, oppositions, and impasses of this period shape the subsequent early modern development of Portugal. What Camões called the "disconcert of the world" in fact described a new epistemology. Diversity and change made possible new forms of knowledge through cross-cultural contacts in such fields as horticulture, pharmacology, and linguistics, whereas tendencies toward authority, conformity, and centralization dictated exclusion and inquisition. Throughout the maritime empire, satire became an antidote to doctrine and expansiveness to the locus of authority. Among the issues that Portugal faced as part of early modern Europe that remain pertinent today are the policy of miscegenation—promulgated in India in 1510 by Afonso de Albuquerque (1461–1515), which produced mixed-race peoples throughout the Portuguese settlements—and emigration, which has led millions of European Portuguese to the communities spread around the globe today. Portugal granted full citizenship rights throughout its empire, and movement throughout its possessions created one of the first modern global cultures.

Sixteenth-century Portuguese theater featured religious allegories staged on board ship, while court theater drew on popular characters and moral conceits. In the *Comedia eufrosina* (1560) by Jorge Ferreira de Vasconcellos (1515–1585), a letter from Goa was read onstage, representative of many true letters commenting on the vicissitudes of life in India. Gil Vicente (c. 1465–c. 1536) wrote and produced some forty-four plays for the Lisbon court from 1502 to 1536, publishing only a few in chapbooks before the incomplete and defective edition compiled and published in 1562 by his son, who divided them arbitrarily into the categories of devotion, farce, comedy, tragicomedy, and lesser works. Characterized by poetic versatility, complexity, and variety of dramatic structure, Vicente's plays satirize the clergy and nobility, as well as local administrators and artisans. The *Auto da Índia* (1509; Play of India) portrays a soldier's wife who enjoys a free life in his absence, while in the farce *Quem tem farelos?* (1508; Who has bran?) the village girl Inês Pereira tries to change her condition through marriage to a feckless squire. In *Juiz da Beira,* an ignorant, half-mad peasant judges normal people, arriving at decisions that are the reverse of the law and the customs of the day.

António Ferreira (1528–1569) represents the apogee of literary classicism and humanism through his use of Italian poetic forms and his defense of the Portuguese language and historical themes. Ferreira's tragedy *Castro* (1587) dramatizes the assassination in 1355 of Inês de Castro who, as lady-in-waiting to her cousin Constance, began an affair with Constance's betrothed, Prince Peter, secretly married him after Constance died, and had four children with him; she was murdered for political reasons by the advisors of his father, King Alfonso IV. Ferreira recast this story with the classical dialogues and choruses of Greek tragedy.

Camões's epic poem in ten cantos, *The Lusiads* (1572), draws together major conflicting forces in Portugal's Renaissance in one of the classic works of Western literature. The theme is drawn from the history of Portugal, recited by Vasco da Gama during his voyage to India. Gama's voyage becomes the advancing line of present time. Progess depends on intrigues among classical gods who observe the voyage, with Venus as protector of the Portuguese and Bacchus opposed. Action is advanced by magical devices, dreams, and intercession of the gods. The poem's interior episodes of "Inês de Castro," "Adamastor," and the "Island of Venus" carry historical action to a pan-erotic plane, suggesting a journey to paradise through sensual desire. The voyage assumes universality as Tethys (wife of Oceanus) and Gama survey the known and future world of the Portuguese from a mountain peak. Full of observation and prophecy, *The Lusiads* is also a naturalist encyclopedia of unusual phenomena. The poetry is dense in musical rhythm and imagery, recalling the visual richness of naturalist painters such as Albrecht Dürer (1471–1528). Achieving unity through diversity, Camões synthesizes the conflicts of a civilization in which he lived as a soldier-poet in Asia and that he incorporated into the ideals of his poetic art.

BAROQUE: BETWEEN SERMON AND SATIRE

The age and style of the baroque was decisive for Portuguese literature in view of the diversity of social forms, peoples, and styles in the overseas empire, whose intercontinental spaces, according to Portuguese literary historian Óscar Lopes, gave rise to an aesthetics of perspective, movement, color, ornamental profusion, modulation, pomp, and external grandeur. The gold and diamonds discovered in Brazil financed a society of spectacle, whereas the period of Spanish Habsburg rule (1580–1640) provided an incentive for popular satires, reaching an apex in the *Arte de furtar* (fraudulently dated Amsterdam, 1652; Art of thieving), an unmasking of the court of John IV (ruled 1640–1656), and the *Obras do diabinho da Mão Furada,* attributed to António José da Silva, the picaresque portrait of a wandering soldier who is tempted by the devil. A cosmopolitan aristocrat, D. Francisco Manuel de Mello (1608–1666), was one of the most varied and versatile writers of his age, publishing lyrical poetry in Portuguese and Spanish, a narrative of the discovery of Madeira, moral works and guides about the ascetic life and duties of wives, as well as comedies and moral letters. He wrote the first critical review of ancient and modern authors and planned a library of modern authors, which was not produced until the following century. Though imprisoned and exiled to Brazil, he returned to represent Portugal in European diplomatic circles.

António Vieira, S.J. (1609–1697), the greatest figure of the era, born in Lisbon and raised in Bahia, Brazil, from the age of seven, won renown as a writer, rhetorician, Jesuit, and man of action. His sermons, in some twenty volumes, expound a brilliant formal rationalism based on biblical texts, with a tendency toward prophetic and messianic interpretations. He spoke out against the enslavement of indigenous Americans, yet defended the unity of the Portuguese throne and church. Vieira's deft style was the most significant contribution to the Portuguese language since Camões.

Corte na Aldeia (1619) by Francisco Rodrigues Lobo (1580–1622) is the principal work on Portuguese baroque style, giving rise to numerous academies as centers of literary endeavor throughout the seventeenth and eighteenth centuries, as in the Academia dos Singulares (1628). Lively doctrinaire panegyrics and allegorical theater by the nuns Sóror Violante do Ceu and Maria do Céu found their satirical counterpoint in the puppet theater of António José da Silva (1705–1739), who was condemned by the Inquisition to be burned in 1739. The great national literary collections of the baroque period are to be found in the first general Portuguese bibliography, compiled 1741–1759 by Diogo Barbosa Machado (1682–1772), and in two massive poetry anthologies, *A fénix renascida* (1716–1728) and *Postilhão de Apolo* (1761–1762).

ENLIGHTENMENT AND EARTHQUAKE

Struggling for liberalization, Portugal turned from its familiar oceanic perspectives to the "foreign" influences of Europe, engendering a new organization of knowledge and pedagogical reforms that pitted Enlightenment against Scholasticism. The great Lisbon earthquake of 1 November 1755 precipitated a massive reorganization and reconstruction of Portuguese letters and society, symbolized by the expulsion of the Jesuits in 1759 by Joseph I's chief minister, Sebastião José de Carvalho e Melo (1699–1782), better known as the Marquês de Pombal, the de facto ruler of Portugal during that period. The founding of the Arcádia Lusitana in 1756 and the Academia das Ciências in 1779 and the creation of autonomous university chairs throughout the country in 1772 represented principal reforms. *Verdadeiro método de estudar* (1746; True method of study) by Luís António Verney (1713–92; pseudonym Barbadinho), after having been banned by its inclusion on the Holy See's *Index librorum prohibitorum* (List of forbidden books), arrived clandestinely in Lisbon in a new edition in 1751 to promote pedagogical reform. His ideas included grammatical analysis in Portuguese instead of Latin, abandonment of obsolete vocabulary, the study of modern languages, the opening of elementary schools, and the teaching of women. The heroic-comic satires of Nicolau Tolentino (1741–1811) were matched by *Os burros ou, O reinado da Sandice*, a "heroic-comic-satiric poem in six cantos" by José Agostinho de Macedo (1761–1831), and by the burlesque poem *O reino da estupidez* (1819) by Francisco de Mello Franco (1757–1823). *Reflexões sobre a vaidade dos homens* (1752) by Matias Aires (1705–1763) addressed a crisis in sensibility and expressed skepticism about human nature. Arcadist poets, including Pedro Antonio Correia Garção (1724–1772), António Diniz da Cruz e Silva (1731–1799), and Francisco Manoel de Nascimento, better known as Filinto Elísio (1734–1819), preceded the Marquesa de Alorna (1750–1839), a celebrated literary muse in Lisbon during the late 1700s, and Manuel Maria Barbosa du Bocage (1765–1805), a poet-wanderer throughout the empire who initiated the modern current of return to the oceanic past.

See also **Academies, Learned; Authority, Concept of; Camões, Luís Vaz de; Colonialism; Dictionaries and Encyclopedias; Drama: Spanish and Portuguese; Europe and the World; Exploration; Gama, Vasco da; Index of Prohibited Books; Inquisition; Jews, Expulsion of (Spain, Portugal); Magellan, Ferdinand; Missions and Missionaries; Portugal; Portuguese Colonies: The Indian Ocean and Asia; Scholasticism; Travel and Travel Literature.**

BIBLIOGRAPHY

Alden, Dauril. *The Making of an Enterprise: The Society of Jesus in Portugal, Its Empire, and Beyond, 1540–1750.* Stanford, 1996.

Anselmo, António Joaquim. *Bibliografia das obras impressas em Portugal no século XVI.* Lisbon, 1926.

Bleiberg, Germán, Maureen Ihrie, and Janet Pérez, eds. *Dictionary of the Literature of the Iberian Peninsula.* Westport, Conn., and London, 1993.

Boxer, Charles R. *The Christian Century in Japan, 1549–1650.* Berkeley, 1951.

———. *João de Barros, Portuguese Humanist and Historian of Asia.* New Delhi, 1981.

———. *The Portuguese Seaborne Empire, 1415–1825.* London, 1969.

Camões, Luís de. *The Lusiads.* Translated with an introduction and notes by Landeg White. Oxford and New York, 1997.

Cooper, Michael S. J. *Rodrigues the Interpreter: An Early Jesuit in Japan and China.* New York and Tokyo, 1974.

Diffie, Bailey W., and George D. Winius. *Foundations of the Portuguese Empire, 1415–1580.* Minneapolis, 1977.

Hart, Henry H. *Luis de Camoëns and the Epic of the Lusiads.* Norman, Okla., 1962.

Hirsch, Elisabeth Feist. *Damião de Góis: The Life and Thought of a Portuguese Humanist, 1502–1574.* The Hague, 1967.

Maxwell, Kenneth. *Pombal, Paradox of the Enlightenment.* Cambridge, U.K., and New York, 1995.

Pinto, Fernão Mendes. *The Travels of Mendes Pinto.* Edited and translated by Rebecca D. Catz. Chicago, 1989.

Russell-Wood, A. J. R. *A World on the Move: The Portuguese in Africa, Asia, and America, 1415–1808.* Manchester, U.K., 1992.

Saraiva, António José, and Óscar Lopes. *História da Literatura Portuguesa.* 17th ed. Porto, 1996.

K. DAVID JACKSON

POSTAL SERVICE. *See* Postal Systems; Communication and Transportation.

POSTAL SYSTEMS. The communications revolution of the early modern period was the result of the first reliable infrastructure of communication introduced at the beginning of the sixteenth century in central Europe. Postal systems were basically systems of portioning the space to create reliable channels of communication. In Renaissance Italy, where messenger systems were developed further than anywhere else in Europe in the late Middle Ages, some princes started experimenting with a division of labor known only from ancient literature or from Marco Polo's (1254–1324) report on China: couriers on horses that changed at regular intervals at fixed points, the posts, and followed fixed courses. However, postal lines were expensive and remained unstable. The most frequent data comes from the wealthier territory of Italy, the duchy of Milan under the Visconti. Milanese *corrieri* seem to have spread the art of effectively transporting information, first throughout Italy (Venice, the papal states) and subsequently throughout Europe. The lingua franca of European communications remained Italian well into the seventeenth century, and some Italian terms (*posta, paccheto, franco, porto*) survive in many languages in the twenty-first century.

PUBLIC ACCESS

The decisive change came when Emperor Maximilian I (German king from 1486, Holy Roman emperor 1493–1519) commissioned the Taxis (or Tassis) family with establishing an effective communication system for the Habsburg dynasty. This proved to be a major challenge because of the far-flung Habsburg marriage associations. Maximilian married Mary of Burgundy (1457–1482), his son Philip I of Castile (ruled 1506) married the heiress of Castile and Aragón, and Maximilian's grandson Charles of Spain (king of Spain 1516–1556; emperor as Charles V 1519–1556) ruled over large parts of Europe from the Netherlands to Sicily with close links to the Austrian Habsburgs who had inherited Hungary and Bohemia.

Unlike in ancient Rome or China, no European ruler was able or willing to finance his or her own postal system. This tension between an obvious demand and a fragile budget was exploited by Francesco de Tassis (1459–1519), by then the head of the northern branch of the Taxis family from Cornello in Lombardy. This family had gained experience in the Milanese and Venetian courier business, the Roman branch actually running the papal messenger system. Francesco de Tassis managed to escape the control of the imperial administration by forging a link to Burgundy (1501) and turning the postal system into a private enterprise based upon a contract among the Taxis company and Burgundy (1505) and Spain (1516).

Unlike in France or England, from then on the postmasters—not the states—were in control of the channels of communication in central Europe and large parts of Italy. The decisive innovations took place there, most importantly that permanent post courses were established around 1510, the service was opened to the public, and periodical post riders were established in 1534 between Antwerp and Venice and three years later between Venice and Rome. The postal systems in Italy, Germany, France, England, and Spain were open to travel as soon as post houses, mostly existing taverns, were fixed. But only within the Holy Roman Empire was the postal system open to the general public. Everybody was entitled to use the post not by privilege but by paying a fee, the *porto*. The post houses, previously only places to change horses, were opened to the public as well and became post offices, where mail, checks, or samples could be dispatched and collected. The postal lines thus became the veins of early capitalism. William Harvey (1578–1657), discoverer of the circulation of the blood, was the son of a postmaster.

Public access to these channels of communication triggered a series of innovations. Within a few years it revolutionized the daily routines of the educated, whose habit it became to use the post, according to its set schedule, for regular correspondence. Public access changed the terms of trade, diplomacy, and politics. From the 1560s weekly written reports were commissioned by princes and leading trading companies, like the Fugger business (collecting, for example, the *Fugger Newsletters*), and commercial newsagents and even news agencies emerged in the imperial city of Augsburg, which lay at the heart of the European postal system, midway between Antwerp and Venice. From the early 1580s these weekly reports were published as newsbooks for the book fairs in Frankfurt and Leipzig (in books called *Messrelationen*). In 1597 a newsagent failed in publishing a monthly newspaper. But in September 1605 Johann Carolus, a newsagent who had become a printer in the imperial city of Strasbourg, succeeded in establishing a weekly newspaper. Both Carolus's *Relation* as well as the second newspaper, the *Wolfenbüttel Aviso* (1609), depended on news from Augsburg delivered by the ordinary post riders of the imperial post.

The invention of the periodical press, a media revolution of prime importance, was thus part of a more general communications revolution. From about 1615 the media revolution gathered momentum, and newspapers were established in a good number of towns within the Holy Roman Empire, some in fact edited by postmasters directly. In 1618, when three publishers were already competing in the imperial city of Frankfurt, this innovation was adopted in the Netherlands. In 1622, presumably not by chance the very year a reliable postal service between Brussels and London was established, the first newspaper attempts started in England, largely depending on news reports from the Continent. Austria and Switzerland followed in 1622, France in 1631, Italy (Florence) in 1636, Sweden in 1645, and Spain and Poland 1661. Only after the collapse of the Licensing Act in 1642 did London become a news capital.

IMPROVED TRANSPORTATION

During the Thirty Years' War (1618–1648) the postal systems of France and England were opened to the general public, and postal networks were introduced in Scandinavia. Around 1630 France succeeded in creating an advanced postal network. The introduction of mail coaches instead of postal riders on all post courses triggered a series of spin-off benefits, such as official printed timetables and the first map indicating existing travel facilities.

Nicolas Sanson's map of 1632 provided the cartographic prototype for scores of postal maps, which were replaced only in the nineteenth century by rail maps and road maps. By 1700 postal maps existed for all European countries and for Europe as a whole, and they offer important insights into the kinds of infrastructures established in different countries. Clearly the postal networks in Italy, Spain, Austria, and Poland had stagnated, whereas in England, France, Belgium, and Germany densely woven networks signaled continuous improvement.

By 1750 European travelers admired the communications system of Britain, although stagecoaches were still run by private haulers and mail coaches were only introduced in 1784. However, the trusts of haulers and innkeepers functioned in a manner not dissimilar to the postal systems of the Continent. Not hampered by the transport of mail, the velocity of British stagecoaches was indeed higher, and new types of coaches were developed, owing to the achievements of the turnpike system of road construction. In contrast to riders, coaches required artificial roads, and systematic road construction was a necessary consequence of the introduction of mail coaches. The post office usually negotiated the building of roads and bridges, and in many countries postmasters were indeed employed as overseers of the roads.

By 1800 the postal networks represented fairly well the progress of industrialization in western Europe, followed by the American East Coast. However, eastern Europe was still undeveloped, and southern Europe had fallen behind. Postal systems also mirrored political structures. The networks in Britain and France were rigorously centralized in the capitals, whereas Belgium, Germany, Italy, and Switzerland were characterized by a more evenly distributed network. Absolutist territories within the Holy Roman Empire, such as Prussia, reveal a centralized pattern also. At the end of the era, postal systems had reached the maximum of their capabilities in western Europe, with seven hundred mail coaches and thirty-three hundred stagecoaches serving in England alone. Clearly the subsequent railway networks were modeled after the postal networks and replaced coaches on the main routes in transporting mail and passengers. This, however, did not mean the end of the mail coaches. The number of mail coaches even rose, since all the rail lines needed reliable suppliers or shuttles. Railways and steamships became parts of the postal systems. However, the importance of the postal systems as institutions declined sharply. Once the universal means of communication, for travel as well as money and letters, the systems' functions disintegrated with the introduction of novel networks, such as telegraphy, railways, telephones, and later cars with motor engines. From about 1850 post offices merely bore the name of the formerly universal institution that had ceased to exist.

The early modern postal system was a reliable medium of communication that triggered a series of media revolutions. The scientific revolution, the industrial revolution, and the political revolutions in England, France, and America took place in the era of the early modern postal systems. The early modern period was a distinctive era in the history of communications molded by the particularities of its communications systems. If one adopts the notion of a communications revolution, one can explain the pattern of all subsequent changes in communication, even to the twenty-first century. The early modern postal systems represented a first universal Internet. Borrowing from Immanuel Wallerstein's description of a "European World System," the early modern postal system could be seen as the grandmother of the World Wide Web.

See also **Communication and Transportation; Industrial Revolution; Industry; Journalism, Newspapers, and Newssheets; Scientific Revolution.**

BIBLIOGRAPHY

Albion, Robert G. "The Communication Revolution." *American Historical Review* 37 (1932): 718–720.

Arbellot, Guy. *Autour des routes de poste: Les premières cartes routières de la France, XVIIe–XIXe siècle.* Paris, 1992.

Beale, Philip. *A History of the Post in England from the Romans to the Stuarts.* London, 1998.

Behringer, Wolfgang. *Im Zeichen des Merkur: Reichspost und Kommunikationsrevolution in der frühen Neuzeit.* Göttingen, 2003.

———. *Thurn und Taxis: Die Geschichte ihrer Post und ihrer Unternehmen.* Munich, 1990.

John, Richard R. *Spreading the News: The American Postal System from Franklin to Morse.* Cambridge, Mass., 1995.

WOLFGANG BEHRINGER

POTOSÍ. Potosí was a city and a region in Upper Peru (modern Bolivia) and was the most celebrated mining district in colonial Spanish America. With the discovery of silver at the Cerro Rico (Rich Hill) in 1545, Spaniards and Andeans rushed to exploit the fabulously rich ores, and the city of Potosí grew.

The first boom ended around 1560 with exhaustion of the rich surface ores that could be refined with indigenous smelting ovens (*guayras*). The next, from the mid-1570s until the early 1600s, began with the introduction of amalgamation, a new technology capable of profitably refining lower-grade ores. Official annual output reached 7 million ounces, and contraband refining added to that. *Vale un Potosí* ("It's worth a Potosí") came to mean something priceless.

To compensate refiners for the cost of underground mining, mills to pulverize ore, and mercury for amalgamation, in 1573 Viceroy Francisco de Toledo adapted the Inca system called *mita* of rotating forced indigenous labor, to provide workers for the mines. It provided Potosí with as many as 13,400 low-paid *corvée* workers per year. Mita workers probably made up half the labor force, with free laborers the remainder. Work at Potosí was dangerous and unhealthy, and the mita disrupted life in indigenous communities.

Despite its altitude, which made it necessary to import basic necessities and luxuries alike, Potosí had more than 100,000 inhabitants by 1600. As silver output declined after 1620 with depletion of its best ores, Potosí's population dropped. After the crown halved the mining tax to a tenth, Potosí experienced a modest revival in the mid-1700s, but it only had 10,000 residents by the end of the colonial period.

Potosí. The title page of a book printed by Richard Ihones in London, 1581, featuring a woodcut of Potosí. ©BETTMANN/CORBIS

Nonetheless, Potosí epitomized the grandeur and brutality of Spain's colonial system. Its silver subsidized Spanish imperialism and helped monetarize the European and world economies.

See also **Coins and Medals; Colonialism; Exploration; Pizarro Brothers; Spanish Colonies: Peru.**

BIBLIOGRAPHY

Bakewell, Peter J. *Miners of the Red Mountain: Indian Labor in Potosí, 1545–1650.* Albuquerque, 1984. Excellent analysis of technological and economic aspects of silver production, as well the *mita* and free labor.

Tandeter, Enrique. *Coercion and Market: Silver Mining in Colonial Potosí, 1692–1826.* Albuquerque, 1993. Traces the crown's attempt to reverse Potosí's decline.

KENDALL W. BROWN

POTTERY. *See* **Ceramics, Pottery, and Porcelain.**

POUSSIN, NICOLAS (1594–1665),

French painter. Poussin is one of the artists most beloved by art historians because his slow but steadily developing talent, combined with his passion for historical accuracy and his reflections concerning the nature and practice of the art of painting that have been extracted from his letters and the comments of others produced profound and beautiful works that rapidly became models for those who followed. Giovanni Pietro Bellori (c. 1615–1696), the esteemed Roman biographer of seventeenth-century Italian painters who thought so highly of Poussin that he (exceptionally) included a study of his life among the Italians, noted that "... his words were very serious, and were listened to attentively; he often talked about art, and with such great knowledge that not only painters, but everyone with a cultivated spirit came to learn from his lips the highest meanings of painting. ...."

Poussin was convinced that he wanted to study painting when Quentin Varin visited his native Les Andelys in 1612. He trained with Georges Lallemant in Paris, and during the early 1620s began his first journey to Rome—a trip that was aborted due to ill health after Poussin reached Florence. He made a second and successful attempt via Venice in the spring of 1624 in the company of the poet Giambattista Marino, who was returning to Italy after a visit to the French capital. Upon their arrival in Rome, Marino introduced Poussin to Cardinal Francesco Barberini and his circle. Poussin soon received a commission from one of the cardinal's most distinguished retainers, the antiquarian Cassiano dal Pozzo, to make drawings after the antique for his celebrated Museo Cartaceo ("Paper Museum"). Cassiano could not have found a better candidate for the task, for investigation of this type of ancient detail would remain important to Poussin throughout his career. Except for a return to Paris for two years (1640–1642), forced upon him by Louis XIII of France and his prime minister, Cardinal Richelieu, Poussin, like his countryman Claude Lorrain, remained in the Eternal City for the rest of his life.

Poussin established his reputation in Rome with his splendid *Death of Germanicus* painted for Barberini in 1627 and delivered in January of 1628 (Minneapolis Institute of Arts), in which the figures are arranged in a frieze-like pattern across the canvas around the draped bed of the dying hero in a spartan, but palatial, interior. By their gestures and expressions it is clear that each of the protagonists is either overwhelmed with grief, overcome with shock, or angrily proclaiming his forthcoming revenge. The historically researched costumes saturated with blues, reds, and yellows reflect the artist's early attachment to Venetian coloring. The enormous success of this canvas led to the distinction of Poussin's receipt of a papal commission for St. Peter's, for which he painted his magnificent *Martyrdom of St. Erasmus* of 1629 (Pinacoteca Vaticana, Rome). After losing the commission to decorate a chapel in San Luigi dei Francesi, the French church in Rome, Poussin abandoned his ambitions to paint grand decorations and turned instead to smaller cabinet pictures, which he continued to produce for a limited number of amateurs in Rome and abroad for the rest of his career.

LATER LIFE AND INFLUENCE

During the 1630s, influenced by an interest in Stoicism, Poussin became increasingly attached to an ascetic way of life and a rigorously disciplined, central Italian approach to art and art theory. These tendencies reveal themselves in his work, where, eschewing the attraction of north Italianate *colore* evident in varying degrees in his earlier Italian works, he turned to a more sober and refined form of classicism that became increasingly distilled and cerebral throughout his maturity. This can be seen at its best in his series of bacchanals commissioned by Cardinal Richelieu (London and Kansas City, Mo.), a series of Seven Sacraments commissioned by Cassiano (Washington, D.C., and Belvoir Castle, Leicester), and in the static and imposing *Miracle of St. Francis Xavier* of 1641 commissioned by François Sublet de Noyers, Surintendant des batiments du roi, for the main altar of the new novitiate of the Jesuits in Paris (Musée du Louvre).

In order to construct his progressively classical compositions in the 1640s, Poussin relied heavily on his skills as a draftsman. As the renowned Poussin scholar Anthony Blunt has noted, Poussin's drawing developed consistently, gaining in expressive power what it lost in elegance and culminating in an elliptical manner appropriate to the poetic and philosophic tone of his later works. Poussin's *Moses*

Nicolas Poussin. *The Poet's Inspiration.* THE ART ARCHIVE/MUSÉE DU LOUVRE PARIS/DAGLI ORTI

and the Daughters of Jethro of c. 1647 (Fogg Art Museum, Harvard University), the final design in a series of studies executed over more than a decade for a lost painting, provides a perfect example of how his exacting and protracted process generated compositions that accentuated the salient didactic elements of a theme with a masterful economy of means. Here, in another frieze-like design, is a counterbalance between the columnar females on the left and the men in the disarray of battle on the right, underscored by the solid architecture on the left and the violent sky and terrain on the right. The careful juxtaposition of wash and blank portions of the sheet to construct their volumes reveals the results of the artist's continued use of props on a

miniature stage of his own construction for the study of physical expression, as well as light and shade. The gestures of the figures not only link the two groups and allow the viewer to read the action across the sheet, they also heighten the integrity of the scene by moving into the third dimension as each of these motions is echoed visually in the planes of the undulating landscape beyond.

Subjects like Poussin's *Infant Bacchus Entrusted to the Nymphs of Nysa* and the *Death of Echo and Narcissus* of 1657 (Fogg Art Museum), commissioned by his close friend, the painter Jacques Stella—a conflation of stories from Ovid's *Metamorphoses,* Philostratus' *Imagines,* and later studies of these texts in a dense allegory that contrasts fertility and sterility—suggest his study of antique literature. Poussin's late landscapes, such as *Autumn* from the series *Four Seasons* of c. 1662 (Musée du Louvre) demonstrate his significant contribution to the classical mode of this genre. Although he clearly benefited from the study of the elements of landscape in the Roman countryside with Claude and others earlier in his career, the disciplined structure of Poussin's stoic vision of nature is markedly different from the sumptuous, pastoral, and idyllic classicism of his fellow expatriate.

The significance of Poussin's processes and achievements are such that it is possible to argue that he became the most influential French painter in history. His name is, indeed, synonymous with French classicism. His art and theories formed the doctrinal foundation of the new Académie, which he declined the offer to direct, and artists from Charles Le Brun and Jacques-Louis David in the seventeenth and eighteenth centuries to Jean-Auguste-Dominique Ingres, Hilaire Germain Edgar Degas, Paul Cézanne, and Pablo Picasso in the nineteenth and twentieth centuries have been compelled to confront his works and thoughts in order to produce a response of their own.

See also **Art: Art Theory, Criticism, and Historiography; Classicism; Claude Lorrain (Gellée); David, Jacques-Louis; Le Brun, Charles; Painting; Rome, Art in.**

BIBLIOGRAPHY

Blunt, Anthony. *The Drawings of Poussin.* New Haven and London, 1979.

———. *Nicolas Poussin.* 2 vols. Bollingen series: 35. Washington, D.C., 1967.

———. *The Paintings of Nicolas Poussin: A Critical Catalogue.* 2 vols. London, 1966.

Bonfait, Olivier, and Jean-Claude Boyer. *Intorno a Poussin: Ideale classico e epopea barocca tra Parigi e Roma.* Exh. cat. Rome, 2000.

Chastel, André, ed. *Nicolas Poussin.* 2 vols. Paris, 1960.

Chomer, Gilles, et al. *Autour de Poussin.* Exh. cat. Paris, 1994.

Cropper, Elizabeth, and Charles Dempsey. *Nicolas Poussin: Friendship and the Love of Painting.* Princeton, 1996.

Fumaroli, Marc. *L'inspiration du poète de Poussin: Essai sur l'allégorie du Parnasse.* Exh. cat. Paris, 1989.

Lagerlöf, Margaretha Rossholm. *Ideal Landscape: Annibale Carracci, Nicolas Poussin, and Claude Lorrain.* New Haven and London, 1990.

Mahon, Denis. "Poussiniana: Afterthoughts Arising from the Exhibition." *Gazette des beaux-arts* 1962 (special issue): 1–138.

Mérot, Alain. *Nicolas Poussin.* New York, 1990.

Rosenberg, Pierre, and Louis-Antoine Prat. *Nicolas Poussin, 1594–1665.* Paris, 1994.

———. *Nicolas Poussin, 1594–1665: Catalogue raisonné des dessins.* Milan, 1994.

Thuillier, Jacques. *Nicolas Poussin.* Paris, 1994.

———. *Poussin before Rome.* Exh. cat. London, 1995.

Verdi, Richard. *Cézanne and Poussin: The Classical Vision of Landscape.* Exh. cat. London, 1990.

Wright, Christopher. *Poussin Paintings: A Catalogue Raisonné.* London, 1984.

ALVIN L. CLARK, JR.

POVERTY. Poverty in early modern Europe was not well understood—at least outside of the biblical conception that the poor will always be with us—and the extent of poverty in the centuries leading up to the industrial revolution has not been well mapped—not by historians, and certainly not by the contemporaries who were confronted by the hungry and diseased, the homeless and fatherless, on their doorsteps. Yet there can be no doubt that both the threat and the reality of poverty were pervasive throughout the early modern period.

The material and spiritual needs of the poor were the subject of endless clerical rumination, which sometimes resulted in actual assistance. The needs of the poor likewise merited the extensive practical consideration of urban magistrates and rural nobility alike, whose best interests often dictated that they do something to lessen, or at least justify, the suffering that they saw around them. Poverty generated responses from the poor ranging from quiet acquiescence and submission to the mercy of God to the violent or coercive appropriation of resources, with a host of possibilities in between. One clear marker of the poor was the need to engage in behaviors intended to ward off hunger, cold, nakedness, or other material deprivation. It is not surprising, therefore, that when historians try to count the poor in early modern Europe, they inevitably begin with the lists of those who applied for and received charity: those who professed in the criminal court records that they turned to theft or prostitution out of desperation; those who sought exemption from the payment of taxes and dues; and those caught participating in bread riots, or myriad other activities located firmly in what historians have to come to refer to as "the economy of makeshifts."

TOWARD A DEFINITION

Any attempt to determine the number of poor in early modern Europe presumes that there exists a clear definition of poverty as well as widely agreed upon indicators of its extent and severity. This is not the case. At the most basic level, the poor were best defined by what they were not. Thus, in early modern Europe poverty could be characterized as the antithetical state either to that of being rich (the most common modern understanding) or that of being powerful (the more typical medieval conception). While power and wealth often travel together, they need not necessarily do so. Certainly the processes of commercialization and urbanization begun in the High Middle Ages and accelerated in the sixteenth and seventeenth centuries, concomitant with the expansion of capitalist economic attitudes and behaviors, worked to increase the importance of money, thereby giving the pecuniary definition of poverty greater cultural resonance over time. But the conflation of the poor with the weak persisted.

This lingering medieval resonance was facilitated in large part by the ongoing influence of the biblical categories of the poor, which consisted especially of widows, orphans, prisoners, and the disabled. All of these groups, which we might now classify as the "structural poor," were likely to suffer from limited resources as well as wielding little political or social power. They are marked by their dependence on others (notably male, be they husbands, fathers, law enforcers, or doctors) for food and shelter, as well as for protection. And it was precisely this dependence that marked them as "deserving"; that is, worthy of receiving the love (caritas) of the community as manifested in material aid. The undeserving poor, by contrast, were believed to be those who were capable of work but who out of laziness or sheer malice refused to earn their own keep. To aid them was not only counterproductive to the health of the economic and social order, it was in fact a sin, and harmful to the soul of both giver and recipient. If the giving of aid indis-

criminately was ever practiced in the medieval past (the evidence is mixed), it was certainly no longer tolerated in the early modern period either by intellectuals or bureaucrats.

This is not to say, however, that exceptions were not made to the biblical rule that the able-bodied who do not work do not eat. Other categories of legitimated poor existed alongside those structurally dependent groups identified in the Bible. The most important of these were the voluntary poor, the shamefaced poor, and what we might now refer to as the cyclical poor. The voluntary poor were those individuals, usually acting in the context of well-established organizations or societies, who had renounced material comforts in favor of a life of humiliation following Christ. The most important of these groups were the mendicant monastic orders that came to prominence in the milieu of urban economic prosperity during the High Middle Ages, most notably the Franciscans and the Dominicans. Their renunciation of material possessions was supposed to be so complete that the only way individual friars could survive was to beg for their bread while they traveled about preaching to souls. The mendicant orders were the subject of heated debates about the spiritual legitimacy of their mission and the social impact of their method, both at the time of their establishment and in the context of the Reformation. Nonetheless, they survived, and even flourished in some parts of Catholic Europe following the Tridentine reforms, remaining an important part of the charitable landscape of early modern Europe.

A less contentious exception to the biblical rule that those who do not work do not eat were the so-called shamefaced poor. This group consisted of members of the ancient nobility who had fallen on hard times economically and could no longer afford the style of life that they were expected to maintain. In truly dire cases they could no longer afford even to support themselves at the margin of subsistence. The source of their distress was often a combination of overspending and the concomitant loss of family land, or the declining profitability of its exploitation by tenant farmers or wage laborers. Because the very definition of nobility precluded members of noble families from working their own land or marshaling their remaining resources to a trade or business, their impoverished condition could only be alleviated by the charitable assistance of others. Moreover, such aid had to be dispensed with discretion in order to avoid any further embarrassment being heaped on the families concerned. In a world in which work was expected of all who were physically able, the shamefaced poor make for an odd exception from the modern perspective. For here was a group whose members were denied the opportunity to work on account of their social status and not their physical attributes. But with the exception of England and the Netherlands, which commercialized early (the Netherlands never having had a strong tradition of local nobility anyway), the shamefaced poor remained an important category of those receiving relief in Europe at least until the social disruptions of the French Revolution. And even in the decidedly bourgeois environment of the Dutch Republic, members of the middling classes (such as urban citizens with corporate rights and artisans with guild memberships) in straitened circumstances received more generous and reliable relief than did the very poor, who could not claim such corporate protections. Downward social mobility, regardless of the level at which one started, was something that all European societies tried to protect against, suggesting that poverty was understood at least as much as a relative state as an absolute one.

The cyclical poor were also made worthy of assistance on account of their changing status over time. Two kinds of cases are especially prominent in this regard. The first included those families that were in the early stages of their household life cycle, with (often many) young children to support and limited access to wage-earning labor. Women's work was poorly remunerated at the best of times, and when pregnant and nursing, women's wages could easily drop to zero. In B. Seebohm Rowntree's classic formulation, the most prosperous time in a family's life was following the mother's child-bearing years, when at least some of the children were old enough to earn wages but not yet old enough to have begun separate households of their own. The other vulnerable group included those families in which the primary wage earner was temporarily un- or underemployed because of either the natural rhythms of the work year or, increasingly, of the business cycle. Until the development of the electrified factory and all-weather transport, winter was a season of slow work at best, not just in agriculture, but in urban crafts and trades as well. And as increasingly more individuals left farming for industrial and service sector occupations, the impact of trade cycles on employment became more severe. Guilds with cash reserves for emergency support were the primary means of defense against trade cycles, for those lucky enough to enjoy membership. The bread and cast-off clothing distributed during the severest parts of the winter had to suffice for the rest. Neither those with young families nor those with unemployed household heads could count on the unqualified charitable support of their larger communities, however. Then as now, families in such circumstances were subject to the moralistic assessments of those in a position to offer relief. Critics pointed to poor families with many children as evidence that the poor were sexually reckless, a view articulated most famously by the English economist Thomas Malthus (1766–1834). Likewise, the able-bodied unemployed generated a great deal of suspicion about how determinedly they were seeking work and whether they were being too choosy about the type of work they would accept, again not unlike the stigma faced by the unemployed in the modern world.

POVERTY AND ECONOMIC DEVELOPMENT
Although, as stated earlier, there are no agreed-upon indicators of the extent and severity of poverty in early modern Europe, many historians have nonetheless felt confident in the belief that a great many Europeans lived either below the poverty line or in imminent danger of dropping below it. This confidence rests in large measure on a commonly shared assumption about the general poverty of all preindustrial economies, in which productivity is low and the probability of risks of all kinds is high. In such an essentially Malthusian world, in which the population constantly threatens to outpace the food supply, the cyclical reappearance of episodes of extreme poverty is guaranteed. Moreover, ways to insure against risk were few or nonexistent. However, despite the attractive logic of the presumption that poverty follows from economic underdevelopment, it suffers from one fundamental inconsistency with the facts: that is, poverty continues to exist in the highly developed, immensely productive, risk-averse, and decidedly non-Malthusian modern first world. Thus the classic narratives about

economic development are insufficient for a true understanding of poverty in early modern Europe.

One striking alternative to the view of poverty as solely a consequence of underdevelopment has been offered by the Marxist historians Catharina Lis and Hugo Soly, who argue that economic development has not only failed to eradicate poverty, it has actually increased the likelihood of it. Specifically, they maintain that the incidence of poverty spread as capitalism developed, first as an agricultural system and later as an industrial system, over the course of the early modern period. The key mechanism they see at work behind this process is that of proletarianization, or the increasing separation of workers from the means of production and thus their forced reliance on wages for their maintenance. They begin their narrative with a fairly dire medieval landscape in which "40 to 60 per cent of western European peasants disposed of insufficient land to maintain a family" (p. 15), and then chart from there what they understand to be the processes of further impoverishment over time: the long-term trend toward diminishment in the size of peasant holdings; the development of social policies that criminalized the poor, thereby permitting the better regulation of the labor market (most notably the Elizabethan Poor Law in England, statues against vagrancy and begging in both Catholic and Protestant Europe, and the institution of workhouses in towns both great and small); and most importantly, the massive shift of the labor force away from small independent holdings and craft workshops toward wage labor in commercial agriculture and industry. While they have supporting evidence of the hardship experienced by particular groups of people and sectors of the economy during this time of radical social and economic change, they fail to make a compelling case for an increase in poverty overall. The spread of capitalist enterprises certainly had its losers, but it had its winners as well. Simply documenting the former in great detail does not demonstrate that the scourge of poverty spread between the end of the Middle Ages and the dawn of the modern era.

Where the classic development story clearly neglects questions of distribution, the Marxist story downplays the importance of massive productivity gains in increasing the pool of material resources to be distributed. Both approaches, then, are inadequate to explain both the origins of poverty in the preindustrial past and its persistence in the face of rapid economic development. If we consider only the material facts of the share of food in the average household budget, lengthening life span, energy available per capita to provide light and heat and perform work, and the remarkable growth of consumables in both number and variety, there can be no doubt that poverty, as understood to be strictly a matter of material deprivation, has decreased precipitously over time, with many of the initial gains achieved over the course of the early modern period. However, poverty is also a relative condition, and it may well be the case that the massive increases in the size of the resource pool have had the counterintuitive effect of highlighting distributional inequities in ways that were not as obvious when the material basis of society was so much lower on average.

The experience of early modern Europe also suggests that poverty is a treatable condition, at least to some extent. Those places that experimented seriously with charitable social policies saw genuine improvements in overall well-being. Two notable examples will have to suffice as evidence for our purposes here. The first is the Tudor-Stuart program of food relief in seventeenth-century England, which demonstrably lowered the variance of wheat prices and contributed to lower levels of non-crisis mortality than in either of the periods before or after the policies were in effect. The second is the strong commitment shown by urban magistrates and guild members in the Dutch Republic to provide outdoor relief for those affected by the cyclical harbingers of poverty, as well as institutional care for the aged, the infirm, and the orphaned, facilitating when possible entry or reentry into the middling world of work. Visitors to the Dutch Republic from all over Europe remarked on the ubiquity and generosity of these institutions and their salubrious effect on the body social. In both of these examples, beneficent social policies traveled hand in hand with economic prosperity, probably as both cause and effect.

See also **Charity and Poor Relief; Orphans and Foundlings; Popular Protest and Rebellions; Public Health; Religious Orders.**

BIBLIOGRAPHY

Abel, Wilhelm. *Massenarmut und Hungerkrisen im vorindustriellen Europa: Versuch e. Synopsis.* Hamburg, 1974.

Boyer, George R. *An Economic History of the English Poor Law, 1750–1850.* Cambridge, U.K., and New York, 1990.

Davis, Natalie. "Poor Relief, Humanism, and Heresy: The Case of Lyon." In *Studies of Medieval and Renaissance History* 5 (1968): 215–275.

Fogel, Robert. "Second Thoughts on the European Escape from Hunger: Famines, Chronic Malnutrition, and Mortality Rates." In *Nutrition and Poverty,* edited by S. R. Osmani, pp. 243–286. Oxford and New York, 1992.

Geremek, Bronislaw. *Poverty: A History.* Translated by Agnieszka Kolakowska. Oxford and Cambridge, Mass., 1994.

Hufton, Olwen H. *The Poor of Eighteenth-Century France, 1750–1789.* Oxford, 1974.

Leeuwen, Marco H. D. van. "Histories of Risk and Welfare in Europe during the Eighteenth and Nineteenth Centuries." In *Health Care and Poor Relief in Eighteenth and Nineteenth Century Northern Europe,* edited by Ole Peter Grell, Andrew Cunningham, and Robert Jütte, pp. 32–66. Aldershot, U.K., and Burlington, Vt., 2002.

———. *The Logic of Charity: Amsterdam, 1800–50.* Translated by Arnold J. Pomerans. London and New York, 2000.

Lis, Catharina, and Hugo Soly. *Poverty and Capitalism in Pre-industrial Europe.* Atlantic Highlands, N.J., 1979.

McCants, Anne E. C. *Civic Charity in a Golden Age: Orphan Care in Early Modern Amsterdam.* Urbana, Ill., 1997.

Pullan, Brian. *Rich and Poor in Renaissance Venice: The Social Institutions of a Catholic State, to 1620.* Cambridge, Mass., 1971.

Rowntree, B. Seebohm. *Poverty: A Study of Town Life.* London, 1901.

Schwartz, Robert M. *Policing the Poor in Eighteenth-Century France.* Chapel Hill, N.C., 1988.

ANNE E. C. McCANTS

PRAGUE. Prague was one of the largest and most influential cities in the Holy Roman Empire and central Europe in the early modern period. It was remarkable for its bilingual and multireligious population of Czech- and German-speaking Catholics, Protestants, and Jews; its distinctive geographic and political landscape; and its Reformation and cultural achievements. It was also the site of events of central importance in the histories of both the Bohemian kingdom and the empire. In reality, Prague was a complex of four legally and politically independent though socially and economically linked cities. The Old and New Cities, on the right bank of the Vltava River, were the center of artisanal and commercial activities. The Castle Hill (autonomous since 1592) and the Small Side, on the left bank, were home to royal and estate governments and were the seat of an archbishopric.

In 1346 Charles IV (ruled 1355–1378), king of Bohemia and Holy Roman emperor, chose Prague as his imperial residence. In 1348 he founded the University of Prague, the first university in central Europe, and he expanded and renovated the city. The new construction included the first stone bridge across the Vltava River and the monumental Saint Vitus Cathedral, which became the seat of a newly established archbishopric. Fifty years later Prague became the birthplace of the religious reform movement centered around Jan Hus (c. 1372–1415), rector of the Bethlehem Chapel in the Old City. In 1419 the reform movement turned into a revolution when a mob threw anti-Hussite councillors out of windows of the New City government building (an event known as the first Prague defenestration). During the Hussite Revolution religious orders and German speakers were forced to flee the city, and churches, monasteries, and other structures were destroyed in direct attacks and battles between competing forces. In the wake of the revolution Prague came into the hands of an Utraquist elite, a religiously and socially moderate group descended from the Hussites. Prague's population began to grow again, and schools and literary brotherhoods flourished in parish churches. Under the reign of King Vladislav II Jagiellon (ruled 1471–1516) Catholic religious orders began to return to the city, and Renaissance architecture first appeared in Bohemia at the Prague Castle. In 1483 the installation of new councillors sympathetic to the king's policies led to a revolt that culminated in a second defenestration of city councillors, this time from both the Old City and the New City government buildings. This revolt paved the way for the 1485 Peace of Kuttenberg, which established legal parity between Roman Catholics and Utraquists (though it forbade other religious groups).

By the beginning of the sixteenth century Prague had a population of about twenty thousand. The arrival of Lutheran ideas in the 1520s assisted in the ongoing development of Utraquism. In 1526 Ferdinand I (ruled Bohemia 1526–1564; ruled the Holy Roman Empire 1558–1564) was elected king of Bohemia. The first years of his reign were marked by maintenance of the status quo in religion and politics. However, in 1547, when the Prague cities refused to send troops to support the Catholic imperial army in the Schmalkaldic War, Ferdinand punished them with sanctions and sent his son, Archduke Ferdinand of Tyrol, to reside in Prague as his viceroy. The residence of the viceroy helped draw Bohemian nobles, artisans, and some foreigners to the city. The mid-sixteenth century also witnessed a flowering of printing houses and literary societies and the spread of Renaissance innovations to noble palaces and burgher houses. In 1555 the first Jesuit college in Bohemia was founded, and in 1561 a new archbishop, who established the foundations of Catholic reform, was installed. In 1583 Rudolf II (ruled 1576–1612), Bohemian king and Holy Roman emperor, moved the imperial court from Vienna to Prague, making the city an imperial capital for a second time. At the Prague court Rudolf assembled a large array of foreign artists, artisans, and scientists. Among these notables were the astronomers Johannes Kepler (1571–1630) and Tycho Brahe (1546–1601), the painters Bartholomeus Spranger (1546–1611) and Giuseppe Arcimboldo (c. 1530–1593), and the sculptor Adriaan de Vries (c. 1560–1626). Rudolf's Kunstkammer, located in the Prague Castle, was the largest art collection in the Europe of that day.

By 1600 Prague had become a major European center of late Renaissance culture and, with a population of about sixty thousand people, the largest city in the empire and in central Europe. Growing tension between Catholics and Protestants within the ruling elite led in 1618 to an Estates revolt, which culminated in a third defenestration. This time Protestant noblemen tossed two Catholic imperial governors from a window in the Prague Castle. Although the men were not badly hurt, this action was the catalyst for the outbreak of the Thirty Years' War (1618–1648). In 1620 the Bohemian

Estates and their Protestant allies were defeated by Catholic imperial troops at the Battle of White Mountain, just outside of Prague. A year later twenty-one leaders of the revolt were executed on Old Town Square, and their heads were displayed on the bridge, an event publicized throughout the empire. The Edict of Restitution in 1629 firmly entrenched Habsburg rule and the Counter-Reformation and resulted in property confiscations and the exile of Protestants from the city. At the same time Prague's baroque culture flowered, which continued into the seventeenth and eighteenth centuries. During the reign of Empress Maria Theresa (ruled 1740–1780) a new wing was added to the Prague Castle. In 1781 the Edict of Toleration of Emperor Joseph II (ruled 1765–1790) brought with it the dissolution of cloisters and monasteries. In 1787 Wolfgang Amadeus Mozart came to Prague for the premiere of *Don Giovanni*, which was widely acclaimed and affirmed Prague's importance as a major cultural center.

See also **Bohemia; Habsburg Dynasty: Austria; Holy Roman Empire; Hussites; Jagiellon Dynasty (Poland-Lithuania); Mozart, Wolfgang Amadeus; Reformation, Protestant; Thirty Years' War (1618–1648).**

BIBLIOGRAPHY

Demetz, Peter. *Prague in Black and Gold: Scenes from the Life of a European City.* New York, 1997.

Fučíková, Eliška, et al., eds. *Rudolf II and Prague: The Court and the City.* Prague, London, and New York, 1997.

Pešek, Jiří. *Měštanská vzdělanost a kultura v předbělohorských Čechách 1547–1620.* Prague, 1993.

Vlk, Jan, and Jaroslav Láník, eds. *Dějiny Prahy* (The history of Prague). 2 vols. Prague and Litomyšl, 1997–1998.

JAMES R. PALMITESSA

PRAGUE, DEFENESTRATION OF.

The humorously complex word *defenestration* simply means throwing someone or something out a window (Latin *fenestra,* 'window'), but in Prague this action came to symbolize a national reaction to foreign or illegitimate rule. The first Defenestration of Prague occurred on 30 July 1419, when radical Hussites, in an action to free several Utraquists imprisoned by the magistrates, killed seven city councillors by throwing them out of the window of the New Town Hall and into the midst of an angry

Hussite mob. Emperor Wenceslas (emperor 1378–1400; Wenceslas IV, king of Bohemia 1378–1419) was so enraged at this event that he died, perhaps of a heart attack. The next year Hussite rebels, led by Jan Žižka (c. 1376–1424), were victorious over the Roman Catholic king (later emperor) Sigismund (emperor 1433–1437; king of Hungary 1387–1437; king of the Romans 1410–1437; king of Bohemia 1419–1437; king of the Lombards 1431–1437) at nearby Vítkov Hill.

The Second Defenestration of Prague triggered the Thirty Years' War (1618–1648). During the stormy reigns of Rudolf II (ruled 1576–1612) and Matthias (ruled 1612–1619), the Bohemian aristocracy had extracted rights to Protestant worship and instruction, most notably the Letter of Majesty of 1609. But when subjects of the archbishop of Prague built a Protestant church at Klostergrab and others a church at Braunau, the archbishop ordered these churches closed. King Matthias brought this crisis to a head by ratifying the archbishop's order. In March 1618 a Protestant assembly protested the emperor's actions in stacking his council with staunch Catholics, but their protest was rejected. The Bohemian Estates, heavily Protestant and zealously protective of their rights to representation, stormed into Prague's Hradczyn Castle on 23 May 1618 and hurled two imperial governors, Jaroslav of Martinic and William of Slavata, along with their secretary out one of the castle windows. Their fall was cushioned by an accretion of refuse at the bottom of the castle wall, so they were not seriously injured by their fifty-foot fall. But peace was at an end. Within months the Estates had raised an army and ordered the exile of the Jesuits from Bohemia along with the confiscation of their property. They elected Frederick V of the Palatinate (elector palatine 1610–1623; d. 1632) as their king. In response, the Habsburg monarch, Ferdinand II of Styria (ruled 1619–1637), laid plans for the subjugation of Bohemia, a goal he effectively achieved at the Battle of White Mountain, 8 November 1620.

Defenestration continued to have such resonance in Czech history that other events, such as the death of Jan Masaryk (1886–1948), have sometimes been called "defenestrations."

See also **Bohemia; Hussites; Prague; Representative Institutions; Thirty Years' War (1618–1648).**

BIBLIOGRAPHY

Sayer, Derek. *The Coasts of Bohemia: A Czech History.* Princeton, 1998.

Teich, Mikulas, ed. *Bohemia in History.* Cambridge, U.K., 1998.

H. C. Erik Midelfort

PREACHING AND SERMONS.

Preaching originates from the ministry of Jesus, the Word of God, and his mandate to "go and make disciples of all nations . . . teaching them to obey everything that I have commanded you" (Matthew 28:19). Saint Paul states, "Faith comes from hearing" (Romans 10:17); the Word is to be preached ceaselessly, "whether the time is favorable or unfavorable; convince, rebuke, and encourage, with the utmost patience in teaching." (2 Timothy 4:2; cf. 3:16) Preaching is proclamation, it is the Good News of "the Kingdom" (Mark 1:14–15; 38–39); it is God's word in human speech.

FORMAT

Scripture provides no instruction on format for preaching but leaves this to the preacher. From the early church to the present, the two principal forms have been the homily *(homilia)*, a simple exposition of Scripture at the liturgy or in private gatherings, used extensively by the Alexandrian theologian Origen (d. 254), and the sermon *(sermo, contio)*, a more formal discourse on a scriptural topic, a religious mystery, theme, custom, event, or saint's life. Variations on these two formats could be considerable.

From the Middle Ages into the early modern era, the more customary form of preaching was the Scholastic, or thematic, sermon, whose intention was primarily teaching. It began usually with a "theme," a short passage from the Gospel read at mass, which was divided into two or three parts, then a protheme, a brief statement of the theme to direct the audience's attention. After a prayer for divine assistance, a repetition of the theme, the preacher gave his sermon in two, sometimes three, parts (corresponding to the elements of the scriptural quotation). In these parts he might give definitions, make distinctions, support points with quotations from Scripture, the church fathers, or other authorities, and give examples. This was followed by a conclusion. As formalistic as this appears, it could be used effectively. It was flexible and could be substantially modified for addressing fellow clergy and religious *(ad cleros)* or "the people" *(ad populum)*. To assist preachers, homiletic materials abounded: sermon collections, *catenae* (compilations of biblical exegesis), florilegia of patristic writers, summae of virtues and vices, books of exempla, the famous *Legenda aurea* (Golden legend) of Jacobus de Voragine (1298), saints' lives whose material preachers could repeat or adapt for preaching, and treatises on preaching *(Artes praedicandi)*, for composing sermons according to the thematic method.

By 1500, the *Artes praedicandi* and the thematic sermon had begun to fall out of favor, or at least undergo significant changes. With the revival of Roman rhetorical education and the rediscovery of the classics, humanist-trained ecclesiastics understood preaching more broadly as "sacred eloquence" and saw it as falling into line with the three aims of classical rhetoric—to move, to teach, to delight *(movere, docere, delectare)*—topics discussed as well by Saint Augustine in book four of *De doctrina Christiana* (397–428). Good preaching was not a Scholastic disputation; it was scriptural, words that touched the heart, called to repentance, and taught matters necessary for salvation. This approach had solid medieval foundations. Franciscan preaching had eschewed the subtleties of Scholastic disputations to shake sinners out of their vices and instill virtue; it aimed at the spiritual needs of town dwellers, adopting their language, images, and stories, as Jesus had done with parables; it shunned "lofty words or wisdom" (1 Corinthians 2:1); it was brief, unostentatious, and scriptural, focused on basic Christian instruction (the Ten Commandments, the Creeds, the Our Father, etc.) and on virtues and vices.

OCCASIONS FOR PREACHING, 1500–1750

Preaching occupied a vast campus. Jesus said, "Wherever two or more are gathered in my name, I am there among them" (Matthew 18:20), and preaching could occur everywhere. In highly formalized settings, as before popes at Solemn High Mass, or before kings at state funerals, sermons marked grand occasions. Apart from regular liturgies, sermons occurred in open air, in city squares, on street corners, at assemblies, at funerals, at the commemorations of saints, victories, and miracles, at Forty Hours (the exposition of the Blessed Sacrament for forty continuous hours in a church), in times of pestilence, famine, and war, in extraliturgical events during Advent and Lent, on holy days and fast days, and in confraternities. It was important that preaching abound. The English cleric Gregory Martin's *Roma Sancta* (1581) describes late-sixteenth-century Rome as bristling with preaching in every church and crosswalk, thereby giving evidence of the city's holiness and the effects of good preaching on a city that years earlier had been sorely criticized for sordid vices. In Protestant circles, the surest sign of the true church was where the Word was preached and baptism and the Eucharist were dispensed. Preaching was the vital activity demonstrating God's intervention. Calvinist preachers preached in open fields and in private homes as well as in church. Because of the Reformation, good preaching became ever more credible evidence of the true church; preaching, too, was a competition, as every denomination knew that so much rested on the eloquence of its minister.

NEW DIRECTIONS IN PREACHING IN THE SIXTEENTH CENTURY

Early-sixteenth-century writers commonly lamented the deplorable condition of sacred oratory, but their words more likely reflect the greater demand for good preaching among educated laity. Much good preaching, in fact, occurred, and ecclesiastical authorities continuously urged homiletic reforms. The Fifth Lateran Council's (1513–1517) decree on preaching, *Circa Modum Praedicandi* (1516) acknowledged abuses, but articulated the direction preaching had already embraced when it demanded that clergy "preach and explain the evangelical truth and Sacred Scripture according to the declaration, interpretation and exposition of the doctors whom the Church or daily use has approved."

The Council of Trent (1545–1563) was the watershed in the reform of Catholic preaching. It defined preaching as the "special duty of bishops" and enjoined them "to preach the holy Gospel of Jesus Christ, to feed the people entrusted to them. . . ." It urged bishops to establish programs for liberal arts and the study of Scripture in their dioceses, which would be the beginning of the seminary system of priestly education, and the formation of excellent preachers. Trent's decree coincided with a revival in preaching that had already made a dramatic impact on Europe. Significantly, the new religious orders (Jesuits, Theatines, Capuchins, etc.) made preaching a priority and in this differed from most clergy. After Trent, few bishops could miss the idea that preaching was crucial; some issued "instructions for preachers" on preaching to the people *(ad populum)*. In Protestant preaching, too, preparation of preachers in biblical studies and languages was paramount; it was the chief work of pastors.

FAMOUS PREACHERS

In the early sixteenth century, scathing criticisms abounded about poor preaching. Erasmus of Rotterdam's (1466?–1536) works, for example, suggest that nearly every contemporary preacher was incompetent or disgraceful. In fact, competent preachers abounded in every confession. Some of the more noted Catholic preachers were Gabriel Biel (d. 1495), Roberto da Lecce, (d. 1495), Girolamo Savonarola (d. 1498), Johann Geiler von Kaisersberg (d. 1510), Bernardino Ochino (d. 1564), Cornelio Musso (d. 1574), Francisco Panigarola (d. 1594), François de Sales (d. 1622), Jean-Pierre Camus, bishop of Belley (d. 1652), Nicolas Caussin (d. 1651), Gian Paolo Oliva (d. 1681), Paolo Segneri (d. 1694), and Jacques-Bénigne Bossuet (d. 1704). Some were known less for their eloquence than for the example they set as preachers, most notably Carlo Borromeo, archbishop of Milan (d. 1584), whose regular preaching made him a model Tridentine bishop.

In Protestant lands, numerous preachers acquired excellent reputations. Among the best known are Martin Luther (d. 1546), Huldrych Zwingli (d. 1531), Théodore de Bèze (d. 1605), John Calvin (d. 1564), Heinrich Bullinger (d. 1575), and William Perkins (d. 1602). Tragically, too few of their sermons survive.

INFLUENCE OF CLASSICAL RHETORIC ON SACRED ORATORY

By 1500, the homily and sermon found new life as humanist-trained preachers returned to the sources *(fontes)* of Christian tradition to acquaint themselves with the eloquence of the Greek and Latin Fathers (Origen, Gregory Nazianzen, Gregory of Nyssa, Basil, John Chrysostom, Ambrose, Augustine, etc.). New editions of the Fathers made clear that the foundations of Christian eloquence lay in classical instruction and study of Scripture.

Erasmus of Rotterdam's groundbreaking and influential treatise on homiletics, *Ecclesiastes sive de Ratione Concionandi* (Ecclesiastes; or, On the Method of Preaching, 1535) codified a method for applying principles of classical rhetoric to preaching. The humanistic method of preaching had been in use at least since the mid-fifteenth century; but Erasmus's approach opened the way for others. Paradoxically, Erasmus himself fell out of favor in Catholic circles, as did his treatise, when his works were placed on the Index of Prohibited Books in 1559 and 1564. His work, however, stimulated a flurry of preaching manuals after the Council of Trent, the "ecclesiastical rhetorics" *(ecclesiastica rhetorica)*, that set standards for preaching for generations, the best known being the *Rhetorica Christiana* (Christian rhetoric, 1579) of Diego Valades; the *De Rhetorica Ecclesiastica* (On Ecclesiastical rhetoric, 1574) of Agostino Valier, bishop of Verona; the *Rhetoricae Ecclesiasticae* (Ecclesiastical rhetoric, 1576) of Luis de Granada, the Modus Concionandi: *De Ratione Concionandi* (The Method Of Preaching, 1576) of Diego de Estella; the *Divinus Orator* (The Divine orator, 1595) of Ludovico Carbone; the *Orator Christianus* (The Christian orator, 1613) of Carlo Reggio; the *De Eloquentia Sacra et Humana* (On Sacred and human eloquence, 1617) of Nicolas Caussin.

Significantly, the new "ecclesiastical rhetorics" defined preaching as "persuasion" *(persuadere)* for moving the heart—instructing the intellect, bending the will, delighting the senses. They explained the genera of discourse—deliberative, demonstrative, and forensic oratory—which humanists saw as corresponding to three types of preaching: in deliberative oratory one urged the shunning of vice and growth in virtues; in demonstrative oratory one extolled the benefits of God, the wonders of the saints, the angels, and the mysteries of the Christian faith. On rarer occasions, a preacher might employ the judicial genus (the type of oratory characteristic of the law courts), though few writers found applications for this. The new manuals also elaborated on the three styles of speaking (the humble, middle, and grand), and on the ways these could be used appropriately; they discussed the parts of oratory, rhetorical devices, ornaments. Above all, they stressed the essential differences between preaching and secular oratory, for in preaching the "salvation of souls" and "the glory of God" are at stake. Classical rhetoric could benefit preachers, but they were about the work of the Lord, not their own aggrandizement.

By 1600, preaching currents across denominations changed dramatically. What Marc Fumaroli has labeled an "Age of Eloquence" in France can rightly be extended to the whole of Europe and to lands beyond, where preachers labored to spread the Gospel.

See also **Rhetoric; Theology.**

BIBLIOGRAPHY

Bayley, Peter. *French Pulpit Oratory, 1598–1650: A Study in Themes and Styles, with a Catalogue of Printed French Pulpit Oratory.* Cambridge, U.K., 1980.

Fumaroli, Marc. *L'age de l'éloquence: Rhétorique et "res literaria", de la Renaissance au seuil de l'époque classique.* 2nd ed. Paris, 1994.

McGinness, Frederick J. *Right Thinking and Sacred Oratory in Counter-Reformation Rome.* Princeton, 1995.

Murphy, James J. *Rhetoric in the Middle Ages: A History of Rhetorical Theory from Saint Augustine to the Renaissance.* Berkeley, 1974.

O'Malley, John W. *Praise and Blame in Renaissance Rome: Rhetoric, Doctrine, and Reform in the Sacred Orators of the Papal Court, c. 1450–1521.* Durham, N.C., 1979.

Ruderman, David B., ed. *Preachers of the Italian Ghetto.* Berkeley, 1992.

Schneyer, Johann Baptist. *Geschichte der katholischen Predigt.* Freiburg, 1969.

Shuger, Debora K. *Sacred Rhetoric: The Christian Grand Style in the English Renaissance.* Princeton, 1988.

Smith, Hilary Dansey. *Preaching in the Spanish Golden Age: A Study of Some Preachers of the Reign of Philip III.* Oxford, 1978.

Taylor, Larissa. *Soldiers of Christ: Preaching in Late Medieval and Reformation France.* New York, 1992.

Taylor, Larissa, ed. *Preachers and People in the Reformations and Early Modern Period.* Leiden, 2001.

FREDERICK J. MCGINNESS

PREGNANCY. *See* **Motherhood and Childbearing; Obstetrics and Gynecology.**

PREINDUSTRIAL MANUFACTURING. *See* **Proto-Industry.**

PRÉVOST D'EXILES, ANTOINE-FRANÇOIS (1697–1763), French ecclesiastic and man of letters. Prévost is best known as the author of the novel *Manon Lescaut* (1731), a love story with tragic overtones in which the hero and heroine, Des Grieux and Manon, are caught and ultimately crushed by the cruel, and at times sordid, social reality of early-eighteenth-century France. The son of a royal magistrate from northern France, Prévost entered the church in 1720 as a novice in the Benedictine congregation of Saint-Maur. His relationship to monastic life was conflicted almost from the beginning. In 1728 he asked to be transferred to a less severe branch of the order, but when his request was denied, he fled dressed as a layman.

The ensuing period of his estrangement from the church was extremely productive from a literary standpoint. Prévost published three volumes of his seven-volume novel, *Mémoires et aventures d'un homme de qualité* (1728–1731; Memoirs and adventures of a man of quality)—the work known today as *Manon Lescaut* is actually the last volume of this multivolume novel—as well as the first four volumes of his second novel, *Cleveland, le philosophe anglais* (1731–1739; Cleveland, the English philosopher), which, although read today only by specialists, also enjoyed great popularity in Prévost's own day.

The same period was disastrous, however, from a financial standpoint. Prévost sought refuge from his creditors in England on two different occasions, but when his financial situation continued to deteriorate, he returned to France in 1734. That same year Prévost formally requested and was granted absolution for his faults and authorized to transfer to a less severe branch of the Benedictine order.

Religion and morality are central concerns in much of what Prévost wrote, but both his contemporaries and his modern readers have tended to be drawn to other aspects of his work. In his *Confessions* (1782), Prévost's illustrious younger contemporary, Jean-Jacques Rousseau (1712–1778), the author of *Du contrat social* (1762; The social contract), wrote of how profoundly his early reading of *Cleveland* had affected him. Many of Rousseau's central themes—especially his views concerning the spontaneity of feeling and its role in defining human nature in ways that conflict with the dictates of social codes and hierarchies—resonate with the discourse and situations of Prévost's characters.

In the twentieth century the influential literary historian Eric Auerbach identified *Manon Lescaut* as one of the most important precursors of the literary realism of the nineteenth century. Other critics have taken up the question of the relationship between Prévost's life and work in order to emphasize the authenticity that they argue his tortured personal existence brought to his fiction. This approach has naturally led them to focus on the perspective and dilemmas of Prévost's male protagonists, but a newer generation of scholars has argued that this focus distorts the deeper implications of his fiction, especially *Manon Lescaut*. For them, the true protagonist of the novel is not Des Grieux but Manon, who seeks pleasure and freedom in a social world constructed on the basis of a hypocritical double standard with regard to women. From a literary standpoint, *Manon Lescaut* is without question Prévost's masterpiece, but his other works are also of interest in that they provide a fascinating depiction of Enlightenment culture, whose major trends they not only reflect but also influenced.

Prévost's knowledge of English and of English culture was virtually unique among his French contemporaries, and he exploited it in a number of ways. He is the author of the French translations of two novels by the eighteenth-century English novelist, Samuel Richardson—*Clarissa* and *Sir Charles Grandison*—which were to influence greatly the development of the novel in France. He edited and served as the major contributor to *Le pour et contre* (1733–1740; The pro and con), a review of English culture written for a French audience. But it was also through Prévost's English contacts that he became the French editor and translator, and eventually (when his English colleagues abandoned the project) the general editor, of the fifteen-volume *Histoire générale des voyages* (1746–1759; A general history of voyages), a compilation and presentation of virtually all the journals authored by the major European explorers of the world outside of Europe.

This highly influential work represented perhaps the most important precursor of Denis Diderot's better-known *Encyclopédie*. More recently, scholars have also insisted on its value as a synopsis of early European ethnography and an indication of the role played by an interest in non-European societies in the creation of the culture of the Enlightenment. It also reflects, however, an interest that was evident in some of Prévost's earliest work, especially *Cleveland*, which contains a detailed fictional portrait of the life of native Americans. Prévost's legacy thus lies not only in the individual works he authored but also in the links he helped establish between various aspects of Enlightenment culture and letters and perhaps, above all, between the exploration of the "inner" worlds of feeling, passion, and thought, and the "outer" worlds defined not only by French society and culture but increasingly by the "new worlds" outside of Europe, which in Prévost's lifetime Europeans were still only beginning to explore.

See also **Encyclopédie; Enlightenment; French Literature and Language; Richardson, Samuel; Rousseau, Jean-Jacques.**

BIBLIOGRAPHY

Primary Source

Prévost, Antoine-François. *Manon Lescaut*. Translated by L. W. Tancock. London, 1949.

Secondary Sources

Auerbach, Eric. *Mimesis: The Representation of Reality in Western Literature*. Translated by W. R. Trask. Princeton, 1968. First published 1946.

Gearhart, Suzanne. "The Sexual Interruption of the Real." In *The Interrupted Dialectic: Philosophy, Psychology, and Their Tragic Other*, pp. 133–156. Baltimore, 1992.

Rabine, Leslie. "Sex and the Single Girl at the Dawn of Liberalism." In *Reading the Romantic Heroine: Text, History, Ideology*, pp. 50–80. Ann Arbor, Mich., 1985.

Segal, Naomi. *The Unintended Reader: Feminism and Manon Lescaut*. Cambridge, U.K., and New York, 1986.

Sgard, Jean. *Prévost romancier*. Paris, 1968.

SUZANNE GEARHART

PRICES AND THE PRICE REVOLUTION. *See* Inflation.

PRIESTLEY, JOSEPH

PRIESTLEY, JOSEPH (1733–1804), English cleric, chemist, historian, theologian, philosopher, and social and political critic. Joseph Priestley, the eldest son of a maker and dresser of woolen cloth, was born in Fieldhead near Leeds, Yorkshire. As a boy, Joseph was exposed to strict Calvinism and tutored by local clergymen. Because his religious Nonconformity barred him from Oxford and Cambridge, his formal education was completed at the dissenting academy at Daventry. However, it was largely through his own efforts that Priestley learned Latin, Greek, French, Italian, German, Hebrew, Chaldean, Syriac, and Arabic.

Over the course of his life, Priestley's religious beliefs evolved from Calvinism to Socinianism (Unitarianism), but religion always remained of pivotal importance. His chief formal occupation was as a minister, and he served liberal congregations in various parts of England. In addition, he taught for six years at the dissenting academy in Warrington, and he tutored private students. During all this time, his prolific pen seldom stopped moving. His collected works fill over twenty-five volumes and include such titles as *A Chart of Bibliography, Rudiments of English Grammar, A Course of Lectures on Oratory and Criticism, An Essay on the First Principles of Government, History of the Corruptions of Christianity, Disquisitions Relating to Matter and Spirit, Institutes of Natural and Revealed Religion,* and *Experiments on Air.*

Although today Priestley is best known for his contributions to chemistry, he was only an amateur scientist. His first scientific publication, *The History and Present State of Electricity* (1767), was stimulated and encouraged by his friend Benjamin Franklin. Priestley reported in his posthumously published memoir that his interest in chemistry was a consequence of living adjacent to a brewery during his ministry at Leeds (1767–1773). His first publication on pneumatic chemistry (1772) provided directions for impregnating water with the "fixed air" generated by fermenting beer. In modern terms, Priestley described the carbonation of water. In addition, he isolated and identified ten gases, most of them previously unknown, and he discovered photosynthesis independently of Jan Ingenhousz.

Joseph Priestley's most famous discovery occurred on 1 August 1774, while he was serving as the "literary companion" of William Petty, the second Earl of Shelburne. On that date, Priestley used a burning glass to focus the rays of the sun on a sample of the red calx of mercury, which evolved a colorless, odorless, and tasteless gas. He ultimately found that this new gas was "between five and six times as good as the best common air" in supporting combustion. The name he chose, "dephlogisticated air," reflects the Phlogiston Theory, an explanation of combustion widely held in the eighteenth century. According to this theory, flammable substances contained phlogiston, the principle of combustibility, which escaped during burning. Air was necessary as a reservoir to absorb the escaping phlogiston, and when the air became saturated with it, burning ceased. Because the newly isolated gas had an enhanced capacity for supporting combustion, Priestley concluded that its phlogiston content must be lower than that of air.

Unbeknown to Priestley, Karl Wilhelm Scheele (1742–1786), a Swedish apothecary, had prepared the same gas in 1771. But the correct interpretation of the essential role of this gas in combustion and in chemistry was one of the major contributions of the French chemist, Antoine Laurent Lavoisier (1743–1794). Lavoisier gave the name "oxygen" to Priestley's dephlogisticated air and included it among the thirty-three simple substances listed in his *Elements of Chemistry* (*Traité élémentaire de chimie*, 1789). Oxygen was literally a key element in the revolution that transformed chemistry and established the modern science, but Priestley never accepted the new "French chemistry."

Priestley's chemical conservatism seems to stand in stark contrast to his religious, political, and social radicalism. He was a severe critic of traditional Trinitarian Christianity, an outspoken advocate of freedom of religion and speech, and an ardent supporter of the American and French Revolutions. It was especially his espousal of the latter cause that led to criticism and caricature in the popular press and to the sacking of his Birmingham home in 1791. Continuing opposition in England contributed to Priestley's decision to move to Pennsylvania in 1794. He and his family settled in the village of Northumberland, where he lived quietly until his death in 1804.

Most modern scholars have found considerable consistency in the great diversity of Priestley's work. The unifying themes are his materialistic world view, his acceptance of a benign form of determinism known as philosophical necessity, his commitment to the power of reason, and his Unitarian beliefs. From this foundation Priestley inferred (in his own words) that "a wise Providence [disposes] everything for the best"; "the human species itself is capable of . . . unbounded improvement"; "the great instrument in the hand of divine providence of this progress of the species towards perfection, is society and consequently government"; and, "the good and happiness of the . . . majority of the members of any state is the great standard by which everything relating to that state must finally be determined." Ultimately, even Priestley's refusal to accept the chemical revolution that he helped start is consistent with his status as an "honest heretic."

See also **Chemistry; Lavoisier, Antoine; Petty, William.**

BIBLIOGRAPHY

Primary Sources

Priestley, Joseph. *Autobiography of Joseph Priestley.* Introduction by Jack Lindsay. Bath, U.K., 1970.

———. *Experiments and Observations on Different Kinds of Air.* 2nd ed. London, 1775.

———. *The Theological and Miscellaneous Works of Joseph Priestley, L.L.D., F.R.S., etc.* 25 vols. Edited by J. T. Rutt. London, 1817–1835.

Secondary Sources

Schofield, Robert E. *The Enlightenment of Joseph Priestley: A Study of His Life and Work from 1733 to 1773.* University Park, Pa., 1997.

Schwartz, A. Truman, and John G. McEvoy, eds. *Motion Toward Perfection: The Achievement of Joseph Priestley.* Boston, 1990.

A. TRUMAN SCHWARTZ

PRIMARY EDUCATION. *See* **Education.**

PRIMITIVISM. *See* **Noble Savage.**

PRINTING AND PUBLISHING. The shift from script to print in early modern communications was both dramatic and gradual. The invention of printing from movable type did produce many more books and led to a steep decline in the production of manuscripts by about 1475. Still, in the seventeenth and eighteenth centuries, three or four hundred years after the introduction of movable type, manuscript was a legitimate form of publication in every field of scientific and literary endeavor. And while official communications from the political and religious spheres more and more began to take printed form, a lively network of clandestine manuscript production allowed unorthodox ideas to circulate outside the purview of the censors. Only by the turn of the nineteenth century did book production begin to assume its modern form. Then, the "typographical old regime," as the previous system is sometimes called, began to be replaced by the structure of an industry, divided into creative, editorial, and publishing sectors, that would emerge during the course of the century as capable of reaching the first mass audiences. Before then, individual entrepreneurs operated myriad relatively small firms in all the major cities without significant legal protection and under a regime of more or less strict political and ecclesiastical control. In spite of these conditions, printing and publishing exercised a profound influence on religious, intellectual, and political life wherever it flourished.

TECHNOLOGY AND MATERIALS

In the generation following Johannes Gutenberg, whose "forty-two-line Bible" was probably completed around 1455, the industry had already begun to take on the features that would characterize it for the next three and a half centuries. A typical operation, under the direction of a master printer, eventually included a compositor who was responsible for composing and justifying the lines of characters in his composing stick. He then tied up the page (i.e., the lead necessary to print a page) and imposed the pages of a sheet, situating the pages of lead so that the sheets would be printed correctly, with the chase and furniture around them, made up a form, and fixed the signatures so the sheets could be folded in an orderly succession when printed. A pressman and his companion were engaged in the actual printing of pages—one was responsible for inking the forms with leather ink balls while the other placed the wet paper upon the tympan, turned the frisket down, moved the carriage in for the correct positioning of the platen, and then pulled the bar two times on one side of a sheet. The whole print run was repeated on the other side for perfecting the sheets. A corrector read proof in the lead characters and then sent his corrections back to the compositor, who reopened the form and reworked the lines. Sixteenth-century printers and publishers formed into guilds, which eventually sought to set standards for the quality of the product and the payment of workers, while governing relations between firms.

The cost of materials, coupled with a primitive system of exchange, powerfully conditioned the average size of pressruns. Well into the eighteenth century, accounts between authors and printers and between printers themselves, often at the trade fairs of Antwerp, Leipzig, Frankfurt, and Lyon, were still being settled by barter of books or paper. To save paper, pressruns rarely exceeded the thousand or so copies that were ordered by authors or their agents, or that printers could be certain of exhausting in a short time. Often this meant the quantity a good pressman could pull in twelve hours of work. Few printers had more than a few type fonts on hand, with rarely enough characters to compose more than a few pages of a book. After several pages had been printed up in predetermined quantities, forms were untied and the type redistributed in the fonts for composing successive pages. Second pressruns thus, in effect, almost invariably entailed new editions.

Established from the outset at a high level of sophistication, the technology of printing evolved slowly. As late as the seventeenth century, the main changes in the wood-and-metal press that had been used by Gutenberg some two hundred years earlier were metal rails to make the carriage slide in and out more smoothly and accurately, and brass bars to connect the platen more firmly to the hose. Type founding became an industry in itself, developed notably by Claude Garamond (c. 1480–1561) in the sixteenth century, whereas the chief advances in the eighteenth century came from such exceptional founder-printers as Giambattista Bodoni (1740–1813) and John Baskerville (1706–1775). The manufacture of paper was also a separate industry, mostly located away from the larger cities, on clear

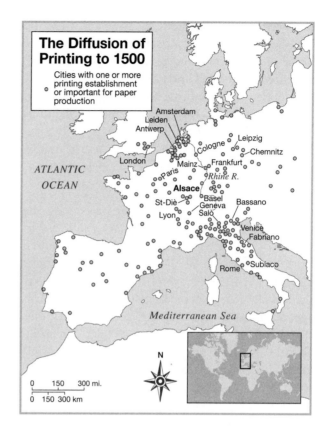

The Diffusion of Printing to 1500

Cities with one or more printing establishment or important for paper production

streams and rivers, in towns like Fabriano and Salò in northern Italy, Chemnitz in Germany, Basel in Switzerland, and in regions like Alsace and the lower Rhineland. Already in the first decades of the sixteenth century, copper plate engraving began to take the place of woodcuts for illustrating works aimed at more cultivated audiences, although woodcuts did not disappear until well into the eighteenth century.

DIFFUSION OF PRINTING

From Gutenberg's operation in Mainz, whether by emigration of personnel or by emulation of technique, the industry soon spread. If Cologne, at least for sheer number of editions, soon emerged as one of the greatest centers in Germany, beginning with the shop of Ulrich Zell (d. 1507), powerful rivals soon appeared across the Rhine. The lure of scholarly publishing may well have inspired Guillaume Fichet and Johann Heynlin to organize production in Paris in 1470; the presence of a commercial fair eventually made Lyon the second printing center of France, beginning with Barthélemy Buyer in 1473. In Westminster, William Caxton brought his experience on the Continent to bear on the project for an

English press in 1476. Between 1465 and 1466 the first shops in Italy were opened in Subiaco outside Rome (Konrad Sweynheym and Arnold Pannartz) and in Rome itself (Ulrich Han). Three years later the debut of Johannes de Spira began the rise of Venice, which in the age of Aldus Manutius (c. 1450–1515) and the Gioliti family of the sixteenth century established its place as the undisputed leader among the 250 or so cities and towns where printing now existed.

By the second half of the sixteenth century, the printing epicenter of Europe began to shift northward. With twenty-four presses and over a hundred workers at the height of his activity, Christophe Plantin (1514–1589), who had offices in Antwerp, Leiden, and Paris, ran the largest printing firm of his age, occupied by, among other commitments, official work for the monarchy of King Philip II of Spain. With a complete type foundry attached to the printing operation, the firm was able to produce 2,450 editions in thirty-four years of activity. A former employee of Plantin, Louis Elzevier (1540–1617), subsequently dominated the market in Leiden.

CULTURAL IMPACT

The vast majority of book production in the early modern period was as uncontroversial as it was unliterary and unscientific. However, almost from the outset, printers became involved in the great cultural movements of the time. Aldus Manutius of Venice was by no means the only humanist who practiced the printing trade, although his case has become paradigmatic. Applying his scholarly knowledge of Latin and Greek, he produced a repertoire of products including the great works of classical antiquity, with text compressed by his innovative italic font, and one work of great beauty, the lavishly illustrated 1499 edition of Francesco Colonna's *Hypnerotomachia Poliphili* (Dream of Poliphilo). The Gioliti family, also based in Venice, contributed to the growing reputation of Italian literature with editions of such authors as Petrarch and Ariosto. In a slightly later period, Robert Estienne, of the Parisian family that moved in circles close to the humanist theologian Jacques Lefèvre d'Étaples (c. 1450–1536), found himself in the midst of the contention between Protestants and Catholics in the Reformation. His celebrated polyglot New Testament, presenting the Vulgate (tradi-

tional Latin), the Greek text, and the Latin translation of the latter by Erasmus, eventually had to be produced in Geneva because of the controversies it aroused in France among authorities in the faculty of theology of the University of Paris.

Wherever important changes were occurring, from Renaissance humanism to the Protestant Reformation, from the birth of modern science to exploration in the New World, the specific role of the press could scarcely be distinguished from the role of other agents of change. Obviously, the printer's art, apart from advantages of speed and diffusion, could be particularly effective for delivering content when combined with various forms of illustration. Almost from the outset, the satiric print, political and religious, and often using primitive xylographic techniques, was a frequent accompaniment to text. Scientific illustration reached a peak of perfection in Basel in 1543 with the publication of Andreas Vesalius's *De Humani Corporis Fabrica Libri Septem* (Seven books on the structure of the human body), setting the standard for later productions such as those by Georges Louis Leclerc, Comte de Buffon (1707–1788). Mapmaking advanced from the *Cosmographiae Introductio* of Martin Waldseemüller, published in 1507 in Saint-Dié (Lorraine) along with a map showing the first depiction of America as such, to the projections of Gerhard Mercator (1512–1594), printed in Amsterdam, to the elaborate editions, printed by the Blaeu family in the same city in the 1640s–1660s, concerning every spot on the known globe.

In the realms of visual arts and music, mechanical reproduction contributed, in ways that still need further study, to education, to the introduction of new categories of leisure-time activities, and even to changing styles. Music printing constituted a particular challenge because notes and other symbols had to be superimposed over a fixed staff. Although the method of movable type, used to particular effect by Ottaviano dei Petrucci in Venice in the early sixteenth century, demanded the extra expense of plural impressions, it spread widely due to the absence of a workable alternative. The engraving of entire sheets of music, first tried in the early sixteenth century, eventually came to be preferred. Still in the eighteenth century, however, important English music publishers like Henry Playford (1657–1709) used the earlier method.

REGULATION

Regulatory mechanisms emerged slowly as officials in church and state began to recognize the potential of the press for ideological purposes—their own and others'. Each new press rule provoked authors, printers, publishers, and purchasers to conceive of new strategies of evasion. Books destined for more tightly controlled markets were shipped in via the free ports or smuggled across political boundaries in shipments of other merchandise. Few dared to suggest, with the early seventeenth-century Italian polemicist Ferrante Pallavicino (1615–1644), that censorship was an advantage; but no one could deny that the demand for certain works was inevitably enhanced by official sanctions.

Preliminary indices of forbidden books drawn up by the faculty of theology of the University of Paris (1540s) and by the Venetian government (1547) in the first decades of the sixteenth century were soon followed by those of Pope Paul IV and the Council of Trent (1564). By the time of the foundation of the Congregation of the Index in 1572, most civil governments had deputed various combinations of churchmen and government representatives to approve manuscripts for publication and oversee book imports.

Censorship was by no means exclusive to Roman Catholic areas, in spite of the relative press freedom advocated by John Milton in his pioneering tract, *Areopagitica,* in 1644. In fact, even in Milton's own thought, press freedom rarely extended to what were unanimously regarded as dangerous matters in religion and politics. Where pre-publication censorship went out of fashion, as it did in Britain after 1695, libel laws continued as an effective method of controlling ideas.

Printers and authors may have regarded piracy as being as serious a problem as censorship. They were fully prepared to protect their vested interest in intellectual property whenever they could. At the local level, they could count on applying for fifteen- or twenty-five-year exclusive privileges to print particular works, enforced by heavy punishments meted out by government agencies. They could also be sure that, if the work was successful, printers in other states would print it with impunity, as no rules had any application outside the state where they were issued. Juan Caramuel y Lobkowitz, Spanish-born cleric and correspondent of Pierre Gassendi

and René Descartes, in his *Syntagma de arte typographica* (1662; Collection concerning the typographical art), condemned the custom of seizing, using, and selling the writings of authors without their permission, citing the only international convention unequivocally binding all humanity—namely, the divine injunction against stealing. His appeal fell on deaf ears.

A WIDER MARKET

Throughout our period, the quantity of printed material increased in absolute terms as well as in proportion to the rising population of Europe. And apart from the now ubiquitous broadsheets in various combinations of text and illustration, new genres emerged for reaching larger audiences. In France, *bibliothèque bleue,* and in England, "chapbooks," referred to cheaply printed pamphlets in small formats with primitive woodcut illustrations that were sold mainly by itinerant hawkers. The first newspapers were produced in Antwerp in 1605, and by mid-century they existed in every major city. Whether privately controlled (as in Germany and England) or sponsored by governments (as in France and certain parts of Italy), they spread widely. The eighteenth century added variety magazines to the growing repertoire of literature on which the middling ranks of people had begun to rely for instruction, information, and entertainment.

A veritable "reading revolution" has been attributed to the eighteenth century, entailing a shift from an "intensive" style (fewer books read carefully) to a more "extensive" style (more books, read carelessly). Whether this was actually true or existed only in the imaginations of contemporary observers and modern scholars is difficult to say. In any case, new genres aiming at larger audiences and new methods of distribution were accompanied by new practices of sociability, especially where coffeehouses, as exemplified in the pages of *The Spectator* (1711–1712) of Joseph Addison and Richard Steele, became places of discussion and cultural exchange. In London, the number of booksellers rose to some six hundred by the end of the century. In eighteenth-century Germany, reading societies and lending libraries fed the appetites of ever larger numbers of readers.

Industry growth and audience development pushed early modern structures to the limits. Subscription publishing allowed printers to plan more carefully for the long term even where credit was tight. Some of the most important works of the eighteenth century were published by this method, including the *Encyclopédie* conceived by Denis Diderot and Jean d'Alembert (35 vols., 1751–1780). Works of imaginative literature were meanwhile published in weekly or monthly installments to sustain reader interest, with considerable influence on the history of the English novel. Freedom to innovate depended to some degree on the abrogation of guild privileges and, in many parts of Europe, the abolition of guilds. The Remondini firm of Bassano took advantage of its location outside the urban epicenter of the Venetian Republic in order to join papermaking operations with type founding, as well as to manufacture a wide variety of print products besides books, including prayer cards, games, and even wallpaper, in a vast strategy to undercut Venetian competitors.

EDITING AND PUBLISHING

By the end of the century, the figure of the editor/publisher, as distinct from the author and the master printer, began to emerge. Charles-Joseph Panckoucke, for instance, undertook such long-term projects as the reprint of the French *Encyclopédie* and the direction of the *Encyclopédie méthodique,* begun in 1781 as a continuation of the former and eventually completed in 166 volumes, along with several newspapers in and around Paris—all before finally purchasing a single press himself. And while John Bell exercised a similar entrepreneurial function in London, publishing several periodicals and newspapers, James Lackington in 1793 opened what may have been the largest book warehouse of the time, including over 500,000 volumes.

Even before mass literacy made a genuine mass market possible in Europe, the premises were laid for transition to a system in which the visual medium, mostly in the form of the products of the printing press, would take the place of speech as the premier method of communicating ideas. The way was prepared, to quote the McLuhanesque phrase, for the irreversible emergence of "typographical man," with all the accompanying cultural consequences that came to define the mental orientation of the modern age.

See also **Antwerp; Bible: Translations and Editions; Caxton, William; Censorship; Dissemination of Knowledge;** *Encyclopédie;* **Gutenberg, Johannes; Index of Prohibited Books; Journalism, Newspapers, and Newssheets; Libraries; Literacy and Reading; Milton, John; Venice.**

BIBLIOGRAPHY

Primary Source

Moxon, Joseph. *Mechanick Exercises: Or, the Doctrine of Handyworks, Applied to the Art of Printing.* Edited by Herbert Davis and H. Carter. London, 1958. Originally published in London, 1683–1684.

Secondary Sources

Chartier, Roger. *The Cultural Uses of Print in Early Modern France.* Princeton, 1987.

Darnton, Robert. *The Business of Enlightenment: A Publishing History of the* Encyclopédie, *1775–1800.* Cambridge, Mass., 1979.

Dooley, Brendan, and Sabrina Baron, eds. *The Politics of Information in Early Modern Europe.* London, 2001.

Febvre, Lucien, and Henri-Jean Martin. *The Coming of the Book: The Impact of Printing, 1450–1800.* Translated by David Gerard. London, 1976. Translation of *L'apparition du livre.* Paris, 1958.

Gaskell, Philip. *A New Introduction to Bibliography.* London, 1972.

Infelise, Mario. *L'editoria veneziana nel '700.* Milan, 1989.

Ing, Janet Thompson. *Johann Gutenberg and His Bible: A Historical Study.* New York, 1988.

Krummel, D. W., and Stanley Sadie, eds. *Music Printing and Publishing.* The Norton/Grove Handbooks in Music. New York, 1990.

Lowry, Martin. *The World of Aldus Manutius: Business and Scholarship in Renaissance Venice.* Oxford, 1979.

McLuhan, Marshall. *The Gutenberg Galaxy: The Making of Typographical Man.* Toronto, 1962.

Voet, Leon. *The Golden Compasses: A History and Evaluation of the Printing and Publishing Activities of the Officina Plantiniana at Antwerp.* 2 vols. Amsterdam, 1969–1972.

BRENDAN DOOLEY

PRINTS AND POPULAR IMAGERY

This entry includes two subentries:
EARLY POPULAR IMAGERY
LATER PRINTS AND PRINTMAKING

EARLY POPULAR IMAGERY

Graphic art is "popular" because it is relatively inexpensive and therefore available to a much wider public than is true of paintings or sculpture. Woodcut, its oldest and most primitive technique, can simply be stamped or rubbed onto sheets of paper, and these began to appear in Europe almost simultaneously with the construction of the first paper mills in northern Europe (France, c. 1348, Germany, 1390), many printed in monasteries as prayer sheets or pilgrim souvenirs.

INDULGENCES, CULTS, AND BROADSHEETS

Indulgenced images were especially popular, since they were presumed to confer on the beholder benefits from the "treasury of grace" (excess grace earned by Christ and the saints) to buy released time from temporal punishment in purgatory. Martin Luther, in his Open Letter to the Christian Nobility of the German Nation (1520), railed against both the abuse of indulgences and the sale of pilgrim sheets: "Ofttimes they [the pope and Rome] issue an indulgence on this same pretext of fighting the Turks, for they think the mad Germans are forever to remain utter and arrant fools, give them money without end, and satisfy their unspeakable greed. . . ." He goes on later to say, "there is a little word commend, by which the pope entrusts the keeping of a rich, fat monastery or church to a cardinal or to another of his people . . . to install some apostate, renegade monk, who accepts five or six gulden a year and sits in the church all day selling pictures and images to the pilgrims, so that henceforth neither prayers nor masses are said there."

The majority of indulgenced images dealt with subjects actually approved by the papacy, for example the engraved pilgrim sheets in three different sizes and price ranges, made for the anniversary of the monastery at Einsiedeln, Switzerland, by Master E. S. (1466). The *sudarium* (veil of St. Veronica, believed to be imprinted with Christ's face) was especially popular, and was depicted even by Albrecht Dürer (c. 1512) and Hans Burgkmair (c. 1505), as well as by Hans Sebald Beham as a close-up of Christ's face alone (*Head of Christ,* 1520).

Well before 1500, however, unscrupulous printmakers were producing images of their own devising, complete with "statistics" regarding released time and/or miraculous effects. A Swabian woodcut of the *Sacred Heart* (Washington, D.C., National Gallery) depicts modules for calculating both "the true length of Christ's corpse," as well as the wound in his side, and as a fringe benefit promises protection from the plague as well as seven years' release from purgatory. Other images with extraordinary properties included depictions of St. Christopher, who could protect one from dying "an evil death" (that is, without the opportunity to make confession), or of the Fourteen Holy Helpers, each of whom was a specialist in protection against a different ailment or dilemma (for example, St. Denis for insanity, St. Erasmus for intestinal problems, and St. Vitus for epilepsy and dog bites). Images of one's own patron saint or guild or city patron were talismanic as well, and depictions of the *noli me tangere* (Christ's appearance to Mary Magdalene, saying "Don't touch me") have been found pasted into the lids of strongboxes and travelers' trunks, where they evidently served as insurance against theft. Woodcuts of the Crucifixion were also pasted into the lids of such boxes, perhaps to serve as portable altarpieces for private meditation.

Practitioners of the *devotio moderna* (a fourteenth-century movement for the personal renewal of spiritual life) could choose from a variety of woodcuts depicting Christ carrying his cross alone—without the usual procession of soldiers, Pharisees and government officials—as a metaphor for patience in bearing one's own burdens in daily life, as taught by Thomas à Kempis's *Imitatio Christi* (Imitation of Christ, 1441). Popular eucharistic images included *Christ in the Winepress,* apparently based on a quotation from St. John Damascene identifying Jesus as "the grape of Life . . . squeezed in the winepress as the grape of the True Vine." A related theme, the Host Mill, explained the miracle of transubstantiation in terms of a flourmill that processes grain into holy wafers. All of these, as well as images of the Mass of St. Gregory, during which the consecrated bread miraculously metamorphosed into the living image of Christ, and series prints of the Twelve Apostles, each labeled with his own supposed contribution to the wording of the Apostles' Creed, were of particular value for the education of the new communicant. Rosary brotherhoods as well as practitioners of the cult of the Five Wounds (of Christ) were similarly educational.

Much less respectable was the short-lived cult of the Beautiful Virgin of Regensburg, whose chapel was built on the site of a synagogue razed in 1519

Prints and Popular Imagery. *The Life and Death of Peter Stump,* broadsheet, 31 March 1590. Thought to be a werewolf and mass murderer, Stump was apprehended, tortured, and executed in 1589. The sensational case is illustrated in this broadsheet. MARY EVANS PICTURE LIBRARY

and whose prayer sheet was an elaborate, multicolored woodcut by Albrecht Altdorfer. Her votive offerings (workmen's tools, wooden legs, crutches, etc.) and ecstatic rites were depicted in a woodcut by Michael Ostendorfer, one impression of which bears an inscription in Albrecht Dürer's hand: "This spectre arose in Regensburg against Holy Writ . . . God help us that we may not dishonor His Holy Mother. Amen."

While prints of all kinds were much less numerous in Italy than in Germany, images of the newly canonized St. Catherine of Siena (1347–1380, canonized 1461) and of the "people's preacher," St. Bernardino of Siena (1380–1444, canonized 1450), and of the fictitious St. Julian the Hospitaler, supposed patron of innkeepers, ferrymen, and circus performers, were among the exceptions. Anti-Semitic woodcuts were produced on both sides of the Alps; those depicting the supposed ritual murder of young Simon of Trent by a group of Jews,

and those referencing "the Jewish sow" were two of the more popular themes.

Broadsheets and single-sheet woodcuts without text appealed both to the illiterate and the semiliterate and could be more or less informative—as in the case of Dürer's woodcut of *The Nativity of Syphilis,* which depicts a man with the symptoms of the new disease, but implies that it was caused by a conjunction of the planets.

Greeting cards constituted another category of popular print, with New Year's wishes showing the infant Christ holding a bird, riding a donkey, or seated inside an image of the heart being most frequently preserved. A unique woodcut is the famous "Power of Venus" valentine (c. 1460, Vienna), depicting a young lover's appeal to "Frau Venus" while surrounded by depictions of human hearts undergoing all sorts of tortures, and accompanied by some of the century's most truly dreadful poetry. This, however, is better classified among the numerous "Power of Women" and "Battle of the Sexes" images that became popular in the late fifteenth and early sixteenth centuries. Such themes include various combinations of unequal lovers as well as the more modern subject of the "Battle for the Breeches."

Decks of playing cards were in great demand, but have survived only when not used for play (for example, the engraved sets by the Master of the Playing Cards, Master PW of Cologne, Telman de Wesel, and Peter Flötner). In some cases in sixteenth-century sets, the face cards included bawdy imagery, which added a new dimension to their use.

CARICATURE AND CONFESSIONAL SYMPATHIES

Signs of the imminent end of the world have always been of popular concern, and in the sixteenth century these included continuing interest in the late medieval concept of the Antichrist, and of the equally venerable theme of the World Upside-Down. The Antichrist survived the Reformation to emerge in Lucas Cranach's Passional, *Christi and Antichrist,* with text by Philipp Melanchthon. Comets were another ill omen, such as the one that marked the 1468 meeting between Pope Pius II and the emperor Frederick III, depicted in a political cartoon of the day. Other such ominous signs included both human and animal misbirths: the Siamese twins who shared a single leg, Dürer's six-legged *Monstrous Sow of Landser,* and the supposed discovery in 1496 of a monstrous creature with a woman's torso, the head of a donkey, one cloven hoof, and an eagle's claw, immortalized in Wenzel von Olmütz's engraving titled *Roma Caput Mundi.* After the dangerous year of 1500—feared by many as the possible end of the world—had safely passed, and been replaced by the issues of the early Reformation, this creature was recycled by the Cranach workshop as *The Papal Ass* (1523), and similar monsters were invented to accompany it, including *The Monk Calf (Das Munchkalb zu Freyberg), The Seven-Headed Dr. Martin Luther,* and *The Two-Headed Cardinal-Fool.* In a similar vein were caricatures of the pope riding a sow, or devouring the dead (gaining from endowed masses and indulgences), the pope as a wild man or as the Harlot of Babylon, and the devil playing a monstrous bagpipe—the tonsured head of a monk (London, British Museum). The time-honored image of the

Ship of Salvation (for example in Nuremberg, 1512) was parodied in imagery inspired by Sebastian Brant's *Ship of Fools* (Basel, 1494) in an unflattering broadsheet, "The Catholic Church as Fishers of Men," which depicts the laity as existing only to be exploited by Catholic clergy. Matthias Gerung (1540) contrasted *The Shipwreck of the Papal Church* with *The Ship of Christ* (London, British Museum). Alternatively, equally tasteless caricatures were produced in the Catholic camp, including *Luther as Winesack* (a rotund Martin Luther with a goblet in one hand, trundling his belly in a wheelbarrow—a reference to his advocacy of communion for the laity in both bread and wine), and *The Two-Headed Luther* (Strasbourg, 1522). When the head is inverted, a second head in a fool's cap appears, in the spirit of Thomas Murner's *Great Lutheran Fool.* A woodcut from the Cranach workshop, on the other hand, personifies Lutheranism by depicting Luther preaching while both bread and wine are administered to the laity, as simultaneously the Catholic clergy—including the pope—fall into a gigantic hell mouth. Trick woodcuts with movable flaps were produced by both Catholic and Lutheran sympathizers to produce indecent exposure on images of, respectively, Luther or a mendicant friar or nun. In addition to those made in Wittenberg under the auspices of the Cranach workshop, many anti-Catholic broadsheets and caricatures were produced in Nuremberg (which lay at the crossroads of the Holy Roman Empire) with the assistance of a ready-made distribution network, a paper mill, a sympathetic city council, and Germany's largest publishing house.

PEASANTS AND SOLDIERS

Nuremberg was also a center of peasant imagery, premiered in its late-fifteenth-century carnival plays and transposed into woodcuts by, among others, the politically radical young Beham brothers. Too expensive by far for the actual peasantry to acquire for themselves, Sebald Beham's *Nose Dance at Fools' Town* (1534), issued with verses by Hans Sachs, his *Large Peasant Kermess* (1535; also known as *The Village Fair*) and *Peasants of Mögelsdorf,* and his brother Barthel's *Peasant Holiday* call attention to inelegant behavior as well as to the consequences of excessive eating and drinking by the peasantry, newly rendered harmless by the suppression of the Peasants' War (1525). Sebald Beham's *Allegory of*

Monasticism, in which a monk rejects Poverty in favor of Pride, Luxury, and Avarice, and his *Christ and the Sheepfold,* with its text by Hans Sachs (based on John 10:1–10) leave no doubt as to the confessional sympathies of his buyers. Leonhard Beck's *The Monk and His Maid* (1523) and *The Monk and the Ass* (1523) make much the same point.

Images of mercenary soldiers, however, could be valorized by both camps, although the living soldiers most highly sought after were Swiss and Protestant. Scenes of mercenaries on parade or in recruitment were treated in sixteenth-century woodcuts, sometimes with Hans Sachs's texts, by Erhard Schön, Sebald Beham, Hans Holbein the Younger, and others, and were a specialty (together with depictions of the inevitable camp followers) of Urs Graf, who was himself a mercenary soldier. Niklas Stör depicted a cobbler and a tailor who each explain the reasons (economic) for deserting their trades in order to become mercenaries. (Urs Graf had been a goldsmith.) Martin Luther, who early on had been critical of the sale of indulgences to finance a papal crusade against the Turks, and who continued to maintain that Christians should not wage war in Christ's name, came to believe by the 1520s that it was fitting and proper that soldiers should go to war if ordered to do so by their ruler ("Whether Soldiers Too Can Be Saved," 1526; "An Army Sermon against the Turks," 1529). The graphic response was Hans Holbein the Younger's woodcut of *Martin Luther as the German Hercules* (1523, Zurich).

See also **Caricature and Cartoon; Catholicism; Dissemination of Knowledge; Dürer, Albrecht; Humor; Luther, Martin; Lutheranism; Marvels and Wonders; Miracles; Peasantry; Popular Culture; Printing and Publishing; Reformation, Protestant.**

BIBLIOGRAPHY

Andersson, Christiane. "Polemical Prints in Reformation Nuremberg." In *New Perspectives on the Art of Renaissance Nuremberg: Five Essays,* edited by Jeffrey Chipps Smith, pp. 41–62. Austin, Tex., 1985.

Dackerman, Susan, and Thomas Primeau. *Painted Prints: The Revelation of Color in Northern Renaissance & Baroque Engravings, Etchings & Woodcuts.* Exh. cat. University Park, Pa., 2002.

Field, Richard. *Fifteenth Century Woodcuts and Metalcuts from the National Gallery of Art.* Washington, D.C., 1965. Catalogue of the collection.

Geisberg, Max. *The German Single-Leaf Woodcut, 1500–1550.* 4 vols. Edited and revised by Walter L. Strauss. New York, 1974.

Goddard, Stephen, ed. *The World in Miniature: Engravings by the German Little Masters, 1500–1550.* Exh. cat. Lawrence, Kans., 1988.

Martin Luther und die Reformation in Deutschland. Exh. cat. Nuremberg, Germanisches Nationalmuseum. 1983.

Moxey, Keith. *Peasants, Warriors and Wives: Popular Imagery in the Reformation.* Chicago, 1989.

Scribner, Robert W. *For the Sake of Simple Folk: Popular Propaganda for the German Reformation.* Cambridge, U.K., 1981.

Stewart, Alison. "The First 'Peasant Festivals': Eleven Woodcuts Produced in Reformation Nuremberg by Barthel and Sebald Beham and Erhard Schön, c. 1524 to 1535." Ph.D. dissertation. New York, 1986.

Zschelletzschky, Herbert. *Die "Drei gottlosen Maler" von Nürnberg.* Leipzig, 1975.

JANE CAMPBELL HUTCHISON

LATER PRINTS AND PRINTMAKING

Alongside the woodcut, engraving emerged in the fifteenth century as another technique for printing images on paper, but one with different historical roots. Engraving on metal for decorative purposes was very old when, some decades after the appearance of the first woodcuts, engraved lines were filled with ink and printed. Unlike woodcut lines, which are produced negatively by cutting away the wood between them, the engraved line is incised directly into a metal plate with a chisel-like tool known as a burin. The direct correspondence between the engraved and the printed line, as well as the greater flexibility and variety of its lines, made engraving more responsive than woodcut to the mimetic and aesthetic goals of early modern artists, and after initially being associated with goldsmiths, it was taken up by painters like Andrea Mantegna (1431–1506) and Martin Schongauer (c. 1430/50–1491). In its size, compositional complexity, and pictorial effects, Schongauer's *Bearing of the Cross* of c. 1475 more nearly resembles a small monochrome painting than a contemporary woodcut.

Although mostly portraying religious subjects, the secular and classical themes of early engravings, such as Mantegna's splendid *Battle of the Sea Gods* (printed from two plates and stretching to nearly three feet in length) point to a more educated and affluent public than that aimed at by woodcuts. With Albrecht Dürer (1471–1528), however, who devoted greater attention to printmaking than any earlier artist, woodcut acquired the sophistication of engraving and engraving attained unprecedented pictorial and plastic force. Dürer's *Apocalypse* of 1498, which joined full-page, woodcut illustrations to the biblical text, was the first book to be designed and published by an artist, a practice also adopted by William Blake (1757–1827) for the pictures and poetry of his "illuminated" books. The *Apocalypse,* along with other sets of prints, as well as single-leaf woodcuts and engravings, were peddled from their native Nuremberg to fairs as far away as Frankfurt by Dürer's mother and wife. Easily transportable, these images on paper traveled widely, enhancing the artist's fame and becoming part of the first print collections.

Prints brought fame not only to their makers, but in an age before photography, to what they represented. Marcantonio Raimondi (c. 1480–c. 1534), who made pirated copies after Dürer's prints, later collaborated with Raphael to reproduce the artist's paintings in engravings. Such reproductive prints, which made an artist's ideas readily accessible to a distant audience, became an increasingly important part of printmaking and were soon joined by representations of architecture and sculpture. By the eighteenth century, cheap copies of reproductive prints were being produced, and William Hogarth (1697–1764) not only issued more expensive and less expensive versions of his works, but was also instrumental in the passage of the Engraver's Copyright Act of 1735, which enabled "Designers, Engravers, Etchers, &c." to protect their work.

The technical mastery achieved by professional engravers like Cornelis Cort (1533–1578) and Hendrick Goltzius (1558–1617) in the later sixteenth century led to remarkable displays of virtuosity. In Claude Mellan's *Veil of St. Veronica* (1649) the swelling and thinning of a single, spiraling line beginning at Christ's nose models the entire face, and in Pierre-Imbert Drevet's *Portrait of Cardinal Dubois* (1724, after Hyacinthe Rigaud) the burin produces the most stunning effects of varied textures.

After the sixteenth century, most artists who worked their own plates preferred etching to engraving. Etched lines are bitten into the plate by acid after the artist scratches through a thin, acid-impervious coating to expose the metal below. The relative ease with which the metal is exposed imparts a greater freedom to the etched line than one finds in the necessarily more formalized and typically geometricized line produced by the engraver's burin. Although Dürer made three etchings and Albrecht Altdorfer (c. 1480–1538) and his followers used the technique for representing the larch-forested landscape of the Danube region, the first artist to exploit the pen-like spontaneity of the etched line was Girolamo Mazzola (called Parmigianino, 1503–1540), whose prints display much of the grace and fluidity of his drawings. Similarly personal and immediate are the open lines and dotted modeling with which Anthony Van Dyck (1599–1641) captured the likenesses of himself and a number of fellow artists (such as Jan Brueghel the Elder, Adam van Noort, Frans Snyders, and others) that later appear in the *Iconography,* a collection of engravings after his portraits of famous men.

More elaborate effects of depth and tone were achieved by Jacques Callot (1592–1635) through multiple bitings and the stopping out or recoating of areas of the plate to prevent further biting. The large number of plates etched by Callot embraces a wide variety of subjects from mostly small representations of beggars, dwarfs, and Morris dancers to more complex scenes of military depredation (*The Miseries of War,* 1633) and large, densely figured compositions like the *Fair at Impruneta* (1620).

Although his early pure etchings owe something to Callot in subject and technique, Rembrandt van Rijn (1606–1669) created what his Italian contemporary, Filippo Baldinucci, described as his own "astonishing style of etching." Through close hatching and the use of drypoint, in which lines are scratched directly into the plate to produce a particularly velvety and luminous tone, Rembrandt subtly modeled everything from his own face to the Dutch landscape, merging the deepest darks with the most brilliant lights of the unprinted paper. In the mid-1630s, in works like the *Annunciation to the Shepherds,* with its radiant glory of angels, dumbstruck shepherds, and stampeding animals, such effects intensify the melodrama, but by the

1640s, the chiaroscuro begins to figure in more interior narratives. In the so-called *Hundred Guilder Print* (c. 1647–1649, from Matthew 19) the sick and the lame stream out of the darkness groping for the light of Christ, while opposite them the Pharisees argue among themselves in the light of day, and in a fourth version of the *Three Crosses* (1653), the violent clash of light and dark at the cataclysmic moment of Christ's death is transformed into darkest mystery and tragedy. As in his paintings, Rembrandt reveals in his prints the utmost sensitivity to the emotional nuances of the narrative and an unequalled capacity for inventing the mimetic and formal means to realize them.

In the eighteenth century, the tonal effects pioneered by Rembrandt dominated printmaking. Although Giovanni Battista Tiepolo (1696–1770) produced lightly bitten, sun-washed fantasies at once classicizing and romantic, Giovanni Battista Piranesi (1720–1778) strengthened the chiaroscuro effect of his architectural views in the forbidding and gloomy interiors of his imaginary prisons (1750). In northern Europe, artists evenly and thickly nicked the surface of the plate, so that if printed it produced a uniform black; burnishing or scraping away the nicks produced lighter shades. These mezzotints, as they are called, were especially popular in England, where they were most often used for reproducing painted portraits and landscapes.

In etching, tone was achieved by biting through a porous, rather than continuous, acid-resistant ground. Perforating the ground in the crayon manner enabled the print to mimic the broken, textured line of the then highly popular chalk drawings, whereas in aquatint the ground itself was given an open, granular structure. Francisco de Goya (1746–1828) used the wash-like shades of aquatint to probe popular superstitions and the darker corners of the human mind in *Los Caprichos* (1799) and to modernize Callot with a surfeit of cruelties and terrors in *Los Desastres de la Guerra,* which were etched in response to the French occupation of Spain from 1808 to 1814. His famous print, *The Sleep of Reason Produces Monsters,* from *Los Caprichos,* illustrates in its aquatint shadows and multiplying night creatures both the Enlightenment's innocent faith in reason and its imminent collapse.

See also **Callot, Jacques; Caricature and Cartoon; Dürer, Albrecht; Goya y Lucientes, Francisco de; Popular Culture; Rembrandt van Rijn.**

BIBLIOGRAPHY

Bartrum, Giulia. *Albrecht Dürer and His Legacy: The Graphic Work of a Renaissance Artist.* Exh. cat. London, 2003.

Bury, Michael. *The Print in Italy, 1550–1620.* London, 2001.

Clayton, Tim. *The English Print, 1688–1802.* New Haven, 1997.

Hinterding, Erik, et al. *Rembrandt the Printmaker.* London, 2000.

Hults, Linda C. *The Print in the Western World: An Introductory History.* Madison, Wis., 1996.

Lambert, Susan. *The Image Multiplied: Five Centuries of Printed Reproductions of Paintings and Drawings.* London, 1987.

Landau, David, and Peter Parshall. *The Renaissance Print, 1470–1550.* New Haven and London, 1994.

Mayor, A. Hyatt. *Prints & People: A Social History of Printed Pictures.* Princeton, 1980.

Reed, Sue Welsh. *French Prints from the Age of the Musketeers.* Exh. cat. Boston, 1998.

GEORGE C. BAUER

PRIVILEGE. *See* **Equality and Inequality.**

PROBABILITY. *See* **Mathematics.**

PROGRESS. The idea of progress, the view that human beings and civilization are improving and advancing toward a better goal, is a very old one. Over the centuries numerous individuals and groups have believed in some form of progress.

In the centuries between 1400 and 1800 many Europeans developed a view of secular progress somewhat different from previous views. This was a secular view of progress divorced from religious, eschatological, and teleological concerns. Intellectuals developed the idea that human civilization had improved intellectually, socially, politically, and in scientific accomplishments. They believed that their own age had made considerable progress in comparison with past epochs and would continue to improve in the future. But there was no definite future point to be reached. Appreciation for the contribution that science had already made and confidence in the future contributions of science and technology played a role. Confidence in what humanity can learn was important, but Europeans had less respect for the achievements of the past. This new, secular, and somewhat different notion of progress was first tentatively formulated in the late Renaissance. It took on greater meaning in the seventeenth century and reached fruition in the eighteenth-century Enlightenment. At the same time, a number of intellectuals strongly denied that their age marked an era of progress.

ANCIENT AND MEDIEVAL BACKGROUND

The Greeks and Romans saw their civilization as better than that of other peoples, whom they characterized as "barbarians," because they lacked Greco-Roman achievements. They sought to spread their civilization to the rest of the world, and this could serve as justification for conquest. Ideas of eschatological religious progress were strong in the Judeo-Christian religious world. The Old Testament chronicled the words and deeds of Jewish prophets who looked forward to the coming of a Messiah, but what would happen then is unclear. One of the most influential expressions of teleological historical progress is found in the Book of Daniel 2:36–45, an historical prophesy of five successive kingdoms. In the view of medieval exegetes and historians, Daniel's interpretation of Nebuchadnezzar's dream indicated that the Kingdom of Babylonia would be followed by that of the Medes and Persians, then that of Alexander the Great (the bronze kingdom), the Roman Empire (called the kingdom of iron), and finally the kingdom of God. In like manner, a fundamental view of medieval Christianity was that history moved in a linear fashion from the birth of Christ to the end of the world. Another manifestation of the idea of religious progress was the New Testament command to teach all nations, which spurred Christians to spread God's word throughout the world.

RENAISSANCE VIEWS

In contrast to medieval teleological ideas of progress, Renaissance intellectuals, especially humanists,

had enormous respect for the ancient world. They greatly respected the achievements of ancient philosophers like Plato (c. 429–347 B.C.E.) and Aristotle (384–322 B.C.E.), ancient scientists like the medical scholar Galen (c. 130–c. 200), and ancient writers such as Cicero (106–43 B.C.E.) and Virgil (70–19 B.C.E.). The humanists were convinced that scholars and even statesmen could achieve great things by carefully studying classical authorities and incorporating their teachings into their own activities. Of course, they knew that fifteenth- and sixteenth-century Europe was not ancient Greece and Rome. But they believed that they could make their own era better by borrowing from and emulating the ancients. In so doing, they held an implicit if incomplete idea of progress because they believed that they were making their own world better than that of the Middle Ages, which they often scorned. They believed that they were creating and entering a new age, a "Renaissance," after the culturally dark Middle Ages. This idea was found in religion as well. The humanist and religious scholar Desiderius Erasmus (c. 1466?–1536) believed that contemporaries who studied the New Testament and the early church fathers such as Jerome and ignored the medieval Scholastic writers would become better Christians and would cleanse the Christian Church of its worldliness. Thus, many Renaissance intellectuals had a limited understanding of human progress, especially cultural and religious progress.

Some Renaissance thinkers went further. After assimilating classical learning in a way medieval scholars were unable to do, they realized that ancient authorities were not always correct. For example, the medical scholar and distinguished anatomist Andreas Vesalius (1514–1564) began as a fervent follower of Galen. But then his own anatomical research led Vesalius to criticize Galen on some points and to assert his own views. He did so, however, in the spirit of correcting with regret, not rejecting, a revered authority. In similar fashion, Nicolaus Copernicus (1473–1543) and Galileo Galilei (1564–1642) concluded that the ancient Greek astronomer Ptolemy (c. 100–170) wrongly stated that the sun revolved around the earth and proposed heliocentric alternatives. But none of these practical men of science formulated theories of progress.

The new understanding of periodization, historical distance, and anachronism of the humanists influenced some Renaissance men to think about progress. Renaissance historians realized better than their medieval predecessors the differences between ancient, medieval, and modern historical eras. Many saw the invention of the printing press as a very positive development of the modern age. Despite these developments, a notion of progress did not develop fully, mostly because of the great respect for the ancient world. The majority of Renaissance historians accepted a cyclical view of history inherited from the ancient world, that is, that history moved in cycles, that bad times followed good times in a regular pattern. This blocked the development of a theory of progress.

SEVENTEENTH CENTURY

A new view began to emerge in the early seventeenth century. Francis Bacon (1561–1626) in his *Advancement of Learning* (1605, expanded edition 1623) and in other works rejected practically all forms of previous reasoning in favor of scientific knowledge discovered through observation and experiment. Scientific knowledge acquired in this way promised dominion over nature, which would be useful to human beings. Although he did not subscribe to a full theory of progress, Bacon was the first to link scientific advancement to utility, an important ingredient in the idea of progress. René Descartes (1596–1650) also enunciated new principles of science and rejected past approaches to science. Philosophy and science were charting a new course, superior to that of the past, according to the followers of Descartes. Admirers of Bacon and Descartes saw the growing number of scientific and technological inventions as signs of progress in civilization. Even more important, they saw the human ability to create inventions as evidence of growing human power over nature, another important theme in the idea of progress.

QUARREL OF THE ANCIENTS AND MODERNS

At the end of the seventeenth century, numerous men and women of letters and arts in France and England (where the quarrel was called "The Battle of the Books") engaged in a spirited debate over the superiority of ancient versus modern authors. In contrast with their predecessors, many argued that modern writers were superior to those of the ancient world. Bernard Le Bovier, Sieur de Fontenelle (1657–1757) in his *Digression sur les anciens et les modernes* (1688; Digression on the ancients and the moderns) saw the moderns as mature in culture and history without suffering a decline in quality. Charles Perrault (1628–1703) in short works of the 1680s and 1690s also argued that the moderns were superior. They did not have more natural talent and intelligence than the ancients. Rather, the moderns were superior because science and the arts depended on the accumulation of knowledge, and the moderns were able to profit from the knowledge acquired over the centuries.

For those who supported the view that the moderns were best, other key arguments were that national vernaculars, especially French, were to be preferred over Latin as the languages for literature and especially for philosophical and scientific communication. Modernist proponents (sometimes lacking knowledge of ancient Greek) attacked Homer for not measuring up to seventeenth-century standards of aesthetic beauty and for his alleged exaggerations and lies. The modernists also pointed out that the ancient world lacked opera, ballet, and the novel. The political and cultural primacy of France under Louis XIV (ruled 1643–1715), the ascendancy of the French language, and the European-wide prominence of French intellectuals lent support to arguments favoring the moderns.

The widely accepted theories of human psychology and development of John Locke (1632–1704) further encouraged many to believe in progress. According to Locke, a person's knowledge depended on the sensations received. A child was an unformed being to be molded through sensory experiences imparted through education. With this view of human psychology, philosophes concluded that better social arrangements in education, social institutions, government, and the economy could make individuals and society better. They viewed human nature with optimism. Freed of the shackles of ignorance and superstition, especially those of organized religion, human beings would follow reason and do better for themselves and others.

ENLIGHTENMENT

While most of the elements—criticism of the past, assertion of the superiority of moderns over ancients, belief that science would improve the lot of humanity, viewing knowledge as cumulative—for a complete theory of secular progress had been proposed by 1700, eighteenth-century French philosophes and English economists, historians, and philosophers brought them together. They believed that reason applied to the problems of the world would yield solutions; they believed that progress could be achieved, was even inevitable; and they were convinced that progress would continue into the indefinite future.

Enlightenment philosophes believed that progress extended to all fields. They articulated a strong faith that reason could make humanity better. They offered concrete proposals for achieving progress, that is, through better education; different governmental arrangements; the spread of rational knowledge through such works as the *Encyclopédie, ou Dictionnaire raisonné des sciences des arts, et des métiers*, seventeen volumes of text and eleven volumes of plates, 1751–1772; and even through the free movement of goods. The Scot Adam Smith (1723–1790) argued in his *Inquiry into the Nature and Causes of the Wealth of Nations* (1776) that individuals acting in their own self-interest will contribute to the general welfare of all. The rejection of a Christian afterlife caused Enlightenment thinkers to place their faith in progress in this life rather than in the next.

Anne-Robert-Jacques Turgot (1727–1781), philosophe and government official, sketched the most systematic argument for a secular and naturalistic theory of progress in works of 1750 and 1751. He brought everything—arts, sciences, government, economics—into his theory of progress. He situated his argument in a universal history, which became a treatise on social evolution. Referring to societies across the globe, he saw humanity's beginnings in barbarism, then steady progress to hunting and pastoralism, then an agricultural era, followed by a commercial-urban stage. Each stage had its own language, learning, and arts. He also charted the progressive development of government, from despotism to greater freedom. He argued that freedom was necessary for all human creativity, including the arts and sciences. Along the way Turgot offered judgments on peoples that had not made as much progress as Europeans, and listed the cultural and social reasons for their failures. Providence

played no role in Turgot's progress; everything came from human actions and occurred in this life. In his *Réflexions sur la formation et la distribution des richesses* (published 1769; Reflections on the formation and distribution of wealth) he argued for an economic system based on individual freedom unchecked by government restrictions.

Turgot had the opportunity to put his theories into practice as intendant of the district of Limoges from 1761 to 1774. He instituted tax reforms, abolished forced labor on the roads by peasants, and made other changes. When he became controller general, the chief financial officer of the monarchy, in 1774, he proposed many more reforms, including abolishing the guilds, liberalizing the grain trade, a system of national education, and assemblies of citizens to advise the government. However, his proposals provoked much opposition, and he was dismissed from government in 1776.

DOUBTS ABOUT PROGRESS

While many believed in progress, some prominent figures expressed doubts. Michel de Montaigne (1533–1592), always ambivalent and individualistic, hailed new inventions such as printing but doubted the ability of human reason to arrive at complete knowledge. In a famous essay *Des cannibales* (1579 or 1580; On cannibals) he noted that although Europeans called New World natives "savages," civilized Europeans were much more barbaric in their behavior. He praised the simple, pure lives of uncivilized natives. The Italian philosopher Giovanni Battista Vico (1668–1744) in his *Scienza Nuova* (1725, revised edition 1730; New science) revived a cyclical view of history. He argued that all societies rise, mature, decline, and fall, in accordance to immutable laws of social development. Early in his career Voltaire (1694–1778) accepted the normative Enlightenment belief of continual secular progress. But in his amusing satirical novel *Candide ou l'optimisme* (published 1759; Candide or optimism) he expressed doubts. The chief characters in *Candide* very optimistically proclaim that the world is a well-ordered and rational place—even while suffering appalling calamities and unjust punishments caused by the misdeeds of eighteenth-century Europeans. Voltaire's doubts about whether history really gave evidence that mankind was making civilized progress grew in his last years.

Jean-Jacques Rousseau (1712–1778) was the most important philosophe to question and redefine progress. Rousseau saw civilization's artifacts, including scientific developments and government, as blocking the road to progress, which was the perfection of humanity. Reconstituting society on the basis of equality would lead to human perfection in his view. Rousseau did not advocate a return to a natural state devoid of civilization. But he wanted his readers to accept as a goal a different and freer human nature and to reorganize society in order to achieve this goal.

CORDORCET

Despite the doubts expressed, the majority of Enlightenment figures strongly believed in their conception of secular progress. The most enthusiastic was Marie-Jean Caritat, marquis de Condorcet (sometimes called Jean-Antoine-Nicolas Caritat; 1743–1794). Cordorcet devoted his life and writings to every cause of the philosophes, from anticlericalism to the abolition of slavery and a call for public instruction. He proposed a system to help representative governments reach rational decisions. And he suited action to words by becoming a member of the National Assembly in the French Revolution. Cordorcet sketched a complete theory of progress in his *Esquisse d'un tableau historique des progrès de l'esprit humain* (written 1793–1794, published 1795; Sketch for a historical picture of the progress of the human mind). Thanks to the growth of reason and scientific advances, humanity was enjoying progressive emancipation from the limits of its physical environment, the superstitions of the past, and ignorance, he wrote. Enlightened laws would eliminate conflicts between individuals and nations. Education would teach individuals their rights and give them the means of improving their lot. Progress would continue indefinitely. "Nature has set no term to the perfection of human faculties . . . the perfectibility of man is truly infinite; . . . the progress of this perfectibility . . . has no other limit than the duration of the globe upon which nature has cast us."

Cordorcet wrote these words while in hiding during the Jacobin Reign of Terror of the French Revolution. Arrested on 27 March 1794, he was found dead in his cell two nights later. Despite what might appear to be evidence contrary to the idea of universal progress during the French Revolution and the Napoleonic period, many European intellectuals of the nineteenth century reaffirmed the idea of inevitable and universal progress. The doubts also persisted. Nineteenth-century Romanticism, which sometimes took the form of nostalgia for the distant past of the Middle Ages, expressed ambivalence about progress. Belief in and pessimism about progress continue to this day.

See also **Ancients and Moderns; Bacon, Francis; Condorcet, Marie-Jean Caritat, marquis de; Copernicus, Nicolaus; Descartes, René; Enlightenment; Galileo Galilei; Locke, John; Montaigne, Michel de; Perrault, Charles; Philosophes; Rousseau, Jean-Jacques; Smith, Adam; Vesalius, Andreas; Vico, Giovanni Battista; Voltaire.**

BIBLIOGRAPHY

Primary Sources

Condorcet, Jean-Antoine-Nicolas de Caritat. *Condorcet: Selected Writings.* Edited by Keith Michael Baker. Indianapolis, 1976. Introduction and selections from his works.

Turgot, Anne-Robert-Jacques. *Turgot on Progress, Sociology and Economics.* Translated, edited and with an introduction by Ronald L. Meek. Cambridge, U.K., 1973. Good introduction and selections from *A Philosophical Review of the Successive Advances of the Human Mind, On Universal History,* and *Reflections on the Formation and the Distribution of Wealth.*

Secondary Sources

Baker, Keith Michael. *Condorcet: From Natural Philosophy to Social Mathematics.* Chicago, 1975.

Bury, J. B. *The Idea of Progress: An Inquiry into its Origin and Growth.* Introduction by Charles A. Beard. New York, 1932. First published in 1920. Although highly opinionated and lacking adequate documentation, this pioneering work remains stimulating.

DeJean, Joan. *Ancients against Moderns: Culture Wars and the Making of a Fin de Siècle.* Chicago, 1997. Studies Perrault and others.

Levine, Joseph M. *The Battle of the Books: History and Literature in the Augustan Age.* Ithaca, N.Y., 1991

Manuel, Frank E. *The Prophets of Paris.* Cambridge, Mass., 1962. Has good chapters on Turgot and Condorcet.

Nisbet, Robert. *History of the Idea of Progress.* New York, 1980. Readable and comprehensive survey but lacking references.

Pollard, Sidney. *The Idea of Progress: History and Society.* London, 1968. Survey, with a long chapter on the Enlightenment.

PAUL F. GRENDLER

PROKOPOVICH, FEOFAN (1681–1736),

was the most influential ecclesiastical official of Russia's Petrine era, who rose to the position of archbishop of Novgorod and vice president of the new Holy Synod, from which he exercised immense authority on behalf of Peter the Great's reforms. One of several prominent Ukrainian clerics (he was born in Kiev) in Peter's service, he first came to Peter's attention as an engaging sermonizer in 1708, and he orated a dramatic panegyric to Peter after the victory at Poltava in 1709.

Feofan is best known for his panegyric sermons and his definitive tracts in defense of Petrine reforms, most famously his justification for Peter's new law on succession of 1722, *The Right of the Monarch's Will,* and the statute setting up the Synodal church, the *Spiritual Regulation.* Although doubts have been raised about Feofan's authorship of these and several other works, most historians attribute them to him. After the incarceration of Peter's son Alexis for treason and his subsequent death in 1718, the tsar was left with no adult male heirs. In response he modified the law to permit the sitting monarch to name a successor. Feofan defended this decision as being consistent with Orthodox principles, the will of God, and common sense.

The *Spiritual Regulation* codified the new administrative structure for the church, the elimination of the patriarchate (which had been vacant since the death of Patriarch Adrian in 1700) and its replacement by a collegial body, the Holy Synod, composed of a mix of clergy and laymen appointed by the tsar. The *Spiritual Regulation* explained what this change meant to the body of the church and to the clergy, especially parish priests, who now became de facto functionaries of the state, and monastic clergy, who saw their numbers and resources dramatically curtailed.

Feofan is also associated with catechization of the parish and parish clergy through the circulation of his booklet, *A Child's First Lesson.* Intended as a literacy primer and a catechism on the Ten Commandments, *A Child's First Lesson* was prescribed for use in the church service, replacing other nonobligatory texts such as those of Efraim the Syrian. This text bore the hallmarks of Feofan's approach to language. Here, and to a lesser extent in his sermons, he consciously adopted a simple and straightforward tone in place of the decorative baroque of high Church Slavonic prose. Writing in the vernacular, he endeavored to employ the language of everyday speech, so that whether spoken aloud or read, the meaning of the text would be accessible directly to the laity. Although it remains unclear whether *A Child's First Lesson* was widely used for literacy instruction, it did circulate very widely in the eighteenth century, running through over a dozen printings and tens of thousands of copies.

During Peter's last years and after his death Feofan played an instrumental role in court politics and may have been crucial in facilitating the elevation of Peter's wife, Catherine, to the throne, thus inaugurating a long period (until 1796) in which female rule was the norm rather than the exception in Russia. Feofan composed the official account of Peter's death and succession, elegies, and the primary panegyrics extolling the post-Petrine political arrangement. He also worked behind the scenes among Russia's fractious court parties and guards' regiments, on behalf of political stability.

See also **Autocracy; Orthodoxy, Russian; Peter I (Russia); Russian Literature and Language.**

BIBLIOGRAPHY

Cracraft, James. *The Church Reform of Peter the Great.* Stanford, 1971.

Lentin, A., trans. and ed. *Peter the Great: His Law on Imperial Succession: The Official Commentary.* Oxford, 1996.

Muller, Alexander V., trans. and ed. *The Spiritual Regulation of Peter the Great.* Seattle, 1972.

GARY MARKER

PROPERTY.

In modern times, "property" generally refers to the ownership of an economic good, such as land or money. During the later Middle Ages and the early modern period, property encompassed a much wider variety of entitlements, including political powers, honorific and useful privileges, and tax exemptions. As one late-seventeenth-century dictionary defined it, property is the mastery of "the resource, the domain, the seigniory of something" (cited in Kaiser, p. 302). Such language reflects the continued influence of later feudal law, which conflated wealth and status and regulated the sale and disposition of property according to the legal standing of its owners and the nature of the property involved.

PUBLIC SEIGNIORY VS. PRIVATE SEIGNIORY

Although adumbrated in medieval jurisprudence, the distinction between public power and property rights, or what the influential early-seventeenth-century French jurist Charles Loyseau termed, respectively, "public seigniory" and "private seigniory," had little practical meaning until a royal state emerged that drained away political powers previously held by noble lords, often referred to as *seigniors*. During the early modern period such a state did gradually emerge in western Europe. Royal legal systems eventually reduced the scope and importance of seignorial justice, while royal armies grew so large that by 1700 the armed units equipped by and loyal to the lords ceased to pose a credible military threat and were disbanded.

Yet the distinction between public and private seigniory by no means disappeared in western Europe, for noble landholders continued to exercise public functions in a variety of ways. In many areas courts run by the seigniors continued to hear cases, some of which involved contests between lords and tenants over land rights. In England noble landlords and their younger brothers translated territorial possession into political power through their heavy representation in Parliament, which after 1688 became the senior partner within the English state. In France the distinction between public and private seigniory was muddied by venal office holding, that is, the practice of selling state offices, including judgeships in the kingdom's superior courts, to private individuals. To be sure, most European peasant and middle-class property owners did not exercise direct political power, but the growth of commerce did expand their access to it, most notably through the purchase of noble landed estates by wealthy merchants. This trend so threatened noble status that kings across Europe outlawed the sale of seigniories to non-nobles, a restriction that was more effectively enforced in eastern Europe than in western Europe, where the middle class was larger and wealthier.

USUFRUCTUARY DOMAIN VS. DIRECT DOMAIN

Although non-landed property expanded greatly during the early modern period, most wealth in early modern Europe still took the form of land and buildings. In areas where Roman law remained strong, such as southern France, land was typically held as freehold, that is, as property that did not require payment of services or dues to a lord. But in most European countries, the majority of peasants held only usufructuary domain over their land, meaning that, even where they had escaped serfdom, as in almost all of western Europe, peasants owed services and dues to a seignior, whose rights over peasant land constituted their direct domain. Beyond direct domain strictly understood, seigniors enjoyed a variety of honorific privileges, such as the right to lead ceremonial processions, and useful privileges, such as the exclusive right to hunt in local forests. In return seigniors were expected to demonstrate paternal concern for their tenants by, for example, providing tenants with occasional gifts and sponsoring village festivals.

In western Europe property ownership became progressively more associated with usufructuary domain during the early modern period, and many labor services were converted into money payments. But these changes did not mean that peasant services and dues, which varied considerably in cost and nature from region to region, were negligible. Thus, whereas in France annual labor services typically required a mere two or three days of work on lands directly farmed by the seignior, in Germany some peasants were required to work for their lords more than three hundred days per year. Labor services in western Europe were usually less onerous than dues, which ranged from rents to obligatory fees for use of the lord's oven and mill to payments on the transfer of land from one tenant to another. Tenants might also be required to pay for the drafting of detailed legal affidavits stipulating their obligations to their lords.

It is unclear whether and to what extent the burden of peasant dues in western Europe grew over the early modern period. But it does appear that western European seigniors became more adept at finding legal pretexts for squeezing more revenue from their tenants, thereby embittering lord-tenant relationships and dispelling the paternalistic aura surrounding them. In England peasants also faced the loss of their land titles as a result of enclosure, the combining of smaller plots into larger, more efficient fields by landlords, a practice that escalated after 1750. Enclosure has been vigorously defended on the grounds that it raised living standards generally by lowering bread prices and that most peasants found new ways to earn a living. At the same time, by allowing larger landlords to dispossess smaller ones, enclosure deprived peasants of the one resource that cushioned them from the vagaries of the market, and it disrupted traditional rhythms of rural life.

In eastern Europe the condition of peasants—most of them enserfed over the previous three centuries—was surely worse than in the West, as evidenced by a wave of peasant rebellions during the later eighteenth century that swept over Bohemia, Russia, and elsewhere. Although the causes of these rebellions were multiple, they generally arose in response to seignorial efforts to exact greater labor services and in some areas to state-supported seignorial efforts to turn serfs into virtual slaves. For despite mild state efforts at moderating such abuses, Russian and Polish seigniors routinely deprived serfs of their land rights, sold them as chattel to other lords, and inflicted brutal corporal punishments and even death sentences upon tenants who resisted the loss of their rights.

WOMEN AND PROPERTY

As in so many other respects, women suffered disadvantages in the matter of property ownership. Generally, the property women brought into marriages and the money they earned as wages legally fell under the control of their husbands. Wives could not normally make binding contracts or sue in court without their husbands' permission. Longstanding misogyny lay behind these limitations, but the need to preserve family unity provided their chief justification, although significant restrictions on female property ownership were not universal. Thus, widows often received and disposed of income accruing from their dead spouse's property, while unmarried women, if the sole living heir, might inherit the estate of their parents. Furthermore, some marriage contracts stipulated that wives retained ownership of their dowries. Despite laws to the contrary, certain cities permitted women to make investments on their own and conduct private businesses. Women also exerted some independence in the deeding of movable property (goods other than land or buildings) to their heirs. In short, despite major legal obstacles in the acquisition and disposition of property, women were by no means entirely dispossessed.

THE GROWING DEBATE ON PROPERTY

During the eighteenth century, seignorialism became the object of a growing debate arising from new political conditions, especially the need for greater state revenues, and the birth of cultural movements, notably the Enlightenment. By 1750 it had become clear that the squeezing of peasants by the seigniors was seriously eroding the state tax base and reducing the incentive of peasants to produce. In some areas of Germany seignorial authority was already declining with the growth of a large number of masterless, landless workers. Influenced by the liberal doctrines of the Enlightenment, German reformers tried to accelerate and regulate this process by limiting seignorial dues and services in hopes that liberation from the most oppressive aspects of seignorialism and a larger stake in the produce of a seigniory would encourage peasants to work harder. A similar attack on seignorialism was launched in France by a group of influential political economists called the Physiocrats. The Physiocrats, too, advocated the gradual scaling back of seignorial dues, as well as the elimination of state-imposed restrictions on the use and disposition of property, which they portrayed as impediments to expanding output. Although they did not deny the legality of seignorial property outright, the Physiocrats undercut its legitimacy by representing seignorial rights as the product of the lords' historic violence and tyranny over the peasantry. Defenders of seignorial rights tried to turn the tables on the Physiocrats by contending that these rights were "natural" properties acquired legitimately through contracts freely entered into by tenants. This counterargument carried little weight after 1789, when the French Revolution, which proclaimed property as an "inviolable and sacred" right, radically scaled back peasant dues, transformed remaining ones into pure rents, and eliminated all the honorific privileges of the seigniors.

By the late eighteenth century, property in western Europe was gradually emerging from its seignorial cocoon, but this did not mean that it had lost all its political significance. On the contrary, as had been the case in England for a long time, property was considered an integral part of one's political personality, particularly insofar as it enabled its owners to resist corruption by "despotic" rulers. The late-seventeenth-century English political philosopher John Locke, in preaching the trinity of "life, liberty, and property" as natural rights of all people, helped make property holding a prerequisite for active citizenship in virtually all states until the later nineteenth century. It was only with the flood tide of democracy that property ownership became legally dissociated from political rights, a dissociation that has lasted until the present day.

See also **Enclosure; Feudalism; Inheritance and Wills; Landholding; Peasantry; Physiocrats and Physiocracy; Serfdom; Serfdom in East Central Europe; Serfdom in Russia; Women.**

BIBLIOGRAPHY

Blum, Jerome. *The End of the Old Order in Rural Europe.* Princeton, 1978.

———. *Lord and Peasant in Russia from the Ninth to the Nineteenth Century.* Princeton, 1961.

Erickson, Amy Louise. *Women and Property in Early Modern England.* New York, 1993.

Kaiser, Thomas E., "Property, Sovereignty, the Declaration of the Rights of Man, and the Tradition of French Jurisprudence." In *The French Idea of Freedom: The Old Regime and the Declaration of Rights of 1789,* edited by Dale Van Kley, pp. 300–339, 418–424. Stanford, 1994.

Markoff, John. *The Abolition of Feudalism: Peasants, Lords, and Legislators in the French Revolution.* University Park, Pa., 1996.

Pocock, J. G. A. *Virtue, Commerce, and History: Essays on Political Thought and History, Chiefly in the Eighteenth Century.* Cambridge, U.K., 1985.

Schlatter, Richard. *Private Property: The History of An Idea.* New York, 1951. Reprint, 1971.

Wright, William. *Serf, Seigneur, and Sovereign: Agrarian Reform in Eighteenth-Century Bohemia.* Minneapolis, 1966.

THOMAS E. KAISER

PROPHECY. Early modern Europeans inherited from their ancient and medieval forebears a vast and complex range of ideas and practices to which the term "prophecy" was, and still is, loosely applied. While prophecy often denotes simply the prediction of future events, the Greek *prophetes* referred more broadly to one who delivered divine messages. The Old Testament prophets warned and consoled through visions that encompassed past, present, and future. Christian prophecy had inherent (if often latent) apocalyptic tendencies, which surfaced when perceptions of crisis evoked urgent efforts to glimpse God's universal blueprint. Medieval and early modern prophecy also incorporated various forms of natural divination and the mantic, or prophetic arts. This entry highlights biblical and spiritual strains and the varied functions of prophecy.

Comprising both divine messages and their interpretation, prophecy was both an inspiration and an art. Prophetic forecasts did not need to be fulfilled in order to be regarded as true, nor did the failure of a particular prophecy make it false, for the prophetic spirit, by foreseeing events, also worked to influence and change them. As Jonah told the Ninevites, true repentance could sway God's will and hence turn away disaster (Jonah 3: 7–9). Here the outward failure of a prophetic expectation was proof of its deeper truth. The most significant and influential messages were at least implicitly connected with divine judgment and the "last things"; such associations allowed prophecy to function as both a weapon of dissent and a shield for the powerful throughout the early modern era.

SOURCES OF PROPHETIC AUTHORITY
The issue of prophetic authority was central to the establishment and maintenance of power well into the early modern period. The central fount of authority lay in Scripture, the interpretation of which could be seen as a prophetic act. In the late Middle Ages the main prophetic texts of the Bible became crucial battlegrounds on which established powers, both sacred and secular, were contested and defended. But the same was true of venerable ancient sources such as the sibylline oracles, numerous pseudonymous texts, and legends such as the predictions of Merlin. Nature presented another key source of prophecy. The reading of wonders, both celestial and terrestrial, became a major obsession by

the sixteenth century; almost anything unusual could be taken to herald war, rebellion, natural disaster, the death of a great prince, or even the Last Judgment. Attention to wonders overlapped closely the various arts of divination, the most pervasive of which was astrology. Moreover, the spirit could communicate to individuals through direct revelation, angels, dreams, or visions.

PROPHETIC HISTORY

The prophetic understanding of history was manifest in several competing schemes, such as the Augustinian six ages corresponding to the ages of man, and the Four Empires of the Book of Daniel. The triadic "Prophecy of Elias," derived from the Talmud, posited three 2000-year periods before, under, and after the Law. More radical was the Trinitarian vision of Joachim of Fiore (c. 1130–c. 1202), in which the world-historical stages of the Father and Son would be followed by that of the Holy Spirit, a time of spiritual fulfillment before the Judgment. Through at least the seventeenth century, thinkers debated these schemes and their application with great intensity. Not only the outlines but also the details of prophetic world-chronology took on immense importance in efforts to legitimize governments, religious movements, and programs of reform.

REFORMATION PROPHECY

The late fifteenth century saw a surging confluence of older currents, evident for instance in the 1488 *Pronosticatio* of Johann Lichtenberger, a grab bag of biblical, astrological, Joachimist, and other ideas. Hopes and fears regarding the fate of the church, the empire, or Christendom fed on one another. Governments worked hard to control the spread of popular prophecies, volatile and dangerous as they often were. Nonetheless, growing lay involvement in all realms of culture brought a proliferation of competing claims to prophetic insight.

The religious explosion of the Reformation saw a dramatic escalation in this contest; the evangelical movement itself was interpreted by Martin Luther as a fulfillment of scriptural as well as extrascriptural prophecies. The reformers placed new emphasis on the prophetic dimensions of preaching and faith. At Zurich, Huldrych Zwingli (1484–1531) introduced a form of public biblical teaching, based on learned discussion, known as "the prophecy." But

did the Spirit speak only through Scripture? The prophet Joel spoke of a general spiritual outpouring in the last days, and many souls felt the flow of a mystical spiritualism that challenged all limits on prophetic inspiration.

The emergence of confessional orthodoxies was partly a reaction to the threatening anarchy of prophetic voices; confessional identities reflected shared prophetic understandings. Protestants almost universally assumed that the Antichrist had been revealed in the Roman papacy. Among Lutherans, apocalyptic expectancy became virtually a mark of true gospel teaching; Luther himself, who denounced many of his enemies as false prophets, became widely viewed as a "last Elijah." Calvinists, though often dispersed and embattled, took a more confident and aggressive stance, buoyed by a sense of God's plan for the elect. Catholic orders such as the Franciscans found missionary inspiration in powerful traditions such as Joachimism.

Early modern concepts of rulership and nationhood had major prophetic dimensions. Well known is the image of Queen Elizabeth as Deborah, prophetess and savior of her people. Conflicts such as the Thirty Years' War and the English Civil War evoked countless prophecies, both political and religious; in fact, the early and mid-seventeenth century appears to mark a peak of stridency in efforts to sanction political goals through Biblical prophecy. Calvinist millenarianism was among the most fertile breeding grounds for a variety of radical political programs.

THE SLOW RETREAT

During this same period, however, a reaction against prophecy set in, moderating this surfeit of the spirit. The slow demise of prophetic history had already begun in the 1560s when Jean Bodin (1530–1596) attacked the traditional scheme of world empires; the dismantling of this framework accelerated in the following century. By 1700 the traditional prophetic worldview was in rapid retreat, at least among intellectuals, along with belief in miracles and most aspects of medieval cosmology. Yet the break between that worldview and a more enlightened outlook was by no means complete. Millenarian hopes, for example, have been convincingly linked to modern conceptions of historical progress as well as to positive attitudes toward the investigation of nature. Similarly, the transition from such prophetic notions as the Quaker "inner light" to the idea of natural reason was subtle, especially in an age when the distinction between nature and spirit was a matter of intense speculation.

While biblical prophecy was broadly attacked and ridiculed in the Enlightenment era, its retreat was both slow and stubborn. Isaac Newton was among the learned figures who worked to pare away the non-biblical accretions to prophecy in order to establish a purer science while preserving true prophecy. Major religious movements of the seventeenth and eighteenth centuries, including Pietism and Methodism, seethed with prophetic conviction. Eighteenth-century rulers and churchmen still had to reckon with perceptions based on long-standing prophetic traditions. The new age of reason was frequently understood in terms of prophetic fulfillment, even if the framework was often no longer biblical. The French Revolution was accompanied by a groundswell of prophetic interpretation and debate, much of which drew directly on the traditional biblical imagery. Certain prophecies had the potential to be self-fulfilling by creating a shared psychological readiness for the predicted outcomes.

Among European elites, however, spiritual prophecy was increasingly relegated to the subjective sphere, in which its public, political role was radically limited. In the eighteenth century spiritual inspiration was already frequently conceived in terms of artistic and literary genius. As biblical and supernatural imagery lost potency, Europeans encountered a world in which the realms of personal and political experience had lost their common prophetic ground.

See also **Apocalypticism; Astrology; Leyden, Jan van; Lutheranism; Magic; Miracles; Reformation, Protestant; Zwingli, Huldrych.**

BIBLIOGRAPHY

Barnes, Robin Bruce. *Prophecy and Gnosis: Apocalypticism in the Wake of the Lutheran Reformation.* Stanford, 1988.

Froom, Le Roy Edwin. *The Prophetic Faith of Our Fathers.* 4 vols. Washington, D.C., 1946–1954. An older but still useful survey by a Seventh Day Adventist. Volume two addresses the early modern era.

Lerner, Robert. *The Powers of Prophecy: The Cedar of Lebanon Vision from the Mongol Onslaught to the Dawn of the Enlightenment.* Berkeley, 1983. Fine survey of a single prophetic tradition.

Niccoli, Ottavia. *Prophecy and People in Renaissance Italy.* Princeton, 1990.

Petersen, Rodney L. *Preaching in the Last Days: The Theme of "Two Witnesses" in the Sixteenth and Seventeenth Centuries.* New York, 1993.

Reeves, Marjorie. *The Influence of Prophecy in the Later Middle Ages: A Study in Joachimism.* Oxford, 1969.

———. *Joachim of Fiore and the Prophetic Future.* New York, 1977. Studies aspects of Joachimism in the sixteenth and seventeenth centuries.

Schwartz, Hillel. *The French Prophets: The History of a Millenarian Group in Eighteenth-Century England.* Berkeley, 1980.

Taithe, Bertrand, and Tim Thornton, eds. *Prophecy: The Power of Inspired Language in History, 1300–2000.* Gloucestershire, U.K., 1997. Includes several helpful articles on the early modern scene.

Wilks, Michael, ed. *Prophecy and Eschatology.* Oxford, 1994.

ROBIN B. BARNES

PROSTITUTION. Between 1450 and 1789, prostitution underwent dramatic changes in organization and policing. Criminalization replaced medieval toleration; a genuine police force appeared in the seventeenth century; and a new attitude toward sex emerged in the late eighteenth century, which pathologized the prostitute and associated her with disease and the urban proletariat.

In the late Middle Ages, prostitution was tolerated. Urban elites in France, Spain, and Germany established municipally owned brothels that were meant to preserve the honor of honest women by satisfying the sexual appetites of the city youth. In the sixteenth century an abrupt change occurred: The municipal houses were closed in Augsburg (1532), Basel (1534), Frankfurt (1560), Seville (1620), and throughout France (1500–1525). The appearance of syphilis (1494) in Europe certainly contributed to this change in attitude. But other forces must have determined it, for between thirty and fifty years elapsed between the arrival of syphilis and the closings of the brothels. Larger, professional armies, the growth of social distinctions, and the Protestant and Catholic Reformations probably led to the demise of toleration. More soldiers made the municipal brothels dangerous, and the strict morality advocated by pastors and priests made whoring shameful. Protestants, like Martin Luther (1483–1546), condemned prostitutes, as did reforming Catholics like Pope Pius V. At the same time, the growth of social distinctions and the spread of better manners caused elite men to seek more refined and exclusive prostitutes or courtesans.

The term "courtesan" originated in the late 1400s at the papal court in Rome, where celibate clerks sought refined female company. In the sixteenth century, Italy had the most accomplished and celebrated courtesans. Venice was famous for its courtesans, and many visiting dignitaries, like the French king Henry III (ruled 1574–1589), sought an evening with one of these beauties. Some courtesans, like the Venetian Veronica Franco (1546–1591) and the Roman Tullia d'Aragona (1510–

1556), frequented men of letters and published poetry in their own right. Others were simply decorative, but all promised a more intimate and socially superior experience to the new elites of Europe.

Paradoxically, at the same time that the courtesan appeared, prostitution was criminalized throughout western Europe. In France, the Orléans ordinance of 1560 made soliciting in Paris a crime. In Rome, Pius V (reigned 1566–1572) repeatedly banished prostitutes. In Spain, Philip IV (ruled 1621–1643) decreed prostitution illegal in 1624. But these new laws had little effect. Early modern monarchs had neither the means nor the desire to hunt down prostitutes. Consequently, prostitution flourished in early modern Europe.

Prostitution. *Transporting Prostitutes to Saltpêtrière Prison,* painting by Étienne Jeaurat, 1757. THE ART ARCHIVE/MUSÉE CARNAVALET PARIS/DAGLI ORTI

Every European army had a host of camp followers, and each city unofficial "hot" streets where prostitutes plied their trade. The tavern was the most common site of prostitution, but soliciting also occurred on bridges, like the Pont-Neuf in Paris, in markets (like London's Covent Garden), and near theaters and opera houses. Both men and women ran brothels, but procuresses were probably more common than pimps. Prostitutes were generally native girls, born within the city walls, between the ages of sixteen and twenty-nine. Some family disruption—the death of a mother or the remarriage of a father—often preceded a girl's drift into prostitution, but the passage of an army was also a major factor. Many women's occupations—linen mender, washerwoman, and street vendor—served as a "cover" for prostitution, and some occupations, like orange sellers in London theaters or bouquet vendors in Paris, were practically synonymous with prostitution. How many prostitutes lived in most early modern cities? It is impossible to say because no police force existed to count or monitor prostitutes.

In 1670, the king of France appointed the first Parisian police chief and gave him broad powers. Small at first, the Parisian police force grew, and by 1700 it was sufficiently large to have an impact on prostitution. Brigades of mounted policemen crisscrossed the city arresting as many as eight hundred women a year. With the Watch Acts of 1751, London too acquired roving watchmen who bound over for trial as many as fifty prostitutes in a night. The most visible form of prostitution, streetwalking, was the target, but the police also monitored brothels and taverns.

The years between 1680 and 1740 were a period of intense repression in cities like Amsterdam and Paris. Prevailing attitudes toward prostitutes remained highly negative: Hogarth's six prints entitled *The Harlot's Progress* (1732) shows the rise of Moll Hackabout, a girl on the town, who is imprisoned and then dies a lonely death of syphilis. The Abbé Antoine-François Prévost d'Exiles's novel *Manon Lescaut* (1731) painted an equally bleak picture of a prostitute's imprisonment and decline, but Manon differed from Moll in that she was the object of the hero's love. Especially after Jean-Jacques Rousseau's novel *Julie; or, the New Héloise* (1761), Europeans came to view romantic love and sexuality

as the very core of the personality, the greatest self-fulfillment. These new attitudes worked against prostitutes, who now appeared to be selling something much more precious than a few moments' pleasure.

While the old religious strictures against prostitution waned, new objections to venal sex emerged. A few authors, including Bernard de Mandeville and Restif de la Bretonne, argued for the legalization and regulation of prostitution, but most thinkers worried about its health consequences. Syphilis and prostitutes were increasingly equated, and physicians began to shape public policy. In 1803, the first dispensary—run by the Paris police—opened in Paris. Here, prostitutes had to register and endure compulsory pelvic examinations. The dispensary evolved into an elaborate and invasive regulatory system that allowed the police to monitor working-class women and incarcerate those, the "rebels," who refused to be registered. In England, the authorities imported the Contagious Diseases Acts (1864, 1866, and 1869) from the colonies, subjecting working-class women in army garrisons and port cities to unprecedented surveillance and punishment. Similar sanitary measures appeared in Italy, Germany, and Russia. Prostitution was now regarded as "the" social evil, and prostitutes were subjected to arbitrary arrest and incarceration. By comparison, the episodic and unsystematic persecution of prostitutes in the early modern period looked benign.

See also **Crime and Punishment; Obstetrics and Gynecology; Police; Public Health; Sexuality and Sexual Behavior; Women.**

BIBLIOGRAPHY

Bénabou, Erica-Marie. *La prostitution et la police des moeurs au XVIIIe siècle.* Paris, 1987.

Henderson, Tony. *Disorderly Women in Eighteenth-Century London: Prostitution and Control in the Metropolis, 1730–1830.* London, 1999.

Perry, Mary Elizabeth. *Gender and Disorder in Early Modern Seville.* Princeton, 1990.

Roper, Lyndal. "Discipline and Respectability: Prostitution and the Reformation in Augsburg," *History Workshop Journal* 19 (1985): 3–28.

Rosenthal, Margaret F. *The Honest Courtesan: Veronica Franco, Citizen and Writer in Sixteenth-Century Venice.* Chicago, 1992.

Rossiaud, Jacques. *Medieval Prostitution.* Translated by Lydia G. Cochrane. New York, 1988.

KATHRYN NORBERG

PROTESTANT REFORMATION. *See* Reformation, Protestant.

PROTESTANTISM. *See* Anabaptism; Calvinism; Church of England; Clergy: Protestant Clergy; Dissenters, English; Huguenots; Lutheranism; Methodism; Moravian Brethren; Puritanism.

PROTO-INDUSTRY.
The term "proto-industry" refers to a form of manufacturing production and organization, and the process of proto-industrialization refers to a historical process and to an economic theory of development. Historians have generally accepted the central features of proto-industrialization as an economic process with deep social ramifications that began around 1650 (there is much more disagreement about when it ended), but they have been more skeptical about the theory as an explanation for the emergence of the industrial revolution.

A SYSTEM OF RURAL MANUFACTURING

As a historical process, proto-industrialization refers to an intensification of rural manufacturing that occurred in various parts of Europe after 1650, above all producing textiles for national and international markets. In other words, quickening demand beyond the immediate vicinity of production, and even overseas, was the fundamental stimulus for expanded production. Production was organized in cottage workshops, and the primary unit of production was the household. Merchants distributed raw materials like wool or flax (for making linen) to peasants. Men and women would spin the raw material into yarn, and merchants would then put the yarn out to weavers working looms in their cottages to produce cloth. Merchants would then distribute the cloth to other cottage workers for bleaching and dyeing and collect it a final time for sale to a whole-saler in a near or distant city. The peasant workers were paid piece rates.

This type of rural manufacturing, sometimes called "the putting-out system," existed at least from the sixteenth century, notably in the Netherlands, as merchants sought cheaper labor than what was available in towns, where cloth workers were well organized to defend their economic interests. Initially peasants engaged in cottage manufacturing to supplement their income from farming, spinning, and weaving in their homes in the intervals between planting and harvesting. As demand for textiles grew after 1650 and above all in the eighteenth century, however, merchants sought more and more cottage workers to produce more and more goods. Proto-industrialization took hold often, although not exclusively, in areas with poor soil, hilly terrain, or concentration of land in a few hands. It reached an unprecedented scale in the eighteenth century, even dominating particular regions in the Netherlands, northern France, the German Rhineland, Belgium, and above all England. Proto-industrialization had important economic ramifications. It strengthened marketing networks as the volume of textiles multiplied and contributed to the accumulation of profit to entrepreneurial merchants who in turn sought further outlets for reinvestment. Moreover, because workers were paid cash for their products, they became increasingly integrated into a cash- and wage-based manufacturing economy. Each of these factors further prepared Europe to make the leap into industrialization.

Contributing to the expansion of proto-industrialization in the eighteenth century were population growth and an increased and better supply of food. More rural workers became available, and expanding commercial farming provided markets with food for them. Proto-industry employed far more people than the traditional cottage industry had, and in some areas peasants gave up farming entirely and became dependent upon "wages" paid by urban merchants. In some rural regions, a majority of the population worked for urban merchants. In England, as commercial and capitalistic farmers purchased and enclosed more and more fields, the population of propertyless rural workers grew more dramatically than anywhere else in Europe.

As proto-industrialization advanced, more peasants were driven into poverty, and landless peasants were more inclined to work for low wages than urban artisans. Merchants, driven by increasing competition in the market and the capitalistic motive to maximize profit by minimizing costs, exploited this source of cheap, unorganized labor. Some historians refer to this process as proletarianization, referring to the transformation of once independent farmer-manufacturers into a class of propertyless, impoverished wageworkers totally reliant upon the merchant-capitalist—and the vagaries of demand in distant markets—for their livelihood. Such developments had deep social, even demographic, consequences. Recent empirical studies show that populations in proto-industrial regions looked very different from those in other rural areas or towns. Marriage ages dropped lower in proto-industrial communities than anywhere else, and fertility rates rose the most and the fastest. Because of the impoverishment that came with proletarianization, poor public health, and rising levels of occupational disease, mortality rates were the highest among these communities as well.

A THEORY OF ECONOMIC DEVELOPMENT

Proto-industrialization describes a historical process, but it also refers to a theory of economic development first advanced by Franklin Mendels in a seminal article in 1972. This theory, subsequently championed by such historians as Peter Kriedte, Hans Medick, and Jürgen Schlumbohm, argues that proto-industrialization had a direct and causal relation to the emergence of factory production, assumed to be the key characteristic of the industrial revolution. Moreover, it focuses almost exclusively upon the woolen, linen, and cotton industries. Empirical studies confirm, as the theory attests, that the first factories were in the countryside and often concentrated the decentralized cottage production in a single building. It is also true that in some areas proto-industrial merchants acquired substantial resources which they later invested in the building of new machines and factories. One can plausibly draw the conclusion, as the proponents of the theory of proto-industrialization have, that cottage manufacturing in both its small traditional form and as proto-industrialization was eventually replaced by factory production. And, of course, it is well known

that the cotton industry was the leader in factory-based industrial development.

The theory of proto-industrialization has as many critics as champions, however, among the earliest being Maxine Berg, Pat Hudson, and Michael Sonenscher. Recent research has demonstrated that industrialization was a slow and protracted process, certainly not complete by 1800, that it did not occur exclusively or even primarily in the countryside, and that it had multiple causes. Moreover, historians are much more inclined today to see the connections between proto-industry and factory production as more geographically limited than the theory originally asserted. Furthermore, studies of the economic functions of cities have shown that, contrary to the assumptions of the theory, cities and towns were not just centers of trade and finance, but were in fact also important manufacturing centers where productive artisans engaged in myriad industrial activities (increasingly supplementing their manual labor with mechanized sources of power as the nineteenth century unfolded), few of which were organized in proto-industrial fashion and even fewer of which evolved into factories.

Perhaps the weakest feature of the theory of proto-industrialization is its overemphasis on the factory in the emergence of industrialism. Research in the last ten years points out that it was only in the second half of the nineteenth century that factory production in textiles truly came to dominate, largely as a result of the widespread installation of power looms. In 1841 in England, for example, scarcely more than half (53 percent) of all cotton workers were employed in factories.

Recent empirical studies have prompted historians to conclude that there were many roads to industrialization, proto-industry and factory production in the countryside being but one, textiles being an important but certainly not the only industry. In fact, much industrialization occurred outside of the factory, notably in metal smelting and mining. A theory like proto-industrialization, therefore, is not so much wrong as limited in its applicability. Indeed, there were many areas of Europe where proto-industries thrived yet did not evolve into factories, nor did these areas sink into "deindustrialized" backwaters, the only two tra-

Proto-Industry. *Workshop of Weavers,* painting by Jacopo Bassano, Italian, sixteenth century. ©CAMERAPHOTO ARTE, VENICE/ART RESOURCE, N.Y.

jectories entertained by the theory of proto-industrialization. Even as some textile manufacturing moved into factories, out-work or cottage work expanded as manufacturers sent work home to be done by workers' families. This was particularly the case in the garment industry, where women did fine needlework and cloth finishing in their homes. Moreover, many other industries besides textiles were proto-industrialized (notably in metalware production), and continued to thrive throughout much of the nineteenth century, even as factory-based industrialization took hold. Indeed, as late as 1851 in England, only 5 percent of the overall industrial workforce worked in factories. Artisanal workshops in the countryside continued to exist and even expand, often as ancillary businesses supplementing the work being done in factories. Skilled machinists and tool and die makers, necessary for the functioning of the machines in the factories, are an illustrative case in point.

See also **Artisans; Capitalism; Commerce and Markets; Guilds; Industrial Revolution; Industry; Laborers; Poverty; Strikes; Textile Industry.**

BIBLIOGRAPHY

Berg, Maxine, Pat Hudson, and Michael Sonenscher, eds. *Manufacture in Town and Country before the Factory.* Cambridge, U.K., and New York, 1983.

Clarkson, Leslie A. *Proto-Industrialization: The First Phase of Industrialization?* Basingstoke, U.K., 1985.

Kriedte, Peter, Hans Medick, and Jürgen Schlumbohm. *Industrialization before Industrialization: Rural Industry in the Genesis of Capitalism.* Translated by Beate Schempp. Cambridge, U.K., and New York, 1981.

Leboutte, René, ed. *Proto-industrialisation: recherches récentes et nouvelles perspectives: Mélanges en souvenir de Franklin Mendels = Proto-Industrialization: Recent Researches and New Perspectives: In Memory of Franklin Mendels.* Geneva, 1996.

Mendels, Franklin F. "Proto-Industrialization: The First Phase of the Industrialization Process." *Journal of Economic History* 32, no. 1 (1972): 241–261.

Ogilvie, Sheilagh C., and Markus Cernan, eds. *European Proto-Industrialization: An Introductory Handbook.* Cambridge, U.K., and New York, 1996.

JAMES R. FARR

PROVIDENCE. Providence is God's foreknowledge, beneficent care, and governance over the universe at large and human affairs in particular. Providence also refers to God himself in his providential aspects, to a person who acts as the means of Providence, and to an act (favorable or unfavorable) witnessing or manifesting God's will. Providence is the hinge that explains and gives moral value to worldly events in terms of religious doctrine. The word derives from the Latin *providentia*, 'foresight'.

Christians, Jews, and Muslims of early modern Europe all prayed to an omnipotent Creator God and all therefore believed in divine Providence. Within this period, however, the concept of Providence was most contested and most invoked in the Latin West. Providence had always been important in Catholic theology, but it rose to greater prominence as the writings and theology of St. Augustine of Hippo (354–430) gained influence among many Catholic thinkers in the high and late Middle Ages. The Augustinian emphasis on the omnipotence of God brought with it linked beliefs that tied an emphasis on Providence to emphases on the importance of God's grace for the human soul's salvation and damnation, predestination, and God's positive responsibility for evil in the world. Augustine's influence was particularly strong among the members of the eponymous Augustinian monastic orders.

When the Augustinian monk Martin Luther (1483–1546) broke with Rome, he took his stand in large part on an Augustinian formulation of the sole power of God's grace to save souls. Huldrych Zwingli (1484–1531), John Calvin (1509–1564), and Théodore de Bèze (1519–1605) successively elaborated upon Luther's revolt by grounding salvation absolutely on the logical sequence of God's absolute sovereignty, God's continuing and providential control of the world, and God's predestining salvation and damnation of human souls. For both Lutheran and Reformed Protestants, Providence therefore assumed a far more central role in their doctrine than it had held for even the most Augustinian of medieval Catholics; for the Reformed, Providence was at the very core of their beliefs. Some of the most intense believers among the Reformed, such as the English Puritans, came to believe that they could discern the predestinate fate of their souls and achieve assurance of salvation by careful scrutiny of the signs of God's Providence in the world. For them, "experimental providentialism" was not only a matter of intellectual doctrine but was also the emotional heart of their practical divinity.

For early modern Catholics, Providence continued to be an important part of their theology. In polemics against Protestants, Catholic controversialists often invoked friendly Providence. Spanish writers referred to Providence to explain their nation's conquest of its New World empire, while Gaelic bards explained the English conquest and settlement of Ireland as God's providential punishment of the Gaels for their sins. Contemplation of the sure working out of God's Providence, manifested in works such as Thomas More's (1478–1535) *De Tristitia Christi* (1535; On the sorrow of Christ), also served to console Catholics during their misfortunes. The Augustinian note resounded among Catholics from the Reformation to the French Revolution.

Yet among Protestants, particularly among the Reformed, providentialism was far more intense, and it permeated their thought and culture. Faith in God's Providence gave the Huguenots the patience to endure massacres and political defeats during the French Wars of Religion, and the Dutch and the English saw the preservation of their political independence and religious liberty through the age of religious wars as providential dispensations to elect nations. Providentialism also united nations internally. In early seventeenth-century England, a popular culture of providentialism united the different Protestant subcultures; likewise, a century later the depiction of the Glorious Revolution (1688–1689) and the Protestant Succession as providential events underpinned the era's Whig political consensus. Providentialism also provided the material for much of the era's literature. Dutch travel accounts, Huguenot poetry, and English history plays—examples include Willem Ysbrantzoon Bontekoe's disaster thriller *The Memorable Account of the Voyage of the Nieuw Hoorn* (1646), Théodore-Agrippa d'Aubigné's epic recapitulation of the French Wars of Religion, *Les Tragiques* (1616), and Shakespeare's depiction of the triumph of Henry Tudor in *Richard III* (1594)—all manifest providential content and structure.

Providentialism could also be revolutionary, despite a tendency for all churches, states, and social orders to justify their establishment by claiming providential dispensation. The Scot John Knox (1506–1572) justified his resistance theory partly in terms of Providence; and a century later English Puritan saints-in-arms justified their actions promoting civil war, revolution, regicide, and an English republic with reference to the doctrine of Providence. Oliver Cromwell's (1599–1658) career provides an excellent case study of how providentialism could inspire military and political actions. Post-Restoration Puritans, chastened by the experience of political defeat, tended to a more fatalistic interpretation of Providence as they moved to the more passive politics of dissent.

Providentialism lessened in rough proportion to the general secularization of Western thought and was progressively supplanted by theories of causation that lessened or removed God's role in worldly events. In the scientific realm, chance, probability, and mechanical laws replaced concepts of providential causation: Pierre Gassendi (1592–1655), Robert Boyle (1627–1691), and Isaac Newton (1642–1727) successively distanced God from the day-to-day operations of the physical universe. In the realm of historical thought, providentialism had been fading since the Renaissance, when classicizing humanists such as Niccolò Machiavelli (1469–1527) reemphasized the pagan, profoundly unteleological concept of Fortune at the expense of Providence. The random purposelessness of history exemplified by Fortune would remain for historians after belief in the personified concept faded. Thomas More, Garcilaso de la Vega (1539–1616), Jacques Bénigne Bossuet (1627–1704), and Daniel Defoe (1660–1731) all upheld more providential

conceptions of history, but the disjunction of Providence from history would prove to be permanent and widening. Giovanni Battista Vico (1668–1744) retained a providential structure in his cyclical conception of human history, but removed it from the details of the historical narrative. Among Enlightenment historians, Voltaire (1694–1778) thought the philosophical historian, not God, gave history its structure and its moral purpose, while Anne-Robert-Jacques Turgot (1727–1781) substituted earthly progress for divine Providence, and thus bequeathed a this-worldly sublimation of providential history to Hegel and Marx.

With regard to Providence, Orthodox Christians responded with particular intensity to the new Protestant doctrines, and Jews with particular intensity to the claims of Newtonianism. Both, however, retained conceptions of Providence largely unchanged during this period.

See also **Bèze, Théodore de; Bossuet, Jacques-Bénigne; Boyle, Robert; Calvin, John; Cromwell, Oliver; Defoe, Daniel; Gassendi, Pierre; Glorious Revolution (Britain); Knox, John; Luther, Martin; Machiavelli, Niccolò; More, Thomas; Newton, Isaac; Puritanism; Reformation, Protestant; Vico, Giovanni Battista; Voltaire; Wars of Religion, French; Zwingli, Huldrych.**

BIBLIOGRAPHY

There are dozens, if not hundreds, of books and articles dealing with Providence in early modern Europe—although the focus is largely upon Providence in England. For theological surveys that include mention of Providence, see Alister McGrath, *Reformation Thought: An Introduction* (Oxford, 1988); George A. Maloney, S. J., *A History of Orthodox Theology since 1453* (Belmont, Mass., 1976); and A. D. Wright, *The Counter-Reformation: Catholic Europe and the Non-Christian World* (New York, 1982). For more specialized books and articles on Providence, see Barbara Donagan, "Providence, Chance and Explanation: Some Paradoxical Aspects of Puritan Views of Causation," *Journal of Religious History* 11 (1981): 385–403; M. A. Fitzsimons, "The Role of Providence in History," *The Review of Politics* 35, 3 (1973): 386–397; Peter Lake, "Calvinism and the English Church 1570–1635," *Past and Present* 114 (1987): 32–76; Keith Thomas, *Religion and the Decline of Magic* (London, 1971), pp. 78–112; Alexandra Walsham, *Providence in Early Modern England* (Oxford, 1999); and Blair Worden, "Providence and Politics in Cromwellian England," *Past and Present* 109 (1985): 55–99.

DAVID RANDALL

PROVINCIAL GOVERNMENT.

PROVINCIAL GOVERNMENT. For the rulers of early modern Europe, maintaining control of vast and often distant territories was a complex task. Communications were slow and it could take weeks, months, or even years for the most basic instructions to be relayed from center to periphery. Indeed, even when orders arrived promptly, there could be no guarantee that they would be carried out by powerful provincial subjects, many of whom were accustomed to self-government and were determined to maintain their own privileges and interests. To ensure obedience and to secure the military, financial, and other resources they required, rulers were obliged to tread carefully, and any attempt to centralize power or to ignore provincial opinion risked provoking opposition and possibly revolt. In order to avoid these pitfalls, it was necessary to employ a variety of strategies, and despite the great increase in state power that was achieved during the early modern period, governing the provinces was still a delicate business on the eve of the French Revolution.

GOVERNORS AND VICEROYS

Although the methods employed varied widely, the key to successful provincial government was cooperation. A consensus was required that would balance the interests of the ruler with those of provincial elites. To achieve that end it was necessary to have effective representatives of princely authority resident in the provinces. Both branches of the Habsburg family faced an immense challenge as they sought to control the constituent parts of their composite empires. As many of these territories, such as Bohemia, Hungary, and Sicily, were kingdoms in their own right, their culture, languages, and institutions had to be treated with respect. Throughout the period it was standard practice for a junior, or female, member of the ruling house to be sent as regent or viceroy to oversee local government. Margaret of Parma, half-sister of Philip II, was thus installed as regent of the Netherlands from 1559 to 1566, while the archduke Leopold, brother of the emperor Joseph II, served as grand duke of Tuscany from 1765 to 1790. When a member of the ruling house was unavailable, the viceroy would be a member of one of the most distinguished aristocratic families from the courts of Madrid or Vienna.

Within the more geographically confined kingdom of France, it was common for the king's cousins, the princes of the blood, or aristocratic grandees to serve as governors of the provinces. Only those of the very highest social station could represent the king, and exalted rank was a necessary prerequisite because of the need for a governor to have higher, or at least equal, rank to that of the most distinguished provincial. To rule effectively, a governor needed to be able to attract the loyalty of local elites, and in this respect the control of patronage was vital. A whole variety of military and civilian offices were distributed with the aim of constructing a loyal clientele whose support would enable the governor to maintain order, collect taxes, and carry out the orders of the king. Ideally the governor was allowed to act with a degree of independence, seeking advice from local elites and wherever possible working with existing institutions. Success depended upon a variety of factors, notably a willingness to allow provincial magnates to participate in government and in the dispensation of patronage.

PROVOKING REVOLT

When rulers forgot or chose to ignore these golden rules, they courted disaster. The Dutch Revolt against Philip II of Spain, which began in 1565–1566, was caused, in part, by the exclusion of local magnates from the regency council. This, combined with the Spanish king's aversion to Calvinism, which was spreading among his Dutch subjects, did much to turn a revolt into a war of independence. Elsewhere Philip II proved more adept, and after securing the Portuguese crown in 1580, he was mindful of the need to woo his reluctant new subjects, whose authority and interests he respected. The lesson was later forgotten by his grandson, Philip IV, whose mishandling of the Portuguese grandees provoked a revolt (1640–1668) that again led to independence. The Austrian Habsburgs faced similar problems, especially when it came to dealing with the effects of the Protestant Reformation. Calvinism inspired the Bohemian revolt of 1618 that detonated the Thirty Years' War, and it contributed to periodic rebellions in Hungary throughout the seventeenth century. Novel religious ideas were not the only cause of dissent, and when Joseph II sought to impose reform upon the Catholic Church in the Austrian Netherlands (modern Belgium) in 1787 he provoked fierce resistance from a local population that was determined to defend traditional practice.

In France, the immense power of the provincial governors could in itself become dangerous if they were tempted to use that authority against the king or his ministers, and between 1560 and 1653 the kingdom suffered periodic bouts of civil war led by aristocratic warlords such as the Condé, the Montmorency, and the Guise. They used their provincial power bases to supply the forces needed to pursue their religious and factional aims, and at times they threatened to tear the kingdom apart. Spain witnessed similar scenes during the reign of the feeble Charles II, and in 1676 a revolt of the grandees resulted in the overthrow of the government led by the queen mother's favorite, Fernando de Valenzuela.

The degree of conflict should not, however, be exaggerated, and revolt was nearly always the last resort, as failure could have very painful consequences. When Valencia and Catalonia rose against Philip V during the War of the Spanish Succession (1701–1714), their subsequent defeat meant that they lost their cherished *fueros* (privileges) as a result. As for the leaders of failed provincial revolts, they often paid with their lives, and the great French aristocrat the duc de Montmorency was beheaded in 1632 after leading an unsuccessful uprising in Languedoc.

CENTRALIZATION

After 1650, the increasing cost and complexity of warfare made revolt a hazardous business, and as the power of the state expanded, the temptation to centralize decision making at the expense of the provinces increased. In France, this process was associated with the intendants, administrators appointed by the king and sent to the provinces with extensive powers to intervene in matters affecting justice, public order, and taxation. The attempt to exercise these responsibilities frequently brought the intendants into conflict with existing institutions and officeholders, but by 1689 an intendant was resident in every French province. Thereafter they gradually expanded their administrative authority, acting as the eyes and ears of the king, levying taxes, overseeing the lives of towns and villages, building roads, encouraging agriculture and commerce, and much else. The dedication of the intendants provided the French crown with loyal and adaptable administrative agents, although to be really effective they were expected to work alongside the governor and to show sensitivity to provincial interests.

When Louis XIV's grandson became Philip V of Spain in 1700, he introduced the intendants as part of a plan to reform Spanish administration. As in France, existing local institutions proved hostile, and it was not until mid-century that the new system put down firm roots. Successive rulers of Russia were also attracted to the model of centralization, but they faced a particularly arduous task given the sheer size of their territories, a problem exacerbated by the almost complete absence of any tradition of independent provincial self-government. Despite the many fine words contained in the local government reforms introduced by both Peter I (ruled 1682–1725) and Catherine II (ruled 1762–1796), provincial administration in their empire consisted of little more than an arbitrary and often brutal struggle to maintain order and extract taxation.

REPRESENTATIVE BODIES

The desire to centralize decision making and to reduce the scope for opposition frequently brought rulers into conflict with the provinces because many possessed parliaments or estates to defend their interests. Most had been in existence since the Middle Ages, and they could usually cite charters or privileges granted by earlier rulers that enshrined the right to participate in government. As a result, such diverse regions as Brittany, Catalonia, Styria, and Zeeland could boast of their own "constitutions," and they claimed the right of consent on crucial matters such as taxation. Although not representative bodies in a modern democratic sense, being generally composed of the wealthy and powerful, they nevertheless defended local interests tenaciously, and their potential as an alternative source of political authority ensured that rulers were tempted to limit their influence or even to end their assemblies. During the seventeenth century, the provincial estates of Guyenne, Normandy, and Dauphiné ceased to meet, as did those of Brandenburg and Bavaria.

Over the period as a whole, the number of representative bodies was in decline, and those that survived have often been treated as medieval relics, to be contrasted with the supposedly more modern centralized administration of the state. In reality, they were usually lively and vibrant institutions, which provided an important forum for negotiation between rulers and their provincial elites. One of the most successful states of the early modern period, the Dutch Republic, was in effect a federation of seven provinces, each with its own Estates that in turn sent representatives to the Estates-General. Local interests were defended fiercely and effectively, and concessions to the center required prior discussion and consent.

Provincial estates in France and the Austrian Habsburg empire were also powerful institutions that were entrusted with the crucial tasks of raising taxation, overseeing local administration, and conscripting men for the army. In Austria there was, however, a movement to strengthen the central authority of governors and their staffs after 1740 as part of a series of reforms designed to meet the challenge of Prussia, a process that accelerated during the reign of Joseph II. In France, on the other hand, the eighteenth century witnessed a movement in the opposite direction, and where Estates survived, as was the case in, for example, the provinces of Artois, Brittany, Burgundy, and Languedoc, they rapidly expanded their administrative competence, assuming responsibility for the tasks performed by the intendants elsewhere. Contemporaries were almost unanimous in declaring that those provinces administered by the Estates were better governed, and the public confidence they acquired proved to be a valuable resource for the state. In the century before 1789, they borrowed millions for the crown at a fraction of the interest rate that the king could command on his own account. Perhaps not surprisingly, there was increasing support for the idea of establishing provincial Estates, or assemblies, throughout France and local government decentralization, in the form of the *départements*, was one of the first and most impressive reforms implemented after 1789.

Other states were also willing to work with representative institutions in the provinces. The Spanish Habsburgs appointed governors to oversee their rule in Milan, but they were always careful not to interfere in the internal affairs of the patricians who dominated the Milanese senate. Their Austrian cousins were generally respectful of the rights of their Hungarian subjects. Local administration in Hungary was controlled by the county assemblies *(congregationes),* where the nobility gathered to discuss public affairs. Austrian rule would have been almost impossible without their cooperation, and when Joseph II imposed a new system of local government that sharply reduced the authority of the county assemblies a major revolt was the predictable result. Finally, in Poland the very weakness of the central government ensured that the localities had considerable autonomy. The nobility regularly gathered in assemblies, known as the *sejmiki,* not only to elect envoys to represent them at the national diet, but also to attend to matters of local interest free of interference from an almost powerless crown.

See also **Dutch Republic; Dutch Revolt (1568–1648); Habsburg Dynasty; Intendants; Representative Institutions; Spanish Succession, War of the (1701–1714); Thirty Years' War (1618–1648).**

BIBLIOGRAPHY

Beik, William. *Absolutism and Society in Seventeenth-Century France. State Power and Provincial Aristocracy in Languedoc.* Cambridge, U.K., and New York, 1985.

Collins, James B. *Classes, Estates, and Order in Early Modern Brittany.* Cambridge, U.K., and New York, 1994.

Friedrich, Karin. *The Other Prussia. Royal Prussia, Poland and Liberty, 1569–1772.* Cambridge, U.K., and New York, 2000.

Israel, Jonathan. *The Dutch Republic: Its Rise, Greatness, and Fall, 1477–1806.* Oxford, 1996.

Kettering, Sharon. *Patrons, Brokers and Clients in Seventeenth-Century France.* Oxford and New York, 1986.

Kivelson, Valerie A. *Autocracy in the Provinces: The Muscovite Gentry and Political Culture in the Seventeenth Century.* Stanford, 1996.

Lynch, John. *The Hispanic World in Crisis and Change, 1598–1700.* Oxford, 1992.

Pörtner, Regina. *The Counter-Reformation in Central Europe: Styria, 1580–1630.* Oxford and New York, 2001.

Swann, Julian. *Provincial Power and Absolute Monarchy. The Estates General of Burgundy, 1661–1790.* Cambridge, U.K., and New York, 2003.

JULIAN SWANN

PRUSSIA. Prussia has become a byword for Germany, but it originally developed on the southeastern Baltic shore distinct from the German-speaking population of the Holy Roman Empire. Prussia's subsequent association with central Europe stems from the Hohenzollern dynasty, which came to rule both it and much of north Germany and helped forged these disparate possessions into a major European power.

CONFLICTING VIEWS OF EARLY MODERN PRUSSIA

Historical writing on Prussia is dominated by two related problems. First, there is the controversy surrounding the region historically known as Prussia that has become enmeshed in political and ideological struggles between Germans and Poles. Second, there is the ambiguous place of the state known more properly as Brandenburg-Prussia in the wider history of Germany and Europe. Historic Prussia lay on the Baltic shore east of the Oder River. German nationalist historians claimed this region for themselves, portraying its conquest by the Teutonic Order after 1222 as a victory for Christian civilization over pagan barbarism. In this story, Germanization was equated with modernization. Polish historians saw the same events as foreign conquest and the brutal repression of an indigenous culture and language. Thanks to its wider international dissemination, the German version of Prussian history remains the most widely known today, with most writers unwittingly adopting the nationalist geographical distinctions of East and West Prussia to label the two parts under German and Polish rule in the early modern period. These terms imply a false unity in the region and suggest the inevitability of German domination over the whole area that came after 1795 and lasted until 1918. While the Polish terms of Ducal and Royal Prussia are more appropriate, Prussian history cannot be interpreted entirely through the lens of later Polish nationalism and should be seen as something both distinct in its own right and intricately connected to the experience of the entire Baltic region.

Prussia's place in German and European history has also been subject to widely differing interpretations. Many German nationalist historians saw it as the embodiment of an ideal social and political order and interpreted all German history from a Prussian perspective. While not uniformly hagiographic, this approach was known as the "Borussian" school and generally stressed that historical events were made by "great men," such as rulers and statesmen.

Military power and authoritarian rule were regarded as essential for Prussia's survival within a hostile international environment and for its "historic mission" to unite the rest of Germany in the nineteenth century. Prussia's influence in the nineteenth century, when it controlled two-thirds of German soil, was projected back into the early modern period when its rulers governed only a tenth of the Holy Roman Empire prior to the mid-seventeenth century and still held no more than a fifth of the entire area in 1806. The empire was largely written out of German history, which was presented as a dualism between Prussia and Austria, prefiguring the struggles over national unification in the mid-nineteenth century. Religious history was woven into this political narrative, portraying Prussia as the Protestant champion against a backward and malevolent Catholic Habsburg Monarchy based in Austria. The experience of two world wars in the twentieth century encouraged significant revisions to this interpretation. Many writers retained the overall Borussian framework, but changed it from a success story to one leading to disaster. This school emphasizes the German *Sonderweg,* or 'special path', and presents Prusso-German development as deviating from a supposedly progressive European pattern and pushing German history down a separate militaristic and authoritarian route.

THE TEUTONIC ORDER

Prussia was not as powerful, advanced, or militaristic and repressive as these interpretations imply. Its early modern history was shaped by the legacy left by the Teutonic Knights. This aristocratic crusading order was founded in 1198 and was sponsored by Polish kings as well as medieval emperors. The Knights created a large state on the southeastern Baltic shore by the fourteenth century. Their conquests were not simply a process of Western Christian conquest since they relied heavily on a local population that was partially assimilated into the order's state. Sections of this population chafed under the Knights' increasingly arbitrary rule, leading to the establishment of the Prussian Estates, or representative assembly, in 1411, one year after the order's defeat by the Polish king at the battle of Tannenberg. Though the Prussian towns were represented, the landed nobility dominated the Estates. The order was unable to stem growing Polish influence and was defeated by a major rebellion after

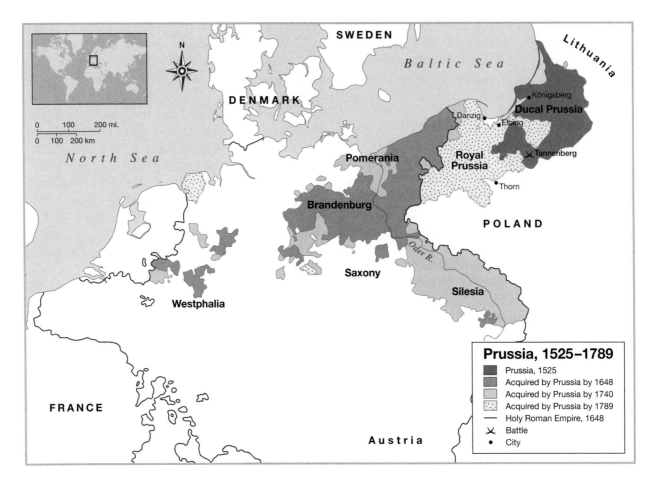

1454, resulting in the partition of Prussia twelve years later. The western half became Royal Prussia under Polish sovereignty and included the important trading cities of Danzig (Gdańsk), Elbing (Elblag) and Thorn (Torun). The order was left with the eastern half, covering 14,270 square miles (36,960 square kilometers), which contained few significant towns other than Königsberg (Kaliningrad). The order's last grand master, Albert von Hohenzollern, tried to reverse this in a new war against Poland from 1519, but only escaped total defeat by secularizing the order's state as a hereditary duchy under Polish overlordship in 1525. Hohenzollern rule lasted until 1918. A remnant of the Teutonic Order regrouped under a new Grand Master, Walter of Cronenberg, who established a new seat in Franconia with a residence in Mergentheim.

ROYAL PRUSSIA

Political separation gradually eroded ties between the two halves of Prussia. Royal Prussia became more closely integrated into the Commonwealth of Poland-Lithuania in the sixteenth century, particularly after 1569 when its nobility secured representation in the Polish Sejm (diet). The three great royal cities of Danzig, Elbing, and Thorn refused to send deputies to the Sejm, but nonetheless saw the commonwealth as protecting their local privileges and autonomy. Together with the nobles, they sought to enhance this autonomy by making Royal Prussia an equal partner with Poland and Lithuania in the commonwealth, but were thwarted by the opposition of the king and the Sejm and had to be satisfied with their own provincial diet. Royal Prussia shared the general development of the commonwealth, participating in its period of cultural and political influence in the later sixteenth and early seventeenth centuries and then declining with the impact of external invasions after 1654. Like the Sejm, the Royal Prussian diet introduced the *liberum veto,* which meant that an objection from one deputy was sufficient to invalidate all legislation passed in one session. This hamstrung the diet between 1713 and 1728 and again between 1735 and 1763. External interference mounted, notably from

Hohenzollern Prussia, polarizing local politics. Self-styled patriots expressed a desire for greater autonomy and used the diet to block reforms proposed by the Polish Sejm after 1764, weakening the commonwealth and precipitating its total collapse between 1772 and 1795.

This collapse saw the reintegration of Royal Prussia into the area ruled by the Hohenzollerns. However, this area had changed fundamentally over the intervening three centuries. Hohenzollern rule was initially very weak. The Teutonic Order retained land within the empire and remained Catholic whereas the new Hohenzollern duke converted to Lutheranism. Because the Prussian lands were not part of the Holy Roman Empire, the empire offered no protection and Albert's possessions in Prussia were not joined immediately to those of the other branch of his family, which had ruled Brandenburg since 1415.

SOCIETY AND ECONOMY

These political divisions did not prevent Hohenzollern Prussia from participating in the general trend to the manorial economy (*Gutswirtschaft*), common to Royal Prussia, Brandenburg, and Poland from the early sixteenth century onward. Farms were consolidated into large estates worked by serfs who were obliged to produce grain that was exported for profit to western European cities. While harsh, this system still allowed limited autonomy to peasant households to organize daily life and labor. As in Brandenburg, the Hohenzollerns intervened from the seventeenth century to divert the lords' profits into their own treasury as taxes. Few nobles could afford to live on agrarian income alone, and most sought military, administrative, or clerical careers. While this inclined many to collaborate with the duke, it would be wrong to see Hohenzollern rule simply as a compromise between crown and nobility at the expense of serfs and urban burghers. Neither was it an exercise in the creation of an impartial, benign government as sometimes implied by Borussian historians. Instead it was a complex, shifting process of bargaining between the crown and key social groups, serfs and burghers included. Like their counterparts in Royal Prussia, the eastern Prussian nobles were not a homogenous social group. Comparatively few corresponded to the archetype of the *Krautjunker,* the boorish back-woods nobleman who directly supervised his estates and spurned wider horizons. Many were at the forefront of agrarian development, particularly in the eighteenth century, when they saw the introduction of wage labor in place of serfdom as a way of boosting their profits. Some gravitated to the world of the Hohenzollern court, embracing Calvinism in the seventeenth century and supporting absolutism. Others favored continued ties to their cousins in Royal Prussia or Poland, sharing their notions of ancient aristocratic freedoms.

HOHENZOLLERN PRUSSIA

The Hohenzollerns made no headway amid this web of conflicting interests and loyalties. The eastern Prussian nobility cooperated with Königsberg in the duchy's own Estates to restrict the duke's income and insist that only locals be appointed to administrative positions. The foundation of a new university in Königsberg in 1544 did little to change this. Albert was bankrupt by his death in 1568 and was followed by the thirteen-year-old Albert Frederick. The new duke suffered from prolonged mental illness and lost control of the government to his Brandenburg relations, who took over as regents in 1605. Thanks to a dynastic inheritance treaty, ducal Prussia passed to Brandenburg on the duke's death in 1618. With the accession of George William in 1619, Brandenburg and Prussia had a common ruler and began their historic association.

Unfortunately for the Hohenzollerns, this coincided with the start of the Thirty Years' War in the empire and renewed conflict between Poland and Sweden. The dynasty was thrown on the defensive, and security rather than expansion remained its overriding concern into the eighteenth century. Their possessions fell into three unequal areas. In addition to ducal Prussia in the east and Brandenburg in the center, they now also held scattered lands in Westphalia close to the Dutch border. Though much smaller than Prussia, these western territories were potentially more important because of their comparatively large populations and active economies. George William's Brandenburg title of elector took precedence over his Prussian title of duke since it was more prestigious and gave him a role in imperial politics.

Borussian historians interpreted Hohenzollern policy as a coherent plan to unite these three areas

Prussia. A map from the April 1757 issue of *General Magazine of Arts & Sciences* showing the location of the action in the Seven Years' War. ("As, according to some late accounts . . . of the Disposition and Motion of the forces of the King of Prussia, we suppose it probable, that the Operations of War will be extended to the Kingdom of Poland. . . . Will enable our readers to view the whole seat of war"). MAP COLLECTION, STERLING MEMORIAL LIBRARY, YALE UNIVERSITY

and establish a uniform, centralized administrative system. Certainly, the dynasty benefited from an unbroken succession of healthy, adult, and generally capable rulers. However, far from shaping history, these rulers responded to pressures that were largely beyond their control. Prussia's growth was uneven and largely unplanned. Its rulers shared the general belief that princes were bound by Christian duty to protect their subjects and promote their well-being. Yet their primary motive remained the enhancement of their dynastic prestige and influence. Territorial expansion was intended to provide security for existing possessions and to bring new titles and resources. The empire remained their primary area of activity until the later eighteenth century, and at no point did they see themselves as the future leaders of a united Germany.

George William was dragged into the Thirty Years' War by 1626. Once involved, he tried to secure the duchy of Pomerania, whose ruling family had died out in 1637, but he was defeated by Sweden. His successor Frederick William (1620–1688; ruled 1640–1688), better known as the "Great Elector," was unable to change this situation after 1640 and was forced to accept Swedish control of the western half of Pomerania in the 1648 Peace of Westphalia. Hoping to deflect Hohenzollern ambitions, Sweden supported Brandenburg claims elsewhere in the empire, increasing the dynasty's territory by a quarter to 40,586 square miles (105,119 square kilometers) with 600,000 inhabitants in 1648.

ABSOLUTISM

Frederick William, the Great Elector, is a pivotal figure in Prussian history. Though not the farsighted modernizer of Borussian legend, he nonetheless forged a minimal level of centralized rule

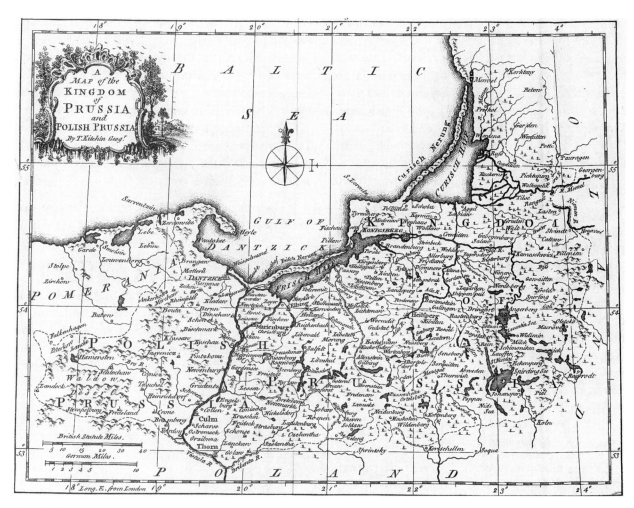

Prussia. From the *London Magazine* of December 1757, this map was designed to inform British readers of the situation in Prussia at the beginning of the Seven Years' War. Map Collection, Sterling Memorial Library, Yale University

necessary for future expansion. He was assisted by the disunity of his possessions, each of which had its own Estates that failed to make common cause with their counterparts elsewhere. By shuttling his troops and key negotiators from one province to another, the elector broke their resistance in turn between 1644 and 1663. The western enclaves and ducal Prussia offered the most resistance. In return for regular taxes, the Hohenzollerns largely left their western provinces alone after the 1660s and extended this light hand to the duchy of East Frisia, which they acquired in 1744, as well as the two margravates of Ansbach and Bayreuth in southwestern Germany, inherited in 1792. By contrast, Prussian opposition was crushed by force, with Königsberg twice being occupied by troops (1663, 1672). The reason for this different approach lies in the Hohenzollerns' relationship to their overlords,

the Holy Roman emperor and the Polish king. As electors under the empire, they enjoyed exclusive jurisdiction only over Brandenburg itself, where they were able to prevent their subjects from appealing to the imperial courts. The Estates in their other German provinces remained free to do this into the late eighteenth century, and while this became more difficult, all their German territories remained part of the empire until 1806. The elector could act differently in Prussia, because he skillfully exploited the Northern War (1655–1660) to force the king of Poland to renounce his sovereignty over ducal Prussia. Prussian nobles were unable to appeal to the commonwealth to protect their liberties after 1660.

Hohenzollern sovereignty over Prussia crushed its nobles' dreams of reunification with Royal Prussia but did not signal a reorientation toward Germany. Instead, the Hohenzollerns drew on local traditions to foster a distinctly Prussian identity that regarded other Germans as "foreign." This was used to support enhanced Hohenzollern status as an equal member of European royalty, no longer mere princes of the empire or vassals of the Polish king. The Great Elector's successor after 1688, Elector Frederick III (ruled 1688–1701), pursued this by developing a lavish court culture in Berlin and his other chief cities. More fundamentally, he avoided challenging the Habsburgs in the empire and supported their claims to the Spanish succession. His reward came at the end of 1700 when Emperor Leopold I agreed that he could crown himself "king in Prussia." Though ridiculed by his successors as an unnecessary extravagance, the lavish coronation ceremony in Königsberg in January 1701 was staged precisely because this new title lacked full international recognition. Now styled Frederick I, the new king continued to support the Habsburgs throughout the War of the Spanish Succession (1701–1714) in order to win acceptance from the other European powers. Since his new royal title took precedence over that of elector, the Hohenzollern monarchy now became known as Prussia.

While minor gains pushed Hohenzollern territory to 46,617 square miles (120,272 square kilometers) by 1720, two-thirds of this still remained within the empire. Frederick's policies reflected this as he looked primarily westward, despite his parallel involvement in the later stages of the Great Northern War (1700–1721) against Sweden. His representatives became more active in imperial institutions, notably taking advantage of the conversion of Elector Frederick Augustus of Saxony to Catholicism in 1697 to wrest the leadership of the German Protestants from the traditional heartland of the Reformation. His successors capitalized on Protestant sympathies in the empire to mobilize support against the Habsburgs, who suddenly realized they could not control their Hohenzollern protégé.

Religion also supplemented loyalty to the dynasty as a bond between the disparate provinces. Frederick and his immediate successor after 1713, Frederick William I (ruled 1713–1740), sponsored the Lutheran spiritual movement known as Pietism, whose values of thrift, obedience, and self-sacrifice dovetailed with their own agenda of a hard-working, loyal population. However, this "Prussian

ethos" was always contradictory and contested, appealing to both its martial king and its pacifist Pietist pastors. Moreover, the dynasty remained uncomfortable with any notion of nationalism defined by language or culture, particularly as their territorial expansion after 1740 added millions of Silesian and Polish Catholics to their subjects. The European Enlightenment took firm hold in Berlin after 1740, but after 1786 the religious establishment turned sharply conservative.

These acquisitions began during the reign of Frederick II, better known as Frederick the Great (1712–1786), who followed his father in 1740. Frederick inherited a kingdom that was still only partially centralized. His father had amalgamated several administrative institutions to form a General Directory as a central coordinating institution in 1723, but much administration remained in the hands of local nobles and magistrates. Later reforms failed to alter this, although the staff became more professional, adopting qualifying entrance exams for senior posts, as well as a more regular salary, promotions, and pension structure. However, Prussian government was not necessarily more advanced or efficient than those in many other German territories.

What impressed contemporaries most about Prussia was its army, which had been established by the Great Elector and increased by each of his successors. Frederick William I expanded it further with a form of limited conscription introduced by 1733. Men were inducted for basic training and then discharged back into the agrarian economy, apart from annual exercises. Many historians see this as the origins of later German militarism since it supported an inflated establishment and encouraged both subservience to authority and the acceptance of war as inevitable. This can be questioned, because the new system also civilianized soldiers, most of whom spent more time working in the fields or as day laborers in the towns than they did drilling on the parade ground.

Military expansion certainly gave Frederick the Great the means to challenge Austria after 1740. The Habsburg Monarchy was uniquely vulnerable in 1740, having just waged two disastrous wars that left its treasury empty and its army disorganized. Moreover, the death of Emperor Charles VI in October 1740 ended an unbroken succession of Habsburg emperors since 1438, opening an international conflict over the Austrian inheritance (War of the Austrian Succession) and denying the dynasty a legal claim on German resources through imperial institutions. Frederick profited from these circumstances to seize the Habsburg province of Silesia between 1740 and 1745. This move dictated policy for the rest of his reign that countered Habsburg attempts to either recover Silesia or find alternative territory elsewhere in Germany. Prussia now had little interest in preserving the empire beyond using it as a framework to immobilize the Habsburgs. While the acquisition of Silesia formally increased its territorial presence within the empire, it shifted Prussian political gravity eastward. This continued with the three partitions of Poland, in which Prussia joined Austria and Russia in annexing the entire Polish Commonwealth between 1772 and 1795. The Hohenzollerns acquired all of Royal Prussia, together with considerable land farther to the south, bringing their total possessions to 119,950 square miles (309,472 square kilometers) and 8.5 million inhabitants. This expansion coincided with ineffective involvement in the war against revolutionary France after 1792, leaving the crown barely able to suppress a Polish rebellion in 1794–1795. Prussia pulled out of the war in the west in 1795, having transformed a treasury reserve of 51 million talers into a debt of 48 million at a time when revenues totaled only 22 million. Discussion of internal reform intensified but failed to produce significant results before old Prussia collapsed in a new war against France in 1806.

See also **Austrian Succession, War of the (1740–1748); Berlin; Brandenburg; Frederick I (Prussia); Frederick II (Prussia); Frederick William I (Prussia); Frederick William II (Prussia); Hohenzollern Dynasty; Holy Roman Empire; Northern Wars; Pietism; Poland-Lithuania, Commonwealth of, 1569–1795; Teutonic Knights; Thirty Years' War (1618–1648).**

BIBLIOGRAPHY

Berdahl, Robert M. *The Politics of the Prussian Nobility: The Development of a Conservative Ideology 1770–1848.* Princeton, 1988.

Burleigh, Michael. *Prussian Society and the German Order: An Aristocratic Corporation in Crisis c. 1410–1466.* Cambridge, U.K., and New York, 1984.

Büsch, Otto. *Military System and Social Life in Old Regime Prussia 1713–1807: The Beginnings of the Social Militarization of Prusso-German Society.* Translated by John G. Gagliardo. Atlantic Highlands, N.J., 1997. Originally published in Berlin, 1962.

Carsten, Francis L. *A History of the Prussian Junkers.* Aldershot, U.K., and Brookfield, Vt., 1989.

———. *The Origins of Prussia.* Oxford, 1954.

Dorwart, Reinhold August. *The Administrative Reforms of Frederick William I of Prussia.* Cambridge, Mass., 1953.

———. *The Prussian Welfare State before 1740.* Cambridge, Mass., 1971.

Dywer, Philip G., ed. *The Rise of Prussia 1700–1830.* Harlow, U.K., and New York, 2000.

Frey, Linda, and Marsha Frey. *Frederick I: The Man and His Times.* New York, 1984.

Friedrich, Karin. *The Other Prussia: Royal Prussia, Poland, and Liberty 1569–1772.* Cambridge, U.K., and New York, 2000.

Gawthrop, Richard L. *Pietism and the Making of Eighteenth-Century Prussia.* Cambridge, U.K., 1993.

Hagen, William W. "The Descent of the *Sonderweg*. Hans Rosenberg's History of Old Regime Prussia." *Central European History* 24 (1991): 24–50.

Harnisch, Hartmut. "Der preußische Absolutismus und die Bauern. Sozialkonservative Gesellschaftspolitik und Vorleistung zur Modernisierung." *Jahrbuch für Wirtschaftsgeschichte* 2 (1994): 1–32.

Hauser, Oswald. ed. *Preußen, Europa und das Reich.* Cologne, 1987.

Hubatsch, Walter. *Frederick the Great: Absolutism and Administration.* London, 1975.

Johnson, Hubert C. *Frederick the Great and His Officials.* New Haven, 1975.

Kathe, Hans. *Preußen zwischen Mars und Musen. Eine Kulturgeschichte von 1100 bis 1920.* Munich, 1993.

Koch, Hans W. *A History of Prussia.* London and New York, 1978.

McKay, Derek. *The Great Elector.* Harlow, U.K., 2001.

Melton, James Van Horn. *Absolutism and the Eighteenth-Century Origins of Compulsory Schooling in Prussia and Austria.* Cambridge, U.K., and New York, 1988.

Midelfort, H. C. Erik. *Mad Princes of Renaissance Germany.* Charlottesville, Va., 1994.

Mittenzwei, Ingrid, and Erika Herzfeld. *Brandenburg-Preußen 1648–1789: Das Zeitalter des Absolutismus in Text und Bild.* Cologne, 1987.

Müller-Weil, Ulrike. *Absolutismus und Außenpolitik in Preußen: Ein Beitrag zur Strukturgeschichte des preußischen Absolutismus.* Stuttgart, 1992.

Rosenberg, Hans. *Bureaucracy, Aristocracy, and Autocracy: The Prussian Experience 1660–1815.* Cambridge, Mass., 1958.

Schieder, Theodor. *Frederick the Great.* Edited and translated by Sabina Berkeley and H. M. Scott. Harlow, U.K., and New York, 1999. Originally published Frankfurt am Main, 1983.

Schissler, Hanna. *Preußische Agrargesellschaft im Wandel. Wirtschaftliche, gesellschaftliche und politische Transformationsprozesse von 1763 bis 1847.* Göttingen, 1978.

Showalter, Dennis E. *The Wars of Frederick the Great.* Harlow, U.K., and New York, 1996.

Streidt, Gert, and Peter Feierabend, eds. *Prussia: Art and Architecture.* Translated by Paul Aston. Cologne, 1997.

Wilson, Peter H. "Social Militarisation in Eighteenth-Century Germany." *German History* 18 (2000): 1–39.

PETER H. WILSON

PSYCHOLOGY. The term *psychology* first appears in the sixteenth century, denoting the study of the human soul (Greek *psyche,* 'soul'), a part of what was then called anthropology: the term is used thus in the first work to use it as a title, Rudolf Goclenius's *Psychologia* of 1594 (the title uses the Greek word). The term continued to be used in this way through the seventeenth century. Only in the early eighteenth century, with the publication of Christian Wolff's *Psychologia Empirica* (1732) and *Psychologia Rationalis* (1734), does it take on its modern sense, supplanting earlier terms like *scientia de anima* ('science of the soul'). The study of the soul, or the mind, did not, of course, begin in the eighteenth century. But it may, with some reason, be said to have begun again in the seventeenth.

ARISTOTELIANISM

From the mid-thirteenth century, when Aristotle's works became the basis of the baccalaureate curriculum in European universities, until the middle of the sixteenth, the starting point for the study of the soul was Aristotle's *De anima.* Hundreds of commentaries on it were published in the sixteenth and early seventeenth centuries. Often they included lengthy disputations on controversial topics, like the immortality of the soul and the nature of the rational soul. In the latter part of the sixteenth century the commentary form began to be abandoned in favor of the systematic textbook, of which Francisco Suárez's *De Anima* (1621; On the soul) is a noteworthy example. A reader of these works would have encountered the major ancient, Arab, and medieval interpretations of Aristotle and a fair helping of empirical observations, mostly from ancient authorities like Pliny and Galen, but also occasionally from such recent authors as Andreas Vesalius (1514–1564), whose *De Humani Corporis Fabrica* (1543) superseded the ancients on anatomical questions.

The subject matter of *De Anima* is life and the functions of life. Aristotle treats not only sensation, memory, imagination, and the intellect, but also what would now be thought of as purely physiological functions like digestion and reproduction. The task of the science of the soul is to define the soul itself and the functions proper to living things, to describe the organs and mixtures of elements that subserve them, and finally to establish the principles on which a classification of plants and animals is to be based.

The soul is what Aristotle calls a "form": it confers on matter the characteristics proper to a certain species of thing—the human, say. Medieval authors called the soul a "substantial form," substantial because like the body it is the bearer of properties. It is not the eye, Aristotle says, but the soul that sees. Every material substance, living or not, has a form; the soul is defined among material forms as that of "an organic body potentially having life." Certain functions are found only in the things we call living; the soul is the form proper to them. Although the soul requires a particular composition and configuration of matter to perform its functions, and some materials like blood and bile are found only in living things, neither the soul nor its functions can be reduced to mere mixtures or concatenations of nonliving stuffs.

The functions of living things were divided into three groups: vegetative, sensitive, and rational. All living things nourish themselves, grow, and reproduce. Animals, but not plants, have senses and can move about. Humans can do all that animals do; moreover, they can reason and exercise free will. The soul is accordingly divided into three parts. Only for the rational part, peculiar to humans, can it be argued that its operations do not require a material organ, and that therefore it can survive the dissolution of the body.

The predominant theory of sensation among Aristotelians was "species theory." Sensing consists in the reception of species (Latin *species,* 'aspect' or 'appearance') in the sense organ. Each sense has its own "proper sensibles"—there are species of color, sound, odor, and so forth. Species from the various senses are combined in the "common sense" *(sensus communis)* and then stored in memory (located in the ventricles of the brain), to be reactivated by recollection, imagination, or the "estimative power" *(vis æstimativa),* which performs such tasks as recognizing that a predator is dangerous, or that grass is food. In humans, sensible species undergo further refinement (the "abstraction from matter," for example, that Aristotle regards as characteristic of mathematics) and become "intelligible species," the raw materials used by reason.

CARTESIANISM

The consensus, never total, established around Aristotle broke down in the early seventeenth century. The stoutest blow was dealt to it by René Descartes (1596–1650). With his work the science of the soul begins to divide into two disciplines: a psychology of ideas and a physiology of the nervous system.

The notion of "idea" and the beginnings of an analysis of ideas are put forward in the *Meditations* (1640). In the *Treatise of Man* (written 1631–1633, published in Latin translation 1662), on the other hand, Descartes, following closely the plan of the relevant parts of *De Anima,* attempts to demonstrate that all the functions hitherto attributed to the souls of animals and plants could be exhaustively accounted for in purely mechanistic terms. The *Description of the Human Body* (1640s, first published in Latin translation 1662) extends that account to reproduction.

The body is for Descartes a hydraulic machine—a connected assemblage of organs whose actions are coordinated by the "animal spirits" (a fluid composed of subtle, fast-moving particles or "corpuscles") that course through the nerves and muscles. Seeing, for a cat, is a sequence of collisions of corpuscles, first of light particles on the nerve-endings in the retina and eventually of the animal spirits with the pineal gland, where they produce "impressions" that in a human body affect the mind to produce sensations of light and color. In human beings alone something more happens. The sight of a rose gives rise to a "mode" or modification of the soul, which for Descartes is a separate, immaterial substance "tightly joined" with the body. If by "seeing" one means 'having a visual sensation', then the cat does not see, only human beings do. Similarly, if "feeling pain" means 'having one's soul modified in the manner we call pain', then animals do not feel pain, only humans do. That consequence of Descartes's dualism excited much controversy from 1650 to 1750, as did the denial of souls to animals.

The human mind is unique. Insofar as psychology is the study of the soul, "animal psychology" is an oxymoron. Psychology comes to devote itself to the study of the operations of the human mind—its faculties and the ideas with which they operate. The essence of mind, according to Descartes, is to think. Occurrent thoughts are modes of *res cogitans,* the "thinking thing," and the "form" of such a mode is what Descartes calls an idea (see Hamilton, Dissertation G). That form can be described in terms of what the idea presents or represents to the mind. Ideas came to be thought of as akin to signs, "representing" concepts or things; whether Descartes and other early users of the term in its new sense regarded them thus is open to question (Yolton, 1984).

Cartesian psychology was not the only option in the seventeenth century. Pierre Gassendi's revival of Epicurean atomism contrasted both with the philosophy of the Schools and with that of his friend and rival Descartes. He retained the notion of an animal soul and considered the human soul to consist effectively of a material soul, similar to those of animals, and an immaterial rational soul (Bloch, p. 368), a view more closely resembling the Aristotelian than the Cartesian, in which the cognitive functions of the sensitive soul are elevated to become part of the single, immaterial human soul.

LOCKE AND THE "WAY OF IDEAS"

The *Port-Royal Logic* (1662) of Antoine Arnauld and Pierre Nicole placed ideas at the center of the study of thought. An idea is simply that which is "in our mind" when we conceive something. To the logical notions of term, proposition, syllogism, and method, there correspond the mental operations of conceiving (an idea), judging, reasoning, and putting arguments in order. Thus the study of language and thought were united into a new discipline at once concerned with the validity of arguments and the nature of the mind.

Cartesian physiology had failed conspicuously to live up to the promises made on its behalf by Descartes. Nicolaus Steno (*Observations Anatomiae*, 1662) and Thomas Willis (*Cerebri Anatomae*, 1664) had shown that Descartes's anatomy was grossly mistaken, and in particular that the pineal gland could not possibly have the functions he ascribed to it. Although anatomists in the early eighteenth century continued to map the brain and nervous system, and to make some headway in localizing functions, it is not surprising that philosophers should have taken to a method that did not require detailed knowledge of the "springs" of thought.

In Descartes's *Rules for the Direction of the Mind* (1626–1628, first published 1684), the "things" with which the philosopher deals are said to be simple or complex. That distinction, not entirely new, was applied to ideas: Arnauld and Nicole, and Leibniz shortly thereafter—both of them having access to the as yet unpublished rules—applied that distinction to ideas. Leibniz in particular is, in the 1670s, proposing the analysis of ideas into what he calls "primitive" ideas, not further analyzable. Locke's *Essay concerning Human Understanding* (1690) deals with the analysis of ideas, or the uncovering of the "original" ideas "from whence all the rest are derived" (p. 286). Those original ideas, few in number, Locke divides into ideas of sense, received from the body, and ideas of reflection, received from the mind.

The analysis and classification of ideas according to their composition from originals provided what could be called their "statics." The "dynamics" was based on the notion of the association of ideas. That one idea might call up another was not at all a new observation. Descartes had taken note of it, and Baruch Spinoza (1632–1677) adverted to it quite often. Locke's contribution was to make it fundamental to a theory of error. Not all connections among ideas arise from association. Some connections are natural (for example, between the idea of red and that of color). Some are artificial, forged by chance or custom, which can bind together any two ideas, however distant. Association became an im-

portant tool. George Berkeley (1685–1753), for example, explains depth perception by reference to a "habitual or customary" connection between the muscular sensations caused by positioning the eyes so as to maintain a single image of an object and the idea of the distance of that object from the viewer (*Essay toward a New Theory of Vision*, 1709).

Locke's *Essay* and the way of ideas were enormously influential through the eighteenth century. Condillac (Étienne Bonnot) in particular devoted his 1754 *Traité des sensations* (Treatise on sensations) to the study of a "statue" having only one of the five senses, and to the proposition that touch teaches vision how to recognize shapes and distances, the conclusion being that all the various faculties of the soul—judgment, reflection, the passions—are nothing other than "transformations" of sensation. (Destutt de Tracy, mentioned below, would later hold that all thought is feeling.) Condillac's claim that touch teaches vision was based in part on descriptions of the experiences of persons blind from birth who recovered their vision, including a famous case described by the London surgeon William Cheselden in 1728. That case seemed to provide an answer to William Molyneux's query to Locke, on whether a person blind from birth would recognize the objects previously known only by touch (see Degenaar).

David Hume (1711–1776) begins his *Treatise* (1739) with a distinction between "impressions" (unlike the impressions made by animal spirits on the pineal gland, these are in the mind) and "ideas," the difference being that impressions are, like Locke's "originals," not derived from other ideas. Ideas of substance and (most famously) cause are analyzed in terms of relations among ideas initiated by association (between resembling ideas) and confirmed into habit. The last concerted attempt to follow the way of ideas was the "ideology" of A. L. C. Destutt de Tracy, presented in his *Idéologie* of 1804. The political importance of Lockeanism is hinted at by noting that Destutt de Tracy was a deputy in the Estates General of 1789, who was arrested under the Terror but survived, and had his commentary on Montesquieu's *Spirit of the Laws* censored by the government of Napoleon in 1806.

MATERIALISM AND PANPSYCHISM

Eighteenth-century materialism was quite distinct from what is now called "physicalism." The physicalist holds that the only properties possessed by concrete substances are those imputed to them by established physical theory. The eighteenth-century materialist, in agreement with the physicalist, denies that the mind is immaterial, but typically sensibility (the basic mental property, as in Condillac and Destutt de Tracy) is treated as a property additional to the basic physical properties of matter, and not reducible to them.

Many eighteenth-century philosophers, among them Denis Diderot (1713–1784) and Pierre Louis Moreau de Maupertuis, attributed a primitive sensibility to small particles of matter, "organic molecules" as Georges Louis Leclerc Buffon called them, from which the more complex capacities of animals and humans are derived. Julien Offroy de La Mettrie is another instance. The title of his best-known work, first published in 1747 (with a false date of 1748), is *L'homme machine* (Man a machine), but in the machine every fiber is endowed with a natural oscillation, proved by, among many other experiments, the continued beating of the hearts of animals after they are removed (1751/1987, 1:104–105; see also *L'homme plus que machine*, 2:159). In the *Rêve d'Alembert* (1769; Dream of d'Alembert), Diderot, following the physician Théophile de Bordeu, likens the organism to a swarm of bees—the "organic molecules." Consciousness and will become "statistical" phenomena, like the changing sentiments of a crowd, a view reminiscent of certain much more recent theories of mental activity.

The end of the early modern period witnessed the discovery by Alessandro Volta (1745–1827) and Luigi Galvani (1737–1798) that nerves conduct electricity. That and the comparative studies of late eighteenth- and early nineteenth-century anatomists, which established, among other things, the independent role of the spinal cord in reflex actions, laid the basis for a neuroscience recognizably like that of today.

Willis, in his "Anatomy," writes that he "addicted my self to the opening of Heads especially, and of every kind" not only in order to found a "more certain Physiologie," but also a "Pathologie of the brain and nervous Stock" ("Anatomy," p. 53; quoted in Frank, p. 108). He went so far as to regard every disease as neural in origin; the resulting "neural pathology" had adherents even in the mid-nineteenth century. At the very end of the period, Philippe Pinel, famous for supposedly setting free the inmates of the Salpêtrière asylum in Paris during the Terror (Weiner, p. 333), published his *Traité médico-philosophique sur l'aliénation mentale* (1801; Medico-philosophical treatise on mental alienation), one of the founding documents of the new discipline of psychiatry.

See also **Aristotelianism; Berkeley, George; Cartesianism; Descartes, René; Gassendi, Pierre; Hume, David; La Mettrie, Julien Offroy de; Leibniz, Gottfried Wilhelm; Locke, John; Madness and Melancholy; Mechanism; Medicine; Spinoza, Baruch.**

BIBLIOGRAPHY

Primary Sources

Bayle, Pierre. *Dictionnaire historique et critique.* 3rd ed. Rotterdam, 1720. 1st ed. Rotterdam, 1697.

La Mettrie, Julien Offroy de. *Oeuvres philosophiques.* 2 vol. Paris, 1987. 1st ed. London, 1751; *L'homme machine* and *L'homme plus que machine* were first published in 1748.

Locke, John. *An Essay concerning Human Understanding.* Edited by Peter H. Nidditch. Oxford, 1975. 1st ed. 1690.

Secondary Sources

Bloch, Olivier René. *La philosophie de Gassendi: Nominalisme, matérialisme et métaphysique.* The Hague, 1971.

Clarke, Edwin, and L. S. Jacyna. *Nineteenth-Century Origins of Neuroscientific Concepts.* Berkeley, 1987.

Degenaar, Marjolein. *Molyneux's Problem: Three Centuries of Discussion on the Perception of Forms.* Translated by Michael J. Collins. The Hague, 1996.

Hamilton, Sir William. "Editor's supplementary dissertations." In *The Works of Thomas Reid, D. D.,* edited by Sir William Hamilton. 7th ed. Glasgow, 1872.

Porter, Roy. "Medical Science and Human Science in the Enlightenment." In *Inventing Human Science: Eighteenth-Century Domains,* edited by Christopher Fox, Roy Porter, Robert Wokler, pp. 53–87. Berkeley, 1995.

Roger, Jacques. *The Life Sciences in Eighteenth-Century French Thought.* Translated by Robert Ellrich. Stanford, 1998.

Rousseau, G. S., ed. *The Languages of Psyche. Mind and Body in Enlightenment Thought: Clark Library Lectures, 1985–1986.* Berkeley, 1990. See, in particular, Frank, Robert G., Jr. "Thomas Willis and His Circle: Brain and Mind in Seventeenth-Century Medicine" and Weiner,

Dora B. "Mind and Body in the Clinic: Philippe Pinel, Alexander Crichton, Dominique Esquirol, and the Birth of Psychiatry."

Wellman, Kathleen Anne. *La Mettrie: Medicine, Philosophy, and Enlightenment.* Durham, 1992.

Yolton, John W. *Perceptual Acquaintance: From Descartes to Reid.* Minneapolis, 1984.

———. *Thinking Matter: Materialism in Eighteenth-Century Britain.* Minneapolis, 1983.

DENNIS DES CHENE

PUBLIC HEALTH. Public health as a concept and as a program of coordinated state or communal action did not exist in early modern Europe. Not until the late seventeenth century did regimes and individuals began to perceive the health of the population as an area of legitimate, ongoing government action. Such realizations eventually led to more concentrated efforts in formulating principles of public health and launching sustained programs designed to improve health and lengthen life. Governments before the eighteenth century were, of course, not oblivious to collective health, but public health initiatives were ad hoc and piecemeal in nature. Public health fell overwhelmingly within the purview of other aspects of governing: the regulation of markets; restrictions on the practice of obnoxious trades such as tanning or slaughtering; the prevention of fires; and the provision of poor relief—to name only the most obvious and significant. Repeated waves of epidemics, especially plague, but also smallpox, syphilis, dysentery, influenza, and perplexing incidents of considerable lethality such as the mysterious English sweat of the 1480s, caused governments to swing vigorously into action to combat them or prevent their spread.

Epidemics as a presence or a threat conditioned many early modern public health responses. The plague of the mid to late 1340s (known since the nineteenth century by the anachronistic name of the Black Death) played a major role in shaping policies. Equally influential was the appearance of syphilis in the late fifteenth and early sixteenth centuries. These two diseases produced a standard set of responses—quarantines, cordons sanitaires, avoidance, flight, closing public baths, shutting up infected houses, and banning assemblages of people—that persisted at least until the eighteenth century and often considerably longer. The steps taken to fight or forestall pestilences depended to a large degree on how people understood their propagation. Since antiquity two concepts of how disease spread competed. Some believed in contagion—that disease circulated through contact with infected people or goods. Others adopted a miasmatic theory—that disease resulted from an insalubrious condition of the environment, a disturbance in the airs, waters, and places described in the ancient Hippocratic corpus. Whereas once historians argued that these two interpretations were mutually exclusive and antagonistic, it is now generally accepted that they could be combined and that both shaped (and still shape) responses to epidemic situations.

Western Europe lived beneath the shadow of plague until 1721 (Brockliss and Jones, 1997), and plague disappeared from eastern Europe and Russia only toward the end of the eighteenth century. Throughout early modern times, public health was intimately concerned with two measures taken to prevent the incursion or recurrence of plague: quarantines and cordons sanitaires. These methods required the coordination of government efforts often crossing territorial borders and covering huge stretches of land. While such cooperation was hardly perfect in an age lacking efficient police forces, evidence suggests that both measures could successfully retard the spread of disease. Once plague struck, however, cities constituted boards of health from their sitting magistracies (choosing, in other words, people with power and status but not necessarily those possessing medical experience or training) for the duration of the emergency. Physicians and surgeons were seldom members of such boards. Although granted wide and expansive powers for a time, boards of health tended to disappear once the threat vanished. Nonetheless, the ordinances that governed city life on a day-to-day basis continued to contain crucial elements of what would later be termed public health. Such regulations pertained not only to cities, of course. Still, evidence is more complete and available for urban sites than for the countryside and control was crisper within still-walled towns. This, too, would change in the late seventeenth and eighteenth centuries. Another institution that we today consider essential to public health is the hospital. Hospitals in early modern times served as multipurpose establishments, although some were set up and run especially for particular patients: those suffering from plague or syphilis, for instance. Hospitals, however, functioned coterminously as places to heal the sick, as homes for the aged or chronically ill, and as refuges for the destitute (and thus, formed a central element of poor relief). Hospitals provided vital economic resources for a community as employers, but also as prominent landowners and even as moneylenders.

Beginning in the late seventeenth century, public health slowly developed a more comprehensive field of action and a more tightly defined program. As states centralized authority and as rulers gathered the reins of power more firmly into their own hands, they and their ministers began to envision the wealth of nations in broader ways. According to the principles of mercantilism and its sister discipline, populationism, the riches of a state could no longer be weighed merely in bullion. Rather the true strength of a polity lay in its productive potential, and that capacity itself depended on the presence of a large, healthy, and industrious population. Thus, advocates of what in German came to be known as *Medizinische Polizei* ('medical police'), denoting a series of policies rather than a police force), foremost among them, Johann Peter Frank (1745–1821), constructed broad programs of public health that ranged from traditional concerns with the fighting of epidemics, the maintenance of hospitals, and the provision of potable water supplies to far more ambitious social policies that included the early education of children and maternal welfare.

In order to formulate rational and purposeful policies, however, it was first necessary to understand which conditions promoted health or caused illness. Thus, medical police stimulated a political arithmetic that amassed and studied information pertaining to commerce, population, and natural resources, as well as vital statistics (birth, death, and morbidity rates). Cities had often collected mortality statistics, especially during epidemic outbreaks. The London Bills of Mortality from the Great Plague of 1665–1666 are perhaps the most famous (but by no means the only or earliest) example of this genre. In the seventeenth and eighteenth centuries, however, the political arithmeticians, such as the Englishman John Graunt (*Natural and Political Observations on the Bills of Mortality*, 1662) or the

German Johann Süssmilch (*Die göttliche Ordnung in den Veränderungen des menschlichen Geschlechts*, 1775 [The godly order in human affairs]) sought to discover patterns of mortality as a basis for the rational planning of state affairs, including but not limited to public health. These advances in political economy paralleled other trends in the eighteenth century: a new valuation on individual worth and a greater tendency to view human happiness, including physical well-being, as a positive good. These perceptions laid the groundwork for the development of public health as a humanitarian enterprise and as an accepted program of state action. Still, it would take several decades and, to some extent, the impact of cholera in the nineteenth century for states to establish health departments as permanent agencies, staffed by professionals possessing strong executive powers, or ones that functioned on a national, rather than merely on a local or municipal level.

See also **Medicine; Plague; Poverty.**

BIBLIOGRAPHY

Primary Sources

Airs, Waters, and Places and Epidemics. Parts of the Hippocratic corpus often attributed to Hippocrates of Cos (460?–377? B.C.E.) but in fact written by a number of Hippocratic authors. A selection of the Hippocratic corpus is available as *The Medical Works of Hippocrates: A New Translation.* Translated from the Greek by John Chadwick and William N. Mann. Oxford, 1950.

Frank, Johann Peter. *A System of Complete Medical Police: Selections from Johann Peter Frank.* Edited by Erna Lesky. Baltimore, 1976. A selection from the eighteenth-century multivolume work *System einer vollständigen medicinischen Polizey.* 9 vols. Mannheim, 1779–1827.

Secondary Sources

Brockliss, Laurence, and Colin Jones. *The Medical World of Early Modern France.* Oxford, 1997.

Cipolla, Carlo. *Miasmas and Disease: Public Health and the Environment in the Pre-Industrial Age.* Cambridge, U.K., 1995.

Lindemann, Mary. *Medicine and Society in Early Modern Europe.* Cambridge, U.K., 1999.

Porter, Roy. *The Greatest Benefit to Mankind: A Medical History of Humanity from Antiquity to the Present.* London, 1997. Chapters 8–10 cover the early modern period.

Riley, James. *The Eighteenth-Century Campaign to Avoid Disease.* New York, 1987.

Rosen, George. *A History of Public Health.* New York, 1958. An old but still useful survey. Also available in an expanded edition, Baltimore, 1993.

MARY LINDEMANN

PUBLIC OPINION. In 1500, the term "public opinion" had no currency in any European language. By 1789, not only had the phrase entered the vocabulary of virtually every language in Europe, but conscious efforts to affect or even control public opinion had come to play a key role in some of the most crucial intellectual and political events of the epoch—the origins of the French Revolution itself being only the most famous case in point. It is hardly surprising, then, that both the idea and the reality of public opinion in the early modern period should have been the object of an exceptional amount of scholarly attention in recent decades.

PRE-HISTORY

The component parts of the term, noun and adjective, had long histories of their own, prior to their union in the modern concept. Descending from classical Latin, *opinio* and its cognates were burdened with a primarily pejorative connotation in the vocabulary of Renaissance humanism. Typically contrasted with "reason," "opinion" tended to designate ungrounded belief, subject to the psychological distortions of the "imagination" and the "passions." The widely circulated humanist cliché, asserting that "opinion governs the world," was thus an expression of regret at the domination of the irrational in human affairs. This negative judgment persisted throughout the early modern period, though the eventual union of "opinion" with the adjective "public" weakened it significantly. "Public," meanwhile, descended directly from the Latin adjective *(publicus)* and noun *(publicum)* used to refer to that which pertained to the state, as opposed to the private household—the collective body of its citizens or its property, above all. For obvious reasons, these terms and their cognates acquired a new currency with the onset of the modern processes of state-building at the end of the Middle Ages. No less important, however, was the eventual extension of the noun, in particular, beyond the boundaries of the state itself. By the end of the seventeenth century, it was possible to refer to a variety of different "publics," in the sense of a critical "audience"—as in the "publics" for plays, music, and novels. As for the actual term *public opinion* itself, finally, the first usages seem to have been in French, in the later sixteenth century: the phrase can be found, for example, in Montaigne's *Essays.* Most authorities agree, however, that the term only really gained currency, in French and in English, about a century later.

PUBLIC OPINION AND THE "PUBLIC SPHERE"

What brought "opinion" and "public" together, to form a new concept? As it happens, nearly all recent research on the topic owes something to a seminal work of social theory that first appeared some forty years ago. *The Structural Transformation of the Public Sphere* (1962) was the earliest major work of the eminent German philosopher and social theorist Jürgen Habermas. Its influence on German-speaking scholarship was immediate, but its greatest impact came with its long-delayed translations into French (1978) and English (1989). The appeal of Habermas's book is not hard to explain, for it offered a sweeping and sophisticated interpretation of the history not just of "public opinion," but of "publicity" itself, from the end of the Middle Ages to the present. A Frankfurt-school Marxist in intellectual background, Habermas traced the origins of a specifically bourgeois "public sphere" to the impact of the transition to market capitalism, on the one hand, and the emergence of the modern sovereign political state, on the other. It was between the two characteristic social institutions produced by these changes—the modern private or "nuclear" family and absolute or divine right monarchy—that a "sphere" for the free exchange of information and opinion developed, sustained by new technologies and institutions of communication, including the newspaper, journal, salon, and Masonic lodge. The heyday of the "bourgeois public sphere," Habermas argued, came in the eighteenth century, when its promotion of the fundamental values of the Enlightenment—liberty, equality, fraternity—brought immense critical pressure to bear on the social and political institutions of the Old Regime. In the long term, however, success ruined the bourgeois public sphere. The spread of representative political institutions in the wake of the American and French Revolutions, and the rise of modern mass media, combined to rob the public sphere of its capacity for autonomous criticism of society. Far from governing the modern world, Habermas concluded, "public opinion" was itself now fully subordinated to the routines of electoral politics and the blandishments of consumer advertising.

PUBLIC OPINION IN THE SIXTEENTH AND SEVENTEENTH CENTURIES

Not surprisingly, Habermas's pessimistic account of the decline of the public sphere in the modern world has proved controversial. His description of its original emergence in early modern Europe, on the other hand, has met with far greater acceptance, although with significant alterations. For one thing, the confident Marxism of Habermas's explanatory framework has tended tacitly to be set aside over time. The adjective "bourgeois," assigning a central role in the story to an emergent social class, has all but disappeared from the recent literature on the "public sphere" and "public opinion." At the same time, the result of several decades of research has been to assign both concepts a rather longer period of gestation than Habermas did in *The Structural Transformation of the Public Sphere*. Habermas did in fact draw attention to the print revolution of the early sixteenth century as a crucial condition of possibility for the emergence of the public sphere. Today, it seems even clearer that both the print revolution and the onset of religious Reformation were watersheds in its development. The breakup of the ideological unity of Christianity unleashed propaganda campaigns, designed to sway opinion in one direction or another, on a hitherto unprecedented scale. The ferocious "religious" warfare that followed in Germany and France was accompanied by equally strenuous struggles in print. By the early seventeenth century, the most advanced political thought in Europe, the "reason of state" traditions in France and Spain, expressly recognized the power of public sentiment, which every ruler ignored to his or her peril. What were once theorized as the first of the great "bourgeois" revolutions—the Dutch Revolt and the English Civil War—brought propaganda warfare of this kind to an even higher pitch, far more explicitly tied to the fates of states than ever before. The condemned king of England made a powerful appeal to the "public" virtually from the scaffold. Less lethally, the end of the seventeenth century saw the arrival of a relatively novel phenom-

enon, secular intellectual controversies in a national context. "Public opinion" itself seems to have entered circulation, in France and England, in the midst of the ideological contests known as the *querelle des anciens et des modernes* in the first, the "battle of the books" in the second.

THE EIGHTEENTH CENTURY: INSTITUTIONS

Despite this long windup, however, Habermas was surely right to insist on the qualitative difference of the role of public opinion in the eighteenth century, when both idea and reality assumed unprecedented forms. Intellectually, there is little doubt that the impact of the Enlightenment was crucial in this respect. Educated elites in Europe were now far more willing than ever before to acknowledge the sovereign power of an anonymous public, in regard to the evaluation of everything from imaginative literature and music to governmental policy itself. At the same time, the expansion in the sway of public opinion in the eighteenth century depended not merely on ideological shifts, but also on the arrival of new modes of communication and social institutions. Probably the greatest contribution of Habermas's work in the long run has been to inspire an extremely lively social history of the technological and institutional underpinnings of public opinion in the age of Enlightenment. On the one hand, the eighteenth century saw a vast expansion in both the production and the consumption of printed matter. The increase in volume was matched by variety, with the full maturation of new forms of literature, from the newspaper, *feuilleton* (serial publication), and periodical, to the novel. "Authorship" itself increasingly came into its own, under the protection of emergent copyright laws and other forms of recognition of literary property; for the first time in European history, the "writing public" came to include significant numbers of women. On the other hand, this whole spectrum of new "reading publics" was sustained by a set of "semi-public" social institutions. Three of these stand out, now the objects of a rich historical literature. One was the literary and intellectual salon, which descended from the Renaissance court to play a pivotal role in promoting Enlightenment values, in France above all; not the least striking feature of eighteenth-century salon culture was the central role assumed by women within it. Secondly, the eighteenth century was the great age of the public drinking establishment, where the commingling of classes and consumption of stimulants encouraged a freer flow of ideas than ever before. The proliferation of taverns, alehouses, wineshops, and cafés was recognized by contemporaries as crucial to the formation of public opinion in the Enlightenment. The same went, finally, for a third institution, Freemasonry, whose spread across Europe in the eighteenth century created sites of egalitarian sociability and communication—with, on occasion, evidence of female participation as well.

PUBLIC OPINION IN ENGLAND

Steadily climbing literacy rates, multiplying reading publics, and the spread of salons, cafés, and Masonic lodges created the conditions of possibility for widespread appeals to public opinion across eighteenth-century Europe. Although few countries were untouched by these phenomena, England and France have attracted the vast bulk of scholarly attention—not least for the contrast between the two. Nearly all authorities agree that the idea of public opinion attracted far more attention in France, and played a more pivotal role in its political history in the eighteenth century, than it did in England. At first glance, the contrast might appear paradoxical. For not only had England made a successful transition from absolute to constitutional monarchy, transferring political sovereignty to a representative institution that, for all of its narrowness, certainly had no equivalent in contemporary France. England, too, enjoyed a far freer press in the eighteenth century, and pioneered many of the most characteristic social institutions of the Enlightenment, including newspaper, café, and Masonic lodge. In fact, the role of public opinion in the political culture of eighteenth-century Britain was far from negligible. Whig control over Parliament down to the 1760s provoked a lively political opposition, centered on a "country" or "patriotic" party, which made a central use of newspapers, periodicals, and books in its appeals to a "political public." The ruling Whigs themselves, meanwhile, orchestrated powerful propaganda campaigns on behalf of British war efforts, promoting an incipient nationalism that reached a kind of climax with the Seven Years' War (1756–1763). Public opinion in England then seems to have come of age with the political radicalism that flowed in the wake of that war, beginning in the 1760s. The Wilkesite

movement marked a watershed in the emergence of a popular radicalism, obsessively focused on manipulating public opinion for its ends. These currents were swelled by the publicity accorded political ideas during and after the American Revolution. By the end of the 1780s, the stage was set for the English reaction to the French Revolution, which involved unprecedented attempts to mobilize public sentiment for geopolitical ends. As many commentators have noted, a key feature of public opinion in Britain was the tendency toward xenophobia—all to be greatly enhanced in the 1790s, of course, by the onset of war with France.

PUBLIC OPINION IN FRANCE

It was in eighteenth-century France, however, that public opinion seems to have enjoyed the greatest fortune as idea—and perhaps as reality—in the early modern period. Everything suggests that this was related to the success of the Bourbon absolute monarchy in avoiding the political revolutions and religious reformation that had transformed its counterpart across the Channel in the seventeenth century. In the context of the High Enlightenment—whose capital, of course, was Paris—appeals to public opinion seem to have compensated for precisely the lack of representative political institutions and civic freedoms enjoyed by the English. In fact, a keen sense of the importance of public sentiment and support to the exercise of political power was a feature of early modern French political theory from the start—strikingly prominent within absolutist apology itself, from Jean Bodin to Jacques-Bénigne Bossuet. By the turn of the eighteenth century, direct appeals to public opinion were to be found in the literature of aristocratic opposition to the regime of Louis XIV. From here, it was a short step to the two major political theorists of the French Enlightenment, each of whom, in their different ways, insisted on the crucial importance of ideological power in political life. In *The Spirit of the Laws* (1748), Montesquieu advanced a theory of the subjective "principles" that gave life to the different forms of government; in *On the Social Contract,* Rousseau advocated a patriotic "civil religion." Meanwhile, practice did not run far behind theory. By the time Rousseau wrote, the Bourbon court had long since begun to lose its grip on political life in France, as one kind of dispute after another spilled into the public sphere. Not all of the contention was owing to the Enlightenment. In fact, the most serious political strife of the period resulted from collisions between the Bourbon monarchy and the parlements or upper law courts, whose magistrats were fired by Jansenism, a crypto-Protestant tradition of resistance to absolutism (religion was a factor curiously marginalized by Habermas in his account of the public sphere). By the time the monarchy attempted—without success—to quell parliamentary resistance by brute force in the early 1770s, however, Jansenist sentiment and Enlightenment values had converged in a single, "patriotic" current of criticism. Far from staying above the fray, the Bourbon monarchy itself now went to the opposite extreme, vying with Jansenist and Enlightenment critics alike in appealing to French public opinion.

CONCLUSION

The most striking sign of the triumph of the idea of public opinion in eighteenth-century France came in 1781. Dismissed as finance minister to the monarchy, the Swiss banker Jacques Necker took the unprecedented step of publishing an account of the royal budget, in violation of every norm of absolutist secrecy. The meaning of this appeal to public opinion over the head of the king was lost on few observers. Eight years later, the bankrupt Bourbon monarchy confirmed this symbolic transfer of sovereignty by summoning the Estates-General, a representative assembly for the expression of public will that had not met for a hundred and fifty years. With the start of the French Revolution, the idea of "public opinion," a gift of a long process of development in the early modern period, was ready to begin its modern career.

See also **Ancients and Moderns; Bourbon Dynasty (France); England; Enlightenment; France; Freemasonry; Jansenism; Journalism, Newspapers, and Newssheets; Salons.**

BIBLIOGRAPHY

Baker, Keith Michael. "Public Opinion as Political Invention." In his *Inventing the French Revolution: Essays on French Political Culture in the Eighteenth Century,* pp. 167–199. Cambridge, U.K., and New York, 1990.

Blanning, T. C. W. *The Culture of Power and the Power of Culture: Old Regime Europe 1660–1789.* Oxford and New York, 2002.

Goodman, Dena. *The Republic of Letters: A Cultural History of the French Enlightenment.* Ithaca, N.Y., and London, 1994.

Gunn, J. A. W. *Beyond Liberty and Property: The Process of Self-Recognition in Eighteenth-Century Political Thought.* Montreal, 1983.

———. *Queen of the World: Opinion in the Public Life of France from the Renaissance to the Revolution.* Oxford, 1995.

Habermas, Jürgen. *The Structural Transformation of the Public Sphere: An Inquiry into a Category of Bourgeois Society.* Translated by Thomas Burger and Frederick Lawrence. Cambridge, Mass., 1989. Translation of *Strukturwandel der Öffentlichkeit* (1962).

Klaits, Joseph. *Printed Propaganda under Louis XIV: Absolute Monarchy and Public Opinion.* Princeton, 1976.

Landes, Joan B. *Women and the Public Sphere in the Age of the French Revolution.* Ithaca, N.Y., and London, 1988.

Melton, James Van Horn. *The Rise of the Public in Enlightenment Europe.* Cambridge, U.K., and New York, 2001.

Ozouf, Mona. "Public Spirit." In *A Critical Dictionary of the French Revolution.* Edited by François Furet and Mona Ozouf, pp. 771–780. Translated by Arthur Goldhammer. Cambridge, Mass., and London, 1989.

JOHNSON KENT WRIGHT

PUBLISHING. *See* **Printing and Publishing.**

PUGACHEV REVOLT (1773–1775).

Emelian Pugachev (1742–1775), a Cossack from the Don region (in contemporary Ukraine), led what would be the last—and arguably the most explosive—of the great Cossack rebellions that plagued the Russian state during the seventeenth and eighteenth centuries. Begun, like so many others, as a frontier rebellion, it engulfed large parts of southeastern Russia and staged a brutal and extended assault on the fortress town of Orenburg between October 1773 and February 1774, and at one point it threatened Moscow itself.

Much of Pugachev's success derived from his use of the pretender myth, that is, his claim to be the avenging reemergent true tsar Peter III, who in reality had been murdered six months after ascending the throne in a coup that brought his wife, Catherine the Great, to power in 1762. Neither the first nor the last such pretender (some surfaced as far away as the Balkans), Pugachev insisted that he was the one true Peter III, who in myth had not died

Pugachev Revolt. A 1775 engraving depicts Pugachev confined in a cage and chained. ©BETTMANN/CORBIS

but had been rescued by loyal Christians. He assembled an army and even something of a campaign court. His goal was nothing short of entering the capital and claiming the Russian throne.

The revolt itself built on a mutiny of the Yaik Cossacks, begun and suppressed in 1772. Pugachev arrived in the Yaik region in November of that year, claiming to be Peter. Soon arrested, he was taken to the city of Kazan' on the Volga river, from which he escaped on 29 May 1773. By early 1774 he had assembled a loose coalition of Yaik Cossacks, Kalmyks, and Tatars, along with a growing number of discontented serfs. At its peak, his forces numbered twenty thousand, organized loosely into Cossack-style regiments. Although effective in the rough and wooded terrain of the Volga frontier, Pugachev's forces had little chance in the long run against the much larger and better-fortified imperial army. Over time this superiority proved decisive, and on 15 September 1774 he was handed over to the authorities by his own Cossacks. Taken to Mos-

cow in an open cage, he was publicly executed on 10 January 1775.

Part of Pugachev's unique appeal was social, in that he fomented a fluid kind of class warfare, pitting serfs against landlords, three thousand of whom are thought to have died during the revolt. Having freed the landlords from compulsory service in 1762, so he claimed, he had intended to free the serfs as well but had been prevented from doing so by disloyal and greedy noble landowners. This claim seems to have resonated with much of Russia's servile population, thus broadening the revolt's base beyond the Cossacks and borderland Turkic minorities, who had predominated in the earlier rebellions of Stepan Razin and Kondraty Bulavin, to include serfs, state peasants, and some homesteading free peasants.

The rebellion generated a new phase of state-building between 1775 and 1785, the period of so-called legislomania. The empress concluded that Russia required a more permanent and extensive administrative presence in the countryside, one that would not be so prone to periodic depopulation or reliant upon unpaid and informal service. The enabling legislation, the Reform of Provincial Administration (1775) and the Reform of Police Administration (1782), greatly increased the size of the standing provincial government, both civil and military, to one sufficient to keep local disorders contained.

See also **Catherine II (Russia); Cossacks; Razin, Stepan; Serfdom in Russia.**

BIBLIOGRAPHY

Alexander, John T. *Emperor of the Cossacks: Pugachev and the Frontier Jacquerie of 1773–1775.* Lawrence, Kans., 1973.

Raeff, Marc. "Pugachev's Rebellion." In *Preconditions of Revolution in Early Modern Europe.* Edited by Robert Forster and Jack P. Greene. Baltimore, 1970.

GARY MARKER

PUNISHMENT. *See* **Crime and Punishment.**

PURCELL, HENRY (1659–1695), English composer. Purcell was born in London in 1659, and died there on 21 November 1695, at the age of 36. His father, also named Henry, was a singer in the choirs of Westminster Abbey and the Chapel Royal. Henry junior was a boy chorister in the Chapel Royal, and his main teachers were John Blow and Christopher Gibbons; Matthew Locke was also a strong influence.

In the early part of his career Purcell was chiefly concerned with church music. He succeeded Blow as organist of Westminster Abbey in 1679 and became a "gentleman" (adult singer) of the Chapel Royal in 1682. In the last years of the reign of Charles II (1660–1685) he composed many "symphony anthems" (with string accompaniment) for use in the Chapel, such as the popular Bell Anthem, "Rejoice in the Lord alway" (1683). When in 1685 Charles II was succeeded by his Roman Catholic brother, James II, this part of Purcell's activities came to a virtual stop and did not fully revive with the accession of the Protestant William and Mary in 1689. He did, however, continue to compose odes for royal events, as well as the moving funeral music for Queen Mary, "Thou knowest, Lord, the secrets of our hearts" (1695).

In 1689 Purcell wrote the miniature opera *Dido and Aeneas* for a girls' boarding school, perhaps modeled on Blow's *Venus and Adonis,* to words by Nahum Tate. This unique, all-sung masterpiece of moderate length and modest forces (voices, strings, and continuo) manages to convey a wide spectrum of human feeling. Dido's tragic pride, already hinted at in her first entries, reaches the height of expression in her famous Lament ("When I am laid in earth"). Both her formal songs are examples of one of Purcell's favorite procedures, the ground bass (a repeating bass on which variations are built). Aeneas's weak indecision is brilliantly conveyed in his one brief dialog with Dido, and Belinda is a well-delineated soubrette. There is still room for extrovert humor (in the sailors' song), tone-painting (in the royal hunt), and blood-curdling (in the witches' scene).

From 1690 onward Purcell was heavily involved in music for the London theaters, composing four full-scale "semi-operas" (also termed "dramatic operas"): *The Prophetess, or The History of Dioclesian*

Henry Purcell. Portrait by John Closterman. LIBRARY OF CONGRESS

(1690); *King Arthur* (words by John Dryden; 1691); *The Fairy Queen* (1692); and *The Indian Queen* (1695). They are hardly operas in the modern sense, for the principal characters speak rather than sing, and they afforded little opportunity for Purcell to develop the powers of characterization he demonstrated in *Dido and Aeneas.* Yet his music for the incidental songs, choruses, dances, and extended scenes is wonderfully fresh and inventive. The promise for a future development of English theater music was denied by his early death, leaving no successors of comparable stature, and by the growing popularity of Italian opera.

Purcell was a master of the English song, already well represented by earlier composers such as John Dowland and Henry Lawes. Many of his best-known songs are taken from his theater music, which included more than forty plays as well as the semi-operas. He wrote three *Odes for St. Cecilia's Day* (for soloists, chorus, and orchestra), and his grand *Te Deum and Jubilate* of 1694 was also in honor of Cecilia, the patron saint of music. He was in great demand as a teacher, and composed much domestic music. His chamber music embraces fantasies for viols, among the last of a genre highly esteemed and cultivated in English domestic circles, but also Italianate sonatas for the newly fashionable violin with harpsichord accompaniment. For drinking clubs he contributed glees (unaccompanied part songs) and catches (rounds), some with bawdy words, others reflecting the turbulent politics of the time.

Like other English composers of his era, Purcell was much influenced by French and Italian styles as well as by older English traditions. He is noted for strong, distinctive harmonies and for his exquisite sensitivity to the rhythms and stresses of the English language. The grand public style of his choral odes and other ceremonial works, such as the 1692 *Ode for St. Cecilia's Day* ("Hail, bright Cecilia") and the *Te Deum and Jubilate,* were certainly models for George Frideric Handel. Purcell challenges William Byrd, Edward Elgar, and Benjamin Britten for the claim of being considered the greatest of English composers.

See also **Handel, George Frideric; Music; Music Criticism.**

BIBLIOGRAPHY

Harris, Ellen T. *Henry Purcell's* Dido and Aeneas. Oxford, 1987.

Holman, Peter. *Henry Purcell.* Oxford, 1994.

Price, Curtis A., ed. *Purcell Studies.* Cambridge, U.K., 1995.

NICHOLAS TEMPERLEY

PURITANISM. A movement within the Church of England, Puritanism called for the church's further reformation in accord with what was believed to be "the best reformed" tradition, which was taken to mean the doctrine and ecclesiology of Protestant Switzerland (Geneva, Zurich), of the Rhineland (Strasbourg in particular), the Palatinate, the Netherlands, and Scotland.

THE EMERGENCE OF THE PURITAN MOVEMENT

Puritanism was born out of dissatisfaction with the Elizabethan Settlement, the ecclesiastical order established by the Acts of Supremacy and Uniformity in 1559 by the young Queen Elizabeth (ruled 1558–1603) and her first Parliament. Many English Protestants who had survived the reign of Catholic Queen Mary I (ruled 1553–1558) and the persecution of Protestants that marked her later years, and many of the more than eight hundred clerics and laymen who had fled abroad, had hoped that Elizabeth would bring a return to the second (more Protestant) Book of Common Prayer of King Edward VI's reign (1547–1553) and to the Reformed Protestant momentum of that king's last years. Exiles, who had experienced the reformed Calvinist order of the churches in Frankfurt am Main, Arau, Strasbourg, Basel, Zurich, and Geneva, returned to England hoping that the English Church would now go beyond the Edwardian reformation and join the ranks of the "best reformed churches."

Although few quarreled with the doctrine set out in 1563 in the Thirty-Nine Articles (Articles XI, Of the Justification of Man, and Article XVII, Of Predestination and Election, were unambiguously in the Reformed camp), some did question whether the retention of the traditional disciplinary machinery of episcopacy and the episcopal and archidiaconal church courts really approximated the structure of the primitive church of the Book of Acts and the early church fathers. More objectionable were the Prayer Book rubrics requiring that parish priests officiate wearing a surplice rather than an academic gown, as worn by ministers in the Reformed Churches of the Continent, and the continued use of the cross in baptism and the ring in marriage. These were admittedly adiaphora (issues not central to a saving faith), but if so, many questioned why their use should be obligatory. Further, in a country that was still largely Catholic, it seemed a mistake to "symbolize" with the old faith, thus leading many of the laity to assume that no substantive change had occurred. Finally, the liturgy of the Book of Common Prayer, although largely written by Archbishop Thomas Cranmer (1489–1556), who was already a Protestant and moving in the direction of the Reformed churches when he wrote the 1552 Prayer Book, allowed little time for the sermon, and preaching had seemingly come to be central to inculcating a true saving faith: the Word preached, rather than the sacraments, was thought to be the principal vehicle of grace for those who were dissatisfied.

The first clash between the clergy who would come to be called "Precisions" or "Puritans" came over the requirement that the minister officiate in a surplice. Edmund Sandys, soon to be one of the new Elizabethan bishops, dismissed the rubric saying, "Our gloss upon this text is that we shall not be forced to use them," but events belied his optimistic view. Although strict uniformity was not enforced at first, in 1566, under pressure from the queen, Archbishop Matthew Parker published his *Advertisements,* which called for decency and uniformity in worship. Ministers were not to preach without an episcopal license, and all ministers were required to wear the surplice when officiating. The Vestiarian Controversy followed, brought to a head by the bishop of London, who convoked the London clergy before him; thirty-seven of the ninety-eight clergy refused to conform and were suspended for refusing to wear what Robert Crowley called "the conjuring garments of popery." As William Cecil (1520–1598), the queen's secretary of state, complained, the consequence of silencing so many "godly men at one instant" was the "utter overthrow [of almost] all exercises . . . of interpretation of Scripture" within the city.

Many of those suspended were subsequently rescued by lay supporters who had the right of presentation to parochial livings, and in a sense the Puritan movement was born from that moment. In 1570 the conflict escalated. In that year, Thomas Cartwright's divinity lectures at Cambridge on the Acts of the Apostles argued that the primitive church had a presbyterian structure and lacked bishops. The issue of governance was no longer academic when, two years later, two young London preachers, John Field and Thomas Wilcox, published *An Admonition to the Parliament,* which called for the abolition of episcopacy and the substitution of a presbyterian structure of church government.

Not all relations between the Puritans and the bishops were as contentious as these measures implied. An overriding problem was the inability of many uneducated parish priests to preach the kind of exegetical sermons many bishops as well as ministers believed the times required, and this perception led to officially sanctioned meetings of local clergy called "prophesyings." During these meetings, typically, two skilled ministers preached upon a biblical text before the assembled local clergy and interested laity, and afterwards the clergy withdrew to discuss the performance. Although Archbishop Edmund Grindal (c. 1519–1583) backed the prophesyings, saying "public and continual preaching of God's word is the ordinary means and instrument of the salvation of mankind," Queen Elizabeth preferred that ministers read the official homilies. Thus in 1576 she ordered Grindal to suppress the prophesyings. Nevertheless, preaching exercises in one form or another, sometimes with episcopal approval (approval of the bishop), survived in many localities into the seventeenth century.

Such cooperation between bishops and the Puritan clergy largely came to an end in 1583, when John Whitgift (c. 1530–1604) succeeded Grindal as archbishop of Canterbury. Whitgift was a disciplinarian after the queen's own heart, and he promptly instituted the three articles of subscription as a means for suppressing Puritan nonconformity. The articles required the unfeigned acknowledgment of the royal supremacy in the church (few Puritans disagreed with that requirement), that the Thirty-Nine Articles were agreeable to the word of God, that nothing in the Book of Common Prayer was contrary to the word of God, and that it should therefore be used without alteration or abbreviation by all ordained ministers. More than three hundred ministers were suspended for refusing subscription, although many subsequently subscribed in some modified form sufficient for reinstatement.

Equipped with the prerogative Court of High Commission, over which Whitgift presided, and with the support of Queen Elizabeth, the archbishop set about enforcing conformity in a series of show trials: three who had separated from the established church in despair of reforming it were executed in 1593. The nascent presbyterian program organized by Field and Wilcox was at an end, and the Puritan clergy, whether supporters of a presbyterian church or not, lost their principal champions at court, including (among others) the earl of Leicester and his brother, the earl of Warwick; Sir Francis Walsingham, the queen's secretary of state; and Sir Walter Mildmay, an old privy counselor, as the first Elizabethan generation died in the late 1580s and early 1590s.

Loss of support at court did not spell the end of Puritanism in the countryside, where many Puritan clergy found support among the local gentry and country peers. Robert Rich, the second earl of Warwick, and his gentry allies in two generations of the Barrington family and their kin turned Essex into one of the principal Puritan strongholds until the episcopal attacks of the later 1620s. These attacks prompted an exodus of clergy and their lay followers to Massachusetts Bay and southern New England. The Knightleys in Northamptonshire and Sir Robert Jermyn, Sir John Higham, and Sir Edward Lewkenor in Suffolk were patrons of Puritan ministers. In the west, Sir Robert Harley and his friends made part of Herefordshire a Puritan haven. In London, where most of the parochial livings were not in the hands of the laity, Puritans found a solution in the lectureship, a minister hired to preach either because the incumbent was not licensed to preach or because the parish vestry wished more sermons than the parish minister could provide. At one time more than one hundred London parishes had preachers paid to give these extra sermons, supported either by collections organized by the vestry or by endowments made by wealthy merchants.

THE PURITAN MOVEMENT IN STUART ENGLAND

When James I (ruled 1603–1625) succeeded to the throne of England, the Puritans briefly hoped for better times; after all, as James VI of Scotland, this king had been brought up in a Presbyterian church. The so-called Millenary Petition, calling for moderate reform, was promptly organized and purportedly signed by one thousand clergymen; James responded by summoning a meeting of bishops and Puritan ministers at Hampton Court. The king was sympathetic to the Puritan demand for a preaching clergy, but he had no sympathy for what he thought might be reform leading to a presbyterian system in England. In the end, little came of Hampton Court except the new translation of the Bible published in 1611, the last official collaboration between Puritan and non-Puritan members of the Church of England. Richard Bancroft (1544–1610), who succeeded Whitgift as archbishop of Canterbury, was as rigorous a disciplinarian as his predecessor. He promulgated a revised set of canons for the church in 1604, which required subscription and conformity,

and in the ensuing five years more than seventy beneficed Nonconformist clergy were deprived, including such Puritan luminaries as Arthur Hildersham and Ezechial Culverwell.

Two issues gained the Puritans support in the wider community in the course of James's reign. Many members of the church favored a rigorous Sabbath that was devoted exclusively to religious activities, and were shocked when King James issued the *Book of Sports* in 1618 in an effort to appease, as it seemed to many, Catholic sensibilities in Lancashire. The *Book of Sports* specifically forbade "Puritans and precisions" from discouraging any "lawful recreations" once the second service was completed on Sunday afternoons. Such lawful recreations included dancing, May games, Whitsun ales, and Morris dances, all of which could now legally take place in the churchyard.

More seriously, many, including Archbishop George Abbot (1562–1633), joined the more incautious Puritan preachers in criticizing King James's pursuit of a Spanish Habsburg wife for Prince Charles, particularly after 1618, when in the early stages of the Thirty Years' War (1618–1648) the Catholic armies of Spain and Bavaria invaded the Protestant Palatinate, the hereditary electorate of Frederick and his wife, Elizabeth, James's daughter. In 1622 James attempted to stop such preaching by promulgating his "Directions concerning Preachers," but in fact the preachers were doing little more than giving voice to popular opinion.

Catholic political and military successes on the Continent were one threat; the rise of Arminianism and ceremonialism at home was even more threatening, for to Puritans and to old-fashioned Calvinists like Abbot, these clerics seemed bent on subverting Protestantism from within. Puritans and non-Puritans alike had shared a common Reformed theology during most of Elizabeth's reign, but beginning in the 1590s anti-Calvinists appeared in the universities, arguing that grace was resistible, that salvation could be lost, which was a denial of predestination, and that the sacraments were more important vehicles of saving grace than the preached Word. Eight Arminians became bishops during James's reign, including his favorite court preacher, Lancelot Andrewes (1555–1626). After 1625, in the reign of King Charles I (ruled 1625–1649), they rapidly came to dominate the church. William Laud (1573–1645) became Charles's chief ecclesiastical adviser and rose to become bishop of London in 1628 and archbishop of Canterbury in 1633. Calvinists were now seen as Puritans, and Puritans as "Brownists," separatists from the Established Church in tendency, if not yet in fact. As Laud preached in a court sermon in 1621, "nothing more needful for . . . State and Church, than prayer," and the peace he sought when he came to power was the peace of silent pulpits.

In 1629 Thomas Hooker, the silenced lecturer at Chelmsford in Essex, preached in his farewell sermon: "God is going, his glory is departing, . . . England hath seen her best days," and shortly after left for Massachusetts; forty-eight Essex ministers had petitioned Laud on his behalf, but to no avail. Others retreated to the Netherlands. Alexander Leighton, a Scottish minister and physician, was tried in 1630 before the Star Chamber for writing against episcopacy, had his ears cropped, and was imprisoned until released by Parliament in 1640; Henry Burton, a minister, John Bastwick, a physician, and William Prynne, a lawyer, suffered a similar fate in 1637. The *Book of Sports* was reissued in 1633 and was required to be read from every pulpit in the land; those ministers who resisted what many regarded as an invitation to profane the Sabbath were suspended from their ministerial duties.

THE PURITAN MOVEMENT AND THE ENGLISH REVOLUTION

The rebellion of the Scots in 1637 over the attempted introduction of an English-style Book of Common Prayer and the summoning of the Long Parliament in November 1640 following two disastrous so-called Bishops' Wars, as Charles tried to bring his rebellious Scottish subjects to heel, brought the downfall of the Caroline regime. Laud was imprisoned in the Tower of London, and the House of Commons entertained petitions against parochial clergy who favored the Laudian regime and, after the civil war began in 1642, those who preached against Parliament and for the king. Puritan clergy who lost their livings behind royalist lines found new pulpits in London and those areas held by Parliament. As Richard Baxter (1615–1691), then a young West Country Puritan divine, later wrote: "Though it must be confessed that the public safety and liberty wrought very much with most, especially with the nobility and gentry who adhered to the parliament, yet was it principally the differences about religious matter that filled up the parliament's armies and put the resolution and valor into their soldiers."

A church settlement proved more difficult for Parliament than military victory. As part of an agreement with the Scots Covenanters, Parliament had summoned the Westminster Assembly of Divines in 1643, but argument over the definition of "the best reformed church" soon revealed a split between the Presbyterian majority, champions of a national church to which all would necessarily belong (similar to the Scots), and the Independent minority (called Congregationalists in America), who insisted on autonomy for gathered, voluntary congregations. The latter had the backing of the Baptists, always outside the national church, and the sectarian radicals in some of the parliamentary regiments. After the creation of the New Model Army in 1645, its success in the second civil war in 1648 and the conquest of Ireland and Scotland, followed by Oliver Cromwell's Protectorate in 1653, the survival of the Independents and the sects was guaranteed by the victorious army. The upshot was a Presbyterian structure without coercive sanctions, Independents and Baptists existing outside its purview, and in the 1650s these were joined by the Fifth Monarchists, Quakers, and other radical groups.

When the Restoration took place in 1660, in part due to the fear of sectarian anarchy, instead of a Puritan movement within the national church that had existed prior to 1640, denominations—Presbyterians, Independents, Baptists, and Quakers—came to exist as persecuted congregations on the outside, and Old Dissent was born. Yet it was in this period of defeat that the two great literary expressions of the Puritan ethos appeared: John Milton's *Paradise Lost* (1667) and John Bunyan's *The Pilgrim's Progress* (1678).

Puritanism, if it failed to create the sought-after City on the Hill, nevertheless was to have a lasting influence on the primacy given to the Bible as the word of God and to a certain type of moral seriousness and Protestant culture pervasive, if not dominant, in the English-speaking world.

See also Baxter, Richard; Bible; Bunyan, John; Calvinism; Charles I (England); Church of England; Cromwell, Oliver; Elizabeth I (England); English Civil War and Interregnum; English Civil War Radicalism; Harley, Robert; James I and VI (England); James II (England); Laud, William; Milton, John; Star Chamber.

BIBLIOGRAPHY

Primary Sources

Baxter, Richard. *The Autobiography of Richard Baxter.* Edited by J. M. Lloyd Thomas. London and New York, 1931.

Dent, Arthur. *The Plaine Mans Pathway to Heaven.* London, 1601.

Hutchinson, Lucy. *Memoirs of the Life of Colonel Hutchinson.* Edited by James Sutherland. London, New York, and Toronto, 1973.

Secondary Sources

Collinson, Patrick. *The Elizabethan Puritan Movement.* Berkeley and Los Angeles, 1967.

———. *Godly People: Essays on English Protestantism and Puritanism.* London, 1983.

Durston, Christopher, and Jacqueline Eales, eds. *The Culture of English Puritanism, 1560–1700.* New York, 1996.

Greaves, Richard L. *Glimpses of Glory: John Bunyan and English Dissent.* Stanford, 2002.

Hill, Christopher. *Society and Puritanism in Pre-Revolutionary England.* London, 1964.

———. *The World Turned Upside Down: Radical Ideas during the English Revolution.* London, 1972.

Lake, Peter. *Anglicans and Puritans? Presbyterianism and English Conformist Thought from Whitgift to Hooker.* London, 1988.

———. *The Boxmaker's Revenge: "Orthodoxy," "Heterodoxy," and the Politics of the Parish in Early Stuart London.* Stanford, 2001.

———. *Moderate Puritans and the Elizabethan Church.* Cambridge, U.K., 1982.

Nuttall, G. F. *Visible Saints: The Congregational Way, 1640–1660.* Oxford, 1957.

Seaver, Paul S. *Wallington's World: A Puritan Artisan in Seventeenth-Century London.* Stanford, 1985.

Spurr, John. *English Puritanism, 1603–1689.* New York, 1998.

PAUL S. SEAVER

PUTTING-OUT SYSTEM. *See* Proto-Industry.

PYRENEES, PEACE OF THE (1659). The struggle between France and Spain that burst out into full-scale war in 1635 was not ended by the Peace of Westphalia in 1648. Instead, the French lost much ground when Spain took advantage of the Fronde, the French civil wars of 1648–1653. Eventually allied with the prince of Condé (1621–1686), one of the leaders of the Fronde, the Spaniards retook earlier French gains, such as Dunkirk, and ended the French-backed rebellion in Catalonia. The end of the Fronde brought little improvement in French prospects, and defeats in 1655–1656 led France to offer terms, only for Philip IV (1605–1665) of Spain to reject them. The French demand that the peace include the marriage of Louis XIV (1638–1715) with Philip's daughter Marie-Thérèse (1638–1683), then first in line in the succession, was unacceptable.

The war ended only after the intervention of English forces on the side of France, under an alliance signed in 1657, tipped the balance in Flanders. English units helped Henri de la Tour d'Auvergne (1611–1675), marshal Turenne, defeat the Army of Flanders at the Battle of the Dunes (14 June 1658). This transformed the strategic situation. Having exploited the victory to capture Dunkirk, Gravelines, Menen, and Ieper (Ypres), La Tour d'Auvergne could threaten an advance on Brussels, the capital of the Spanish Netherlands.

This led to the Peace of the Pyrenees of 7 November 1659, signed at the Isle of Pheasants at the western end of the mountain chain. Important French gains in the war, Artois in the Low Countries and Roussillon at the eastern end of the Pyrenees, were ceded by Spain. However, the peace was more of a compromise than is usually appreciated, and this reflected the outcome of the war. The French had failed to drive the Spanish from the southern Netherlands or Italy as had been planned, and as a result the Spaniards retained their territories in Italy as well as most of the Spanish Netherlands. The Spanish Empire remained the largest in western Europe.

The marriage of Louis XIV and Marie-Thérèse as part of the settlement was now acceptable to Spain because Philip now had a son, a reminder of the role of dynastic fortune. As an indication, however, of the extent to which policy was debated and thus of the danger of treating states as unproblematic building blocks, the negotiations were opposed by the queen of Spain, who wanted Marie-Thérèse to marry Emperor Leopold I (1640–1705), and by courtiers concerned to secure better terms for Condé. Dunkirk, a major naval base on the North Sea, was ceded to England, but the recently restored Charles II (1630–1685) sold it to Louis XIV in 1662.

When Louis married Marie-Thérèse in 1660, she renounced the right of succession on the Spanish inheritance, both for herself and for her heirs. However, it was by no means clear how acceptable this was to Spanish custom and law. Indeed at the time of the marriage her renunciation was regarded as a matter of formality, entered into in order to allay international mistrust. It gave Louis and the Bourbon dynasty a claim to the Spanish inheritance, which was pushed when Philip IV died in 1665. Louis claimed Brabant, Antwerp, Limburg, and parts of Franche-Comté and Luxembourg from the inheritance, leading to the War of Devolution in 1667–1668. After gains then, including Lille and Tournai, he won more, including Franche-Comté and parts of the Spanish Netherlands, in the Dutch War of 1672–1678. More seriously, the death of Philip's son, Carlos II (1661–1700), led to the War of the Spanish Succession (1701–1714) as the inheritance of the whole succession by Louis's second grandson, Philip V of Spain (1683–1746; ruled 1700–1746), was contested by Britain, Austria, and the Dutch.

The Peace of the Pyrenees is sometimes seen as setting the seal on the decline of Spain. This is misleading. It was no more than a stage in the long-running saga of relations. Spain proved a robust power possessing great resilience in the 1640s and 1650s. Subsequent Spanish difficulties owed more to contrasting domestic developments in the 1660s. The vigorous Louis XIV took personal charge of France on the death of Cardinal Jules Mazarin (1602–1661) in 1661, while in Spain the physically and mentally impaired Carlos II (ruled 1665–1700) could not provide the necessary leadership.

See also **Condé Family; Devolution, War of (1667–1668); Fronde; Louis XIV (France); Netherlands, Southern; Philip IV (Spain); Spain; Spanish Succession, War of the (1701–1714).**

BIBLIOGRAPHY

Méndez de Haro, Luis. *Letters from the Pyrenees: Don Luis Méndez de Haro's Correspondence to Philip IV of Spain, July to November 1659.* Edited by Lynn Williams. Exeter, U.K., 2000. A crucial source.

JEREMY BLACK

PYRRHONISM. *See* **Skepticism: Academic and Pyrrhonian.**

QUAKERS. Quakers (Religious Society of Friends) emerged in the north of England in the early 1650s as one of the many sects spawned by the Puritan revolution. George Fox (1624–1691), the most prominent early leader, after seeking for certainty among many religious groups, experienced what he and other Friends described as the Inward Light of Christ, an unmediated contact with God. Quakerism was an attempt to communicate and institutionalize this encounter with divinity that was available to all women and men. Worship consisted of meetings held in silence in an unornamented room with preaching or prayer spoken under the guidance of the Light. There was no educated and ordained clergy, no liturgy, hymns, or Bible reading to come between a person and God. Friends refused to pay tithes, take oaths, or show deference to social superiors and denounced all other forms of worship as corrupt.

Early Friends attracted the middling classes and few of the very rich and powerful or the poor. Traveling ministers (persons recognized as able to preach the new faith) brought the movement by 1654 to London, Bristol, and Norfolk and soon after to the West Indies, Ireland, and North America. The rapid spread and religious and social radicalism of many early Friends brought sporadic persecution, even under Oliver Cromwell (ruled 1653–1658).

The Restoration in 1660 brought twenty-four years of occasional persecution by royal and Anglican authorities who saw Friends as threatening religious uniformity and social order. Friends also experienced internal divisions occasioned by Fox's effort to organize a hierarchy of meetings, including separate gatherings for women. Robert Barclay's (1648–1690) *Apology for the True Christian Divinity* (1678) provided a theological framework, and William Penn (1644–1718) emerged as an advocate for religious toleration for all Dissenters and Roman Catholics.

After the Revolution of 1688, Friends repudiated their social radicalism and became respectable dissenters. No longer openly challenging church or state, Friends enjoyed toleration, accepted distraints for tithes, and sought to ensure their survival by concentrating upon family nurture and preserving distinctive customs of dress, speech, and endogamous marriage (that is, marriage with other Friends). Their primary impact on England came through innovations in technology, industry, and finance, for example the Darbys and Lloyds in iron and Barclays and Lloyds in banking.

Outside Britain, the primary concentrations of Friends were in Rhode Island, Maryland, and North Carolina, where inhabitants converted, and New Jersey and Pennsylvania, which were settled by Quaker immigrants. In 1681 William Penn obtained a charter for Pennsylvania, and colonization began the next year. Penn's law guaranteed religious liberty, created a representative assembly, ended capital punishment for most crimes, and instituted a strict moral code. Quakers dominated the assembly until the eve of the American Revolution. Conflict with the proprietors, first with Penn and then with his sons, became characteristic as Quakers sought political power and won every assembly election until 1775 on a platform of low taxes, no established church, and no militia. Pennsylvania and Friends prospered, and Philadelphia became a cosmopolitan town with Quakers supporting the American Philosophical Society, the Pennsylvania Hospital, and the Library Company.

The French defeat of a British force in 1755 near present-day Pittsburgh brought a major transformation of Quakerism. Blaming the war on their own moral failures, Quakers now pronounced slavery a moral evil, initiated an Indian rights movement, questioned the legitimacy of their exercising political power and paying war taxes, and tightened the enforcement of testimonies on all Friends. The reform movement eventually spread to meetings throughout the colonies and Great Britain.

American Friends supported the protests against British taxation beginning in 1765 until they concluded that the agitation was leading to war. After 1774, Quakers began withdrawing from politics and opposing the movement toward independence. In 1776 they proclaimed neutrality between the two warring parties and noninvolvement in politics, required all members to free their slaves, and disowned members who served in the military or occupied political office. They also began the international antislavery movement taken up by British Friends after 1783. In the new Republic, Friends saw it as their role to be advocates for American Indians and African Americans.

See also **American Independence, War of (1775–1783); Cromwell, Oliver; Dissenters, English; English Civil War Radicalism; Puritanism.**

BIBLIOGRAPHY

Barbour, Hugh, and J. William Frost. *The Quakers.* New York, 1988.

Ingle, H. Larry. *First among Friends: George Fox and the Creation of Quakerism.* New York, 1994.

Larson, Rebecca. *Daughters of Light: Quaker Women Preaching and Prophesying in the Colonies and Abroad (1700–1775).* New York, 1999.

Marietta, Jack. *The Reformation of American Quakerism, 1748–1783.* Philadelphia, 1984.

Moore, Rosemary. *The Light in Their Consciences: The Early Quakers in Britain, 1646–1666.* University Park, Pa., 2000.

Tolles, Frederick. *Meeting House and Counting House: The Quaker Merchants of Colonial Philadelphia, 1682–1763.* New York, 1963; first published 1948.

J. WILLIAM FROST

QUEENS AND EMPRESSES. As women situated at the top of the social hierarchy, all of the queens and empresses of the early modern era were far from sharing the same fate. Depending on the state and the period, they could live relatively low-profile lives or, on the contrary, have a major political role to play. Although most of these women were the wives of kings or emperors, some of them nevertheless reigned in their own names whenever the rules of succession in their state authorized this, and they then conducted themselves as the equals of kings. It is therefore important to distinguish between kings' wives, whose titles as queen derived solely from their marriages and who generally lived apart from the political stage, and women who acceded to power by virtue of hereditary rights and exercised sovereign authority as head of state. Like all the empresses in the early modern era, the vast majority of queens fall into the first category, women who succeeded to the throne being quite rare.

RULES OF SUCCESSION

The living conditions of queens thus depended very largely on the rules of succession that determined the degree to which they enjoyed a share of power. Although all kingdoms show a marked preference for men in the line of succession, some admitted females when there were no males in the direct line. Most heads of state were therefore men, by virtue of natural law as the texts put it, but it was not unknown for a woman to take the throne. It happened in England with the reigns of Mary I (Mary Tudor, ruled 1553–1558), Elizabeth I (ruled 1558–1603), and Anne Stuart (ruled 1702–1714); in Scotland with Mary Stuart (1542–1587); in Sweden with Queen Christina (ruled 1632–1654); and in Hungary and Bohemia, two realms that were the hereditary dominions of the Austrian Habsburgs and to which Maria Theresa of Austria (ruled 1740–1780) acceded by virtue of the Pragmatic Sanction (1713) before becoming empress in 1745 with the election of her husband Francis I (ruled 1745–

1765). We find the same thing in eighteenth-century Russia: both Elizabeth Petrovna (ruled 1741–1762), the daughter of Peter the Great, and especially Catherine II (known as Catherine the Great; ruled 1762–1796), who took power to the detriment of her husband Peter III (1728–1762), had a profound effect on the age of Enlightenment. Denmark also allowed for female sovereigns and was ruled by queens in the Middle Ages, although it has always had male rulers in the modern era. Many small European states, minor independent principalities, similarly permitted female succession. They are not considered here because these women were not of royal status. However, the principles governing devolution of the throne, and the living conditions of women in these princely courts, were not fundamentally different from those of major states.

In certain monarchical states women were not allowed to rule but could nevertheless transmit their rights to the crown to their male descendants. Spain and Portugal underwent dynastic changes that were brought about by female transmission. The heads of state in these countries were necessarily men, but they nevertheless sometimes owed their throne to a grandmother: Spain fell into the hands of Philip V (ruled 1700–1746), a Bourbon prince, thanks to the rights of his grandmother Marie-Thérèse (María Teresa de Austria; 1638–1683); and Portugal was for a time united with the Spanish crown by virtue of the same principle. These rules of succession had an important role to play in the choice of partners because the marriage of every princess capable of passing on the crown meant that the throne could potentially pass into another family line. Foreign sovereigns sought marriage with crown princesses above all others.

That France was exceptional in this respect (Savoy alone was in the same situation, though not a kingdom) placed it in a position of power on the European scene. Salic law (the law of the French monarchy) totally excluded women from transmission; they could neither inherit the throne directly nor transmit it to their descendants. The marriage of a French princess thus implied no risk of transferring the crown to another family line, whereas kings could wed crown princesses and thus obtain new lands or even a new crown. The choice of alliances was directly conditioned by the laws governing succession.

ROYAL MARRIAGES

The priority that governments accorded to boys meant that girls became the object of matrimonial transactions; they were exchanged and, once married, had to leave their homeland to live in a new kingdom. Princesses by birth, they thus became the queens of countries to which their fate was intimately linked.

Three priorities governed the choice of a queen: ideally she should be a foreigner, a woman from a sovereign house, and an older daughter who was better placed in the order of succession. To the alliances contracted between states on the occasion of royal weddings we must also add dynastic considerations: as the daughters of kings, queens could bring the paternal succession in their inheritance. But although these young queens were generally foreigners, more often than not they were also cousins. Sovereign houses were none too plentiful, and social endogamy led to marriages between close relatives. It was not infrequent for the bride and groom to share at least one grandparent. Thus Louis XIV (ruled 1643–1715), an extreme case indeed, married his paternal and maternal first cousin Marie Thérèse.

The choice of a princess was not always an easy matter because eligible candidates were sometimes rare, particularly because, in addition to the social origins of the princess, her religion and age at time of marriage also had to be taken into account. Kings' daughters generally married quite young, but they had to have reached the age of puberty and thus be able to produce heirs rapidly. This consideration could even be decisive: Marie Leszczynska, a minor Polish princess, was married to Louis XV of France (ruled 1715–1774) specifically because she came from a large family and was therefore expected to produce many children. Hopes for a long line thus compensated for the relative mediocrity of the match.

Dynastic questions were of primordial importance in royal marriages, with the arrival of a son guaranteeing the union of the paternal and maternal inheritances; it was through descendants that two crowns could one day be united on the same head. This explains why both sides discussed the terms of the marriage contract so carefully. For the queen, the contract was of decisive importance because it established the conditions of her future life: the amount of her dowry, the constitution of her household, the dower she would receive in the event of being widowed were all defined on this occasion, as well as any rights to an inheritance from her parents. The wedding ceremony itself was nothing very spectacular. More often than not, the couple was united in a proxy marriage before they had even met, and the religious ceremony in the presence of the bride and groom reiterated the Christian principles whereby the union of two people made them into one flesh. On this occasion the princess contracted her husband's status, assumed the rank and title of queen, and in so doing passed from her father's authority into that of her husband. For the new queen, this stage was of fundamental importance because it sanctioned the passage from the state of daughter to that of wife, from princess to sovereign.

LIFE AT COURT

Transferred to a strange new house, a royal wife had to renounce her origins and erase all traces of her foreign extraction. The metamorphosis had to be all the more complete as it was, in theory at least, definitive. Only widowed queens with no children could conceivably return to their country of origin. Upon arrival in her new realm, the queen adopted the local customs and the language and etiquette of the court. Her role was essentially symbolic: as the incarnation of monarchical grandeur, she had to reflect it in the splendor of her household (consisting of hundreds of servants), the sumptuousness of her clothing, and the value of her jewelry. In this respect, she was treated magnificently well. The transition, however, was not always easy. Language, in particular, could continue to be an obstacle: Catherine de Médicis (1519–1589), an Italian princess who arrived in France at the age of fourteen, kept her strong accent throughout her life and continued to make mistakes whenever she spoke or wrote in French. Conversely, Catherine II of Russia, who was of German origin, very quickly adapted to the court of the tsars and soon spoke fluent Russian.

Although it is true that the importance accorded to the queen varied from one kingdom to another, she nevertheless always represented the monarchy, and the evolution of courtly life in Europe tended to place queens in the forefront of the royal stage. The majority of them were very well educated, particularly those who might be expected to rule in their own name. Elizabeth I of England spoke no fewer than seven languages, including Latin and Greek. Christina of Sweden (ruled 1632–1654) corresponded with René Descartes (1596–1650), whom she invited to her court, and Catherine II maintained epistolary relationships with philosophers such as Voltaire (1694–1778) and Jean Le Rond d'Alembert (1717–1783).

As a focus of attention, queens had to be able to maintain a dazzling court: because political power was traditionally in the hands of men during the *ancien régime,* domestic activity, which bore on the organization of the royal court, naturally fell into the hands of women. The distribution of social space did not therefore deprive women of political responsibility: the splendor of the court was also an expression of sovereign power. Royal patronage, which queens exercised just as much as kings, was another reflection of this power.

MOTHERHOOD AND POWER

In addition to this symbolic role, it was the wife's duty to provide successors and to ensure the continuation of the family line. Mainly, she was expected to produce sons, but also daughters in order to negotiate dynastic alliances. Motherhood guaranteed the queen a stronger position in the court and a more reliable future in the kingdom. Although marriage was theoretically indissoluble, a sterile princess was always in danger of losing her eminent position. In France the marriage between Henry IV (ruled 1589–1610) and Margaret of Valois (1553–1615) was declared null for reasons of sterility, and queens Catherine de Médicis and Anne of Austria (1601–1666), both of whom were slow to produce offspring, were not secure in their royal position until they gave birth to sons. In England, the notorious memory of Henry VIII (ruled 1509–1547), who married no fewer than six wives in order to ensure his succession, demonstrates the importance of these questions. However, the arrival of a son transformed these princesses into full-fledged queens.

As the mother of the crown prince, the queen could wield power one day in the name of her son. This considerably increased her influence in the court. When the king was worried about maintaining political continuity, he sometimes even prepared her for this role. She was then introduced into the royal council in order to familiarize her with the affairs of government. It is true, however, that by virtue of their influence over their husbands, some royal wives exercised political power while their husbands were still alive, regardless of whether they were mothers. By virtue of the role she played in the affairs of her husband, Sigismund I (ruled 1506–1548) of Poland, Bona, princess of Milan and Bari, introduced the Renaissance into Poland in the first half of the sixteenth century. In the seventeenth century Louise Marie de Gonzague-Nevers played an essential role: twice queen of Poland, thanks to her support, her brother-in-law John II Casimir Vasa, later her husband, was elected king of Poland (ruled 1648–1668). In Spain, Maria Anna of Bavaria Neuburg (1667–1740) took advantage of the weakness of her husband, Charles II (ruled 1665–1700), to favor Austrian interests in the matter of Spanish succession, and in France Marie Antoinette (1755–1793) was accused of giving bad advice to King Louis XVI (ruled 1774–1792). For better or worse, the political role of the wives of kings was generally not well known, except when a regency made it official.

REGENCIES

It was essentially by virtue of their being mothers that queens actually gained access to power in the event of a royal minority, in which case they ruled in the names of their sons. When a king died leaving an heir who was too young to govern, a regency was organized. The queen thus reached the peak of her glory, conducting affairs of state either alone or with the dignitaries and princes of the realm. Although regencies were theoretically a form of collective rule, they were very often personal in practice, the queen making it her business to rule without interference. Thus Catherine de Médicis, Marie de Médicis (1573–1642), and Anne of Austria, all three queens of France who are known essentially for their political action during royal minorities, eliminated all rivals to their authority as soon as their husbands died. Catherine de Médicis, mother of three successive kings—Francis II (ruled 1559), Charles IX (ruled 1560–1574), and Henry III (ruled 1574–1589)—managed to retain her power beyond the legal end of the royal minority (French kings reached their majority at the age of fourteen) by virtue of her influence over her children. Marie de Médicis also continued in government well beyond the majority of Louis XIII (ruled 1610–

1643). Anne of Austria, however, widow of Louis XIII, stepped aside in 1661 when her son Louis XIV decided to rule alone. He was already more than twenty years old, and the queen mother was prepared to relinquish the major political role she had played for nearly seventeen years. Other regencies were very long indeed: when the Scottish queen Mary of Guise (1515–1560) was widowed in 1542, her daughter Mary Stuart (1542–1587), heir to the throne, was only seven days old. When the little queen left Scotland to marry the French dauphin and future Francis II, her mother ruled as regent until her death in 1560, a period of nearly eighteen years. Mariana de Austria (1634–1696), widow of Philip IV of Spain (ruled 1621–1665), exercised power for ten years (1665–1675) in the name of her son, Charles II. In Sweden, Hedwig-Leonora, widowed at the age of twenty-four, found herself in charge of the government when her son, Charles XI (ruled 1660–1697), who was barely four years old, succeeded to the throne. The country had already been through a female regency some thirty years earlier when the young Queen Christina inherited her father's throne in 1632.

All of these examples, which are significant though not exhaustive, show that regency was a classic mode of administration in the absence of royal authority. The longest and most famous examples of female rule took place during royal minorities. A regency could also be organized in the absence of a king (away at war) or in the event of illness. The wives or mothers of the sovereign thus replaced the person who legally held royal authority but was unable to wield it. By doing so, they ensured political stability while maintaining dynastic continuity.

The political role of the wives of kings was therefore not negligible. Of course it did not compare with the role of queens reigning in their own name and inscribed in the long list of European sovereigns. But these regents also left their mark on their country of adoption. The same cannot be said for queens who disappeared without trace, dying young or widowed without children, and who hardly had the chance to exercise their political talents. Others had an even more tragic fate: Anne Boleyn (1507?–1536), queen of England, was condemned to death by her husband Henry VIII. Mary Stuart was executed by order of her cousin Elizabeth I of England; Marie-Antoinette, queen of France, died a victim of the French Revolution.

See also **Absolutism; Anna (Russia); Anne (England); Anne of Austria; Catherine de Médicis; Catherine II (Russia); Christina (Sweden); Court and Courtiers; Elizabeth I (England); Elizabeth (Russia); Isabella of Castile; Marguerite de Navarre; Maria Theresa (Holy Roman Empire); Marie Antoinette; Marie de Médicis; Mary I (England); Regency.**

BIBLIOGRAPHY

Cosandey, Fanny. *La reine de France: Symbole et pouvoir, XV–XVIIIe siècle.* Paris, 2000.

De Madariaga, Isabel. *Russia in the Age of Catherine the Great.* New Haven, 1981.

Dickens, A. G., ed. *The Courts of Europe: Politics, Patronage and Royalty, 1400–1800.* New York, 1977.

Frazer, Antonia. *Marie Antoinette: The Journey.* New York, 2001.

Hanley, Sarah. "The Monarchic State in Early Modern France: Marital Regime Government and Male Right." In *Politics, Ideology, and the Law in Early Modern Europe: Essays in Honor of J. H. M. Salmon,* edited by Adrianna E. Bakos, pp. 107–126. Rochester, N.Y., 1994.

Hopkins, Lisa. *Women Who Would Be Kings: Female Rulers of the Sixteenth Century.* London, 1991.

Kaiser, Thomas E. "Who's Afraid of Marie-Antoinette? Diplomacy, Austrophobia, and the Queen." *French History* 14, no. 3 (2000): 241–271.

Watkins, John. *Representing Elizabeth in Stuart England: Literature, History, Sovereignty.* New York, 2002.

FANNY COSANDEY
(TRANSLATED FROM THE FRENCH BY LIAM GAVIN)

QUIETISM. Quietism is a form of spirituality that emphasizes a direct relationship with God in a state of quietness of the soul (Latin *quies*). The ideas behind Quietism are to be found in many religions of the world. In the West, they influenced the mysticism of the Christian Middle Ages, notably that of the *devotio moderna* (modern devotion) movement. Quietist ideas reappeared during the sixteenth century in the *alumbrados* (illuminism) movement, which greatly worried the Spanish authorities. These notions reemerged in Italy in the 1680s when religious groups, self-proclaimed *quietisti,* promoted transformation in God and total spiritual passivity. The famous Spanish theologian Miguel de Molinos (1628–1696) encouraged these ideas in *La guia espiritual* (1675; The spiritual guide), ideas that were soon condemned because they seemed not only to call into question the hierarchy, authority, and dogma of the Roman Catholic Church but also to tolerate a dangerous moral bent toward sin—for committing sin could not trouble Quietism's intimate relationship with God. Molinos was tried by the Holy Office in 1685, and his teachings were condemned in 1687 by Pope Innocent XI for their Quietist negation of human powers and for what were regarded as their injurious theological and moral consequences. In Italy, works suspected of Quietism were included in the Index of Prohibited Books, and many trials followed. The hunt for *Quietisti* soon expanded all over Europe and contributed to the eighteenth-century waning of the mystical movement in France, Italy, and Spain.

In France, opponents of mysticism used the Roman condemnation to fight leading mystical figures such as Jeanne-Marie Bouvier de la Motte Guyon (Madame Guyon du Chesnoy; 1648–1717), the Barnabite preacher known as Father La Combe (1640–1715), and François de Salignac de La Mothe Fénelon, archbishop of Cambrai (1651–1715). They were all accused of suspicious links with the Italian *Quietisti,* of doubtful morality, and of disturbing theological concepts. First, La Combe was charged and imprisoned, then Guyon was condemned. Influenced by the Spanish mystic John of the Cross (1542–1591), Guyon actively promoted a mysticism based on the annihilation of the soul in *Les torrents spirituels* (1682; Spiritual torrents) and in *Moyen court et très facile pour l'oraison* (1685; Short and easy method to pray). Appealing at first to Parisian *dévot* circles and to the Marquise de Maintenon, the second wife of Louis XIV, she saw her writings condemned for their Quietism and found herself imprisoned many times between 1688 and 1703. Nevertheless, her ideas influenced various European audiences: Catholics and deists from France, Protestants from England, Scotland, and Switzerland, German Pietists, as well as the founder of Methodism, John Wesley (1703–1791), all claimed to be her disciples. The charges against Madame Guyon served also to put on trial Archbishop Fénelon to the point that his doctrine of Pure Love was equated with Quietism (he was on trial not only for being associated with Madame Guyon but also for political reasons). Fénelon promoted an unconditional love for God, so detached from any expectation of reward that one freely accepts to love God, even though convinced of one's own damnation. Fénelon, who had taken not only the side of Madame Guyon against her detractors, but also a political stand against Louis XIV's absolutism, was in turn accused of Quietism. Fénelon's formidable opponent, Bishop Jacques-Bénigne Bossuet, openly accused him of Quietist views and bad morality, leading to his condemnation and silencing in 1699. But, as French historian Jacques Le Brun notes, nothing was farther from Fénelon's austere doctrine of Pure Love and perfect charity than the accusation of total passivity.

See also **Bossuet, Jacques-Bénigne; Catholic Spirituality and Mysticism; Fénelon, François; Index of Prohibited Books; Inquisition; Methodism; Pietism.**

BIBLIOGRAPHY

Armogathe, Jean-Robert. *Le quiétisme*. Paris, 1973.

Beaude, Joseph, et al. *Madame Guyon*. Grenoble, 1997.

Cognet, Louis. *Crépuscule des mystiques: Bossuet–Fénelon*. Paris-Tournai, 1991.

Gondal, Marie-Louise. *Madame Guyon (1648–1717): Un nouveau visage*. Paris, 1989.

Laude, Patrick D. *Approches du quiétisme: Deux études suivies du* Moyen court et très facile pour l'oraison *de Madame Guyon (texte de l'édition de 1685)*. Paris, Seattle, and Tübingen, 1991.

Le Brun, Jacques. *Le pur amour de Platon à Lacan*. Paris, 2002.

Lehmann, Hartmut, et al. *Jansenismus, Quietismus, Pietismus/im Auftrag der Historischen Kommission zur Erforschung des Pietismus*. Göttingen, 2002.

Meyer, Jean. *Bossuet*. Paris, 1993.

Richardt, Aimé. *Fénelon*. Ozoir-la-Ferrière, France, 1993.

Thompson, Phyllis. *Madame Guyon, Martyr of the Holy Spirit*. London, 1986.

DOMINIQUE DESLANDRES

RABELAIS, FRANÇOIS (c. 1483–1553), French writer. Little is known about Rabelais's early life; even the year of his birth remains uncertain. He was born near Chinon, in the Loire valley, and refers affectionately to the region in his work. As a young man Rabelais joined the Franciscans (c. 1510), studied both theology and law, and frequented or corresponded with leading humanist scholars of the day. By 1521 he had become a priest and acquired the reputation of being both an excellent scholar of Greek and a troublemaker, as his Franciscan superiors confiscated his Greek books. By the early 1530s, having first left the Franciscans for the Benedictines, and then left monastic life entirely to become a secular priest, he was a prominent physician living in Lyon, the cultural (and publishing) capital of France at that time. There he took up a position at a hospital, began a correspondence with Desiderius Erasmus, and published several medical texts.

In the fall of 1532, Rabelais published a very different sort of text: *Pantagruel,* the first of the comic works to which he owes his fame. The book's considerable commercial success did not keep it (or Rabelais's subsequent works) from being condemned by the Sorbonne, whose faculty of theology acted as the church's office of censorship. Nonetheless, Rabelais's patrons shielded him well enough that he could follow up on *Pantagruel's* success by publishing *Gargantua* in late 1534 or early 1535. *Gargantua* was in its turn both successful and highly controversial; Rabelais chose, in the increasingly dangerous politico-religious climate of the mid-1530s, to publish less and to avoid France as much as possible. He spent a great deal of time in Italy in the late 1530s and early 1540s, often with members of the powerful du Bellay family, who continued to protect him. After twelve years of intermittent exile and silence, Rabelais published, in 1546, the *Tiers Livre.* Given the controversy it excited, Rabelais judged it prudent once again to leave town, taking refuge this time in Metz. In 1548 he returned to Rome at the request of Cardinal Jean du Bellay, along the way leaving an incomplete draft of the *Quart Livre* with his publisher in Lyon. The latter printed it immediately, perhaps to the annoyance of Rabelais, who did not produce the final version until January 1552. The *Quart Livre* was, like Rabelais's previous volumes, promptly attacked by the Sorbonne, but thanks to the author's fame and connections the censors could not prevent publication. Rabelais died in the early 1550s, probably on 9 April 1553. A *Cinquième Livre,* published several years after Rabelais's death, in 1564, is of dubious, or at best partial, authenticity.

The four authentic books together constitute a comic masterpiece of the first order, unique in Western literature. *Pantagruel,* in appearance a mass-market book, a parody of popular chivalric romances filled with superhuman heroes, fabulous monsters, and often obscene humor, is in fact an immensely complex work, combining features of popular literature with deep learning, topical satire, and enthusiasm for the ideals of Renaissance humanism. *Gargantua,* the story of Pantagruel's father, shares features (for example, its narrative tra-

François Rabelais. THE ART ARCHIVE/MUSÉE DU CHÂTEAU DE VERSAILLES/DAGLI ORTI

jectory) with its predecessor but is more sophisticated, eschewing at least some of *Pantagruel's* raw slapstick in favor of elaborate political and religious satire, a clearer commitment to a tolerant Erasmian Christianity, and a not entirely unironic reexamination of the humanist project. The *Tiers Livre* is the least overtly comic of the four books; it is dominated by the contrast between the humanist sage Pantagruel and his irrational, appetite-driven sidekick Panurge (from the Greek, in the sense of 'one willing to do anything'), who consults a series of more-or-less outlandish "experts" in order to find out whether he should marry. This opposition continues into the *Quart Livre,* in which Pantagruel, Panurge and his companions embark on a sea voyage to visit the oracle of the *Dive Bouteille* ('holy bottle'). The islands they visit are populated by a range of odd beings ludicrously secure in their own varieties of folly, and the voyage thus represents to the reader the limits of human understanding, and the consequent (and dangerous) absurdity of any claim to definitive interpretation or knowledge, especially in matters of faith.

Rabelais is perhaps the most difficult of French authors. His immense learning, richness of language, and intense engagement with the literary, religious, and political issues of his day produce a density and complexity of allusion and linguistic play that demand great effort from the reader. This was true even for Rabelais's contemporaries, most of whom nonetheless recognized him to be a writer of the first rank, although some were repelled by his uncompromisingly graphic humor. He fell from favor in the seventeenth century, not least because his linguistic exuberance was at odds with the more severe aesthetic of the day. For many in the eighteenth and nineteenth centuries he was more talked about than read, a mere name representing at best drunken good humor, at worst coarse literary debauchery. The twentieth century saw a resurgence of interest in Rabelais, and, as a result of actually reading what he wrote, a truer appreciation of his immense accomplishment. As the twenty-first century begins, the enthusiasm and controversy excited by Rabelais show no signs of diminishing. In particular, the tensions between the serious and the comic in his work continue to provoke lively critical debate.

See also **Erasmus, Desiderius; French Literature and Language.**

BIBLIOGRAPHY

Primary Sources

Rabelais, François. *Complete Works.* Translated by Donald M. Frame. Berkeley, 1991.

———. *Oeuvres complètes.* Edited by Mireille Huchon. Paris, 1994.

Secondary Sources

Bakhtin, Mikhail. *Rabelais and His World.* Translated by Hélène Iswolsky. Bloomington, Ind., 1984.

Cave, Terence C. *The Cornucopian Text. Problems of Writing in the French Renaissance.* Oxford and New York, 1979.

Defaux, Gérard. *Rabelais Agonistes: du rieur au prophète.* Geneva, 1997.

Duval, Edwin M. *The Design of Rabelais's* Pantagruel. New Haven, 1991.

Jeanneret, Michel. *Le défi des mots: Rabelais et la crise de l'interprétation à la Renaissance.* Orléans and Caen, 1994.

Rigolot, François. *Les langages de Rabelais.* 2nd ed. Geneva, 1996.

Screech, Michael. *Rabelais.* Ithaca, N.Y., 1979.

Tournon, André. *"En sens agile": Les acrobaties de l'esprit selon Rabelais.* Paris, 1995.

DAVID M. POSNER

RACE, THEORIES OF. After Portuguese, Spanish, Italian, and French sailors discovered in the fourteenth and fifteenth centuries both hitherto unknown oceanic wind flows and how to find their bearings in the open sea, Europeans began to cross the oceans and interact with West African, South and East Asian, and American peoples—peoples of whom the ancient geographies had been ignorant or whom they simply disregarded or treated as monstrous races. Medieval accounts of fantastic beings located in faraway, mythical places receded, giving way to excruciatingly detailed descriptions of the mores and religions of African, American, and Asian peoples. Newly acquired ethnographic sensibilities stemmed from the need to rule colonies and conduct foreign business. Expansion overseas, however, overlapped with the consolidation of new, relatively large dynastic states such as England, France, and Spain. These states sought to introduce religious and linguistic uniformity into maddeningly complex and ethnically heterogeneous worlds. In early modern Europe, understanding ethnic distinctions overseas became as important as comprehending cultural variations at home.

Ancient and medieval categories helped early modern intellectuals grapple with their growing awareness of ethnic differences. To catalog these differences scholars turned to the age-old genre of "natural history." Yet a commitment to the historicity and veracity of the Bible made it difficult to pigeonhole others as separate species (monstrous races, natural slaves) or to explain away differences simply as the result of independent godly creations (polygenism). Such restrictions forced intellectuals to find in Galenic and Hippocratic notions of temperaments and complexions, and in Aristotelian psychology and Ciceronian jurisprudence, the tools to make sense of bodily and behavioral differences between groups. Climate and the environment, it was widely believed, accounted for variations in political systems and skin color. Thus it was thought that, say, colder places made peoples dull, white, and democratic, whereas tropical ones rendered them intelligent, dark, and subservient. Seemingly whimsical customs first introduced by cultural heroes, it was also argued, launched peoples into divergent paths of development. As these mores hardened over time into laws and traditions, peoples developed collective behaviors ("second nature") that were almost impossible to transform.

Fifteenth- and sixteenth-century Europe was a harsh place for outsiders. Christians raided and enslaved Muslims from the Mediterranean to the Indian Ocean (and vice-versa). Jews continued to be persecuted, and in Spain experienced mass expulsion. Enslaved blacks arrived by the thousands in European ports. Slavs on the eastern and Irish peoples on the western margins of the European continent continued to endure intolerable conditions. This harsh world, however, seemed not to have room for the concept of race. Cultural and bodily identities remained porous. As in the ancient Roman world, assimilation rather than exclusion was the norm. To be sure, some outsiders, particularly Jews, were deemed hereditarily prone to resist assimilation. Yet even boundaries between "black" and "white" bodies remained difficult to pinpoint. The age-old theory of cross-color generation, for example, held that white mothers, if exposed to certain thoughts and visions during copulation, could naturally have black children (and vice-versa). In this mongrel world, race was a category often used to discriminate against insiders, not outsiders. Early modern just as much as medieval Europe was a hierarchical society in which the nobility often took peasants to be an altogether different race.

These classical and medieval sensibilities gave way to new ideas as slavery, colonization, and state-building developed unrelentingly. Oddly, new concepts of race developed more rapidly in those societies that were more economically vibrant. One of the great paradoxes of the modern age is that some of the harshest forms of slavery ever witnessed existed in the colonies of those societies that enjoyed the "freest" labor markets at home. Although Iberians in the islands off the coast of Africa first introduced plantation economies, and although millions of African slaves wound up laboring and dying under miserable conditions in their American colonies, slaveholding was typical of both metropolis and peripheries in the Portuguese and Spanish empires. This contributed to keeping boundaries between blacks and whites porous (through manumission and miscegenation). In the British-American Atlantic, however, free labor became the rule in the metropolis while chattel slavery flourished on the periphery. The growing polarization between freedom and slavery led to the hardening of "white" and "black" identities, which came to be seen as fixed and inherited, as well as to a poverty of categories to deal with hybrid conditions.

The mounting popularity of the theory of polygenism typified this growth of white and black racialized identities. Over the course of the seventeenth and eighteenth centuries, as the Bible steadily lost ground to more secular historical accounts, the idea that all human groups descended from a common ancestral pair (Adam and Eve) began to be called into question. The theory of polygenism held that different peoples had different primeval ancestors. Climate alone, it was now believed, could not explain the origins of differences in skin color. That blackness and whiteness were rapidly becoming rigid bodily and behavioral attributes was also reflected in the demise of theories of cross-color generation. By the eighteenth century it was no longer thought feasible that white mothers whose imagination had been jolted during copulation could have black children. The racialization of identities was also reflected in changing interpretations given to the biblical story of the curse of Ham. According to this story, Noah cursed the descendants of one of his sons, Ham, to a life of toil and slavery after the latter had found Noah naked and drunk. Since antiquity this story had helped justify the subordinate status of a variety of groups, particularly the European peasantries. Yet by the seventeenth and eighteenth centuries the curse became firmly and exclusively associated with the fate of African blacks.

RACE AND EARLY MODERN SCIENCE

The coming of age of the concept of race has been attributed to the rise of new forms of science, particularly Enlightenment natural history. It is clear that in the eighteenth century naturalists were fond of devising new taxonomies to classify not only plants but also peoples. Collecting and measuring skulls and dissecting blacks and apes became fashionable in efforts to explain the origins of racial differences.

Scientific racism made further inroads in the nineteenth century as a result of major political transformations. As old political orders based on social estates, hereditary privileges, and religion came tumbling down in the age of revolutions, and as new social formations built on the principles of citizenship, natural rights, and secular political authority emerged, white European males located in science (of race and sex) the ideological justification to prevent women, Jews, slaves, and non-Europeans from sharing in their newly acquired political rights. This dominant account of the origins of scientific racism, however, is not entirely accurate.

The science of race arose in the seventeenth century in the New World. British colonists schooled in the new mechanical philosophy came up with representations of Indians' bodies as innately inferior—weak and predisposed to diseases. Such scientifically racialized views helped colonists not only to explain the demographic collapse of native peoples in the wake of the arrival of new European diseases but also to claim for themselves the identity of Americans—individuals providentially destined to occupy the land that had once belonged to the now quickly disappearing Indians. Other forms of the science of race developed in the Spanish colonies. Here Creole colonists responded to disparaging European views on the climate and constellations of Spanish America as threatening and degenerating by suggesting that bodies were immune to climatic and environmental influences, thus rejecting long-held theories on temperament and complexion. Their new version of ancient astrological and medical theories also allowed them to claim that the natives were innately inferior. In this *ancien régime* colonial society Indians came to inhabit the same niche that peasants had long occupied in the imagination of the European elites—that is, they were an altogether different race.

See also **Class, Status, and Order; Colonialism; Ethnography; Exploration; Slavery and the Slave Trade.**

BIBLIOGRAPHY

Braude, Benjamin. "The Sons of Noah and the Construction of Ethnic and Geographical Identities in the Medieval and Early Modern Period." *William and Mary Quarterly* 54 (1997): 103–142.

Cañizares-Esguerra, Jorge. "New World New Stars: Indian and Creole Bodies in Colonial Spanish America, 1600–

1650." *American Historical Review* 104 (1999): 33–68.

Chaplin, Joyce. *Subject Matter: Technology, the Body, and Science on the Anglo-American Frontier, 1500–1676.* Cambridge, Mass., 2001.

Eltis, David. *The Rise of African Slavery in the Americas.* Cambridge, U.K., and New York, 2000.

Fredrickson, George M. *Racism: A Short History.* Princeton, 2002.

Freedman, Paul. *Images of the Medieval Peasant.* Stanford, 1999.

Friedman, John Block. *The Monstrous Races in Medieval Art and Thought.* Cambridge, Mass., 1981.

Hannaford, Ivan. *Race: The History of an Idea in the West.* Washington, D.C., and Baltimore, 1996.

Pagden, Anthony. *The Fall of Natural Man: The American Indian and the Origins of Comparative Ethnology.* Cambridge, U.K., and New York, 1982.

Peabody, Sue. *"There Are No Slaves in France": The Political Culture of Race and Slavery in the Ancien Régime.* New York, 1996.

JORGE CAÑIZARES-ESGUERRA

RACINE, JEAN

RACINE, JEAN (1639–1699), French playwright and author. Racine was born in La Ferté-Milon, northeast of Paris. His parents died when he was very young, and he was therefore raised mostly by his maternal grandmother, Marie Desmoulins. As his mother's family had close connections with the Jansenists of Port-Royal, Racine came under their influence from an early age, and their rigorous Augustinian theology would be central to his work. After beginning his education at the Collège de Beauvais, he studied at the Petites Écoles de Port-Royal, where he absorbed both Jansenist doctrine and a solid classical education, becoming a particularly fine scholar of Greek. From 1658 Racine began to lead a more worldly life, rejecting his austere upbringing in favor of writing poetry and party-hopping with his cousin Nicolas Vitart, the writer of fables Jean de La Fontaine (also a distant relation), and other figures on the Parisian literary scene. His family sent him (1661–1663) to Uzès in an effort to make a churchman of him, but his letters from this time show us how little this sort of life appealed to him. By 1663 he was back in Paris, where he met Molière and Nicolas Boileau-Despréaux, and (despite criticism from his family) began to write for the theater.

Racine's first play to be produced was *La Thébaïde* (The Thebiad), which had its premiere on 20 June 1664, inspiring both popular and critical acclaim. This was followed by *Alexandre le grand* (1665), in whose preface Racine somewhat ungratefully repudiated his teachers at Port-Royal. The first few performances were given by Molière's theater company; then, however, Racine took both the play and its leading lady, Thérèse du Parc, away from Molière, and arranged for further performances to be given by the rival troupe of the Hôtel de Bourgogne, a move that Racine thought (correctly) would augment both his fame and his box-office receipts. Such machinations made Racine few friends, and indeed he seems to have been, at least in his professional life, a difficult man: vain, humorless, quick to take offense, and ungenerous toward fellow artists, even if his scathing attacks on his enemies were sometimes justified.

There followed Racine's first real masterpiece, *Andromaque* (1667, written for Du Parc); his only comedy, *Les plaideurs* (1668; The litigants); *Britannicus* (1669); *Bérénice* (1670); *Bajazet* (1672); and Louis XIV's personal favorite, *Mithridate* (1673, the year in which Racine was elected to the Académie Française). Du Parc having died in 1668, by 1670 Racine had joined the crowd of lovers of another leading actress, Marie de Champmeslé, for whom he wrote the title roles of *Bérénice* and his two last plays on classical subjects, *Iphigénie en Aulide* (1674) and *Phèdre* (1677). After *Phèdre* he suddenly abandoned the theater, probably less because of any spiritual crisis than because Louis XIV made him (with Boileau, one of the few friends Racine had managed to keep) his official historiographer. He married Catherine de Romanet, a distant relation by marriage, and settled down to a life as a respectable courtier and the devoted father of seven children. For the next twelve years Racine busied himself with his official duties, only returning to the theater in 1689 at the request of Louis's wife Madame de Maintenon, for whose girls' school at Saint-Cyr he wrote *Esther* (1689) and *Athalie* (1691). In 1695 he produced his *Cantiques spirituels* (Spiritual songs), and thereafter entered semi-retirement, interpreted by some as the result of falling from Louis's favor. After writing the *Abrégé de*

Jean Racine. LIBRARY OF CONGRESS

l'histoire de Port-Royal (Summary of the history of Port-Royal), which was not published until 1767, Racine died on 21 April 1699.

Racine's theater uses extreme economy of means to generate an intensity of tragic feeling rivaled only by his classical Greek models and by Shakespeare. The unusually small vocabulary of the plays (just under 3,000 words) and his strict adherence to the three unities (codified by his rival Pierre Corneille) give his tragedies the sharpest possible focus. He is a poetic craftsman of the first order, and the austere, oblique elegance of his verse serves to heighten, through ironic contrast, the horror of his characters' torments. His themes and plots, too, while more varied than commonly supposed, are rigorously organized, and their inexorable unfolding shows how well he has absorbed both the theatrical technique and the tragic outlook of the Greeks; but the ruthlessness of his tragedy often surpasses even that of Sophocles or Euripides. This is because Racine adds to the tragic equation a harsh pessimism, derived from Jansenist theology, according to which humans are not merely liable to error, but doomed to self-destructive transgression. In the absence of redemptive grace, even the greatest and

noblest souls are driven by their own passions—incestuous lust, hunger for power, murderous vengefulness, sadistic cruelty—to crimes that destroy victim and perpetrator alike. Racine displays an almost clinical fascination with this process, especially as embodied in his tormented female protagonists. Of the sufferings of an Iphigénie or a Phèdre, perhaps none is more exquisite than their terrible lucidity, their claustrophobic awareness of a fate they can do nothing to avoid. The psychological complexity Racine gives to these roles has made them coveted by generations of actresses.

In the immaculate music of his verse, Racine expresses passions of a perverse, even blasphemous ferocity; the result is powerful theater that has continued to fascinate audiences and scholars alike from the seventeenth century to the present. Save for a period of disfavor in the nineteenth century, when the Romantics preferred Shakespeare, Racine's work has remained the benchmark for tragic theater, in France and elsewhere. He claimed to be writing for the sophisticated few, but his immense success belies his intention. The literature on Racine is enormous and still growing; historicists, Marxists, psychoanalytic critics, poststructuralists, and the philosophically or theologically inclined all find that Racine has as much to say as ever.

See also **Boileau-Despréaux, Nicolas; Classicism; Corneille, Pierre; French Literature and Language; Jansenism; La Fontaine, Jean de; Molière.**

BIBLIOGRAPHY

Primary Sources
Racine, Jean. *Andromache, Britannicus, Bérénice.* Translated by John Cairncross. Baltimore, 1967.

———. *Five Plays.* Translated by Kenneth Muir. New York, 1960.

———. *Iphigenia, Phaedra, Athaliah.* Translated by John Cairncross. Baltimore, 1963.

———. *Oeuvres complètes.* Edited by Raymond Picard. 2 vols. Paris, 1950–1966.

———. *Oeuvres complètes.* Edited by Georges Forestier. Paris, 1999–.

Secondary Sources
Barthes, Roland. *On Racine.* Translated by Richard Howard. New York, 1964.

Bénichou, Paul. *Morales du Grand Siècle.* Paris, 1948.

Goldmann, Lucien. *The Hidden God: A Study of Tragic Vision in the* Pensées *of Pascal and the Tragedies of Racine.* Translated by Philip Thody. London, 1964.

Jasinki, René. *Vers le vrai Racine.* Paris, 1958.

Picard, Raymond. *La carrière de Jean Racine.* Paris, 1961.

Pommier, Jean. *Aspects de Racine, suivi de l'histoire littéraire d'un couple tragique.* Paris, 1954.

Rohou, Jacques. *Avez-vous lu Racine? Mise au point polémique.* Paris, 2000.

Viala, Alain. *Racine, la stratégie du caméléon.* Paris, 1990.

DAVID M. POSNER

RÁKÓCZI REVOLT. After the reconquest of Hungary from the Ottomans in the war of 1684–1699, Vienna treated the Hungarians as unreliable rebels and their country as conquered territory that could now be integrated into the monarchy according to Vienna's design. However, the harsh measures to subdue, exploit, Catholicize, and Germanize the country triggered unrest that culminated in a full-scale uprising in May 1703. Led by Ferenc Rákóczi II (1676–1735), the wealthiest aristocrat in Upper Hungary, who had been raised as a loyal Habsburg subject by the Jesuits following his stepfather's (Imre Thököly) and mother's (Ilona Rákóczi) failed struggle against the Habsburgs, the insurrection aimed at restoring Hungary's independence. By early 1704, since the best of the Habsburg forces were occupied in the War of the Spanish Succession, Rákóczi controlled almost the entire country. However, the country was unable to finance the insurgent, or *kuruc,* army of 70,000 men, its generals were inexperienced, and Rákóczi, who was elected prince of Transylvania (1704) and of Hungary (1705), himself proved to be a better diplomat and statesman than a battlefield commander. After successive defeats, most of the aristocrats returned to the Habsburgs, deposed by the diet of 1707. While Rákóczi was seeking foreign aid in Poland, his general, Sándor Károlyi, signed the peace treaty of Szatmár (1711). Although accused of "treachery" by nationalist historians, Károlyi attained the best possible compromise, given the unfavorable military and diplomatic situation for the insurgents. While the Habsburgs reestablished royal authority over Hungary, the insurgents were given general amnesty and a pledge from their ruler that their constitutional and religious rights would be restored. More importantly, the treaty opened the way for a peaceful reconstruction of the country after three decades of war. Rákóczi rejected the amnesty and died in exile in Tekirdağ (Rodosto), Turkey in 1735.

See also **Habsburg Dynasty: Austria; Hungary.**

BIBLIOGRAPHY

Ingrao, Charles W. "Guerilla Warfare in Early Modern Europe: The Kuruc War (1703–1711)." In *War and Society in East Central Europe,* edited by Béla K. Király and Gunther E. Rothenberg, vol. 1, pp. 47–66. New York, 1979.

Köpeczi, Béla, ed. *History of Transylvania.* Budapest, 1994.

Rácköczi, Ferenc II. *Mémoirs du Prince François II Rákóczi sur la guerre de Hongrie.* Edited by Béla Köpeczi. Budapest, 1978.

GÁBOR ÁGOSTON

RAMEAU, JEAN-PHILIPPE (1683–1764), French composer and theorist. For much of the reign of Louis XV (1715–1774), Rameau dominated the French musical scene: several of his contributions to the Opéra were the most successful of the time and continued to be performed long after his death. He was particularly favored by the court, and, as a "rationalist" thinker, he engaged vigorously in Enlightenment intellectual debates.

Son of an organist, Rameau early showed musical gifts. At eighteen he went to Italy for study, and on his return, he was appointed organist at the cathedral in Avignon and then in Clermont (1702). His surviving early compositions for the church, *grands motets,* and for the chamber, *cantates* and pieces for solo harpsichord, as well as later contributions in these genres and works for harpsichord and violin (or flute) and bass viol (or second violin), are popular with performers today.

After a brief stay in Paris (1706–1709), Rameau returned to Dijon (where he succeeded his father as cathedral organist) and then moved to Lyons before returning to Clermont in 1715. In 1722 he went back to Paris, where he published his second (1724) and third (1728) harpsichord books and his *Traité de l'harmonie* (1722; Treatise on harmony). He also held several posts as organist, but he was determined to conquer the operatic stage. After contributions (now lost) to several *opéras-comiques* for Fair theaters, Rameau made a stunning debut—at the age of fifty—at the Académie Royale de Musique (the Opéra) with his *Hippolyte et Aricie* (1733). The public saw in it a direct challenge to the *tragédie en musique* as established by Jean-Baptiste Lully (1632–1687), whose works were still an important part of the Paris repertoire. Some, the "Lullistes," were askance; others, "Ramistes," or even more descriptively, *ramoneurs,* 'chimney sweeps', viewed Rameau's heightened emphasis on the drama and a more direct presentation of emotions as positive.

Not content with reorienting conceptions of this genre, in his next work for the Académie, the composer turned his attention to the other genre that had been popular there from the time of the Regency: the ballet (now generally referred to as *opéra-ballet,* as it includes both dancing and singing). In *Les Indes galantes* (1735) Rameau (with the librettist Louis Fuzelier, who was one of his collaborators at the Fair) adopted the typical structure of prologue and acts, or *entrées,* each of which explored a common theme, in this case the imagined customs of love and courtship, and appealed to the audience's interest in the exotic (Peru, Turkey, Persia). With its many revisions, including the addition of the act "Les sauvages" (set in the Americas and reflecting Rousseauesque Enlightenment views of the "noble savage"), it proved an enduring work. While magnificent and imaginative costumes and stage sets and impressive effects, such as the volcanic explosion in the act called "Les Incas de Pérou," certainly contributed to its success, Rameau's theatrical score surely takes pride of place.

Castor et Pollux (1737, revised 1754) differs from the great majority of *tragédies en musique* in that it celebrates not principally the relationship of two conventional lovers, but rather the strong bonds between brothers, each ready to sacrifice himself for the other. (This reflects a theme dear to Freemasons. *Zoroastre* [1749, revised 1756], among other Rameau works, also shows the influence of Freemasonry.) The choruses are unusually varied, from the people's religious dirge at Castor's death, "Que tout gémisse," to the deliberately unmelodic demons of "Brison tous nos fers." The *divertissement* in the Elysian Fields, featuring the Blessed Spirits in chorus and dance, achieved an

Jean-Philippe Rameau. LIBRARY OF CONGRESS

appropriately ethereal quality admired by contemporaries and later by Gluck, as *Orphée et Euridice* (1744) makes clear. *Castor et Pollux* remained in the Opéra's repertory until 1785. In 1791, at the administration's request, Pierre Candeille undertook a new setting, which retained the best-loved pieces of Rameau's original, among them Télaïre's moving lament, "Tristes apprêts," though reorchestrated. In this guise, the Parisian public still heard some of Rameau's music until 1817.

The composer also broke conventional genre boundaries at the Académie Royale in works such as *Platée,* a *ballet bouffon* (1745 at court, 1749 in Paris), whose heroine, an ugly nymph *(en travesti),* with her frog followers, and hero, Jupiter, whose transformations include becoming an ass and an owl, are hardly the typical depictions of gods and demigods expected there. Rameau exploited the element of farce to the full and often showed himself a remarkable orchestrator (even requiring violinists to slide quarter tones to imitate an ass and oboists, deliberately out of tune, to represent croaking frogs). In all, he wrote or substantially revised about thirty works for the Paris Opéra in less than thirty years—works that constituted the core of the late baroque repertory there.

Rameau was also the court composer par excellence during the reign of Louis XV. He celebrated the king's victories (*Le temple de la Gloire*, 1745, and *Naïs* 1749), the marriages of his son and heir (*La princesse de Navarre*, 1745, and *Les fêtes de l'Hymen et de l'Amour; ou Les dieux d'Egypte*, 1747), and, in his *Cantate pour le jour de la fête de Saint Louis* (1730s), the king's name day. The *concerts de la Reine*, under the aegis, of course, of Queen Marie Leszczyńska, frequently featured his music, and yet, he also pleased the *maîtresse en titre*, Mme de Pompadour, by writing *Les surprises de l'Amour* (1748), which featured her as an operatic performer, for the Théâtre des Petits Cabinets. He was well rewarded: he was named compositeur de la chambre du Roi in 1745 and ennobled shortly before his death (1764).

As a theorist, Rameau revolutionized the concept of chords by establishing the primacy of the triad and seventh chords whose roots became the *basse fondamentale* and relating the myriad of other chordal formations recognized in earlier thorough-bass manuals to inversions of the basic types. He also offered a more rational approach to harmonic progression. Influenced by René Descartes's mechanistic model, Rameau emphasized the importance of dissonance and resolution, strong bass movements, often by perfect fifth, and a hierarchy of cadences crucial to the structure of tonal composition. In his writings, however, the "scientific" approach and what he called "the judgment of the ear" were complementary. Early in his career influential philosophes supported him; Jean Le Rond d'Alembert, for example, presented his ideas in a more readable form in *Éléments de musique théorique et pratique selon les principes de M. Rameau* (1752), but they later parted company. The Rousseau-Rameau aesthetic debate over the primacy of melody (choice of the Italophile Rousseau) or harmony (Rameau's position) enlivened the mid-century *Querelle des Bouffons* (on the superiority of Italian *opera buffa* or French *tragédie en musique*). Nonetheless, Rameau's approach to chordal analysis, tonal definition, and other theoretical issues proved an enduring legacy.

See also **Lully, Jean-Baptiste; Music; Opera; Rousseau, Jean-Jacques.**

BIBLIOGRAPHY

Bouissou, Sylvie, gen. ed. *Jean-Philippe Rameau: Opera Omnia*. Paris, 1996–.

Christensen, Thomas. *Rameau and Musical Thought in the Enlightenment*. Cambridge, U.K., 1993.

Dill, Charles W. *Monstrous Opera: Rameau and the Tragic Tradition*. Princeton, 1998.

Foster, Donald H. *Jean-Philippe Rameau: A Guide to Research*. New York, 1989.

Green, Thomas R. *Early Rameau Sources: Studies in the Origins and Dating of the Operas and Other Musical Works*. Ph.D. diss., Brandeis University, 1992.

Jacobi, Erwin R., ed. *Jean-Philippe Rameau: The Complete Theoretical Writings*. 6 vols. Rome, 1967–1972. Facsimiles of eighteenth-century editions.

La Gorce, Jérôme de. *Jean-Philippe Rameau: Colloque international organisé par la Société Rameau, Dijon, 21–24 septembre 1983*. Paris, 1987.

Rice, Paul F. *The Performing Arts at Fontainebleau from Louis XIV to Louis XVI*. Ann Arbor, Mich., 1989.

Sadler, Graham, and Thomas Christensen. "Rameau, Jean-Philippe." In *The New Grove Dictionary of Music and Musicians*. 2nd ed. London, 2001.

Saint-Saëns, Camille, general ed. *Jean-Philippe Rameau: Oeuvres complètes*. 18 vols. Paris, 1895–1924. Reprint New York, 1968.

Verba, Cynthia. *Music and the French Enlightenment: Reconstruction of a Dialogue, 1750–1764*. Oxford, 1993.

M. ELIZABETH C. BARTLET

RAMUS, PETRUS

RAMUS, PETRUS (1515–1572), French humanist philosopher, educator, and communicator. A controversial figure in sixteenth-century Europe, Petrus Ramus used the lecture hall and the printing press to oppose the educational establishment of his day. His goals were to reform the teaching of grammar, redistribute and refashion the functions of logic and rhetoric, add physics and metaphysics to the liberal arts, and place more value on mathematics. Reconstructing the university curriculum, he argued with passion that all knowledge was available to those willing to use the correct method to obtain it. His message was that there was only one method in true learning, and that it was based on a new dialectic, his own. Challenging the authority of Aristotle, Cicero, and Quintilian, he furthered the work of the Dutch philosopher Roelof Huysman (Rodolphus Agricola, 1443/44–1485) and the early humanists who sought to simplify the world of Aristotle's dialectics.

Baptized Pierre de La Ramée, Ramus was born into a poor farming family at Cuts in the province of Picardy. He went to Paris as a valet for wealthy students in 1523, entering the College of Navarre in 1527. His M.A. thesis (1536) argued the falsity of Aristotle's doctrines. Among his colleagues and friends were future bishops and cardinals, which figured in his appointment as an instructor at the College of Mans in 1537. His lectures were well attended and he quickly established a reputation as a vociferous critic of Aristotle. Moving to the College of Ave Maria around 1540, he worked with a team of colleagues who included Omer Talon, his major collaborator, and Nicolaus Nancel, his later biographer. In 1543 he published his two defining works: *Dialecticae Institutiones* (Training in dialectic) and *Aristotelicae Animadversiones* (Remarks on Aristotle). In 1544 a royal commission forced Ramus into a debate with Antonio de Gouveia, defender of the Aristotelian tradition. The commission denounced Ramus for attacking the art of logic accepted by all nations, and banned him from teaching. However, his friend Charles de Guise, cardinal of Lorraine, procured his appointment as principal of the College of Presles in 1545, and had the ban lifted by the new king, Henry II, in 1547.

Over the next quarter century Ramus gained in girth as in stature. Appointed royal lecturer at the College of France (the Sorbonne, Paris) in 1551, his lectures were said to have drawn thousands. Meanwhile, he continued to publish a work or two a year. A major event was his conversion to the Protestant faith in 1561, an act that broke his relationship with the church and with patrons. With the outset of the Wars of Religion in 1562, he withdrew to Fontainebleau with the king's protection. The wars caused him to be on the move between France, Germany, and Switzerland, although he became dean of his college in 1565. During these turbulent years he published perhaps his greatest work, the *Scholae in Liberales Artes* (1569; Lectures on the liberal arts) in 1,166 columns. He returned to the College of Presles in 1570 and in 1572 was condemned by the Synod of Nîmes for advocating secular views of church government. That same year,

hunted by assassins hired by his longtime academic adversary Jacques Charpentier, he was murdered in his rooms on 26 August in the midst of the Saint Bartholomew's Day Massacre.

Ramus was one of the most prolific writers of his time. He published over fifty works in Latin and French, and many unpublished manuscripts were looted from his study after his death. There were over two hundred editions of his *Dialectic* alone in the sixteenth century, in numerous languages and versions. Colleagues and devoted students typically worked with Ramus in his "laboratory" as unnamed collaborators, complicating the issue of authorship. In addition, Ramus frequently revised his books and papers. By 1650, there were over eleven hundred printings of his works in Europe, and hundreds of authors who wrote about him. The influence of his group spread to Germany, Switzerland, Denmark, Poland, the Low Countries, Scotland, and England by the early seventeenth century, and to New England.

The purpose of Ramism was to establish a Socratic superiority that would invalidate Aristotle and all of medieval scholasticism, supplanting it with a new and simple method that would be applicable to all the arts and sciences. Logic (dialectic) comprised the two functions of invention (finding arguments to answer problems) and judgment, or disposition (arranging arguments to reach conclusions). The result was a godly law of truth for each problem resolved.

The largest influence was in religion, literature, and the sciences; the wider goal was to spur people to challenge authority, and to think, write, and create in their own vernacular languages in an era when Latin still predominated. While Ramus may be remembered by academics as a key figure in the history of the new philosophy and Protestant theology, by linking philosophical to mechanical theory, he often saw his own legacy as one for astronomers, geographers, engineers, and mathematicians, as well as architects, carpenters, and carvers (one of his works, translated in 1636, is titled *The Way to Geometry*). He was, in this way, a child of the Renaissance.

See also **Aristotelianism; Humanists and Humanism; Logic; Mechanism; St. Bartholomew's Day Massacre.**

BIBLIOGRAPHY

Feingold, M., J. S. Freedman, and W. Rother, eds. *The Influence of Petrus Ramus Studies in Sixteenth and Seventeenth Century Philosophy and Sciences.* Basel, 2002. The most recent evaluation of Ramus and Ramism by European scholars.

Grafton, Anthony, and Lisa Jardine. *From Humanism to the Humanities: Education and the Liberal Arts in Fifteenth- and Sixteenth-Century Europe.* Cambridge, Mass., 1986. The best modern work on dialectics and its context.

Howell, Wilbur S. *Logic and Rhetoric in England, 1500–1700.* Reprint. New York, 1960. The most lucid description of his logic and rhetoric and of their history in England.

Ong, Walter J. *Ramus and Talon Inventory: A Short-Title Inventory of the Published Works of Peter Ramus (1515–1572) and of Omer Talon (c. 1510–1562) in Their Original and Variously Altered Forms with Related Material.* Cambridge, Mass., 1958. Reprint Folcroft, Pa., 1970.

———. *Ramus, Method, and the Decay of Dialogue: From the Art of Discourse to the Art of Reason.* Reprint. New York, 1974. The most complete study of his work.

LOUIS KNAFLA

RAPHAEL (Raffaello Sanzio; 1483–1520), Italian painter and architect. The importance of the sixteenth-century artist Raffaello Sanzio to the subsequent development of European culture can be gauged by the fact that only three Italian artists were ever glorified by receiving anglicized versions of their names: Raphael, Titian (Tiziano Vecellio), and "Michael Angelo" Buonarroti. Raphael's father, Giovanni Santi, worked as a court painter to the duke of Urbino; his colorful style owed a great deal to the area's lush, hilly landscape and to the spiritual legacy of St. Francis, whose native Assisi bordered Urbino. Giovanni Santi also nourished literary ambitions (expressed in a long history written in vernacular verse) as did his talented relative Donato Bramante (1444–1514), a painter, architect, and musician who eventually moved to Milan. Raphael himself would one day try his hand at writing vernacular sonnets.

Raphael's mother supposedly cared for her infant son herself rather than sending him out to a wet nurse, and the close relationship with his parents was invoked by contemporaries as the reason for his sweet disposition. Sweet he may have been, but he was also talented to an extraordinary extent, with ambitions to match. He learned the elements of painting from his father and the local painter Timoteo Viti, but was soon apprenticed in Florence to Italy's most successful painter of the time, Pietro di Vannucci, nicknamed Perugino (c. 1450–1523), "the man from Perugia."

The Florence in which Raphael served his apprenticeship was a republican city (the Medici had been expelled in 1494) that celebrated its cultivation of ancient Roman virtues in diplomacy, in rhetoric, and in public works of art. The most famous of these is Michelangelo's *David* of 1504. Among painters, Perugino stood at the height of a long, successful career, his soft, colorful Umbrian style underpinned by a stately grandeur that lent his paintings some of the authority of ancient Roman monuments. Perugino's soft contours and bright primary colors had introduced what proved to be a popular contrast with the more linear "dry" style of Florentine painters like Botticelli and Pollaiuolo, and Raphael's earliest work shows the strong influence of his master. In 1503 Raphael worked in Siena with another popular Umbrian painter, Bernardino Pinturicchio (c. 1454–1513), on the frescoed walls of the Piccolomini Library of Siena's Duomo.

Already, however, the young painter stood out among these two established masters for his sheer dexterity: his brushwork was finer, his textures more meticulous, and his ability to suggest depth by layering different colors of paint was comparable only to the treasured oil paintings imported from northern Europe. Once again, the talented young painter contemplated a change of venue. This time the opportunity came from Rome, through the good offices of Bramante.

ROMAN COMMISSIONS AND MICHELANGELO

In 1507, Pope Julius II Della Rovere (reigned 1503–1513) decided to move the papal apartments upstairs and to commission a new decorative scheme for their walls; this was the commission for which Bramante procured Raphael's participation as part of a team of painters drawn from all over Italy to work in competition with one another. Quickly, however, Raphael's ability to put the pope's ambitions into powerful imagery earned him the entire commission. This suite of rooms, now called the

Raphael. *Alba Madonna*, c. 1510. ©Francis G. Mayer/Corbis

Vatican Stanze, would occupy him for the next several years. At the same time, Raphael made several important contacts among the people who comprised the intimate circle of Julius II: his brilliant, eccentric librarian, Tommaso Fedro Inghirami, his banker, Agostino Chigi, and his favorite theologian, Egidio da Viterbo. Despite their widely differing roles in the Julian court, each of these men shared the pope's deep commitment to an ideal view of Rome as a renewed capital city for a renewed Catholic Church, and they worked with remarkable zeal to see that ideal made concrete. Raphael's own work reflects his contacts with each of them; Chigi soon became his most important private patron.

Raphael also confronted, for the first time, a serious rival to his skill. When Raphael arrived in 1508 to join the team of painters assigned to the Stanze, Pope Julius had entrusted the greatest painting commission in the city, the Sistine Chapel ceiling, to a sculptor, Michelangelo Buonarroti (1475–1564). By 1510, when Bramante procured Raphael entrance into the unfinished chapel, the young painter from Urbino took in all of Michelangelo's epic grandeur and strange, luminous color. Michelangelo would later claim that he himself had taught Raphael all he knew about painting. Still, when Michelangelo finished the chapel in 1512, the older painter hurried back to Florence, leaving

Raphael as Rome's undisputed master painter, just as Bramante had become the city's supreme architect.

By this time, however, Raphael had begun to diversify his operations. He became an early proponent of engraving as a new medium with potentially wide appeal, and he also began to work as an architect under Bramante's expert tutelage. The press of his commissions compelled him to assemble a workshop of variously talented assistants; he ran his artistic business with a good deal of the acumen gleaned from his patron Agostino Chigi.

The deaths of Julius II in 1513 and Bramante in 1514 led Raphael into ever closer collaboration with Julius's successor, Pope Leo X (reigned 1513–1521). Together with the venerable architect Fra Giovanni Giocondo (c. 1433–1515) and Bramante's young assistant Antonio da Sangallo the Younger, Raphael took over the post of architect for St. Peter's. Raphael and many of his associates, among them Tommaso Inghirami, Egidio da Viterbo, and Agostino Chigi, survived the transition from one papacy to the next and continued to exert their influence on their artistic friends and on the papal court. Raphael's circle of acquaintances widened to include Leo's private secretary, the Venetian writer Pietro Bembo, and the papal functionary Angelo Colocci, an antiquarian and book collector of deep learning. Raphael's most inspired work in this period was done not for the pope but for Chigi, whose fiscal genius was accompanied by a bold, innovative taste in art.

Unable to build a new Rome to rival the old, Leo instead commissioned Raphael to draw a reconstruction of the ancient city, which the artist undertook together with an investigation of the work of the Roman architectural writer Vitruvius. In this undertaking Fra Giocondo and Angelo Colocci would exert profound influence on the depth of Raphael's architectural insight, already refined by his long association with Bramante, who had been a remarkably insightful interpreter of ancient architecture.

With the spread of his own reputation, Raphael began to cultivate international connections, taking orders from the king of France and other heads of state. His death of a sudden fever on 11 April 1520, his thirty-seventh birthday, came as a surprise to everyone. Four days later, Agostino Chigi followed him to the grave. Both men were mourned extravagantly in Rome.

Raphael's many unfinished projects were carried out by his efficiently diversified workshop; but not even the artist's most gifted associates could provide either Raphael's inventiveness or his painterly technique. Furthermore, they lacked their master's fierce dedication; their humor was more flippant, their monsters more monstrous, their conceits more conceited, their erotica more pornographic. As painters, engravers, and architects, Giulio Romano, Gianfrancesco Penni, and Marcantonio Raimondi owed an immense debt to Raphael, but the harmonious order of his style gave way to more extreme effects, presented most powerfully in the art of the elderly Michelangelo.

Already in their own day, Raphael and Michelangelo had acquired the personae by which they are still known today: Raphael as the angel called too early back to heaven, Michelangelo as the rugged, struggling hero. Their relative fortunes have varied somewhat with changing tastes, but their stature has never been seriously called into question. Each, however, partakes of the other: Michelangelo's *Pietà* is as intimately moving as a Raphael Madonna, and some of Raphael's frescoes show the muscular monumentality of Michelangelo.

See also **Art: Artistic Patronage; Florence; Florence, Art in; Julius II (pope); Michelangelo Buonarroti.**

BIBLIOGRAPHY

De Vecchi, Pierluigi. *Raphael.* New York, 2002.

Hall, Marcia, ed. *The Cambridge Companion to Raphael.* Cambridge, U.K., and New York. Forthcoming.

Jones, Roger, and Nicholas Penny. *Raphael.* New Haven and London, 1983.

INGRID ROWLAND

RAY, JOHN (or Wray, 1627–1705), British natural historian and natural philosopher. The son of a blacksmith, John Ray was born in Black Notley, Essex. He received his early education at the Braintree grammar school and was admitted to Catherine Hall at Cambridge University in 1644. In 1646 Ray transferred to Trinity College, from which he graduated with bachelor's (1648) and master's (1651) degrees; he was elected a fellow of the college (1649–1662). Ray, who was ordained as a clergyman in the Church of England (1660), resigned his fellowship in 1662 rather than take the oaths required by the Act of Uniformity. In 1667, he was elected a fellow of the Royal Society and continued his beloved studies of natural history through the generosity of his friend and patron, Francis Willughby (1635–1672).

Sometimes called the "father of natural history," Ray was the most influential natural historian of early modern Britain. He was a leader in the establishment of an expert community of naturalists who had as their central aim the firsthand observation of creation and its systematic organization. Through his efforts, a technical vocabulary for communicating the increasingly specialized material for standardized plant descriptions was stabilized, and many of these terms are still used in botany. An array of observational practices, methodological techniques, and textual protocols were also introduced by Ray and became culturally dominant within the discipline.

Ray authored or edited numerous books that cover the full spectrum of natural history. However, it is as a botanist that he is best remembered; his three-volume *Historia Plantarum* (1686–1704) and his *Synopsis Methodica Stirpium Britannicarum* (1690) remained standard botanical texts in Britain for much of the eighteenth century. In his plant taxonomy, Ray sought to define obviously natural groups of species and to classify them according to their maximum natural affinities. Accordingly, members of any two groups of plants showing a high degree of similarity in an array of physical characteristics would be assumed to be related and would be grouped together. His first formal statement of plant classification, the *Methodus Plantarum Nova* (1682), assigned taxonomic standing to the number of seed leaves produced by the embryo, providing the foundation to distinguish the major classes of flowering plants into monocotyledons and dicotyledons. This innovation was adopted by Antoine Laurent de Jussieu in the *Genera Plantarum* (1789), which gradually replaced the artificial classification system of Linnaeus.

Ray's popular and frequently reprinted *Wisdom of God Manifest in the Works of Creation* (1691) and his *Miscellaneous Discourses concerning the Dissolution of the World* (1692) are paradigmatic examples of British natural theology. Founding these on evidence drawn from his experience of natural history, Ray sought to provide rational arguments for the existence of God and to demonstrate God's providential activity in the world. Ray's natural theological works also served to publicize contemporary views on such controversial topics as spontaneous generation and the organic nature of fossils, which had theological implications as well as scientific importance in the early modern period. Ray's natural theology ultimately made the study of natural history an acceptable and pious practice for Anglican gentlemen and for Anglican divines.

See also **Botany; Church of England; Linnaeus, Carl; Natural History.**

BIBLIOGRAPHY

Primary Sources

Ray, John. *Historia Plantarum.* London, Vol. I, 1686; Vol. II, 1688; Vol. III, 1704.

———. *Methodus Plantarum Emendata et Aucta.* London, 1703.

———. *Methodus Plantarum Nova Brevitatis et Perspicuitatis causa Synoptice in Tabulis Exhibita.* London, 1682.

———. *Miscellaneous Discourses Concerning the Dissolution and Changes of the World.* [Later editions entitled *Three Physico-Theological Discourses.*] London, 1692.

———. *Synopsis Methodica Stirpium Britannicarum.* London, 1690; 2nd ed., 1696; 3rd. ed. 1724.

———. *The Wisdom of God Manifested in the Works of Creation.* London, 1691.

Willughby, Francis. *Francisci Willugbeii Armig. de Historia Piscium.* 2 vols. Oxford, 1686.

———. *The Ornithology of Francis Willughby of Middleton.* London, 1678.

Secondary Sources

Cain, A. J. "John Ray on 'Accidents.'" *Archives of Natural History* 23 (1996): 343–368.

Gillespie, Neal C. "Natural History, Natural Theology and Social Order: John Ray and the 'Newtonian Ideology.'" *Journal of the History of Biology* 20 (1987): 1–49.

Keynes, Sir Geoffrey. *John Ray, 1672–1705: A Bibliography, 1660–1970: A Descriptive Bibliography of the Works of John Ray, English Naturalist, Philologist and Theologian, with Introductions, Annotations, Various Indexes.* Amsterdam, 1976.

McMahon, Susan. "John Ray (1627–1705) and the Act of Uniformity 1662." *Notes and Records of the Royal Society of London* 54 (2000): 153–178.

Raven, Charles R. *John Ray: Naturalist. His Life and His Works.* 2nd ed. Cambridge, U.K., 1950; reprinted 1986.

SUSAN MCMAHON

RAZIN, STEPAN (known as Stenka; 1630?–1671), leader of one of the more destructive Cossack rebellions in Russian history. Razin was born near Cherkassk on the southern Don around 1630. His father was a prominent figure within the Don Cossack Host, his mother a Turkish or Tatar captive; Host hetman Kornilo Iakovlev was his godfather. In 1658 Stepan Razin was among a delegation of Cossacks sent from the Host to the Ambassadors' Chancellery in Moscow. He subsequently played an important role in negotiations with the Kalmyks on behalf of the Host and the Ambassadors' Chancellery.

By the mid-1660s Muscovite military colonization of the southern frontier districts of the Belgorod Line had produced a cascade migration of thousands of deserters and fugitive peasants southward into the Don Host. Moscow's semiannual cash, grain, and gunpowder subsidies to the Host were not increased accordingly, however, and Cossack impoverishment on the upper Don was further exacerbated by harvest failures. Furthermore, the Don Host now faced fewer Moscow-sanctioned opportunities to plunder the Crimean Khanate and Ottoman towns on the Black Sea coast, for Moscow was trying to rein in the Host to convince the Ottoman Sultan to restrain the Crimean Tatars from further raiding in Ukraine.

In 1667–1669 some eight hundred Don Cossacks desperate for plunder defied Moscow's ban and followed Stepan Razin on a campaign of piracy in the Caspian and raids in Daghestan and northern Persia. They successfully overcame halfhearted attempts by Muscovite troops from the lower Volga garrison towns to block their access to the Caspian. This appears to have convinced Razin he was unlikely to receive the tsar's pardon, but also that he had little to fear from the weak Muscovite garrisons on the Volga.

Stepan Razin. A late-seventeenth-century print depicts Stepan Razin being conveyed to his execution. ©AUSTRIAN ARCHIVES/
CORBIS

Upon his return to Cherkassk in April 1670 Razin defied efforts to arrest him, killed the Muscovite envoy to the Host, and exploited his newfound popularity among rank-and-file Cossacks to turn against Hetman Iakovlev and form his own renegade Host, which soon attracted about seven thousand followers. In March 1670 Razin's forces began pushing up the Volga; by autumn they had captured Astrakhan, Tsaritsyn (Volgograd), Saratov, and Samara. Razin's addresses to his council *(krug)* of Cossack lieutenants allegedly proclaimed his intention of marching on Moscow itself to punish particular powerful boyars and chancellery directors as oppressors of the people, and for a while he kept in his entourage a pretender tsarevich and impostor patriarch. His forces did find some support among the lower clergy, townsmen, garrison musketeers, burlak boatmen, peasants, and the Chuvash and Mordvin ethnic minorities. But Soviet historiography exaggerated in painting the Razin insurgency as an emerging general antifeudal class war; Razin's probable objective was, rather, to seize garrison re-

sources on the lower Volga and expand the scale of Cossack piracy in the Caspian region.

Razin's forces failed to take control of the Volga north of Samara; Simbirsk and Kazan' did not fall to them. Detachments under his brother Frolka unsuccessfully tried to carry the war to the eastern end of the Belgorod Line (September–October 1670). In late 1670 Stepan Razin fell back to the lower Don. He tried but failed to overthrow Hetman Iakovlev and bring the rest of Don Host under his control. Iakovlev's Cossacks finally captured Razin at Kagal'nik in April 1671. In June 1671 Razin was executed at Moscow.

See also **Cossacks; Russia.**

BIBLIOGRAPHY

Avrich, Paul. *Russian Rebels, 1600–1800.* New York, 1972.

Chistiakova, E. V., and V. M. Solov'ev. *Stepan Razin i ego soratniki.* Moscow, 1988.

Khodarkovsky, Michael. "The Stepan Razin Uprising: Was It a 'Peasant War'?" *Jahrbücher für Geschichte Osteuropas* 42, no. 1 (1994): 1–19.

BRIAN DAVIES

READING. *See* **Literacy and Reading.**

REASON. For many in the sixteenth and early seventeenth centuries, reason was understood as "right reason." It was a human faculty, divinely founded, that uncovered the world by revealing it, because it was part of the world. Reason was an ontological property of a divinely ordered cosmos, an innate virtue that directed right behavior and served as the source for civil and social law and order. It was not an introspective activity separate from, and thus searching for, certain laws and principles about the world. This it was to become over the next two centuries as epistemology became separated from ontology, as knowing became separated from the world to be known. During this process, the history of the idea of reason became the history of a search for certainty and authority about the natural and, increasingly, also the cultural world. From being a human faculty that was ontologically part of God's world, reason was reconceptualized as a methodology that was epistemologically apart from the world.

An integral feature of this methodological transformation was widespread skepticism about the power of reason, even as reason began to serve, in one fashion or another, as the foundation for authoritative knowledge about the world. Recognizing reason's limits while searching for certainty furthered the secularizing process Europe underwent during these centuries. In the realms of religion, philosophy, and science, the power and limits of reason were constantly discussed and debated.

REASON AND SKEPTICISM

Perhaps the most famous opponent of reason at the beginning of the early modern period was the instigator of the Protestant Reformation, Martin Luther (1483–1546). A mighty haranguer, Luther often referred to reason as a "harlot" and spoke of Aristotle's works as either a scourge of God let loose upon humankind, as punishment for its sins, or as the cunning ploy of the devil, meant to confound humans and steer them away from Scripture. Bombast aside, Luther built upon a tradition of thought that had been developing since the late Middle Ages, and which was most popularly identified with the English Franciscan thinker William of Ockham (c. 1285–1347/1349), who separated reason and faith according to the respective realms to which they applied, the earthly and the heavenly. Luther, and after him the French reformer John Calvin (1509–1564), sought to highlight the inadequacy of natural reason to comprehend God, especially God's actions. God was inaccessible by reason, and those who sought to reason their way to him would fail. All natural reason could do was to recognize God's omniscience and omnipotence. While it would always stop short of understanding God, Luther did not reject reason in all cases. Indeed, he advocated the use of reason—that is, deductive logic—as a tool to understand and evaluate the things of this world.

The separation of faith and reason, of the heavenly and the earthly, inspired various strategies for negotiating life. If Luther stressed faith, others focused more attention on this world. Skepticism about the ability of reason to attain certain knowledge characterized both approaches. At the end of the sixteenth century the French writer Michel de Montaigne (1533–1592), in a series of autobiographical essays (*Essais*, 1580–1588), promoted a cautious skepticism. Neither God nor the natural world could be known with certainty. With regard to each, Montaigne believed, reason teaches us humility and shows us its own limitations.

Montaigne was one of the first to see reason as a process of reasoning, and he also linked it to experience. It was still part of the given, natural world, but now both the world and reason were seen to be in flux, rather than displaying a static, divine order. Reason could not provide definitive conclusions; it could only guide us to assess our experiences and govern our natural passions. This, for Montaigne, was virtue. Montaigne sensed the psychological burden of negotiating an ontologically destabilized world. Faith provided security for some; the rest, he noted, were driven by a desire for knowledge. Yet given its nature, reason failed to offer fixed truths. Montaigne recognized that in such a world habit accustoms people to change and variety, and that routine is practically reasonable.

REASON AND METHODOLOGY

The seventeenth and eighteenth centuries debated means for instrumentalizing reason and instituting it authoritatively in order to do just what Montaigne knew it could not: to discover definitive and fixed truths about the world. Such debates were primarily methodological and led to the establishment of reason as the foundation for knowledge. The important question was whether one should follow René Descartes (1596–1650) and reason to truth intuitively and deductively, or whether one should proceed inductively, as Francis Bacon (1561–1626) would have it, moving from "facts" gleaned about the natural world to general principles in order to come up with certain truths or natural laws. In either case, the world was epistemologically dualistic, with objective and subjective and external and internal realities that could only be reasoned about and known dialectically.

Descartes separated matter from mind, or what he called extension from thought, and based certainty upon the reasoning (that is, the doubting) self. Authority as rationalism was thus subjective; it moved from within to without. But even as this means of achieving certain knowledge deified reason and the power of the human mind, knowledge rested upon doubt and skepticism. Like Descartes, Bacon recommended starting out by doubting all previous knowledge, but he sought a more stable support structure than rationalism for building new truths. His goal was to connect human reason to accurate information about nature, to marry the rational and the experimental. As he opined in his essay "Of Truth," "The first creature of God, in the works of the days, was the light of the sense; the last was the light of reason." Ultimately, Bacon aimed at nothing less than the reformation of knowledge.

For Bacon, reason was not the traditional "right reason" that revealed and participated in the natural order. But neither was it fully a methodological intervention into a neutral, objective world. Bacon's reason was, rather, a construction supported by observations about the natural world, and he believed that it could help reform the relation between mind and nature, between knowing and being, and consequently improve human life. Reason, then, was

becoming materialistic, becoming what mattered, so that if properly exercised, it could generate useful knowledge about nature.

The accomplishments of the seventeenth-century scientific revolution owed much to the combination of Descartes's deductive, mathematical rationalism with Bacon's inductive empiricism. The eighteenth-century Enlightenment, which popularized these accomplishments and applied their underlying premises to efforts at social and political reform, emphasized the Baconian tradition, especially as refined by John Locke (1632–1704). Locke's epistemological arguments in fact made it plausible and useful to link Cartesian and Baconian methods. In his *Essay concerning Human Understanding* (1690), Locke established his sensory epistemology and his famous concept of the *tabula rasa,* the clean slate. Humans were born empty, so to speak, and objects from the natural world impressed themselves on their senses. Subsequently, the mind reasoned about these sensory impressions and through its reasoning established the probability or certainty of propositions deduced from them. Knowledge according to Locke was built upon such sensory impressions, and there were no innate ideas. Reasoning was concerned with a limited number of things and limited to objective reality.

Even though Locke referred to reason as "natural revelation" and concluded that it should be the "last judge and guide in everything," he acknowledged its limits to a greater extent than did Descartes. By linking reason to mind and nature, Locke in effect built certainty upon reason's very limits. Even as it doubts and criticizes, reason can only work upon received sensory impressions; in doing so it also recognizes, reflexively and self-evidently, its own methodological structure and truth. Locke rescued reason from uncontainable skepticism and thus provided the impetus for the Enlightenment's methodological revolt against rationalism, a revolt waged in the name of reason.

REASON AND THE ENLIGHTENMENT

The Enlightenment was critical in furthering the process, begun three centuries earlier, that altered the understanding of reason and, by empirically connecting it to nature, established reason as the alternative authority to both Christian revelation and speculative, metaphysical theory. The so-called Age of Reason may thus be described as a methodological revolution that, in effect, redeemed reason's authority by countering rationalism. Reason was set apart from the natural world so that it might observe and know it, and the method of knowing, in turn, was itself key in shaping the world one knew. More completely than before, Enlightenment thinkers separated the natural world, which they could observe, reason about, and know authoritatively, from the supernatural world, of which humans could have no certain knowledge. Authority, based on experience and a reason guided by the senses, was limited—or even, as some claimed, arbitrary—but it had thereby become less susceptible to skepticism.

As this new view of reason and knowledge developed, the modern sciences and social sciences began to establish themselves as sources of authority about physical, social, and even emotional reality and as means of furthering human progress. By practically combining British empiricism and French rationalism, Enlightenment thinkers sought to ascertain universal truths about human, social, political, and economic nature, cautiously expecting that they could then be used to ameliorate society. Reason would lead to truth, to natural laws that would serve as the foundation for a new political and social morality.

Used appropriately, reason was seen as an instrument of virtuous action, and it was thus linked to developing concepts of freedom and responsibility. As Immanuel Kant (1724–1804) argued in his essay *Was ist Aufklärung?* (1784; What is enlightenment?), the free and courageous use of reason was a sign of humanity's moral maturation. A free individual was a rational one, and in fact humans were obliged to exercise their reason in order to ensure their own freedom. The modern Western concept of rights rests upon this articulation of reason's ability to uncover natural laws. Voltaire (1694–1778) claimed in his *Traité sur la tolérance* (1763; Treatise on toleration) that reason builds virtue and motivates freedoms. Jean-Jacques Rousseau (1712–1778) maintained that rational principles provide the only proper foundation for social and political order. Denis Diderot's (1713–1784) essay "Natural Law," written for the *Encyclopédie* (1755), contained perhaps the clearest statement of

this position. According to Diderot, reason could uncover natural rights, and in fact humans had a moral obligation to use it to uncover such truths and then to help society conform to them.

REASON AND PROGRESS

Awaiting his death by decapitation during the French Revolution's Reign of Terror (shortly after the celebration in Paris of the Festival of Reason, 10 November 1793), Marie-Jean Caritat, the marquis de Condorcet (1743–1794) completed his multipart *Esquisse d'un tableau historique des progrès de l'esprit humain* (1795; Sketch of a historical picture of the progress of the human spirit). Condorcet divided human history into ten stages, identifying the future—stage ten—as the age of the "liberated mind." In boldly reductive fashion he summed up his century's flirtation with reason as the instrument of human perfectibility and progress. Intoxicated with optimism, Condorcet imagined the future as a "heaven created by reason."

Earlier in the century, Rousseau had more soberly investigated the relationship between human reason and progress. In so doing he highlighted the complicated character of each and provided a framework for critical reflection on the emerging new concept of reason. For Rousseau, the more arts and sciences advanced, the more humans became corrupted. By corruption Rousseau meant the alienation or estrangement of humans from what characteristically makes them human. For Rousseau, what made humans human was their sociable and sentient nature, not their rationality. Reflection, Rousseau argued, was in fact antithetical to nature. It led one self-consciously to differentiate self from other, forming a false sense of identity premised upon individuality. Yet humans inherently sought improvement and perfectibility, as individuals and as a species. Thus Rousseau's argument incorporated a paradox. Rationalization led to specialization, which simultaneously marked indefinite progress and estrangement from nature.

Rousseau's criticism of reason and reflection needs to be considered in the context of the long and rich historical discussion about the power and limits of reason and its relationship to nature. As this discussion proceeded during the seventeenth and eighteenth centuries, it increasingly became a methodological discussion, a debate about what humans could know with any certainty, how they could best go about knowing, and ultimately, how such knowledge could be used to improve society. Rousseau's claims attacked the very reason that, separated from the natural world, was increasingly advanced as the authoritative source of knowledge.

At the same time a related critique emerged, which opposed reason's increasingly instrumental character. Building directly or indirectly on Rousseau's assertions, thinkers from Kant to the English Romantic poet William Blake (1757–1827) sought to resurrect humanity's sense of creative freedom and moral authority against the prevalent vision of a mechanistic universe running on rationalized, causal, and deterministic laws. The Scotsman David Hume (1711–1776) had challenged the confidence in reason by ascertaining that while empiricism was indeed the only method for gaining knowledge about nature, it was custom and habit rather than reason that made this method successful. Truth was wholly experiential and thus wholly arbitrary. For Kant, empiricism was an insufficient guide to either knowledge or morality. In his *Kritik der reinen Vernunft* (1781; Critique of pure reason) he began to establish his sense that a priori knowledge (knowledge that precedes experience of the world) existed in humans, and that without such knowledge empiricism would in fact be impossible.

By the end of the eighteenth century, reason's future was fairly well laid out. The Enlightenment had methodologically focused seventeenth-century attempts to gain knowledge about the world. Reason replaced revelation and tradition as the primary authority. In the process, it became disembodied and disengaged from the objective world, which it could now authoritatively know. As rational doubt increasingly undermined ontological security, instrumental reason was increasingly used in an epistemological attempt to establish control over the world. And at the same time, a tradition took root that highlighted the alienating consequences of using instrumental reason to negotiate social and emotional reality and criticized the reductive linking of morality and freedom with reason.

See also **Bacon, Francis; Descartes, René; Empiricism; Enlightenment; Epistemology; Hume, David; Idealism; Kant, Immanuel; Locke, John; Philosophy; Scientific Revolution; Skepticism: Academic and Pyrrhonian.**

BIBLIOGRAPHY

Beiser, Frederick C. *The Sovereignty of Reason: The Defense of Rationality in the Early English Enlightenment.* Princeton, 1996.

Bronowski, J., and Bruce Mazlish. *The Western Intellectual Tradition: From Leonardo to Hegel.* New York, 1960.

Butterfield, H. *The Origins of Modern Science, 1300–1800.* New York, 1957.

Collins, Stephen L. *From Divine Cosmos to Sovereign State: An Intellectual History of Consciousness and the Idea of Order in Renaissance England.* New York, 1989.

Gay, Peter. *The Enlightenment: An Interpretation.* Vol. 1, *The Rise of Modern Paganism.* New York, 1967.

——. *The Enlightenment: An Interpretation.* Vol. 2, *The Science of Freedom.* New York, 1969.

Giddens, Anthony. *The Consequences of Modernity.* Stanford, 1990.

Hunt, Lynn, ed. and trans. *The French Revolution and Human Rights: A Brief Documentary History.* Boston, 1996.

Owen, David. *Hume's Reason.* Oxford and New York, 1999.

Taylor, Charles. *Sources of the Self: The Making of Modern Identity.* Cambridge, Mass., 1989.

Willey, Basil. *The Seventeenth Century Background: Studies in the Thought of the Age in Relation to Poetry and Religion.* New York, 1977.

STEPHEN L. COLLINS

RECREATION. *See* **Gambling; Games and Play; Popular Culture; Sports.**

REFORMATION, CATHOLIC. In their attempts to characterize the nature of early modern Catholicism, historians have utilized the terms "Counter-Reformation" and "Catholic Reformation," which convey different understandings of the church's attempts at reform in the sixteenth and seventeenth centuries. The former term views religious renewal within Catholicism as a reaction against the challenges posed by the Protestant reformers. Consequently, the Counter-Reformation is understood as repressive, seeking to reemphasize Catholic dogma, to reassert Catholic liturgical life, and to win back those who accepted the Protestant faith. "Catholic Reformation" highlights the existence of a spontaneous reform within the church itself that sought to revitalize religious life through the improvement and application of Gospel teachings to the life of both the individual and the institution. This movement predates Martin Luther and represents the culmination of medieval reform efforts. The goal of the Catholic Reformation was to reform the existing institutional church by fostering a renewal of its spiritual life and mission.

HISTORIOGRAPHICAL ORIGINS

Within Protestant scholarship, the term "Reformation" had, by the seventeenth century, become part of the vocabulary of historians. Consequently, Protestant historians began to look at sixteenth-century Catholicism from this perspective. The term "Counter-Reformation" was used for the first time by a Lutheran legal historian, Johann Stephan Pütter (1725–1807) in 1776 in his edition of the Augsburg Confession. By this phrase, Pütter meant the forced return of Lutherans to Catholicism in those regions that had accepted the Lutheran confession. As a result, the Counter-Reformation was associated with military and political measures utilized by Catholic princes against the German Lutherans. The term came into general historical use in the nineteenth century with Leopold von Ranke (1795–1886), whose use of the term suggested a unity within Catholicism that he saw emerging after 1555 from the Council of Trent, the Jesuits, and the papacy.

The term "Catholic Reformation" also originated within Protestantism. In 1880 the Lutheran Wilhelm Maurenbrecher (1838–1892) spoke of a Catholic Reformation when describing the various efforts at reform within the late medieval church. This understanding of Catholicism was given currency by Ludwig von Pastor (1854–1928), who demonstrated that Catholic reform was a spontaneous and independent movement, accelerated but not caused by Protestantism, because it arose and consolidated itself in areas where there was no religious dissent to react against.

Thus, the terms "Counter-Reformation" and "Catholic Reformation" derive from contrasting interpretations of the same historical process, and were often used to the exclusion of the other. This changed with the historian Hubert Jedin (1900–1980) who, in 1946, sought to bring some order to the debate over terminology. For Jedin, Catholicism in the sixteenth century could only be prop-

erly understood by utilizing both "Counter-Reformation" and "Catholic Reformation." Catholic Reformation not only predated the Counter-Reformation but also for Jedin was its animating and motivating force. Jedin holds that the Catholic revival of the sixteenth and seventeenth centuries sprang from two sources—the Council of Trent (which gave legislative form to reform) and the struggle against Protestantism (embodied in the work of the Jesuits). He calls the former "Catholic Reform" and the latter "Counter Reform." However, they ought not to be seen as two separate realities, since Jedin sees them as closely interwoven in their historical evolution. Jedin considers the Council of Trent (1545–1563) and the Jesuits as much a part of the Catholic Reformation as they are of the Counter-Reformation. While the Catholic Reformation arose independently of Protestantism, Jedin also contends that it only won over the papacy and prevailed after Luther's challenge, which awakened the leaders of the church to the urgency of reform. Consequently, the Catholic Reformation was able to extend itself throughout the church because it became in part a Counter-Reformation.

While Jedin's understanding of these terms remains standard, the debate continues, giving rise to new terminology such as "Tridentine Reformation," "Confessional Catholicism," and most recently, "Early Modern Catholicism" advanced by John O'Malley.

THE NATURE OF CATHOLIC REFORM

At the end of the Middle Ages, the church was, institutionally and spiritually, in a state of decline. Corruption and abuse had set in on all levels—unworthy men held office in the church; politics came to dominate the papacy; bishops did not reside in their dioceses; priests were uneducated; monastic discipline was lax. It was clear that the church was in urgent need of reform, yet the cry for a "reformation in head and members" went unanswered "from above." There was, however, a movement for reform "from below" led by individuals who sought not rebellion but restoration. These reformers, scattered throughout Europe, did not desire to inaugurate a new way but rather to return to the origins of the Christian religion. Regardless of the form that these individual efforts took, the aim was the spiritual renewal of the individual and the purification of the church. Thus, the Catholic Reformation would be marked by reformed congregations of the leading monastic and mendicant orders; reform-minded bishops who resided in their dioceses personally looking after the religious lives of their flock; and groups of clergy and laity devoted to personal sanctification and the works of mercy.

Noteworthy among the reformers of the late fifteenth and early sixteenth century was Cardinal Francisco Jiménez de Cisneros (1436–1517) of Spain. His reform efforts impacted the entire Iberian Peninsula. A member of the Franciscan order, Cisneros, from 1495 until his death in late 1517, restored discipline and enhanced the quality of the Spanish church. He enjoined his priests to high standards in their own lives, in caring for the souls entrusted to them, and in performing their duties to preach the gospel. The pastoral mission of the church was at the heart of his reform efforts. Cisneros, however, was not simply concerned with the immediate needs of the church, but rather recognized the importance of ensuring the future of the church by preparing its future leaders. Consequently, Cisneros founded the University of Alcalá de Hénares in 1499 for the purpose of educating the clergy.

Italy also provides numerous examples of individuals who became leaders in the reform of the church. Foremost among these was the Venetian senator Gasparo Contarini (1483–1542), one of the most impressive personalities of the Catholic Reformation. He wrote several treatises calling for meaningful reforms and moral rejuvenation. His most significant treatise was *On the Office of Bishop* (1516). Based on patristic ideals, the first section of the treatise explained the virtues that a good bishop must possess, while the second illustrated how a bishop should conduct himself and carry out his duties. Contarini stressed the importance of residency for bishops and chastised bishops for neglecting their duty to preach.

Gian Matteo Giberti, bishop of Verona (reigned 1524–1543) embodied the ideas expressed in Contarini's treatise. His diocesan reforms and his role as a conscientious bishop were his chief contributions to the reform movement. Giberti revived the pastoral mission of the bishop who personally dedicated himself to the care of souls. Giberti's efforts led to a thorough renewal and reform of his diocese that proved to be a model and inspiration for later bishops. In addition, his diocesan regulations regarding clerical life served as a model for many of the reform decrees of the Council of Trent.

Religious orders also experienced a renewal that restored them to their original pristine state. The Benedictine abbot Gregorio Cortese (1483–1548) initiated a program of renewal that rested on the principles and ideals of humanism. The Franciscans, under the inspiration of Matteo da Bascio (1495–1552), saw the emergence of the Capuchins, who sought to return to the primitive simplicity and poverty of St. Francis of Assisi, while also devoting themselves to the work of preaching the gospel and caring for the poor and the sick.

Several brotherhoods devoted to regulating and spiritualizing the lives of the laity and the clergy alike emerged in the early sixteenth century. The earliest and most important was the Oratory of Divine Love, founded in Genoa in 1497 by Ettore Vernazza (1470–1524), who had been influenced by the charitable work of St. Catherine of Genoa (1447–1510). The fundamental aim of the members of the Oratory was the inner renewal of the self through the practice of good works on behalf of others, such as the care of the sick and orphans. The example of a life rooted in charity would pave the way for the reform of the church, since such reform emerged from personal sanctification. The most significant offshoot of the Genoese Oratory was the Roman Oratory, founded sometime between 1514 and 1517, which has often been seen as the initiation of effective Catholic reform within the church. This group dedicated itself to combating the abuses which had developed in Rome. The Roman Oratory gave birth in 1524 to the Theatine Order, priests who lived in community under a rule but also undertook an active apostolate.

The most significant of the new religious orders to emerge at this time was the Society of Jesus, founded by Ignatius Loyola (1491–1556). It was never the intention of Ignatius, nor the aim of the society itself, to defend the Catholic cause against Protestantism, although they did become involved in combating its spread. Rather, it was Ignatius's aim to provide a spiritual ideal and method capable of changing lives that would bring about the personal reform of the individual. Based on his own experience of conversion, Ignatius hoped to effect a similar change of heart in others. The Jesuits sought to work for the advancement of souls in Christian life and doctrine wherever the need arose. Upon their approval in 1540 by Paul III (reigned 1534–1559), the Jesuits became involved in numerous religious and scholarly activities, all of which reflected a highly active spirituality. Some were missionaries, others theologians, still others schoolteachers, yet all sought to live a religious life based on an interior conversion to Christ and active service in his name.

Of equal importance was the founding of the Company of St. Ursula in 1535 by Angela Merici (1474–1540). Concerned primarily with the education of young girls, the Ursulines were the first teaching order of women to be established. While the nuns observed the canonical hours and took vows of chastity and obedience, they were not cloistered and often taught in the homes of their pupils. After Angela's death, the papacy introduced changes within the Ursulines, first requiring the nuns to wear a habit and second imposing enclosure. Nevertheless, Angela Merici set the pattern for the future education of young girls within the church.

PAPALLY SPONSORED REFORM

While the spontaneous reform "from below" was fruitful, its impact was limited. The scattered efforts of individual bishops, clerics, and laity were unable to effect a general reform of the church, which would only occur with coordination "from above." In order for any reform effort "from above" to be truly effective, the head had to play a dynamic role. A pope was needed who would lead the reform movement himself. Many believed that Leo X (reigned 1513–1521), whose election was greeted with a renewed sense of hope by those desirous of reform, would be such a pope. He reconvened the Fifth Lateran Council (1512–1517), begun by his predecessor, which represented the last major effort at reform within the church prior to the Reformation. However, the decrees of the council failed to initiate any effective reform because of Leo X's lack of enthusiasm in their implementation.

In 1522 hope for a reform movement led by the papacy was rekindled with the election of Adrian VI. Adrian saw his task of initiating reform as a pastoral obligation intimately connected with his apostolic office. Unfortunately, Adrian died in 1523, before any effective reform could be initiated. His successor, Clement VII (reigned 1523–1534), spent most of his pontificate trying to avoid summoning a General Council, which was increasingly being called for by many within the church, including Emperor Charles V (ruled 1519–1556).

It was not until the election of Paul III in 1534 that strong leadership directed toward reform was restored to the papacy. Catholic reform came to pervade Rome during Paul's pontificate. The first papal-sponsored reform plans and projects were formulated and debated. Commissions dealing with specific abuses in the church were appointed. Outstanding men known for their support of reform were elevated to the college of cardinals and summoned to Rome to initiate and carry out reform. Recognizing the need for a General Council, Paul III created a nine-man commission in 1536 under the presidency of Gasparo Contarini to draw up a reform program that would serve as a foundation for conciliar discussions. The formation of this commission was a significant step toward Catholic reform as it sought to elevate the spiritual and moral life of the church and its clergy. In 1537, the commission issued its report, the *Consilium de Emendanda Ecclesia* (Advice on reform of the church), one of the great documents of Catholic reform. The document outlined in vivid frankness the problems and abuses in the church and clearly set forth recommendations to alter the existing conditions. The *Consilium* began by boldly affirming an exaggerated use of papal authority as the underlying problem in the church. Having stated this, the reformers highlighted specific abuses that they felt needed immediate attention, among them the state of religious orders and episcopal residency.

These first years of Paul III's pontificate witnessed the most earnest effort that was made to carry out a reform under papal initiative. With men such as Contarini in Rome efforts were made to reform the Curia, to renew theology and the life of the church, and to reconcile with the Protestants. These efforts failed, however, and in 1542 Paul III established the Roman Inquisition to check the spread of Protestantism, almost exclusively in Italy. It also became clear to Paul III that the only means of reforming the church and answering the Protestant challenge was that of a council.

THE COUNCIL OF TRENT

In 1544 Paul III issued a bull that convoked a General Council to meet in Trent. The Council of Trent was in session, with two lengthy adjournments, between 1545 and 1563. The council had three main objectives—to effect needed reform within the church, to clarify and define disputed doctrine and condemn heresy, and to restore the peace and unity of the church. The council was unable to accomplish this final goal since the split between Protestantism and Catholicism was now too deeply rooted. Thus, the council was confined to the Catholic world and functioned not as an instrument of reconciliation or reunion, but as a body legislating and defining for those who continued to profess the Catholic faith. It undertook this task from the outset, treating questions of doctrine and reform simultaneously.

In the area of doctrine, the council reaffirmed the authority of apostolic tradition as well as that of the Bible. It also declared the authenticity of the Vulgate but did not forbid critical editions in the original languages or vernacular translations. The most important of the doctrinal decrees was that on justification. It declared that humans are justified and saved only through God's grace freely bestowed on those who are baptized and have faith, but it insisted that humans participated in the process through a disposition for grace and a voluntary reception of it. The decree stressed the need for good works and observance of God's commandments. The council also issued dogmatic decrees on the seven sacraments, the Mass, purgatory, and the invocation of the saints. The decree on the Mass, affirming its sacrificial character, is second in importance only to the decree on justification among the council's declarations.

In the area of reform, the council focused on four basic problems that touched upon the pastoral mission of the church—the training of priests, the duty of preaching the gospel, the jurisdiction of bishops, and the obligation of residency for bishops and pastors. These decrees were the chief contribution of the Council of Trent to Catholic reform.

Focusing especially on the role and responsibility of the bishop, the council affirmed the obligation of bishops to reside in their dioceses and gave bishops greater authority and powers over the clergy and religious orders in their diocese. The administrative responsibility of the bishop was substantially restored at the same time that his primary role as pastor and teacher of his flock was strongly emphasized. Bishops were also obliged to establish seminaries for the training of future priests.

The Council of Trent clarified and defined many disputed doctrines, legislated reforms, and strengthened the church. The implementation of the decrees was left to the papacy. Pius IV (1559–1565) in 1564 approved and published the Tridentine decrees and created a committee to oversee their implementation and interpretation. At the same time that he proclaimed the Tridentine Profession of Faith, he issued a revised Index of Forbidden Books, which modified the more severe and rigid index issued by Paul IV (1555–1559) in 1559. Pius V (reigned 1566–1572) completed the work of the council by issuing a standard catechism in 1566, a uniform Breviary in 1568, and a uniform Roman Missal in 1570. The strong leadership of Pius V, Gregory XIII (reigned 1572–1585), and Sixtus V (reigned 1585–1590), which spanned the years 1566 to 1590, firmly established the papacy as the agent of Catholic reform.

Implementing the Tridentine decrees on the local level was not always easy and met with frustration. While theologians and church leaders anticipated that the implementation of the council would be met with great enthusiasm, the reality was far different. This situation arose as a result of an erroneous assumption that Catholic Reformation Catholicism would supersede the distinct flavor and traditions of local Catholicism that had developed over centuries. While the church did achieve some success in implementing reform along Tridentine lines, Catholicism would retain an element of local flavor both in Europe and the New World.

CONCLUSION

Certain basic characteristics stand out in the Catholic Reform movement from the time of Cisneros to the end of the Council of Trent: awareness of the need for reform and the serious efforts made to achieve it; preoccupation with individual and personal reform; and concern for the restoration and renewal of the Church's pastoral mission. Thus, Catholic reform was marked by a personal and pastoral orientation.

See also **Ignatius of Loyola; Jesuits; Leo X (pope); Paul III (pope); Pius IV (pope); Pius V (pope); Trent, Council of.**

BIBLIOGRAPHY

Primary Sources

The Canons and Decrees of the Council of Trent. Translated by H. J. Schroeder. Rockford, Ill., 1978.

Olin, John C. *Catholic Reform: From Cardinal Ximenes to the Council of Trent, 1495–1563. An Essay with Illustrative Documents and a Brief Study of St. Ignatius Loyola.* New York, 1990.

Olin, John C., comp. *The Catholic Reformation: Savonarola to Ignatius Loyola: Reform in the Church, 1495–1540.* New York, 1992. A collection of documents dealing with aspects of the Catholic reform movement.

Secondary Sources

Bireley, Robert. *The Refashioning of Catholicism, 1450–1700: A Reassessment of the Counter-Reformation.* Washington, D.C., 1999. Looks at the forces that shaped early modern Catholicism.

Black, Christopher F. *Italian Confraternities in the Sixteenth Century.* Cambridge, U.K., and New York, 1989.

Cesareo, Francesco C. *Humanism and Catholic Reform: The Life and Work of Gregorio Cortese, 1483–1548.* Bern and New York, 1990.

———. *A Shepherd in Their Midst: The Episcopacy of Girolamo Seripando, 1554–1563.* Villanova, Pa., 1999.

Comerford, Kathleen M., and Hilmar M. Pabel, eds. *Early Modern Catholicism.* Toronto, 2001. A collection of essays on various aspects of Catholicism in the early modern period.

DeMolen, Richard L., ed. *Religious Orders of the Catholic Reformation.* New York, 1994. A collection of essays on nine religious orders.

Evennett, H. Outram. *The Spirit of the Counter-Reformation.* Cambridge, U.K., 1968.

Gleason, Elisabeth G. *Gasparo Contarini: Venice, Rome, and Reform.* Berkeley, 1993.

Hsia, R. Po-chia. *The World of Catholic Renewal, 1540–1770.* Cambridge, U.K., and New York, 1998. Presents a synthesis of the scholarship on Catholic renewal in Europe and on Catholic missions in the non-European world.

Hudon, William V. *Marcello Cervini and Ecclesiastical Government in Tridentine Italy.* DeKalb, Ill., 1992.

Jedin, Hubert. *A History of the Council of Trent.* 2 vols. Translated by Ernest Graf. London, 1957–1961. A translation of two of the four volumes published in German.

Mullett, Michael A. *The Catholic Reformation.* London and New York. 1999.

O'Malley, John W. *The First Jesuits.* Cambridge, Mass., 1993. A comprehensive survey of the early Society of Jesus, spanning 1540–1565.

———. *Trent and All That: Renaming Catholicism in the Early Modern Era.* Cambridge, Mass., 2000. Historiographical survey of the way in which early modern Catholicism has been understood by historians.

Prosperi, Adriano. *Tra evangelismo e controriforma: G. M. Giberti (1495–1543).* Rome, 1969. A study of the reform efforts of Gian Matteo Giberti as bishop of Verona.

Rummel, Erika. *Jiménez de Cisneros: On the Threshold of Spain's Golden Age.* Tempe, Ariz., 1999.

Tedeschi, John. *The Prosecution of Heresy: Collected Studies on the Inquisition in Early Modern Italy.* Binghamton, N.Y., 1991.

FRANCESCO C. CESAREO

REFORMATION, PROTESTANT.

The term *Reformation* refers in general to the major religious changes that swept across Europe during the 1500s, transforming worship, politics, society, and basic cultural patterns. One key dimension was the Protestant Reformation, the movement that began in 1517 with Martin Luther's critique of doctrinal principles and church actions in Germany and that led to the establishment of new official churches—the Lutheran, the Reformed or Calvinist, and the Anglican. These were separate from the Latin Catholic Church in organization and different from it in theology. Many other dissident groups and individuals, collectively known as the Radical Reformation, also emerged during the turmoil of the 1520s and 1530s, building communities despite frequent persecution. Ongoing efforts to reform the old church took on new urgency in response to these challenges, leading to a distinct Catholic Reformation. The Protestant Reformation affected patterns of change in Europe through Protestant theology's shifting theological emphases, through Protestant piety's emphasis on reading and knowledge, and through new alignments between organized churches and politics.

Because of the complex course and multiple outcomes of the Reformation movements, historians today speak of multiple Reformations during the first two-thirds of the 1500s—the Protestant, the Radical, and the Catholic; the urban, the peasants', and the princely; or the German, French, and British. The Protestant Reformation was embedded in larger processes that included the emergence of national states, new encounters with the outside world, and deep socioeconomic shifts. The breakdown of religious unity and the establishment of multiple churches in this era highlights the central role that religion played in early modern European self-understanding. Doctrinal and ceremonial changes had consequences for every aspect of society, from family life and gender roles to art and philosophy. As we learn more about different historical actors and their varying goals, we can no longer view the Reformation as a single conflict between Luther and the popes or as a single movement, positive or negative. Rather, we must approach the Reformation by looking carefully at the spiritual aspirations, the cultural frameworks, and the material circumstances of the people whose lives it transformed.

The idea of reformation had a long history in Western thought before 1500, with two main meanings: to modify in general (to reform) and to improve something by returning it to its original state (to re-form, or restore). St. Augustine's statement that "man is not able to reform himself as he is able to deform himself" durably connected reformation with individual conversion and divine grace, although during the Middle Ages the word could refer to any systematic change. Because the term implied renewal or even rebirth, it could also be associated with the renaissance of classical learning. By the late 1300s, the "reformation" of monasteries became a central goal of the Observant movements that sought to restore the principles of their orders' founders, and by the 1400s, calls for a "reformation in head and members" of the entire church had become loud.

When evangelical thinkers in the early 1500s called for radical changes in the church, they too described their project as a "reformation," as did those who sought to improve the church from within. Most sixteenth-century reformers hoped that a single purified church would be the outcome,

while others saw religious division as a sign of the imminent Apocalypse. Only after 1600, when it became clear that the division among western European Christians was permanent, did the term "Reformation" become the name for the movements that created the division as well as for the period during which the division took place.

ANTECEDENTS OF THE REFORMATION

Scholars have pointed to several developments during the 1400s as possible forerunners of the Protestant Reformation. Developments in formal theology, in broader cultural life, and in different European regions all confirm the continuity between the Reformation and earlier historical processes. For example, disputes among academic theologians raised issues similar to those later addressed by Luther and other Reformation thinkers. Late medieval followers of St. Thomas Aquinas's *via antiqua* ('old path') argued against adherents of the *via moderna* ('new path') developed by William of Ockham (1280–1349), while mystical thinkers sought to bypass the confining procedures of Scholastic theology entirely. Particularly in the 1400s, learned churchmen disagreed about such fundamental issues as God's sovereignty, the place of human effort in gaining salvation, and the effects of sin and grace on the human soul. With the growth of universities and the spread of printed books around 1500, many more thinkers became aware of these debates about the fundamentals of Christian faith, setting the stage for Reformation controversies.

Other scholars point to the Renaissance and particularly to humanist philology as preparing the ground for religious turmoil. Although few historians today see the Renaissance as the birth of modern individualism, the recovery of Greek and Latin texts on philosophy and philology during the 1400s did spur intellectuals to look at the writings of the church fathers and the Bible in new ways. Even when motivated by orthodox zeal, careful printed editions and new translations of sacred texts raised new questions about the way the church interpreted its mission. Italian humanists such as Lorenzo Valla led the way in applying the new philology to sacred texts, but the humanist with the greatest impact in northern Europe was Erasmus of Rotterdam. In addition to editing both classical literature and the church fathers, Erasmus in 1516 issued the first

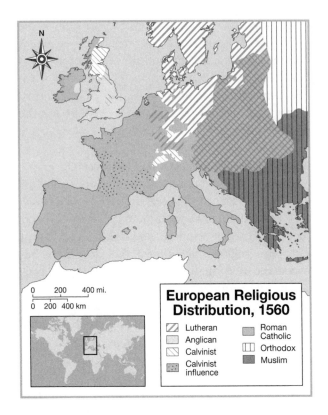

European Religious Distribution, 1560

▨ Lutheran	▨ Roman Catholic
▦ Anglican	▥ Orthodox
◩ Calvinist	▥ Muslim
⠿ Calvinist influence	

0 200 400 mi.
0 200 400 km

printed edition of the New Testament in Greek, together with a new Latin translation that changed the meaning of several key passages. Erasmus was also a best-selling author of Latin textbooks—such as *Encomium Moriae* (1511; English translation, *In Praise of Folly,* published 1549)—that savagely mocked popular superstitions and greedy clergymen.

Finally, the Protestant Reformation shared important features with the Hussite movement that swept through Bohemia in the early 1400s. The teachings of Jan Hus contained several ideas that Luther later engaged: an emphasis on God's grace over human works in salvation, a harsh critique of the papacy, and a call for lay Bible reading in local vernaculars. Moreover, Hus's ideas gained support in Bohemia from a coalition of burghers, nobles, and peasants who combined Czech resentment of German dominance with aspirations for a just Christian society. Anger about the special privileges that priests enjoyed and about the fiscal impact of an international church on local societies heightened anticlerical feelings across Europe at this time. Luther's recognition that he shared Hus's ideas accelerated his break with the papacy, and Protestant propaganda later named Hus among its martyrs.

Although the Hussite movement was limited to Bohemia after Hus's execution for heresy in 1415, it revealed how potent the combination of anticlericalism, lay enthusiasm for new ideas, and effective preaching could be.

EARLY PROTESTANT MOVEMENTS IN GERMANY

All across Europe after 1500, reformist clerics sought to reform church organization, to purify religious practice, and to intensify individual piety. In Italy educated priests such as Gasparo Contarini combined prayer and study while organizing groups to improve church services for the laity. In France a group around Jacques Lefèvre d'Étaples also called for an evangelical renewal of the church. They, like John Colet in England, turned to the Epistles of St. Paul in their efforts to better understand God's will, as would Luther. Among all these groups, humanist ideas and connections played an important role. Evangelical ideas were therefore widespread in Europe, yet the course of reform differed enormously from place to place. To understand this variation, argues historian Euan Cameron, we must analyze the different coalitions that formed and sometimes dissolved around evangelical ideas.

The emergence of separate Protestant churches could not have taken place without the movement's early breakthrough in the Holy Roman Empire, where Martin Luther was the critical figure. Luther's doctrinal views took shape during the 1510s, but the Protestant Reformation as a movement began with the response that he evoked among German clergy, nobles, and common people in the 1520s. This response grew rapidly because of the force of Luther's writing and because evangelical texts were printed not just in Latin but also in pithy German summaries and in illustrated versions. Moreover, criticism of the Roman church was already widespread in Germany, as were lively popular piety and interest in correct religious practice. Many early adherents saw Luther as a German champion against a corrupt Roman hierarchy and its financial abuses, and approved of his attacks on the special status of the clergy; others found spiritual consolation in his understanding of salvation, thought that his calls for "spiritual freedom" would bring about a just world with lighter burdens, or shared his belief in an imminent Apocalypse. Luther's precise theological arguments about justification and grace, meanwhile, mostly influenced engaged clerics and other spiritually focused individuals.

After 1519 another evangelical center emerged in Zurich, where Huldrych Zwingli began preaching sermons that combined humanist critiques of the church and its ceremonies with theological ideas similar to Luther's. Zwingli's ideas quickly became popular in south German cities and in parts of the Swiss Confederation. Although the southern movement remained separate from Luther's, ultimately giving rise to the Reformed and Calvinist churches, both spread evangelical ideas throughout German society. The earliest representatives of the Radical Reformation also emerged during the early 1520s from the circles around Luther and Zwingli; while they joined Luther and Zwingli in attacking the existing church, they often called for radical reform of society and eventually diverged on key doctrinal issues as well.

Political and social tensions converged with new religious ideas to produce a mass movement in the empire, partly because many German and Swiss towns and even villages enjoyed considerable autonomy. During the decisive years between 1518 and 1521, moreover, political circumstances in Germany delayed action against Luther. Luther had powerful supporters among both churchmen and lay leaders, including his lord Frederick the Wise of Saxony, whereas the death of Emperor Maximilian and the struggle to elect his successor Charles V preoccupied the imperial authorities. By the time Luther was excommunicated in 1520 and banned by the empire in 1521, he had already become a national hero. The early Reformation coalitions in Germany thus included clergy, some nobles, and many townspeople and peasants.

After Luther refused to recant at the Diet of Worms in 1521, ordinary people in many German towns called for "preaching the pure Gospel." They enjoyed support from committed members of the local elites—often younger men with humanist educations. Through the 1520s, many German cities edged cautiously toward open rejection of Rome, and by 1530, a substantial majority had joined the Lutheran or Zwinglian "Reformation in the cities." It is striking how radically new converts during these years rejected practices such as the veneration of images, in which they had often participated right

Protestant Reformation. *The Pope/Antichrist Selling Indulgences,* woodcut by Lucas Cranach the Elder from Luther's pamphlet *Passional Christ und Antichristi,* 1521. ©THE PIERPONT MORGAN LIBRARY/ART RESOURCE, N.Y.

up to the introduction of evangelical ideas. Adopting the Reformation brought about sharp changes in daily ritual that everyone could see.

The German peasants also hoped that "Godly law" would help liberate them from their burdens. In 1525 during the German Peasants' War, many of them refused to pay dues, sacked monasteries and castles, and gathered into huge armed bands. Hundreds of peasant communes formulated demands that were ultimately distilled into the Twelve Articles of the Swabian Peasantry. These demanded the "pure Gospel," local election of priests, an end to serfdom, and free access to commons and forests. Specific Bible verses justified each of the articles, thus linking spiritual renewal to social change. Although poorer townspeople joined the movement in some areas, the German nobility brutally suppressed the uprising. Luther too condemned the peasants, although he had initially recognized the justice of some of their demands. The defeat of the "common man" in 1525 shifted Reformation coalitions in Germany toward urban elites and the territorial nobility, decisively shaping later developments.

For defenders of the old church, the Peasants' War proved that the evangelical movement was subversive. Luther's supporters among Germany's princes and magistrates also sought to control popular turmoil. They faced the challenge of rebuilding territorial church organization in a way that reflected the new teachings while taking account of social and political pressures. This required both gaining legal recognition for their faith and establishing a clearer definition of what they believed. Luther and his key supporter Philipp Melanchthon drew up a comprehensive statement of Lutheran principles, the Augsburg Confession of 1530, and published new catechisms to instruct the laity. The process of consolidation led to heightened repression against dissenters of all kinds. Fearing that Satan sought to destroy the Gospel by encouraging fanaticism, Luther supported the organization of new hierarchical churches under princely control.

After it became clear that neither church would gain a clear majority among the princes, prelates, and towns in the empire, both sides built up alliances, such as the Schmalkaldic League, which linked princely territorial ambitions with the defense of Lutheran doctrine. In 1546 the emperor sought a military solution in the Schmalkaldic War. The effects of his initial victory quickly evaporated amid political maneuvering, however, creating a deadlock that led to the Religious Peace of Augsburg in 1555. The peace decreed that political rulers within Germany could choose between the Catholic and Lutheran faiths for their entire territories: dissidents had to depart or face official persecution. The dynamic evolution of Reformation coalitions thus left the German-speaking world mixed in religious confession, with decisive power over religion in the hands of territorial rulers. Confessional division had a deep and lasting effect on German identity, churches, and politics.

PROTESTANT MOVEMENTS
OUTSIDE GERMANY

The Protestant Reformation followed diverse paths outside the Holy Roman Empire, generally as a minority movement. The first adherents were often intellectuals who read Luther's Latin writings. With few exceptions, those in charge of both churches and governments remained hostile to the Reformation for at least a generation, rigorously persecuting those who sought to introduce it from Germany. Even where Roman authority was rejected early, as in England, Reformation coalitions appeared later, grew more slowly, and attracted fewer influential patrons than in Germany. Partly because of this delay, the form of Protestantism that had the greatest impact outside Germany was based on John Calvin's views rather than on Luther's.

The historian Heiko Oberman suggests that we view the Reformation outside Germany as a "reformation of the refugees," since so many leading figures had to flee from persecution. Calvin himself was a refugee who left France in 1534 during an early crackdown against French evangelicals. During stays first in Strasbourg and then in Geneva, he developed views that differed in important ways from the Lutheran tradition. Calvin shared Luther's belief in justification by faith but adopted a different interpretation of Communion. Calvin and his followers also wanted churches that were more independent from secular control than the Lutheran territorial churches. After Zwingli died in battle against the Catholic Swiss in 1531, his successor Heinrich Bullinger also sought to clarify the doctrine that separated the Zurich church from Catholics and Lutherans. Discussions among Bullinger, Calvin, and other Reformed theologians produced the Second Helvetic Confession of 1566 and the Heidelberg Catechism of 1562, important models for later Calvinist confessions of faith. In his *Institutes of the Christian Religion,* Calvin produced a systematic Reformed guide to doctrine. Calvinism expanded into France after the 1550s and spread through parts of Germany, the Netherlands, and eastern Europe. It also predominated in the theology (but not the organization) of the Anglican Church in England after 1558.

The emergence of new churches and the consolidation of a reformed Catholic Church confronted Europeans after the 1530s with a complex spiritual landscape. To understand how different Reformation coalitions formed, evolved, and sometimes collapsed, we need to consider the social position of early adherents, the political system, the nature of earlier heretical or anti-Roman ideas, and the international pressures each region faced. The

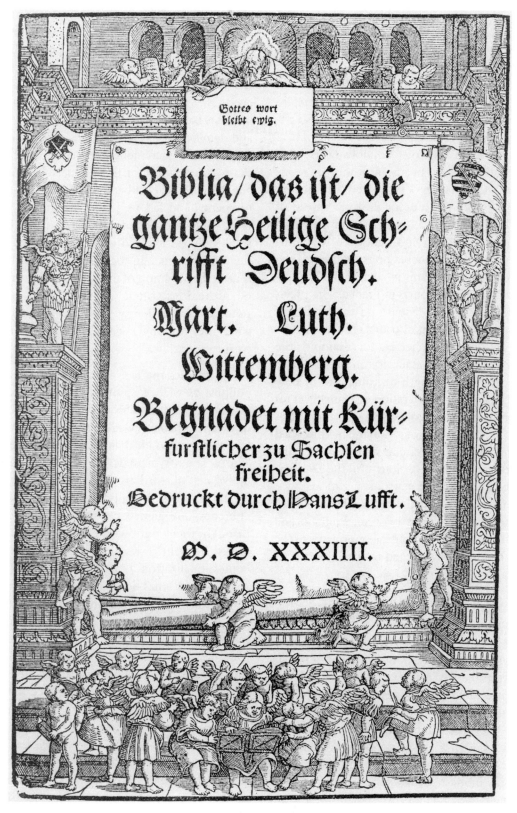

Protestant Reformation. Frontispiece for the 1534 Luther Bible by Hans Holbein the Younger. ©FOTO MARBURG/ART RESOURCE, N.Y.

Reformation outside Germany generally lacked peasant participation. It was an urban and professional movement whose most important early activists came from the younger clergy. In France the decision of some nobles to protect Reformation thinkers allowed the movement to grow despite harsh persecution. However, noble support also entangled evangelical religion with factional political disputes that led to vicious religious wars after 1560. In northern Europe the attitudes of monarchs were critical: Henry VIII's decision to break with Rome opened the way for the later spread of Protestantism in England, as did Gustav I Vasa's combination of Swedish independence with Lutheran conversion. Elsewhere, kings suppressed the Reformation using mechanisms such as the Inquisition in Spain or special courts in France. The previous history of religious dissent and the vitality of local humanist movements also affected local Reformation coalitions. In Bohemia, for example, the surviving Hussite church made common cause with the Reformers. The strength of humanism in Italy ensured that serious consideration of evangelical reform within the church continued into the 1550s under the protection of humanist-influenced bishops. Finally, external circumstances shaped the different Reformation coalitions. In the Netherlands, Calvinism became part of a national war against Spanish rule, while the Reformation in Scotland depended on relations between England and France. In eastern Europe political opponents of the Habsburg dynasty often turned to the Lutheran or Calvinist faiths.

SIGNIFICANCE OF THE REFORMATION

Scholarly views of the Reformation have often reflected religious and ideological perspectives. Protestant historians portrayed it as a moment of heroic recovery from medieval "corruption," while some Catholic historians attacked it as a catastrophic outbreak of undisciplined individualism. Nineteenth-century liberal descendants of Protestantism argued that Martin Luther's appeal to conscience represented the "birth of individual liberty," and saw the origins of the modern secular state in conflicts over the free practice of religion. Marxist historians argued that the popular appeal of Luther made him part of an "early bourgeois revolution," while the rebellious peasants were proletarians before their time.

Recent studies of the Reformation more often emphasize its social dimension, going beyond the doctrinal issues that divided Europeans. Because religion helped shape every aspect of European life, the practices of the new churches caused major changes. Sacramental ceremonies from baptism to last rites had long marked key moments in the lives and families and communities. By abolishing or changing the sacraments, Protestantism challenged the social meaning of these rituals. The Protestant attack on clerical celibacy emptied monasteries and nunneries and led to a married clergy. This shattered older understandings about sexuality and personal holiness and led to intensified debate about the role of women in society. New ideas about piety caused the abolition of many public festivals in Protestant regions, often against popular resistance. Poor relief and charity meant something different when they no longer served as rich people's way to perform penance.

In politics the fact that the church had been a political as well as spiritual power led to realignments at every level from villages to international diplomacy. Religious adherence became an important factor in political alliances until the end of the Thirty Years' War in 1648. The emerging Protestant states of northern Europe were strengthened by the windfalls of property they seized from their churches, and gained new authority over daily life through their tight control over the Protestant clergy. Current research concentrates especially on confessionalization, that is, the organizational consolidation of churches and identities along confessional lines. Of particular interest is the question of whether the Reformations—Catholic and Protestant—opened the way for European states to impose new standards of ethical and sexual behavior on their populations. Among intellectuals, debates among the emerging faiths challenged fundamental understandings about the relation of the individual conscience to God, about how sinful humans should live together in ordered societies, and ultimately about the sources of truth and authority. The confidence of the early reformers gave way later in the 1500s to bitter debates among theologians about ever smaller matters on the one hand, and to calls for the forcible reimposition of unity on the other. In contrast, arguments for greater toleration of dissent and skepticism about whether humans

Protestant Reformation. A woodcut from *Foxes Acts and Monuments of the Church,* 1583, depicts the execution of Hugh Latimer and Nicholas Ridley, English Protestant clergymen who refused to convert to Catholicism during the reign of Queen Mary. THE ART ARCHIVE

could really know God's will were met with repression throughout the 1500s.

Some thinkers have looked to the Reformation to explain the profound transformation of Europe between 1500 and the present. Notably, the sociologist Max Weber proposed that the religious culture of Protestantism, with its emphasis on Bible reading and ethical self-scrutiny, had produced habits that favored the emergence of modern capitalism, especially among Calvinists. Many other thinkers have probed the contrast between a Protestant "religion of the Word" and a Catholic religion focused on action and emotion, often suggesting that Protestant or radical views "disenchanted" the world to produce a more modern worldview. Today, most historians who study the cultures of Protestant and Catholic Europe are more cautious.

Major cultural changes did not correlate in a simple way with religious difference. Moreover, recent research has demonstrated that the larger population only slowly absorbed the formal agendas of Protestantism and renewed Catholicism. It therefore seems unlikely that differences in religious doctrine can entirely explain later developments. Instead, current research seeks to include both the spiritual meaning and the social consequences of Europe's Reformations in efforts to explain Europe's early modern history.

See also **Augsburg, Religious Peace of (1555); Bullinger, Heinrich; Calvin, John; Calvinism; Charity and Poor Relief; Church of England; Clergy: Protestant Clergy; Huguenots; Inquisition; Luther, Martin; Lutheranism; Melanchthon, Philipp; Peasants' War, German; Reformation, Catholic; Reformations in Eastern Europe: Protestant, Catholic, and Ortho-**

dox; Schmalkaldic War (1546–1547); Theology; Thirty Years' War (1618–1648); Wars of Religion, French; Zwingli, Huldrych.

BIBLIOGRAPHY

Benedict, Philip. *Christ's Churches Purely Reformed: A Social History of Calvinism.* New Haven, 2002. Definitive study of the Reformed and Calvinist developments from the perspective of social history.

Brady, Thomas A., Jr., Heiko A. Oberman, and James D. Tracy, eds. *Handbook of European History, 1400–1600: Late Middle Ages, Renaissance, and Reformation.* Leiden and New York, 1994. Scholarly assessments of major issues in European history during this period.

Cameron, Euan. *The European Reformation.* Oxford and New York, 1991. Comprehensive survey suitable for advanced readers, emphasizing the importance of varying coalitions.

Dickens, A. G., and John Tonkin. *The Reformation in Historical Thought.* Cambridge, Mass., 1985. Reprint 1999. Explores changing perceptions of the Reformation's course and significance.

Gordon, Bruce. *The Swiss Reformation.* Manchester, U.K., and New York, 2002. Best survey of the Protestant movements in German-speaking Switzerland.

Karant-Nunn, Susan C. *The Reformation of Ritual: An Interpretation of Early Modern Germany.* London and New York, 1997. Explores how changes in ritual transformed religious life in Germany after 1520.

McGrath, Alister. *Reformation Thought: An Introduction,* 3rd ed. Oxford, 1999. An accessible introduction to Protestant theology with emphasis on key doctrinal issues.

Oberman, Heiko A. *Luther: Man between God and the Devil.* Translated by Eileen Walliser-Schwarzbart. New Haven, 1989. Sets Luther's career in context of late medieval developments and later interpretations.

O'Malley, John W. *Trent and All That: Renaming Catholicism in the Early Modern Era.* Cambridge, Mass., and London, 2000. Explores changing understandings of reform and Reformation in a Catholic context.

Scribner, Robert W. *For the Sake of Simple Folk: Popular Propaganda for the German Reformation.* 2nd ed. Oxford, 1994. Pathbreaking study of visual propaganda.

Scribner, Robert W., Roy Porter, and Mikulás Teich, eds. *The Reformation in National Context.* Cambridge, U.K., 1994. Concise introductions to the course of the Reformation in Western and Eastern European contexts.

Tracy, James. *Europe's Reformations, 1450–1650.* Lanham, Md., 1999. Comprehensive survey, suitable for all readers, reflecting latest research and perspectives.

RANDOLPH C. HEAD

REFORMATIONS IN EASTERN EUROPE: PROTESTANT, CATHOLIC, AND ORTHODOX.

The Reformation first came to Poland-Lithuania in its Lutheran form soon after 1517, finding sympathizers among the German burghers in the cities of Royal Prussia. By 1522 calls for the introduction of the new religion had arisen in Gdańsk against the background of social unrest. King Sigismund I the Old banned the possession and reading of Lutheran books in 1520, and in 1526 he restored order in Gdańsk, reiterating the ban, although some burghers may have continued to practice the religion covertly. In 1525 Königsberg, the capital of the newly secularized Ducal Prussia (a fief of the Polish crown), became a center for Lutheran propaganda in the area (print shop from 1530, university from 1544). Polish and Lithuanian students attended the university, and religious propaganda was printed in their languages. Polish magnates of Great Poland began to serve as patrons of Lutheranism in the 1530s, offering protection to non-nobles on their estates. A few individual voices were heard in Vilnius in the same decade, but pioneering Lithuanian Lutherans such as Abraomas Kulvietis and Stanislovas Rapalionis were forced to seek protection in Königsberg. Another center of the Polish Reformation grew up in the 1520s and 1530s around humanistic circles at the Cracow Academy, at the center of which stood Jakub of Iłża the Younger (member of the Collegium Minor 1518–1535; documented Reformation activity from 1528). It was here that conditions were created for the first propagation of the new religion in Polish society, and there is some justification in calling Little Poland the "cradle of the Polish Reformation."

REFORMATION

All of these activities either remained largely covert or depended upon the protection of the nobles until the reign of Sigismund II Augustus (1548–1572), who, although remaining Catholic, was more open to the new ideas. He corresponded with Philipp Melanchthon and John Calvin (who dedicated his 1549 *Commentary on Hebrews* to him), and he appointed the patron of Lithuanian Calvinism, Mikołaj Radziwiłł the Black, as Lithuanian grand chancellor (1550–1565). The transformation of the Polish-Lithuanian Reformation from a clandestine

Protestant, Catholic, and Orthodox Reformations in the Commonwealth of Poland-Lithuania

— International border, 1582
- - - Polish-Lithuanian border before 1589
A Anti-Trinitarian institution
C Catholic institution
J Jesuit institution
L Lutheran institution
O Orthodox institution
R Reformed institution

movement into an open, organized church with public services and synods dates from about 1550, when Protestant gentry began to form a majority in the lower house of the parliament. Protestant magnates were a majority in the upper house from the 1560s. Between 1552 and 1565, only Protestants were elected as marshals presiding over sessions of parliament. In 1552 the diet vacated decisions of the ecclesiastical courts against tithe-resisters and heretics, and in 1555 it declared a Polish interim, guaranteeing religious toleration for nobles until a general council could meet. In 1559 Sigismund II granted religious liberty to Prussian towns, approving the Augsburg confession that had been adopted by the Royal Prussian Diet.

In the years 1556–1560 a reformed church of Little Poland began to take shape as an overt organization, with a presbyterial governing structure and a Calvinist-Zwinglian doctrine. Leaders of the movement included Francesco Lismanini (1504–1566), the Franciscan provincial of Poland and confessor of Sigismund II Augustus's mother, Queen Bona Sforza, and the Erasmian Jan Łaski (Joannes à Lasco, 1499–1560), who returned to Poland after a seventeen-year exile in December 1556.

The Reformation in Poland-Lithuania quickly underwent fragmentation. The Brest Bible—the first printing of the entire Holy Writ by Polish Protestants—was a joint project of the Reformed churches of Poland and Lithuania. Its financial patron was Mikołaj Radziwiłł the Black. By the time it was printed in 1563, many of its sponsors and translators, led by such Italian refugees as Giorgio Biandrata (c. 1515–1588), had made moves in the direction of Anti-Trinitarianism, forming a volatile and loosely organized "Minor church" (as opposed to the still Calvinistic "Major church").

In 1570 the Calvinists, Lutherans, and the Czech Brethren living in exile in Great Poland (the latter had been in communion with the local Calvinists since the Union of Kominek in 1555) met at a synod of concord at Sandomierz and produced a *Confessio Sandomirensis,* agreeing to hold joint synods, although they actually met jointly only four times between 1570 and 1595. The Minor church, which was excluded from those deliberations, experienced a period of great internal turmoil in the 1570s and 1580s. The social radicals of Little Poland established centers in Raków and Lublin. Their leaders, such as the "pope of Lublin" Marcin Czechowicz (1532–1613), argued for pacifism and a withdrawal from the state. Lithuanian Anti-Trinitarians, such as Szymon Budny (c. 1530–1593), wrote in defense of the *jus gladii* ('office of the sword') but took much more radical ("non-adorantist") stances on Christological questions. Compromise positions were worked out by the Italian refugee Fausto Sozzini (Socinus), and the "Arians" at Raków published their *Confessio Racoviensis* in 1605, dedicating the work to King James I of England.

As the tiny but intellectually prominent groups of Polish Anti-Trinitarians were conducting their intensive debates on religion and society, the mainstream Reformation in Poland-Lithuania began to decline. The signs of weakness were already visible as the Polish Reformation reached its zenith in the 1573 Confederation of Warsaw. This document was worked out during the interregnum after the death of the last Jagiellonian king, Sigismund II (d. 1572), and from then on the elected kings of Poland were required to sign *pacta conventa* based on it and guaranteeing mutual toleration among dissidents in religion.

COUNTER-REFORMATION

In the original formulation of the Confederation of Warsaw, all, including Catholics, were seen as in a state of "dissidence." Catholic clergy, however, opposed the Confederation and were soon mounting a successful restoration. Cardinal Stanisław Hosius, bishop of Warmia (1504–1579), had presided over the proceedings of the Council of Trent in 1562–1563. He introduced the Jesuit order into Poland in 1564. Jesuit colleges quickly arose (Braniewo, 1565; Vilnius, 1570; Poznań, 1573) and became important tools in the Catholicization of Protestants and Orthodox.

Part of the weakness of the Reformation in Poland-Lithuania stemmed from its late introduction, internal fragmentation, lack of cadres of clergy and attractive schools, the general weakness of the cities, and the fact that it remained largely an affair of the nobles, for whom its use as a political tool may already have run its course by 1573. The fragmentation in mainstream Protestantism was between a largely German burgher Lutheranism and a Polish and Lithuanian noble Calvinism. But it was also between the Calvinist middling gentry and the magnates, whose mutual antagonism brought the latter more and more into political alliance with the crown. By 1582 the only remaining Protestant senators were from Lithuania. The practice of Sigismund III Vasa (ruled 1587–1632) of appointing only Catholics to office encouraged magnate reconversions. The Zebrzydowski rebellion of 1606–1607 marked the end of the widespread political influence of Protestant nobles.

ORTHODOX REFORM

Both Protestants and Catholics had made proselytizing among the Orthodox of Poland-Lithuania one goal of their confessional propaganda. The future Antitrinitarian Szymon Budny published a Ruthenian-language version of Luther's catechism at Niasvizh (Nieśwież) in 1562. The Jesuits published a Ruthenian catechism at Vilnius in 1585. The Union of Brest of 1596 gave rise to a situation in which two Ruthenian camps laid exclusive claims to the patrimony of Kievan Orthodoxy, and both sought, using the tools of Reformation and Counter-Reformation—through brotherhoods, schools, printing houses, and monasteries—to restore the church to its pristine form. In addition to fearing loss of souls to the other side, Uniates and Orthodox were troubled by conversions from within their ranks in a trajectory that often led first to Calvinism and then to Catholicism (and later directly to Catholicism).

An Orthodox hierarchy was "illegally" restored in 1620. A decade of pamphlet wars, followed by the death of Sigismund III in 1632, led to the temporary consolidation of a Protestant-Orthodox camp during the negotiations behind the election of the late king's son Władysław IV as king of Poland and grand duke of Lithuania. The new monarch recognized the status quo, granting legality to both Uniate and Orthodox hierarchies. On the eve of the Khmelnytsky Uprising (1648) we can discern three programs for a Ruthenian church and people: one Uniate and two Orthodox, the first orthodox program led by hierarchs such as Peter Mohyla and the nobles, and the second by the lesser clergy and Cossacks.

DENOUEMENT

By 1600 there was no Protestant church within the walls of Cracow. In 1627 the last urban Protestant church in the crown lands (at Lublin) was destroyed, as was the Anti-Trinitarian center at Raków in 1638. The wars of the mid-century with the Orthodox Cossacks, Lutheran Sweden, and Orthodox Muscovy helped to establish the equation of Pole and Catholic. In 1658 the Polish parliament made Anti-Trinitarianism illegal, giving the Polish Arians a choice of conversion to Catholicism or emigration. The Treaty of Andrusovo (1667) ceded Kiev and left-bank Ukraine to Muscovy, removing the Orthodox spiritual center and many Orthodox inhabitants from the lands of the Commonwealth. Nonetheless, Lutherans and Calvinists were still present, and Uniates and Orthodox still made up a considerable portion of the population in the eastern lands. And although the magnates were almost exclusively Catholic by around mid-century, all four non-Catholic confessions could still look to patrons among the middling gentry. Thus the story in Poland-Lithuania was one of a relatively peaceful Catholic restoration and a toleration of the other confessions, now rendered unthreatening through increasing restrictions, dwindling numbers, and growing incentives to conform to a Polish Catholic norm.

See also **Belarus; Lithuania, Grand Duchy of, to 1569; Lithuanian Literature and Language; Orthodoxy, Russian; Poland-Lithuania, Commonwealth of, 1569–1795; Poland to 1569; Polish Literature and Language; Ukraine; Ukrainian Literature and Language; Uniates; Union of Brest (1596).**

BIBLIOGRAPHY

Eberhard, Winfried. "Reformation and Counterreformation in East Central Europe." In *Handbook of European History, 1400–1600: Late Middle Ages, Renaissance,* and Reformation. Vol. 2, *Visions, Programs, and Outcomes,* edited by Thomas A. Brady, Jr., Heiko A. Oberman, and James D. Tracy, pp. 551–584. Leiden and New York, 1994–1995.

Frick, David. *Meletij Smotryc'kyj.* Cambridge, Mass., 1995.

Gudziak, Borys A. *Crisis and Reform: The Kyivan Metropolitanate, the Patriarchate of Constantinople, and the Genesis of the Union of Brest.* Cambridge, Mass., 1998.

Jobert, Ambroise. *De Luther à Mohila: La Pologne dans la crise de la Chrétienté, 1517–1648.* Paris, 1974.

Schramm, Gottfried. *Die polnische Adel und die Reformation.* Wiesbaden, 1965.

Sysyn, Frank E. *Between Poland and the Ukraine: The Dilemma of Adam Kysil, 1600–1653.* Cambridge, Mass., 1985.

Tazbir, Janusz. *A State without Stakes: Polish Religious Toleration in the Sixteenth and Seventeenth Centuries.* Translated by A. T. Jordan. New York, 1973.

Williams, George Huntston. *The Radical Reformation.* 3rd ed. Kirksville, Mo., 1992.

DAVID FRICK

REFUGEES, EXILES, AND ÉMIGRÉS.

Many of the most important changes of the early modern period—including the European discovery of America, the growth of the sovereign nation-state, the Protestant Reformation, and the rise of absolutism—led to migrations, both forced and voluntary. The phenomenon of removal and banishment of groups was already widespread during the Middle Ages, as in the case of the expulsion of the Lombards from France in 1268 and of the Jews from England in 1290. It intensified during the early modern period, when the rise of the territorial church and the nation-state spurred a large number of expulsions and migrations. Most significant among these were the 1492 expulsion of the Jews and Muslims from Spain, followed by the expulsion of the Moriscos in the early seventeenth century; the seventeenth-century migration from England to North America of Puritans, Catholics, and Quakers; and the migration of French Huguenots during the Wars of Religion (1562–1598), and after the revocation of the Edict of Nantes in 1685. Early modern Europeans conceived of church and state as integrally and inevitably united. The rise of the nation-state therefore often led to the exclusion—and in many cases expulsion—of those who seemed to disrupt this cherished unity.

The dramatic increase in forced and voluntary migration during the early modern period was tied closely to the development of absolutist regimes. The best example of seventeenth-century absolutism is Louis XIV (ruled 1643–1715), known as *le Roi Soleil*, or 'the Sun King'. In such regimes as his, absolute sovereignty was invested in the person of the king, who was considered above the law *(princeps legibus solutus est);* the king's will was in fact identified with the law. The absolutist aspirations of monarchs were compounded by the struggle between Catholics and Protestants, which during the Protestant Reformation grew out of the struggle between centralized regimes and the proponents of traditional, local liberties. During the Reformation in England Henry VIII abolished the local liberties and particular rights—financial, political, and social—of the clergy. The same applied to the Huguenots in France. Secular rivalries became inseparable from religious ones, and religious beliefs were closely intermingled with social and political ones. Hence the civil and religious wars of the sixteenth and seventeenth centuries—the French Wars of Religion (1562–1598) between Catholics and Huguenots; the English Civil War (1642–1651) between Puritans and Loyalists; and the Thirty Years' War (1618–1648) between the forces of the Protestant and Catholic Reformations. All of these struggles and conflicts resulted in large numbers of refugees, exiles, and émigrés throughout Europe.

Absolute monarchs pursued policies of *une foi, un loi, un roi* (one faith, one law, one king), striving for complete social, political, and religious unification of their territories, driving out dissenting religious groups as well as alien ethnic groups who seemed to endanger their efforts at consolidation. The secular authority assumed religious functions and was thus responsible for religious unity, uniformity, and conformity within the realm, as can be seen in Spain after the Reconquista of 1492, in England after Henry VIII's break with Rome in 1534, and in France after the Wars of Religion.

The Spanish monarchs Ferdinand and Isabella, after successfully accomplishing the Reconquista (reconquest) of Spain from Muslim rule in 1492, demanded that both Jews and Muslims convert to Christianity and forced those who refused into exile. Accordingly, between 100,000 and 200,000 Jews were forced to leave Spain in 1492. Later, in 1609–1614, some 275,000 Moriscos, Muslims who had converted to Christianity, were likewise expelled—mainly for keeping their Muslim faith in secret. In England the absolutist policy of the Stuart kings, James I (ruled 1603–1625) and his son Charles I (ruled 1625–1649), drove some 20,000 Puritans into exile in New England during the 1630s; many Catholics and Quakers also left for North America, where they established, respectively, the colonies of Maryland (1634) and Pennsylvania (1681). Similarly, during the French Wars of Religion about 200,000 Huguenots (Protestants) fled the country; the revocation of the Edict of Nantes in 1685 by Louis XIV, which ended toleration of Protestants in France, led to further mass migrations, estimated at between 400,000 and 1 million Huguenots.

Geography had a significant impact on the fates of refugees, exiles, and émigrés in early modern period. Until European explorers reached the Americas, dissenting religious groups faced persecution or even annihilation, as was the case with the Waldenses, who fled to the Piedmontese Alps for shelter from the papal Inquisition and crusade in 1209, or the Albigenses of southern France, against whom the papacy launched a crusade in 1208–1218. The New World, and especially the English settlements in North America, opened up possibilities for many persecuted Christian movements to maintain their religious faith and practices by going into exile there. Thus Puritans, Catholics, Quakers, and Huguenots, to name only a few, found shelter and refuge in the British colonies in America.

In spite of the terrible agony and suffering on the part of the displaced peoples themselves, migration had a lasting influence on Europe's historical development in the early modern and modern periods. The expulsion of Jews from Spain—once the world's most vibrant Jewish center—led to the development of important Jewish centers in the Netherlands, Germany, Poland, and Italy, as well as in other parts of Europe and the Ottoman empire. The migration of Puritans, Catholics, and Huguenots greatly transformed the European colonial enterprise during the seventeenth century and contributed much to the rise and development of the Atlantic world during the seventeenth and eighteenth centuries.

Equally important, the flight of many dissenting religious groups to colonial British America during the seventeenth and eighteenth centuries led to the rise of religious pluralism and eventually to the triumph of religious freedom and liberty in the United States. The religious map of British North America shows how the long struggle over religion in Europe led directly to the migration of wide range of religious groups. While European absolutist regimes did not allow religious freedom, in British North America religious liberty and pluralism became the norm from the outset, as Puritans, Catholics, Quakers, and other religious groups settled there and maintained their religious faith and practices in peace and liberty. This toleration was then enshrined in the constitution of United States, upon their independence from Britain.

Refugees, exiles, and émigrés greatly contributed to the establishment of European culture in countries outside Europe. Their physical displacement thus illuminates the important processes of transfer, diffusion, and accommodation of European culture throughout the world. For the people involved, displacement meant that, with regard to their mother country, their cause was lost; at the same time, they gained the opportunity to transfer their culture to new places, where they would be able to live according to their ideals. Thus, while English Puritan exiles lost the battle for the soul of the English people, in New England they were free to establish their grand vision of a godly, Christian society; similarly, only in Philadelphia were the Quakers able to realize their vision of a society built around "brotherly love." Many other religious and ethnic groups, such as the Huguenots who emigrated to South Africa and colonial America in the seventeenth century and the Shakers in the eighteenth century, had analogous experiences of migration.

See also **Absolutism; British Colonies: North America; Dissenters, English; English Civil War and Interregnum; Huguenots; Jews and Judaism; Mobility, Geographic; Moriscos, Expulsion of (Spain); Wars of Religion, French.**

BIBLIOGRAPHY

Clark, J. C. D. *The Language of Liberty 1660–1832: Political Discourse and Social Dynamics in the Anglo-American World.* Cambridge, U.K., and New York, 1994.

Elliot, J. H. *Spain and Its World, 1500–1700: Selected Essays.* New Haven, 1989.

Greenfeld, Liah. *Nationalism: Five Roads to Modernity.* Cambridge, Mass., 1992.

Prestwich, Menna, ed. *International Calvinism, 1541–1715.* Oxford, 1985.

Scott, Jonathan. *England's Troubles: Seventeenth-Century English Political Instability in European Context.* Cambridge, U.K., and New York, 2000.

Zakai, Avihu. *Exile and Kingdom: History and Apocalypse in the Puritan Migration to America.* Cambridge, U.K., and New York, 1992.

AVIHU ZAKAI

REGENCY. A regent took the place of a monarch when the latter departed the realm, suffered incapacity, or succeeded to the throne at an age too young to rule. In the best circumstances, the king himself, prior to his final illness or on the eve of a departure, designated the regent, ordinarily favoring his mother or his queen or another close relative. In medieval England, however, even a high administrator or esteemed noble could serve. Although barons and royal councils in England and France, the most developed monarchies, might temper the regents' powers, tradition and precedent eventually accorded them the same powers as a king, no matter that they ruled temporarily. In early modern Europe, France experienced the most, and the most consequential, regencies, starting with the reign of Francis I (ruled 1515–1547). Preparing to wage war in Italy, Francis assigned the regency to his mother, Louise of Savoy, in keeping with what was then a long tradition. Louise served longer than Francis anticipated, because after his defeat at Pavia (1525), the king underwent captivity in Italy and Spain. Despite the ensuing pressure, Louise governed capably in 1525–1526, defending the realm against military threats and scoring diplomatic successes.

Catherine de Médicis, queen of France by virtue of her marriage to Henry II (ruled 1547–1559), became regent in 1560 when their son, and Henry's successor, Francis II (ruled 1559–1560), fell ill and died. Serving until 1564, when her second surviving son, Charles IX (ruled 1560–1574), came of age, she experienced a turbulent regency, marked by a deepening religious crisis, intensified by the court struggles between such great families as the Catholic Guise and the Calvinist Bourbons. But she at least preserved the fullness of royal power during a difficult time.

Henry IV (ruled 1589–1610) named his queen, Marie de Médicis, as regent just before his planned departure for a military campaign in 1610. Her regency began almost at once, however, because Henry died unexpectedly at the hands of an assassin. Once again, domestic and international pressures threatened the kingdom, if not the monarchy itself. But Marie and her councillors improved relations with Spain, the strongest European power, gaining a respite from war; conciliated and bought off the great nobles, without yielding to their larger ambitions; and preserved royal power intact during the Estates-General of 1614–1615. The coup d'état of 1617 by which her son Louis XIII (ruled 1610–1643) terminated, and thus tarnished, her government, obscured her achievements among historians for some time.

As his death approached, Louis XIII established his queen, Anne of Austria, as the regent apparent. Her regency lasted from 1643 to 1651, although her son Louis XIV (ruled 1643–1715) left her and her first minister, Jules Mazarin, in charge of affairs until 1661. This regency, the most troubled in French history, coincided with the final stages of the Thirty Years' War (1618–1648) and then the domestic upheaval and civil war known as the Fronde (1648–1653), when the absolute monarchy teetered on the verge of collapse. But, once again, the resolution of the queen regent, and this time the cunning of Mazarin, brought the monarchy through another crisis.

Louis XIV outlived his queen, Marie-Thérèsa, by thirty-two years and at his death in 1715 left the regency to his nephew, Philippe, duke of Orléans (1674–1723). In French history, this regency (1715–1723) stands out as the most successful and Philippe II as the regent par excellence. Philippe was articulate, affable, even irresistibly charming, and intellectually gifted. He was a discriminating connoisseur of painting and music and experimented with chemistry. Although physically unimpressive and acutely nearsighted, he proved his courage on the battlefield. Along with his gifts, however, Philippe suffered from the defect of irresolution that, more than his sexual appetite, which he indulged to the point of debauchery, threatened his regency.

At the death of Louis XIV, France had just emerged from more than twenty years of ruinous war; and it remained to be seen if the recent peace was merely a truce. Because of the wars, Philippe inherited a depleted treasury and a mountain of debt. The Parlement of Paris, along with its provincial counterparts, had grown restless under the repression of Louis XIV and hoped for a political comeback. Religious tensions now centered upon Jansenism, a version of Catholicism that church authorities deemed heretical. Philippe himself, despite his personal charm, had over the years antagonized some very important people. Many of these, especially his great rival, Louis-Auguste de Bourbon, the duke of Maine, the natural son of Louis XIV, now sat on the regency council, where Philippe had to cope with factions arrayed against him.

Louis de Rouvroy Saint-Simon, his lifelong friend, whose memoirs of the late reign and ensuing regency retain their literary and historical value, at first feared that Philippe, uncertain and anxious to avoid conflict, underestimated the perils that he, and France, faced. In fact, the regent, rising early and working late, was supremely dedicated to his duties and to the five-year-old Louis XV. He soon displayed a resolution that shocked enemies and friends alike.

After a period of compromise and deference, which only emboldened the parlement, Philippe asserted his authority over the tribunal and frightened it back into political submission. At the same time, he drove Maine out of the regency council and overcame the opposition factions there. He restored the late king's unitary council, discarding his experiment with multiple councils *(polysynodie)* staffed by great nobles. After administering a near-bankruptcy, the regent gave control of finances and the economy to the Scottish financier John Law of Lauriston (1671–1729), whose experiment with paper currency and banking reform, despite its ultimate failure, lightened the debt load and prepared the way for the commercial prosperity of the new century. The regent, tolerant in matters of religion, dampened the Jansenist dispute. While he did fight a brief (and successful) war against Spain, he also arrayed France diplomatically with the maritime powers Great Britain and the Dutch Republic, a new orientation.

Philippe died in 1723, leaving to Louis XV (1715–1774) a France in better condition than in 1715, as historians came to see. In addition to maintaining royal authority, Philippe's regency embraced economic and political ideas that pointed distinctly to the future. These achievements, in addition to the cultural glories symbolized by the mature work of the painter Antoine Watteau and the plays and poetry of the emerging Voltaire, best mark his regency.

See also **Catherine de Médicis; France; Fronde; Henry IV (France); Louis XIII (France); Louis XIV (France); Louis XV (France); Marie de Médicis; Mazarin, Jules; Saint-Simon, Louis de Rouvroy.**

BIBLIOGRAPHY

Le Roy Ladurie, Emmanuel, and Jean-François Fitou. *Saint-Simon and the Court of Louis XIV.* Translated by Arthur Goldhammer. Chicago and London, 2001.

Leclercq, Henri. *Histoire de la régence pendant la minorité de Louis XV.* 3 vols. Paris, 1921–1922.

Meyer, Jean. *Le régent, 1674–1723.* Paris, 1985.

Petitfils, Jean-Christian. *Le régent.* Paris, 1986.

Saint-Simon, Louis de Rouvroy. *Mémoires de Saint-Simon.* Edited by Arthur André Gabriel Michel de Boislisle. 41 vols, plus index. Paris, 1879–1928.

Shennan, J. H. *Philippe, Duke of Orléans: Regent of France, 1715–1723.* London, 1979.

JOHN J. HURT

RELIGIOUS ORDERS.

A religious order within the Catholic Church is an organization of persons, either men or women, who profess the three evangelical vows of poverty, chastity, and obedience and live that obedience under a superior within a community structure in accordance with a specific rule of life. Religious were frequently referred to as "regulars" from the Latin *regula*, 'rule', because they followed a specific rule. Benedict of Nursia (c. 480–547) is considered the father of religious life in the Western tradition, as all religious rules have been influenced in part by the rule he composed from 530 to 540. The many religious orders within the Catholic Church and their differ-

ent ways of life reflect the specific recommendations and practices suggested by their founders regarding the best way to live their vows in response to the needs and contingencies of the times. There were periods of great revival within religious life, such as the Cluniac reform of the Benedictines in the early tenth century and the creation of the Dominicans and Franciscans in the thirteenth century. The beginning of the sixteenth century saw another revival of religious life and the creation of new religious orders. It was also a time when the condition of clerics and religious life received its severest criticism, especially from evangelical reformers, who hurled their strongest diatribes against the wrongdoing within convents and monasteries. Catholic reformers likewise criticized those monastic communities that showed little regard for the vowed life.

Amid all this controversy a flowering of religious life also occurred, its growth nourished by roots that grew deep in the Middle Ages. The sources that nourished this revival included the Modern Devotion *(Devotio Moderna)* established by Gerhard Groote (1340–1384) and a mid-fifteenth-century book accredited to Thomas à Kempis (1379 or 1380–1471), *The Imitation of Christ,* which grew out of this tradition. Likewise, the Oratory of Divine Love, founded in Genoa in the late fifteenth century, gained inspiration from the Modern Devotion and encouraged many future reformers. These and other movements fostered a deeper devotion to the person of Jesus, greater participation in the sacraments of confession and Communion, an emphasis on techniques of prayer and Scripture reading, and an encouragement to perform corporal works of charity among the sick, homeless, and dying.

REFORM OF RELIGIOUS ORDERS FOR MEN

By the end of the fifteenth century several religious instigated reforms within their own orders. Luigi Barbo (died 1443) led a reform of the Benedictines that later became institutionalized through the creation of an alliance of communities known as the Cassinese Congregation (1515). The Augustinians experienced reforming fervor under the direction of Giles of Viterbo (1469–1532), who while prior-general of the Augustinians (1507–1518) enforced existing rules by establishing representatives with powers to remove ineffective superiors and to enforce the rules of community life. Giles's inaugural address at the Fifth Lateran Council (3 May 1512) demonstrated that his concerns went beyond the specific needs of the Augustinian order when he raised issues that would be acknowledged at the Council of Trent thirty years later. Tommaso de Vio (1469–1534), known as Cajetan, while serving as master-general of the Dominicans (1508–1518), stressed reform, studies, and a greater adherence to the common life. The Franciscan community attempted reform, but disagreements concerning the interpretation of poverty culminated in 1517 with a division between Conventuals and Observants, who by that year numbered twenty-five thousand and thirty thousand respectively. Further desires for a stricter observance of poverty and greater reforms further split the Observants into four major Franciscan reform groups: the Discalced, Recollects, Reformed, and Capuchins, of whom the Capuchins exercised the greatest influence.

The Capuchin branch began in 1525, when the Observant friar Matteo Serafini da Bascio (c. 1495–1552) desired to live a more austere life, one he believed conformed to the original rule of Francis of Assisi (1181 or 1182–1226). Soon others joined him, among them Ludovico da Fossombrone (died 1555?), another Conventual. Thanks to the interest and insistence of Caterina Cibo, the second cousin to Pope Clement VII (reigned 1523–1534), Ludovico's codifications of Matteo's ideals received papal approval in 1528. In 1542 the famous preacher and vicar-general of the Capuchins, Bernardino Ochino (1487–1564), left the order and embraced Protestantism, causing the Capuchins to nearly collapse. Only after a few decades did the order regain the papacy's trust. Surmounting this and other difficulties, the Capuchins became one the most important religious orders in promoting reform. The largest order, its membership numbered 8,003 in 1600 and 27,336 in 1700.

NEW RELIGIOUS ORDERS FOR MEN
New religious orders formed alongside the older, reforming orders. A technical point may be made that not all these groups, when first formed, were actually religious orders. True membership in a religious order, in its strictest sense, meant professing the evangelical vows and living under obedience to a superior other than a bishop. Some of the new "orders" of the sixteenth century and early seventeenth century did not at their inceptions require their members to profess the evangelical vows; hence they were not strictly religious orders. This essay, however, considers the establishment of movements that eventually became orders, whether they were strictly "orders" at their foundations or not.

In 1524 Pope Clement VII approved the Congregation of Regular Clerics, established under the guidance of Gian Pietro Carafa (1476–1559), the future Pope Paul IV (reigned 1555–1559); Bonifacio de'Colli (died 1558); and Paulo Ghisleri (1499–1557). Carafa, the first superior of the group, was bishop of Chieti, *Teate* in Latin, hence the attribution of the more common name of Theatines to the group. These founders, deeply influenced by the spirituality of the Oratories of Divine Love, dedicated themselves to works of mercy, a rejection of benefices, and a revitalization of clerical life. By 1600 they numbered four hundred, and by 1700 they numbered seventeen hundred.

In 1530 Pope Clement VII approved a religious order founded by Antonio Maria Zaccaria (1502–1539). Abandoning the possibilities of a lucrative career as a medical doctor, Zaccaria worked with the poor, taught the catechism, and was ordained a priest in 1528. Officially named the Clerics Regular of Saint Paul, the group became known as the Barnabites, a name taken from their mother church of Saint Barnabas in Milan. The Barnabites, taking Saint Paul as their model, preached, heard confessions, and performed acts of public penance in an attempt to reform the corrupt morals of the time. In 1607 the group had 320 members; a century later it had increased to 726 members.

In 1540 Pope Paul III (reigned 1534–1549) approved the Society of Jesus—the Jesuits. Founded by Ignatius of Loyola (1491–1556), a Spanish Basque nobleman and former soldier, the Jesuits advanced reform by means of education and preaching in urban, rural, and foreign missions. The Jesuits were known as the "schoolmasters of Europe," their system of education admired by Catholics and Protestants alike. By 1615 the Jesuits supported 372 colleges. By the first quarter of the seventeenth century Jesuit missionaries were located in North and South America, India, China, and Japan. In all their ministries the Jesuits promoted a greater participation in the sacraments of confession and Communion, suggesting reception of communion twice a month, an extraordinary frequency for the times. The Jesuits played a crucial role in the implementation of the ideals of the Council of Trent, as they directed most seminaries in Europe, guided the consciences of many Catholic monarchs, and were influential preachers and educators. In 1600 there were 8,519 Jesuits; by 1700 their number had increased to 19,998.

In the same year as the official establishment of the Jesuits, Pope Paul III approved the Clerks Regular of Saint Maol. Jerome Emiliani (1486–1537) established this group initially for the care of orphans. Emiliani was the only founder of a religious order who lived and died a layman. Like other reformers of the period, Emiliani was a member of the Oratory of Divine Love. The order's members became known as the Somachi, named after the town of Somasca, Italy, where their founder died. In 1547 Pope Paul IV, the former Gian Pietro Carafa and cofounder of the Theatines, attempted to merge the Theatines and the Somachi into one group. The union lasted until 1555. An attempt was made to unite the Somachi with the Jesuits, but this also failed. In 1568 Pope Pius V (reigned 1566–1572) raised the status of the Somachi to a religious order. By 1600 they numbered 438 members, and by 1700 they numbered 450 members.

In response to the sickness and mortality rampant in late-sixteenth-century Rome, Camillo de Lellis (1550–1614) organized a group of men dedicated to the care of the sick and dying around the year 1582. In 1591 the papacy elevated the organization to a religious order. At the death of Camillo, the order had 330 members living in fifteen communities throughout Italy.

In 1588 Pope Sixtus V (reigned 1585–1590) approved the Order of Clerks Regular Minor, commonly referred to as the Caracciolins after one of their founders, Ascanio Caraccioli (1563–1608). This new order practiced works of charity and was especially active in promoting devotion and adoration of the Blessed Sacrament. By 1700 this order numbered five hundred.

John Leonardi (1541?–1609) founded the Clerks Regular of the Mother of God in Lucca,

Italy, in 1574 which received papal approval as an order in 1595. Leonardi advocated a way of life that promoted secluded contemplation and active works of charity. At the death of Leonardi, the order had only two communities, one in Lucca, the other in Rome. They did not extend beyond the Alps until 1800.

The Spaniard José Calasanz (1556–1648) in 1597 gathered a group of men, the Poor Clerks Regular of the Mother of God, who were approved by the church hierarchy as a religious order in 1617. The Piarists, as they became known, took as their only work the education of poor children. Although the Jesuits advanced free education, their emphasis on higher education and its necessary requirement of fluency in Latin made such an education impossible for the poor, who could not afford a good (Latin) grammar school education. The Piarists received official papal approval as a religious order in 1621. In 1646 the Piarists numbered five hundred in thirty-seven communities.

A former Portuguese soldier, John of God (Juan Ciudad; 1495–1550), established a hospital in Granada for the poor in 1537, and a community formed around this effort. After the founder's death, Pope Sixtus V approved the community as a full religious order in 1596. The Brothers Hospitallers, as they were known, expanded throughout Europe and Latin America. In 1600 they numbered 626 members; in 1700 there were 2,046 Hospitallers.

The Oratorians, founded by Philip Neri (1515–1595), were not established as a religious order. They were secular priests who formed a congregation (from the Latin *congregare*, 'to gather') for the purposes of spiritual growth and to serve as a model for other priests. Pope Gregory XIII (reigned 1572–1585) approved their rule in 1575. These associations or oratories became particularly strong in France, especially under the direction of Pierre de Bérulle (1575–1629), through his work in seminary education.

RELIGIOUS ORDERS FOR WOMEN

During the same time women reformed their existing religious orders and created new ones. In 1536 Teresa of Ávila (Teresa de Cepeda y Ahumada; 1515–1582) entered the Spanish Carmelite convent in Ávila. At this time Carmelite convents were microcosms of Spanish society, with particular attention to title, wealth, and status. After twenty years Teresa rejected this style of living and advanced a stricter observation of the Carmelite rule. Fundamental in her reform was the removal of all the privileges of class status, the implementation of begging, and the elimination of all endowments that provided a stable income. As a symbol of this new austerity, the sisters wore sandals and thus were shoeless or "discalced." To be discalced became synonymous with Teresa's reform project. Although cloister was strictly enforced, Teresa recommended that the sisters' prayer life have a missionary focus, the prayer of the contemplative providing spiritual support for missionaries and those working in Protestant countries. Teresa established the first convent manifesting these reforms in 1562. Inspired by her reforms, the Spaniard John of the Cross (1542–1591) established a discalced monastery for men in 1568. Both efforts at reform came under suspicion from religious and civil authorities, but the persistence of their founders extended the discalced reform throughout the Old and New Worlds.

In the sixteenth and seventeenth centuries new religious orders for women were created, though they were not as numerous as their male counterparts. In 1535 Angela Merici (1470 or 1474–1540), on the feast of Saint Catherine Alexandria (25 November), gathered twenty-eight women around her under the dedication of Saint Ursula. They made private promises to live the evangelical vows and to perform works of charity. Identifying her group with Ursula (fourth century?), a female saint known and respected for her work outside the cloister wall, and Catherine of Alexandria (died early fourth century), who professed total dedication to the person of Jesus with the promise of chastity, Angela attempted to create a rule in which the women combined a celibate life with activities outside the cloister. At the founding of the order the Ursulines were not a religious order, as their promises were private and the organization not officially approved; the women lived at home under the protection of their parents. The idea of consecrated virgins outside of cloistered life did not appeal to church authorities, and after Merici's death, and in spite of efforts by her followers to adhere to the original ideal, the church authorities implemented Tridentine regulations concerning strict adherence to cloister for female religious.

Jeanne-Françoise de Chantal (1572–1641) established a way of life for women in France that was less cloistered and placed greater emphasis on the active apostolate. Under the spiritual direction of François de Sales (1567–1622), Chantal's rule was a type of middle way for women who desired neither married life nor the rigors of strict monastic enclosure envisioned by the discalced reform. The Visitation sisters (Visitandines) did not take public vows; instead, they consecrated themselves as brides of Christ and lived under the authority of the local bishop. Such an arrangement did not meet with approval. Parents questioned the welfare of such an arrangement, since it lacked stability and financial security for their daughters' futures. Church authorities disapproved of the looser interpretation of cloistered life. In 1618 the papacy legislated that the Visitation sisters embrace the rule of Saint Augustine and strict monastic enclosure. By 1700 there were sixty-five hundred sisters.

Mary Ward (1586–1646) in England advanced the most radical rule for women who desired to live the vowed life outside the cloister. Ward argued that English Catholics could be best served by women who could move about society freely and unrecognized by authorities and therefore could not live in a cloister or wear a habit. Taking as a model the Jesuits, the English Ladies—or the Institute of Mary—desired to have no authority other than the pope. The idea of uncloistered women religious moving freely across the English countryside did not sit well with the papacy. Although their foundation received papal approval in 1616, they were suppressed in 1631.

COMMON THEMES
Simple conclusions and summaries cannot be made concerning the religious orders of early modern Europe. Jesuits wanted to be known for their strict obedience, the Oratorians stressed individuality, and Teresa of Ávila espoused a "holy freedom" for her sisters in their selection of a confessor and spiritual guide. Some common themes, however, are discernable. All new and reformed orders found inspiration in late medieval spirituality, particularly the Modern Devotion. Religious embraced the vow of poverty with new vigor. These orders placed a

great emphasis on education and care for the sick, a response to the demographic increase in the sixteenth century and the growing poverty and illiteracy of the lower classes. All the new orders and some of the reformed desired to transcend the traditional monastic enclosure in some manner. This was particularly true of the Jesuits and other male religious and was attempted by female religious, such as Mary Ward and Angela Merici. Although women religious were subject to strict enclosure, Teresa of Ávila insisted that their prayers breach the convent wall in support of missionary efforts throughout the known world. Active life outside the cloister for women religious had to wait until after the French Revolution.

See also **Catholic Spirituality and Mysticism; Clergy: Roman Catholic Clergy; Confraternities; Jesuits; Reformation, Catholic; François de Sales.**

BIBLIOGRAPHY

Cistellini, Antonio. *San Filippo Neri: L'oratorio e la congregazione oratoriana: Storia e spiritualità.* Brescia, 1989.

DeMolen, Richard L., ed. *Religious Orders of the Catholic Reformation.* New York, 1994. The best survey on the subject. The bibliographies are helpful for further investigations.

Devotio Moderna: Basic Writings. Preface by Heiko Oberman. Translated by John van Engen. New York, 1988.

Hudon, William V., trans. and ed. *Theatine Spirituality.* New York, 1996.

Mariani, Luciana, Elisa Tarolli, and Marie Seynaeve. *Angela Merici: Contributo per una biografia.* Milan, 1986.

Martin, Friancis X. *Friar, Reformer, and Renaissance Scholar: Life and Work of Giles of Viterbo, 1469–1532.* Villanova, Pa., 1992.

Nimmo, Duncan. *Reform and Division in the Medieval Franciscan Order, from Saint Francis to the Foundation of the Capuchins.* Rome, 1987.

Pelliccia, Guerrino, and Giancarlo Rocca, eds. *Dizionario degli istituti di perfezione.* Rome, 1974–1988. The term "institutes of perfection" covers not only religious orders but also all organizations attempting to implement a more devout life. A crucial reference work.

Polgár, László. *Bibliographie sur l'histoire de le compagnie de Jésus, 1901–1980.* Rome, 1981–1990.

Ponnelle, Louis, and Louis Bordet. *St. Philip Neri and the Roman Society of His Times (1515–1595).* Translated by Ralph Francis Kerr. London, 1979. Originally published in 1932.

MICHAEL W. MAHER

RELIGIOUS PIETY. The word "piety" has its roots in the ancient Latin *pietas,* a term that implied filial duty and respect for elders, obligations that were religious duties in antiquity. The word has long been used as well to describe the rites and devotions people practiced in their daily religious observances in the medieval and early modern periods and to describe more specifically the ways in which they worshiped Christ and venerated the Virgin Mary and the saints.

PROBLEM

Scholars have long spoken of "Marian piety," "christocentric piety," or "saintly piety." In tracing the contours of religious piety, historians have also been concerned to delineate the differences between the religion of Europe's masses on the one hand and the official religion of the church on the other. Obvious differences have long been noted between these two kinds of religious experience. The official teachings of the medieval church were fashioned by highly literate elites who often shared a common outlook created by academic training in canon law and theology. The piety of Europe's peoples, by contrast, was rooted in the concerns of village life and in the issues that surrounded an overwhelmingly agrarian existence. Beyond such distinctions the attempt to try to isolate a "popular piety" distinct from the official church is problematic since, at the dawn of the early modern period, elites and people shared many religious assumptions. The European clergy of the time was not a hereditary caste, but was recruited anew in each generation from the laity. For much of the fifteenth and sixteenth centuries, few clergymen had much formal theological training since the seminary came to play an important role in clerical education only at the end of the sixteenth century. Its rise helped to create a wider gap between the intellectually rigorous, highly structured religions promoted by the Protestant and Catholic Reformations and the cycles of religious rituals and beliefs that were popular in towns and countryside. This divide became one of the defining features of European life in the nineteenth and twentieth centuries and helped to sponsor the notion of the "superstitious folk," as well as the presumption that European history represented a gradual triumph of rationality and secularity over popular magic. For most of the early modern period this thesis cannot be applied without significant cautions because, particularly in the years between 1450 and 1650, both elites and people appear, to modern observers, to share many superstitions. The thesis of gradual secularization and rationalization has, as a result, been more recently challenged even as historians have continued to be concerned with charting the importance of piety as a dynamic factor in forging early modern societies.

CHARACTER

In the early modern world religion was not a separate sphere or dimension of existence. While modern intellectuals assume a dichotomy between sacred and secular, religion functioned in premodern Europe as a "sacred canopy," to use a term coined by the sociologist Peter Berger. Religious explanations for existence and its rituals permeated every dimension of life. At the dawn of the early modern period the church's teachings provided an explanation for the sinner's place in a larger drama of forgiveness and redemption in the afterlife. The piety of the people, on the other hand, was frequently more practical in orientation, concerned with the "here and now" instead of the hereafter. Under the best of circumstances, demographic, economic, and material realities were bleak for most Europeans in the early modern centuries, and scores of rituals were used to try to control life's harsh circumstances. Many practices common throughout Europe explicitly violated longstanding church prohibitions against the use of magic, but they were, nevertheless, firmly ensconced in society through centuries of usage. Women fearing the pains of childbirth, for example, relied on amulets and spells to protect themselves as they approached the day of delivery. Peasants protected their livestock with similar practices, just as they tried to prevent headaches, toothaches, and all sorts of personal ills through various rituals. Rites intended to ensure the fruitfulness of the fields, the marriage bed, and the barnyard were common, just as specific feast days were considered auspicious times for gathering herbs and other plants for combating diseases and fashioning potions that might protect against bad weather. In these and many other ways people used rituals and objects to combat the evils that threatened everyday living. Even when these practices did not explicitly violate church prohibitions, they sometimes subtly altered Christian teaching to suit

purposes other than those originally intended. Examples of this tendency can be seen in the widespread popularity of sacramentals and benedictions in Europe around 1500. Sacramentals were lesser rites of the church that often had their origins in the sacraments themselves. They included a range of services like the blessing of water, a practice that originally developed from the sacrament of baptism; and the consecration of candles, palm leaves, and other objects used in church liturgies. These rituals were not sacraments per se, and thus were not dependent upon the ministration of a priest. At the same time they were thought to be beneficial to body and soul, and for this reason laypeople adapted them for their own use. Peasants ground up consecrated bread, palm leaves, and other blessed objects, casting the residue on their fields, or they sprinkled holy water on their doorsteps, beds, and homes. Benedictions were another widely popular custom, with prayers commonly being offered to God and the saints to protect against threatening circumstances. Despite the attempts of early modern Protestant and Catholic reformers to curtail the abuse of many of these practices, they often persisted unchanged in European societies into the nineteenth and twentieth centuries.

THE SAINTS

Perhaps no other dimension of piety had such a long history as the veneration of the saints. From early Christian times the cult of the saints had played an important role in spreading Christianity, and the popularity of the saints had long been sustained through a steady stream of miracles. The missionaries who had journeyed to northern Europe in early medieval times often came with relics of the saints in hand and, until the twelfth century, the cult they nourished remained intently focused on physical objects. During the later Middle Ages (twelfth to fifteenth centuries) successive waves of change had introduced new subjective elements into Western religion as Europeans came increasingly to venerate images and statues of the saints alongside their ancient relics: the images were no longer the direct, physical relict of the saint but only represented the saint's presence. Christians now focused their devotion more decidedly on the Virgin Mary and on saints common to the entire church rather than on the graves of holy men and women from their own regions. While this broad snapshot holds true generally, saintly veneration was amazingly complex and continued to display many local variations in the early modern period. Local saints and relic cults survived at this time, often flourishing alongside Marian shrines and international saints common to the entire church. In sixteenth-century Spain, for example, hundreds of shrines dedicated to the Virgin Mary and to local and international saints were present throughout the peninsula, and the power of the image, statue, or relic that was revered at each of these places was perceived to be distinctive, with the patron of a specific shrine often acquiring a special ability to combat certain diseases. Many people appealed to a broad spectrum of the saints for aid throughout their lives, and a rich lore circulated about local shrines as people traded tales of successful intercessions worked by a specific shrine's patron. The clergy fed a popular appetite for miracles by regularly publicizing intercessions the saints had worked. While most of the thousands of shrines that attracted the faithful in Europe were quite small and drew people from nearby, the faithful also traveled to great international shrines. Places like Santiago de Compostela in Spain, Mont Saint Michel in France, Canterbury in England, and, above all, Rome were great transregional centers of devotion. These sites became more important on the religious landscape during the fifteenth century as a result of the collapse of the Byzantine Empire and the rise of the Turks in the eastern Mediterranean, events that cut off the Holy Land as a destination for all but the most resourceful of European pilgrims.

THE CHURCH

While many rituals were practiced beyond its control, the church was nevertheless a vital force in the religious piety of Europeans around 1500. Through its system of seven sacraments the Catholic Church dispensed divine grace to the faithful, even as certain of the sacraments played a role in marking life's rites of passage. The sacraments of baptism, confirmation, and extreme unction (the last rites) were universally received by both laypeople and clergy alike, and while they were important religious ceremonies, these rituals also functioned with a large social purpose, admitting those who received them into new life stages. Rich traditions of godparentage, for example, had grown up over the centuries around baptism, and at the beginning of the early modern period the rite retained an important communal

dimension, as parents sometimes named scores of godparents for their children, hoping in this way to establish a protective network for them as they matured. The early modern world knew its share of lax or indifferent Christians. For most of the fifteenth and sixteenth centuries, most Europeans rarely received the sacraments of penance and the Eucharist more than once each year, although devout Christians attended the Mass and other services of the church more frequently, their attendance being a sign of their devotion. Even the devout, however, rarely received Communion more than two or three times a year. Instead, most practiced the custom of adoring the Eucharist at the moment of its consecration in the Mass, or in the tabernacles where it was kept in every church between services. This visual piety inspired the commissioning of enormous tabernacles for displaying the Eucharist, some of which rose to more than forty feet in Europe's major churches. The importance of viewing religious objects also nourished the custom of displaying saints' relics on important feast days. Passive activities like this were important to the devout, but late medieval and early modern religion also offered many opportunities for participation. Confraternities provided a vital avenue for those seeking to deepen their faith. These brotherhoods and sisterhoods of laypeople and clergy met regularly to say prayers and perform good works. Their members sometimes practiced ascetic regimens that imitated the disciplines of monastic life, including self-flagellation, the wearing of hair shirts, and other acts of self-denial that were designed to overcome the needs or desires of the body. Since the Mass was believed to be beneficial to the souls of both the living and the dead, the endowing of Masses was a pious good work, held in high repute throughout Europe. Fasting, dietary restrictions, and other good works like the giving of alms to the poor were also widely practiced by those anxious to live more perfect lives.

THE CHURCH AND SOCIAL LIFE

The church also played a key role in defining social life and in structuring the passage of time through the observance of its liturgical seasons and holidays. The penitential seasons of Advent and Lent were particularly important to those who were interested in a diligent observance of the church's teachings. In these seasons the devout abstained from sexual activity, from the eating of meat and all its byproducts, while they intensified their prayers and attendance at Mass. For society at large, feasting was more cherished than fasting, and the often raucous celebrations of Carnival that preceded Lent were vital releases that prepared the way for the rigors that followed. Many religious holidays were commemorated each year, and they were commonly celebrated with religious processions, dances, and feasts. These celebrations were usually crowded into the late spring and summer months when the weather was more favorable for outdoor activity. The Feast of the Ascension and Pentecost (also called Whitsunday in England), the commemoration of the founding of the Christian Church, occurred in May or June, and were followed by the Feast of Corpus Christi, a celebration of the Eucharist and of Christian community as "the Body of Christ." Huge bonfires lit on the Feast of St. John the Baptist in late June often became the scenes of revelry, dancing, and brawling, while the commemoration of the Assumption of Mary in mid-August rounded out the cycle of major summer religious observances before the harvests of the early fall. During the summer months many parishes and confraternities also made processions to local shrines, and in Europe's villages, the season was often marked by the observance of the kermis or fête, an anniversary celebration of the local church's consecration. Lay leaders in the parish staged these celebrations, and thus the kermis became an opportunity for them to demonstrate their important status in the community, even as the celebration provided all villagers with another occasion for entertainment.

REFORMATION

In the years following his 1517 attack on indulgences, Martin Luther developed a new theology centered on the concept of justification by faith alone. Luther's doctrinal insight denied that good works played any role in human salvation, and as a result he came to reject many traditional religious teachings. During the 1520s he reduced the number of sacraments from seven to two (baptism and the Eucharist) and denied that the Mass was a sacrifice beneficial to the living and the dead. The beliefs in purgatory, the effectiveness of pilgrimage, and the intercession of the saints were similarly rejected; clerical celibacy and the many privileges long accorded the clergy were similarly abolished. The de-

veloping Reformation came to emphasize humankind's utter helplessness in the process of salvation and the life-changing experience of a faith that was given as a free gift of God's grace. In Germany, this new Evangel came to be the standard by which traditional religious practices were judged. Luther and his evangelical supporters were uncompromising in opposing those practices that seemed to promote a belief in the saving benefit of good works. At the same time they also tried to eliminate rituals intended to control life's harsh circumstances and to secure earthly rewards, denouncing the seeming effectiveness of many of these practices as the "work of the devil." While uncompromising in their attitude toward many longstanding customs, Luther and his followers permitted many traditional practices provided they were adapted to a church centered on the Gospel. Other reformers who rose to prominence around the same time did not share this tolerant attitude. At Zurich in Switzerland, Huldrych Zwingli promoted reforms that attempted to clear away more than a thousand years of religious rituals and to replace them with a dramatically simplified religion subjected to biblical teaching and the example of the ancient church. While he relied on governmental authority at Zurich to accomplish his reforms in an orderly fashion, radical reformers elsewhere nourished demands for social as well as religious change. Their demands erupted in the great Peasants' War of 1524–1525, and in its wake, both religious reformers and state officials moved to institutionalize the Reformation and to adopt educational schemes to indoctrinate the young in the new teachings.

CATECHISM

The educational programs fostered by the Reformation were also inspired by a series of inspection tours of local religious life that were known as visitations. On their journeys through the German countryside, state and religious officials discovered a remarkably low level of knowledge about Christian doctrine among the people. State and church leaders came to concentrate their efforts on catechizing the young, a plan to which Luther himself contributed by the publication of his famous German catechism in 1529. In the coming decades his statement of key Christian teachings and evangelical doctrines was adopted in Lutheran Germany in many primary educational schemes, even as his practice of catechism was soon to be imitated by all kinds of Christians, both Protestant and Catholic, anxious to foster a higher level of religious knowledge. Catechisms were usually taught to children in weekly sessions conducted by village priests and ministers. Their appearance was important because in the heated world of Reformation and Counter-Reformation debate, printed catechisms and other confessions of faith were seen as important ways to inoculate the laity against competing religious positions. But the long-term effectiveness of these campaigns remains highly debatable. Filled with dry formulas, the catechisms were often mastered merely through rote memorization. After a century of intensive efforts to educate the young, both Protestant and Catholic officials continued to discover remarkably low religious knowledge in the countryside. Yet at a more fundamental level the rise of catechisms and confessions points to a development that was to intensify in the coming centuries. Increasingly, church and state officials judged a person's mastery of doctrinal formulas as an indication of their piety and devotion. The notion that religion was an ideology that might be defined intellectually thus came to compete against the rich world of devotional and protective practices that had largely defined piety for most Europeans in 1500.

MORAL REFORM

Educational schemes were the first prong of Protestant and Catholic attempts to reform piety and were soon to be followed by a broad campaign to elevate moral behavior. In traditional religious life, festive and pious elements had long flourished side by side, with dancing, drinking, and revelry occurring along with the Mass and processions at the commemoration of major feasts and holidays. The religious life of Europe had long oscillated, moreover, between periods of self-denial and raucous celebration, with the festive releases of Carnival preceding the ascetic fervor of Lent. Now both Catholic and Protestant moralists came to promote a new serious moral tone they hoped might pervade the entire year, not just the penitential seasons long promoted by the church. The efforts to raise moral standards were most pronounced in those societies that adopted Reformed Christianity, the pattern of Reformation teachings that had first begun to emerge in the work of figures like Huldrych Zwingli, and which later came to be dominated by John Calvin's influence.

But in Catholic, Lutheran, and Anglican societies the campaign to raise moral standards was present as well, intensifying in particular during the later sixteenth and seventeenth centuries. At this time Protestant and Catholic Reformers set themselves with greater determination to the task of ridding the countryside of rites they judged magical and superstitious, even as they tried to enforce more uncompromising moral standards. In Calvinist, Lutheran, and Anglican societies prayer, frequent church attendance, Bible reading, and family devotions were imposed as replacements for traditional rituals, benedictions, and sacramentals. Among Catholics, attendance at Mass and frequent reception of the sacraments of penance and the Eucharist were intended to forge a similar determination to achieve moral perfection. The new puritanism of the age inspired many attempts to outlaw dancing, blasphemous language, and prostitution as well as all forms of sex outside of marriage. This moral order was best achieved on a small scale, that is, in a medium-size city like Calvin's Geneva, where religious and civic officials joined forces to scrutinize the populace's activities quite closely. Yet as territorial princes and their state and church officials adopted the heightened moral tone of the age, they tried to foster a similar observant climate in the countryside, often to the chagrin and outright resistance of rural people. The ideals of religious devotion these early modern moralists most often favored were a sober, prayerful attitude; a diligent observance of Christianity's moral teachings; and frequent worship and participation in the life of the parish. This emphasis on parochial life flourished in all the major religions that developed as a result of the sixteenth-century Reformations, and it spelled key changes for piety since it fixed people's attentions ever more intently on the local institutions of the church, rather than on the broad range of communal rites and personal rituals that had played such a large role at the dawn of the sixteenth century.

CULTURAL SYMBOLS

The processes unleashed by the Protestant and Catholic Reformations also heightened the importance that certain religious practices played in the creation of Catholic and Protestant cultural identities. The intense biblicism of Calvinism, for example, led outsiders to identify the religion's followers as a "people of the book" who favored restraint in church decoration and an unadorned style of worship. By contrast, Lutherans and Anglicans retained much of the substance of the medieval Mass, while translating that service into the native tongue. In both these traditions a rich musical life was just one of the many new cultural developments that came to play a key role in sustaining the popular appeal of these religions and in creating their early modern identity. The singing of chorales and other musical innovations in Lutheranism afforded the laity a rich avenue of participation in the worship of the church, as did the service music and anthems of Anglicanism. For Catholics, many traditional rituals of the medieval church lived on, even as they came to be subjected to subtle modulations. The popularity of pilgrimage, the cult of the saints, and the intensely visual character of late medieval religion survived into the seventeenth and eighteenth centuries but were now subjected to the more vigorous disciplines of parish life, even as they were wedded to a heightened emphasis on penance and moral perfection. Devotion to the Eucharist and the Virgin Mary similarly intensified, even as new images of the Virgin like the Madonna of Victories came to express her increasingly important role as a triumphant standard bearer for Roman Catholicism. In these and numerous other ways the institutional changes in early modern religious life left their mark on European piety down to the present day. At the same time these forces proved insufficient to obliterate the rich, varied substratum of popular beliefs and rituals that had long played a vital role as a force for negotiating the problems of daily existence.

See also **Calvin, John; Calvinism; Carnival; Catholic Spirituality and Mysticism; Church of England; Luther, Martin; Lutheranism; Magic; Pietism; Puritanism; Reformation, Catholic; Reformation, Protestant; Reformations in Eastern Europe: Protestant, Catholic, and Orthodox; Theology; Zwingli, Huldrych.**

BIBLIOGRAPHY

Berger, Peter L. *The Sacred Canopy: Elements of a Sociological Theory of Religion.* New York, 1967.

Bossy, John. *Christianity in the West, 1400–1700.* London and New York, 1985.

Brown, Peter. *The Cult of the Saints: Its Rise and Function in Latin Christianity.* Chicago, 1981.

Cameron, Euan. *The European Reformation.* London and New York, 1991.

Châtellier, Louis. *The Europe of the Devout: The Catholic Reformation and the Formation of a New Society.* Translated by Jean Birrell. Cambridge, U.K., and New York, 1989.

Christian, William A., Jr. *Local Religion in Sixteenth-Century Spain.* Princeton, 1981.

Cressy, David. *Birth, Marriage and Death: Ritual, Religion, and the Life-Cycle in Tudor and Stuart England.* London and New York, 1997.

Hsia, R. Po-Chia. *The World of Catholic Renewal, 1540–1770.* Cambridge and New York, 1998.

Scribner, Robert W. *Popular Culture and Popular Movements in Reformation Germany.* London and Ronceverte, W.Va., 1988.

Strauss, G. *Luther's House of Learning. Indoctrination of the Young in the German Reformation.* Baltimore, 1978.

Thomas, Keith. *Religion and the Decline of Magic: Studies in Popular Belief in Sixteenth and Seventeenth-Century England.* London and New York, 1971.

PHILIP M. SOERGEL

RELIGIOUS SOCIETIES. *See* **Confraternities; Jesuits.**

REMBRANDT VAN RIJN (1606–1669), Dutch artist. Known for his portraits, history paintings, and graphic works that display an affecting empathy for his subjects, Rembrandt Harmensz van Rijn was born on 15 July 1606 in the university town of Leiden. The ninth child of a baker's daughter and the well-to-do owner of a malt mill, "De Rijn," the young Rembrandt must have attended the local Latin school because on 20 May 1620, at the age of 14, he enrolled at Leiden University, where he remained for only a short time. Rembrandt may have started his artistic studies with a Leiden painter unknown to us today. Between 1619 and 1622 he began a three-year apprenticeship with Jacob Isaacsz van Swanenburgh (1571–1638) whose painted scenes of hell left no trace in the work of his famous pupil. In 1623 or 1624 Rembrandt moved to Amsterdam to study with Pieter Lastman (1583–1633), the city's leading history painter. After about six months Rembrandt left Lastman's studio and, rather than travel and study in Italy (as had van Swanenburgh, Lastman, and many of his fellow artists), he returned to Leiden as a master and probably moved into the studio of another Lastman pupil, Jan Lievens (1607–1674). Here Rembrandt began examining his face and emotional expression in painted and etched self-portraits and produced a series of small-scale history paintings in whose choice of subject matter and composition one can see both the influence of Lastman and an artistic dialogue with Lievens.

REMBRANDT'S EMERGING STYLE

Rembrandt's earliest known dated painting, *The Stoning of St. Stephen* (1625; Musée des Beaux-Arts, Lyon), recalls the horizontal format and dramatic gestures of Lastman's work. It also shows evidence of his own emerging artistic qualities, including a greater focus on the central subject and a variety of emotional responses to an event. In his early twenties Rembrandt came to the attention of Constantijn Huygens, the influential secretary to Frederik Hendrik, prince of Orange. Huygens praised the dramatic emotional tenor of his *Repentant Judas Returning the Thirty Pieces of Silver* (1629; private collection, England). Over the course of the following decade he received through Huygens a number of commissions from Prince Frederick Hendrick, including a portrait of the prince's wife and a series of Christ's Passion.

EARLY YEARS IN AMSTERDAM

By about 1631 Rembrandt had begun receiving portrait commissions from prominent Amsterdam citizens, and in 1632 he moved to the thriving metropolis. As exemplified in the single-figured *Nicholas Ruts* (1631; Frick Collection, New York) and the *Anatomy Lesson of Dr. Nicolaes Tulp* (1632; Mauritshuis, The Hague), these works transformed the portrait tradition by displaying figures caught in actions that imply an inner life of thought and feeling. Rembrandt's history paintings from this period similarly show motion and psychological drama, from his lyrical *Danaë* welcoming Jupiter as a shower of golden light (c. 1636 and early 1640s; The Hermitage, St. Petersburg) to the high theatricality of *The Blinding of Samson* (1636; Städelsches Kunstinstitut, Frankfurt) that depicts the gruesome moment a dagger is plunged into Samson's eye.

During his first years in Amsterdam, Rembrandt, lodged with the art dealer Hendrick Uylenburgh, who may have brokered some of the artist's early portrait commissions. In 1634 Rembrandt both joined the Amsterdam Guild of St. Luke and married Uylenburgh's niece Saskia, the daughter of a wealthy burgomaster of Leeuwarden. From early in his career, Rembrandt self-consciously fabricated an artistic persona. Throughout his life he produced an unprecedented number of drawn, etched, and painted self-portraits (of which about 80 survive), and even occasionally inserted his own face into his history paintings. Beginning in 1633, in contrast to most of his contemporaries, he signed his works with his given name, emulating such Italian predecessors as Raphael, Titian, and Leonardo. By 1639 Rembrandt could afford to purchase an expensive house, complete with studio.

Rembrandt's *Self-Portrait* of 1640 (London, National Gallery) depicts a self-confident artist at the height of his powers. Its pose and composition recall two Italian Renaissance portraits known to Rembrandt: Titian's so-called *Portrait of a Man*, at the time believed to represent the poet Ariosto (c. 1512; National Gallery, London), and Raphael's portrait of the courtier and author Baldassare Castiglione (c. 1514–1515; Musée du Louvre, Paris). In doing so, Rembrandt created a "paragone," a classic rivalry, between himself and his Renaissance forebears, two painters and two poets. In his most famous work, *The Militia Company of Captain Frans Banning Cocq*, better known today as *The Night Watch* (1642; Rijksmuseum, Amsterdam), Captain Banning Cocq strides beside his smartly dressed lieutenant and, gesturing with a sweep of his left hand, gives the order for his men to march out behind him. With its implied narrative, lively movement, and varied psychological response to the occasion, the conceit was unprecedented in Dutch group portraiture.

SETBACKS AND LATER SUCCESSES

Also in 1642, Rembrandt's beloved wife Saskia died. He took into his bed his son's nurse, Geertge Dircks, and subsequently Hendrickje Stoffels, who, pregnant, in 1654 was called before the Reformed Church council for "having committed whoredom" with the artist. About this time Rembrandt began to suffer economic setbacks, in part due to his own poor financial decisions and to the general economic slowdown that accompanied the Anglo-Dutch war of 1652–1654. On 14 July 1656, facing bankruptcy, the artist applied for a *cessio bonorum*,

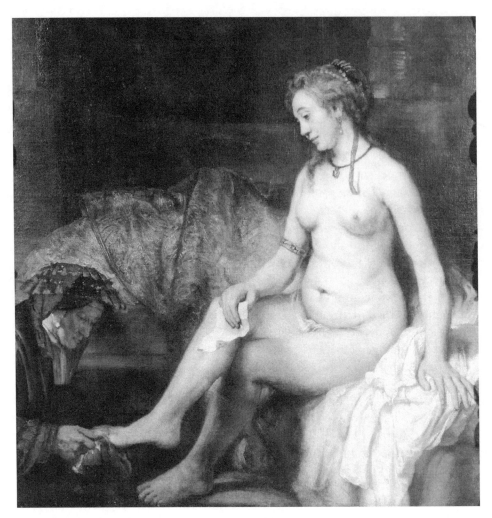

Rembrandt van Rijn. *Bathsheba with King David's Letter.* ©Giraudon/Art Resource, N.Y.

surrendering the control of his large house, its contents, and his possessions to the Chamber of Insolvent Estates. These stresses may be responsible, in part, for the intensely meditative turn of his works. His *Bathsheba with King David's Letter* (1654; Musée du Louvre, Paris) depicts the young woman in deep reflection, while his great *Portrait of Jan Six* shows the regent lost in thought as he pulls on a glove (1654; Foudation Six, Amsterdam).

Throughout his life, Rembrandt experimented with print media, from early studies of his face dating from the late 1620s through charming etchings of family life, landscapes, genre images, and biblical scenes—many displaying a beguiling intimacy, freshness, and spontaneity. He tried various effects of ink, pulled impressions on different kinds of paper, and avidly reworked his conceptions: Rem-

brandt developed his masterful drypoint *Ecce Homo* (also called *Christ Presented to the People,* 1655) through eight different states. The title later given to an image depicting several episodes from chapter 19 of the Gospel of Matthew, *The Hundred Guilder Print* (c. 1642–1649), attests to the value collectors attached to the master's prints.

His magnificent *Self-Portrait* of 1658 (Frick Collection, New York) presents the master as confident of his artistic powers. Gold light bathes a garment set off by a red sash. A fur-trimmed cloak drapes his shoulders, and he holds his painter's mahlstick as if it were a king's scepter. However, not all of the commissions he received during the last decade of his life were trouble-free. His *Oath of the Batavians to Claudius Civilis,* commissioned for the Amsterdam Town Hall, was removed after only a few months (c. 1661–1662; Nationalmuseum, Stockholm). The taste of many Dutch patrons and art theorists had turned toward classicistic painting, while Rembrandt's work moved in another direction and featured freely worked surfaces, glowing colors, and profoundly contemplative subjects. Nonetheless, the fact that writers occasionally singled out the master for derision confirms the hold he and his work had on the century's imagination. Rembrandt continued to receive important commissions, including the *Syndics of the Drapers' Guild* of 1662 (Rijksmuseum, Amsterdam), while his late history paintings, such as *The Return of the Prodigal Son* (c. 1666–1668; The Hermitage, St. Petersburg) are among the most personal and moving images produced in his time.

See also **Art: The Conception and Status of the Artist; Netherlands, Art in the; Painting; Prints and Popular Imagery.**

BIBLIOGRAPHY

Bruyn, Josua, et al. *A Corpus of Rembrandt Paintings.* 3 vols. The Hague, 1982–1989.

The Rembrandt Documents. Edited by Walter L. Strauss and Marjon van de Meulen. New York, 1979.

Schama, Simon. *Rembrandt's Eyes.* New York, 1999.

Schwartz, Gary. *Rembrandt: His Life, His Paintings.* New York, 1985.

Westermann, Mariët. *Rembrandt.* London, 2000.

Wetering, Ernst van de. *Rembrandt: The Painter at Work.* Amsterdam, 1997.

ANN JENSEN ADAMS

RENAISSANCE. The Renaissance is one of the most interesting and disputed periods of European history. Many scholars see it as a unique time with characteristics all its own. A second group views the Renaissance as the first two to three centuries of a larger era in European history usually called early modern Europe, which began in the late fifteenth century and ended on the eve of the French Revolution (1789) or with the close of the Napoleonic era (1815). Some social historians reject the concept of the Renaissance altogether. Historians also argue over how much the Renaissance differed from the Middle Ages and whether it was the beginning of the modern world, however defined.

The approach here is that the Renaissance began in Italy about 1350 and in the rest of Europe after 1450 and that it lasted until about 1620. It was a historical era with distinctive themes in learning, politics, literature, art, religion, social life, and music. The changes from the Middle Ages to the Renaissance were significant, but not as great as historians once thought. Renaissance developments influenced subsequent centuries, but not so much that the Renaissance as a whole can be called "modern."

THE RENAISSANCE VIEW OF THE RENAISSANCE

The term "Renaissance" comes from the Renaissance. Several Italian intellectuals of the late fourteenth and the early fifteenth centuries used the term *rinascità* ('rebirth or renaissance') to describe their own age as one in which learning, literature, and the arts were reborn after a long, dark Middle Ages. They saw the ancient world of Rome and Greece, whose literature, learning, and politics they admired, as an age of high achievement. But in their view, hundreds of years of cultural darkness followed because much of the learning and literature of the ancient world had been lost. Indeed, Italian humanists invented the concept of the "Middle Ages" to describe the years between about 400 and 1400. Scholastic philosophy, which the Italian humanists rejected, and a different style of Latin writing, which the humanists viewed as uncouth and barbarous, prevailed in the Middle Ages. But Italian humanists believed that a new age was dawning. In the view of the humanists, the painter Giotto (d. 1337) and the vernacular writer and early humanist Francesco Petrarch (1304–1374) led the rebirth or Renaissance. Most Italian intellectuals from the mid-fifteenth century on held these views.

Northern Europeans of the sixteenth century also reached the conclusion that a new age had dawned. They accepted the historical periodization of ancient, medieval, and Renaissance and added a religious dimension. Desiderius Erasmus (c. 1466–1536), the great Dutch humanist, and his followers looked back to two ancient sources for inspiration: the secular learning of ancient Greece and Rome, and Christianity of the first four centuries. The former offered models of literature, culture, and good morality, while the New Testament and the church fathers, such as Sts. Augustine (354–430) and Jerome (c. 347–419/420), combined pristine Christianity with ancient eloquence. But then barbarous medieval culture replaced ancient eloquence, and, in their view, the theological confusion of medieval Scholasticism obscured the message of the New Testament. Erasmus and his followers dedicated themselves to restoring good literature, meaning classical Greek and Latin, and good religion, meaning Christianity purged of Scholastic irrelevance and clerical abuses. They believed that Christians could best live moral lives and attain salvation in the next life by following both Cicero and the New Testament. They believed that there were no real differences between the moral precepts found in the pagans of ancient Greece and Rome and the Bible.

CHRONOLOGY

A cluster of dates marks the beginning of the Renaissance era. The majority of scholars view the early humanist and vernacular writer Petrarch as the first important figure. He strongly criticized medieval habits of thought as inadequate and elevated ancient ideals and literature as models to emulate. By the period 1400 to 1450 numerous Italian intellectuals agreed with Petrarch's criticism of the Middle Ages and support for a classical revival. The result was the intellectual movement called humanism, which came to dominate Italian Latin schooling, scholarship, ethical ideas, and public discourse and spread to the rest of Europe in the late fifteenth and early sixteenth centuries. Both contemporaries and modern historians also see the Great Plague of 1348 to 1350, with its huge demographic losses (30 to 50 percent in affected areas) and psychological impact as another dividing point between Middle Ages and Renaissance. Next, a series of major political changes between 1450 and 1500 marked a new political era that was uniquely Renaissance. Spain, France, and England emerged as powerful territorial monarchies in the last quarter of the fifteenth century. Their quarrels with each other and interventions in the affairs of smaller states through the next 150 years dominated European politics. Finally, the invention of movable type in the 1450s by Johannes Gutenberg (c. 1398–1468) created a break with the medieval past in the production and dissemination of books that was so great that it is difficult to measure. By the end of the year 1470, some nineteen towns had printing presses; by 1500 some 255 towns had presses, and the spread of printing was far greater in the sixteenth century. An efficient system of distribution and marketing spread printed books to every corner of Europe. The greater availability of books had an impact on practically every area of life, especially intellectual and religious life, so immense as to be beyond measurement.

HUMANISM

Humanism was the defining intellectual movement of the Renaissance. It was based on the belief that the literary, scientific, and philosophical works of ancient Greece and Rome provided the best guides for learning and living. And humanists believed that the New Testament and early Christian authors offered the best spiritual advice.

The nineteenth century invented the term "humanism." But humanism is based on three Renaissance terms. *Studia humanitatis* meant humanistic studies, which were grammar, rhetoric, poetry, history, and moral philosophy based on study of the standard ancient authors of Rome and, to a lesser extent, Greece. This is the famous definition presented in 1945 by the eminent historian Paul Oscar Kristeller (1905–1999) and now widely accepted. The Renaissance also used and praised *humanitas,* an ancient Latin term meaning the good qualities that make men and women human. And the Renaissance invented a new term, *humanista.* It first appeared in Italian in a University of Pisa document of 1490. By the end of the sixteenth century it had spread to several European vernacular languages and was occasionally used in Latin. A *humanista* was a student, teacher, or scholar of the humanities.

Humanism became institutionalized in society as a new form of education. Around 1400 a number of Italian pedagogical leaders decided that the traditional medieval curriculum for Latin schools, consisting of studying medieval authors and a few ancient poetic classics, or portions of them, and learning to write formal letters in Latin according to nonclassical rules, was inadequate. They proposed a new curriculum and approach. Pier Paolo Vergerio (c. 1368–1444) wrote the first and most important humanist pedagogical treatise, called *De Ingenuis Moribus et Liberalibus Studiis Adulescentiae* (On noble customs and liberal studies of adolescents) in 1402 or 1403. He argued that the best way to foster good character, learning, and an eloquent Latin style in speech and writing was to teach humanistic studies. He gave pride of place to history, moral philosophy, and eloquence, a novel emphasis. Boys trained in humanistic studies would be ready to become honorable leaders in society as adults. Vergerio's treatise had enormous resonance: More than one hundred manuscripts can be found in Italian libraries, and Italian presses produced more than thirty incunabular (printed before 1501) editions. It enjoyed similar diffusion in northern Europe.

Humanism was more than skill in Latin. It tried to teach the principles of living a moral, responsible, and successful life on this earth. Parents came to believe that a humanistic education would best prepare their sons, and a few daughters, for leadership positions, such as head of a family, member of a city council, judge, administrator, or teacher. Humanistic studies provided the fundamental education. Training in the specialized disciplines of law, medicine, philosophy, or theology came later for those needing them. By about 1550 the English clergyman, the French lawyer, the German knight, the Italian merchant, and the Spanish courtier shared a common intellectual heritage. They could communicate across national frontiers and despite linguistic differences. They shared a common fund of examples, principles, and knowledge derived from the classics. Humanism brought intellectual unity to Europe.

Humanism also included a sharply critical attitude toward received values, individuals, and institutions, especially those that did not live up to their own principles. The humanists' study of ancient Rome and Greece gave them the chronological perspective and intellectual tools to analyze, criticize, and change their own world. Humanists especially questioned the institutions and values inherited from the Middle Ages. They found fault with medieval art, government, philosophy, and approaches to religion. Once the humanist habit of critical appraisal developed, many turned sharp eyes on their own times. And eventually they turned their critical gaze on the learning of the ancient world and rejected parts of it.

SCIENTIFIC AND PHILOSOPHICAL LEARNING

Renaissance scholars inherited from the Middle Ages intellectual views and approaches in philoso-

phy, medicine, and science, and challenged almost all of them. In astronomy they inherited a conception of the universe originating in Ptolemy (c. 100 C.E.–c. 170 C.E.) of the ancient world that the sun revolved around the Earth. Nicolaus Copernicus (1473–1543) in his *De Revolutionibus Orbium Caelestium* (1543; On the revolutions of the heavenly orbs) argued the reverse, that the Earth and other planets revolved around the sun. Despite bitter opposition from both Catholic and Protestant religious authorities, his views prevailed with most astronomers by the early seventeenth century. Galileo Galilei (1564–1642) absorbed Aristotelian science and then rejected it in favor of a mathematically based analysis of physical reality, the modern science of mechanics. And along the way he offered evidence that Copernicus's daring view was not just mathematical hypothesis but physical reality. Another mathematical achievement affecting Europe and the rest of the world in future centuries was calendar reform. Renaissance Europe inherited the Julian calendar of ancient Rome, which was ten days in arrears by the sixteenth century. Pope Gregory XIII (reigned 1572–1585) appointed a team of scholars to prepare a new calendar and in 1582 promulgated the Gregorian calendar still used today.

Renaissance medical scholars inherited an understanding of the human body and an approach to healing based on the ancient Greek physician Galen (c. 129–c. 199 C.E.), Aristotle (384–322 B.C.E.), and medieval Arab medical scholars. But a group of medical scholars called "medical humanists" by modern scholars challenged and altered received medical knowledge. Led by Niccolò Leoniceno (1428–1524), who taught at the universities of Padua and Ferrara, they applied humanistic philological techniques and ideological criticism to both medieval and ancient medical texts, found them wanting, and proceeded to investigate the human body anew. As a result, Andreas Vesalius (1514–1564) through his anatomical studies, William Harvey (1578–1657) through his study of the circulation of the blood, and other scholars revolutionized medical research and instruction. Several Renaissance medical scholars gave their names to parts of the body; for example, the eustachian tube between the ear and the nose is named for Bartolomeo Eustachi (1500/10–1574), and the fallopian or uterine tubes are named for Gabriele Falloppia (1523–1562).

Most of the innovative research in science, medicine, philosophy, and law came from universities. The Renaissance saw a great expansion in the number and quality of universities. It inherited twenty-nine functioning universities from the Middle Ages in 1400, then created forty-six new ones by 1601, losing only two by closure in between. This left Europe with sixty-three universities, more than double the medieval number. Demand for new universities came from several directions. Most important, increasing numbers of men wanted to learn. Society also needed more trained professionals. Monarchs, princes, and cities required civil servants, preferably with law degrees. A medical degree enabled the recipient to become a private physician, a court physician, or one employed by the town. The Protestant and Catholic Reformations stimulated the demand for theology degrees.

Universities provided stipends and other support for scholars. Since the universal language of learning was Latin and the printing press could publish new information, scientific communication was rapid and overcame the religious division of sixteenth-century Europe. University students to a lesser extent also crossed religious frontiers. The adoption of Roman law in central Europe created a demand for lawyers and judges trained in this field, which meant that both Catholic and Protestant Germans continued to study in Italian universities, the centers for the study of Roman law.

RENAISSANCE POLITICS

Renaissance states had three basic forms of government: princedoms, monarchies, and oligarchies, which the Renaissance called republics.

Princedoms. A prince was an individual, whether called duke, count, marquis, or just signore (lord), who ruled a state, usually with the support of his family. The term "prince" meant the authority to make decisions concerning all inhabitants without check by representative body, constitution, or court. But the source of the prince's power and the nature of his rule varied greatly. He often had displaced another ruler or city council by force, war, assassination, bribery, diplomacy, purchase, marriage, or occasionally because the city invited him in

to quell factionalism. Most often a prince came to power through an adroit combination of several of these. Once in control, he promulgated laws of succession to give himself a cloak of legitimacy so that his son or another family member might succeed him. Indeed, some inhabitants of the state would see him as legitimate and be content to be ruled by him.

Princely power was seldom absolute. Most princes depended on some accommodation with powerful forces within the state, typically the nobility or the merchant community. Many small princedoms depended on the good will of more powerful states beyond their borders to survive, and this limited options in foreign policy. And the prince's rule was always uneasy, which was one reason he relied on hired mercenary troops in war, instead of a militia created from his subjects. However achieved, what mattered most was that the prince possessed effective power to promulgate and enforce laws, to collect taxes, to defeat foreign invaders, and to quell rebellion. If the prince commanded the affection and loyalty of his subjects, this made his task easier. Italy and central Europe had an abundance of princedoms, including the states of Ferrara, Mantua, Milan, Parma, Piedmont-Savoy, and Urbino in northern Italy, and Bavaria, Brandenburg, Burgundy, Brunswick-Lüneberg, Luxembourg, the Palatinate, Albertine and Ernestine Saxony, and Württemberg in central Europe.

Monarchies. A monarchy was a princedom sanctioned by a much longer tradition, stronger institutions, and greater claims of legitimacy for its rulers. The majority of monarchies (for example, England, France, Portugal, Scotland, and Spain) were hereditary, while Poland, Hungary, Bohemia, and the Holy Roman Empire were elective. Monarchies typically were larger than princedoms and ruled subjects speaking multiple languages and dialects. Monarchies usually had developed laws and rules that determined the succession in advance. Only when the succession was broken through the lack of a legitimate heir, a bitter dispute within the ruling family, or overthrow by a foreign power was a monarch displaced by another.

Monarchies grew in power and size in the Renaissance. The creation of the dual monarchy of Ferdinand of Aragón and Isabella of Castile between 1474 and 1479 created a powerful Spain that ruled the entire Spanish peninsula except Portugal, and Portugal as well from 1580 to 1640. The Tudor monarchy of England (three kings and two queens from 1485 to 1603) made England, previously a small, strife-torn, and remote part of Europe, into a major force. After the conclusion of the Hundred Years' War with England (1337–1453), France under the Valois dynasty (ruled 1328 to 1589) became a powerful and rich state. Conflicts between territorial monarchies dominated international politics and war in the Renaissance.

Republics. The smallest and most unusual political unit was the city-state consisting of a major town or city and its surrounding territory of farms and villages. Oligarchies, usually drawn from the merchant elite of the town, ruled republics. Flanked by the professional classes, the merchant community first dominated the commerce of the city. Then in the Middle Ages they threw off the authority of prince, king, or emperor. In their place the merchants created a system of government through interlocking and balanced councils. Large deliberative assemblies, comprising of one hundred, two hundred, or more adult males, elected or chosen by lot, debated and created laws. Executive committees, often six, eight, or a dozen men elected for two to six months, put the laws into action. Short terms of office and rules against self-succession made it possible for several hundred or more adult males to participate in government in a few years. The system of balanced and diffused power ensured that no individual or family could control the city. It was a government of balanced power and mutual suspicion.

Borrowing terminology and legal principles from ancient Roman law and local tradition, the men who formed oligarchies called their governments "republican" and their states "republics." They believed that their rule was based on the consent of the people who mattered. But they were still oligarchies, because only 5 to 20 percent of the adult males of the city could vote or hold office. Members of government almost always came from the leading merchants, manufacturers, bankers, and lawyers. Some republics permitted shopkeepers and master craftsmen to participate as well. But workers, the propertyless, clergymen, and other middle and low groups in society were excluded. Occasionally the laws conceded to them extraordinary powers in times of emergency. Those living in the countryside and villages outside the city walls had neither a role in government nor the right to choose their rulers. Indeed, the city often exploited them financially and in other ways. Venice, Genoa, Lucca, Florence, Pisa, and Siena in Italy, and Augsburg, Nuremberg, Strasbourg, and the Swiss cantons were republics. Some city-state republics were small in comparison with monarchies and princedoms. But the Republic of Venice commanded an overseas empire of considerable size and commercial importance, while Florence's merchants and bankers played a large role in international trade, and the city participated forcefully in Italian politics.

Renaissance Europe presented a constantly shifting political scene. No government escaped external threats and very few avoided internal challenge. The numerous weak small states tempted powerful rulers and states. Despite their eloquent proclamations in defense of the liberty of states and citizens, republics were just as aggressive in conquering their weaker neighbors as were princedoms, while monarchies were always on the watch for another princedom, landed noble estate, or republic to absorb. It was the same within the state. Some powerful group or individual within the state would attempt through force or stealth to take control and change its nature. Many succeeded. The maneuvering for advantage, the shifting diplomatic alliances, plots, threats of war, and military actions made Renaissance politics extremely complex.

Two broad political developments prevailed. Princedoms grew in number and strength, and more powerful states, especially monarchies, absorbed smaller states. Republican city-states became princedoms, as a powerful individual or family within the city took control while maintaining a facade of republican institutions and councils. The gradual transformation of the Republic of Florence into a princedom ruled by members of the Medici family is the classic example. Meanwhile, princedoms fell into the hands of monarchies through military action or dynastic marriages. Three examples will suffice. France and the Habsburgs divided the Duchy of Burgundy between them when its duke, Charles the Bold, was killed in battle in 1477, leaving no male heir; Spain took control of the Kingdom of Naples by military force in 1504; and

Spain absorbed the Duchy of Milan as the result of an alliance when the Duke Francesco II Sforza died without an heir in 1535. Strong republics also grew at the expense of their neighbors. The Republic of Venice conquered almost all the independent towns and small princedoms in northeastern Italy in the first half of the fifteenth century in its successful drive to create a mainland state. Small states survived at the price of careful neutrality, which avoided giving offense to more powerful neighbors, or by aligning themselves with larger powers. Such alliances came at a price. The small state lacked an independent foreign policy and might itself become a victim if the larger state fell.

DIPLOMACY AND POLITICAL THOUGHT

The very complex and ever-shifting political reality stimulated the rapid development of diplomacy. The resident ambassador, that is, a permanent representative of one government to another, was a Renaissance innovation. He went to live in the capital city or court of another state where he conveyed messages between his government and the host government. Or to use the words that Sir Henry Wotton (1568–1639), the English ambassador to Venice, supposedly wrote in 1604, "a resident ambassador is a good man sent to tell lies abroad for his country's good." Perhaps more important than the messages, or lies, was the information that the resident ambassador and his staff gathered about the host country. Ambassadorial reports full of every kind of information are invaluable sources for modern scholars studying the Renaissance. The reports of papal nuncios and Venetian ambassadors are particularly useful.

The instability of forms of government, the many wars, and the fluidity of international politics stimulated an enormous amount of discussion about politics, including several masterpieces of political philosophy. Niccolò Machiavelli (1469–1527), having observed both, wrote about princedoms in his *Il principe* (*The Prince,* written in 1513), and on republics in *Discorsi sopra la prima deca di Tito Livio* (Discourses on the first ten books of Titus Livy, written 1514–1520). Numerous humanists wrote treatises advising a prince or king how he might be a good prince, work for the good of his people, and, as a result, see his state and himself prosper. Erasmus wrote the most famous one, *Insti-*

tutio Principis Christiani (1516; Education of a Christian prince). Jean Bodin (1530–1596) argued that state and society needed the stability that only a sovereign and absolute power can provide, and that this must be the monarchy, in his *Six livres de la république* (1576; Six Books on the commonwealth; in Latin, 1586).

VERNACULAR LITERATURE

Vernacular literatures flourished in the Renaissance even though humanists preferred Latin. In 1400 standard English, French, German, Portuguese, Spanish, and other vernaculars did not exist. People spoke and sometimes wrote a variety of regional dialects with haphazard spelling and multiple vocabularies. Nevertheless, thanks to the adoption of the vernacular by some governments, the printing press, and the creation of literary masterpieces, significant progress toward elegant and standard forms of modern vernaculars occurred.

German was typical. German-speaking lands inherited many varieties of German from the Middle Ages. In the fifteenth century some state chanceries began to use German instead of Latin. Hence, versions of German associated with the chanceries of more important states, including the East Middle Saxon dialect used in the chancery of the electorate of Saxony, became more influential. Next, printing encouraged writers and editors to standardize orthography and usage in order to reach a wider range of readers. Most important, Martin Luther (1483–1546) published a German translation of the Bible (New Testament in 1522; complete Bible in 1534), which may have had three hundred editions and over half a million printed copies by 1600, an enormous number at a time of limited literacy. And many began to imitate his style. Since he wrote in East Middle Saxon, this version of German eventually became standard German. Literary academies concerned about correct usage, vocabulary, and orthography rose in the seventeenth century to create dictionaries. A reasonably standardized German literary language had developed, though the uneducated continued to speak regional dialects.

Similar changes took place in other parts of Europe, with the aid of Renaissance authors and their creations. In Italy three Tuscan authors, Dante Alighieri (1265–1321)—medieval in thought but using Tuscan brilliantly—Petrarch, and Giovanni

Boccaccio (1313–1375) began the process. Literary arbiters, such as Pietro Bembo (1470–1547) insisted on a standard Italian based on the fourteenth-century Tuscan of Dante, Petrarch, and Boccaccio. Major sixteenth-century writers, including Ludovico Ariosto (1474–1533), Baldassare Castiglione (1478–1529), and Torquato Tasso (1544–1595), agreed. None of the three was Tuscan, but each tried to write, and sometimes rewrote, their masterpieces in a more Tuscan Italian. Then the *Accademia della Crusca* (founded in Florence in the 1580s) published a dictionary. Tuscan became modern Italian. William Shakespeare (1564–1616) and three English translations of the Bible, that of William Tyndale (printed 1526 and 1537), the Geneva Bible of 1560, and the King James Bible of 1611, had an enormous influence on English. The writers and dramatists of the Spanish Golden Age, particularly Miguel de Cervantes Saavedra (1547–1616), did the same for the Castilian version of Spanish.

ART

Art is undoubtedly the best-loved and -known part of the Renaissance. The Renaissance produced an extraordinary amount of art, and the role of the artist differed from that in the Middle Ages.

The Renaissance had a passion for art. Commissions came from kings, popes, princes, nobles, and lowborn mercenary captains. Leaders commissioned portraits of themselves, of scenes of their accomplishments, such as successful battles, and of illustrious ancestors. Cities wanted their council halls decorated with huge murals, frescoes, and tapestries depicting great civic moments. Monasteries commissioned artists to paint frescoes in cells and refectories that would inspire monks to greater devotion. And civic, dynastic, and religious leaders hired architects to erect buildings at enormous expense to beautify the city or to serve as semipublic residences for leaders. Such art was designed to celebrate and impress.

A remarkable feature of Renaissance art was the heightened interaction between patron and artist. Patrons such as Lorenzo de' Medici (1449–1492) of Florence and popes Julius II (reigned 1503–1513) and Leo X (reigned 1513–1521) were active and enlightened patrons. They proposed programs, or instructed humanists to do it for them, for the artists to follow. At the same time, the results show that they did not stifle the artists' originality. Men and women of many social levels had an appetite for art. The wealthy merchant wanted a painting of Jesus, Mary, or saints, with small portraits of members of his family praying to them, for his home. A noble might provide funding to decorate a chapel in his parish church honoring the saint for whom he was named. Members of the middle classes and probably the working classes wanted small devotional paintings. To meet the demand, enterprising merchants organized the mass production of devotional images, specifying the image (typically Mary, Jesus crucified, or patron saint), design, color, and size. It is impossible to know how many small devotional paintings and illustrated prints were produced, because most have disappeared. Major art forms, such as paintings, sculptures, and buildings, have attracted the most attention, but works in the minor arts, including furniture, silver and gold objects, small metal works, table decorations, household objects, colorful ceramics, candlesticks, chalices, and priestly vestments were also produced in great abundance.

The new styles came from Italy, and Italy produced more art than any other part of Europe. Art objects of every sort were among the luxury goods that Italy produced and exported. It also exported artists, such as Leonardo da Vinci, who died at the French court.

The ancient world of Rome and Greece, as interpreted by the humanists, greatly influenced Renaissance art. Artists and humanists studied the surviving buildings and monuments, read ancient treatises available for the first time, and imbibed the humanist emphasis on man and his actions and perceptions, plus the habit of sharp criticism of medieval styles.

Stimulated by the ancients, Renaissance artists were the first in European history to write extensively about art and themselves. Leon Battista Alberti (1404–1472) wrote treatises on painting (1435) and on architecture (1452); Raphael wrote a letter to Pope Leo X (c. 1519) concerning art. Giorgio Vasari's (1511–1574) *Lives of the Artists* (first edition 1550, revised edition 1568) was a series of biographies of Renaissance artists accompanied by his many comments about artistic styles. It was the first history of art. The silversmith Benvenuto Cellini (1500–1571) wrote about artistic practices and much more about himself, much of it probably fictitious, in his *Autobiography,* written between 1558 and 1566.

The social and intellectual position of the artist changed in the Renaissance. The artist began as a craftsman, occupying a relatively low social position and tied to his guild, someone who followed local traditions and produced paintings for local patrons. He became a self-conscious creator of original works of art with complex schemes, a person who conversed with humanists and negotiated with kings and popes. Successful artists enjoyed wealth and honors, such as the knighthood that Emperor Charles V conferred on Titian (Tiziano Vercelli, c. 1488–1576) in 1533.

SOCIETY

The Renaissance was a hierarchical age in which the social position of a child's parents largely determined his or her place in society. Yet it was a variegated society, with nobles, commoners, wealthy merchants, craftsmen, shopkeepers, workers, peasants, prelates, parish priests, monks in monasteries, nuns in convents, civil servants, men of the professional classes, and others. It was an age of conspicuous consumption and great imbalances of wealth. But Renaissance society also provided social services for the less fortunate. Ecclesiastical, lay, and civic charitable institutions provided for orphans, the sick, the hungry, and outcast groups, such as prostitutes and the syphilitic ill. Although social mobility was limited, a few humble individuals rose to the apex of society. Francesco Sforza (1401–1466), a mercenary soldier of uncertain origins, became duke of Milan in 1450 and founded his own dynasty. The shepherd boy Antonio Ghislieri (born 1504) became Pope Pius V (reigned 1566–1572).

UNITY AND DISINTEGRATION

Renaissance Europe had considerable cultural and intellectual unity, greater than it had in the centuries of the Middle Ages or would again until the European Economic Union of the late twentieth century. A common belief in humanism and humanistic education based on the classics created much of it. The preeminence of Italy also helped because Italians led the way in humanism, art, the techniques of

diplomacy, and even the humble business skill of double-entry bookkeeping.

The prolonged Habsburg-Valois conflict, often called the Italian Wars (1494–1559) because much of the fighting occurred in Italy, and, above all, the Protestant Reformation began to crack that unity. Moreover, many typical Renaissance impulses had spent their force by the early seventeenth century. The great revival of the learning of ancient Greece and Rome had been assimilated, and humanism was no longer the driving force behind philosophical and scientific innovation. Italy no longer provided artistic, cultural, and scientific leadership, except in music, as a group of Florentine musicians created lyric opera around 1600.

Europe began a new age on the eve of the Thirty Years' War (1618–1648). More powerful monarchies with different policies ushered in a different era of politics and war. Exuberant baroque art and architecture of the seventeenth century were not the same as the restrained, classicizing art of the previous two centuries. Galileo Galilei and René Descartes (1596–1650) discarded Renaissance Aristotelian science in favor of mathematics and mechanics. The universities of Europe were no longer essential for training Europe's elite and hosting innovative research. France would be the military, literary, and stylistic leader of the different Europe of the seventeenth century.

See also **Art; Bible: Translations and Editions; Cellini, Benvenuto; Copernicus, Nicolaus; Education; English Literature and Language; Erasmus, Desiderius; Galileo, Galilei; German Literature and Language; Humanists and Humanism; Italian Literature and Language; Leo X (pope); Medici Family; Monarchy; Political Philosophy; Printing and Publishing; Republicanism; Spanish Literature and Language; Universities.**

BIBLIOGRAPHY

Brand, Peter, and Lino Pertile, eds. *The Cambridge History of Italian Literature.* Rev. ed. Cambridge, U.K., 1999. See articles on Renaissance authors and genres.

Burns, J. H., ed., with the assistance of Mark Goldie. *The Cambridge History of Political Thought, 1450–1700.* Cambridge, U.K., 1991.

Copenhaver, Brian P., and Charles B. Schmitt. *Renaissance Philosophy.* Oxford and New York, 1992. Excellent one-volume survey.

Elton, G. R. *England under the Tudors.* 3rd ed. London, 1991. Standard study.

Ferguson, Wallace K. *The Renaissance in Historical Thought: Five Centuries of Interpretation.* New York, 1948. Classic study of the concept of the Renaissance from the fourteenth century to the twentieth.

Grendler, Paul F. *Schooling in Renaissance Italy: Literacy and Learning, 1300–1600.* Baltimore and London, 1989. Explains humanistic education.

———. *The Universities of the Italian Renaissance.* Baltimore and London, 2002. Survey of all sixteen universities and curriculum changes, 1400–1600.

Grendler, Paul F., et al., eds. *Encyclopedia of the Renaissance.* 6 vols. New York, 1999. Nearly 1,200 articles and 800 illustrations on every aspect of the Renaissance.

Hall, A. Rupert. *The Revolution in Science, 1500–1750.* 3rd ed. London and New York, 1983. Good survey.

Hardin, James, and Max Reinhart, eds. *German Writers of the Renaissance and Reformation, 1280–1580.* Detroit, 1997.

Hays, Denys, and John E. Law. *Italy in the Age of the Renaissance, 1380–1530.* London and New York, 1989.

Hirsch, Rudolf. *Printing, Selling and Reading, 1450–1550.* 2nd printing with a supplemental annotated bibliographical introduction. Wiesbaden, 1974. Excellent short account of the first century of printing.

Kristeller, Paul Oskar. *Renaissance Thought: The Classic, Scholastic, and Humanist Strains.* New York, 1961. Pioneering account of humanism by the most important twentieth-century scholar of the Renaissance.

Lynch, John. *Spain under the Habsburgs.* Vol. 1, *Empire and Absolutism, 1516–1598.* Oxford, 1965.

Mattingly, Garrett. *Renaissance Diplomacy.* Boston, 1955, with many reprints. Classic study not yet superseded.

McFarlane, I. D. *Renaissance France, 1470–1589.* London and New York, 1974. Survey of French literature.

Paoletti, John, and Gary Radke. *Art in Renaissance Italy.* 2nd ed. New York, 2002.

Rabil, Albert, Jr., ed. *Renaissance Humanism: Foundations, Forms, and Legacy.* 3 vols. Philadelphia, 1988. Articles on humanism everywhere in Europe.

Schmitt, Charles B., et al., eds. *The Cambridge History of Renaissance Philosophy.* Cambridge, U.K., 1988. Comprehensive coverage.

Snyder, James. *Northern Renaissance Art: Painting, Sculpture, the Graphic Arts from 1350 to 1575.* New York, 1985.

Stephens, John. *The Italian Renaissance: The Origins of Intellectual and Artistic Change before the Reformation.* London and New York, 1990.

Turner, Jane S., ed. *Encyclopedia of Italian Renaissance and Mannerist Art.* 2 vols. New York, 2000. Part of the 34-volume *Dictionary of Art* (1996).

Wear, A., R. K. French, and I. M. Lonie, eds. *The Medical Renaissance of the Sixteenth Century.* Cambridge, U.K., 1985.

PAUL F. GRENDLER

RENTIERS. Rentiers—men and women who relied on government bonds and other securities for substantial parts of their incomes—became a significant social group in mid-sixteenth-century France, and they remained a presence in French society through the twentieth century. Comparable groups emerged everywhere in early modern Europe, but nowhere else did they have so profound an effect on their societies' economic values and political evolution. As a result, some historians have argued that the rentiers' taste for the low but safe returns offered by government bonds permanently diminished French economic dynamism. Although these claims seem overstated, a high percentage of early modern French capital remained tied up in long-term loans, and many French bourgeois preferred them to the perils of entrepreneurship.

The rentiers' emergence resulted from basic governmental needs. All sixteenth-century states had to raise more money than their predecessors, and with its grandiose international ambitions, France had especially pressing fiscal problems. Government borrowing offered a way to meet some of these, but kings were unattractive debtors. They had the power to manipulate currency values, thus unilaterally diminishing what they owed lenders, and royal bankruptcies were frequent; in any case lending at interest was condemned by the Catholic Church. In 1522 the government of Francis I (ruled 1515–1547) devised bonds guaranteed by the Paris city government (*rentes sur l'hôtel de ville de Paris*) as a way to meet all these objections. Against church prohibitions of usury, the rentes were defined not as a loan but as a sale of property. In exchange for a cash payment from the buyer-lender, the king was to make fixed yearly payments at an interest rate set out in the initial contract. So long as the interest was paid, reimbursement was entirely at the borrower's discretion, making the transaction a sale of income not unlike the fixed feudal rents found throughout

France. Against lenders' doubts about the king's reliability, the transaction used the city's good credit, and high interest rates—8.25 percent in Paris, 10 percent in some of the provinces—allayed fears of currency manipulation.

The rentes proved a popular device for many purposes beyond state finance. Often, through the mediation of local notaries, private borrowers made similar arrangements to meet cash flow problems, and families used them to ease transactions among heirs. Kings remained unreliable, occasionally defaulting on obligations or arbitrarily lowering interest rates on existing loans. But both public and private rentes were attractive enough that members of the middle class continued buying them, and the government could slowly lower interest rates; by 1665 rentes could find buyers at 5 percent, and most bourgeois portfolios included an array of them. The early eighteenth century brought shocks to this credit system. John Law's (1671–1729) introduction of paper money in 1717–1718 provoked a burst of inflation and allowed debtors to pay off loans with depreciated currency, and more flexible instruments of credit emerged. As a result, the classic rente tended to disappear. But the mind-set that it had engendered—a concern for safety and a willingness to tie up funds for long periods—continued to characterize the French bourgeoisie throughout the nineteenth century.

See also **Interest; Law's System.**

BIBLIOGRAPHY

Hoffman, Philip T., Gilles Postel-Vinay, and Jean-Laurent Rosenthal. *Priceless Markets: The Political Economy of Credit in Paris, 1660–1870.* Chicago, 2000.

Schnapper, Bernard. *Les rentes au XVIe siècle: Histoire d'un instrument de crédit.* Paris, 1957.

JONATHAN DEWALD

REPRESENTATIVE INSTITU-TIONS.

Europe in the early modern period can be thought of as a patchwork of representative institutions—local, regional, and national—from parish vestries, juries, and village or town councils to parliaments, Cortes, *Stände, sejm,* diets, and *zemsky sobors.* The only part of the Continent where representative institutions were not important was the Ottoman-ruled Balkans. This discussion is limited to the most politically significant bodies: Estates and city or town governments.

THE BUSINESS OF ESTATES

The regional and national assemblies collectively labeled Estates differed enormously. They included the Estates of tiny Gex, a poor territory on the French-Swiss border, and the Imperial Diet of the Holy Roman Empire, where electors and princes sat alongside the representatives of some sixty-six imperial cities. A few assemblies met almost annually, like the Polish *sejm;* the majority met intermittently, and might almost be called events rather than institutions. Most Estates had three houses—for clergy, nobles, and townsmen—but Sweden and the kingdom of Aragón had four; England, Ireland, Poland, and Hungary had only two; and Scotland's Parliament was unicameral. In Poland and Hungary, the upper house was reserved for magnates, the lower for gentry, while in England, whose legislature originated as a feudal court, the bishops (and some abbots, before the Reformation) were integrated into a House of Lords that met alongside a Commons dominated by lesser landowners. In the Estates of Holland, by contrast, the nobility were granted only one seat. Some Estates that are hardly remembered today—those of Sicily, Upper Austria, and East Prussia—were full of energy and initiative in the early modern period. By the eighteenth century, many Estates were moribund, but, with the exception of those of Scotland and the crown of Aragón, no national Estates were abolished before 1789.

The number and variety of the Estates of early modern Europe indicate that they did not have a common origin. They were established between the twelfth and fifteenth centuries because of particular circumstances such as fiscal or constitutional emergencies, and they served specific purposes. While they were often created at the command of a ruler, and could be seen as an extension of his or her council, the members of Estates in many parts of Europe did not hesitate to assert an authority that arose from society as a whole. So whom did they represent, and how?

Today, we see political representation as flowing from direct elections. In early modern Europe, however, representation was an amorphous state of affairs in which an individual claimed to speak for others by virtue of some process of legitimation. None of the Estates was fully elective, and none was chosen by more than a small fraction of the population for which they spoke. The powerful provincial Estates of the United Provinces of the Netherlands were elected by 2,000 individuals. About 300,000 men voted for the British Parliament in 1714, but this was only 5.5 percent of the population. Everywhere in Europe, the vast majority of men excluded from voting were peasants or rural laborers. They had formal representation in a few places: the Alpine regions of Austria, Germany, and Switzerland (although Swiss townsmen began to chip away at peasant rights after 1653); in the Dutch province of West Friesland; in Denmark until 1627; in Sweden if they were living on royal estates; and in Russia's *zemsky sobor* if they paid taxes. Some constituencies of the French Estates-General allowed peasants to participate in 1560–1561, many more in 1789. A national system of universal male suffrage was not contemplated until the eighteenth century. As for female suffrage, it remained theoretically unthinkable.

Clearly, the Estates of Europe did not directly reflect the political will of the majority of the people, but were chosen by various types of privileged groups. What, then, set them apart from other nonelected assemblies or councils? It was not their purpose or their makeup. Rather, it was their legal, historical, or traditional claim to represent the nation or the people. Separately, they were the privileged few; collectively, they stood for the homeland or *patria*, an imagined community that might be a kingdom, a nation, or a province. Ideally, they spoke not for themselves but for the good of the whole.

The business of Estates was fiscal, legislative, and administrative. Many of them also retained judicial functions, such as receiving petitions, creating special courts, and giving pardons. The fiscal role of Estates, their ability to grant or refuse taxes, has rightly been considered crucial to their survival. It kept the Estates strong in Languedoc, where representatives not only voted on royal revenues, but also collected them; it weakened the Imperial Diet, which had too little authority to deliver on any promises of revenues it made to the emperor. Where fiscal control was lacking, as in Russia or the French

pays d'élection (provinces that had no Estates; instead, they had courts called Élections), it was not necessary to summon the Estates except in situations of political crisis.

The Estates with the greatest control over finances, however, were not necessarily the most likely to thrive. A strong monarchy would try to suppress them; a weak monarchy would be threatened by their power. The English Parliament, seen by many as the most successful of all Estates, was normally willing to compromise with the crown. After 1660, it granted an annual civil list to cover royal expenses. Parliament scrutinized accounts, but did not run the fiscal bureaucracy except during the brief Commonwealth period (1649–1660). The Castilian Cortes, on the other hand, made royal revenues conditional on mutual contracts, and itself administered the main excise tax, known as the *millones* because it was calculated in millions of ducats. The Cortes was too strong for a debilitated crown, which felt obliged to transfer the administration of the *millones* to city councils in 1658, and did not dare summon the Cortes of Castile again. By the late seventeenth century, in fact, many of the Estates of western and central Europe had been too successful for their own good in the sphere of fiscal control. Rulers had decided to cease consulting them and to live off revenues that did not require their approval. The Estates of Brandenburg, for example, became fiscally irrelevant after 1667 when the elector secured an excise tax with the support of the towns. To avoid begging favors from the tumultuous East Prussian Estates, the elector allowed the city of Königsberg to choose its own method of raising taxes.

The second important role of the Estates was legislative. Their approval for the promulgation of new laws was fixed in the privileges of the crown of Aragón, the 1505 *Nihil Novi* ('nothing new') constitution of Poland (which forbade the introduction of new laws without the approval of the *sejm* and senate), and the 1576 Union of Utrecht that created the United Provinces. In England, it became impossible, during the course of the seventeenth century, for the ruler to impose a law without consulting Parliament. James II tried this in 1687 with his Declaration of Indulgence (calling for religious toleration), and the results were disastrous. Legislation by the Estates was not fully established in Sweden until the reign of Queen Christina (1640–1654); it was then self-curtailed in 1680, revived in 1720, and revoked in 1772. Elsewhere, the Estates might be consulted on big changes—the Reformation and the Royal Law in Denmark, the Tridentine decrees (issued by the Council of Trent and central to the Counter-Reformation) in France, or the Russian legal reforms of 1648–1649—but new laws were not regularly submitted to them. The actions of the enlightened monarchs of eighteenth-century Europe were hardly ever approved by representative bodies. Joseph II (ruled 1765–1790), unlike James II (ruled 1685–1688), was not seriously challenged by the Estates of the Habsburg lands when he proclaimed his own Edict of Toleration in 1781. The emperor told the Estates of Brabant in 1789: "I do not need your consent to do good."

The administrative role of Estates was significant in parts of France, Germany, and the Habsburg lands. There the Estates had their own salaried bureaucracies, which in the Austrian archduchies outweighed those of the ruler until the late eighteenth century. Throughout central Europe, local "dietines" (*sejmiki* in Poland, *landfridy* in Bohemia) were responsible for collecting taxes, maintaining roads and bridges, repairing fortifications, and even raising troops. In Bohemia after 1627, the dietines carried on these functions in the absence of the crown Estates. The Estates of Britanny actually increased their administrative duties in the eighteenth century. (Historians who argue for the decline of Estates should consider such activities more carefully.)

In general, the fiscal and legislative authority of European Estates peaked in the fifteenth and sixteenth centuries as the result of dynastic changes, the Reformation, and the financial demands of monarchs. The huge costs of war and heightened religious tensions put enormous pressure on the Estates in the 1600s. Some failed to meet it and were no longer summoned; others rebelled, with mixed results. By the eighteenth century, they were either entrenched in power or viewed as useless.

Even the most abject of Estates, however, retained a ceremonial importance as the symbolic "point of contact" between ruler and people. The elaborate rituals that opened and closed their meetings served to emphasize the point. In addition, their sessions usually entailed social events and conspicuous consumption that bound elites together and provided a healthy stimulus to the economies of towns in which they gathered.

ESTATES AND POLITICS

The Estates in many parts of early modern Europe played a vital part in governance. This was true in kingdoms where royal dominion was limited (where it was "political and regal," to use the term coined by the English chief Justice Sir John Fortescue [c. 1394–1476]), but it also applied to purely "regal" kingdoms with no clear limits on royal power, like Castile or France. It was chiefly as a result of religious conflict that the Estates acquired a higher theoretical significance. The political writers known as "monarchomachs" claimed that the Estates exercised greater and more ancient authority than that of the king, and were usually ardent Calvinists; for example, François Hotman (*Francogallia*, 1573), Hubert Languet and Philip Duplessis-Mornay (*Vindiciae contra Tyrannos* [Revenge against tyrants], 1579) in France; Théodore de Bèze (*The Right of Magistrates*, 1573) in Geneva; and John Althusius (*Politics*, 1603) in Germany. They argued that rulers should be responsible to magistrates (Althusius called them "ephors," using the term for the powerful ancient Spartan officials), and Hotman was explicit in identifying this sovereign body with the Estates-General of France. The aim of the monarchomachs was to question the authority of kings who were hostile to Calvinism; Hotman even changed his mind about the supremacy of Estates when a Protestant, Henry of Navarre (ruled 1589–1610), became heir to the French throne. Their opponents maintained that kings held sovereignty either by patriarchal right (Jean Bodin [1530–1596]) or by an irrevocable grant from the people (Hugo Grotius [1583–1645], Thomas Hobbes [1588–1679]). However, none of the critics of the monarchomachs went so far as to claim that representative institutions were unnecessary.

The monarchomachs had considerable influence on Dutch political writers, as well as on John Locke (1632–1704). Althusius was widely cited in Sweden. He influenced both the rebellious Lower Austrian Estates in 1618 and the authors of the 1638 Scottish National Covenant. Yet for most members of Estates, the theories of the monarchomachs were irrelevant. They had no intention of challenging the basis of royal authority, although they might oppose the ruler on specific points. The sort of political writing that most impressed them was not theoretical but historical, like John Selden's (1584–1654) researches into parliamentary privileges or Francisco Gilabert's (d. 1552) vindication of the constitutional autonomy of Catalonia. The investigation of the legal rights of the Estates of the Holy Roman Empire preoccupied generations of German public lawyers, down to John Jacob Moser (1701–1785).

When serious confrontations occurred between ruler and Estates, it was because some extraordinary factor had been introduced into their working relationship. In the revolt of the Netherlands against Philip II (ruled 1556–1598), the factor was religion. This also disturbed the French Estates-General that met at Blois in 1588. Dominated by the Catholic League, it bitterly opposed the succession of the Protestant Henry of Navarre. Five years later, the Estates-General were irregularly convoked by the league in order to sanction the choice of an alternative Catholic monarch. Not surprisingly, the Bourbons never regained confidence in the national legislature. The 1618 rebellion of the Bohemian Estates was largely inspired by religion, as were the English Civil Wars (1642–1651) between king and Parliament. The causes of the 1640 rebellion in Catalonia were primarily financial, although they were aggravated by Catalan patriotism. The *Diputació,* the standing committee of the Cortes, opposed the imposition by the crown of military billeting and sharing of the tax burden; it then summoned the Estates, which took the lead in a rebellion lasting twelve years. In contrast, in Sweden it was Queen Christina herself who encouraged the *Riksdag* to attack the authority of her aristocratic councillors in 1650.

The Estates did not always emerge weaker from these confrontations. The Dutch provincial Estates (which chose the Estates-General) became the most powerful element in the new national polity. A purged English Parliament put the king to death and governed a republic from 1649 to 1653; after the Restoration, in 1660, it recouped its strength as an ally of the crown and the established church. Its opposition to the succession of a Catholic heir allowed Parliament to become the mainstay of royal government after the Glorious Revolution of 1688. The Swedish *Riksdag* cemented its relationship with the monarchy by supporting the *reduktion* ('restitution') of crown lands in 1680. Between 1720 and 1772, it exercised greater authority than the ruler, to the point of creating a secret committee to which the monarch had to report. In Catalonia, a major rebellion against the Spanish monarchy, led by the Cortes, broke out in 1640. Although it eventually failed, the *Diputats* ('commissioners') of the Cortes continued to play a crucial administrative role. They were abolished in 1716 after making the serious mistake of backing the losing claimant in the War of the Spanish Succession (1701–1714). Even the French Estates-General were summoned again in the crisis of 1614; elections were held in 1649 and 1651, during the Fronde, but no further session took place until 1789. Only the Bohemian Estates lost completely: except for attendance at coronation ceremonies, they were not summoned by the Habsburg kings for the remainder of the early modern period.

Enough has already been said here to cast doubt on the thesis that the Estates were generally in decline. Yet by the eighteenth century many of them had ceased to meet (the combined Cortes of Castile and Aragón was summoned only three times after 1716), and others had become rubber-stamp assemblies, especially those whose authority was vested in a standing committee, as in Bavaria. Only a few, like the British Parliament, the Dutch Estates-General, the Swedish *Riksdag,* and the Polish *sejm,* continued to control finances and legislation. In the rest of Europe, rulers were able to override the Estates. Maria Theresa of Austria (ruled 1740–1780) completely ignored the Carinthian Estates in imposing a hefty annual contribution for the support of the army in 1750, and her military governors in Transylvania and Croatia ran roughshod over the Estates there. Nevertheless, the empress was careful to win passage of the contribution through the other Austrian Estates, which were more compliant, and she put up with a great deal of obstruction from the powerful Diet of Hungary. As always, monarchs were willing to consult Estates when they felt sure of a friendly reception, or were afraid to do without them. Frederick II (ruled 1740–1786) did not have to cope with Estates in his Prussian kingdom, but a nobleman once told him to his face that his refusal to hold a diet did not mean he enjoyed unlimited power. The Estates of Königsberg were gone, but not forgotten. Representative bodies had not lost their legitimating power, as the autocratic Russian tsars were well aware. Peter I (ruled 1682–1725) brought into being a consultative Senate in 1711, and Catherine the Great (ruled 1762–1796) created provincial assemblies of nobles in 1785.

By the late eighteenth century, the threat to Estates came as much from patriotism as from monarchical despotism. Gustavus III (ruled 1771–1792) exploited patriotic sentiments in clipping the authority of the Swedish *Riksdag* in 1772. George III of Great Britain (ruled 1760–1820) also played the patriot king in challenging his faction-ridden Parliaments. Some of his subjects adhered to a patriotism that was critical of both monarchy and Parliament. These radical patriots began to demand reform of a legislative system that was seen as unrepresentative of the people. Inspired by writers such as James Burgh (*Political Disquisitions,* 1774–1775) and John Cartwright (*Take Your Choice!,* 1776), the reformers became more vocal during the crisis of the War of American Independence (1775–1783), and formed a network of associations that rivaled Parliament itself as a reflection of the national will. Similarly, in the United Provinces after the ousting of the *stadtholder* (leader of the United Provinces of the Netherlands) in 1785, and in Poland after the first partition, radical patriots began to discuss an assembly representing the whole people, but Prussian and Russian cannon silenced such proposals. Belgian patriots established an Estates-General early in 1789 and drew up a constitution based on the American Articles of Confederation. Democrats, led by the lawyer J. F. Vonck (1743–1792), called for suffrage reform, but they were suppressed by the clergy and the Habsburg authorities.

In France, the British model of representative government had been admired by Montesquieu (1689–1755) and Voltaire (1694–1778), although the latter gently mocked its partisan divisions. By the 1760s, the younger philosophes (French intellectuals of the French Enlightenment), like Denis Diderot (1713–1784) or the Swiss-born democrat Jean-Jacques Rousseau (1712–1778), had little good to say about the "corrupt" British parliamentary system. Rousseau argued for the sovereignty of a "general will" that was the sum of all individual wills. Meanwhile, French politics was convulsed between 1749 and 1774 by the claims of the parlements, the supreme law courts, to represent the nation. In the early 1760s, the parlements backed the Estates of Brittany against an authoritarian provincial governor. Exhausted by such resistance, and facing bankruptcy, the ministers of Louis XVI (ruled 1774–1792) drafted a proposal to set up new assemblies in provinces that had none. The plan was rejected by the parlements, and the king was obliged in 1789 to convoke the national legislative body, the Estates-General of France. When it declared itself a national assembly, it sent a message to Estates throughout Europe that they must either represent the "general will" or admit that they were merely bastions of aristocratic privilege. Within the next century, all of them either reformed or became defunct.

CITY AND TOWN GOVERNMENTS

Alongside the Estates stood a vast range of municipal and communal institutions that can be regarded as representative of local interests. The most celebrated of them were the Italian city-states. While they did not adhere to a single form of government, most of the city-states combined aspects of the guild-based, quasi-democratic medieval communes with councils of wealthy citizens who regarded themselves as the equivalents of Roman senators. The political decline of the city-states was once a standard assumption among historians, but it has now been qualified. Those cities whose constitutions were revised in the early sixteenth century (Genoa, 1528; Venice, 1528–1529; Lucca, 1532; Florence, 1532; Milan, 1541) tended to survive in this form throughout the early modern period. Aspects of representative government through councils of leading citizens persisted even in Florence under the Medici dukes, or in Milan under its imperial governor. Throughout Italy, the representative principle continued to be important in town government, even in areas subject to the dominion of a hereditary prince. Towns from Vicenza to tiny San Ginesio in the Marche drew up constitutions for municipal governance that included representative institutions. Many were quite democratic. For example, in the Tuscan town of Montepulciano, all male heads of household who were natives or long-term residents were admitted to the *parlamento.*

In Germany, as in Italy, representative institutions endured in the cities and many small towns throughout the early modern period, but they became increasingly oligarchic. The Imperial Free Cities, which were subject only to the Holy Roman emperor, were governed by patriciates that dominated the municipal councils. At Nuremberg, a list of families whose members were eligible for civic office was drawn up in 1521 and adhered to thereafter. In smaller German cities, however, oligarchy did not preclude fairly broad representation. One in ten male citizens of Weissenburg served on the town councils during the eighteenth century, although the chances of serving were far higher if one's name was Roth, Preu, or Oberdorfer. Guilds were active in many small German towns (not at Nuremberg, where they had been abolished), and they were often formally represented on town councils. In some areas of Germany, representative institutions extended into the countryside as well. In Württemberg, after the Thirty Years' War (1618–1648), adult males in every village elected a *Schultheiss* ('chief administrator'), a *Bürgermeister* ('mayor'), a *Gericht* ('administrative committee'), and a *Rat* ('deliberative council'), along with representatives to the Estates. Württemberg's highly conservative governing bodies were intended mainly to preserve public order and moral discipline, yet in many respects the duchy became the most perfect example in Europe of a state based from top to bottom on representative institutions.

The German model of urban oligarchy, occasionally combined with guild representation, extended into the Baltic, Poland, Austria, Bohemia, the United Provinces, and Switzerland (at Bern, only 250 families were legally *regimentsfähig* ['qualified to rule']). It was in such self-governing towns that Protestantism, with its promise of release from clerical interference, made rapid gains in the sixteenth century. Capital cities within monarchical states, however, often endured more direct control from the ruler.

Stockholm, like any other German imperial city, had a burgomaster and council, but they were royally appointed. On the other hand, it also had an assembly of elders that could resist the crown's fiscal demands. In the countryside, moreover, the Swedish peasants could assemble at a traditional *häradsting* ('district court') at which jurymen, assisted by the public, made decisions about issues of local concern.

The political institutions of English borough towns were uniquely linked to those of the central state, and depended on royal charters to escape the control of landowners. Their right to send representatives to Parliament meant that their affairs were always of interest to the crown. National events like the Reformation (sixteenth century), Civil Wars (1642–1651), Exclusion Crisis (1678–1683), or Glorious Revolution (1688) could result in wholesale changes in their governing personnel. It was not until the early eighteenth century that most English towns could sink into the political torpor that their leading families craved. Guilds were of little significance in England, with the notable exception of London, where company freemen elected a common council that shared power with an oligarchic court of aldermen. London was strongly parliamentarian in the Civil War, and firmly Whig in 1688. Its politics thereafter were marked by factionalism, and after 1760 by the efflorescence of various radical movements, usually short-lived.

England had towns without royal charters where governance was essentially manorial or parochial. Scotland, too, had "private burghs," and in France many small municipalities remained in aristocratic control, such as Angers, where the *seigneur* ('lord') nominated the town council. Poland's "private towns" were created by noblemen and entirely lacked representative institutions. In contrast, Polish peasants had the right to elect village councils.

In France and Spain, town government was profoundly affected by the sale of offices. French magistrates could purchase their positions from the crown, and in some cases, such as Paris after 1581, they had the right to pass them on to their heirs. In Spain, resident aristocrats bought town offices and passed ordinances to prevent those of lesser status from sharing their power. They could also resign in favor of a designated successor. In both kingdoms, elections were usually held only for the lowest administrators, such as market or police officials.

However undemocratic they may have been, urban institutions did serve to protect municipal liberties and privileges. Such independence came under increasing attack after 1660. Louis XIV (ruled 1643–1715) made a concerted attempt to transfer urban authority to provincial *intendants* ('administrative officials'). In newly conquered Alsace, the liberties of towns like Strasbourg were stripped away by the French government, and the Spanish Bourbons initiated a similar policy of appointing royal administrators to take charge of urban affairs. The Austrian Habsburgs took away the fiscal powers of Bohemian towns and shifted policing throughout the hereditary lands to the central government. In Prussia and Italy, bureaucrats increasingly usurped municipal duties or filled civic offices. Yet Peter I, who tolerated no challenges to his absolute authority, saw the lack of representative bodies in Russian towns as a weakness. He attempted, without much success, to create town councils in 1699 and 1721, in exchange for regular taxation. Finally, Catherine II decreed in 1785 that all chartered towns would have a council elected by male householders.

There was no real contradiction between the actions of the Russian tsars and those of the rulers of other lands. All monarchs perceived urban government as an administrative tool to be altered according to circumstances. Fiscal policies often required consultation with town magistrates; on other matters, they could be bypassed. Most civic leaders consented to this approach. They had little desire for town councils to become legislatures, or to provide a voice for the people.

Still, there were always those who felt that towns should represent more of their citizens. Whether motivated by religion or patriotism, egalitarianism or opportunism, complaints about urban oligarchy were consistently expressed throughout the early modern period. In Frankfurt, they resulted in a popular and anti-Semitic revolt in 1614 (the so-called Fettmilch uprising, named after its leader, Vincent Fettmilch), as well as a series of political confrontations in 1705–1732. Agitation against the ruling families of Geneva began in 1707 and culminated in a brief takeover by the opponents of oligarchy in 1782. Before 1789, however, no significant or long-lasting reform took place in civic institutions anywhere in Europe, with the exception of Russia, where it was carried out by the monarch. Urban democracy would begin with the communes of the French Revolution.

See also **Democracy; Estates-General, French; Intendants; Law; Parlements; Parliament.**

BIBLIOGRAPHY

Carsten, F. L. *Princes and Parliaments in Germany, from the Fifteenth to the Eighteenth Century.* Oxford, 1959. Detailed treatment of a neglected subject.

Evans, R. J. W., and T. V. Thomas, eds. *Crown, Church, and Estates: Central European Politics in the Sixteenth and Seventeenth Centuries.* New York, 1991. Important essays on Estates in Habsburg lands.

Graves, Michael A. R. *The Parliaments of Early Modern Europe.* Harlow, U.K., 2001. Comparative survey of Estates down to late seventeenth century.

Hoffmann, Philip T., and Kathryn Norberg, eds. *Fiscal Crises, Liberty, and Representative Government, 1450–1789.* Stanford, 1994. Essays on England, the Netherlands, Castile, and France.

Jago, Charles. "Habsburg Absolutism and the Cortes of Castile." *American Historical Review* 86 (1981): 307–326. Important article on the continuing significance of the Cortes.

Koenigsberger, H. G. *Estates and Revolutions: Essays in Early Modern European History.* Ithaca, N.Y., 1971. Essays on Sicilian, Piedmontese, and Netherlandish Estates.

———. *Politicians and Virtuosi: Essays in Early Modern History.* London, 1986. Contains an influential article on "dominium regale" and "dominium politicum et regale."

Major, J. Russell. *Representative Government in Early Modern France.* New Haven, 1980. Thorough narrative of history of provincial Estates as well as Estates-General.

Myers, A. R. *Parliaments and Estates in Europe to 1789.* London, 1975. Still a valuable source of information.

Parliaments, Estates, and Representation 1– (1980–). Journal devoted to the history of representative institutions.

Walker, Mack. *Johann Jakob Moser and the Holy Roman Empire of the German Nation.* Chapel Hill, N.C., 1981. Biography of leading public lawyer and defender of Estates.

PAUL MONOD

REPRODUCTION. *See* **Sexual Difference, Theories of; Sexuality and Sexual Behavior.**

REPUBLIC OF LETTERS. The "Republic of Letters" *(Respublica Literarum),* a term apparently coined by the humanist Francesco Barbaro in 1417, was first intended to designate the community of early modern scholars who restored the ancient "Orators, Poets, Historians, Astronomers, and Grammarians" who would otherwise have been lost forever; but the term later encompassed other writers in the emergent public sphere of early modern Europe. Also connected to the term was the international network of the European university, which was a basically ecclesiastical foundation, but which, through the faculties of arts and law, contributed also to a large secular intelligentsia. Between the fourteenth and sixteenth centuries, hundreds of thousands of students flocked to the eighty or ninety universities in Europe, thousands of them as foreigners in the "nations" of Paris, Bologna, Prague, Oxford, and Cambridge. For example, in Paris in the second quarter of the sixteenth century, 1,500 or more students registered annually in the arts faculty of the university there, including, contemporaneously, François Rabelais, John Calvin, and Ignatius of Loyola, who each had an extraordinary impact on public opinion in their century and long afterwards.

The humanist movement, which continued traditions of disputation and learned pilgrimages beyond the university, expanded this increasingly secular intelligentsia through book-hunting travels and epistolary exchange. The correspondence of Desiderius Erasmus and Nicolas-Claude Fabri de Peiresc, for example, added to and consolidated the information and "good letters" that print culture made available to the growing community of scholars. The printed book was at once a divine gift, invaluable for spreading religious truth, and a devilish invention, open likewise to the dissemination of heresy and treason. What mainly held this "republic" together was not virtue but learning, including a common language (a more or less classical Latin, with its treasury of topics and tropes), a common, if highly disputed, view of the Christian past, and a devotion to the literary tradition essential for communication and meaningful disputes between contemporaries and between "ancients and moderns."

The Republic of Letters had its own special history and mythology. As Noel d'Argonne wrote in the seventeenth century, "The Republic of Letters is of very ancient origin . . . and existed before the Flood. It embraces the whole world and is composed of people of all nations, social conditions, ages, and sexes, neither women nor even children being excluded. All languages, ancient and modern, are spoken. Arts are joined to letters, and the mechanical arts also have their place in it." This republic was coterminous with Christendom, he continued, but differed from it in political as well as ecclesiastical terms. "The politics of this State consists more in words, in maxims and reflections, than in actions and in accomplishments. People take their strength from eloquence and reasoning. Their trade is entirely spiritual and their wealth meager. Glory and immortality are sought above all things. . . ."

That is not to say that he neglected the negative side of the Republic. In contrast to the medieval ideal of religious and political unity, d'Argonne argued, concerning the Republic of Letters, "its religion is not uniform, and its manners, as in all republics, are a mixture of good and bad, both piety and libertinage being found. Sects are numerous, and every day new forms appear. The whole State is divided among philosophers, medical doctors, jurists, historians, mathematicians, orators, grammarians, and poets; and each has its own laws." For d'Argonne, most divisive of all was the art of criticism, which recognized no superior in things literary or philosophical, and which set itself up as the final arbiter of meaning: "Justice is administered by the Critics, often with more severity than judgment. . . . They cut, slice up, or add as they please, and no author can escape once he falls into their hands."

The Reformation and Counter-Reformation exploited the printing press and promoted monumental works of cooperative scholarship as well as bitter controversies. Yet the negative and positive aspects of the new invention expanded the Republic of Letters through doctrinal debates, incentives to scholarship, and efforts to reach a wider public and popular culture. Though signaled normally by mastery of ancient languages, membership was eventually extended to writers in modern languages, since the community itself was referred to in the vernacular: "Deutsche Republik der Gelehrten," "Republyk der Geleerden," "Republique des lettres," "República literaria," and "Republic of Letters." There were also analogous and overlapping learned international groups, such as the community of jurists (*respublica jurisconsultorum*), that

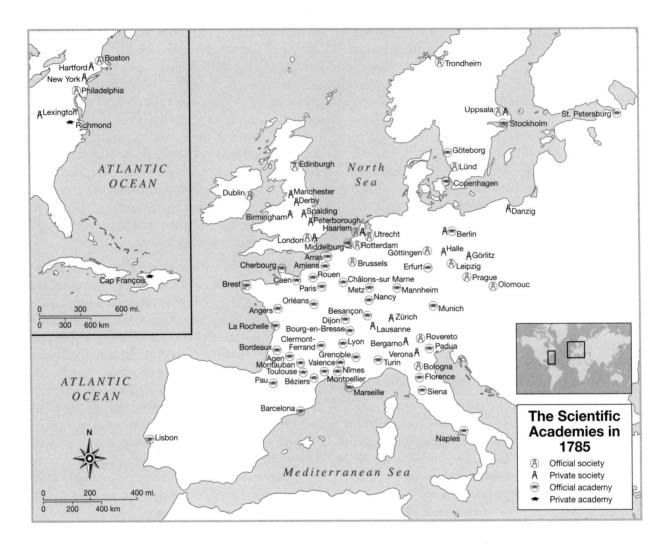

The Scientific Academies in 1785

Ⓐ Official society
Ⱥ Private society
⊕ Official academy
🐦 Private academy

gave further coherence to the community of "intellectuals," as it would be called in later generations.

The foundations of this international intelligentsia were laid by the media of largely printed communication, including correspondence, books, and especially journals, which represented the avantgarde as well as the rear guard of doctrinal and scholarly accomplishment and conflict. The *Journal des savants* (1665), the *Philosophical Transactions* (1665), the *Giornale de' letterati* (1668), the *Acta Eruditorum* (1682), and especially Pierre Bayle's *Nouvelles de la République des lettres* (1684) established the forum for exchanges among men and women of letters, from Lorenzo Valla and Erasmus to Voltaire, Jean-Jacques Rousseau, and Madame Necker. These periodicals contained not only articles but also book reviews, open letters, obituaries, and other genres of learned exhange, which, in the face of growing practices of censorship and suppression, constituted the material base for the critical discourse of the Enlightenment and its revolutionary aftermath.

In the Republic of Letters the stress was normally on the "public" aspect of intellectual exchange and propagation of ideas, but the intimidation of authority and institutions of censorship encouraged another dimension of discourse: "forbidden best-sellers" (investigated by Robert Darnton) and especially "clandestine literature" (revealed by Richard Popkin and others). In recent years scholars have uncovered a vast amount of anti-Christian literature, in which skepticism, libertinism, free thought, naturalism, "atheism," Judaism, and Spinozism commingled in a counterculture based on the circulation of published and manuscript materials—most spectacularly the quasi-legendary treatise on the "Three Impostors" (Moses,

Jesus, and Muhammad). This was a whole world of subversion in the Republic of Letters which is still in the process of being mapped, though the old questions remain, including (as Darnton writes): Do books cause revolutions?

See also **Academies, Learned; Ancients and Moderns; Bayle, Pierre; Erasmus, Desiderius; Humanists and Humanism; Journals, Literary; Latin; Peiresc, Nicolas-Claude Fabri de; Public Opinion.**

BIBLIOGRAPHY

Primary Sources

d'Agonne, Noel. *Mélanges d'histoire et de literature.* 4th ed. Paris, 1740, pp. 166–167.

Goodhart, Gordon, Phyllis Walter, ed. and trans. *Two Renaissance Book Hunters: The Letters of Poggius Bracciolini to Nicolaus de Niccolis.* New York, 1974.

Secondary Sources

Berti, Silvia, Françoise Charles-Daubert, and Richard H. Popkin, eds. *Heterodoxy, Spinozism, and Free Thought in Early-Eighteenth-Century Europe: Studies in the Traité des trois imposteurs.* Dordrecht, 1996.

Bots, Hans, and Françoise Waquet. *La république des lettres.* Paris, 1997.

Darnton, Robert. *The Literary Underground of the Old Regime.* Cambridge, Mass., 1982.

Goodman, Dena. *The Republic of Letters: A Cultural History of the French Enlightenment.* Ithaca, N.Y., 1994.

Grimm, Gunter E. *Literatur und Gelehrtentum in Deutschland.* Tübingen, 1983.

Israel, Jonathan. *Radical Enlightenment: Philosophy and the Making of Modernity 1650–1750.* Oxford, 2001.

Jaumann, Herbert. "Ratio clausa: Die Trennung von Erkenntnis und Kommunikation in gelehrten Abhandlungen zur *Respublica literaria* um 1700 unter der europäische Kontext." In *Res Publica Literaria,* edited by Sebastian Neumeister and Conrad Wiedemann, pp. 409–429. Wiesbaden, 1987.

Levine, Joseph M. *The Battle of the Books: History and Literature in the Augustine Age.* Ithaca, N.Y., 1991.

McKenna, Antony. "Spinoza in Clandestine Manuscripts: A Bibliographical Survey of Recent Research." In *Disguised and Overt Spinozism around 1700,* edited by Wiep van Bunge and Wim Klever. Leiden, 1996.

Ruegg, Walter, ed. *A History of the University in Europe.* 2 vols. Cambridge, U.K., 1992–1996.

Wacquet, Françoise. *Latin, or the Empire of a Sign: From the Sixteenth to the Twentieth Century.* Translated by John Howe. London, 2001.

DONALD KELLEY

REPUBLICANISM. Broadly defined, republicanism means a preference for nonmonarchical government and a strong dislike of hereditary monarchy. Narrowly defined, and in its early modern context, it means self-government by a community of citizens in a city-state.

Republicanism is a prominent concept in the history of political thought. Republican ideology claimed that citizens of republics enjoyed a liberty unknown to the subjects of monarchies because they were bound by laws that they themselves had made, not the personal whim of an individual monarch. In the early modern period, republicanism had special relevance in Italy (where Florence and Venice became the most famous republics in early modern history), Switzerland (a federation of autonomous rural and urban cantons that had never been effectively governed by a monarch), Germany (where many free imperial cities maintained a high degree of autonomy within the Holy Roman Empire), the Netherlands (where a new state, the Dutch Republic, was born in the sixteenth century out of a revolt against the Spanish monarchy), England (where, in the mid-seventeenth century, a revolt against the monarchy led to a short period of kingless government that paved the way for parliamentary government under a constitutional monarchy), and the United States of America (which revolted against the British monarchy and became a federal congressional republic in the 1770s). Early modern theorists whose writings are relevant to republicanism include Niccolò Machiavelli (1469–1527), Francesco Guicciardini (1483–1540), Thomas More (1478–1535), Thomas Hobbes (1588–1679), John Milton (1608–1674), John Locke (1632–1704), Algernon Sidney (1622–1683), Charles-Louis de Secondat de Montesquieu (1689–1755), and Jean-Jacques Rousseau (1712–1778). What follows is an introduction to republics and republicanism, not a survey of thinkers or their ideas. Three institutional levels within republican government will be distinguished: the voting assembly, the intermediate council, and the executive magistracies. The differences between three models will also be emphasized: direct democracy, republicanism, and parliamentary representation.

ANCIENT AND MEDIEVAL BACKGROUND

Greek city-states, when not ruled by tyrants, governed themselves by some form of direct democracy: an assembly of all the adult male citizens, meeting and voting frequently to pass legislation, make decisions, act as a high court, and elect (from their own ranks) the short-term members of the intermediate councils and holders of magistracies and military commands. The Greek model of direct democracy was replicated in European history only at the village level, notably in Switzerland, and in the imaginations of Jean-Jacques Rousseau and the proto-Romantics.

In contrast, the Roman republican model became prominent in later European history. Compared to direct democracy, it was marked by greater social stratification and the dominance of (largely hereditary) elites. Livy's history of the early Roman republic depicted the foundation of the republic in 753 B.C.E. as a revolt in the name of liberty by members of leading families against a primeval monarchy. The earliest group of ruling families, and the clans they spawned, called themselves "patricians" and formed a hereditary status group that attempted to monopolize political power against the rest of the population—the plebeians. Livy records and dramatizes bitter social and political conflict between the patricians and the plebeians, but the latter succeeded over several centuries in breaking the patrician monopoly on the political institutions, so that the political elite included members of both groups.

Instead of a simple voting assembly, Rome had a complicated system of assemblies in which individual preferences were combined into bloc votes, with preponderant weight given to the blocs in which men of higher status and higher socioeconomic class were enrolled. There was a semi-formal nobility consisting of families whose members, past and present, patrician or plebeian, had competed successfully in the annual elections of magistrates in the assembly, and entry by "new men" (ones without an office-holding ancestor) into the nobility was possible, though never easy. The nobility governed the republic through an intermediate council that had no real precedent in Greek history and became one of the most famous political institutions of all time: the Roman Senate. All former magistrates were senators, and though they often stood for election and left the Senate for a year to hold a magistracy or a military command, they always returned to it at the end of their term: membership was for life. The Senate was the locus of debate and decision making in Rome. Many of Cicero's most famous works are political speeches delivered during deliberations in the Senate or prior to a vote in one of the assemblies.

Social conflict never disappeared from the Roman republic, but that did not prevent its armies of citizen-soldiers from making it the greatest conquest state in European history. The Roman republic ended in chaos and was transformed into an empire ruled by a monarchical emperor, but the Senate survived for as long as the empire did; its members, though, became a hereditary status group, no longer the winners of electoral contests held in a voting assembly. The historian Tacitus (c. 55–c. 117 C.E.) vividly described the despotic behavior of the early Roman emperors, the corrupt courts that surrounded them, the servile and fearful behavior of the Senators, and the decline of free debate in the Senate.

The European cities of the medieval and early modern periods were born as communes: sworn associations of male heads of households who collectively claimed freedom from feudal overlordship. The primordial institution of the commune was the assembly of all the citizens, as in the ancient Mediterranean cities. Each commune was a small republic, and the story of republicanism in Europe is largely the story of Europe's cities. Europe was the only area of world civilization in which so many and such autonomous city republics emerged. In every communal city of Europe, as in the ancient Mediterranean, citizenship was a privileged hereditary status to which newcomers were not granted easy or automatic access. In each city, families belonging to the earlier strata tried to monopolize political power, like the Roman patricians, and were challenged from below by ambitious families and rising status and socioeconomic groups. In each there was a complex structure of councils and executive committees, but the primitive communal institution, the voting assembly of all the citizens, ceased to be summoned regularly in most cities.

The European cities were the motor of a dynamic European economy based on free rather than slave labor; this was a fundamental difference between the city-states of the ancient world and the European cities. In Italy a number of cities (Milan was an example) went from republican (or "communal") government to monarchical rule by a princely family at the close of the Middle Ages, but in others, like Florence and Venice, republican structures persisted. Florence and Venice were not the only republican city-states in Italy, but they were the only ones to conquer not just the adjacent countryside but many other smaller cities as well, thereby building up large territorial states.

Elsewhere in Europe, and even in some parts of the Italian peninsula, the feudal system was giving birth to a type of political institution unknown to the ancient world or the republican tradition: the feudal parliament or meeting of the Estates, an assembly of representatives delegated by the various social strata and localities in the lands of a monarch to represent them. But the conquered subjects of Florence and Venice were not represented in any parliament, and thus had no institutional recourse against harsh exploitation. Parliamentary government in nation-states was the way of the future; republican government in city-states had, by the close of the early modern period, come to the end of its historical course.

FLORENCE

Florence was one of the centers of Renaissance humanism, a movement that began in the late thirteenth century and flourished in the fifteenth, aiming to revive the use of classical Latin and knowledge of all aspects of Greek and Roman antiquity. The Roman writers with the greatest prestige and influence had lived in the late republic (Cicero, Sallust) or under the early empire (Livy, Tacitus), and this gave a superficial republican ethos to Renaissance humanism, which is seen in the realms of political thought and artistic imagery. The city of Florence took particular pride in regarding itself as the daughter and heir of the Roman republic and Roman liberty.

There are objective parallels between the history of the Roman republic and empire in the ancient world and Florence in the early modern period. In the fourteenth and fifteenth centuries, Florence, despite its wealth and control of much of Tuscany, was made turbulent by the struggle for political power

between older and more recent factions of powerful families and their clienteles. Only adult male guild members were entitled to hold office, and the complex guild-based constitutional machinery of Florence produced the same result as the machinery of the Roman republic: a steep stratification of political power based on status and socioeconomic class. There was rapid rotation through the small executive committees in which the power of government was concentrated, and individuals were chosen to hold office randomly, through a lottery (the drawing of names from a bag of eligible candidates). Legislation was ratified in a couple of intermediate councils that also had rotating membership.

From the 1430s to 1494, the Medici family controlled Florence, although formally their status was no different from that of any other great family. They manipulated the constitution in at least three ways: by controlling the lottery process so that names were no longer drawn at random; by the abuse of emergency powers; and by creating new, smaller, more permanent councils whose members were carefully screened for loyalty to the Medici. The Florentines called this "narrow government." From a favorable standpoint (that of the Medici, their clientele, and the top families allied to them), narrow government was more efficient and consistent than the "wide government" of the past, in which many more citizens had rotated through the offices, ruling and being ruled in turn. But "wide government" was traditionally seen as the essence of Florentine liberty, so from an unfavorable standpoint (that of the rival families excluded from power, as well as the many families of middling status whose ambition to participate in government was being frustrated), the Medici regime was an assault on Florence's traditional republican liberty.

In the revolution of 1494 the Medici were driven from Florence. There followed a political struggle over the constitution, with the leading families striving to keep it as narrow as possible (aristocratic, but not princely), and a popular movement led by Girolamo Savonarola (1452–1498) that demanded a return to wide government. The latter prevailed, and thus there began a unique eighteen-year period in the history of Florence (and republicanism): the republic of 1494–1512. This republic was ended by the return of the Medici, who set about establishing princely rule. The Florentines revolted against them and revived the republic between 1527 and 1530, but after that the Medici proceeded to make themselves hereditary grand-dukes of Florence and Tuscany, in a historical parallel to the establishment of the Roman Empire on the ruins of the Roman republic. Niccolò Machiavelli, the first great political thinker of modern times, had all of his direct experience of political and military affairs as a senior administrator and diplomat for the republic of 1494–1512, and many other Florentines also participated in political life and composed political treatises (long and short, practical and theoretical) between 1494 and the 1530s. At no other place or time in Europe did political thought about republics (and the alternative form, monarchy, or as Machiavelli called it, "principality") flourish with the same intensity.

In the Florentine republic of 1494–1512 and 1527–1530, the direct voting assembly of all the citizens was revived. Over 3,000 male scions of families whose members had held office in the past became permanent members of the assembly; although this was still only a fraction of the entire population, it represented an extraordinarily high degree of political participation in the context of Europe at that time. (The members of the Florentine voting assembly were not modern liberal democrats though, and like virtually every other status group that won political entitlement in the history of ancient and modern republics, they wanted admission to the assembly in the future to be limited to their own male descendants.) There was also an intermediate council, which in Florence had little importance, and the typical array of small executive committees. Throughout the period 1494–1512 the families of high status never ceased to press for more narrow government, in which their putative expertise and insight would prevail over the inexperienced and inept majority; their ideal was to govern aristocratically, like Roman senators. Many of these families defected from the republic and supported the return of the Medici in 1512, and again in 1530.

The internal politics of republican Florence were not Machiavelli's main concern when, in forced retirement after 1512, he became a writer on politics. Machiavelli did not believe that the Florence he had served, or any other modern republic, was a model for imitation, because all had been corrupted by Christianity. His model for analysis

and imitation in his major work, the *Discourses,* was the Roman republic, where there had been a fruitful tension between the competitive drive of a small number of individual nobles to dominate their rivals and win glory, and the opposing desire of the mass of the citizens to enjoy the spoils of conquest and check the imperiousness of the nobles. It was this tension, directed outward against neighboring peoples, that had made Rome the greatest of all conquest states. Since Machiavelli believed that the same two conflicting impulses were present and active in all societies, whether they were governed as principalities or republics, his basic vision of political life was republican, even in his famous short treatise *The Prince.*

Many other Florentines did ponder the problems and fate of their own republic more closely than Machiavelli. One was Francesco Guicciardini (1483–1540), and another was Donato Giannotti (1492–1573), a strong proponent of wide government who wrote the treatise *Republica Fiorentina* in the 1530s to describe what had gone wrong with the Florentine republic and how it could have been preserved. Giannotti was also the author of an influential description of the Venetian system of republican government.

VENICE

Venice was the clearest example of the explicit hierarchical correlation between social status and political participation that differentiated republicanism from ancient (and modern) democracy, and was considered a miraculous example of social and political stability. In 1297 a group of Venetian families achieved what the patricians of ancient Rome and the politically active families of Florence had always dreamed of: a constitutional limitation of political participation to themselves and their male descendants. These families also came to be called "patrician," and although new families were admitted in every generation, the Venetian patriciate was essentially composed of the same families for centuries. Not all of them were rich and powerful, but all enjoyed the same exclusive right to have their sons admitted to the voting assembly, which was roughly the same size as the one in Florence.

The offspring of the political elite, a small number of rich and powerful families, sought to ascend through elections held in the assembly to membership in the intermediate council, the Senate—a locus of prestige and power comparable to the Roman Senate itself—and from there to the array of small committees that made up the executive. The head of state and government, the doge, was elected for life but did not have what we would call presidential powers, for the Venetian leadership was essentially collective. The most feared and powerful committee of the Venetian executive was actually the Council of Ten, which attended to state security. They worked in secret, received anonymous denunciations, had, or were believed to have, informants everywhere, and could make "enemies of the state" disappear. Hence there arose a "black legend," a negative image of life in Venice that contrasted with the positive image of Venetian republican liberty.

PATRICIAN CITIES

Florence and Venice were exceptional because they were fully sovereign and were capitals of territorial states. But there were many other cities in Europe, especially in Italy and Germany, which never conquered large territorial states of their own, but which continued to govern themselves as republics while retaining a high degree of autonomy within larger (and by later standards, looser) state frameworks. Over the span of time from the Middle Ages to the early modern period, social and political mobility gradually dwindled in all these cities, and they evolved into patrician republics governed by narrow oligarchies. The families whose male members had a claim to a seat on the city council became a hereditary, and largely closed, status group, visibly distinguished by their style of dress, their titles, and their membership in exclusive dining and drinking clubs. Frankfurt, Augsburg, Nuremberg, and Hamburg were renowned patrician city-states in the Holy Roman Empire. There is a vast literature on these and many other European cities, tracing the social and political history of each in detail, and seldom making any reference to republicanism as a concept, although it is in these cities that republicanism lived out the last phase of its history. Internally there was little or no republican liberty left (no more freedom to participate in politics, that is, except for the patrician elite) but externally the patricians were adept at defending another kind of republican liberty (the local autonomy of their cities) against centralized control by the larger state structures into which their cities were integrated.

The city of Bologna, which was part of the large Papal State of central and northern Italy, is a good example: its liberty was based on the pact it made with Pope Nicholas V (reigned 1447–1455) when it submitted to the papacy in 1447. This was a contract that bound both parties and was renegotiated with every new papacy. The Bolognese patriciate used it to protect their autonomy for the next three hundred years, in what can be seen from one standpoint as stubborn particularism, preserving entrenched local privilege against the bureaucratic rationalization of the modern state, and from another as the proud defense of local tradition, local jurisdiction, and control of the local treasury against arbitrary centralism.

It was in defense of similar contractually protected local rights that the northern provinces of the Netherlands rebelled against Spain in the late sixteenth century and formed a new state, the Dutch Republic, that became a beacon for opponents of monarchy (republicans in the broad sense) during the seventeenth and eighteenth centuries. The Netherlanders repeatedly fended off attempts by the house of Orange to establish a new regal dynasty, and adopted a confederal system of government with strong local autonomy and weaker authority at the higher levels. Towns governed by local patriciates dominated the provinces, there was a parliament (an "Estates") for each province attended by local delegates, and there was an Estates-General for the whole federation, attended by provincial delegates. Thus the Dutch Republic was a fusion of the republican and the parliamentary-representative models.

ENGLAND AND THE UNITED STATES OF AMERICA

Because the English civil war between parliamentary and royalist forces in the mid-seventeenth century led to regicide and ten years of kingless government, and because the United States of America was an antimonarchical offshoot of the civilization of the British Isles, there is a large scholarly literature attempting to trace the influence of republicanism in Britain and its rebellious colonies. Controversy and debate abound in this field, for in Britain there had never been an actual republican city-state, so scholars are left to deal with language, concepts, and ideas. Britain actually led European civilization down the road to a different destination: government by parties holding parliamentary majorities, with loyal opposition from opposing parties—a structure of government foreign to the republican tradition. It also led Europe in the development of liberalism as a set of political and economic ideas, especially through the influence of John Locke. In eighteenth-century Britain and its American off-shoot, republican ideas formed a counterpart to liberal ones in political thought, and republicanism and liberalism are seen as conflicting intellectual influences on the founders of the American republic. The values of liberalism include economic individualism and constitutional limitation on the power of government to invade the sphere of private life, while republicanism (in this context) stands for the disinterested devotion of individual citizens to the common good, and their willingness to set aside private concerns and participate in public debate and decision making.

See also **American Independence, War of (1775–1783); Divine Right Kingship; Dutch Republic; Dutch Revolt (1568–1648); English Civil War and Interregnum; Florence; Free and Imperial Cities; Guicciardini, Francesco; Hobbes, Thomas; Locke, John; Machiavelli, Niccolò; Milton, John; Monarchy; Montesquieu, Charles-Louis de Secondat de; Parliament; Political Philosophy; Rousseau, Jean-Jacques; Switzerland; Venice.**

BIBLIOGRAPHY

Primary Sources

Chambers, David, and Brian Pullan, eds. *Venice. A Documentary History, 1450–1630.* Oxford and Cambridge, Mass., 1992.

Giannotti, Donato. *Republica fiorentina.* Edited by Giovanni Silvano. Geneva, 1990.

Guicciardini, Francesco. *Dialogue on the Government of Florence.* Edited by Alison Brown. Cambridge, U.K., and New York, 1994.

Harrington, James. The *Commonwealth of Oceana and a System of Politics.* Edited by J. G. A. Pocock. Cambridge, U.K., and New York, 1992.

Kohl, Benjamin G., and Ronald G. Witt, eds. *The Earthly Republic.* Philadelphia, 1978.

Kraye, Jill, ed. *Cambridge Translations of Renaissance Philosophical Texts. Volume 2: Political Philosophy.* Cambridge, U.K., and New York, 1997.

Machiavelli, Niccolò. *The Prince.* Edited by Quentin Skinner and Russell Price. Cambridge, U.K., and New York, 1988.

Machiavelli, Niccolò, and Francesco Guicciardini. *The Sweetness of Power: Machiavelli's Discourses and Guic-ciardini's Considerations.* Translated with introduction by James B. Atkinson and David Sices. DeKalb, Ill., 2002.

More, Thomas. *Utopia.* Edited by George M. Logan and Robert M. Adams. Cambridge, U.K., and New York, 2002.

Sharp, Andrew, ed. *The English Levellers.* Cambridge, U.K., and New York, 1998.

Sidney, Algernon. *Court Maxims.* Edited by Hans W. Blom, Eco Haitsma-Mulier, and Ronald Janse. Cambridge, U.K., and New York, 1996.

van Gelderen, Martin, ed. *The Dutch Revolt.* Cambridge, U.K., and New York, 1993.

Wootton, David, ed. *Divine Right and Democracy. An Anthology of Political Writing in Stuart England.* Harmondsworth, U.K., 1986.

Secondary Sources

Berengo, Marino. *L'Europa delle città. Il volto della società urbana europea tra Medioevo ed Età moderna.* Turin, 1999. See especially ch. 4, "I cittadini e la vita pubblica," and ch. 5, "Patriziato e nobiltà."

Blickle, Peter. *Obedient Germans? A Rebuttal. A New View of German History.* Translated by Thomas A. Brady. Charlottesville, Va., 1997.

Bock, Gisela, Quentin Skinner, and Maurizio Viroli, eds. *Machiavelli and Republicanism.* Cambridge, U.K., and New York, 1990.

Bouwsma, W. J. *Venice and the Defense of Republican Liberty.* Berkeley, 1968.

Burns, J. H., ed. *The Cambridge History of Political Thought, 1450–1700.* Cambridge, U.K., and New York, 1991.

Cooper, Roslyn Pesman. "The Florentine Ruling Group under the Governo Popolare." *Studies in Medieval and Renaissance History* 7 (1985): 71–181.

De Benedictis, Angela. *Repubblica per contratto. Bologna: una città europea nello Stato della Chiesa.* Bologna, 1995.

Fasano Guarini, Elena. "La crisi del modello repubblicano: Patriziati e oligarchie." In *La Storia,* vol. 3, *L'Età moderna, i quadri generali.* Edited by Nicola Tranfaglia and Massimo Firpo, pp. 553–584. Turin, 1987.

Finlay, Robert. *Politics in Renaissance Venice.* London and New Brunswick, N.J., 1980.

Gelderen, Martin van. *The Political Thought of the Dutch Revolt 1555–1590.* Cambridge, U.K., and New York, 1992.

Gelderen, Martin van, and Quentin Skinner, eds. *Republicanism: A Shared European Heritage.* 2 vols. Cambridge, U.K., and New York, 2002.

Grendler, Paul F. "The Leaders of the Venetian State, 1540–1609: A Prosopographical Analysis." *Studi Veneziani* 19 (1990), pp. 35–85.

Guidi, Guidubaldo. *Lotte, pensiero, e istituzioni politiche nella repubblica fiorentina dal 1494 al 1512.* 3 vols. Florence, 1992.

Hankins, James. "Humanism and the Origins of Modern Political Thought." In *The Cambridge Companion to Renaissance Humanism,* edited by Jill Kraye, pp. 118–141. Cambridge, U.K., and New York, 1996.

Koenigsberger, Helmut, ed. *Republiken und Republikanismus im Europa der frühen Neuzeit.* Munich, 1988.

Lane, Frederick C. *Venice. A Maritime Republic.* Baltimore, 1973.

Mansfield, Harvey C. *Machiavelli's Virtue.* Chicago, 1996.

McCuaig, William. *Carlo Sigonio: The Changing World of the Late Renaissance.* Princeton, 1989. Chapters 2 and 3 deal with the Roman republic as it was understood in Europe from the sixteenth to the mid-eighteenth centuries.

Pangle, Thomas L. *The Spirit of Modern Republicanism: The Moral Vision of the American Founders and the Philosophy of Locke.* Chicago, 1989.

Pocock, J. G. A. *The Machiavellian Moment: Florentine Political Thought and the Atlantic Republican Tradition.* Princeton, 1975.

Rahe, Paul A. *Republics Ancient and Modern: Classical Republicanism and the American Revolution.* Chapel Hill, N.C., 1992.

Rössler, Helmuth, ed. *Deutsches Patriziat 1430–1740.* Limburg, 1968.

Rubinstein, Nicolai. "Politics and Constitution in Florence at the End of the Fifteenth Century." In *Italian Renaissance Studies,* edited by E. F. Jacob, pp. 148–183. London, 1960.

Silvano, Giovanni. *La "Republica de' Viniziani." Ricerche sul repubblicanesimo veneziano in età moderna.* Florence, 1993.

Stephens, J. N. *The Fall of the Florentine Republic, 1512–1530.* Oxford, 1983.

Stolleis, Michael, ed. *Recht, Verfassung, und Verwaltung in der frühneuzeitlichen Stadt.* Vienna, 1991.

von Albertini, Rudolf. *Das florentinische Staatsbewusstsein im Übergang von der Republik zum Prinzipat.* Bern, 1955. Italian translation, Turin, 1970.

Wootton, David, ed. *Republicanism, Liberty, and Commercial Society, 1649–1776.* Stanford, 1994.

WILLIAM MCCUAIG

RESISTANCE, THEORY OF.

The development of the theory of resistance in the early modern period was complex and was based in large part on the political, philosophical, and legal arguments of French authors during the religious wars in the sixteenth century. Their arguments in turn were a development of three earlier theories based on Roman, canon (church), and medieval law: the right to defend oneself and one's property, the contractual relationship between the ruler and the people, and the just war theory. The sixteenth-century authors took the earlier justification of an individual's right to use violence in self-defense, added just war theory, and turned them into a justification for using violence to resist the ruler's authority when he violated the contractual relationship on which he based his power.

RIGHT OF DEFENSE

The Roman law maxim *vim vi repellere licit* (force may repel force) formed the basis of the concept of justified defense against violence. Laws and statutes permitted violent defense against aggression because it was generally believed that both natural law (*ius naturale*) and human law (*ius gentium*) granted the individual a right to defense. Roman and medieval law limited this violence by requiring that the defense was immediate and the force used was moderate. Medieval scholars developed these two concepts of immediacy and moderation from simple self-defense into the area of defending one's property, including one's rights.

CORONATION: CONSENT AND CONTRACT

The idea of popular sovereignty had become increasingly common with the medieval revival of Roman law. Writers commenting on the Roman civil law interpreted passages of Justinian's Digest as meaning that the emperor's or king's authority originally came from the people. The sixteenth-century coronation ceremonies in many countries supported this interpretation because they contained a *consensus populi* (consent of the people) clause that suggested election. This was applied by proponents of the resistance theory.

Others saw the question not as one of elective elements in the coronation oath, but of contractual ones. The feudal contract, like any contract, carried rights and duties for all parties. As a contract between a king and his people, the coronation oath bound both parties. The king had to observe the oath unless the people released him from it. In this feudal view of kingship, royalty was not absolute and the king was only the administrator, not the owner, of the kingdom. In his coronation oath the king swore to obey the law, defend the faith, and protect his subjects and their property. The inclusion of his duty to defend the faith obligated him to fight heresy, which could also mean to maintain order, since heresy was seen as a threat to the peace of the kingdom. In addition, since the king was supposed to protect the faith, any challenge to that faith became a kind of treason. Numerous canon law precedents also justified the use of force against heretics and the confiscation of their property.

JUST WAR AND RESISTANCE

The Christian theory of just war was developed from the works of a number of medieval theologians, including St. Augustine (354–430) and St. Thomas Aquinas (1225–1274). In this theory there were three conditions necessary for a war to be a just war: a legitimate ruler had to order the war, there had to be a just cause (the enemy had to have done something wrong), and the declarers of the war had to have good intentions, to be fighting for the repression of evil, not for revenge. By the sixteenth century the king's commitment in his coronation oath to defend religion and the concept of the consent of the people led to the development that protecting religion was a legitimate reason for a just war.

FRENCH WARS OF RELIGION

The theory of resistance was developed fully by sixteenth-century French political theorists. Théodore de Bèze (1519–1605) implied in his *Du droit des magistrats* (1574; Right of magistrates) that the kingship still could be elective, and he reminded his readers that the French kings still took an oath when they were anointed at their coronation. In *Vindiciae contra Tyrannos* (1579; Judgment against tyrants) the pseudonymous author Étienne Junius Brutus (probably Philippe Duplessis-Mornay, but also attributed to Hubert Languet) claimed that a twofold covenant was made at the coronation: the first part among God, the king, and the people, and the second between the king and the people. The latter stipulated that the people would obey the king if he were a proper ruler. These oaths may have been more myth than history, as in the case of the Aragónese oath, "We who are worth as much as you, take you as our king, provided that you preserve our laws and liberties, and if not, not," but their power to influence the popular mind and political theory was strong nevertheless.

The sixteenth-century activists recognized the necessity of remaining within the prescribed limits of the law when advocating or using violence. The ethical and practical issues they faced paralleled those Roman law writers had raised concerning self-defense and canonists and theologians had raised while developing the arguments for just war. First the Huguenots in 1562 and then the Catholics in 1576 justified arming themselves against the king's will with the argument that they were taking arms not against the authority of the king, but against heresy and evil counselors of the king. They claimed to be doing this in defense of themselves, their property, their king, and their religion. They appealed to the king based on his legal duties and obligations under the coronation oath: his promises to obey the law, defend the faith, and protect his subjects and their property. A breach of those promises could, according to some theorists, justify correction of a ruler by the lesser magistrates (civil officials, including members of the city governments and officials of the central government) with the power to administer the law. The personal responsibility of the magistrates for their own actions as well as for those of the king seems to have been widely accepted during the sixteenth century, although earlier medieval theorists (such as Marsilius of Padua [c. 1280–c. 1343] and John of Salisbury [1115 or 1120–1180]) had not named any representative group as having such responsibility.

The massacre of Huguenots on St. Bartholomew's Day in 1572 forced the Huguenot theorists into a new position. They continued to use the constitutional and historical arguments and the legal precedents, but now they used the new arguments to reason that true sovereignty belonged to the community and enabled its representatives to discipline, depose, or even assassinate the ruler. In this way, Francis Hotman (1524–1590) in his 1573 work *Francogallia* reminded his readers that the Parlement of Paris had to approve the king's laws and edicts before they had any force, and Bèze claimed that it was the duty of the lesser magistrates to resist tyranny and safeguard the people until the Estates-General, or whoever held the legislative power of the kingdom, could provide for the public welfare. Bèze went further and claimed that the Estates-General had the authority to appoint and to depose the chief officers of the crown, or at least to supervise the king in doing so. Arguing from the law of fiefs, Bèze declared that since a lord lost his fief for committing a felony against his vassal, a king must also lose his fief, or kingdom, for committing a felony against his subjects.

This feudal basis for forfeiture of the kingdom was repeated in *Judgment against Tyrants* and tied to the covenant made at the coronation ceremony. The author of *Judgment* took this another step toward legitimate resistance to and rebellion against the king when he claimed that a king who committed a felony against his people also committed treason *(lèse majesté)* against the kingdom and was no better than any other rebel. These ideas were not unanimously accepted. For example, Jean Bodin (1530–1596) argued in his *Les six livres de la république* (1583; Six books of the republic) that the king was restricted by natural law to respect his subjects' liberty and property, but his violations of these restrictions did not justify resistance by his subjects because the king answered only to God.

LATER DEVELOPMENTS

Hugo Grotius (1583–1645), a Dutch scholar and jurist, recognized in his 1625 work *De Jure Belli ac Pacis* (The law of war and peace) that the individual had a right to resist injury, but he also stated that society had an obligation to maintain order and could limit that right of resistance. Extreme cruelty or injustice could justify resistance by individuals or groups, but a primary consideration for him was whether that resistance itself would be more destructive or harmful to the state than the original injustice.

John Locke (1632–1704), on the other hand, argued in his *Second Treatise of Civil Government* (1690) that although the contract made between the sovereign and the people is binding, a ruler who misused the authority or broke the contract could be resisted, even to the point of removing that ruler and restoring the governing power to the people. A ruler who acted arbitrarily was not fulfilling his duty, and the people could assume governing power in order to restore their rights.

The theory of resistance has continued to develop. It remains an important part of modern popular revolutions and arguments for just war.

See also **Authority, Concept of; Bèze, Théodore de; Bodin, Jean; Grotius, Hugo; Law; Locke, John; Wars of Religion, French.**

BIBLIOGRAPHY

Primary Sources

Constitutionalism and Resistance in the Sixteenth Century: Three Treatises by Hotman, Beza, & Mornay. Translated and edited by Julian H. Franklin. New York, 1969. English translations of key excerpts from their major works on resistance, with an introduction.

Hotman, François. *Francogallia.* Variorum edition. Latin text by Ralph E. Giesey. Translated by J. H. M. Salmon. Cambridge, U.K., 1972.

Secondary Sources

Gelderen, Martin van. *The Political Thought of the Dutch Revolt.* Cambridge, U.K., 1992.

Giesey, Ralph E. *If Not, Not: The Oath of the Aragónese and the Legendary Lives of Sobrarbe.* Princeton, 1968.

———. "The Monarchomach Triumvirs: Hotman, Beza, and Mornay." *Bibliothèque d'humanisme et Renaissance* 32 (January 1970): 41–56.

Hanley, Sarah. "The French Constitution Revised: Representative Assemblies and Resistance Right in the Sixteenth Century." In *Society and Institutions in Early Modern France,* edited by Mack P. Holt, pp. 36–50. Athens, Ga., 1991.

Jackson, Richard A. "Elective Kingship and Consensus Populi in Sixteenth-Century France." *Journal of Modern History* 44 (June 1972): 155–171.

Johnson, James Turner. *Ideology, Reason, and the Limitation of War: Religious and Secular Concepts, 1200–1740.* Princeton, 1975.

Parrow, Kathleen A. *From Defense to Resistance: Justification of Violence during the French Wars of Religion.* Philadelphia, 1993.

KATHLEEN A. PARROW

RESTITUTION, EDICT OF (1629).
See **Thirty Years' War (1618–1648).**

RESTORATION, PORTUGUESE WAR OF (1640–1668). In December 1640 a palace coup in support of the duke of Bragança and his acclamation as King John IV restored the

Portuguese monarchy and ended sixty years of rule by the Spanish Habsburgs. From 1641 to 1668 the two nations were at war, with Spain seeking to isolate Portugal militarily and diplomatically and Portugal hoping to find the resources to maintain its independence through political alliances and colonial income.

The military aspects of the war fall into three periods: an early stage when a few major engagements demonstrated that the Portuguese could not be easily returned to submission; a long second period (1646–1660) of military standoffs characterized by small-scale raiding, while Spain concentrated on its military commitments elsewhere in Europe; and a final period (1660–1668) during which the Spanish king Philip IV unsuccessfully sought a major engagement that would bring an end to hostilities.

Spain in early 1641 faced a war with France as well as rebellions in both Catalonia and Portugal. Hoping for a quick victory in Portugal, Spain immediately committed seven regiments to the Portuguese frontier, but delays by the count of Monterrey, a commander more interested in the comforts of camp than of the battlefield, lost any immediate advantage. A Portuguese counter-thrust in late 1641 failed, and the conflict soon settled into a stalemate, especially after a major column under the Neapolitan marquis of Torrecusa was stopped at Montijo in 1644 by the Portuguese under the Brazilian-trained Matias de Albuquerque, one of a number of experienced Portuguese colonial officers who rose to prominence during the war. Shortly thereafter, in November 1644, Torrecusa crossed from Badajoz in a rare winter campaign to attack Elvas, where he suffered heavy losses and was forced to retreat back across the border.

The war now took on a peculiar character as a frontier confrontation, often between local forces that knew each other well, but whose familiarity did not diminish the destructive effects on either side. The bloody nature of the combat was often exacerbated by the use of foreign troops and mercenaries. Incidents of singular cruelty were reported on both sides as the Portuguese settled old animosities, while Spanish commanders often took the view that their opponents were disloyal and rebellious sub-jects, not an opposing army entitled to the rules of combat.

Three theaters were eventually opened, but most activity focused on the northern front and on the frontier between Portuguese Alemtejo and Spanish Extremadura. The southern front in Spanish Andalusia was a logical target for Portugal, but it never bore the full weight of Portuguese attack, probably because the Portuguese queen, Luisa de Gusmão (Guzmán), was the sister of the duke of Medina Sidonia, the leading noble of Andalusia. Spain at first made the war defensive. Portugal, for its part, felt no need to take Spanish territory in order to win, and it too was willing to make the war a defensive one. Campaigns typically consisted of *correrias,* or 'cavalry raids', burning fields, sacking towns, and appropriating large herds of enemy cattle and sheep. Soldiers and officers primarily interested in booty and prone to desertion were poor instruments for the conduct of serious war. For long periods, without men or money, neither side mounted formal campaigns, and when actions were taken, they were often driven as much by political considerations, such as Portugal's need to impress its potential allies, as by clear military objectives. Year by year, given the transportation problems of campaigning in winter and the heat and dry conditions of summer, most fighting was limited to the spring and fall.

The war settled into a pattern of mutual destruction. As early as December 1641 there were Spanish complaints that "our Extremadura is finished." Tax collectors, recruiting officers, the billeting of soldiers, and depredation by Spanish and foreign troops were feared as much by the Spanish population as the destructive raids of the enemy. In Extremadura, local militias bore the brunt of the fighting until 1659, and this was destructive to agriculture and local finances. Since there was often no money to pay or support the troops or to reward commanders, the crown turned a blind eye to the contraband, disorder, and destruction on the frontier. Similar conditions also existed among the Portuguese forces.

The war was also expensive. In the 1650s there were over 20,000 Spanish troops in Extremadura alone, compared to 27,000 in Flanders. Between 1649 and 1654 about 29 percent (over six million ducats) of Spanish defense spending went to Portugal, a figure that rose during the major campaigns of the 1660s. Portugal was able to finance the war because of its ability to tax the spice trade from Asia and the sugar trade from Brazil, and because of support from the European opponents of Spain, particularly Holland, France, and England.

The 1650s were indecisive militarily but important on the political and diplomatic fronts. The death of John IV, the former duke of Bragança, in 1656 brought the regency of his wife, followed by a succession crisis and a palace coup (1662). Despite these domestic problems, the expulsion of the Dutch from Brazil (1654) and the signing of a treaty with England (1654) improved Portugal's diplomatic and financial position for a while and gave it needed protection against a naval attack on Lisbon. Nonetheless, the major goal of a formal pact with France continued to evade Portugal, whose weakness and isolation had been driven home by its virtual exclusion at the negotiations for the general European peace of Westphalia (1648). With that treaty and the end of hostilities in Catalonia in 1652, Spain was again ready to direct its attention against Portugal but faced a lack of men, resources, and especially good military commanders.

By 1662 Spain committed to a major effort to end the rebellion. Don Juan José de Austria, Philip IV's illegitimate son, led some 14,000 men into Alemtejo and in the following year succeeded in taking Évora, the major city of the region. The Portuguese under the marquis of Marialva and the German soldier of fortune Friedrich Hermann von Schönberg, the duke of Schomberg, who had been contracted along with other foreign officers to bolster the Portuguese forces, were able to turn the tide. They defeated the Spanish in a major engagement at Ameixial (8 June 1663), forcing Don Juan José to abandon Évora and retreat across the border.

The Portuguese now had some 30,000 troops in this theater, but they could not draw the Spanish into a major engagement until June 1665, when a new Spanish commander, the marquis of Caracena, took over Vilaviciosa with about 23,000 men, including recruits from Germany and Italy. The Portuguese relief column under Schomburg met them

at Montes Claros (17 June 1665). The Portuguese infantry and gun emplacements broke the Spanish cavalry, and the Spanish force lost over 10,000 men as casualties and prisoners. This was the last major engagement of the war. Both sides returned to skirmishing campaigns. Portugal, with the intercession of its English ally, had sought a truce, but after the Portuguese victory at Montes Claros and with the signing of a Franco-Portuguese treaty in 1667, Spain finally agreed to recognize Portugal's independence (13 February 1668).

The war proved costly to both sides. Portugal won its independence at a high price in terms of concessions it made to forge the alliances needed for its political survival. Its economy was damaged by reduced access to Spanish-American silver and colonial losses. The effect on Spain was difficult to calculate. The economy of Spanish Galicia and especially Extremadura were devastated, and the reputation of Spanish arms suffered badly. The war drained resources and men for almost three decades. It may well be true, as the historian R. A. Stradling has said, that the war with Portugal, "ended contributing more than any other single factor to the final dissolution of Spanish hegemony."

See also **Portugal; Spain.**

BIBLIOGRAPHY

Bouza Álvarez, Fernando. *Portugal no tempo dos Felipes.* Lisbon, 2000.

Livermore, H. V. *A History of Portugal.* Cambridge, U.K., 1947.

Magalhães Godinho, Vitorino. "1580 e a restauração." In *Ensaios*, 3 vols. Vol. 2, pp. 255–292. Lisbon, 1968.

Stradling, R. A. *Europe and the Decline of Spain: A Study of the Spanish System, 1580–1720.* London and Boston, 1981.

Valladares, Rafael. *La rebellion de Portugal, 1640–1680.* Valladolid, Spain, 1998.

White, Louise. "War and Government in a Castilian Province: Extremadura, 1640–1668." Ph.D. diss., University of East Anglia, 1985.

STUART B. SCHWARTZ

REVOLUTIONS, AGE OF.

REVOLUTIONS, AGE OF. At the end of the eighteenth century a series of revolutions broke out on both sides of the Atlantic. In the 1960s the historians R. R. Palmer and Jacques Godechot argued that these were not discrete revolutions but manifestations of a single democratic revolution common to the entire Atlantic world. In fact, eighteenth-century revolutions shared a common language but little else, and each had significant unique features. Moreover, once the Revolution of 1789 broke out in France, the democratic features of this supposedly single Atlantic revolution ebbed away. The French Revolution was not inherently more radical than any of the others, but it did face entrenched and determined opposition from a very early stage, which forced the revolutionaries to violate their own principles and institute terror. Finally, once the French began to expand and annex surrounding countries and principalities, they transformed local democrats into unpopular collaborators and provoked much of the same kind of opposition as they had faced at home, and often for the same reasons. The repression in occupied territories was just about as brutal as anything that had been witnessed in France itself during the Terror. Such patterns of opposition and repression played themselves out throughout Europe, until the age of revolution ushered in an age of counterrevolution, a counterrevolution that was popular and enduring.

Partisans of change certainly had a common language, which had developed over the course of the eighteenth century, and a powerful sense of transnational solidarity. Phrases like "patriot," "liberty," "aristocrat," and "democrat" and symbols like the liberty tree, the eye of vigilance, and so on, cropped up in most of these revolutions. There was also widespread sympathy among European intellectuals, and later among journalists, for the "patriots" in various struggles. Enlightenment writers such as Voltaire, Jean Le Rond d'Alembert and Jean-Jacques Rousseau all celebrated the revolution against the oligarchs in Geneva (1760s–early 1780s). The struggles of the Dutch patriots and certainly the American patriots also had extensive support. The journalist Camille Desmoulins (1760–1794) called his first newspaper *Révolutions de France et de Brabant* (Revolutions of France and Brabant).

THE STRUGGLE AGAINST OLIGARCHY

Palmer was certainly right to call attention to the eighteenth-century struggles against oligarchies in various parts of Europe, but these oligarchies differed in their nature and in the ways they held power, and despite the common language of liberty among their opponents, the struggle against oligarchy took various forms. Geneva, whose revolution began in the 1760s, illustrates this point. By 1768, the majority *natifs* (those born in the city but with no political rights) had forced the ruling patricians to share power. By 1781 the citizenship was extended, again under pressure from the *natifs*—and under the banner of equality of rights. This was too much for the French, who intervened in 1782 to restore the settlement of 1768.

The struggles in Geneva reassembled those that broke out later in France itself over the issue of municipal citizenship and access to office. The conflict in the United Provinces, however, was more complex. Here the Amsterdam oligarchy of merchants, who called themselves "republicans" and later "patriots," was pitted against the Orangist party, which supported the stadtholder and was backed by plebeian and noble elements as well as the more rural provinces. The Amsterdam merchants favored an alliance with France and, through France, support of the American rebels in their war for independence from Great Britain, while the Orangists favored the traditional alliance with Britain. In 1780 the merchants prevailed and went to war with Britain. Opinion blamed the stadtholder for the disastrous campaigns that followed. The fear of the prince's army provoked the formation of the Free Corps, which soon numbered some twenty-eight thousand volunteers. At the same time many municipal councils revolted against the prince's power of appointment, and some began to adopt the elective principle. The Prussians intervened in 1787 to restore the old order, while many patriots fled to the Austrian Netherlands or to France.

Meanwhile, the reforms of Holy Roman Emperor Joseph II (ruled 1780–1790) threw huge areas of the Austrian empire into turmoil. Like the other "enlightened despots," Joseph was motivated in part by the desire to improve his finances and his military after Austria's mediocre performance in battle under his mother, Maria Theresa. Unlike his "enlightened" counterparts, he did not believe that further exploitation of his subjects was desirable. Instead, Joseph's policies borrowed from many of the nostrums of the intellectuals of his day. Thus his tax reforms were based on a thorough land survey that evaluated real resources, and they also annulled the exemptions for nobles and certain corporate bodies. He promulgated religious toleration for Protestants (but not for Jews or Muslims). He also suppressed the contemplative orders of the Roman Catholic Church, which he considered useless, and seized their property.

These measures provoked massive disturbances throughout Joseph's realms. Peasants in the Tyrol rebelled against the suppression of their monasteries, while the Hungarian nobility flirted with treason over the loss of their privileges. The most prolonged resistance originated in the Austrian Netherlands (roughly modern Belgium), where the numerous provincial Estates were upset that the new tax reforms had been introduced without their consent. Eventually, the Estates were simply replaced with a set of "rational" administrative bodies responsible to the emperor's officials in Brussels. Meanwhile, peasants in the Flemish-speaking regions revolted against the religious reforms. The war on the Turks delayed repression, but when repression came in mid-1789, it was met with widespread resistance. In a phenomenon that became common elsewhere, excitable priests and monks did everything they could to stir up opinion by claiming that "religion" was threatened. The patriots' civilian militias—contemptuously referred to as the "Army of the Moon" by the Austrians, who grossly underestimated them—met with considerable success, and their victories encouraged further rebellion. Finally, having routed the Austrians, the Estates General declared independence and the formation of a United States of Belgium in December 1789.

THE FRENCH REVOLUTION

It is seductive to see parallels between the revolution in France and the revolutions in these other countries. After all, as in the Austrian Netherlands, the government in France needed to reorganize the fiscal system in order to compete with its great-power rivals. In France as elsewhere, oligarchs struggled among themselves for control of state power. But in Belgium, traditional society exerted itself against princely power, and so privilege protected all of society against despotism. In France, patriots saw privilege and despotism as one and the

same. Furthermore, unlike in Geneva, the Dutch Republic, or Belgium, the repression from outside came very late in the French case, well after the revolution had defined itself. European powers initially interpreted the French Revolution as a collapse of French power and saw no reason to intervene; rather, they saw limitless advantage in letting France immolate itself. In short, because a revolution had broken out in a great power, other powers were bound to treat it differently. For that reason alone, the revolution in France followed a different course.

With the Declaration of the Rights of Man and Citizen (26 August 1789) the Revolution declared its principles: liberty under the law, due process, religious toleration, and protection of property. It took more than a year to work out the implications of these principles, but they were by any standard a radical departure from the recent past. The Constitution of 1791 established a unicameral legislature elected by an indirect but very wide male suffrage. The king was to have extensive executive powers over foreign relations and the military, as well as a veto over any legislation, one that could not be overridden easily. The constitution failed to provide for a speedy resolution to a clash between the legislature and the executive, leaving force as the only solution should such a conflict arise.

By the new constitution, the old division of France into provinces was abolished and replaced by eighty-three territorial entities called "departments." Although theoretically responsible to the national government, the department administrators were not paid officials but elected volunteers. Government was henceforth in the hands of at least a million enthusiastic citizens, who often governed in their own way, frequently ignoring direct orders from Paris.

FISCAL CRISIS

The revolutionary crisis had begun over the insolvency of the crown, and the Constituent Assembly inherited huge problems of public finance. Its attempts to resolve these problems were disastrous. In a series of laws, the Assembly seized the property of the church and sold it at auction. But the church had much less property and many fewer resources than contemporaries imagined. Church land comprised about 3 to 4 percent of the national patri-

Age of Revolutions. Undated engraving of the Tennis Court Oath. Meeting in an indoor tennis court on 20 June 1789, the self-proclaimed National Assembly of France vowed not to disband until a constitution had been written and accepted by King Louis XVI. The king agreed but was ultimately overthrown as the revolution progressed to its anti-monarchical republican stage. ©BETTMANN/CORBIS

mony, not 10 to 15 percent as had been thought. Moreover, the Assembly's decision to issue non-interest-bearing bonds (paper money, in other words) called *assignats* turned out to be calamitous. *Assignats* amounted to a loan that was supposed to be retired as the church lands (termed *biens nationaux*) were sold. But this did not happen. The economist and deputy Antoine-Laurent Lavoisier pointed out that *biens nationaux* were worth far less than they seemed, because the Assembly also assumed responsibility for the church's massive debt and the payment of clerical salaries. The value of the *assignat* against gold therefore began to fall almost immediately. There were more and more *assignats* in circulation that were not backed by the mass of *biens nationaux*. Thus in January 1791, the *assignat* had lost 10 percent of its value, and a year later, nearly 40 percent.

The consequences of this monetary disaster reverberated throughout the country and abroad. Farmers refused to bring grain to market if they were going to be paid in the deteriorating currency. The result was endless rioting from 1791 until 1795. Smart citizens paid their taxes in *assignats,* when they paid at all. Not only did the state lose, so did private individuals. Holders of government bonds, among whom the high nobility was well represented, had their fortunes wiped out. Landlords who received rents in cash were also big losers. The falling *assignat* even affected how the French fought their wars for the rest of the decade.

One of the biggest demands in the summer of 1789 was for fiscal equality. With the outbreak of the Revolution, the implicit assumption was that the destruction of fiscal privilege would lower the tax burden. This did not happen. Estimating whether the new regime's citizens paid more than the Old Regime's subjects is tricky, but it is certain that the Revolution did not effect much, or even any, transfer of wealth. By law, landlords were allowed to add the equivalent of the defunct tithe to leases. A rise in rents would have happened regardless—because of the intense land hunger in France—and the rise in rents exceeded the former tithe and former seigneurial dues combined. Indeed, the higher rents gave landlords some compensation for the loss of their fiscal privileges. But the state was the main beneficiary, since the increase in taxes gouged landlords. In Brittany, for instance, large landowners paid roughly 15 percent of their incomes in taxes under the Old Regime, but 40 percent during the Revolution. Under Napoleon Bonaparte, this percentage was cut by half. No wonder the emperor was popular. Nobody had anticipated that fiscal equality would mean higher taxes.

It was in this context of monetary crisis, continuing economic inequality, and rising rents and taxes that the French were asked to express their loyalty to the Revolution, and the result in many areas of the country was disturbing to the new regime. The regime attempted to regulate the relations between church and state by means of a new law, the Civil Constitution of the Clergy (12 July 1790). Unlike the Americans, the revolutionaries in France did not believe in the separation of church and state. Instead, they envisioned the clergy as proselytizers for the revolutionary regime, and the Civil Constitution was supposed to promote this new role. When the upper clergy balked, the Constituent Assembly added an oath of loyalty to the Civil Constitution. About 60 percent of French parish priests took the oath, but in large parts of the country, especially in the west and south, huge numbers of clerics refused it. In many cases, they had the support of their parishioners, many of whom had gotten nothing from a revolution that had once been so promising. Many of the supporters of the refractories, as those who refused the oath were called, were women who had deep emotional attachments to their parish priests, many of whom had long attended to their families. Still others supported the refractories simply because these clerics were overtly defiant of the bourgeois revolutionaries who, many felt, had deceived them.

THE END OF THE MONARCHY

A Revolution that should have been over at the end of 1789 thus proved impossible to conclude because of the unforeseen consequences of the Constituent Assembly's policies. National politics aggravated this turmoil immeasurably. On 20 June 1791, Louis XVI and his family fled Paris for the eastern frontier. What the king hoped to accomplish is unclear, and perhaps he did not know himself. The next day he was apprehended at Varennes and brought back to Paris. The flight to Varennes had enormous consequences. At first the politicians in the Constituent Assembly were masters of the situation. They had no intention of deposing the king and preferred to believe he had been kidnapped. Their determination to preserve the monarchy probably cut short a drift to republicanism in the provinces, and in the capital republicanism was dealt a violent blow in the Champ de Mars massacre (17 July 1791).

Nonetheless, restoring Louis XVI to the throne was a huge error. Many disgusted patriots, including the radical journalist Jacques-Pierre Brissot, began to demand a war on the hereditary enemy, Austria, to smoke out, as they said, the "great treasons." The question of war and the defense of the Revolution dominated the new Legislative Assembly (October 1791–September 1792). According to Brissot, war would define loyalties clearly, and Louis XVI had shown where he stood by vetoing several laws penalizing the refractory clergy and émigrés, those who had fled abroad.

The vetoes not only revived the democrats in Paris, who began to denounce the king; they also galvanized the provinces. Democrats in the provinces had expressed their dismay at the king's betrayal following the flight to Varennes but had largely demurred on the issue of a penalty for his attempted escape. After the vetoes, many provincial administrations and many Jacobin clubs went far beyond the demands of the radicals in Paris. They illegally interned refractory priests, invoking a justification often heard later, during the Terror, that the safety of the people is the supreme law. They also demanded, well ahead of Paris, the suspension of the king. By mid-summer of 1792 dozens of National Guard battalions, including that of Marseille, converged on Paris, singing the hymn that later became the national anthem.

On 10 August 1792 the provincial National Guards, with some help from Parisian radicals, overthrew the monarchy. But this did not neutralize the immediate threat. The internal enemy—the supporters of the refractory priests—was as dangerous as ever. Furthermore, Brissot finally persuaded the Legislative Assembly to declare war on Austria (20 April 1792). Prussia soon allied with Austria, and the Prussians were indeed the first to cross the frontier. Shortly after the fortress of Verdun surrendered to the Prussians, the September Massacres (2–6 September 1792) began in Paris. About 1,400

people were murdered in this appalling episode, in which murderers methodically dragged prisoners from their cells, set up kangaroo courts, and murdered the "guilty" in the streets. The most prominent victim was the Princesse de Lamballe, an intimate of Marie Antoinette, whose head and body parts were paraded through the Marais section of Paris.

The overthrow of the monarchy was also the death of the Constitution of 1791. Consequently, a new body, the National Convention, was elected to replace the Legislative Assembly. The Convention declared France a republic on 20 September 1792. Military victories at Valmy and Jemappes forced the Prussians out of France and allowed the French to occupy Belgium. The Convention also decided to put Louis XVI on trial. It ignored the fact that he was immune for all political acts under the Constitution of 1791. Despite widespread charges that the king was guilty of treason (a charge that many historians continue to repeat), the Convention failed to produce any evidence that he had betrayed his country in wartime.

Even so, the Convention found Louis guilty, and he was executed on 21 January 1793. The men of the Convention were convinced that they were living through a great moment in human history. They were right, but not for the reasons they imagined. They thought they had founded the republic of universal happiness, that the sacrifice of their king had made them true republicans, that spilling the blood of Louis the Last had sacralized the republic. It did none of this. Indeed, the republic succumbed to a dictatorship eleven years later, in part because of what they had done. In effect, the execution of the king provoked the counterrevolution, in the person of the king's brother, the new self-proclaimed regent. He vowed that a successful counterrevolution would demand the execution of the regicides. The execution of Louis XVI therefore rendered impossible any compromise between revolutionary and counterrevolutionary France.

THE CRISIS OF 1793
The death of the king solved none of the pressing challenges before the Convention. In February and March, the Convention declared war on Great Britain, Holland, and Spain. Every great power except Russia was now at war with France. Moreover, the

spring military campaign went badly. A renewed Austrian offensive forced the French into retreat. Worse still, one of the French generals, Charles-François du Périer Dumouriez, tried to turn his troops on Paris to "restore the sane part of the Convention." He failed, but his treason fueled the revolutionaries' already powerful conviction that conspiracy was everywhere and no one could be trusted.

The economy, meanwhile, teetered on the brink of collapse. By January 1793 the *assignat* was at half its original value. There were riots in several major cities, particularly in Paris, where journalists and demagogues demanded a law prescribing death to hoarders. The Convention balked at that, but it did decree a "maximum," a law fixing the price of grain. The maximum did little for the cities, but it

did fix the price the government would pay for grain for the swelling armies of the republic.

Alongside foreign war and economic chaos, the third dimension of the crisis of 1793 was counter-revolutionary insurrection in the west of France. The first riots were spread over fourteen departments in Normandy, Brittany, Maine, Anjou, and Poitou. The revolutionary army and local National Guard put down most of the rebellion, but they failed to do so in four departments south of the Loire, known as the "Vendée *militaire*" or simply the "Vendée." This was easily the most extensive and enduring peasant rebellion of the entire Revolution. It began as a protest over the recruiting law of 24 February 1793, whereby the Convention conscripted 300,000 young men into the army. But whole communities, upset over higher taxes, higher rents, and the disruption of their spiritual life by the

Age of Revolutions. A contemporary engraving depicts the execution of Louis XVI of France, 1793. ©BETTMANN/CORBIS

Civil Constitution of the Clergy, soon joined the young men. By July, noble leaders, often impressed into service by their former "vassals," had formed a "Catholic and Royal Army of the West" and sent out emissaries to seek out British arms and money.

The Convention responded with the first steps toward the Terror. It established a Revolutionary Tribunal in Paris, whose initial purpose was to punish traitors like Dumouriez, and a Committee of Public Safety to take whatever measures were necessary to save the young republic. It also established revolutionary committees to arrest suspects, that is, anyone thought to be a potential enemy. And it passed the law of 10 March 1793, which established revolutionary tribunals that reduced enormously the protections for the accused as guaranteed in the Declaration of the Rights of Man and Citizen. Finally, it authorized its own members, known as "representatives on mission," to fan out over the provinces to supervise conscription and the application of revolutionary laws in general.

These early measures of defense provoked widespread resistance, especially in the cities of the south. Because local Jacobins took these measures even further than the Convention intended and threatened a bloodbath of their enemies, many in the south rebelled under the banner of "federalism." The federalists had little contact amongst themselves and not much of a program beyond resistance to the Jacobin vision of the future, but one by one they took over many cities in the region. These cities, Lyon, Marseille, Toulon, Bordeaux, and some smaller ones such as Arles and Aubagne, had all experienced lynchings the previous summer. Like the September Massacres in Paris, these lynchings had never been punished.

THE TERROR

Federalism and the Vendée were defeated, at least militarily, by the end of 1793. At the same time, the purge of Brissot's friends from the Convention (31 May–2 June 1793), the accession of Maximilien Robespierre to the Committee of Public Safety (27 July 1793), and the murder of the journalist-deputy Jean-Paul Marat in his bath by Charlotte Corday (13 July 1793) all combined to ratchet up a will to destroy the enemies of the Revolution.

These events led France to the Terror, the most violent and also one of the most misunderstood

episodes of the Revolution. Most of the victims of the Terror were found guilty of counterrevolutionary acts, but in fact their trials were too short to establish guilt or innocence: in Marseilles they averaged twenty minutes each, in Lyon seventy-two seconds. Around Nantes, one tribunal passed 666 death sentences in three days. Among the victims were numerous women, priests, and children. In any case, the language of Terror was not defensive, and it was deliberately horrible and cruel. "The guillotine awaits its game birds," said the representative on mission in Arras, Joseph Le Bon. According to the representatives in Lyon,

> Our enemies need a great example, a terrible lesson to force them to respect the cause of Justice and Liberty. All right then! We are going to give it to them. . . . All their allies at Liberated City [Lyon] must fall before the thunderbolts of justice and their bloodied corpses, tossed into the Rhône, offer from its two banks until its mouth, under the walls of the infamous Toulon, to the eyes of the cowardly and ferocious English, the impression of horror and the image of the all powerful French people.

The Terror had many purposes, but one of the most common justifications at the time was that it was needed to purge the nation of corrupting influences and to regenerate the citizenry, to make it worthy of the egalitarian republic. Hence the necessity to make executions as spectacular as possible and hence, too, the frequent ceremonies, often known as dechristianization, to exorcize the Christian, royalist, and feudal past. The Terror was intended to purge the Old Regime from people's minds.

The Terror as mass execution, of course, failed, and it formally came to an end with the execution of Robespierre and his faction on 28 July 1794. But the successor regimes, known as the Thermidorean Convention (after the month in the revolutionary calendar when the Terror ended) and the Directory (the government established by the Constitution of the Year III, or 1795) nonetheless remained revolutionary regimes. They, too, aimed to produce a new republican man animated by public virtue, through reforms in the school curricula and lengthy, didactic public ceremonies. They were enthusiastically anticlerical and maintained the death penalty for returned refractory priests and émigrés. Finally, they established exceptional military commissions from time to time, whose legal basis and procedures were scarcely different from revolutionary courts of the Terror.

EXPORT OF THE REVOLUTION

Thus, when the French expanded into western Europe, they brought with them not the promise of 1789—a regime based upon the rights of man, fraternity, and limited government—but rather revolutionary regimes, which they imposed upon the newly liberated peoples. Moreover, they exported not only policies, but also stubborn habits of mind. French authorities viewed all opposition as the result of conspiracy, and religious dissidence as the work of refractory priests. They believed foreigners unworthy to receive the blessings of liberty, since they had been corrupted by centuries of despotism. The same attitudes had played themselves out in France itself; abroad, the result was the same: repression followed by resistance.

The pattern of repression and resistance appeared almost everywhere as people protested the French-imposed reforms of the Catholic Church. In France, strong anticlerical surges throughout the 1790s provoked an equally powerful response, including talk of apparitions of the Virgin in sacred oak trees, pilgrimages to holy fountains and wells to ward off divine wrath, stories about the end of days, pilgrimages to the Holy Land to establish the "Republic of Jesus Christ," and so on. The rest of Europe was no different. On the left bank of the Rhine, for instance, although the monasteries were left alone for a while, the invaders imposed the revolutionary calendar, forbade pilgrimages, suppressed outdoor religious ceremonies, deported unruly priests, and took other similarly repressive measures. The response in the Rhineland was similar to that in France. Around Aachen, one widely distributed pamphlet denounced "all enemies of the saints, of their images and of their solemn veneration . . . all harbingers of the Anti-Christ . . . O Lord, be gracious unto us! At a time when many carry the mark of the beast." In Italy, there were stories of miraculous appearances of the Virgin in lonely dilapidated chapels, stories of miraculous cures at her shrines, stories of her statues weeping, blinking, falling over, or speaking. The French, like the Tridentine reformers before them, deplored the reports as senseless superstition and tried to suppress them, but in driving such sentiments underground,

they made the faithful cling to their traditions even more. As in France, clerics who had once condemned such enthusiasms as aberrations began to see their value as stimulants to faith, and the church entered the new century with priests and laity more in harmony than they had been in centuries.

Another reason for discontent was that the French occupiers did not bring liberty to Europe's oppressed for free. Not only did they expect the natives to sustain the occupation and tolerate pillage, they also expected indemnities. When the republican armies overran Belgium, the Dutch Republic, and the left bank of the Rhine in late 1794–early 1795, they made the price clear. In the former Dutch Republic they established the first of the "sister republics," the Batavian Republic, and staffed it with Dutch patriots. But they also imposed an indemnity of 100 million florins, and over a fifth of the new republic's expenditure was for the upkeep of French troops. One of the reasons for the invasion of Switzerland was to loot the treasury of the city of Bern in order to finance Bonaparte's Egyptian campaign. General Guillaume Brune levied an indemnity of five million livres and took hostages among the patricians to ensure compliance. One commissioner threatened to toss the patricians into the nearby lakes as fish food. In the Kingdom of Naples, ordinary people welcomed the French because they believed their liberators would abolish all taxes. Instead, they levied an indemnity of 2.5 million ducats as well as a separate indemnity on Bari of 40,000 ducats. Royalist opponents of the French, in turn, got a great deal of traction by promising a moratorium on all taxes for ten years.

Resistance against the French emerged almost everywhere. Although the particular motivating factors varied from place to place, rebellion usually had to do with increased taxation, conscription, and religious innovation. In Belgium, for instance, the French definitively abolished the old institutions of estates and provinces that had recently defied the Austrian "despotism," creating instead nine new subservient departments. Many priests refused yet another oath of loyalty, and nearly five hundred were deported to Guienne or the islands of Ré and Oléron off the Atlantic coast. In December 1798, a "War of the Peasants" broke out on both sides of the Flemish-Walloon linguistic line to protest conscription. Young men; the rural poor, now desperate because of the abolition of traditional relief; and the socially marginal, including demobilized imperial soldiers and men the French called "brigands," took up all manner of farm tools and tore down liberty trees, burned vital statistics registers, robbed tax offices, and welcomed refractory priests. One band called itself the "Catholic Army of Brabant," while others shouted their support for George III, the prince of Orange, or the Austrian emperor. Many of these same people had rebelled against the innovations of Joseph II nine years before. French repression was far more successful than Austria's had been; some five to ten thousand Belgians were arrested, and nearly two hundred were shot by military commissions.

In the vastly over-taxed Batavian Republic, the Dutch navy mutinied during the Anglo-Russian invasion of August 1799, but the rebellion did not spread, possibly because the Orangist pretender remained an uncompromising enemy of the former patriots, now Jacobins, just as he had been in the 1780s. There were also significant disturbances in Switzerland. Many could see little point in the "Helvetic Republic," with its modern and expensive government, its requisitions, and its military drafts. People in the more remote cantons had never paid taxes of any sort and had certainly never been drafted (there were similar conditions in many of the tiny German statelets, where the knights of the Holy Roman Empire lived off their own resources and made no demands on their subjects). Everywhere the French tax system was disruptive, since the Swiss had never known a direct land tax. As in France and elsewhere, in Switzerland protests based on religion were dismissed as the work of fanatics, and in one rising nearly four hundred were killed.

In Italy there was counterrevolutionary resistance almost from the beginning of the French invasion in March 1796. There were irregulars operating against the Army of Italy in Lombardy, Liguria, Romagna, and Tuscany. The "Jacobins" who accepted positions of authority in the sister republics—the Ligurian (Genoa, June 1797), Cisalpine (Milan, July 1797), Roman (February 1798), and Parnethopean or Neapolitan (January 1799)—had very little popular following and were always threatened with insurrection. There was a major counterrevolutionary rising in the Ligurian Republic as early as September 1797, which the French saw as a clerical and noble-inspired rising (like previous risings in France) to restore the Genovese oligarchy using religion as a pretext. In fact, French anticlericalism had outraged local religious sensibilities. Around Rapollo some peasants wished to plant "a tree with the banner of the Madonna" to counter the French liberty trees. Nearby, the "low people" decided to "raise the Genovese standard, reinforced with the image of the Immaculate Virgin." In a rising in Ferrara, one rebel leader said he was a "captain of the Emperor." In Nice and western Piedmont, a particularly vicious guerilla movement, known as the *barbets* or *barbetti*, murdered "the French" and bragged about eating their livers and bread soaked in their blood. They frequently decapitated their victims and took the heads with them.

There was a major insurrection in Rome on 25 February 1798, in which up to two hundred French may have been killed. Earlier, General André Masséna had been accused of being the Antichrist. On the eve of the declaration of the Roman Republic, "around 90,000 faithful, covered with the grime of penitents, implored divine help." The occasion for the rising itself was the decision of the republic to abolish the Jewish ghetto and free Jews from the obligation to wear a yellow symbol. Jews could now wear the republican tricolor, which raised fear and suspicion that they supported the French. The rebellion was quickly suppressed and on 27 February alone, thirty rebels were executed after sentencing by a military commission. Over the next two years over eighty people were executed.

The year 1799 witnessed generalized insurrections throughout the peninsula. These had begun in Piedmont, in the valley of the Aosta, the previous December; in February 1799 they spread to the Neapolitan Republic, and they became general with the Austro-Russian invasion. The Russian commander Aleksandr Suvorov entered Milan on 28 April, whereupon the Cisalpine Republic collapsed. Turin fell a month later. This encouraged the counterrevolution throughout Italy. In the Alpine villages, the local captains of the irregulars were parish priests who had swords and pistols stuffed into their cassocks. The most dramatic and bloody rebellion occurred in the Neapolitan Republic. In February 1799, Cardinal Fabrizio Ruffo, a former official in the papal curia, set out from Sicily and landed in Calabria with just four men. Gradually, he gathered more and more forces to his movement, the Santa Fede or 'Holy Faith'. Officially, he called his army the "Most Christian Armada of the Holy Faith," although it was less an army than a constantly changing series of formations of local irregulars. On 13 June, the Santafedisti entered Naples and began an orgy of revenge and bloodletting. Ruffo himself watched with despair. As an enlightened reformer, he had gnawing misgivings about the crude faith of his followers, but he contributed to the lawlessness by promising them confiscated Jacobin estates. Indeed, authority collapsed to such an extent, and the restored Bourbons and their advisor Lord Horatio Nelson were in such a vindictive mood, that the vendetta killings continued for another year. Brigandage remained a problem in the kingdom for decades afterward.

NAPOLEON AND THE END OF THE REVOLUTION

The French Revolution destroyed the ancient institutions of old Europe, institutions that had kept an uneasy and not always successful balance between despots and subjects. The consequence of this destruction was the Napoleonic despotism and, in response, a revival of the Catholic enthusiasm that the Tridentine reforms had tried to contain over two hundred years before. No one could have anticipated such an end to the Revolution back in the summer of 1789, amid the blissful hopes for a humanity reborn.

See also **American Independence, War of (1775–1783); Ancien Régime; Dutch Republic; Enlightened Despotism; Estates-General, French: 1789; France; Geneva; Italy; Joseph II (Holy Roman Empire); Louis XVI (France); Marie Antoinette; Patriot Revolution; Popular Protest and Rebellions.**

BIBLIOGRAPHY

Baker, Keith Michael. *Inventing the French Revolution: Essays on French Political Culture in the Eighteenth Century.* New York and Cambridge, U.K., 1990.

Baker, Keith Michael, ed. *The Old Regime and the French Revolution.* Chicago, 1987.

Bergeron, Louis. *France under Napoleon.* Translated by R. R. Palmer. Princeton, 1981.

Blanning, T. C. W. *The Culture of Power and the Power of Culture: Old Regime Europe, 1660–1789.* New York and Oxford, 2002.

Blum, Jerome. *The End of the Old Order in Rural Europe.* Princeton, 1978.

Doyle, William. *The Oxford History of the French Revolution.* 2nd edition. New York and Oxford, 2002.

Doyle, William, ed. *Old Regime France, 1648–1788.* New York and Oxford, 2001.

Furet, François. *Interpreting the French Revolution.* Translated by Elborg Forster, Cambridge, U.K., 1981.

———. *Revolutionary France, 1770–1880.* Translated by Antonia Nevill. Cambridge, Mass., and Oxford, 1992.

Furet, François, and Mona Ozouf, eds. *A Critical Dictionary of the French Revolution.* Translated by Arthur Goldhammer. Cambridge, Mass., 1989.

Hunt, Lynn. *The Family Romance of the French Revolution.* Berkeley, 1992.

———. *Politics, Culture, and Class in the French Revolution.* Berkeley, 1984.

Lefebvre, Georges. *The Coming of the French Revolution, 1789.* Translated by R. R. Palmer. Princeton, 1967. First published 1947.

Nicolson, Harold. *The Congress of Vienna: A Study in Allied Unity, 1812–1822.* New York, 1946.

Palmer, R. R. *The Age of the Democratic Revolution: A Political History of Europe and America, 1760–1800.* 2 vols. Princeton, 1959–1964.

Schama, Simon. *Citizens: A Chronicle of the French Revolution.* New York, 1989.

———. *Patriots and Liberators: Revolution in the Netherlands, 1780–1813.* New York, 1977.

Sheehan, James J. *German History, 1770–1866.* Oxford, 1989.

Sutherland, D. M. G. *France 1789–1815: Revolution and Counter-revolution.* New York, 1986.

Tackett, Timothy. *Becoming a Revolutionary: The Deputies of the French National Assembly and the Emergence of a Revolutionary Culture (1789–1790).* Princeton, 1996.

DONALD SUTHERLAND

REYNOLDS, JOSHUA (1723–1792), English portrait painter and theorist. Sir Joshua Reynolds's critical role in the development of British art from the eighteenth century lay both in his painting practice and his position as the first president of the Royal Academy. As the leading painter of aristocratic and intellectual society in the second half of the eighteenth century, Reynolds looked to classical and Old Master models to endow his "great style" portraits and his own reputation with art historical seriousness. He articulated his method for raising

the social status of the artist in theoretical form with the fifteen lectures (known as the *Discourses on Art*) he delivered between 1769 and 1790 to the students and members of the Royal Academy that he helped found in 1768.

Born in Plympton, where his father, an Oxford fellow, was master of the local grammar school, Reynolds began his London career as an apprentice to fellow Devonshire-born portrait painter Thomas Hudson in 1740. After three years (although he had been indentured for four), Reynolds began his independent practice in London and Devonshire. To complete his artistic education, he sailed with his friend Commodore Augustus Keppel to Italy, where he studied in Rome between April 1750 and April 1752.

On his return to London at the end of 1752, Reynolds set up his studio near Covent Garden, the neighborhood then popular with artists. His second portrait of Keppel (c. 1753–1754; National Maritime Museum, London) in the pose of the Greek sculpture *Apollo Belvedere* demonstrates Reynolds's study of the antique statues in Rome, as well as the heroic figures of Michelangelo. As his future student James Northcote related, Reynolds's success was consolidated with his commissions of "several ladies of high quality, whose portraits the polite world flocked to see." Reynolds's hectic schedule of sittings (in 1758 he had sittings every day of the week) provided the income necessary for his move to a larger house in Leicester Fields in 1760.

That year also marked the initial exhibition of the Society of Artists, which was the first public exhibition of paintings to be held in England. Reynolds contributed four portraits, including the classicizing full-length portrait of Elizabeth Gunning, duchess of Hamilton (1758–1759; Lady Lever Art Gallery, Port Sunlight). Reynolds continued to exhibit at the Society of Artists; however, he socialized with men of letters, such as Samuel Johnson, Oliver Goldsmith, and Edmund Burke, and was a founding member of the Literary Club in 1764.

Soon after his two-month trip to Paris, the Royal Academy was founded, in December 1768, and Reynolds was elected its first president. It was for the academy rooms that he painted his only portraits of King George III and Queen Charlotte. Although he never succeeded in winning royal patronage, Reynolds was knighted in April 1769 and named principal painter in 1784 on the death of Allan Ramsay.

The following two decades of Reynolds's career revolved around his dual role as painter and theoretician at the Royal Academy. At the annual exhibitions, Reynolds displayed his most ambitious works, such as *Mrs. Siddons as the Tragic Muse* (1783–1784; Huntington Library Art Collections, San Marino, Calif.), in which the dramatic actress is seated in the pose of Michelangelo's prophet Isaiah from the Sistine Chapel ceiling.

Presented annually for the first five years and then every other year at the academy's annual awards ceremony, Reynolds's *Discourses on Art* were not only a prescriptive course of study for aspiring artists, but also presented the president's case for the intellectual status of the artist in society. In his stated theory of beauty in Discourse IX, Reynolds's emphasis on the cerebral is clear: "The beauty of which we are in quest is general and intellectual; it is an idea that subsists only in the mind."

Although Reynolds's dictate to artists urging inventiveness may seem at odds with his own borrowing of poses from antique sculpture and Old Master paintings, his allusions to great works from the past are in keeping with the theory he outlines in Discourse XII: "The daily food and nourishment of the mind of an Artist is found in the great works of his predecessors. There is no other way to become great himself." To this end, Reynolds recommends the "great style" of the Roman and Bolognese schools, as opposed to the "ornamental" approach of the Venetians.

Reynolds's own attempts to achieve the richness of color of Titian and the Venetian school led him to experiment with mixtures of varnish, turpentine, bitumen, and other unconventional ingredients that often caused irreparable damage to his paintings. To Northcote he confessed that "I had not an opportunity of being early initiated in the principles of Colouring." Reynolds stopped painting upon the deterioration of his eyesight in 1789. On his death in 1792, he was buried in the crypt of St. Paul's Cathedral. In his eulogy, Edmund Burke took up Reynolds's own insistence on the intellectual role of the artist, noting that "he was a profound and penetrating philosopher."

Joshua Reynolds. *Mrs. Siddons as the Tragic Muse,* in the Henry E. Huntington Library and Art Gallery, San Marino, California. ©Francis G. Mayer/Corbis

See also **Academies of Art; Art: The Conception and Status of the Artist; Britain, Art in; Gainsborough, Thomas.**

BIBLIOGRAPHY

Primary Sources

Northcote, James. *Memoirs of Sir Joshua Reynolds: Comprising Original Anecdotes of Many Distinguished Persons, His Contemporaries, and a Brief Analysis of His Discourses.* London, 1813.

Reynolds, Sir Joshua. *Discourses on Art.* Edited by Robert R. Wark. New Haven and London, 1975.

———. *The Letters of Sir Joshua Reynolds.* Edited by John Ingamells and John Edgcumbe. New Haven and London, 2000.

Secondary Sources

Mannings, David. *Sir Joshua Reynolds. A Complete Catalogue of His Paintings.* New Haven and London, 2000.

Penny, Nicholas, ed. *Reynolds.* London, 1986.

ELIZABETH A. PERGAM

RHETORIC. The term "rhetoric" refers to the art of persuasive discourse or to the presence of rhetorical elements in prose, poetry, or oratory.

THE HERITAGE OF THE MIDDLE AGES

As a discipline, rhetoric crowned education in the culture of ancient Greece and Rome and served in the Middle Ages as one of the three liberal arts of the *trivium:* grammar, logic, and rhetoric. Even though occasions for the practice of live oratory in judicial courts and political forums declined in the medieval period, rhetoric supplied theoretical principles for the arts of preaching, letter writing, and poetry.

RENAISSANCE RECOVERY OF CLASSICAL LITERATURE

Humanists in fourteenth-century Italy began to study newly recovered classical manuscripts, including previously unknown rhetorical works, histories, and other literary texts. At the same time the advent of printing carried forward the pedagogical influence of the most ubiquitous rhetorical manuals of Roman antiquity: *De inventione* (On invention) by Cicero (106–43 B.C.E.) and the anonymous *Rhetorica ad Herennium* (Rhetoric for Herennius). The recovery of *De institutio oratoria* (On the education of the orator) by Quintilian, a first-century Roman teacher of rhetoric, reinforced and expanded the content of the early works. All of these depicted rhetoric as including five parts or canons: invention, arrangement, memory, delivery, and style; and all envisioned three kinds of oratory: political, judicial, and ceremonial (epideictic).

The discovery around 1400 of Cicero's *De oratore* (On oratory), a dialogue, and many of his orations and letters to friends inspired scholars to imitate his Latin and to regard as inadequate the medieval form inherited from the Scholastics. Ciceronianism, as the new movement was called, had its critics, who argued against excessive imitation of the vocabulary and syntax of Cicero.

Interest in the language and literature of ancient Greece also arose in the fifteenth century when Greek scholars came to reside in Italy, bringing with them Greek manuscripts of works unknown for centuries. Among these scholars were Manuel Chrysoloras (c. 1353–1415), who taught Greek in Florence, and George of Trebizond (1395–1486), author of a popular rhetoric incorporating the Greek and Byzantine tradition and a translator of Aristotle's *Rhetoric* into Latin. His was the first of many translations that made Aristotle's teachings available once more.

Prominent among the manuals of rhetoric reviving the whole classical tradition were George of Trebizond's *Rhetoricorum Libri V* (c. 1433; Five books on rhetoric); Guillaume Fichet's *Rhetorica* (1471); Lorenzo Guglielmo Traversagni's *Nova Rhetorica* (1478; New rhetoric); Johannes Caesarius's *Rhetorica* (1542); and the Jesuit Cipriano Soarez's *De Arte Rhetorica* (1562), which was reprinted continuously into the eighteenth century. Some very popular textbooks of the Renaissance were devoted entirely to invention and some solely to style.

THE CHIEF ELEMENTS OF RENAISSANCE RHETORIC

As occasions for the use of rhetoric in the city-states of Italy increased at the beginning of the Renaissance, so too did interest in the elements of the art. Invention, the technique of developing arguments on both sides of a subject, was deemed critical to persuasive speech or prose. Rhetoric shared with logic (or dialectic) the need for invention, but dialectic debated philosophical questions while rhetoric argued matters of public concern in order to persuade a general audience.

Invention aided orators in creating arguments when certain knowledge could not be attained, when one could argue only from what seemed probable. The ancient dialectical method of assessing probabilities, "the topics," was used to probe a subject systematically by asking for its genus, species (or definition), accidents, and properties (and its similarities, opposites, and relationships). Rhetorical texts added to the topical lore of invention the topics of persons (ancestry, education, appearance, and character) and action (manner of life, deeds, words). Collectively these were referred to as "commonplaces" in English, *koinoi topoi* in Greek, and *loci communes* in Latin. In sixteenth-century England students kept "commonplace books" in which they recorded topical arguments, memorable sayings, and set pieces of eloquence. The topical method permeated creative efforts in poetry and literary prose as well as public discourse. Closely linked to the topics was the canon of style. Its concern with levels of discourse, tone, and the fecundity of figures of speech inspired even more interest than invention in the Renaissance. The figures or "colors" were exploited extensively in oratory, prose, and poetry to appeal to the emotions.

The lines between the provinces of dialectic and rhetoric began to break down in the sixteenth century when more and more philosophical subjects came to the attention of an increasingly educated public. The scope of rhetoric was thus widened beyond the three traditional kinds.

HUMANISM AND CURRICULAR REFORM

The recovery of Quintilian's *De institutione oratoria* in 1416 confirmed humanists in their efforts to revamp the curriculum to emphasize both literary and practical concerns. The *studia humanitatis,* which soon replaced the *trivium* in most Italian schools, included grammar, poetics, rhetoric, history and moral philosophy. Logic was deleted from the new curriculum in reaction to what was deemed Scholastic preoccupation with syllogistic reasoning.

Among the later humanists, Desiderius Erasmus (1466?–1536) was probably the best known in his lifetime. His influence spread across the Continent to England, where his *De Ratione Studii*

(1512; On a course of studies) and *De Copia* (1512; On copiousness), a treatise on style, were adopted by John Colet (1467–1519) for use in St. Paul's School in London. Juan Luis Vives (1492–1540), educated at the University of Paris, also carried humanist studies to England. Soarez's *De Arte Rhetorica* (1562), mentioned earlier, circulated from Portugal to Italy and to Jesuit schools throughout the world. Philipp Melanchthon's (1497–1560) rhetorical works extended his humanistic approach to Germany and other northern areas.

RISE OF THE VERNACULAR

Although Latin remained the predominant language for scholarly communication, during the sixteenth century the vernacular increasingly became the preferred medium for familiar letters, preaching, publications, and oratory aimed at a general audience. As consciousness of national differences increased in the sixteenth and seventeenth centuries, so also did attention to the perfection of national languages and a desire to make them equal to classical Latin. Textbooks of rhetoric soon appeared in the vernacular, for example, Thomas Wilson's *The Art of Rhetorique* (1553) in English and Bartolomeo Cavalcanti's *La retorica* (1555) in Italian.

RAMISM

The Dutch humanist Rudolph Agricola (1444–1485) and the French scholar Petrus Ramus (1515–1572) suggested changes in the curriculum that reversed earlier humanist alterations. Teaching at the University of Paris, Ramus followed the lead of Agricola in returning attention to the study of dialectic, making it the master discipline. Attempting to eliminate overlap in the curriculum, he allocated invention, organization, and memory to dialectic and gave style and delivery to rhetoric. The effect was to attribute to dialectic his own methods of analysis and composition and to equate rhetoric with stylistic artifice, neglecting entirely its aim of persuasion. Ramism was most popular in northern Europe and England during the last half of the sixteenth and early seventeenth centuries.

SCIENCE AND RHETORIC IN THE SEVENTEENTH CENTURY

The rise of interest in scientific induction and experiment in the seventeenth century brought with it a concern for clearer, more succinct prose. Francis

Bacon (1561–1626) called for a more analytic approach to the coloration of meaning in expression. René Descartes (1596–1650) and John Locke (1632–1704) deplored stylistic artifice. Invention, which Bacon saw as primarily associated with science, diminished in importance. Emphasis in teaching style moved from stress on elegant figures and extensive elaboration to that on precision in diction and clarification of meaning in open, familiar expression.

EIGHTEENTH-CENTURY TRENDS IN RHETORIC

Four major and enduring trends in the study of rhetoric can be discerned in the eighteenth century: neoclassicism, elocution, belletrism, and philosophical-psychological theory. Neoclassicism and elocution both flourished in the first part of the century. Neoclassicism called for renewed study of the Greek and Latin classics of rhetoric. Bernard Lamy (1640–1715) and François Fénelon (1651–1715) in France and John Lawson (1709–1759) and John Ward (1679?–1758) in England were foremost in this movement. Elocution, the old canon of delivery concerned with voice and gesture, came into vogue as a separate art because critics believed that proficiency in pulpit and political oratory had seriously declined. Thomas W. Sheridan (1719–1788) successfully promoted this new trend in education.

The latter half of the eighteenth century saw the rise of belletrism and the philosophical-psychological approach to rhetoric. Neither of these retained invention, their focus being analysis of the written word. Growing out of the Scottish Enlightenment, the belletristic movement engaged such disparate figures as Henry Home, Lord Kames (1696–1782), Adam Smith (1723–1790), Edmund Burke (1729–1797), Joseph Priestley (1733–1804), George Campbell (1719–1796), and Hugh Blair (1718–1800). They stressed interpretation of literary texts and such concepts as taste, the sublime, and the beautiful. George Campbell approached the study of rhetoric from the standpoint of the new theories of the human mind, termed faculty psychology. His *Philosophy of Rhetoric* (1776) treats the aims of discourse and the creation of effects on the mind. All four of these views of rhetoric were transported to North America.

See also **Descartes, René; Education; Erasmus, Desiderius; Humanists and Humanism; Locke, John; Melanchthon, Philipp; Ramus, Petrus.**

BIBLIOGRAPHY

Fumaroli, Marc. *L'age de l'éloquence: rhétorique et "res literaria" de la Renaissance au seuil de l'époque classique.* Geneva, 1980.

Howell, Wilbur S. *Logic and Rhetoric in England, 1500–1700.* New York, 1961.

Kristeller, Paul Oskar. *Renaissance Thought: The Classic, Scholastic, and Humanist Strains.* New York, 1961.

Miriam Joseph, Sister. *Rhetoric in Shakespeare's Time: Literary Theory of Renaissance Europe.* 1947. Partial reprint, New York, 1962.

Ong, Walter J. *Ramus: Method and the Decay of Dialogue from the Art of Discourse to the Art of Reason.* Cambridge, Mass., 1958.

Vasoli, Cesare. *La dialettica e la retorica dell'Umanesimo: "Invenzione" e "Metodo" nella cultura del XV e XVI secolo.* Milan, 1968.

Vickers, Brian. *In Defence of Rhetoric.* Oxford, 1988.

JEAN DIETZ MOSS

RICHARDSON, SAMUEL (1689–1761),

English novelist. Samuel Richardson was born at Mackworth in Derbyshire. His father was a joiner, and his family were farmers. Richardson's poverty precluded a classical education, and he went to a common school. Apprenticed for seven years to a printer, John Wilde, Richardson became a Freeman of the Stationers' Company and of the City of London in 1715. He married his employer's daughter, Martha, in 1721, and they had six children, all of whom died in childhood.

Hardworking and diligent, Richardson established himself as a prosperous stationer and printer in 1721 near St. Bride's Church off Fleet Street, London. Renowned for his charity and generosity, he printed the novels *Moll Flanders* and *Roxana* by Daniel Defoe, the duke of Wharton's periodical the *True Briton,* and works by the philosopher Francis Hutcheson. Characterized as an extreme Tory printer, he was impeached by the secretary of state in 1722. Two years after his wife's death in 1733, Richardson married Elizabeth Leake; they had four daughters, Mary, Martha, Anne, and Sarah. He moved his business to Salisbury Square, which became his home until his death, and did not travel far outside of London.

Richardson's first work was *The Apprentice's Vade Mecum; or, Young Man's Pocket Companion* (1733), a book of letters of advice on model behavior for apprentices. Addressed to his own nephew and apprentice, Thomas Richardson, the book expounds on the importance of the moral duties between employer and employee, especially obedience and mutual respect. In 1735 he printed the progovernment *Daily Gazetter*. Richardson's revisions and prefaces to Defoe's *The Complete English Tradesman* and *Tour thro' the Whole Island of Great Britain* display his interest in the cultural aspects of Britishness. Richardson was asked by the Society for the Encouragement of Learning to write a book of model letters on how to act morally in different situations.

Richardson's first novel *Pamela; or, Virtue Rewarded* (1740–1741) developed from a further morally improving project called *Letters Written to and for Particular Friends on the Most Important Occasions* (known as *Familiar Letters* and published in 1741). One of the letters, "A Father to a Daughter in Service, on Hearing of Her Master's Attempting Her Virtue," inspired Richardson to explore "practical examples, worthy to be followed in the most critical and affecting cases" (*Pamela,* Preface). Pamela writes to her parents about her master, Mr. B., who locks her up and tries to rape her. She evades this fate by marrying him. A critical success and praised for its heroine's steadfast virtue, *Pamela* was reprinted four times in 1741 and inspired imitations, a play by Henry Gifford, and Pamela merchandise including wax dolls. Novelist Henry Fielding, however, denounced *Pamela* as an opportunistic example of virtue and parodied the novel with *Shamela* (1741). Responding to this criticism, Richardson published *Pamela in Her Exalted Condition* (1741), but the sequel was less successful. That year also saw Richardson elected to the Court of Assistants of Stationers' Company.

Written "in a double yet separate correspondence," (*Clarissa,* Preface) Richardson's epic novel *Clarissa* (published in installments between 1747 and 1748) allows him as self-styled editor to effectively depict the subtleties of the voices of the four principal characters, reflecting their unfolding emo-

tional states. Begun in 1744, the novel explores the interior life of the bourgeois paragon Clarissa Harlowe, who is disowned by her family after not marrying the man of their choosing. Duped by the aristocratic rake Robert Lovelace, whom she loves, she believes she can "rescue" him to virtue, but he deceives her, imprisoning her in a brothel and raping her. Her hopelessness causes her death, and Lovelace dies in a duel with her cousin. Instantly successful, the novel was translated into French by writer and priest Abbé Antoine François Prévost d'Exiles; with *Pamela*, Richardson founded the sentimental novel.

Richardson encouraged women's writing among his fellow novelists and friends, Sarah Fielding, Frances Sheridan, and Charlotte Lennox, and engaged in extensive literary and moral debate with women. Shocked by female readers' attraction to the character of Lovelace, he revised the novel in the 1750s and extracted "instructive" passages from it for publication.

The History of Sir Charles Grandison (1753–1754), his last novel, creates a virtuous male equivalent of Clarissa, who is desired by two very different women. The novel's light satire of "vicious" individuals influenced novelist Jane Austen. Richardson died in July 1761 and is buried in St. Bride's Church in London.

See also **Advice and Etiquette Books; Defoe, Daniel; English Literature and Language; Printing and Publishing.**

BIBLIOGRAPHY

Primary Sources

Richardson, Samuel. *Clarissa; or, The History of a Young Lady.* Edited by Angus Ross. Harmondsworth, U.K.; New York, 1985.

———. *Pamela.* Edited by Thomas Keymer and Alice Wakely. Oxford and New York, 2001.

Secondary Sources

Blewett, David. *Passion and Virtue: Essays on the Novels of Samuel Richardson.* Toronto and Buffalo, 2001. Fourteen essays on two of the most central concerns of Richardson's fiction by leading Richardsonian scholars.

Eaves Duncan, T. C., and Ben D. Kimpel. *Samuel Richardson: A Biography.* Oxford, 1971. The most comprehensive and standard biography.

Gwilliam, Tassie. *Samuel Richardson's Fictions of Gender.* Stanford, 1993. A stimulating investigation of how

Richardson's fiction exposes the instability of eighteenth-century gender models.

Keymer, Tom. *The Life of Samuel Richardson*. Oxford, 2002. A biography contextualizing Richardson's life and works within literary and political developments and examining the relationship between literary form and unresolved ideological conflicts in Richardson's beliefs.

MAX FINCHER

RICHELIEU, ARMAND-JEAN DU PLESSIS, CARDINAL (1585–1642),

French ecclesiastical and political figure. Richelieu was the youngest son of a middle-ranking noble family from Poitou, whose father enjoyed short-lived prominence as grand provost of France under Henry III (ruled 1574–1589), but whose early death and bankruptcy (1590) spelled possible disaster for his widow and young children. The support of patrons, new and old, and the goodwill of King Henry IV (ruled 1589–1610) enabled Armand-Jean, after foreshortened theology studies in Paris, to become a very young bishop of Luçon by 1606. Although a neglected and unattractive diocese with well-entrenched Protestant communities, Luçon could afford wider career prospects to an ambitious cleric. This and several years of active pastoral activity in Luçon gradually drew him into contact with the royal court during a time of political—especially ministerial—instability following Henry IV's murder in 1610. This context, rather than his role at the 1614 Estates-General, explains his appointment in 1615 as grand almoner to Louis XIII's (ruled 1610–1643) young queen, Anne of Austria, and then secretary of state in November 1616, but he was rapidly swept out of office (April 1617) with the assassination of his first patron, Concino Concini, the Italian favorite of the queen mother, Marie de Médicis. Alone among Concini's protégés to make a political comeback, Richelieu survived seven turbulent years during which he honed his political skills as he was successively sent into internal exile, recalled, and finally made a cardinal despite the deep-seated reluctance of Louis XIII and his ministers. Well before 1624, when he was made a minister again, he had become Marie de Médicis's right-hand man and the principal beneficiary of her insistence on playing a political role throughout the 1620s.

THE KING'S MINISTER

Richelieu's new position, which would gradually evolve toward that of a "principal" minister, struck most contemporaries as that of a conventional royal favorite. But despite the enormous power and influence he enjoyed until his death, he never became Louis XIII's favorite in the accepted sense. From the outset, his relations with Louis were tense and difficult, and they remained so even after the political ménage à trois with Marie de Médicis finally ended with her disgrace and exile abroad in 1630–1631. Until then, Richelieu's ministry had been highly vulnerable: he depended mainly on Marie and her supporters, the *dévots,* at a time when the overlapping of domestic and foreign questions created acute problems of political management. Protestant and aristocratic rebellion was an enduring feature of the 1620s, and could sometimes play havoc with pursuing a foreign policy that, because it aimed at containing Habsburg expansionism, required alliances with certain Protestant states. This required considerable dexterity, and laid Richelieu—a cardinal of the Roman church, after all!—open to accusations of being a disciple of Machiavelli. The ending of Protestant revolt in 1629 was the only major success of this period, while France's military efforts against the Habsburgs were limited to intervention in northern Italy, when the real threat was building up elsewhere, in the empire. King and minister agreed fully on the need to oppose it, but were wary of precipitous action while aristocratic revolt and provincial discontent were still serious domestic threats.

Richelieu, whose essential duty was to articulate and manage foreign policy, fell foul of Marie and her *dévot* supporters, who were deeply hostile to Protestant alliances and wanted peace in order to pursue internal reforms. He barely survived the ensuing crisis, known as the Day of the Dupes (November 1630), although it took at least two more years to deal with the aftershocks from it. This partly explains the caution of foreign policy and the preference for fighting the Habsburgs using proxies like Denmark or Sweden. Thus full-scale war was postponed until it became unavoidable, in 1635. The king and minister's optimism about an early victory and peace was rudely shattered, so that the final years of Richelieu's ministry were dominated by the unending burdens of organizing and financing armies, coaxing allies, cajoling military commanders to fight—all with very mixed results—and, finally, framing plans for a peace that would only materialize in 1648.

THE PLENITUDE OF POWER

Richelieu's position as chief minister took final shape during the 1630s, when his attention was devoted primarily to war and foreign affairs. After Marie de Médicis's fall, he no longer needed to fear opposition within the ministry itself, since all of the ministers were now clients of his who could work well together and who recognized their dependence on him. Internal affairs were, consequently, largely devolved to them, and the main changes to royal government resulted more from the pressures of war than from conscious plans for reform or centralization, plans that Richelieu progressively jettisoned by the late 1620s. His relations with Louis XIII could still be strained, thus offering hope to assorted royal favorites and conspirators to plot his downfall. The last of these, the famous Cinq-Mars conspiracy (1642), may even have had some royal sympathy and ended only months before Richelieu's own death. But Louis's waverings were always effectively countered by Richelieu's astute realization that all important decisions be taken explicitly by the king, thus making it virtually impossible for him to disown them later. The main opponents of Richelieu's accumulation of power and influence came from within the royal family and certain great noble houses. But a general assault on them was scarcely possible, given the wider political context, and Richelieu himself was no sworn enemy of the higher nobility. The best he could do was to win over as many of them as possible through offices, military commands, or advantageous marriage alliances, but some, like the Guise and the Montmorency, would not play the game by his rules, and suffered disgrace, exile, or even execution. Moreover, this policy of "divide and rule" was itself limited in its potential scope: it worked far better in peacetime than during war, when the crown depended more heavily on aristocratic goodwill. Some of Richelieu's strongest enemies had to be given army commands after 1635, and at least one used his army to provoke a rebellion in 1641. The cardinal's most spectacular success lay in turning the previously rebellious Bourbon-Condé family into allies, even to the extent of securing the marriage of

Cardinal Richelieu. Engraving after the painting by Philippe de Champaigne. LIBRARY OF CONGRESS

its heir, the future "great" Condé, to his niece in 1641. Richelieu made additional enemies and critics by the way he used his immense power to restore and extend his family's fortunes, a sometimes ruthless process in which his wealth consolidated his power, and vice versa. His power was not confined to the "four square feet of the king's study" or council chamber but extended into the provinces, thanks to provincial and town governorships as well as tenure of the admiralty of France. When he died, he was not only Louis XIII's richest subject, but he had secured three duchies for members of his extended family, who were now well integrated into the upper reaches of the French nobility.

POWER AND IDEAS

Richelieu's many offices, his great wealth (which included works of art, precious stones, and châteaus) and his many buildings (the Palais-Royal, Richelieu town and château in Poitou, the new Sorbonne college) all show him behaving as a Renaissance-style cardinal was expected to do. But neither wealth nor office alone could sustain political power, especially when it was as bitterly contested as his was. His early years in politics convinced him that cultural patronage, beginning but not ending with political propaganda, was indispensable.

From the early 1620s, he recruited writers into his service and initially used them to undermine existing favorites and ministers of Louis XIII—a dangerous game, which he learned to play effectively. Back in office, he needed propagandists to defend often unpopular policies. He quickly saw the advantages of crown-sponsored newsletters and gazettes, not to mention quasi-official histories of his own time. Thus, crown policies would be stoutly defended in print, successes publicly celebrated by every means available. Even the foundation of the Académie Française (1635) and Imprimerie Royale (1640), both important milestones in the French monarchy's attempts at cultural absolutism, were not divorced from such political considerations. Many of Richelieu's other projects, such as founding special academies to educate the nobility, were frustrated by the imperatives of war. Finally, as befitted a university theology graduate with enduring intellectual aspirations, he wrote extensively throughout his career on religious matters—pastoral instructions, a catechism, treatises on the conversion of France's Protestants and on Christian perfection. These works may not bear comparison with those of his greatest contemporaries (François de Sales, Pierre de Bérulle), but they show a genuine desire to apply religious precepts to the daily life lived by ordinary mortals. In theological terms Richelieu was essentially a Thomist who, despite being influenced by neo-Stoic ideas, never shared the Augustinian pessimism of contemporaries like Bérulle or Saint-Cyran. Psychologically and intellectually, he was comfortable with a relatively optimistic view of humankind as inhabited by a God-given reason. It may be claimed that his *Political Testament,* the most problematic of his works but not published in his lifetime, was itself typical of this lifelong didactic passion, and it was aimed at the Christian—as exemplified by his master, Louis XIII—rather than the Machiavellian prince.

See also **Absolutism; Louis XIII (France); Mantuan Succession, War of the (1627–1631); Marie de Médicis; Provincial Government; Thirty Years' War (1618–1648).**

BIBLIOGRAPHY

Bergin, Joseph. *Cardinal Richelieu: Power and the Pursuit of Wealth.* New Haven and London, 1985.

———. *The Rise of Richelieu.* New Haven and London, 1991.

Church, William F. *Richelieu and Reason of State.* Princeton, 1972.

Elliott, J. H. *Richelieu and Olivares.* Cambridge, U.K., and New York, 1984.

Levi, Anthony. *Cardinal Richelieu and the Making of France.* London and New York, 2000.

Ranum, Orest A. *Richelieu and the Councillors of Louis XIII: A Study of the Secretaries of State and Superintendents of Finance in the Ministry of Richelieu, 1635–1642.* Oxford, 1963.

JOSEPH BERGIN

RIGHTS, HUMAN. *See* **Rights, Natural.**

RIGHTS, NATURAL. The idea of natural rights is inseparable from the doctrine that all human beings, regardless of extrinsic differences in circumstance (nationality, class, religion) or physical condition (race, gender, age, etc.), share an identical set of powers, freedoms, and/or competencies. Scholars have customarily treated natural rights theory as a hallmark of modern legal and political thought, although one with roots in preceding intellectual traditions. In particular, the idea of natural rights has been contrasted with earlier teachings about natural law that were grounded in more robust principles of reason and natural or divine teleology. Many important thinkers of early modern Europe subscribed to a version of natural law without endorsing a doctrine of natural rights.

Central to the concept of natural rights is the view that every human being enjoys a complete and exclusive dominion over his or her mental and bodily facilities—and the fruits thereof—in the form of personal property. Thus, a natural rights theory entails a conception of private ownership grounded on the subjective status of the individual human being. The rights arising from such human subjectivity are both inalienable and imprescriptible in the sense that any attempt to renounce or extinguish them would constitute at the same time the cessation of one's personhood. Thus, for example, natural rights theory renders incoherent arguments for slavery based on alleged natural inequalities of intellect or physique.

Consequently, an important feature of the fully developed idea of natural rights is its direct and immediate political bearing. Given that natural rights may not be curtailed or eliminated without the denial to a person of his or her very humanity, any government that attempts to suppress them without due process has no claim on the obedience of its citizens. Natural rights always take precedence over artificial communal or public rights that might be imposed by political institutions. In this way, the doctrine of natural rights circumscribes political power and may even generate a defense of resistance to or revolution against systems of government that violate the rights of individuals.

The assertion of the modernity of natural rights theory must be qualified by the recognition that many of its characteristic elements were present in and elaborated by earlier theorists. For instance, scholars have found in Aristotle (384–322 B.C.E.) the logical rudiments of natural rights theory, albeit imperfectly articulated and applied. The language of rights was first clearly expressed in the teachings of classical Roman lawyers, for whom *ius* ('right' or 'law') constituted the basis of law and persons were fundamentally bearers of rights derived from law. Likewise, medieval canon (church) lawyers and Scholastic philosophers insisted that God endowed human beings with basic rights to themselves and to those goods that they required to preserve their divinely created lives.

Many attempts have been made to identify the "first" theorist of natural rights. In addition to Aristotle, the Scholastic philosopher/theologians Jean de Paris (c. 1240–1306; also known as John of Paris), William of Ockham (c. 1285–1349), and Jean de Gerson (1363–1429) have been nominated. Several of the participants in the fourteenth-century controversy between the papacy and the members of the spiritual wing of the Franciscan Order over the status of voluntary ecclesiastical poverty also moved the debate about the naturalness of property ownership in the direction of a theory of rights. Yet in each instance, some of the ingredients central to the fully "subjective" or individualistic doctrine of natural rights doctrine associated with modern thought are absent.

It is perhaps best to examine the development of the theory of natural rights after 1450 as an incremental process. Various thinkers contributed important dimensions to its history without necessarily enunciating the idea in its final form or perhaps even appreciating the wider significance of their particular contributions. One such source may be found in the work of a group of theologians of a Thomist orientation working at the University of Paris in the later fifteenth and early sixteenth centuries, most prominently Conrad Summenhart (c. 1455–1502), John Mair (c. 1468–1550), and Jacques Almain (c. 1480–1515). In a number of writings, these authors equated *ius* with *dominium* ('lordship' or 'ownership'), which was understood to reside in people naturally and to license in them the power or faculty of acquiring those objects necessary for self-preservation. Their argument was as much theological as legal or philosophical: just as God enjoyed ultimate ownership of the earth and the rest of his creations by virtue of his will, so human beings, in whom God's image resided, could claim dominion over themselves and their property.

The Reformation brought further refinement and application of the idea of natural rights. On the Protestant side, rights theory became a major element of late sixteenth-century Huguenot efforts to ground the justification of resistance to governments that imposed doctrinal conformity upon religious dissenters. While the earliest generations of Reformers had looked toward duty to God in order to justify acts of political disobedience, a noticeable change in language and concepts occurred in the wake of the St. Bartholomew Day's Massacre of 1572. In their reactions to the massacre, Théodore de Bèze (1519–1605) and Philippe du Plessis Mornay (1549–1623; also known as Duplessis-Mornay), as well as the authors of a large body of anonymous texts, argued for a condition of natural liberty—a privilege of nature whose rightful withdrawal is impossible—that precedes the creation of political society. Hence, any subsequent government must result from, and must be consonant with, the basic natural state of humanity. And those who would use political power to deny to human beings the exercise of their liberty—including the freedom of conscience to dissent from the established Roman Church—may properly and licitly be challenged with forms of resistance to their tyranny. The Huguenots stopped short, however, of advocating popular rebellion. Instead, they looked to so-called intermediary magistrates as the appropriate instigators of resistance to tyrannical conduct. Hence, in the hands of sixteenth-century Reformers, the idea of natural rights became a stimulus for a religio-political movement that directly opposed forms of religious intolerance and suppression of dissent.

The Counter-Reformation produced its own version of natural rights theory that developed out of the language and concepts pioneered by the Parisian theologians Mair and Almain. This is especially evident in the work of the so-called second Scholastic thinkers associated with the School of Salamanca, such as Francisco de Vitoria (c. 1480–1546), Domingo de Soto (1494–1560), and Francisco Suárez (1548–1617). Vitoria had been trained at Paris and returned to Spain to disseminate the ideas to which he had been exposed there. Although Vitoria himself wrote nothing, leaving only lecture summaries, his immediate students and their intellectual progeny produced some of the fullest and most enthusiastic elaborations of natural rights. In particular, Vitoria and de Soto explored the complexities of rights theories, moving away from the traditional Thomistic conception of rights as objective duties required by reason. Vitoria's work seems to have contained two differing conceptions of subjective natural rights—one connected with individual *dominium,* the other defined in relation to communal law. Each position involved notable limitations and flaws, a fact that led de Soto to attempt to resolve them into a coherent picture of rights that incorporated both public and private dimensions. Suárez added further to the picture by identifying *ius* with self-preservation and drawing from this some, albeit limited, political implications. He held that a natural right existed to resist extreme forms of tyranny, construed as those circumstances in which the survival of the community as a whole was endangered. Otherwise, the misbehavior of government was to be tolerated lest communal destruction result from acts of disobedience and resistance.

While the School of Salamanca remained steeped in the neo-Aristotelian doctrines of the medieval past, other thinkers attempted to replace this framework with a paradigm for natural rights rooted purely in legal principles. Especially celebrated in this regard were Hugo Grotius (1583–1645) and John Selden (1584–1654). Grotius proposed that rights should be grounded solely upon the universality of the propriety of human self-preservation, thus placing self-interest at the center of a natural system. He reasoned that human beings enjoy *dominium* over those goods that are immediately necessary in order to preserve themselves: rightful private ownership is directly licensed as a natural right. Moreover, he attacked the Aristotelian doctrine of the naturalism of political society. For Grotius, social order was voluntary, and the only reason that people joined into civil society was for self-protection. As a consequence, the individual does not surrender natural rights by entering into a communal arrangement and indeed might resist a direct attack on those rights by a magistrate. While Selden enunciated a sustained critique of Grotius, he ultimately embraced an account of natural rights derived from his adversary. Selden pushed the devaluation of reason understood as a moral force with the power to bind and compel the actions of individuals. Rather, he stressed that natural rights were directly correlated to natural liberty, such that the only basis for individual obligation could be free assent to contracts and compacts, which, once agreed to, had to be maintained without exception. Hence, for Selden, unlike for Grotius, natural liberty itself could be renounced by a valid act of human will.

Selden's best-known follower was Thomas Hobbes (1588–1679), who developed the insights of the former into a powerful individualist theory of natural rights. In his major works, culminating in *Leviathan* (1651), Hobbes ascribes to all human beings natural liberty as well as equality, on the basis of which they are licensed to undertake whatever actions are necessary in order to preserve themselves from their fellow creatures. Such self-preservation constitutes the indispensable core of human natural rights. Adopting a position radically opposed to the Aristotelian teaching of political naturalism, Hobbes maintained that the exercise of one's natural liberty leads directly to unceasing conflict and unremitting fear, inasmuch as nature confers upon each individual the right to possess everything and no legitimate limitation on one's freedom to enjoy this right. Unalloyed nature yields a state of chaos and warfare and, as a result, a "solitary, poor, nasty, brutish, and short" life, the avoidance of which leads human beings to authorize a single sovereign ruler in order to maintain peace. The exchange of natural freedom for government-imposed order, constructed through a social compact, requires renunciation of all claims on rights that humans possess by nature (except, of course, for the right of self-preservation itself) and voluntary submission to any dictate imposed by the sovereign. In this way, Hobbes seconded Selden's defense of absolute government, yet upheld the basic right to self-preservation. Moreover, under the terms of Hobbes's absolute sovereignty, the subject was still deemed to retain the right to chose for himself concerning any and all matters about which the ruler had not explicitly legislated.

John Locke (1632–1704) crystallized the preceding conceptions of natural rights into the quintessential statement of the modern idea. He began his major work of political theory, the *Two Treatises on Government* (written c. 1680; published 1689), with the postulation of the divinely granted natural rights of individuals, understood in terms of the absolute right to preserve one's life and to lay claim to the goods one requires for survival. Arguing against the patriarchal doctrine of Sir Robert Filmer (c. 1588–1653), Locke insisted that no natural basis—neither paternity nor descent—justifies the submission of one person to another. Rather, all people are deemed sufficiently rational, as well as free and equal, in their natural condition that they can govern themselves according to a basic cognizance of moral (natural) law, and thus will generally respect the rights of others. In contrast to Hobbes, then, Locke maintained that the condition of perfect natural liberty does not represent a state of war. In the state of nature, human beings can enjoy unimpeded rights to acquire private property, the ownership of which is asserted on the basis of the admixture of their labor (the natural talents and industry of their bodies) with the physical world. Indeed, Locke's state of nature resembles nothing so much as a fully functioning commercial society, which has introduced a system of exchange relations

and money, all perfectly consonant with the recognition of the natural rights of individuals.

For Locke, then, there is no pressing necessity for people living in the state of nature to eschew this condition for formalized communal life. Hence, should they chose to enter into bonds of civil society by means of a contract, the sole reason that they do so is to avoid the "inconveniences" and inefficiency of the pre-civil world. This does not require parties to the contract to surrender any of their natural rights. Indeed, the only government worthy of authorization is that which strictly upholds and protects the rights that persons possess by nature. According to Locke, any magistrate that systematically denies to his subjects the exercise of their natural rights to their life, liberty, and estate is tyrannical and unworthy of obedience. Locke closes the *Second Treatise* with a discussion of the dissolution of government. In his view, a regime that violates systematically natural rights places itself in a state of war with the members of civil society, who severally and individually may renounce allegiance to it and may vote to establish a new government. Some have viewed Locke as justifying revolution on the basis of natural rights, but his actual point seems to be less extreme: the retention of one's natural rights in civil society affords one the ability to protect oneself from those (whether housebreakers or magistrates) who would try to take one's property or limit one's proper sphere of liberty. Locke's resistance theory represents a chastened, but nonetheless genuine, defense of natural rights.

Locke's theory, then, stated an integrated position that drew upon many of the earlier strands of natural rights thought. In turn, the eighteenth century would see the extension, refinement and, in some respects, radicalization of the fundamentals of the Lockean doctrine. Locke's language was adopted, for instance, by both theorists and polemicists who sought to halt Europe's complicity in the global slave trade. Likewise, defenders of the equal rights of women to political and social power, such as Mary Wollstonecraft (1759–1797), framed their ideas in the language of rights. And critics of natural nobility and other claims to in-born human inequality invoked the universality of rights as the basis of their assertion of the equal worth and dignity of all people, regardless of birth, class, or occupation. The elaboration of the Lockean stance during the eighteenth century perhaps enjoyed its European apotheosis in the Revolutionary French Declaration of the Rights of Man and the Citizen. The Declaration, which forms perhaps the major source for all later declarations of human rights, proclaims that the aim of civil life is "the preservation of the natural and imprescriptible rights of man"—they nearly included woman, too—including political, economic, social, religious, and cultural rights as well as resistance to tyranny. Of course, Lockean natural rights received their share of criticism during the eighteenth century as well, whether from communalist democrats such as Jean-Jacques Rousseau (1712–1778) or from more individualistic proponents of political economy like Adam Smith (1723–1790). But in general, the 1700s may well be regarded as the European "century of natural rights."

See also **Enlightenment; Feminism; Grotius, Hugo; Hobbes, Thomas; Locke, John; Natural Law; Political Philosophy; Revolutions, Age of; Rousseau, Jean-Jacques; Salamanca, School of; Scholasticism; Smith, Adam.**

BIBLIOGRAPHY

Primary Sources

Hobbes, Thomas. *Leviathan.* Edited by Edwin Curley. Indianapolis, 1994.

Locke, John. *Two Treatises of Government.* Edited by Peter Laslett. Cambridge, U.K., 1988.

Vitoria, Francesco de. *Political Writings.* Edited by Anthony Pagden and Jeremy Lawrence. Cambridge, U.K., 1991.

Secondary Sources

Brett, Annabel S. *Liberty, Right, and Nature: Individual Rights in Later Scholastic Thought.* Cambridge, U.K., 1997.

Haakonssen, Knud. *Natural Law and Moral Philosophy: From Grotius to the Scottish Enlightenment.* Cambridge, U.K., 1996.

Miller, Fred D., Jr. *Nature, Justice, and Rights in Aristotle's Politics.* Oxford, 1995.

Skinner, Quentin. *The Foundations of Modern Political Thought.* 2 vols. Cambridge, U.K., 1978.

Tierney, Brian. *The Idea of Natural Rights: Studies on Natural Rights, Natural Law, and Church Law, 1150–1625.* Atlanta, 1997.

Tuck, Richard. *Natural Rights Theories: Their Origin and Development.* Cambridge, U.K., 1979.

CARY J. NEDERMAN

RITUAL, CIVIC AND ROYAL. The words "ritual" and "ceremony" are here used interchangeably because separating them would be anachronistic and would suggest distinctions that people did not make until near the end of the early modern period. By the nineteenth century, the words had come to denote the ostentation of power and superstitions and the exotica of non-Western or illiterate societies. The words first gained currency in the sixteenth century to disparage heretical religious and extravagant political practices. Before this time, rituals or ceremonials were not concepts as much as books of practices that gave some precision to the places, costuming, and gestures in processionals and assemblies, as seen in the late-fourteenth-century Roman *clerici cerimoniarum* or the *Libro Ceremoniale* (1475) of Florence. Despite sixteenth-century print culture's derogatory usage of the terms, cities and kingdoms staged lavish and magnificent processions and urban pageantry—productions in which hundreds and often thousands participated. These large-scale performances frequently placed religious, royal, and civic-legal rituals on the same plane.

With the growth of the state in the late sixteenth and early seventeenth centuries, the most powerful element and participants were those intent on expanding their spheres of influence in the government. As arguments about national character and divisions of power continued, these interested parties invested in rituals to strengthen—or on occasion to question or to redirect—governmental authority and their status or rank within it. Courtiers, nobles, judges, wealthy townsmen, and others dependent on the resources and patronage of princes sought to define in their favor the overall meaning of ritual or ceremonial performances and to represent in them their personal or official status in the state. Thus, the terms "ritual" and "ceremony" came to describe the highest performances of princely and royal celebrations. By 1619, the French royal historiographer and *parlementaire* Théodore Godefroy entitled his collection of royal public performances *Le cérémonial de France.* In it, he published historical accounts of the ranking and actions of officials and courtiers in rituals-with-the-king, which he presented according to the prescriptions of an encompassing political theory of hierarchy and kingship. The collection also incorporated many el-

Civic and Royal Ritual. Charles V entering Bologna for his coronation by the pope, 1530, painting by Juan de la Corte. THE ART ARCHIVE

ements of traditional legal protocols and religious acts. In 1649 Godefroy, with the aid of his son Denis, expanded the work into the two-volume *Le cérémonial françois.* In these collections, rituals and ceremonies supplied essential cultural components for the practice of what we call "politics" and what early modern people thought of as mysteries of governance.

Rituals and ceremonies bound together the societies of medieval and early modern Europe; they occurred any place where a group of people claimed a particular purpose, legitimacy, and identity. Townsmen, judges, English common lawyers, and princes self-consciously expanded the scale, rhetoric, and publicity of civic and royal events as rites of passage and of government, which served for the sanctification, legitimization, and continuity of communal and national authorities. According to their needs and the circumstances, fifteenth- and

sixteenth-century governments appropriated ritual practices and ideas from religious, classical, feudal-military, and legal-constitutional traditions. Public participation—even in the roles of spectator or reader—was extended over time, space, and social groups through processional rankings, symbols, medallions, program books, special costumes, reenactments, and ritual theater. By 1600, and certainly under the influence of earlier Italian rulers (like the Sforza of Milan, the Medici of Florence, and the doges of the Venetian Republic), royal rituals in England, France, and Germany exalted the ruler from a symbol of state and society to its actual embodiment, and the ceremonies frequently equated these kings with pagan rulers or gods. In early-seventeenth-century Stuart England (1603–1649) and Louis XIV's France (1643–1715), rituals were staged as dramas of state. They encouraged obedience within the political hierarchy and obligated nobles, royal officials, and subjects to act out their parts in that order, and they centralized the king and his royal court as the source of privilege and honor. Similarly, in guild elections, funerals, or pageant-laden communal processions, western European cities staged rituals to reinforce sociopolitical hierarchies and to connect individuals to the larger community.

HISTORICAL CONTEXT OF A RITUAL MENTALITY

For royal ceremonies, the European monarchies, particularly those of France and England, perpetuated in a new key the medieval ritual expressions of Christian sanctity, while Renaissance Italy added strikingly new artistic and theatrical effects and iconologies. Many early modern Europeans held the medieval belief of the "king's two bodies," that is, kingship was represented in a unique royal person who possessed both a natural, mortal body and a mystical, immortal, political one. According to this belief, the king, in ritual, became the intermediary who joined God's working in the world and his justice with the preservation of a people as a unique body politic. In studying the belief in French and English kings' ability to heal scrofula by touching people with the disease, Marc Bloch's groundbreaking study *The Royal Touch* traced how "rather vague ideas" based on a general belief in the supernatural character of royalty "crystallize in the eleventh and twelfth centuries into a precise and stable institution" that lasted for seven centuries. The ritual of the royal touch developed into frequent public demonstrations of the miraculous results of coronation rites, in which kings were both anointed with holy oil and crowned. Bloch traced the vicissitudes of the ritual among the divergent explanations of eight centuries of writers. By 1500, the coronation mattered less than the evidence of the king's unique nature as a royal person. French kings performed the ritual until the Revolution; the practice ended in England with the death of Queen Anne in 1714.

The belief in the power of the royal touch emphasizes the notion that the king was a "mixed person"—part sacred and part layperson. Although the essentially religious attributes of this notion are related to the concept of the "king's two bodies," they should not be confused with it. The latter concept has a larger scope than the particular ambience and rites around the king's person and finds its fullest development in juridical thought and

ceremonies that emphasized the king as image or embodiment of justice: justice being, after truth (religion in medieval Christian thought), a permanent part of God's creation. In the fifteenth and sixteenth centuries, lawyers, officials, and corporate bodies claimed rights in this divine creation according to the notion of legal fictions: that is, that towns or institutions have rights in law as do persons. Ceremonies with kings and princes articulated these rights and mirrored right order in secular titles, offices, and institutions. Among the people participating in political life, rituals complemented and represented constitutional developments over which the seventeenth-century French were best positioned to assert hegemony as model builders. Other national histories took different turns: in Spain the isolationist policies of the monarchy starting with Philip II (ruled 1554–1598) prevented foreign ideas and innovations in state rituals; in Germany independent imperial principalities limited the spread of royal ceremonies; in England royal ceremonies took shape bounded by the weakness of the monarchy and growth of parliamentary power; in Italy the Habsburgs, papacy, and princely dynasties favored the new inventions of political spectacles over rituals that contained residues of civic traditions; and throughout Europe Reformation and Counter-Reformation churches were attentive to maintain the purity of religious ceremonies from secular pollution. Through symbolic forms and performances, early modern rituals placed one's sense of status and civic consciousness within a framework of loyalty to national monarchy or state identities.

RITUAL AS MODELS OF KINGSHIP

Ralph E. Giesey has argued that the ever-changing "event-filled [European] history" requires a constitutional explanation of rituals in contrast with the "affective comprehension of kingship that anthropologists apply so well when studying societies that have no thick transcription of their 'constitution.'" Rituals are historical sources for a society's temper, presenting comparative indices for understanding continuity and changes in the ways that societies constitute themselves around the central agent of legitimate power, the king. Four major French state ceremonies represent the models of European rulership. "Sacral kingship" associated with coronations was joined by the new form of "juristic kingship" as dramatized in royal funeral ceremonies.

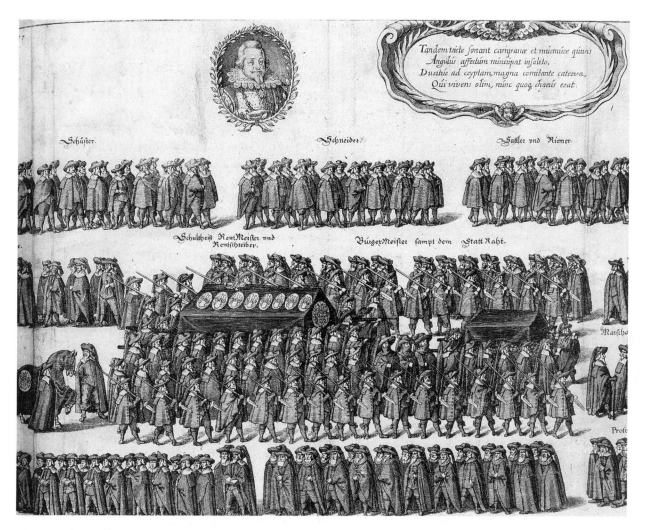

Schuster.   Schneider.   Sattler vnd Riemer.

Schultheiß RentMeister vnd
Rentschreiber.   BürgerMeister sampt dem Statt Raht.

Marscha

Profe

Civic and Royal Ritual. A late-seventeenth-century German engraving depicts the funeral of a prince. THE ART ARCHIVE/
BIBLIOTHÈQUE DES ARTS DÉCORATIFS/DAGLI ORTI

Royal entries advanced a civic and secular model of "humanistic kingship." The *lit de justice* ceremony with the king in solemn assembly with the Parlement of Paris portrayed "constitutional kingship." By 1700, the court-centered "rites of personality" exemplified by Louis XIV (1638–1715) had depreciated these traditional ritual models for enacting kingship.

Each ceremonial model of rulership had its own forms and venue. The coronation took place in great churches where the clergy and magnates of the kingdom had major roles in the ritual drama, which was replete with royal paraphernalia including the crown, holy oil, scepter and sword of state, gloves, slippers, and robes. The ritual entailed an undressing, anointing, redressing, and crowning of

the king. The English Queens Mary (ruled 1553–1558), Elizabeth (ruled 1558–1603), Mary (ruled 1689–1694), and Anne (ruled 1702–1714) had coronations like kings, but issues of Protestantism and revolution—more than sex—gave occasion to changes in the liturgy, language, and scenic effects of the English ceremony. The Spanish did not have a coronation ceremony, since their king ruled over an Iberian monarchy with regional inaugural rites, of which the most noted in the early modern period was the Oath of Aragón. While Holy Roman emperors had elaborate coronations, imperial elections demystified the rituals and placed attention on politics of the empire. Through a combination of rituals, legends, and myths, the French king's coronation came to be seen as sacred in character, ancient in the continuity of its liturgy, and most prestigious in its divinely chosen dynasty.

In France, royal funeral ceremonies developed an influential style and unique interregnum practices, such as the display of a lifelike effigy along with the corpse in its coffin and the disappearance from public duties of the heir until after the funeral. This was done to call attention to the undying part of the king's two bodies as the source of justice. By the time of Philip II's 1598 funeral, the Spanish had fully accepted the notion of *rey muerto, rey puesto,* that is, after a king dies, another immediately replaces him. The funeral celebration focused on services before a magnificent catafalque with thousands of candles built within the church; the funeral served as an occasion for the court hierarchy to reassert itself in the form and order of its mourning. Other elite groups mourned in satellite celebrations

before catafalques in churches throughout the king's domain.

From the fourteenth century, royal entry ceremonies into cities gave kings and subjects occasion to acknowledge the reciprocal obligations between them, particularly the king's charge to preserve justice and confirm corporate liberties and the people's duty to demonstrate obedience and devotion. By the fifteenth century, Italian city-states such as Florence and Venice had appropriated processions to celebrate local saints into rituals that became "the principal mechanism for representing governmental authority," as Edward Muir writes. In London and Paris, royal entries were distinctly political by 1500. Their rites aimed to balance the tensions inherent between the dual desire to preserve local liberties and to give unconditioned loyalty to the sovereign. In London, guilds lined the streets in their livery as

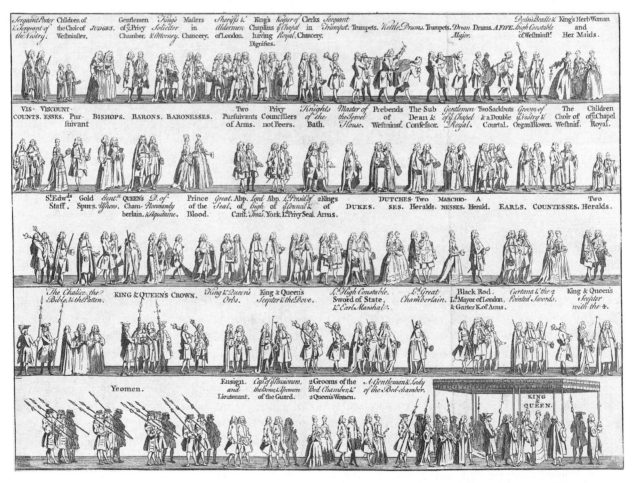

Civic and Royal Ritual. Engraving showing the order of the coronation procession, Britain, eighteenth century. ©Hulton-Deutsch Collection/Corbis

the new ruler and his entourage viewed street plays while en route to the coronation at Westminster. In Paris, the king returning from his coronation appeared on horseback under a canopy carried by guild members. He processed with his royal robe, hat, helmet, gauntlets, and sword displayed before him. From 1484, the royal seal and the chancellor of France preceded the king to accentuate the legal nature of the ceremony. Likewise, the Parlement of Paris in robes of office closed the ranks of several thousand liveried urban groups. Thousands of splendidly costumed lords and nobles followed the Parisians as part of the royal procession. The Parisians had exited from the city to submit to the king and to lead the march into the city, where the king slowly made his way among *tableaux vivants* and street plays to a banquet at the Palais de Justice, residence of the Parlement of Paris.

Other towns staged entries and progresses, but metropolitan and royal ceremonies tended to establish the norm in terms of rank and privilege within kingdoms. In Italian cities, despots and princes transformed the style and ultimately the meaning of entry pageantry from reciprocal ceremonies between rulers and cities to celebrations of power. By the 1600s, northern cities appropriated Italian monumental architecture, classical symbolism, and awesome images of the Roman triumph to their royal entries. In the process, they replaced the ceremonial image of the ruler as judge and arbitrator of a unified body politic with that of sovereign and absolute ruler. In the fifteenth century, French kings replaced royal robes of office with armor of parade. By 1660, Louis XIV began his Parisian entry seated on an especially built royal throne to receive the kneeling representatives of all major Parisian institutions, including the Parlement of Paris. Like the submission of the Parlement of Paris in the entry, the *lit de justice* ritual came to dramatize the king's absolute power and not the court's pretensions of partnership in governing.

RITUALS, CIVILITY, AND MANNERS

Public political ceremonies declined after about 1650. In England after the Glorious Revolution of 1688 and the subsequent advancement of parliamentary power, royal ceremonies became shadows of their earlier magnificence and suggested constitutional restraints. The Spanish Habsburg Monarchy

since Philip II had eschewed public state ceremonies, and royal rituals were performances of conduct and protocol within the relative privacy of the Spanish royal court. By the eighteenth century, most European rulers followed France's example of emphasizing "rites of personality" and frequent ceremonies around the king's body to punctuate every royal accomplishment, such as awakening *(lever)*, dining *(diner)*, retiring *(coucher)*, and other events in the life of the prince. If the ruler were sacred in one place, like the coronation, he was now seen as sacred in all places and at all times. Thus, with the centering of princely activities in their courts, particularly Versailles, the minutiae of daily rituals inundated and depreciated traditional one-time or occasional state ceremonies. Seventeenth-century ceremonial researchers culled the rules governing the ranks, protocol, and conduct of subjects and those in royal service from the historical records of monarchical ceremonies. In many cases these were precarious, occasional, and random examples of behavior or acts that promoters of monarchical absolutism succeeded in ossifying into rules of deportment in a society based on ranks, orders, and honors. Rituals performed very occasionally in past centuries supplied the foundations for a perpetual etiquette at the royal court.

Rituals that today appear to have been for minute distinctions—such as a system of seating and standing based on rank—were fundamental to the thought and habits of court and political society. The king's power to rule was partly grounded in the belief that he had a sacred duty to preserve the rituals that symbolized the honor and hierarchy of his nobility. Royal ceremonies marked the degree of honor possessed by any individual and his or her family. They set standards of deference for a code of courtesy, which guided both noble and bourgeois into new forms of civility. Ritual was refashioned into conduct, forms of association, and practices of disassociation.

See also **Absolutism; Court and Courtiers; Festivals; Monarchy; Ritual, Religious; State and Bureaucracy.**

BIBLIOGRAPHY

Primary Sources

Godefroy, Théodore. *Le cérémonial français.* 2 vols. Paris, 1649. The collection that rationalized its taxonomy in terms of exalted royalty and unique national ceremonies.

Graham, Victor E., and W. McAllister Johnson, eds. *The Royal Tour of France by Charles IX and Catherine de'Medici: Festivals and Entries, 1564–66.* Toronto, 1979. One of several contemporary accounts of entries and ceremonies extensively annotated by Graham and Johnson. This one shows rituals of the monarchy in different regions of France.

Mösenedor, Karl. *Zeremoniell und monumentale Poesis: Die "Entrée solenelle" Ludwig XIV, in Paris.* Berlin, 1983. A facsimile of the program for Louis XIV's Parisian entry as well as a study of its place in the literary culture of the period.

Nichols, John. *The progresses and public processions of Queen Elizabeth. Among which are interspersed other solemnities, expenditures, and remarkable events during the reign of that illustrious princess. Collected from original manuscripts, scarce pamphlets, corporation records, parochial registers.* . . . 3 vols. London, 1823 [reprint]. The title gives an exact account of this useful antiquarian collection. Nichols's views are those of a distant age.

———. *The progresses, processions, and magnificent festivities of King James the First, his royal consort, family, and court; Collected from original manuscripts, scarce pamphlets, corporation records, parochial registers.* . . . 4 vols. New York, 1968 [reprint of 1828 edition]. The title gives an exact account of this useful antiquarian collection. Nichols's views are those of a distant age.

Secondary Sources

Bak, János M., ed. *Coronations: Medieval and Early Modern Monarchical Ritual.* Berkeley, Los Angeles, and Oxford, 1990. Collection of recent scholarship on European royal rituals. Bak has a very useful introduction to approaches to coronation studies.

Bertelli, Sergio. *The King's Body: Sacred Rituals of Power in Medieval and Early Modern Europe.* Translated by R. Burr Litchfield. University Park, Pa., 2001. A study in rich detail of the sacred rituals of power, greatly emphasizing the early modern religious nature of kingship at the expense of other important aspects of royalty. The work does not place itself in the historiography of royal imagery and ceremony, particularly the seminal study of Ernst Kantorowicz.

Bloch, Marc. *The Royal Touch: Sacred Monarchy and Scrofula in England and France.* Translated by J. E. Anderson. London, 1973. French publication of 1924 was the first to move from apologetics, polemics, or positivist interpretations of monarchical customs and ceremonies and apply the insights of ethnography and anthropology to interpreting historical sources. Essential for studying medieval and early modern ceremonies.

Bryant, Lawrence. *The King and the City in the Parisian Royal Entry Ceremony: Politics, Ritual, and Art in the Renaissance.* Geneva, 1986. Reaching beyond positivist

history, this study aims to place the entry's development into a major royal ceremony within the changing political and cultural worlds that created it.

———. "Making History: Ceremonial Texts, Royal Space, and Political Theory in the Sixteenth Century." In *Changing Identities in Early Modern France,* edited by Michael Wolfe, pp. 26–46. Durham, N.C., and London, 1997. Considers the sixteenth-century rise of magnificent ceremonies in regard to humanist rhetoric, sixteenth-century historiography, royal ideology, and politics.

Burke, Peter. *The Fabrication of Louis XIV.* New Haven and London, 1992. An imaginative and highly informed study of the vast enterprise entailed in the making and promoting of Louis XIV's royal image from 1660 to 1715. Essential for understanding how royal power does not just happen but is fabricated.

———. *The Fortunes of the Courtier: The European Reception of Castiglione's* Cortegiano. University Park, Penn., 1996. Studies the *Cortegiano* as the stimulus to a series of discourses that contributed to codifying the social imagery and ideals of life among the early modern European aristocracy.

Elias, Norbert. *Court Society.* Translated by Edmund Jephcott. New York, 1983. Highly influential, sociologically based study of the court of Versailles as a model of aristocratic behavior and shaper of modern codes of conduct.

Elliott, J. H. "Philip IV of Spain: Prisoner of Ceremony." In *The Courts of Europe: Politics, Patronage, and Royalty,* edited by A. G. Dickens, pp. 169–190. London, 1977. Basic source for the workings of Spanish royal ceremony. Dickens's edition has other useful studies of European courts as well.

Geertz, Clifford. *The Interpretation of Cultures: Selected Essays.* New York, 1973. A work of extraordinary influence in the study of rituals that gives European history an anthropological frame for more contextualized studies.

Giesey, Ralph E. "Models of Rulership in French Royal Ceremonial." In *Rites of Power: Symbolism, Ritual, and Politics since the Middle Ages,* edited by Sean Wilentz, pp. 41–64. Philadelphia, 1985. An overview of four major royal ceremonies that reveals access—which escapes positivist-minded historians—to institutions, events, and political history. The chronology of the rising and ebbing of a model offers a way to understand changes in the thought and practice of politics. The introduction and other essays in Wilentz's edition are also of interest to ritual studies.

———. *The Royal Funeral Ceremony in Renaissance France.* Geneva, 1960. A foundational study of the culture and mentality that animated this royal ceremony and made its imagery expressions of royal political thought.

Hanley, Sarah. *The Lit de Justice of the Kings of France: Constitutional Ideology in Legend, Ritual, and Discourse.* Princeton, 1983. For histories of ceremonies and political thought, this extraordinarily original study places the rise of a new form of constitutional discourse in the mentality of Parisian *parlementaires'* ceremonial practices when they invented a tradition to strengthen their claims to co-guardianship of the crown against the innovations of the king.

Harding, Vanessa. *The Dead and the Living in Paris and London, 1500–1670.* Cambridge, U.K., 2002. A comparative study of funerary rituals that demonstrates their utility in preserving the civic hierarchy and reinforcing orderly behavior.

Jackson, Richard. *Vive le Roi! A History of the French Coronation from Charles V to Charles X.* Chapel Hill, N.C., 1984. Shows that ritual and interpretations of this central royal ceremony changes as the ideas and needs of the rulers change.

Kantorowicz, Ernst. *The King's Two Bodies: A Study in Medieval Political Theology.* Princeton, 1957. From the medieval period through seventeenth century, a foundational study of royal and (due to the influence of Roman Law) civic political thought (or, as he calls it, political theology) as revealed in a synthesis of religious liturgies and processionals, canon and civil law, processions, iconography, and ceremonies. His paradigm of transitions from Christ-centered kingship to law-centered and man-centered rulership remains essential for any history of European monarchies and their ceremonies.

Le Roy Ladurie, Emmanuel. *Saint-Simon, and the Court of Louis XIV.* Translated by Arthur Goldhammer. Chicago and London, 2001. A study of court and aristocratic society and *mentalités* that centers on careful analysis of ideological models detected in Saint-Simon's writing. An impressive and persuasive revealing of the mind of an age in which royal ceremonies were critical in sustaining the power of the state and defining status, honor, and worth. Calls for a different outlook on the cultural influence of court society from that of Norbert Elias.

Mitchell, Bonner. *Italian Civic Pageantry in the High Renaissance: A Descriptive Bibliography for Triumphal Entries and Selected Other Festivals for State Occasions.* Florence, 1979. The major source for grasping the scale and contents of Italian civic ceremonies.

Muir, Edward. *Ritual in Early Modern Europe.* Cambridge, U.K., 1997. Impressive synthesis of the many studies and various types of rituals in early modern Europe and the beginning point for all new studies. Of particular importance for this article's topic are the chapter and bibliography on "Government as a ritual process" (pp. 229–268).

Smuts, R. Malcolm. *Court Culture and the Origins of a Royalist Tradition in Early Stuart England.* Philadelphia, 1987. Valuable both for understanding ceremonial politics of the period and for its bibliography.

———. "Public Ceremony and Royal Charisma: The English Royal Entry in London, 1495–1642." In *The First Modern Society: Essays in English History in Honour of Lawrence Stone,* edited by David Cannadine and James M. Rosenheim, pp. 65–94. Cambridge, U.K., 1989. Latest and insightful study of the London entries.

Strong, Roy. *Art and Power: Renaissance Festivals, 1450–1650.* Berkeley, 1984. Among the earliest of Strong's many studies into political festivals, art, and ceremony in the period.

Texler, Richard C. *Public Life in Renaissance Florence.* New York, 1980. A groundbreaking study on public rituals and conduct in public and political life.

Wortman, Richard S. *Scenarios of Power: Myth and Ceremony in Russian Monarchy.* Vol. 1. *From Peter the Great to the Death of Nicholas I.* Princeton, 1995. Essential for understanding early modern Russian rituals and political symbolism.

LAWRENCE M. BRYANT

RITUAL, RELIGIOUS.

Ritual is one means by which a society expresses its beliefs both symbolically and explicitly. In the late medieval and Reformation era, the performance of religious rites reconfirmed traditional precepts and instructed each new generation afresh. Whatever a church's intentions were, such ceremonies did not remain static, but evolved. We can assume that as conditions changed the meanings that people attributed to such acts also altered.

Religious ritual and ecclesiastical ritual overlapped, but they were not synonymous. The former expressed people's views of the supernatural world and its bearing on daily life, as by praying and crossing oneself before going to bed or saying grace at the table. These might be far more than ritualized behaviors; they could be fairly elaborate and regular, like going on a pilgrimage to a nearby (or more distant) shrine in order to be healed of an illness. Ecclesiastical ritual was presided over by a priest or, later, a pastor and usually took place within or in proximity to a church. It adhered to more and more narrowly prescribed models. During the sixteenth and seventeenth centuries, Catholic and Protestant authorities strove for uniformity and precision in the rubrics they introduced.

Prior to the Reformation, the division between these two kinds of religious ritual was blurred. A great strength of the Catholic Church during the centuries of its gradual conversion of most western Europeans was its tolerance of folkish elements and its willingness to express by means of its ceremonies the telluric concerns of the unlettered masses. It gladly lent the strength of the Mass, via the priest's blessing, to water, salt, wax candles, bread, and crops. People could bear the more portable items home to radiate their heightened benefits upon all who used or consumed them. In June, during Rogation Days, the priest led peasants out to their fields and blessed their crops. At other times, he sprinkled holy water on their houses, and in Germany, he often received a loaf of bread from each household in recompense. On Corpus Christi the elaborate circumambulation of parts of the city by clergy, magistrates, and guilds, besides displaying the Host, implicitly told the populace of the protective powers of the Body of Christ. No church building alone contained all ecclesiastical ritual.

In the performance of their holy ritual offices, priests were, and within Catholic Reform remained, charged personages. On those occasions when they said or sang a full Mass (rather than a so-called dry Mass or *missa sicca*), they entered the sanctuary in procession, garbed in vestments that were sometimes elaborately embroidered with symbols, with acolytes bearing the emblems of their functions and their special connection with God. Their signal capacity lay in transubstantiating the bread and wine, by means of the verbal formulae *Hoc est corpus meum* and *Hic est sanguis meus,* into the true body and blood of Christ. So potent was this veritable miracle that every person and object associated with the Mass acquired some degree of sanctity.

In a number of respects, the Protestant Reformation in its several salient forms has been shown to rely on late medieval precedents. This is only relatively true of the celebration of the Eucharist. To be sure, voices against the powers of the Mass could be heard in the fourteenth and fifteenth centuries, but they were muted. The Reformers as a group broke radically with the assumptions underlying the Mass. Because the messages it conveyed symbolically were now rejected, the symbolic acts and artifacts were themselves eliminated. Protestant groups as they emerged nevertheless took varying stances on particular aspects of the Lord's Supper. Luther's theology of consubstantiation left intact the Real Presence even as it demolished the priest's sacral power

of producing Christ's body for the communicants' ingestion. The sacral space, whether intentionally or not, remained quite highly decorated with biblically attested stories depicted in altarpieces and other paintings, colored windows, and crucifixes. Organists and choirboys, along with congregational singing, made a joyful noise, and church bells continued to toll. Luther himself permitted the elevation of the Host and the Chalice until 1542, and although he preferred a simple choir robe when presiding at services, by the end of the century Lutheran divines might again be decked out in admirable vestments even though not cloth of gold. By century's end, all pastors faced their congregations and had added Communion tables at the outer edge of the altar dais, from which males and females, at their respective corners, received the dual elements of the sacred meal.

Followers of Huldrych Zwingli and John Calvin—those of the latter including Puritans and Dutch Reformed—decisively rejected the doctrine of Christ's physical ubiquity and conveyed their conviction fittingly, in the radical simplification of ritual space. Zwingli's Eucharist was strictly commemorative, and Calvin wrote of spiritual nourishment. Determined to abolish "idolatry," the Genevan reformer followed Zwingli in recommending the removal of every possible decorative accompaniment to worship—statues, stained glass, paintings, altars together with their daises and niches, candelabra, monstrances, pyxes, thuribles, rich chalices and patens, baptismal fonts, church bells (except in France), organs, and all singing except the unison intoning of metrical Psalms. Occasionally, a tablet displaying the text of the Ten Commandments hung over the Communion table, which was now often at the foot of the pulpit. Where new churches could be built, their architecture avoided a place for an altar. The whitewashed walls in both old and new churches provided an interplay of light and shadow that attracted many painters of Dutch interiors. These seem to signify God as a spirit, for they offer no place for the eye to rest.

Protestant innovators retained baptism as the second biblically validated sacrament. Luther pared down but still retained exorcism, which some, but not all, of his followers abolished late in the century. Zwingli and Calvin removed this act from the rite, along with the sign of the cross, immediately. They also insisted that infant consecration take place before the gathered congregation and that biological fathers be present beside the godparents. Luther advocated, but the Swiss reformers rejected, the emergency baptism of infants in the birthing chamber, and the same respective opinions determined the preservation or abolition of the churching of women after childbirth.

When the Reformation began, only nobles, magistrates, and sometimes nursing mothers and elderly women had seats in churches. Throughout the later sixteenth and on into the seventeenth century, pews appeared everywhere, including Catholic churches. They should be regarded as an aspect of ritual in that they held the people's bodies in place and directed their attention more pointedly to the drama of the ceremony, including preaching. Pews also expressed the new Protestant requirement that the laity attend church. Because people sat in the same places, any absence could be detected.

Binding all wings of the Reformation together, from Canterbury to Lund and from Geneva to Königsberg, was the centrality of the sermon. The preached Word took the place of the transubstantial moment as the ceremonial pièce de résistance. Pulpits replaced altars as the focal point in sanctuaries. By the seventeenth century, some formal training in homiletics, an extension of the humanist curriculum in rhetoric, was a requirement for entering the clergy. The hearing of the Word was often a prerequisite of enjoying Communion, having one's infant baptized, or getting married; visitation records and other assessments of lay behavior record people's coming to church only after the sermon, a serious but ultimately irremediable transgression. Preaching was regarded as crucial because it enabled the Holy Spirit to fructify the faith of the elect. Promoting this function was surely one factor encouraging the printing presses from the mid-sixteenth to the mid-eighteenth century to pour forth sermons in tangible, legible rather than audible form. Throughout northern and central Europe, households of adequate substance acquired small numbers of such books for the edification of their increasingly literate members, and for "house-fathers" to read in family devotions. Whereas the Mass had lent its power to the community by means of priest-blessed objects, the sermon extended its benefits via the printed book.

Post-Tridentine Catholicism adhered to medieval liturgical patterns even though, in 1588, the church founded the Sacred Congregation of Rites and Ceremonies. After 1614 and the publication of the Rituale Romanum, the central hierarchy urged adherence to its new standard upon all quarters. Regional and local tropes and altarpiece representations of unattested saints were to be cleansed from the churches. No study exists of the extent to which local and regional churches complied. Certainly there was much resistance, even if for political reasons, to the decrees of Trent. Carlo Borromeo (1538–1584), Archbishop of Milan (from 1560), provided detailed instructions for the administration and elaborate decoration of churches in his archdiocese. His influence, via his *Instructiones* and other writings, was broad. He urged catechetical instruction for all children, which might have provided the laity with a better basis for understanding Catholic ritual. He is credited with introducing the confessional box as we know it today and with promoting frequent confession.

The Catholic Church in the age of the baroque everywhere adopted a Protestant stress upon preaching. Even though the sacrifice of the Mass remained central, the proliferation of baroque high pulpits throughout Catholic Europe bears witness to the integration of the sermon into the service. Members of the Capuchin and Jesuit orders turned preaching into a high art, the outcome of concerted training in homiletics. In the Catholic world, too, the sermon gradually became a ritual artifact. Holy Week preaching marked the apogee of the annual cycle and was designed, along with the late-emerging Stations of the Cross, to move the faithful to tears. Ritual repentance as contained in the sacrament of penance was closely tied to this affect, for a sense of personal complicity in bringing about Christ's torment was to produce frequent—more frequent than the once-yearly enumeration of sins demanded by the Fourth Lateran Council—resort to auricular confession.

Catholicism continued to regard marriage, the anointing of the dying (extreme unction), and priestly ordination as sacraments. Confirmation, long officially of sacramental status yet neglected, underwent a revival as the church acknowledged the need to better inculcate its precepts via the catechism upon each new generation.

Nowhere were liturgical practices more contested than in the British Isles. The ambiguity of the Anglican Church's early history permitted varied preferences to be expressed. On the return of the Marian Exiles at the accession of Elizabeth, a so-called Puritan party gradually appeared with its pro-Genevan inclination toward spare and didactic liturgy. Puritan divines objected to the ornate traditionality (which is to say, at least the potential idolatry) of the forms provided in the Edwardian prayer books. They objected to the outpouring of cathedral music during the Restoration. Like their confreres on the Continent, they would not brook funeral sermons, for these elevated individual human beings, the deceased, to an undeserved height. They objected to clerical vestments, wedding rings, and churching. As heirs of Calvin, the Puritans stressed interiority and cared little for outward ritual acts. Their services intentionally bespoke the unworthiness of humans and the omnipotence and separateness of God. In Scotland, Presbyterian leaders, too, favored the utmost simplicity. Under pressure during the English Revolution, the Reformed creeds accepted compromise among themselves in adopting *A Directory for Publique Worship in the Three Kingdoms* (1644). Although disputed, in Low Church parishes this rubric would remain a basic guide for centuries. On the High Church side, the Book of Common Prayer of 1662 restored some of the language (priest instead of minister) and practice of Catholicism but avoided extremes. Owing to its bifurcated past, the Anglican Church down to today affords its adherents a spectrum of liturgical choices, from Protestant plainness to near-Catholic elegance.

Two contrasting trends characterize the late seventeenth and eighteenth centuries: the heightened mysticism visible in Pietism and the Catholic baroque, and the rational approach to religion claimed by leaders of the Enlightenment. Most ordinary Christians would not have been conscious of the qualitative changes effected at theologians' behest. Johann Sebastian Bach's (1685–1750) music finely embroidered Lutheran worship and moved hearts by its own devices; Philipp Jakob Spener (1635–1705) verbally urged the imitation of Christ and a heartfelt longing for moral improvement as a precondition of the experience of God's presence. Everywhere the states' ties to their territorial churches found expression in the nobility's elaborate grave monuments within and near sanctuaries and in longer prayers for the well-being of rulers. Educated city dwellers of means could espouse Enlightenment calls for the daily, practical application of ethical and neighborly principles. This class might be persuaded by voices critical of the irrational, "superstitious" dimensions of all religion. However, the masses uncritically entered their local churches as always and participated in the ceremonial patterns established in the sixteenth century, or, in the case of Catholicism, long before. Eighteenth-century urban congregations did begin to feel the effects of the state's withdrawal as an enforcer of religious conformity. Increasingly, people could select from more than one theological position. Available positions were most immediately communicated by means of liturgy. Throughout the early modern period, ceremony informed even the unlettered laity and involved it in the tacit affirmation of the tenets on which it was based.

See also **Calvin, John; Calvinism; Church of England; Luther, Martin; Lutheranism; Pietism; Puritanism; Reformation, Catholic; Reformation, Protestant; Zwingli, Huldrych.**

BIBLIOGRAPHY

Christian, William A., Jr. *Local Religion in Sixteenth-Century Spain.* Princeton, 1981.

Coster, Will. *Baptism and Spiritual Kinship in Early Modern England.* Aldershot, U.K., 2002.

Cressy, David. *Birth, Marriage and Death: Ritual, Religion, and the Life-Cycle in Tudor and Stuart England.* Oxford and New York, 1997.

Davies, Horton. *Worship and Theology in England.* 3 vols. Reprint, Grand Rapids, Mich., 1996.

Ditchfield, Simon. "Giving Tridentine Worship Back Its History." In *Continuity and Change in Christian Worship,* edited by R. N. Swanson, pp. 199–226. Woodbridge, U.K., and New York, 1999.

———. *Liturgy, Sanctity, and History in Tridentine Italy: Pietro Maria Campi and the Preservation of the Particular.* Cambridge, U.K., and New York, 1995.

Duffy, Eamon. *The Stripping of the Altars: Traditional Religion in England, c. 1400–c. 1580.* New Haven, 1992.

Eire, Carlos M. N. *War against the Idols: The Reformation of Worship from Erasmus to Calvin.* Cambridge, U.K., and New York, 1986.

Finney, Paul Corby, ed. *Seeing Beyond the Word: Visual Arts and the Calvinist Tradition.* Grand Rapids, Mich., 1999. Numerous fine articles.

Gordon, Bruce. "Transcendence and Community in Zwinglian Worship: The Liturgy of 1525 in Zurich." In *Continuity and Change in Christian Worship,* edited by R. N. Swanson, pp. 128–150. Woodbridge, U.K., and New York, 1999.

Karant-Nunn, Susan C. *The Reformation of Ritual: An Interpretation of Early Modern Germany.* London and New York, 1997.

———. "'Suffer the Little Children to Come unto Me, and Forbid Them Not': The Social Location of Baptism in Early Modern Germany." In *Continuity and Change: The Harvest of Late-Medieval and Reformation History,* edited by Robert J. Bast and Andrew C. Gow, pp. 359–378. Leiden, 2000.

Michalski, Sergiusz. *The Reformation and the Visual Arts: The Protestant Image Question in Western and Eastern Europe.* London and New York, 1993.

Muir, Edward. *Ritual in Early Modern Europe.* Cambridge, U.K., and New York, 1997.

Myers, W. David. *"Poor, Sinning Folk": Confession and Conscience in Counter-Reformation Germany.* Ithaca, N.Y., 1996.

Nischan, Bodo. *Lutherans and Calvinists in the Age of Confessionalism.* Aldershot, U.K., and Brookfield, Vt., 1999. Contains a number of key articles on ritual.

Old, Hughes Oliphant. *The Shaping of the Reformed Baptismal Rite in the Sixteenth Century.* Grand Rapids, Mich., 1992.

Scribner, R. W. *Popular Culture and Popular Movements in Reformation Germany.* London and Ronceverte, W.Va., 1987. Several crucial articles on ritual.

Senn, Frank C. *Christian Liturgy: Catholic and Evangelical.* Minneapolis, 1997.

Spinks, Brian. "Evaluating Liturgical Continuity and Change at the Reformation: A Case Study of Thomas Müntzer, Martin Luther, and Thomas Cranmer." In *Continuity and Change in Christian Worship,* edited by R. H. Swanson, 151–171. Woodbridge, U.K., and New York, 1999.

Swidler, Leonard J. *Aufklärung Catholicism, 1780–1850: Liturgical, and Other, Reforms in the Catholic Aufklärung.* Missoula, Mont., 1978.

Wandel, Lee Palmer. *Voracious Idols and Violent Hands: Iconoclasm in Reformation Zurich, Strasbourg, and Basel.* Cambridge, U.K., and New York, 1995.

White, James F. *Roman Catholic Worship: Trent to Today.* New York, 1995.

SUSAN C. KARANT-NUNN

ROADS AND ROADBUILDING. *See* **Communication and Transportation.**

ROBERTSON, WILLIAM (1721–1793), Scottish historian, clergyman, and educator. William Robertson was born on 8 September 1721 in Borthwick, Midlothian, where his father, William, was a parish minister in the Church of Scotland. The Robertson name was descended from the Robertsons of Gladney in Fifeshire and, more distantly, from the Robertsons of Struan in Perthshire. His mother, Heleanor, was the daughter of David Pitcairn of Dreghorn and Mary Anderson. The eldest of eight children, Robertson was educated in the Borthwick school and in nearby Dalkeith. In 1733, his father was called to Edinburgh as minister of Lady Yester's Church, and two years later Robertson entered the University of Edinburgh. According to his biographer Dugald Stewart, his dedication as a student was aptly demonstrated by his prefixing to his commonplace books the motto *vita sine literis mors est* (life without literature is death). As was typical of many students at the time, Robertson did not take a degree, but in 1740–1741 he studied divinity and subsequently took his examinations to become a minister of the Church of Scotland. In 1744 he was ordained minister of Gladsmuir, and seven years later he married his cousin Mary Nisbet, daughter of James Nisbet, minister of the Old Church, Edinburgh, and Mary, daughter of David Pitcairn. Together they had six children.

In 1758 Robertson, like his father, was called to Lady Yester's Church. Before arriving in Edinburgh, Robertson had already begun to establish himself as a leader in the church, joining a group of ministers, eventually to be known as the Moderates, who advocated church reforms, and publishing a well-regarded sermon, "The Situation of the World at the Time of Christ's Nativity" (1755), which prefigured his historical interests. He had also completed much of the work on his first book, *The History of Scotland during the Reigns of Queen Mary and King James VI.* Published in 1759, the book was a great success, going through some thirteen editions in his lifetime. As a result of this success, Robertson received several appointments, the most notable coming in 1762 when he was named principal of the University of Edinburgh, a post that he would hold until his death.

During his years as an administrator, Robertson made substantial contributions to the stature of the university, improving the library, strengthening the medical school faculty, and lobbying for new buildings (a dream that only became reality beginning in 1789). In assuming the position, Robertson relinquished some of his parish duties, though he remained a minister, moving from Lady Yester's to Old Greyfriars in 1761. Robertson also exercised leadership in the Church of Scotland's General Assembly during the 1760s and 1770s, championing the Moderate Party's often controversial policies of patronage and toleration, together with a demand for a more educated clergy.

In 1769 he published *The History of the Reign of the Emperor Charles V* in which he studied the development of the European state system and the concept of the balance of power by tracing the career of the most notable Habsburg ruler of the sixteenth century. He was unable to include discussion of the Spanish conquests in the Americas because he believed they would dilute the focus of his history, and this omission gave rise to his next project. In 1777 he published *The History of America,* describing the Spanish exploration of the fifteenth and sixteenth centuries in Mexico and South America. He had intended this history to be part of a general history of European colonization in the Americas, but after *America* he was only able to complete a small portion concerning English colonization (published posthumously in 1796). His work was interrupted by a physical breakdown, manifested in chronic congestion and increasing deafness during the late 1770s and early 1780s. He retired permanently from church leadership in 1780. By 1785, however, his health had revived sufficiently for him to undertake a complete revision of his historical works (published in 1787–1788) and to write *An Historical Disquisition concerning the Knowledge Which the Ancients Had of India* (1791), a discussion of European contacts with India up to the sixteenth century, with clear implications for contemporary British involvement in the area. In 1792, however, his health once again began to fail, and, after enduring considerable pain, he died on 11 June 1793. He is buried in Old Greyfriars churchyard.

See also **Charles V (Holy Roman Empire); Edinburgh.**

BIBLIOGRAPHY

Brown, Stewart J., ed. *William Robertson and the Expansion of Empire.* Cambridge, U.K., 1997. Collection of essays by various scholars on Robertson's work as historian and writer, with a bibliography of writing about him from 1755–1996.

Horn, David Bayne. *A Short History of the University of Edinburgh, 1556–1889.* Edinburgh, 1967. A concise history of the university assessing Robertson's role as principal.

Sher, Richard B. *Church and University in the Scottish Enlightenment: The Moderate Literati of Edinburgh.* Princeton, 1985. Groundbreaking study of the careers of Robertson and four other Moderates.

Sher, Richard B., ed. *The Works of William Robertson.* 12 vols. London, 1996. The most complete edition including, in Vol. 12 (edited and introduced by Jeffrey Smitten), his miscellaneous works and the important early lives by John Erskine, Dugald Stewart, and Henry Brougham.

Smitten, Jeffrey. "Selected Bibliography: William Robertson." Web site at http://www.c18.org/biblio. A bibliography of secondary sources, regularly updated.

JEFFREY SMITTEN

ROCOCO. A style of art characteristic of the eighteenth century, its focal point was France, where it was the dominant style during the first half of the century, although it enjoyed manifestations throughout Europe. Etymologically, "rococo" probably derived from a combination of the first two syllables of the French words *rocaille* (a form of rockwork found in architectural ornament and decorative arts) and *coquillage* (a shell motif that accompanied the *rocaille*). Coined in the 1790s by students of the neoclassical French painter Jacques-Louis David (1748–1825), "rococo" began as a pejorative expression. In an ironic twist of history, however, the earliest instance of the term's recorded usage applied it to David, rather than to a rococo artist properly speaking (such as Antoine Watteau, 1684–1721, or François Boucher, 1703–1770). A group of David's students (he called them his "Greeks"), finding his *Intervention of the Sabine Women* (1799) not Greek enough, judged his masterpiece "[Charles André] Van Loo, [Madame de] Pompadour, rococo." Originally then, the term was studio slang that involved critical judgments about aesthetic taste in general and about painting in particular, rather than a designation for stylistic tenden-

Rococo. The Würzburg Palace, designed by Johann Balthasar Neumann and built 1720–1744. THE ART ARCHIVE/DAGLI ORTI

cies in decorative arts, interiors, or architectural ornament (what the eighteenth century called *le rocaille* or *le genre pittoresque*, which rococo now denotes in its strictest usage). This account of the word's origin (which comes from David's student, Etienne Delécluze) also suggests that from the start "rococo" was a critical term bound up conceptually with issues of gender and class—hence the synonymity between rococo and Madame de Pompadour (1721–1764), the longtime favorite of Louis XV (ruled 1715–1774).

Until the end of the nineteenth century "rococo" was not widely used as an art historical term, except in Germany. For the French it remained a general label for the taste that was fashionable during the reign of Louis XV. As early as the 1840s the French also commonly applied it to anything that was old-fashioned, as did the English. By then Jacob Burckhardt had begun to use it as a generic art historical term for the decadent phases of all period styles (he described a "rococo" in Romanesque, Gothic, and Hellenistic art). Soon thereafter other German art historians began to use rococo as a formal classification of the general period and style of Louis XV, and it was they who inaugurated the first critical analyses of the style. Though recognizing rococo as a mode of decoration that originated in France, these scholars were concerned largely with theorizing the style in relation to baroque architecture in Germany and Italy. The Residenz in Würzburg, designed by Balthasar Neumann (1687–1753), is a magnificent example of German rococo architecture.

Since Fiske Kimball's foundational book, *The Creation of the Rococo* (1943), the term has been used most commonly to name an indigenously French style of decoration, marked by asymmetry and motifs both fanciful and naturalistic, that was distinct and separate from the baroque and was developed by a small number of designers, ornamentalists, and architects during the first half of the century (these included Gilles-Marie Oppenord, Nicolas Pineau, Juste-Aurèle Meissonier, and Jacques de Lajoüe). In the meantime, the word has continued to be used variously as a designation for a broad historical period spanning the decades from the Regency to the reign of Louis XVI (ruled 1774–1792), known as the "Rococo Age," or a pan-European style "capable of suffusing all spheres of art." Some scholars have argued that it was the first "modern" style; others have denied that it qualifies as a style at all. Lately it has become possible to speak of rococo as a cultural mode of being, thought, and representation rather than exclusively as a formal idiom.

See also **Baroque; Boucher, François; David, Jacques-Louis; France, Art in; Louis XV (France); Pompadour, Jeanne-Antoinette Poisson.**

BIBLIOGRAPHY

Delécluze, E. J. *Louis David, son école, et son temps: Souvenirs.* Paris, 1983.

John, Richard. "Rococo." In *The Grove Dictionary of Art Online,* edited by L. Macy. Available at http://www.groveart.com.

Kimball, Fiske. *The Creation of the Rococo.* Philadelphia, 1943.

Minguet, J. Philippe. *Esthétique du Rococo.* Paris, 1979.

Park, William. *The Idea of Rococo.* Newark, Del., and Cranbury, N.J.: 1992.

Roland Michel, Marianne. *Lajoüe et l'art rocaille.* Neuilly-sur-Seine, France, 1984.

Schönberger, Arno, and Halldor Soehner. *The Age of Rococo.* Translated by Daphne Woodward. London, 1960.

Sedlmayr, Hans, and Hermann Bauer. "Rococo." In *The Encyclopedia of World Art.* New York, 1966.

Semper, Gottfried. *Der Stil in den technischen und tektonischen Künsten, oder, praktische Aesthetik: Ein Handbuch für Techniker, Künstler, und Kunstfreunde.* 2 vols. 2nd rev. ed. Munich, 1878–1879.

MELISSA HYDE

ROMA (GYPSIES).

The Roma, or Romani, entered southeastern Europe via the Byzantine Empire in the late Middle Ages from India. Early chronicles referred to the Roma as *ÆEgyptians,* hence the name *Gypsies.* However, in much of Europe they are referred to as *Zigeuner, cigán, cigány,* or *tsiganes,* which are derived from the Byzantine Greek word *Atsínganoi,* 'itinerant soothsayers and wanderers'. Most members of this diverse ethnic group prefer to be called Roma, 'group', or Romas, the adjectival form being Romani.

By the beginning of the early modern period, there were Roma scattered throughout the Balkans. While most lived as nomads, those in Walachia and Moldavia (modern Romania), traditionally the Eu-

Roma. *Washerwomen and Gypsies in a Grotto*, seventeenth-century painting by David Teniers II the Younger. THE ART ARCHIVE/
MUSÉE FABRE MONTPELLIER/DAGLI ORTI

ropean homeland of the Roma, had been enslaved by the boyars (nobility). Initially the Roma were respected for their skills as metalsmiths, gunsmiths, equine specialists, and musicians. As the Ottoman Turks gradually took over other parts of the Balkans, the Roma were subject to a growing body of prejudice that sought to restrict their settlement patterns or force them into a more permanent nomadic status.

Some Roma who tried to seek refuge in central and western Europe met with similar prejudice, particularly in the Holy Roman Empire. By the beginning of the early eighteenth century, Habsburg rulers threatened nomadic foreign Roma with branding, torture, and execution if they were caught. Such policies changed during the Enlightenment, particularly under Maria Theresa (ruled 1740–1780) and her son Joseph II (ruled 1780–1790). They adopted new policies designed to force the Roma to assimilate into Habsburg society; this included kidnapping Roma children, who were then placed into foster Catholic homes. They also ordered that wheels be taken off Roma wagons, and they limited the number of horses that a Roma family could own. Most of these policies failed, and many Habsburg Roma resumed their nomadic ways. One of the few good results of these policies was a series of extensive Habsburg Roma censuses detailing Roma life at the end of the Enlightenment.

The plight of the Roma in the rest of the Balkans was not much better, particularly in Walachia and Moldavia, where the Roma remained slaves until 1864. The Roma suffered from similar discrimination in other parts of Europe during this period. They had entered France as early as the fifteenth century and also moved out of the Balkans into the German states, Scandinavia, the British Isles, and Russia, although the bulk of Europe's Roma remained in the Balkans.

While most of Roma history in the early modern period tends to focus on various aspects of the discrimination they faced, the Roma contributed significantly to the history and culture of Europe during this period, particularly in the fields of music and literature. They formed the modern basis of Russian choral music and Spanish Flamenco and inspired some of Europe's most prominent writers.

See also **Balkans; Holy Roman Empire; Persecution; Romania.**

BIBLIOGRAPHY

Crowe, David M. *A History of the Gypsies of Eastern Europe and Russia.* New York, 1995.

Fraser, Angus. *The Gypsies.* Oxford, 1992.

DAVID M. CROWE

ROMAN LAW. *See* **Law: Roman Law.**

ROMANIA. The principalities of Walachia and Moldavia, formed in the fourteenth century, were the nucleus of what would become modern Romania in the nineteenth century. Their populations were ethnically the same, spoke the same language, and professed the same Orthodox faith; and their political institutions, culture, and historical development throughout the early modern period were similar. They were situated at the crossroads of East and West: their Latin heritage linked them to Rome; their religion drew them to Constantinople.

The decisive force in the international relations of the principalities from the middle of the fifteenth to the end of the eighteenth century was the Ottoman Empire. Despite the heroic efforts of princes such as Stephen the Great of Moldavia (ruled 1457–1504) to defend their independence, both countries were eventually forced to recognize Ottoman suzerainty, Walachia between 1420 and 1480 and Moldavia between 1484 and 1498. Under the terms of *ahd-names* (treaties) granted by the sultans, they accepted vassal status and agreed to pay an annual tribute, to participate in Ottoman military campaigns, and to sever direct political relations with foreign countries. But both principalities avoided occupation by the Ottoman army and the settlement of Muslims on their territory, and they preserved their political institutions, laws, and economic and social structures, thus escaping the incorporation into the Ottoman Empire to which the peoples south of the Danube had been subjected. Their relationship with the Ottoman Empire constantly evolved and became increasingly restrictive and burdensome. By the eighteenth century the sultans were treating the principalities as mere provinces and their princes as Ottoman functionaries. Yet the heaviest burdens they bore were economic and fiscal, as the Ottomans continually increased the amount of the tribute, the number and size of bribes, and the quantities of foodstuffs to be delivered at fixed prices.

Opposition to the Ottomans was constant, but the majority of princes were realists. Aware that their countries were too weak to challenge Ottoman supremacy directly, they looked for support to Poland, the Habsburg empire, and Russia. Theirs was the classic strategy of playing powerful neighbors off against one another, thereby securing independence. One of the high points of this delicate game was the reign of Michael the Brave of Walachia (ruled 1593–1601), who allied himself with the Habsburgs and won several significant victories over Ottoman armies, notably at Calugareni in 1595. He also brought Moldavia and the principality of Tran-

sylvania under his rule for a brief time, but his enemies prevailed, and the Ottomans regained their predominance over the principalities. Other significant attempts to throw off Ottoman rule occurred a century later. Constantin Brâncoveanu of Walachia (ruled 1688–1714) cooperated with Austria, and Dimitrie Cantemir of Moldavia (ruled 1710–1711) turned to Peter the Great of Russia to regain independence, but neither alliance was successful, and both princes lost their thrones.

The Ottomans, convinced that they could no longer trust native princes, dispensed with elections altogether and appointed princes mainly from among important Greek families of the Phanar (Lighthouse) district of Constantinople. During the so-called Phanariot regime, which lasted until 1821, Ottoman political interference in the principalities' internal affairs, economic and fiscal exploitation, and corruption reached its height. Yet it was also an

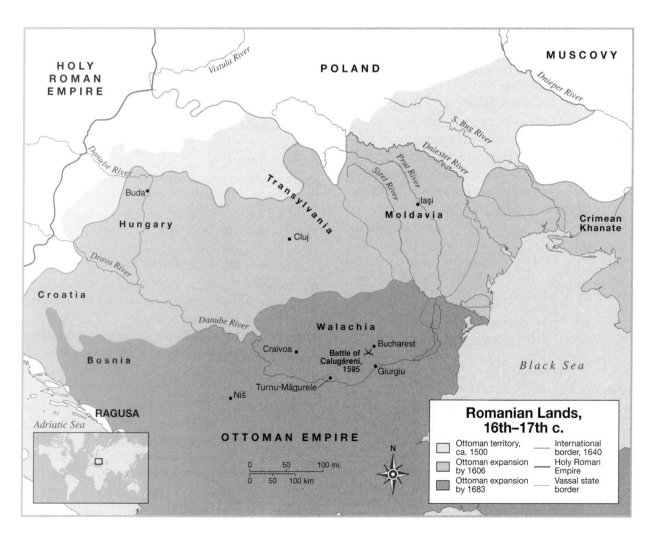

Romanian Lands, 16th–17th c.

era of significant reforms under forward-looking princes such as Constantin Mavrocordat (ruled six times in Walachia and four times in Moldavia between 1730 and 1769), who reorganized administrative, judicial, and fiscal institutions and abolished serfdom in Walachia in 1746 and in Moldavia in 1749, and Alexandru Ipsilanti of Walachia (ruled 1774–1782, 1796–1797) and Moldavia (ruled 1786–1788), who introduced new governmental reforms and undertook the codification of laws. In the latter decades of the eighteenth century, the striving for independence became more intense and was led by the *boiers* (nobles). Their efforts coincided with Russia's own policy of aggrandizement against the Ottomans and brought an easing of Ottoman rule. The Treaty of Kuchuk Kainarji (1774) required the sultan to respect the autonomy of the principalities guaranteed in the *ahd-names* and enabled Russia to intervene regularly on their behalf.

The economy of the principalities rested on agriculture. Production was organized around large estates controlled by the *boiers* and the monasteries, which were worked by peasants, many of whom were serfs (before 1746 and 1749) or were dependent in some other way. There were also free peasants who had their own holdings, but their numbers steadily declined. Artisan crafts were practiced in villages as well as towns, where they were organized into guilds; production was mainly consumed locally. Local commerce was carried on by small merchants, artisans, and peasants, while long-distance and transit trade was mainly in the hands of foreign merchants. Among the main exports of the principalities were foodstuffs, timber, and salt, the bulk of it going to the Ottoman Empire, which monopolized their foreign trade.

Society was dominated by the *boiers,* who formed a hereditary estate and owed their status to control of land and to posts in government. The great majority of the population (about 600,000 in Walachia and 400,000 in Moldavia in 1700) consisted of peasants, who bore the greatest share of taxation and other public burdens but had few civil or political rights. The native middle class was small, mainly because of the modest level of urbanization, the artisan industry, and commerce, and it exercised little influence in public affairs. The clergy of the Orthodox Church, to which the great majority of

Walachians and Moldavians belonged, was the primary spiritual force, especially in the villages.

Cultural and intellectual life until the eighteenth century reflected the principalities' primary orientation toward the Byzantine-Orthodox world. Education was the province of the church, and monasteries were the centers for the copying and diffusion of manuscripts, which were almost all religious in nature. The majority of books, the printing of which began in 1508 with a liturgy book, were also religious. Slavonic persisted as the official language of the church and the princes' chancelleries until the seventeenth century. But influences came from the West, too. The Reformation stirred religious debate and hastened the replacement of Slavonic by Romanian. Contacts with Western scholarship helped transform chronicles into true histories, as in the works of Miron Costin (1633–1691), which revealed a new, secular consciousness of man's destiny. The Enlightenment brought the elites still closer to Europe and provided them with the analytical tools they needed to define their condition and chart their future. By the end of the eighteenth century, the transition from a medieval to a modern society was underway.

See also **Balkans; Habsburg Dynasty: Austria; Orthodoxy, Russian; Ottoman Empire; Poland; Russia.**

BIBLIOGRAPHY

Duțu, Alexandru. *Romanian Humanists and European Culture: A Contribution to Comparative Cultural History.* Bucharest, 1977.

Hitchins, Keith. *The Romanians, 1774–1866.* Oxford, 1996.

Iorga, Nicolae. *Histoire des Roumains et de la Romanité orientale.* Vols. 4–7 (10 Vols.). Bucharest, 1937–1940.

Maxim, Mihai. *Tările Române si Înalta Poartă. Cadrul juridic al relatiilor româno-otomane în Evul Mediu.* Bucharest, 1993.

Mihordea, V. *Mâitres du sol et paysans dans les Principautés Roumaines au XVIIIe siècle.* Bucharest, 1971.

Pippidi, Andrei. *Traditia politică bizantină în Tările Române în secolele XVI–XVIII.* Bucharest, 1983.

KEITH HITCHINS

ROMANOV DYNASTY (RUSSIA).

The Romanov family was one of the old boyar families in Moscow, but its fortunes really began in 1547, when Anastasiia Romanovna Iur'eva married Tsar Ivan IV. Her relatives remained prominent boyars throughout the reign and suffered little from Ivan's suspicions and resultant executions. Anastasiia's nephew, Fedor Nikitich Romanov, received boyar rank in 1586 and played a major role in the politics of the court of Ivan's successor Fedor. The election of Boris Godunov as tsar in 1598 was a defeat for the Romanovs, and in 1600 Boris sent Fedor Romanov and his wife into exile. They were forced to enter monastic life, taking the names Filaret and Marfa. During the Time of Troubles Filaret as metropolitan of Rostov helped overthrow the first False Dmitrii (ruled 1605–1606) and fought against Tsar Vasilii Shuiskii (ruled 1606–1610). He supported the election of Władysław, the son of King Sigismund III of Poland, to the Russian throne. When negotiations with Poland broke down in 1610, Sigismund threw Filaret in prison.

Back in Russia Marfa looked after their son Michael (born 1596) in Kostroma. The defeat of the Poles in 1612 led to the calling of an Assembly of the Land in 1613, which elected Michael tsar. He ruled until his death in 1645, at first under the influence of his mother and then after 1619 of his father Filaret, who was elected patriarch of Moscow on his return in that year.

In the reign of Tsar Michael Russia slowly recovered from the devastation of the Time of Troubles, repopulating the center and west of the country and expanding settlement south and east. The government returned to normal and slowly expanded in size, aided by the relative peace at court among the boyar factions. An unsuccessful attempt to regain losses to Poland in the Troubles was balanced by the successful construction of extensive fortifications and garrisons on the southern frontier that guarded against Crimean raids.

Michael's son Alexis Mikhailovich (ruled 1645–1676) was far more successful. The long war with Poland brought back the lost territories and also the Ukrainian Hetmanate as an autonomous unit within Russia. Internal disputes in the church led to much reform but also to the schism of the Old Belief by 1667. For most of his reign Alexis was content to balance the boyar factions and rule by consensus, a system interrupted by the ambitions of Patriarch Nikon (reigned 1652–1658), which led

to Nikon's eventual downfall. By the end of the reign Alexis relied more and more on his favorite, Artamon Sergeevich Matveev.

The male children of Alexis by his first wife Mariia Miloslavskaia, whom he married in 1648, were not a healthy lot. The first heir Alexis died in his teens, and his brother Fedor was ill (probably with scurvy) from childhood. A younger son, Ivan, was also sickly and partly blind. The daughters flourished, but according to Russian custom could not rule. The second marriage of Tsar Alexis in 1671, to Nataliia Naryshkina, produced another daughter but also a healthy son, the future Peter the Great.

At Alexis's death in 1676 the throne went to Fedor, who was too young and sickly to rule until 1680, two years after which he died. After the revolt of the musketeers in 1682, Alexis's daughter Sofiia ruled as regent for the young Peter and his brother Ivan. Peter and his allies at court overthrew her in 1689, inaugurating thirty-six years of deep transformation of the Russian state and Russian culture. By his death in 1725 Peter had made Russia a major regional power, built a European absolutist state, and brought Russia into the circle of European culture. He did not, however, secure the succession. The conflict in 1718 with his son Alexis led him to decree that the tsar could choose his successor, but he did not do so. Thus on his death the Russian elite chose his wife to rule as Catherine I.

The death of Catherine I in 1727 threw the succession back to Peter II, the son of the unfortunate Alexis Alekseevich. Peter II died suddenly of smallpox in 1730, and the elite this time chose Anna, the daughter of Peter the Great's co-tsar Ivan and widow of the duke of Courland, to be the empress. She ruled with the help of her Courland favorite Ernst Johann Bühren (known in Russia as Biron) until 1740. As she had no children, the succession was again in question. Anna's desire was to leave the throne to her infant grand-nephew in the maternal line, Ivan VI, the son of the duke of Brunswick-Lüneburg. The inevitable regency was unpopular, and in 1741 the ruling elite and the guards overthrew Ivan and his family and placed on the throne Peter's daughter Elizabeth.

Elizabeth restored a sense of legitimacy to the throne and the dynasty. She reestablished harmony at the court by returning Anna's enemies from exile and pursued the building of the Russian state, economy, and culture, including the founding of Moscow University in 1755. Russia's armies defeated Frederick the Great of Prussia in the Seven Years' War (1756–1763). Elizabeth's secret morganatic marriage to Aleksei Razumovskii produced no heirs, so she arranged the succession of the duke of Holstein-Gottorp, the son of Peter the Great's daughter Anna. As Peter III he took the throne on Elizabeth's death in 1762, but he was soon overthrown in favor of his wife, Catherine II.

Catherine, born Sophie of Anhalt-Zerbst, ruled from 1762 to 1796 and was one of Russia's greatest rulers. Her defeats of the Ottomans, the attendant conquest of the north Black Sea coast, and the partitions of Poland made Russia a great power in Europe. At the same time her rationalization of provincial and town administration, with the granting of limited participation to merchants and gentry, strengthened legal order and added new dimensions to Russian administration. The Charter of the Nobility (1785) for the first time spelled out the rights and obligations of the gentry. Her promotion of education and Enlightenment culture spread new political ideas among the gentry. Later liberal opposition to the monarchy sprang from these ideas.

In her memoirs Catherine said that it was her first lover, Sergei Saltykov, rather than Peter III, who was the father of her son Paul. Paul came to the throne in 1796 during the European crisis sparked by the French Revolution. Alarmed by its success, Paul briefly joined the anti-French coalition and reversed many of his mother's reforms. Elite discontent led to his murder in March 1801. Ironically, his succession decree of 1797 allowed for an orderly succession to his son, Alexander I, for the first time in over a century.

See also **Alexis I (Russia); Anna (Russia); Autocracy; Boris Godunov (Russia); Catherine II (Russia); Elizabeth (Russia); Michael Romanov (Russia); Nikon, patriarch; Old Believers; Orthodoxy, Russian; Paul I (Russia); Peter I (Russia); Russia; Russian Literature and Language; Russo-Polish Wars; Russo-Ottoman Wars; Sofiia Alekseevna; Time of Troubles (Russia).**

BIBLIOGRAPHY

Alexander, John T. *Catherine the Great: Life and Legend.* Oxford, 1989.

Ansimov, Evgeny V. *Empress Elizabeth: Her Reign and Her Russia 1741–1761.* Trans. by John T. Alexander. Gulf Breeze, Fla., 1995.

Hughes, Lindsey. *Peter the Great: A Biography.* New Haven and London, 2002.

Longworth, Philip. *Alexis, Tsar of all the Russias.* New York, 1984.

McGrew, Roderick E. *Paul I of Russia 1754–1801.* Oxford, 1992.

PAUL BUSHKOVITCH

ROMANTICISM. According to most definitions, Romanticism begins sometime around or after 1789, the terminal date of this encyclopedia and the moment of the French Revolution. 1789 has been the key date in a good many historical narratives, the point at which everything is thought to have changed forever. But much of what we recognize as Romantic was in place before the Revolution. Confusion arises from the way in which scholars and critics have understood Romanticism as both a period (somewhere between 1760 and 1850) and an attitude or disposition whose priorities include (but are not limited to) emotionalism, excessive self-consciousness, respect for the dignity of childhood, a critique of neoclassicism, an interest in folk culture and primitive origins, a preference for rural life, and a high valuation of private reading over public performance. Artists or writers who foreshadow these concerns before 1789 are likely to be called "Preromantics" (Brown, 1991) or to be assigned to the "age of sensibility" (Hilles and Bloom). The poet George Crabbe (1754–1832) is squarely within the Romantic period but is anti-Romantic because he opposes the spirit of the age. Some writers, like Johann Wolfgang von Goethe (1749–1832), go through Romantic and anti-Romantic phases; others, like Lord Byron (1788–1824), appear throughout as excessively Romantic in some ways (the melodramatic hero) and doggedly antagonistic in others (the decision to use neoclassical rhyming couplets).

Romanticism can be politically radical and democratic (as it was held to be in Britain among the poetic avant-garde in the 1790s) or reactionary and traditional (as it mostly was in France). Often it can be somewhere in between, leading to a lively controversy about, for example, the politics of William Wordsworth's (1770–1850) poetry. National chronologies also vary significantly. British and German Romanticisms are held to be well under way in the 1790s; French and other European Romanticisms come later, in the 1800s and after; and American Romanticism comes later still. Romanticism also varies according to the forms and genres we examine. Ludwig van Beethoven (1770–1827) and Franz Schubert (1797–1828) are Romantics; there are Romantic painters (Francisco Goya [1746–1828], James Mallord William Turner [1775–1852], and Eugène Delacroix [1798–1863]); but there is no familiar concept of Romantic architecture (Gothic revival comes closest). There is lots of Romantic literature, especially poetry.

Intellectual historians have often favored explanations relating both the Revolution and Romanticism to preexisting conditions, and in this they repeat a common assumption of the 1790s whereby massive historical changes were attributed to the power of ideas. Commentators of both left and right blamed or praised Voltaire (1694–1778), Denis Diderot (1713–1784), and Jean-Jacques Rousseau (1712–1778) for historical events that none of them lived to see. Many recent interpreters have assimilated Romanticism into a "long eighteenth century" starting around 1690 and extending well into the 1800s, making it central to our understanding of modernity as a whole. Others retain an allegiance to the idea of a clear break between a "classical" eighteenth century and a "modern" worldview. Michel Foucault took the second position in describing the emergence of the "sciences of man," for which biocultural life is both the origin and the object of knowledge. The compulsive reflexivity and often anxious self-consciousness emanating from this sense of temporality can also be traced in historically earlier forms, though we might agree that it comes to be dominant and impossible to ignore in the Romantic period and the Romantic attitude. Debates between the so-called ancients and moderns throughout the eighteenth century had taken up the question of how much we could expect to understand in the literature of the past, given its different conditions of production and reception. Some felt that truth was transhistorical and natural, others that meaning could only be recovered by careful and patient research (Levine).

The 1700s also saw the emergence of a biblical hermeneutics (science of interpretation) concerned to establish the origins and relative authenticities of the various parts of the Bible (Frei): the sacred book was given human time and place. Again, the Romantic interest in folk and popular culture emerged from a preexisting tradition of antiquarianism that was already implicated in a nationalist-imperialist agenda, one that became even more urgent during the European and world wars that dominated the years between 1793 and 1815. Romanticism embodies a north European, Gothic primitivism that could be invoked to support both popular democracy and the monarchist alliance against Napoleon, as well as a liberal-classicist, cosmopolitan admiration of the pagan Mediterranean that was used to critique the restorations of 1815 (Butler, ch. 5). We can look to Romanticism as containing forms of resistance to the "civilizing process" described by Norbert Elias, evident, for example, in the revolt of Lord Byron, Robert Burns (1759–1796), and Gérard de Nerval (1808–1855) against the rituals of bourgeois self-discipline. However, it includes also those forms of acutely anxious self-examination, as in William Wordsworth's or John Keats's (1795–1821) poetry, which are so clearly coincident with the taming of social violence and the internalization of revolt that Elias traced in the evolution of modern manners.

Romanticism has mostly been a polemical and politicized construction, whether in the interpretations of latter-day scholars (Simpson, 1993, 2000) or in the earliest inventions of the category itself. Hegel gave us the most forceful early definition in positing Romanticism as marked by a turn from the external to the internal, spiritual world and the afterlife. He saw this beginning in the Christian Middle Ages and intensifying in later centuries. His Romanticism is thereby somewhat coincident with the royalist, Christian, antirevolutionary movement typified by François René Chateaubriand (1768–1848) and Victor Hugo (1802–1885). A chronologically more contained Romanticism has been based on the Byronic hero, with its obvious allusions to the figure of Napoleon in its liberating as well as its tyrannical incarnations. Still another can be based on the new interest in folk culture (Johann Gottfried von Herder [1744–1803], William Wordsworth, Robert Burns, and Sir Walter Scott

[1771–1832]). Romanticism has been identified with both religion (orthodox and nonconformist) and atheism, with the political right and left, with progressive optimism and besetting nostalgia, according to the needs of its various interpreters. It is perhaps best understood as an assembly of all of these tendencies (and others) within a loosely understood historical period, giving us the tools for setting about a study of individual artists or movements without imposing a prescriptive boundary.

See also **English Literature and Language; French Literature and Language; German Literature and Language; Goethe, Johann Wolfgang von; Goya y Lucientes, Francisco de; Herder, Johann Gottfried von; Revolutions, Age of.**

BIBLIOGRAPHY

Brown, Marshall. *The Cambridge History of Literary Criticism.* Vol. 5, *Romanticism.* Cambridge, U.K., 2000.

———. *Preromanticism.* Stanford, 1991.

Butler, Marilyn. *Romantics, Rebels and Reactionaries: English Literature and its Background, 1760–1830.* New York and Oxford, 1982.

Elias, Norbert. *The Civilizing Process.* Translated by Edmund Jephcott. Oxford, 1994.

Foucault, Michel. *The Order of Things: An Archaeology of the Human Sciences.* New York, 1973.

Frei, Hans W. *The Eclipse of Biblical Narrative: A Study in Eighteenth and Nineteenth-Century Hermeneutics.* New Haven and London, 1974.

Hegel, G. W. F. *Aesthetics: Lectures on Fine Art.* Translated by T. M. Knox. Oxford, 1975.

Hilles, Frederick W., and Harold Bloom. *From Sensibility to Romanticism: Essays Presented to Frederick A. Pottle.* London, Oxford, and New York, 1965.

Levine, Joseph M. *The Battle of the Books: History and Literature in the Augustan Age.* Ithaca, N.Y., and London, 1991.

Simpson, David. "The French Revolution." In *The Cambridge History of Literary Criticism.* Vol. 5, *Romanticism,* edited by Marshall Brown, pp. 49–71. Cambridge, U.K., 2000.

———. *Romanticism, Nationalism and the Revolt against Theory.* Chicago and London, 1993.

DAVID SIMPSON

ROME. From 1500 to 1789, Rome's population grew from about 50,000 to over 160,000. A small civic government maintained some autonomy well into the seventeenth century, but the papacy increasingly controlled local and regional administration, even as its own role in European politics declined. As the center of Catholic Christendom, Rome remained the focal point for the church hierarchy, for numerous religious orders, and for pilgrims. From the 1540s on, concern for doctrinal orthodoxy circumscribed written and artistic expression, but for another two centuries the city of the popes remained a site of cultural creativity and accomplishment, particularly in architecture.

ECONOMY AND GOVERNMENT

In 1500, papal revenues still came primarily from dioceses and church landholdings throughout Europe. After the Protestant Reformation diminished that source, the popes relied more upon heavy taxation of their territories in central Italy, known as the Papal States. A funded debt established in 1526 helped rationalize the curial economy. By 1600, Rome's administration of its territories was arguably as sophisticated as that of any other European state, but its failure to develop new sources of wealth meant reliance upon deficit spending and foreign patronage. The economy of the city beyond the Curia, built largely around the annual influx of pilgrims, perennially lacked a strong industrial or agricultural base. Bad harvests could readily lead to famines, as happened in 1763–1764.

Whereas sixteenth-century popes such as Julius II (reigned 1503–1513) and Paul III (reigned 1534–1549) engaged in wars with powerful Roman families such as the Colonna, over time the local nobles were subsumed into the church hierarchy. A civic government, the Senate and People of Rome, retained some judicial powers and provided a forum for rallying public opinion. It had influence particularly during periods of vacant see (i.e., between popes). But by 1600 all top state officials were churchmen: a cardinal-chamberlain *(camerlengo)* headed administration of the papacy's temporal domain, with cardinal-legates governing different regions and a cardinal serving as secretary of state. Thereafter, Roman nobles played an essentially ceremonial role, except to the extent that family members obtained high curial offices.

FOREIGN RELATIONS

By 1500, Italian politics were being transformed by the presence of French and Spanish armies. Pope

Rome. When Giambattista Nolli published his famous twelve-sheet plan of Rome in 1748 he included a reduced reproduction of Leonardo Bufalini's 1551 woodcut map of the city. Bufalini's map represented a major advance over its medieval and Renaissance predecessors, which were usually odd collections of buildings drawn in elevation or oblique view with inconsistent topography. The drawing here is meticulous and complete, with every street clearly depicted. MAP COLLECTION, STERLING MEMORIAL LIBRARY, YALE UNIVERSITY

Julius II played the two against each other while strengthening his economic and political hold on the Papal States. By the mid-1520s, however, the might of Spain and the Holy Roman Empire, united in the person of Charles V (ruled 1519–1556), became decisive. Clement VII (reigned 1523–1534) sought intermittently to form alliances to contain imperial power on the peninsula, but the League of Cognac (formed 22 May 1526), in which the pope joined forces with Venice and France, was too disunified in purpose to prevent an imperial army from sacking Rome on 6 May 1527. Clement VII ultimately made peace with Charles V, and he officially crowned Charles emperor in Bologna in February 1530.

Thereafter, Spanish sovereigns often proved critical in defending Rome and in furthering papal goals beyond Italy. Paul IV (reigned 1555–1559)

bucked this trend, forming with France an alliance designed to drive the Spaniards from Italy, but the strategy backfired when an imperial army under the duke of Alba encamped near Rome in 1557, forcing the pope to make peace. French defeats soon led to the Treaty of Cateau-Cambrésis (1559), following which Spain enjoyed a uniquely privileged relationship with Rome: Spanish kings exerted influence in the papal court and gained control over substantial church revenues in Spain. In turn, the kings generously endowed religious institutions in Rome and provided military support to the papacy. Meanwhile, the Vatican diplomatic service grew more complex and systematic, especially under Gregory XIII (reigned 1572–1585) and Clement VIII (reigned 1592–1605), and it came under official control of cardinals.

By the 1620s, the balance of power between Spain and France shifted temporarily in the direction of the latter, and Urban VIII (reigned 1623–1644) was elected pope with strong support of French cardinals. Spain remained influential throughout the century, particularly during the pontificate of Alexander VII (reigned 1655–1667). But following the Peace of Westphalia (1648), which ended the Thirty Years' War, religion became sharply less important in European politics, and so Rome ceased to be as critical to dynastic strategies.

THE URBAN LANDSCAPE

Although the building of Renaissance Rome was well under way by 1500, Pope Julius II gave it added impetus. Seeking to make the city suitably dignified for his ambitions, he sponsored construction projects including the Via Giulia and St. Peter's Basilica (begun 1506). Paul III enhanced the fortifications of the Vatican, employed Michelangelo to restore the city capitol (the Campidoglio), and saw to the construction of major urban thoroughfares. Subsequent pontiffs, notably Sixtus V (1585–1590), further edified and embellished the city. Classical models inspired both urban design and the building of suburban villas with gardens.

The seventeenth century saw the addition of massive baroque structures, many designed by Francesco Borromini (1599–1667) and Gian Lorenzo Bernini (1598–1680). Commissioned in 1638 to build the Church of San Carlo alle Quattro Fontane, Borromini later designed its imposing curved facade. Bernini's projects included overseeing the completion of St. Peter's and designing the colonnade that surrounds its square (completed 1667).

In the eighteenth century, elaborate new facades for churches and other buildings transformed the appearance of existing squares and streets. Wealthy families such as the Corsini and the Doria Pamphili commissioned private palaces whose facades vied for attention in the public theater of the city. There was more practical construction, as well: some structures were divided into private apartments of varying size to house the burgeoning ranks of mid-level papal officials, and new buildings were erected for oratories, monasteries, convents, and charitable institutions. By the later eighteenth century, construction was curtailed amidst economic crises, but there was by then a dense core of buildings in central Rome, surrounded on the outskirts by the villas of the wealthy.

RELIGIOUS AND CULTURAL LEADERSHIP

Although the Protestant Reformation cut into the papacy's prestige and revenues, Rome remained the world center of the Catholic faith. Starting in the pontificate of Paul III, it was also a center of reform. When the papacy convened the Council of Trent (1545–1563), which enacted extensive doctrinal and institutional reforms, new religious groups had already emerged, including the Capuchins (1528) and the Society of Jesus, or Jesuits (1540). The latter's zealous and at times controversial promotion of the faith, which could threaten secular rulers' prerogatives, led in 1773 to its temporary suppression by Pope Clement XIV (reigned 1769–1774). Beginning in the mid-sixteenth century, the Roman Inquisition and the Index of Prohibited Books (first promulgated in 1559) limited the scope of acceptable theological expression but did not entirely stifle other forms of intellectual creativity. The University of Rome, strong before the Sack of 1527, had to shut down for eight years. After reopening, it had mainly regional importance, educating lawyers, mid-level papal and civil officials, and some doctors. Bologna remained the premier university in papal territories. Within Rome, religious orders' schools, especially the Jesuits' Collegio Romano (established 1551), dominated theological education. Literary, scientific, and archaeological culture flourished in the later sixteenth century and beyond, when private collections of manuscripts and antiquities became increasingly fashionable. The constraints of orthodoxy limited radical religious expression, at times forcefully, as in the case of Giordano Bruno, who was burned at the stake in Rome in 1600. Philosophical, scientific, and literary pursuits that did not directly contravene church dogma flourished, especially in academies such as that of the Lincei (1603–1630) and the Arcadia, founded in 1690 by scholars who had enjoyed the patronage of Queen Christina of Sweden (d. 1689), who had converted to Catholicism.

The early sixteenth century, a peak period for artistic creativity in Rome, encompassed Michelangelo's painting of the Sistine Chapel ceiling (1508–1512) and Raphael's work in the Vatican stanze (begun 1509). Later influential contributions in-

Rome. *A View of Rome with the Bridge and Castel St. Angelo by the Tiber* by Gaspar van Wittel. ROY MILES FINE PAINTINGS/
BRIDGEMAN ART LIBRARY

cluded Michelangelo's *Last Judgment* (completed 1541), and around 1600 Rome still drew major painters like Annibale Carracci (1560–1609) and Caravaggio (1571–1610). Achievements in architecture reached new heights the following century in the works of Borromini and Bernini, the latter of whom also made enduring contributions to baroque statuary, notably his *Ecstasy of St. Theresa* (1652) in the church of Santa Maria della Vittoria, and the Fountain of the Four Rivers (1651) in the Piazza Navona. In the eighteenth century, public spaces were redesigned with an eye to theatricality. Major projects included the Spanish Steps (1723–1726), the Piazza Sant' Ignazio (1727–1735), and Nicola Salvi's design for the Trevi fountain (mid-1730s), which still today dominates its piazza.

By 1789, Rome had ceased to be a center even of architectural innovation. Still, prints designed and compiled by the architect and engraver Giovanni Battista Piranesi (1720–1778) helped disseminate abroad an appreciation for the city's cultural riches, as did its distinction as the final stop on European aristocrats' grand tour. Although Rome's cultural role had waned, the Renaissance, Reformation, and baroque ages would bequeath a rich legacy to future generations, much as the culture of antiquity had done for them.

See also **Art: The Conception and Status of the Artist; Catholicism; Christina (Sweden); Jesuits; Papacy and Papal States; Rome, Architecture in; Rome, Art in; Rome, Sack of; Trent, Council of.**

BIBLIOGRAPHY

Dandelet, Thomas James. *Spanish Rome, 1500–1700.* New Haven and London, 2001.

Gross, Hanns. *Rome in the Age of Enlightenment: The Post-Tridentine Syndrome and the Ancien Regime.* Cambridge, U.K., and New York, 1990.

Partner, Peter. *Renaissance Rome, 1500–1559: A Portrait of a Society.* Berkeley and Los Angeles, 1976.

Signorotto, Gianvittorio, and Maria Antonietta Visceglia, eds. *Court and Politics in Papal Rome, 1492–1700.* Cambridge, U.K., and New York, 2002.

KENNETH GOUWENS

ROME, ARCHITECTURE IN. In the early sixteenth century, the architectural development of Rome was spurred by a campaign to reclaim the city as the *caput mundi,* while the century closed with the more pragmatic goal of providing Catholic pilgrims with a coherent and forceful spiritual experience as they moved about the city. Early-seventeenth-century efforts celebrated what was hailed as a triumph for the Catholic Church over the Protestant Reformation, but by the early eighteenth century, as the power of the Church waned and the papal budget for building flagged, triumph turned to a hope that Rome would become a destination on the grand tour of Europe. On more than one occasion over this span of 300 years, observers commented that the city itself resembled one big construction site, as architecture became the visible sign of these shifting goals.

THE SIXTEENTH CENTURY

Two projects—one sacred and one secular—spanned much of the sixteenth century. Reconstruction of the church of St. Peter's began in 1506 at the command of Pope Julius II Della Rovere (reigned 1503–1513) on the design of Donato Bramante (1444–1514), who projected a Greek-cross plan with a massive central dome, a radical departure in design from the Latin-cross plan of the original fourth-century foundation of Old St. Peter's marking the burial site of Peter, the first pope. The scheme was fantastic and promised to rival the scale of Roman imperial public architecture. Although the massive piers for the crossing were begun according to Bramante's design, the plan was revised repeatedly after his death—by Raphael (1483–1520), by Baldassare Peruzzi (1481–1536),

by Antonio Giamberti da Sangallo the Younger (1483–1546), and finally, beginning in 1546, by Michelangelo Buonarroti (1475–1564), who simplified the plan by embedding the Greek cross in a square, capped with a magnificent double-shelled dome offering a striking skyline image for this, the city's most important pilgrimage destination. The great sculptor turned architect was also responsible for the restructuring of the Campidoglio, the civic center atop the Capitoline Hill, close by the Tabularium and Forum Romanum of the ancient city. Beginning in 1539, the work was carried out in phases (Palazzo Nuovo was not even begun until 1603), but Michelangelo's mark is apparent in the brilliant design of the oval space, focused on the ancient equestrian statue of emperor Marcus Aurelius and framed by the angled placements of the flanking structures.

Highlights of private building in the city include Bramante's Palazzo Caprini (c. 1501–1510), an elegant townhouse design that spawned a new category of urban domestic architecture. In contrast, the majestic Palazzo Farnese, built over time on designs by Sangallo, Michelangelo, and Giacomo della Porta (c. 1537–1602), established the aristocratic Roman palace type. In the category of church building, noteworthy developments include experimentation with oval designs, such as S. Anna dei Palafrenieri, Vignola (begun 1565) by Giacomo Barozzi (1507–1573) and S. Giacomo degli Incurabili, Volterra (begun 1592) by Francesco Capriani (c. 1530–1594). In contrast, the newly sanctioned Society of Jesus, founded by Ignatius of Loyola and headquartered in Rome, built the church of Il Gesù (begun 1568), designed by Barozzi, financed by Pope Paul III Farnese (reigned 1534–1549) and responsive in its architecture to the reforms called for at the close of the Council of Trent (1563). Strategically located in the city center, the church is Latin-cross in plan, with a shallow transept and a broad nave, devoid of side aisles, but with a series of discrete side chapels. The unified interior space was to accommodate large crowds with good acoustics for preaching, while the side chapels provided individual altars for serving the requisite daily masses. Likewise, the facade, designed by Della Porta, established a new type of aedicular composition with two stories of unequal width reflecting the elevation of the church. The

Architecture in Rome. This is a reproduction of the lower-right corner of Giambattista Nolli's magnificent twelve-sheet 1748 plan, which also features elaborate symbolic scenes. In this scene, the Christian character of the city is emphasized. The inscription above the seated figure refers to Pope Clement XII (reigned 1730–1740), and the map was dedicated to his successor Benedict XIV (reigned 1740–1758); both did much to beautify Rome. Architectural monuments are also depicted. MAP COLLECTION, STERLING MEMORIAL LIBRARY, YALE UNIVERSITY

plan, the interior articulation, and the facade of the Gesù were widely imitated; notable among these offspring are the churches of S. Maria in Vallicella (begun 1575), S. Andrea della Valle (begun 1591), and S. Susanna (begun 1595).

In the same spirit of reform, the century drew to a close with the election of Pope Sixtus V Peretti (reigned 1585–1590) who instituted, with his architect Domenico Fontana (1543–1607), an urban scheme to unify the city by establishing a network of straight streets and vertical markers, ancient Roman commemorative columns, and ancient Egyptian obelisks, each topped with Christian symbols. The Sistine plan for the city, aimed at pilgrims in anticipation of the holy year of 1600, served to link the city center with the outskirts where the early Christian basilicas—obligatory stops on the pilgrimage route—were located. In this way, Sixtus stimulated growth of the city and established a framework for its later urban development.

THE SEVENTEENTH CENTURY

The expansion of St. Peter's to form a Latin-cross plan and the completion of its facade, all at the direction of Pope Paul V Borghese (reigned 1605–1621) on designs by Carlo Maderno (1556–1629), opened the seventeenth century on a note of celebration. This tone is evident in both private and public architecture, where new forms and hybrid solutions abound. The grand tradition of Palazzo Farnese was transformed in the designs of Palazzo Borghese (Maderno; 1605–1614), Palazzo Barberini (Maderno and Bernini; 1628–1638), Palazzo Pamphili at the Piazza Navona (G. Rainaldi and Borromini; 1646–1647) and Palazzo Chigi-Odescalchi (Bernini; 1664–1667), each a palace of family members of the reigning pope. What had appeared as formidable blocks showing reserved faces to the city grew into organic structures with facades replete with arcades and orders orchestrating opened and closed wall segments in response to the immediate urban context and the larger

Architecture in Rome. *The Piazza San Pietro,* painting by Gaspare van Wittel, showing St. Peter's Basilica and the Bernini colonnades. ©CHRISTIE'S IMAGES/CORBIS

cityscape. Likewise, church architecture attained new levels of invention, both in plan as well as in elevation. Central plans attracted renewed attention, as for example in Pietro da Cortona's SS. Martina e Luca (begun 1635) and Francesco Borromini's S. Carlo alle Quattro Fontane (begun 1638). Facades that were planar as aedicular compositions (horizontal elements that support a vertical element), stemming from the Gesù, grew increasingly complex with heavily tectonic designs marked by a dramatic repetition of the columnar order in planes that break forward into space, as for example at SS. Vincenzo ed Anastasio (M. Longhi the Younger; 1646–1650), S. Maria in Campitelli (C. Rainaldi; begun 1662), and S. Marcello (C. Fontana; 1682–1683). These inventions, with their marked attraction to the dramatic in purely architectural terms, define what we mean by the term "baroque."

Nowhere is this baroque mentality more apparent than in the architectural works of the triumvirate of design personalities—Francesco Borromini (1599–1667), Pietro da Cortona (1596–1669), and Gian Lorenzo Bernini (1598–1680)—and their papal sponsors, Urban VIII Barberini (reigned 1623–1644), Innocent X Pamphili (reigned 1644–1655), and Alexander VII Chigi (reigned 1655–1667). At S. Ivo della Sapienza (1640–1660), Borromini offers a purely architectural composition celebrating the theme of wisdom, appropriate to the

chapel of a university and revealed in the highly unusual star-hexagon plan, the undulating walls, the pleated dome, and the extraordinary lantern. Cortona's facade design for S. Maria della Pace (1656–1661) involved formation of an urban setting, a small polygonal opening carved into a dense neighborhood that not only facilitated access to the church by carriage, but also offered a dramatic setting for the semicircular portico of the facade that ironically seems to fill the open space as the church aggressively seeks its visitor. Bernini's S. Andrea al Quirinale (1658–1676) offers a stage like architecture that begins on the street with its grand, one-story aedicular facade announcing the aedicule of the altar opposite where the crowning pediment opens to reveal Andrew in his ascent to the heavenly dome where his fellow fishermen await him. The drama of the sculptural event in this small oval church highlights Bernini's role as impresario and his manipulation of the viewer for whom he stages spectacular events, whether in his design of the Baldacchino (1624–1633) at the crossing of St. Peter's, in the Cornaro Chapel (1645–1652) in S. Maria della Vittoria, or in the monumental Piazza S. Pietro (1656–1667). The Piazza S. Pietro, the crowning achievement of the papacy of Alexander VII, completed the campaign to rebuild St. Peter's. Here, the defining lines of the giant colonnades unite the opposing forms of the latitudinal oval, a gathering space for the faithful, and the trapezoid, a funnel-like space leading to the church. These spaces also function to frame the ritual appearances of the pope in the Benediction Loggia at the center of the church facade and in his apartment at the upper story of the papal palace to the north. In each case the architects of baroque Rome focus on the participant and in so doing offer exciting challenges fraught with subtleties of scale, of surface, of space, and of time.

THE EIGHTEENTH CENTURY

Although the pace of building in Rome slowed at the end of the seventeenth century, the eighteenth century brought an interesting combination of architectural styles, stemming from the baroque, while also offering a contemporary aspect. The classical strain of architecture, employed for official commissions, recalls Bernini's (and even Michelangelo's) architecture and reflects the growing fascination among her tourists with Rome's ancient past. The more playful rococo style, apparent in urban planning and smaller church and domestic architecture and spawned by the fanciful creations of Borromini, offered an important foil, yet the two strains seem perfectly compatible. On the one hand, new facades for S. Giovanni in Laterano (Galilei; 1733–1736) and S. Maria Maggiore (Fuga; 1741–1746) demonstrate both the severity as well as the drama of the classical style in which the wall has been eliminated to reveal dark recesses in space while the order alone remains to define the skeletal structure of the whole. On the other hand, the curvilinear shapes of the open-air designs of the Spanish Steps (De Sanctis; 1723–1726) and Piazza S. Ignazio (Raguzzini; 1727–1735) offer an alternative sensibility of refinement and elegance suitable to a new leisure class of Romans as well as to tourists drawn to Rome to study both ancient and contemporary art and architecture. On occasion, the two styles merge in monuments such as the Fontana di Trevi (Salvi; 1732–1762), where the classical language furnishes a luxurious backdrop for the extraordinary sculptural display and waterworks, and the main facade of Palazzo Doria-Pamphili (Valvassori; 1730–1735), where the skeletal aspect of the classical conjoins with the decorative and curvilinear elements of the rococo.

The appeal of this architecture, beginning in the early sixteenth century and continuing well into the eighteenth century, is its grandeur and drama, aspects that enjoyed success whether in the service of the church, of public institutions, or of individuals. The wonder of this architecture lies not only in the sheer number of buildings that were built, but also in the staggering variety of these buildings that together created Rome's marvelously variegated and unified urban fabric.

See also **Architecture; Art: Artistic Patronage; Baroque; City Planning; Classicism; Grand Tour; Rococo; Sculpture.**

BIBLIOGRAPHY

Ackerman, James S. *The Architecture of Michelangelo.* 2 vols. Rev. edition. London, 1964–1966.

Bruschi, Arnaldo. *Bramante.* Translated by Peter Murray. London, 1977.

Curcio, Giovanna, and Elisabeth Kieven, eds. *Storia dell'architettura italiana: Il settecento.* Milan, 2000.

Del Pesco, Daniela. *L'architettura del seicento.* Turin, 1998.

Lotz, Wolfgang. *Architecture in Italy, 1500–1600.* Introduction by Deborah Howard. New Haven, 1995.

Marder, Tod A. *Bernini and the Art of Architecture.* New York, 1998.

Varriano, John. *Italian Baroque and Rococo Architecture.* New York and Oxford, 1986.

Waddy, Patricia. *Seventeenth-Century Roman Palaces: Use and the Art of the Plan.* New York, 1990.

Wittkower, Rudolf. *Art and Architecture in Italy, 1600–1750.* 3 vols. Revised by Joseph Connors and Jennifer Montagu. New Haven, 1999.

DOROTHY METZGER HABEL

ROME, ART IN. Like the art and architecture of the early modern city, the art of ancient Rome was largely produced by ambitious immigrants: ever since the legendary early days when Rome welcomed Etruscan kings and Sabine women, its culture had always been both international and eclectic. But art in early modern Rome was eclectic in a highly particular sense, incorporating influences from vastly different times as well as different cultures. Even after the Vandal invasions of the sixth century cut the ancient aqueducts and reduced the Roman population to a fraction of its million inhabitants, artists in Rome were compelled to face the imposing physical legacy of the ancient city: its monumental ruins, its fading frescoes, ancient buildings that had never gone out of use (like the Pantheon, some early Christian basilicas, and many humbler structures), and a population of statues that sometimes rivaled the numbers of the living. The legacy of Roman grandeur and Roman style persisted in the work of later artists and architects, who often adapted a set of columns, a statue, or a marble inlay for their own projects. A pair of lions from the twelfth-century cloister of the basilica of Saint John Lateran feature Egyptian *nemes* head-dresses like those of the ancient sphinxes their sculptors must have seen in the ruins of the Temple of Isis. A statue of Saint Helen from the church of Santa Croce in Gerusalemme, itself built into a vaulted hall of Helen's Sessorian Palace, has been cleverly recarved from an ancient image of the goddess Juno. Medieval Rome was filled with colonnaded porches, porphyry inlays, gilt mosaics and marble statuary all directly inspired by—and often made of—the physical remains of the ancient city. Medieval Roman painters like Pietro Cavallini (c. 1250–c. 1330) gave their figures the same majestic solidity they must have seen in ancient frescoes.

THE ALLURE OF THE ANCIENT

By Cavallini's time, however, the Roman economy lagged far behind that of emerging merchant republics like Pisa, Siena, and Florence; the presence of the pope and his curia could not compensate for the lack of a thriving merchant class to attract and nurture artists and architects with a range of plentiful, competitive commissions. Visitors described medieval Rome as a landscape of ruins: the Forum was called Campo Vaccino (cow pasture) and the Capitoline, site of ancient Rome's most glorious temple, had become Monte Caprino (goat hill). The huge basilicas of Christianity, themselves relics of late Roman antiquity, crumbled in squalor as vendors hawked souvenirs and straw pallets to the pilgrims who bedded down within their huge, shabby porticoes. Yet the columns and statues strewn among Rome's ruins also seemed to contain the mysteries of perfect proportion, known to the ancients and lost in later eras—a perfection based on the harmony between the human body and the divine cosmos. Ancient Latin and Greek inscriptions expressed their own version of this divine order in the stately forms of their lettering. Thus, in their tantalizing incompleteness, the monuments of Rome

came to excite the early modern artistic imagination, spawning ideas of a scope and daring that no "complete" city could ever have inspired. The idea of restoring Rome to its ancient splendor had seemed an impossible vision to Petrarch when he visited in the mid-fourteenth century. The papacy had recently moved to Avignon, further crippling the feeble Roman economy, and Petrarch worried that the spark of ancient inspiration had gone out for good. During the first half of the fifteenth century, however, the popes gradually returned from Provence, trailing cardinals, curates, and bankers. To reinforce the permanence of their return to Rome, the fifteenth-century popes and their courts began to speak openly about renewing the city or, more radically, fostering its rebirth. Because of Rome's unique political structure, its history, and its physical presence, this culture of renewal also took on its own distinctive characteristics. In the first place, the papacy, with its theocratic monarchy, deliberately drew inspiration from the ancient Roman Empire rather than from the preceding republic. When republican ideals took hold in Rome, as they did on occasion, the result, until the Italian unification late in the nineteenth century, was almost invariably chaos. Second, the brooding presence of ancient ruins gave Renaissance Rome's sense of the ancient past an urgent physical immediacy. The architects of Renaissance Rome could hardly resist emulating the grand proportions of ancient buildings. Through painstaking study, they eventually came to understand, and then to apply, the ancient Romans' subtle system of aesthetic refinement, deployed with their inspired sense of freedom, and governed by the same rigor. But they also looted the fallen portions of the Colosseum to erect the walls of *palazzi* whose forms were themselves eloquent reworkings of the Colosseum's facade. The sheer complexity of Renaissance Rome's position between ancient past and imaginative present meant that the city's revival fostered an unusual degree of collaboration. The culture that resulted from the collaboration of these sometimes unlikely groups of friends represented an unusually broad population by comparison with Florence, where the Medici dictated intellectual and artistic fashion for generations, or Naples, with its Spanish-centered court, or even Venice, with its broad-based but carefully regimented civic life. The cultural life of fifteenth- and sixteenth-century Rome eventually thrived in a wide variety of places such as the *palazzi* of cardinals, businessmen, and papal bureaucrats as well as the Apostolic Palace. For even if the popes commanded spiritual as well as temporal power during their reigns, the reigns were often quite short—popes, like Venetian doges, tended to be elected as old men. The cultural life of the city therefore became unusually adaptable and always maintained a certain degree of diffuse independence from its one dominant figure.

RENEWAL OF ROME

The initial stages of Rome's artistic renewal were dominated by Tuscan artists. (Tuscans also dominated the curia to the extent that the Roman dialect changed in these years from a distinctively southern to a central Italian vernacular.) Masolino da Panicale created a fresco cycle for the Dominican church of San Clemente in the 1430s. Twenty years later, Pope Nicholas V invited the Florentine painter Fra Angelico (Guido di Pietro, c. 1400–1455) to decorate his private chapel in the Vatican Palace. In both cases, the renowned Tuscan painters brought their native style to Rome, but Rome exerted its own suggestive power over that style; in the shadow of the Colosseum, the Palatine palace, and the great Roman baths, their work took on a new gravity, their compositions became more architectonic, and architecture itself came to figure prominently in the paintings. As late as 1481, when Pope Sixtus IV gathered a team of painters to decorate the walls of his new chapel in the Vatican, he summoned them from Florence. Yet the frescoes produced by that team of Florence-based Tuscan and Umbrian artists on the Sistine Chapel walls entirely reflected their Roman setting: triumphal arches and Roman-style basilicas dominate the background, and even the famously sinuous figures of Botticelli and Ghirlandaio acquired the grandeur of Roman historical relief. Melozzo da Forli's (1438–1494) fresco honoring Sixtus's chartering of the Vatican Library in 1475 (finished 1476) ranges the pope, his librarian, and his nephews within a spacious marble hall. The most majestic of these figures, the cardinal Giuliano della Rovere (the future Pope Julius II) is ranged against a classical column as if he is literally a pillar of the library—as indeed he was. The bronze tomb designed for Sixtus by the Florentine artist Antonio Pollaiuolo reflects his acute awareness of Etruscan and Roman

bronzes. Similarly, the Florentine painter Filippino Lippi's frescoes for the chapel of Cardinal Oliviero Carafa in Santa Maria Sopra Minerva are focused compositionally on grand architectonic structures and move with the measured deliberation of an ancient Roman procession. Two Umbrian painters, Pietro Perugino and Bernardino Pinturicchio, and a Tuscan, Luca Signorelli, dominated painting in Rome at the turn of the fifteenth century. All three had been at work in Rome off and on since the 1480s, and for them the city's ruined buildings, statues, paintings, and stucco reliefs provided an inescapable stimulus to paint more grandly, with more clearly articulated spaces, more substantial figures, sturdier architecture. Pinturicchio's scenes from the life of Saint Bernardino of Siena for the Bufalini Chapel in Santa Maria in Aracoeli, his decorations for the Vatican apartments of Pope Alexander VI Borgia, and his ceiling for the choir of Santa Maria del Popolo are especially remarkable. Indeed, all three of these talented masters would have a far greater reputation today if it were not for what happened in Rome during the first decades of the sixteenth century. In December of 1503, Cardinal Giuliano Della Rovere was elected Pope Julius II (reigned 1503–1513), a man of enormous vision and implacable temper who took the project of Rome's renewal to heart with a vehemence that swiftly eclipsed the work of his active uncle Sixtus IV. He sought out Donato Bramante (1444–1514), a mature artist born in Urbino and recently arrived in Rome from Milan, who had begun to make his mark as an architect in the classical style. Together, the two of them embarked on an ambitious plan to raze the tottering early Christian basilica of St. Peter's, develop the Vatican Palace around a huge internal garden that would house the papal art collections, and transform the city itself into a model metropolis of broad, straight thoroughfares, glorious new buildings, and bustling river traffic. A perceptive collector of ancient sculpture, Julius also made contact with a young Florentine sculptor, Michelangelo Buonarroti (1475–1564), whom he set to work on designing his tomb beneath the crossing vault of Bramante's new St. Peter's. By 1507 Julius had decided to decorate his private apartments as well. Following the successful stratagem of Sixtus IV, he called in a team of illustrious painters from central Italy to execute the project, including a young relative of Bramante's named Raffaello

Sanzio (Raphael, 1483–1520). Raphael's first two frescoes proved so evocative, however, that Julius assigned him the whole commission. A host of other artists flocked to Rome in the early days of Julius's reign: the Tuscan sculptor Jacopo Sansovino, the dynasty of architects known as the Sangallo (after their neighborhood in Florence), the Tuscan painters Antonio Bazzi (called Il Sodoma) and Baldassare Peruzzi. Most of the Sangallo clan returned to Florence when it became clear how entirely Bramante would dominate architectural commissions in the city. Antonio da Sangallo the Younger, who remained in Rome, began to work his way through the ranks on the St. Peter's project in hopes of eventually setting up on his own. Pope Julius commissioned two elaborate marble tombs of Sansovino for the choir of Santa Maria del Popolo; one of these, the tomb of Cardinal Ascanio Sforza (1505), is remarkable for the lively reclining figure of that lean, sophisticated Milanese prelate. Other commissions followed from wealthy members of the curia. Sodoma and Peruzzi were taken up by the Sienese banker Agostino Chigi, who was rich enough in 1503 to have provided Cardinal Giuliano Della Rovere with the bribe money that secured his election as pope, and who became richer than ever once he and Pope Julius began to pilot the economic course of the papacy. The unerring artistic instinct that prompted Julius II to see a painter in the sculptor Michelangelo inspired the irascible pontiff to push the equally irascible artist into replacing the gilt stars and blue background of the Sistine Chapel ceiling with a design that began as a depiction of the twelve apostles and eventually expanded dramatically to trace the history of the papacy back to the creation of the universe. It took Michelangelo only four years, from 1508 to 1512, to cover the chapel's ceiling with his broad, sure brushstrokes. Two muscular marble statues from the papal collections, the Belvedere Torso and the Laocoön (the latter discovered in 1506), inspired the epic physiques of Michelangelo's figures, but his extraordinary colors—purple and orange and sea green—seem to have been his own invention, and all at once they changed the palette of Italian art. Raphael, the most attentive of painters, had already absorbed Michelangelo's grand figure style and novel color schemes long before the Sistine Chapel ceiling was unveiled; Bramante, to Michelangelo's chagrin, had let him in for a preview. The results can

be seen in Raphael's *School of Athens* (1510–1511), his *Isaiah* in Sant' Agostino (1511–1512) and his *Galatea* (c. 1512–1514), painted for Agostino Chigi. When Julius died in 1513 and was succeeded by the Florentine pope Leo X, a distinctive Roman style had already been established in painting, sculpture, and architecture, characterized by powerful, elegant human figures, high contrasts of light and dark, strong architectural lines, mastery of space, and strange, brilliant colors. There was even a distinctive papal style for architecture: Doric triglyph-and-metope friezes, Tuscan columns, and rusticated masonry, devised by Bramante for St. Peter's and the unbuilt Palazzo dei Tribunali on the Via Giulia, one of the long, straight boulevards that formed an important part of the pope's city planning. Pope Leo and successors like his cousin Clement VII (reigned 1523–1534) and their contemporary Paul III (reigned 1534–1549) continued to foster this grand, colorful Roman style for projects like the Villa Madama, Palazzo Farnese, Michelangelo's Campidoglio, and the seemingly never-ending project of St. Peter's. Before his death in 1520, Raphael had established a flourishing workshop; furthermore, thanks to his association with the penetratingly insightful Bramante, he lent a strong theoretical instinct to the creation of art, so that onetime associates like Antonio da Sangallo the Younger, Perino del Vaga, and Giulio Romano could continue creating works of art and architecture along the same basic lines. In many ways, these were the same lines adopted by Michelangelo, an equally thoughtful student of ancient Rome—and an equally independent flouter of the compositional principles he observed in ancient art. Like the ancient Roman architect and writer Vitruvius, who used two-story columns to "lend authority" to the interior of the basilica he designed in the city of Fano, Bramante, Raphael, and Michelangelo all used giant orders of columns to bind together huge facades, none so brilliantly as Michelangelo for the Palazzo dei Conservatori (c. 1537) on the Capitoline Hill and for the exterior walls of St. Peter's. The dome of Hadrian's Pantheon inspired Bramante, Raphael, Michelangelo, and finally Giacomo della Porta in their successive designs for the dome of St. Peter's; it was della Porta who elongated the profile to its present graceful shape. Raphael's workshop's rediscovery of the formula for ancient stucco in about 1518 allowed architecture to merge with sculpture, and sculpture with painting, as in Raphael's Vatican Logge for Pope Leo X, his workshop's Palazzo Madama, and his facade for Palazzo Branconio dell'Aquila. The melding of stucco work and architecture reached its apogee with the facade of Palazzo Spada in 1550.

By the middle of the sixteenth century, the Protestant Reformation had provoked Pope Paul III to convene the reforming Council of Trent, which closed in 1563 after a quarter century of wrangling. Its call for a newly persuasive religious art did not produce immediate effects on the look of art in Rome; the distinctive, sophisticated local tradition had become too strong to change immediately. In the very last years of the sixteenth century, however, a Milanese painter named Michelangelo Merisi da Caravaggio (1573–1610) suddenly gave forceful new expression to Trent's call for a simple, persuasive religious art: his paintings, with their dramatic contrasts of light and dark and their apparently down-to-earth figures (many of them drawn from ancient models) brought the stories of the Bible dramatically into the here and now. In their effect, they were sermons in paint, performing exactly the same devotional service as the priest's homily at mass. Roman painting now began to show an apparent split between dramatic, even grubby naturalism and sophisticated classical style, but these poles were never truly opposed. Caravaggio's *Deposition* in the Vatican (1602–1604), however dirty its figures' feet, adopts the poses of an ancient Roman sarcophagus, and there is no more grittily rustic peasant than the arch-classicist Annibale Carracci's *Bean Eater* (c. 1585) in the Galleria Colonna.

THE SEVENTEENTH CENTURY

Caravaggio's stark lighting affected later artists like Guercino (Giovanni Barbieri, 1591–1666) and Mattia Preti (1613–1699), their dramatically posed figures emerging from deep shadows; silvery flesh tones and a loose brushwork gave their large paintings an added vibrancy. The versatile Orazio Gentileschi (c. 1562–c. 1647) and his daughter Artemisia (c. 1597–after 1651) also worked occasionally in this style, as did the popular Guido Reni (1575–1642) for his *Crucifixion of St. Peter* in the Vatican Museum. Soon, however, the spareness and

restricted color of Caravaggio gave way in Rome to a more elaborate, colorful taste in painting.

The classical whimsy of Annibale Carracci's ceiling frescoes for the Galleria in Palazzo Farnese added new life—and lightness—to the stately, architectonic quality of monumental painting in Rome, so that an important commission like Pietro da Cortona's ceiling fresco for the grand entrance hall of Palazzo Barberini (1631) could amuse as well as celebrate the family by showing their coat of arms, a trio of gigantic bees, buzzing in formation into the heavens. The same kind of virtuoso whimsy assured the popularity of Gian Lorenzo Bernini (1598–1680), whose phenomenal ability to carve marble was matched by the fertility of his imagination. His series of early works for Cardinal Scipione Borghese, *Apollo and Daphne* (1622–1625), *David* (1623–1624), and *Pluto and Persephone* (1621–1622) seemed to turn stone into living flesh where Pluto's fingers press into plump Persephone, where Daphne's fingers sprout leaves and her toes take root, and where David (a self-portrait of the artist) bites his lip in concentration. Bernini's later commissions often combined sculpture with architecture, from the Baldacchino in St. Peter's (1633) to the Throne of St. Peter (1657) in the same basilica, to the tombs of Popes Urban VIII (1647) and Alexander VII (1672–1678), this last with a gilt skeleton struggling to free itself from a red jasper curtain that symbolizes—all too literally—the flesh. Bernini's sheer technical skill and his lively compositions set the standard for all other sculptors in Rome. His fountains still dot the city: the Fountain of the Four Rivers in Piazza Navona (1651) incorporates an ancient Egyptian obelisk into its complicated symbolism of life's instability and religion's offer of eternity, contrived with the help of the Jesuit scholar and philologist Athanasius Kircher (1601–1680). A century later, Nicola Salvi's Trevi Fountain (1732–1762) would look to Bernini's masterwork for its chief inspiration, just as Andrea Pozzo's altars to Saint Ignatius Loyola and Francis Xavier in the church of Il Gesù (1695) ultimately owe both the upward sweep of their design and the daring richness of their lapis lazuli decoration to Bernini's designs for St. Peter's and the Jesuit church of Sant'Andrea al Quirinale (1658–1670), where he designed both the architecture and the

Art in Rome. The Ganges sculpture of the *Fountain of the Four Rivers,* created by Gian Lorenzo Bernini in the Piazza Navona, Rome, 1651. ©MIMMO JODICE/CORBIS

sculptural decoration, which merge into one another seamlessly.

The creation of art in seventeenth-century Rome was a matter of intense intellectual discussion, and conspicuously learned artists who worked there included the young Fleming Peter Paul Rubens (1577–1640), destined to become both painter and diplomat after his studies in Rome in 1601–1602 and 1605, and the Frenchman Nicolas Poussin (1594–1665), whose theories about color and classicism injected a stately sobriety into the painting of his adopted city. Yet the same collectors who assembled Poussin's myths and allegories also collected paintings of flowers, peasants, and landscapes, all separate genres in the burgeoning seventeenth-century art market (as was the venerable art of portraiture). Raphael had already excelled at por-

trait painting in the early sixteenth century, and his image of a pensive *Pope Julius II* (1511–1512) may have been in the mind of the Spanish painter Diego Velázquez when he created his glorious portrait of a gimlet-eyed *Innocent X* more than a century later (c. 1650). The contrast between Raphael's meticulously fine brushwork and Velázquez's commanding sweeps of raw paint could not be greater, but they share the gift of psychological insight. The eighteenth century in Rome would add a new kind of portrait to the traditional repertoire of churchmen, nobles, merchants, and courtesans: the so-called swagger portraits of English "grand tourists" who had begun to flock to Rome and felt that they could not leave until they had been immortalized, striking a pose in a recognizably Roman setting, by Pompeo Batoni (1708–1787).

Raphael also had been a pioneer as a print-maker, with the help of the engraver Marcantonio Raimondi, and as a result most painters and sculptors from the sixteenth century onward came to rely on prints as a vital means by which to illustrate works in other media as well as a cheap, attractive art form in their own right. But Rome had never seen anything like the prints that began to emerge in the eighteenth century from the burin of Giovanni Battista Piranesi (1720–1778): monumental visions of Roman ruins, intricate, surreal prisons (in his *Carceri d'invenzione*, 1749–1750), fireplace designs based on Egyptian and Etruscan as well as classical motifs, all executed with a sureness of touch equaled in the history of the medium only by Albrecht Dürer. Piranesi's exaggeratedly tiny human figures, his tempestuous skies, and the wayward smoke of his fireplaces give his designs a haunting immediacy.

In the eighteenth century, the aesthetic theories of Johann Joachim Winckelmann (1717–1768), secretary in Rome to Cardinal Alessandro Albani, began to encourage painters like Anton Raphael Mengs (1728–1779) to work in a more restrained, classical style inspired by Raphael (for Mengs, the similarity in their names also acted as a stimulus); Winckelmann also amassed an impressive collection of ancient sculpture for the cardinal. In 1791, inspired by the same movement, the successful but restless sculptor Antonio Canova (1757–1822) undertook a design for the tomb of Pope Clement XIII in St. Peter's Basilica that was radical enough to make the apprehensive artist attend its unveiling in disguise. With its simplified neoclassical forms and its now-famous weeping lions, the massive white marble tomb marked a sharp departure from the legacy of Bernini. Canova had exchanged the rich textures and headlong movement of the baroque for the calm and clarity that he, like Winckelmann before him, had observed in ancient art. Canova quickly dropped his disguise; the Romans immediately loved his new work, indicating that their tastes, like those of Europe as a whole, were shifting toward a different understanding of the ancient classical ideal—neoclassicism—that would soon transform all the arts.

See also **Ancients and Moderns; Art: Artistic Patronage; Baroque; Bernini, Gian Lorenzo; Caravaggio and Caravaggism; City Planning; Gentileschi, Artemisia;** **Julius II (pope); Michelangelo Buonarroti; Prints and Printmaking; Raphael; Rome; Rome, Architecture in; Sculpture; Winckelmann, Johann Joachim.**

BIBLIOGRAPHY

Barkan, Leonard. *Unearthing the Past: Archaeology and Aesthetics in the Making of Renaissance Culture.* New Haven and London, 1999.

Bowron, Edgar Peters, and Joseph J. Rishel, eds. *Art in Rome in the Eighteenth Century.* Philadelphia, 2000.

Brown, Beverly Louise, ed. *The Genius of Rome, 1592–1623.* New York, 2001.

Hall, Marcia. *After Raphael: Painting in Central Italy in the Sixteenth Century.* Cambridge, U.K., 1998.

Haskell, Francis. *Patrons and Painters: A Study in the Relations between Italian Art and Society in the Age of the Baroque.* New Haven and London, 1980.

Haskell, Francis, and Nicholas Penny. *Taste and the Antique: the Lure of Classical Sculpture, 1500–1900.* New Haven and London, 1981.

Magnuson, Torgil. *Rome in the Age of Bernini.* Atlantic Highlands, N.J., 1982–1986.

Partridge, Loren. *The Art of Renaissance Rome, 1400–1600,* New York: Abrams, 1996.

Rowland, Ingrid D. *The Culture of the High Renaissance: Ancients and Moderns in Sixteenth-Century Rome.* Cambridge, U.K., 1998.

Shearman, John. *Only Connect . . . : Art and the Spectator in the Italian Renaissance.* Princeton, 1992.

Stinger, Charles. *The Renaissance in Rome.* Bloomington, Ind., 1998.

Wilton, Andrew, and Ilaria Bignamini, eds. *Grand Tour: The Lure of Italy in the Eighteenth Century.* London, 1996.

INGRID ROWLAND

ROME, SACK OF.

The conquest of Rome on 6 May 1527 by troops of the Holy Roman emperor Charles V (ruled 1519–1556) has traditionally been viewed as a turning point in the history of papal Rome and in Renaissance culture. While recent research has highlighted economic, political, and social continuities between pre- and post-sack Rome, a consensus remains that the event, which occurred during the Italian Wars of 1494–1559, had cultural repercussions of lasting significance.

The conquest itself was brief. Around dawn on 6 May 1527, an imperial army composed primarily of Spanish and German troops besieged the poorly defended city. Their commander, Charles de Bourbon-Montpensier (1490–1527), died in the initial assault, but by sunset virtually all of Rome had fallen to his men. His successor, Philibert of Orange-Châlon (1502–1530), could not control the victorious troops, who proceeded to spend months desecrating sacred objects, ransacking the city, and torturing its citizens in order to extract ransoms. Pope Clement VII (Giulio de' Medici; reigned 1523–1534), who had taken refuge in the Castel Sant'Angelo, formally capitulated on 5 June, and remained a captive there until early December. Only in February 1528 did the occupying army leave Rome.

The sack resulted most immediately from Clement VII's decision to join with Florence, France, Milan, and Venice in the League of Cognac (22 May 1526), an alliance formed to limit Charles V's power on the Italian peninsula. As Bourbon-Montpensier's army advanced southward, the particular goals of the Venetians and the French had come to outweigh the interests they shared with the papacy. In March 1527, the pope had agreed to a truce with Charles de Lannoy, the imperial viceroy of Naples, but Bourbon-Montpensier and his men had refused to honor it. Historians disagree about whether or not Charles V authorized the attack on Rome; certainly he abhorred the atrocities that followed. Meanwhile, Clement discovered that he could not count on the league's armies either to come to his rescue or to mount a coherent counteroffensive. Having been effectively abandoned, in 1529 the pope made peace with Charles V, whom he crowned as Holy Roman emperor in Bologna in February 1530. Thus, he adjusted with some success to the emperor's now decisive hegemony on the peninsula.

The cultural impact of the sack was felt acutely throughout Europe. Many artists and architects, including Rosso Fiorentino (Giovanni Battista di Jacopo, 1494–1540) and Sebastiano Serlio (1475–1554), sought safety and patronage elsewhere, and in so doing promoted the diffusion of High Renaissance Roman culture. In humanists' rhetoric, claims that the papacy would soon initiate a golden age perforce gave way to more modest expectations. Religious interpretations of the event varied, but there was a widespread consensus—shared even by Pope Clement himself—that moral failings of the clergy were in part to blame for the catastrophe. His successor, Paul III (reigned 1534–1549), did much to restore the papacy's prestige, political influence, and cultural centrality, but any optimism was tempered by a new awareness of political contingency and by nostalgia for an idealized age of cultural efflorescence that was widely perceived to have already passed.

See also **Charles V (Holy Roman Empire); Italian Wars (1494–1559).**

BIBLIOGRAPHY

Primary Sources

Guicciardini, Francesco. *The History of Italy.* Translated and edited by Sidney Alexander. New York, 1969. Translation of *La storia d'Italia*, Book 18, first printed in 1564, includes an account of the sack.

Guicciardini, Luigi. *The Sack of Rome.* Translated and edited by James H. McGregor. New York, 1993. Translation of *Historia del sacco di Roma*, Paris, 1664. Adequate English rendition marred by a misleading critical apparatus.

Secondary Sources

Chastel, André. *The Sack of Rome, 1527.* Translated from the French by Beth Archer. Princeton, 1983.

Gattoni, Maurizio. *Clemente VII e la geopolitica dello Stato Pontificio.* Vatican City, 2002.

Hook, Judith. *The Sack of Rome, 1527.* London, 1972.

KENNETH GOUWENS

ROSICRUCIANISM. Rosicrucianism is the ideology of the Rosicrucians, a mysterious, possibly apocryphal, religious sect announced in early-seventeenth-century Germany. The existence of a secret Brotherhood of the Rosy Cross, the Rosicrucians, was proclaimed in *Fama Fraternitas* (Rumor of the brotherhood), a short treatise that circulated in manuscript several years before it was published by Wilhelm Wessel in Kassel in 1614. Further details about the brotherhood followed in the *Confessio Fraternitatis* (1615; Confession of the brotherhood), ostensibly the secret society's manifesto. A spate of "Rosicrucian" treatises ensued, written by a cadre of radical reformers associated with several princely courts and universities of Germany and published mainly in Kassel, Frankfurt, and Danzig.

Although these earliest treatises were anonymous, it appears that the *Fama* was written, perhaps as early as 1608, by Tobias Hess (1558–1614) and circulated by Adam Haslmayr (1588–1602) and Benedict Figulus (1567–1624). These three appear to have played key roles in codifying the fundamentals of Rosicrucianism from the philosophical and theological ideas of the German reformer Paracelsus, but drawing on material from John Dee (1527–1608), Cornelius Agrippa (1486–1535), and other "Hermetic" authors. The religious teachings of Paracelsus (1493–1541), who despaired of the institutionalized church and urged focus on a German mystical, inner realization of divinity, were especially amenable to Protestants who felt that the Reformation had stopped short and abandoned its original principles. This same impulse had produced numerous radical sects, but the especially attractive claim of the Rosicrucians was their call for a reform of all society to bring it a unified ideology based on a true, irenic (peaceful) religious movement, and a scientific and technological enlightenment.

Many of the Rosicrucian ideas and mode of expression are chemical in nature, clearly evident in Johan Valentin Andreæ's (1586–1654) *Chemical Wedding of Christian Rosencreutz* (1616; *Chymische Hochzeit Christiani Rosencreutz*) and blended readily with Hermetic philosophy and religion in treatises like the *Secretioris Philosophiæ Consideratio Brevis* (1615; Brief consideration of the very secret philosophy) of Philip a Gabella (a pseudonym, possibly for Raphael Eglinus or Johannes Rhenanus), which was largely extracted from works by John Dee, Sendivogius (1556–1636), and other Paracelsian writers. The Rosicrucians' calls for a refounding of society along radical Calvinist and natural philosophical lines struck a chord with a broad audience, piquing the curiosity of the Danish physician Ole Worm (1588–1654) and the Englishman Robert Fludd (1574–1637), a contemporary of William Harvey (1578–1657) and fellow member of London's elite Royal College of Physicians. Men such as these sought further information about the brotherhood or, in the case of Fludd, promoted its aims through his own Hermetic publications and correspondence.

Soon, too, a number of condemnations arose, penned by those fearful that the Rosicrucians presented a real threat to the status quo, or merely convinced that they were yet another heretical sect bent on contributing to Europe's disquiet in the tumultuous years leading up to the Thirty Years' War (1618–1648). Chief among these from the scientific community was Andreas Libavius (1560–1616), who attacked the Rosicrucians as heretics and proponents of false, Paracelsian chemical philosophy. But theological censure was particularly energetic, coming from all orthodoxies. A well-known episode, the "Rosicrucian furor" that erupted in Paris after the discovery of publicly posted Rosicrucian placards in the summer of 1623, is now known to have been the work of a cabal of French Jesuits, who sought to link dissident, free-thinking libertines with Hermetic and Rosicrucian heresies of the sort promoted by Rudolph Goclenius, Jr. (1547–1628), painting them as the dangerous devil-spawn of Lutheranism.

Efforts to see in the Rosicrucians a specific political movement centered on the Calvinist Palatinate aiming to wrest the kingdom of Bohemia from the Catholic Holy Roman emperor have now been discredited, as it is evident that the main actors were not in Heidelberg, but in other courts. The question of the Rosicrucians' contribution to the development of modern science is still unresolved. While the Hermetic and Calvinist ideas they promoted encouraged the development and deployment of technology for social betterment, an idea taken up and publicized by Francis Bacon (1561–1626), the historical connections remain to be clarified. Likewise, their ideas on the importance of fathoming the divine mind by empirical study of creation and experimentation with natural processes must be discerned from contemporary attitudes among Lutherans and other denominations. Yet it is undeniable that many of the champions of scientific reform, particularly the influential Hartlib Circle (a group of scientists and philosophers that formed around Samuel Hartlib [1640–1656]) and its Continental correspondents were keenly interested in finding and studying the Rosicrucian tracts. Continuity between the seventeenth-century Rosicrucians and the eighteenth-century Freemasons and modern Rosicrucianism has been adduced, but the historical connections have not been convincingly teased out.

See also **Alchemy; Bacon, Francis; Calvinism; Dee, John; Freemasonry; Hartlib, Samuel; Hermeticism; Mag-**

ic; Occult Philosophy; Paracelsus; Reformation, Protestant; Theology.

BIBLIOGRAPHY

Gilly, Carlos. "'Theophrastia Sancta'—Paracelsianism as a Religion, in Conflict with the Established Churches." In *Paracelsus: The Man and His Reputation, His Ideas and Their Transformation*, edited by Ole Grell, pp. 151–185. Leiden, 1998.

Kahn, Didier. "The Rosicrucian Hoax in France (1623–24)." In *Secrets of Nature: Astrology and Alchemy in Early Modern Europe*, edited by William R. Newman and Anthony Grafton, pp. 235–344. Cambridge, Mass., 2001.

Montgomery, John Warwick. *Cross and Crucible: Johann Valentin Andreae (1586–1654), Phoenix of the Theologians.* 2 vols. The Hague, 1973.

Moran, Bruce T. *The Alchemical World of the German Court: Occult Philosophy and Chemical Medicine in the Circle of Moritz of Hessen (1572–1632).* Stuttgart, 1991.

Yates, Frances. *The Rosicrucian Enlightenment.* London, 1972.

JOLE SHACKELFORD

ROUSSEAU, JEAN-JACQUES (1712–1778),

French philosopher and writer. Rousseau is widely viewed as the greatest social, political, and pedagogical philosopher of the French Enlightenment. He gives education the task of transforming naturally self-loving egoists animated only by their own "particular wills" into polis-loving citizens with a civic "general will" ("the will one has as a citizen"). For Rousseau, the "Great Legislator" (more accurately the great civic educator) must "change the nature of man" by turning self-lovers into "Spartan mothers" (who ask not whether their own sons have survived battles but whether the "general good" of the city still lives). Rousseau also insists that education, however "denaturing," must finally produce autonomous adults who can ultimately say to their teachers (with Émile), "I have decided to be what you made me" (Foxley translation, p. 435).

Jean-Jacques Rousseau was born in the Calvinist stronghold of Geneva on 28 June 1712, the second son of the watchmaker Isaac Rousseau and his wife Susan; both were "citizens" of Geneva, and Rousseau styled himself *citoyen de Genève* until his final renunciation of citizenship in 1764. Rousseau's mother died ten days after his birth. With his father the child read (and then perpetually cherished) *Plutarch's Lives* of the greatest Greeks and Romans. Later he was brought up by a puritanical aunt who (he admitted in the *Confessions*) did much to warp his sexuality. In 1722 Isaac Rousseau fled Geneva after a quarrel, and the ill-educated Jean-Jacques had to be apprenticed, first to a notary, then to an engraver.

In March 1728 Rousseau missed the Genevan city curfew, found himself locked outside the gates, and wandered on foot to Annecy in Savoy, where he was taken in by Mme de Warens, who became his protector and then (1733–1740) his lover. In the provincial salon of Mme de Warens ("Les Charmettes"), Rousseau acquired the education he had lacked in Geneva (Plutarch apart). One gets some sense of his autodidactic passion from his poem, "Le Verger des Charmettes," in which he declares his debt to Gottfried Wilhelm von Leibniz, Nicholas de Malebranche, Isaac Newton, and John Locke.

Mme de Warens, who specialized in finding Catholic converts, sent the young Rousseau to Turin, where he renounced his inherited Calvinism and converted to the Roman Church; he even briefly attended a seminary for priests, until a Catholic ecclesiastic attempted to seduce him. Returning to Les Charmettes, he lived with de Warens ("Maman"), completed his education, and undertook his earliest writings, including the remarkable *Chronologie universelle* (c. 1737), with its eloquent praise of Fénelon's charitable moral universalism.

In 1740 Rousseau began to serve as a tutor, moving north to Lyon and living in the house of M. de Mably, whose children he instructed. However, in Lyon he met M. de Mably's two elder brothers, Étienne Bonnot (later the Abbé de Condillac, with Voltaire the greatest "Lockean" in post-Regency France) and the Abbé de Mably. This was the beginning of Rousseau's connection to the Paris philosophes, with whom he would later have a love-hate relationship. At this same time Rousseau became a considerable composer, music theorist, and copyist; in later years he would represent himself as a simple Swiss republican who earned a living as a musical craftsman.

In 1742 Rousseau moved definitively northward to Paris, carrying with him a new system of musical notation, a comedy, an opera, and a collection of poems. In Paris Rousseau eked out a precarious living by tutoring, writing, and copying music; for a brief period (1743–1744) he served, not very happily, as secretary to the French ambassador in Venice—an interlude that he described in his later *Lettres écrites de la montagne* (1764). He also met and befriended Denis Diderot, soon-to-be editor of the great *Encyclopédie,* who would ultimately commission Rousseau's first great writing on civic "general will," the *Économie politique* of 1755.

It was while visiting Diderot in prison (for alleged impiety) in 1749 that Rousseau decided to write an essay for a prize competition sponsored by the Académie de Dijon, dealing with the question whether morals had been harmed or advanced by the rebirth (renaissance) of the arts and sciences. Rousseau won the prize with *Discours sur les sciences et les arts* (Discourse on the arts and sciences), the so-called First Discourse, in which he defended Spartan-Roman civic *généralité* against the Athenian literary "tyranny" of poets and orators. The *Discourse* made his European reputation, even attracting the criticism of the king of Poland, and from this period forward Rousseau was a leading citizen, however reluctantly, of the *République des lettres* (as Voltaire maliciously reminded him).

In 1752 his opera, *Le devin du village* (The village soothsayer), was performed at the court of Louis XV at Versailles; at roughly the same time his black comedy *Narcissus, the Lover of Himself* was given in Paris at the Theatre français. As a good *citoyen de Genève,* Rousseau refused a royal pension, continuing his republican self-support as a musician by publishing *La lettre sur la musique française* (Letter on French music) in 1753, which, with its strong defense of Italian simplicity against French elaborateness, led to a collision with Jean-Baptiste Rameau, the greatest French composer of the day.

Rousseau's *Discours sur l'origine et les fondements de l'inégalité parmi les hommes* (Discourse on the origins of inequality among men) was completed in May 1754. The most radical of his works, this so-called Second Discourse urges that existing government is a kind of confidence trick on the part of the rich, who persuade the poor that it is universally and equally advantageous to be subjected to law and to political order. In June 1754 Rousseau left Paris for a visit to his native Geneva, where he reconverted to Calvinism and had his civic rights restored and where, in 1755, he published his *Inégalité* and the *Économie politique* (the Third Discourse). In 1756 he moved to the countryside, taking up residence at l'Hermitage, the country seat of Mme d'Epinay (inspiring Diderot's sarcastic epigram, "a fine citizen a hermit is"), a move that marked the start of the weakening of Rousseau's ties to the philosophes—a process accelerated by his 1758 *Lettre à d'Alembert,* which opposed the latter's scheme to found a theater in Geneva. (Plato-like, Rousseau urged that such a theater would be inimical to civic virtue and good morals and that Molière's *Misanthrope* would have a deleterious effect.)

In 1758, too, Rousseau began *L'état de guerre* (The state of war), his most brilliant and scathing critique of Thomas Hobbes and Hobbism. Taking over observations first made by René Descartes and Gottfried Wilhelm von Leibniz (*Essais de théodicée,* 1710), Rousseau insists that Hobbes has simply mistaken badly socialized, ill-educated Englishmen for "natural" men, leading to Hobbesian unquestionable "sovereignty" as the only antidote to rapacious appetite: Looking out his London window, Hobbes "thinks that he has seen the natural man," but he has really only viewed "a bourgeois of London or Paris." Hobbes, for Rousseau, has simply inverted cause and effect, mistaking a bad effect for "natural" depravity.

In the late 1750s Rousseau labored on (but never published) the *Lettres morales* (for Sophie d'Houdetot) and then produced his vast epistolary novel, *Julie, ou la Nouvelle Héloïse* (published 1761), with its celebrated account of a small ideal society, Clarens, superintended by the godlike, all-seeing M. de Wolmar. The novel was a runaway best-seller, the greatest literary success since Fénelon's *Telemachus, Son of Ulysses* in 1699.

In May 1762 Rousseau brought out two of his greatest but most ill-fated works: *Du contrat social* (The social contract) and *Émile, ou Traité de l'éducation* (both focusing on transformative, "denaturing" education). Both were condemned and publicly burned in Paris at the behest of Archbishop Christophe de Beaumont (and with the acquiesence of the Parlement of Paris); Rousseau, under order of arrest, fled to Geneva (only to find the same works condemned and burned there). Against charges of impiety leveled by the Genevan public prosecutor—alleging the danger of Rousseau's "natural" theology in Émile's "Profession of Faith of the Savoyard Vicar"—Rousseau composed and published his trenchant *Lettres de montagne* (Letters written from the mountain), in which he defended ancient "civic" religion and insisted that Christianity produces good men whose other-worldliness makes them "bad citizens." This of course only increased the furor against him, and he took refuge in the Prussian enclave of Neuchâtel (Switzerland). Renouncing his Genevan citizenship definitively, Rousseau occupied himself by writing a constitution for recently liberated Corsica; increasingly threatened, his paranoia aggravated by genuine danger, Rousseau accepted the offer of British refuge from David Hume, although he soon came to see the benevolent Scot as part of the "league of malignant enemies" bent on his destruction. After an unhappy period in England, Rousseau returned incognito to France, living under the assumed name of Renou. While living under this name, Rousseau finally married his longtime companion, Thérèse Levasseur, by whom he had fathered—if the *Confessions* are to be believed—five children, all supposedly abandoned in a foundling hospital.

The *Confessions* themselves increasingly occupied Rousseau's time, and he often read substantial fragments of this work in progress in sympathetic aristocratic salons. In 1772 he produced the remarkable *Gouvernement de Pologne* as part of an effort to avert partition by Prussia, Austria, and Russia; the book combines intelligent constitutional reforms with Rousseau's most glowing account of Spartan and Roman-republican civic virtue. In the same year he wrote (without publishing) the brilliantly innovative *Rousseau juge de Jean-Jacques,* in which he bifurcated himself and had one half comment on the other half—schizophrenia turned into a literary genre.

In 1777 Rousseau wrote his last great confessional work, *Rêveries d'un promeneur solitaire* (The reveries of a solitary walker), which begins with the celebrated words, "Here I am, then, alone on the Earth, no longer having any brother, or neighbor, or friend, or society except myself." A year later, while in refuge on an aristocratic estate at Ermenonville (north of Paris) and while engaging in his beloved botanical studies, Rousseau died quite suddenly on 2 July 1778. He was originally buried in a quasi-Roman sarcophagus on the Isle of Poplars at Ermenonville, but at the height of the French Revolution his ashes were translated, in a dramatic torchlight procession, to the Pantheon in Paris and placed next to the remains of his nemesis Voltaire (1794).

See also **Diderot, Denis;** *Encyclopédie;* **French Literature and Language; Hobbes, Thomas; Philosophes.**

BIBLIOGRAPHY

Primary Sources

Rousseau, Jean-Jacques. *The Collected Writings of Rousseau.* Edited by Roger D. Masters and Christopher Kelly. 9 vols. to date. Hanover, N.H., and London, 1990–.

———. *Confessions.* Translated by J. M. Cohen. Harmondsworth, U.K., 1954.

———. *Correspondance complète de Jean-Jacques Rousseau.* Edited by R. A. Leigh. 51 vols. Geneva and Banbury, U.K., 1965–1995.

———. *The Discourses and Other Early Political Writings.* Translated and edited by Victor Gourevitch. Cambridge, U.K., 1998.

———. *Émile; or, On Education.* Translated by A. Bloom. New York, 1979. Reprint, London, 1991.

———. *Oeuvres complètes.* Edited by Bernard Gagnébin, Marcel Raymond, et al. 5 vols. Paris, 1959–1995. The "standard" edition.

Secondary Sources

Charvet, John. *The Social Problem in the Philosophy of Rousseau.* Cambridge, U.K., 1974.

Hendel, Charles William. *Jean-Jacques Rousseau, Moralist.* 2 vols. London, 1934.

Riley, Patrick. "General Will." In *Blackwell Encyclopedia of Political Philosophy.* Edited by A. Ryan, et al. Oxford, 1988.

———. *The General Will before Rousseau: The Transformation of the Divine into the Civic.* Princeton, 1986.

Shklar, Judith N. *Men and Citizens: A Study of Rousseau's Social Theory.* Cambridge, U.K., 1969. Reprint, 1985.

Starobinski, Jean. *Jean-Jacques Rousseau: La transparence et l'obstacle.* Paris, 1971. Translated into English as *Transparency and Obstruction* by Arthur Goldhammer. Chicago, 1988.

Wokler, Robert. *Rousseau.* Oxford, 1995.

PATRICK RILEY

ROYAL TOUCH. *See* **Ritual, Civic and Royal.**

RUBENS, PETER PAUL (1577–1640), Flemish painter. Peter Paul Rubens became the most influential northern artist in seventeenth-century Europe. His prolific production included religious, historical, and mythological paintings as well as landscapes and portraits. In his idealized figural paintings Rubens brought the artistic traditions of the Netherlands, early modern Italy, and classical antiquity into an unprecedented harmonious synthesis.

BIOGRAPHY AND DEVELOPMENT

Rubens received his professional training in Antwerp, the art center of northern Europe, where his most influential teacher was the learned Otto van Veen. Stylistically, Rubens's works before about 1600 resemble his generalized forms. From 1600 to 1608 Rubens lived in Italy, where the stylistic diversity of his production testifies to his intense viewing of classical remains and works by Renaissance and contemporary artists (for example, Michelangelo and Titian, Caravaggio and Annibale Carracci). He also successfully pursued a professional career, working as court painter to the duke of Mantua, but also portraying nobility in Genoa and painting altarpieces in Rome (such as the prestigious commission for Sta. Maria in Valicella).

In 1608 Rubens hurried back to Antwerp at the belated news of his mother's fatal illness. He remained there, living in a splendid house that accommodated a large library, extensive art collection, and a spacious studio. Stylistically, Rubens shifted to a less individualized technique with smooth surfaces, clear contours, and local colors. This style looked more traditional to local patrons and also proved accessible to the studio assistants who helped with the execution of various paintings. With studio help Rubens carried out extensive commissions as court painter to the regents of the Southern Netherlands, Archduke Albert and Archduchess Isabella, and for other patrons in the Southern Netherlands, Spain, France, England, Germany, and Italy. An allegory about Europe's plight, *The Horrors of War* (1638; Florence, Pitti Museum), exemplifies how Rubens increasingly loosened his paint technique, which

Peter Paul Rubens. *The Miracle of Saint Ignatius Loyola,* oil sketch. This sketch served as a compositional model for the finished work, shown on p. 271. ©ERICH LESSING/ART RESOURCE, N.Y.

enabled him to suggest optical effects of soft light and atmospheric conditions.

During his last decade Rubens resided half of each year at his country house. There he painted more landscapes, such as the panoramic, light-filled *Landscape with Château Steen,* based on his own estate (circa 1631; London, National Gallery).

WORKING METHOD

The artist rightly regarded an ability to work on a huge scale as his special talent. "I confess I am by natural instinct better fitted to execute very large works than small curiosities" (letter, 13 September 1621). Yet despite this preference for a life-size or larger scale, Rubens believed in correlating subject matter with size. "As for the subject, it would be best to choose it according to the size of the picture" (letter, 25 July 1637).

The sensual impact of huge rippling forms and coloristic richness camouflages the intellectual component in works by this exceptionally erudite artist, who was respected as an equal by other scholars. Rubens's learning and intelligence are especially evident in his choice and interpretation of literary subjects for paintings, tapestries, and the title pages he designed in his free time for the Plantin-Moretus publishing house in exchange for books.

Rubens's deep familiarity with classical literature is matched by his intimate knowledge of classical art. Quotations from classical authors fit seamlessly into the content of letters written in Italian, French, or Flemish, and probably no other artist so frequently quoted or paraphrased figures from classical and early modern art, subtly using the associations that clung to the borrowing to amplify the meanings of his own works.

Some paintings are entirely autograph, such as *Pelzchen* (The fur coat; circa 1638; Vienna, Kunsthistorisches Museum), which portrays his young second wife as Venus. By contrast, pupils and assistants executed all or part of many large-scale paintings (for example, Medici cycle, circa 1622–1625; Louvre, Paris, originally Luxembourg Palace). For practical reasons, and to raise the status of his profession, Rubens organized his workshop to separate invention from much of the manual execution. He planned works by making compositional drawings and studies from the model, but also, untraditionally, through oil sketches on oak panels. The oil sketches served as both compositional models for assistants and colorful demonstration pieces for patrons. No previous artist had given such sketches a large role in the working process. Rubens often retouched finished paintings so that weaker execution by studio assistants did not spoil his invention, for example, in *The Miracles of St. Ignatius* (1617–1618; Vienna, Kunsthistorisches Museum). Both sketch and altarpiece originally hung in St. Charles Borromeo, the new Jesuit church in Antwerp. Although Rubens never worked as a sculptor, he furnished designs for sculptures, such as the reliefs on the facade of St. Charles Borromeo. Victory-like angels transform its doorway into a triumphal arch through which one originally entered an interior whose decoration included thirty-nine ceiling paintings by Rubens and his studio as well as two altarpieces in sculptural frames of Rubens's own de-sign. The ensemble exemplified his persuasiveness as a propagandist for the Roman Catholic Church.

For economic and perhaps aesthetic reasons Rubens also worked extensively with collaborators who painted the landscapes and still-life portions in various works, such as the eagle in *Prometheus* (finished by 1618; Philadelphia Museum of Art) by the animal specialist Frans Snyders. When painting figures in landscapes and interiors by Jan Bruegel the Elder, however, Rubens adjusted his sweeping style to his older friend's miniaturized, delicate approach (as in *The Earthly Paradise,* circa 1625; The Hague, Mauritshuis).

Printmakers, among them Lucas Vorsterman, also played an important role because prints made after the paintings circulated Rubens's "inventions" through and beyond Europe.

SOCIAL HONORS

Ennobled in 1624 for his artistic achievements, Rubens received knighthood in 1630 from Charles I of England and in 1631 from Philip IV of Spain. Although he had carried out extensive commissions for both kings (ceiling paintings in Whitehall Banqueting House, London, circa 1629–1634; series for a hunting lodge, Torre de la Parada, circa 1636–1638, now in Madrid, Prado), they knighted Rubens explicitly for his political activity as a diplomat who worked to promote peace in Europe.

See also **Bruegel Family; Caravaggio and Caravaggism; Michelangelo Buonarroti; Netherlands, Art in the; Titian (Tiziano Vecelli).**

BIBLIOGRAPHY

Primary Source

Magurn, Ruth Saunders, trans. and ed. *The Letters of Peter Paul Rubens.* Cambridge, Mass., 1955. Annotated English translations of selected letters.

Secondary Sources

Corpus Rubenianum Ludwig Burchard. London, Oxford, and New York, 1968–. A thematically organized series in English with volumes by different authors.

Held, Julius S. *The Oil Sketches of Peter Paul Rubens: A Critical Catalogue.* Princeton, 1982. General essays about the oil sketches followed by catalogue entries discussing each known individual sketch.

White, Christopher. *Peter Paul Rubens: Man and Artist.* New Haven and London, 1987.

ZIRKA ZAREMBA FILIPCZAK

Peter Paul Rubens. *The Miracle of Saint Ignatius Loyola,* oil on canvas, 1617–1618. ©ERICH LESSING/ART RESOURCE, N.Y.

RUDOLF II (HOLY ROMAN EMPIRE) (1552–1612; ruled 1576–1612), Holy Roman emperor and Habsburg monarch.

Rudolf II was a controversial figure during his lifetime and has remained one for historians since. He has many claims to fame and infamy. His political and religious policies led to his ouster as ruler by members of his own family and contributed to the outbreak of the Thirty Years' War (1618–1648), one of the most destructive wars in European history. He became a believer in and practitioner of the occult, promoting alchemy, pursuing research into the Cabala, and seeking truth in various mysteries and superstitions. And he was one of the great patrons of the arts and letters, financing the work of scientists such as Tycho Brahe (1546–1601) and Johannes Kepler (1571–1630), commissioning artists and engravers of remarkable skill, and collecting fine works throughout Europe.

Rudolf possessed an unstable personality and suffered serious physical and psychological upheavals in 1578–1580 and 1599–1600. In response to the latter, Rudolf retreated to his castle in Prague and became somewhat of a recluse, focusing his attention on the occult. In some ways his breakdowns and his internal struggles can be attributed to the two heavy burdens that tormented his reign—the increasingly divisive struggle between Catholics and Protestants and the threat to his lands posed by the Ottoman Empire.

Regarding the first, Rudolf and his brothers were educated at the leading Roman Catholic center of power in Europe, the court of Philip II (ruled 1556–1598) of Spain, who was the cousin of their father, Emperor Maximilian II (ruled 1564–1576). In Spain they observed the implementation of Philip's belief that political and social strength can only come through religious conformity—in this case Catholicism—and likewise observed the destructive impact sectarian violence could have in the war in the Netherlands. Their father, unlike Philip, was perfectly willing to tolerate Protestantism, and some historians have argued that he was in fact a closet Lutheran. By the time Maximilian died, a majority of Habsburg subjects had adopted Lutheranism, and some had converted to Calvinism or one of the other Protestant movements. Likewise the Estates of most of the Habsburg lands had become strongholds of Protestantism.

Scholars have argued that, given his upbringing, Rudolf believed it his task to restore Catholicism to his patrimony. He invited the Jesuits into his lands, and they worked hard to reconvert Protestants. That action got him into trouble with the Protestant Estates. In 1606 the Estates of Hungary, Austria, and Moravia voted to turn him out and recognized his brother, Matthias (ruled 1612–1619), as ruler. That in turn prompted Rudolf to issue in 1609 what became the famous Letter of Majesty to the Estates of Bohemia, promising them religious toleration if they would retain him as sovereign. That did not work, and just before Rudolf's death in 1612 the Bohemian Estates themselves recognized Matthias. The perceived infringement of the Letter of Majesty in 1618 inspired the Bohemian Estates to reject Habsburg rule altogether and to engage in those events that precipitated the Thirty Years' War.

Rudolf's foremost biographer, R. J. W. Evans, has argued that Rudolf's religious beliefs were by no means so solid. In fact he did not like Catholicism because of the power of its clergy, and he particularly distrusted the papacy. Yet he also had no affinity for Protestants because of their tendency to divide endlessly into sects and squabbles. In the end he was uncertain about religion and whether or not it did any good. Evans has argued that in many ways Rudolf reflected doubts about religion found elsewhere in Bohemia and has compared him to his distant successor Joseph II (ruled 1765–1790), who was a tolerant Catholic but suspicious of the church. Rudolf's doubts about religion encouraged his forays into the occult and the mysterious in hopes of finding a different truth that underlay life. Thus the Catholic-Protestant divide deepened not because of his actions but because of his inability to take action.

Rudolf's other deep concern was the threat from the Turks. In large part because of that threat, Rudolf moved the capital of the Habsburg lands from Vienna to Prague, which became under his aegis a cultural capital of Europe. Brahe and Kepler did their work there, and Rudolf employed many of Europe's brilliant architects and artists there. He brought much art to the city. His wars with the

Turks lasted until 1606, ending with the Treaty of Sitvatorok, an obscure treaty but the first in which the Turks acknowledged the Habsburgs as their equals in international diplomacy. By that time the radicalizing of the Catholic-Protestant split, Rudolf's seclusion, the growing opposition to him among the Estates, and the discontent of his family members had created an atmosphere that would no longer tolerate him as ruler. Stripped of power, Rudolf died in 1612.

See also **Bohemia; Habsburg Dynasty; Holy Roman Empire; Matthias (Holy Roman Empire); Maximilian II (Holy Roman Empire); Prague; Thirty Years' War (1618–1648).**

BIBLIOGRAPHY

Evans, R. J. W. *Rudolf II and His World: A Study in Intellectual History, 1576–1612.* Oxford, 1973.

Fučíková, Eliška, et al., eds. *Rudolf II and Prague: The Court and the City.* London, 1997.

Kaufmann, Thomas DaCosta. *The School of Prague: Painting at the Court of Rudolf II.* Chicago, 1988.

KARL A. ROIDER

RURAL LIFE. *See* **Agriculture; Peasantry; Villages.**

RUSSIA. Russia emerged as a state at the end of the fifteenth century on the northeastern periphery of Europe, with a thin population spread over the forest belt of the east European plain. Never having seen either feudalism or serfdom, its society was different from that of western Europe. Its Christianity came from Byzantium, which further set it apart from its western neighbors. During the sixteenth to eighteenth century Russian society changed rapidly, with the appearance of serfdom, economic growth, and expansion south into the steppe and east to Siberia. The Russian state grew in size and sophistication, especially after the reign of Peter I the Great (ruled 1682–1725). Peter inaugurated a vast cultural revolution, bringing European secular culture to Russia and thus including Russia in the circle of European civilization.

GROWTH OF THE STATE

The core of the Russian state was the Moscow principality, which gained control of the original Russian ethnographic territory with the annexation of Novgorod (1478), Pskov (1510), and other neighboring regions. Essentially a household state managed by a few secretaries and the boyar elite, the Russian state began to acquire the trappings of state administration in the reign of Ivan IV, "the Terrible" (ruled 1533–1584). The growth of the state in the center was not matched by a corresponding development in local administration. The abolition of "feeding," direct payments in kind from local areas to provincial governors, occurred in the 1540s. From then on the treasury paid local officials, but tax collection remained largely in the purview of the local communities, which collected the dues as a service to the crown. Thus the grand claims of the tsars to autocracy met very sharp limits in the small size and limited competence of administration, especially local administration.

In the seventeenth century the central apparatus grew swiftly, reaching some two thousand officials and scribes by the 1680s. Again provincial administration lagged behind, with huge areas managed only by a governor with a staff of some five to ten clerks and scribes and little or no armed force. Even the cadastres that registered landholdings and tax obligations of the rural population were compiled almost entirely on the bases of the village communities' own reports of their population and holdings. These cadastres allowed the state to collect an annual tax on peasant households, mainly to support the army. The collections were also in the hands of the village communities, which meant that collection was slow and often in arrears. The state did have some more effective tools for raising revenue, such as the sales tax and the vodka monopoly. Older systems persisted, such as the expectations that musketeers would live partly from trade and handicrafts and that the gentry cavalry would live from their estates, both serving in the military only during the summer months. These methods were enough to ensure Russia success in some wars and expansion to the south and east. At the same time the state had little effective control over the countryside. Confronted with popular unrest, as in 1604–1605, 1648–1650, and 1671–1672 (the great Cossack revolt of Stepan Razin), the tsar could do little more

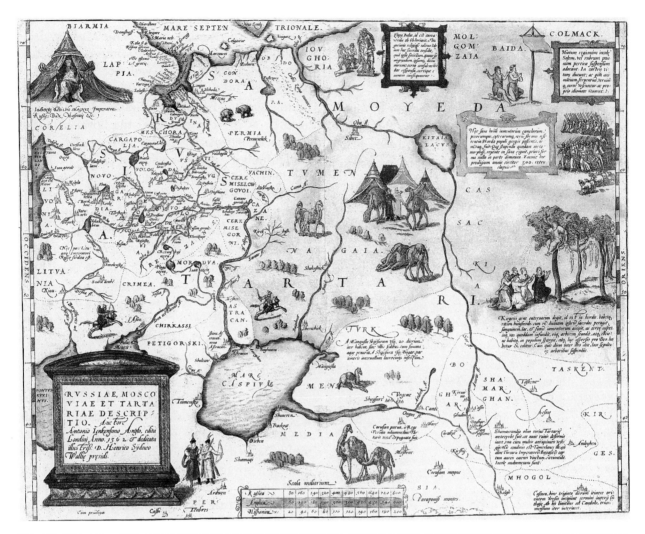

Russia. This map, which appeared in editions of Abraham Ortelius's *Theatrum Orbis Terrarum* from 1570 to 1612, was based on a lost map by the Englishman Anthony Jenkinson, an agent of the Muscovy Company who traveled in Russia from 1557 to 1660. At that time Ivan IV (the Terrible) was gradually expanding Russian territory and had recently seized the southern Volga regions of Kazan and Astrakhan, providing Russia with access to the Caspian Sea. MAP COLLECTION, STERLING MEMORIAL LIBRARY, YALE UNIVERSITY

than call out the army and hope that it could restore order.

Administrative reform. Ultimately, the existing forms proved inadequate in the face of the larger aims of Peter the Great. Peter transformed the Russian state. After several experiments, he established the Senate to coordinate government and take the routine tasks away from the tsar, eleven colleges or ministries headed by a committee for central administration, a reorganized local administration, and the Table of Ranks (1722) to regulate promotions and status in the army and civil service. His army was a permanent body, living in barracks and ready to fight at any time of the year. He shifted the burden of taxes further onto the peasantry by the introduction of the "soul tax," levied on individuals, not households. He attempted to increase the size and effectiveness of provincial administration, but here he was less successful. Some of his measures in this area had to be rescinded as too complex and expensive.

Catherine II the Great (ruled 1762–1796) and her son Paul I (ruled 1796–1801) continued the reordering of the state along European lines. Catherine redrew internal boundaries into more easily administered provinces, increasing the size and rationalizing the structure of provincial governments. She also introduced modest participation by the gentry into the judicial system, as well as similar forms of participation in the courts for the urban elites. Her Charter to the Nobility (1785) specified the rights and obligations of the gentry, for the first time introducing such formulations into Russian legislation. The outcome was a great increase in efficiency in the provinces, but the neglect of the central administration. Her son Paul recentralized government in the 1790s. Both reigns prepared the way for a more modern central state after 1801. The result was a relatively modern government in St. Petersburg, still resting on thin foundations in the provinces. If to a lesser extent than in the sixteenth century, the autocracy of the tsars still meant grand claims and more limited reality. Society was only in part subject to state direction.

SOCIAL STRUCTURE AND ECONOMY

For the whole of the early modern period Russia remained an agrarian society. In the sixteenth century Russian peasants inhabited settlements often of two to four small households, widely scattered along the rivers and lakes of the central and northern forest zones. While the peasants of the center and northwest cultivated grain and raised livestock in modest quantities, northern peasants derived most of their livelihood from hunting and selling furs and obtaining other forest products as well as preparing salt from saline springs. The life of the Russian peasantry changed fundamentally at the end of the sixteenth century with the appearance of serfdom. Unfortunately little is known about the process and causes of enserfment. The law regulated only peasant movement, at first allowing landlords to bring back peasants who left the estates within five years, but by 1649 allowing them to do so in perpetuity. The restrictions on peasant mobility, though difficult to enforce in practice, corresponded to the state's need for a stable tax base and populated land to reward the gentry cavalrymen.

By the mid-seventeenth century a bit over half of the Russian peasants were serfs of secular landlords, about a fifth serfs of the monasteries and bishops, and another fifth, concentrated in the north, the Urals, the Volga region, Siberia, and the southern border, remained free and normally without gentry or ecclesiastical landlords. The north

prospered in these years, especially as the increasing trade with Holland and England opened new markets for furs and other forest products and the expansion of population in Russia itself meant a growing market for salt. The population of Russia grew rapidly after recovery from the Time of Troubles (1598–1613), reaching about eleven million by the 1670s. Much of the increase came from colonization of new land in the south and the Volga region.

Among the peasants of Russia who were not serfs, nearly half were also non-Russian in ethnicity. The largest groups lived in the middle Volga region, the descendants of the peoples of the Kazan' Tatar khanate. The Muslim Tatars lived in villages around Kazan', while the Bashkir pastoralists occupied the steppe to their southeast toward the southern Urals. To the north, east, and west of these Turkic-speaking peoples were other, smaller Turkic and Finnic groups, animists in religion. All of them paid a tax to the state called *yasak* and were not enserfed. Similarly, the incorporation of the Ukrainian Cossack Hetmanate into Russia as an autonomous unit brought in Ukrainian peasants who were legally free (mainly as Cossacks), and more than half of whom also owned their own land.

Among peasants and townspeople, households were small, comprising the nuclear family and occasionally a relative. Better-off townspeople and northern peasants might have a servant or two in addition, while the nobles maintained large staffs of house servants, artisans, and stewards. Some of the latter were bondsmen in the sixteenth and seventeenth century, a status that merged with serfdom in the early eighteenth century. The greatest aristocrats maintained huge establishments in Moscow, with hundreds of servants as well as a large body of administrators for their vast estates. Toward the very end of the seventeenth century the aristocrats began to build the first country houses, mostly within a few hours' ride of Moscow.

The ruling elite of Russia was organized in a system of court and military ranks, at the top being the Duma ranks—boyar; *okol'nichii*, a sort of junior boyar; Duma gentleman; and Duma secretary—in all about a hundred men from some two hundred families by 1600. They formed the pinnacle of the sovereign's court, and in turn the core of the Moscow ranked gentry. Below them were the provincial gentry, organized for purposes of military service around provincial towns or forts, more or less coinciding with residence and landholding patterns. Men with Duma ranks, especially the two highest, held all important household positions at the court, military commands, and provincial governorships, and in the seventeenth century also headed almost all chanceries *(prikazy)*. Immensely wealthy, the boyars also provided the inner circle of advisers, formally through the Duma or tsar's council and informally as friends or favorites of the tsar. Other than the tsar's relatives by marriage, powerful men from outside this circle were extremely rare.

In elite families women were secluded in separate parts of the houses and did not join in the all-male banquets that were the staple of elite socialization. Women of all classes were expected to dress modestly, in the voluminous traditional Russian clothing and with their hair covered, and to obey fathers and husbands. But women also owned and managed property, including tax obligations to the state. This was particularly true of the mothers and wives of the gentry, whose men were often away with the army every summer for years in a row. In merchant families the men traveled to distant markets while the women stayed home and ran the business as well as the household.

Social control. The inability of the state to regulate social life to the extent of Western societies placed a premium on various forms of communal solidarity.

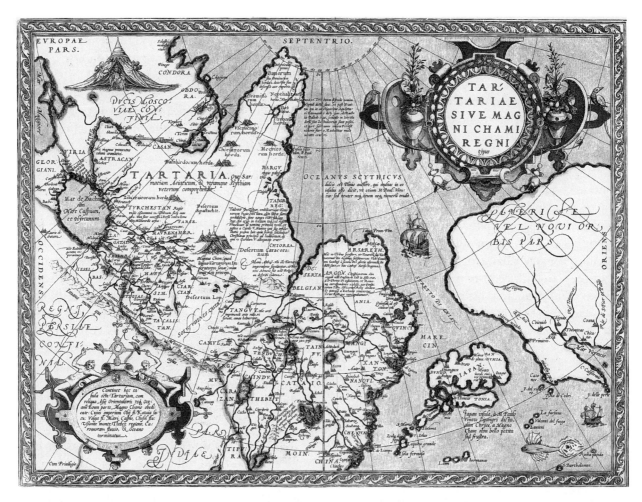

Russia. First published in Abraham Ortelius's *Theatrum Orbis Terrarum* in 1570, this map of "Tartary or the Land of the Great Khan" shows Siberia, China, and Japan, as well as the unexplored northwest coast of America. The Great Khan is shown in the upper left corner, seated in front of his splendid tent. Often considered the earliest printed map of Siberia, this is also one of the first depictions of the Strait of Anian between Siberia and North America. MAP COLLECTION, STERLING MEMORIAL LIBRARY, YALE UNIVERSITY

The urban and peasant communities collected taxes themselves and judged many petty crimes and civil disputes. The absence of any police or military force over large areas meant that even serious crimes (murder, rape, banditry) were often left to local communities, rather than to state authorities as required by law. The local communities had a conception of what sort of actions by administrators were incorrect and petitioned the tsar or revolted if these were violated. Sometimes state and community norms coincided. Many disputes over slander, verbal arguments, and insults were settled in state courts as disputes over honor. Everyone in the Russian state, even slaves and serfs, had honor, and an insult to that honor was punished by fines or, if the victim was higher in rank, by beating, prison, or various rituals of humiliation. Repeated violations of the community and state norms of honor put the offender outside the protection of his neighbors, as did witchcraft (the majority of accused witches were male).

RELIGION AND CULTURE

Until the very end of the seventeenth century, culture in Russia was essentially equivalent to religion. Though the predecessors of the Russian princes had received Orthodox Christianity from Byzantium, Russia did not inherit the secular culture of Byzantium, with its ancient Greek classics. The language of the church was not Greek but Church Slavonic, a dialect of early medieval Bulgaria. Thus the religious literature of Russia had its foundation in Slavonic translations of the church fathers and some later Byzantine theological and devotional literature.

Until 1448 the Orthodox church in Russia was under the jurisdiction of the patriarch of Constantinople, who appointed the metropolitan of Kiev and later of Moscow. Most of the metropolitans were thus Greeks or southern Slavs, and the Moscow princes had little say in their appointment. At the council of Ferrara-Florence (1438–1445), however, the Greek metropolitan of Moscow, Isidoros, went over to Rome, and the Russian church and the Moscow prince deposed him, appointing the Russian Iona in his place. The Orthodox church thus became in fact autocephalous. Even after the restoration of Orthodoxy in Constantinople, the Russians continued to select their own metropolitan.

Conflicts between the princes and tsars and the metropolitans were inevitable, especially as the tsars tried to increase their power over the church in the course of the centuries. If Metropolitan Makarii was an ally to Ivan the Terrible, his successors were expected to obey, and Metropolitan Filipp was murdered for opposing Ivan in 1569. The elevation of the metropolitan to the rank of patriarch by the Greeks in 1589 regularized Russia's relations with the Greek church, but the new patriarch, Iov, was very much the tsar's man.

Structurally the church in Russia differed in some ways from the Byzantine model. In place of the many small eparchies in the former Byzantium, the sees of Russian bishops were very extensive, and bishops were few in number and controlled little landed wealth, except for the metropolitan (later patriarch) of Moscow. The monasteries, in contrast, were as great and wealthy as those of the Greeks, if not more so. Collectively they were the lord of at least a fifth of the peasantry, more in central Russia. They were also the spiritual centers of Orthodoxy, producing almost all the saints and the devotional literature, original and translated from Greek. Only the metropolitan of Moscow himself, and to some extent the archbishop of Novgorod, had comparable spiritual authority and power at the start of the sixteenth century.

Laymen came to the monasteries for occasional spiritual advice, but also for pilgrimages to the burial places of holy monks and saints. They came for cures at the many shrines, both relics of saints and miracle-working icons. The elite and the provincial gentry tried to bury their dead in the monastery cemeteries and pay for liturgies for the dead. Particular monasteries became the objects of charity of particular clans and families, who endowed them with land, money, and valuable vestments, books, and even whole churches. Most larger monasteries enjoyed valuable immunities from taxation as well as from local judges and administrators. The parish clergy of the sixteenth century largely served churches created by private foundations and were subject to the founders' jurisdiction. They lived poorly on small parcels of land or meager income from services and gifts from parishioners. The clergy was not yet a hereditary caste, though most parish clergy were of humble origin, while monks were usually lesser gentry landholders. The ruling elite almost never entered monastic life voluntarily, though they gave generously to support it and buried their dead at the great monasteries.

Religious life for the laity in the sixteenth century revolved around the celebration of the liturgy in daily life, observation of the many fasts, and processions and pilgrimages to local shrines and monasteries. Preaching was virtually nonexistent, and the spiritual and moral direction came mainly from the clergy as spiritual fathers of laymen, each parish priest and sometimes monks taking on a group of families to follow through life.

Reform within the church. In the seventeenth century the Orthodox church saw many changes. The increasing influence of Kiev and the Ukrainian church under Polish rule played a major role. The Orthodox church in Kiev retained its dogmatic beliefs but also began to present them in the neo-Scholastic forms of Catholic theology. The basis of learning was no longer the fathers but Latin grammar and the Jesuit curriculum in language and philosophy. Preaching became a prominent part of religious life, while miracle cults and shrines were secondary and mainly served the purpose of confessional propaganda. Simultaneously in Russia reformers among the parish clergy called for greater propagation of Orthodox teaching and stronger discipline, coming to influence Tsar Alexis I (ruled 1645–1676) on these matters. In 1649 the tsar invited the first of a series of Kiev-trained clergy to Moscow to aid in translation of religious texts. They also preached in and around the court, giving a strong impulse to native reformers.

Earlier in the century Patriarch Filaret (d. 1633) had been a powerful figure, dominating his son, Tsar Michael (ruled 1613–1645), as long as he was alive, but his power came more from his position as the tsar's father than from his position in the church hierarchy. In 1652 Nikon, one of the reformers, was selected patriarch by the reformers in the church, with the informal pressure of the tsar. Besides taking a crucial role in secular politics, Nikon introduced liturgical reforms that ultimately caused a schism in the church. He left the office in 1658 over a quarrel with the tsar, a dispute only resolved by his deposition at the council of 1666–1667. The later patriarchs Ioakim (reigned 1674–1690) and Adrian (1690–1700) reinforced the power of the patriar-

chate and the clergy, striving especially hard and largely successfully to remove the parish clergy from the power of gentry church founders and place them under ecclesiastical jurisdiction.

In the later seventeenth century the impulses from Kiev grew stronger every decade, reinforced by the establishment in 1687 of the first real school in Russia, the Slavonic-Greek-Latin Academy in Moscow. Though its teachers were Greeks, they were Italian-educated and relied exclusively on Jesuit textbooks. These changes in the church, supported by the increasing flow of secular texts from the west, especially from Poland, changed the culture of the court and ruling elite, taking them away from traditional Orthodoxy with its monastic orientation toward a lay religion that included a much stronger moral element as well as some elements of secular culture. Greater changes were ahead.

Cultural change and secularization. These changes came from Peter the Great, who vastly accelerated the pace and scope of change. Culturally, his reign was a revolution. He sent young noblemen abroad to study languages, mathematics, and other subjects. He ordered the printing presses to produce a long series of texts basic to secular culture, elementary reading texts, introductions to history, architecture, mathematics, geography, and military sciences. He reoriented the ritual of the court away from the pilgrimages and virtually daily attendance at liturgy to secular celebrations of great victories and name-days and birthdays of the tsar's family and favorites. His new city of St. Petersburg was a port city with European-style architecture and only one monastery, in contrast to the dozens in and around Moscow. By the end of his reign the basic ideas of European politics, art, and learning were available in textbooks translated into Russian. In thirty-six years, the old exclusively religious culture came to an end.

The church also changed rapidly in Peter's time. At the death of Patriarch Adrian Peter appointed a Ukrainian, Stefan Iavorskii, as *locum tenens* of the patriarchate. Throughout his reign he preferred Ukrainians to Russians as bishops, a practice that continued until the 1760s. Eventually Peter abolished the patriarchate altogether and established in its place the Holy Synod, a board composed of laymen and clergy appointed by the tsar to run the

Russia. A late-eighteenth-century French map of southern European Russia during the reign of Catherine the Great (ruled 1762–1796). Under Catherine, Poland was partitioned, the Crimea was annexed, and vast territories in the south and west were taken from the Ottoman Empire, including Belarus, parts of Ukraine west of the Dnieper River, and the Black Sea shores. MAP COLLECTION, STERLING MEMORIAL LIBRARY, YALE UNIVERSITY

church. The monasteries came to play a very subordinate role. In the later seventeenth century their revenues had already been placed under state control, and Peter reestablished that policy, hoping to use them as hospitals and schools rather than centers of ascetic spirituality.

BUILDING A MODERN STATE

Peter's political and administrative measures were not as radical, but they nevertheless had major effects. They produced a European style of absolutism in the central government, though still without sufficient apparatus outside the capital. Combined with

victory over Sweden and the acquisition of a Baltic seacoast and new capital, Peter's state-building made Russia a major regional power, and one with a European culture. His successors in the eighteenth century continued to reorder and build the state, maintaining Russia's power as well. In the 1730s Empress Anna (ruled 1730–1740) upheld Russian influence in Poland and retained a foothold on the Black Sea. Russia was an active participant in the Seven Years' War (1756–1763), emerging with no concrete gains but considerable prestige owing to the defeat of Frederick the Great of Prussia. It was Catherine the Great who made Russia a great power in Europe, with two successful Turkish wars (1768–1774, 1787–1792) and the partitions of Poland (1772, 1793, 1795). These victories moved Russia's borders far to the west, incorporating most of Ukraine, Belarus, and Lithuania and conquering Crimea and the whole of the northern Black Sea coast.

While the years from Peter's death until the middle of the reign of Elizabeth (ruled 1741–1762) were devoted to court intrigues and succession struggles, the 1750s saw the resumption of policies designed to modernize state and society. Under the influence of her favorite, Count Ivan Ivanovich Shuvalov, Elizabeth founded Russia's first university in Moscow (1755) and encouraged other cultural projects, such as Russian-language theater at court. Other measures included fostering trade and industry, the abolition of internal tolls, and other economic projects. Plans to free the nobility from obligatory military service and to confiscate monastery lands came to fruition only after Elizabeth's death.

Catherine's reign saw more extensive political projects in the Legislative Commission (1767) and reorganization of provincial as well as central administration. These measures included a certain element of participation by the nobility and urban elites, as well as the delineation of their rights and privileges in law. By the end of her reign the issue of serfdom arose, most sharply in the work of Aleksandr Radishchev, who condemned the institution on moral and economic grounds. Catherine herself was by then alarmed at the French Revolution and sent Radishchev to prison, but his ideas, like her own measures, were typical products of the European Enlightenment.

RUSSIAN CULTURE IN THE AGE OF ENLIGHTENMENT

The Enlightenment was the first European current of thought to be fully received in Russia. Peter's cultural revolution had laid a foundation not only by example but through new institutions as well. His plan for an Academy of Sciences was realized in 1725, after his death. The academy brought scientists and scholars of European reputation to St. Petersburg, where they not only pursued their researches but also taught Russian students. The Noble Cadet Corps, based on the European noble

academies, came into being in 1731, teaching young noblemen a curriculum that emphasized modern languages, law, history, and the sciences as well as proper behavior at court. Few formal schools followed its example, but private tutors among the gentry and private gymnasia supplemented the few state schools. The theater, dramatic and musical, flourished at the court, joined in the 1750s by a Russian-language dramatic theater and even theaters outside the capital. The Academy of Arts (1758) trained Russian painters to supplement the few Western and Western-trained artists already at work. Catherine founded a Society for the Translation of Foreign Books in 1768, which merged into the Academy of Letters in 1783. St. Petersburg evolved into a city of largely baroque and classical architecture, built by Italians and Germans. Even in Moscow and the provinces classical palaces sprang up alongside ancient churches and monasteries in the older Russian styles.

Both within the framework of these institutions and outside of them, Russians absorbed European thought and culture with great speed. Most of the well-known European writers of the time appeared in Russian translation—all of Jean-Jacques Rousseau, for instance, except *Du contrat social* (1762; Social contract), had appeared by 1780. Works that remained untranslated nevertheless circulated widely, since the elite generally knew either German or French by mid-century. Russia contributed little that was original to European culture in the eighteenth century. Its art and literature followed European patterns, as with Aleksandr Petrovich Sumarokov's (1717–1744) tragedies, based on the models of Jean Racine and Voltaire. Even the church followed European patterns, in spite of the turn toward Russian rather than Ukrainian bishops in the 1760s. Earlier in the century the seminaries and other church schools continued the seventeenth-century Jesuit curriculum inherited from Kiev, but gradually other trends emerged. Pietism was a major influence after about 1750, with Johann Arndt's *Vier Bücher vom wahren Christentum* (1605–1609; True christianity) a work widely read, even by such luminaries as St. Tikhon Zadonskii. The great preachers of Catherine's time, such as Metropolitan of Moscow Platon Levshin, followed Lutheran models, preaching a mildly rationalized Christianity and sentimentalizing morality.

Political thought stayed within the framework created elsewhere by Voltaire, Charles-Louis de Secondat de Montesquieu, and others, propounding ideas of enlightened absolutism, aristocratic rights and privileges, and the need to create legal order. Radishchev was unusual in his radicalism in the face of serfdom, but he too borrowed his theoretical arguments from European writers on slavery, such as the abbé de Raynal. The importance of the eighteenth century lay not in original contributions but in the thorough integration of European thought and art into Russian culture.

SOCIAL AND ECONOMIC CHANGES AND IMPERIAL EXPANSION

Underneath the intellectual growth and ferment Russian society moved within the inherited framework of serf agriculture, but some new phenomena emerged. The settlement of the southern steppe with its rich black earth soil continued, especially after the Turkish wars and the defeat of Crimea. The southern steppe zone gradually became an area of great estates worked mainly by labor services, which diminished or disappeared in central Russia. The new ports on the Black Sea gave an outlet to grain from the steppe, while central Russia turned more to market gardening, crafts, and seasonal labor such as transport on the great rivers. The result was a boom for the gentry, who began to build great country houses on their estates, even those far from the cities. Nobles tried to use the latest ideas in European agrarian practices to enhance their incomes. In Peter's reign noblewomen had emerged from seclusion to mix freely with men and women outside the family at home and at court. They retained more property rights and played a larger role in estate management than women farther west. For non-elite women, however, little changed.

The serf peasants of central Russia found themselves neighbors of the "economic peasants" when monastic lands were confiscated in 1764 and put under the College of the Economy. Many of the former monastery villages were great centers of crafts and trade, producing dynasties of wealthy merchants. In these villages and those of great noblemen the crafts began to turn into more modern enterprises. In the Sheremetev villages of Ivanovo and Voznesensk serf entrepreneurs built cotton textile factories and hired their fellow serfs as laborers. The Urals, with more primitive technology but low costs, became a major iron producer. By the 1760s St. Petersburg was the center of Russian trade in the Baltic, as Peter had hoped, becoming the home of an international business community of Russians, Germans, Swedes, Britons, Dutch, and other commercial peoples. In the Volga area the growing trade with Persia and Central Asia came to a large extent into the hands of the Kazan' Tatars, giving them a new significance in the area and incidentally a leading role among Muslims in Russia. The conquest of the south and the foundation of Odessa in 1794 gave rise to a new port and new trade, dominated by Greeks, Jews, Bulgarians, Poles, and even some Russians, exporting grain to western Europe and trading with the Ottoman Empire. In remote Siberia, the Russian-American Company entered the fur trade in Alaska.

Russia's population grew rapidly, reaching some thirty-six million by 1800, of which only about six million came from territorial annexation. This demographic expansion, which continued into the twentieth century, provided an important stimulus to economic growth and to colonization of the southern steppe as well as eastern regions. If the center and south of Russia prospered, the north went into decline, resulting from the decline of the northern salt industry and the shift of the fur trade ever farther east. The Siberian economy was hampered by low population, but the discovery of silver and gold in the 1720s laid the foundation for a new and increasingly important industry, one largely under state control.

The expansion of the empire brought in new peoples. The nomadic Bashkirs, Kalmyks, and Tatars were now fully inside Russian borders in the south. The partitions of Poland brought most of the Ukrainian people into Russia, as well as Lithuanians and Belarusians. In the vast formerly Polish territories the nobility was almost entirely Polish, and initially Russia maintained Polish local gentry institutions, placing them under Russian governors. The towns in this area were largely Jewish in population, bringing another new people into the Russian orbit. As with the Polish nobility, Russian policy initially preserved preexisting community structures. In the old Ukrainian Hetmanate, the defection of Hetman Ivan Mazepa to Sweden in 1708 led Peter to appoint his own hetman and later abolish the office. Local institutions and laws remained, however, until the 1780s, when Catherine's reform of provincial administration meant the end of the Hetmanate's remaining autonomy. It also meant the integration of the Cossack nobility into the Russian imperial nobility, reflected in high positions in the army and government. Similarly, the German nobility of the Baltic provinces retained local rights and elected institutions until the 1780s, while Baltic German families played an increasingly central role in St. Petersburg. As many conservative Polish magnates chose to serve the tsars as well after 1796, the Russian ruling elite took on an increasingly multiethnic character, with Germans, Poles, and Ukrainians prominent in all spheres of the government and military services.

At the end of the eighteenth century Catherine's son Paul, frightened by the French Revolution, satisfied his conservative instincts by a re-centralization of government, paradoxically coupled with some restoration of local gentry rights in the Baltic provinces and elsewhere. His eccentric personality, however, led to his assassination on 11 March 1801, ushering in a new century and a return to more liberal measures under his son Alexander I. Russia's society, state, and especially culture changed rapidly in the early modern era, but not enough to erode the basic structures. Those would have to wait for more powerful forces still to come.

See also **Alexis I (Russia); Anna (Russia); Autocracy; Avvakum Petrovich; Black Sea Steppe; Boris Godunov (Russia); Catherine II (Russia); Elizabeth (Russia); False Dmitrii, First; Fur Trade: Russia; Ivan III (Muscovy); Ivan IV, "the Terrible" (Russia); Law: Russian Law; Michael Romanov (Russia); Morozova, Boiarynia; Nikon, patriarch; Old Believers; Oprichnina; Orthodoxy, Russian; Paul I (Russia); Peter I (Russia); Pugachev Revolt; Razin, Stepan; Romanov Dynasty (Russia); Russian Literature and Language; Russo-Ottoman Wars; Russo-Polish Wars; Serfdom in Russia; Sofiia Alekseevna; Time of Troubles (Russia); Vasilii III (Muscovy).**

BIBLIOGRAPHY

Avrich, Paul. *Russian Rebels 1600–1800.* New York, 1972.

Bushkovitch, Paul. *Peter the Great.* Lanham, Md., 2001.

———. *Religion and Society in Russia: The Sixteenth and Seventeenth Centuries.* New York, 1992.

Cracraft, James. *The Petrine Revolution in Russian Architecture.* Chicago, 1988.

Crummey, Robert O. *Aristocrats and Servitors: the Boyar Elite in Russia 1613–1689.* Princeton, 1983.

———. *The Formation of Muscovy 1304–1613.* London and New York, 1987.

DeMadariaga, Isabel. *Russia in the Age of Catherine the Great.* New Haven, 1981.

Dixon, Simon. *The Modernization of Russia 1676–1825.* Cambridge, U.K., and New York, 1999.

Dukes, Paul. *The Making of Russian Absolutism 1613–1801.* London and New York, 1990.

Garrard, J. G., ed. *The Eighteenth Century in Russia.* Oxford, 1973.

Hartley, Janet. *A Social History of the Russian Empire 1650–1825.* London, 1999.

Hughes, Lindsey. *Russia in the Age of Peter the Great.* New Haven, 1998.

Kollmann, Nancy Shields. *By Honor Bound: State and Society in Early Modern Russia.* Ithaca, N.Y., 1999.

LeDonne, John P. *Absolutism and Ruling Class: The Formation of the Russian Political Order 1700–1825.* New York and Oxford, 1991.

Marker, Gary. *Publishing, Printing, and the Origins of Intellectual Life in Russia 1800–1800.* Princeton, 1995.

Martin, Janet. *Medieval Russia 980–1584.* Cambridge, U.K., and New York, 1995.

Moon, David. *The Russian Peasantry 1600–1930: The World the Peasants Made.* London and New York, 1999.

Platonov, S. F. *Moscow and the West.* Trans. by J. Wieczynski. Hattiesburg, Miss., 1972.

Raeff, Marc. *Understanding Imperial Russia: State and Society in the Old Regime.* New York, 1984.

Thyret, Isolde. *Between God and the Tsar: Religious Symbolism and the Royal Women of Muscovite Russia.* DeKalb, Ill., 2001.

PAUL BUSHKOVITCH

RUSSIA, ARCHITECTURE IN.

Construction in old Russia was principally of horizontal logs from trees abundantly available in the forested zones where most Russians lived. Floor plans of log structures were typically combinations of square or rectangular cells, whether the structures were houses, palaces, fortification towers, or churches. In church architecture, carpenters reproduced the two basic plans inherited from Byzantine (Eastern Roman) Christian masonry churches: an extended east-west plan of sanctuary, nave, and narthex, or a centrally oriented plan of a square or octagon of logs, sometimes with extensions built around a central nave. Several open-air museums of

Architecture in Russia. This image is part of a very large and elaborately decorated nine-sheet map of St. Petersburg produced by the Russian Academy of Sciences in 1753. Dedicated to Elizabeth I, who reigned from 1741 to 1762, the sheet shows the base of a statue of the empress and some of the architectural features of the city. The inscription reads ''Capital City of St. Petersburg. Dedicated to Elizabeth I, Empress of All Russia, Daughter of Peter the Great.'' MAP COLLECTION, STERLING MEMORIAL LIBRARY, YALE UNIVERSITY

traditional wooden architecture have been established in Russia, among them Suzdal', Novgorod, Kostroma, Kizhi, Arkhangel'sk, and Lake Baikal.

Wood and masonry architecture influenced one another in numerous ways. In wooden log churches, for example, the curve of a masonry apse is imitated by a half-octagon of shortened logs. The "storied" effect of some masonry churches (for example, the Church of the Intercession at Fili, 1690s, Moscow) is copied from log churches surmounted by tiers of receding log octagons (for example, the wooden Church of the Transfiguration, eighteenth century, Museum of Wooden Architecture, Suzdal'). Especially popular in village wooden church architecture was a tent-shaped superstructure, usually with eight slopes arising from an octagonal drum. The drum in turn was placed on one or more square or octagonal bases (for example, the wooden Church of the Dormition from the village of Kuritsko, 1595, Novgorod open-air museum). A masonry imitation is the brick Church of the Ascension at Kolomenskoe, 1532, Moscow.

St. Basil's Cathedral (sixteenth to seventeenth centuries) on Red Square in Moscow represents a sort of encyclopedic combination of elements from both wooden and masonry architecture. Its central chapel, for example, imitates a log tower/tent structure, topped by an onion dome. The Russian onion-shaped dome was functional in design—to shed rain and prevent snow buildup—and also symbolic; its shape was likened to a candle flame of faith reaching up to heaven. Among masonry influences, St. Basil's has exterior ornamentation borrowed from the walls and churches of the nearby Italian-built Kremlin.

A major building project in Moscow in the late fifteenth to early sixteenth centuries was the reconstruction of the Kremlin, the central citadel of the city. Because of the lack of experience and skill among native builders, architects from northern Italy were imported for the task. Italians designed and built the present red brick-faced Kremlin walls, the Cathedrals of the Dormition and the Archangel Michael, the Palace of Facets, and the Great Ivan Bell Tower and adjacent Dormition Belfry. Least Italianate in the appearance of these structures is the Dormition Cathedral (1470s) by Aristotele Rudolfo Fioravanti, an engineer who copied—as instructed—the cubic mass surmounted by five domes of the twelfth-century Dormition Cathedral in Vladimir. Most importantly, Fioravanti and his colleagues introduced Russian builders to better brick and mortar construction techniques, making possible an unprecedented building boom throughout Russia in the sixteenth and seventeenth centuries.

Standing on Cathedral Square in the Kremlin, one can identify architectural elements that mirror the political and territorial rise of Muscovite Russia: architectural compositions and ornamentation from regions incorporated into Muscovy (Pskov, Novgorod, Vladimir), from village wooden architecture, and from Italy. In turn, given the prestige of major buildings in the capital city, Kremlin structures became models for buildings throughout Russia. For example, the Dormition Cathedral became an oft-repeated model for subsequent major cathedrals (Novodevichii Convent in Moscow, Vologda, Kostroma, the Trinity-St. Sergii Monastery outside Moscow, Rostov Velikii, and others).

THE BAROQUE AND WESTERN INFLUENCE

If Muscovite architecture achieved a synthesis of regional, village, and Italian influences in the fifteenth and sixteenth centuries, that synthesis was shattered in the seventeenth century when west European influences entered Russia from Ukraine, a portion of which was incorporated into Muscovy in the mid-seventeenth century. A so-called Moscow baroque decorative style characterized many churches and palaces in the second half of the seventeenth century (the Church of the Trinity in the Nikitniki Courtyard, mid-seventeenth century, Moscow, is an example), but aside from baroque decorative elements, these structures show little of the balance and symmetry of the baroque style of Western Europe. Several regional centers developed their own schools of architecture, notably Iaroslavl', northeast of Moscow, whose seventeenth-century churches are crowned by elongated slender drums under the domes.

Building and design in Muscovy was typically a family affair: a builder would pass on his skills to his sons (although none of them might be literate) and design plans might not be drawn up in advance of a construction project. With the founding and buildup of St. Petersburg, beginning in the early eighteenth century, the old Muscovite building trade became the new "science" of *arkhitektura*, studied in special new schools where pupils were taught foreign languages, mathematics, and classical architecture. Teachers and textbooks first came from west Europe but were quickly followed by newly trained Russian masters and Russian translations. A Chancellory of Construction was established which supervised training and construction, first for St. Petersburg, then later in the eighteenth century for cities throughout the country.

Beginning with Peter I the Great (ruled 1682–1725), west European architectural trends determined the overall style of "high" architecture—almost all significant government and private construction—and the personal taste of the ruler determined the current style employed. Peter's favorite architect, Domenico Trezzini, employed the restrained baroque of northern Europe, for example in his 400-meter-long Twelve Colleges Building, 1722–1742, St. Petersburg. The very existence of such a large government building, the likes of which did not exist in Moscow at the time, indicates a new and major investment by the government in an extensive administrative system. The planned design of St. Petersburg, with its neat grids and patterns of streets, regular building heights and setbacks, wide avenues, and huge squares and public spaces, brings to mind another eighteenth-century city planned from scratch and designed to impress citizens and foreigners alike: Washington, D.C.

Major architectural styles after Peter were a fancy baroque, or rococo during the reign of Elizabeth Petrovna (ruled 1741–1762), exemplified by the works of Bartolomeo Francesco Rastrelli (Winter Palace, Smolnyi Convent, Catherine Palace at Tsarskoe Selo), and classical or neoclassical in the reign of Catherine II the Great (ruled 1762–1796), for example the Hermitage Theater by Giacomo Quarenghi, the Great Palace at Pavlovsk by Charles Cameron and others, and the Marble Palace by Antonio Rinaldi.

The "St. Petersburgization" of architecture in other cities—in particular, the dispersion of classical or neoclassical norms—gained momentum during Catherine's reign and continued to influence Russian architecture throughout the imperial period. An early example of classical architecture in Moscow is the Pashkov House, attributed to V. I. Bazhenov (1780s), now a part of the Russian State Library, formerly the Lenin Library.

See also **Architecture; Baroque; Catherine II (Russia); City Planning; Moscow; Neoclassicism; Peter I (Russia).**

BIBLIOGRAPHY

Brumfield, William Craft. *A History of Russian Architecture.* Cambridge, U.K., 1993.

Cracraft, James. *The Petrine Revolution in Russian Architecture.* Chicago and London, 1988.

Hamilton, George Heard. *The Art and Architecture of Russia.* 3rd ed. New York, 1983.

JACK KOLLMANN

RUSSIA, ART IN.

RUSSIA, ART IN. Formal art in fifteenth- and sixteenth-century Muscovite Russia (the principality of Moscow) was concentrated in the Russian Orthodox Church and consisted principally of icons, frescoes, and manuscript illuminations. Most artists were monks or closely associated with the church, typically trained in monastic painting workshops. To be an artist was considered a holy calling. Instructions for artists were essentially identical with those for scribes copying religious texts: "copy exactly from holy models, changing absolutely nothing." And yet, no two painted scenes or hand-copied manuscripts are alike: local preferences varied in subject matter, style, and coloration; the availability of natural pigments varied locally; training was not standardized; no cartoon books existed before the seventeenth century (the "holy model"

at hand might vary drastically from place to place); and finally, each artist differed in taste and talent.

FROM BYZANTINE TO MUSCOVITE

A famous example of Byzantine art that influenced Russian art is the icon of the *Vladimir Mother of God,* thought to have been painted in Constantinople in the early twelfth century (State Tretyakov Gallery, Moscow), and often copied in Russia. From Byzantine and early Russian regional schools, notably that of Novgorod, Moscow synthesized artistic styles and subjects. As Moscow absorbed the other eastern Slavic principalities and city-states, it acquired the best of their art and architecture.

Two additional trends distinguished Muscovite art. First, the introduction of Moscow-specific themes, frequently imbued with political significance. Moscow was not the first to insert Russian themes into church art. The "schools" of the merchant city states of Novgorod and Pskov introduced local themes: a locally revered saint (for example, St. Paraskeva-Piatnitsa, patroness of Friday market day) or a local event (the miracle of the saving of embattled Novgorod by the palladium icon of Novgorod). The appearance of Russian saints (and the report of their miracles) in Russia provided artists with new material beyond the confines of Byzantine tradition, amplifying their role beyond that of mere copyists. One of the more notable examples of Moscow patriotic art is the 12-feet-long mid-sixteenth-century icon of *The Church Militant,* or *Heavenly Forces* (Tretyakov Gallery), thought to be an allegory of the conquest of Kazan' (1552). It depicts the Moscow grand prince (possibly Tsar Ivan IV, "the Terrible") and the Archangel Michael leading columns of current and historical Russian princes and troops toward the heavenly city, where the Christ child, sitting on his mother's lap, hands out crowns of glory.

A second major trend in Muscovite art was the literal rise of the iconostasis. From the Byzantine and early Russian tradition of placing icons singly or in a row before the sanctuary, the Muscovite church expanded the icons upward and outward, creating a wall of images that reached toward the ceiling vaults and spread across the nave and into the side aisles. Standing before it, even the illiterate churchgoer is instructed visually in the teachings of the church, because the meaning of each icon is explained in services on relevant days in the church calendar.

The "classical" period of Muscovite icon painting (late fourteenth and fifteenth centuries) is exemplified in works attributed to the monk and artist Andrey Rublyov (c. 1360/70–c. 1430), who was named by the 1551 Stoglav ("hundred chapters" church council) as a model for artists to emulate. The icon of the *Old Testament Trinity* (Tretyakov Gallery) attributed to him is especially harmonious, with its pastel colors and circular composition of the three angels who visit Abraham and Sarah (Genesis 18).

The Muscovite synthesis of regional themes and styles achieved in the fifteenth and sixteenth centuries was shattered in the seventeenth century. The acquisition of left bank Ukraine in the mid-seventeenth century led to an influx into Moscow of Ukrainian clerics and scholars who had been exposed to western European Renaissance, Reformation, and Counter-Reformation culture via Poland. Among changing trends in seventeenth-century Muscovite art were the following: western European post-Renaissance perspective and three-dimensional illusionism (for example, the use of chiaroscuro) began to supplant the traditional use of inverse perspective and two-dimensional treatment of figures and scenes; engravings in western European publications, such as the Dutch Piscator Bible, provided fresh subject matter and stylistic ideas to artists, notably teams of painters who created a remarkable series of frescoes in churches in Yaroslavl', Rostov Velikii, Kostroma, Vologda, and elsewhere; icons began to be produced in small sizes (rectangles whose vertical height was frequently no more than twelve to sixteen inches) for personal and home use by individuals (for example, in the Stroganov School, commissioned initially by that wealthy family); Moscow political themes became more overt; the artist began to sign work which had previously been left anonymous, and increasingly it was expected that he would imbue his work with his own individual, recognizable style.

Of some 2,800 names recently published in a dictionary of Russian icon painters of the eleventh through seventeenth centuries, approximately 95 percent worked in the seventeenth century. Exem-plary among these was Simon Ushakov (1626–1686). In his icon of the *Vladimir Mother of God and the Tree of the Muscovite State* (Tretyakov Gallery), Ushakov "updates" the twelfth-century icon with profuse references to the glory of Moscow; in his *Old Testament Trinity* (State Russian Museum, St. Petersburg), he alters the simplicity of Rublyov's icon with extraordinary detail and the use of chiaroscuro to suggest three-dimensional faces on the three angels. Both works by Ushakov are signed and dated.

PORTRAITS AND SCULPTURE

Portrait painting arose in the seventeenth century, partly under Polish influence via Ukraine, but overtly western European post-Renaissance subjects and principles came to characterize Russian art only in the eighteenth century. Peter I the Great (ruled 1682–1725), who imported western European culture wholesale for his new city of St. Petersburg, had his portrait painted scores of times by foreign and domestic artists—and in oil paint, which lends itself better to chiaroscuro than does the egg tempera medium of traditional icons. European artists were imported to record the buildup of the city, decorate the interiors of buildings, and train Russian students. Some Russian art students were also sent abroad for training. During the eighteenth century, the Academy of Fine Arts, founded by Empress Elizabeth Petrovna (ruled 1741–1762) and funded significantly beginning with Catherine II the Great (ruled 1762–1796), dominated art training. Leading eighteenth-century Russian artists include Dmitry Levitsky (1735–1822), whose portraits of aristocratic girls at Catherine the Great's Smolny Institute show great skill, Vladimir Borovikovsky (1757–1825), who broke new ground with his relatively informal study of Catherine walking her dog in a park (copies in Tretyakov Gallery and State Russian Museum), and Ivan Argunov (1729–1802), who was born a serf yet rose to become one of the founders of the Academy of Fine Arts in 1758. His career demonstrates that in post-Petrine Russia advancement could be based on merit and not on privileged birth alone.

In sculpture, the adoption of western European neoclassical traditions paralleled developments in painting. Fedot Shubin's (1740–1805) numerous plaster and marble busts of aristocratic patrons show

Nicolas Poussin. *The Death of Germanicus,* 1627, reflects Poussin's passion for historical accuracy. This painting, completed during his early years in Rome, established his reputation there and led to a papal commission. ©ERICH LESSING/ART RESOURCE

RIGHT: Raphael. *Veiled Woman (La Velata),* c. 1513. Rivaling Michelangelo as one of the most talented artists of the High Renaissance period, Raphael executed a number of portraits which are considered to have set the standard for subsequent Renaissance portraiture. ©SCALA/ART RESOURCE, N.Y.

BELOW LEFT: Raphael. *The Transfiguration,* 1519–1520. Left unfinished at his death, this altarpiece is one of Raphael's many explorations of the meaning of the Incarnation. ©SCALA/ART RESOURCE, N.Y.

BELOW RIGHT: Renaissance. *The School of Athens,* mural in the Vatican Palace by Raphael, c. 1509. This section of the mural, considered a masterpiece of perspective drawing, reflects the burgeoning interest in classical learning typical of the period. ©ERICH LESSING/ART RESOURCE, N.Y.

ABOVE RIGHT: Joshua Reynolds. Portrait of Sir Banastre Tarleton, 1782. Reynolds was the first president of the Royal Academy of Art and the leading painter of aristocratic London during the second half of the eighteenth century. His numerous portraits reflect classical and Old Master models. ©NATIONAL GALLERY COLLECTION; BY KIND PERMISSION OF THE TRUSTEES OF THE NATIONAL GALLERY, LONDON/CORBIS

BELOW RIGHT: Rococo. *The Rape of Europa* by François Boucher, 1747. Boucher's rococo style is here exemplified in exuberant use of color and playful eroticism. THE ART ARCHIVE/MUSÉE DU LOUVRE, DAGLI ORTI (A)

RIGHT: Scientific Illustration. Albrecht Dürer's *Large Piece of Turf,* watercolor on paper, 1503. ©Erich Lessing/Art Resource, N.Y

BELOW: Peter Paul Rubens. *The Horrors of War,* 1638. This allegory of the plight of Europe, torn by religious and political conflicts, is representative of Rubens's style in its massive figural forms and rich colors. ©Nimatallah/Art Resource

OPPOSITE PAGE: Rachel Ruysch. *A Carnation, Morning Glory, and Other Flowers* is representative of the later works of Ruysch, who was one of the most successful women artists of the early modern period. ©Christie's Images/Corbis

RIGHT: Art in Spain. *The Immaculate Conception,* 1676–1679, by Bartolomé Esteban Murillo. Murillo painted in Seville, and by the 1640s he had become the dominant artistic figure in that city. His works were created primarily for religious patrons and appealed in their idealized depictions to the religious imagination of his society. ART ARCHIVE/MUSEO DEL PRADO MADRID/DAGLI ORTI (A)

BELOW: Suleiman I. The Seige of Vienna, 1529, as depicted in *Hunername,* a 1588 manuscript written by Sayyid Lokman, one of Suleiman's official court historians. ©GIRAUDON/ART RESOURCE, N.Y.

Art in Russia. An icon of the holy doors showing Metropolitan Peter and Alexius, with the Annunciation above, sixteenth century. THE ART ARCHIVE/KIZHI MUSEUM/NICHOLAS SAPIEHA

the fruits of his six years of study in Paris. St. Petersburg's most famous statue, the equestrian *Bronze Horseman of Peter the Great,* was commissioned by Catherine and designed by the Frenchman Étienne-Maurice Falconet (1716–1791) and his pupil and mistress, Marie-Anne Collot (1748–1821).

Space does not permit discussion of folk art, which flourished largely apart from the formal trends identified here. Folk art influenced formal art before the eighteenth century to some extent, but less so beginning with the westernization of formal art.

See also **Catherine II (Russia); France, Art in; Peter I (Russia); Russia.**

BIBLIOGRAPHY

Bird, Alan. *A History of Russian Painting.* Boston, 1987.

Cracraft, James. *The Petrine Revolution in Russian Imagery.* Chicago and London, 1988.

Hamilton, George Heard. *The Art and Architecture of Russia.* 3rd ed. New York, 1983.

Milner, John. *A Dictionary of Russian & Soviet Artists, 1420–1970.* Woodbridge, U.K., 1993.

JACK KOLLMANN

RUSSIAN LITERATURE AND LANGUAGE.

The category of "old Russian literature," however enduring, constitutes little more than an omnibus retrospection of almost all prose native to Rus' and written in Slavonic or Russian prior to the eighteenth century. It marks the mythic boundary between antiquity and modernity in Russian culture and includes heroic tales and epics, compendia of saints' lives (*chet'i minei, prologi,* etc.), chronicles *(letopisi),* general Christian histories *(khronografy),* and numerous individual codices *(sborniki)* compiled from a wide range of materials, usually by anonymous monastic bookmen.

From the end of the twentieth century scholarship increasingly replaced this confining typology of an undifferentiated old Russian culture with more nuanced and fragmented constructs that posit inner tensions, regional variations, and epistemic shifts over the centuries between the fall of Kiev and Peter the Great's assertion of Russian modernity. Such tensions and variations were particularly marked during the late sixteenth and seventeenth centuries,

thanks in large measure to a cultural influx from Poland and Ukraine. Another major stimulus came from the schism within Russian Orthodoxy in the 1650s, out of which emerged the movement known as Old Believers or Old Ritualists. Edifying vitae soon appeared for many of the movement's early martyrs, including Boiarynia Feodosiia Morozova, Ivan Neronov, and Iuliana Lazarevskaia. The most outstanding of these was the autobiographical account of the leader of the Old Believers, the archpriest Avvakum Petrovich. Told in earthy and vivid prose, *The Life of the Archpriest Avvakum* (1672–1673) marked the beginning in Russia of a vernacular form of autobiographical writing, penned by an identified author and directed at a broad literate audience who read outside of the church service. All of these lives were widely known, at least among religious dissenters, and their abiding tropes of civic powerlessness and suffering for one's faith later became commonplaces of eighteenth-century memoirs and autobiographies.

At the same time Russia was developing a new "high" literature beyond the narrowly devotional, including highly literary sermons, religious poetry, drama, and an ever growing corpus of tales and fables, translated in large measure from Polish. Most scholars tie these innovations to the courts of Tsar Alexis I Mikhailovich (ruled 1645–1676) and, especially, his daughter Sofiia, who was the de facto regent between 1682 and 1689. Starting in 1672 the Muscovite court housed an intermittent theater whose repertoire mixed biblical tales (such as that of Artaxerxes) with Greek fables and dramas based on saints' lives (for example, of St. Catherine).

Another important new genre of literary expression was the sermon, a rarity in Russian culture before the mid-seventeenth century. The central figure in this trend was the monk Simeon Polotskii, who moved from Belarus to Moscow in 1660. During the final few decades of the seventeenth and throughout the eighteenth century, several other religious hierarchs, almost all of them Ukrainians linked to the Kremlin or important monasteries near Moscow, were active in sermonizing. Although subject to severe restrictions in form, theme, and structure, sermons afforded these clerics the opportunity to create new texts, many of which were subsequently published in collections, and to be recognized as their authors.

CIVIL ORTHOGRAPHY, PRINT, AND THE NEW LITERARY LANGUAGE

Peter the Great's new civil orthography of 1707 and his aggressive deployment of print initiated new explorations toward a distinctly civil Russian (as opposed to Slavonic) literary language. Most scholars now believe that this discourse did not arise in a linguistic vacuum, but that the developments of the late-seventeenth century as well as the evolution of what is sometimes termed "chancellery (*prikaznyi*) writing" set the context for the reforms. During the 1730s, Vasilii Trediakovskii, Antiokh Kantemir, and Mikhail Lomonosov debated furiously about the shape of this literary language. At issue were the use of arcane constructions and "pure" slavonicisms versus the construction of something more in line with contemporary European literature. All three of the principals, but especially Trediakovskii and Lomonosov, chose the medium of literary translation as their linguistic laboratory, often creating texts that were stilted and idiosyncratic but nonetheless literary. A noted example is Trediakovskii's rendering of Paul Tallemant's *Le voyage à l'isle d'amour de Lycidas*.

Along with the new orthography and the nascent literary language, the institutionalization of literature benefited from the proliferation of lay publishing, primarily at educational institutions. Drawing from a mixture of foreign scholars, professional translators, and a handful of brilliant former seminarians and cadets (including Trediakovskii, Lomonosov, and Sumarokov), the Academy of Sciences during the second quarter of the eighteenth century acted as midwife for the birth of a lay print culture, producing small runs of poetry, tales, and translated opera librettos. Exceedingly modest in volume when compared to the rest of Europe, this work was nonetheless momentous for creating what we would now call Russian literature, as a creative, public, accessible, lay discourse for private reading and pleasure.

Mid-century witnessed several new publishing houses, primarily at Moscow University and the Cadet Academies; together these presses provided an institutional setting for young—mostly noble—literati to engage in literary pursuits and develop a public voice. Virtually every luminary of the Elizabethan and Catherinian eras—including Mikhail Kheraskov (1733–1807), Denis Fonvizin (1745–

1792), Ippolit Bogdanovich (1744–1803), Gavrila Derzhavin (1743–1816), Aleksandr Radishchev (1749–1802), and several others—participated in this collective endeavor of literary and institutional creation. In most cases these writers earned little or nothing from their original works (a bit more from translations), and the great majority maintained commissions in state service. Derzhavin, for example, had been in an elite guards' regiment, and he ultimately became a full-time civil administrator, rising to the very high position of provincial governor. Some, however, including Nikolai Novikov (1744–1818) and Nikolai Karamzin (1766–1826), became something approaching professional intellectuals in that they devoted all their time to intellectual pursuits, sometimes, as with Novikov, resigning their commissions. During the last quarter of the eighteenth century the life of literature and literary production developed very rapidly, thanks to the growth in secondary education, both secular and religious, which produced an exponential rise in the number of writers and readers, as well as the easier access to print, especially after 1783, when the decree on private presses made publishing much simpler.

GENRES

In addition to the profusion of literary translation, poetry provided some of Russia's most important writing during this period. Especially significant were the lyric and religious poetry of Trediakovskii, the epic poetry of Kheraskov (the "Russian Homer" and author of the lengthy *Rossiiada*), and, above all, the reflective and highly personal verses of Derzhavin. As was true throughout Europe, travel literature, recounting journeys both real and imaginary, proved to be a particularly effective medium for combining entertainment with cultural commentary. Karamzin's *Letters of a Russian Traveler, 1789–1790* (1797), although often fanciful, nevertheless offered entertaining glimpses of the mores Karamzin observed during his European grand tour of 1789–1790, and it situated Russia in the European context and oriented the reader's sense of national identity and civility. The genre also lent itself to severe social commentary, most famously in Radishchev's novel, *A Journey from St. Petersburg to Moscow*. Taking advantage of lax censorship, Radishchev published this savage critique of serfdom and Russia's lack of freedom in 1790, much to the outrage of the empress Catherine II, who ordered all copies confiscated and the author jailed. Dramatic as this episode was, Radishchev's pained voice of political and social opposition remained the exception for the eighteenth century, as few of his contemporaries expressed—or apparently held—views in opposition to the political status quo.

Beginning in the mid-1750s and especially from the late 1760s onward, literary and philosophical journalism became the medium of choice among aspiring literati. Few of these ventures lasted longer than several months, and most could count their readerships in hundreds rather than thousands. But these journals came out frequently and regularly, and as one folded others took its place. Essayists and translators, as often as not still unidentified by name, could pool their resources and energies and use periodical publication to construct the rudiments of an engaged textual community, playing off of other journals to establish a clear field of discourse. The prime example comes from the so-called satirical journals of 1769–1774. During this period, journals linked to Novikov *(The Painter, The Drone, The Tattler)* parried with others associated with the empress *(Bits of This and That),* who was herself an avid author and essayist. As was true elsewhere, editors employed public subscription campaigns to generate a reader base and to inscribe a public onto their enterprises. Some of these campaigns, such as Novikov's solicitation for his pietistic journal *Morning Light* (1777–1780), were quite successful, generating hundreds of subscribers (who thereby subsidized Novikov's new charity schools) from towns throughout the empire and from social groups, such as clergy and merchants, well beyond the omnipresent cosmopolitan audience. Most journals, however, attracted several dozen to about a hundred subscribers, almost 90 percent of whom derived from the hereditary nobility.

MODES OF SOCIABILITY

The intimate and largely male world that produced Russia's lay literati led easily into a proliferation of small societies, translation groups, student seminars, private lending libraries, reading circles, and eventually salons, at which women often were in attendance. By far the most popular sites of sociability, though, were Masonic lodges, which in Russia were quintessentially masculine in outlook and membership. During the Catherinian period as many as three thousand Russian subjects belonged to dozens of lodges, most of which combined a vaguely Neostoic sense of public improvement with the conviviality of brotherhood. Some scholars have seen the lodges as the beginnings of a Russian public sphere, while others have emphasized their secrecy, exclusivity, and sense of hierarchy. But there is no doubt that the lodges became centers of sociability that encouraged the fusion of literary activity and an increasingly ritualized politesse, which reached its apotheosis during the era of Aleksandr Pushkin in the 1830s. Although they were typically not oppositional, their combination of fraternity, secrecy, and commitment to moral improvement evoked periodic suspicion from officialdom, leading to periodic censure and closures in the latter fifteen years of the eighteenth century and again during the early 1820s.

See also **Alexis I (Russia); Avvakum Petrovich; Catherine II (Russia); Enlightenment; Journals, Literary; Novikov, Nikolai Ivanovich; Old Believers; Orthodoxy, Russian; Peter I (Russia); Printing and Publishing; Sofiia Alekseevna.**

BIBLIOGRAPHY

Primary Sources

Avvakum Petrovich, Protopope. *The Life of Archpriest Avvakum by Himself.* Translated by Jane Harrison and Hope Mirrlees. London, 1924.

Segel, Harold B., ed. and trans. *The Literature of Eighteenth-Century Russia: An Anthology of Russian Literary Materials of the Age of Classicism and the Enlightenment from the Reign of Peter the Great, 1689–1725, to the Reign of Alexander I, 1801–1825.* 2 vols. New York, 1967.

Secondary Sources

Levitt, Marcus C., ed. *Early Modern Russian Writers, Late Seventeenth and Eighteenth Centuries.* Vol. 150 of *A Dictionary of Literary Biography.* Detroit, 1995.

Newlin, Thomas. *The Voice in the Garden: Andrei Bolotov and the Anxieties of Russian Pastoral, 1738–1833.* Evanston, Ill., 2001.

Raeff, Marc. *Origins of the Russian Intelligentsia: The Eighteenth-Century Nobility.* New York, 1966.

Reyfman, Irina. *Vasilii Trediakovsky: The Fool of the New Russian Literature.* Stanford, 1990.

Rogger, Hans. *National Consciousness in Eighteenth-Century Russia.* Cambridge, Mass., 1960.

Schönle, Andreas. *Authenticity and Fiction in the Russian Literary Journey, 1790–1840.* Cambridge, Mass., 2000.

GARY MARKER

RUSSIAN ORTHODOXY. *See* Orthodoxy, Russian.

RUSSO-OTTOMAN WARS (1710–1711; 1736–1739; 1768–1774; 1787–1792).

The first Russo-Ottoman War of the eighteenth century occurred during the expansion era of Peter I, also known as Peter the Great (ruled 1682–1725), who stopped paying tribute to the Khan of the Crimea, an Ottoman vassal, when he became tsar in 1683. He staged attacks on the Perekop Isthmus in the 1680s and Azov in 1695 because the Russians viewed the Crimea as a haven for Tatars who continually raided Russian areas to seize captives, property, and livestock. In 1696, Peter mounted the first successful attack on Azov, using the new flotilla he had built. In a 1700 Russian-Ottoman peace treaty, Russia was permitted to keep Azov and had the cancellation of its tribute payment to the Crimean khans formally recognized.

RUSSO-OTTOMAN WAR OF 1710–1711

Sultan Ahmet III (ruled 1703–1730) initially looked favorably on the Russians because one of his grand viziers, Chorlulu Ali Pasha, cultivated good relations with them to prevent Ottoman entanglement in European politics. Russia's overwhelming victory against the Swedes at Poltava in 1709 has been attributed to the fact that Ali Pasha kept Crimean troops from intervening against Russia.

Ali Pasha was soon dismissed, though, when the mood of religious officials in Constantinople was swayed by the anti-Russian sentiment of the Crimeans. Also, the Swedish King Charles XII (ruled 1697–1718) had fled to the Ottomans from his failed encounter with Peter I and worked to stir up anti-Russian sentiments even more. When it appeared that after their Poltava triumph the Russians were getting ready to attack the Crimea, the Ottomans preemptively declared war on them. A Russian army led in person by Peter and his wife, Catherine I, invaded Moldavia for the first time in centuries, attempting to secure it before Ottoman forces could arrive.

However, the Russians ran into severe food shortages there, and a large Ottoman army proved to be close by. When the Russians were suddenly surrounded at a place on the Pruth tributary of the Danube on 21 July 1711 by regular Ottoman forces on one side and Tatars on the other, they had to surrender to avoid annihilation. Peter agreed to give back Azov, demolish his fortresses in its vicinity, release Ottoman prisoners, and allow Charles XII safe passage to Sweden. This swift Russian agreement to favorable terms for a time convinced the Ottomans that the Russians were not a serious threat. The final peace treaty (1713) pushed the Russians back as far north as the Orel River and required Peter to evacuate Poland within two months. Its terms would constantly be challenged over the next few years as Peter continued to modernize and expand his nation, which aroused Ottoman suspicions of Russian intentions.

Notwithstanding these tensions, both took advantage of the turmoil produced by the 1722 Afghan conquest of Iran to occupy Iranian territory in Azerbaijan and the Caucasus. The Russians and the Ottomans signed an agreement in 1724 that recognized each other's recent acquisitions in Iran. The agreement called for the restoration of the Shi'ite Safavids instead of the Sunni Afghans as the rulers of Iran—a curious stance for the Ottomans, quintessential defenders of Sunni Islam against Shi'ism. This agreement, too, proved fleeting when a new Iranian monarch, Nadir Shah (ruled 1736–1747), drove both the Russians and the Ottomans out of their occupied territories.

RUSSO-OTTOMAN WAR OF 1736–1739

The next Russo-Ottoman conflict broke out in 1736, when Russia determined to put a stop to Crimean Tatar attacks on its territories and finally to establish a presence on the Black Sea. After Russia had resolved its then outstanding conflicts with other European nations, the tsar denounced Ottoman negligence of the Treaty of Pruth as a pretext for war. Encouraged by the French, the Ottomans declared war on both Russia and Austria in May 1736 to protest the placement of a pro-Russian candidate on the Polish throne.

The first result was that the Russians, who were better mobilized, invaded the Crimea and took Azov within three months. However, they soon had to withdraw because of poor logistics. Russia then shifted focus to Moldavia and Walachia when its ally Austria captured Niš in 1737. Soon, though, the Austrians were pushed back so decisively that they were forced to sign a treaty with the Ottomans in 1739 at Belgrade, giving up most of the territory they had been assigned at Passarowitz in 1718.

As this agreement was being signed, the Russians were in the midst of trying to incite a Balkan Christian revolt against the Ottomans, had advanced deep into Moldavia, and were preparing to conquer Walachia, but news of the treaty ended these plans. With Austrian assistance gone, the Russians also signed an agreement with the Ottomans and relinquished Azov again.

RUSSO-OTTOMAN WAR OF 1768–1774

In 1768, when Catherine II, also known as Catherine the Great (ruled 1762–1796), revived Peter's imperialist projects and began interfering in Polish affairs again, the sultan declared war on Russia. Because internal Crimean politics and severe logistical difficulties had greatly weakened the Ottoman military, the Russians advanced swiftly into Moldavia and Walachia. They decimated a huge Ottoman army at Kartal in 1770. The Russians also finally took Crimea and came to dominate naval warfare in the Black Sea and even in the Aegean. In this conflict, Austria actually restrained Russia because it worried about excessive Russian influence in Poland.

Following a significant number of Russian victories, the 1774 Treaty of Kuchuk Kainarji allowed the Ottoman sultan to remain the religious leader, or caliph, of the Crimean Muslims, who were declared politically autonomous. Russia then took much of the northern Black Sea coast and received a large war indemnity from the Ottomans. A Russian cathedral was built in Constantinople, which was later construed to mean that the tsar was the protector of all Ottoman Orthodox Christians.

RUSSO-OTTOMAN WAR OF 1787–1792

In 1787, Catherine developed a scheme to expel the Ottomans from Europe and divide their European territories between Russia and Austria. The Otto-

man reaction was to wage war to regain the Crimea. The war reached a critical stage in 1789 when the Austrians conquered Belgrade and the Russians took Walachia. Just as the two were set to advance on Constantinople, other European powers persuaded them to end the war in order to help contain the tide of revolution sweeping across Europe from France. The Russians finally signed the 1792 Treaty of Jassy, by which they extended their control of the Black Sea coast and declared that henceforth Russia was the sovereign of the Crimea. In effect, the Black Sea, too, now passed into Russian hands.

See also **Austro-Ottoman Wars; Catherine II (Russia); Charles XII (Sweden); Ottoman Empire; Peter I (Russia); Russia.**

BIBLIOGRAPHY

Fisher, Alan. *The Crimean Tatars.* Stanford, 1978.

Goffman, Daniel. *The Ottoman Empire and Early Modern Europe.* Cambridge, U.K., and New York, 2002.

Kurat, A. N., and Bromley, J. S. "The Retreat of the Turks, 1683–1730." In *A History of the Ottoman Empire to 1730,* edited by M. A. Cook, pp. 178–219. Cambridge, U.K., and New York, 1976.

Shaw, Stanford J. *History of the Ottoman Empire and Modern Turkey.* Cambridge, U.K., and New York, 1976.

ERNEST TUCKER

RUSSO-POLISH WARS.

From the 1480s to 1667 Muscovy fought a series of devastating wars along its western frontier, first with the Grand Duchy of Lithuania and then with the Polish-Lithuanian Commonwealth. Muscovy's wars with Lithuania had four principal causes: disputed claims over the right to collect tribute and taxes in border districts and competition for the fealty of influential Orthodox princes; the question of ecclesiastic jurisdiction over Lithuania's large Orthodox population; Muscovy's gradual absorption of the Republic of Novgorod; and involvement in the struggle between the Crimean Khanate and the Golden Horde over the Pontic Steppe.

The 1480s saw a series of border clashes between Lithuania and Muscovy, particularly along the Novgorod-Pskov front. The death of the Polish king and Lithuanian grand duke Casimir finally gave Muscovite Grand Prince Ivan III the opportunity to launch a major invasion of Lithuania (1492–1494). Casimir's successor was forced to renounce his claims to Novgorod, Pskov, and Tver' and to cement the peace by taking Ivan's daughter Elena in marriage. But the peace did not last. In the Second Muscovite-Lithuanian War (1500–1503) Muscovite armies seized about a third of Lithuania—most of the former principalities of Chernigov (Chernihiv) and Novgorod-Seversk and about half of the Smolensk region. One crucial objective eluded Ivan III, however: the capture of the Lithuanian fortress of Smolensk, which commanded the roads and waterways to Moscow, Kiev, and Riga. Grand Prince Vasilii III therefore resumed the struggle for mastery of Smolensk in a Third Muscovite-Lithuanian war (1512–1522). Smolensk fell to Muscovite forces in 1514, but the war wound down in stalemate.

The Muscovites invaded Lithuania again in the second phase (1563–1571) of Tsar Ivan IV's Livonian War. Ivan's objective was to seize control of the entire course of the Western Dvina in order to blockade Riga into submission, but he also hoped to force King Sigismund II Augustus of Poland to cede him the rest of Livonia in exchange for his withdrawal from Lithuania. The Muscovite invasion instead had the effect of finally pushing the Lithuanian nobility into accepting Sigismund's proposal for the union of Lithuania and Poland in a Commonwealth (1569). Sigismund's successor Stephen Báthory drove the Muscovites from Livonia and Lithuania (1579–1580) and invaded northwestern Muscovy, forcing Ivan to cede Livonia to the Commonwealth and Sweden in exchange for an armistice (1582, 1583).

Polish-Lithuanian intervention in Russia's Time of Troubles initially took the form of private adventurism by magnates and border governors who perceived in the political upheaval an opportunity to recover some of the borderlands lost in 1503 and 1522. They abetted the two False Dmitriis (1603–1606, 1607–1610). After the defeat of the second, his Muscovite supporters and some powerful boyars decided to overthrow Tsar Vasilii Shuiskii and place King Sigismund III's son Władysław on the Russian throne. Shuiskii's overthrow in July 1610 permitted Polish forces to enter Moscow, but the resulting Polish military dictatorship provoked several Muscovite provincial governors and gentry leaders to

join with Cossack elements in a national liberation army, which defeated the Poles in October 1612. Three months later Michael Fedorovich Romanov was proclaimed tsar. Eventually the Treaty of Deulino (1618) established an armistice in exchange for the return of Smolensk, Chernigov (Chernihiv), and Seversk to the Commonwealth.

Michael's government, intent on recovering these territories, invaded eastern Lithuania in 1632 with an army of 33,000 men. This war (1632–1634) marked the largest experiment to date with Russian troops in reorganized Western-style "new formation regiments" trained and officered by Swedish, Dutch, and English mercenary officers. Some twenty towns fell to the Russian army, but their long siege of Smolensk failed and their commanders were forced to sue for armistice in exchange for safe evacuation.

From the mid-1630s Ukrainian churchmen and Cossack leaders had pleaded for Russian support for their rebellion against the Commonwealth. Moscow held back until 1654, when Bohdan Khmelnytsky agreed to place the Zaporozhian Host and the territories it held—Kiev and all Ukraine east of the Dnieper—under the tsar's protection. But the greater inducement to military intervention was the opportunity to recover Smolensk. The Treaty of Andrusovo, ending the Thirteen Years War (1654–1667), partitioned Ukraine along the Dnieper and restored the Smolensk region to Russia. This was the last great war fought between Russia and the Commonwealth, in large part because of the rising danger to both from the Ottoman Empire; the two signed an "eternal peace" in 1686.

See also **Cossacks; False Dmitrii, First; Ivan III (Muscovy); Ivan IV, the "the Terrible" (Russia); Khmelnytsky, Bohdan; Khmelnytsky Uprising; Lithuania, Grand Duchy of, to 1569; Livonian War (1558–1583); Lublin, Union of (1569); Michael Romanov (Russia); Poland to 1569; Poland-Lithuania, Commonwealth of, 1569–1795; Russia; Sigismund II Augustus (Poland, Lithuania); Stephen Báthory (Poland); Time of Troubles (Russia); Ukraine; Vasilii III (Muscovy).**

BIBLIOGRAPHY

Fennell, John Lister Illingworth. *Ivan the Great of Moscow.* London, 1961.

Ignatev, A. V., ed. *Istoriia vneshnei politiki Rossii, konets XV–XVII vek: Ot sverzheniia ordynskogo iga do Severnoi voiny.* Moscow, 1999.

Platonov, S. F. *The Time of Troubles: A Historical Study of the Internal Crises and Social Struggle in Sixteenth- and Seventeenth-Century Muscovy.* Translated by John T. Alexander. Lawrence, Kans., 1976.

BRIAN DAVIES

RUYSCH, RACHEL (1664–1750), Dutch painter. One of the most successful women artists of early modernity, Ruysch was born in The Hague. While growing up, she assisted her father, Frederik Ruysch, a professor of anatomy and botany, by recording the appearances of the exotic plants he studied. The resulting works may have encouraged her father, who was also an amateur painter and collector, to apprentice his fifteen-year-old daughter to the Amsterdam still life painter Willem van Aelst (1627–c. 1683). While it was uncommon for a girl to train for a profession outside the home, painting still lifes posed fewer obstacles than other genres because, for example, she was spared drawing from nude models—an activity deemed inappropriate for women until well into the twentieth century.

In her earliest works, Ruysch closely followed the dramatically lit woodland scenes of the Dutch painters of the previous generation, Otto Marseus van Schrieck and Abraham Mignon (1640–1679). In paintings like *Arrangement of Flowers by a Tree Trunk* from the 1680s (Glasgow Art Gallery and Museum), Ruysch depicted forestal vignettes complete with small-scale creatures. Characteristically, Ruysch repeats Schriek's motif of the lizard with a butterfly perched in its open mouth, but minimizes the menacing import of such a creature by reducing its scale and by relegating it to the fringe of the composition. Mignon's influence is more noticeable in *Floral Still Life* from 1686 (Memorial Art Gallery, University of Rochester), which replicates the right half of a Mignon painting in Vaduz Castle. Ruysch adopted Mignon's practice of placing cultivated plants in natural settings, but she omitted Mignon's signature goldfinches and other latent Christian symbols. By choosing to stress decorative effects over iconographic details in both the Glas-

Rachel Ruysch. *Bouquet of Flowers*, 1706. ©ALI MEYER/ CORBIS

gow and Rochester paintings, Ruysch limits symbolic interpretations of her paintings.

In 1693 Ruysch married Mignon's adopted son, the portrait painter Juriaen Pool. Despite the demands of raising ten children, Ruysch remained active as a painter, becoming a member of the Confrerie Pictura in 1701 and later joining the painter's guild in The Hague in 1709. Shortly thereafter, Ruysch and Pool relocated to Düsseldorf, where they became court painters to the elector palatine John William.

In her mature works Ruysch increased the decorative and theatrical aspects of her compositions, presumably to suit her patron's sense of refinement. While her early endeavors represented floral groupings as they occurred in nature, she later experimented with juxtapositions of cultivated and wild plants in vased bouquets. Ruysch also explored fruit assemblages as pendants to her floral pieces. One sees all of these elements combined in *Fruit and Flowers in a Forest* from 1714 in Augsburg. This piece, which originally hung in the elector's bedroom, shows Ruysch's skill in rendering the vibrant flowers' fragility to contrast with the lusciously firm fruits strung across the forest floor, a motif that recalls her earlier woodland vignettes. Ruysch deliberately composed the scene, imposing her own order upon the natural world with the floral arrangement occupying the upper register across the stone ledge, the fruit closer to the Earth, and the requisite insects and reptiles framing the scene from the periphery. In the Augsburg painting, as in her entire oeuvre, Ruysch retained the dark, moody lighting of her early manner, yet heightened the vibrancy of individual elements. For example, while at the elector's court, she began to employ the newly discovered pigment Prussian blue, an inexpensive means of summoning luminous blues. Similarly, Ruysch utilized a smooth touch to craft crystal-clear surfaces. When Ruysch and Pool returned to Amsterdam in 1716, Ruysch brought her aristocratically fostered aesthetic with her and continued to paint elegant still lifes such as *Still Life with Flowers on a Marble Table Top*, now in the Rijksmuseum, Amsterdam. Here, Ruysch replicated the supple textures of the petals and crafted a subtle play of pinks against the dark backdrop and cobalt vase, as she had done in Düsseldorf, but restricted the scope to a moderately sized bouquet. Ruysch painted works of this type for gentrified Dutch burghers until she was well into her eighties.

Ruysch's work found a receptive audience and contemporary writers praised her extensively. Such esteem was admirable for any painter, but especially so for a woman. As Johan van Gool wrote in *De nieuwe schouburg der Nederlandtsche kunstschilders en schilderessen* in 1750, her artfulness "was all the more astonishing and to be praised in women, who by nature are destined to other occupations"(vol. 2, p. 541). Despite such gendered trepidations, Ruysch earned international renown for her expertly wrought and pleasingly arranged creations.

See also **Netherlands, Art in the; Women and Art.**

BIBLIOGRAPHY

Berardi, Marianne. *Science into Art: Rachel Ruysch's Early Development as a Still-life Painter*. Ph.D. diss., University of Pittsburgh, 1998.

Gool, Johan van. *De nieuwe schouburg der Nederlandtsche kunstschilders en schilderessen*. 2 vols. The Hague, 1750. Reprinted Soest, 1971.

Harris, Ann Sutherland, and Linda Nochlin. *Women Artists 1550–1950*. New York, 1984.

Still-Life Paintings from the Netherlands 1550–1720. Edited by Alan Chong and Wouter Kloek. Amsterdam and Cleveland, 1999.

CHRISTOPHER D. M. ATKINS

SACHS, HANS. *See* **Drama: German; German Literature and Language.**

SACRAMENTS. *See* **Ritual, Religious.**

SADE, DONATIEN-ALPHONSE-FRANÇOIS DE (1740–1814), French writer. Belonging to one of France's most ancient noble families, the marquis de Sade attended Paris's rigorous Louis-le-Grand lycée as a youth and then a light cavalry academy that would steer him toward a military career. At the age of sixteen he was commissioned as a lieutenant and standard bearer in the Carabiniers, a prestigious military unit of armed officers, and he took part in the war against Prussia. By early 1759, when he was eighteen years old, Sade was nominated captain in the Burgundy cavalry. Early in his military career Sade had earned a reputation with his peers as a gambler and a ladies' man, and the young officer often lamented both his lack of motivation to do the things required to succeed and the absence of close, sincere friends in his life. When the Seven Years' War ended in 1763, Sade's family began marriage negotiations with the Montreuil family, petty nobility of the robe who were nevertheless extremely wealthy. Sade resisted his family's wishes that he marry, but when the woman with whom he was in love scorned him, Sade returned to Paris from Provence four days before his

wedding in May 1763 and married Renée-Pélagie de Montreuil, whom he did not meet until the day before the wedding.

Five months later, the marquis was imprisoned in the Vincennes dungeon for licentiousness and blasphemy. This first of his many incarcerations resulted from the violence he meted out to the young Jeanne Testard, whom he had paid to spend the night with him in small rented quarters in Paris which, like a number of aristocrats, the marquis kept for occasional trysts. During his encounter with Testard, the marquis first asked the young woman whether she believed in God, and then proceeded to desecrate a number of crucifixes and other religious objects. He asked the young woman to beat him with a red-hot whip and pressed her to choose the whip with which he would flagellate her. Testard made a deposition to the commissioner of police, Sade was arrested, and taken to Vincennes, an ancient fortress on the southeast edge of Paris. Sade remained there for less than a month, but would return to Vincennes or to the Bastille on numerous other occasions for similar acts of blasphemy and sexual violence. (He spent a total of about thirty years, including the years from 1801 to the end of his life, in prison.) Sade wrote most of the works for which he is best known while incarcerated. His first significant piece is the *Dialog between a Priest and a Dying Man,* probably composed in 1782 while he was imprisoned in Vincennes. The dialogue treats some standard eighteenth-century views on religion, philosophy, materialism, and reason, and the dying man concludes that it is the latter faculty,

Donatien-Alphonse-François de Sade. Engraving
depicts a demonic young de Sade. ©CORBIS

more than faith in God, that leads to human happiness. Shortly after Sade finished the short philosophical piece, authorities confiscated all the prisoner's books because they appeared to give him inappropriate ideas. In the remaining years of the decade Sade wrote *The 120 Days of Sodom, The Misfortunes of Virtue,* and *Aline and Valcour,* a semi-autobiographical novel. Other major works consist of a number of short stories and plays.

The marquis de Sade's novels combine a philosophical interest in materialism, an intense examination of the extent and limits of human reason, and an extremely vivid, often overwhelming, depiction of graphic sexual violence. All of the major novels revolve around the planning, narration, and carrying out of elaborate, often implausible acts of torture and mutilation, many of which involve religious motifs. Most often, a sophistic diatribe

concerning, among other things, the absurdity of virtue in a class-based society accompanies the consummation of the violent acts. The libertines who inflict the violence in Sade's novels engage in a nonstop philosophical conundrum in which they attempt to locate the limits of language, power, bodily existence, and domination. Repeatedly attempting to physically and subjectively annihilate their victims, they rely all the more on those whom they would destroy for their own identities in their attempts to do, say, and be all. The dialectic Sade constructs throughout the better part of his fiction interrogates the possibility of unmediated access to such ostensibly natural phenomena as the body, pleasure, pain, and intersubjective violence.

Virtually all of Sade's works have been reviled and censored since their very first appearances, and even as late as 1956 the publishing firm Pauvert was fined for printing the complete works. Nevertheless, Sade has had considerable influence in artistic and philosophical circles. André Breton (1896–1966) and the surrealists, in particular, found in his work liberating ideas for thinking about reason and sexuality.

See also **Enlightenment; French Literature and Language; Pornography.**

BIBLIOGRAPHY

Primary Sources

Sade, marquis de. *The Complete Justine: Philosophy in the Bedroom and Other Writings.* Compiled and translated by Richard Seaver and Austryn Wainhouse. New York, 1965.

———. *The Crimes of Love.* Translated and edited by Margaret Crosland. London, 1996.

———. *Dialogue entre un prêtre et un moribond.* Paris, 1926.

———. *The 120 Days of Sodom and Other Writings.* Translated and edited by Austryn Wainhouse and Richard Seaver. New York, 1987.

Secondary Sources

Frappier-Mazur, Lucienne. *Writing the Orgy: Power and Parody in Sade.* Translated by Gillian C. Gill. Philadelphia, 1996.

Lély, Gilbert. *The Marquis de Sade: A Biography.* Translated by Alec Brown. New York, 1970.

Lever, Maurice. *Sade: A Biography.* Translated by Arthur Goldhammer. New York, 1993.

THOMAS DIPIERO

ST. BARTHOLOMEW'S DAY MAS-SACRE.

Early on the morning of 24 August 1572 (St. Bartholomew's Day by the Catholic Church calendar), French Catholic troops began to slaughter unarmed Protestants who had gathered in Paris for a royal wedding. The wave of popular violence that followed resulted in the death of some two thousand persons in Paris and another three thousand in other French cities. Known collectively as the St. Bartholomew's Day Massacre, these events constitute the most infamous episode in the French Wars of Religion and a turning point in these wars. Scholars continue to debate the questions of who authorized the killings and why, who took part in them, and what they tell us about the nature of religious intolerance.

Although some contemporaries believed the massacre to be the product of a conspiracy plotted during Queen Mother Catherine de Médicis's 1565 meeting with Spanish emissaries at Bayonne, most scholars now regard it as a more immediate response to deteriorating relations between Huguenots and

the crown in the aftermath of the Peace of Saint-Germain, which ended the third religious war in August 1570. Popular opposition to the measures of toleration accorded the Protestants made the peace difficult to enforce, and yet Protestant leader Admiral Gaspard de Coligny continued to press for full enforcement. He further irritated Catherine by attempting to convince her son, the young King Charles IX, to send troops to aid Dutch Protestants in their revolt against Spain. Some historians believe that Catherine, jealous of Coligny's growing influence over Charles IX, tried to have the admiral assassinated on 22 August 1572. Others have blamed members of the Ultra-Catholic Guise family for the attempt, which wounded but did not kill Coligny. This was the view of the Huguenot leaders, who had assembled in Paris to celebrate the wedding of Henry of Bourbon, king of Navarre, to the king's sister, Marguerite of Valois. Their demand for revenge appears to have sparked both a popular outcry and a defensive reaction on the part of the king and queen mother, who feared a Protestant coup.

St. Bartholomew's Day Massacre. Painting by eyewitness François Dubois. THE ART ARCHIVE/MUSÉE DES BEAUX ARTS LAUSANNE/DAGLI ORTI

A secret meeting in the Louvre on the night on 23 August resulted in the order to eliminate the Huguenot leadership. We do not know how many persons were to be killed or how willingly the king consented to the plot, but it is clear that in the aftermath of the order the killings took on a life of their own. The duke of Guise's men first dispatched the admiral and then hunted down other Huguenot leaders. Overhearing Guise remind his troops that they killed at the king's command, militiamen posted about the city to ensure its defense began to take part in the violence. Private citizens joined in, and the murders spread to encompass ordinary men, women, and children. Looting was common, and some of the victims' corpses were mutilated or subjected to crude parodies of judicial and religious rites. Some Protestants saved their lives by recanting their faith; others were hidden by charitable friends until they could secretly flee. It took more than a week to recover order in Paris, by which time the killing had spread to other French cities.

In some towns the killing began as soon as word arrived of the massacre in Paris. In other cases, a precarious peace was maintained until local events touched of a wave of murders several weeks later. At least twelve cities, including the provincial capitals of Lyon, Rouen, Bordeaux, and Toulouse, experienced significant levels of violence. All were predominantly Catholic cities that had once harbored sizeable Huguenot minorities, and all witnessed the same popular participation and ritualistic murders as Paris. In each, moreover, participants appear to have shared a common belief that the king had authorized the killing.

While surviving Protestant leaders fled to the west and launched a fourth religious war, Huguenot propagandists publicized the murders in order to gain international support for their cause. Articulating new theories of political resistance, François Hotman, Théodore de Bèze, and other Huguenot writers defended the right of subordinate magistrates to withdraw obedience from a tyrannical monarch who would permit such atrocities against his subjects. Shock and horror at the extent of the killing prompted some moderate Catholics to oppose the renewal of war and advocate further compromises in order to secure a lasting peace. Although this policy ultimately triumphed with the Edict of Nantes in 1598, the immediate result of the moderates' defection was rather to encourage Ultra-Catholics to demand that the king act more decisively to eliminate the Protestant heresy. Saint Bartholomew's Day thus initiated the last, radical phase of the religious wars, at the same time that it seriously traumatized the Huguenot faithful and permanently undermined the Protestant movement in France.

See also **Bèze, Théodore de; Coligny Family; Guise Family; Henry III (France); Henry IV (France); Huguenots; Nantes, Edict of; Resistance, Theory of; Wars of Religion, French.**

BIBLIOGRAPHY

Benedict, Philip. "The Saint Bartholomew's Massacres in the Provinces." *Historical Journal* 21 (1978): 205–225. The best study of the provincial massacres.

Diefendorf, Barbara B. *Beneath the Cross: Catholics and Huguenots in Sixteenth-Century Paris.* Oxford and New York, 1991. Focuses on the circumstances that led up to the massacre in Paris.

Holt, Mack P. *The French Wars of Religion, 1562–1629.* Cambridge, U.K., and New York, 1995. Sets the massacre into the broader context of the religious wars.

Kingdon, Robert M. *Myths about the St. Bartholomew's Day Massacres, 1572–1576.* Cambridge, Mass., 1988. How the massacres were used for propaganda purposes.

BARBARA B. DIEFENDORF

ST. PETERSBURG. Founded in 1703 and by 1712 already the capital of Russia, St. Petersburg existed in the mind of Peter the Great (ruled 1682–1725) and on the planning boards of his architects almost before construction began—"the most abstract and intentional [or, 'premeditated'] city in the whole world," in the words of Dostoevsky (*Notes from Underground,* 1864). In contrast to Moscow, which grew organically over the centuries in concentric circles, St. Petersburg was planned from scratch (like Washington, D.C.) by west European architects who attempted to impose geometric street patterns on the swampy delta of the Neva River. Echoes of the city's planned origins are preserved in the not-so-romantic names of several north/south streets on Vasilii Island: Second/Third Line Street, Fourth/Fifth Line Street, and so forth (each of these streets was originally intended to be a canal, with a numbered line of houses on each side of the canal).

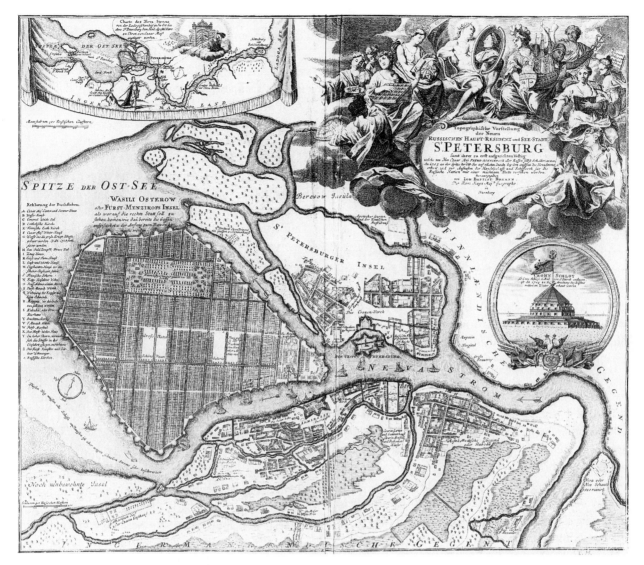

St. Petersburg. Johann Baptist Homann's map appeared in 1718, not long after the city was founded by Peter the Great in 1703. It reflects the plan developed by French architect Jean-Baptiste Leblond who proposed making Vasileyev Island (on the left) the city center with a formal pattern of streets and canals. Instead only the right tip of the island was developed in the eighteenth century, and the whole map shows a St. Petersburg largely imagined, not as it really existed at this time. MAP COLLECTION, STERLING MEMORIAL LIBRARY, YALE UNIVERSITY

LOCATION

St. Petersburg is located far to the north, at about 60 degrees latitude, above the middle of Hudson's Bay in Canada and slightly above that of Juneau, Alaska. It is situated on the Gulf of Finland in the Baltic Sea in the delta of the Neva River, which flows from Lake Ladoga forty-six miles to the east. Though short, the Neva carries a large volume of water (sixth largest in Europe) and its currents are strong. Winding through St. Petersburg, the Neva divides at the tip (*strelka,* or 'arrow point') of Vasilii Island, the Large Neva to the south, the Small Neva

to the right. Some one hundred islands dot the delta. The largest, Vasilii Island, was originally envisioned as the future city center, but security and supply considerations prompted a shift to the left bank. The left bank itself is not "mainland": several rivulets, notably the Moika and the Fontanka, flowed through the area and were preserved as canals in the city center. Because the flat territory of the city is close to the level of the Gulf of Finland (only six feet above it at the western end of Vasilii Island), and because storms and tides sometimes combine to back up water in the entire delta, low-lying areas of the city periodically flood. In 1703, as Peter the Great was starting to build the city's fortress (a not unwise choice, given that the area belonged to Sweden at the time), a flood carried off construction materials. In 1777 a major flood destroyed buildings and some fifty fountains in the Summer Gardens. The gardens were restored, but not the fountains; the adjacent Fontanka River/Canal was named for the fountains. Snow lies on the ground some five months a year, and the river and nearby gulf typically freeze over for two to four months each year. Nevertheless, prevailing winds from the west over the Baltic have a slight moderating effect on the climate. There is no good building stone in the area. In the early eighteenth century, a stone levy was placed on carts and boats entering the city, each one required to bring in stone for building foundations. As in Venice, many buildings in eighteenth-century St. Petersburg were set on wooden pilings driven into the mud.

PETER THE GREAT'S MOTIVES

Why did Peter persist in building the city in this inhospitable location? He had first tried to gain access to the Black Sea in the south, but he failed militarily to hold a position there. In any case, the Neva and the Gulf of Finland promised more direct contact with the countries of northern Europe with which he wanted to communicate and trade. From his youthful experiences among foreigners in Moscow and his two trips to western Europe, Peter was enamored with the accomplishments of west Europeans in science, industry, military and naval technology and training, and political administration. Sea power and maritime commerce captured his attention, and he determined to gain access to the sea for Russia by establishing a port city like Amsterdam. Moscow, with its narrow winding streets of logs or mud, its buildings of wood that fueled the city's frequent fires, its traditional culture, was for Peter—to use a modern term—backward and underdeveloped. "Sanktpiterburkh"—as he named the city in a Germano-Dutch spelling—was his initial experiment in transforming Russia into a sea power and giving his new Russian Empire an impressive European capital. In the twenty-one-year-long Great Northern War (1700–1721), Peter defeated Sweden's army and naval forces and formally annexed territory on the Baltic.

ST. PETERSBURG IN 1725

The rapidity with which St. Petersburg was created is remarkable. As of 1703, when the city was founded, there was one Swedish fortress in the immediate area and a few modest fishing villages. By 1725, when Peter died, St. Petersburg had some forty thousand residents and over six thousand buildings. James Cracraft, in his authoritative study *The Petrine Revolution in Russian Architecture,* lists the reasons why the city was built up so quickly: the government commanded the resources of the entire nation to be devoted to the cause; conscripted and convict labor was used; foreign architects and artisans were imported; Russian students were trained in architecture and building in St. Petersburg and abroad; training and city planning were standardized and coordinated by newly established government offices; and factories were established for bricks and other building materials. The costs were high; thousands of laborers perished in the harsh conditions. While St. Petersburg acquired the epithet of "Venice of the north," it was also described as "built on bones."

ARCHITECTURE

For Peter, architectural style per se did not matter much, but he admired the sober practicality of north European restrained baroque, and he recognized that the Dutch use of brick as a construction material was appropriate for St. Petersburg. In any case, architecture was an integral part of the west European cultural package that he sought to implant in St. Petersburg (minus restraints on the ruler's authority). His chief architect, Domenico Trezzini, a Swiss-Italian, created most early structures: the Fortress of St. Petersburg (later called the Peter and Paul Fortress, after the name of its cathedral, which Trezzini also designed), the Summer Palace and Gardens, the Twelve Colleges government administrative building, the Alexander Nevsky Monastery, and others. Peter's daughter, Empress Elizabeth (ruled 1741–1762) and her favorite architect, Bartolomeo Francesco Rastrelli, added extravagant rococo concoctions (the Winter Palace, Smolnyi Convent, the Catherine Palace at Tsarskoe Selo). During Empress Catherine II the Great's reign (ruled 1762–1796), the city acquired numerous neoclassical ensembles designed by west Europeans, including the Hermitage Theater and State Bank by Quarenghi, the Marble Palace and

St. Petersburg. Engraving of the Winter Palace, built 1754–1762 as a royal residence for Elizabeth Petrovna, daughter of Peter the Great; it is now part of the Hermitage Museum. ©REPRODUCED BY PERMISSION OF THE STATE HERMITAGE MUSEUM, ST. PETERSBURG, RUSSIA/CORBIS

Sliding Hill Pavilion at Oranienbaum by Rinaldi, the Cameron Gallery at Tsarskoe Selo and Great Palace at Pavlovsk by Charles Cameron. In addition, Russian architects, trained in west European neoclassical principles, made contributions, notably I. E. Starov, who built the Tauride Palace and rebuilt the Trinity Cathedral in the Alexander Nevsky Monastery.

Catherine's most famous contribution to the city is the equestrian statue of Peter the Great, designed by the Frenchman Étienne-Maurice Falconet, later called the "Bronze Horseman," after Pushkin's poem (1833) of that name. St. Petersburg symbolizes Russia's turn to Western culture, and, as such, is a historic rival of Moscow, which symbolizes traditional Muscovite culture.

See also **Catherine II (Russia); Elizabeth (Russia); Moscow; Northern Wars; Peter I (Russia); Russia; Sweden.**

BIBLIOGRAPHY

Brumfield, William Craft. *A History of Russian Architecture.* Cambridge, U.K., 1993.

Cracraft, James E. *The Petrine Revolution in Russian Architecture.* Chicago, 1988.

Egorov, Iurii Alekseevich. *The Architectural Planning of St. Petersburg.* Translated by Eric Dluhosch. Athens, Ohio, 1969.

Hamilton, George Heard. *The Art and Architecture of Russia.* 3rd ed. London, 1983.

Shvidkovsky, Dmitri. *St. Petersburg: Architecture of the Tsars.* Translated from French by John Goodman. Photographs by Alexander Orloff. New York, 1996.

JACK KOLLMANN

SAINT-SIMON, LOUIS DE ROUVROY (1675–1755), duke and peer of France, whose memoirs depict courtly life and politics during the reign of Louis XIV and the regency. Saint-Simon was the offspring of a favorite of Louis XIII.

Having lost his father at the age of eighteen, he served in the army and tried to gain prominence at the court. Soon, however, disappointed by Louis XIV's perceived neglect of the nobility, he retired from the military and incurred the king's disfavor. Instead of a promising career, he thus embarked upon the path of a clandestine and critical observer of the court.

Although removed from the king's favor, Saint-Simon had powerful allies and informants: his beloved wife, Marie-Gabrielle de Lorges, duchess of Saint-Simon, who remained in Louis XIV's closest circles in spite of her husband's precarious position, and to whom he owed regular invitations to the much coveted royal secondary residence at Marly; Philippe II, the duke of Orléans, the king's nephew and future regent; a state chancellor; several ministers who formed with François Fénelon the circle of Louis, duke of Bourgogne, heir to the crown and its would-be reformer. Thus Saint-Simon gained close knowledge of state politics in which he even participated briefly during the regency. Living at the court from 1691 through Louis XIV's death in 1715 to the regent's in 1723, he saw, listened, and took secret notes at night, in a small dressing cabinet behind his Versailles apartment. He composed numerous genealogies, timely memos to influence decisions of etiquette and rank politics, and even a bitterly critical anonymous letter to Louis XIV that he had the courage to circulate during the monarch's lifetime, in spite of a recognizable personal style of writing.

After he retired from the court, Saint-Simon came upon a detailed journal kept by the well-known courtier Philippe de Courcillon (the marquis of Dangeau). Shocked by its boundless flatteries and "lies," he reread and annotated it between 1729 and 1739 and, at the age of sixty-four, set out to write his own journal, a truthful "history of his time." His monumental *Mémoires,* 2,754 manuscript pages narrating court intrigues and crown politics over thirty-two years (1691–1723), encompass over seven thousand characters depicted with inimitable insight and wit, and lament the chaos introduced into the kingdom by absolutism and predict its demise. The narrative was destined by its author to "remain under the safest locks" for at least fifty years after his lifetime. His wish was granted: a first, incomplete, version was published in 1788, and not until 1829–1830 did a first complete edition appear in French. By presenting a unique backstage view of Versailles, in spite of a certain partiality admitted by the author and due to his distinct noble ethos, his memoirs give an exact picture of daily life at court and of its factions and intrigues, and constitute an important source for court sociologists and historians. Testifying to Saint-Simon's unique vision and style, his memoirs have also inspired French novelists including Stendhal and Marcel Proust, and they remain a masterpiece of early modern French literature and of the memoir genre as a whole.

See also **Biography and Autobiography; Court and Courtiers; Louis XIV (France); Versailles.**

BIBLIOGRAPHY

Primary Sources

Saint-Simon, Louis de Rouvroy. *Les additions de Saint-Simon au journal de dangeau.* Edited by Yves Coirault. Paris, 1965.

———. *Ecrits inédits de Saint-Simon.* 8 vols. Paris, 1880–1893.

———. *Grimoires de Saint-Simon: Nouveaux inédits.* Edited by Yves Coirault. Paris, 1975.

———. *Hiérarchie et mutations: Écrits sur le kaléidoscope social.* Edited by Yves Coirault. Paris, 2002.

———. *Historical Memoirs of the duc de Saint-Simon: A Shortened Version.* Edited and translated by Lucy Norton. 3 vols. London, 1999–2000.

———. *Mémoires.* 8 vol. Edited by Yves Coirault. Paris, 1983.

———. *Papiers en marge des Mémoires.* Edited by François-Régis Bastide. Paris, 1954.

———. *Traités politiques et autres écrits.* Edited by Yves Coirault. Paris, 1996.

Secondary Sources

Auerbach, Erich. *Mimesis: The Representation of Reality in Western Literature.* Translated by Willard R. Trask. Princeton, 1968.

Coirault, Yves. *L'optique de Saint-Simon.* Paris, 1965.

De Ley, Herbert. *Saint-Simon Memorialist: "Un enchaînement si singulier . . ."* Urbana, Ill., 1975.

Elias, Norbert. *The Court Society.* Translated by Edmund Jephcott. Oxford, 1983.

Le Roy Ladurie, Emmanuel, with Jean-François Fitou. *Saint-Simon and the Court of Louis XIV.* Translated by Arthur Goldhammer. Chicago, 2001.

Stefanovska, Malina. *Saint-Simon, un historien dans les marges.* Paris, 1998.

MALINA STEFANOVSKA

SALAMANCA, SCHOOL OF. A group of sixteenth-century Spanish moral theologians, also sometimes called the Neoscholastics, centered at the universities of Salamanca and Alcalá de Henares. Largely members of the two most powerful religious orders, the Dominicans and the Jesuits, they were concerned with political rule, tyranny, morals, law, economics, and the justice of war and conquest. Their writings, though steeped in Aristotle, St. Augustine, and St. Thomas of Aquinas, engaged directly with the imperial, political, and economic challenges of the sixteenth century. The outstanding Neoscholastics were the Dominicans Francisco de Vitoria (1492–1546), Domingo de Soto (1495–1560), and Melchor Cano (1509–1560), followed a few decades later by the Jesuits Luis de Molina (1535–1600), Francisco Suárez (1548–1617), and Juan de Mariana (1535?–1624). Several of the movement's leading figures represented Spain at the Council of Trent.

The tension between the Gospel and the flow of silver and gold from America was important to the Dominicans, a mendicant order. Commerce seemed to be replacing land as the source of wealth, which some called ultimately impossible, and others called simply pernicious. The Dominicans believed economics was a human activity whose objective must be to satisfy needs without sacrificing morality. They were concerned not with how well the economy was running but with how fair it was, and some of their fiercest debates concerned price ceilings and the just price. Buying and selling, in short, were matters of justice and equality.

Vitoria, who taught in Paris, Valladolid, and Salamanca, is often considered to have established the foundations of international law, which later would be elaborated upon by Hugo Grotius (1583–1645). Vitoria's starting point was the conquest of America, a testing ground for *dominium.* In 1539, in lectures entitled *De Indis* and strongly influenced by Aristotle, Vitoria argued that the Indians were rational, and therefore the crown had no right of sovereignty or property rights over them. Vitoria further rejected the notion that Indians were what Aristotle called slaves by nature. A public debate on the matter with one of his contemporaries, Juan Ginés de Sepúlveda (Charles V's tutor and his generation's supreme authority on Aristotle), was held in Valladolid in 1550–1551. It was also attended by the Indians' great defender, Bartolomé de las Casas (1484–1566), who proclaimed the Indians' innocence and their eagerness to become Christians.

In the political realm, the Neoscholastics elaborated upon natural law theory, building upon Aquinas and Aristotle to construct a plausible and moral basis for human law. In particular, Soto, in his six-volume *De la justicia y del derecho* (1556), offered guidelines for ensuring that justice and the common good were the ultimate arbiters of rule. All the Salamanca thinkers believed a king was bound by the rule of law, and at one time or another considered such controversial issues as tyrannicide and popular representation.

The Jesuits were less bound than the Dominicans to the teachings of Aquinas, and the two orders sometimes clashed on theological issues, particularly about metaphysics, predestination, and will. Both Molina's work on grace (1588) and Suárez's *Disputationes metaphysicae* (1597) were highly influential throughout Europe.

See also **Grotius, Hugo; Las Casas, Bartolomé de; Sepúlveda, Juan Ginés de; Trent, Council of.**

BIBLIOGRAPHY

Fernández-Santamaría, J. A. *The State, War and Peace: Spanish Political Thought in the Renaissance.* Cambridge, U.K., 1977.

Grice-Hutchinson, Marjorie. *The School of Salamanca: Readings in Spanish Monetary Theory.* Oxford, 1952.

Hamilton, Bernice. *Political Thought in Sixteenth-Century Spain: A Study of the Political Ideas of Vitoria, De Soto, Suárez, and Molina.* Oxford, 1963.

Hanke, Louis. *Aristotle and the American Indians.* Bloomington, Ind., 1959.

Pagden, Anthony. *Spanish Imperialism and the Political Imagination.* New Haven, 1990.

RUTH MACKAY

SALONS. The salon was a venue for intellectual sociability that took form in the seventeenth century and flourished in the eighteenth but only acquired its name in the nineteenth, after it had been supplanted at the heart of the world of letters and ideas by more democratic, masculine, and politically oriented institutions. In the seventeenth century the gatherings later classified as salons were called *ruelles* (after the corridor beside the bed on which the hostess received her guests) or *réduits* (alcoves) or, as would be most common in the eighteenth century, were referred to simply by the day of the week on which they took place: Mademoiselle de Scudéry had her "Saturdays," Madame Geoffrin her "Mondays," and so on.

Those assemblies recognized in retrospect as "salons" differed from other forms of social and intellectual exchange in well-recognized ways: by gathering intellectuals and socially prominent men and women on a regular basis in a woman's home for conversational exchanges on issues of mutual interest. But the fact that this venue for intellectual sociability lacked a name during the period when its importance was most evident and its influence strongest suggests some of the ambiguities attached to this unofficial social form.

Which among the assemblies that aspired to offer both pleasure and instruction should be considered salons? At what point did an assembly veer so far toward gaiety in one direction or high-mindedness in the other as to blur the boundaries with parties at one extreme or professional meetings at the other? How widespread was the phenomenon? Relatively few of these assemblies managed enough longevity and appeal to be truly important, but how many other salons or would-be salons met briefly or in obscurity, and to what effect? A salon was easy to establish—there being no formal prerequisites to meet or permissions to acquire—yet difficult to pull off. What blend of ingredients—the intangibles of the hostess's personality and the participants' chemistry, the tangible patronage available to be dispensed there—made for success? Though it was by definition hosted by a woman in her private quarters, how central or marginal was the *salonnière* (another term of nineteenth-century invention) to its intellectual pursuits? As in any leisure entertainment, the hostess was understood to direct her guests' activities, yet the serious business of the evening turned, as did the meetings of academies and male coteries, on the attending men of letters who were her guests. It might even turn on the husband in the late eighteenth century, when several salons were led by a married couple (Condorcet, Helvétius, Suard), though the fact that the masculine construction *salonnier* was never coined implies the continuing identification of the venue with its female host.

Salons flourished in France, especially in Paris, but they could also be found in the French provinces and elsewhere in Europe, notably in Berlin. For antecedents one can point in the sixteenth century to intellectual coteries surrounding Marguerite de Navarre and other learned women at the French court as well as to occasional urban literary circles such as the one held in Poitiers by Madeleine and Catherine des Roches. But the first fully developed salon is generally held to be that founded by Catherine de Vivonne, marquise de Rambouillet, in the 1630s at her home, the Hôtel de Rambouillet, in Paris. In her *chambre bleue* she orchestrated light entertainments, poetry readings, serious discussions, even dramatic productions.

Later in the seventeenth century, influential venues that likewise centered their sociability on literary pursuits were established by such talented women as Mademoiselle de Scudéry, Madame de La Fayette, Mademoiselle de Montpensier, Madame de La Suze, Madame de Sablé, and Ninon de Lenclos. Writers including La Rochefoucauld, Paul Pellisson, Gilles Ménage, Charles Perrault, and Charles de Saint-Évremond offered up their own works in these salons, and amateurs among the *gens de bonne compagnie*, men and women alike, tried their hand at composing literary pieces, often as a collective activity. Several original genres emerged in the salon to shape the development of French literature generally: the word portrait that was so influential in creating a new language of emotions and character psychology, *précieuses* verses and allegories (such as Mademoiselle de Scudéry's *Carte de Tendre*) that enriched the French language with new concepts and purged it of old usages, neochivalric romances, and other brief fictional narratives that evolved into the modern novel.

The participation of women in these early salons reflected the vast expansion of the literary field effected by the new print capitalism. Women probably accounted for at least an equal proportion of the increase in readers and writers over the course of the century. As a cultural venue sharply divergent from the masculine world of humanist erudition, the salon seemed to promise that men and women would advance side by side as creators and interpreters of modern literature. Late in the century, however, as the literary field coalesced once again in a hierarchical and masculine structure, women were increasingly steered into minor genres (occasional poems, fairy tales) and into marginal roles as consumers rather than producers of culture, inspirations to creativity rather than the inspired.

The prominence of literary pursuits in the early salons has led some to see them, quite incorrectly, as apolitical and as distinguishable on those grounds from the overtly politically oriented salons of the eighteenth century. These early salons were deeply, though subtly, political in original ways. Intertwined with the new literary genres they pioneered, seventeenth-century salons incubated a discourse of innovative ideas—*honnêteté,* meritocracy, and feminism—that acknowledged and celebrated the distinctive kind of community they constituted and the transformations in social practice being effected by the dynamics of salon society. Both this discourse and those dynamics would have far-reaching consequences on social organization in the longer term. This tripartite discourse was political in the sense not of formal politics but of asserting claims about power relationships in the salons where they were articulated and, by extension, in the world of absolutist authority in which salons dwelt.

The ideal of *honnêteté,* 'politesse', prescribed a model of sociable behavior *(moeurs)* that was refined, orderly, moderated, lofty in spirit but (unlike family, state, and corporate society) nonhierarchical. Its quintessential discursive practice was reciprocal conversation among equals rather than disquisition or prescription by superiors. In the case of the *honnête homme* or the *honnête femme,* disciplined behavior emanated from inward character rather than being imposed by external constraint.

Within salons ruled by *honnêteté,* character and manners were said to count more than the criteria of social status operative in Old Regime corporate society. The person of whatever rank or lineage whose personal and intellectual qualities (his or her "merit") were pleasing in company was preferred to the person of even the loftiest birth but rough manners. This evocation of meritocracy expressed a reality of salon life. The women who hosted salons, as well as the men and women who attended them, might come from traditionally dominant noble families, but just as often they were recently ennobled or non-nobles who were distinguished for their wealth or wit. By mixing individuals of varied statuses, salons fostered a new pattern of egalitarian relations within the very heart of hierarchical society. Salons, then, provided a way for aristocratic society to absorb newly powerful individuals and families into the Old Regime elite without overturning established hierarchy.

A third discourse emerging from the very nature of the salon reimagined gender difference in ways that contested received notions of hierarchy between women and men, feminine and masculine. Some salon writings claimed that observable differences between men's and women's behavior were not innate or "essential" but merely socially prescribed, the effect of "custom." Others accepted gender differences as "natural" but deemed them complementary in ways that advantaged women. Either way, women were seen as suited for spheres of activity broader than household and family.

Again, this discourse expressed a reality of salon life, for the salon was the one intellectual space to which women were admitted and in which they might exercise informal cultural authority. There, they read and wrote, voiced their judgments, granted or refused patronage to men and women of letters, contributed orally and through letter writing to networks of opinion. Women's authority in salons was most commonly grounded in a gendered sense that feminine qualities—sensibility, delicacy, and intuition—grasped the rules of polite conversation and reciprocity better than masculine reason and so could insulate intellectual sociability from practices of contestation that structured male domains (intellectual and military).

The prominence of women in salons, however, generated tension within the world of letters and sociability about the part women should play in society and culture. It made women vulnerable to insult or mockery, wrath or scorn from those who decried the three revisionary salon discourses and their revisionary social underpinnings. From Molière's *Les précieuses ridicules* (1659) through Nicolas Boileau's "Satire on Women" (1694) to Jean-Jacques Rousseau's *Émile* (1762), commentators denounced women who aspired to cultural authority as agents of corruption in the literary world, in society, and in their neglected families.

The renowned salons of the eighteenth century adapted the main structuring features of the early salons to evolving intellectual, social and political contexts. There were still salons, such as Madame de La Ferté-Imbault's, that played rhetorical and chivalric games. But as Enlightenment thought developed its critical edge, as the philosophes set out (in the words of the *Encyclopédie*) "to change the common way of thinking," discussions in salons turned critical as well. The marquise de Lambert, Madame Geoffrin, Julie de Lespinasse, Madame Du Deffand, Madame Necker, and Madame d'Epinay hosted centers where disparate philosophes could form an intellectual community with one another as well as a community of discourse and manners with persons of education and power. In salon conversations, reformist ideas were introduced, reshaped, and disseminated to those who might enhance them in theory or apply them in practice.

The ties between the Enlightenment and salons far transcended the mere presence of philosophes in them: new visions of society diffused by the Enlightenment bore the imprint of the sociable norms and social dynamics that lay at the heart of salon society from its beginnings. The salon norm of *honnêteté* and moderated exchanges of views broadened into a claim that civil society ought to conform to the practices and norms of sociability and that societies should be judged by the refinement of their *moeurs*, their "civilization." The meritocratic and universalistic rhetoric of the salons ripened into a new vision of social relations as egalitarian rather than hierarchical or corporate. In the privacy of the salon, outside the political space defined by absolutism, a reconfigured "public" learned to form and express opinions on political matters. In short, the salon emerged in the eighteenth century as one of the institutions of the "public sphere" that prepared a new kind of political participation for an expanded elite.

Enlightenment salons continued to serve as places where women could educate themselves, participate in literary and intellectual life, and form networks of friendship and correspondence. The character of salons as women's networks became particularly salient in the *salonnière-protégée* networks that abounded there. Madame de Tencin initiated Madame Geoffrin, who trained both her own daughter, Madame de la Ferté-Imbault, and Madame Necker; the last apprenticed her own daughter, Germaine Necker, later to gain fame as the Romantic writer Madame de Staël. Yet one of the puzzles about salons as women's institutions is the fact that whereas the ideals of sociability ("fraternity") and social egalitarianism would be enshrined by the Revolution, neither gender equality nor the participation of women in the public political sphere would accompany those other major features of salons into the new social order.

The need to explain why women's roles in salons did not translate into rights of citizenship in the modern liberal state continues to prompt reexaminations of salon history: the extent to which the roles women played in salons were integral to the formation of opinion; how notions of gender difference, upon which women's authority in salons had rested, came to justify exclusion of women from modern politics; whether salons, despite their independence from absolutism's political space and despite their egalitarian rhetoric, were yet institutions bred by and limited to aristocratic forms of society that, like salons, fell to the margins as the eighteenth century came to an end. Such issues make the history of salons important for understanding both the Old Regime and the origins of modernity.

See also **Enlightenment; Feminism; Geoffrin, Marie-Thérèse; Holbach, Paul Thiry, baron d'; La Fayette, Marie-Madeleine de; La Rochefoucauld, François, duc de; Marguerite de Navarre; Perrault, Charles; Philosophes; Scudéry, Madeleine de; Sévigné, Marie de; Women.**

BIBLIOGRAPHY

Bodek, Evelyn Gordon. "Salonières and Bluestockings: Educated Obsolescence and Germinating Feminism." *Feminist Studies* 3 (1976): 185–199.

Chartier, Roger. *The Cultural Origins of the French Revolution.* Translated by Lydia G. Cochrane. Durham, N.C., 1991.

DeJean, Joan. *Tender Geographies: Women and the Origins of the Novel in France.* New York, 1991.

Goldsmith, Elizabeth C., and Dena Goodman, eds. *Going Public: Women and Publishing in Early Modern France.* Ithaca, N.Y., and London, 1995.

Goodman, Dena. *The Republic of Letters: A Cultural History of the French Enlightenment.* Ithaca, N.Y., 1994.

Gordon, Daniel. *Citizens without Sovereignty: Equality and Sociability in French Thought, 1670–1789.* Princeton, 1994.

Hertz, Deborah. *Jewish High Society in Old Regime Berlin.* New Haven, 1988.

Kale, Steven D. "Women, the Public Sphere, and the Persistence of Salons." *French Historical Studies* 25 (2002): 115–148.

Lougee, Carolyn C. *Le paradis des femmes: Women, Salons, and Social Stratification in Seventeenth-Century France.* Princeton, 1976.

Melton, James Van Horn. *The Rise of the Public in Enlightenment Europe.* Cambridge, U.K., and New York, 2001.

CAROLYN C. LOUGEE

SALZBURG EXPULSION. On 11 November 1731 Leopold Anton von Firmian, the Catholic archbishop of Salzburg (reigned 1727–1744), ordered the expulsion of all Protestants from the archbishopric. Poor and landless Protestants were ordered to leave within the week; householding Protestants were given two months. The order affected more than twenty thousand peasants, mostly from the Pongau region (about thirty miles south of Salzburg)—the largest religious deportation in early modern European history after the expulsion of Huguenots from France at the revocation of the Edict of Nantes in 1685.

For decades Protestantism had flourished almost unencumbered among the peasants in the alpine valleys south of Salzburg. Not long after his election as archbishop in 1727, Firmian tried to exert stronger administrative and pastoral control over the remoter regions of his see. His efforts provoked resistance, which became widely publicized throughout Germany with the publication, in June 1731 in Nuremberg, of a document purportedly stating the grievances of nineteen thousand oppressed Salzburg Protestants, a considerably larger number than Firmian had anticipated when he began his re-Catholicization campaign. The growing regional rebelliousness and the surprisingly large size of the Protestant minority prompted Firmian to turn to expulsion as a solution.

The first exiles left Salzburg at the end of November. They spent the winter wandering in southern Germany, unable to find a permanent home. When the bulk of the householders were expelled in April 1732, the king of Prussia offered his lands as a destination for the refugees. East Prussia was relatively unpopulated, and King Frederick William I (ruled 1713–1740) was happy to have immigrants to populate it. Prussia administered a convoy system to transport immigrants to their new homes. By 1734 twelve thousand refugees were settled in East Prussia.

One consequence of the expulsion was that Prussia solidified its identity as the political bulwark of German Protestantism, which it had first achieved by receiving Huguenot refugees in 1685. A massive outpouring of sermons and pamphlets by politically active Protestants drew attention to the plight of the emigrants as they made their way to Prussia. The expulsion was therefore a public relations disaster for political Catholicism in Germany. The "legend" of the Salzburg expulsion was as potent in the cultural clash between German Protestantism and Catholicism in the nineteenth century as it was in the eighteenth.

See also **Frederick William I (Prussia); Nantes, Edict of; Prussia; Reformation, Catholic; Reformation, Protestant.**

BIBLIOGRAPHY

Walker, Mack. *The Salzburg Transaction: Expulsion and Redemption in Eighteenth-Century Germany.* Ithaca, N.Y., 1992.

JOHN THEIBAULT

SANITATION The word "sanitation" only entered the English language in the nineteenth century, and the term is inextricably linked with integrated water and sewer systems. Lacking such technologies, early modern Europeans are often reckoned to have lived without sanitation. Their epidemiology of the time might seem to support this contention: three out of every ten babies born in Geneva between 1580 and 1739 died by their first birthday and the infant mortality rate in late seventeenth-century London was over one in four. Many of these deaths were caused by dirt-related infections like infantile diarrhea—what contemporaries termed "griping in the guts." Moreover, there are many vivid complaints of noxious conditions in early modern cities—one account of 1670s Edinburgh, for instance, claimed that one could not step anywhere in the streets without treading on turds.

Appearing in an Englishman's denunciation of all things Scottish, this claim was designed to promote prejudice. The charge also reveals how early modern people did indeed discriminate between cleanliness and dirt. Their sanitary technology rarely consisted of more than cesspits, chamber pots, and carts to carry ordure from their communities, but early modern Europeans possessed notions of public health and collective salubrity. Furthermore, scholars are now revealing the extent to which they sought to regulate and cleanse their environments.

URBAN DIRT AND URBAN ORDER

Such efforts were rarely entirely successful—early modern utopian writing appreciatively delineated the cleanliness of the ideal community—but civic authorities regularly commanded that streets be swept and nuisances removed. Such sanitary regulation was linked to wider conceptions of order. Noxious wastes shaped social and symbolic geographies. Offensive trades such as butchers and tanners were generally confined to particular districts, often downstream or outside city walls. In Paris the bodies of condemned criminals were buried in the municipal dump at Montfaucon. In central Europe the emptying of cesspits and the removal of waste were associated with other "dishonorable" trades. Between the sixteenth and nineteenth centuries, for instance, the "night-king" (chief latrine-cleaner) of Augsburg had to share a residence with the city executioner. Furthermore, precepts for cleansing streets often coincided with drives to rid communities of vagrants and "disorderly persons."

MIRE AND MEDICINE

Medical beliefs further encouraged sanitary care. Throughout the early modern period it was generally believed that plague and other epidemic diseases were caused or spread by corrupt airs or miasma produced by rotting organic matter. Environmental regulation thus sought to prevent evil smells. Perfumes and fumigants were used to purify infected spaces; street cleaning often intensified in periods of epidemic. In late-sixteenth- and early-seventeenth-century London, for instance, householders were required to sweep in front of their houses every morning and evening. During the early seventeenth century the boards of health of northern Italian states energetically sought to remove dunghills and other sources of miasma from the towns and villages under their jurisdiction.

Early modern doctors knew of "miasma" from a range of classical works, especially those of the ancient Greek physician Hippocrates. From the mid-seventeenth century medical authors became preoccupied with one strand of his work—the relation between epidemics and the airs, waters, and weather of particular places. Population statistics derived from bills of mortality and parish registers revealed geographical variations in the incidence of fevers and other fatal diseases; eighteenth-century analyses of air by natural philosophers like the English chemist Joseph Priestley sought to isolate mephitic substances that caused disease. Many eighteenth-century doctors proposed ways of reducing mortality by draining marshes, ventilating buildings, and reorganizing the environments and the ways in which people lived. Such interventions in the physical environment were often associated with proposals for the police of national populations. The term "police" had wider connotations than does its modern usage. It expressed a desire for the regulation of all aspects of life in order to achieve a smoothly functioning polity and (crucially) a healthy and productive population. The work of the German professor Johann Peter Frank exemplified the scale of this concept. His six-volume *System of Medical Police* (1779–1817) recommended the regulation of everything from midwifery and marriage to water supply and street cleaning.

The impact of medical police was less than the ambition of its advocates. Nevertheless, eighteenth-century Europe did see medically inspired reforms of daily life. In the 1750s, for instance, the British physicians Stephen Hales and John Pringle oversaw the installation of ventilators in the notoriously disease-ridden London prison of Newgate. In the 1780s the French Royal Society of Medicine not only declared that the Cemetery of the Holy Innocents in Paris was so full that it was a threat to public health but also had it closed and all human remains removed from it. More generally there was a considerable extension of new forms of sanitation, bathing and hygiene in hospitals, barracks, and similar institutions.

WATER SUPPLIES

These reforms were restricted by the general scarcity of water in preindustrial Europe. Clearly, this was a pressing problem in arid regions like southern Spain, where elaborate systems of water regulation were developed during the Middle Ages. But water was also a limited and costly resource in northern European communities not associated with drought. In eighteenth-century Paris, for example, a cubic meter of water would have cost a laborer more than two days' wages. Households spent much time and energy fetching water from rivers, streams, and wells. Communal life literally revolved around water sources. In larger urban centers public authorities maintained wells and sponsored schemes to pipe water to public fountains or conduits. In 1585–1587, for instance, Pope Sixtus V established the Acqua Felice, redeveloping the waters of an ancient aqueduct, the Aqua Alexandrina, in order to supply the eastern districts of Rome. Princely and aristocratic fountains like those at Louis XIV's palace of Versailles were, by contrast, ostentatious displays of conspicuous consumption.

The comparative scarcity of water remained a structural characteristic of European society throughout the early modern period. However, the sixteenth and seventeenth centuries saw the establishment of the first water companies piping supplies to the houses of private paying customers. The London Bridge Water Company (established 1582) and New River Company, which began supplying London in 1613, were among the first such concerns. They soon had imitators. By around 1700 one could rent a piped water supply in nine of the ten largest English provincial towns. Such companies were unevenly spread across Europe—no water

company operated in Paris until after the French Revolution—and the supplies they offered were unreliable and intermittent. However, they did pioneer new technology. Eighteenth-century water companies were among the first users of steam power, and thus laid the foundations for the subsequent industrialization of urban water supplies. In the nineteenth century the intellectual heritage of medical police combined with such technological developments to produce the public reforms that are conventionally associated with the term sanitation.

See also **City Planning; Public Health.**

BIBLIOGRAPHY

Corbin, Alain. *The Foul and the Fragrant: Odor and the French Social Imagination.* Cambridge, Mass., 1986.

Jenner, Mark S. R. "From Conduit Community to Commercial Network? Water in London 1500–1725." In *Londinopolis: Essays in the Cultural and Social History of Early Modern London.* Edited by Paul Griffiths and Mark S. R. Jenner. Manchester, U.K., and New York, 2000.

Riley, J.C. *The Eighteenth-Century Campaign Against Disease.* Basingstoke, U.K., and London, 1987.

Roche, D. "Le temps de l'eau rare: Du Moyen Age à l'Epoque Moderne." *Annales: Economies, sociétés, civilisations* 39 (1984): 383–399.

Rosen, George. *A History of Public Health.* Reprint. New York, 1993. Chaps. 3–5.

Stuart, Kathy. *Defiled Trades and Social Outcasts: Honor and Ritual Pollution in Early Modern Germany.* Cambridge, U.K., and New York, 1999.

For a website devoted to the history of the water supply of the city of Rome: http://www.iath.virginia.edu/waters/.

MARK JENNER

SANTA CRUZ, ÁLVARO DE BAZÁN, FIRST MARQUIS OF (1526–1588), Spanish admiral.

Born in Granada to Álvaro de Bazán the elder, who contracted and commanded both Atlantic squadrons and Mediterranean galleys, the younger Bazán began early to serve alongside his father and, in 1543, fought at Muros Bay against the French. In 1554, he sailed in the armada that took Philip II of Spain to his marriage with Mary Tudor of England. On the death of the elder Bazán in 1555, he assumed command of his Atlantic squadron. With peace in 1559, Bazán took command of eight galleys to patrol the Strait of Gibraltar. In the war on corsairs, he closed the harbor of Tetuán, aided by engineers, and in 1564 participated in the capture of Peñón Vélez de la Gomera, an island off the coast of northern Morocco. In 1565 he joined García de Toledo's armada for the successful relief of Malta, under siege by the Turks. Philip II promoted Bazán to command the Neapolitan galleys, and in 1569 made him Marquis of Santa Cruz de Mudela. On his estates in La Mancha, Santa Cruz constructed at Viso del Marqués an Italianate palace decorated with murals of his naval triumphs.

At the Battle of Lepanto in 1571, Santa Cruz proved brilliant in command of the Holy League rearguard and countered an attempted Turkish rally to ensure the league's victory. In 1572 he captured a Turkish galley and liberated its slaves, an episode related in *Don Quixote* by Miguel de Cervantes, a Lepanto veteran who called Santa Cruz "that thunderbolt of war . . . and never defeated captain." Interested in shipbuilding, Santa Cruz designed six galleasses (large warships using oars and sails) for Naples.

In 1578 he took command of the royal galleys of Spain. His quick response to the defeat and death of Dom Sebastian in Morocco saved Portugal's remaining strongholds at Tangier and Ceuta. For Philip's annexation of Portugal in 1580, Santa Cruz assembled a vast armada at Cádiz for a joint campaign with the duke of Alba. Alba invaded from Badajoz and marched to the sea at Setúbal. Santa Cruz sailed with his armada, assisted the duke of Medina Sidonia in the subjection of the Algarve, and met Alba. He loaded Alba's army aboard his armada and landed them at Cascais, downriver from Lisbon. The forces of Dom António, Philip's rival, had to abandon their positions upriver to face the invaders. Alba, supported by Santa Cruz's galleys, routed them, capturing Lisbon and the Portuguese navy.

Backers of Dom António, with covert aid from France and England, gained control of the Azores, save for São Miguel. Terceira was their stronghold. In 1582 Santa Cruz assembled an armada against the Azores and in July sailed from Lisbon. Off São Miguel, he encountered French admiral Philip Strozzi and the Portuguese count of Vimioso with thirty large and over thirty small armed vessels. He had twenty-five big ships, including two Portuguese galleons. After several days of maneuvering, on 26 July Strozzi forced the Atlantic's first big blue-water battle. After a hard fight, Santa Cruz emerged victorious. In 1583 he returned with an invasion force and conquered Terceira. Triumphant, he suggested that he invade England, which backed Dom António and Dutch rebels. Philip made Santa Cruz Captain General of the Ocean Sea and a grandee, but shelved the suggestion and allowed Santa Cruz's armada to dwindle.

In 1585 war erupted between Philip and England. Francis Drake attacked Vigo in Spain, then sacked Santo Domingo and Cartagena in the Caribbean. Philip ordered Santa Cruz to collect an armada of thirty-four ships to pursue Drake and asked him to submit a plan for the Enterprise (invasion) of England. Santa Cruz proposed an armada of more than 500 ships, large and small, to carry an invasion force from Spain. Philip decided on a smaller armada that would support an invasion army from the Spanish Netherlands.

In April–May 1587 Drake attacked Spanish preparations at Cádiz and the Algarve. Unprepared, Santa Cruz did not sail till July. He met the homeward-bound treasure fleets in the Azores, but on his return his armada was battered by storms. In Lisbon he found new orders to sail with 6,000 reinforcements to join Parma in the Narrows and cover his invasion of England. Storm damage, shortages, and foul weather held him to port, despite Philip's repeated demands that he sail. Under criticism and in failing health, he died on 9 February 1588. An aggressive and innovative commander, he might have succeeded, Spaniards believed, had he lived long enough to command the armada he had created.

See also **Alba, Fernando Álvarez de Toledo, duke of; Armada, Spanish; Lepanto, Battle of; Medina Sidonia, Alonso Pérez de Guzmán, 7th duke of; Parma, Alexander Farnese, duke of; Philip II (Spain).**

BIBLIOGRAPHY

Altolaguirre y Duvale, Angel de. *Don Álvaro de Bazán, primer marqués de Santa Cruz de Mudela.* Madrid, 1888.

Herrera Oria, Enrique. *Felipe II y el marqués de Santa Cruz en la empresa de Inglaterra: según los documentos del Archivo de Simancas.* Madrid, 1946.

Pierson, Peter. "Thunderbolt of War," *MHQ: Quarterly Journal of Military History* 13, no. 4 (Summer 2001): 54–63.

PETER PIERSON

SARMATISM. Sarmatism grew out of Renaissance theories about the genealogy of the Slavs. It developed into a peculiarly Polish-Lithuanian way of viewing the world and the place of the Commonwealth in it, and in the seventeenth and eighteenth centuries it came to describe aspects of a way of life associated with the gentry. Sixteenth-century Polish historians, drawing on classical and medieval notions of geography and cartography, elaborated a myth of the Sarmatian homeland of the Slavs in general and the Poles in particular. The myth came to have several components; it identified Sarmatia with the Jagiellonian Commonwealth of the Two Nations and prized the Commonwealth's political system as superior to all others, and it limited the Sarmatian ethnogenesis to the political nation, that is, the gentry (or *szlachta*) of Poland-Lithuania, thus excluding the burghers and peasants, who were seen in extreme cases as members of another "nation."

Polish Sarmatism passed through a number of phases. In its initial period, from the reign of Stephen Báthory (ruled 1575–1586) to the death of Władysław IV (ruled 1632–1648), the original Renaissance components focusing on the historical genealogy of the Sarmatians were reworked in a new, baroque context. At first, Sarmatism—which divided the gentry from all other inhabitants of the Commonwealth—served to unite a multiethnic and multiconfessional "noble nation." We soon find, however, the beginnings of a new divide between the "foreign," cosmopolitan culture of the magnates and the nativist, peculiarly Sarmatian identity of the gentry, especially the middling and poorer gentry. This division would deepen in the second, peak period of the development of Sarmatism (from 1648 to the death of King John III Sobieski in 1696), with the growing servitude of the peasantry and the further weakening of the cities. In this period, the Sarmatian myth was consolidated, taking on mystical and messianic colorations. Sarmatism now became the way of life and the worldview of a traditional, exclusive, xenophobic, more decidedly Catholic landed gentry. It emphasized gentry hospitality, patriarchal values, grandiloquence, and ostentation. There were certain paradoxes here; for one, a nation that saw itself as the bulwark of Christendom *(antemurale christianitatis)* eagerly adapted eastern (Turkish or Tatar) elements in custom, dress, lifestyle, and language.

The zenith of Sarmatism coincided with the beginning of the decline of the Commonwealth. In fact, some later blamed the fall of Poland-Lithuania on certain aspects of Sarmatian culture—gentry anarchy, the overly jealous defense of personal freedom at the expense of royal power and the common weal, even gentry ostentation and love of speechifying. The rule of the Saxon kings Augustus II the Strong and Augustus III in Poland-Lithuania (1697–1763, a period later known as the "Saxon Night") was characterized by a certain "Sarmatian degeneracy." Reactions against Sarmatism that began in the 1740s (with Stanisław Konarski and other Piarists, as well as the Jesuit Franciszek Bohomolec) gained momentum under Poland's last king, Stanisław II August Poniatowski (ruled 1764–1795). There was a growing division between a western-looking reform movement, which followed models of the Enlightenment and included burghers and peasants in its purview, and a traditional, now backward, gentry, which still equated Sarmatian values with patriotism. The latter group was exemplified by the participants in the Confederation of Bar in 1768–1772.

Sarmatism lived on after the partitions, especially in petty gentry circles in the east (in Lithuania and Belarus, but also Ukraine), and it became the object of romantic nostalgia following the failed November Uprising (1830). Some still find elements of Sarmatian mentality in modern Polish worldviews.

See also **Aristocracy and Gentry; Augustus II the Strong (Saxony and Poland); National Identity; Poland-Lithuania, Commonwealth of, 1569–1795; Poland to 1569; Poniatowski, Stanisław II Augustus.**

BIBLIOGRAPHY

Cynarski, Stanisław. "The Shape of Sarmatian Ideology in Poland." *Acta Poloniae Historica* 19 (1968): 5–17.

Ulewicz, Tadeusz. *Sarmacja: Studium z problematyki słowiańskiej XV i XVI w.* Cracow, 1950.

DAVID FRICK

SARPI, PAOLO (PIETRO) (1552–1623),

Italian theologian, scientist, and historian. Paolo Sarpi became notorious as the defender of Venice against the papacy during the Venetian Interdict of 1606 and as the author of a controversial history of the Council of Trent. Before 1606 he was an obscure ecclesiastic, a member of the Servite order; after 1606 he was known throughout Europe. Before this turning point, Sarpi was free to cultivate a range of intellectual interests, as his *Pensieri*, a collection of aphoristic notes on scientific and philosophical topics, demonstrate. The ones on religion are written from a notably detached and strictly philosophical point of view. The *Pensieri*, which only began to be studied thoroughly in the twentieth century (the complete corpus was only published in 1996), have had great influence on the scholarly interpretation of the "private" Sarpi. He was certainly abreast of the most advanced scientific and philosophical ideas of the time and was a leading member of the milieu of Galileo Galilei (1564–1642). He was also, to say the least, indifferent to formal religion except as an instrument of social and political organization, and many see him as a libertine and a virtual atheist.

In the 1590s and the early 1600s the level of jurisdictional and political conflict between Venice and Rome was rising. Venice claimed to control navigation in the Adriatic, Rome (backed by the Habsburgs of Spain and Austria) claimed freedom of navigation there; Venice had friendly contacts with non-Catholic states; in 1604 Venice forbade the construction of any new churches or shrines without permission from the state; in 1605 Venice forbade any further transfers of real property to ecclesiastical institutions without permission from the state; and in the summer and autumn of 1605 Venetian authorities arrested two delinquent clerics in mainland cities. In the late spring of 1606 Pope Paul V (reigned 1605–1621) excommunicated the Venetian leadership and interdicted all clergy in the Venetian dominion from performing their functions. Venice defied the interdict and ordered all clergy to continue in their duties, and the affair rapidly escalated into a European crisis. Sarpi was recruited by the Venetian government to act as adviser and publicist, and he wrote many effective memoranda and works for publication in defense of Venetian jurisdiction. After much hard negotiation,

in which Sarpi was closely involved, the interdict was lifted in April 1607. Sarpi was excommunicated in early 1607 and, targeted for assassination, was almost killed in October. But he retained his post and his influence on government policy for the rest of his life and became a prolific writer on church-state relations. He also maintained a network of epistolary and personal contacts with many influential individuals throughout Europe, Catholic and Protestant, as a way of acquiring support for Venice and reinforcing opposition to Rome and the Habsburgs.

As a young man Sarpi obtained firsthand information from a number of ecclesiastics who had participated in the Council of Trent (1545–1563) and had access to some of the private correspondence between Rome and the papal legates who had steered the sessions of the council, as well as other unpublished sources. Long before beginning his history of the council in the 1610s, Sarpi was convinced that the papacy had manipulated it to thwart Catholic sovereigns like Charles V (1500–1558), defeat the movement for internal reform, and reinforce its own preponderance in the Catholic world. Some historical narratives of the general history of the sixteenth century were in print, as were the decrees on doctrine and ecclesiology passed by the council. But the normal process by which these decrees would have been subjected to open debate and interpretation by competent specialists had been explicitly forbidden by Rome in 1564, as had the publication, which would also have taken place in the normal course of events, of the acta, or "acts," of the council (the record of the deliberations and proceedings; publication of them began only in the late nineteenth century). In result the history of the Council of Trent was more or less an arcanum until the publication of Sarpi's celebrated *Istoria del concilio tridentino* (History of the Council of Trent) in London in 1619. This work was considered poisonous and scandalous at Rome and has been challenged consistently by Catholic historiography. It is indeed moderately tendentious, as Sarpi fully intended it to be, but overall its veracity and its classic status are not in doubt. The influence it had on the perception of the papacy in Europe throughout the early modern period is incalculable.

See also **Papacy and Papal States; Paul V (pope); Trent, Council of; Venice.**

BIBLIOGRAPHY

Primary Sources

Sarpi, Paolo. *Opere.* Edited by Gaetano Cozzi and Luisa Cozzi. Milan, 1969. Contains selections from Sarpi's works and the fullest modern interpretive biography.

———. *Paolo Sarpi.* Edited by Corrado Vivanti. Rome, 2000. The complete annotated text of *Istoria del concilio tridentino* and a selection of shorter pieces. Vivanti's earlier edition of *Istoria del concilio tridentino* (Turin, 1974) is also of value.

———. *Pensieri naturali, metafisici e matematici.* Edited by Luisa Cozzi and Libero Sosio. Milan, 1996.

Secondary Sources

Frajese, Vittorio. *Sarpi Scettico: Stato e Chiesa a Venezia tra Cinque e Seicento.* Bologna, 1994.

Wootton, David. *Paolo Sarpi: Between Renaissance and Enlightenment.* Cambridge, U.K., 1983.

WILLIAM MCCUAIG

SAVOY, DUCHY OF. Situated in the western Alps with its capital at Chambéry, the duchy of Savoy began as a county of the Holy Roman Empire in the Middle Ages. During the reign of Amadeus VIII (1391–1436), the duchy acquired significant territory in Piedmont, east of the Alps, and its ruler was promoted to the status of duke by the Holy Roman emperor in 1416. In the fifteenth century, the duchy of Savoy included both Nice and Geneva, but by the sixteenth century the focus of the duchy turned east of the Alps. Savoy and the other western territories were difficult to defend against the powerful neighbor state of France. The plains of Piedmont offered more fertile land, greater population, and more possibility of expansion. Turin, the largest city in Piedmont, became the capital of the duchy in 1560.

The survival of the duchy as an independent state was precarious throughout the sixteenth century. Riddled by factions of *savoiardi* and *piemontesi* internally, it was also subject to the whim of its more powerful neighbors, France in the west, and the Habsburg domains in the east. Although Savoy had strategic importance as the "gatekeeper of the Alps," it could not stand up to the major powers by itself. Rather, it could only be a useful ally to further the aims of one or another power. In general, France and Spain recognized that Savoy provided an important buffer between their states, and the game of diplomacy often worked well for Savoy. At others times, it caused disaster. During the Italian Wars of the sixteenth century, France overran and occupied the state in 1536. Duke Emanuel Filibert, through an alliance with Spain, managed to reconstruct the Savoyard state in 1559 in the peace of Cateau-Cambrésis. Subsequent dukes were less successful, and once again, Savoy was reduced to the status of a French satellite until the late seventeenth century.

The turning point for the state of Savoy in the early modern era was the reign of Victor Amadeus II (1675–1730). Not only did this ruler manage to reacquire the territories lost to Savoy-Piedmont in the preceding century, but he also carried out reforms that would make Savoy a model of efficient government in the eighteenth century. Due to his participation in the War of the League of Augsburg (1688–1697) and the War of the Spanish Succession (1701–1714), Victor Amadeus II was awarded the island of Sicily in the Peace of Utrecht in 1713. Although Sicily was later exchanged for Sardinia, both islands brought the dukes of Savoy the title of king. In the nineteenth century, the western Savoyard territories were finally absorbed into the French state. The kings of Piedmont-Savoy would be compensated by the crown of the newly unified kingdom of Italy.

ECONOMY

As an Alpine region, Savoy lacked many natural resources and fertile land. Its main importance stemmed from the fact that it held the main mountain passes between France and the Italian peninsula. Although towns such as Susa and Chambéry were significant entrepôts between Italian and French cities, the majority of the revenue from this trade went to foreign rather than Savoyard merchants. The territories of Savoy on the western side of the Alps were economically backward throughout the early modern era. The economy there was primarily based on subsistence agriculture. In a mountainous environment, this meant frequent shortages. Feudal lords subjugated the peasantry. On the eastern side of the Alps, however, the territory of Piedmont had fertile plains and a significant silk industry in Turin. The main importance of Turin, however, was not economic but political. As the center of government, Turin held the most lucrative offices in the government administration.

Economic differences exacerbated social and cultural tensions between the two sides of the Alps. The old nobility of Savoy in the west spoke French and leaned toward France in alliances that often challenged the legitimacy of the central government. In contrast, most of the regions in the east spoke Italian, and often leaned toward the empire. Conflicts between the Savoyard nobility in the west and the central government in the east increased when Victor Amadeus extended greater state control over Savoy, abolishing ancient governmental institutions in Chambéry and ending feudal dues by the middle of the eighteenth century.

RELIGION

In terms of religion, the dukes of Savoy were loyal supporters of the Roman Catholic Church. One of the greatest figures of the Catholic Reformation, François de Sales, was a native of Savoy and became the archbishop of Geneva (situated in Annecy after the loss of the city). The author of the influential introduction to the *Devout Life,* de Sales worked ceaselessly to convert the Savoyard territories surrounding the Protestant Swiss cantons to Catholicism, advocating persuasion rather than force as a means of conversion. He was canonized in 1661. A noteworthy exception to the Catholic majority in Savoy was the enclave of Protestant Vaudois in the mountains outside of Turin. The remnants of the Waldensian heresy going back to the 1100s, the Vaudois were grudgingly tolerated with the exception of major persecutions in 1487, 1551, 1655, and 1663. Victor Amadeus II carried on a war of extermination against the Vaudois from 1684 to 1687, executing or exiling and dispersing the entire community, and resettling the area with Catholics. Despite the loss of many thousands, the community somehow managed to survive.

STATE BUILDING AND MILITARY CULTURE

The state of Savoy provides historians with an interesting example of absolutism and state building in the early modern era. Without an abundance of natural resources, the state survived through its ability to play the major European powers off each other in complex diplomatic maneuvering. However, the strength of the state was also due to its efficient centralization and peculiarly militaristic culture. Although the institutions of state were in large part established under Emanuel Filibert in the

late sixteenth century, the major phase of state building took place under the reign of Victor Amadeus II one hundred years later. An energetic ruler who led his troops into battle, Victor Amadeus mobilized his small state for war to an extraordinary extent. His reforms included tax reforms based on meticulous land surveys, and state-run systems of education and poor relief. He established an increasingly professional bureaucracy that included provincial intendants, government officials who made sure that the provinces were acting in accord with the central government. Such reforms ensured the greatest amount of revenue for the centralized state. The Savoyard government was admired as a model of efficiency throughout Europe. In addition, Victor Amadeus made Turin a showplace of state power. Miles of elegant baroque arcades linked the splendid royal palace to government institutions. The architect Juvarra was commissioned to build the great basilica of Superga, on the highest hill in Turin. Visible for miles, the enormous domed structure commemorated the victorious battle of Turin (1706) that ensured the survival of the state, and it stood as a monument to the glory of Victor Amadeus II and the house of Savoy.

The centralization of Savoy has been the subject of extensive historiographical debates. Jean Nicolas has seen it as a reaction to a resurgent aristocracy in the seventeenth century. Geoffrey Symcox attributes it to the desire of Victor Amadeus for absolute power. Others, such as Samuel Clark and Christopher Storrs, have seen Savoy as a perfect model of state building in the service of war. In their view, success in war ensured the continuation of the state, and the efficient mobilization of resources for war created state institutions that in turn were a byproduct of the war effort.

Savoy was an unusually militaristic society. Per capita, it had the largest army of any major European state. From the sixteenth century on, it had conscripted a peasant militia with legal rights. The nobility, unique among Italian states, maintained its militaristic identity throughout the early modern era. Very often when the nobles were not fighting in the army of Savoy, they were fighting in the armies of foreign states. Contemporaries frequently noted the quality of Savoyard soldiers and their loyalty to the state. This militaristic culture, along with efficient administration and astute diplomacy contributed to the success of the Savoyards in maintaining an independent state throughout the early modern era.

See also **Cateau-Cambrésis (1559); François de Sales; Italian Wars (1494–1559); League of Augsburg, War of the (1688–1697); Spanish Succession, War of the (1701–1714); Utrecht, Peace of (1713).**

BIBLIOGRAPHY

Barberis, Walter. *Le armi del Principe: La tradizione militare sabauda.* Turin, 1988.

Castelnuovo, Guido. *Ufficiali e gentiluomini: La società politica sabauda nel tardo medioevo.* Milan, 1994.

Clark, Samuel. *State and Status: The Rise of the State and Aristocratic Power in Western Europe.* Montreal, 1995.

Guichonnet, Paul, ed. *Histoire de la Savoie.* Toulouse, 1973.

Nicolas, Jean. *La Savoie au 18e siècle: Noblesse et bourgeoisie.* 2 vols. Paris, 1977–1978.

Storrs, Christopher. *War, Diplomacy and the Rise of Savoy, 1690–1720.* Cambridge, U.K., and New York, 1999.

Symcox, Geoffrey. *Victor Amadeus II: Absolutism in the Savoyard State, 1675–1730.* Berkeley, 1983.

REBECCA BOONE

SAXONY. The rise of Saxony dates from 1423, when the Holy Roman emperor Sigismund gave the electorate and duchy of Saxony to Margrave Frederick of Meissen of the Wettin dynasty. The gift was consequential, unifying the regions of Thuringia and Saxony under the House of Wettin. In return, the strengthened Wettin princes were to guard the Bohemian border during the Hussite wars and protect the Holy Roman Empire's northeastern frontier against the Ottoman Empire. Saxony also possessed parts of the province of Meissen, of the Vogtland, of the Ore Mountains, and that portion of Franconia south of Schwarzburg.

POLITICS

The elector of Saxony was one of seven princes with constitutional authority to elect new emperors and was also the imperial vicar and president of the Imperial Council of Regency, making him second only to the emperor in terms of constitutional power within the empire. Saxon rulers, possessing lucrative salt and mineral mining rights, became financially powerful in the early modern era. This wealth, combined with the Wettins' ability to inte-

grate lesser nobles and cities into their territorial system, made them the strongest of all north German princes by the late fifteenth century. Saxony's location on the northeastern fringe of the empire protected it from direct imperial and papal influence; indeed, the emperor and pope relied on Saxony to guard the Bohemian border.

Saxony was divided in 1485 by the ducal brothers Albert and Ernest. The partition left the dynasty in a perilous condition but can be explained by the fact that fifteenth-century princes regarded their lands as patrimonies and tended not to think territorially. The major towns in Albertine Saxony included Dresden, Leipzig, and Freiberg. Important towns located in the Ernestine portion included Zwickau, Torgau, and Wittenberg. During the sixteenth century none of these achieved a population over ten thousand. Because the electoral title was attached to the possession of territory around Wittenberg, the Ernestine branch retained (until 1547) the electoral dignity. Both lines passed laws that guaranteed the indivisibility of their domains and the succession of the eldest son. Neither line, however, was able to create an enclosed state. Contained within Saxon borders were a plethora of independent territories. These included the domains of the counts of Henneberg, Schwarzburg, and Mansfeld, the city of Erfurt, imperial abbeys, powerful monasteries, and wealthy bishoprics. Indeed, Lutheran visitation committees sent out in the 1520s to consolidate the Reformation often had to ask peasants whether their village lay within Saxony.

Ernestine Electors John the Constant (ruled 1525–1532), and his son, John Frederick the Magnanimous (ruled 1532–1547; died 1554), were devoted Lutherans who exercised less caution in the religious-political realm than had their predecessor Frederick the Wise (ruled 1486–1525), the elector famed for protecting Luther. At the Imperial Diet of Augsburg (1530), electoral Saxony led a group that presented a summary of Lutheran religious beliefs that is now called the Augsburg Confession. The inability of this diet to resolve religious differences and the perceived threat to national institutions within the empire encouraged John the Constant to form the Schmalkaldic League in 1531. This "defensive" league consolidated the gains of the Lutheran movement.

During the time of the league's ascendancy, the Holy Roman emperor, Charles V, had been preoccupied with external dangers presented by the Turks and by France. Peace with France (1544) and the Turks (1545), combined with a grant of money and troops from Rome, allowed Charles to confront the Protestant threat. In June 1546, Duke Maurice of Albertine Saxony, himself Lutheran, committed his domain and forces to the imperial cause against his cousin and rival. The decisive battle of the Schmalkaldic War (1546–1547), fought in April 1547 at Mühlberg, resulted in defeat for the league. The Wittenberg Capitulation (May 1547) transferred most of the Ernestine lands, and the electoral dignity, to Maurice. The Ernestine line was left scant territory around Weimar, Gotha, Eisenach, and Coburg, and a ducal title. Charles's decision to preserve the Ernestine line and his annexation of certain Wettin territories from Electoral Saxony indicated the rise of imperial might and foreshadowed the decline of Electoral Saxony as a political force.

In 1618 Elector John George I rejected approaches to become king of Bohemia. He continued instead a policy of helping the emperor maintain the empire's constitutional foundation, seeking to preserve his power as elector. As war loomed, John George, an enemy of Calvinism, pledged Saxony's support to the Catholic emperor. The first phase of the Thirty Years' War resulted in a persecution of Protestants throughout the empire. Though Saxony absorbed nearly 150,000 Bohemian refugees who had been forced into exile, its position within the Protestant world was compromised. In 1631 Saxony and Sweden allied against the empire, resulting in an invasion of Saxony. After a devastating defeat at Nördlingen, Saxony made peace with the empire in 1635. Saxony was not spared: until 1648 Swedish armies used it as their base and plundered it.

The Peace of Westphalia (1648) created a system that encouraged rivalries of power, and Saxony was quickly eclipsed by Austria, Bavaria, and Prussia. Both Frederick Augustus I (Augustus the Strong; ruled 1694–1733) and Frederick Augustus II (ruled 1733–1763) realized Saxony had to expand outside Germany to survive; each had himself elected king of Poland in an unsuccessful effort to broaden the Wettin dynasty's lands. The Saxon-Polish union did not elevate Saxony's power; rather, its economy declined due to the cost of assuming the Polish crown twice and of establishing a permanent standing army. Saxony's involvement in eighteenth-century conflicts like the Seven Years' War exposed its military frailty and contributed to further decline. Under the regency of Maria Antonia (1763–1768) and during the reign of Frederick Augustus III (1763–1827), Saxony benefited from enlightened reforms, fiscal responsibility, and a prudent foreign policy based on maintaining deferential relations toward greater powers.

ECONOMY

Between 1300 and 1600 Saxony had a diversified and robust economy. Mining, metallurgy, and smelting were crucial industries. Cobalt, tin, zinc, bituminous coal, iron, silver—all indispensable commodities—were mined in the Ore Mountains (Erzgebirge). Copper was plentiful in parts of Thuringia, as was iron ore in eastern Saxony. The growing mining industry absorbed workers, sparing Saxony the destabilizing effects of the fifteenth century's rapid population growth. Sixteen new towns with populations over five thousand were founded in this era. A significant smelting industry existed in the Thuringian Forest. Merchants from southern Germany's wealthy cities were eager to invest in Saxony; the Fuggers of Augsburg established an important foundry at Georgenthal and a smeltery at Hohenkirchen. Lucrative salt mining operations also existed in Thuringia. Because mining in Saxony did not depend on a single mineral, the boom receded slowly.

Textile manufacturing provided another crucial segment of Saxony's economy. An internationally important flax and linen industry developed in southern Saxony, centered around Chemnitz. Over three hundred villages in Saxon-controlled Thuringia specialized in cultivating woad, a plant from which a valuable blue dye was extracted. These towns enjoyed a woad monopoly and, as a result, they prospered economically. A highly developed woolen industry also contributed to Saxony's economic strength. Moreover, Saxony was advantageously situated at the center of international trade routes. Leipzig emerged by the sixteenth century as the principal entrepôt in central Europe and hosted numerous international fairs. One of Europe's largest international cattle markets took place at Buttstädt.

Several factors allowed Saxony to limit the social unrest that befell other parts of Germany in the late fifteenth and sixteenth centuries. Though impartible inheritance was practiced east of the Saxon Saale River, the mining boom minimized the economic difficulties that this custom generated elsewhere. Labor-intensive viticulture along the Elbe River around Meissen and along the Unstrut River also absorbed excess population. Saxony thus suffered less from the strains of overpopulation than did other German parts of the empire. The Wettin lords successfully subordinated local nobles into a network of territorial estates, forestalling potential rivalries, and concurrently expanding the state's administrative apparatus in the countryside. Saxony also benefited from an "intermediary" system of landlordship, one based on both wage labor from free peasants and forced labor services performed on large demesnes. This unique form of landlordship kept the organization of rural communes at a rudimentary level and served to mitigate conflicts associated with the "crisis of feudalism." With the noteworthy exception of mining areas in Thuringia and the Ore Mountains, Saxony escaped the violence generated by the Peasants' War of 1524–1525 and avoided the rural unrest that plagued Upper Germany after 1570.

CULTURE

Saxony possessed impressive educational institutions: influential universities at Leipzig (1409), Wittenberg (1502), and Jena (1588); a number of remarkable secondary schools *(Lateinschulen)* for the privileged and gifted; and, after the Reformation, schools throughout the land to teach every boy and girl reading and writing. Leipzig also was an early center for book publishing (1480s) and for book trading. Humanist circles, encouraged by Duke George of Albertine Saxony (reigned 1500–1539) and Elector Frederick the Wise, emerged in Leipzig and Wittenberg. Thinkers such as Martin Luther, Philipp Melanchthon, and Agricola made Saxony a leading center for humanism in Germany. All these factors were instrumental in making Saxony the birthplace of the Reformation and the home to its crucial events. Early modern Saxony's contribution to world culture cannot be underestimated: Lucas

Cranach, Johann Sebastian Bach, George Frideric Handel, Gottfried Wilhelm Leibniz, Gotthold Ephraim Lessing, and Johann Gottfried von Herder were either born in Saxon lands or developed their talents within them.

See also **Augsburg; Augustus II the Strong (Saxony and Poland); Bach Family; Cranach Family; Dresden; Handel, George Frideric; Herder, Johann Gottfried von; Holy Roman Empire; Humanists and Humanism; Leibniz, Gottfried Wilhelm; Leipzig; Lessing, Gotthold Ephraim; Luther, Martin; Lutheranism; Melanchthon, Philipp; Reformation, Protestant; Schmalkaldic War (1546–1547); Thirty Years' War (1618–1648); Universities; Westphalia, Peace of (1648).**

BIBLIOGRAPHY

Blaschke, Karlheinz. *Sachsen im Zeitalter der Reformation.* Gütersloh, 1970.

Gagliardo, John G. *Germany under the Old Regime: 1600–1790.* London and New York, 1991.

Holborn, Hajo. *A History of Modern Germany. The Reformation.* Princeton, 1959.

Hughes, Michael. *Early Modern Germany: 1477–1806.* Philadelphia, 1992.

Karant-Nunn, Susan C. *Zwickau in Transition, 1500–1547: The Reformation as an Agent of Change.* Columbus, Ohio, 1987.

Scott, Tom. *Society and Economy in Germany, 1300–1600.* New York, 2002.

Wilson, Peter H. *The Holy Roman Empire, 1495–1806.* New York, 1999.

JAMES GOODALE

SCARLATTI, DOMENICO AND ALESSANDRO

(Pietro) Alessandro (1660–1725) and (Giuseppe) Domenico (1685–1757), members of a renowned family of musicians, originally from Sicily. Alessandro has traditionally been credited as the founder of the Neapolitan school of opera; his son Domenico was a noted harpsichordist and composer. Not much is known about Alessandro's parents except that they were involved in Palermo's musical life and that his father, Pietro, was a tenor. Alessandro proved to be a gifted young musician and continued his studies in Rome, where he moved with his mother and several siblings in 1672.

Alessandro Scarlatti. ©BETTMANN/CORBIS

Alessandro cultivated his musical skills as well as an influential circle of friends in Rome. In April 1678 he married Antonia Anzaloni, and in the same year he was appointed *maestro di capella* of the church of San Giacomo degli Incurabili and also composed his first opera, an untitled work, for Filippo Bernini, son of sculptor Gian Lorenzo Bernini (1598–1680). Two years later, Alessandro's short comic opera *Gli equivoci nel sembiante* (1679) not only established him as one of Rome's leading operatic composers, but also introduced him to his most famous patron, Queen Christina of Sweden (ruled 1632–1654), who was living there in exile. He served as her *maestro di capella* until 1683, and she sponsored private productions of several of his operas. In Rome during this period, operas were presented only occasionally and in private to the aristocracy and to foreign ambassadors, since public opera and theater performances were banned under Innocent XI (reigned 1676–1689), who closed Rome's first public opera house three years after it had opened.

Desiring more artistic freedom, Alessandro accepted a commission from Domenico Marzio Carafa, the viceroy of Naples, and moved there in 1684, becoming *maestro di capella* at the vice-regal court at the age of twenty-four. The following year, his sixth child, Domenico, was born. As master of the royal chapel in Naples until 1702, Alessandro composed nine oratorios and sixty-five cantatas, and composed and produced more than eighty operas. His most successful operas from this period were *Il Pirro e Demetrio* (1694), his only opera to be produced internationally during his lifetime; *La caduta de' Decemviri* (1697), the first piece to employ a three-part rather than two-part Italian sinfonia; and *Tito Sempronio Gracco* (1702), one of his most financially successful endeavors. Significant during Scarlatti's tenure in Naples is the change from the five-act opera popular in Rome to works of three acts. He also maintained his contacts in Rome, returning there occasionally for performances of cantatas and oratorios and to put on new operas for private patrons such as Cardinal Pietro Ottoboni (1667–1740) and Cardinal Benedetto Pamphili. At the weekly concerts established by Ottoboni, he met virtuosos and composers including Arcangelo Corelli (1653–1713). One of Scarlatti's operas, *La Statira* (1690), was even given a public performance in Rome when Alexander VIII (reigned 1689–1691), Cardinal Ottoboni's uncle, reopened the theater that Innocent XI had closed; but Alexander's successor, Innocent XII (reigned 1691–1700) renewed the ban on public opera productions and finally dismantled the theater in 1697.

In 1702, with the position of the Neapolitan nobility becoming insecure due to the onset of the War of the Spanish Succession (1701–1714), Alessandro and his family left Naples and went to Florence, where he sought work for himself and Domenico from Prince Ferdinand de' Medici. Receiving commissions for several operas but no full-time job there, he took his family back to Rome, where he accepted an appointment as assistant *maestro di cappella* at the church of Santa Maria Maggiore, composing motets and masses. He remained in Rome until 1708, supplementing his income with commissions from Cardinals Ottoboni and Pamphili, and from a new patron, Marquis Ruspoli, as well as from Prince Ferdinand. In 1706 he was elected, along with Corelli and Bernardo

Pasquini (1637–1710), to the Arcadian Academy, a circle of poets and musicians devoted to a classical aesthetic modeled on Greek antiquity, and he must have met George Frideric Handel (1685–1759) at one of the Arcadians' gatherings in 1707. With the papal ban on public opera still in effect in Rome, he concentrated on oratorios, serenatas, and cantatas, although he wrote four operas for Ferdinand in Florence during this period and in 1707 went to Venice to direct two new five-act operas, which were not successful there. He returned to Rome briefly as *maestro di cappella* at Santa Maria Maggiore, but when he was offered his old position in Naples in 1708 by the new Austrian viceroy there—that city having come under Austrian occupation—he accepted it. Naples remained his center of activity for the rest of his life, as a composer and a teacher (with such students as Hasse and Quantz), although he made periodic visits to his patrons in Rome, where he was able to produce some of his finest late operas, including his last, *La Griselda* (1721).

Oratorios at that time were a substitute for opera during the seven-week period of Lent, and Alessandro wrote approximately forty of them, including *La Giuditta* (1697), based on the biblical account of Judith of Bethulia. He also wrote at least twenty-two serenatas, large festive cantatas on secular themes, often political in nature, written to commemorate important events and performed in open-air theaters. Among the more politically oriented serenatas was *Pace, amor, e providenza* (1714), composed for the nameday of Emperor Charles VI to celebrate the 1714 Treaty of Rastatt, one of several treaties comprising the Peace of Utrecht, which ended the War of the Spanish Succession. The libretto's allegorical figures each claim responsibility for Charles's diplomatic triumphs. Among Alessandro's most celebrated compositions are his more than six hundred chamber cantatas, both sacred and secular, most set for solo soprano accompanied with basso continuo, with lyrical poetic texts frequently focused on the theme of love. Alessandro's church music, including masses, motets, and psalm settings, spans both the *stile antico* and the *stile moderno*. He also wrote purely instrumental music, including seven toccatas for harpsichord, and twelve concerti grossi in the style of Corelli.

Domenico Scarlatti.

Alessandro Scarlatti's reputation rests largely on his dramatic compositions for the stage. The opening sinfonias of these works are of particular importance. The majority of his approximately 114 operas can be categorized as *drammae per musica* (musical dramas); many are based on ancient history (sometimes apocryphal). Some use literary subjects as their basis, such as *La Griselda*, which draws its libretto from Boccaccio; others can be classified as *commedie in musica*, or *pastorales*. The three-part Italian sinfonia, consisting of an introductory Allegro, followed by a slower contrasting section, and concluding with a fast movement in triple meter, was the precursor to the classical symphonies of Wolfgang Amadeus Mozart (1756–1791) and Franz Joseph Haydn (1732–1809).

The most famous of Alessandro Scarlatti's children was Domenico, born in 1685, the same year as Handel and as Johann Sebastian Bach (1685–1750). His keyboard-playing talent was recognized at an early age; he may have studied harpsichord with Pasquini or Gaetano Greco (1657–1728) in

Rome. Alessandro helped him procure the position of composer and organist at the Cappella Reale in Naples in 1700 when Domenico was fifteen. After a brief period in Florence with his father, he returned to Naples to take over his father's duties for the 1703–1704 season while Alessandro was in Rome and then was sent by his father to Venice, where he was "escorted only by his own ability" (as Alessandro wrote to Ferdinand de' Medici in 1705). Domenico returned to Rome in 1707, where he is reported to have entered a keyboard competition under the auspices of Cardinal Ottoboni in 1708 or early 1709. Among the contestants was Handel, who was judged Domenico's equal on the harpsichord, but whose organ skills surpassed those of Scarlatti. In 1713 and 1714, Domenico was appointed to two of the most important positions in Rome: first as *maestro di cappella* in service to Maria Casimira, the exiled dowager queen of Poland, and then as chapelmaster of the Cappella Giulia at St. Peter's. Both titles afforded him financial security. In addition to the seven operas Domenico composed from 1710 to 1714 while in Rome, it is believed that he went briefly to England in 1719 to revise an earlier work, which Handel produced at Drury Lane in 1720.

In 1719, Domenico finally freed himself from his father's control when he was granted legal independence from Alessandro and resigned his positions in Rome. His most important position came soon after that, when he was appointed *mestre de capela* in Lisbon, where he also oversaw the education of John V's younger brother, Don Antonio, and John's daughter Maria Barbara. He returned to Rome for a visit in 1728 to marry the sixteen-year-old Maria Catarina Gentili. In 1729, when Princess Maria Barbara married the Spanish crown prince and became queen of Spain, Domenico followed her to Seville, and then in 1733 to Madrid, becoming her *maestro da cámera* and spending the rest of his life there. His wife died in 1739, and sometime before 1742 he married Anastasia Maxarti Ximenes.

Most of his approximately 550 keyboard works were written at the Portuguese and Spanish courts, and many of these reflect an influence of Iberian folk-music idioms. Known for his ability to improvise at the harpsichord, Domenico did not write down his compositions until 1738, when he published his first collection of keyboard pieces, thirty

Essercizi per gravicembalo. He was knighted by John V that same year, and in return he dedicated the *Essercizi* to the king.

Domenico organized a large number of his harpsichord works into two volumes (1742, 1749) and presented them to Maria Barbara. It was through this patron that he met the famous castrato Farinelli (1705–1782), who inherited several volumes of the composer's keyboard manuscripts after the queen's death. Between 1752 and 1757, Domenico composed an additional 200 keyboard suites (or sonatas, as he called them), which he compiled and edited for publication, possibly with the assistance of one of his students, Catalan composer Antonio Soler (1729–1783), as his copyist.

Domenico Scarlatti's compositions include fourteen operas, over seventy cantatas, several serenatas (of which only two have survived, including the *Festeggio armonico*, written in 1728 for the engagement of Maria Barbara to the Spanish crown prince), and various sacred pieces. He is best remembered for his large output of single-movement keyboard sonatas, which place him as one of the founders of modern keyboard technique. Scarlatti's sonatas are technically innovative in their use of hand crossings, quickly repeated notes, and wide leaps, requiring a high level of technical proficiency. The sonatas skillfully utilize the harpsichord to its fullest capacity and demonstrate the composer's gift of melodic and harmonic invention. The elegance and graceful ornamentation of these works epitomize the refined qualities of the early rococo style. The binary structure of Scarlatti's sonatas is noteworthy; an antecedent to sonata form, it is similar to the Italian sinfonias of his father, in that both were influential to the development of later Classical-period music. The sonatas have remained an integral part of the keyboardist's repertory.

See also **Handel, George Frideric; Music; Opera.**

BIBLIOGRAPHY

Boyd, Malcolm. *Domenico Scarlatti—Master of Music.* London, 1986.

Grout, Donald J. *Alessandro Scarlatti: An Introduction to His Operas.* Berkeley, 1979.

Pagano, Robert, and Malcolm Boyd. "Scarlatti, Alessandro." In *The New Grove Dictionary of Music and Musicians,* 2nd ed., edited by Stanley Sadie, vol. 22, pp. 372–396. London, 2001.

———. "Scarlatti, Domenico." In *The New Grove Dictionary of Music and Musicians,* 2nd ed., edited by Stanley Sadie. Vol. 22, pp. 398–417. London, 2001.

GREGORY MALDONADO

SCHILLER, JOHANN CHRISTOPH FRIEDRICH VON

(1759–1805), German dramatist, poet, historian, and philosopher. Born on 10 November 1759 in Marbach, in Württemberg, the only son of a low-ranking army officer, Schiller was educated from 1773 to 1780 at the military academy founded by Karl Eugen, duke of Württemberg (1728–1793). His first play, *Die Räuber* (1781; The robbers), premiered at the Mannheim National Theater in 1782. Forbidden by the duke to pursue his literary work, he absconded from Württemberg later that year, and after serving as resident playwright at Mannheim for one year, he moved to Dresden and Leipzig and then in 1787 to Weimar, home of several leading literary figures, chiefly Johann Wolfgang von Goethe. In 1789 he was appointed professor of history at the University of Jena, on the strength of his *Geschichte des Abfalls der vereinigten Niederlande von der spanischen Regierung* (History of the revolt of the United Netherlands from Spanish rule, 1787).

Schiller married Charlotte von Lengefeld in 1790. After a serious illness in 1791 he remained a semi-invalid for the rest of his life. In 1794 he formed a friendship and alliance with Goethe based on shared convictions about the enduring validity of classical principles in art and about the centrality of art as a human activity. Their correspondence, along with their joint essays and projects, had a lasting impact on German literary debate and practice. In 1799 Schiller moved from Jena to Weimar, and he died there on 9 May 1805.

Schiller's work as a poet and dramatist falls into two distinct periods: before 1789 and from the mid-1790s to his death. His first three plays, *Die Räuber, Die Verschwörung des Fiesko zu Genua* (1783; The conspiracy of Fiesko at Genoa), and *Kabale und Liebe* (1784; Intrigue and love) owe much in style and spirit to the short-lived but influential avant-garde literary movement of the 1770s, the Sturm und Drang. Written in vigorous prose and showing the impact of the Sturm und Drang generation's

reception of William Shakespeare, the plays explore flawed idealism, the charismatic leader, social divisions, and the impatience of the young with the imperfections of the world. They also bear the imprint of Schiller's medical training at the military academy and in particular of his interest in the problem of mind-body relationships. His fourth play, *Don Carlos, Infant von Spanien* (1787; Don Carlos, infante of Spain), anticipates his later dramas in its use of blank verse and concern with historical and public themes.

The compositional difficulties Schiller encountered with *Don Carlos* provoked a creative crisis, and though he wrote two seminal poems in 1788, "Die Götter Griechenlandes" (The gods of Greece) and "Die Künstler" (The artists), he turned away for almost a decade from creative writing, with the purpose of clarifying his thoughts on art in general and tragedy in particular. In 1791 he turned to the German philosopher Immanuel Kant's philosophy. Kant's dualism, according to which human beings belong to the realm of nature but also partake through reason in the realm of freedom, became fundamental to Schiller's thinking on aesthetics, for he saw art as a means of reconciling the tensions between nature and reason. His theory of the sublime in tragedy claims that tragedy mediates an experience of transcendence derived from the awareness that human beings may assert their moral freedom even while being physically destroyed (see in particular "Über das Pathetische" [On tragic pity]). In his influential treatise *Über die ästhetische Erziehung des Menschen in einer Reihe von Briefen* (1794; On the aesthetic education of man in a series of letters), he argues that beauty as "living form" symbolizes and helps bring about the ideal harmony of sense and spirit to which human beings aspire. His notion of beauty as play and of aesthetic semblance have been important in later discussions of aesthetics. His final major treatise, *Über naive und sentimentalische Dichtung* (1795; On naive and sentimental poetry), defines the problem of the modern ("sentimental") writer's divided consciousness.

During 1795 Schiller started again to write poetry. In 1799 he completed his greatest drama, *Wallenstein* (published 1800). A rapid succession of verse plays followed up to his death: *Maria Stuart* (1801; Mary Stuart), *Die Jungfrau von Orleans* (1802; The maid of Orleans), *Die Braut von*

Messina (1803; The bride of Messina), *Wilhelm Tell* (1804; William Tell), and *Demetrius* (unfinished). Each signals a new departure in style. Together they reflect Schiller's preoccupation with some of the pressing themes of the age of the French Revolution: legitimacy of government, conscience versus political calculation, and the individual within the tide of events. His later poetry encompasses the more popular in style (for example, his ballads and "Das Lied von der Glocke" ([The song of the bell]), but he also used poetry as a meditation on the nature of art (for example, in "Das Ideal und das Leben" [The ideal and life] and "Der Tanz" [The Dance]).

The action-filled plots, strong characters, and thrilling encounters of Schiller's plays have not only guaranteed their continued place on the world stage but have inspired numerous opera composers, Giuseppe Verdi being the most prominent.

See also **Drama: German; German Literature and Language; Goethe, Johann Wolfgang von.**

BIBLIOGRAPHY

Primary Sources

Dewhurst, Kenneth, and Nigel Reeves. *Friedrich Schiller, Medicine, Psychology and Literature: With the First English Edition of His Complete Medical and Psychological Writings.* Berkeley, 1978.

Schiller, Friedrich. *Don Carlos and Mary Stuart.* Translated by Hilary Collier Sy-Quia. Adapted in verse drama by Peter Oswald. New York, 1996.

———. *Five Plays.* Translated by Robert David MacDonald. London, 1918.

———. *On the Aesthetic Education of Man, in a Series of Letters.* Edited by Elizabeth M. Wilkinson and Leonard A. Willoughby. Oxford and New York, 1967.

———. *Schillers Werke. Nationalausgabe.* Edited by Julius Petersen, Liselotte Blumenthal, et al.; from 1992 by Norbert Oellers. 44 vols. Weimar, 1943–.

———. *Wallenstein.* Translated by Charles E. Passage. New York, 1958.

———. *Werke und Briefe.* Edited by Otto Dann et al. 12 vols. Frankfurt am Main, 2000–.

———. *Wilhelm Tell.* Translated and edited by William F. Mainland. Chicago, 1972.

Secondary Sources

Koopmann, Helmut, ed. *Schiller-Handbuch.* Stuttgart, 1998.

Reed, T. J. *Schiller.* Oxford and New York, 1991.

Sharpe, Lesley. *Friedrich Schiller: Drama, Thought and Politics.* Cambridge, U.K., and New York, 1991.

LESLEY SHARPE

SCHMALKALDIC WAR (1546-1547).

The Schmalkaldic War (fought between July 1546 and April 1547) was a short-lived military victory by the Holy Roman emperor Charles V (ruled 1519–1556) over the forces of the Lutheran princes and cities of the Schmalkaldic League (1531–1547). The history of the league and the survival of Protestantism after such decisive military defeat reflect both the strengths and weaknesses of the Holy Roman Empire.

HISTORY OF THE SCHMALKALDIC LEAGUE

The Schmalkaldic League was a German Protestant military federation based on an agreement made at Schmalkalden in Thuringia in December 1530 and ratified in February 1531. The original members of the league included the two military commanders Elector John Frederick of Saxony and Landgrave Philip of Hesse; the northern princes of Anhalt-Bernburg and Mansfeld-Hinterort; the northern cities of Lübeck, Magdeburg, and Bremen; and the southern cities of Strasbourg, Ulm, Memmingen, Konstanz, Biberach, Lindau, and Isny. The presidency of the league alternated between the elector and the landgrave.

The league differed from previous federations, including the Swabian League (1488–1534), in both its defined purpose and scope. The purpose of the league was the defense of religion in addition to traditional aims of mutual defense. The defense of the evangelical movement brought together powers, such as the ruling families of Strasbourg and the elector of Saxony, who had no other interests in common. Unlike the Swabian League with its strictly upper German focus, the Schmalkaldic League was imperial in scope, eventually stretching from east to west from Pomerania to Strasbourg and from north to south from Oldenburg to Konstanz. Although the league tried to break out of the imperial borders through attempted alliances with Henry VIII of England and Francis I of France, these efforts ended in failure.

The league, originally formed for six years, ratified a fixed constitution at Schmalkalden on 23 December 1535, which was almost immediately revised in October 1536 because of the growth in league membership. The cities of Esslingen, Brunswick, Goslar, Einbeck, and Göttingen all joined the league between 1531 and 1535. In 1535 the dukes of Pomerania and Württemberg, the count of Pfalz-Zweibrücken, two princes of Anhalt-Dessau, and the cities of Frankfurt am Main, Kempten, Hamburg, and Hannover all joined the league. Under the new constitution the league was divided into two "circles": a northern, "Saxon" circle and a southern, "upper German" circle.

The league faced the same political and constitutional problems that plagued the empire. The league's tax structure and sole means for financing its military force mirrored the imperial tax structure. Despite the efforts of many leaders from the southern cities (in particular, Jakob Sturm von Sturmeck [1489–1553]), the league consistently defeated proposals to reform and streamline its collection of revenue.

The principle success of the league was its defense of the Protestant cause against the emperor, the Imperial Diet, and the Imperial Chamber Court. The league's first victory was its successful campaign to suspend all suits by Catholic clergy for the restitution of ecclesiastical property seized by evangelical cities and territories. Charles V's policy of toleration, however, required the league's support for and participation in his wars with the French and the Ottoman Turks as well as a series of theological colloquies at Hagenau, Regensburg, and Speyer.

The league had no fixed seat but it did meet some twenty-six times over the course of its sixteen-year history, over a more extensive area than did the Imperial Diet (which met only once in the same period). The league also had no chancery or league court or any official means of mediating disputes among its members and was, therefore, unable to agree upon a common ecclesiastical constitutional, or liturgical, policy for ecclesiastical properties.

The politics of particularism also hindered the league's effective unity—especially in the case of the northern cities (the southern cities largely continued their long-standing practice of mutual consulta-

tion). Originally possessing four of nine possible votes and later six of thirteen votes in the league, the cities in general also found themselves in a long familiar position of minority status in relation to the princes. The confessional nature of the league, based as it was upon the religious conflict between the Catholic and Protestant camps within western Christianity—and the distractions of Charles V in the Mediterranean and of Ferdinand I of Austria with his Jagellon territories and Turkish incursions—estranged the cities from their traditional alliances with the crown against the princes. For example, in 1534 Philip of Hesse was able to restore the (Lutheran) duke Ulrich of Württemberg in his territories with the support of Bavaria, France, and Strasbourg, over the opposition of the Saxon elector and most of the imperial and free cities.

CAUSES OF THE WAR

The underlying causes of the Schmalkaldic War were the ambitions of the leading princes of the league, particularly Landgrave Philip of Hesse and Elector John Frederick of Saxony, and the imperial effort to bring the territories and cities of the league to heel confessionally. The ambitions of the nobles and their limitations as political and military strategists can be clearly seen in the political offensive led by Elector John Frederick to secure the North German prince-bishoprics for the evangelical cause.

In 1542 the league successfully invaded the last remaining Catholic lay territory in northern Germany, the Duchy of Brunswick-Wolfenbüttel, but in 1543 the league failed to come to the aid of the elector's brother-in-law, Duke William of Cleves-Jülich, against Charles V. The southern cities of the league viewed these campaigns as of little lasting value and approved the Brunswick-Wolfenbüttel campaign reluctantly. The perception among the cities that they were bearing more than their fair share of the costs of the league's military operations began to foment open dissent, and left the league in enough political disarray that its reratification would have been in doubt even without its military defeat by the imperial forces.

The need to justify resistance to imperial authority was a standing issue for Protestant rulers and their advisers. As a result, beginning with Martin Luther's own volte-face in 1531 in favor of active resistance against an unjust emperor, Lutheran theologians, lawyers, and counselors were under constant pressure to portray their resistance against the empire in a positive light. By the time the city of Minden was outlawed in the autumn of 1538, Wittenberg theologians judged that a preemptive attack by the league in defense of Minden would be a "defensive" first strike under the terms of the league's charter.

The Schmalkaldic League did not intend to undermine any territorial sovereign. In 1543–1544 the Protestant community of Metz in Lorraine petitioned the league for admission. Although Martin Bucer and the senate of Strasbourg supported the Metz Protestants, Elector John Frederick, on the advice of the Wittenberg theologians, blocked their bid for admission on the grounds that they were dissident subjects of a legitimate government. Nonetheless, the league ignored concerns for legitimacy in the case of the city of Brunswick when it admitted that city as a member even though it was still ruled by Duke Henry the Younger, a Catholic.

The proximate cause of the war was the rejection by the members of the league of the conditions under which Charles convened the Diet of Regensburg in June of 1546. The immediate circumstances that finally allowed Charles to act against the Lutherans were the conclusion of peace treaties with France (the Peace of Crespy on 18 September 1544) and with the Ottoman Turks (on 10 November 1545), the successful negotiation of the participation of papal troops in a campaign against the league, as well as free passage for these troops through the Bavarian territory of Duke William, and the tacit support of Duke Maurice of Saxony against his cousin John Frederick upon Maurice's withdrawal from the league in 1542. Despite careful imperial preparations for a confrontation with the league, the initial league offensive caught Charles off guard in Regensburg with only a small number of Spanish and German troops.

PROGRESS OF THE WAR

Among the league's initial advantages were successful attempts to reinforce its field army with experienced mercenaries, who had been released recently from French service, and the recruitment of the famous mercenary captain Sebastian Schertlin von Burtembach as a field commander. Official command, however, remained in the inexperienced and

clumsy hands of the princes, especially Elector John Frederick. The elector's imperial counterpart, Fernando Álvarez de Toledo, duke of Alba, was one of the finest military commanders of the sixteenth century. In short, John Frederick was no match for Alba or Charles.

There were two distinct phases to the war. In the first phase, in the south, the imperial troops under Charles and Alba escaped from Regensburg by outmaneuvering the league's forces and then joined forces with papal troops from Italy via Bavaria and with heavy cavalry from the Netherlands under Egmont, count of Buren. The indecisiveness of the league's war council caused Schertlin to be called off just when he could have cut off the papal reinforcements in the mountains and destroyed them piecemeal. The ability of the imperial troops to avoid a decisive engagement along the Danube, coupled with the failure of John Frederick to seize the initiative, precipitated a financial and political crisis within the leadership of the league.

Duke Maurice's attack on electoral Saxony began the second phase of the war and shifted the front to the north. Electoral troops broke off contact with imperial forces along the Danube and marched home, where they successfully counterattacked and overran much of Maurice's ducal Saxony and defeated an imperial relief force under Albert of Culmbach. During this phase of the war, however, the revelation of Philip of Hesse's scandalous bigamy effectively removed him from the military and diplomatic fray. Meanwhile, since most of the league's forces were defending electoral Saxony, Alba and Charles were unopposed as they neutralized the southern cities and then moved north to reinforce Maurice on the northern front.

John Frederick's fatal strategic miscalculation of advancing to the south away from easily defended locations proved to be the beginning of the end for the league. Upon realizing his error, John Frederick attempted to keep the Elbe River between the league's forces and the imperial forces, but Alba's scouts discovered a ford and the imperial infantry was able to force its way across the Elbe, across the Protestant line of retreat. During the battle on 24 April, now known as the Battle of Mühlberg, the imperial troops gradually destroyed the scattered Protestant formations and captured John Frederick.

PROTESTANTISM AND THE WAR

In the aftermath of his victory, Charles stripped both John Frederick and Philip of Hesse of their domains, installed Maurice as ruler of all of Saxony, and proclaimed the institution of Catholic religious conformity with the Augsburg Interim. However, Charles's triumph proved to be short-lived. After sixteen years of protection provided by the Schmalkaldic League, the Protestant cause was now strong enough to survive politically even after a sound military defeat.

The Gnesio-Lutheran stronghold of Magdeburg was a center of resistance after the league's defeat. Lutheran clergy (led by Nickolaus von Amsdorf, Matija Vlačic [Matthias Flacius Illyricus], and Nikolaus Gallus, among others) continued to develop a constitutionalist theory of resistance by so-called inferior magistrates against the empire. In both formal publications and pamphlet campaigns this political innovation proved to be influential in other confessionally based political resistance movements, such as the Huguenot Monarchomachs and the Reformed Dutch revolt against the Spanish, and among the English Marian exiles and political theorists opposed to the claims of absolutism, such as Johannes Althusius (Althaus).

The so-called Prince's Revolt and the Treaty of Passau in 1552 ensured the survival and even official recognition of the Lutheran cause. These events culminated in the Religious Peace of Augsburg (1555), which placed a territory's confessional allegiance squarely in the hands of its ruler.

See also **Alba, Fernando Álvarez de Toledo, duke of; Augsburg, Religious Peace of (1555); Charles V (Holy Roman Empire); Lutheranism.**

BIBLIOGRAPHY

Brady, Thomas A., Jr. "Phases and Strategies of the Schmalkaldic League: A Perspective after 450 Years." Archiv für Reformationsgeschichte 74 (1983): 162–181.

———. *Protestant Politics: Jacob Sturm (1489–1553) and the German Reformation.* Atlantic Highlands, N.J., 1995.

Fischer-Galati, Stephen A. *Ottoman Imperialism and German Protestantism, 1521–1555.* Cambridge, Mass., 1959.

Hartung, Fritz. *Karl V. und die deutschen Reichsstände von 1546 bis 1555.* Darmstadt, reprint 1971; original edition 1910.

Haug-Moritz, Gabriele. *Der Schmalkaldische Bund, 1530–1541/42: Eine Studie zu den genossenschaftlichen Strukturelementen der politischen Ordnung des Heiligen Römischen Reiches Deutscher Nation.* Leinfelden-Echterdingen, 2002.

Held, Wieland. *1547, Die Schlacht bei Mühlberg/Elbe: Entscheidung auf dem Wege zum albertinischen Kurfürstentum Sachsen.* Beucha, 1997.

Maltby, William S. *Alba: A Biography of Fernando Álvarez de Toledo, Third Duke of Alba, 1507–1582.* Berkeley, 1983.

Oman, Sir Charles. *A History of the Art of War in the Sixteenth Century.* Repr. Elstree, U.K., 1987.

Schlütter-Schindler, Gabriele. *Der Schmalkaldische Bund und das Problem der causa religionis.* Frankfurt am Main and New York, 1986.

Wunder, Gert. "Sebastian Schertlin: Feldhauptmann und Kriegsunternehmer, 1496–1577." In *Lebensbilder aus Schwaben und Franken.* Vol. 13, edited by Robert Uhland, pp. 52–72. Stuttgart, 1977.

THOMAS E. RIDENHOUR, JR.

SCHOLASTICISM. In the early modern period the term "Scholasticism" denoted the systematization of learning in schools and universities, mainly in philosophy and theology, occasionally extended to law and medicine. It may be characterized by its distinctive method and language and by its elaboration into competing systems of thought.

SCHOLASTIC METHOD

What is called "scholastic method" started with the disputations that were held in the schools of the Middle Ages. A disputation began with the posing of a question that could be answered either affirmatively or negatively. It involved two interlocutors, one on each side, and the method of arguing was basically that explained in the *Topics* of Aristotle (384–322 B.C.E.). The topics or problems were drawn from a teaching text, usually in philosophy or theology, and expressed in Latin. The rules of reasoning were those concerned with concepts, propositions, and arguments and contained in other logical works of Aristotle. The proponent of the affirmative, called the defendant, stated his thesis in the form of a proposition, and then proceeded to develop arguments that supported his thesis. In response, the proponent of the negative, called the objector, developed counterarguments that disproved the defendant's thesis. To these counterarguments the defendant then replied by reformulating his initial arguments, introducing distinctions of meaning to meet the opponent's objections. The argument went back and forth in this form until either the objector was convinced that his difficulties had been met and he conceded the thesis, or the defendant was unsuccessful in his defense of the thesis and conceded defeat.

Scholastic method grew out of this procedure. Its basic instruments were definition, distinction, and argumentation, and its ideal goal was certain truth, although frequently it could reach only probable conclusions. By the time of the Renaissance a stylized format had been developed for meeting these objectives. First the thesis was stated, usually as a universal affirmative proposition. Then three steps were commonly envisaged, consisting of prenotes, proofs, and difficulties that might be brought against the thesis. In the prenotes the proponent provided definitions of the terms in the thesis, distinctions relating to them, and different positions being held on the thesis. Then various proofs were offered, first from authority, such as the Bible or a noted philosopher, then from reason, using varieties of argument. Finally, objections against the thesis were restated and resolved, usually on the basis of distinctions introduced earlier in the presentation.

MEDIEVAL SCHOOLS

The development of Scholasticism coincided with the founding of universities in the late twelfth century and of religious orders such as Dominicans and Franciscans in the early thirteenth century. In the universities newly translated texts of Aristotle provided the basis for a system of thought known as Aristotelianism. Additionally, religious orders had their favorite doctors, whose teachings were also systematized. Dominicans followed Thomas Aquinas (1225–1274), whose system was called Thomism, and Franciscans followed Duns Scotus (1266?–1308) and William of Ockham (c. 1285–1347), whose systems were called Scotism and Ockhamism, respectively. A feature of medieval universities was public disputations in which doctors of these schools debated before the student body. Different though their systems were, the discourse was made possible by the participants' reliance on Aristotle's method of logic.

The language of Scholasticism was a technical Latin, with specialized vocabularies suited to particular subject matters. Geographically, Scholasticism flourished in Italy and on the Iberian Peninsula, in France, Germany, the Low Countries, and in the British Isles. The leading schools were the University of Oxford, noted for philosophy, the University of Paris, for theology, and the University of Bologna, for law and medicine.

In the late twelfth and thirteenth centuries Augustinianism, a theological form of Neoplatonism advanced by Augustine of Hippo (354–430), was influential. In the thirteenth and fourteenth centuries, Latin Averroism, a teaching of Averroës (Ibn Rushd; 1126–1198) that denied the immortality of the human soul, assumed importance, mainly at the University of Padua. Ockham's insistence that universal natures cannot be known in things, but only their names *(nomina)*, led to his system's being known as nominalism. The opposing systems, which held that natures could be known to be real *(realia)*, were then seen as various forms of realism. Debates between realists and nominalists were frequent in university disputations.

THE RENAISSANCE

Scholasticism reached its highest state of development during the Renaissance, roughly from about 1450 to about 1650. The first phase, to the mid-sixteenth century, was focused in Italy and Spain and is known to historians as "Second Scholasticism." The second phase saw its development by the Jesuits and its extension to the schools of northern Europe, Protestant as well as Catholic.

In the first phase Thomism, Scotism, and nominalism developed extensively. Thomism was advanced mainly by Dominicans, of whom the most significant were the Italians Tommaso de Vio Cajetan (1469–1534) and Giovanni Crisostomi Javelli (1470–c. 1538), and the Spaniards Francisco de Vitoria (c. 1486–1546) and Domingo de Soto (1495–1560). Cajetan was the most profound synthesizer of St. Thomas's theology, whereas Javelli is best known for his teaching manuals in philosophy. Vitoria and Soto worked extensively on social and political thought, arguing that natives in America had souls and therefore had the same rights as Europeans.

Scotism was largely the preserve of the Franciscans, who adopted Scotus as their order's doctor in 1539. Before that, a revival of Scotist teachings had been promoted by the French Peter Tartaretus (d. c. 1532), and the Italian Antonio Trombetta (1436–1517). Trombetta was a critic of Cajetan and is known especially for having combated Averroism at Padua.

A nominalist revival radiated out from the University of Paris to other countries, including Spain and the Low Countries. Its chief promoters were Gerard of Brussels (d. 1502) and the Scot John Major (1469–1550), both teaching at Paris, and Johannes Eck (1486–1543), whose career was mainly in Germany. Among Major's students were Pedro Ciruelo (1470–1554) and Gaspar Lax (1487–1560), the latter well known for his manuals in logic. Major's school made significant contributions to the study of motion and prepared the way for the scientific revolution of the seventeenth century.

The second phase of the Renaissance began with the founding of the Jesuit order in 1540. Jesuits blended humanism with Scholasticism and introduced methods of teaching that had profound effects throughout Europe. In general, they subscribed to Thomism but introduced variations within that system. Their most important school was the Collegio Romano, located in Rome, which was staffed initially by Iberians, notably Franciscus Toletus (1532–1596) and Gabriel Vázquez (1549–1604), who wrote influential textbooks. Their most outstanding teacher was Francisco Suárez (1548–1617), whose version of Thomism is referred to as Suarezianism.

Although Martin Luther (1483–1546) held a disputation against Scholasticism in 1517, it came to occupy a central place in Protestant universities within a hundred years. This was true whether the universities leaned to Calvinism, as in Heidelberg and Marburg, or to Lutheranism, as in Wittenberg, Altdorf, and Helmstedt. The basic approaches were those of Philipp Melanchthon (1497–1560), who composed textbooks on physics, psychology, and ethics at Wittenberg, and Jacob Schegk (1511–1587), who commented on Aristotle's logic and natural philosophy at Tübingen.

For metaphysics, Jesuit textbooks, particularly Suarez's, were used initially but were later replaced by Protestant manuals. Johannes Caselius (1535–1613), working at Helmstedt, wrote early texts in the Aristotelian tradition pioneered by Schegk. Works showing Suárez's influence include those of Jakob Martini (1570–1649) at Wittenberg and Christoph Scheibler (1589–1653) at Giessen, the latter called the Protestant Suárez. For systematic thought, notable works are those of Bartholomaeus Keckermann (1571–1608), who taught at Heidelberg and Gdańsk and wrote manuals for all of philosophy and science. Johann Heinrich Alsted (1588–1638) followed Keckermann's teachings with his own *Encyclopediae* in 1620 and 1630. At Leiden, Franco Burgersdijk (1590–1635) wrote similar compendia for Scholastic philosophy that were widely used throughout Protestant Europe.

LATER PERIOD

By the seventeenth and eighteenth centuries, Scholasticism had run its course. The way of thought it had spawned, with its many "-isms," had become overburdened and toppled of its own weight. Disputations that had earlier held great interest had by then degenerated into making subtle distinctions and quibbling endlessly over terms. Scholastic method continued to be employed in religious houses of study and in universities, however, though in the latter it gradually gave way to new methods based on experimentation and mathematical reasoning. This transition is seen graphically in the early writings of Galileo Galilei (1564–1642) and Isaac Newton (1642–1727). Galileo's Latin notebooks on logic and natural philosophy, written at Pisa between 1588 and 1592, were couched in the language of Scholastic disputations. The same can be said of Newton's Trinity notebooks, written at Cambridge in the early 1660s.

Scholasticism was transplanted to the New World by religious orders in time for the founding of institutions of higher learning in North and South America and the Philippines. Those in Mexico and the Philippines followed the teachings of Spanish Scholastics, mainly from Salamanca and Alcalá, whereas American colleges, such as Harvard, Yale, and William and Mary, reflected teachings current in Protestant universities in England, Scotland, Germany, and the Low Countries.

See also Aristotelianism; Galileo Galilei; Humanists and Humanism; Jesuits; Newton, Isaac; Renaissance; Universities.

BIBLIOGRAPHY

Marthaler, Berard, et al., eds. "Scholastic Philosophy," "Scholastic Terms and Axioms," and "Scholasticism." In *New Catholic Encyclopedia*. 2nd ed. Vol. 12, pp. 749–779. New York, 2003. Very complete treatment.

Nauert, Charles G., Jr. *Humanism and the Culture of Renaissance Europe*. Cambridge, U.K., 1995.

Rummel, Erika. *The Humanist-Scholastic Debate in the Renaissance and Reformation*, Cambridge, Mass., and London, 1995.

Wallace, William. "Newton's Early Writings." In *Newton and the New Direction in Science: Proceedings of the Cracow Conference, 25 to 28 May 1987*, edited by George V. Coyne et al., pp. 23–44. Vatican City, 1988.

———. "Scholasticism." In *Encyclopedia of the Renaissance*, edited by Paul F. Grendler, vol. 5, pp. 422–425. New York, 1999. See also the same author's entries on "Aristotle and Aristotelianism," vol. 1, pp. 107–113, and "Logic," vol. 3, pp. 443–446.

Wallace, William, trans. *Galileo's Early Notebooks: The Physical Questions*. Notre Dame, Ind., 1977.

Wallace, William A. "Aristotle in the Middle Ages." In *Dictionary of the Middle Ages*, edited by Joseph R. Strayer, vol. 1, pp. 456–469. New York, 1989.

WILLIAM A. WALLACE

SCHÜTZ, HEINRICH (1585–1672), German composer.

Heinrich Schütz was the most important German composer of vocal music in the seventeenth century. For much of his long career, Schütz was kapellmeister (music director) to the elector of Saxony at the Dresden court, as well as serving in the court of Christian IV of Denmark. A student of the Venetian masters Giovanni Gabrieli (1557–1612) and Claudio Monteverdi (1567–1643), Schütz synthesized Italian and German procedures in an unprecedented manner that was to have a profound influence on the course of German baroque music.

Schütz was born in Kösteritz near Gera (Saxony) and baptized 9 October 1585. At the age of four his musical talent attracted the attention of Landgrave Moritz of Hessen-Kassel, who persuaded Schütz's parents to send him to his court for further education in music and art. He was an apt pupil who excelled in languages, and also studied law at the University of Marburg. However, with the landgrave's support, he traveled to Venice to study with Giovanni Gabrieli. Here he received training in Renaissance polyphony as well as the polychoral innovations favored at San Marco, and published a set of five-voice madrigals in 1611.

Upon his return to Germany around 1613, Elector Johann Georg I of Saxony requested Schütz's service for the Dresden court. Schütz obtained his release from Moritz after several years of complex negotiations, arriving in Dresden in 1615, becoming the vice-kapellmeister in March 1617 and kapellmeister in 1619, although he only received this title officially in 1621 after the death of Michael Praetorius (1571–1621). The Dresden court maintained a large musical establishment, and Schütz's extensive duties included the training of choirboys, hiring personnel, staffing, and the producing of secular and sacred music for all civic and religious occasions. Music in Dresden flourished prior to that city's belated involvement in the Thirty Years' War, as did Schütz's productivity and fame. His *Psalmen Davids sampt etlichen Moteten und Concerten* (1618), the first important collection of German church music, reflected the influence of Gabrieli's *Symphoniae Sacrae* and exploited the lavish vocal and instrumental resources at the Dresden court and the sonic potential of the elector's chapel. The originality of this enterprise is apparent in the detailed instructions included in the preface, which describes the proper size, makeup, and position of the forces, and other aspects of performance practice.

In addition to sacred compositions in a variety of genres, including biblical dramas and Latin motets, Schütz composed what is usually regarded as the first German opera, *Apollo und Dafne*, which has not survived. A second trip to Italy in 1628—and studies with Claudio Monteverdi—introduced Schütz to the most recent Italian innovations in dramatic music, in particular the techniques for expressive solo singing associated with the *seconda prattica* (second practice). Schütz's first set of *Symphonie Sacrae* (1629) integrates this revolutionary new approach to text setting with the impressive use of instrumental colors and vocal sonorities gleaned from Gabrieli.

Heinrich Schütz. GETTY IMAGES

The last decades of Schütz's career at Dresden were marked by the economic pressures of the Thirty Years' War, which Saxony entered in 1631, and the meager vocal and instrumental forces he used in the compositions from this period, such as the first two sets of *Kleine geistliche Konzerte* (Little spiritual concertos), dating from 1636 and 1639, reflect the severe economic conditions in Germany. He twice journeyed to Copenhagen to compose music for the court of Christian IV (to whom he would dedicate his second set of *Symphoniae Sacrae* [1646]) and served several other prominent North German courts. In failing health, Schütz was finally permitted to take partial retirement in 1656, although he continued to advise the court on musical matters as kapellmeister. During the 1660s, he also composed a biblical drama based on the Christmas story (*Historia . . . der . . . Geburth . . . Jesu Christi* [1664]) of three Passions: St. John, St. Matthew, and St. Luke, all performed in Dresden in April 1666. These intense, personal works are noteworthy because of their stark, highly dramatic quality, the fidelity to the text of the Gospels, and the use of a different mode for each to accentuate the individual nature of the utterances. Schütz died on 5 November 1672, and his funeral was held at Dresden's Frauenkirche on 17 November.

Although little of Schütz's secular music has survived, he left an impressive body of sacred works in numerous genres that range from sober expressions of Lutheran piety to full-bodied, dramatic manifestations of unmatched sonic splendor. The essence of Schütz's style is an extraordinary synthesis of German and Italian techniques—the grand approach of Gabrieli and the expressive text-setting and sense of drama that distinguishes Monteverdi's compositions, combined with the contrapuntal integrity and innate serious tone that was part of Schütz's German training and heritage. It is this genius that would find expression in the high German baroque through the music of Johann Sebastian Bach (1685–1750) and George Frideric Handel (1685–1759).

See also **Bach Family; Dresden; Handel, George Frideric; Monteverdi, Claudio; Music.**

BIBLIOGRAPHY

Primary Source
The Letters and Documents of Heinrich Schütz 1656–1672: An Annotated Translation. Edited by Gina Spagnoli. Ann Arbor, Mich., 1990. Translations of letters and important documents with extensive commentary about Schütz's career and style.

Secondary Sources
Breig, Werner. "Heinrich Schütz's Musikalische Exequien: Reflections on Its History and Textual-musical Conception." In *Church, Stage, and Studio: Music and its Contexts in Seventeenth-Century Germany,* edited by Paul Walker, pp. 109–225. Ann Arbor, Mich., 1990.

Frandsen, Mary. "Allies in the Cause of Italian Music: Schütz, Prince Johann Georg II and Musical Politics in Dresden." *Journal of the Royal Musical Association* 125 (2000): 1–40.

Moser, Hans Joachim. *Heinrich Schütz: His Life and Works.* Translated by Carl F. Pfatteicher. St. Louis, 1959. Translation of *Heinrich Schütz: Sein Leben und Werk* (1959).

Smallman, Basil. *Schütz.* Oxford, 2000. Excellent overview of life and musical style, with complete works list and chronology.

WENDY HELLER, MARK KROLL

SCIENTIFIC ACADEMIES. *See* Academies, Learned.

SCIENTIFIC CLASSIFICATION. *See* Linnaeus, Carl.

SCIENTIFIC ILLUSTRATION.

The development of scientific illustration in early modern Europe paralleled a rising interest in studying, collecting, and classifying the natural world. These practices gave rise to new methods of documenting and displaying nature and its products. Although early modern European artists and naturalists did not deliberately set out principles or rules for creating scientific images, a common set of practices emerged during the period that formed the foundation of scientific illustration into the modern period.

From the late medieval period pictorial techniques designed to convince viewers that an image contained an exact record of the artist's observation were increasingly employed in the illustration of botanical and medical texts, as well as in illuminated manuscripts. To convey the impression of accuracy and lifelikeness, artists often depicted objects against a plain background and offered highly detailed renderings of surfaces and textures. Such images functioned variously as practical aids to identification and study, as delightful entertainments, and as symbolic representations of religious and philosophical ideas. The plants and other minute objects represented in the margins of illuminated books of hours inspired readers to marvel at both the complexity and beauty of the natural forms and the artist's skill. During the early modern period images of the natural world continued to be characterized by a dual capacity to delight and instruct the viewer. Leonardo da Vinci's (1452–1519) pen-and-ink studies of plants, animals, and the human body combined meticulous observation of natural structures with idealized forms and harmonious compositions. Albrecht Dürer's (1471–1528) plant and animal studies treated subjects similar to those found in the borders of illuminated manuscripts but focused on previously "marginal" subject matter as the main subject of the compositions. The two major botanical publications of the sixteenth century, *Herbarum Vivae Eicones* (1530–1536) by Otto Brunfels (c. 1488–1534) and *De Historia Stirpium* (1542) by Leonhard Fuchs (1501–1566), exemplify one of the central problems of scientific

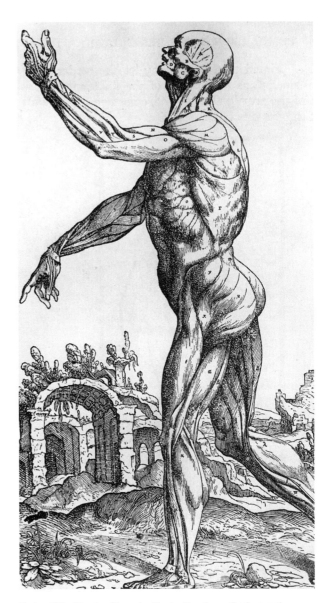

Scientific Illustration. An illustration from *De humani corporis fabrica* by Andreas Vesalius, 1543. GETTY IMAGES

illustration. The illustrations in both publications rely on empirical observation but reflect differing ideas about the meaning of accuracy and lifelikeness in images. The images of plants in Brunfels are individualized portraits containing signs of decay and features unique to a particular specimen, whereas the images in Fuchs attempt to capture the general characteristics of the species by presenting perfect, idealized specimens.

Other early modern European artists highlighted the ambiguous relationship between visual images and the reality they purport to represent.

Joris Hoefnagel (1542–1600) often depicted imaginary creatures in a meticulous and convincing visual style, while the deep hues, intense luminosity, and sculptural forms of Jacopo Ligozzi's (1547–1627) botanical drawings create a profound material presence that in some cases may have surpassed that of the actual specimen. By the end of the seventeenth century, artists such as Maria Sibylla Merian (1647–1717) incorporated the meticulous style perfected by Dürer, Hoefnagel, and Ligozzi into vibrant compositions of living creatures in their natural habitats competing with one another for survival.

Scientific illustration in early modern Europe was closely connected to the collecting practices of the period, particularly in the field of natural history. Collectors such as Ulisse Aldrovandi (1522–1605) and Conrad Gessner (1516–1565) assembled exotic objects from the New World, Asia, the Middle East, and Africa into cabinets of curiosities, the forerunners of modern museums, and published copiously illustrated natural histories based on their collections. Illustrations were used to document and supplement existing collections, and in some cases functioned as collections in and of themselves.

Close connections between artistic and scientific practice were also evident in the area of anatomical illustration. Andreas Vesalius (1514–1564) worked with artists from Titian's (1488 or 1490–1576) workshop to produce the illustrations for his *De Humani Corporis Fabrica* of 1543, in which human figures in various stages of dissection were depicted in poses derived from ancient sculpture. Early modern scientific illustration also treated technical and mechanical subjects, making use of visual forms used in botany, natural history, and anatomy, as well as diagrams, used by astronomers and mathematicians to describe movement and abstract ideas. Over the course of the seventeenth century optical instruments such as the telescope and the microscope were used to investigate previously invisible structures and phenomena, and illustrations were used to communicate these discoveries to others. Galileo Galilei's (1564–1642) *Sidereus Nuncius* of 1610 made use of both diagrams and illustrations to convey new knowledge gained through the use of the telescope about the surface of the moon and the newly discovered moons of Jupiter. Robert Hooke's (1635–1703) *Micrographia* of 1665 presented readers with meticulously crafted illustrations of magnified objects and creatures observed with a microscope.

See also **Anatomy and Physiology; Hooke, Robert; Merian, Sibylla; Museums; Natural History; Vesalius, Andreas.**

BIBLIOGRAPHY

Primary Sources

Hooke, Robert. *Micrographia*. London, 1665.

Richter, Jean Paul, ed. *The Notebooks of Leonardo da Vinci*. 2 vols. New York, 1970.

Vesalius, Andreas. *De Humani Corporis Fabrica*. Basel, 1543.

Secondary Sources

Edgerton, Samuel Y., Jr. *The Heritage of Giotto's Geometry: Art and Science on the Eve of the Scientific Revolution*. Ithaca, N.Y., 1991.

Kemp, Martin. *The Science of Art: Optical Themes in Western Art from Brunelleschi to Seurat*. New Haven and London, 1990.

Koreny, Fritz. *Albrecht Dürer and the Animal and Plant Studies of the Renaissance*. Translated by Pamela Marwood and Yehuda Shapiro. Boston, 1988.

JANICE L. NERI

SCIENTIFIC INSTRUMENTS. The early modern period saw the use of devices both to advance scientific research (such as the telescope and the microscope) and those of a more practical nature that embodied scientific knowledge (such as the astrolabe and the thermometer). Because scientific instruments are typically made by specialized craftsmen who produce improvements in design and effectiveness through technical means, their production may also be considered as a discrete technology.

Although in the Middle Ages there had been specialized craftsmen who made astrolabes and, later, clocks, the emergence of a specialized craft for the production of a line of scientific instruments with distinct functions first emerged (in England, at least) in the 1540s, in response to the need for more accurate measurement in navigation, surveying, and astronomy. In England, the multiple forces of population growth, agricultural expansion, and, later, the draining of The Fens, stimulated the development of professional surveying, which required instruments for making angular measurements. The age of discovery, moreover, expanded the market for navigational instruments at a time when the "lunar distance" method (involving difficult observations of the distance between the Moon and a designated star, the use of tables, and calculation) was the predominant method of navigation. At the same time, in the course of the sixteenth century, practical mathematics was developed and then diffused in printed manuals. The primary measurements involved in describing the use of such instruments themselves required instrumentation, as did the mathematical manipulation of observations made by using such manuals. The emergence of a scientific-instrument craft in the 1540s was the result of the interaction of all of these factors.

THE TELESCOPE

Once eyeglasses came into common usage toward the end of the thirteenth century, it was just a matter of time until two such lenses were combined to produce either a telescope or a microscope. That insight, however, took quite a long time to realize. The telescope is first documented in Holland in the fall of 1608, when at least three different craftsmen, including a maker of spectacles, were manufacturing them. Because the principles involved were widely known, the telescope is a good example of invention appearing simultaneously in different places. Galileo Galilei heard of the Dutch instruments by the summer of 1609 and made his own version, with a diverging eye lens and a converging (convex) object lens. These early examples had magnifications of two or three, but within a year Galileo, who ground his own lenses, achieved magnifications of twenty and thirty and objectives with increasingly long focal lengths. The Englishman Thomas Harriot heard of the Dutch instruments in the same period and was drawing maps of the Moon in August 1609, before Galileo's most significant research had begun. Galileo published his first telescopic results in March 1610 in his famous *Sidereus nuncius* (Starry messenger) and by the end of the year Johannes Kepler had published two little books on the results of telescopic research, without having done any yet himself. (Kepler's contribution was a telescope with both eyepiece and objective converging, which made it possible to create a real, though inverted, image and project it onto a screen beyond the ocular, which became the normal way of observ-

ing the Sun.) As is frequently the case with recognizably important inventions (the automobile, the airplane), the invention and innovation of the telescope caused a quickening of communication among scientists and stimulated simultaneous excitement in countries widely removed from one another.

Galileo's earliest telescope observations—of the lunar landscape, the satellites of Jupiter, and the Milky Way—caused a sensation. The satellites of Jupiter, moreover, revealed that Earth was not the only planetary center of rotation, which worked against Aristotelian cosmology and in favor of that of Nicolaus Copernicus, as did Galileo's subsequent description of the phases of Venus. The discovery of sunspots also contradicted the Aristotelian axiom of the unchangeable nature of celestial bodies. In the hands of Galileo alone, the telescope changed the nature of planetary astronomy, both how it was conceptualized and how it was observed.

One of the problems of early telescopes was that the objective caused the images to appear with extraneous colors. The solution was the achromatic lens, developed in England in the 1730s. To avoid such coloring and other distortions, seventeenth-century telescopes had very small apertures and long focal lengths. The eventual solution was a two-component objective, with two lenses of different density in contact with one another, worked out by Parisian craftsmen in 1763, and then by John Dolland in England. This was the most popular telescope until William Herschel (1738–1822), toward the end of the century, invented a reflecting telescope with a large mirror that made possible the gathering of enough light to be able to examine much fainter celestial objects.

The telescope's impact was sudden, immense, and rippled across the length and breadth of cultures, affecting scientific theory and method, of course, but also theology, philosophy, literature, and art. In particular, Galileo's depiction of a jagged, rough, and crater-pocked lunar surface threatened a whole range of entrenched cultural conventions, including the Aristotelian perfection of heavenly bodies and the pure, diaphanous quality of the Moon, which was theologically associated with the purity of the Immaculate Virgin. Galileo himself had had training in art and interacted with artists, many of whom had observed the Moon tele-

Scientific Instruments. Isaac Newton's telescope, the first reflecting telescope, made in 1668, in front of a corresponding drawing from the *Principia Mathematica.* ©JAMES A. SUGAR/CORBIS

scopically with reference to specific paintings. Ever since Plutarch wrote his essay on the face that seemingly appeared on the Moon's surface, it had been common to refer to the lunar facade as similar to the surface of a painting, and in the seventeenth century writers conventionally likened the dark and light sides of the Moon to painted pigments. The Virgin was, for theological reasons, conventionally painted in the presence of a crystalline moon. In his *Inmaculada* of 1619, Diego Velázquez depicted the Virgin standing on a textured moon, the image he had almost certainly seen for himself through a telescope in Seville.

THE MICROSCOPE

The success of the telescope and consequent diffusion of its optical principles led quickly to the appearance of the first compound microscopes between 1612 and 1618. Galileo himself had one, but until the second half of the seventeenth century they seem to have been more a curiosity than an active research tool. The main technical problems of microscopes were to illuminate the substance under observation effectively and to produce a small lens that could provide a sharp image. Large magnifications tended to yield blurry images. Microscopy really got under way with the publication of Robert Hooke's *Micrographia* (1665) and Jan Swammerdam's general history of insects in 1669. In the early 1670s they were joined by contributions from Marcello Malpighi (1628–1694) and Antoni van Leeuwenhoek (1632–1723).

The earliest microscopes looked like telescopes: the lenses were set in wooden rings mounted on the ends of cardboard tubes, the one that held the ocular fitting inside the tube with the objective. Hooke used a compound microscope with a double-convex lens objective and a complicated three-lens eyepiece. By this time, however, improvements in grinding techniques had produced simple microscopes with much higher powers of magnification, the kind used by Leeuwenhoek. Sold in large numbers at the end of the seventeenth century, this was the instrument that popularized microscopy.

NAVIGATIONAL, SURVEYING, AND PRACTICAL INSTRUMENTS

In the late Middle Ages and early modern times, the so-called mariner's astrolabe was used for telling time: by lining up the site with the Sun the user could read the time of day directly from a dial on the instrument. But the device had no use in practical navigation. The most common nautical instruments were the cross-staff, the back-staff, and the quadrant, reasonably simple handheld devices for measuring the altitude of stars but which could not easily be used to measure the angle between two stars from a moving boat. These instruments were all abandoned in the 1770s, replaced by John Hadley's reflecting quadrant, or octant, which eventually gave rise to the sextant, still in use today. With it, the navigator could bring the Moon's reflection down to the horizon, where the image would remain immovable, no matter how violently the ship was rolling.

Folding rules could be used by surveyors, gunners, or carpenters for small-scale plotting of terrain, or to estimate heights and depths, and were engraved with useful information like timber and board measures. A sector was a jointed rule with two radial arms engraved with a graduated scale. With the invention of logarithms (1614), the sector gave rise to the slide rule. Such ruled instruments were only as accurate as their graduations. Various methods of graduation, constantly improved, such as subdividing a scale by transverse lines that could be read to the one-hundredth part of quite small units, depending on the quality of the engraving, allowed the direct reading of angles, to an accuracy of five or ten seconds. Such graduation schemes became increasingly geometrical in the course of the eighteenth century and finally machines were devised for engraving linear scales.

There were also instruments of a practical nature designed to be carried by ordinary citizens. One such was the compendium, a pocket-sized brass gadget made for personal use that typically included an equinoctial sundial, religious calendars, a table of latitudes, a magnetic compass, a nocturnal (to determine time at night), a tide computer, and a table for establishing ports.

PHYSICAL INSTRUMENTS

Thermometers based on a variety of principles and materials were built as curiosities in the seventeenth century. It was not until the German physicist Daniel Gabriel Fahrenheit began to use mercury systematically in the 1720s that the thermometer design stabilized, even though competing models used other kinds of liquid. Most used alcohol, which was cheaper, but the reading of the scale varied with the concentration of alcohol. The Fahrenheit thermometer (with two fixed points, the freezing [32°] and boiling [212°] points of water, respectively) was adopted in England, Germany, and the Netherlands; France used René-Antoine Ferchaulte de Réaumur's scale, where 0° was the freezing point of water.

Robert Hooke devised a barometer to measure atmospheric pressure based on the variation of a column of mercury; Christiaan Huygens made a similar model but, following an idea of René Descartes, it used two liquids, mercury and water. The only barometer widely used around 1700 was that of Evangelista Torricelli, a tube plunged into a container of mercury. At issue was how to achieve consistent variations in the height of the mercury column, how best to contain the mercury, and what kind of scale could be devised (in the end, a metal casing placed around the glass tube bore the graduation marks). The hygrometer, to measure humidity, presented similar difficulties. The problem was to find an appropriate substance that was sturdy yet suitably sensitive to humidity. Finally, around 1783, Horace-Bénédict de Saussure perfected a model in which a hair held by a clamp at one end was attached at the other to a silver thread which, as it wound around a horizontal axis, caused a pointer to move across a 360° graduated dial. In the case of all three of these instruments, there was a century-long process whereby scientists devised workable instruments through the trial-and-error methods of empirical craftsmen.

ELECTRICAL MACHINES
Benjamin Franklin's discoveries made electrical machines and demonstrations fashionable after 1750. A variety of machines featuring the production of electrical current with a hand crank were made in the first half of the eighteenth century; but they were not generally produced until the English instrument maker Jesse Ramsden's plate machine of 1766, which was equipped with an electrometer to measure the charge produced. Subsequently, all such machines had electrometers because they were useful in measuring the shock applied to patients undergoing electric-shock therapy. Such machines could be connected to Leyden jars serving as batteries.

SPECIALIZED WORKSHOPS
Specialized workshops making and selling scientific instruments proliferated in England and in France in the eighteenth century. Some of the earlier ones specialized either in navigational or surveying instruments, on the one hand, or physical instruments, especially barometers, on the other. The first large instrumentation workshop in England was that of George Adams founded in 1735, identified by a sign of Tycho Brahe's head in Fleet Street, London. Brahe (1546–1601), of course, was a pre-telescopic astronomer famous for his design and use of huge, finely calibrated observational instruments using the unaided eye alone, and thus became an apt symbol for the craft of instrumentation. Microscopes were Adams's specialty, as well as mathematical instruments of all types. John and Peter Dolland, father and son, opened an optical shop in London in 1752. The Dollands made quadrants, telescopes, and other observational instruments in large numbers. Of all the English instrument makers of the period, Jesse Ramsdem (1735–1800) was said to be the best mechanician and optician. He was famous for large-scale astronomical and geodesic instruments, built telescopes for European observatories, and was elected a fellow of the Royal Society. In Holland, Jan van Musschenbroek, himself an important popularizer of Newtonian physics, had a famous workshop (in which he made instruments for his brother Pieter), as did Fahrenheit, a German born in Danzig who lived and worked in Amsterdam. Fahrenheit specialized in glass instruments, particularly the thermometer whose scale he established, and the barometer.

In France, the great instrument makers of the late eighteenth century tended to work for institutions. The Mégniés (probably two brothers) were associated with the Academy of Sciences, where they built chemical apparatuses for Antoine-Laurent Lavoisier (1743–1794), as well as telescopes and other optical instruments. Étienne Lenoir (1822–1900) worked mainly for the Weights and Measures Commission, where he built the apparatus that French expeditionaries used to measure the meridian.

INSTRUMENTS AND IMPERIAL RIVALRIES
As the expeditions sent out by European powers to the Pacific came increasingly to focus on scientific matters, they began to take on the guise of floating

laboratories, equipped with instrument collections that increased in size with each succeeding expedition. In the last quarter of the eighteenth century, numerous expeditions tested the marine chronometer devised by John Harrison (1693–1776) for the determination of longitude at sea. The instrument was a matched set of clocks, one set to the prime meridian, the other to local time. The difference in hours multiplied by fifteen yields the degree of longitude. On his 1772–1775 voyage, Captain James Cook tested four English chronometers, one by Harrison and three by John Arnold. He quickly determined that with accurate chronometers longitude could be determined within 1.5 degrees of accuracy, and more importantly, he let it be known publicly that he was abandoning the complex and tedious "lunar distance" method for determining longitude in favor of chronometers.

The role that scientific instrumentation played in imperial rivalries of the late eighteenth century can be appreciated in the provisioning of the expedition that the Italian captain Alessandro Malaspina led for the Spanish crown between 1782 and 1794. For the procuring of scientific instruments, the Spanish navy had an agent in London and another in Paris. The instrument makers were anxious to place their wares on spectacular expeditions such as the one being planned, because the performance of the instruments was highly publicized after the voyage in the string of memoirs by officers and naturalists sure to follow. Malaspina carried seven sets of chronometers, four made by Arnold and three by Ferdinand Berthoud. Alexander Dalrymple, who supplied Malaspina with English instruments, had close connections with Arnold's shop, as a result of which Malaspina offered to provide Arnold with systematic comparisons of the longitude results given by Arnold's instruments and those obtained simultaneously by astronomical methods. In this way, detailed field results were fed back to the manufacturer, who could then make the necessary corrections in future models. Malaspina's judgment was that an Arnold chronometer was the best of the six, a Berthoud almost as good; the others ran too fast. The rest of Malaspina's apparatus was heavily English: an astronomical pendulum invented by George Graham, two Dolland achromatic telescopes with triple objectives, and thermometers from the houses of Nairne and Blunt, respectively.

INSTRUMENT COLLECTIONS

As a result of the scientific revolution, collections of scientific instruments emerged in all of the centers of the Western world. Some collections were formed at universities and other teaching institutions for didactic purposes; others fulfilled the whims of wealthy scientific amateurs. Popularizers of Isaac Newton, who diffused the results of the scientific revolution in public lectures in the early eighteenth century, required a large number of instruments with which to conduct experiments or illustrate scientific principles during their presentations. The prototypes of much of this Newtonian demonstration apparatus were built by Pieter van Musschenbroek at the request of Willem J. s'Gravesande. The entire collection, including pulleys, weights, pendulums, pumps, and machines for illustrating specific concepts of physics is still preserved in Holland. In the second half of the eighteenth century, electrical apparatus was added to the repertory of demonstration equipment. The reputation of lecturers on physics depended in great part on the quality of their apparatus. Instrumentation became so expensive that private institutions like the Royal Society were dependent on patrons to supply them with instruments. The collection of the German counts of Hesse in the early eighteenth century had 57 telescopes and 32 microscopes. To own such instruments was a mark of culture. The collection of the kings of France at Versailles contained 245 instruments, including 52 pieces of electric apparatus, at the time of its confiscation during the French Revolution. In Madrid, the Spanish crown established in 1791 a Royal Machine Museum (Real Gabinete de Máquinas), a collection of 270 models of different kinds of machines. Private collectors of the same period, whose collections we know through inventories included in their wills, inevitably owned electrical machines and air pumps. Franklin's experiments had made the former a symbol of scientific progress, and air pumps, as a kind of prototypical machine, though of a size manageable for demonstrations, were a convenient symbol of the incipient industrial revolution and could be used to run a multiplicity of experiments.

See also **Astronomy; Barometer; Biology; Brahe, Tycho; Chronometer; Copernicus, Nicolaus; Galileo Galilei; Hooke, Robert; Huygens Family; Lavoisier, Antoine; Malpighi, Marcello; Optics; Scientific Revolution; Shipbuilding and Navigation; Surveying.**

BIBLIOGRAPHY

Bradbury, S. *The Evolution of the Microscope.* Oxford and New York, 1967.

Daumas, Maurice. *Scientific Instruments of the Seventeenth and Eighteenth Centuries and Their Makers.* Translated and edited by Mary Holbrook. London, 1989.

Glick, Thomas F. "Imperio y dependencia científica en el XVIII español e inglés: La provisión de los instrumentos científicos." In *Ciencia, vida y espacio en Iberoamerica,* edited by José L. Peset, vol. 3, pp. 49–63. Madrid, 1989.

North, John. *The Norton History of Astronomy and Cosmology.* New York, 1994.

Reeves, Eileen. *Painting the Heavens: Art and Science in the Age of Galileo.* Princeton, 1997.

Ruestow, Edward G. *The Microscope in the Dutch Republic: The Shaping of Discovery.* Cambridge, U.K., and New York, 1996.

Turner, Gerard L'E. *Elizabethan Instrument Makers: The Origins of the London Trade in Precision Instrument Making.* Oxford and New York, 2000.

THOMAS F. GLICK

SCIENTIFIC JOURNALS. *See* Communication, Scientific.

SCIENTIFIC METHOD.

Methods for investigating the natural world were transformed in the early modern era, leading to a variety of approaches that emerged from diverse philosophical orientations. To call these diverse methodologies "scientific" is a convenience but one that entails anachronistic usage. The Latin word *scientia,* meaning, broadly, 'knowledge', has none of the methodological implications of the modern term *science.* Early modern investigators called themselves philosophers, natural philosophers, physicians, and experimental or mathematical philosophers rather than scientists. Methodological issues often were the focus of lively discussions and bitter disputes. By the end of the era, approaches to investigating the natural world had undergone profound changes that historians traditionally have called the "scientific revolution."

ARISTOTELIANISM

The predominant methodology inherited by early modern learned culture was Aristotelian. The writings of Aristotle became the basis of the medieval university curriculum and remained so well into the seventeenth century. For Aristotle, knowledge (*epistēmē* in Greek, *scientia* in Latin) was universal and necessary. The goal of natural philosophy was to grasp the principles and natures of natural substances and to understand their causes. The method was a logical one based on syllogistic reasoning. If A equals B and B equals C, then A equals C. The four Aristotelian causes comprised the material cause (what a thing is made of), the formal cause (what kind of thing it is), the efficient cause (what made it), and the final cause (its purpose or goal), this last being most important. Demonstration was a process whereby a syllogistic proof of an effect was constructed through an analysis of its causes.

In the mid-sixteenth century at the University of Padua, traditional Aristotelian logic began to provide a renewed methodological basis for investigating the natural world. The most important figure in this development was Jacopo Zabarella (1533–1598). Remaining within an Aristotelian framework, the new logic asked how investigators got from sense perception to demonstrable truth. They discussed "demonstrative regress, a logical technique permitting the scholar to reason from an observed effect (fact) to its proximate cause and then to reason back (regress) from the cause to the effect where the reasoning began" (Grendler, p. 263). These methodological explorations influenced Galileo and other investigators until the mid-seventeenth century when Aristotelianism itself declined in influence.

HUMANISM AND NEOPLATONISM

Without replacing Aristotelianism, new approaches developed in the fifteenth and sixteenth centuries that emphasized particulars. Humanism was a broad intellectual movement that engaged in the reform of Latin and the rediscovery of ancient texts. Humanists criticized the logical approach of Scholasticism and often focused upon individuals in specific times and places, utilizing the dialogue and letter as literary forms that allowed the expression of individual points of view. They also studied and edited ancient texts, many of which became significant for the investigation of the natural world.

Renaissance Neoplatonism emerged as a result of this humanist textual work. A key figure is Marsilio Ficino (1433–1499), who during the second half of the fifteenth century translated and edited the writings of Plato, Neoplatonic philosophers such as Plotinus (205–270 C.E.), and the Hermetic corpus. The latter consisted of a group of writings actually dating from late antiquity that Ficino and his contemporaries believed were written before the time of Moses by one Hermes Trismegistus. They considered that the Hermetic corpus comprised a synopsis of ancient theology *(prisca theologia)*. Ficino and his many successors in the sixteenth and seventeenth centuries believed in the reality of magic and in occult powers because they viewed the universe as a spiritual unity connected in all its various parts by sympathies and antipathies. The magus or magician could influence remote parts of the cosmos by manipulating these connections, and he or she did so to influence worldly matters, such as sickness and health. The operational aspects of Neoplatonic magical traditions may have influenced the development of experimentation, a methodology that entailed the active manipulation of the natural world.

Neoplatonic doctrines also influenced notions about experience and its role in investigating nature. One example entails the doctrine of signatures and illumination. In one version, that of the sixteenth-century physician Paracelsus (1493/94–1541), experience is framed by the biblical context of the Fall. Humans after their expulsion from paradise no longer had direct access to the Word of God or direct knowledge of the world of nature. Yet because God had put the light of nature *(lumens naturalis)* in them they could overcome their fallen state. The light of nature awakened in their minds, so they were able to see signs stamped on natural things. Directly experiencing such things, they could thereby see God's "signatures," which were external signs that pointed to the internal nature of things.

MEDICINE AND ALCHEMY

Within the discipline of medicine, interest in particulars and a validation of individual experience developed in a variety of ways. In the fourteenth century a branch of medicine known as *practica* emerged that concerned the particulars of disease and treatments. By the sixteenth century the writings of the ancient physician Galen (129–c. 199 C.E.) had become widely influential, particularly with respect to

his empirical orientation and his practice of dissecting animals. Human dissection was taken up as part of the medical curriculum in the late medieval universities. Initially dissections were carried out in formal, public settings in which a high-status, learned doctor stood on a podium to read an authoritative text on anatomy, while a low-status person performed the handwork of dissection. In his famous *De Humani Corporis Fabrica* (On the fabric of the human body) published in 1543, Andreas Vesalius (1514–1564) advocated hands-on dissection by the high-status physician as well as careful observation and the visual depiction of body parts. Vesalius criticized but was also indebted to Galen. His famous treatise is part of a rich tradition of anatomical study that continued through the eighteenth century. This tradition notably includes the experimental work of William Harvey (1578–1657) in the 1620s on the circulation of the blood.

Alchemy represents a distinct discipline that developed in early modern Europe after the medieval transmission of key texts from the Islamic world. Alchemists often undertook hands-on, laboratory operations entailing separations, distillations, and the like. In the seventeenth century alchemy and related fields developed genuine experimental procedures. Jean Baptiste van Helmont (1579–1644) carried out numerous careful determinations of specific weights of substances he produced in his laboratory. George Starkey (1627–1665) undertook thousands of experiments to discover a single method of changing all sulfurs into medicines. The laboratory experiments of Robert Boyle (1627–1691) were influenced by this work. Scholars have investigated these seventeenth-century developments in detail and have traced their influence on eighteenth-century chemists, such as Antoine Lavoisier (1743–1794). This scholarship has brought into question the traditional sharp distinction between early modern alchemy and modern chemistry.

MECHANICAL ARTS

The mechanical arts entailed skilled craft work, including carpentry and weaving, but also arts that are now considered fine arts, such as painting and sculpture. The influence of artisanal craft values on early modern scientific methodology has been a longstanding topic of discussion in the history of science. The Viennese scholar and refugee Edgar Zilsel

(1891–1944) argued that artisanal values that appreciated hands-on experience and craft work influenced the emergence of an experimental methodology in the seventeenth century. Subsequent scholarship has shown that the fifteenth- and sixteenth-century proliferation of writings on mechanical arts transformed the practical knowledge of the crafts into discursive subjects worthy of the attention of learned persons. Painters and other practitioners wrote books in which they articulated the value of practice and direct experience as crucial for obtaining knowledge of the natural world.

MATHEMATICS AND MECHANICS

Practical problems in the mechanical arts increasingly came to be analyzed in mathematical terms. The ancient mathematician Archimedes (c. 287–212 B.C.E.), who had applied geometric analysis to problems of statics (the science of weights), came to be highly influential. In the sixteenth century Niccolò Tartaglia (1499–1557) published the first Latin treatises of Archimedes and also wrote books in which he mathematically analyzed practical problems, such as the trajectory of cannonballs. Later in the same century authors, such as the nobleman and patron of Galileo, Guidobaldo del Monte (1545–1607), wrote treatises on machines and mechanics in the context of theory and mathematics.

This sixteenth-century tradition preceded the development of the new science of motion developed by Galileo Galilei (1564–1642). Galileo worked out the mathematical kinematics of motion. Disregarding air resistance, he concluded that all bodies fall in uniformly accelerated motion and that velocity increases in proportion to time elapsed. He went on to deduce the mathematical results of this conclusion, for instance, that the distance increases in proportion to the square of time. Following Galileo, Christiaan Huygens (1629–1695) worked out the mathematics of the pendulum and of circular motion. Near the end of the seventeenth century, in *Philosophiae Naturalis Principia Mathematica* (1687; Mathematical principles of natural philosophy), Isaac Newton (1642–1727) created a system of terrestrial and celestial dynamics in which he demonstrated mathematically a large array of propositions concerning natural phenomena. In these and many other examples in the seventeenth and eighteenth centuries, the aim of natural and experimental philosophers was to describe motion by means of mathematics. This project was possible because of simultaneous developments within mathematics itself, culminating in the invention of calculus by Newton and by Gottfried Wilhelm Leibniz (1646–1716) at the end of the seventeenth century.

INSTRUMENTATION AND EXPERIMENTATION

During the sixteenth and seventeenth centuries the use of instruments to measure and investigate the natural world came to be increasingly important. The Danish nobleman Tycho Brahe (1546–1601) is considered the greatest observational astronomer before the invention of the telescope. For twenty years, from his Uraniborg observatory, Brahe made systematic observations of the moon, the planets, and other phenomena, such as the comet of 1577. He used these observations not only to correct and improve available data but to investigate and develop theories about the nature of the heavens and the structure of the cosmos.

Observational astronomy changed with the invention of the telescope. With this new instrument Galileo made detailed observations of the moon and the stars of the Milky Way. He further discovered the four moons of Jupiter (the Medicean Stars). In *The Sidereal Messenger* (1610) he described these discoveries with both text and drawings. Galileo's conclusions were by no means instantly accepted. He had to persuade his contemporaries that his instrument produced valid data, not optical illusions. Like Brahe and others of his predecessors, Galileo produced new data, but he also used that data to make novel claims about the nature of the cosmos.

Instruments and devices became especially significant in the seventeenth and eighteenth centuries. Among these devises were "philosophical" machines especially devised to investigate the natural world. A prominent example of such a philosophical machine was the air pump, used by Boyle to investigate the nature of air. The pump was difficult to build and to use. Nevertheless, it was key to a whole series of experiments concerning air carried out in the mid-seventeenth century.

In seventeenth-century England the notion of the reliable witness to experiments emerged. Such a witness was an honorable person, preferably a gentleman (therefore immune from the self-interest of the artisan), who could attest to the accuracy of the stated results of a given experiment. Valid experimental results came to be tied to the social requirements of gentlemanly honor. By the eighteenth century, however, learned visitors interested in natural philosophy who came to London often visited the shops of instrument makers to purchase instruments but also to discuss philosophical and experimental issues. By this time the instrument maker's shop had become a space for philosophical discourse, while the status of certain kinds of craft practitioners had risen.

The use of instruments to investigate nature had important methodological implications because it challenged the notion of Aristotelian common experience. For Aristotelians common experience was valid because all reasonable people without question agreed that a particular claim was true. In contrast, truth derived from experimentation, and instrumentation depended on the manipulation of a device that was only available to particular individuals. Such individuals had to have access to the device itself and had to possess particular skills to use it. Aristotelian common experience and seventeenth-century experiment represented opposing methodologies. Further the use of instrumentation to investigate nature challenged the Aristotelian separation of the categories of *technē* (material production and reasoning about that production) and *epistēmē* (certain knowledge of unchanging truths).

BACONIAN EMPIRICISM AND NATURAL HISTORY

The English jurist and philosopher Francis Bacon (1561–1626) proposed a new methodology that aimed to bring about a continuous flow of new facts about the natural world. Bacon's most significant methodological work was *Instauratio Magna* (1620–1626; The great instauration), which included *Novum Organum* (1620; New instrument). Bacon rejected syllogistic logic, pointing out that the premises of the syllogism could be in error. His own method entailed gathering a large amount of data on a variety of subjects and applying that data to the development of axioms. His goal was to account for the many particular things in nature in all its diversity. Yet his method entailed more than the simple collection of sense experiences, for Bacon believed the senses could deceive. Rather, in the

creation of axioms he took into account the "maker's knowledge," that is, the presuppositions necessary for the fabrication of a thing. To gather data, Bacon proposed a cooperative effort to write "histories of the trades," detailed accounts of the essential operations of productive arts, such as silk textiles, mining, printing, papermaking, and agriculture, as well as "natural histories" on topics such as snakes, birds, and metals.

In the sixteenth and seventeenth centuries, particularly in Italy, natural history was the focus of growing interest. The creation of natural history collections by naturalists, such as Ulisse Aldrovandi (1522–1605) and Athanasius Kircher (1601–1680), and the intense study of the specimens in those collections became an important aspect of the investigation of nature. Museums became "laboratories of nature" (Findlen, p. 154), where investigations entailing testing, dissection, and distillation occurred. In some instances the collection of specimens was accompanied by the creation of detailed drawings based on careful observations. Collecting specimens, examining them, and having them drawn or painted became important modalities for the study of nature. Federico Cesi (1585–1630) and other members of the Academy of the Lincei, a scientific society founded in 1603, were particularly active in this form of investigation of the flora and fauna of Italy.

DESCARTES AND THE MECHANICAL PHILOSOPHY

The methodological writings of René Descartes (1596–1650) laid the foundations for the "mechanical philosophy." Descartes's famous dictum *"Cogito ergo sum"* ('I think therefore I am') is the basis for his notion that mind is a thinking substance and is to be excluded from the physical world entirely. That world, composed of particles of matter, is characterized by extension. These particles move only by virtue of mechanical necessity. Their motions produce all the variety of natural phenomena. Descartes eliminated spiritual or mental qualities from the material world, leaving the thinking subject (the "I" of the cogito) as the discoverer of the clear and certain truths of nature. That natural world, characterized by extension, is ordered by mathematical relationships. For Descartes certain knowledge could be obtained by applying mathematical rules to the world of nature.

CONCLUSION

Investigations of the rich methodological cornucopia that characterizes the early modern period have been guided by several general principles. First, early modern thought is studied on its own terms, not according to the values of modern scientific methodology. Second, the wide-ranging connections of methodological thought to contemporaneous language and meaning on the one hand and to social and cultural conditions on the other are being explored in depth. Finally, studies have followed the sources, whatever that content might be. As a result, natural history has taken its place beside physics. The doctrine of signatures has been studied as thoroughly as the laws of planetary motion. Such contextual approaches have greatly expanded knowledge of early modern methodologies for investigating the natural world.

See also **Alchemy; Aldrovandi, Ulisse; Astronomy; Bacon, Francis; Boyle, Robert; Brahe, Tycho; Descartes, René; Galileo Galilei; Harvey, William; Helmont, Jean Baptiste van; Hermeticism; Huygens Family; Kircher, Athanasius; Leibniz, Gottfried Wilhelm; Mathematics; Natural History; Nature; Neoplatonism; Newton, Isaac; Paracelsus; Scientific Revolution; Vesalius, Andreas.**

BIBLIOGRAPHY

Primary Sources

Aristotle. *The Complete Works of Aristotle: The Revised Oxford Translation.* Edited by Jonathan Barnes. 2 vols. Princeton, 1984.

Galilei, Galileo. *Sidereus Nuncius; or, The Sidereal Messenger.* Translated by Albert van Helden. Chicago, 1989. An English translation that reproduces all of Galileo's drawings. Contains an extensive and useful introduction and notes.

Newton, Isaac. *The Principia: Mathematical Principles of Natural Philosophy.* Translated by I. Bernard Cohen and Anne Whitman. Berkeley and Los Angeles, 1999. Translation of *Principia*, 3rd ed. (1726). The translation to use. Contains an extensive and useful guide by Cohen.

Secondary Sources

Applebaum, Wilbur, ed. *Encyclopedia of the Scientific Revolution: From Copernicus to Newton.* New York, 2000.

Bennett, James A. "Shopping for Instruments in Paris and London." In *Merchants and Marvels: Commerce, Science, and Art in Early Modern Europe,* edited by Pamela H. Smith and Paula Findlen, pp. 370–395. New York, 2002.

Bono, James J. *The Word of God and the Languages of Man: Interpreting Nature in Early Modern Science and Medicine.* Vol. 1, *Ficino to Descartes.* Madison, Wis., 1995.

Dear, Peter. *Discipline and Experience: The Mathematical Way in the Scientific Revolution.* Chicago, 1995.

Des Chene, Dennis. *Spirits and Clocks: Machine and Organism in Descartes.* Ithaca, 2001.

Findlen, Paula. *Possessing Nature: Museums, Collecting, and Scientific Culture in Early Modern Italy.* Berkeley and Los Angeles, 1994.

Freedberg, David. *The Eye of the Lynx: Galileo, His Friends, and the Beginnings of Modern Natural History.* Chicago, 2002.

Grant, Edward. *The Foundations of Modern Science in the Middle Ages: Their Religious, Institutional, and Intellectual Contexts.* Cambridge, U.K., 1996.

Grendler, Paul F. *The Universities of the Italian Renaissance.* Baltimore, 2002.

Lindberg, David C., and Robert S. Westman, eds. *Reappraisals of the Scientific Revolution.* Cambridge, U.K., 1990.

Long, Pamela O. *Openness, Secrecy, Authorship: Technical Arts and the Culture of Knowledge from Antiquity to the Renaissance.* Baltimore, 2001.

Newman, William R., and Lawrence M. Principe. *Alchemy Tried in the Fire: Starkey, Boyle, and the Fate of Helmontian Chymistry.* Chicago, 2002.

Pérez-Ramos, Antonio. *Francis Bacon's Idea of Science and the Maker's Knowledge Tradition.* Oxford, 1988.

Shapin, Steven, and Simon Schaffer. *Leviathan and the Air-Pump: Hobbes, Boyle, and the Experimental Life.* Princeton, 1985.

Siraisi, Nancy G. *Medieval and Early Renaissance Medicine: An Introduction to Knowledge and Practice.* Chicago, 1990.

Wallace, William A. *Galileo's Logic of Discovery and Proof: The Background, Content, and Use of His Appropriated Treatises on Aristotle's Posterior Analytics.* Dordrecht, 1992.

PAMELA O. LONG

SCIENTIFIC REVOLUTION.

The scientific revolution took place from the sixteenth century through the seventeenth century and saw the formation of conceptual, methodological, and institutional approaches to the natural world that are recognizably like those of modern science. It should not be seen as a revolution in science but a revolution in thought and practice that brought about modern science. Although highly complex and multifaceted, it can essentially be seen as the amalgamation of what was called natural philosophy with various so-called subordinate sciences, such as the mathematical sciences, astronomy, optics, and geography, or with separate traditions, such as those of natural magic and alchemy. The traditional natural philosophy, institutionalized in the universities since their foundation in the thirteenth century, was almost entirely based upon the doctrines of Aristotle and followed rationalist procedures. When those trained in natural philosophy began to recognize the power of alternative traditions for revealing truths about the physical world, they increasingly incorporated them into their natural philosophies. In so doing, these natural philosophers inevitably introduced different methods and procedures to complement and refine the earlier rationalism. To fully understand the scientific revolution, however, requires consideration not only of what happened but also of why it happened. Before looking at this, it is necessary to consider the status of the scientific revolution as a historiographical category.

HISTORIOGRAPHY AND THE SCIENTIFIC REVOLUTION

The *scientific revolution* is the historians' term and should be seen as a shorthand way of referring to a multitude of historical phenomena and processes, not all of which were directly related to one another. Although potentially misleading in so far as there were not, for example, defining moments when the revolution can be said to have begun or to have ended nor a recognizable body of revolutionaries who were all self-consciously affiliated with one another, it continues to be recognized as a valid label. The lengthy time span of this revolution might also seem anomalous, but this is easily outweighed by the undeniable fact that approaches to natural knowledge in 1700 were completely different from those deployed in 1500 and that there is no exaggeration in calling these changes revolutionary. Those historians who have chosen to emphasize the undoubted continuities between the thought of the scientific revolution and medieval thought nevertheless concede that, by the end of the period, things were completely different from the way they had been at the beginning. It is perfectly possible, for example, to see Nicolaus Copernicus (1473–1543), who first suggested that Earth was not stationary in the center of the universe but was re-

volving around the Sun, not as the first modern astronomer but as the last of the great medieval astronomers. Far from being an indefensible position, this is the only way to fully understand what Copernicus did and how he did it. Nevertheless it remains true to say that the switch from an Earth-centered universe to a Sun-centered planetary system had revolutionary consequences that cannot possibly be denied.

An important indicator of the persuasiveness of the notion of a scientific revolution is its role in one of the most influential works in the modern philosophy of science, Thomas Kuhn's (1922–1996) *Structure of Scientific Revolutions* (1962). Inspired chiefly by the Copernican revolution (which he made the subject of an earlier book) and its far-reaching aftermath, Kuhn developed a theory about the nature of scientific progress based upon radical innovations that mark a revolutionary disruption from earlier thinking. Kuhn's influence has been greatest among philosophers and sociologists of science concerned with understanding the nature of scientific innovation and advance, but his ideas were directly inspired by and modeled upon the historiography of the scientific revolution.

Given the importance of this historiographical category, it is hardly surprising that it has attracted a number of attempts to provide a simple key for understanding it. Two of the most serious attempts to explain its origins are the so-called scholar and craftsmen thesis and the Protestantism (or even Puritanism) and science thesis. Deriving essentially from Marxist assumptions, the scholar and craftsmen thesis takes for granted the idea that modern science is closer to the work of elite craftsmen and skilled artisans than it is to the ivory tower philosophizing of the medieval university. All that was required to bring about the scientific revolution therefore was a realization by educated scholars, provoked by the economic stimulus of the incipient capitalism of the Renaissance period, that artisans were producing accurate and useful knowledge of the physical world. This thesis is untenable on a number of grounds. Among the more wide-ranging are the fact that it pays insufficient attention to the continuities between the natural philosophy of the scientific revolution and medieval natural philosophy and the obvious fact that craftsmen and artisans do not, as a rule, rely upon, much less produce, scientific thinking while doing their work. There is too much reliance in these Marxist accounts on glib talk to the effect that experimentation is manual work, craftsmen indulge in manual work, therefore craftsmen do experiments. Nonetheless it is certainly true that scholars began to pay attention to the work of technical artisans in the Renaissance, and this no doubt owed something to economic factors. But the scholars took this craft knowledge and turned it into something closer to modern science; the artisans themselves were not already in possession of scientific knowledge.

The Protestantism and science thesis, based more on statistical claims that Protestants play a disproportionate role in the development of modern science than on causative explanation, is also problematic but much harder to dismiss. Although it is quite clear that Roman Catholic thinkers, notably Copernicus, Galileo Galilei (1564–1642), and René Descartes (1596–1650), played a major role in the early part of the scientific revolution, the later period does seem to be dominated by developments in Protestant countries, even though the Protestant population as a whole remained the minority in Europe. Nevertheless the reasons advanced to explain why this might be so remain unconvincing. One of the most powerful refinements of this thesis, by the American sociologist Robert K. Merton (1910–2003), seeks to explain the culmination of the scientific revolution in late-seventeenth-century England, with the formation of the Royal Society and the appearance of its most illustrious fellow Isaac Newton (1642–1727), as the result of the rise of Puritanism in the civil war period. Here the statistics have proved much less satisfactory, since it is virtually impossible, without merely begging the question, to say who was a Puritan and who was not. Moreover the suggested reasons seem to apply equally to all English Protestants, not just Puritans, and indeed in some cases to European Catholics as well. The starting point for these explanations is the claim of the German sociologist Max Weber (1864–1920) that the ''spirit'' of capitalism is linked to the Protestant work ethic. Again it is difficult to accept the suggested reasons for this link, and yet, as a result of collective prosopography, a feeling remains that there must be some truth in it.

Another influential historiographical claim about the scientific revolution, but this time one that does not seek to explain its origins but its cultural impact, links the development of the scientific revolution with a vigorous reassertion of patriarchal values and the subjection of women. Based on a historiography that presents premechanistic worldviews as holistic, organic, vitalistic, and feminine, the mechanical philosophy of the scientific revolution (see below), by contrast, is shown to be manipulative, exploitative, and aggressively masculine. Supported by pointing to the routine use of sexual metaphors by the new natural philosophers in which the investigator is recommended to subdue, constrain, and bind into service Mother Nature in order to facilitate penetrating her inner secrets, feminist historians have seen these attitudes as a reason for the gendering of science that persists into the twenty-first century. There seems to be a prevailing assumption that science is a masculine pursuit and that women are somehow mentally unsuited to it. This is a legacy not of the ancient period or of the Middle Ages, feminists claim, but of the new approach to the natural world developed during the scientific revolution. Although there is some interesting and undeniable evidence for this general view, the claim that earlier natural philosophy was in some way feminine or feminist seems merely tendentious. The magical worldview, for example, was exploitative and manipulative for centuries prior to the scientific revolution. What's more, traditional natural philosophy excluded women throughout the Middle Ages.

If the historians' concept of a scientific revolution remains indispensable for understanding the origins of modern science, it raises another important set of historiographical issues. Why did the scientific revolution occur when it did (at the end of the Renaissance and the beginning of the early modern period)? Why did it occur only in western Europe? More to the point, why did it not occur in ancient Greece, early imperial China, medieval Islam, or Byzantium, where there is enough historical evidence to suggest it might have occurred? To what extent was the scientific revolution responsible for the subsequent cultural dominance of the West? Debates on these issues continue in the twenty-first century. Requiring a wide-ranging familiarity with the history of diverse cultures as the basis of comparison and an enlightened caution against chauvinistic assumptions that Western culture is somehow innately superior, there has so far been little or no consensus. It seems likely, however, that this aspect of the historiography of the scientific revolution will grow as awareness of the need for multicultural perspectives to reach a full understanding of the past increases.

THE RENAISSANCE AND THE SCIENTIFIC REVOLUTION

In its origins the scientific revolution can be seen as another outcome of that sea change in European life and thought known as the Renaissance. In particular the new emphasis by intellectuals on the *studia humanitatis,* the 'study of humanity', with its concomitant concern for the *vita activa,* the 'active life' lived for the public good, as opposed to the traditional religious emphasis upon the contemplative life, stimulated new attitudes toward natural knowledge. Traditional natural philosophy had always been seen as a "handmaiden" to theology, the queen of the sciences, and as such it was a contemplative pursuit concerned with understanding God's creation for its own sake. The Renaissance humanists, concerned with living the active life, increasingly looked to alternative intellectual traditions with more pragmatic aims, in particular the mathematical sciences and the traditions of what was called natural magic.

These changes in attitude toward knowledge and what it was for went hand in hand with revelations emerging from the rediscovery of ancient wisdom. Humanist scholars systematically searched monastery libraries all over Europe for any surviving copies of ancient Roman and subsequently ancient Greek writings. Previously the only body of writing on natural philosophy available to Western scholars was that of Aristotle (384–322 B.C.E.), but for the first time it was possible to read the works of Plato (c. 428–348 or 347 B.C.E.), Epicurus (c. 341–270 B.C.E.), the Stoics, various Pythagorean or Neoplatonic writers, and others. Plato proved especially influential, and this boosted the importance of the later Pythagorean and Neoplatonist writers who were seen to be his followers. Since these writers tended to see mathematics and especially geometry not merely as human constructs but as reflections of the divine mind, the principles of which had been built into the world in Creation, they stimulated humanist scholars to see mathematics as a legitimate and powerful means of discovering truths about the natural world. This was in stark contrast to the prevailing Aristotelian view of mathematics, which was dismissed as essentially irrelevant for understanding nature because it was abstracted from physical considerations and did not provide explanations in terms of causes.

Similarly, the discovery of a body of writings attributed to Hermes Trismegistus (Thrice-Great Hermes), who was assumed to be an ancient sage deified by the Greeks, gave a new legitimacy and intellectual kudos to magical traditions. Although actually written in the second and third centuries C.E., the Hermetic writings were assumed to be contemporary with Moses and his writing of the Pentateuch. Since these works were highly magical, it now seemed that magic was part of ancient wisdom, the wisdom known to Adam that gradually became forgotten after the Fall. Throughout the Middle Ages the church had condemned magic, declaring it to be entirely dependent upon demonic intervention. After the discovery of the Hermetic writings, for a brief period magic was seen as a powerful system of knowledge that exploited the natural qualities and powers of bodies to recover the dominion over all things that God had offered to Adam (Genesis 1:28).

The elevation of the intellectual status of mathematics and natural magic had far-reaching effects. Large numbers of mathematical practitioners of various kinds were quick to extol the virtues of their practice in terms of its certainty (unlike the speculative natural philosophy) and its pragmatic usefulness. The result was an increasing mathematization of the world picture, culminating at the end of the seventeenth century in the supreme achievement of Newton. The title of his great book, *Philosophiae Naturalis Principia Mathematica* (1687; The mathematical principles of natural philosophy), still widely regarded in the twenty-first century as one of the most important scientific books, sums up the change from an Aristotelian natural philosophy where mathematics had no role to a physics dependent upon mathematics. Other salient points in this transformation were Copernicus's insistence in 1543 that Earth must move, in spite of the lack of compelling physical reasons for its movement, simply because the mathematics of a heliocentric system was more elegant and coherent, and the belief of the astronomer Johannes Kepler (1571–1630) that the world can be understood in geometrical terms because "Geometry, which before the origin of things was coeternal with the divine mind and is God himself . . . supplied God with patterns for the creation of the world" (1619; *Harmony of the World* [*Harmonices Mundi*], p. 304). The great Italian mathematical physicist Galileo claimed that the book of nature "is written in the language of mathematics . . . without which it is humanly impossible to understand a single word of it" (*The Assayer*, 1622, in *Discoveries and Opinions*, p. 238).

The increased concern with the practical utility of knowledge of the Renaissance humanists ensured that practitioners of occult arts, like alchemy, astrology, sympathetic magic, and what was called "mathematical magic" (the construction of technological devices and machines—regarded as occult because their operations could not be explained in Aristotelian terms), also earned enhanced intellectual status. The most important outcome of the rise of magic was an appropriation of one of its chief methods of exploration—the experimental method—and a far-reaching reassessment of the concept of so-called occult qualities.

The use of the experimental method in natural philosophy is undoubtedly a characterizing feature of the scientific revolution, but the method itself was not newly invented in this period. It was simply incorporated into the previously entirely speculative natural philosophy from the natural magic tradition. Alchemists and those seeking supposed sympathetic effects of one substance on another, in order to bring about desired ends, had long since developed and continued to use techniques of experimental manipulation. The most prominent figure in the scientific revolution responsible for promoting the experimental method was the English statesman and philosopher Francis Bacon (1561–1626), but it is perfectly clear that he took his inspiration from the magical tradition. Similarly William Gilbert (1544–1603), an English physician and author of a seminal book on magnetism generally seen as the first scientific book based almost entirely on the experimental method, was directly influenced by a medieval magical treatise. It used to be assumed by historians that Gilbert's *De Magnete* (1600; On the magnet) took its experimental method from craftsmen and artisans working with iron or manufacturing magnetic compasses, but all the features of his

experimental method are in a *Letter on the Magnet*, written by the natural magician Petrus Peregrinus de Maricourt (fl. 1269) and first published in 1558.

The issue of occult qualities came to prominence as a result of increasing dissatisfaction with Aristotelian matter theory and emerging awareness of alternative magical accounts. The aim of Aristotelian natural philosophy was to explain everything in terms of easily understood and obviously true factors. Accordingly, it tried to account for physical changes in terms of changes in the four manifest qualities, hot, cold, wet, and dry, all of which were obvious to the senses. In many cases, of course, a certain amount of ingenuity was required to refer changes back to these four qualities. A change from roughness to smoothness, for example, would be explained as a change from dryness to wetness. When ingenuity failed, however, there was often nothing for it but to admit that occult qualities were at work—qualities that could not be referred back to the manifest qualities but whose effects were undeniable to the senses. The classic occult quality is magnetism—the lodestone's ability to attract iron does not seem to be reducible to the action of heat or any other manifest quality, but its effect, the movement of a piece of iron, is visible for all to see.

It was common in the magical tradition to assume that some bodies could act upon others by inherent sympathies or antipathies, a notion that was dismissed by Aristotelians as an "asylum of ignorance" because it explained nothing. As the experimental method became increasingly accepted as a legitimate aspect of natural philosophy, however, it became possible to demonstrate the operation of sympathies or antipathies experimentally (consider any of the phenomena, for example, that modern chemists refer to as elective affinities between chemical compounds) and to consider them as operationally defined. This in turn led to speculations about causes. Either bodies could act on one another at a distance, or there was some form of invisible interaction. For some, particularly those in England who were influenced by Bacon's emphasis upon experiment devoid of speculation, it was possible to accept action at a distance merely on empiricist grounds and forego further speculation. For others, however, this was too magical to concede, and it was assumed that effects must be brought about by invisibly small particles streaming between bodies. This strategy was favored by those aware of the alchemical tradition, which had a long history of explanation in terms of invisibly small corpuscles, and was further reinforced by the revival of ancient atomism as the result of the rediscovery of the writings of Epicurus and of the summary of Epicurean principles by Lucretius (c. 100 or 99–c. 55 B.C.E.) in his *De Rerum Natura* (On the nature of things).

At its extreme the attempt to explain all physical phenomena in terms of the interactions of invisibly small particles led to a vigorous denial of occult qualities. Descartes, the French mathematician and philosopher, believed that his system was capable of explaining all phenomena without recourse to occult qualities and that all occult qualities themselves, including magnetism, were reducible to the motions of invisibly small particles. In England, by contrast, the Cartesian system was seen as unacceptably speculative and not always supported by the evidence. This was particularly apparent in what would now be thought of as chemical reactions (about which Descartes was largely silent) and in the case of gravitational attraction. If gravity was caused, as Descartes suggested, by continual streams of descending particles pushing things to Earth, why was it not possible to shield a body from these streams and keep it suspended? It is surely historically significant that the universal principle of gravitation, seen as an occult force capable of acting across vast distances of empty space, was developed by an English alchemist working within the tradition of Baconian empiricism—Newton.

The new importance of matter theory in understanding the nature of the physical world is another characterizing feature of the scientific revolution. These variations on the use of invisibly small particles, their motions, and their interactions were generally referred to as the mechanical philosophy, a term first coined by the English experimental natural philosopher Robert Boyle (1627–1691). Although only the systems developed separately by Descartes and Thomas Hobbes (1588–1679) could be said to be strictly mechanical in the sense that they assumed particles of matter to be completely passive, capable of acting only by virtue of impact in collision with other particles, there was a range of other mechanical philosophies, such as those of Pierre Gassendi (1592–1655), Robert Hooke (1635–1703), and Newton, where particles were

held to be endowed with various inherent principles of activity ("seminal powers" or "internal faculties" in Gassendi, for example, and gravitational attraction in Newton).

The mechanical philosophy went hand in hand with two other innovations still seen as characteristic of modern science. Although the concept of laws of nature is as old as natural philosophy itself and can be found among the ancient Greeks, they were only invoked in a nonspecific, even vague way as principles of regularity in nature. The sun rises, for example, in accordance with a law of nature. Because Descartes was concerned with explaining all phenomena in terms of the motions of invisibly small particles out of which all gross bodies were composed and those motions were said to be the result of earlier collisions and could only be passed on by further collisions, he needed to be able to codify precisely how motions were passed on. This need for precision was also inspired of course by his background in mathematics and the rise in the belief that the world itself was mathematical through and through. Accordingly Descartes based his system of natural philosophy on three precise and carefully defined laws of nature supplemented by seven rules of impact (to clarify exactly what happens in different kinds of collision). Although now seen to be misconceived, Descartes's laws had an enormous influence and seemed to his contemporaries to be the major factor in radically transforming natural philosophy from a speculative to a certain, physically and mathematically grounded enterprise. This confidence in the new mechanical philosophy was fully justified not long after, when Newton's *Principia* established three revised laws of motion, which proved to be the correct basis for a highly successful mathematical physics until the advent of relativity and quantum theories in the early twentieth century.

Descartes was also aware that, in stark contrast to Aristotelian philosophy, which was supposedly based on common sense, his philosophy explained the world in ways that were not only contrary to sense impressions but were in principle undiscoverable by the senses. What the senses revealed was mere appearances; the underlying reality was one of crowding and jostling particles too small ever to be seen. Even light itself, according to Descartes and the other mechanical philosophers, was not what people might think. Either pressure pulses in the intervening medium between the eye and the thing observed or streams of invisible particles flowing into the eye, light and color were subjective experiences, the reality of which was different. This fundamental belief was open to different interpretations and gave rise to differing opinions. Where Descartes believed people could infer the reality underlying appearances by essentially rationalist procedures, others took a more skeptical line. Out of these debates the English philosopher John Locke (1632–1704) initiated the philosophical position known as British empiricism. Locke insisted, against Descartes, that one can never be sure about the nature of the substance underlying the subjective experience of reality and must rely on empirical investigation rather than potentially misleading rational reconstruction. Subsequent thinkers took even more radical positions. For instance, the Anglo-Irish philosopher and divine George Berkeley (1685–1753), later bishop of Cloyne, said that all people can know is what they perceive, and they cannot even know that there is an underlying reality. British empiricism is a movement in philosophy rather than in science, but the distinction between what are called primary qualities (the qualities of the invisibly small particles, like size, shape, motion) and secondary qualities (subjective qualities, like taste, color, temperature) remains an important distinction in modern science.

THE WIDER CULTURE AND THE SCIENTIFIC REVOLUTION

Although it is possible to present the major innovations of the scientific revolution, that is, the mathematization of the world picture, the experimental method, and the concern for a practically useful knowledge, as well as their development into the mechanical philosophy, as direct outcomes of the humanist movement in the Renaissance and its concern with the active life, there were other important elements in the historical context. As is well known, the Renaissance was also the period that saw the rise of city-states and regional and national principalities, to say nothing of wealthy mercantilist corporations, all of whom had not only the wealth but also their own reasons for patronizing various enterprises. The role of patronage in the fine arts is well known, and its effects on the more realist nature of Renaissance art compared to medieval art and its

frequently more secular subject matter are plain to see. The role of secular patronage in changes in natural philosophy has not yet been fully explored, but it is already clear that this played a major part in the emphasis upon practically useful knowledge.

Royal courts employed mathematicians and natural magicians before they employed natural philosophers. Furthermore this kind of patronage led to the establishment of the first alternative institutional setting for learning about the natural world since the formation of the universities. At the Platonic Academy in Florence, under the patronage of Cosimo de' Medici (1389–1464), Marsilio Ficino (1433–1499) first translated not only the works of Plato into Latin but also those works attributed to Hermes Trismegistus. Subsequently, royal patrons began to support academies devoted directly to the investigation of the natural world, such as the Accademia dei Lincei (Academy of the Lynxes) supported by Federico Cesi (1585–1630) that grew around the famous natural magician Giambattista della Porta (1535?–1615) but later included Galileo among its members.

The importance of these academies and of the individual patronage of leading thinkers like Galileo (by Grand Duke Cosimo II de' Medici, 1590–1621) or Kepler (by the Holy Roman emperor Rudolf II, ruled 1576–1612) can be seen from the fact that virtually every conceptual or methodological innovation in the scientific revolution was introduced by thinkers working outside the university system. The most successful of these scientific research institutions were the Royal Society of London, founded in 1660, and the Académie des Sciences in Paris, set up in 1666, both of which consisted of the leading natural philosophers in their respective countries.

The universities should not be overlooked entirely, however. Although there was little innovation in the arts faculties where natural philosophy was taught, it was sometimes different in the medical faculties, where there was always a greater concern with the practical usefulness of knowledge. Most famous is the medical faculty at Padua, where Andreas Vesalius (1514–1564) revolutionized the traditional teaching of human anatomy by performing the dissections himself. More usually a lower-status surgeon performed the dissection for the class while the medical professor simply read from the relevant work of the ancient medical authority Galen (c. 130–201 C.E.). By performing the dissections himself, Vesalius claimed to have discovered over two hundred errors in Galen's anatomical works. In particular Vesalius established that there was something seriously wrong with Galen's account of the heart and the movement of the blood. This led to the discovery of the lesser circulation of the blood (its circulation from the right ventricle to the left ventricle of the heart by crossing the lungs) by another professor at Padua, Realdus Columbus (1510–1559), in 1553 and the discovery of the full circulation by William Harvey (1578–1657), a former student at Padua, in 1628.

The medical faculties sometimes provided the institutional setting for advances in knowledge about the so-called *materia medica,* medicinal minerals, plants, animals, or parts of animals, although they had to compete for honors with the so-called cabinets of curiosities gathered by wealthy collectors that can be seen as the origins of modern museums. In many cases a wealthy patron not only set up a cabinet of exotic specimens from the natural world but also employed a learned curator, who then became well placed to revise current knowledge of flora and fauna. For example, Pierandrea Mattioli (1500–1577), curator of Archduke Ferdinand of Tyrol's (1529–1595) collection, became one of the leading naturalists of the age.

Generally speaking, of course, university-trained medical practitioners were able to make a good living, and many were able to pursue further study independently. Medical practitioners form the single biggest group of contributors to the scientific revolution. But it was not always university men who made the greatest contributions. The itinerant Swiss autodidact who called himself Paracelsus (c. 1493–1541) developed a new system of medicine and therapeutics based on assumptions about the alchemical nature of the whole of Creation, the macrocosm and the microcosm of the human being. Physiological processes were seen as alchemical processes within the body, and it was assumed that alchemically produced medicines could be as efficacious as traditional herbal remedies if not more so. Accordingly Paracelsians used far more mineral-based medicines than had been usual previously. Although Paracelsian methods were always controversial, some notable therapeutic successes (and the inadequacy of traditional cures) ensured that it was widely adopted by numerous followers throughout Europe.

Responses to Paracelsianism point to another important aspect of the reform of natural knowledge. For many contemporaries the radical and iconoclastic nature of Paracelsianism was seen as subversive of orthodoxy. Traditional Galenic medicine, like Aristotelian natural philosophy, was seen as guaranteeing what were regarded as traditional verities enshrined in university curricula and confirming the old authorities. More to the point, it was seen as all of a piece with orthodoxy in religion. In Catholic countries Paracelsus was regarded as the Luther of medicine, as subversive to the health of the body as the religious reformer Martin Luther (1483–1546) was to the health of the believer's soul. Paracelsianism tended to flourish therefore in societies riven by religious and concomitant political factionalism. In France it was promoted by the Protestant Huguenots, in Germany it flourished in the Protestant states, and in England after the Civil War it was promoted by parliamentarian physicians, who saw Galen as a tyrant in medicine who had to be deposed as Charles I (ruled 1625–1649) had been.

The most famous aspect of the alliance between traditional authority in natural knowledge and orthodox religion is, of course, the alliance between Aristotelianism and Roman Catholicism, particularly as manifested in beliefs about the stationary position of Earth. But the situation was significantly different from the response to Paracelsianism. Perhaps because astronomy was of less concern to people in their everyday lives than was medicine, little attention was paid to the innovations of Copernicus when they were first published in 1543. Only after Galileo widely publicized discoveries he had made by turning the newly invented telescope to the heavens in 1610 did the Catholic Church begin to take notice. Galileo's telescopic innovations could do nothing to prove the truth of Copernican astronomy, but they could and did show that Aristotle's ideas were significantly wrong. Galileo used his considerable rhetorical skills to imply that Aristotelian cosmology should be replaced by Copernicanism. Unfortunately, Galileo's rhetorical strategy included a widely circulated letter to Grand Duchess Christina (1615; the dowager duchess was the mother of Galileo's patron Cosimo de' Medici) in which he suggested that certain biblical passages should be reinterpreted to make them compatible with Copernican theory. The Catholic Church could not let this intervention by a layman into matters of scriptural interpretation pass and made a ruling in 1616 that confirmed the traditional, geostatic interpretation of Scripture and condemned Copernicanism as erroneous and heretical.

It is significant that the Protestant churches, usually more concerned with biblical literalism than the Catholic Church, took no comparable action against Copernicanism. The fact that the Catholic Church took no action until Galileo made the religious implications of Copernicanism highly public, some seventy years after the publication of Copernicus's book, suggests that analyses that have emphasized the local contingencies in the Galileo affair are correct and that it is wrong to use this affair to argue that science and religion are irreconcilable worldviews.

Indeed, most of the evidence from the scientific revolution points the other way, showing a strong alliance at this period between science and religious belief. The end of the sixteenth century saw the beginnings of atheism in Europe, arising at least partly out of a skeptical crisis among intellectuals as a result of the newly discovered alternatives to Aristotle from ancient thought, including ancient skeptical writings. It seems clear that early atheists (for the most part they covered their tracks well—atheism was, after all, a capital offense) used their interpretations of natural philosophy (at first Aristotelianism and subsequently the mechanical philosophy) to promote irreligion. Nevertheless, all the major contributors to the development of the scientific revolution seem to have seen themselves as "priests of the Book of Nature," to use Kepler's phrase. The starting point of Descartes's system of natural philosophy was an argument he saw as undermining any skeptical position, his famous argument, "I think, therefore I exist." And his next move was to prove the existence of God before going on to build up his rational system of nature. Once again the culmination of this line is in the work of Newton, who privately admitted, "When I wrote my treatise about our system, I had an eye upon such principles as might work with considering men for the belief of a Deity; and nothing can

rejoice me more than to find it useful for that purpose" (Letter to Dr. Richard Bentley, December, 1692, in *Papers and Letters,* p. 280). Accordingly, in the second edition of the *Principia* (1713), he publicly declared that "to treat of God from phenomena is certainly a part of natural philosophy" (p. 943).

If modernity is associated with the advent of secularism, therefore, the role of early modern science is by no means unambiguous. On the one hand, the tradition of natural theology, that is, using the principles of science and close observation of the natural world to suggest that the world shows signs of intelligent design, can be seen as an attempt to resist secularization of the world picture. On the other hand, however, this same movement led believers away from Scripture and revelation to a rationalist and intellectual approach to God that ultimately came to seem indistinguishable from a science-based atheism. Similarly, although some early modern scientists used the limitations of the mechanical philosophy to point to the need to accept the existence of a spiritual realm, using accounts of witchcraft and ghosts to make their points, others insisted on the reality of the immaterial rational soul but proceeded to explain as many mental phenomena as possible in terms of a material "animal soul." Eventually the new science contributed to the movement toward secularization, but the process was not fully accomplished until the Enlightenment, the age succeeding that of the scientific revolution.

See also **Bacon, Francis; Berkeley, George; Boyle, Robert; Copernicus, Nicolaus; Descartes, René; Galileo Galilei; Gassendi, Pierre; Gilbert, William; Harvey, William; Hermeticism; Hobbes, Thomas; Hooke, Robert; Kepler, Johannes; Locke, John; Matter, Theories of; Nature; Newton, Isaac; Paracelsus; Scientific Method; Vesalius, Andreas.**

BIBLIOGRAPHY

Primary Sources

Bacon, Francis. *Novum Organum* (1620). Translated and edited by Peter Urbach and John Gibson. Chicago, 1994.

Descartes, René. *Discourse on Method and Related Writings* (1637). Translated with an introduction by Desmond M. Clarke. Harmondsworth, U.K., 1999.

————. *The World and Other Writings.* Translated and edited by Stephen Gaukroger. Cambridge, U.K., 1998.

Galilei, Galileo. *Discoveries and Opinions of Galileo*. Translated and edited by Stillman Drake. Garden City, N.Y., 1957.

Harvey, William. *An Anatomical Disputation concerning the Movement of the Heart and Blood in Living Creatures*. Translated by Gweneth Whitteridge. Oxford, 1976.

Kepler, Johannes. *The Harmony of the World*. Translated into English with an introduction and notes by E. J. Aiton, A. M. Duncan, and J. V. Field. *Memoirs of the American Philosophical Society*. Vol. 209. Philadelphia, 1997.

Newton, Isaac. *Papers and Letters on Natural Philosophy and Related Documents*. Edited by I. Bernard Cohen. Cambridge, Mass., 1978.

———. *The Principia*. Translated by I. Bernard Cohen and Anne Whitman. Berkeley, 1999.

Secondary Sources

Cohen, H. Floris. *The Scientific Revolution: A Historiographical Inquiry*. Chicago, 1994.

Cohen, I. Bernard. *Revolution in Science*. Cambridge, Mass., 1985.

Cohen, I. Bernard, ed. *Puritanism and the Rise of Modern Science: The Merton Thesis*. New Brunswick, N.J., 1990.

Dear, Peter. *Revolutionizing the Sciences: European Knowledge and Its Ambitions, 1500–1700*. Princeton, 2001.

Debus, Allen G. *Man and Nature in the Renaissance*. Cambridge, U.K., 1978.

Henry, John. "Animism and Empiricism: Copernican Physics and the Origins of William Gilbert's Experimental Method." *Journal of the History of Ideas* 62 (2001): 1–21.

———. *The Scientific Revolution and the Origins of Modern Science*. 2nd ed. Basingstoke and New York, 2002.

Keller, Evelyn Fox. *Reflections on Gender and Science*. New Haven and London, 1985.

Kuhn, Thomas S. *The Copernican Revolution: Planetary Astronomy in the Development of Western Thought*. Cambridge, Mass., 1957.

———. *The Structure of Scientific Revolutions*. Chicago and London, 1962.

Lindberg, David C., and Robert S. Westman, eds. *Reappraisals of the Scientific Revolution*. Cambridge, U.K., 1980.

Merchant, Carolyn. *The Death of Nature: Women, Ecology, and the Scientific Revolution*. San Francisco, 1980.

Merton, Robert K. *Science, Technology, and Society in Seventeenth Century England*. New York, 1970.

Rossi, Paolo. *Francis Bacon: From Magic to Science*. London, 1968.

Thorndike, Lynn. *A History of Magic and Experimental Science*. 8 vols. New York, 1923–1958.

Webster, Charles. *From Paracelsus to Newton: Magic and the Making of Modern Science*. Cambridge, U.K., 1982.

Weeks, Andrew. *Paracelsus: Speculative Theory and the Crisis of the Early Reformation*. Albany, N.Y., 1997.

Westfall, Richard S. *The Construction of Modern Science: Mechanisms and Mechanics*. Cambridge, U.K., 1977.

Zilsel, Edgar. *The Social Origins of Modern Science*. Dordrecht, 2000.

JOHN HENRY

SCOTLAND. In 1500 Scotland was a small, poor, and peripheral country on the northern fringe of Europe. Its economy was largely agricultural, its religion unremarkably Catholic, its political leanings toward France, its military and commercial significance minor, its people largely illiterate. By 1800 Scotland was a European leader in the fields of agriculture and commerce; it had long been self-consciously, perhaps aggressively, Protestant; its philosophers had changed the face of European thought; its inhabitants, by now among the best educated in Europe, saw themselves as Scots, but also as Britons; its people, practices, and ideas had left a stamp on the whole British, European, and Atlantic world.

RELIGION AND POLITICS

The first step in this progression was the Reformation. Politically it was made by Scotland's separate Parliament, at grass roots principally by urban middle classes, and in popular memory by John Knox (1513–1572). Where the Scandinavian and German lands espoused the Word according to Martin Luther, Scotland followed the Swiss model of John Calvin, which also appealed to the northern Netherlands and certain parts of what is now France. To make a political statement against Mary Queen of Scots (1542–1587) and her French connections, Scotland's Parliament introduced in 1560 an assertive Calvinist Confession of Faith. Within a generation or two, Protestantism's institutions were firmly established in the Lowlands, and within three or four generations it had become the faith of most of the country.

Pockets of Catholicism survived into the eighteenth century, but the principal religious battles in the generations after the Reformation were fought over church organization: should it be presbyterian or episcopalian? Bishops and presbyteries coexisted unhappily from 1560 until 1689. The Scottish Revolution of 1638, which eventually led to an invasion of England and the overthrow of Charles I, and the "Glorious Revolution" of 1688–1689 were sparked by Presbyterians; powerful ties existed between Scottish Presbyterians and radical English Puritans in the period up to 1646. Late-sixteenth- and early-seventeenth-century Scotland was a hotbed of revolutionary religious and political ideas.

The political origins and standing of the Church of Scotland gave it power almost unique in Europe, for example allowing it to control the moral and religious behavior of all Scots through parish "kirk sessions." Yet this was fatally weakened by a Toleration Act in 1712 and by further splits between Protestant denominations (for example, in 1733), which

continued to fragment the faith into the mid-nineteenth century. Vocal and sometimes violent anti-Catholicism also persisted throughout the early modern period.

Calvinist reformers placed education at the top of their agenda. A national system of parish schools was established by Parliament during the seventeenth century, giving Lowland Scots among the highest literacy levels in Europe by the mid-eighteenth century. Scots came to value education highly. Around 1790 Scotland had the highest ratio of universities per million inhabitants in Europe (3.3 per million; the figure was 0.2 for England, Wales, and Ireland, 0.9 for France). Early growth in university numbers was fueled by demand for training in Protestant theology, while its eighteenth-century expansion was principally associated with legal and medical education—Scotland's universi-

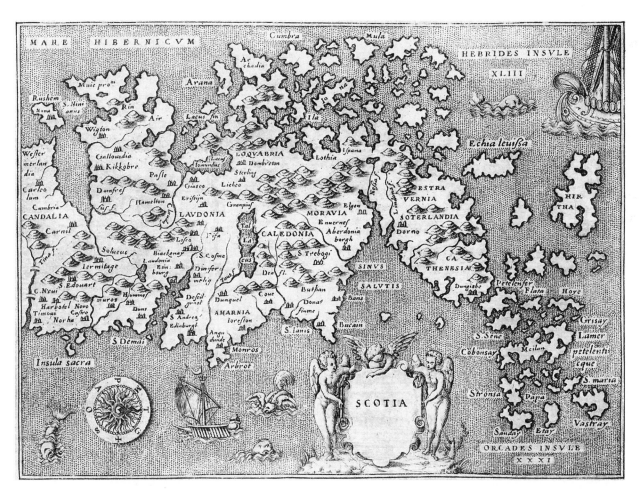

Scotland. A miniature map of Scotland originally engraved for Thomas Porcacchi's *Isole piu famose del mundo* [The most famous islands of the world] first published in 1572. MAP COLLECTION, STERLING MEMORIAL LIBRARY, YALE UNIVERSITY

ties produced nine out of ten British medical graduates between 1750 and 1800. Student numbers rose from just over 1,000 to 4,400 between 1700 and 1820. Young men were attracted to Scotland's institutions of higher learning by important changes in teaching methods and curricula, and by the fact that Scotland was almost the only country in Europe where it became cheaper in real terms to attend university over the course of the eighteenth century. Thus Scotland's universities were much less elitist than Oxford or Cambridge and were becoming more socially inclusive during the eighteenth century.

Scotland's eighteenth-century universities represented the country to the world. Yet from the 1707 Union of Parliaments until 2000, Scotland had no representative assembly. At one level the Union of 1707 was part of a process of growing integration with and dependence on England. Links with England, regarded since the Middle Ages as the "auld [old] enemy," had been enhanced by the Union of the Crowns in 1603. James VI of Scotland (ruled 1567–1625) became James I of England (ruled 1603–1625) after the extinction of the Tudor dynasty with the death of Elizabeth I. James left the old royal palace of Holyrood in Edinburgh for the decidedly more lavish setting of London. From 1603 to 1714 the house of Stuart reigned over Scotland (as it had since 1371), England, Wales, and Ireland, albeit with a shift in the line of succession in 1689 when James VII of Scotland (James II of England) fled to France. The Union of the Crowns brought about important changes in the status of the border counties of England and Scotland, pacifying and integrating them into unified government structures, but in all other regards the nations remained distinct. The most important

Scotland. This is another miniature map from Poracacchi's book, showing northern Scotland and the Hebrides and Orkney Islands. MAP COLLECTION, STERLING MEMORIAL LIBRARY, YALE UNIVERSITY

event integrating them was the Union of Parliaments in 1707.

Earlier attempts at integration, for example by the crown with its disastrous attempt to impose an Anglican prayer book on Scotland in 1637–1638 and by the Republican Oliver Cromwell with his forced union in the 1650s, had met with failure. In the early 1700s the mood of Scots remained decidedly Anglophobic, and the Union was constructed by elements of the ruling elite. "We are convinced that an Union will be of great advantage to both. The Protestant religion will be more firmly secured, the designs of our enemies effectually disappointed, and the riches and trade of the whole island advanced." So argued supporters of the Union. In exchange for giving up their own Parliament, they got 45 members in the 513-strong House of Commons and 16 representative peers in the House of Lords, both in London. Scotland was thereafter part of the "United Kingdom of Great Britain" and was managed by a succession of aristocratic patrons, notably the dukes of Argyll. For all that Scots prized an egalitarian ethos, theirs was not a politically democratic society. Scotland had only 3,000 county electors in 1788, and the burgh franchise was confined to town councils; Edinburgh's member of Parliament was elected by just thirty-three men.

While Queen Mary (wife of William of Orange and co-ruler with him 1689–1702) was a Stuart, the change of monarch in 1689 left many Scots (and some English) uneasy, feelings accentuated by the arrival of a Hanoverian monarch (George I) in 1714. This discontent provided support for the Jacobite rebellions of 1715 and 1745. Glorious failures as they may have been, the rebellions bound Scotland ever more closely into the political, military, and imperial destiny of her nearest neighbor.

SOCIETY
The defeat of the '45 also signaled important social changes. Lowland society had long been a "modern" one. Landowners were the elite. Landownership was concentrated in a few hands, and the "lairds" dominated the hierarchies of wealth, status, and political power. The men who attended Scotland's Parliament until 1707 were members of the landed nobility. Beneath them in the social hierarchy came the tenant farmers, along with their subtenants or "cottars" and servants, who worked

the land that provided the bulk of wealth and well-being. In the Lowlands approximately a fifth of late-seventeenth-century rural dwellers were craftsmen and tradesmen. Until the eighteenth century the "middle class" was made up of prosperous tenants and small landowners in the countryside and the merchants of the larger towns. Then professionals came into their own—lawyers, doctors, and educators—along with the increasingly confident merchants and manufacturers spawned by the industrial and commercial revolutions.

Highland society was distinctive until the eighteenth century. The structure of landholding was superficially similar, but Highland society was based on very different premises, which were increasingly alien to Lowlanders and to the English. Highland nobles were not just landlords, but also chiefs, in charge of clans built on the bonds created by feuding and feasting. The crown used clan rivalries to extend its hold on the Highlands, most notably in the notorious massacre of MacDonalds by Campbells at Glencoe in 1692. Weakened by political and economic change since the sixteenth century, the cultural framework of clans was not finally dismantled until after the failure of the 1745 Jacobite rising. In its aftermath the wearing of Highland dress and the carrying of bagpipes were banned, except for Highland regiments abroad.

The early modern Highlands were densely peopled, and indeed the distribution of Scotland's population was very different from that of the present day. As late as the mid-eighteenth century more than half of Scotland's people lived north of an imaginary Highland Line drawn from just south of Aberdeen to just north of Glasgow. In common with most northern Europeans except the Dutch, Scots were country dwellers. Just 3 percent lived in towns of 10,000 or more in 1500. However, the rate of urbanization was the fastest in Europe in the eighteenth century. Just one Scot in twenty lived in a large town in 1700, compared with one in six by 1800. The most rapid eighteenth-century growth occurred in Glasgow and neighboring towns in the west-central Lowlands, the former on the back of the colonial tobacco trade, the latter mostly thanks to textile manufacturing.

Until the eighteenth century population figures are largely guesswork. Scotland may have had

700,000 people around 1500 and perhaps one million by about 1700, though most of the growth probably took place between about 1540 and 1640; the first accurate census in 1801 showed there were 1.6 million people. Scotland's population growth rate was slower than elsewhere in the British Isles—strikingly so in the eighteenth century because Scottish women married later than did their English and Irish counterparts, and a larger proportion never married during their childbearing years. Slow growth occurred despite the fact that adults began to live much longer in the eighteenth century. Life expectancy at the age of twenty-five years rose from twenty-eight years in the early seventeenth century to thirty-eight years by the end of the eighteenth century. Apart from low fertility and high mortality, the other reason was substantial emigration, this usually of young men for military or mercantile service. The North Sea and Baltic countries had always been important destinations for Scots (as had England), but the main goal in the seventeenth century was Ireland and in the eighteenth the Atlantic and Caribbean colonies.

The redistribution of population to the west central Lowlands in general and the rise of Glasgow in particular marked a profound shift in the economic focus of Scotland's wealth and overseas trade. In the Middle Ages both had centered on the east coast, Scots looking to the North Sea and the Baltic; then the emphasis changed to the west, focusing on the Atlantic economies. Scotland's agriculture had always been less developed than that of England, but the second half of the eighteenth century saw dramatic improvements in arable farming, which brought rural productivity onto a par with the best in Europe. Industry, until then located mainly in the countryside, became more identifiably urban and began to diversify from textiles and other "organic" economies (using, for example, leather and wood) into mineral-based production of coal and metals. Scotland had already become more dependent on her southern neighbor for trade by the end of the seventeenth century, and experienced agricultural and industrial revolutions at the same time as England a century later.

Yet for all the convergences of experience, Scotland was in many ways a very different country from England even in 1800. There was fiscal integration with England from 1707, but Scotland's legal systems, educational framework, religious establishment, and even currency—the pound (£) Scots was worth about one twelfth of the pound (£) sterling and the Bank of Scotland was a separate foundation in 1695. The trading privileges of her royal burghs were preserved distinct from England's at the Union of Parliaments. Key social institutions also differed. For example, poor relief was discretionary and recipients had less clearly defined rights than in England; it was usually supplementary and therefore meager; there were fewer institutions like workhouses, which existed mainly in some of the larger towns.

CULTURE

Within Scotland's borders considerable social and cultural diversity also persisted. Highland literacy was much lower than Lowland because most people there spoke Gaelic, not Scots (a West Germanic tongue similar to English). Gaelic was the first language of half of Scotland in the fifteenth century, a third in 1689, but just a fifth in 1806. Linguistic variety did not end there, for all of Scotland was becoming more Anglicized. Scots itself had flourished as a literary medium in the late Middle Ages (c. 1480–1520) but was in retreat thereafter as standard court Scots fragmented into regional dialects after the departure of James VI in 1603. Anglicization of language and culture proceeded in the eighteenth century. The literati of Enlightenment Edinburgh aspired to pronunciation and orthography that conformed to the best London practice, and it was English rather than Scots that became the tongue of Scotland's landed, professional, and aspirant mercantile classes.

Edinburgh was the crucible of the Scottish Enlightenment, which also flourished in the universities, drawing rooms, and clubs of Glasgow and Aberdeen. Scotland's enlightened thinkers and writers—Adam Smith and David Hume, to name but two—were of worldwide significance, bound together by a shared faith in the improvability of individual and society through education, reason, and discussion. They celebrated and promoted commercial change, including an early consumer revolution, by arguing that economic cooperation and exchange would promote sociability, refinement, and "taste." Scotland's Enlightenment was far more vigorous, socially diverse, and influential than England's.

While Scotland ended the early modern period closely integrated with England and tied up in its industrial, commercial, and imperial future, its independent evolution and effects on England (and Ireland) in the early modern period illustrate that different parts of the United Kingdom influenced each other's development. Through contacts with Europe and the Atlantic world, Scotland also exerted a wider influence over space and time. Aspects of the educational system developed in the seventeenth century, political theories expounded at the Reformation and after, the ideas aired in the Scottish Enlightenment, and Scotland's interpretation of Calvinist theology and some of the practices of church organization and discipline are all examples of an enduring international impact of her early modern development.

See also **Calvinism; Edinburgh; England; Hume, David; Knox, John; Jacobitism; James I and VI (England and Scotland); Puritanism; Smith, Adam; Stuart Dynasty (England and Scotland).**

BIBLIOGRAPHY

Houston, R. A., and W. W. J. Knox, eds. *The New Penguin History of Scotland: From the Earliest Times to the Present Day.* London, 2001. A comprehensive, up-to-date and readable overview.

R. A. HOUSTON

SCUDÉRY, MADELEINE DE (1607–

1701), French novelist, philosopher, and moralist. One of five children born in Le Havre to a noble family of relatively modest means, Mlle de Scudéry was one of the most influential and popular novelists of the seventeenth century. She spent most of her youth in Rouen, where she received a better education than that of most girls of her social background and time. In 1637 she joined her brother Georges in Paris, and together they frequented the thriving literary salons of the Marais district. The two siblings worked together on works of fiction that enjoyed immediate success. In 1641 Madeleine published her first novel, *Ibrahim ou l'illustre Bassa,* under her brother's name. This practice of using the name of her brother as her pseudonymous signature was one that she continued for most of her prolific career as a

writer, despite the fact that her own authorship was openly acknowledged in the gazettes, memoirs, and letters of the time. Although the precise nature of his contributions is uncertain, Georges did clearly collaborate to some extent with his sister in the writing of her novels, and he wrote the prefaces to several of her books.

Artamène, ou Le Grand Cyrus, Madeleine de Scudéry's second novel, published in ten volumes between 1649 and 1653, assured her celebrity both in France and abroad. It was translated into English, German, Italian, and Arabic. The French civil wars known as the Fronde were coming to a close during this same period, and Scudéry dedicated the novel to the duchess of Longueville, who had been a leader in the uprisings against the throne. Although its characters were drawn from historical sources and the setting was remote, *Artamène, ou Le Grand Cyrus* was a roman à clef in which most of the major characters could be identified with real people among Scudéry's contemporaries. She included a character sketch of herself as the Greek poet Sappho, expounding with her friends on platonic love and the life of the intellect. While she was writing the novel, Scudéry established her own literary coterie known as the *samedi,* named for the day of the week on which she received her guests, and modeled after the famous Rambouillet salon gatherings that Madeleine and her brother had frequented in the 1630s.

In her later works Scudéry focused increasingly on the philosophical discussions of salon society. The most famous episode in her third novel *Clélie, histoire romaine,* published between 1654 and 1660, concerns an allegorical map of the human heart, called the *Carte du pays de Tendre* (Map of the land of tenderness). The conversations generated by the map elaborate a theory of love that values reason over passion and discourages marriage. This led to Scudéry's novels being labeled as subversive by some, including the theorist of neoclassicism Nicolas Boileau-Despréaux, who published a harsh satire on novels in which *Clélie* and the *Carte du pays de Tendre* were targeted as fostering waywardness among women and contributing to the decline of marriage as a social institution.

In the 1660s Scudéry moved away from the heroic novel genre and turned to shorter narrative forms, publishing three novellas, *Célinte, nouvelle première* (1661), *Mathilde d'Aguilar* (1667), and *La promenade de Versailles* (1669). These works were more realistic than her novels and were situated in modern times, and their action took place in locations that would have been familiar to her readers. But Scudéry continued to portray characters who themselves were captivated by the epic plots of heroic novels, thus focusing on the strong influence of novels on the collective imagination of her own social world. The 1660s were difficult years for many of Scudéry's circle, following the disgrace of her protector and patron Nicolas Fouquet, the superintendent of finances (1615–1680). Madeleine and her friend the historian Paul Pellisson (1624–1693) were among the small number of authors who dared to write appeals to Louis XIV on behalf of Fouquet, and Pellisson was imprisoned from 1661 to 1666. Although in 1671 Scudéry received the first prize awarded to authors by the Académie Française, she ceased to publish for the next nine years, until the appearance of the first of her collections of conversations, *Conversations sur divers sujets* (1680).

The last phase of Scudéry's career as a writer was devoted to ten more volumes of collected conversations, many of them excerpted from her novels. These were regarded by her contemporaries as representing the best of her writing, and unlike her earlier works, they were published under her own name. They reflected the collective efforts of Scudéry's milieu to cultivate the art of talk and develop a new aesthetic and practice of conversation. Translated almost immediately into English, they contributed to a body of literature describing new "French" styles of living that were imitated by elite circles in England, Germany, Italy, and Spain.

See also **Bossuet, Jacques-Bénigne; French Literature and Language; Fronde; Salons.**

BIBLIOGRAPHY

Primary Sources

Scudéry's works were translated in the seventeenth century, but few of her works are available in English today. Two new translations are *The Story of Sapho*, edited and translated by Karen Newman, Chicago, 2003; and *Selected Letters, Orations and Rhetorical Dialogues,* edited and translated by Jane Donawerth and Julie Strongson, Chicago, 2003.

Secondary Sources

Aronson, Nicole. *Mademoiselle de Scudéry.* Translated by Stuart Aronson. Boston, 1978.

Munro, James S. *Mademoiselle de Scudéry and the Carte de Tendre.* Durham, U.K., 1986.

ELIZABETH C. GOLDSMITH

SCULPTURE. By 1500 in Italy, the recovery of classical antiquity permeated all aspects of art and culture. In Padua, Mantua, and Florence, sculptors like Riccio, Antico, and Verrocchio revived the small bronze in exquisite tabletop figures of satyrs, gods, goddess, emperors, and heroes of ancient Rome that evoked the ethos of antiquity. In Rome, however, the Renaissance manifested itself on a larger scale. Here, the young Michelangelo Buonarroti (1475–1564) carved a remarkable life-sized marble statue, *Bacchus* (1496). Not even in antiquity had the god of wine been shown like this: pudgy, tipsy, lascivious, mouth open and eyes glazed in Dionysiac abandon, the very embodiment of wine's intoxicating effects and the ancient world's appeal to the carnal senses. If *Bacchus* represented the epitome of worldly classical values, then Michelangelo's *Pietà* (1499) in St. Peter's was its Christian counterpart. The young Madonna looks down pensively at the nude, lifeless body of her crucified son. Carved to anatomical perfection and brought to a high polish, the body of Christ holds an irresistible appeal for the beholder. The *Pietà* was recognized both as a masterpiece and a powerful spiritual icon created in the new idealized vocabulary of classical antiquity, yet infused with Christian piety.

POWER AND THE FORMS OF SCULPTURE

Both sculptures were created in Rome, capital of the ancient Roman Empire, seat of the papacy, and center of humanistic literary and artistic study. Pope Julius II della Rovere (reigned 1503–1513) accelerated earlier campaigns of urban renewal in his strong desire to return the Eternal City to its ancient glory. During his reign, Julius II also ruthlessly reestablished the papacy as a major secular power by militarily reuniting far-flung papal territories. Yet consolidation of political power and association with the prestige of imperial Rome was the goal not only of Spanish, French, and English monarchs but that

Sculpture. The tomb of Lorenzo de' Medici in the San Lorenzo church, Florence, sculpted by Michelangelo, c. 1520–1534.
©SCALA/ART RESOURCE

of the Holy Roman emperor as well. These rulers sought to express their power and garner prestige in major sculptural projects meant to glorify their persons and dynasties.

In Germany, Holy Roman Emperor Maximilian I (ruled 1493–1519) gave sculptural form to his political, dynastic ambition with plans for a colossal, multi-figured bronze tomb begun in 1502. Despite its medieval style, its size and conception rivaled the tombs of the ancient Roman emperors. Maximilian planned to erect this monumental structure in a specially designed church in Innsbruck. It featured a bronze, life-sized kneeling effigy situated atop a large, high free-standing rectangular structure decorated around the sides with reliefs showing important events from his life. In it, forty life-sized bronze statues of Maximilian's ancestors (both men and women, beginning with Julius Caesar and ending with Ferdinand the Catholic of Spain), thirty-four bronze busts of Roman emperors beginning with Julius Caesar, and a hundred statuettes of Habsburg saints were to accompany the emperor. The ambitious program, only partially realized, genealogically linked the Holy Roman emperor, his ancestors, and his future heirs to the imperial legacy and glory of Emperor Julius Caesar.

However, Pope Julius II's commission for his tomb to Michelangelo (1505) unified in form and content the legacy of ancient art with the pope's dynastic, political, and spiritual needs. Designed as a huge, freestanding three-storied marble structure (roughly 23 by 36 feet), with niches for statues and terms on the first level in front of which were bound prisoners, the plan called for forty allegorical marble statues and numerous bronze reliefs celebrating the pontiff's achievements and virtues. Now only the statue of *Moses* on the much-reduced tomb in San Pietro in Vincoli provides a clue to its original splendor. Formally it evoked not so much the tombs of Julius's papal predecessors as ancient Roman imperial monuments. Although never realized on this scale, the *Julius Tomb* nonetheless set an ambitious standard for dynastic sepulchral monuments.

The return of the Medici to power in Florence in 1512 and the election of Giovanni de' Medici as Pope Leo X in 1513 (reigned 1513–1521) led to a Medici funerary chapel at San Lorenzo, Florence, designed by Michelangelo (1519–1534). The pope's dream of dynastic supremacy in Italy, and the end of foreign intervention, was shattered by the premature deaths of the young Lorenzo and Giuliano de' Medici (1519, 1516). In their marble effigies, seated pensively above sarcophagi upon which recline representations of the times of day, Michelangelo subtly transcended dynastic panegyric, creating a poetic meditation upon the meaning of life, fame, and art itself.

In 1529, Henry VIII of England commissioned from the Italian sculptor Benedetto da Rovezzano (1474–1554) a tomb with numerous bronze statues and statuettes, one of the most ambitious sculptural projects ever conceived (abandoned in 1536). Later, Henry II of France planned at St. Denis a great chapel and tomb dedicated to the Valois dynasty. However, Philip II of Spain erected the most majestic tomb of all by building the Escorial (1563–1584), thus fulfilling his father's request (Holy Roman Emperor Charles V, reigned 1519–1556). At the sides of the Capilla Mayor's high altar, Leone Leoni's (1509–1590) over-life-sized gilt bronze and enameled effigies of Charles V, Philip II, and family members kneel facing the chapel's majestic sacrament tabernacle in perpetual adoration. Here was an eternal demonstration of Habsburg piety, sacramental devotion, and divine dynastic favor.

Throughout the sixteenth century, sculpture embellished civic spaces throughout Italy. The first and most important example is Michelangelo's colossal marble *David* erected in 1504 outside the Palazzo Vecchio, Florence. The *David* represented not only an emblem of republican liberty but also a fundamental psychological shift that merged Christian spirituality with worldly, man-centered values of antiquity. After the return of the Medici to power in Florence, Baccio Bandinelli carved his muscular, marble giant *Hercules and Cacus* to flank the *David*, an authoritarian antidote to *David*'s republican sentiments. Cellini's bronze *Perseus and Medusa* soon rose on the Loggia dei Lanzi along with Giambologna's serpentine, three-figured group *The Rape of the Sabines*. Giambologna's elegant, mannered style was disseminated throughout Europe via exquisite small bronzes frequently presented as diplomatic gifts establishing him as the most influential artist of the last third of the sixteenth century. His legacy was carried forward by Antonio Susini and Adrien de Vries.

Sculpture. *Samson Slaying a Philistine,* by Giambologna, c. 1578.
©VICTORIA & ALBERT MUSEUM, LONDON/ART RESOURCE, N.Y.

Sculpture. *Pluto and Proserpina (The Rape of Persephone),* 1622, by Gian Lorenzo Bernini. ©Scala/Art Resource, N.Y.

BERNINI AND ROME

Widespread political and religious conflicts generated by the Reformation and the Catholic Counter-Reformation wracked Europe, and Renaissance worldly values ebbed in favor of a purified Christian spirituality. In the arts, the Catholic Counter-Reformation spurred the reform of Italian painting toward the end of the sixteenth century. However, sculpture awaited the appearance of Gian Lorenzo Bernini (1598–1680) who became the most renowned artist of the seventeenth century. During the course of his long and incredibly productive career, Bernini changed Rome through commissions for churches, palaces, fountains, statues, chapels, monuments, and tombs. Orchestrating a small army of artists and workmen, Bernini dominated the artistic scene. His combination of painting, sculpture, and architecture into one unified and dramatic whole was a major influence in the

development of the baroque style that soon spread throughout Italy and Europe.

Like Michelangelo, the young Bernini immersed himself in the study of ancient sculpture. His first large-scale statues for Cardinal Scipione Borghese reflected years of intense analysis. These dramatic marbles stunned Bernini's contemporaries. *Pluto and Proserpina* (1621–1622, Galleria Borghese, Rome) presents an explosive combination of motion and emotion. The large, muscular Pluto, inspired by the ancient Roman *Hercules and the Hydra* (Museo Capitolino, Rome), hefts the distraught and struggling girl on his hip as he strides vigorously forward across the threshold of the underworld symbolized by the snarling, three-headed dog Cerberus. Proserpina's soft flesh yields to the god's violent grasp, her braids spin out into space, and marble tears course down her smooth cheeks. The over-life-sized group's startling impact and compelling naturalism is all the more remarkable as Bernini set it on a low pedestal against a wall, creating a commanding frontal view and strong physical presence directly to the viewer.

Apollo and Daphne (1622–1624, Galleria Borghese), inspired by a passage in Ovid's *Metamorphoses,* represents the instant that the fleeing Daphne's prayers are answered and she is turned into a laurel tree as she tries to escape the pursuing Apollo. The startled god (inspired by the *Apollo Belvedere* in the Vatican but in this instance running madly) appears as amazed as we are to witness the transmutation of Daphne's flesh (marble) into leaves, roots, bark, and cloth. This hallucinatory realism was made all the more shocking by the way that Bernini orchestrated the visitor's perception of the group. When in its original position in the villa, the approaching viewer saw only Apollo's back. As the visitor moved into the room, the drama unfolded in real time and space until reaching its crescendo. In this way, Bernini controlled the viewer's experience, as he did on a much larger scale in St. Peter's.

It is at St. Peter's that Bernini's mark is firmly implanted. The church is defined from beginning to end by Bernini. St. Peter's Square and the curved *Colonnade's* embracing arms greet the visitor; at the crossing, under the dome in four pier niches, colossal marble saints—Longinus, Andrew, Veronica, and Helen—activate the crossing by looking upward or seeming to move toward the immense bronze *Baldachin,* whose four spiral bronze columns and canopy mark the high altar and the tomb of the First Apostle. In the apse, the majestic bronze reliquary containing the throne of St. Peter—the *Cathedra Petri*—has descended from heaven accompanied by the Holy Spirit and its golden light burst. Cloud-borne and surrounded by a host of angels, the *Cathedra Petri* hovers miraculously above the apse altar, steadied by colossal bronze statues of the two Greek and two Latin church fathers. A shimmering apparition, the *Cathedra Petri* is a dramatic artistic culmination of the church's image and visible proof of the papacy's divinely endowed power.

The *Triton Fountain,* the *Elephant Obelisk,* and the stupendous *Four Rivers Fountain* at the center of Piazza Navona are but three of Bernini's best known sculptural landmarks, each offering novel interpretations of well-known types. However, it is the Cornaro Chapel (1647–1652, Santa Maria della Vittoria) that remains Bernini's most famous and potent symbol of seventeenth-century spirituality. Cardinal Federigo Cornaro commissioned a funerary chapel to commemorate seven other members of his family and to honor St. Teresa of Avila, the sixteenth-century Spanish mystic and reformer canonized in 1622. Into the existing architecture of the left transept chapel Bernini wove a related order of pilasters and entablature. Above the altar he placed a pedimented tabernacle framed by double columns into which the marble group of St. Teresa and the angel was set below a hidden window providing illumination. The altar frontal is decorated with a gilt bronze relief of the Last Supper; in choir boxes at each side, four members of the Cornaro family are engaged in discussion, or reading. Two skeletons in roundels on the floor look upward in prayer and wonder as they seemingly rise from their graves. At the apex of the vault is a fresco of the dove of the Holy Spirit, accompanied by a multitude of cloud-borne angels. The frescoed clouds cover a portion of the vault window and the actual architecture of the chapel, creating the illusion of an arriving heavenly host. This unity of painting, architecture, and sculpture focuses on the altarpiece, the *Ecstasy of St. Teresa.* Here Bernini depicted her rapture: the moment when an angel appeared with a golden

Sculpture. Bust of Molière by Jean Antoine Houdon, 1778. ©BURSTEIN COLLECTION/CORBIS

spear with a point of fire. In her own words, ". . . With this he seemed to pierce my heart several times so that it penetrated to my entrails. When he drew it out, I thought he was drawing them out with it and he left me completely afire with a great love for God." In his sculpture, Bernini alluded to other mystical events described by Teresa (and others) in their writings: her levitation upon receiving the Eucharist, her mystic marriage to Christ, and her death when, though old, she became young and lovely.

Indeed, the entire program revolves around the action taking place at and above the altar. The dead rise ecstatically from their graves through the chapel floor; members of the Cornaro family bear fervent witness to the portentous significance of this proof of divine love; the Holy Spirit and angels descend into the chapel in celebration of Teresa's union with God. The banderole carried by angels at the apex of the chapel bears God's message: "If I had not created heaven, I would create it for you alone." Teresa appears as an example of faith, as intercessor and emblem of God's love for all mankind, and of his promise of eternal salvation through the Eucharist. Bernini's seamless visual logic gathers and unites the spiritual themes into an instant of stunning clarity focused on St. Teresa and the angel. This programmatic and aesthetic unity represents the culmination of Bernini's career, a perfect unity of form and content, and the artistic zenith of the Counter-Reformation.

Although Bernini's chief rival, Alessandro Algardi (1598–1654), labored in his shadow, he was an artist of immense talent. As a portraitist, Algardi was much admired for the sensitive handling of marble and the psychological depth he imparted to the sitters. The monumental marble relief in St. Peter's, *The Encounter of St. Leo the Great and Attila* (1646–1653), a sculptural tour-de-force, initiated a new genre for baroque art that would be emulated into the eighteenth century. The doubled life-sized marble group the *Beheading of St. Paul* (1634–1644, San Paolo Maggiore, Bologna) is set above the altar and seen in the round. The composition captures the moment before the executioner's raised sword strikes and displays Paul's peaceful, spiritual resignation in the face of imminent death.

The influence of Bernini's baroque style extended to the end of the seventeenth and well into the eighteenth century. The *Altar of St. Ignatius Loyola* at the Gesu in Rome (1695–1699) was designed by Andrea Pozzo and executed by a number of sculptors including Pierre Legros. A marble, gilt bronze, and frescoed confection on a truly monumental scale, it was designed to overwhelm by size, opulence, and the extravagant use of colored marbles. Herein lay the seeds of the decline of the baroque style, for the deep personal piety that vivified Bernini's art was not evident in that of his followers. With the advent of the Age of Reason in the eighteenth century and the concomitant decline in the status of the church, art theorists scorned baroque illusionism and its exuberant emotionalism as an affront to reason.

Slowly taste turned, favoring the restrained aesthetic of ancient Greek art for what Johann Joachim Winckelmann called its "noble simplicity and calm grandeur." Rome still attracted sculptors from all over Europe but they began to seek different ways of expressing the time's new ideas. The young Jean-Antoine Houdon's statue *St. Bruno* (1766–1767, Santa Maria degli Angeli) pointed the way with still, smooth vertical draperies, a closed profile, and placid, meditative calm. His portrait busts are a marvel of natural observation that ennobles the sitters' intellectual traits. Yet it was an Italian sculptor, Antonio Canova (1757–1822) who created what we now think of as the first neoclassical sculpture, *Theseus and the Minotaur* (1781, Victoria and Albert Museum, London). His subsequent works, such as *Cupid and Psyche* (1787–1793, Louvre, Paris), *Perseus* (1804–1806, Metropolitan Museum of Art, New York), *Paolina Borghese as Venus Victorious* (1804–1808, Galleria Borghese) and *The Three Graces* (1815–1817, London), recouped the artistic and ethical purity of Greek art and inspired artists on two continents, initiating the century-long reign of neoclassicism.

See also **Baroque; Bernini, Gian Lorenzo; Michelangelo Buonarroti; Rome; Rome, Art in.**

BIBLIOGRAPHY

Avery, Charles. *Giambologna: The Complete Sculpture.* Mt. Kisco, N.Y., 1987.

Boucher, Bruce. *Italian Baroque Sculpture.* London, 1998.

Enggass, Robert. *Early Eighteenth Century Sculpture in Rome: An Illustrated Catalogue Raisonné.* 2 vols., University Park, Pa., and London, 1976.

Hibbard, Howard. *Bernini.* New York, 1990; 1st ed. 1965.

———. *Michelangelo.* 2nd ed. Cambridge, Mass., 1985.

Lavin, Irving. *Bernini and the Unity of the Visual Arts.* 2 vols., New York, 1980.

Licht, Fred. *Canova.* New York, 1983.

Pope-Hennessy, John. *Donatello.* New York, 1993.

———. *Italian High Renaissance and Baroque Sculpture.* 4th ed. London, 1996.

———. *Italian Renaissance Sculpture.* 4th ed. London, 1996.

MICHAEL P. MEZZATESTA

SEA BEGGARS. The Sea Beggars were pirates who made a living in the 1560s from capturing North Sea shipping. On 1 April 1572, six hundred Sea Beggars seized by surprise the small harbor city of Brill. It turned out to be a turning point in the history of the Netherlands, the beginning of what later nationalist historians have coined the "heroic phase of the Dutch Revolt," with its epic sieges of Haarlem, Alkmaar, and Leiden. The Sea Beggars were thus inextricably bound up with the genesis of the Dutch nation. Until 1572, they had been ordinary privateers, confining themselves to disrupting maritime traffic, raiding the coast of the Netherlands, plundering monasteries, and pillaging supplies of the Spanish troops, but with their seizure of Brill and its aftermath, they had become part of national history and memory.

In May 1568, during his invasion of Friesland, Louis of Nassau (1538–1574), the youngest brother of William of Orange (1533–1584), needed a small fleet to defend his supply routes to Emden. He called on the assistance of John Abels, a local corsair, and formed a fleet of fifteen ships. The military role of these newly formed Sea Beggars was, however, short-lived. After the failure of Louis's invasion in July 1568, because they lacked a harbor of their own, they were forced to piracy. William of Orange discerned their importance for his own military plans but could not afford to pay them properly. Instead, he provided them with letters of marque, which allowed them to attack hostile ships. Operating out of the communities of exiled Calvinists from the Netherlands in Emden and the English Channel ports, the Sea Beggars performed their acts of piracy and planned their raids of the Netherlands. In the spring of 1571 their force amounted to some thirty ships.

Their disruption of maritime traffic, however, more and more annoyed the authorities in Emden and England. On 1 March 1572, Queen Elizabeth I denied them admittance to English ports. Cruising aimlessly in the English Channel, they decided to seize Brill, hoping to find a new base for their undertakings. The news of the seizure took William of Orange by surprise and complicated his own plans for an invasion of the Netherlands. In the following months, however, one after another the towns of Holland and Zeeland opened their gates to the Sea Beggars. At last, William of Orange had his base in the Netherlands.

The Sea Beggars never proved to be a reliable armed force. Consisting mainly of fortune seekers and Calvinist exiles and commanded by such first-generation rebels as Lumey van der Marck and William Blois of Treslong, who had consciously broken with their pasts to revolt, the Sea Beggars cultivated an ethos that differed markedly from that of professional soldiers. They believed themselves to be God's elect and fought with the bitterness of the exile, and this made them hard to control. Their military advance in Holland and Zeeland was accompanied by the murder of priests, raping of nuns, and plundering of monasteries. Fearing that this behavior would alienate the moderate citizenry and town councils, William of Orange dismissed obstinate commanders such as Lumey and incorporated the ordinary men into a new, more professional army.

See also **Dutch Republic; Dutch Revolt (1568–1648); Elizabeth I (England); William of Orange.**

BIBLIOGRAPHY

de Meij, J. C. A. *De Watergeuzen en de Nederlanden, 1568–1572.* Amsterdam and London, 1972. The most important study.

Parker, Geoffrey. *The Dutch Revolt.* London, 1977.

van Deursen, Arie Theodorus. "Holland's Experience of War during the Revolt of the Netherlands." In *Britain and the Netherlands,* edited by A. C. Duke and C. A. Tamse. Vol. 6 of *War and Society,* pp. 19–53. The Hague, 1977.

PAUL KNEVEL

SECRETS, BOOKS OF. One of the most popular genres in early modern science publishing, the collections of recipes known as "books of secrets" began to stream from the presses in the mid-sixteenth century and were printed continuously down to the eighteenth century. These popular works contained hundreds of medical recipes, household hints, and technical recipes on metallurgy, alchemy, dyeing, and the making of perfume, oil, incense, and cosmetics. The books of secrets supplied a great deal of practical information to an emerging new middle-class readership, leading some historians to link them with the emerging secularist values of the early modern period and to see them as contributing to the making of an "age of how-to."

However, the books of secrets were not merely "how-to" books. They were also intended as serious contributions to the study of natural philosophy, as science was then called. Underlying the books of secrets was the premise that nature was a repository of hidden forces that might be discovered and manipulated by using the right techniques. Unlike the recondite contemporary treatises on magic and the occult arts, the books of secrets were grounded upon concrete, experimental trials. At the same time, the books of secrets popularized the emerging experimental method and attitudes to the lay public.

The most famous sixteenth-century book of secrets was a work attributed to Alessio Piemontese, *I Secreti del reverendo donno Alessio Piemontese* (1555; The secrets of Alessio). Alessio's *Secreti* went through more than a hundred editions and was still being reprinted in the 1790s. The humanist Girolamo Ruscelli (1500–1566), the real author of the *Secreti*, reported that the work contained the experimental results of an "Academy of Secrets" that he and a group of humanists and noblemen founded in Naples in the 1540s. Ruscelli's academy is the first recorded example of an experimental scientific society. The academy was later imitated by Giambattista Della Porta, who founded an *Accademia dei Secreti* in Naples in the 1560s.

Alessio Piemontese was the prototypical "professor of secrets." The description of Alessio's hunt for secrets in the preface to the *Secreti* gave rise to a legend of the wandering empiric in search of technological and scientific secrets. Its enormous popularity made the work play a key role in the emergence of the conception of science as a hunt for the secrets of nature. The concept of science as a hunt pervaded experimental science during the scientific revolution.

In the books of secrets, experimental science shaded into natural magic. Giambattista Della Porta's famous *Magia Naturalis* (1558; Natural magic) deployed practical recipes in an effort to demonstrate the principles of natural magic. Other books of secrets, such as Isabella Cortese's *Secreti* (1564), a compilation of alchemical recipes, disseminated experimental techniques and practical information to a wide readership. Recent research has suggested that the books of secrets played an important role in the emergence of early modern experimental science, acting as intermediaries between the private and esoteric "secrets" of medieval alche-

mists and magi and the public Baconian "experiments" that characterized the research programs of the Royal Society of London and other seventeenth-century experimental academies.

See also **Alchemy; Astrology; Magic; Medicine; Natural History; Scientific Revolution.**

BIBLIOGRAPHY

Eamon, William. *Science and the Secrets of Nature: Books of Secrets in Medieval and Early Modern Culture.* Princeton, 1994.

Ferguson, John K. *Bibliographical Notes on Histories of Inventions and Books of Secrets.* 2 vols. London, 1959.

WILLIAM EAMON

SEIGNEURIALISM. *See* Feudalism.

SEMINARY.

The Council of Trent (1545–1563) required the creation of diocesan seminaries with the canon *Cum Adolescentium Aetas,* adopted during the council's twenty-third session in 1563. It became compulsory for every diocese to erect a seminary for the purpose of educating the local clergy.

Some historians claim that this legislation was fundamentally a return to the concept of cathedral school, where, from the beginning of Christianity, young men were prepared for priesthood. It was thus conceived as a restoration and renovation of the traditional way in which priests received their training. In its original design, the Tridentine seminary legislation was influenced by three factors. First, petitions coming from Italy, France, and the Holy Roman Empire had highlighted abuses in the education of the clergy, and had proposed either the reformation of cathedral schools or the erection of special schools attached to cathedral churches. Second, the Society of Jesus insisted on the necessity of providing adequate means for clerical education, and had already pursued this aim in founding and running colleges, including the famous Germanicum, founded in Rome by the Jesuit Claude Le Jay in 1552. Finally, the synodal legislation, promulgated for England by Cardinal Reginald Pole (1500–1558) in his *Reformatio Angliae* (1556), was taken as a model. Pole's solution was to cure the carelessness of the clergy by erecting seminaries at every cathedral church. This directly inspired the fathers of the council in their writing of the Tridentine decree.

According to this decree, the diocesan colleges were to be *seminaria* ('breeding grounds') for the future priests. The students were to be adolescents at least twelve years of age, who were born of lawful wedlock and were already able to read and write. They also had to show a sincere desire to dedicate themselves to the service of the church. Under the local bishop's control, students were to receive a liberal education first, then an ecclesiastical one. The young men were thus to study letters, humanities, chant, liturgy, sacred scripture, and dogmatic, moral, and pastoral theology. Their spiritual formation included daily attendance at Mass and monthly confession. However, the decree did not specify that all priests should pass through the seminaries. On the contrary, the seminary seemed rather a means to help poor but deserving young people to become priests. The rich could be admitted on the condition that they paid for their education. In fact, what is most important in this decree is that it placed the formation of future priests, or at least a good number of them, under the direct responsibility of the bishops. The local bishop, as the chief administrator of the school, had to have an eye on the content of the courses and the quality of the professors who provided them. The rest of the diocesan clergy was also closely associated in the project. Not only was it asked to finance the seminary, in paying a special tax imposed on its revenues, but it also had to delegate four of its members to help in the administration of the new institution.

The creation of seminaries became the main concern not only of the popes attached to the Catholic Reformation, such as Pius V and Gregory XIII, but also of the political powers (principally the Catholic sovereigns and sometimes the local authorities) who saw in this measure a good way to reinforce the expansion and the control of higher education. The number of seminaries expanded quickly in Europe under these conditions. Two small Italian dioceses disputed the honor of having founded the first Tridentine seminary in 1564, Larino in Umbria and Rieti in the kingdom of Naples. The seminary of Milan, founded by Archbishop Cardinal Carlo Borromeo, followed shortly,

a year before his uncle Pope Pius IV founded the Collegio Romano. A great many seminaries were created in Italy but their spread was uneven. In fact, certain large dioceses, such as those of Genoa and Florence, had to wait until the seventeenth and even the eighteenth century before being endowed with a seminary.

Pope Pius IV and his successors worked hard to implement the Tridentine decision in countries where Catholics were in a majority. Thus, from 1564 onward, the number of seminaries spread quickly. In the German countries, seminaries were founded in Eichstätt, Breslau, Würzburg, Bamberg, Trier, Salzburg, Gurk, and Graz. Poland opened its first seminary in 1564 (Poznan, Warmia) and Hungary in 1567 (Tyrnau). However, the colleges established in Rome such as the Germanicum and the Hungaricum (united in 1580) had more impact on the formation of priests than the diocesan seminaries created in central Europe.

In the Netherlands, the development of seminaries progressed more slowly because of the 1566 uprising against the religious policies of Spanish king Philip II. These troubles led in 1579 to the revolt of the Calvinist provinces of Holland and Zeeland against Spanish domination and ended in 1609 with the independence of the United Provinces. Tridentine seminaries were thus erected almost exclusively in the southern provinces, in cities such as Ypres (1565), Namur, Bruges, Liège, and Malines.

Contrary to other countries, Spain had already secured training for its priests through a solid network of university colleges. Some of them, such as those of Grenada, Malaga, and Sigüenza, were used as diocesan seminaries. However, most of the Spanish bishops were willing to obey the Tridentine decree. At least twenty new seminaries were founded from 1565 onward, among them Burgos (1565) and Teruel (1566). In 1651, twenty-six out of fifty-four Spanish dioceses had a seminary. However, the expansion was not without difficulties. Because of hostility from the local chapters, many seminaries were short of financial and human resources. The need for training of the local clergy was also felt in the Spanish colonies. It took only ten years before the first seminary was founded in Antequera in Mexico (1574). Before the end of the sixteenth century, under the initiative of Saint Toribio, archbishop of Lima, the seminaries of Santiago de Chile, Lima, Bogota, Cuzco, and Sucre were created.

It is clear that there was a great desire among European bishops to apply the decree of the council, even in France, which had not yet officially accepted the council's decisions. In effect, many French bishops bypassed the offical position against Rome and tried to implement the Tridentine Reformation, especially the decree concerning the training of the local clergy. This explains why as early as 1567, Charles de Guise, the cardinal of Lorraine, founded the first seminary in Reims. However, because of the Wars of Religion, it was difficult to gather the necessary money for the founding of seminaries. After the wars ended, competition with colleges (which had chairs of theology) and universities impeded the growth of seminaries, which still remained optional for the aspiring priests. All this explains why, between 1580 and 1620, only sixteen seminaries were created in a country that counted 108 dioceses. The number increased from 1641 onward, however, and in 1790, most French dioceses had a seminary. This development was due to astounding founders of new orders for secular priests, such as Pierre de Bérulle, Vincent de Paul, Jean-Jacques Olier, and Jean Eudes, who founded, respectively, the seminaries of the Priests of the Oratory, the Lazarists, the Sulpicians, and the Society of the Sacred Heart. These institutions were to have considerable influence later in the erection of similar houses in the British Isles, Canada, and the United States.

Most of the Tridentine seminaries were modeled on that created in Milan by Cardinal Borromeo. He first opened a major seminary, that of St. John the Baptist, with facilities for 150 students. But recognizing that all candidates did not have the intellectual capacity to be admitted to this institution, he established La Canonica, a preparatory school for about sixty students who would receive a basic education about the care of souls, through classes on holy Scriptures, cases of conscience, and Roman catechism. He then founded three preparatory seminaries: one for younger boys, another for adolescents, and a third for older students. From these three institutions the candidates were to pass either to the major seminary or to La Canonica. Borromeo also wrote rules dictating students' life

and piety, which were adopted by almost all the European seminaries. Most of them also adopted the Milanese way of giving the management of the study program to the Jesuits. In reality, the majority (excepted that of Pavia) were closely associated with the local Jesuit college. They ended up being boarding houses that lodged a rather small number of young men (sometimes fewer than ten, through lack of money) who attended classes with the Jesuits. In fact, the existence of these first seminaries was often brief and always difficult because of financial and political problems. In the seventeenth century, their failure was imputed to the young age of the students. Catholic reformers such as Vincent de Paul promoted the education of adults rather than that of adolescents with the "seminaries for ordinands," centered on a more practical religious education and destined for grown men ready to take the orders.

In fact, if the intellectual and moral qualities of the European clergy were stronger in the seventeenth and eighteenth centuries, that strength was due less to the Tridentine seminary training than to a better selection of candidates and better control of the local priests (by the bishop's visit and by the frequent holding of synods). Above all, the improved qualities were due to the Jesuit colleges, who trained a growing part of the European clergy. A strict schedule, tamed behavior and attitudes, the practice of prayer, the conferences about piety and spiritual examinations, the weekly confession and communion, all this prepared the priest to live and behave as dictated by the Council of Trent.

See also **Clergy: Roman Catholic Clergy; Education; Jesuits; Reformation, Catholic; Trent, Council of.**

BIBLIOGRAPHY

Broutin, Paul. *La réforme pastorale en France au XVIIe siècle. Recherches sur la tradition pastorale aprés le Concile de Trente* 2 vols. Tournai, 1956.

Darricaud, Raymond. *La formation des professeurs de séminaires d'après un directoire de M. Jean Bonnet (1664–1735), supérieur de la congrégation de la mission.* Piacenza, 1966.

———. "Le traité des séminaires d'Antoine Godeau et la formation des premiers séminaires français." In *Antoine Godeau, 1605–1672, de la galanterie à la sainteté: actes des journées commémoratives, Grasse, 21–24 avril 1972.* Edited by Yves Giraud, pp. 167–187. Paris, 1975.

Degert, Antoine. *Histoire des séminaires français jusqu'à la Révolution*. 2 vols. Paris, 1912.

Julia, Dominique. "L'éducation des ecclésiastiques en France au XVIIe et au XVIIIe siècle." In *Problèmes d'histoire de l'éducation. Actes des séminaires organisés par l'école française de Rome et l'Università di Roma-La Sapienza, janvier–mai 1985*. Rome-Paris, 1988, pp. 141–204.

———. "Le prêtre." In, *L'homme des Lumières*. Edited by Vovelle Michel, pp. 391–429. Paris, 1996.

O'Donohue, J.-A. *Tridentine Seminary Legislation: Its Source and Its Formation*. Louvain, 1957.

Quéniart, Jean. *Les hommes, l'Église et Dieu dans la France du XVIIIe siècle*. Paris, 1978.

Tallon, Allain. *Le concile de Trente*. Paris, 2000.

Taveneaux, René. *Le catholicisme dans la France classique: 1610–1715*. 2 vols. Paris, 1980.

Venard, Marc. "Les séminaires en France avant saint Vincent de Paul." In *Vincent de Paul (colloque de Paris, 1981)*, pp. 1–17. Paris, 1983.

DOMINIQUE DESLANDRES

SENSATIONALISM. *See* Empiricism.

SENSIBILITY.

During the eighteenth century, cultures of sensibility came into general existence in several European countries and colonies; they persisted well into the nineteenth century, and while they have been fragmented as coherent middle-class cultures, the values they embodied have persisted into the twenty-first century. In their intense interest in the operation of the mind and in interpersonal relations, these cultures displayed the rise of what we think of as modern consciousness and, within it, psychology. Their context was the time and space that newly developing consumer economies first afforded significant numbers of women and men, and they were preoccupied with pleasure and pain, as more and more people found themselves able to choose more of the former and to transcend more of the latter. How widespread the culture was in any nation depended, therefore, on the extent of the consumer revolution in the eighteenth century and thereafter. Cultures of sensibility existed in such urban centers as Edinburgh and Paris, but appear to have been most widespread in England, Holland, and the British colonies that became the United States. They both displayed transnational characteristics (among multilingual and often well-traveled elites) and reflected local ones, as people drew upon their language and other modes of expression—tears above all, but other physiological signs (legible to other people of sensibility), such as blushes and trembling—in response to their own thoughts, to interpersonal exchanges, to the "distress" of others, and to "sublime" natural phenomena.

The word "sensibility" denoted the receptivity of the senses and referred to the psycho-perceptual scheme systematized in the late seventeenth century in the nerve theory of Isaac Newton and the environmental psychology of John Locke, both of whom were influential, not only in their native England, but in European philosophical thought in general. Sensibility (and "sensible" and "sentiment") connoted the operation of the nervous system, the material basis for consciousness. By the mid-eighteenth century, "sensibility" stood for a widely held body of beliefs signifying a particular kind of heightened consciousness of self and others, and incorporating a "moral sense"—a conscience, but also something thought to be an equivalent of the other senses, like sight and touch. The coexistence of reason and feeling was assumed, but the proportion of each was endlessly debated, above all because of what many saw as the dangers of unleashed feelings.

Notable eighteenth-century expositions of sensibility's operation ranged from the philosophical publications (1711) of the third earl of Shaftesbury (1671–1713) and those of his disciple, the Scot Francis Hutcheson (1694–1746), in the 1720s; to Abbé Prévost's novel *Manon Lescaut* (1731); to the internationally influential novels of Samuel Richardson (1689–1761), published 1740–1754; to the neurology (published 1751) of another Scot, Robert Whytt (1714–1766), and that (published 1753) of the Swiss, Albrecht von Haller (1708–1777); to *The Theory of Moral Sentiments* (1759) by Adam Smith (1723–1790); to *Julie, ou la Nouvelle Héloïse* (1761) by Jean-Jacques Rousseau; and to Johann Wolfgang von Goethe's *Die Leiden des jungen Werthers* (The sorrows of young Werther, 1774). The latter two demonstrated the sexually subversive possibilities in the responsiveness of sensitive nerves and the aggrandizement of feeling. Much the same can be said of two playful novels by Lawrence Sterne, *The Life and Opinions of Tristram Shandy* (1759–1767) and *A Sentimental Journey* (1768). The consequences of these sexual potentials were emulation and recoil, heightening tensions over the value of sensibility. From the 1740s the boundaries of sensibility and satire were crossed and recrossed frequently.

The French Revolution was a turning point in the history of sensibility because its opponents attributed it in part to the emotional abandon of Rousseau. Indeed, its ideology, like that expressed by the American Declaration of Independence (1776), did manifest some of sensibility's values. The debate over the proportions of reason and feeling in persons of sensibility was politicized, and the need for women to channel their feelings toward moral and domestic goals was reemphasized. The word "sentimental," which had been used positively, became a label for "excessive sensibility" and self-indulgence.

Sensibility and sentimentalism continued to flourish at all levels through the nineteenth century, both on the Continent and in the New World, developing into or accompanying Gothic, anti-Gothic, romantic, and realistic forms through the nineteenth century. The tradition extended through antislavery narratives and sentimental novels (Harriet Beecher Stowe), reform-oriented novels (Charles Dickens), and in popular and religious forms (Gustave Flaubert). While there were significant changes in the language of sensibility over time, its major terms and values were still important to the exquisitely conscious upper-class Europeans and Americans described by Henry James at the turn of the twentieth century. Mark Twain continued to place central value on heightened consciousness and on the morality of inner feeling even while he replaced the language of sensibility with fresh democratic forms.

The continuing persistence of this tradition through the nineteenth century, however, is remarkable only if one neglects its deep popular appeal and its links to consumerism. As the word "culture" implies, the phenomenon was by no means limited to intellectual and literary expressions. Its different origins had included the code of behavior of the Renaissance courts of Italy and France, subsequently imitated by aristocrats and would-be aristocrats throughout Europe, then absorbed by upwardly mobile groups below them in the social pile, in accordance with "the civilizing process" described by Norbert Elias. Also key had been changes of religious thought (to which Newton and Locke were connected) in England, as well as in France and Holland. Some of the ideals and corresponding behavior were absorbed by evangelized working-class audiences, as well as by the increasingly literate bourgeoisie. That the culture's chief feature was the elevation of pleasurable feelings meant that it held appeal for all, including those who had been denied literacy, let alone formal theological and intellectual, training—those who now found value in the "heart" alone, and an empowering sense of victimization and of moral superiority. Thus sensibility can be detected in overlapping Christian, bourgeois, and reformist ideologies and identities, as well as in mere fashion, but could also sponsor, even revolutionize, individual consciousness.

SENSIBILITY, RELIGIOUS BELIEF, AND CONSUMERISM

Both elite and popular thought reimagined God to reflect the more positive reconceptualization of human nature that had arisen amid gentler material circumstances. God was now seen to be benevolent and responsive to the same signals of human wishes and needs as men and women of sensibility, although representations of the older God of inflexible justice and condemnation persisted. Religious campaigns for "the reformation of manners," from the later seventeenth through the nineteenth centuries, aimed at inculcating, in objects from upper-class debauchees, working-class males, and uncouth frontiersmen to frivolous women, the non-European colonized, and the enslaved, the habits Max Weber (1864–1920) was to call the "Protestant ethic" (although subsequent scholars have pointed out such an ethic was not limited to Protestants). During the eighteenth century one sign of such reformation was a feeling heart. Colin Campbell has shown that the religious traditions explored by Weber had in fact incorporated the emotional materials from which sensibility and consumer psychology were developed; complacent religious feelings, first stimulated by a sense of religious goodness, were extended to embrace the pleasures derived from consumer goods.

"Taste" in goods expressed sensibility (and was identified with morality), but unsuccessful struggles by elites to maintain standards demonstrated that aesthetic dikes could not prevail against the flood of consumer and producer desires. Home was where new objects (from novels to tea sets, more elaborate cuisine to chamber pots) were primarily enjoyed, and where their owners expressed the feelings with which they were invested. Sensibility was generated in more sentimental families, where children were nurtured in more indulgent, future-oriented ways. Women became more central as consumers as well as mothers; their demand was crucial to the new economies. But new male capitalists had their own interests (in addition to religious imperatives and those emanating from their wives and mothers) in internalizing, or at least displaying, sensibility as they pursued commercial ends rather than the warrior and knightly ideals of the feudal past. Liberated commerce was seen as a reform integral to the "civilizing process," albeit susceptible to the corruptions of ambition, greed, and insincerity at the hands of unfeeling men. Extending from cities to international and imperial horizons, it required the reputation and trustworthiness manifested by sensibility, although men might feel threatened in that sensibility by the charge of effeminacy, to which they were vulnerable because they now shared much with women. Their new, related republican ideologies embodied values that overlapped with those of cultures of sensibility.

SENSIBILITY, WOMEN, AND HUMANITARIANISM

The empowerment of bourgeois women extended from home to public heterosocial spheres beyond the traditional churchgoing to shopping, visits, assemblies, dances, and even masquerades, where fashions and manners transmitted sensibility. In entering the new culture women were not limited by class (although enjoyment of the range of possibilities was); in daily working relations with employers, in their exposure to sensibility's religious outlets, and motivated by their own interests at home, particularly in the challenge of reforming men, they seized new opportunities. Increasingly women became literate, writing in a wide range of forms, from private letters to published poetry and novels, specializing in the sentimental.

These and other kinds of female self-assertion provoked powerful opposition. Sensibility was thus of ambiguous value to women; it could be deemed the cause of nervous disorders and sexual corruptibility as well as the source of moral superiority. A major symbol of sensibility was the often feminized figure of "virtue in distress," archetypically Richardson's heroine in *Clarissa*, drugged and raped by Lovelace. Women and their male allies elevated sensibility as a standard, demanding that unfeeling men of archaic or new, competing cultures, reform themselves and their treatment of women. If one root of feminism lay in that empowering sense of victimization and the "relief" (a common term in women's sentimental writings) brought out by its private and public expression, another lay in criticism of the disabling effects of gendered sensibility exaggerated at the expense of intellect. The most developed argument here was Mary Wollstonecraft's (1759–1797) *Vindication of the Rights of Woman* (1792), which aimed to reform women's manners, which she said were utterly sensitized to pleasing men.

We can see the efforts to soften men as women's chief expression of the application of sensibility to reform. But both sexes also worked (although usually separately) in humanitarian efforts. "Humanity" became synonymous with the sympathy automatically stimulated in the nervous system of people "of feeling," and it was a nongendered term; indeed, it was a term intended to undermine all invidious distinctions, even though humanitarians often marked their efforts with condescension and racism. "Humanitarianism" is an umbrella term for a startling variety of reforms, some of which had been attempted from the very beginning of the eighteenth century. Most of these focused on the abuses of the bodies of human beings (some were concerned with animals, too); this preoccupation mirrored the physicality of the sensibility of the reformers themselves. Instances of humanitarian targets were the physical abuse of enslaved Africans, the flogging of children, sailors, and criminals, judicial torture, and the seduction and abandonment of women.

The sympathy that cultivators of sensibility felt for such victims (Adam Smith's 1759 *Theory of Moral Sentiments* took for its opening model the irresistible sympathy he argued human beings felt for their "brother" on the rack) was the expression of the transcendence of age-old deprivations and sufferings on the part of those who were now consumers. An essential condition for the rise of cultures of sensibility, however, was the unevenness and inequity of the consumer revolution—indeed, that it depended on the exploitation of others. If eighteenth-century people, developing their consciousnesses and indulging their delicate feelings in conditions of comfort, remained aware at some level of the harsh circumstances of their predecessors, more immediate was the contrast between prosperous consumers and those around them still living in misery. Contrasts were central to the self-conception of women and men of sensibility and included art versus nature; rural life versus the city; the past versus the present; private, domestic retreats versus the bustling, public "world"; and most fundamental, pleasure versus pain. All of these contrasts stimulated feelings of sensibility, from schadenfreude (taking pleasure in another's pain) to nostalgia, from self-indulgence to sympathy. Men and women of feeling, finally, were preoccupied with their own sincerity and insincerity—a debate over the culture of sensibility that continues today.

See also **Consumption; Goethe, Johann Wolfgang von; Haller, Albrecht von; Locke, John; Newton, Isaac; Passions; Prévost d'Exiles, Antoine-François; Revolutions, Age of; Richardson, Samuel; Rousseau, Jean-Jacques; Sade, Donatien-Alphonse-François de; Smith, Adam; Sterne, Laurence; Sublime, Idea of the; Women.**

BIBLIOGRAPHY

Barker-Benfield, G. J. *The Culture of Sensibility: Sex and Society in Eighteenth-Century Britain.* Chicago, 1992.

———. "The Origins of Anglo-American Sensibility." In *Charity, Philanthropy, and Civility in American History.* Edited by Lawrence J. Friedman and Mark D. McGarvie. Cambridge, U.K., and New York, 2003.

Brissenden, R. F. *Virtue in Distress: Studies in the Novel of Sentiment from Richardson to Sade.* London, 1974.

Campbell, Colin. *The Romantic Ethic and the Spirit of Modern Consumerism.* Oxford and New York, 1987.

Elias, Norbert. *The Civilizing Process.* Translated by Edmund Jephcott. Oxford and Cambridge, Mass., 1994.

Fiering, Norman S. "Irresistible Compassion: An Aspect of Eighteenth-Century Sympathy and Humanitarianism." *Journal of the History of Ideas* 37 (1976): 195–218.

Schama, Simon. *Citizens: A Chronicle of the French Revolution, 1789–1799.* New York, 1989.

———. *The Embarrassment of Riches: An Interpretation of Dutch Culture in the Golden Age.* London and New York, 1987.

Todd, Janet. *Sensibility: An Introduction.* London and New York, 1986.

G. J. BARKER-BENFIELD

SEPÚLVEDA, JUAN GINÉS DE

(1490?–1574), Spanish humanist scholar and philosopher. Juan Ginés de Sepúlveda was a distinguished university professor possessed of a mastery of Latin style. In 1515 he moved from Córdoba to Italy, where he was accepted into the Spanish College in Bologna. Working under the direction of the eminent Pietro Pomponazzi (1462–1525), Sepúlveda developed into one of the leading scholars in Italy. By 1526 he had become the official translator of Aristotle's writings for the papal court. During his twenty years in Italy he worked to recover the "true" Aristotle. He compiled and published in Paris a Latin translation of the *Politics* that for centuries was an indispensable work. Upon his return to Spain he translated Aristotle's *Ethics* into Castilian for the Habsburg Monarchy.

In 1542 the king of Spain, Charles V of the Holy Roman Empire (ruled 1519–1556), signed the "New Laws," which prohibited the enslavement of Indians. The king ordered in 1550 that conquests in his name cease until the Council of the Indies should decide upon the justness of Spain's conduct. Sepúlveda's opinions were solicited by the president of the Council of the Indies. Sepúlveda was an ardent nationalist, much impressed by his compatriots' conquests in the Americas described in Gonzalo Fernández de Oviedo's (1478–1557) writings, which belittle aboriginal peoples. Never having visited the territories under question or having met a native, Sepúlveda had no personal or fiscal stake in his theoretical arguments.

Sepúlveda produced *Democrates Alter sive de justicis beli causis apud Indios* (Concerning the just cause of the war against the Indians; first published in Latin 1545 with a Spanish apology published in 1550 and the definitive version finally published in 1554). In this dialogue, Demócrates, a spokesman for the author, convinces Leopoldo, a German with Lutheran tendencies, that war against Indians is the just and necessary preliminary to their conversion. Sepúlveda's request that the Latin manuscript be published was denied, and the university faculties of Alcalá and Salamanca also recommended against granting permission. A committee of government officials, scholars, and theologians was formed in response to Sepúlveda's insistence that there be a debate over the merits of his argument. The committee's deliberations at Valladolid began in 1550 and reconvened the following year.

To Sepúlveda the Spanish were obviously champions of an advanced civilization. He believed that hierarchy, not equality, was the natural condition of human society. This argument mirrors Aristotle, who maintained, rather inconsistently, that some humans are by nature slaves and others masters. Natural slaves are persons of inborn rudeness and inhuman and barbarous customs, and those who exceed them in prudence and talent, even if physically inferior, are their natural lords. Sepúlveda's variant is: "If you know the customs and nature of the two peoples, that with perfect right the Spaniards rule over these barbarians of the New World and adjacent islands. . . . There is as much difference between them as there is . . . between apes and men . . . . And if they refuse our rule, they may be compelled by force of arms to accept it" *(Demócrates Secundus)*.

Sepúlveda claimed that every native was barbarous. Thus their natural condition was to obey a superior because they committed crimes against natural law by eating human flesh, offering human sacrifice, and worshiping "demons." War may thus be justly waged and should be waged against these infidels in order to prepare the way for preaching the True Faith.

Sepúlveda next abbreviated his principal arguments for his *Apología* (1550). This time he focused on the bulls of Pope Alexander VI (reigned 1492–1503), which he claimed gave Spain entire authority over the Indies. According to the laws of both nations and Nature, to the victor belong the spoils. Although Sepúlveda published the *Apología* in Rome, it was never made widely available in Spain, where it was confiscated by royal authority.

The committee next heard from Father Bartolomé de Las Casas, who took five days to read from an enormous manuscript. One of the committee's members then condensed the long argument for Sepúlveda, who wrote a point-by-point refutation of the positions held by the Dominican "Defender of the Indians." The two contenders did not debate face to face, and the proceedings proved inconclusive since the committee never produced a final report.

Sepúlveda's views about the inferiority of the Indians became well known and largely prevailed in the Western Hemisphere, where his stance was popular with the colonists. The municipal council of Mexico City sent Sepúlveda a letter of congratulations and thanks. From a theoretical viewpoint, however, Sepúlveda lost the debate because his manuscript was not published in Spain, where the government rejected his central argument that it was just to wage war against the Indians.

See also **Colonialism; Las Casas, Bartolomé de; Natural Law; Natural Rights; Spanish Colonies; Toleration.**

BIBLIOGRAPHY

Primary Sources

Losada, Ángel, ed. *Juan Ginés de Sepúlveda a través de su "Espistolaro" y nuevos documentos.* Madrid, 1973.

Sepúlveda, Juan Ginés de. *Demócrates Secundo o De la justas causas de la guerra contra los indios.* Madrid, 1951. Spanish translation of *Demócrates Alter sive de justicis beli causis apud Indios.*

Secondary Sources

Bell, Aubrey G. F. *Juan Ginés de Sepúlveda.* London, 1925.

Hanke, Lewis. *Aristotle and the American Indians.* London, 1959.

———. *"All Mankind Is One": A Study of the Disputation between Bartolomé de Las Casas and Juan Ginés de Sepúlveda in 1550 on the Intellectual and Religious Capacity of the American Indians.* DeKalb, Ill., 1974.

MARVIN LUNENFELD

SERBIA. The kingdom of Serbia disappeared from the map of Europe in the fifteenth century, following defeats at the hands of the Ottoman Empire beginning with the Battle of Kosovo in 1389. The Ottoman conquest socially leveled Serbia. The Serbian aristocrat either converted to Islam, lost his lands and privileges, or was killed. The result was a society consisting of peasants. However, the memory of independence was kept alive by the Serbian

Orthodox Church. A Serbian archbishopric had been founded in 1219 thanks to the initiative of the monk Sava (Rastko Nemanjic, a son of Nemanja, the founder of the Nemanjic dynasty). The archbishop had been raised to the level of patriarch by Stefan Dušan in 1346. Although this patriarchate did not survive him, a Serbian church remained and continued to define the Serbian population culturally. The Ottomans restored the Serbian patriarchate in 1557 at Peć, a city in modern northwestern Kosovo. It lasted until 1766, when fears of collusion with Ottoman enemies convinced the government to abolish it. The church, ministering to its peasant flock via its peasant clergy, nourished the continued existence of a Serbia not as a state, but as an identity.

SERBIA UNDER THE OTTOMANS

Most of medieval Serbian territory fell to the Ottoman province of Rumeli, which extended from the Peloponnese to the Danube; Serbian populations also inhabited the provinces of Bosnia, Kanije, and Temeşvar, until the latter two were taken by the Habsburg Monarchy in wars of the seventeenth century. The notable towns of the Serbian kingdom now became Ottoman garrisons. Belgrade, not a part of Stefan Dušan's Serbia in any case, had up to 40,000 inhabitants in 1632, but was down to 15,000 in 1838. Niš, Kruševac, Peć, and other important towns in Serbia withered. As inhabitants of the Ottoman Empire, Serbs both suffered and benefited. Many Serbs chose to convert to Islam, in which cases they instantly became members of the favored faith and thus part of the ruling class. It is true that Orthodox Christian Serbs were subject to taxes and levies that Muslims did not pay, but those burdens were potentially balanced by the fact that Christians did not have to fight in Ottoman armies. Above all, though, the fact remains that the Orthodox Christians of the Ottoman Empire were administered via the millet system, by which they were governed by their own church hierarchy.

The millet system was established in 1453 as a result of a decree by Sultan Mehmed II (ruled 1444–1446, 1451–1481). It reflected the Ottoman belief that one's identity is fundamentally religious. Thus, while one had the option to convert to Islam and enjoy the fruits of that conversion, one also had the right to maintain one's faith. Thus, the Ottomans administered their subjects as religious beings, and the Orthodox patriarch in Istanbul was given responsibility for the Orthodox Christians of the empire. On the local level, where contact between the believer and the church was most common, the parish priest was of the ethnicity of the flock. The church was made responsible for marriage, divorce, and the collection of dues to the church as well as to the state. The millet system thus ameliorated some of the effects of the Ottoman conquest. Serbian statehood was gone, but a Serbian, Orthodox Christian identity was maintained through what many Serbs see as a "dark age" thanks to a system that allowed a degree of self-administration.

Over the course of the Ottoman conquest and in subsequent centuries, many Orthodox Christians migrated northward and westward under the pressure of the Ottoman advance. Thus, a large Serbian presence was established in the Habsburg Monarchy. Population movements began in earnest after the Battle of Smederevo in 1459, and by 1483, up to two hundred thousand Orthodox Christians had moved into central Slavonia and Srijem. The final major population shift occurred in the 1690s, following an Austro-Ottoman war, when at least 30,000 Orthodox Serbs, led by Patriarch Arsenije III Crnojevic, made their way from Kosovo north to southern Hungary. The center of authority in the Serbian Orthodox Church moved with the migrants. The Patriarchate at Peć, which would finally be extinguished by the Ottomans in 1766, was essentially replaced by the Metropolitanate of Sremski Karlovci, in Croatia. Through the late nineteenth century, two institutions, the military frontier and the metropolitanate, would define Serbian life in the Habsburg Monarchy. The military frontier would exist until 1881. The Orthodox Christians who had made their way from Ottoman territories to the Habsburg Monarchy were given certain privileges, usually including a plot of land, freedom from taxation by the local aristocracy, and freedom of worship, but they paid for these privileges with military service in times of crisis. Individual agreements, the most famous of which was the Statuta Valachorum, issued in 1630 by Emperor Ferdinand II (ruled 1619–1637), regulated the obligations of the Orthodox Serbian population. Settlement patterns, with Banija, Kordun, and Lika in the west, and parts of Slavonia in the east, heavily populated by Serbs, were a result of these agreements.

ORIGINS OF THE INDEPENDENCE MOVEMENT

Although the Serbian population of the Habsburg Monarchy was more advanced economically and educationally, the origins of a modern Serbian state can be traced to the late eighteenth century in the *pašalik* (Turk., *pashalik*) of Belgrade, the northernmost reach of the Ottoman Empire in Europe. This region, south of the Danube and Sava rivers and east of the Drina River, would become the geographic core of modern Serbia. The first stirrings of rebellion among the Serbs of the region followed the Austro-Ottoman War of 1788–1791, during which Serbs had fought for the Austrian empire. Thereafter, the Serbs of the region were left to their own devices by the Austrians, who had lost the war. In spite of their disloyalty to the sultan, the Serbs as well as the Ottomans desired stability in the region. However, in the ever-weaker Ottoman Empire, the borderlands had come under the sway of local janissaries, and the *pašalik* of Belgrade was no exception. The sultan and his Serbian subjects had a mutual interest in destroying the destabilizing influence of the janissaries, and the roots of the Serbian independence movement were thus paradoxically to be found in an alliance of local Serbian headmen with the Ottoman central government. The revolution of 1804 thus began as a movement for economic and political stability within the Ottoman Empire rather than as a romantic-nationalist movement for independence.

See also **Austro-Ottoman Wars; Balkans; Ferdinand II (Holy Roman Empire); Ottoman Empire.**

BIBLIOGRAPHY

Lampe, John R., and Marvin R. Jackson. *Balkan Economic History, 1550–1950.* Bloomington, Ind., 1982.

Pavlowitch, Stevan K. *Serbia: The History of an Idea.* New York, 2002.

Sugar, Peter F. *Southeastern Europe under Ottoman Rule, 1354–1804.* Seattle, 1977.

NICHOLAS J. MILLER

SERFDOM. Serfdom was a status of legal bondage, almost invariably referring to peasants in en-forced dependence on seignorial overlords. Serfdom could be an inherited, personal status (serfs of this sort were known as neifs in English, *hommes de corps* in French, and *Erbuntertanen* in German) or the consequence of the tenure of servile land (serfs of this sort were known as villeins in English, *serfs de la glèbe* in French, and *Gutsuntertanen* in German). During the early modern period serfdom encompassed a wide variety of conditions and social relations. Generally speaking, however, serfdom was a more recent, more widespread, and more onerous phenomenon in eastern than in western Europe, although even here there were important regional variations.

West European serfdom was of diverse and often obscure origin. In some places it developed out of the late Roman colonate (peasant tenants who were legally tied to the land during the fourth and fifth centuries); in others it was the result of self-commendation by peasants to powerful landlords in exchange for protection. Particularly important was the extension of the private jurisdictions of landlords at the expense of public systems of justice during the tenth and eleventh centuries, a process often accompanied by the imposition of fees and labor services on the peasantry. Finally, at the frontier between Christendom and the Islamic world, serfdom was also spread through military conquest. Thus in Sicily, which was seized by Norman adventurers between 1061 and 1091, most serfs were Muslims.

LEGAL STATUS OF SERFS

By the twelfth and thirteenth centuries, serfdom in western Europe had acquired a more precise legal definition, and was associated with a fairly standard series of legal disabilities. Particularly prominent was the obligation to provide *corvées,* or labor services, for the lord, ranging from a few days a year in southern France and the Mediterranean to one to two days every week on the northern European plain and in England. Serfs were forbidden to live outside the seignorial territory, and had to pay fines to marry the serf of another lord *(merchet, formarriage, Ungenossame).* Serfs were also subject to a characteristic set of fees, including poll taxes or annual recognition fees (tallage, *chevage*), fees at the commencement of tenancy (entry fines, *Handlohn, Erdschatz*), and death duties (heriots, *mainmorte,*

Todesfälle). Finally, serfdom often entailed disqualification from public office or exclusion from public jurisdiction.

Nevertheless, serfs were not slaves, but persons with rights in law. Only rarely could serfs be sold apart from their land; most "sales" of serfs in western Europe represented only the transfer of jurisdictional rights from one overlord to another with no physical movement of the peasants concerned. Moreover, de facto control of the means of production (the tenanted land) gave the serf leverage to bargain, and over the course of the Middle Ages, most of the rents, fees, and charges associated with serfdom became fixed by custom, while labor services tended to be commuted into cash payments. Serfs always retained extensive potential to resist seignorial pressure, either actively, through negotiation, protest, flight, and revolt, or passively, through foot-dragging and pilfering. Western European serfs also became adept at manipulating royal courts and other systems of public justice, despite seignorial efforts to impede their access to external legal authorities. Furthermore, it should be kept in mind that the serf's material circumstances were by no means necessarily inferior to those of the free peasant, as the legal encumbrances of servility were often counterbalanced by the greater size of servile, as opposed to free, landholdings. The English "Hundred Rolls" of 1279–1280 indicate that the average villein landholding was twice the size of its free counterpart, and similar patterns emerge from mid-sixteenth-century Swabian tax registers.

Serfdom was never a universal condition of the West European peasantry. It was insignificant in Scandinavia and most of the Iberian Peninsula (Catalonia being the main exception). Even in England, where servility assumed much greater significance, free peasants made up fully 50 to 60 percent of the rural population during the High Middle Ages. Furthermore, from the thirteenth century serfdom began to decline in significance throughout western Europe. Sometimes this happened through formal decrees of enfranchisement, as at Bologna (1257) and Florence (1289), or through mass sales of freedom, as in the Paris region from 1246. During the later Middle Ages serfdom also became a subject of several peasant protest movements, most notably the so-called Jacquerie in northern France (1358), the Peasants' Revolt of 1381 in England, and the

German Peasants' War of 1524–1526. Almost all of these uprisings failed to secure a formal abolition of servile status, and instead were brutally suppressed by the authorities. The one great exception to this pattern occurred in Catalonia, where a series of revolts beginning in the 1370s culminated in the Peasants' War of 1462–1486 and ended with the suppression of serfdom by the Sentence of Guadalupe (1486). Despite the limited immediate successes of these rural rebellions, serfdom was in fact fatally undermined in western Europe by the plagues of the fourteenth century and by the ensuing late medieval agrarian depression.

The wave of epidemics that commenced with the Black Death of 1347–1351 and persisted into the fifteenth century created an acute labor shortage throughout the European continent, and the peasantry was able to capitalize on this situation by extracting major concessions from overlords. Initial efforts to enforce strict pre-plague wage and labor conditions, such as the English Statute of Laborers (1351) and the German Golden Bull of Charles IV (1356) foundered on economic realities and peasant resistance, and serfdom began to wither away through the practical modification of tenurial arrangements, rather than through formal abolition (that serfdom declined primarily in this way underscores the fact that most west European peasants incurred serfdom through villeinage rather than neifty). Landlords began to abandon the direct exploitation of seignorial reserves, which had required the mobilization of considerable labor services, and instead began parceling out their demesnes to the peasants in tenancy. Labor services and servile disabilities were gradually abandoned or (more commonly) commuted into fixed monetary payments and made incidents of land tenure, while peasant property rights grew more secure and increasingly heritable. In England, where the phenomenon has been particularly well studied, bondland was transformed over the course of the later Middle Ages into secure "customary" tenure, with robust rights of inheritance, conveyance, and mortgage. The tenant's rights were formalized in the manorial court roll, and a copy of the entry was issued to the tenant (hence the alternative appellation "copyhold" tenure). From the fifteenth century disputes over copyhold land could be appealed to royal courts, and by the 1580s English common law even upheld the copyholder's right to sublet such property to third parties. A similar pattern obtained in Germany, where the fourteenth and fifteenth centuries saw the spread of heritable tenancy *(Erblehenrecht)* with extensive rights of conveyance, and guaranteed by the issue of parchment charters authenticated by seal.

By the beginning of the sixteenth century, therefore, the burdens of servility had been "tenurialized" in most of western Europe, thereby disarming serfdom as a status of legal bondage. In France, even tenurial serfdom was largely confined to the eastern regions of Burgundy and Franche-Comté, where one-third to one-half of the population remained serfs until the institution was abolished by the French revolutionaries on 3 November 1789. In England, serfdom was still mentioned in the grievance lists of Kett's Rebellion (1549), and crown serfs were manumitted as late as 1575, but as far as contemporary commentators like Thomas Smith (1581) and William Harrison (1577) were concerned, neifty had ceased to exist, while villeins were "so fewe . . . it is not almost worth the speaking" (quoted in Hilton, 56). The most significant exceptions to this trend in western Europe were the German-speaking lands of the Holy Roman Empire, where serfdom remained a vital institution throughout the early modern period.

The persistence, indeed intensification, of serfdom in Germany at the end of the Middle Ages was in part a reaction to the late medieval agrarian crisis. Thus, in the German southwest, ecclesiastical lordships in particular began to impose new mobility restrictions and extend the scope and weight of death duties during the later fourteenth and early fifteenth centuries in order to retain control over the thinning ranks of the tenantry. This seignorial reaction ultimately collapsed because of determined peasant resistance—most spectacularly the aforementioned Peasants' War of 1524–1526—and most lordships came to an accommodation with their subjects guaranteeing peasant inheritance rights and capping the disabilities imposed by servility. More significant changes flowed from the second impetus for the revival of serfdom in Germany (again, especially in the southwest), namely the drive for territorial centralization. During the later fifteenth and well into the sixteenth centuries, rural lordships, territorial princes, and even free imperial cities began systematically exchanging rights with neighboring territories over "foreign" serfs in order to create exclusive jurisdictions free of legal claims from external authorities. Territorial serfdom of this sort did also entail some fiscal burdens and marriage and mobility restrictions, but the former were not especially onerous and the latter could always be waived for a moderate fee. By the early seventeenth century serfdom had ceased to occasion widespread complaint in Germany (with the notable exception of a protracted conflict in Hauenstein, in the southern Rhine Palatinate, between 1725 and 1745), and the institution persisted in its tenurial and territorial forms until abolished in the various German states over the years between the revolutions of 1789 and 1848.

EASTERN VERSUS WESTERN EUROPEAN SERFDOM

In eastern Europe serfdom had a rather different history from patterns in the west, although historians now characterize the east-west contrast as a gradual and varied transition, rather than in terms of a sharp demarcation along the river Elbe. Serfdom appeared only at the end of the fifteenth and especially during the sixteenth century in Eastern Europe, and was closely associated with intensified seignorial jurisdiction (often called *Gutsherrschaft*) and the spread of vast demesnal economies predicated on large-scale inputs of labor service (often called *Gutswirtschaft*). Explanations for the rise of *Gutsherrschaft* and *Gutswirtschaft* remain controversial, but most accounts stress a combination of factors, including the relative sparseness of population (which increased the appeal of a dependent labor force), the sixteenth-century boom in cereal prices as a result of both local and international demand, and the relative weakness of village communities, which were less able (though by no means utterly incapable) of resisting seignorial pressure than their counterparts in western Europe.

Eastern European serfs were subjected to the same kinds of disabilities as in the west, including the obligation to provide labor services, and restrictions on mobility and outmarriage. Eastern European serfdom also recognized the distinction between tenurial and personal serfdom, with the former pattern predominating in the lands of the Austrian Habsburgs and Prussian Hohenzollerns, and the latter obtaining in Poland, Hungary, and

Russia. On the other hand, serfdom tended to be introduced in eastern Europe by governmental decrees forbidding peasants from leaving the jurisdiction or territory of their landlords, rather than spreading piecemeal as a result of the policies of individual overlords (as in the west). Decrees of this sort were first passed in Bohemia (1487) and Poland (1496), and thereafter in Hungary (1514), Prussia (1526), Brandenburg (1528), upper Austria (1539), Pomerania (1616 and 1645), Russia (1649), and Mecklenburg (1654).

Eastern European serfdom has often been characterized as more oppressive than its western counterpart because of the intensity of labor services demanded (three, four, and in some cases up to six days of work per week), the denial of a serf's right of appeal against the lord to royal or other public courts, and the fact that serfs could be sold apart from their land in the east (thousands of such cases have been documented for Poland alone). Although this contrast is broadly true, it is subject to important qualifications. First of all, a great deal of time often elapsed between a royal proclamation of serfdom and the full elaboration of seignorial jurisdiction and demesnal economies. In the Russian case it seems that it was only in the later eighteenth century that the system of servile dependency implied by the 1649 law code was actually enforced. Moreover, in some parts of eastern Europe (in particular Prussia and the Austrian Habsburg lands), the steady intrusion of royal courts into seignorial jurisdiction during the eighteenth century created a significant avenue for the mitigation of serfdom, as peasants were able to appeal to the crown for redress. Nevertheless, serfdom lasted much longer in eastern than in western Europe, and was only abolished over the course of the nineteenth century, beginning in Prussia (1807), and then later Austria (1848), Hungary (1853), Russia (1861), and Romania (1864).

See also **Agriculture; Class, Status, and Order; Enclosure; Feudalism; Laborers; Landholding; Peasantry; Peasants' War, German; Plague; Serfdom in East Central Europe; Serfdom in Russia.**

BIBLIOGRAPHY

Aston, T. H., and C. H. E. Philpin, eds. *The Brenner Debate: Agrarian Class Structure and Economic Development in Pre-Industrial Europe.* Cambridge, U.K., and New York, 1985.

Bloch, Marc. *Slavery and Serfdom in the Middle Ages: Selected Essays.* Translated by William R. Beer. Berkeley, 1975.

Blum, Jerome. *The End of the Old Order in Rural Europe.* Princeton, 1978.

Bush, M. L., ed. *Serfdom and Slavery: Studies in Legal Bondage.* London and New York, 1996.

Freedman, Paul. *The Origins of Peasant Servitude in Medieval Catalonia.* Cambridge, U.K., and New York, 1991.

Hilton, R. H. *The Decline of Serfdom in Medieval England.* London and New York, 1969.

Hoch, Steven L. *Serfdom and Social Control in Russia: Petrovskoe, a Village in Tambov.* Chicago, 1986.

Luebke, David Martin. "Serfdom and Honour in Eighteenth-Century Germany." *Social History* 18, no. 2 (1993): 143–161.

Scott, Tom. *Society and Economy in Germany, 1300–1600.* Houndmills, U.K., and New York, 2002.

Scott, Tom, ed. *The Peasantries of Europe: From the Fourteenth to the Eighteenth Centuries.* London and New York, 1998.

GOVIND P. SREENIVASAN

SERFDOM IN EAST CENTRAL EUROPE.

From the sixteenth to the seventeenth centuries, peasants in Poland, Ukraine, Hungary, and Bohemia were gradually subjugated to their landlords. This subjugation, usually referred to as the "second serfdom," had three aspects: economic, by virtue of the peasant's use of the lord's land; judicial, whereby peasants fell under the landlord's jurisdiction; and personal, in that peasants now needed their lords' permission in order to leave their villages. Enserfed peasants owed goods and services to their lords, including tribute in kind (usually grain, dairy products, or poultry), rent in money, and above all labor, or *corvée,* on the lord's lands (the demesne or *folwark*). Beyond the above-mentioned countries, aspects of the "second serfdom" were also seen in Russia and Prussia.

As landlords expanded their demesnes during the early modern period, *corvée,* initially limited to several days a year, increased to a few days a week. Peasants worked their lord's estates using their own plow oxen and farm implements or, lacking those, simply their hands and bodies. *Corvée* often involved the most arduous work of farming a large estate, and eventually the burden of the demesne's production costs was shifted onto the peasants' shoulders. Serfs were also bound to do additional work, such as providing transport and helping during the harvest. They were often also constrained by the landlord's monopoly on the production and/or sale of wine, beer, and spirits. The monopoly gave landlords an outlet for excess grain when market conditions were unfavorable, as in the second half of the seventeenth and the first half of the eighteenth centuries, as well as providing additional income from the sale of alcohol. Peasants were in most cases forbidden to produce alcohol themselves, and they were required to purchase it at their lord's tavern. In Hungary, while peasants were allowed to produce wine, they could sell it only to their lords. The limitation on the peasant's right to leave the village was also often extended to his family. In some cases serfs were de facto bought and sold, as when an estate or part of an estate was sold along with its residents, or when a landlord who had taken in a runaway peasant offered monetary compensation to the original owner in lieu of returning the runaway.

The "second serfdom" has been variously interpreted. Some scholars have stressed the legal aspects of enserfment, while others have analyzed the social or economic aspects. Some of the interpretations put forward have had a distinctly ideological character. Marxist historiography (especially in Soviet-bloc countries) saw the enserfment of the peasantry in the early modern period as contributing to a "refeudalization" of society and sometimes even the return to a natural economy. The "second serfdom" was, according to this view, a return to the most primitive form of peasant service (*corvée*) and a retreat from a market-based and money-based economy. Marxist historians further argued that it led to the gradual destruction of both peasant and urban economies, because by hampering the growth of an affluent rural population and by fostering the self-sufficiency of landed estates, it deprived urban craftsmen of markets for their products. Generalizations about "refeudalization" have not gained lasting acceptance, but historians continue to react negatively to the second serfdom, particularly when comparing developments in eastern Europe with the social and economic structure of western European countries during the same period. The second

serfdom is seen to reflect the underdevelopment of eastern Europe.

One can date the beginning of the second serfdom in Poland to the end of the fifteenth century and the beginning of the sixteenth, when the first limits on a peasant's right to leave the village were imposed (1496) and a parliamentary decree mandated one obligatory day of *corvée* a week from each full peasant allotment, or *laneus* (1520). One can also connect the beginnings of enserfment with the 1423 decree giving landlords the right to buy the office of village administrator (Latin *scultetus*) and subordinate villages directly to themselves. It is generally held that these developments were related to the enlargement of the landlord's demesne, as landlords sought to produce more grain to meet market demand. The growth in grain exports through Gdańsk, along with the price revolution in Europe, created greater opportunities for landlords to sell their grain. From the sixteenth to the first half of seventeenth century the burden of *corvée* grew significantly heavier. By the second half of the sixteenth century it had reached three to four days a week per allotment, even though most peasants had only half of a full allotment (*laneus*). The peasant could, however, realize substantial profits as the result of the growth of grain prices and the lease of supplementary lands (without giving *corvée*); he could also send his servants (farm hands) to implement the *corvée* on the landlord's demesne.

The burdens entailed by enserfment and the deficit of manpower in the country were such that the frequency of peasant flight increased steadily in this period. Ukraine was a particularly popular destination, as services were less burdensome there, and landlords rarely demanded *corvée*. The situation of the peasantry took a sharp turn for the worse after the wars of the mid-seventeenth and early eighteenth centuries. Peasants' farms grew smaller, the grain market shrank, and the landlord's demesne asserted an ever tighter monopoly over the production and sale of beer, the staple drink of the region. The effort to replace *corvée* with rent during the eighteenth and nineteenth centuries failed. But reforms granting peasants personal freedom, independent jurisdiction, and even the right to vote were introduced after the second (1793) and third (1795) partitions of Poland in the territories annexed by Austria, Prussia, and Russia.

In Hungary, after the 1514 peasant uprising led by György Dózsa, the parliament consolidated the lord's right to land and introduced an obligatory *corvée* of one day per week. Although Hungarian landlords were unable to export grain, their demesnes started to develop markedly between 1530 and 1540 (in Slovakia c. 1550). *Corvée* reached two to three days a week only in the second half of sixteenth century, and it became widespread in the seventeenth century. Because of the Turkish conquest and the ravages of war, the agrarian economy was forced to evolve; the steppe regions shifted from grain to cattle breeding and the export of livestock, while the northern regions moved to viticulture. In these conditions, and because the agrarian economy was more diversified, serfdom could not be fully enforced. Landlords tried instead to take over peasants' wine production. In Hungary the heyday of the second serfdom was the seventeenth century, and it can be said to have ended in 1767, when the empress Maria Theresa limited peasants' labor services. Her son Joseph II went further in 1785 when he abolished the personal subordination of peasants to their lords.

In Bohemia early steps toward enserfment were taken in the fifteenth century. The parliament limited the peasant's right to leave the village, and later in the century it passed further regulations against peasant flight. But historians consider the years 1530–1540 to be the beginning of the development of the demesne and the concomitant intensification of enserfment. Since the market for Bohemian grain was limited to Bohemia's urban population, landlords looking for additional revenue tried to take over and monopolize the production and sale of beer and to breed fish on their demesnes. In such conditions the demand for peasant labor services grew rather slowly. In some places *corvée* reached two to three days a week by the second half of the sixteenth century, but this became common only after the defeat at White Mountain in 1620. In 1680 *corvée* was fixed at three days a week from each allotment *(laneus)*. Thus in Bohemia the second serfdom did not fully establish itself until the seventeenth century. Its end came with the peasant uprising of 1775 and the abolition of personal serfdom by Emperor Joseph II in November 1781.

The notion of the "second serfdom" is misleading, for it gives the impression that east central European peasants had been relatively free during the late Middle Ages—while their counterparts in western Europe toiled under the "first" serfdom. According to this view, before the early modern imposition of the "second serfdom," east European peasants enjoyed the right to leave the village, rendered their services in money instead of *corvée,* and were under the jurisdiction of village administrators who represented the village self-government rather than the lord. But a closer look at these circumstances undermines the notion that late medieval east European peasants were free. The right to leave the village was in fact limited, because labor was more valued than land. Even in free villages, the village administrator was the lord's official and judged on his behalf, not on behalf of the community. Finally, it can be doubted that peasants ever paid services in money ("rent"), since there were few cities where peasants could sell their goods to obtain money. The earlier serfdom did lack the extended labor services that characterized serfdom in the early modern period, but this was because landed estates were autarkic and could serve the landlord's community without recourse to the market. The relation between these estates and the larger economy changed, and early modern east European serfdom should thus be seen as not a new, "second" serfdom but rather as a continuation of medieval serfdom, as adapted to the conditions of the agrarian market economy that arose during the period.

See also **Agriculture; Bohemia; Hungary; Peasantry; Poland-Lithuania, Commonwealth of, 1569–1795.**

BIBLIOGRAPHY

Andrasfalvy, B., et al. *Magyarország agrartörténete.* Budapest, 1996.

Ihnatowicz, Ireneusz, et al. *Społeczeństwo polskie od X do XX wieku.* 3rd corr. ed. Warsaw, 1996.

Klima, Arnost. "Agrarian Class Structure and Economic Development in Preindustrial Bohemia." *Past and Present* 85 (1979): 49–67.

Kula, Witold. *An Economic Theory of the Feudal System: Towards a Model of the Polish Economy, 1500–1800.* Translated by Lawrence Garner. New ed. London, 1976.

Maczak, Antoni, Henryk Samsonowicz, and Peter Burke, eds. *East-Central Europe in Transition from the Four-*

teenth to the Seventeenth Century. Cambridge, U.K., and New York, 1985.

Makkai, Laszlo. "Neo-Serfdom: Its Origin and Nature in East-Central Europe." *Slavic Review* 34, no. 2 (1975): 225–238.

Prus, Jaroslav, and Miroslav Kropilák, eds. *Přehled dejin Československa.* 2 vols. Prague, 1980–1982.

Topolski, J. *Gospodarka polska a europejska w XVI–XVII wieku.* Poznań, Poland, 1977.

Wyczański, Andrzej. "Gospodarka wiejska w Polsce XIV wieku w ujęciu liczbowym (Proba oceny)." *Roczniki Dziejow Spolecznych I Gospodarczych* 62 (2002): 167–187.

Zimányi, Vera. *Economy and Society in Sixteenth and Seventeenth Century Hungary (1526–1650).* Translated by Mátyás Esterházy. Budapest, 1987.

ANDRZEJ WYCZAŃSKI

SERFDOM IN RUSSIA.

The origins of serfdom as a form of migration control can be seen in mid-fifteenth-century documents that restricted peasant movement to the period on or around St. George's Day in November. By the early 1580s decrees proclaiming "forbidden years," which prohibited all peasant movement for specific periods, were already functioning in certain districts, and they were extended to the rest of the realm in the reign of Fyodor Ivanovich (ruled 1584–1598). By 1597 the state instituted central registration of deeds and documents—*kreposti*, the root of *krepostnichestvo*, or 'serfdom'—regulating various kinds of dependency. Although Muscovite slavery was also regulated by government officials, slaves belonged to a separate juridical category denoted by the Russian term *kholop*, which could refer to various forms of indentured servitude and debt bondage as well as to chattel slavery. The majority of slaves were Russian males of diverse social origins, primarily employed in nonagricultural occupations.

Serf legislation developed primarily in the core lands of the Muscovite state in order to secure labor for estates belonging to elites and military servitors. Beginning in the sixteenth century the majority of dependent peasants came under the control of individuals and families in state service. Two forms of landholding predominated in the rural economy of early modern Russia. Hereditary properties *(votchina)* could be sold or transferred to kinsmen, while usufruct or conditional land grants *(pomest'e)* were revocable grants of lands and their revenues awarded to individuals in return for fulfillment of military service. In order to preserve their revenue and military potential, conditional lands could not originally be donated to the church or sold, nor could they be passed on to heirs without government authorization.

The supply of service lands expanded as Moscow conquered neighboring political structures, most notably Novgorod in 1478 and Kazan' in 1552. Lands annexed along the southern steppes also fueled the growth of a significant class of provincial cavalrymen supported by the labor of a small number of dependent peasant households. By the mid-sixteenth century retention of all lands was made contingent upon service, and by the early decades of the seventeenth century the stark distinctions between the two forms of landholding were eroding, and service tenure lands were being acquired, exchanged, and passed on to heirs like hereditary lands. The combining of both forms of landholding into a single category was recognized de jure in 1714.

Competition for a limited supply of peasant labor and endemic peasant flight and relocation drew the government into recording, regulating, and policing the relations between agricultural laborers and their masters. Decrees specifying a limited period of years (five at the turn of the seventeenth century and ten by mid-century) after which peasants could not be returned to their former masters particularly hurt provincial gentry. As early as 1637 they petitioned for an end to such restrictions, and in January 1649 the limitations on returning fugitives were abolished throughout Russia. By the turn of the eighteenth century serfs could be moved, bought, and sold, and by the 1720s the legal distinctions between serfs and slaves were eliminated.

At the end of the first quarter of the eighteenth century, the overwhelming majority of peasants were enserfed to private masters. Many landowners merely extracted resources from their serfs, allowing serfs to work only their own lands or ply other trades in exchange for cash *(obrok)* payments. Others sought to develop their estates by issuing detailed instructions on the management of their properties to stewards and attempting to control various aspects of the rural serf economy, from land tenure to marriage. Around the same time formerly free groups of militiamen from the southern frontier and some non-Russian groups were equated in status with the tax-paying *(chernososhnye)* peasant communities of the Russian north and Siberia and were reclassified as state peasants. By the mid-eighteenth century over fifty thousand state peasants were forced to work in factories in the Urals region and Siberia, and a growing number of private serfs were also put to work in industrial enterprises.

Under serfdom the peasant commune *(mir)* coalesced into a distinct labor and fiscal unit. The available evidence does not clearly outline the features of the peasant commune until the seventeenth century. Institutions of community suretyship over and collective responsibility for the actions and obligations of individuals were a significant feature of the early modern Russian rural economy. Government taxation and fiscal policies also significantly shaped household and village structures. By the last decades of the seventeenth century sources record certain contours of the *mir* and its communal gathering *(skhod)* that show how it assigned lands and apportioned shares of the collective fiscal burden to its individuals. In the first half of the eighteenth century, elected representatives of the *mir* often worked jointly with government officials and landowners to ensure that villages and their inhabitants fulfilled their economic obligations to the state and/or to their landlords, in addition to providing recruits for the army. The *mir* could function as both a rapacious institution of communal control over individuals and a vehicle for negotiating communal interests and voicing them to the wider world. Active resistance by serfs was primarily realized through flight, suggesting that the government's attempts to wholly regulate movement were not always effective in practice. Serfs frequently joined rebellions instigated by Cossacks along the southern frontiers in the seventeenth and eighteenth centuries.

See also **Landholding; Peasantry; Pugachev Revolt (1773–1775); Razin, Stepan; Russia; Slavery and the Slave Trade.**

BIBLIOGRAPHY

Aleksandrov, V. A. *Sel'skaia obshchina v Rossii (XVII– nachalo XIV.)* Moscow, 1976.

Blum, Jerome. *Lord and Peasant in Russia: From the Ninth to the Nineteenth Century.* Princeton, 1961.

Hellie, Richard. *Enserfment and Military Change in Muscovy.* Chicago, 1971.

BRIAN BOECK

SERVANTS. Domestic service, often ignored in the first decades of research into the social history of early modern Europe, has recently benefited from greater scholarly attention. Investigation has made it clear that a knowledge of master-servant relations provides essential insights into the larger relationships of elite and popular classes and into the unexpected elasticity of the boundaries of public and private spheres in this period. Since servants were considered part of the family, at least until family values began to emphasize privacy and affection around the middle of the eighteenth century, their history also adds depth to efforts to understand the evolution of family structures over time. Yet far more is unexplored than is known about the domestic servant population, particularly since most researchers have focused on England and France, with some initial surveys of Renaissance Italy and the Dutch Republic.

The major obstacle to achieving a better understanding of the roles of servants in the past is the difficulty of finding documentary sources with useful information. Servants were not members of a corporate group that might have maintained records on their numbers, their wages, or the terms and conditions of hire. In a time when censuses were rarely taken, the presence of servants in a household was seldom systematically noted. They were occasionally considered a luxury item and hence taxable, notably in Holland in the 1740s and in England in 1777. Despite this, government records rarely provide much data on the servant population. Servants produced little in the way of autobiographies, and any letters they might have written were not addressed to families that had the resources to preserve them. While criminal court records do contain some interesting information, they cannot support conclusions about the larger population of law-abiding servants. The picture we have of servants' lives then is based on a diverse assemblage of household account books, wills, servants' ordinances, and similar local records. These establish that servants' experiences varied not only over time but according to the sizes of the households in which they worked, the households' wealth and location in urban or rural settings, and the work servants were expected to do.

FUNCTIONS OF DOMESTIC SERVICE

Servants were a practical necessity in an era before labor-saving appliances; they freed the mistress of a household to cultivate social networks or to participate in the family business. Domestic service enabled poor and unskilled people to survive. It was usually a temporary occupation, especially for women, who might save their wages toward the dowries that would enable them to make respectable marriages.

But as an institution, domestic service filled many more roles in early modern Europe. It bridged the worlds of workers and elites. Servants initiated into the manners, the values, and the fashions of the elites transmitted that culture to the laboring classes. They were the most regular contacts members of the middling and elite groups had with working people, so such relationships helped form class attitudes. In supervising domestics, bourgeois housewives learned managerial skills. And retinues of liveried men were a public and visible sign of wealth and status for members of the nobility.

HOUSEHOLD AND HOUSEWORK

Contemporaries certainly noticed the ubiquity of servants in their communities. In his *Letters on the Importance of the Rising Generation of the Laboring Part of Our Fellow-Subjects* (1767), Jonas Hanway estimated that one in thirteen Londoners was a domestic, and Sébastien Le Prestre de Vauban gave the same figure for France in *Projet d'une dixme royale* (Plan for a royal tithe) in 1707. Historical demographers have confirmed the guesses made by an earlier generation. Most studies have concluded that servants comprised roughly 7 to 15 percent of the population.

Servants were so important in early modern Europe that they were employed in any household that could afford their upkeep. Indeed possessing at least one live-in domestic acted as a marker indicating that a family could claim respectability and status in the community. Estimates of the percentages of households employing servants hover around 23 percent, though it could range much higher in towns that were judicial or administrative centers.

The most common form of domestic servant was a maid of all work, often the only servant in a household, whose work included whatever errands, cleaning, food preparation, or child care tasks a family required. The larger the establishment, the more specialized the servants became, as families hired cooks, coachmen, valets to attend to the masters' wardrobes and personal needs, dress maids to do the same for the mistresses, nursemaids, governesses and tutors, and ultimately platoons of male lackeys, postilions, and footmen, whose presence shielded employers from contact with commoners. The establishment of any truly grand seigneur required some fifty servants, according to Audiger's *La maison reglée et l'art de diriger la maison d'un grand seigneur & autres* (1700; The ordered house and the art of directing the house of a great lord and others).

In the countryside servants in husbandry added to the variety of occupations considered domestic service. A dairymaid was a servant even if the family marketed its cheese. Indeed Europeans did not make sharp distinctions between workers hired for domestic labor on the one hand and for productive labor on the other until the eighteenth century—and in some places well beyond that time. An apprentice might be required to accompany his or her mistress to market, while a girl hired to keep the family home tidy might find herself scrubbing the shop floor as well as the kitchen floor. The salient feature that defined the nature of domestic service to contemporaries was dependence. From an archbishop's secretary to an orphaned scullery maid, all were dependents and hence servants.

WHO BECAME SERVANTS?

Much of the evidence to date has concluded that the majority of servants were young, unmarried migrants who traveled from rural villages to larger towns and cities for work. Some were poor relatives of their employers. Historians of domestic service have engaged in a debate over the ratios of men to women employed as household servants. Some have identified a process of "feminization" of domestic service, in which the numbers of men employed as domestics declined in relation to the numbers of women during the course of the eighteenth century. Two trends are said to have produced this shift. As middle classes or bourgeoisies replaced the aristocracies in roles of political and economic leadership, status markers no longer emphasized splendor and public display. The demand for male servants decreased. At the same time, changing attitudes about gender roles emphasized independence and autonomy for men, making service less desirable for them.

Other historians, however, have challenged feminization as a means of analyzing shifts in the structure of domestic service. The majority of domestic workers were always women, they argue. The apparent trend is the result of a focus on researching the largest establishments of the wealthy, which gives too much importance to the roles played by menservants. The boundaries of the public sphere or of the domestic sphere were perpetually shifting, so what appears to be feminization could be more the result of a redefinition of work roles than it was of occupational demographics.

"Live-in" servants were not married. Employers wanted people in their service who would surrender their own interests to those of the householder, and married couples did not meet that condition. At the same time, early modern servants rarely saw their jobs as lifetime occupations. The point of entering service was to escape from it. Women sought marriage with a partner who offered financial security and a home of their own. Men looked for the contacts who could provide them a means of earning an independent living. But there were no guarantees that such ambitions could be fulfilled, particularly when employers restricted their servants' opportunities of meeting people outside the household.

CONDITIONS OF SERVICE

Servants who lived under the same roofs as their employers had little in the way of private lives. Their time was not their own. They were expected to be working before their employers rose from bed, and those in attendance on their masters or mistresses had to remain awake late into the night if their employers had gone out to a social event. Time off was a matter of individual arrangements; some servants might receive an afternoon once or twice per month, while others had to apply for each rare hour off. Many had no leisure time at all. Employers discouraged servants from socializing in their homes. Local laws in some parts of the Dutch Republic actually made servants' social use of their employers' food a criminal act. Employers considered their domestics' time to be their property, and unauthorized socializing represented the theft of that property. Socializing also provided opportunities for domestics to spread gossip about the family and might lead to maidservants becoming pregnant out of wedlock. Hence many elite employers absolutely refused to give their domestic workers any leisure time.

Wages earned by servants were low. Very young, inexperienced, or unskilled servants might receive only room and board. Domestics received their earnings no more frequently than semiannually and in many cases received nothing until they left the household. Wages varied by location, and they varied depending on the skill level of the worker. Male servants were always paid more than female ones, even when the type of work was the same. (Cooking and gardening, for example, were less sex-linked than other tasks.)

But historians have emphasized that the rewards of service included far more than the wages paid. Room and board itself might be of better quality and quantity than that which a servant who otherwise would have been a pauper might have enjoyed. During inflationary periods such payments-in-kind meant that servants' remunerations effectively kept pace with the rise in prices, something wageworkers did not enjoy. Custom called for servants to be remembered in their employers' wills, although the tradition was not universally honored. Other rewards included cash gifts at holidays, tips, and "vails"—guests staying for a holiday at an upper-class home in England were expected to provide gratuities to their hosts' servants when they departed. Servants who accompanied their employers in public wore liveries, uniforms decorated to indicate the identities of their masters. Personal domestics so often received their employers' hand-me-down clothing that many considered it a "right," according to their testimony before courts when they were prosecuted for theft after they had helped themselves to items they thought were worn out. The maids and valets who obtained the fine clothes of their employers—either with or without their approval—could supplement their income by re-selling the articles through second-hand clothes dealers.

Sexual harassment represented one of the greatest perils of service. Young, unmarried girls, isolated from family and friends, were vulnerable to their employers, their employers' sons and male guests, as well as to male servants. Whether quartered in common areas or attic rooms, they could not put a locked door between themselves and sexual predators. Gentlemen seeking a sexual outlet found their household domestics convenient, easy to pressure or to seduce using threats or promises. A maidservant who became pregnant, whether as the result of rape or a voluntary relationship, faced disaster: immediate dismissal without the good reference that any other employer would require and, as a woman who had lost her virtue, little or no prospect of making a respectable marriage. Yet it would be a mistake to believe that all sexual relationships involving female domestics were the result of rape or harassment. Deliberately confined in their workplaces, some maidservants found sex within the household offered their only opportunities for affection and physical relief and so undertook such relationships willingly.

SHIFTING ATTITUDES: THE QUESTION OF PATERNALISM

Prescriptive literature in household manuals, confessional guides, and religious tracts defined an ideal of master-servant relations that historians have termed "paternalist." Linked to the authoritarian stage in the evolution of the family among Europeans, the paternalist ideal defined a standard of reciprocal obligations between masters and servants in which servants were bound to loyalty, obedience, and diligence in the service of their masters, while the latter were held responsible for the moral and physical welfare of their domestic workers, just as they were responsible for their own children's welfare. This ethos required employers to care for servants who became sick, to support those who had grown old in the service of their masters, and to provide for all servants' religious educations. As a set of values governing master-servant relations, the paternalist ideal had disappeared by the early nineteenth century if not before, replaced by a contract mode of relations based on the exchange of work for money. But historians still debate the timing and the causes of this shift, which varied from one location to another. These arguments notwithstanding, other historians doubt that reciprocity was ever characteristic of the reality of most master-servant relationships.

CONCLUSION

Two decades of efforts to rescue the domestic servant from historical oblivion have demonstrated that there are few if any features that can be considered universal of the institution in early modern Europe. Researchers have grown quite critical of work that accepts stereotypes and generalizations about servant and employer demographics, the sexual division of labor, and overall trends in the evolution of master-servant relationships. Only with additional research will enough data emerge to support broad generalizations about servant life in early modern Europe.

See also **Aristocracy and Gentry; Class, Status, and Order; Family; Serfdom.**

BIBLIOGRAPHY

Primary Sources

Ashford, Mary. *Life of a Licensed Victualler's Daughter, Written by Herself.* 1844.

Gourville, Jean Hérault de. *Mémoires de Monsieur de Gourville, concernant les affaires ausquelles il a été employé par la cour, depuis 1642, jusqu'en 1698.* 2 vols. Paris, 1724.

Legrain. "Souvenirs de Legrain, valet de chambre de Mirabeau." *Nouvelle revue rétrospective I.* Paris, 1901.

Secondary Sources

Carlson, Marybeth. "A Trojan Horse of Worldliness? Maidservants in the Burgher Household in Rotterdam at the End of the Seventeenth Century." In *Women of the Golden Age,* edited by Els Kloek et al., pp. 87–96. Hilversum, 1994.

Fairchilds, Cissie. *Domestic Enemies: Servants and Their Masters in Old Regime France.* Baltimore, 1984.

Gutton, Jean-Pierre. *Domestiques et serviteurs dans la France de l'ancien régime.* Paris, 1981.

Hecht, J. Jean. *The Domestic Servant Class in Eighteenth-Century England.* London, 1956.

Hill, Bridget. *Servants: English Domestics in the Eighteenth Century.* Oxford, 1996.

Kent, D. A. "Ubiquitous but Invisible: Female Domestic Servants in Mid-Eighteenth Century London." *History Workshop Journal* 28 (1989): 111–128.

Kussmaul, Ann. *Servants in Husbandry in Early Modern England*. Cambridge, U.K., 1981.

Maza, Sarah C. *Servants and Masters in Eighteenth-Century France: The Uses of Loyalty*. Princeton, 1983.

McIntosh, Marjorie K. "Servants and the Household Unit in an Elizabethan Community." *Journal of Family History* 9 (1984): 3–23.

Meldrum, Tim. *Domestic Service and Gender, 1660–1750: Life and Work in the London Household*. New York, 2000.

Romano, Dennis. *Housecraft and Statecraft: Domestic Service in Renaissance Venice, 1400–1600*. Baltimore, 1996.

MARYBETH CARLSON

SEVEN YEARS' WAR (1756–1763).

Encompassing conflict in Europe, North America, the Caribbean, and India, the Seven Years' War resulted from a collision between two very different international problems. First, there was the growing colonial and imperial friction between Britain and France, which became acute in the early 1750s as the French authorities and the British colonists in North America began staking out rival claims to the Ohio River Valley. Open warfare then erupted in the backcountry during 1755, and this was followed by repeated British seizures of French shipping in the North Atlantic. In response Louis XV despatched Louis Joseph, marquis of Montcalm, with reinforcements for the French colonial forces, to take military command in New France (Quebec) in April 1756.

Second, the Seven Years' War stemmed from Austria's refusal to accept the loss of Silesia to Frederick II of Prussia during the War of the Austrian Succession, and from Russian determination to humble Prussia. The Peace of Aix-la-Chapelle (1748) had merely suspended Austro-Prussian conflict over Silesia. While Austria carried out internal reforms to her administration, Count Wenzel Anton von Kaunitz, one of Maria Theresa's inner councillors who became chancellor in 1753, pursued the possibility, remote at first, of a French alliance against Prussia. Nevertheless, during 1755–1756 his patience and hard work began to pay dividends. Great Britain, anxious about the security of George II's German domains and no longer able to rely on Austrian support, secured Russian guar-

antees in September 1755 for George's electorate of Hanover in exchange for promised subsidies. This Anglo-Russian agreement in turn prompted a fearful Frederick II of Prussia to manage a reconciliation with Britain in January 1756 in the shape of the defensive Convention of London. But the unforeseen consequence was the "diplomatic revolution." A furious Russia all but repudiated her agreement with Britain and tightened her alliance with Austria, and both powers prepared for a combined war against Prussia. Now bereft of allies, Louis XV took up Kaunitz's proposal of an end to 250 years of Franco-Habsburg antagonism, and on 1 May the defensive first Treaty of Versailles was signed between France and Austria (Russia acceded to this treaty in January 1757). Two weeks later, after France invaded British-ruled Minorca, war broke out between the two states. Frederick II, now acutely aware of the forces gathering against him, felt he had no choice but to launch a preemptive strike in August to seize Saxony and take over its army, causing France to activate its Austrian alliance.

PRUSSIA'S STRUGGLE FOR SURVIVAL

Not until the summer of 1757 did the triple alliance launch an assault on Prussia, after France and Austria concluded the offensive second Treaty of Versailles (1 May) with the purpose of dismembering Frederick's state. Frederick's invasion of Bohemia was halted, and the Russians invaded East Prussia, but more damaging was the neutralization of the trapped Anglo-Hanoverian army by the French at Kloster-Zeven in early September. In the face of such a crisis, Frederick fought a campaign of strategic brilliance. First he crushed the poorly commanded and logistically weak Franco-Imperial army at Rossbach (5 November), deploying the greatly improved Prussian cavalry under Friedrich Wilhelm von Seydlitz and moving his infantry swiftly across the battlefield in echelon, rather than linear, formation. Then he followed this up with the defeat of the Austrians at Leuthen, two hundred miles to the east and exactly a month later, using the "oblique order" in an attack on the enemy right flank. After Rossbach, George II repudiated the convention of Kloster-Zeven, and Anglo-Hanoverian operations resumed under the command of Frederick's protégé Ferdinand of Brunswick-Wolffenbüttel. Moreover, thanks to William

Pitt's return to power in June 1757, Britain began subsidizing both the Hanoverian forces and, from April 1758, Frederick's Prussia. With the odds evened up, Austria henceforth sought to wear Prussia down by a process of attrition, but this presupposed a certain strength within the triple alliance that itself was fading.

In 1758 the French were pushed back over the Rhine by Ferdinand, while the emerging dominance within the French government of Étienne-François, duke of Choiseul, produced in March 1759 the third Treaty of Versailles, in which France reduced her role in the continental war to that of an Austrian auxiliary, and concentrated instead on trying to force Britain into peace. Yet when the French returned to Westphalia in 1759, Ferdinand of Brunswick smashed them at Minden on 1 August. The principal burden of attacking Prussia had in fact passed in 1758 to the Russians, a symptom of their growing strength and stamina. Königsberg, in East Prussia, was captured in January, forcing this kingdom under Russian occupation for the rest of the war. However, in his Brandenburg heartland, Frederick II defeated the Russians in the bloody battle of Zorndorf in August, while an Austrian surprise attack at Hochkirch in October failed to loosen his control of Saxony and Silesia. Despite the apparent stalemate, the Austrians and Russians made a further joint offensive against Prussia during 1759, in which Frederick suffered his worst defeat ever, at Künersdorf, forcing him to abandon Saxony and Silesia. The following year saw victories on both sides, but Frederick's success against the Austrians at Torgau was bought with greater casualties than were suffered by the vanquished (3 November), and Russian troops even reached Berlin and held it to ransom.

How was it, though, that the three greatest military powers on the Continent failed to crush Frederick's Prussia? To begin with, Austria and Russia both suffered from sluggish systems of planning and logistics that impeded offensive operations. Furthermore, their leading generals were cautious, unimaginative, and relatively uncooperative, and in the French case frequently incompetent. Maria Theresa and her advisers displayed poor strategic sense, waging a war of aggressive intent in a largely defensive and attritional fashion that allowed Frederick to deal with his enemies in turn in each campaign.

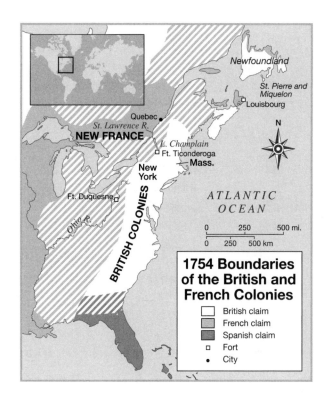

1754 Boundaries of the British and French Colonies

British claim
French claim
Spanish claim
□ Fort
• City

Elizabeth of Russia was similarly unable to provide clear strategic direction after her stroke in 1757 allowed a major split to open up in her council. Related to this, the aims of the three powers diverged sufficiently to impede any overriding common purpose of destroying Prussian power. All this combined to prevent Frederick's enemies from holding the initiative for any length of time, and from following up their military successes.

The weaknesses of the triple alliance were matched by the remarkable resilience of Prussia. Britain's financial support of Prussia and Anglo-Hanoverian military protection of Brandenburg from the west enabled Frederick to concentrate his forces against only two enemies after late 1757: Austria and Russia. Frederick's strategic, operational, and tactical skill, while by no means flawless, enabled a united Prussian command, and a heavily centralized and obedient state, to take full advantage of the deficiencies in the triple alliance's war effort. If Prussia was exhausted financially and materially, with underage and substandard recruits filling the army's ranks by 1760, the Austrians and the French were also incapable of further offensive action.

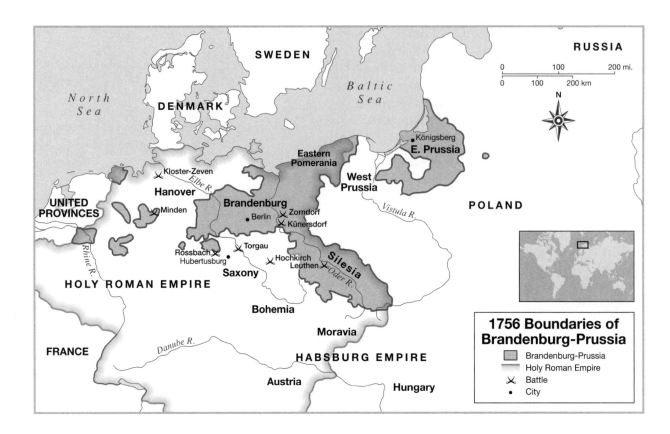

THE ANGLO-FRENCH IMPERIAL STRUGGLE 1755–1760

While the war in Europe produced stagnation, the Anglo-French conflict was vastly more decisive, in large part because Pitt was determined to destroy as much of France's overseas power as possible. In India, Robert Clive's skillful handling of indigenous auxiliary troops and combined operations with the navy allowed him to recapture Calcutta from the Nawab of Bengal in March 1757 after its loss the previous year; and he followed this by gaining control of all Bengal after his victory at Plassey (26 July). But in North America things were going considerably less well for the British. Montcalm made much progress in the backcountry in 1756–1757, but this only forced the British commanders to reconsider their strategy and plan instead for a full assault on New France up the Saint Lawrence River, for which they requested massive land and sea reinforcements from London.

They were fortunate that Pitt endorsed their request, and in early 1758 the issues that had bedeviled relations between the regular forces and the colonies were resolved to the satisfaction of the colonists, unlocking colonial military resources im-

mediately. As if to prove the need to attack New France by sea, in July 1758 Montcalm blocked the British advance at Fort Ticonderoga at the foot of Lake Champlain, but the same month the French were unable to prevent a British amphibious seizure of their fortress of Louisbourg on Cape Breton Island. Four months later the British also reduced Fort Duquesne at the forks of the Ohio, and the cumulative effect of these successes was to neutralize the American Indian nations, who now came to an accommodation with the British colonial authorities. In the meantime, during 1758 Pitt launched a series of diversionary amphibious attacks on the French Atlantic coast, the mere threat of which pinned down French forces so they could not be deployed either against Hanover or in the colonies.

Worse was to come for Louis XV in 1759. Montcalm's forces in New France were suffering from a lack of supplies and dwindling manpower, in spite of the mass mobilization of the colony's adult males. Britain, by contrast, sent out eight thousand fresh troops under James Wolfe, who in June sailed up the Saint Lawrence with twenty-two ships of the line to Quebec City, which soon found itself cut off and with dwindling supplies. While Amherst captured Ticonderoga, securing New York and Massachusetts, in September Wolfe provoked Montcalm into a battle just outside Quebec where both commanders were killed, but the British were victorious. Although Quebec surrendered, remnants of the French army managed to escape, and, reinforced to seven thousand men, marched on Quebec to attempt its recapture in April 1760. Yet Lévis's victory over a British force just outside the city walls could not prevent the abandonment of the siege in the face of British relief, and in September the French governor, Pierre François de Rigaud, marquis of Vaudreuil, surrendered the rest of New France. But in spite of this vigorous campaign, the outcome in North America had, in reality, been determined the previous year at sea, when the British had destroyed one French battle fleet off Lagos (Portugal) on 17 August, and defeated the other at Quiberon Bay off the coast of Brittany (20 November). Not only did

this dash Choiseul's serious hopes of an invasion of Britain; it also assured Britain command of the Atlantic and English Channel, allowing the blockade of French ports and cutting off the French overseas from the homeland. In June 1761 Britain even managed to capture Belle-Isle, dominating the southern coast of Brittany.

DOMESTIC POLITICS AND THE ENDING OF THE WAR

However, by the end of 1760 there was a general war-weariness among all the belligerents, even the British, whose economy was flourishing. Indeed, during 1761 Anglo-Prussian relations deteriorated largely because Frederick II refused to consider any concessions to his enemies, culminating in the curtailment of British subsidies in April 1762. All this notwithstanding, the hostility of Elizabeth of Russia to Frederick II, and Pitt's determination to wring a "Carthaginian peace" out of France pro-

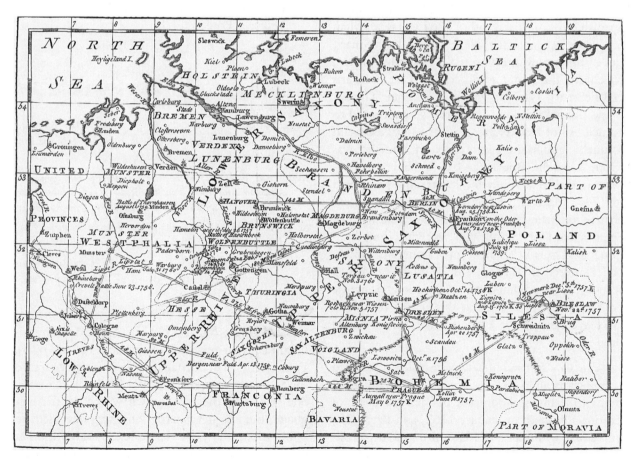

Seven Years' War. A map from John Entick's *General History of the Late War,* a British account of the Seven Years' War, showing the theater of war in the German states. The battles marked with a "K" indicate the presence ("The King in Person") of Frederick II the Great of Prussia. MAP COLLECTION, STERLING MEMORIAL LIBRARY, YALE UNIVERSITY

longed the conflict. What pushed the great powers toward peace was not victories or defeats but rather changes in their domestic political configurations.

George III's accession in October 1760 produced a notably more pacific tone in the British government, driving Pitt out of the ministry a year later. France sought to profit from this, ratcheting up demands in peace negotiations. Louis XV forged a third Family Compact in August 1761 with the anglophobe Charles III of Spain, who had acceded to his throne in 1759. This produced in January 1762 a Spanish declaration of war against Britain, ostensibly to protect Charles's New World economic interests, but Charles's rash decision was soon repented, as Britain captured both Havana (August) and Manila (October) in successful amphibious operations. That same year, the British also captured the islands of Martinique, Saint Lucia, Saint Vincent, Grenada, and Tobago from France, to add to earlier seizures of Guadeloupe in 1759 and La Gorée in West Africa (1758). The Franco-Spanish position at the end of 1762 was worse than it had been a year earlier. Nevertheless, John Stuart, earl of Bute, now directing the British government, concluded the unnecessarily lenient Peace of Paris (10 February 1763) in which Martinique, Guadeloupe, Saint Lucia, and La Gorée were returned to France. All of New France, except Saint Pierre and Miquelon and fishing rights off Newfoundland, was retained by the British, and in India France was permitted to retain only the five trading posts held in 1748; Minorca was returned to Britain in exchange for Belle-Isle. To recover Cuba and Manila, Spain ceded Florida to Britain, receiving compensation from Louis XV in the form of Louisiana. Britain had shattered the French empire, and France had seen her armies humiliated (with serious domestic political consequences), but the French territories George III handed back to Louis XV were the most productive.

Prussia's survival intact, with peace concluded at Hubertusburg (15 February 1763), equally owed much to changes in domestic politics: the death of Tsarina Elizabeth in January 1762, and Peter III's immediate withdrawal of Russia from the triple alliance. Catherine II, after her usurpation of the throne six months later, maintained Russian neutrality but refused to assist Frederick as her husband had wished to do. With the treaty, Europe reverted to the status quo ante bellum. By merely carrying on the war, and regularly defeating his enemies against massive odds, Frederick II acquired the sobriquet "the Great" for himself and Prussia's recognition as a great power by the other states. Austria had failed dismally in the attempt to regain Silesia, prompting a further bout of administrative reform that, in less than a decade, increased the quality and quantity of her armies. Yet Russia, in spite of making no territorial gains from the war, emerged as the arbiter of eastern Europe, in part through her military performance but also thanks to the new tsarina, Catherine II, who was determined that Russia would henceforth act to maintain its newly acquired pivotal role.

See also **Austrian Succession, War of the (1740–1748); British Colonies: The Caribbean; British Colonies: North America; Catherine II (Russia); Elizabeth (Russia); Frederick II (Prussia); French Colonies: The Caribbean; French Colonies: North America; Louis XV (France); Maria Theresa (Holy Roman Empire); Pitt, William the Elder and William the Younger; Prussia.**

BIBLIOGRAPHY

Anderson, Fred. *Crucible of War: The Seven Years' War and the Fate of the Empire in British North America, 1754–1766.* London, 2000.

Dorn, Walter L. *Competition for Empire, 1740–1763.* London and New York, 1963. See chapter 8. Still the best narrative of the war.

Middleton, Richard. *The Bells of Victory: the Pitt-Newcastle Ministry and the Conduct of the Seven Years' War, 1757–1762.* Cambridge, U.K., and New York, 1985.

Scott, H. M. *The Emergence of the Eastern Powers 1756–1775.* Cambridge, U.K., and New York, 2001.

GUY ROWLANDS

SÉVIGNÉ, MARIE DE (Marie de Rabutin-Chantal, marquise de Sévigné; 1626–1696),
French letter writer. Madame de Sévigné occupies a special position in the history of French literature. She is one of the best-known writers in the language, but she never wrote anything intended for publication. Her fame derives exclusively from her correspondence, made up of thousands of letters that were first published after her death. She was born in Paris to a mother from a wealthy bourgeois family and a father who was a titled nobleman from

Burgundy. Orphaned at a young age, she grew up in the large and affectionate household of her maternal grandparents. She received an education under their guardianship that emphasized broad readings in French and Italian literature and in religion. Her paternal grandmother was Jeanne de Chantal, founder, with François de Sales, of the religious order of the Visitation.

After her marriage in 1644 to Henri de Sévigné, a young nobleman, Marie had two children: Françoise-Marguerite, born in 1646, and Charles, born in 1648, and the family moved to the Sévigné estate in Brittany. She was widowed after seven years of marriage when her husband was killed in a duel fought over a mistress. She then moved back to the Marais district in Paris, where she had spent her youth, and where she was quickly assimilated into the elite social circles of court and city. As a widow of some means who enjoyed the support of her extended family, Madame de Sévigné had considerable freedom in the conduct of her life. She never remarried, but enjoyed a lifetime of close friendships with many of the principal figures on the French literary, cultural, and political scene: Marie de La Fayette, Madeleine de Scudéry, François, duc de La Rochefoucauld, Jean François Paul de Gondi, cardinal de Retz, and Jean de La Fontaine. Sévigné's close ties with the circle patronized by Nicolas Fouquet (1615–1680), minister of finance in the first years of Louis XIV's reign, drew her into the debates that polarized Parisian high society during Fouquet's trial for treason in 1664. Her letters written during the trial offer a subtle interpretation of political events and a lively, dramatic narrative.

As time went on, Sévigné was to see other close friends suffer disgrace or exile. Her letters invited her far-flung correspondents to continue their participation in social conversations and remain, at least through writing, on the "inside." In her letters to her cousin Roger de Rabutin, comte de Bussy, who spent most of his adult life trying in vain to regain favor at court, she regularly reported how his letters were read aloud, absorbed into social dialogue, and given real power in a world where gossip and political action were never very far apart. To other correspondents who spent periods away from the capital she became a prized source of information, and her own letters were circulated, read and admired by many readers, who valued them for their witty and

Marie de Sévigné. Portrait by Claude Lefevre. ©ARCHIVO ICONOGRAFICO, S.A./CORBIS

conversational style as much as for the news they contained. Sévigné's principal correspondent was to be her daughter, Françoise-Marguerite, who in 1671 moved to Provence with her new husband, the comte de Grignan. Three-fourths of the letters of Madame de Sévigné that we know today were written from mother to daughter. They reveal an intense, often contradictory relationship. Madame de Grignan's move to the provinces precipitated a profound sense of isolation in her mother, an experience that was new to this woman known by all to be a paragon of sociability. In the process of building her correspondence with her daughter, Sévigné discovered her vocation as a writer. Her letters written from Paris are rich personal chronicles of behind-the-scenes events in an extremely volatile social milieu. Her letters written from her family property in Brittany evoke more intimate memories that she can share with her daughter. She fills her descriptions of the woods and the familiar property with allusions to their shared taste for pastoral romance, and invites her correspondent to imagine herself with her in the same stable company of their favorite landscapes and books. During the winter and spring of 1696, while Sévigné was visiting her daughter in Grignan, Françoise-Marguerite suffered a lengthy illness. Her mother exhausted herself in attending to her. In April the older woman fell ill, and died two weeks later.

Mother and daughter visited each other for lengthy periods, but their repeated experience of separation and reunion inspired Sévigné's ongoing struggle as a writer to find words to express her passion. The theme of the inadequacy of language for communicating love recurs throughout Madame de Sévigné's correspondence. To put her maternal feeling into words, she drew on a multitude of discourses from her culture—the language of prayer, erotic love, and myth—and in so doing she designed an image of a mother's passion that has become an important model for literary, historical, and psychological discussions of the mother-daughter bond. As the intimate and articulate record of a long life fully lived, Sévigné's letters have been the favorite reading of great writers from Voltaire to Virginia Woolf.

See also **François de Sales; La Fontaine, Jean de; La Rochefoucauld, François, duc de; Scudéry, Madeleine de.**

BIBLIOGRAPHY

Primary Sources

Sévigné, Marie de. *Letters from Madame la marquise de Sévigné.* Edited and translated by Violet Hammersley. New York, 1956.

———. *Selected Letters.* Translated by Leonard Tancock. Harmondsworth, U.K., and New York, 1982.

Secondary Sources

Farrell, Michèle Longino. *Performing Motherhood: The Sévigné Correspondence.* Hanover, N.H., 1991.

Mossiker, Frances. *Madame de Sévigné: A Life and Letters.* New York, 1983.

ELIZABETH C. GOLDSMITH

SEVILLE. The Andalusian city of Seville, located fifty-four miles inland from the Atlantic Ocean, was the hub of the Spanish empire for much of the early modern era. In 1503, Isabella of Castile and Ferdinand of Aragón established the Casa de Contratación (House of Trade) in Seville and thereby launched the ascent of this provincial capital. The number of households doubled between the censuses of 1534 and 1565, and the local population was amplified by droves of foreign traders, sailors, and slaves. The population peaked at over 100,000 at the end of the sixteenth century, making Seville one of the three largest metropolises of Europe and the single most populous city in Spain. A catastrophic plague in 1649 reduced that population by almost half, and it would not recover until the early 1800s. Seville's preeminent position within the empire formally ended in 1680 when the monarchy named the coastal city of Cádiz as the official port for the Indies trade. In its imperial heyday, Seville was notorious for its ostentatious public displays and for the active underworld described so vividly in Golden Age classics by Mateo Alemán (*Guzmán de Alfarache,* 1599), Miguel de Cervantes (*Rinconete and Cortadillo,* 1613), and Tirso de Molina (*El burlador de Sevilla,* 1630).

Seville lies along the east bank of the southwesterly flowing Guadalquivir River, which empties into the Gulf of Cádiz. A countryside rich in natural resources produced high-quality olive oils, wines, and citrus fruits for export to Europe and the Americas, while pine trees provided raw materials for local shipbuilding. The main industries of early modern Seville—soap and ceramics—were located in Triana, a neighborhood across the river, connected to the city center by a single wooden bridge laid atop a string of boats. Triana also housed the castle of the Inquisition, which was founded in Seville in 1480. In the eighteenth century, tobacco production flourished at Seville's Royal Tobacco Factory (1757), the setting for Bizet's *Carmen* (1873–1874) and the current site of the University of Seville.

Royal interests were represented in Seville by an official called the *Asistente* and by a royal tribunal *(Real Audiencia).* Honored by four royal visits in the sixteenth and seventeenth centuries, Seville was transformed into the court for five years under the first Bourbon, King Philip V (ruled 1700–1746). Local government was led by an aristocratic *ayuntamiento* ('city council') comprising thirty-six *veinticuatros* and fifty-six lesser-ranked *jurados.* The council's jurisdiction extended over many neighboring towns and villages, although Seville's territory shrank considerably as the Habsburg kings sold independent status to many of those towns and

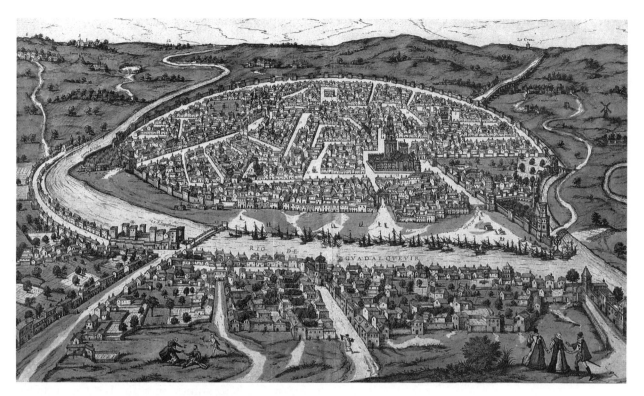

Seville. A late-sixteenth-century engraving by Braun. THE ART ARCHIVE/MUSEO DE LA TORRE DEL ORO SEVILLE/DAGLI ORTI

villages for much-needed cash. The most serious challenge to local authority took place in 1652, when a popular uprising began with bread riots and ended in a bloody crackdown. Seville was the seat of a wealthy archbishopric and a powerful cathedral chapter, and perpetual tension existed among the city's religious, municipal, and royal authorities.

Seville's enormous Gothic cathedral (completed 1506) dominated urban life, and its Giralda—a minaret redesigned as a bell tower—symbolized the city. Until the 1500s, Seville had retained its medieval Islamic character, but the urban fabric changed dramatically as the imperial metropolis burst the seams of the old medieval city. New neighborhoods developed outside the old walls, city gates were expanded, and wide, straight avenues replaced narrow, twisting lanes. In 1572 the Casa Lonja (House of Trade, the present-day Archive of the Indies) was built to store New World goods. The Lonja joined the cathedral, Alcázar ('royal palace'), and archbishop's palace as the physical center of power. The Plaza de San Francisco was another important urban nucleus, as the site of the main Franciscan monastery (now destroyed), the Royal Audiencia, the city jail, and the town hall

begun in 1527 in the elaborately decorative Plateresque style. Seville's sixteenth-century humanists found inspiration in the Roman ruins of nearby Itálica, and grand urban projects (notably the Casa de Pilatos and the Alameda de Hércules) completed Seville's conversion from an Islamic to a Renaissance city.

Urban development was predominantly religious in the 1600s, a century marked by the founding of dozens of new religious institutions, by the growing popularity of Holy Week and Corpus Christi, and by wide popular support promoting the cause of the Immaculate Conception. The baroque church of San Salvador was begun in 1674, and the 1670s also saw the construction of two spectacular hospitals for the poor, the Hospital de los Venerables and the Hospital de la Santa Caridad, both founded by noble patrons with fortunes from New World trade. The new architecture of Counter-Reformation Seville was filled with masterworks by the local painters Francisco de Zurbarán (1598–1664), Bartolomé Murillo (1617–1682), and Juan de Valdés Leal (1622–1690) and the sculptors Juan Martínez Montañés (1568–1649) and Pedro Roldán (1624–1700).

See also Cádiz; Cervantes, Miguel de; Ferdinand of Aragón; Inquisition; Isabella of Castile; Murillo, Bartolomé Esteban; Zurbarán, Francisco de.

BIBLIOGRAPHY

Primary Sources

Caro, Rodrigo. *Antigüedades, y principado, de la ilustríssima ciudad de Sevilla.* Seville, 1998. Facsimile of the 1634 edition.

Ortiz de Zúñiga, Diego. *Anales eclesiásticos y seculares de la muy noble y muy leal ciudad de Sevilla, metrópoli de la Andalucía.* 5 vols. Seville, 1988. Facsimile of the 1795–1796 edition.

Secondary Sources

Clarke, Michael, ed. *Velázquez in Seville.* Edinburgh, 1996.

Dominguez Ortiz, Antonio, and Francisco Aguilar Piñal. *El barroco y la ilustración.* Vol. 4 of *Historia de Sevilla.* Seville, 1976.

Morales Padrón, Francisco. *La ciudad del Quinientos.* Vol. 3 of *Historia de Sevilla.* 3rd rev. ed. Seville, 1989.

Pike, Ruth. *Aristocrats and Traders: Sevillian Society in the Sixteenth Century.* Ithaca, N.Y., 1972.

AMANDA WUNDER

SEXUAL DIFFERENCE, THEORIES OF.

Historians agree about two things: that sexual differences were carefully marked in the early modern period, and that theories of difference underwent significant changes in the late seventeenth and eighteenth centuries. How these differences were marked and how they changed, however, are the subject of much scholarly debate.

For much of the early modern period, theories of sexual difference derived from those of classical antiquity. Humoral theory, the basis of learned and lay medical thinking, explained that everyone was made up of four humors (yellow bile, black bile, phlegm, blood), but that men and women differed constitutionally. Men tended to be hotter and drier than women. Two strands of classical thought described the creation of sexual difference. Aristotle argued that male seed acted on female matter in the womb to create a new being. Because matter strove toward perfection, the ideal was always male, but sometimes inadequate heat or weak seed resulted in a female. In this model, males are the default setting and females are the result of some failure or deficit. The Hippocratic model was more generous: males and females contributed seed to make a new being, and the shape of the resulting offspring was due to the interaction of both seeds.

Galen's (129–c. 199 C.E.) ideas about sexual anatomy also portrayed the male as the more perfect specimen. Male and female reproductive parts were the same, but located in different arrangements in the body. The penis and the scrotum were like the womb and vagina turned inside out; the male body's greater heat and perfection pushed these internal organs outside. Renaissance anatomists highlighted these similarities in their illustrations. The historian Thomas Laqueur has described this as the "one-sex" model, meaning that sexual difference was a matter of degree rather than kind. He has emphasized that male and female sexual desire and fulfillment were thought to be necessary for reproduction; only in the heat of orgasm could a new person be created.

If male and female bodies were thought to be so similar, Laqueur argues, then the burden of difference was borne by gender, that is, by social and cultural arrangements. Biblical authority was constantly invoked to remind women that they were the daughters of Eve, and legal proscription attempted to constrain the desires of what was thought to be the lustier sex. Women's history provides a wealth of examples to illustrate the maintenance of difference by means of patriarchy. In England, for example, men who murdered their wives were guilty of homicide and hanged, but women who murdered their husbands were guilty of the far more serious crime of petty treason and burned at the stake.

Historians have argued about the extent to which Laqueur's model truly dominated discussions of sexual difference. Lyndal Roper, for instance, has highlighted the significance of maternity, arguing that the corporeality of women's repeated experiences of pregnancy and lactation emphasized the radical differences between male and female bodies to both sexes. Recent work has also suggested that Renaissance anatomists were fascinated by manifestations of sexual difference, although they often highlighted sexual dimorphism in features that we no longer see as sexually specific.

By the end of the eighteenth century, ideas about sexual difference had changed. Broadly speaking, historians agree that by the late eighteenth century differences rather than similarities between male and female bodies came to be emphasized; that women were no longer thought to be the lustier sex; and that sexual difference permeated the entire body, not just the arrangement of the genitals.

Laqueur dates this larger shift as occurring around 1780–1820, and he connects the development of the "two-sex" model to social and political change. He suggests that contract theories of government and redefinitions of the political subject created an imperative to define women as categorically different from men. He emphasizes the work of thinkers such as Jean-Jacques Rousseau, who declared in 1762 that a man is only a man occasionally, but a woman is a woman for her whole life, by which he meant that men usually functioned as gender-neutral subjects while women were constantly marked as different and, therefore, as incompetent to function as political subjects.

Anthony Fletcher dates this shift toward greater difference earlier in England, describing a move from scriptural to secular patriarchy. By the later seventeenth century, Fletcher suggests, gender difference was rooted in beliefs about women's innate modesty and godliness, rather than the older view that saw them as sinful and disorderly. Female chastity was the natural result of women's lack of sexual desire and their investment in motherhood rather than passion. For Fletcher, such differences were understood in bodily terms—women were "naturally" different from men—but those corporeal differences were not highly articulated.

Randolph Trumbach complicates this picture by reminding us that same-sex desire shaped ideas about gender relations. He suggests that with the late-seventeenth-century development of "molly houses" in Amsterdam and London—clubs frequented by men who had sex with other men—masculine and feminine roles became more tightly defined as a third sex—the molly, or effeminate man—was imagined, represented, and lived. Such a suggestion resonates also with the work of Henry Abelove, who suggests that the range of usual sexual behaviors between English men and women narrowed to focus on the reproductive act sometime in the early eighteenth century.

Other interpretations focus on changing views of the nervous system. Popular medical works by the physician George Cheyne (1671–1743) and novels by Samuel Richardson (1689–1761), grounded in John Locke's psychological theories, portrayed the human body as a creature of sensation. Nerves mediated a person's relationship to his or her surroundings, but nerves were not gender-neutral. Women's nerves tended to be finer and more delicate than those of men, whose grosser nerves demanded more stimulation (often in the form of sex and alcohol). Women's more refined nerves made them the moral center of the domestic sphere, but also made them prey to a range of ailments.

All of these interpretations suggest that difference became more fully embodied in the eighteenth century. None of these, however, grounds that change in scientific developments. Instead, historians see scientific work as culturally shaped, part and parcel of larger social changes.

See also **Citizenship; Education; Equality and Inequality; Feminism; Gender; Homosexuality; Literacy and Reading; Locke, John; Marriage; Medicine; Midwives; Obstetrics and Gynecology; Passions; Prostitution; Richardson, Samuel; Rights, Natural; Rousseau, Jean-Jacques; Scholasticism; Sexuality and Sexual Behavior; Virtue; Witchcraft; Women.**

BIBLIOGRAPHY

Primary Sources
Rousseau, Jean-Jacques. *Émile.* Amsterdam, 1762.

Sharp, Jane. *The Midwives Book, Or, the Whole Art of Midwifry Discovered* (1671). Edited by Elaine Hobby. Oxford, 1999.

Secondary Sources
Abelove, Henry. "Some Speculations on the History of Sexual Intercourse during the Long Eighteenth Century in England." *Genders* 6 (1989): 125–130.

Fletcher, Anthony. *Gender, Sex, and Subordination in England 1500–1800.* New Haven, 1995.

Laqueur, Thomas W. *Making Sex: Body and Gender from the Greeks to Freud.* Cambridge, Mass., 1990.

Maclean, Ian. *The Renaissance Notion of Woman: A Study in the Fortunes of Scholasticism and Medical Science in European Intellectual Life.* Cambridge, U.K., and New York, 1980.

Roper, Lyndal. *Oedipus and the Devil: Witchcraft, Sexuality, and Religion in Early Modern Europe.* London, 1994.

Stolberg, Michael. "A Woman Down to Her Bones: The Anatomy of Sexual Difference in the Sixteenth and

Seventeenth Centuries." *Isis* 94 (June 2003). See also the rebuttals, Thomas Laqueur, "Sex in the Flesh," and Londa Schiebinger, "Skelettestreit," that follow.

Trumbach, Randolph. *Sex and the Gender Revolution.* Chicago, 1998.

MARY E. FISSELL

SEXUALITY AND SEXUAL BEHAVIOR.
Since the 1970s, new approaches to the history of sexuality have combined to transform understanding of early modern sexual practices and beliefs. Social historians began by recovering sexualized aspects of the life cycle such as marriage and childbirth. Historians of women and gender examined longstanding patterns of sexual socialization relative to such issues as coerced sex and arranged marriage and the patterns of community response to such sexually marked populations as prostitutes and nuns. Michel Foucault's *Histoire de la sexualité* (1978; History of sexuality) provided a new intellectual framework for sexuality studies by arguing that modern sexuality ought to be understood as discursively organized and marked by technologies of power. That is, patterns of language such as confession and silencing around sexual acts operate in complex ways within structures of power (such as the family, church, state, and science) to form sexual identity. Foucault's work stimulated and reformulated questions and approaches to the history of sexual behavior even as he was criticized both for the lack of historical specificity in his account of ancient sexuality and for contending that the beginning of the modern notion of sexuality was fundamental to identity in eighteenth-century Europe.

Since Foucault, much empirical historical work on sexuality has filled gaps in his chronology and challenged a number of his particular assertions. Nonetheless, the work of historians of sexuality on such issues as birth control, prostitution, pornography, and homosexuality remains indebted to Foucault for his insights regarding the patterns of meaning and significance with respect to sexuality and sexual behavior. What follows takes into account both the empirical and the discursive understandings of the history of sexuality and sexual practices in early modern Europe. For purposes of clarity, "sex" throughout refers to sex acts, while "biological sex" refers to male or female bodies.

"Sexuality" refers to the complex of ideas associated with sex and often inflected by "gender," by which is meant the cultural meanings attached to biological sex.

SEXUAL PRACTICES
From the emergence of Catholic Christianity in late antiquity, suspicion of corporeal matters as detracting or distracting from the Christian's duty to focus on eternal salvation was especially strong with regard to sex. Procreation was permitted, but pleasure was generally frowned upon by the church. Persistent beliefs and strictures indicate that fears of sexuality remained very much in play throughout the Middle Ages. Theologians were adamant that sex was primarily procreative and ought to be confined to legitimate marriage. In general, any sort of sex in which procreation was impossible (anal, oral, homosexual) or even made difficult (by means of withdrawal, for instance) was regarded as "against nature." Although other factors were not entirely excluded, strictures regarding marital sex reflected the predominance of procreation to the exclusion of other factors. Couples were not supposed to have sex when the woman was already pregnant, since the sexual act could not possibly produce children. Men were supposed to be on top during the act in part because of the belief that if the woman was on top, the man's seed would spill out, preventing conception. As long as procreation was the aim and a reasonable expectation, sex was permissible.

Procreation as the goal did not eliminate the understanding that sex was an important form of marital intimacy. From St. Paul and medieval theologians, early modern Europeans inherited the concept of the marriage debt, which was seen as a crucial element in the maintenance of marriage. Tensions over the marriage debt are manifest in the extensive discussions about mutual obligation and exceptions to it. While both partners were expected to provide sex on demand, most assumed that men would be more demanding, despite the widespread cultural belief that women were the lusty sex because of their inferior capacity for reason. The marriage debt was enforceable, but it also could be evaded. Women resisted unwanted marital sex by observing church-defined days and periods of abstinence. Three days of abstinence were required on either side of participation in the sacrament of Communion. The penitential season of Lent was a period of sexual abstinence. Sexual relations were also forbidden before a woman was blessed by a priest after childbirth in a "churching" ceremony. These evasive strategies functioned in effect as birth control and supported the cultural climate that regarded sex as inferior to chastity and devotion to God.

Sex and medicine. Medical knowledge about sex was largely organized around procreation. The understanding and treatment of diseases of both men and women centered around making certain that their bodies were properly balanced for insemination, conception, and pregnancy. Ancient medical authorities remained a significant source of (often dubious) knowledge about sexuality in the early modern period. Greco-Roman humoral theory continued to dominate thinking about conception and pregnancy, with women described as cold and wet, while men were dry and hot. Following Galen in particular, early modern medical practitioners believed that failure to conceive was often the result of an imbalance in the fluids—blood, black bile, bile, and phlegm—that corresponded to the humors (hot-wet, cold-dry, hot-dry, and cold-wet, respectively). Medical intervention for complaints such as irregular menstrual cycles, improper configuration of the womb for conception, and lack of sperm of the proper consistency and potency was organized around making certain that the humors were properly balanced within each partner and between the partners. While historians have been careful for lack of direct evidence, Roy Porter and Lesley Hall have argued that sex advice was used both positively and negatively. An explanation of the best conditions for conception, for instance, implied that the converse might prevent conception. Advice to prevent miscarriages by avoiding spicy foods, heavy lifting, and jumping suggested what exactly to do in order to induce a miscarriage.

Humoral theory was combined with assumptions about gender hierarchy inherited from the ancients as well. From elaborate potions and poultices to reminders that women should lie on the right side and avoid sneezing after intercourse, advice manuals, herbal recipe books, and medical texts were replete with ways to facilitate conception. Since Aristotle had defined male qualities as superior, and because men were generally considered more valuable and of higher status than women,

many questions about sex revolved around making certain that proper humoral balance would result in male children. Failure to conceive, in the Aristotelian tradition was entirely the woman's fault, but popularizers of medical knowledge in the Renaissance were not so certain. Experts contended that factors such as uterine environment, physical conditions during intercourse, and frequency of intercourse could influence the biological sex of the child. While medical writers such as Laurent Joubert (*Erreurs populaires* [1578; Popular errors]) and Giovanni Marinello (*Delle medicine partenenti all'infermità delle donne* [1563; Medicine for the infirmities of women]) debated who was responsible for the biological sex of the offspring, they accepted the Aristotelian claim that only men produced seed thought to produce the infant's soul. Women were thought to provide only the matter necessary to produce the baby. Others agreed with Galen that women provided a necessary seed of their own that joined with the male seed to form a fetus.

Information about dysfunction was abundant; consensus was not. Consider impotence, a topic of central importance, as family lineages depended on successful reproduction. Causes and cures of impotence, male and female, filled thousands of pages of commentary. Numerous, exceedingly complicated recipes claimed to help men enhance desire, sustain erections, and produce high quality sperm. Following humoral theory quite literally, some thought excessive coldness or dryness in a man caused impotence, and advised adding heat or moisture. If the specified imbalance was corrected and the impotence remained, perhaps the problem was a penis either too short or too long. For the latter condition, the advice was to choose a tall bride. No advice was forthcoming for the man with a small penis. Others looked to the *Malleus Maleficarum* (c. 1486; The hammer of witches), blaming witchcraft for male impotence. For women too, the range of possibilities was vast. Diets, baths, and douches in a bewildering array were prescribed for sterile women. If these remedies were unavailing, one might try remedies to alter the shape or orientation of the uterus. Issues of sexual mood and timing mattered as well: if the woman was not sufficiently aroused, her seed would not be released. The husband was advised to engage in foreplay to make certain that this did not happen. The air of desperation in the range of remedies was in part because failure to reproduce disrupted social norms. But the remedies themselves—both in their complexity and their vast number—only increased anxiety about sex.

Indeed, the failure of medical authorities to reach consensus contributed to the development of scientific efforts around sexual issues. While physicians like Leonardo Fioravanti in his 1564 *Dello specchio di scientia universale* (Mirror of universal science) started publicly rejecting the established medical wisdom about sex, others sought to utilize debate to further sexual knowledge. Anatomists, for instance, engaged in controversies, particularly over female sexual anatomy: whether the womb was stationary or mobile; if it could be influenced by smells; whether the hymen existed; and also whether the penis was made of ligaments, muscles, or cartilage. As strictures on dissecting human bodies loosened, such questions could increasingly be answered by reference to empirical evidence. Gradually, such empirical efforts started to replace the medieval and Renaissance habit of fitting observed data into predetermined frameworks formulated by ancient authors and shaped by the need to reconcile pagan knowledge with Christianity.

One key idea that shifted with the development of science was about the relationship of the biological sexes. Thomas Laqueur has argued that medieval Christians generally accepted the Aristotelian hypothesis of one sex—male—with women as inferior and inverted versions of men. Anatomists and physicians beginning in the early modern period increasingly allowed that men and women were sexually distinct. Some contended that men and women constituted two sexes designed to complement each other. This more egalitarian image of sexual biology competed with the older, hierarchical model until the Enlightenment, and even then, remnants of the one-sex model remained. Laqueur's account has been criticized as overly schematic. But as with other aspects of sexual knowledge, the lack of fixity about sexual difference prompted investigations that increased the information available about male and female sexual anatomy.

Disease and adultery. The gradual increase of knowledge about sex and sexuality was slow to allay everyday sexual anxieties and ambiguities. While sex was believed to have positive effects—doctors allowed that sex combated melancholy and stimulated the senses—commentators were in rare agreement that too much sex was harmful. Frequent intercourse supposedly drained a man of his vital fluids, resulted in weak or degenerate offspring, and even caused death. For women, too much sex could contribute to excessive moist, cold humors. There was, however, little consensus on what was meant by "frequent." Similarly, old people were told to avoid sex for the most part, but texts rarely agreed on what constituted "old" and varied on whether sex ought to stop entirely or just happen less often. With the emergence of syphilis in the late fifteenth century, anxiety about venereal disease ran high as well. As the origins of syphilis were unclear, national groups blamed each other for the disease (the French called it the "Neapolitan pox," and the Italians, the "French pox"), and some claimed women who mixed the seed of several men in their wombs were responsible for the disease.

By far the most prominent anxiety was the fear of adultery. Fictional texts, legal tracts, and abundant case law warned that uncontrolled female lust could destroy the household: the wife would exhaust her husband, and then seek her pleasures elsewhere. Early modern commentators maintained the story from Hippocrates that women imprinted what they saw on the child developing in the womb. A woman could get pregnant by any man and pass the child off as her husband's as long as she thought about her husband during intercourse. As the jurist Jacques Buchereau noted in his 1580 commentary on the Institutes of Justinian *(Les Institutes imperiales de Justinian)*, adultery provisions in legal codes typically penalized adultery with confiscation of goods, corporal punishment, and banishment. These penalties weighed more heavily on women, however, because of their more limited resources. Jurists considered the disproportional punishment of women to be reasonable because women could introduce illegitimate offspring into the family lineage.

GENDER ASYMMETRY

That the penalties for male cheating were rarely so severe points to the enormous asymmetry in power relations between men and women where sex was concerned. Seemingly benign manifestations included the tendency to sequester women in the home, with greater seclusion for women of higher socioeconomic status. In Venice, respectable middle-class and noble women left their homes to go to church, but otherwise hardly at all. Lower-class women could move more freely but were often subject to sexual violence. In some Italian cities, gangs of young men raped unprotected women, and isolated peasant women in the countryside were similarly vulnerable to sexual violence. Sexual honor for women centered on chastity and sexual fidelity, while (in addition to factors such as prowess in war) male honor included acquiring and maintaining sexual mastery over women. Sexual insults, even if completely untrue, could destroy a woman's reputation and make her effectively unmarriageable. Slander cases often included disputes over one party calling a woman a whore or a slut. Sexual honor, lost through words or deeds, might be regained if a woman could prove she had been tricked into sexual relations, but generally only if the man married her. Men lost some sexual honor if they were thought to be out of control sexually or if they allowed themselves to be treated as the passive partner. A man who was thought a cuckold was regarded as having failed to control, or worse, having failed to satisfy his wife sexually. These were serious complaints, but where sexual honor was primary to a woman's reputation, it was only one of several components of male identity.

The combination of cultural anxiety, increased availability and spread of information, and lack of consensus about sex figured prominently in the early modern organization of families. Freedom in terms of choosing marriage partners was virtually nonexistent for men, but was especially unavailable for women. As Christiane Klapisch-Zuber noted regarding Renaissance Florence, men defined membership in "houses," or families. This was true throughout Europe, as male family members controlled most aspects of economic, legal, and political life. Women brought goods into the family lineage in marriage, managed the household, and were necessary for reproduction, but the family lineage passed through husbands and fathers to sons, rather than to daughters, who married into other families. One implication of this configuration was the sharp difference in age of marriage: men were often in their late twenties or thirties, while women were usually in their teens when first married. Men had to be relatively secure financially to start a new household, while the desire to be certain of chastity and purity made early marriage more likely for women. Women who survived childbirth were often widowed, and often while still young and with small children because of the age differential at marriage. Whether a woman could remarry was determined by negotiation between her marital family and her family of birth. Especially if she had children, the marital family would try to keep the woman and her dowry within their family, but the birth family might return her to the family home and seek a new marital alliance with another lineage.

The sexual pressures on women were in many ways far more extensive than those on men. A woman could lose her sexual honor even if she was raped, especially if she got pregnant: common belief held that conception was only possible if the woman felt pleasure. Finally, female sexuality was heavily subject to familial strategies organized by male family members, often throughout a woman's life cycle.

DISCIPLINE AND DEVIANCE

Catholics and Protestants alike measured sexual transgressions against a combination of theological and communal standards upheld by church courts, the family, and state institutions. Together these loci of power defined sexual behavior in such a way that non-normative sexual behavior was subject to scrutiny and even criminal penalties.

Catholic theology as confirmed at the Council of Trent (1545–1563) retained marriage and holy orders as sacraments, and the notion that marriage was the best state for those who did not take vows of celibacy remained implicit in Catholic belief. Protestants rejected both holy orders and marriage as sacraments on the grounds that they lacked scriptural warrant, but the main Protestant groups (Lutherans, Calvinists, and Anglicans) continued to emphasize marriage as a means of controlling sexuality. More radical sects (such as Anabaptists) were sometimes persecuted because of their rejection of the dominant sexual mores. Catholic ecclesiastical courts and Calvinist consistory records are among the richest sources regarding regulation of sexuality. Fornication was especially prominent in these records, but issues surrounding marriage, illegitimacy, and sexual violence also appear regularly.

The immediacy of the parish in the life of virtually all Europeans meant that religious courts and strictures had much more influence than state efforts to regulate sexuality, but states engaged in efforts to control sexuality as well. The patriarchal and hierarchical structure of society meant that state legislation and jurisprudence tended to uphold paternal power in matters of sexuality. The most common areas of state intervention were around clandestine marriage, adultery, rape, fornication, and prostitution. Across Europe, parental consent was generally required for marriage. The French monarchy produced a series of ordinances against clandestine marriage, beginning with Henry II's 1556 edict condemning it as a crime against God and king. In 1579, the penalty was changed from disinheritance to death for those convicted of "rapt" (abduction or seduction of a minor for purposes of clandestine marriage). Ordinances in 1639, 1697, and 1730 upheld the state's interest in marriage, utilizing the language of the king's sacred authority, even as the monarchy encroached on areas traditionally reserved to the church and its courts.

State intervention in cases of rape and fornication tended to vary by social status, marital status, and reputation. Seduction of a woman of high status typically received greater penalties than if the woman was of lower status. Virginity raised the stakes, with jurisdictions often willing to force the man either to marry the deflowered woman or provide her with sufficient dowry to enable her to marry respectably. Monetary penalties in many Italian cities were graded explicitly by social status, with the most vulnerable population—female servants—virtually unprotected. State authorities generally did not intervene when men attacked women who were at a comparative social disadvantage.

The efforts of the state with respect to prostitution were often complicated by the mixed inheritance from the Middle Ages and the practical needs of particular jurisdictions. While the church regarded sex as distracting from salvation, it grudgingly allowed unmarried men recourse to prostitutes on the grounds that fornication under controlled circumstances was less sinful than allowing sexual urges to spill over into violence. Because women were regarded as lustier by nature than men, prostitutes were often seen as women indulging their carnal desires. Few recognized the economic pressures on poor women. Many municipalities, moreover, regarded brothels as revenue sources. Brothels and prostitutes were regulated by such measures as special clothing to distinguish prostitutes from "respectable" women, limits on access to prostitutes, and bans on freelance prostitution. As Reformation and Catholic Reformation rhetoric about morality took hold, municipal brothels gradually disappeared, while religious foundations to redeem repentant prostitutes, such as the Convertite House in Venice (founded in 1552) and the Magdalen Hospital in London (founded in 1758), sprang up.

State attempts to control prostitution were generally ineffective. The focus on the prostitute as a fallen moral agent rather than on the economic problems that produced prostitution, combined with the inattention to male customers, ensured that prostitution flourished. The major change resulting from state antipathy was the decline in management of prostitution by women and the rise of the pimp. This made prostitutes increasingly vulnerable to violence and economic exploitation. States often accepted more or less open prostitution in less respectable parts of towns. To satisfy moral crusaders such as the Society for the Reformation of Manners (founded in the early 1690s in London), states engaged in or allowed occasional raids of such areas, but generally allowed business as usual, as long as order was not routinely disrupted. Higher class prostitutes (courtesans) were often prominent culturally as mistresses of kings and courtiers. Vulnerable to the vagaries of favor, such women were hardly subject to state pressure. By the outbreak of the French Revolution (1789), prostitution was much more "illegal" than it had been at the beginning of the Renaissance, but it remained a prominent feature of the sexual landscape.

Cross-dressing, infanticide, and sodomy were also subject to state regulation. While early modern jurists did not use the vocabulary of gender, these crimes were all violations of gender norms. Cross-dressing threatened the social hierarchy that presumed that men and women were in a stable relation to each other by virtue of biology. Men who cross-dressed were deemed effeminate, while women who did so were regarded as unnatural and were pressured to conform. By the eighteenth century, cross-dressing men who frequented private clubs, notably in London, were subject to police harassment and prosecution. Prison terms, fines, and periods of standing in the pillory were often the penalties for those caught and convicted. Infanticide was punishable by death, but lesser penalties (fines, banishment) were often substituted. Women accused of infanticide were regarded as unnatural mothers who violated the primary purpose of their sex. Statutes required unmarried women to declare their pregnancies or risk being charged with infanticide if the baby died. Many women convicted of infanticide had tried to hide their pregnancies with the help of clandestine networks in larger European cities.

Sodomy was more complicated in that it meant a number of things. Sodomy was "sinning against nature," and it encompassed nonreproductive sexual techniques such as masturbation, sex between two men, between human and animal, or between a man and woman in such a way that conception was impossible. Sodomy was associated with weakness, and passive male sodomy was often seen as resulting from a deficiency of proper male gender characteristics. But male homosexual sodomy, as Michael Rocke has argued, was a significant mode of political socialization in Renaissance Florence, and the efforts to prosecute it suggest that it was widely practiced. Officially, sodomy often carried the death penalty, but this seems to have been carried out primarily against socially disadvantaged individuals. By the eighteenth century, the state occasionally attempted to disrupt the meeting places of "sodomites," particularly when pressured by moral crusaders. The social pattern of prosecutions persisted as members of the elite caught in raids were usually fined, while harsher penalties were reserved for poorer men.

While Foucault asserted that sexual identity categories only developed in the nineteenth century, historians such as Alan Bray have argued that the earlier emergence of identifiable homosocial institutions such as "molly houses" (private residences where men could meet other men for sex) created a sense of sexual difference. Where Foucault contended that Europeans thought in terms of sexual acts rather than identities marked by systematic sexual preferences, his critics argue that institutional settings, linguistic practices such as pet names for those "in the know," and sartorial indicators

formed basic elements of sexual identity. In the face of official hostility, deviant practices had some organizational structures that made it easier for those who participated in them to recognize themselves as different from the dominant sexual ethos.

THE MEANINGS OF SEX

Both church and state maintained that sex was procreative in purpose, but sex had a number of other meanings. The infusion of classical texts in the Renaissance increased the prominence of secondary meanings. Over the course of the early modern period, these additional ideas threatened aspects of the religious and cultural hegemony of Christianity.

The association of sex with pleasure was not new in the early modern period, but the idea that pleasure was a positive good received several endorsements, beginning in the Renaissance. The revival of Plato, especially by Marsilio Ficino (1433–1499) and his followers, suggested that sexual pleasure was an important aspect of love. Since Neoplatonic theory held that love was the means to salvation, carnal love had a significant role to play. While most Neoplatonists tried to downplay the corporeal elements, every important thinker who advocated Neoplatonic notions of love addressed pleasure as an element of sex and love. Protestants such as Lutherans, Calvinists, and Anglicans allowed that sexual pleasure within marriage created stronger emotional ties between husband and wife. Rather than distracting from salvation, in Protestant thought sexual pleasure facilitated harmonious relations that enabled men and women to focus on matters of grace, faith, and scriptural knowledge. The Protestant rejection of non-biblical sources of doctrine downplayed the ascetic tradition that regarded pleasure as dubious.

The printing revolution was crucial to Renaissance humanism and the Protestant Reformation, but it also played a significant role in disseminating ideas regarding sexual pleasure. Sexual poetry and prose were not invented in the Renaissance, but both the recovery of ancient writers of sexually explicit material such as Catullus and Juvenal and the development of hermeneutical techniques that allowed for new readings of old texts brought the issue of pleasure to the fore. Ovid's *Metamorphoses* had been read allegorically before Renaissance humanists developed critical techniques to situate ancient texts in context and recover the range of explicit sexual behavior in antiquity. Figures like Pietro Aretino (1492–1556), notorious for sexually explicit poetry and ribald dialogues, took advantage of the openness of humanist culture to ancient sexual ideas and texts. Aretino utilized the print medium to disseminate erotic and pornographic materials, and generations of imitators produced images and texts in the same vein. "Aretino's Postures" (c. 1524) —sexually explicit engravings by Giulio Romano based on ancient images to which Aretino appended even more explicit, very raunchy sonnets—took the "high culture" of humanism and put it in the comparatively accessible format of the cheap print. Often regarded as a precursor to modern pornography, Aretino's work loomed large throughout Europe as the paradigm of sex emphatically devoted to pleasure. Audience demand for explicit sexual material grew to such an extent that novels like John Cleland's *Fanny Hill, or Memoirs of a Woman of Pleasure* (1748–1749) remained perennial popular sellers despite official censorship.

The valorization of pleasure had proponents whose ideas expanded into a full-scale challenge to Christian orthodoxy, with sexual pleasure as a core element. Libertines as described by Molière in his 1665 play *Don Juan* were amoral and atheistic. The title character married or promised to marry women indiscriminately, and left one as soon as another caught his eye. Don Juan's pursuit of pleasure leads to his death in Molière's play, and more famously in Wolfgang Amadeus Mozart's opera, *Don Giovanni* (1787). Libertine men who rejected the notion of familial domesticity in favor of homosocial gatherings that celebrated sexual pleasure often also rejected Christian sexual mores. Groups like Sir Francis Dashwood's Dilettanti Society (established in 1732) were organized ostensibly to share research about ancient Greece and Rome. Members of the society undertook to reconstruct the supposed rites of Priapus, a minor Roman deity famous for his oversized, perpetually erect penis. Libertine organizations remained small in size, but their ideas about sexual pleasure in place of marriage and advocacy of pagan sexual ideas over Christian ones impressed and shocked mainstream European society. The fear of libertine influence often made their ideas more prominent because of their shock value.

The early Enlightenment libertines like Dashwood still drew on Renaissance modes of producing meaning. That is, they looked to the ancients for information and for authority for their own ideas. Later Enlightenment libertinism, partly in reaction to the growing popularity and hegemony of sentimental domesticity, advocated most famously by Jean-Jacques Rousseau (*Émile*, 1762), made a rather different case for libertine sexual ideas. Following the lead of materialist philosophers like the physician Julien Offray de la Mettrie (*L'homme machine* [1747; Man a machine]), pornographers increasingly described sex through reference to materialist philosophy, which posited that everything, including human beings, was simply matter. The extreme version of this tendency is exemplified in the works of the Marquis de Sade. His *Philosophy of the Bedroom* (1795) took Enlightenment language about reason and nature to the logical extreme. Any form of pleasure, even if it involved pain or death, was justified as reasonable and natural. Because pleasure was naturally occurring, Sade explicitly rejected any other criteria for evaluating sexual acts. Sade was, and to many still is, outrageous for his exploitative view of human behavior and sexual violence, in part because he effectively yoked sexual pleasure to reason and nature within an Enlightenment intellectual scheme.

The significance of libertine discourse in early modern Europe underscores the shift between the Renaissance and the Enlightenment in terms of the meanings of sex. In keeping with the larger cultural understandings of the production of knowledge, Renaissance advocates of pleasure as a central meaning of sex looked to the ancients. Enlightenment thinkers, generally dubious about tradition as well as religious belief, framed sexual pleasure in terms of reason and nature. Sade's version was extreme to be sure, but the notion that pleasure was a natural part of sex permeated much Enlightenment thinking.

The other side of Enlightenment thinking about sex—the association of sexuality with gender roles in ways that presume men to be sexually aggressive and women passive—has remained more prominent. The Enlightenment inheritance has in fact included both the assumptions about gender roles and the multiple logics that resulted from the application of reason to nature and sexuality. The family, church, state, and science were not replaced by Enlightenment reference to reason, but rationality, largely envisioned on a personal level, shifted assessments of sexual behavior to the individual. Sexuality as a matter of preference or desire could then much more easily be imagined as integral to the self. But modern sexual identity was, and is, clearly built on the structures and habits of early modern European society.

See also **Biology; Divorce; Enlightenment; Family; Gender; Homosexuality; Humanists and Humanism; Marriage; Medicine; Pornography; Prostitution; Rousseau, Jean-Jacques; Sade, Donatien-Alphonse-François de; Sexual Difference, Theories of; Women.**

BIBLIOGRAPHY

Bell, Rudolph M. *How to Do It: Guides to Good Living for Renaissance Italians*. Chicago, 1999.

Bray, Alan. *Homosexuality in Renaissance England*. New York, 1995.

Brown, Judith C., and Robert C. Davis, eds. *Gender and Society in Renaissance Italy*. New York and London, 1998.

Farr, James R. *Authority and Sexuality in Early Modern Burgundy (1550–1730)*. New York, 1995.

Flandrin, Jean-Louis. *Families in Former Times: Kinship, Household and Sexuality*. Translated by Richard Southern. Cambridge, U.K., and New York, 1979.

Foucault, Michel. *The History of Sexuality*. Translated by Robert Hurley. New York, 1978.

Hunt, Lynn, ed. *The Invention of Pornography: Obscenity and the Origins of Modernity, 1500–1800*. New York and Cambridge, Mass., 1993.

Ingram, Martin. *Church Courts, Sex, and Marriage in England, 1570–1640*. Cambridge, U.K., and New York, 1987.

Klapisch-Zuber, Christiane. *Women, Family and Ritual in Renaissance Italy*. Translated by Lydia Cochrane. Chicago, 1985.

Laqueur, Thomas. *Making Sex: Body and Gender from the Greeks to Freud*. Cambridge, Mass., 1990.

McLaren, Angus. *A History of Contraception: From Antiquity to the Present Day*. Oxford and Cambridge, Mass., 1990.

Merrick, Jeffrey, and Bryant T. Ragan Jr., eds. *Homosexuality in Early Modern France: A Documentary Collection*. New York, 2001.

Migiel, Marilyn, and Juliana Schiesari, eds. *Refiguring Woman: Perspectives on Gender and the Italian Renaissance*. Ithaca, N.Y., 1991.

Moulton, Ian Frederick. *Before Pornography: Erotic Writing in Early Modern England*. Oxford and New York, 2000.

Porter, Roy, and Lesley Hall. *The Facts of Life: The Creation of Sexual Knowledge in Britain, 1650–1950*. New Haven, 1995.

Rocke, Michael. *Forbidden Friendships: Homosexuality and Male Culture in Renaissance Florence*. New York, 1996.

Ruggiero, Guido. *The Boundaries of Eros: Sex Crime and Sexuality in Renaissance Venice*. New York, 1985.

Soman, Alfred. "Anatomy of an Infanticide Trial: The Case of Marie-Jeanne Bartonnet (1742)." In *Changing Identities in Early Modern France*, edited by Michael Wolfe. Foreword by Natalie Zemon Davis. Durham, N.C., 1997.

Talvacchia, Bette. *Taking Positions: On the Erotic in Renaissance Culture*. Princeton, 1999.

Trumbach, Randolph. *Sex and the Gender Revolution*. Chicago, 1998.

KATHERINE CRAWFORD

SHABBETAI TZEVI

SHABBETAI TZEVI (also Sabbatai Sevi, Zevi, or Zebi, 1626–1676), Jewish rabbi of the Ottoman Empire whose messianic claims and abrupt conversion to Islam in 1665–1666 convulsed Jewish communities in Europe and the Near East. The widespread appeal of his messiahship establishes the movement as the most significant millenarian outpouring in modern Jewish history. The crypto-Jewish sect known in Turkish as *Dönme*, 'convert (to Islam)', refers to a minority of devotees who clung to belief in Tzevi as messiah and followed his lead in converting. Although "Shabbetean" principally denotes believers in Tzevi's messiahship, the term also can apply to currents and sympathies among nonadherents, especially regarding the movement's mystical (Cabalist) conceptions.

FAMILY AND EARLY CAREER

Many of the details of Shabbetai Tzevi's life have been clouded by partisanship and Tzevi's own self-representations. He was born in Ottoman Izmir (Smyrna) in 1626, the son of Mordecai Tzevi, a merchant broker recently arrived from Salonika. Both his mother, Clara, and his father died before his famous movement. After a period of study in Izmir, Tzevi was ordained as a rabbi when he was eighteen (Scholem, p. 111). Tzevi's early inclinations toward Cabala, or Jewish mysticism, are unclear. In his subsequent travels, he studied the Lurianic teachings (after Isaac Luria, 1534–1572) that permeated contemporary Cabalism. The revelations and prophecies of his eventual movement are deeply imprinted with Cabalist thought. He was pious and ascetic for the most part, but his behavior could also be bizarre and unpredictable. Observers saw in his eccentricities everything from madness and blasphemy to genius and divine blessing. In 1648, his behavior, which included messianic utterances, led to chastisement by the rabbinic authorities and, in the early 1650s, expulsion from Izmir. His transgressions at the time are not known, but in the following years he was reprimanded for saying aloud the divine name and for parodying religious rituals.

FROM OUTCAST TO MESSIAH

For a number of years Tzevi lived in a succession of Jewish communities in Ottoman Europe, but he was expelled from both Salonika and Istanbul and returned to Izmir in 1658. After three years he decided to travel to Palestine. However troubling his reputation may have been at this point, when he arrived in Jerusalem in 1662 he was well received by the rabbinic leadership and was even employed as their agent to gather Egyptian contributions for the city. In Egypt in 1664, Tzevi married Sarah, a young woman who had been orphaned by the massacres in Poland of 1648–1649. Until then his messianic claims had been cryptic and inconsistent, but that changed in 1665 when he formed a relationship with a famed Cabalist, Nathan Ashkenazi of Gaza. Buoyed by Nathan's zeal, Tzevi proclaimed himself messiah in May 1665 (Scholem, pp. 220–221) Nathan's letters of announcement and the rumor of miracles soon stirred messianic fervor from Gaza deep into Europe. The promise of imminent redemption and retribution took on a life of its own. European Christian millenarians shared in the enthusiasm, predicting the fall of the Ottomans and Islam. Given the recent Jewish massacres in Europe and the memory of the expulsion from Spain, the movement's own retributive focus fell more on Christendom than on Muslims or the Ottoman Turkish Empire (Scholem, pp. 349–350).

In December of 1665, Tzevi and his adherents fought their way into the main opposition synagogue in Izmir, and the movement had its greatest triumph to date. Congregations all over the eastern Mediterranean were in an uproar. As Tzevi attempted to land at Istanbul in February 1666, the

Ottomans arrested and imprisoned him, first at Istanbul, then later and more comfortably at Gallipoli. Tzevi's opponents and the rabbinic authorities in the capital, skeptical of Tzevi and fearful of repercussions from the Ottomans, no doubt had a role in his detention, but the movement among the masses continued to grow. With pilgrims from as far away as Poland converging upon Gallipoli and partisan clashes disrupting life in the cities, the central government acted again. In September 1666 Tzevi was brought to the imperial palace at Edirne for interrogation by the grand vizier Ahmed Köprülü and Mehmed IV's chief preacher Vani Efendi, among others. Faced with the prospect of execution, probably for encouraging mayhem, Tzevi denied his messianic mission and, to gain the sultan's mercy, agreed to convert to Islam. With a new name (Aziz Mehmed), a Muslim turban, and a paid appointment in the palace service, Tzevi was pardoned. His renunciation of Judaism was a calamitous shock to the Jewish community, especially when Tzevi began to proselytize on behalf of Islam.

Although some Shabbeteans, including Tzevi's wife, also converted, Tzevi was not a convincing Muslim for long. In 1672 he was banished to Dulcigno in Albania, where he died in 1676. Many believers clung to the hope that his conversion had been part of the messianic plan or a sacrifice in their interests. In the 1680s and 1690s, hundreds of Jews converted to Islam, most of them as members of the Donme sect. The rabbinical leadership sought to restore the community by erasing memory of the episode, but its effects were too profound to forget.

See also **Jews and Judaism; Messianism, Jewish.**

BIBLIOGRAPHY

Barnai, Jacob. "Messianism and Leadership: The Sabbatean Movement and the Leadership of the Jewish Communities in the Ottoman Empire." In *Ottoman and Turkish Jewry: Community and Leadership,* edited by Aron Rodrigue. Bloomington, Ind., 1992.

Benbassa, Esther, and Aron Rodrigue, eds. *The Jews of the Balkans: The Judeo-Spanish Community, 15th to 20th Centuries.* Oxford, 1995.

Idel, Moshe. *Messianic Mystics.* New Haven, 1998.

Levy, Avigdor. *The Jews of the Ottoman Empire.* Princeton, 1994.

Scholem, Gershom. *The Messianic Idea in Judaism, and Other Essays on Jewish Spirituality.* New York, 1971.

————. *Sabbatai Sevi: The Mystical Messiah, 1626–1676.* Translated by R. J. Zwi Werblowsky. Princeton, 1973.

MADELINE C. ZILFI

SHAKESPEARE, WILLIAM (1564–1616),

English playwright, poet, and actor. Shakespeare is universally recognized as the foremost writer in the English language to date. The thirty-seven plays associated with his name, including the major tragedies *Hamlet, King Lear, Othello,* and *Macbeth,* and his romances and comedies, *Twelfth Night* and *A Midsummer Night's Dream* among them, have been translated into many languages and have crossed all kinds of cultural divide. His poetry, in particular his intricately woven and fiercely passionate love sonnets, have stirred the senses of reader and critic alike for generations past and will do so for generations to come.

Shakespeare was born in Stratford-upon-Avon in Warwickshire, England, and he was probably educated in the 1570s at the free grammar school there known as the King's New School. His father, John Shakespeare, has been described as a glover or whittawer, which means someone who works with animal skins. Shakespeare's mother, Mary Arden, was from a noted local family, the daughter of Robert Arden, John Shakespeare's landlord. At some point, perhaps in 1568 when his father was high bailiff (mayor) of the town and responsible for Stratford's entertainment, Shakespeare must have first seen actors perform as traveling players visiting on tour.

In about 1582, Shakespeare married Anne Hathaway, a rich yeoman's daughter. The marriage was undertaken during a notable downturn in the affairs of Shakespeare's father. Having been a respected and confident town official during Shakespeare's earliest years—initiating an application for gentry status in 1576, for example—during 1586 John Shakespeare's alderman status was withdrawn. Although controversy surrounds the possible reasons for Shakespeare's marriage to a woman who was eight years his senior, three children were produced from the marriage. Susanna was the first-born in 1583 with a pair of twins produced in 1585—a son, Hamnet, who died in childhood, and a daughter, Judith.

William Shakespeare. AP/WIDE WORLD

LONDON ACTOR, PLAYWRIGHT, AND POET

Whether Shakespeare had to leave Stratford for some reason, or whether he joined a visiting touring company such as the Queen's Men, we first hear of him as a London playhouse personality seven years after the birth of the twins. This is when he is mentioned in a pamphlet called *A Groatsworth of Wit Bought with a Million of Repentance* (1592) written by a writer and playwright named Robert Greene. This text was written while the writer knew that he was dying, and in it he urged his fellow well-educated peers, Christopher Marlowe, Thomas Nashe, and George Peele, to forsake the stage. "For there is an upstart crow, beautified with our feathers," Greene wrote, "that with his 'Tiger's heart wrapped in a player's hide' supposes he is as well able to bombast out a blank verse as the best of you, and [. . .] is in his own conceit the only Shake-scene in a country." We know this allusion is directed toward Shakespeare, not only because of the play on his name and profession as a "Shake-scene," but also because of the misquotation from one of his *Henry VI* plays: "O Tiger's heart wrapped in a woman's hide!" (Part III, act 1, scene 4, line 138).

By this time, scholars believe that the player Shakespeare had not only embarked on his English history cycle with the three *Henry VI* plays, but had also presented the highly successful if violent *Titus Andronicus* as well. In this play a woman is raped, has both her hands cut off and her tongue cut out, and a queen unknowingly eats her own children, baked in a pie. However, in a matter of a few years Shakespeare was also provably capable of writing the extraordinarily poised and tragic *Romeo and Juliet*. Here two young lovers, divided by their families' antagonism to one another, meet, marry, and die while speaking the most beautiful words of love written for the English stage.

By 1595, Shakespeare, as a sharer member of the acting company called the Lord Chamberlain's Men, was entitled to a portion of the company's takings. This status was acquired through his investment in things for the company like costumes, playbooks, and props. However, there is some evidence to show that Shakespeare wanted to be perceived more as a serious poet than as either an actor or a playwright. In 1593 and 1594 he published his two narrative poems, *Venus and Adonis* and *The Rape of Lucrece*, both dedicated to his supposed patron Henry Wroithesley, 3rd earl of Southampton. This period also marks the time when it is believed he had begun his 154 sonnets, published as a collection in 1609, with Southampton a candidate for the "Fair Youth" to whom the first 126 possibly allude. The fourteen-line sonnet, quietly evolving in form since its first emergence in fourteenth-century Italy, had reached England through poet-courtiers such as Sir Thomas Wyatt and the earl of Surrey earlier in the sixteenth century. In the hands of Shakespeare, many sonnet conventions were challenged, questioning the poetic expectation of comparing one's lover to nature, for example. "My mistress' eyes are nothing like the sun" is the bold opening of Number 130, for example. Thus Shakespeare chose to use the sonnet to engage, not only with the passions and intellect of the person to whom the sonnet is addressed, but even with poetry itself. It is interesting that Greene chose to mark out Shakespeare's verse as his primary objection to him as an "upstart." Shakespeare indeed wrote much of his drama in blank verse, the flexible iambic pentameter form of unrhymed poetry, again used by Henry Howard, the earl of Surrey, and taken on by dramatists such as Christopher Marlowe. However, Shakespeare's energy when approaching his plays did not hold back on inventiveness and variety. The blank verse form reached its apotheosis with Shakespeare, but a few of his early plays contain sonnet moments too. The Prologue to *Romeo and Juliet*, given by the Chorus, is a sonnet, and later in this lovers' play, one is interwoven through the dialogue when the protagonists first speak together (act 1, scene 5, lines 90–113).

By the turn of the seventeenth century, the Lord Chamberlain's Men had rebuilt their Shoreditch amphitheater (called the "Theater") as the Globe on London's Bankside (the south bank of the Thames). They were now the most well established of the city's playing companies. By this time Shakespeare had begun to write his heavyweight tragedies for them, beginning with *Hamlet* published in 1603. If *Titus Andronicus* was violent, and *Romeo and Juliet* tragically romantic, *Hamlet* was Shakespeare's play concerned with the human mind. The eponymous prince of Denmark, whose father's ghost tells him how he was murdered by Hamlet's uncle, sets out on a course of revenge, while at the same time, as the philosopher prince studying at Wittenburg University, he questions life and death and any decision involving them. Shakespeare is creative with the revenge tragedy form, using the vengeful mindset of the main character to explore highly philosophical questions. 'What a piece of work is man!' (act 2, scene 2, lines 293–300) and 'To be, or not to be, that is the question' (act 3, scene 1, lines 58–90) are two lines from speeches of profound mental depth. *Hamlet* is the most widely quoted and most investigated of Shakespeare's plays, attracting a phenomenal amount of scholarly study, just as much because of the questions it poses as because of the answers it fails to give.

THE JACOBEAN SHAKESPEARE

In 1603, after the death of Queen Elizabeth and the accession of James I, the company were renamed the King's Men, acquiring royal patronage status. In 1608 they also acquired a new, small, more select playhouse known as the Blackfriars that was to be used alongside the Globe, the public playhouse. Shares in this venture, which company members were given, were very lucrative acquirements for the actors—including Shakespeare. This period marked the writing of plays such as *Othello*, first performed 1603–1604 and published in the 1620s, *King Lear* of 1606, published in 1608, and *Macbeth,* again c. 1606 but first published in the collected First Folio of Shakespeare's works of 1623. The plot lines and characters of these tragedies continued to demonstrate the extraordinary range of Shakespeare's mind as he dealt with, for example, jealousy and deception in *Othello;* madness, mercy, and true filial love in *King Lear;* and the dangers of encouraged ambition in *Macbeth.* In about 1613, however, at the peak of his writing powers, Shakespeare was to give up his career on London's stage.

SHAKESPEARE THE STRATFORD MAN

By 1616, Shakespeare had returned to Stratford and the substantial home called New Place that he had bought for his family. It was there that he was to die in 1616 of a fever, reputedly after a rowdy visit from his friend and colleague Ben Jonson. He died where he began, therefore, not in London where he made his name, but in the Stratford of his birth. Back in 1596, gentry status had finally been achieved for his family, and the payee for this was likely to have been William. He died, therefore, not only rich, but respected and esteemed in his community, to become later in the minds of many the man most associated with the finest use of poetic English.

In the historical context of his day-to-day existence as an actor and a companyman, Shakespeare's significant output as a dramatic writer can be interpreted as simple good business sense that resulted in his family's bettered status at home. By writing good plays he drew audiences to playhouses in which he had financial interests. Shakespeare's plays did not, in fact, belong to him, but were the property of his company. Despite evidence that Shakespeare was involved in the printing of his poetry, there is no proof of authorial concern with the printed publication of his plays. His dramas were only collected as serious "works" seven years after his death in 1623 for what we now know as Shakespeare's "First Folio," put together by his fellow actors. A man of extraordinary talent, however, at a time when there were no rulebooks for the English language or its lexicon, his contribution to what we now perceive as beauty through dramatic story and words is inestimable.

See also **Beaumont and Fletcher; Drama: English; English Literature and Language; Jonson, Ben; Marlowe, Christopher.**

BIBLIOGRAPHY

Primary Sources

Shakespeare, William. *The First Folio of Shakespeare.* Norton facsimile, prepared by Charlton Hinman. 2nd ed. New York and London, 1996.

————. *The Norton Shakespeare.* Edited by Stephen Greenblatt, Walter Cohen, Jean E. Howard, and Katharine Eisaman Maus. New York and London, 1997. Based on the Oxford Edition.

————. *Shakespeare's Sonnets.* Edited by Stephen Booth. New Haven, 1997.

Secondary Sources

Dobson, Michael, and Stanley Wells, eds. *The Oxford Companion to Shakespeare.* Oxford, 2001.

Gurr, Andrew. *The Shakespearean Stage, 1574–1642.* 3rd ed. Cambridge, U.K., 1992.

Jones, Peter, ed. *Shakespeare, the Sonnets: A Casebook.* London, 1977.

Kermode, Frank. *Shakespeare's Language.* New York, 2001.

Schoenbaum, S. *Shakespeare's Lives.* Rev. ed. Oxford and New York, 1991.

EVA GRIFFITH

SHERIDAN, RICHARD BRINSLEY

(1751–1816), Irish playwright, theater manager, and politician. Sheridan was born in Dublin shortly before 4 November 1751, the day when he was baptized. His father was Thomas Sheridan, an Irish Protestant actor and theater manager; his mother was Frances Sheridan, who became well known as a writer of novels, including *The Memoirs of Miss Sydney Biddulph* (1761) and the Oriental tale *The History of Nourjahad* (1767).

The family moved to England, where Sheridan attended, and disliked, Harrow School, until 1770 when he left and moved, again with his family, to Bath. Early efforts at writing included *Jupiter,* a farce that prefigures *The Critic* and that was rejected for production by Sheridan's future colleague David Garrick; verse for the *Bath Chronicle;* and fragments of political essays. In Bath he met and eloped with the singer Eliza Linley (1754–1795), but the validity of their marriage was contested by both families and by another admirer of Linley's with whom Sheridan fought two duels. Although the families eventually dropped their opposition to the marriage, Sheridan remained very short of money, having moved to London to study law in 1773.

His first play was the comedy *The Rivals,* staged at Covent Garden in January 1775. It is a polished and urbane "comedy of manners" whose satirical targets include the corruption of language by Mrs. Malaprop (who famously describes another character as "as headstrong as an allegory on the banks of the Nile"), and the corruption of morals in the contemporary cult of "sentimentality." After a near failure on the first night, it went on to achieve spectacular success and to bring Sheridan both money and aristocratic contacts. Sheridan went on to write a string of brilliant and successful comedies: The farce *St. Patrick's Day* was produced in May 1775 and *The Duenna,* an operatic play, followed in November 1775. In 1776 Sheridan became manager and part-owner of the Drury Lane Theatre. *A Trip to Scarborough,* a loose adaptation of John Vanbrugh's comedy *The Relapse,* was staged there in 1777, followed in May of that year by the classic comedy *The School for Scandal* in which a hypocritical "man of feeling" is contrasted with his rakish but good-hearted younger brother in a comedy set in the world of newspaper columns and society gossip. In 1779 Sheridan became the sole owner of the Drury Lane Theatre, where he produced *The Critic, or A Tragedy Rehearsed* in the same year.

1780 marked a turning point in Sheridan's career: he spent over £1000 securing election as a member of Parliament for Stafford and ceased to write for the theater. A political ally of Charles James Fox and the Whigs, he joined the government in 1782 as the undersecretary of foreign affairs, and in 1783 became secretary of the treasury. His most famous parliamentary interventions, however, related to the impeachment of Warren Hastings, governor of India. A particular facet of the case related to the Begums of Oude, whom Hastings was alleged to have unlawfully deprived of their property: Sheridan discussed the case in a five-hour speech on 7 February 1787 that even his opponents acknowledged as "the most splendid display of eloquence and talent which has been exhibited in the House of Commons during the present reign" (Bingham, p. 237). Politically, Sheridan also argued against the Act of Union, and against press censorship.

However, Sheridan himself was sinking into debt. The Drury Lane Theatre was declared unsafe in 1792 and had to be demolished; Sheridan himself borrowed the money for the building of a new theater on the site. After the death of his first wife, Sheridan married in 1795 the nineteen-year-old Esther Ogle, daughter of the dean of Winchester. In 1799 Sheridan even returned to dramatic writing, and his tragedy *Pizarro,* an adaptation from August Friedrich Ferdinand von Kotzebue's *The Spaniards in Peru,* earned enough money to gain him a brief financial reprieve; but in 1802, with debts on all sides, the Drury Lane Theatre went into receivership. At the same time, his political career was stalling.

In the 1806 "ministry of all the talents," Sheridan was made treasurer of the navy, but this relatively minor post did not carry cabinet rank. In 1809 the new Drury Lane Theatre burned down. Although, characteristically, he was able to joke about it—he is said to have watched from a nearby coffeehouse, remarking, "a man may surely be allowed to take a glass of wine by his own fireside"—the fire made his financial ruin unavoidable and marked the end of his ownership of the theater. Sheridan had been a friend of Prince George (later King George IV) and should have benefited from George's elevation to Prince Regent in 1811, but the prince's favor proved short-lived. The following year Sheridan lost his seat in Parliament, and although the prince supplied him with £3000 to buy his way back in, Sheridan spent the money clearing personal debts. In 1813 Sheridan was again imprisoned for debt. He lived in poverty and alcoholism until his death on 7 July 1816.

See also **Drama: English; English Literature and Language; Hastings, Warren.**

BIBLIOGRAPHY

Primary Sources

Sheridan, Richard Brinsley. *The Dramatic Works of Richard Brinsley Sheridan.* Edited by Cecil Price. 2 vols. Oxford, 1973.

——. *The Letters of Richard Brinsley Sheridan.* Edited by Cecil Price. 3 vols. Oxford, 1966.

Secondary Sources

Bingham, Madeleine. *Sheridan: The Track of a Comet.* London, 1972.

Morwood, James, and David Crane, eds. *Sheridan Studies.* Cambridge, U.K., and New York, 1995.

O'Toole, Fintan. *A Traitor's Kiss: The Life of Richard Brinsley Sheridan, 1751–1816.* London, 1997.

MATTHEW STEGGLE

SHIPBUILDING AND NAVIGATION.

A revolutionary change in the design and construction of seagoing sailing ships occurred around 1400. The two established European shipbuilding traditions, one Mediterranean and the other northern, merged in the production of the full-rigged ship. From the north the rounded tubby hull form of the cog, the sternpost rudder, and the large square sail for driving the ship were combined with the abutting or carvel hull planking and the lateen sail of the south. Full-rigged ships carried three masts with a large square sail on the mainmast, a triangular lateen sail on the mizzen, and a small square sail on the foremast to balance the lateen at the stern. The square sails provided power while the lateen made the ship more maneuverable. Relying on the internal frame for strength—necessary if the hull planks did not overlap but instead abutted one another—made for lower initial construction costs, though such a hull required more repair and maintenance.

The carrack was the most prominent example of the new type, but there were smaller versions that were also capable of more reliable passages and over longer distances at lower cost than before. The higher carrying capacity per sailor gave these vessels much more range than did any of their predecessors, while the rig made it possible for them to survive more dangers. The most impressive accomplishment of the new merged type was its ability to carry Europeans on voyages across the oceans and, ultimately, around the world.

The change in construction also meant a change in the organization of work in shipbuilding. There was a growing distinction between the master builder, who drew the lines, and so designed the ship, and the carpenters who formed the wood according to his directions. Once established, the design of the full-rigged ship was far from static. Shipbuilders experimented with variations and explored the potential of the new design.

Late medieval northern European cargo ships were about three times as long as they were wide, and deep, with high freeboard. The tendency through the fifteenth and sixteenth centuries was to reduce height while increasing length. Oared ships—galleys—did not disappear and their length-to-breadth ratios of 6:1 or more probably served to influence the design of cargo ships. In the state shipyards of the Mediterranean region, most notably the Arsenal at Venice, oared ships such as the heavy galleass and the more common light lower galley continued to be produced. Only governments built those types, for use against similar ships in war, because they were no longer useful for carrying cargo.

Oared warships changed in response to the introduction of gunpowder arms on board. The galleon, built in a number of places in southern Europe from the 1530s on, may have been an effort to get the most from both the new full-rigged design and heavy cannon. The type had a low beak and carried heavy armament in the bow like a galley, but the rest of the ship was like other full-rigged ships, the exception being a relatively high length-to-breadth ratio. Modified over time, the galleon proved to be an effective carrier of expensive goods. In some cases builders added a fourth mast, a bonaventure mizzen, with a second lateen sail to increase speed and maneuverability.

The galleon and other similar sixteenth-century types proved that the future of naval warfare belonged to the sailing warship armed with cannon. There would be mistakes in developing and exploiting the new technology, mistakes that now provide invaluable information through the work of underwater archeologists. The English *Mary Rose* sank in 1545 when the overmanned vessel took in water through gunports no one had thought to close, despite what was an obvious danger. The Swedish *Gustavus Vasa* sank in Stockholm harbor in 1628 on a shakedown cruise, one that the builders did not want to attempt because they knew the ship was unstable and needed modification. Political authorities insisted on the ill-fated voyage because the warship was a symbol of royal power as well as a vehicle for battle at sea. In each case the difficulties of dealing with novelty were obvious.

The diffusion of new techniques was often slow. The durability of medieval types of construction features continued into the eighteenth century. Ship-

Shipbuilding and Navigation. *Table of the Mechanical Arts: Shipbuilders for the Arsenal of Venice,* seventeenth-century Italian painting. ©ARCHIVO ICONOGRAFICO, S.A./CORBIS

building was typically conservative, given the high cost of error, so shipbuilders were often reluctant to adopt new methods. Old designs and types persisted for centuries, especially in smaller craft and riverboats. New composite or bastard types appeared when builders tried to exploit some of the advantages from the new improvements without giving up what they knew.

Builders and captains changed the sail plan of the full-rigged ship further, exploiting the advantages of combined rig. The general tendency was toward a more divided sail plan. They added new sails, a square sail above the mainsail and a square sail under the bowsprit, and even a square sail above the square sail on the foremast. The greater number of sails meant that sailors could work on each one separately. Captains enjoyed greater choices in de-

ploying canvas and owners enjoyed lower labor costs. Because the individual sails were smaller than the single mainsail on the mainmast had been, the maximum effort required to handle sails decreased, and with it the size of the crew needed to man the vessel. To further reduce crew, masts were made simpler and rigging reduced so that more of the work of handling the sails could be done from the deck. That, in turn, reduced dangerous time aloft for the crew and further decreased the labor requirement.

The advances in the building of cargo ships came together in the highly efficient *fluyt,* developed in Dutch yards in the late sixteenth century. It had a length-to-beam ratio of 5:1 or 6:1 and a low bow with a tapered or fluted stern. It carried little or no armament and a simplified rig. The vessel was

Shipbuilding and Navigation. In June 1667, at the end of the Second Anglo-Dutch War (1665–1667), Dutch admiral de Ruyter conducted a daring raid on the English fleet at Chatham, near the mouth of the River Thames, destroying several British ships and capturing the flagship Royal Charles. This map, with a portrait of De Ruyter in the upper left, shows the Dutch fleet and the attacks on Queenborough and Sheerness on the Isle of Sheppey, as well as the action off Chatham. MAP COLLECTION, STERLING MEMORIAL LIBRARY, YALE UNIVERSITY

suited for the carriage of bulk goods such as grain and salt between the Baltic and western Europe. Because it traveled in peaceful waters, it required a smaller crew. The *fluyt* was slow but it offered relatively low costs, and it became a critical factor in the rapid growth of Dutch shipping and trade in the seventeenth century.

Builders modified the *fluyt* for use in different waters or for special purposes, and in its various forms the fluyt was widely used throughout Europe. Cargo ships required protection in wartime, so the diffusion of the *fluyt* promoted the use of convoys and an enduring distinction between ships for trade and ships for fighting. Because the number built was so large, Dutch builders were, to some degree, able to standardize parts. They also centralized much

new construction in shipyards along the Zaan River just to the north of Amsterdam, where the wharves were permanent. The presence of a sizable skilled labor force and of complementary industries—such as sawing and canvas and rope making—made it possible to produce ships quickly and less expensively. The pattern in the Zaanstreek was followed, perhaps to a lesser extent, in a number of places such as the lower Thames in England and the lower Tagus in Portugal.

For many trade routes in the eighteenth century, the sailing packet proved superior, especially for transporting more costly goods over long distances. The packet carried full rig, although on the mizzen there was now a spritsail, a true fore-and-aft sail, which was easier to handle than a lateen.

Whereas the giant carracks that the Portuguese used for trade to India in the sixteenth century reached 2,000 tons and more, the *fluyt* proved that for most trades the most efficient size was significantly smaller. The packet was typically about 500–600 tons, the optimum economic and technical size for a sailing cargo ship.

There were variations in size and in design to suit specific trades or functions. There were lighter variants for safe trades similar to the *fluyt* and its descendants, and there were heavier variants such as the East Indiaman produced by the yards of the national trading companies in the Dutch Republic and England, which carried enough weaponry to make them similar to warships. Competition for the packet in the north came increasingly from two-masted ships such as brigs and snows. Builders found ways to make those types larger, nearly the optimum size of a full-rigged ship, while reducing crew size. Two-masted ships became especially popular for regional trades. In the Mediterranean, smaller types, for example, the polacre and the felucca, which retained traditional triangular sails, survived in short distance and coastal commerce. State shipbuilding yards in the south still produced galleys at the end of the eighteenth century, but their numbers were small and declining.

At the same time that oared ships were disappearing, improvements in metallurgy—among the first signs of the industrial revolution—led not only to better and more reliable tools for shipbuilding but also to the introduction of iron for major framing and supports. Such composite construction was the first step toward the iron, and then steel, ships of the nineteenth century. Like cargo ships, warships tended toward greater standardization over time. With vessels built to fight, government agencies made the decisions about design so that limitations on design were much stricter. By the eighteenth century, navies had their vessels divided into specific rates, each with its own form of hull and rig and level of armament. The distinction between warships and cargo ships was by 1750 virtually complete, in sharp contrast to the years through about 1600. With no value as traders, warships were built exclusively in government yards that also typically served as bases with all the necessary stores and spare parts needed for the operation of those ships.

In the late Middle Ages sailors came to use a method of finding their way at sea that relied on the use of compass bearings and estimates of speed. Such dead reckoning could replace the traditional combination of experience, some stargazing, and the use of lead and line to find out about depth and the nature of the bottom. Portolan books, available in several languages by the sixteenth century, were compilations of data on sailing along coasts with directions, distances, and warnings about dangers. The pilots who worked along portions of coast in the Mediterranean and western Europe used them. From the thirteenth century they also had portolan charts, which visually represented the knowledge in the books. It is likely, though, that pilots and captains did not abandon the use of stars as a guide. Dead reckoning made possible impressive navigational feats. Long-distance voyages across the open sea, far out of sight of land and around the world, presented very different navigational problems from sailing along or near coasts. Still, navigators like Columbus found their way to, and, more importantly, their way back from, sites consistently, all that before the growth in astronomical knowledge that precipitated and was part of the scientific revolution. The influence of the new knowledge on navigation in the short term was small. It did, however, generate increasing interest in research on the movement of the stars and planets and in the potential of using observations of the heavens to aid navigation. For most of the voyages undertaken in early modern Europe, however, other information, such as prevailing wind directions or dangers of specific coastal features, was more critical for sailing.

As part of the exploration of the west African coast, Portuguese sailors developed ways to measure latitude—the distance they were south of Lisbon. Already discussed and formalized in the fifteenth century, the measurement of latitude was normal by the eighteenth century. What was lacking was a way to measure longitude. It was not until the perfection of an accurate chronometer by John Harrison in the second half of the eighteenth century that it was possible to establish the position of a ship at sea with accuracy. The diffusion of the more sophisticated navigational techniques was slow and, in 1800, sailors still commonly used lead and line and dead reckoning to find their way at sea, especially on shorter voyages in smaller vessels. Even if old techniques persisted in both shipbuilding and navigation into the nineteenth century, advances from the late Middle Ages on made possible the massive increase in trade and commerce that was the hallmark of the society and economy of early modern Europe. They also made possible the sharp increase in the productivity of workers on board ship, a success that translated into improvements in welfare, not just for sailors but for all people touched by waterborne transportation.

See also Astronomy; Atlantic Ocean; Barometer; Cartography and Geography; Chronometer; Clocks and Watches; Commerce and Markets; Communication and Transportation; Consumption; Earth, Theories of the; Engineering: Military; Europe and the World; Exploration; Galleys; Industrial Revolution; Industry; Navigation Acts; Navy; Pacific Ocean; Scientific Revolution; Shipping; Technology.

BIBLIOGRAPHY

Gardiner, Robert, ed. Cogs, Caravels, and Galleons: The Sailing Ship, 1000–1650. London, 1994.

———. The Heyday of Sail: The Merchant Sailing Ship, 1650–1830. London, 1995.

———. The Line of Battle: The Sailing Warship 1650–1840. London, 1992.

Lucassen, Jan, and Richard Unger. "Labour Productivity in Ocean Shipping, 1500–1850." International Journal of Maritime History 12 (2000): 127–141.

Unger, Richard W. Ships and Shipping in the North Sea and Atlantic, 1400–1800. Basingstoke, U.K., 1998.

Williams, J. E. D. From Sails to Satellites: The Origin and Development of Navigational Science. Oxford and New York, 1992.

RICHARD W. UNGER

SHIPPING. Shipping went through a radical transformation between the fifteenth and eighteenth centuries, a transformation that eventually had extensive influence on most aspects of the lives of Europeans. Shipping was the economic activity of the period with the greatest potential for growth. The merchant marine experienced a rise in tonnage per capita of more than 400 percent from 1500 to 1800. The productivity of sailors manning that tonnage rose dramatically, faster than in virtually all other major occupations. The range of government efforts to promote shipping, a bundle of policies often lumped together under the omnibus term "mercantilism," indicates that Europeans realized the possibilities created by improvements in water, especially ocean, transport. It was not just the increasing scale but also the scope of shipping that made it so important to early modern Europe. Adam Smith (1723–1790) in the late eighteenth century attributed some of the greatest strides in improving the wealth of nations to shipping, both over short distances and across the Atlantic. Even in art and literature there was recognition that shipping was a part of life going through dramatic changes and thus worthy of consideration. Seascapes became standard fare for painters, and by around 1800 the romance of ships and sea travel had made its way into fiction.

VESSELS, ROUTES, AND CARGOES
Beginning in the late thirteenth century Europeans were at last able to connect the shipping regions of the Mediterranean on the one hand and the North and Baltic Seas on the other. The contrary currents and winds of the Strait of Gibraltar had made sailing out into the Atlantic from the Mediterranean all but impossible before around 1270. It was then that ships from Italy made regular voyages back and forth between the north and the south. Great galleys with two or three triangular lateen sails were the vehicles for the scheduled trips by Venetians and later by Florentines. Large tubby two-masted carracks, principally from Genoa, soon joined the galleys. This new type combined the hull form of the northern cog with the abutting hull planking of Mediterranean ships. It also combined the large square sail on the mainmast with a lateen sail on a second or mizzenmast. The carrack was more maneuverable, and the addition of a small square sail on a foremast to balance the lateen mizzen created an even more versatile vessel. The new full-rigged ship, also called a carrack in its largest version, made possible the efficient carriage of luxury goods in ever-increasing volume between northern and southern Europe.

The development of the full-rigged ship also made possible the opening of new all-sea routes outside of Europe at the end of the fifteenth century. Christopher Columbus (1451–1506) had intended to open direct trade with Asia by sea but instead found lands to colonize. In the New World, he quickly adopted the model of settlement and exploitation already established on Atlantic islands like the Canaries and Azores, which Iberian sailors had opened to shipping over the previous 150 years. As in those cases, trade with the New World soon developed in colonial agricultural goods. They were followed by shipment to Europe of the products of mining. The direct sea route to India, first exploited by Portuguese sailors making trips contemporaneous with Columbus's voyages, proved to be extremely long. The distances involved and the routes chosen meant that shipping around the Cape of Good Hope was slow to develop in the sixteenth century. Alternative routes overland in Asia and then by water from the eastern Mediterranean to Europe proved to be as effective in getting such oriental goods as spices to Europe.

While the fifteenth century was characterized by revolutionary changes in ships and routes, the sixteenth century was a period of gradual exploitation of those revolutionary changes. The tonnage deployed and volume of goods transported along internal European routes expanded in the wake of growth in population and in the production of goods. Contributing the most to increased tonnage and the increase in the average size of cargo ships during this time was the rise in the carriage of bulk goods, that is, those with low value for each unit of volume. The most obvious case was the rising trade in grain. While the shipping of wheat from Crimea to Italy, a route in place in the High Middle Ages, might have decreased because of wars generated by Turkish expansion, the carriage of grain from the Baltic to northwest Europe grew dramatically as the century went on. Supplies were large enough and shipping efficient enough that by around 1600 Dutch shippers carried Baltic grain to Italian ports in years of shortage in the Mediterranean. The carriage of other bulk goods, like fish, cured and packed in barrels, salt, and wood for building, also contributed substantially to the growth in shipping through the sixteenth century. The result within Europe was an increase in the volume of shipping and an even greater increase in the exchange of knowledge. Avenues for the transfer of commercial information became more plentiful and, along with the rise in the volume of trade, led to the more efficient exploitation of ships. Those valuable capital goods could be kept at sea for a greater part of the year if captains knew when and where they could

find cargoes. That knowledge generated a greater return on the sizable investment that was the cargo ship. To meet the need to carry bulk goods in northern Europe, shipbuilders developed new types of vessels, often elaborating on existing designs. The most obvious case was the *fluyt,* a relatively long three-masted ship with a boxlike cross section, first built in the Netherlands at the close of the sixteenth century. It was well suited to shipping cargoes back and forth between the Baltic and western Europe; variants soon emerged that were designed for moving wood from Norway or traveling to the Mediterranean from the Low Countries.

European shipbuilders designed special vessels to deal with the various distances and dangers involved. The giant carracks of Portuguese trade to India were the largest wooden ships ever built. The galleons, originally warships for battles in European waters, were adapted to handle the carriage of silver from the New World to Spain. While emphasis within Europe was on shipping bulk goods, in extra-European trade the cargoes were typically luxury items. Among the luxuries shipped were tropical goods that could not be produced in Europe. Human beings as settlers or slaves were taken to the New World, and soldiers, merchants, and officials were taken to Asia. The volumes of goods shipped were small compared with those carried over much shorter distances in and around Europe. Trade outside of Europe tended to be controlled and regulated by governments, which directed investment and routes used. Shippers had to sacrifice flexibility but received in exchange security and some predictability of profits in trade that involved high levels of risk.

In the seventeenth century, shipping continued to evolve along established lines, but there were some setbacks. The grain trade from the Baltic expanded, reaching its peak in mid-century, but stabilization, or in some regions a fall, in population led to a shrinking demand for food grains and so in turn in demand for transportation. Efficiency improvements in shipping largely compensated for those pressures in the second half of the seventeenth century. There were no major changes in ship design nor the opening of any new categories of trade, factors that had been the basis for earlier growth. The use of routes through the southern Indian Ocean made possible faster and more frequent trips to the Far East, engendering increased shipping to Asia. The agents of that growth were the Dutch and English East India Companies, which made even more clear over time that ships and shipping were the foundations of European colonization. Meanwhile, within Europe, the elaboration of earlier practices, both in shipping and shipbuilding, laid the groundwork for the great expansion in shipping that was to occur in the eighteenth century.

The pattern of trade established in the Baltic and North Seas in the sixteenth century—the carriage of bulk goods and the reliance on agents to assemble cargoes and pass along commercial intelligence—spread throughout the world from the late seventeenth century on. Shipbuilders found ways to get the most from the three-masted ship, constructing a packet boat in the range of 500 to 600 tons, a size found to be the optimum for most long-distance trades. A vessel of that size and design could carry out a range of tasks and do so at lower risk. Two-masted vessels like barks and snows came to compete with the three-masted sailing ships for the carriage of bulk goods in regional trades, such as moving grain, wood, and coal around the North Sea. The rapid growth in English coal production and the rising demand for the fuel in urban centers made a significant contribution to the growth in shipping and to the use of barks and other colliers. The two-masters, larger than in the past, needed fewer sailors per ton than three-masted ships and increased flexibility in deploying shipping services. As in the north, in the Mediterranean two-masted ships or ones smaller than the sailing packet, like the polacre and the felucca, found increasing use in regional trades. The rising exchange in bulk goods like fish between northern and southern Europe, however, generally meant employment for three-masted ships. Large three-masters in trade to the Far East, the East Indiamen, proved effective in carrying the increasing volume of goods imported into Europe. The volume of shipping in extra-European trades in general and to the New World in particular increased dramatically in the eighteenth century. Improvements in production as well as falling shipping costs led to a collapse in prices of sugar, followed by coffee, tea, tobacco, rice, and other agricultural products most economically grown in the New World or South and Southeast Asia. Lower prices, in turn, led to dramatic increases in demand

in Europe. Both the quantity and the range of commodities shipped grew. That made possible the regular and predictable marshaling of goods to be sent out. Though such changes may have decreased the urgency of gaining commercial information, the greater frequency of travel and the development of newspapers, often created for people involved in shipping, made access to the latest news easier. The larger populations of Europe, the increasing production of goods, the greater demand for commodities, and especially the rapidly falling shipping costs of the late eighteenth century led to more rapid and dramatic growth in the shipping sector than ever before.

COMMERCE AND WARFARE

Shipping was not merely about the carriage of goods. There were always many interconnected activities that depended on and facilitated shipping. That became most obvious in the eighteenth century with the overall growth in commerce. The trading markets, the bourses for exchange of various goods, were also sites for arranging the financing and insurance of shipping. Shipbuilding and ship repair and related industries like rope and sail making were necessary to shipping. More generally, the growth in the size and wealth of port towns in early modern Europe indicated the long-term success of shipping and the interconnected nature of the shipping enterprise. In itself shipping was not the largest sector of the economy. That was always agriculture. But the contribution of shipping to the economy was sizable and growing throughout the period. Its value was not just in opening new possibilities but also in its rapid development, probably more rapid than any other sector.

By the late eighteenth century, European shipping encompassed interconnected routes around the world. There were regular sailings with something close to predictable travel and movement of what was, compared with earlier years, a mass of a broad range of goods. Governments relied heavily on the income generated by taxes on shipping and commerce. Political and economic advantages fell to states that enjoyed the most successful shipping sectors. Venice and Genoa set the pattern first in the late Middle Ages. Spain and Portugal followed in the sixteenth century and then the Dutch Republic in the seventeenth. The success of France in the eighteenth century, thanks to government promotion of shipping, and of the Scandinavian kingdoms at end of the century was eclipsed by the even greater success of Great Britain. It was no coincidence that some wars of the eighteenth century were fought by navies over the control of shipping routes. Improvements in the sailing qualities of warships in Europe paralleled those in cargo ships. The introduction of cannons on board beginning late in the thirteenth century led to the building of specialized warships by the sixteenth century. The process of division between fighting ships and cargo carriers was expedited by the falling prices of guns and their increasing reliability in the second half of the sixteenth century. The protection of shipping with warships built for that purpose became a proper function of government. By the end of the eighteenth century, the quality of one's navy could mean the difference between winning and losing a war. The ability of a state to protect its shipping was vital to its ability to wage war, if for no other reason than that government needed the income from shipping to sustain any military effort.

CONCLUSION

Shipping changed probably more than any other sector of the early modern European economy. Technical changes improved the ships. Organizational changes on shore in the assembling, handling, and distribution of cargoes created greater efficiencies. Developments in shipping made significant contributions, most obviously to the economy in increased production, but also in lowering costs of supplies to producers as well as opening new markets for their goods. Improvements in shipping expanded the scope of goods available to consumers and allowed governments to extend their authority. Much of the transformation of the economy and many aspects of politics and to a lesser extent society in Europe can be traced to changes in shipping between 1450 and 1789.

See also **Commerce and Markets; Communication and Transportation; Mercantilism; Navy; Shipbuilding and Navigation; Trading Companies.**

BIBLIOGRAPHY

David, Ralph. *The Rise of the English Shipping Industry in the Seventeenth and Eighteenth Centuries.* London and New York, 1962.

Glete, Jan. *Warfare at Sea, 1500–1650: Maritime Conflicts and the Transformation of Europe.* London and New York, 2000.

Lucassen, Jan, and Richard Unger. "Labour Productivity in Ocean Shipping, 1500–1850." *International Journal of Maritime History* 12 (2000): 127–141.

Shepherd, James F., and Gary M. Walton. *Shipping, Maritime Trade, and the Economic Development of Colonial North America.* Cambridge, U.K., 1972.

Tracy, James D., ed. *The Rise of Merchant Empires: Long-Distance Trade in the Early Modern World, 1350–1750.* Cambridge, U.K., and New York, 1990.

Unger, Richard W., ed. *Ships and Shipping in the North Sea and Atlantic, 1400–1800.* Basingstoke, U.K., and Brookfield, Vt., 1997.

van Tielhof, Milja. *The Mother of All Trades: The Baltic Grain Trade in Amsterdam from the Late Sixteenth to the Early Nineteenth Century.* Leiden and Boston, 2002.

RICHARD W. UNGER

SHOPS AND SHOPKEEPING. In the late seventeenth century, it is estimated that there were about forty thousand shopkeepers in England and Wales, most of them based in towns. Though identified as grocers or drapers, they operated what were, to judge from their inventories, general stores, selling whatever they could. So understood, shopkeeping is a form of retailing: the selling of merchandise in individual units or small lots by a business established for that specific purpose. In the broader sense of a full-time mercantile activity, its history reaches into the past to peddlers hawking their wares and marketplaces drawing sellers and buyers together. In the narrower sense—retailing carried out in a specialized, permanent structure—its history is relatively limited.

Whichever sense—narrow or broad—is preferred, the origins of shopkeeping are unknown. The first shopkeepers to sell from permanent structures, thus competing with marketplaces and fairs, were probably artisans. Producers sold their products from the windows of their workshops in the intervals between market and fair days. Such sales are probably as old as artisanal production itself. Most European cities reveal traces of this activity in their topography. Shops—and, therefore, the trade in certain goods—tended to cluster in particular neighborhoods, leaving traces in the architecture and names on the streets. Baker Street and Tanners Alley are not uncommon examples.

The first true shopkeepers appear somewhat later, perhaps as early as the eleventh century. They were not producers but rather middlemen of exchange between producers and consumers, who confined their activities to buying and selling. Throughout the Middle Ages, shopkeeping was distinct from other forms of retail. Peddlers walking the streets or vendors setting up stalls in marketplaces carried out the majority of retail selling. According to the 1296 City Law of Augsburg, for example, the sale of goods that "one must weigh with a scale," apart from the annual markets, was open only to shopkeepers operating out of permanent shops. This law captures a tension that was present and that created conflict in all towns and cities in the Middle Ages as well as the early modern period, the distinction and competition between shops and marketplaces on the one hand and between specialized and nonspecialized shops on the other hand. Being bound to stable structures in fixed locations separated these merchants from itinerant peddlers and other vendors. Market vendors were allowed to erect their stalls only in areas designated as marketplaces. Certain trades, for example, bakers and smiths, congregated in particular neighborhoods, often located on the edge of the city, for safety reasons or because such locations made it easier to get needed supplies. Shopkeepers, in contrast, scattered freely, and opened their doors anywhere and everywhere in the city.

Their shops offered a variety of goods to a variety of customers. Some sold necessities of limited value, catering to the needs of a poorer clientele. It is thought that the well-to-do of medieval cities visited local markets to purchase from foreign merchants, who could supply higher-quality goods in larger quantities over longer periods of time. Some shopkeepers, however, imported wares of various sorts: spices, wax, metalwares, faience, and silks. Their shops tended to be general stores that offered luxury commodities to wealthier patrons. The tremendous variation in quality and quantity of wares led to a no less tremendous variation in income and status among the shopkeepers of any given city. In Augsburg, once again, analysis of tax records from the early seventeenth century indicate that shopkeepers were distributed evenly across the economic scale, from 13 percent reckoned "have-nothings" to 11 percent reckoned wealthy. A similar range of income distribution has been identified for shopkeepers in seventeenth-century Dutch cities, including Amsterdam, as well as mercers in eighteenth-century Paris. It stands to reason that shops providing luxury goods to elite customers would be more profitable than their common counterparts, trading in daily or popular items. Nor would such distinctions be limited geographically.

Given the wide variation in degrees of prosperity among shopkeepers, it is not surprising to find hierarchies developing among them. Nor were these limited to their wealth or the quality of their wares and patrons. Unlike many craft and trade guilds, shopkeepers were a diverse group. Economic development during the late Middle Ages and early modern period created ever more distinctions based on ever-greater specialization. In general, there was a clear line of demarcation between shopkeepers and grocers, retailers who trafficked in foodstuffs. Shopkeeping tended to resolve itself further into various subspecialties based on types of commodities: those who trafficked in herbs and spices, in cloth and clothing, or in iron and metal. They began to discriminate among themselves according to sale by weight as opposed to measure. Further divisions arose between those who sold new and those who sold used goods. This internal differentiation, which becomes visible in the late fifteenth or early sixteenth century, eventually separated the various specialty shops from one another, ironmongers from apothecaries and so forth. The tendency toward specialization should not distract from the general observation that most early modern shopkeepers, whether rich or poor, sold whatever they could.

Generally speaking, however, whether a shopkeeper was impecunious or prosperous, his wares cheap or expensive, his customers poor or rich, his specialty one thing or nothing, he was not allowed to sell locally produced goods, a ban that preserved the rights of local producers to sell their own products. This prohibition was commonly placed on shopkeepers and indicates the near universal competition between local producers and retailers, a competition that led to frequent conflicts in the late Middle Ages and early modern period. The necessary engagement of some shopkeepers in the import trade, to say nothing of the relative prosperity some achieved, has led some scholars to postulate the origins of international commerce in domestic shopkeeping. Superior shopkeepers, acting for themselves or as factors for consortia of shopkeepers, visited foreign marketplaces and fairs to buy goods wholesale while other household members minded their shops.

Shops and shopkeeping expanded significantly in the early modern period, a reflection of the general development of the economy toward increased production, distribution, and consumption of goods that has led scholars to speak of a retail revolution or a consumption revolution in early modern Europe as a whole. The increasing number of shops was often the most tangible evidence of economic growth and social change to early modern Europeans. In 1606, the Spanish playwright Lope de Vega's observation that in Madrid "everything has become shops" took note of this development. In London, Daniel Defoe observed that "mercers" (sellers of expensive fabrics) had increased "monstrously" from roughly fifty to as many as four hundred in the second half of the seventeenth century. By 1789, excise commissioners reckoned that Britain possessed over 141,000 retail outlets, of which all but 21,600 were located in London. In 1774, Justus Möser cited the increase in the number of mercers in the German city of Osnabrück by a factor of three, while the number of artisans had decreased by half, as evidence of economic modernization, the transition from an economy marked by local self-sufficiency to one of market connection. Similar increases occurred in Holland and France, more specifically Amsterdam and Paris.

This growth has attracted new attention and appreciation among scholars. The growth of the European population spurred a corresponding growth in the European economy. As the supply of goods and the number of consumers increased, retailers recognized the advantages of fixed points of distribution. These made possible longer business hours, stable customer relations, and improved business communication, among other things. As a result, distribution networks became more extensive and the distribution of goods became more intensive. Abraham Dent of Kirkby Stephen in Westmorland, for example, drew goods from 190 suppliers in 51 locations. By so doing, he and his peers throughout Europe provided access to goods

and services that would otherwise be available only in major cities. As John Brewer noted, "Shopkeepers linked market towns and local communities to a network of markets that stretched beyond the nation's boundaries and across oceans and continents." Shops and shopkeeping contributed directly, therefore, to the growth of the European economy by providing sales outlets for increasingly efficient forms of production and by promoting consumption even at the lowest levels of society. They provided the necessary infrastructure for a consumer revolution that reached all parts of early modern Europe and linked those parts to a wider world.

They provided another crucial service as well. Shopkeepers were an essential source of credit for individual consumers. Indeed, they existed in a unique credit nexus. On the one hand, shopkeepers received credit from wholesalers, whom they paid in installments for purchased inventories. At the same time, they granted credit to customers, who were forced to run a "tab" between paydays. Living on and off credit made shopkeeping a risky business. Should a customer fail to pay on time, or a distributor demand payment in advance, the entire fragile complex could come crashing down. There is some evidence to suggest that many early modern bankruptcies involved shopkeepers caught in such ruptures. Shops and shopkeeping nonetheless played a crucial role in supplying credit to consumers who might otherwise have been unable to make purchases. By so doing, they further increased the speed and extent of the circulation of goods. Yet next to nothing has been written about it. As important as they are now understood to be in the larger history of European economic development, as crucial as they were in promoting demand—that is, in shaping taste—shops and shopkeeping await a history of their own. Too little is known about the wholesale networks that supplied these fixed points of sale. If these shops trafficked only in imported goods, in order to protect local producers, who were the wholesalers and what was their place in local and regional economies? Too little is known about the expansion of shopkeeping itself. The established explanation reads like the triumph of modern consumption and convenience. Could the rise of shopkeeping have another side?

Shopkeeping was a far easier trade to enter than other sectors of the manufacturing economy. Because it required no artisanal skills, no laborious period of training and certification was necessary, and little start-up capital was needed. Any ground-floor space, including a rented room, might serve, and inventories could be obtained with no money down and payment by installments. And, it required a relatively low level of experience to operate, though a great deal of experience to operate successfully, allowing a shopkeeper's family to lend a hand in a wide range of shopkeeping activities. The efforts of women and children, often extended by the presence of servants in the more prosperous houses, kept the shops running in the all-too-frequent absence of the shopkeepers. Shopkeeping provided, therefore, an important by-employment for many households. In Holland, sailors' families often ran shops to provide income while their men were at sea. Likewise, it provided a source of employment for households headed by females. Studies of eighteenth-century Amsterdam reveal that one in seven households were headed by women, some 30 percent of whom were shopkeepers. Taking these conditions into account might explain why the trade of shopkeeping expanded so rapidly. In a growing economy that displaced so many people, retail selling attracted many economically marginal individuals. They could afford it: they needed no particular skills, no particular resources. That same marginality may explain the extraordinary number of failures. They could not afford it for long without good skills and good fortune: the least bad luck or bad management could drive them into default.

The general rise of shopkeeping—whether the result of economic growth or ease of access or both—meant that the number of shopkeepers rose in most cities and towns. Numbers gave them a political potency beyond the relative prosperity of individuals. In many cities, shopkeepers, together with members of other trades that involved more specialized forms of retailing, such as the hatters, cutlers, purse makers, lace makers, and brush makers, formed one of the largest and, therefore, most influential guilds. Paris on the eve of the French Revolution was home to no fewer than four thousand mercers. Nor was their political role necessarily limited to guild representation or population size.

General stores served a social as well as an economic function. People gathered in them not only to buy but also to meet. They took care of their daily needs and exchanged the daily news. Shops provided a place for a wide range of interaction and exchange, including political discussion. It should not be surprising, therefore, if shopkeepers played a prominent role in the rebellions and revolutions that rocked early modern Europe. The sans-culottes, for example, recruited heavily from among Parisian shopkeepers during the French Revolution. Although the political function of coffeehouses and taverns is well known, a corresponding history of shops and shopkeeping has yet to be written.

See also **Artisans; Capitalism; Clothing; Commerce and Markets; Consumption; Guilds; Mobility, Social; Political Secularization; Sumptuary Laws; Trading Companies.**

BIBLIOGRAPHY

Alexander, David. *Retailing in England during the Industrial Revolution.* London, 1970.

Below, Georg von. *Probleme der Wirtschaftsgeschichte: Eine Einführung in das Studium der Wirtschaftsgeschichte.* Tübingen, 1920.

Braudel, Fernand. *The Wheels of Commerce.* Translated by Siân Reynolds. 3 vols. London and New York, 1982.

Brewer, John. *The Sinews of Power: War, Money and the English State, 1688–1783.* New York, 1989.

Brewer, John, and Roy Porter, eds. *Consumption and the World of Goods.* London, 1993.

Bücher, Karl. *Die Berufe der Stadt Frankfurt am Main im Mittelalter.* Leipzig, 1914.

Clasen, Claus-Peter. "Arm und Reich in Augsburg vor dem Dreißigjärigen Krieg." In *Geschichte der Stadt Augsburg: 2000 Jahre von der Römerzeit bis zur Gegenwart,* edited by Gunther Gottlieb, Wolfram Baer, and Josef Becker, pp. 312–336. Stuttgart, 1985.

Davis, Dorothy. *A History of Shopping.* London, 1966.

Defoe, Daniel. *The Complete English Tradesman.* New York, 1970.

De Vries, Jan, and Ad van der Woude. *The First Modern Economy: Success, Failure and Perseverance of the Dutch Economy, 1500–1815.* Cambridge, U.K., 1997.

King, Gregory. "Natural and Political Observations and Conclusions upon the State and Condition of England." In *Two Tracts by Gregory King.* Edited by George A. Barnett. Baltimore, 1936.

Lütge, Friedrich. *Deutsche Sozial- und Wirtschaftsgeschichte: ein Überblick.* Berlin, 1952.

Mauersberg, Hans. *Wirtschafts- und Sozialgeschichte zentraleuropäischer Städte in neuerer Zeit.* Göttingen, 1960.

Soboul, Alfred. *Les sans-culottes parisiens en l'an II: Mouvement populaire et gouvernement révolutionnaire, 2 juin 1793–1799, Thermidor An II.* Paris, 1958.

Sombart, Werner. *Der moderne Kapitalismus.* 2 vols. Munich and Leipzig, 1916–1919.

Wrightson, Keith. *Earthly Necessities: Economic Lives in Early Modern Britain.* New Haven, 2000.

THOMAS MAX SAFLEY

SICKNESS AND DISEASE. *See* Medicine; Public Health.

SIDNEY, PHILIP (1554–1586), English poet, courtier, and statesman. Born at Penshurst (Kent) to Sir Henry Sidney, viceroy of Ireland, and Lady Mary Dudley, sister of Queen Elizabeth's favorite, the earl of Leicester, Sidney was educated at Shrewsbury and Christ Church, Oxford, and then sent on a three-year tour of the Continent in 1572. In Paris he made the acquaintance of Sir Francis Walsingham, the English ambassador (whose daughter Frances he was to marry in 1583), and of Hubert Languet, an older Huguenot political observer who became his friend and mentor. Narrowly escaping the St. Bartholomew's Day Massacre of 24 August 1572, Sidney spent a year at the University of Padua, and then traveled the Continent from Florence to Cracow.

Back in England (1575), he represented his father at court, and in 1577 was chosen to head a congratulatory embassy to the new Emperor Rudolph II, secretly exploring possibilities for a Protestant coalition against the pope's Holy League. That project came to nothing, but Sidney acquitted himself brilliantly.

The next few years saw him cutting a dash at court and writing a masque, *The Lady of May* (1578), with Queen Elizabeth in a deciding role (the masque was written in such a form that at the end the queen was given the role of deciding which suitor the Lady of May should accept). When in 1579 Spanish successes revived the project of the queen's French marriage, the court's alarmed Prot-

estants chose Sidney to write an open letter dissuading her from wedding the duke of Alençon. He also quarreled with the dissolute earl of Oxford, one of the marriage's supporters, was rebuked by the queen on grounds of rank (even though Sidney was in the right, in a quarrel with an earl, a mere gentleman should give way), and withdrew for a year to Wilton, the country manor of his sister Mary, the countess of Pembroke. Here he began his three major literary works, the treatise *A Defence of Poesy,* the prose romance *Arcadia,* and the sonnet sequence *Astrophil and Stella.* ("Astrophel" is the spelling long used, but the consensus among most modern scholars is that the double pun of "Astrophil" is too good not to have been intended. He is the "Astro-phile"—the Star-Lover—and his name is "PHIL-ip.")

The graceful *Defence* (c. 1580, published 1595; also called *The Apologie for Poetrie*) adapts Continental literary concepts to English conditions. Imitating a legal speech for the defense, it claims for "poesy" (imaginative writing) the highest role in moral education, and passionately defends the poet's faculty of "invention" which makes poesy, alone among human arts and sciences, the equal of creating Nature, under the overall authority of God.

Astrophil and Stella (c. 1581, published 1591), based upon but not tied to Sidney's love for Penelope Devereux, Lady Rich, uses the *Defence*'s principle of energia (liveliness or poesy's power to "move" its readers) dramatically to revive the 250-year-old Petrarchan sonnet sequence. Its rhetoric movingly dissects the way esteem becomes love, love becomes desire, and desire eventually undermines true love. Its vitality created a wave of English sonnet sequences and influenced John Donne (1573–1631) and his followers George Herbert, Henry Vaughan, Richard Crashaw, Thomas Traherne, Thomas Carew, and Andrew Marvell.

The *Arcadia,* begun in 1580 and written initially for his sister Mary, also adapts Continental models, especially Jacopo Sannazaro's "Arcadia" (1504) and Jorge de Montemayor's "Diana" (c. 1559). Its adventures of two princes, Musidorus and Pyrocles, in combat and in love (with the princesses Pamela and Philoclea), are interspersed with eclogues in which shepherds' singing matches become virtuoso poetic experiments. This first version, now known as the *Old Arcadia,* only circulated in manuscript, and was then lost until 1908.

Sidney's later revision, now known as the *New Arcadia,* remained unfinished at his death. It was subsequently completed with the ending of the old and issued as a composite (1593): this became the *Arcadia* read until the twentieth century. The *New Arcadia* consistently moves toward greater narrative complexity and less frivolity: it is a more "serious" work, concerned with principles of both public and private (self-) government.

The early 1580s saw Sidney engrossed in preparations for war with Spain and writing more religious works: he versified the first forty-three Psalms (later magnificently completed by his sister Mary), and began a translation of Guillaume de Salluste du Bartas' *La semaine* (1578; The week) on the Creation (since lost), as well as an English version of his French friend Philippe Duplessis-Mornay's work *The Trewnesse of the Christian Religion* (completed by Arthur Golding).

As Spain advanced in the Netherlands, Elizabeth finally sent troops; in return for English military aid, the queen and her government asked for three forts and fortified towns to be garrisoned by English troops and held as sureties for the repayment. In 1585, Sidney was made governor of Flushing, chief of these three cautionary places. With Prince Maurice of Orange, Sidney stormed the town of Axel, and in the autumn of 1586 helped besiege Zutphen, on the Spanish supply corridor that ran from Franche-Comté through Burgundy to the Netherlands. On 22 September 1586, against heavy odds the English attacked a Spanish column that was coming to relieve Zutphen. Sidney was wounded in the thigh, and three weeks later, at the age of thirty-one, he died of gangrene at Arnhem. He became an instant hero and in February 1587 was buried in St. Paul's Cathedral in London, receiving the grandest funeral of any private Englishman until Winston Churchill's in 1965.

Sidney, the statesman, courtier, and convinced Protestant, is most remembered as a poet. He was a profoundly serious man, yet of great charm; a passionate man, yet deeply religious and filled with the morality of politics; a reflective man, yet a skilled and daring soldier when the occasion came. His friend Duplessis-Mornay's motto *Arte et Marte* ("by art and Mars") applies equally to Sidney.

See also **Elizabeth I (England); English Literature and Language.**

BIBLIOGRAPHY

Primary Sources

Sidney, Sir Philip. *The Countess of Pembroke's Arcadia: The New Arcadia.* Edited by Victor Skretkowicz. Oxford, 1974.

——. *The Countess of Pembroke's Arcadia: The Old Arcadia.* Edited by Jean Robertson. Oxford, 1973.

——. *Miscellaneous Prose.* Edited by Jan van Dorsten and Katherine Duncan-Jones. Oxford, 1973.

——. *The Poems of Sir Philip Sidney.* Edited by William A. Ringler, Jr. Oxford, 1962.

Secondary Sources

Hamilton, A. C. *Sir Philip Sidney: A Study of His Life and Works.* Cambridge, U.K., and New York, 1977. Classic study of both life and work, and of their interaction.

Kalstone, David. *Sidney's Poetry: Contexts and Interpretations.* Cambridge, Mass., 1965. Well-balanced analysis of the secular poetry.

Stewart, Alan. *Sir Philip Sidney: A Double Life.* London, 2000. Excellent study especially of Sidney's political career.

ROGER KUIN

SIGISMUND II AUGUSTUS (POLAND, LITHUANIA)

(1520–1572; ruled 1530–1572), last of the Jagiellon kings of Poland and grand duke of Lithuania (from 1529). Under pressure from his parents, King Sigismund I the Old and Bona Sforza, Sigismund was made grand duke of Lithuania and elected king of Poland (coronation on 20 February 1530) in his father's lifetime, which was contrary to the law then in force. In 1543 he was married to Elizabeth of Habsburg (daughter of the emperor Ferdinand I), who suffered from epilepsy and died childless in 1545. In 1543–1548 he stayed in the Grand Duchy of Lithuania, dealing with the problems of that country and hunting with relish. It was then that he fell in love with Barbara Radziwiłł and married her secretly (1547), which provoked a hostile response in the country. After the death of his father (1548) he returned to Cracow and took up his royal duties. At the Sejm held in 1548–1549 a conflict arose between the king and some magnates and nobleman over his marriage to Barbara.

Throughout the 1550s the king, supported by the most powerful magnate families, opposed the nobility's call for the enforcement of laws demanding a ban on the holding of multiple public offices by one person (the so-called *incompatibilitas*); the return of royal estates given away or pawned by previous rulers, mainly to magnates (which had impoverished the state treasury and led to the amassing of enormous fortunes); freedom of religion; and the unification of the laws of Poland and the Grand Duchy. The king was also against a stronger union between Poland and the Grand Duchy of Lithuania. It was only in the 1560s that he changed his internal policy; this was partly due to the impending war with Russia, which required joint Polish-Lithuanian military measures and the support of the nobility. From 1562 to 1569 the Sejm, supported by the king, passed several significant resolutions: most importantly, it concluded a Polish-Lithuanian Union (1569); other resolutions provided for the return of royal estates, reformed the financing of the standing army, and curbed the holding of multiple offices of state.

Sigismund also concurred with politicians and humanists who proposed to guarantee religious toleration; this was reflected in the edict banning trials for heresy (1570) and, after the king's death, in the Compact of Warsaw (1573), which guaranteed peace between followers of different religions and granted dissidents equal rights with Catholics. Sigismund was the first European ruler to accept the decisions of the Council of Trent (1564), although the Sejm did not confirm them until 1577. He also deserves credit for a great land reform carried out in the royal estates in the Grand Duchy of Lithuania in 1557–1566.

Sigismund strengthened relations with the Habsburgs by the treaty of Prague (1549) and in 1553 concluded a peace with Turkey. Livonia became an important question for the king's policy; after the secularization of the Order of the Brothers of the Sword, which ruled there, he took Livonia under his rule and protection. In 1563 a war for Livonia broke out with Russia; it was brought to an end by an armistice (1570), but the conflict was not resolved. Sigismund also took part in the rivalry for

the Baltic, and during his reign the nucleus of a royal navy was created, and a Maritime Commission, the first Polish maritime office and law court, was set up (1568). Sigismund committed a grave mistake, however, and one with far-reaching consequences, when he granted the Brandenburg line of the Hohenzollerns the right of succession to the Duchy of Prussia (1563).

Sigismund Augustus was a patron of writers, a music lover, a collector of arrases, and the founder of the first large royal library in Poland. After the early death of Barbara (1551), the king, pressed by advisers who wanted to see an heir to the throne, married Catherine of Austria, daughter of the emperor Ferdinand I; this was an unhappy, childless marriage, ending in separation in 1563. Sigismund's death meant the extinction of the male line of the Jagiellonian dynasty. He was buried in the cathedral on Wawel Hill.

See also **Jagiellon Dynasty (Poland-Lithuania); Livonian War (1558–1583); Lublin, Union of (1569); Poland-Lithuania, Commonwealth of, 1569–1795; Reformations in Eastern Europe: Protestant, Catholic, and Orthodox.**

BIBLIOGRAPHY

Cynarski, Stanisław. *Zygmunt August*. Rev. ed. Wrocław, 1997.

Kolankowski, Ludwik. *Zygmunt August, wielki książę Litwy, do roku 1548*. Lwów, 1913.

Sucheni-Grabowska, Anna. *Zygmunt August, król polski i wielki książę litewski, 1520–1562*. Warsaw, 1996.

MARCIN KAMLER

SILESIA. Because of their considerable regional variety, the principalities of Silesia became important locations for power politics, and Silesia played an integral role in the political, economic, and cultural systems within the lands governed by the crown of Bohemia. It is possible to understand many of the integrating and disintegrating trends in European history through the example of Silesia. Its history contains many parallels with the development of Bohemia, but it also has important differences. For a long period the interests of the Piast, Jagiellon, Přemysl (Opava), Luxembourg, Habsburg, and Hohenzollern dynasties in the region complicated Silesia's relationship with the Bohemian crown.

In the late Middle Ages the seemingly marginal Silesian territory demonstrated its economic and strategic importance and highlighted the extent of the religious and political changes taking place in the northern part of the Czech state. Many Silesians wielded extraordinary political influence in central Europe (for example, Prince Casimir II, duke of Teschen; Victor, duke of Münsterberg; Frederick II, duke of Legnica; George, duke of Brandenburg-Ansbach-Krnov; George John Brandenburg-Krnov; John II, duke of Opole; Charles, duke of Münsterberg). On the other hand, the princes of Silesia were feudal subjects of the Bohemian king, and at times their differences with the crown drew them into the camp of Bohemia's Czech adversaries. In the sixteenth century a clear turn took place in the policy of Silesian princes and estates in their relations with the kingdom of Bohemia and the margravate of Moravia, leading to various kinds of cooperation. By compromising on religious differences (there was a religious allowance between Catholic Silesia and Hussite Bohemia), Bohemia gradually escaped from its post-Hussite provincial isolation in all spheres of life. In the power struggle against Hungarian and Polish interests, Silesia in the end maintained its constitutional place among the lands of the crown of Bohemia.

The turbulent social and political history of the estates of Bohemia involved Silesia as well. The tensions between the Habsburg Catholic minority and the Protestant opposition of the estates found expression in nearly all of the Silesian principalities, and as a result the traditional hierarchical principles of Bohemian and Silesian society and the rules of political engagement were disrupted. When Ferdinand I mounted the throne of Bohemia in 1526, Silesia was undergoing a wave of religious reformation, which, unlike the Hussite movement, was fully accepted by the majority of the population. A major role in this process was played by certain princes (the Krnov Hohenzollerns and the Piasts of Legnica-Brzeg), who through the descendants of George of Podebrady (ruled 1458–1471) aspired to the throne of Bohemia. In 1537 they concluded an important family contract with the Hohenzollern elector of Brandenburg to secure inheritance and cooperation in protecting the Protestant religion.

After 1523 the Breslau town council also introduced Lutheran preachers into the town's churches. Considered politically, these religious changes aligned Silesia with the Bohemian "heretics."

Of the Silesian princes, by the mid-sixteenth century only the bishop of Breslau, resident in Nysa, remained loyal to the Catholic faith, and he mainly concentrated on the struggle with the Polish churchmen in Gniezno to achieve the independence of his diocese. In competition with the Protestant princes, the bishops of Breslau lost their position of power at the turn of the seventeenth century, and it was only after the Thirty Years' War that they regained their preeminence.

After the uprising of the Bohemian estates in 1618–1620 (the Bohemian War that marks the beginning of the Thirty Years' War), and especially after the Danish units were defeated in Silesia, major social changes erupted, even at the periphery of a Bohemia that was now dominated by Habsburg absolutism, centralism, and Catholicism. The new Silesian power elites were recruited from the bureaucracy, the army, and the imperial court (such as Charles, duke of Liechtenstein; John Weikhard, duke of Auersperg; and Albrecht Wallenstein/Waldstein). For more than a century the tone of political life was set by representatives of these newly successful noble families, who patiently built up their wealth and who even more importantly had no ties to the rebellious and centrifugal noble estates of prewar Silesia-Bohemia.

From the late Middle Ages on, the cultural and religious development of Silesia was strongly influenced by German scholars and artists and by those from other neighboring countries, including Martin Luther, John Calvin, Philipp Melanchthon, Balthasar Hubmaier, and Jan Hus. A decisive role was also played by the economic and social network of an area which, along with the regional capital of Breslau, was one of the most important parts of the Czech state. A wide range of religious opinions existed side by side, along with a rich variety in the realms of art and literature based on the cultural maturity of the German, Jewish, Polish, and Czech populations. Silesia's literary and artistic production testified to the fact that its society was open to the outside world, enabling it to contribute considerably to the treasury of European civilization.

The margraves and electors of Brandenburg introduced a split in Silesia during the early modern period. The Hohenzollerns of Brandenburg wanted to rule Lower Silesia and the region of Crossen, while the Ansbach line of the same house struggled to form a family enclave in the territory of Upper Silesia, especially in the regions of Opole, Racibórz, Krnov, Bytom, and Bohumín. The creation of Hohenzollern possessions in Silesia and their stabilization alongside the properties of the Opava Přemysl family, the Saxony Wettins, the Silesian Piasts, and the descendants of King George of Podebrady became a political reality. In the first half of the sixteenth century, it could not have been foreseen that the existence of the Hohenzollern power in the Oder region would become a stepping-stone for Prussian militarist expansion in the eighteenth century under Frederick II and would eventually lead to the division of Silesia after 1740 in the Wars of the Austrian Succession.

See also **Bohemia; Frederick II (Prussia); Hohenzollern Dynasty; Hussites.**

BIBLIOGRAPHY

Bahlcke, Joachim, ed. *Schlesien und die Schlesier*. Munich, 1996.

Grünhagen, Colmar. *Geschichte Schlesiens*. 2 vols. Gotha, Germany, 1884–1886. Reprint, Osnabrück, Germany, 1979.

Maleczyński, Karol, ed. *Historia Śląska*. 3 vols. Wrocław, Warsaw, and Cracow, 1961–1963.

Petry, Ludwig, ed. *Geschichte Schlesiens*. 2 vols. Sigmaringen, Germany, 1988.

Weber, Matthias, and Carsten Rabe, eds. *Silesiographia: Stand und Perspektiven der historischen Schlesienforschung*. Würzburg, Germany, 1998.

RADEK FUKALA

SILESIAN WARS. *See* **Austrian Succession, War of the (1740–1748).**

SINAN (Sinan bin Abdulmennan, c. 1489–1588), chief court architect of the Ottoman dynasty from 1538 until his death; his works defined the architectural style of the Ottoman Empire in the sixteenth century. Born to Greek parents in a central Anatolian village, he converted to Islam and was recruited into the elite Ottoman janissary corps in the 1510s and trained as a carpenter. In his autobiography he noted that the military campaigns he took part in founded his architectural knowledge. In these campaigns he worked on the construction of several military structures, and he learned from the architectural monuments he encountered.

The fifty years that composed Sinan's career as chief court architect correspond to the reigns of three sultans, Suleiman (ruled 1520–1566), Selim II (ruled 1566–1574), and Murad III (ruled 1574–1595), and to the peak of Ottoman political power. As builder of the major architectural monuments of the Ottoman dynasty and ruling elite, he helped to create and spread the imperial court culture that was consolidated throughout the second half of the sixteenth century.

As chief architect, Sinan was designer and overseer of all building activity of the centralized Ottoman court, hence the large number of buildings (between 344 and 422) he claimed to have built. Although Sinan's many imperial, religious, educational, commercial, and civic structures were dispersed throughout the vast empire and made a myth out of his long career, his major works are located in Istanbul, the Ottoman capital, and in Edirne and Damascus, cities of importance to the dynasty.

Ottoman architecture inherited architectural typologies from the medieval Islamic world. It also reflected aspects of the Greco-Roman and Byzantine architectural legacies of western Asia Minor from the previous two centuries: a cellular and additive notion of design, based on domed cubic volumes, shaped buildings of ashlar (a type of hewn stone) and masonry in various scales. Sinan transformed this legacy. His centralized schemes integrated various volumes through a complex interplay of architectural elements. A hemispherical dome supported by half domes, smaller domes, and vaults defined the superstructure; this system of vaulting determined the external massing and the interior space of the building. A masterly use of windows allowed natural light to accentuate all of these features. Externalization of the structural order and exploration of the plastic possibilities of stone marked important Sinan buildings.

The three buildings that Sinan singled out as his masterworks also marked important stages in his career; these buildings exhibit Sinan's relationship with a series of architectural traditions and concepts of design. The Şehzade Mosque (1548–1549), built for the crown prince Mehmed, son of Suleiman the Magnificent, features a perfectly centralized scheme of a square prayer hall covered by a hemispherical dome rising on four half domes in a quatrefoil design reminiscent of Leonardo da Vinci's drawings for centralized churches. The mosque of Suleiman the Magnificent (1557), centerpiece of the largest socioreligious compound in Istanbul, is an Ottoman interpretation of the Hagia Sophia. The Selimiye Mosque in Edirne (1574–1575), with its immense dome held by an octagonal support system, sums up a career of explorations with domed spaces wherein attached or freestanding piers disengage a domed canopy from surrounding walls, turning the latter into luminous membranes pierced by numerous windows.

While monumental mosques were the primary symbols of Ottoman power, and therefore constitute Sinan's primary works, a series of lesser structures embody other aspects of his architectural style. Dynastic mausoleums exhibit novel interpretations of polygonal, double-shelled commemorative structures from the early Islamic era and medieval Iran; a hospital and a college, built for Suleiman's wife Haseki Hurrem and the grand vizier Rustem Pasha, interpret a fifteenth-century scheme with an octagonal courtyard. A number of aqueducts reflect Sinan's engineering skills and mastery in sculptural articulation. The Çoban Mustafa Pasha Bridge in Svilengrad (1529) and the Drina Bridge in Visegrad (1578) are among his important engineering works in the Balkans.

Sinan's contribution to the urban environment was his method of relating buildings to their immediate urban context as well as to the larger cityscape. His building complexes were laid out in multiaxial arrangements that offered multiple views of urban space, creating varying spatial experiences and dramatic encounters with buildings. These buildings also contributed to the creation of Istanbul's imperial image, as the city's famed silhouette was consolidated through these constructions.

Sinan was called the "Euclid of the times" by his contemporaries. Modern commentators have noted the rational architectural sensibility and predilection for centralized schemes he shared with architects of the Italian Renaissance.

See also **Constantinople; Janissary; Ottoman Dynasty; Ottoman Empire.**

BIBLIOGRAPHY

Primary Source

Sai Mustafa Çelebi. *Mimar Sinan and Tezkiret-ül Bünyan.* Edited by Metin Sözen and Suphi Saatçi. Translated by Georgina Özer. Istanbul, 1989. Translation of *Tezkiretü'l-Bünyan.*

Secondary Sources

Kuban, Doğan. *Sinan's Art and Selimiye.* Istanbul, 1997.

Kuran, Aptullah. *Sinan: The Grand Old Master of Ottoman Architecture.* Washington, D.C., and Istanbul, 1987.

Necipoğlu, Gülru. "Challenging the Past: Sinan and the Competitive Discourse of Early Modern Islamic Architecture." *Muqarnas: An Annual on Islamic Art and Architecture* 10 (1993): 169–180.

ÇIĞDEM KAFESCIOĞLU

SIXTUS V (POPE) (b. 1520, reigned 1585–1590), Felice Peretti, born 13 December at Grottammare, near Montalto, March of Ancona. A farmer's son, educated by the Conventual Franciscans at Montalto, he joined the order at age twelve and received training at Fermo, Ferrara, Bologna, Rimini, and Siena before his ordination in 1547; he received a doctorate in theology from Fermo in 1548. Peretti's Lenten preaching at Rome in 1552 brought him notoriety, and he entered papal service as a member of Paul IV's (pope 1555–1559) reform commissions. During his service as inquisitor for Venice (1557–1559), he so vigorously enforced the Index of Prohibited Books of Paul IV that he was forced to flee the city. Appointed consultor of the Roman Inquisition in 1560, made vicar-general of the Franciscans and bishop of Sant'Agata dei Goti in Benevento in 1566, he was elevated to cardinal by Pius V (pope 1566–1572) in 1570 and transferred to become bishop of Fermo (1571–1577). Because of disagreements with Gregory XIII (reigned 1572–1585), Peretti (now known as Cardinal Montalto) withdrew to the Esquiline Hill, where he worked in obscurity on an edition of St. Ambrose's writings.

Supported by a strong minority of reform-minded cardinals, he was elected pope on 24 April 1585.

Sixtus's five-year pontificate was significant internationally for his support of Catholic monarchs against Protestantism and for rallying (unsuccessfully) Christian princes against the Turks to recapture the Holy Land. He promised Philip II of Spain (ruled 1556–1598) monetary aid for his invasion of England, but after the Armada's ruin in 1588, he reneged and battled him, diplomatically at least, until the end of his life. Sixtus refused to recognize the right to the throne of French king Henry of Navarre (Henry IV, ruled 1589–1610), whom he excommunicated in 1585, as long as the king remained a Huguenot; Sixtus later encouraged Henry to return to Catholicism to resolve the religious wars in France. In Poland, he assisted Stephen Báthory (ruled 1575–1586) against Russia, and Sigismund III Vasa (ruled 1587–1632) of Sweden as Báthory's successor. His relations with the Holy Roman emperor Rudolf II (ruled 1576–1612) deteriorated, though he succeeded in putting in place a plan for the restoration of Catholicism in the empire.

Sixtus ruled the Papal States with severity, extirpating bandits, executing them publicly and punishing their protectors; but his severity also roused the anger of many fellow Franciscans, clergy, Romans, and others. He established public funds (monti) for carrying out public works; he drained swamps, promoted the wool and silk industries and agriculture, increased taxation, and reduced expenses. At his death he left over five million scudi in the papal treasury.

Sixtus is perhaps best remembered for his reorganization of the administration of the Curia Romana into fifteen congregations (nine for the spiritual affairs of the church, the others for the administration of Rome and the Papal States). He fixed the number of cardinals at seventy. The result made clear that the Sacred College's function was to offer advice and help, not to corule with the pope. Sixtus mandated that bishops visit Rome and submit regular reports on their dioceses. At Rome, his massive public works included road construction linking the seven pilgrimage churches, setting them off with obelisks crowned with crosses, the most prominent being that erected in Saint Peter's

Square by Domenico Fontana (1586). He continued work on Saint Peter's Basilica, refurbished the Lateran Basilica and the Quirinal Palace, built the new wing for the Vatican Library, rejuvenated the University of Rome (Sapienza), repaired the aqueduct of Alexander Severus to bring fresh waters (aqua felice) to the Esquiline, and saw the completion of Michelangelo's dome for Saint Peter's. Sixtus died on 27 August 1590. His remains lie in the Basilica of Santa Maria Maggiore, where they were translated on 26 August 1591.

See also **Index of Prohibited Books; Inquisition, Roman; Papacy and Papal States.**

BIBLIOGRAPHY

Pastor, Ludwig von. *The History of the Popes from the Close of the Middle Ages.* Vols. 21 and 22. Translated by Ralph Francis Kerr. St. Louis, 1952.

Schiffmann, René. *Roma felix: Aspekte der städtebaulichen Gestaltung Roms unter Papst Sixtus V.* Bern and New York, 1985.

FREDERICK J. McGINNESS

SKEPTICISM: ACADEMIC AND PYRRHONIAN.

Skepticism dogged claimants to knowledge and truth throughout early modern Europe. In its most general sense it refers to uncertainty, doubt, disbelief, suspension of judgment, and rejection of claims to knowledge. It is characterized by its opposition to dogmatism, which means the holding of firm beliefs (from Greek *dogmata*) about truth and reality. As a philosophical stance it is best understood as the outcome of two traditions in ancient Greek philosophy. Academic skepticism was attributed to Socrates and to Plato's successors at the Academy in Athens (fifth to second centuries B.C.E.), and Pyrrhonism was traced back to Pyrrho of Elis (c. 365–275 B.C.E.).

ACADEMIC SKEPTICISM

Roman statesman and philosopher Marcus Tullius Cicero (106–43 B.C.E.) is our chief source for Academic skepticism. In his *Academica* (45 B.C.E.) he reported on the teachings of Arcesilaus (315–240 B.C.E.) and Carneades (214–129 B.C.E.), who were heads of the Academy, and he claimed allegiance to the Academic school. St. Augustine's earliest extant work was entitled *Contra Academicos* (386 C.E.;

Against the academics), and this polemic was an important source of knowledge about Academic skepticism.

Placing Socrates at the origins of skepticism turns on the argument that he only asked questions and did not teach positive doctrines. Plato and Aristotle strayed from the path when they claimed to know the truth. Arcesilaus gave renewed vigor to skepticism, arguing against the opinions of all men, as Cicero put it. But he also showed that skeptics could make choices by relying on the *eulogon* (the reasonable) in the absence of truth. Carneades, who was also a master of arguing on both sides of every issue, refined this into the standard of the *pithanon* (the credible). In Cicero's translation into Latin, this became *probabile,* which set the stage for the skeptics' claim to live by the probable in the absence of truth.

Cicero's *Academica* was read by some thinkers in the Middle Ages but does not seem to have had a major impact. It was first printed at Rome in 1471, and numerous commentaries and annotations followed. More than one hundred editions had been published by 1600.

One of the first to take Academic skepticism seriously was Dutch Humanist Desiderius Erasmus (1466?–1536), who expressed admiration for the Academics in his *Praise of Folly* (1511), provoking opposition from Christian scholars like Philipp Melanchthon (1487–1560). Gianfrancesco Pico della Mirandola's *Examen Vanitatis* (1520) drew on both Cicero and Sextus Empiricus. Omer Talon emphasized the philosophical freedom from dogmatism of the Academics in his *Academia* of 1547, and Petrus Ramus praised their style and rhetoric in *Ciceronianus* of 1557. Both of these were attacked by Pierre Galland and Guy de Brués. Giulio Castellani defended Aristotelianism against Academic skepticism in *Adversus . . . Ciceronis* (1558), partly by showing empirically that disagreement was not as widespread as the skeptics claimed it was. Johannes Rosa published the most substantial early commentary on the *Academica* in German-speaking Europe in 1571, and Pedro de Valencia reconstructed Academic skepticism in his own *Academica* of 1596, showing that these ideas were available in Spain.

The publication of the works of Sextus Empiricus in the 1560s replaced Cicero's writings as the chief source of knowledge about ancient skepticism. In the following centuries most authors drew their inspiration from both sources to the extent that it is hard to speak of purely Academic skeptics after that point. One exception is David Hume (1711–1776), who has sometimes been called an Academic skeptic because—among other reasons—one of the characters in his *Dialogues concerning Natural Religion* (1779) takes the role of an Academic. There has also been scholarly debate about whether other individual early modern figures were Academic skeptics or Pyrrhonians, but in this period the two traditions were often run together, and few, if any, authors made a clear distinction between them.

PYRRHONISM

Our chief source for ancient Pyrrhonism is the work of the Alexandrian Greek physician Sextus Empiricus (second century C.E.), including *Outlines of Pyrrhonism* and *Against the Mathematicians.* A few manuscripts of Latin translations of Sextus Empiricus existed in medieval collections, and more came from Byzantium in the mid-fifteenth century. Florentine religious reformer Girolamo Savonarola (1452–1498) used Sextus to combat pagan philosophy. But the printing press made for the most influential dissemination of these texts. Latin translations by Henri Estienne (Stephanus) (1562) and Gentian Hervet (1569) provided the stimulus for a widespread "skeptical crisis."

As Sextus explained it, skepticism was not a philosophy but rather a way of life in which one opposed all philosophical claims with equal opposite claims (equipollence). He laid out standard tropes or formula arguments which could be used against any certainty or truth and which he attributed to Greek philosophers Aenesidemus (first century B.C.E.[?]) and Agrippa (first century B.C.E.[?]). The result was that one would suspend judgment and then find oneself in *ataraxia* or tranquillity, no longer disturbed by philosophical disputes. One would live in accordance with the phenomena or appearances without taking a stand on the truth or reality behind them, and one would follow one's natural impulses as well as local customs and laws.

Michel de Montaigne (1533–1592) was the most influential of the early writers to draw on the writings of Sextus, in his *Essais* (1580–1595). In a long chapter entitled "Defense of Raymond

Sebond," Montaigne retailed most of the skeptical tropes and all of the skeptical vocabulary from Sextus Empiricus. Here and in other essays he demolished any pretensions to human knowledge and argued both sides of almost every issue. And yet he never despaired; rather, he showed people how to live a happy life in the face of skepticism, which may explain why his writings were so popular.

Later philosophers often started from Montaigne. One who went far beyond in posing questions of skepticism was René Descartes (1596–1650). Without specific sources in the ancient materials, he set out to answer the skeptical idea that there could be an all-powerful *malin genie* or evil demon that controls our perceptions and reasoning and fools us about the world. His conclusion was that we know we exist because we can think—the famous "I think therefore I am." Pressed for an explanation as to why our perceptions of thinking could not be a deception, Descartes asserted that God would not allow such deception. Thus, religion is invoked to certify truth. Later skeptics would worry about a deceiving God.

Bishop Pierre Daniel Huet (1630–1721) and Huguenot refugee Pierre Bayle (1647–1706) have been described as the "master skeptics." Huet invoked Sextus Empiricus in great detail against Descartes and many other dogmatic philosophers in his *Traité de la foiblesse de l'esprit humaine* (1723; Tract on the weakness of the human mind). Bayle's massive works attacked all previous philosophy and historical scholarship.

David Hume expressed the skeptical challenge in ways that made him central to philosophical discussion up to and including our own day. His *Treatise of Human Nature* (1739–1740) argued for skepticism about both facts and reason. His critique of our ideas of causation reduces them to little more than a habit based on constant conjunction. And yet in typical skeptical fashion he showed how people could live with skepticism on the basis of probabilities and custom.

Immanuel Kant (1724–1804) was called the "all-destroyer" in his own day because of his rejection of so many other dogmatic philosophies. He adopted skeptical Greek vocabulary when he argued that we could have no knowledge of the noumena—the reality behind appearances—but

only of the phenomena. He saved free will and morality from scientific determinism only by reducing our knowledge of them to faith rather than knowledge. Other skeptics writing in German in his time included Salomon Maimon (1753–1800) and Gottlob Ernst "Aenesidemus" Schulze (1761–1833). When Carl Friedrich Stäudlin's *Geist und Geschichte des Skepticismus* (History and spirit of skepticism) of 1794 showed Hume facing Kant on the title page, it became clear these two thinkers had posed the skeptical challenge for the age: Stäudlin decried an unphilosophical skepticism even as he showed that the philosophical skeptics could not be refuted.

SKEPTICISM IN SCIENCE AND MEDICINE

Francis Bacon (1561–1626), who was chancellor of England from 1618 to 1621, served as a spokesman for early natural philosophy, convinced that the experimental method would produce absolute certainty. Skeptics like François de La Mothe le Vayer (1585–1672) used many of the skeptical tropes to show that science could not produce certain knowledge. Other natural philosophers such as Marin Mersenne (1588–1648) and Pierre Gassendi (1592–1655) in France dispensed with the need for absolute certainty and defended experimental science on the ground that it could produce useful knowledge, in accordance with the phenomena, even without certainty. This attitude prevailed at the Royal Society in London as well. Skepticism could be used to sweep away the pretensions of Aristotelians and other dogmatists while leaving experimental scientists free to continue their work. In this spirit Robert Boyle (1627–1691) named his spokesman "Carneades" in *The Sceptical Chymist* (1661), and Joseph Glanvill (1636–1680) titled one of his books *Scepsis Scientifica* (1665).

Of all the fields that we now consider sciences, medicine was especially intertwined with skepticism. Sextus Empiricus was a practicing physician whose work influenced his philosophy, and each of the ancient schools of medicine had taken positions for or against philosophical dogmatism or skepticism. Ancient Hippocratic sources stressed the importance of skeptical observation and experience and the dangers of dogmatic theory in medicine. In early modern Europe the writings of Hippocrates (c. 460–c. 377 B.C.E.) and Galen (c. 129–c. 200

C.E.) were an important part of medical studies, and they introduced the student both to dogmatic medicine and to the skeptical critique.

Several prominent early modern physicians contributed to the literature on skepticism and medicine. Toulouse professor Francisco Sanches (c. 1550–c. 1623) called himself "Carneades philosophus" and attacked Aristotelian science in his book *Quod Nihil Scitur* (1581; That nothing is known). The English physician and philosopher John Locke (1632–1704) may have picked up some of the skeptical elements in his philosophy from skeptical physician Thomas Sydenham (1624–1689). Martín Martínez (1684–1734), royal physician and president of the Royal Academy in Seville, was the author of *Medicina Sceptica* (1722–1724), which attacked dogmatic Galenism, and *Philosophia Sceptica* (1730), which introduced Gassendi and Descartes to Spain. Ernst Platner (1744–1818) was a German physician whose skeptical writings were influential in Kant's time.

SKEPTICISM, HISTORIOGRAPHY, AND POLITICAL THOUGHT

Especially in the seventeenth century, skepticism made its way into historiography as writers began to question the received accounts of history. La Mothe le Vayer's *On the Small Amount of Certainty in History* (1668) and Pierre Bayle's *Historical and Critical Dictionary* (1697–1702) brought numerous historical errors to public attention. The only lasting solution was to learn to live with the appearances and accept lower standards for practical purposes instead of absolute certainty, as in natural science.

Throughout the early modern era skepticism was used to justify a wide variety of political stances, from quietist conservatism to radical activism.

SKEPTICISM AND RELIGION

The historical scholarship of Isaac la Peyrère (1596–1676), Baruch Spinoza (1632–1677), and Richard Simon (1638–1712) contributed to skepticism about the Bible. In response, throughout the early modern period it was common to accuse skeptics of atheism, libertinism, and immorality. But skeptics were not necessarily atheists. In fact, one of the most common uses of skepticism was its use by the self-described orthodox against pagan claims to

truth, by the Lutherans and Calvinists against Catholic claims to infallibility, and by Catholics against Protestant claims to truth. Many religionists believed that their own truth was immune from skepticism, but one argument was that if all claims to truth can be demolished, one should accept traditional religion on faith. This position is known as fideism.

Various versions of fideism were widespread. Thinkers from Montaigne to Huet and Bayle to many figures in the eighteenth century wrote that skepticism cleared the way to faith by removing rationalist objections. Blaise Pascal (1623–1662) in France in the seventeenth century and Jean de Castillon (1709–1791) in Berlin in the eighteenth century Christianized skepticism by showing that, properly understood, it set the scene for Christianity. In the *Critique of Pure Reason* Kant famously wrote that he had had to deny knowledge in order to make room for faith (Preface to Second Edition [1787], B, xxx). Whether each such figure was sincere or was using fideism as a defense against possible persecution for heresy has been the subject of debate ever since.

See also **Atheism; Bayle, Pierre; Descartes, René; Humanists and Humanism; Hume, David; Kant, Immanuel; Montaigne, Michel de; Pascal, Blaise; Spinoza, Baruch.**

BIBLIOGRAPHY

Borghero, Carlo. *La certezza e la storia: Cartesianesimo, pirronismo e conoscenza storica.* Milan, 1983.

Floridi, Luciano. *Sextus Empiricus: The Transmission and Recovery of Pyrrhonism.* New York, 2002.

Laursen, John Christian. *The Politics of Skepticism in the Ancients, Montaigne, Hume, and Kant.* Leiden and New York, 1992.

Popkin, Richard H. *The History of Skepticism from Savonarola to Bayle.* 4th edition. New York and Oxford, 2002.

Schmitt, Charles B. *Cicero Scepticus: A Study of the Influence of the* Academica *in the Renaissance.* The Hague, 1972.

Van Leeuwen, Henry G. *The Problem of Certainty in English Thought 1630–1690.* The Hague, 1970.

JOHN CHRISTIAN LAURSEN

SLAVERY AND THE SLAVE TRADE.

Slavery has existed throughout history. Most societies have made provisions for it within their structure, and most peoples have been sources of slaves at one time or another. The expansion of slavery was often a by-product of empire building as a dominant power turned its prisoners of war into slaves through conquest. However, from empire to empire there was considerable variation in slaves' legal status and prospects for incorporation into the polity; likewise, within a given society or state, there could be a wide range of status, labor, and opportunities among different slaves.

Indeed, a precise definition of slavery that will fit all societies is difficult to present. Most forms of slavery share the following characteristics: (1) slaves are obliged to live their lives in perpetual service to their master, an obligation that only the master (or the state) can dissolve; (2) slaves are under the complete power of their masters, although the state or community may impose certain restrictions upon the master's treatment of the slave; (3) slaves are property, which may be sold or passed along as an inheritance at the master's discretion; and (4) the condition of slavery is transmitted from parent to child.

Historians often distinguish between "slave societies" and "societies with slaves," based upon the centrality of slavery to the economy. Ancient Rome and the plantation colonies of Brazil, the Caribbean, and the American South were "slave societies"; during the early modern period, most European countries and many Latin and North American colonies were merely "societies with slaves."

The question of who can legitimately be enslaved in any society often boils down to a definition of who constitutes an "insider" and who is fundamentally excluded from a society. Over the course of the early modern period, these lines shifted from religious to somatic categories, thus creating the relatively new category of "race." Thus, fifteenth-century Christians justified the enslavement of non-Christians on fundamentally religious grounds. In some contrast to the Russian and Ottoman empires, by the seventeenth century all western European powers defined Africans as peculiarly destined to enslavement, an opinion that was often justified by the biblical account of the curse upon Noah's sons. As Enlightenment secularism and materialism became influential in the eighteenth and nineteenth centuries, a new, biologically justified discourse of

racism was buttressed by the pronouncements of science. Some theorists, including those in nations with no direct ties to the slave trade, embraced these attitudes. For example, the German Enlightenment thinker Immanuel Kant cited with approval David Hume's characterization of blacks as highly superstitious, overly talkative, lacking intelligence, and ungifted in the arts. Various forms of racism—scientific, institutional, and cultural—outlived the institution of slavery and persist in Europe today.

ROOTS OF EARLY MODERN SLAVERY

While slavery was a significant feature of ancient Greek and Middle Eastern societies, the direct roots of Europe's early modern traffic in slaves can be traced to ancient Rome and to early Islam. At the height of its power (c. 200 B.C.E.–200 C.E.), the Roman republic depended upon perhaps 2 million slaves (or about a third of its population) to perform every kind of labor, from agricultural production and domestic service to military command and political advising. Many of these slaves were taken from the communities and cultures at the empire's periphery and pressed into service where, through trade networks, they relocated throughout the lands under Roman imperial control.

With the collapse of the Roman Empire in the late fourth century, slavery became much more marginal in most European regions. While some families continued to maintain small numbers of slaves, often as domestic servants, widespread agricultural slavery generally gave way to serfdom, especially in northern and western Europe (including England, Scandinavia, and France). The chief difference between serfs and slaves was that serfs were bound to the land—they could not be traded away from the manorial estate to which they were born. Slaves, by contrast, were chattel property that could be bought and sold; their legal existence was mediated through their masters. By 1086, when William the Conqueror ordered the survey of the lands of England commonly known as the Domesday ("Doomsday") Book, only about 10 percent of the English population was counted as slaves, and the proportion continued to decline after that. Regions with stronger ties to the Byzantine Empire (for example, Russia) and Muslim northern Africa (for example, Sicily) had greater access to slave markets, and slavery continued as a minor but persistent feature of southern and eastern European medieval societies.

Islam, being religiously and linguistically distinct from Christian Europe, expanded a preexisting slave system in the seventh and eighth centuries during its major conquests from Europe's Iberian Peninsula (Spain and Portugal) to the frontier of China. The Islamic empire, like Rome, allowed for the integration of conquered people into its own population through various assimilation mechanisms, including slavery. The Arabic language—the dominant language of the original Muslims—provided bureaucratic and cultural unity to elites while many vernacular languages and customs persisted. Yet the religion of Islam gave legal, cultural, and linguistic unity—at least at the elite administrative level—to a diverse and cosmopolitan empire.

Slavery under Islamic regimes, however, differed from Roman slavery in certain ways. First, it was not a central feature in agricultural production, as slavery had been to the Italian peninsula; most slaves held by Muslims were employed in domestic service. Second, the great majority of slaves in early Islamic states were women and children—male prisoners of war who resisted were more likely killed than enslaved. However, male slaves came to be used by the thousands as soldiers and administrators in later empires, like those of the Mamluks of Egypt and of the Ottomans.

Another important feature of Islamic slavery, from the perspective of early modern Europe, is the development of trans-Saharan slave routes and an emerging discourse associating blackness with slavery. While Muslims enslaved an extremely diverse range of peoples, from the blond and blue-eyed Caucasians to the ebony-skinned Zanj of East Africa, a literary trope emerged around 675–725 under the Umayyad dynasty, connoting inferiority to those with dark skin. The Muslim world also supplied the Iberian Peninsula with slaves, so that by completion of the Reconquista in the fifteenth century, there was a stable community of several thousand blacks of sub-Saharan African descent in the major cities of Portugal and Castile.

Constantius II (ruled 337–361), the Christian emperor of Rome, had decreed in 339 that Jews were not permitted to hold Christians as slaves. During the Middle Ages a new policy barring the

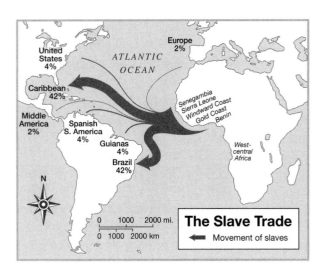

enslavement of fellow Christians—possibly in imitation of similar Muslim prohibitions against the enslavement of coreligionists—served to win pagan converts to the expanding Christian feudal order. Most of the western European languages' words for slave are etymologically related; "slave" (English), *Sklave* (German), *esclave* (French), *esclavo* (Spanish), *schiavo* (Italian), and even the Arabic *saqaliba* are all based upon the ethnic term "Slav" and refer to the southern Balkan peoples who were one of the chief sources of slaves during the ancient and medieval periods.

EUROPEANS AS SLAVES

Europeans were not only slaveholders in the early modern period; they were also slaves. From at least the sixteenth century, thousands of Europeans were captured by Muslim privateers in or along the coasts of the Mediterranean Sea, Atlantic Ocean, or North Sea and sold into slave markets from Alexandria, Egypt to Meknes, Morocco. Seamen, fishermen, traders, travelers, and soldiers were the most vulnerable to seaborne raiders. On land, with the expansion of the Ottoman Empire into Europe, peasant families were just as subject to enslavement as were combatant soldiers. Some Christian captives converted to Islam and made new lives for themselves, others were ransomed by their relatives, escaped, or died in captivity. Some were pressed into service as galley slaves on Muslim ships. Many observers noted that their treatment there was better than on the French, Italian, or Spanish galleys. In general, slavery in the Ottoman Empire was reportedly milder than slavery elsewhere, and manumission (the individual freeing of slaves) was a common, even expected, form of charity for observant Muslims.

In the second half of the seventeenth century, Jean-Baptiste Colbert, the chief minister to France's king Louis XIV (ruled 1643–1715), expanded a system of galley slaves as punishment for many different kinds of crimes. More than 1,500 Protestant dissenters were condemned to the French galleys. During the same period, the Habsburg emperor Leopold I (ruled 1658–1705), in conjunction with Louis XIV, suspended the religious freedom guaranteed by the Hungarian constitution and sent some sixty Protestant ministers to be sold to the Spanish galleys; twenty-six surviving prisoners were released in 1676. The French galley penal system continued until 1748.

In the same period, from the end of the seventeenth century until the end of the eighteenth, the seizure of war captives for ransom or labor became a fixture of warfare between the Russian and Ottoman empires. However, in contrast to the Ottomans, whose slaves were overwhelmingly non-Muslim outsiders, Russia drew most of its slaves from its own domestic population, many of whom sold themselves to escape famine or destitution.

Slavery persisted in Russia until the early eighteenth century, when the tsarist state redefined domestic slaves as serfs so that they might be taxable. The line between serf and slave, however, was often blurred in practice. Slavery in Ottoman Europe continued in reduced form through the nineteenth century until its formal abolition at the end of the century.

EUROPE AND THE TRANSATLANTIC SLAVE TRADE

The roots of Europe's slave colonies in America can be found in Portugal's fifteenth-century exploration of the western coast of Africa. Upon conquering the Muslim fortress of Ceuta in North Africa in 1415, Portuguese rulers turned their attention to the trade goods being delivered across the Sahara desert. By skirting the coast, royally sponsored explorers hoped to trace the supplies of gold and other precious goods to their source, thus bypassing the costs of the middlemen traders. By the mid-1450s, the Portuguese had begun to purchase slaves along the West African coast, establishing contracts with Wolof, Mandinga, and Bati rulers to exchange gold, cotton, ivory, and slaves for horses, red cloth, and iron. In the 1480s, the Portuguese established the entrepôts of São Tomé and Elmina to serve the regular trade routes from Congo and Benin. At the same time, following the medieval model of sugar production in North Africa and several Mediterranean islands, the Portuguese established plantations on the Atlantic islands of Madeira, the Cape Verde islands, and the Canaries, and they increasingly worked them with slaves imported from Africa.

Though some African slaves arrived in America along with Spanish conquistadors as early as 1502, most early colonial labor needs in the New World were initially met by Amerindians. The Spanish rulers replicated the feudal tribute system of *encomienda* in their New World colonies, compelling Amerindians to produce staples such as corn, beans, and cotton, as well as luxury products, including gold and silver. Due to this exploitation, susceptibility to Old World diseases, and perhaps, in some regions, an environmental crisis of soil depletion, native populations died at appalling rates: in the highly populated Mexican basin, 90 percent of the population died within a century of conquest. A confluence of this labor shortage with ready supplies of African slaves from the entrepôts in the western and central African regions of Senegal, Elmina (along the Gold Coast), Angola, and Congo facilitated Spanish colonies' experimentation with the importation of African slaves to the Caribbean, Mexico, and Peru. By 1580, some 74,000 Africans had been shipped from Africa for the Americas, while some 232,000 Spanish and Portuguese left for the Americas during the same period.

From 1580 until 1700, the relative proportion of emigration from Africa and Europe reversed. Approximately 1,531,000 Africans left Africa for the Americas (though an average of 20 percent perished during the grueling Middle Passage), while during the same time only about 944,000 Europeans ventured out for the New World, primarily to Spanish and British colonies. Key in this transformation was the introduction of sugar cultivation, first in Portuguese Brazil, then in the Caribbean. Unlike tobacco, another exotic product grown in America for export to Europe, sugar required a large labor force to process the ripe sugarcane on site before it rotted.

Colonial planters sought economy of scale by consolidating large plantations, with gangs of 20 to 200 slaves staying up through the night to feed the proto-industrial sugar mills and tend the refining vats.

Also in the seventeenth century, the Dutch took over much of the Portuguese empire, conquering trading posts in Africa and Brazil and confiscating the lucrative transatlantic slave trade. Meanwhile, English and French colonists began to encroach on the Iberian colonial monopoly in North America, the Antilles, and coastal Guyana. At first, the favored commodity in Virginia and the Caribbean was tobacco, grown primarily with indentured servants from Europe, but gradually this was overtaken in the tropics by sugar and indigo, and it was supplemented by coffee and cotton. These crops accelerated the colonial demand for slave labor so that from 1700 to 1760, some 2,775,000 Africans were shipped for the New World, while only 891,000 Europeans departed for the same destination.

In this way, a "triangle of trade" emerged, linking the continents of Europe, Africa, and the Americas. Slave traders from Portugal, the Netherlands, England, and France brought raw and manufactured materials (such as iron, glass, guns, cloth, and horses) to African traders. African rulers profited from this trade, waging war on neighbors or requiring tribute in the form of slaves, which they, in turn, bartered to Europeans for the exotic luxury items they supplied. European traders packed slaves into sailing ships for the notorious Middle Passage, which averaged two to three months in the sixteenth century but could be completed in as little as 20 to 40 days by the nineteenth century. Survivors of the transatlantic voyage were sold to slaveholders for sugar, gold, tobacco, and rum, which in turn were sold in Europe.

The royally sponsored Portuguese trade was eclipsed in the seventeenth century by the Dutch, English, and French trading companies, each with exclusive national privileges, or charters, to trade between specific regions. Yet many colonists chafed against these mercantilist restrictions, and smuggling was widespread, especially outside the central commercial hubs. By the mid-eighteenth century, the English and French dominated the Atlantic slave trade.

SLAVERY AND THE ECONOMY OF EUROPE

The effect of Atlantic slavery on Europe's economies has been a matter of considerable debate since the 1944 publication of Eric Williams's *Capitalism and Slavery*. As part of his argument about the rise and fall of Atlantic slavery, Williams asserted that the Atlantic slave system created the export demand, the trading network, and one of the main streams of capital that fueled England's industrial revolution. Williams's claims have been challenged, however, by a generation of historians, such as Roger Anstey and Seymour Drescher, who have argued that profits from the slave trade were never sufficient to be a significant source of capital for the industrial revolution, and that the slave colonies, rather than generating substantial profits, were actually a net loss for the metropole.

Still, the complex economic relationships established within and between Europe, Africa, and the Americas during the early modern period make it difficult to isolate Europe's economic developments from the American slave complex. Some historians continue to argue that African slaves were responsible for about 75 percent of the American products that fed the seventeenth- and eighteenth-century commercial revolution, which in turn contributed to Britain's urbanization, creation of markets, export manufacture, and shift to industrial production after 1750. Others suggest that the concentration of capital, technological innovation, and organization of labor for efficiency in the colonial sugar plantations were models for the industrialization of the European textile industries.

SLAVERY AND THE LAW

Slave law, as with law more generally, encompasses positive law (statutes), jurisprudence (legal philosophy), and case law. While knowledge of the statutes is necessary to know the prescriptive status of slaves in any given jurisdiction, a better understanding of their actual condition in any community can be found through an examination of the judicial cases concerning slaves, as well as those concerning former slaves or "freedmen."

Roman slave law, codified in Justinian's sixth-century *Corpus juris civilis*, influenced most continental European legal systems, although as slavery became economically important to American colonies the law was modified to reflect local interests.

Several characteristics of Roman law were fundamental to later jurists, including manumission practices, civil status, and criminal law. For some purposes, the law treated slaves as though they were human beings, for others, as things.

Roman law facilitated manumission, or individual freeing of slaves, and slaves' entry into the populace as citizens. Although manumitted slaves did not enjoy all the rights of freeborn Roman citizens, their freeborn children did. Slaves, like freeborn sons or daughters of Roman citizens, could not own property in their own right until the death of the master/patriarch. However, Roman law allowed for the creation of a savings fund, or *peculium*, which—though technically the property of the master—was administered by the slave within the constraints dictated by the master. Thus slaves were permitted to purchase their freedom through accumulated savings, with the permission of, and at the price set by, the master.

The emperor Justinian introduced a range of procedures that, if enforced, would moderate the slave system from the point of view of the slave. For example, Justinian's code held that a master could not kill his slave with impunity and, in cases of extreme abuse, a slave could seek the protection of the emperor or the church. And while the late Roman republic (c. 50 B.C.E.) had recognized only three avenues to freedom—manumission by enrollment on the census, manumission by testament, and proceedings whereby liberty was restored to a free person who had been wrongfully held as a slave—under Justinian, additional means of manumission were recognized, including a letter signed by five witnesses, manumission in the Christian church, and official recognition by a master that a slave was his son.

Yet under Roman law, slaves could not be parties to civil lawsuits, nor accusers in criminal cases, nor under Roman law could they marry. Their testimony could, under certain conditions, be accepted, but not against their masters. In those instances where their testimony was authorized, they were required to undergo torture. At the same time, it was perfectly legitimate to try slaves as defendants in criminal cases. Escaped slaves were not punished by the state, but, if caught, were subject to the master's discipline.

Most of the judicial courts of western Europe absorbed Roman law as part of their legal culture, yet innovated according to their own customs and conditions through the medieval and early modern eras. For Castilian Spain, *Las siete partidas,* a compilation consolidated under Alfonso X (ruled 1252–1284) around 1265 (and promulgated in 1348) integrated Roman features with Visigothic codes and medieval practices. The new Spanish law recognized slave marriages, even over a master's opposition, and masters would be penalized for fostering a clandestine marriage between their own slave and that of another. Portugal's *Ordenaçoes Filipinas,* promulgated by Philip II (ruled 1556–1598) and confirmed by the Portuguese king John IV (ruled 1640–1656) in 1643, established general slave laws for Portuguese territories past Brazilian independence in 1822, but these were supplemented explicitly by the *Corpus juris civilis* until 1769, when Roman precedents were discarded for natural law principles of the Enlightenment. In many regards, including manumission, Portugal's laws were therefore identical with Rome's. While France's *Code noir* of 1685 strongly reflected Louis XIV's desire to make Catholicism the sole religion of the kingdom (an innovation over Roman traditions), many of the French law's provisions mirrored the ancient Justinian code.

Despite these continuities with Roman law, the new Atlantic slave experience generated new legal customs and, eventually, statutes. In French Caribbean colonies, the *Code noir* contained a provision, apparently following local custom but no doubt sanctioned by the church, to the effect that any master who sired a child with his slave concubine would bear a hefty fine and the slaves would be confiscated for the state, unless the master married the slave in question, whereupon both mother and child would be thereby recognized as free. When the *Code noir* was reissued for the new colony of Louisiana in 1724, however, this provision was omitted and a new one explicitly forbade marriages between whites and blacks.

The most striking innovations were apparent in England and its colonies, where neither Roman legal traditions, nor the practice of enslavement, carried through the Middle Ages into the early modern period of Atlantic colonization. England's colonial assemblies were authorized to make local law distinct from that of the metropole; hence each colony developed its own unique statutory and case law with regard to the status and treatment of slaves and freedmen. During the late seventeenth and eighteenth centuries, British American colonies passed increasingly harsh measures regulating slaves and free blacks. For example, a Virginia statute of 1682 held that if a slave died resisting the force of his master, the master would not be liable for felony charges since "it cannot be presumed that [premeditated] malice should induce any man to destroy his own estate [property]."

The written law of Spain mutated further in the colonial settlements of the New World. For example, slaves were sometimes permitted to testify in court and a master's privilege of re-enslaving an ungrateful freedman fell into disuse. One of the most significant customary innovations in slave law was the practice of *coartación,* which developed in eighteenth-century Spanish America. On the basis of *coartación,* a slave who presented a fair price to his master could achieve his freedom—with or without the master's consent. This factor, along with demographics, economic conditions, and cultural reasons, helps to explain why people of color made up a larger proportion of the free population in many Latin American colonies.

ANTISLAVERY AND ABOLITION

The movement to abolish slavery has roots in European urban culture, elite European religious and intellectual movements, and African-American slave resistance. Yet it was not until the late eighteenth century that all of these forces combined to create a sustained attack on the institution of slavery itself, and not until the nineteenth century that the Atlantic slave trade, and then American slavery, were finally abolished.

Since at least the thirteenth century, urban centers in France, such as Toulouse and Pamiers, became refuges from the most extreme forms of bondage by adopting charters that freed slaves upon entrance to the village. In England, a Russian slave was freed in 1567 on the grounds that "the air of England is too pure for a slave to breathe." In seventeenth-century France, local traditions supporting liberty were extended to the French kingdom in the maxim, "All persons are free in this

kingdom; and as soon as a slave had arrived at the borders of this place, being baptized, is freed."

As the Atlantic slave system began to expand, some critics argued for limitations on the excesses of slavery and the slave trade throughout the early modern period. In sixteenth- and seventeenth-century Spain and Spanish America, some Catholic clergy voiced their concerns, including Bartolomé de Las Casas (1474–1566), who opposed the enslavement of Indians, and Tomás de Mercado and Alonso de Sandoval, who challenged the most extreme cruelties of the slave trade. In 1646, the Capuchin missionary order was expelled from the French Antillean colony of Saint-Christophe, allegedly because they preached the idea that once baptized, blacks could no longer be held as slaves since "it is an unworthy thing to use one's Christian brother as a slave." In 1688, several Dutch-speaking Quakers of Germantown, Pennsylvania, chastised their coreligionists for owning and trading slaves, for they "have . . . as much right to fight for their freedom as you have to keep them as slaves." Yet many Christians also stressed the virtue of slaves' obedience to their masters, and the suspension of reward until the hereafter, thus implicitly sanctioning slavery and inequality in the here and now.

In the eighteenth century, more secular voices began to critique slavery on the grounds of natural law and the linkage of personal slavery with political despotism. Scottish Enlightenment writers Francis Hutcheson and George Wallace were among the first to attack both slavery and the slave trade as violations of "natural justice" and "humanity." French philosopher Jean-Jacques Rousseau (1712–1778) drew directly from Wallace to challenge the right of slaves to sell themselves into bondage in his *On the Social Contract.* By 1762, there was a sufficient body of antislavery thought for the Pennsylvania Quaker Anthony Benezet to publish the first title devoted solely to the abolition of slavery and the slave trade, a collection he titled *A Short Account of That Part of Africa Inhabited by Negroes,* which was widely read on both sides of the Atlantic.

The third source of abolitionism was the actions taken by slaves themselves to resist slavery. In the Americas, slaves who ran away, known as "maroons," established independent communities in the regions beyond direct colonial power, such as the canyons of Jamaica, the mountains of Guadeloupe, the *sertão* of Brazil, and the swamps of Florida. Some of the maroon communities were so powerful militarily that they established treaties with the local European colonial powers, as in Surinam.

From as early as 1527 and throughout the expansion of plantation slavery in the seventeenth, eighteenth, and nineteenth centuries, slaves plotted and revolted against masters. Most such revolts were small-scale events, with the aim of seeking local justice. Whether they were enacted on the individual or communal scale by the maroons, or in the wider arena of revolt or revolution, slaves overcame tremendous odds in seeking autonomy for themselves and, when possible, in extending that freedom to others. The 1791 slave revolt in northern Saint Domingue that escalated into the Haitian Revolution articulated a strong antislavery ideology and effected the first universal emancipation (of French colonies, in 1794) and the first independent republic established by former slaves (Haiti, 1804).

The end of the eighteenth century also marks the beginning of the bourgeois Atlantic abolition movements. Granville Sharp, an eccentric and pious Englishman, took up the cause of a slave who had been kidnapped and beaten by his master in England in 1765. Sharp's research into the law convinced him the English constitution was antithetical to slavery. English abolitionists had their first major success when they rallied to the support of the slave Somerset, whose master attempted to expel him from England on a ship bound for Jamaica in 1772. Though the extent of Judge Mansfield's decision in the *Somerset* case has been debated by historians, it was widely interpreted at the time as effectively abolishing slavery within England, and Scottish courts soon followed suit with an even broader pronouncement against slavery in 1778.

In North America, patriots of the American Revolution equated British political tyranny with slavery and offered proposals to ban the slave trade. Some extended the critique to slavery itself, though antislavery and antiblack sentiments were sometimes intertwined. Vermont prohibited slavery in its 1777 constitution while Pennsylvania, Rhode Island, and Connecticut all adopted emancipation statutes. Judges in Massachusetts and New Hamp-

shire issued decisions similar to England's *Somerset* decision, thus establishing these territories as free states. In the North, only New York and New Jersey, both with sizable slave populations, maintained a legal apparatus permitting the continuation of slavery, yet these states also generated active, if elitist, abolitionist societies.

Sharp was soon joined by other antislavery activists in England, including the Methodist founder John Wesley, who preached against the evils of slavery on both sides of the Atlantic. Quakers, Methodists, Sharp, and others formed the Society for Effecting the Abolition of the Slave Trade in 1787 and set about lobbying the British Parliament for their cause. Thomas Clarkson was the society's full-time organizer and propagandist. Within months, the group had collected more than 10,000 signatures on an antislavery petition from the city of Manchester alone, comprising half of the adult male population. Former slaves, including Olaudah Equiano (Gustavus Vassa) and Ottobah Cugoano penned their life stories and went on the lecture circuit to rally audiences to the cause. William Wilberforce, an influential member of Parliament, translated the antislavery sentiment into legislative initiatives. The first of these was defeated by pro-slavery opponents in 1791. Petition drives increased, with nearly 400,000 signatories in 1792. At this same time, the Danish government announced that it would abolish its own slave trade within ten years.

In France, the outbreak of the French Revolution in 1789 and the Saint Domingue slave revolt of 1791 made it expedient for the French antislavery association, the Amis des noirs, to focus on mulatto rights. In 1794, the French Convention ratified the republican commissioners' offer of freedom to slaves who would fight against the royalists in Saint Domingue, and they extended it as a universal emancipation to slaves in all other colonies still under French control. However, Napoleon's forceful reimposition of slavery to the Caribbean colonies in 1802 precipitated Haitian independence and postponed French abolition until 1848.

The French and Haitian revolutions proved a setback to the British abolitionist movement, as conservative forces asserted that the popular classes were incapable of self-rule. It was not until 1808 that the Atlantic slave trade was formally abolished by Britain and the United States, with Britain policing the seas in an attempt to prevent Spanish and Portuguese trade to the Caribbean and Central and South America. It would take another thirty years for Britain's abolitionists to eliminate slavery within its remaining colonies (for example, Jamaica and Barbados), and not until 1888 was slavery abolished within the last American state, Brazil.

Though slavery was officially abolished in the Americas in the nineteenth century, it expanded in some parts of Africa as a direct result of Euro-American abolition. Slavery and related forms of coerced labor still exist today in many countries of the world. Women and children are especially vulnerable.

See also **Africa; Equality and Inequality; Industry; Laborers; Race, Theories of; Serfdom; Servants.**

BIBLIOGRAPHY

Anstey, Roger. *The Atlantic Slave Trade and British Abolition, 1760–1810.* Atlantic Highlands, N.J, 1975.

Blackburn, Robin. *The Making of New World Slavery: From the Baroque to the Modern, 1492–1800.* New York, 1997.

———. "The Old World Background to European Colonial Slavery." *William and Mary Quarterly* 3rd ser. 54, no. 1 (January 1997): 65–102.

———. *The Overthrow of Colonial Slavery, 1776–1848.* London, 1988.

Braude, Benjamin. "The Sons of Noah and the Construction of Ethnic and Geographical Identities in the Medieval and Early Modern Periods." *William and Mary Quarterly* 3rd ser. 54, no. 1 (January 1997): 103–142.

Cotter, William R. "The Somerset Case and the Abolition of Slavery in England." *History* 79, no. 255 (1994): 31–56.

Davis, David Brion. *The Problem of Slavery in the Age of Revolution, 1770–1823.* Ithaca, N.Y., 1975.

———. *The Problem of Slavery in Western Culture.* Ithaca, N.Y., 1966, reissued 1971.

———. *Slavery and Human Progress.* New York, 1984.

Drescher, Seymour. *Econocide: British Slavery in the Era of Abolition.* Pittsburgh, 1977.

———. *From Slavery to Freedom: Comparative Studies in the Rise and Fall of Atlantic Slavery.* New York, 1999.

Drescher, Seymour, and Stanley L. Engerman, eds. *A Historical Guide to World Slavery.* New York, 1998.

Eltis, David. *The Rise of African Slavery in the Americas.* Cambridge, U.K., 2000.

Epstein, Steven A. *Speaking of Slavery: Color, Ethnicity, and Human Bondage in Italy.* Ithaca, N.Y., 2001.

Finley, Moses I. *Ancient Slavery and Modern Ideology.* London, 1980.

Gerzina, Gretchen. *Black London: Life before Emancipation.* New Brunswick, N.J., 1995.

Hellie, Richard. *Slavery in Russia, 1450–1725.* Chicago, 1982.

Karras, Ruth Mazo. *Slavery and Society in Medieval Scandinavia.* New Haven, 1988.

Klein, Herbert S. *African Slavery in Latin America and the Caribbean.* New York, 1986.

Lewis, Bernard. *Race and Slavery in the Middle East: An Historical Enquiry.* New York, 1990.

Lind, Vera. "Privileged Dependency on the Edge of the Atlantic World: Africans and Germans in the Eighteenth Century." In *Interpreting Colonialism,* edited by Byron Wells and Philip Stewart. Studies on Voltaire and the Eighteenth Century. Forthcoming.

Mintz, Sidney W. *Sweetness and Power: The Place of Sugar in Modern History.* New York, 1985.

Patterson, Orlando. *Slavery and Social Death: A Comparative Study.* Cambridge, Mass., and London, 1982.

Peabody, Sue. *"There Are No Slaves in France": The Political Culture of Race and Slavery in the Ancien Régime.* New York, 1996.

Phillips, William D., Jr. *Slavery from Roman Times to the Early Transatlantic Trade.* Minneapolis, 1985.

Restall, Matthew. "Black Conquistadors: Armed Africans in Early Spanish America." *The Americas* 57, no. 2 (2000): 171–205.

Saunders, A. C. de C. M. *A Social History of Black Slaves and Freedmen in Portugal, 1441–1555.* Cambridge, U.K., and New York, 1982.

Shyllon, F. O. *Black People in Britain, 1555–1833.* London, 1977.

Tannenbaum, Frank. *Slave and Citizen: The Negro in the Americas.* New York, 1946.

Thornton, John. *Africa and Africans in the Making of the Atlantic World, 1400–1800.* 2nd ed. Cambridge, U.K., 1998.

Toledano, Ehud. *The Ottoman Slave Trade and its Suppression, 1840–1890.* Princeton, 1982.

United Nations Office of the High Commission for Human Rights. *Fact Sheet No. 14: Contemporary Forms of Slavery.* Geneva, June 1991. Available online at: 193.194 .138.190/html/menu6/2/fs14.htm.

Vitkus, Daniel J., ed. *Piracy, Slavery, and Redemption: Barbary Captivity Narratives from Early Modern England.* Introduced by Nabil Matar. New York, 2001.

Walvin, James. *Black Ivory: A History of British Slavery.* Washington, D.C., 1994.

Watson, Alan. *Slave Law in the Americas.* Athens, Ga., 1989.

Williams, Eric. *Capitalism and Slavery.* Chapel Hill, N.C., 1944.

SUE PEABODY

SLEIDANUS, JOHANNES (Johannes Philippi; 1506–1556), German historian. Johannes Sleidanus was a diplomat, scholar, translator, historian, and finally official historiographer of the Lutheran party—that is, of the Schmalkaldic League—who left the most authoritative account of the Lutheran Reformation in its political as well as religious aspects.

Johann Philipson (son of Philipus, a merchant), was born in 1506 in Schleidan and, along with his friend Johann Sturm, studied first at the school of Johann Neuburg in that Rhineland town, then in Liège with the Brothers of the Common Life and at the academy of Cologne, later rejoining Sturm at Louvain. Sleidanus served Count Dietrich IV of Manderscheid, a moderate Catholic, as tutor to his son. In 1533 Sleidanus moved to France, where he remained until 1542, studying law briefly at the University of Orléans, publishing a translation of Jean Froissart's *Chroniques* (1537), and entering into the service of Cardinal DuBellay, who was engaged in pressing the German Protestants into an alliance with King Francis I. In this cause Sleidanus, in the company of Lazare de Baif, attended the religious colloquy in Hagenau in 1540, but his mission was unsuccessful, as were those to the colloquy of Regensberg the next year, to England in 1545, and to the Diet of Augsburg in 1547. Sleidanus was in a difficult position, poised between Emperor Charles V and the French king (who had only a political interest in the Lutherans and who had begun to persecute the French Protestants), and in 1544 he returned to Strasbourg, where he continued his scholarly as well as his political work, beginning with his "Zwei Reden an Kaiser und Reich" (Two orations on the emperor and the empire.) In 1546 he was married to Iola Nidbruck, who bore him three daughters, and he was appointed a "civil servant" to the Strasbourg council, a post that included being liaison to the French population as well as composing his history.

Throughout his intellectual life Sleidanus was interested in the writing of contemporary history. He expressed this first in his Latin translations of Philippe de Commynes's *Mémoires* (1537), of Froissart's chronicles, and of Claude de Seyssel's *Monarchy of France* (1548), dedicated to King Edward VI of England, but most comprehensively in his extensively documented history of the Reformation. In 1545, with the support of Martin Bucer (1491–1551) and Jacob Sturm, he began negotiations with the Schmalkaldic League for this project, which he had begun as early as 1539. This book Sleidanus had first conceived as a "history of the restored religion" *(historia restauratae religionis, histori der ernewter religion)*, but he later included the political dimension as well. "In the history of religion," Sleidanus wrote in the preface to his *De Statu Religionis et Reipublicae Carlo Quinto Caesare Commentarii,* "I would not omit what concerned the civil government because they are interwoven with the other, especially in our times, so that it is not possible to separate them." In this effort Sleidanus was diligent in the collecting of manuscript and archival as well as published materials and careful to preserve an impartial stance, as befitting a moderate Protestant, residing in Strasbourg and situated between German, French, and English parties. Published in 1555, the work offered a comprehensive survey of European history from All Saints' Eve 1517 to February 1555, that is, from Luther's appearance on the public scene at Wittenberg on All Saints' Eve 1517 to the retirement of his great nemesis Charles V in February 1555. His last major topic was the Diet of Augsburg of 1555, which put an end to the first phase of the Reformation, but the book (translated soon into English, French, and German) was extended in later editions, from Sleidanus's own notes, to September 1556, when the author died.

Sleidanus was a major contributor to the Renaissance "art of history." As a larger background to his epic survey Sleidanus also published a small textbook surveying "the first four great empires of the world," of which, through the principle of *translatio imperii,* Sleidanus's own sovereign, Emperor Charles V, was the last beneficiary. Reactions to Sleidanus's work were extreme, ranging from the adulation of friends, Calvinists as well as Lutherans, to the denunciation of enemies, Protestants as well as Catholics. Sleidanus answered with an "apology," which posthumously made public his historiographical confession of faith and in which he concluded by declaring that "I am the enemy of all falsehood and do not boast when I affirm that I would rather die than say, still less write, anything without proof." Leopold von Ranke (1795–1886), though not impressed with Sleidanus's critical abilities, would not object to his claim to be the "father of Reformation history."

See also **Charles V (Holy Roman Empire); Historiography; Reformation, Protestant; Schmalkaldic War.**

BIBLIOGRAPHY

Primary Sources

Ioannis Sleidani de Statu Religionis et Reipublicae Carlo Quinto Commentarii. Strasbourg, 1555.

De Quatuor Summis Imperiis. London, 1584.

Secondary Sources

Dickens, A. G., "Johannes Sleidanus and Reformation History." In *Reformation, Conformity and Consent: Essays in Honour of Geoffrey Nuttall,* pp. 17–43. London, 1977.

Kelley, Donald R., "Johann Sleidan and the Origins of the Profession of History." *Journal of Modern History* 52 (1980): 973–998.

Vogelstein, Ingeborg Berlin. *Johann Sleidan's Commentaries: Vantage Point of a Second Generation Lutheran.* Lanham, Md., 1986.

DONALD KELLEY

SMITH, ADAM (1723–1790), Scottish economist. Along with figures like his teacher Francis Hutcheson (1694–1746) and his best friend David Hume (1711–1776), Smith was one of the principals of a period of astonishing learning that has become known as the Scottish Enlightenment. He is the author of two books: *The Theory of Moral Sentiments* (1759) and *An Inquiry into the Nature and Causes of the Wealth of Nations* (1776). His first book brought him considerable acclaim during his lifetime and was quickly considered one of the great works of moral theory—impressing, for example, such people as Immanuel Kant (1724–1804), who called Smith his *Liebling,* or 'favorite', and Charles Darwin (1809–1882), who in his *Descent of Man* (1871) adopted some of Smith's argument and

called his moral thought "striking." The book went through fully six revised editions during Smith's lifetime. Since the nineteenth century, however, Smith's fame has largely rested on his second book, which must be considered one of the most influential works of the past millennium.

Smith matriculated at the University of Glasgow at the age of fourteen in 1737. He considered his instruction at Glasgow, which was heavy in the classics, quite good; the influence of Hutcheson—whom Smith later referred to as "the never to be forgotten Dr. Hutcheson"—was pronounced. After Glasgow, Smith studied at Balliol College, Oxford, with whose level of instruction Smith was not so impressed: "In the university of Oxford, the greater part of the publick professors have, for these many years, given up altogether even the pretence of teaching" (*Wealth of Nations,* Liberty Fund edition, p. 761). Smith made good use of the libraries at Oxford, however, studying widely in English, French, Greek, and Latin literature. He left Oxford and returned to Kirkcaldy in 1746.

In Edinburgh (1748) Smith began giving "Lectures on Rhetoric and the *Belles Lettres,*" as Kames's biographer Alexander Tytler reports, focusing on literary criticism and the arts of speaking and writing well. It was during this time that Smith met and befriended Hume, who was to become Smith's closest confidant and greatest philosophical influence. Smith left Edinburgh to become professor of logic at the University of Glasgow in 1751 and then professor of moral philosophy in 1752. The lectures he gave there eventually crystallized into *The Theory of Moral Sentiments.*

In his *Theory of Moral Sentiments* Smith argues that human beings naturally desire a "mutual sympathy of sentiments" with their fellows, which means that they long to see their own judgments and sentiments echoed in others. Because we all seek out this "sympathy" or harmony, much of social life is a give-and-take whereby people alternately try to moderate their own sentiments so that others can "enter into them" and try to arouse others' sentiments so that they match their own. This market-like negotiation results in the gradual development of shared habits, and then rules, of judgment about moral matters ranging from etiquette to moral duty. This process also gives rise,

Smith argues, to an ultimate standard of moral judgment, the "impartial spectator," whose perspective we routinely seek out in judging both our own and others' conduct. When we use it to judge our own, it is what constitutes our conscience. We consult the impartial spectator simply by asking ourselves what a fully informed but disinterested person would think about our conduct. If such a person would approve, then we may proceed; if he would disapprove, then we should desist.

Morality on Smith's account is thus an earthly, grounded affair. Although he makes frequent reference to God and the "Author of Nature," scholars disagree over to what extent such references do any real work in his theory—and thus to what extent Smith's theory of moral sentiments is a relativistic account, eschewing reliance on transcendent, objective rules of morality.

In 1763, Smith resigned his post at Glasgow to become the personal tutor of Henry Scott, the third duke of Buccleuch, whom Smith accompanied on an eighteen-month tour of France and Switzerland. It was during his travels with the duke that Smith met François Quesnay (1694–1774), Jacques Turgot (1727–1781), and others in France called Physiocrats, who were publicists arguing for a relaxation of trade barriers and for laissez-faire economic policies. Although Smith had long been developing his own, similar ideas, frequent conversations with the Physiocrats no doubt helped him refine and sharpen his ideas. In 1767, Smith returned to Kirkcaldy to continue work on what would become his *Wealth of Nations.*

In *The Wealth of Nations* Smith argues against the mercantilists that wealth is not mere pieces of metal: it is rather the ability to satisfy one's needs and desires. Since each person wishes to "better his own condition," the argument of *The Wealth of Nations* is that those policies should be adopted that best allow each of us to do so. It turns out, Smith argues, that markets in which the division of labor is allowed to progress, in which trade is free, and in which taxes and regulations are light are the most conducive to this end. Smith argues that in market-oriented economies based on private property, each person working to better his own condition will increase the supply, and thus lower the price, of whatever good he is producing; this means

that others will be in a better position to afford his goods. Thus each person serving his own ends is led, in Smith's famous phrase, "by an invisible hand" simultaneously to serve everyone else's ends as well. Much of *The Wealth of Nations*'s 1000-plus-page bulk is concerned with providing historical evidence supporting this theoretical argument.

By the middle of the nineteenth century, *The Wealth of Nations* was regularly cited in the British Parliament—for example, in the Corn Law debates—and its recommendations of free markets and free trade went on to have great influence in the subsequent political and economic developments not only of the British Isles, but also of most of the Western and even parts of the Eastern world. Smith's influence on the founding of the United States was also great. Among his readers were Benjamin Franklin (1706–1790), George Washington (1732–1799), Thomas Paine (1737–1809), and Thomas Jefferson (1743–1826). When compiling a "course of reading" in 1799, Jefferson included *The Wealth of Nations* along with John Locke's *Second Treatise of Government* (1690) and Marie-Jean Caritat de Condorcet's *Equisse d'un table historique des progrès de l'esprit humaine* (1793; Sketch of the progress of the human spirit) as the essential books. The English historian Henry Thomas Buckle (1821–1862) wrote that *The Wealth of Nations* "is probably the most important book that has ever been written," including the Bible. Today most countries in the world either rely on some version of Smithian market-based economies or are in the process of creating them.

Smith remained in Kirkcaldy until 1777, when he left to become commissioner of customs in Edinburgh. During this time he visited regularly with friends—including Edmund Burke (1729–1797), the chemist Joseph Black (1728–1799), the geologist James Hutton (1726–1797), the younger William Pitt (1759–1806), and Lord North (1732–1792)—and he took active roles in learned organizations like the Poker Club and the Oyster Club. He also extensively revised his two books for new editions, while additionally working on a "theory and history of law and government." The latter work was never published, however. One week before he died, Smith summoned Black and Hutton to his quarters and asked that they burn his unpublished manuscripts, a request they had been resisting for several months. This time Smith insisted. They reluctantly complied, destroying sixteen volumes of manuscripts. It is probable that Smith's theory and history of law and government were among the works that perished in that tragic loss.

Smith was a true polymath: he was master of several languages and their literatures, a historian of the ancient and modern worlds, a philosopher in his own right, and a brilliant observer of human society and behavior. Although he is known today principally as the father of the discipline now known as economics, given the scope and breadth of his work, he is probably better considered the father of sociology.

See also **Capitalism; Enlightenment; Hume, David; Liberalism, Economic; Physiocrats and Physiocracy; Scotland.**

BIBLIOGRAPHY

Primary Source

Smith, Adam. *The Glasgow Edition of the Works and Correspondence of Adam Smith.* Edited by R. H. Campbell and A. S. Skinner. 6 vols. Oxford, 1976–1977. The definitive edition of Smith's collected works, including student notes on his lectures on jurisprudence, his smaller essays, and his letters. Also published in paperback by the Liberty Fund, Inc. (Indianapolis, 1981–1987).

Secondary Sources

Campbell, R. H., and A. S. Skinner. *Adam Smith.* New York, 1982.

Campbell, T. D. *Adam Smith's Science of Morals.* London, 1971.

Griswold, Charles L., Jr. *Adam Smith and the Virtues of Enlightenment.* Cambridge, U.K., and New York, 1999.

Haakonssen, Knud. *The Science of a Legislator: The Natural Jurisprudence of David Hume and Adam Smith.* Cambridge, U.K., and New York, 1981.

Heilbroner, Robert L. *The Worldly Philosophers: The Lives, Times, and Ideas of the Great Economic Thinkers.* 7th ed. New York, 1999. See chapter 3, "The Wonderful World of Adam Smith."

Muller, Jerry Z. *Adam Smith in His Time and Ours: Designing the Decent Society.* New York and Toronto, 1993.

Otteson, James R. *Adam Smith's Marketplace of Life.* Cambridge, U.K., and New York, 2002.

Rae, John. *Life of Adam Smith.* London and New York, 1895.

Raphael, D. D. *Adam Smith.* Oxford and New York, 1985.

Ross, Ian Simpson. *The Life of Adam Smith.* Oxford and New York, 1995.

Skousen, Mark. *The Making of Modern Economics: The Lives and Ideas of the Great Thinkers.* Armonk, N.Y., 2001.

Winch, Donald. *Adam Smith's Politics: An Essay in Historiographic Revision.* Cambridge, U.K., and New York, 1978.

JAMES R. OTTESON

SMOLLETT, TOBIAS (1721–1771), Scottish novelist, translator, and periodicals editor. Smollett is perhaps best known as the author of the hugely successful picaresque novel *Roderick Random* (1747), as an editor of the monthly magazine *The Critical Review,* and the patriotic periodical *The Briton* (1762–1763), and the xenophobic travel book *Travels through France and Italy* (1766), which details his own experiences of traveling in Europe. He was born Tobias George Smollett in Dumbarton, the son of a Scottish laird, attended Glasgow University to read medicine, and was subsequently apprenticed to a surgeon to learn the trade. In 1741 he traveled to the West Indies as a surgeon's mate in the navy, where he met his wife, Anne Lassells, the daughter of a wealthy plantation owner in Jamaica. He returned with her to London in 1744 to establish himself as a surgeon in Downing Street.

Smollett's career as a surgeon did not flourish. In order to supplement his income, and to satisfy an urge that had inspired him to produce the play *The Regicide* in 1739, he undertook editing, translating, and, subsequently, writing. In 1746 he produced "The Tears of Scotland," a poem in support of Scottish tolerance after the Jacobite uprising of 1745. As a Scot and lifelong supporter of the British union, Smollett was not afraid to court controversy or to be outspoken in his opinions. Indeed, he declared in the preface to his first novel that his "avowed purpose" in writing was to arouse "generous indignation against cruelty and injustice" wherever possible.

Smollett anonymously published his first novel, *Roderick Random* (2 volumes), in 1747 to enormous public and critical approval. As a picaresque tale, a form that Smollett himself believed to be best for a novel, *Roderick Random* has a rambling structure detailing the life of a hapless, outcast naval surgeon seeking his fortune and a wife, who ultimately emerges at the end of the novel wealthy and married, despite an eventful and at times violent series of events. Following Smollett's success with this novel, he wrote two more tales in a similar style, including *The Adventures of Peregrine Pickle* (2 volumes, 1751 and 1758), which contained many savage caricatures of contemporary figures, including Henry Fielding; and *The Adventures of Ferdinand Count Fathom* (2 volumes, 1753), the story of a charming but treacherous con man in search of a fortune. Neither of these tales enjoyed the success of his first novel, however, leading him to engage in other literary ventures in addition to writing novels.

In 1755, Smollett translated Cervantes's seventeenth-century romance *Don Quixote*, and, in the following year, cofounded *The Critical Review*, which, though not a commercial success, ran for seven years and placed Smollett at the heart of literary London. In the late 1750s, Smollett turned his attention to nonfiction and published *A Compendium of Authentic and Entertaining Voyages* (7 volumes, 1756) and his own *A Complete History of England* (4 volumes, 1757–1758), which sold well and made him financially secure. His fourth novel, *The Adventures of Sir Launcelot Greaves*, appeared serially in *The British Magazine* in 1760.

In the 1760s, after he had suffered with consumption (tuberculosis) for a number of years, Smollett's health began to deteriorate. Despite his ill health, however, he embarked on a new project, *The Briton*, a pro-union periodical that he wrote and edited in the years 1762–1763, but that was eventually killed off by a rival publication, the satirical *North Briton*, edited by John Wilkes. In the same year that his periodical was taken off the press, his only child died suddenly, and Smollett headed for France and Italy, hoping the change of climate would restore both his mind and body. Returning to London in 1765, he published the story of his journey through Europe as a series of anonymous letters in *Travels through France and Italy* (1766), a book that was condemned for its xenophobic portrayal of the French, and prompted Laurence Sterne to rename its author Smelfungus in 1768, but also admired for its frank reporting of his own experiences and his detailed observations of life in the French town of Nice. Smollett returned to France in

1768. Before his death in Livorno in 1771 he wrote and published two further novels, the anonymous and bizarre *The History and Adventures of an Atom* (1786) and, perhaps his most respected work, *The Expedition of Humphry Clinker* (1771), a comic epistolary novel that tells the story of a family's tour through Great Britain.

See also **Burney, Frances; Defoe, Daniel; English Literature and Language; Fielding, Henry; Jacobitism; Scotland; Sensibility; Sterne, Laurence.**

BIBLIOGRAPHY

Primary Sources

Smollett, Tobias. *The Adventures of Ferdinand Count Fathom*. Edited by Paul-Gabriel Boucé. London, 1990.

———. *The Adventures of Peregrine Pickle in which are included Memoirs of a Lady of Quality*. Edited by James L. Clifford. London and New York, 1969.

———. *The Adventures of Roderick Random*. Edited by David Blewett. London, 1995.

———. *A Compendium of Authentic and Entertaining Voyages*. 7 vols. London, 1756.

———. *A Compleat History of England*. 4 vols. London, 1757–1758.

———. *The Expedition of Humphry Clinker*. Edited by Angus Ross. London, 1977; reprinted 1985.

———. *Fénelon's Adventures of Telemachus*. 2 vols. London, 1776. Translation.

———. *The History and Adventures of an Atom*. Edited by O. M. Brack. Athens, Ga., 1989.

———. *Le Sage's Adventures of Gil Blas*. 4 vols. London, 1749. Translation.

———. *The Letters of Tobias Smollett*. Edited by Lewis M. Knapp. Oxford, 1970.

———. *The Life and Adventures of Sir Launcelot Greaves*. Edited by Peter Wagner. London, 1988.

———. *Poems, Plays, and* The Briton. Edited by O. M. Brack. Athens, Ga., 1993.

———. *The Present State of all Nations*. 8 vols. London, 1764.

———. *Travels through France and Italy* 2 vols. London, 1766.

Smollett, Tobias, with Thomas Francklin. *The Works of M. de Voltaire*. 38 vols. London, 1761–1774. Translation.

Secondary Sources

Bourgeois, Susan. *Nervous Juyces and the Feeling Heart: The Growth of Sensibility in the Novels of Tobias Smollett*. New York, 1986.

Douglas, Aileen. *Uneasy Sensations: Smollett and the Body*. Chicago, 1995.

Grant, Damian. *Tobias Smollett: A Study in Style*. Manchester, U.K. and Totowa, N.J., 1977.

Kelly, Lionel, ed. *Tobias Smollett: The Critical Heritage*. London, 1987.

Rousseau, G. S. *Tobias Smollett: Essays of Two Decades*. Edinburgh, 1982.

Spector, Robert Donald. *Smollett's Women: A Study in an Eighteenth-Century Masculine Sensibility*. Westport, Conn., 1994.

Wagoner, Mary. *Tobias Smollett: A Checklist of Editions of his Work and an Annotated Secondary Bibliography*. New York, 1984.

ALISON STENTON

SMOTRYTSKYI, MELETII

SMOTRYTSKYI, MELETII (c. 1577–1633), Orthodox archbishop of Polatsk, bishop of Vitsyebsk and Mstsislaŭ, archimandrite of the monastery of the Vilnius Orthodox Brotherhood of the Descent of the Holy Spirit; subsequently, following his conversion to the Uniate church, archbishop of Hierapolis and archimandrite of the Uniate monastery in Volhynian Derman'; philologist and polemical writer.

Smotrytskyi was born into one of the first documented families of a burgeoning Ruthenian Orthodox intelligentsia: his father Herasym, a client of the palatine of Kiev Kostiantyn Ostrozkyi, was one of the editors of the 1581 Ostrih Bible, the first printing of Holy Writ in Church Slavonic. Meletii's educational path took him from the Orthodox "Academy" at Ostrih to the Jesuit Academy in Vilnius (late 1590s), and then to Protestant universities of western Europe (including Leipzig and Wittenberg in the years around 1606, when he served as preceptor to a young Orthodox nobleman).

Smotrytskyi likely experienced the Union of Brest (1596) while a student of about nineteen years at the Vilnius Jesuit Academy, and his entire career unfolded in the context of the debates that agitated Rus' and the Polish-Lithuanian Commonwealth in the early seventeenth century. He had returned to Lithuania by 1610, when his *Threnody* appeared at the Orthodox Brotherhood press in Vilnius. The work became a battle cry for the Orthodox, and it brought about royal warrants to arrest the anonymous author and printer and close the Vilnius printing shop.

In the 1610s Smotrytskyi worked on two major projects of "national education," a Ruthenian-language Homiliary Gospel, a sort of Orthodox postil intended to supplant existing Protestant and Catholic versions in Polish (1616), and a grammar of Church Slavonic (1618–1619), the liturgical language of the Orthodox Slavs, which would be supplanted as a textbook only at the beginning of the nineteenth century.

By 1618 Smotrytskyi had become a monk at the Vilnius Orthodox Brotherhood Monastery of the Descent of the Holy Spirit, and in 1620 he was made archbishop of Polatsk, when Patriarch Theophanes of Jerusalem, returning home from a sojourn in Muscovy, consecrated seven bishops to "vacant" Orthodox sees. The sees were in fact occupied by bishops who had joined the Union in 1596, and thus the consecrations were viewed as illegal by Polish-Lithuanian authorities. From his seat in Vilnius (he had also become archimandrite of the influential Brotherhood Monastery in 1620), Smotrytskyi became the leading spokesman in defense of the new Orthodox hierarchy, publishing five lengthy polemical tracts in the years 1621–1623.

From 1623 to 1625, Smotrytskyi made a controversial pilgrimage to the Holy Land, where he encountered Kyrillos Loukaris, one of his former teachers (perhaps at Ostrih), now patriarch of Constantinople. After returning to the Commonwealth, Smotrytskyi began seeking ways to reunite the "Ruthenian nation," and he became a covert Uniate. He was "unmasked" at a Ruthenian Orthodox Church synod held in Kiev in August 1628. He retreated to his new seat as archimandrite of the Volhynian Derman' monastery, where he wrote four major polemical works in the years 1628–1629, now propagating the Union as true Ruthenian Orthodoxy and unmasking the Orthodox intellectual elite (including his own former literary incarnations and Loukaris) as heretics and even crypto-Protestants. On 5 June 1631 Pope Urban VIII made Smotrytskyi archbishop of the "Church of Hierapolis, which is *in partibus infidelium*, under the patriarchate of Antioch." Smotrytskyi died at Derman' in December 1633.

See also **Mohyla, Peter; Orthodoxy, Russian; Poland-Lithuania, Commonwealth of, 1569–1795; Reformations in Eastern Europe: Protestant, Catholic,** and Orthodox; Ukraine; Uniates; Union of Brest (1596).

BIBLIOGRAPHY

Frick, David. *Meletij Smotryc'kyj.* Cambridge, Mass., 1995.

Frick, David, trans. and ed. *Rus' Restored: Selected Writings of Meletij Smotryc'kyj (1610–1630).* Cambridge, Mass., forthcoming.

DAVID FRICK

SMYRNA (İZMIR). İzmir (the Greek Smyrna), nestled at the eastern end of a gulf along the central western Anatolian coast, remained the only port town to escape the Ottoman ruler Bayezid I's hands when he conquered the rest of western Anatolia in 1390. It was not until 1424 that the Ottomans finally absorbed the town. In the subsequent five centuries, İzmir became transformed several times.

A combination of events and structural changes caused these dramatic alterations. In the years immediately before the Ottoman takeover, İzmir was a town divided between a Turkish-Muslim settlement in and around a hill castle, Kadifekale, and a Latin Christian settlement in the small harbor below. In such circumstances, the site could not thrive, and the Ottomans inherited an almost deserted place in 1424. Nor, without a potent navy, could the authorities do much to revitalize the port thereafter. A Venetian raid in 1474 exposed its vulnerability.

The creation of an eastern Mediterranean Pax Ottomanica in the early sixteenth century did little for İzmir. The conquest of Constantinople in 1453 had led to an Ottoman policy that envisioned western Anatolia as a provisioning zone. As part of its strategy, the government discouraged international commerce in İzmir. A reflection of this policy was an almost exclusively Turko-Muslim population of no more than two thousand in 1575.

The combination of new European trading companies and Ottoman political decentralization in the seventeenth century stimulated İzmir's growth. The weakness of the Ottoman center eased foreign manipulation of provincial economies and societies in general. İzmir itself became a "new port city," created by the combined interests of foreign traders and local Ottoman elites. By 1630, İzmir's diverse population of perhaps fifty thousand Turkish-Muslims, Armenians, Jews, Greeks, and foreigners had fashioned a cosmopolitan frontier entrepôt, whose wealth was based upon trade in silk, dried fruits, grains, and other goods.

The Ottoman government set out to tame the place. In about 1659, the grand vizier Köprülü Mehmed had a castle, Sancakburnu Kalesi, built at the narrow entrance to the Gulf of İzmir in order to oversee naval activity and shipping. During the following decades, his successors constructed a customs shed, aqueducts, public bath, and other edifices. İzmir maintained much of its autonomy, however. French, English, Dutch, and other foreign communities had carved out such a strong presence in the town that not only did its most vital district become known as "Franks Street," but foreign representatives also shared more and more municipal power with town notables.

The city quickly rebuilt after a calamitous earthquake in 1688. In the eighteenth century, French and British traders used the influence of their ambassadors in Istanbul to hold the central Ottoman government at bay, and negotiated with local notables and native merchants to better their positions in İzmir and its hinterland. As the century progressed, İzmir became a nexus of Mediterranean and European commerce and culture. Its population also remained diverse, and its physical appearance more and more resembled other world cities.

İzmir is at the center of several historiographical debates. Among these are the causes for the city's sudden emergence in the early seventeenth century, its characteristics as an Ottoman, a Mediterranean, or a world city, and its role in the "world economic system."

See also **Mediterranean Basin; Ottoman Empire.**

BIBLIOGRAPHY

Eldem, Edhem, Daniel Goffman, and Bruce Masters. *The Ottoman City between East and West: Aleppo, İzmir, and Istanbul.* Cambridge, U.K., and New York, 1999.

Frangakis-Syrett, Elena. *Commerce of Smyrna in the Eighteenth Century (1700–1820).* Athens, 1992.

Goffman, Daniel. *İzmir and the Levantine World, 1550–1650.* Seattle, 1990.

Kütükoğlu, Mübahat S. *XV ve XVI. asirlarda İzmir kazasinin sosyal ve ikisâdi yapisi.* 2 vols. İzmir, 2000.

DANIEL GOFFMAN

SOCIAL MOBILITY. *See* Mobility, Social.

SOCIAL STATUS. *See* Class, Status, and Order.

SOCIETY OF JESUS. *See* Jesuits.

SOFIIA ALEKSEEVNA (1657–1704; ruled 1682–1689), regent of Russia.

The daughter of Tsar Alexis I and his first wife Mariia Miloslavskaia, Sofiia spent her life until 1682 in the privacy of the women's quarters of the Kremlin palace with her sisters and aunts. She seems to have been well educated by the standards of the time for women. She emerged into view during the confusion after the death of her brother Tsar Fedor III in 1682. The boyars and the patriarch had proclaimed Peter Alekseevich (Peter the Great) tsar over his sickly elder brother Ivan. The musketeers objected and rioted, killing Peter's uncle and several other boyars. Sofiia emerged as the central figure among Peter's opponents, as the representative and leader of the Miloslavskii clan, the family of her mother and of Tsar Ivan V (d. 1696). The struggle ended when both boys were proclaimed co-tsars, with Sofiia as regent. In the course of the summer of 1682, she managed to neutralize and suppress a bid for power by the favorite of the musketeers, Prince Ivan Khovanskii, whom she arrested and executed in the fall. For the next seven years she ruled the country as de facto regent with her favorite, Prince Vasilii Vasilevich Golitsyn. Peter's mother Nataliia Naryshkina and her clan remained unreconciled to the new regime, providing a source of instability at court.

Sofiia was the first woman to rule Russia, if only as regent. In decrees and official rescripts her name came after those of Ivan and Peter, but from 1686 she, too, was usually accorded the title "autocrat."

Beginning with the audience for the Swedish ambassador in May 1684 she took a more public role in political matters. The exact nature of her personal relationship with Golitsyn has been the subject of romantic fancy, but evidence is sparse. What is certain is that she, not the favorite, made the final decisions.

Sofiia maintained peace with Sweden, and her emissaries negotiated the treaty of Nerchinsk with China, setting the border in Siberia for the next century and a half. After complex negotiations, Russia joined the Holy League of Poland, Austria, Venice, and the papacy against the Ottoman Empire, completing the transition of Russian policy away from concentration on the rivalry with Poland. Two Russian military expeditions against the Crimean Khanate in 1687 and 1689 were unsuccessful and ultimately led to Sofiia's downfall. In the meantime, her government continued most of the policies of her predecessors.

One exception was in religious affairs. The penalties for religious dissidents (the Old Believers) were drastically strengthened, and the Protestant mystic Quirinus Kuhlmann was arrested and condemned to death. In contrast, foreign Catholics received permission for the first time ever to open churches and bring priests to Russia. Two Jesuits were allowed to come to Moscow to serve the various needs of the foreign Catholic community (Protestant foreigners had long had these rights). The price of these concessions was the alienation of Patriarch Ioakim, the powerful and vigorous head of the church. Ioakim pursued his own agenda of elevating the educational level of the clergy and ultimately secured Sofiia's support for the Slavonic-Greek-Latin Academy, founded in 1687. Nevertheless, the patriarch remained a supporter of Sofiia's opponents, the Naryshkin clan and its allies.

Sofiia's brief regency was also a period of incipient cultural transition, as baroque architecture, knowledge of Polish and Latin, and an acquaintance with the religious culture of Ukraine began to spread among the elite. Sofiia and Golitsyn both encouraged these trends.

The failure of the Crimean campaigns undermined the credibility of Golitsyn and Sofiia, and after the return of the army in 1689, the Naryshkins saw their moment. By that time not only Ioakim supported them, but also the court of Tsar Ivan. Fearing a possible plot against him in August, Peter and his court went to the Trinity Monastery, where their allies joined them. Peter's camp blamed the secretary Fedor Shaklovityi for this alleged plot and demanded his arrest. In the course of the next weeks Sofiia realized that her support among the boyars and the army had evaporated, and by early September she surrendered. Shakolovityi was executed, and Sofiia was sent to the Novodevichii convent. There she remained until 1698, when Peter interrogated her about the musketeer revolt of the previous summer. Peter believed that she had been involved in the rebellion, and from then on until her death, Sofiia lived in virtual isolation from her sisters and associates. Her irregular status as regent and Golitsyn's military failures ensured her fall.

See also **Alexis I (Russia); Old Believers; Peter I (Russia); Russia.**

BIBLIOGRAPHY

Hughes, Lindsey. *Sophia, Regent of Russia, 1657–1704.* New Haven, 1990.

O'Brien, Carl Bickford. *Russia under Two Tsars, 1682–1689: The Regency of Sophia Alekseevna, 1682–1689.* Berkeley, 1952.

Solov'ev, Sergei M. *History of Russia.* Vol 25, *Rebellion and Reform: Fedor and Sophia 1682–1689.* Gulf Breeze, Fla., 1989.

PAUL BUSHKOVITCH

SONGS, POPULAR. The popular song in early modern Europe was a melody, usually widely known in society, that was set to a poetic text and communicated either in private or public performance or in print. The melodies had origins variously in folk music, tavern singing, comic opera, or vaudeville, all-sung opera, or even hymn singing. In fact, they moved back and forth between such contexts, being set to new words. In this period "vaudeville" had different meanings in different countries, referring to courtly songs in France and "country" ballad or song in England.

Here "popular" should be taken to mean "general" culture, part of what almost everyone was assumed to know, rather than an idiom that was distinctive of the lower classes or was seen on a lesser cultural level.

In such countries as France, England, and Germany, popular songs were disseminated during the sixteenth and seventeenth centuries chiefly by men who both sang and sold them in fairs, most notably on the Pont-Neuf in Paris. The *chansonnières* were part of the *charlatans,* unlicensed trades such as jugglers, magicians, or vendors of medical or cosmetic items. Essential to the *chansonnières'* business was the maintenance of a wide network of connections and news by which to write ballads on topics of general interest. They also formed part of small companies that put on skits in fairs. Editions of songs, which were numerous beginning in the early seventeenth century, became closely linked with political dispute, as in the *Recueil general des chansons de la Fronde* (General collection of songs of the Fronde) of 1649.

In the early eighteenth century the song became institutionalized within the musical theater known variously as opera buffa, *opéra comique,* vaudeville, *Singspiel,* and what was called either English or ballad opera. Their productions combined songs with a spoken text, the latter usually linked to the former in mood rather than plot line. The same songs were attached to dramas in the licensed theaters; by 1700 London playwrights had become concerned that much of the public went to Drury Lane more for the songs than the plays. In both Paris and Vienna some works in these idioms—most notably *Die Entführing aus dem Serail* and *Die Zauberflöte* by Wolfgang Amadeus Mozart (1756–1791) and *Le Déserteur* by Pierre-Alexandre Monsigny (1729–1817)—were by 1789 thought to stand on a level of sophistication equal to that of all-sung opera.

Writing texts for songs became an extremely important aspect of both amusement and politics during the eighteenth century. Robert Darnton shows that chansons evolved in a process of successive, collective authorship that was deeply rooted in aspects of sociability. It served as a central means by which news was spread, became interpreted, and thereby influenced public life anew. A leading aficionado of chansons was Jean-Frédéric Phélypeaux, comte de Maurepas (1701–1781), minister to Louis XV; his collection was published in Émile Raunié's *Chansonnier historique du XVIIIe siècle*

(1879–1884). Some men of letters, most notably Charles Collé (1709–1783), made a career out of writing chansons.

By 1750 editions of the songs in a well-known work that had been done by a famous singer became a major commercial component of music publishing. Tendencies of mass marketing can be detected by 1800 in the production of songs designed to be easy to appreciate by the expanding ranks of people playing and singing at home. Publishers in Britain and Germany pressured composers to write songs on supposedly Irish or Scottish themes that came to be seen as mere fashion and hype in some quarters.

See also **Hymns; Mozart, Wolfgang Amadeus von; Music; Popular Culture.**

BIBLIOGRAPHY

Darnton, Robert. "An Early Information Society: News and the Media in Eighteenth-Century Paris." *American Historical Review* 105 (2000): 1–35.

Duneton, Claude. *Histoire de la chanson française.* Vol. 1, *Des origines à 1780.* Paris, 1998.

Schwab, H. W. *Sangbarkeit, Popularität und Kunstlied Studien: Zu Lied und Liedästhetik der mittleren Goethezeit.* Regensburg, 1965.

WILLIAM WEBER

SOUTH SEA BUBBLE. *See* **Economic Crises.**

SOVEREIGNTY, THEORY OF. The modern concept of sovereignty owes more to the jurist Jean Bodin (1530–1596) than it does to any other early modern theorist. Bodin conceived it as a supreme, perpetual, and indivisible power, marked by the ability to make law without the consent of any other. Its possession by a single ruler, a group, or the entire body of citizens defined a commonwealth as monarchy, aristocracy, or popular state. Without it a commonwealth was not properly a state at all. In his *Six livres de la république* (1576; Six books of the commonwealth) Bodin came to favor absolute monarchy, but the legacy of medieval juristic ideas and the political conflicts of his time led him into some contradictions and changes of front.

In the sixth chapter of his *Methodus ad Facilem Historiarum Cognitionem* (1566; Method for the easy comprehension of histories) Bodin first discussed the nature of sovereignty, which he called in Latin *suverenitas.* Using a comparative historical method, he classified past and present states and empires and reviewed the opinions of Roman law jurists on the meaning of such terms as *summum imperium* (the highest authority) and *merum imperium* (unqualified authority). He insisted that the mixed state was an impossibility, but at this stage he did not stress the legislative function. It was listed as only the second of five functions of sovereignty, the others being creating magistrates, declaring war and peace, hearing judicial appeals in the last resort, and deciding on life or death where the latter was the prescribed penalty. In *The Commonwealth* making and unmaking law became the sole function, engrossing all the rest. Here Bodin was influenced by Roman law traditions that saw legislative power as command or will, as expressed in the maxim "what pleases the prince has the force of law" *(quod principi placet legis vigorem habet).* His term for sovereignty became *souveraineté* in French and *majestas* in Latin.

The main reason for Bodin's change of heart was probably the desire to outflank theories of legitimate resistance to the French crown advanced by Protestant writers in the contemporary civil wars. However, he did suggest certain limitations on the power of what he termed "royal monarchy," as distinct from lordly and despotic types of rulership where power knew few or no boundaries. In a royal monarchy, such as France, England, Scotland, and Spain, the sovereign was bound to observe divine and natural law; he could not tax his subjects without their consent; he should keep contracts with his subjects; and he was unable to alter certain fundamental laws, such as the laws of succession to the throne. Despite these limitations, the power of a royal sovereign was termed "absolute," and this is not surprising, since Bodin undermined most of these constitutional reservations. The sovereign was the sole judge of divine and natural law; he could tax without consent in emergencies; and he could decide that contracts were no longer operative when, in his view, a subject had ceased to benefit from them. An additional novelty was introduced in *The Commonwealth.* While continuing to insist on the indivisibility of sovereignty and the impossibility of the mixed state, Bodin made a distinction between the form of the state and the method of its administration. A sovereign might choose to administer his realm using officials of aristocratic or popular origin, thus giving the false impression of mixture.

BODIN'S INTERPRETERS

In the seventeenth century Bodin's idea of absolute sovereignty became influential throughout most of Europe. In France it was absorbed into the prevailing doctrine that kings were appointed by God and responsible to him alone, but its juristic elements remained important and were even strengthened in some respects. The jurists Charles Loyseau (1564–1627) and Cardin Le Bret (1558–1655), for example, eliminated Bodin's view that the sovereign should normally obtain consent to taxation in their respective treatises *Traité des seigneuries* (1608; On lordships) and *De la souveraineté du Roi* (1632; On royal sovereignty). Le Bret invented the celebrated phrase that sovereignty was as indivisible as a point in geometry.

Bodin, whose *Commonwealth* was translated into English in 1606, was often cited in political discourse in England during the early part of the reign of Charles I (1625–1648), but it was not until war broke out between the king and the Long Parliament in 1642 that his concept of sovereignty seemed relevant to English conditions. The militant pamphleteer who later made his peace with the Stuarts, William Prynne (1600–1669), adapted Bodin to claim sovereignty for Parliament without the king in *The Soveraigne Power of Parliaments and Kingdomes* (1643). He also enlisted French sixteenth-century resistance theorists in the parliamentary cause, associating the underlying authority of the people with sovereign power in a way that would have been anathema to Bodin. Opposing polemicists referred at times to Bodin in support of Stuart absolutism, but the general policy of Charles I's advisers was to assert that it was Parliament that had broken the mixed English constitution by asserting a superior authority.

In Germany Johannes Althusius (1577–1638), professor of law at Herborn (Nassau) and syndic of Emden, had close ties to the resistance to Spanish rule in the Netherlands and sympathized with French resistance literature. Like Prynne forty years later, he linked these ideas with the Bodinian definition of sovereignty, but in a much more logical fashion. His *Politica Methodice Digesta* (1603; Politics systematically analyzed) concluded that in every state Bodinian sovereignty reposed inalienably in the community as a whole, and that rulers and magistrates were mere delegates of the people. This, he asserted, was what Bodin had implied when he held that fundamental constitutional laws belonged to the sovereignty and not to individuals who ruled in name.

Other German jurists resented Bodin's classification of the Holy Roman Empire as an aristocracy and of the emperor as no more powerful than the doge of Venice. Some ingeniously exploited Bodin's qualifications to his theory to make it fit the complexities of the German constitution. Henning Arnisaeus (1576/1579–1636), a physician who acted as political adviser to the king of Denmark, criticized Althusius and defended monarchical sovereignty in a manner closer to Bodin's intentions. His best-known theoretical work, *De Jure Majestatis* (1610; On the right of sovereignty), not only defended Bodin's denial of the mixed state, but refused to admit its equivalent through Bodin's distinction between form of state and method of government. However, the complications in imperial institutions led Arnisaeus to suggest that the attributes of sovereignty could be distributed among several authorities.

Another German theorist, the Hebrew scholar Bartholomäus Keckermann of Gdańsk (1571–1608), used the distinction between form and method to argue in his *Systema Disciplinae Politicae* (1606; System of political science) that the empire was monarchic in form but aristocratic in governance. Perhaps the most discerning German commentator on Bodin's theory of sovereignty was Christoph Besold (1577–1638), who taught jurisprudence at Tübingen and Ingolstadt. He adopted the theory of double sovereignty, in which personal sovereignty (*majestas personalis*) resided in the ruler or in a corporate entity of unequal parts (such as the emperor and the diet), while real sovereignty (*majestas realis*) lay permanently in the community as a whole. The latter, however, could only be exercised as a constituent power when government collapsed and a new constitution was needed. These views were expressed in *Politicorum Libri Duo*

(1618; Two books on politics). Besold also remarked that, if personal sovereignty was shared among several persons in an aristocracy, it was pointless to deny the possibility of the mixed form.

GROTIUS AND PUFENDORF

The idea of constituent power was also implied by the influential Dutch statesman and jurist Hugo Grotius (1583–1645). Although he had some constitutional reservations, Grotius strongly admired Bodin's view of monarchical sovereignty. His best-known work was *De Jure Belli ac Pacis* (1625; On the law of war and peace), in which he preferred the Roman law term *summum imperium* to *majestas*. He suggested two possessors of sovereignty, the proper owner *(subjectum proprium)* and the communal owner *(subjectum commune)*, but denied that the latter could be invoked to support resistance. It resembled a theory propounded by Arnisaeus, who held that the whole community or *civitas* existed as a latent corporation to protect property rights.

In 1672 Samuel Pufendorf (1632–1694), a Saxon jurist at Heidelberg who entered the service of the king of Sweden, published his *De Jure Naturae et Gentium* (Of the law of nature and nations), a book comparable with Grotius's *War and Peace*. A student of the German constitution, he was more critical of Bodin than was Grotius, and he generally found German institutions too complex to fit the straitjacket of any political theory. Nevertheless, he described sovereignty in terms of a legal fiction as "a composite moral person *(persona moralis composita)* whose will . . . is deemed the will of all; to the end that it may use and apply the strength and riches of private persons towards maintaining the common peace and security."

HOBBES, BOSSUET, AND ROUSSEAU

Thomas Hobbes (1588–1679), perhaps the most logical of all the theorists of sovereignty, achieved a level of abstraction in his masterpiece, *Leviathan* (1651), which ignored historical facts and previous thinkers with equal disdain. Superficially, Hobbes's concept of sovereignty appears similar to Bodin's in terms of absolute power, indivisibility, and the voluntarist view of law, but its premises are entirely different. Human beings were not, in terms of Aristotelian organicist imagery, by nature social and political animals: they were egotistical beings whose

mutual hostility had created a savage state of nature from which they were obliged to escape by agreeing with each other to surrender all their rights to a sovereign for the sake of security. Thenceforth the sovereign represented all citizens separately, and in a sense they became the authors of all his acts. They could not, it is true, renounce the right of self-defense, but all the corporate resistance and contract theories of the past were refuted by this new and ruthless doctrine of absolute sovereignty.

The personal rule of Louis XIV (ruled 1643–1715; took personal charge of the government of France from 1661) seemed to contemporaries to incarnate absolute monarchical sovereignty. Indeed the king himself, preparing his memoirs in 1666, said that kings were absolute sovereigns controlling all the property of their subjects, whether clerical or lay, for the needs of the state. Elements of the juristic tradition of sovereignty lay behind this attitude, but the ideology that dominated the reign was that of the divine right of kings. Its principal spokesman was Jacques-Bénigne Bossuet (1627–1704), bishop of Meaux. His *Politique tirée des propres paroles de l'écriture sainte* (composed 1670, published 1709; Politics drawn from the very words of Holy Scripture) expounded this doctrine, but also stressed that the king owed a duty to his subjects and pointed out that his power was absolute but not arbitrary.

In the eighteenth century the concept of absolute sovereignty began to be replaced by a theory of checks and balances defined by Charles-Louis de Secondat, baron de La Brède et de Montesquieu (1689–1755). However, a new kind of sovereignty was devised by the proto-Romantic writer Jean-Jacques Rousseau (1712–1778) in *Du contrat social* (1762; The social contract). Rousseau had read Hobbes closely and, like him, based his doctrine on multiple agreements between primitive people to escape the state of nature. At the same time Rousseau detested both Hobbes's premises and his conclusions. Instead of postulating a presocial people involved in a brutal war for survival, Rousseau believed moral sentiment and a desire for the common good had moved humankind to renounce the state of nature. Instead of agreements to surrender individual rights to an absolute ruler, Rousseau proposed primeval agreements to merge all particular rights in a democratic corporate community whose general will (*la volonté générale*) was the sovereign. Since the general will was always devoted to the common good, its decisions must always be morally right: "Now, as the sovereign is formed entirely of the individuals who compose it, it has not, nor could it have, any interest contrary to theirs. . . . The sovereign by the mere fact that it is, is always all that it ought to be."

Rousseau's formula bore the shades of earlier theorists of sovereignty. It reflected Bodin's indivisibility and legislative power, Althusius's communal sovereignty, and even Pufendorf's "composite moral person whose will is deemed the will of all" (see above). The problem was that Rousseau had no clear idea of how the general will could be determined. He did not believe in representation, and he regarded majority decisions with suspicion. His theory seemed to make sense only in the context of an ancient Greek city-state society, where the free citizen could realize his full potential. This was not the way his ideas were applied in the French Revolution, where Jacobin demagogues declaimed that they alone were the bearers of the nation's general will.

See also **Absolutism; Aristocracy and Gentry; Authority, Concept of; Autocracy; Bodin, Jean; Bossuet, Jacques-Bénigne; Democracy; Divine Right Kingship; Grotius, Hugo; Hobbes, Thomas; Law; Louis XIV (France); Monarchy; Montesquieu, Charles-Louis de Secondat de; National Identity; Natural Law; Political Philosophy; Republicanism; Rousseau, Jean-Jacques; Tyranny, Theory of.**

BIBLIOGRAPHY

Primary Sources

Althusius, Johannes. *Politics.* Translated and abridged by Frederick S. Carney. Boston, 1964.

Bodin, Jean. *Method for the Easy Comprehension of History.* Translated by Beatrice Reynolds. New York, 1945.

———. *On Sovereignty: Four Chapters from* The Six Books of the Commonwealth. Edited and translated by Julian H. Franklin. Cambridge, U.K., and New York, 1992.

Bossuet, Jacques-Bénigne. *Politics Drawn from the Very Words of Holy Scripture.* Translated and edited by Patrick Riley. Cambridge, U.K., and New York, 1990.

Grotius, Hugo. *The Rights of War and Peace.* Edited by Jean Barbeyrac. London, 1738.

Hobbes, Thomas. *Leviathan: Or, the Matter, Forme, and Power of a Commonwealth, Ecclesiasticall and Civil.* Edited by Michael Oakeshott. Oxford, 1946.

Pufendorf, Samuel. *Of the Law of Nature and Nations: Eight Books.* Translated by Basil Kennet. London, 1717.

Rousseau, Jean-Jacques. *The Social Contract.* Edited and translated by Maurice Cranston. Baltimore, 1968.

Secondary Sources

Dufour, Alfred, "Pufendorf." In *The Cambridge History of Political Thought, 1450–1700.* Edited by J. H. Burns. Cambridge, U.K., and New York, 1991.

Franklin, Julian H. *Jean Bodin and the Rise of Absolutist Theory.* Cambridge, U.K., 1973.

Jouvenel, Bertrand de. *Sovereignty: An Inquiry into the Political Good.* Translated by J. F. Huntington. Chicago, 1957.

Salmon, J. H. M. "The Legacy of Jean Bodin: Absolutism, Populism, or Constitutionalism?" *History of Political Thought* 17, no. 4 (1996): 500–522.

Tuck, Richard. *Philosophy and Government, 1572–1651.* Cambridge, U.K., and New York, 1993. See Chapter 5 on Grotius (pages 154–201) and chapter 7 on Hobbes (pages 279–345).

J. H. M. SALMON

SPAIN. Although the term "Spain," from Latin *Hispania,* had long been used to refer to the greater part of the Iberian Peninsula, that nation did not become a political reality until the marriage of Isabella of Castile (1474–1506) to Ferdinand of Aragón (ruled 1479–1516) united the kingdom of Castile and León with the crown of Aragón. Castile added the Canary Islands during the fifteenth century, Granada in 1492, Melilla in 1497, and most of Navarre after 1512. The crown of Aragón possessed the kingdoms of Aragón and Valencia, the county of Barcelona (Catalonia), and the Balearic Islands. Between 1707 and 1716, Philip V (ruled 1700–1746), first king of the Bourbon dynasty, unified these regions into the single kingdom of Spain, with its sole capital at Madrid.

Prior to the War of the Spanish Succession (1701–1714), the crown of Aragón also held the Mediterranean kingdoms of Sardinia (after 1323), Sicily (from 1409), and Naples (from 1443). Castile, beginning in 1492, acquired a vast empire in the Americas and the Philippine Islands, along with a few towns and forts on the North African coast.

GEOGRAPHY

Spain occupies 85 percent of the Iberian Peninsula. It borders France to the north, the boundary defined since 1659 by the crest of the Pyrenees, following Spain's cession to France of Roussillon and most of Cerdagne. To the west Spain borders Portugal, with the boundary running through rugged, sparsely inhabited country save in its southern reaches, where the Rio Guadiana defines it. For the rest, Spain is surrounded by sea: its northwest and southwest coasts face the Atlantic, its east coast, the Mediterranean. Some eleven miles of the Strait of Gibraltar separate Spain from North Africa.

Spain is mountainous, and its climate, apart from the rainy northwest, ranges from Mediterranean to semiarid. Much of Castile is a high tableland, known as the *meseta*. Barely half Spain's terrain was historically productive, only a fraction rich. Four important rivers, the Duero, Tagus, Guadiana, and Guadalquivir, flow west to the Atlantic. None is navigable for other than small craft until it nears the sea. Each defines a valley with mountains separating it from the others. Of the rivers that flow east, only the Ebro is long, allowing barge traffic in its lower reaches. Shorter rivers that flow east water fertile soils in Catalonia and Valencia and irrigate semiarid *vegas* ('fertile plains') in Murcia and eastern Granada.

For most of the early modern period the historic kingdoms and principalities of Spain defined its political geography. The largest kingdom, Castile, incorporated many others: Galicia in the northwest; the principality of Asturias and the Basque lordships of Vizcaya and Guipúzcoa facing the bay of Biscay; a third Basque lordship, Álava, inland of them; León and Old Castile in the Duero valley; the kingdom of Badajoz, today's Extremadura; New Castile, often called the kingdom of Toledo; the kingdoms of Jaén, Córdoba, and Seville along the course of the Guadalquivir; and, in the mountainous southeast, the kingdoms of Granada and Murcia. The Bourbon King Ferdinand VI (ruled 1746–1759) replaced Castile's historic kingdoms with twenty-four provinces in 1749, each based in a populous capital. In 1799, further subdivision increased the number to thirty-two.

POPULATION AND LANGUAGES

The first attempt at a modern census occurred in 1768. Earlier population figures derive from counts of heads of household *(vecinos)*, usually undertaken by bishops. Sometimes their figures are precise, more often they are rounded guesses. Demographers use multipliers that range from 4 to 6, with 4.5 most common. Philip II (ruled 1556–1598) undertook a detailed census, the *Relaciones topográficas,* but data for only a few regions were actually collected. His counselors thought Castile had about 1,250,000 households. Around 1500 there may have been 6,000,000 Castilian subjects, another 100,000 in Navarre, 300,000 in Aragón, 400,000 in Catalonia, and 600,000 in Valencia. Most were Roman Catholics. In 1492 at least 40,000 Jews, of a population that had numbered over 200,000, chose to leave rather than accept Christianity. The rest became or had earlier become "New Christians," mainly under pressure, and were known as *Conversos*. Many Muslims left after 1500, when Islam was proscribed; most, however, some 400,000, remained and accepted Christianity, as often as not superficially, and became Moriscos.

During the sixteenth century Spain's population grew until checked in the late sixteenth century by agrarian crises and recurring epidemics that decreased it by as much as 20 percent by 1660. In 1609–1611, over 200,000 Moriscos were expelled to North Africa. Economic shifts depopulated many northern Castilian cities, even as Madrid and Seville grew. Emigration to the Americas attracted a few thousand each year, while endless foreign wars took more. Growth in population did not return till after 1680, and the 7,500,000 estimated for the early eighteenth century matched the figure for the sixteenth. By the end of the eighteenth century, Spain's population had reached 11,000,000, with much of the growth in Catalonia, Valencia, the Basque Country, and Andalusia. Apart from the overpopulated capital of Madrid and its vicinity, the Castilian heartland recovered more slowly.

Spain's people spoke several languages. Castilian in its several dialects prevailed in Old and New Castile, Andalusia, Murcia, old Aragón, and most of Navarre. In Galicia people spoke Gallego, a dialect very close to Portuguese. In Catalonia, Valencia, and the Balearics, people spoke Catalan. All these were Romance languages and mostly mutually intel-

Bay of Biscay

FRANCE

La Coruña
Santander

Asturias
CANTABRIAN MOUNTAINS
•Bilbao •San Sebastián
Santiago de
Compostela
Vizcaya Guipúzcoa
PYRENEES
Galicia
León•
Álava
•Pamplona
Navarre
Llobregat
River
Ter R.
Gerona
Pisuerga
River
Burgos•
Ebro River
Catalonia
Old Castile
Zaragoza•
•Lérida
Valladolid
Toro•
Tordesillas•
Duero River
Aragón
•Barcelona
Tormes R.
Salamanca•
Segovia•
CENTRAL MTS.
•Tarragona
Ávila•
IBERIAN MTS.
El Escorial
⊛ Madrid
Turia River
PORTUGAL
Tagus River
Aranjuez•
Cuenca•
•Valencia
Toledo•
MONTES DE TOLEDO
Valencia
Extremadura
New
Castile
BALEARIC ISLANDS
•Ciudad Real
Badajoz•
Guadiana River
La Mancha
SIERRA MORENA
•Murcia
Mediterranean Sea
Córdoba•
Guadalquivir River
Jaén•
•Cartagena
Tinto
River
Seville•
Genil River
Granada•
Huelva•
Andalucía SIERRA NEVADA
Almería•
Sanlúcar de Barrameda•
Málaga•
ALGERIA
Cádiz•
Gibraltar•
Strait of Gibraltar
•Ceuta
ATLANTIC
OCEAN
•Melilla
N
Spain
—— International border
⊛ National capital
• Other city
MOROCCO
0   50   100 mi.
0 50 100 km

ligible. In the Basque Country and parts of Navarre. people spoke Basque, a unique language with no relation to the Romance languages. At court, for government, in correspondence, printing, and literature, Castilian came to dominate. Antonio de Nebrija published a grammar for Castilian in 1492, but, until the establishment of the Royal Academy in 1713, spelling continued to vary widely. Catalan and Galician literature, rich in the Middle Ages, would experience a revival in the nineteenth century.

ECONOMY

Most Spaniards worked the soil and lived at a subsistence level. They dwelled communally in villages, towns, and cities. Many peasant proprietors were found across northern Spain, but in the south large estates *(latifundia)* prevailed, owned by a few and worked by landless laborers. In the seventeenth century high taxes and hard times forced many from the land, and Spain had a conspicuous number of vagabonds. Where lands were arable, cereal crops predominated, save in Valencia, where rice provided an alternate staple. Maintained close to dwellings, gardens provided vegetables and fruit, and poultry provided meat and eggs. Orchards were widespread and Spanish citrus fruit, fortified wines, and olive oil proved profitable exports. While scrub woods suited pigs, much of Spain's land was suitable only for grazing cattle and sheep. Wool provided a major export. Each year vast flocks of sheep walked from winter pastures in southern New Castile and Andalusia to summer pastures in Spain's northern mountains. In a trade that had its ups and downs, Burgos became the center for shipping wool to the

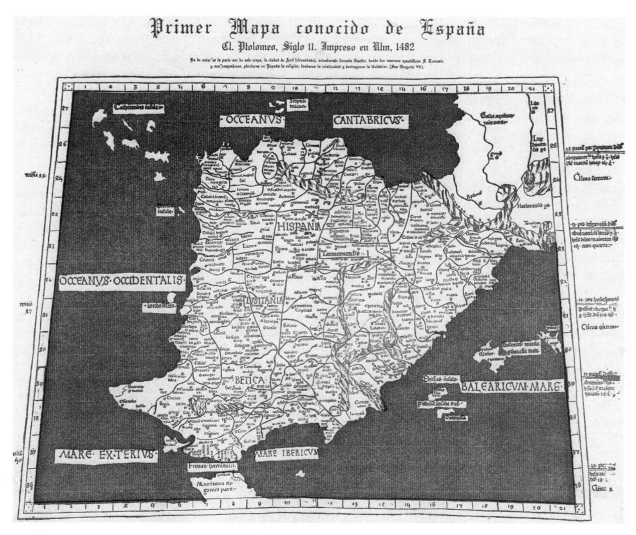

Primer Mapa conocido de España

Cl. Ptolomeo, Siglo II. Impreso en Ulm, 1482

Es de notar en la parte sur de este mapa, la ciudad de Acci (circundada), actualmente llamada Guadir, donde los varones apostólicos S. Torcuato y sus compañeros, plantaron en España la religión, fundaron la cristiandad y destruyeron la idolatría. (San Gregorio VII).

Spain. A reproduction of the first printed map of Spain, from the 1482 edition of Ptolemy's *Geographia* published in Ulm, Germany. It was the first edition to contain woodcut maps, which were drawn by Nicolas Germanus, a Benedictine monk. Ptolemy's work was translated from Greek to Latin in 1406 and disseminated throughout Europe. Early Renaissance geographers used it as their model, adding new maps to the Ptolemaic maps of the classical world. Map Collection, Sterling Memorial Library, Yale University

mills of northwest Europe. Wool shipments to Italian looms were also considerable.

Given Spain's topography, cities of 20,000 people and more, or towns greater than 10,000, generally stood thirty to forty miles distant from one another. Each served as the economic, political, and ecclesiastical hub for its surrounding villages, and provided a focus for the larger regional economy. The lack of navigable rivers and the many mountain barriers limited long-distance transport as well as communication. Most transported goods rode the backs of pack animals. Before the serious improvement of roads in the eighteenth century, wagon

transport seldom left its home region. Until that century, little was done for inland water traffic, despite discussion and periodic planning.

The chief regional economies were those of the major river valleys, the valleys of Catalonia and Valencia, and the maritime economies of the north coast, the gulf of Cádiz, and the coasts of Granada, Murcia, Valencia, and Catalonia. Barcelona, a great medieval commercial center, had been devastated by fourteenth-century plagues, and not till the eighteenth century did it reach its former prosperity. Until that century, local privilege in Castile and the Aragonese realms added further restrictions to internal commerce. Thereafter, Spain's maritime regions became more closely linked, with a revived Catalonia and the Basque Provinces leading.

Manufacture was chiefly limited to local markets. In ironware, military hardware, and shipbuilding, the Basque Provinces dominated, although ships were built along the entire north coast. Old Castile for a long time had a lively textile industry, but that declined in the seventeenth century because foreign goods were cheaper. In the eighteenth century textiles revived, but mainly in Catalonia and Valencia. Catalonia also built ships, though primarily for the Mediterranean. In the sixteenth century Barcelona's arsenal built Spain's Mediterranean galleys, and Málaga founded bronze cannon.

With the opening up of the Americas, their commerce became an important element in Spain's economy and fed many exaggerated notions of Spain's wealth. The crown made Seville the center of American commerce in 1503, but it soon became a clearinghouse. The influx of treasure in the sixteenth century drove Spanish prices up till Spain could only compete through tariffs and restrictions. Other parts of Europe, with longer experience and better resources, produced cheaper goods that came to dominate the American trade, so long as they cleared Seville. By the mid-seventeenth century, Spain could not even provide sufficient shipping for its American trade.

The European wars of the Habsburg dynasty, a heavy tax burden, and the diversion of treasure, goods, and people to warfare abroad, were the chief causes of Spain's economic woes. In the seventeenth century, inflation was compounded by the debasement of currency. In finance and banking, foreigners, above all the Genoese, supplanted less-experienced Spaniards and took their cut. Though popular theorists known as *arbitristas* proposed plans for economic reform, many of them harebrained, little was achieved before the eighteenth century, when Spain made a remarkable economic recovery under more efficient government, even if its Bourbon rulers continued to go to war.

The recovery was most marked on the periphery, where population and industry grew in what became a relatively free market. Influenced by Enlightenment ideas, many of Spain's elite formed societies of *amigos del país* ('friends of the country') and stimulated improvements in education, local industry, and agriculture, while the crown promoted agricultural colonies in long-deserted areas. Economic recovery enabled Spain to tighten control over commerce with its empire, which, along with positive results, bred Spanish-American resentment and inflamed aspirations for independence after 1800.

SOCIETY

Spanish society was based on the three Estates: clergy, nobles, and commoners. The clergy was entered by vocation, the others by birth, although service or money might bring a commoner noble status. Spanish religious life was strong, and the church rich, attracting some 200,000 men and women to the clergy at any time. For ambitious people of humble origins, it offered an avenue to fortune and power. In annual income Spain's primate, the archbishop of Toledo, was second only to the pope.

Perhaps 400,000 Spaniards claimed noble status. At the top stood the grandees, whose number grew from twenty-five in 1520 to 119 by 1787. With great wealth and often great debts, they maintained their domains through *mayorazgo* ('primogeniture'), and dominated provincial life. Like the number of grandees, the number of other nobles with titles grew from perhaps a hundred in 1500 to 585 in 1787. The Bourbon monarchs after 1700 opened a new round in the creation of titles to reward those who served them. With few exceptions, Spanish titles were personal, usually based on one of the holder's domains. Alba de Tormes, from which the duke of Alba's title comes, is simply a lordship, not a duchy. Many without titles possessed domains and were known simply as *señores de vasallos,* 'lords of vassals'. The term *vassal* in Spain, where vestigial feudalism was limited to Aragón and Catalonia, meant anyone under a lord's jurisdiction.

For those claiming noble status, but without domains, the terms *hidalgo* ('nobleman') and *caballero* ('knight') were loosely applied. One was born a *hidalgo;* the king could create a *caballero,* most often as a reward for military service. All natives of some regions, most notably Guipúzcoa, Vizcaya, and Navarre, claimed *hidalgo* status.

Most Spaniards, at whatever economic level and whether they lived in town or country, were com-

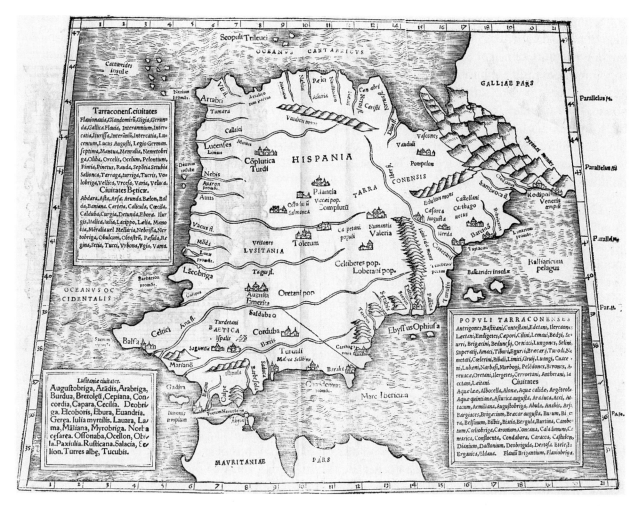

Spain. This Ptolemaic woodblock map of Spain is from Sebastain Münster's 1542 edition of the *Geographia*. At the time of this map, Spain was completing a long process of unification. The last Moorish kingdom, Granada, was conquered in 1492 and the expulsion of the Jews followed soon after. The "Lusitania" on the map is the historic name for Portugal, independent since the twelfth century but claimed by Spain during the Spanish Captivity of 1580–1640. MAP COLLECTION, STERLING MEMORIAL LIBRARY, YALE UNIVERSITY

moners. Unlike the clergy and nobility, they were subject to direct taxes and were often referred to as *pecheros* ('taxpayers').

GOVERNMENT

A monarchy, Spain came under royal jurisdiction. The crown provided justice, made law, organized defense, upheld the church, and collected taxes. From the early sixteenth century, Spanish rulers resided chiefly in Castile and appointed viceroys to their Aragonese and other dominions. To assist the sovereign at court, a system of councils developed that continued through the seventeenth century. The Council of State advised on high policy for all the sovereign's possessions. For Spain there were councils for Castile and Aragón that dealt with administration and law. The Council of War handled military and naval matters. Spain's overseas empire was the business of the Council of the Indies. As Castile provided most of the revenues, its Council of Finance set fiscal policy, largely a matter of struggling with crown debts. The poorer Aragonese realms contributed little, and that with strings. A Council of Military Orders, of which the king became grand master, managed the orders' properties. Most notorious was the Supreme Council of the Inquisition, established in 1480, with jurisdiction over Christians throughout Spain, an organization suspected of being used for political as well as religious ends.

Spain's Bourbon kings after 1700 eliminated the councils, regarded as clumsy and dilatory, save for an honorific Council of State. In their place they appointed responsible ministers for justice, finance, foreign affairs, interior, army, navy, and overseas possessions. Captains general replaced viceroys in the former Aragonese realms and Navarre. In Castile, hereditary offices were suppressed and captaincies general of maritime regions became appointive.

If the sovereign ruled all Spain, at the bottom, in villages, towns, and cities, noble and taxpaying householders elected councils on which both commoners and nobles served. While female heads of household with underage children might not hold office, they enjoyed limited voting rights until they remarried or a son came of age.

Into the major cities of Castile that came directly under its jurisdiction, the crown sent *corregidores* ('magistrates') to look after its interests. Most *corregidores* were well trained in law, and tended to dominate elected counselors, part-timers who had their own private interests to look after. In fortress towns, the *corregidor* was often a soldier, who was assisted by a legist (a specialist in civil law). In the Aragonese kingdoms cities retained greater autonomy until Spain's Bourbon rulers introduced *corregidores* into them. Everywhere they increased *corregidores'* powers, and later appointed intendants (governors) to each province with even greater authority.

Smaller towns and villages might come under the crown's jurisdiction, or that of an ecclesiastical or secular lord, or the nearest city. It was jurisdiction that defined a seignorial domain and produced income through offices, taxes, dues, and fines. Both jurisdictions and offices were often for sale. The lord of a domain, whether king, churchman, or noble, usually owned some lands and businesses in it, but hardly all. Most belonged to vassals, whether noble or common. Much land, especially pastures and woods, was considered common, and there were understood rights to grazing, cutting wood, hunting, and fishing. In Castile *señores* might appoint their own *corregidores* to villages. Villages often sought greater liberty with payments to crown or lord.

In the provision of justice and making of law, Spain's sovereign was in theory absolute, bound only by divine and natural law, and the fundamental laws of Spain, such as the right of female succession. Legal advisers assisted the sovereign. Two chancelleries, in Valladolid and Granada, served Castile as high appellate courts, with broad authority to supervise municipal and seignorial courts. *Audiencias,* lesser appellate courts, existed in Seville and elsewhere. The Aragonese realms had their own appellate system, and Aragón itself had a *justiciar,* who might challenge the king's rulings. After the Chief Justiciary in Saragossa joined a revolt in 1590, the office was suppressed. Under the Bourbon dynasty, Spain's court system was centralized and further refined.

The church served in many respects as a branch of government. The pulpit was the surest way to reach the entire population. The church was also a great landholder. Churchmen served in high office for the crown. Through concordats with the papacy, the crown gradually gained the right to nominate Spain's bishops for papal approval. Education, hospitals, and feeding the poor were the church's business. In theory, Spaniards tithed, though a third of the tithe went to the crown.

For revenues the crown derived many rights from Roman law, including customs and the royal fifth of minerals, which extended to the gold and silver mines of the Americas. Some rights to salt flats and customs duties had been transferred to nobles during the later Middle Ages, but from the reign of Philip II the crown gradually recovered them. Much of the historic crown domain had been transferred as well, but by Ferdinand and Isabella's acquisition of the grand masterships of the Military Orders of Santiago, Calatrava, Alcántara, and Montesa, the crown regained extensive, though seldom rich, domains. These soon became encumbered with debts.

On Castile, richer than the Aragonese realms at the time of union, fell the chief burden of direct taxes till the advent of the Bourbons. After 1538 nobles no longer sat in the Castilian Cortes ('parliament'), which voted subsidies and approved tax increases. Only thirty-six delegates, two each from eighteen royal towns, attended. While stubborn, they generally yielded to the crown's demands.

Spain. This curious map of the Iberian Peninsula is from Edward Wells's atlas *A New Sett of Maps Both of Ancient and Present Geography* published in a number of editions in the early eighteenth century. An Oxford geographer, Wells intended the atlas as an instructional tool for students, perhaps explaining the stylized printing and relative lack of interior detail. Wells was also a tutor to young William, duke of Gloucester, hence the dedication in the title cartouche. MAP COLLECTION, STERLING MEMORIAL LIBRARY, YALE UNIVERSITY

From Moorish times the crown held the right to the *alcabala,* in theory a ten-percent tax on sales and business transactions. Its actual rate was lower and required bargaining with the Cortes for its collection by municipal corporations, and increasingly by royal tax collectors and agents of creditors. Only reluctantly, because of mounting debt and repeated bankruptcies, did the crown agree to levies on basic foodstuffs. The Cortes also granted periodic subsidies in addition to the sums raised through the *alcabala.* As the delegates to the Cortes largely came from the elite, the tax burden fell unduly on the poor. Church wealth provided another big source of royal revenue, mainly arranged through

the papacy, on the argument that Spain crusaded against infidels and heretics.

The Bourbon dynasty, which summoned the Cortes only to acclaim succession to the crown, proved unable to overhaul the Castilian tax structure, but, by eliminating regional privileges in the Aragonese realms, it increased revenues from Catalonia and Valencia as prosperity returned to those areas. From the mid-seventeenth century, corporations of tax farmers undertook much of the revenue collection. Beginning in the early eighteenth century, government finances improved and debt began to decline. Ferdinand VI, whose reign was peaceful, saw a surplus. Mexican silver financed the wars of Charles III (ruled 1759–1788), but with the coming of the French Revolutionary and Napoleonic Wars, debt mounted and government finances turned chaotic.

EDUCATION AND CULTURE

Education was in the hands of the church. Colleges and universities, established in the Middle Ages, concentrated on theology and canon and civil law. To career-oriented students law had the greatest appeal. Science was pursued largely outside the university. Interest in navigation led to an academy of mathematics in Madrid in 1582, while the exotic plants of empire encouraged botanical studies. Though Philip II brought anatomist Andreas Vesalius (1514–1564) to Spain, Spanish medicine remained undistinguished before the work of Andrés Piquer (1711–1772) at the University of Valencia.

Spanish literature of the "Golden Age" peaked with *Don Quixote* by Miguel de Cervantes (1547–1616). Theater flourished with Lope de Vega (1562–1635), Tirso de Molina (1583–1648), and Calderón de la Barca (1600–1681), poetry with St. John of the Cross (1542–1591) and Luis de Góngora (1561–1627). Tomás Luis de Victoria (c.1548–1611) proved a giant of Renaissance music. The Cretan El Greco (1541–1614) caught Spain's religious fervor in paint, while Diego de Velázquez (1599–1660) took painting to unsurpassed levels. For all its renewed prosperity, however, the eighteenth century produced little remarkable, apart from the powerful art of Francisco de Goya (1746–1828), and some good music, with that of Antonio Soler (1729–1783) perhaps the best.

POLITICAL HISTORY, 1474–1516

Ferdinand and Isabella put an end to endemic civil war, restored government, and in 1492 completed the seven-hundred-year "reconquest" of Spain from the Moors with the conquest of Granada. They expelled Spain's Jews, avowedly to prevent those Jews who had become Christian from backsliding. Also in 1492 Isabella commissioned Christopher Columbus to seek Asia by sailing west. His discoveries brought an American empire to Spain.

Rebellion by the Muslims of Granada brought expulsion after 1500 of those who did not accept Christianity. Perhaps 400,000 remained in Spain as New Christian Moriscos, suspected nevertheless by Old Christian Spaniards of insincerity and collaboration with Barbary corsairs and the Ottoman Turks.

Ferdinand's foreign policy led to the dynastic marriage of Princess Joanna to Archduke Philip, son of the Habsburg Holy Roman emperor Maximilian I. The deaths of her only brother Juan, older sister Isabel, and Isabel's infant son made Joanna her parents' heir. When Isabella died in 1504, Queen Joanna (1504–1555) and her consort, Philip I, succeeded to Castile. Philip died in 1506 and Ferdinand became regent for Joanna, who was known as *la loca* ('the Mad'), deemed unfit to rule and confined to a palace at Tordesillas.

HABSBURG SPAIN, 1516–1700

When Ferdinand died in 1516, Joanna's Habsburg son Charles (Carlos I, ruled 1516–1556) succeeded to Castile, Aragón, and the Italian possessions. Born in the Low Countries, which he inherited from his father, Charles also inherited the Austrian lands on Maximilian's death in 1519, and was elected Holy Roman emperor Charles V (ruled 1519–1558). Dunning Spain for money, Charles hurried to Germany in 1520, provoking many Castilian towns to rise in the revolt of the *Comuneros*. Feeling threatened, the landed nobility rallied to Charles and crushed the revolt. A revolt in Valencia that mixed urban grievances and hostility to Moriscos was also crushed by the nobility.

Charles bequeathed his Austrian inheritance to his brother Ferdinand in 1522 and returned to Spain to restore his rule, yet after 1530 he spent little time in Spain. Wars with France in defense of his Low Countries and Italian possessions, with German Lutherans and the Ottoman Turks, drained his energies and increased Spain's debts. In 1556 he abdicated to his Spanish-born son Philip II (ruled 1556–1598). Philip wished to improve government in Spain, but became embroiled in foreign wars. He began his reign with a bankruptcy in 1557 that allowed him to renegotiate his debts. Gaining an edge on France at the battle of St. Quentin (1557), he achieved a favorable peace at Cateau-Cambrésis (1559). Both he and the king of France feared the spread of Protestant heresy. Extirpated by the Inquisition in Spain, Protestantism would prove the chief issue in the Low Countries, where growing unrest led to open revolt in 1568. By 1580 the Low Countries had divided into a Protestant, Dutch-dominated United Netherlands in the north and the "Spanish" Netherlands in the south. Battling the Dutch Revolt proved a drain on both the Spanish treasury and manpower.

In the same years, Ottoman Turkish ambitions fired conflict in the Mediterranean, and in 1568–1571 the Moriscos of Granada rebelled. Though Philip's half-brother Don Juan of Austria crushed the Morisco revolt and, in league with the pope and Venice, defeated the Turkish navy at Lepanto (1571), Philip could not sustain simultaneous wars in the Mediterranean and Low Countries. In 1575 he declared bankruptcy again, and in 1578 achieved a truce with the Turks.

In 1580 he annexed Portugal when its legitimate male line died out, and acquired Portugal's Asian empire with its African way stations. Increasingly fearful of his power, both Protestant England and Catholic France fed the Dutch revolt and attacked Philip's overseas empire and treasure routes. In 1588 Philip launched his great armada to overthrow Queen Elizabeth and restore England to Roman Catholicism, or at least compel her to cease aiding the Dutch. The armada was defeated, but an English attack on Portugal in 1589 also failed. That year Protestant Henry IV succeeded to the French throne. Philip encouraged Catholic rebels and sent his army of Flanders into France against Henry. In 1590, local issues led to a brief revolt in Aragón. By 1595, Philip was at war with the Dutch, England, and France. In 1596 an Anglo-Dutch fleet sacked

Spain. This map was published by Jan Jansson in Amsterdam about 1626. Around the top and bottom borders of the map are several views of Spanish cities (and a portrait of Philip III), while the side borders contain illustrations showing the dress of the Spanish nobility, merchant class, and peasants. MAP COLLECTION, STERLING MEMORIAL LIBRARY, YALE UNIVERSITY

Cádiz. Philip vainly counterattacked with armadas in 1596 and 1597, and again declared bankruptcy. In 1598 he made peace at Vervins with Henry IV, now Catholic, and tried to separate the Low Countries from Spain by bestowing them on his daughter Isabel and her husband, Archduke Albert.

Though disease and famine racked Spain in 1599–1601, Philip III (ruled 1598–1621) persisted in war with England and the Dutch. Winning no advantage, he made peace in 1604 in London with James I of England, and in 1609 accepted a Twelve Years' Truce with the Dutch, but refused to relinquish his claims on their lands. Blame for Spain's shortcomings fell on his *valido* ('favorite'), Francisco Gómez de Sandoval y Rojas (1553–1625), duke of Lerma. Unsuccessful abroad and facing economic problems at home, Spain's government expelled the Moriscos, who did not seem sufficiently assimilated and were suspected of conspiring with North Africa. In 1618, war in central Europe involving the Austrian Habsburgs sucked in Spain as well.

In 1621 Philip III died, the Low Countries reverted to the Spanish monarchy when Albert died childless, and the truce with the Dutch expired. Sixteen-year-old Philip IV (ruled 1621–1665) ascended the throne, while a new *valido*, Don Gaspar de Guzmán (1587–1645), count-duke of Olivares, acquired direction of policy. He determined to make Philip IV the greatest of sovereigns, though most Spaniards had become disillusioned by endless wars, heavy taxes, and relentless recruiting. Olivares knew that Castile bore a disproportionate share of the monarchy's burdens and called for a Union of Arms, which would require more from the Aragonese realms and Portugal. Opposition proved immediate. After early victories, the tide of war turned against the Spanish and Austrian Habsburgs. In 1628 the Dutch captured a treasure fleet, impairing Spain's credit even as Olivares pushed into the Mantuan succession crisis that brought war to Italy. In 1635, France openly joined the anti-Habsburg forces it had long aided, and in 1639 the Dutch shattered Spain's last great armada in the battle of the Downs.

Early in 1640 Olivares's policies provoked rebellion in Catalonia. At the end of that year Portugal, its empire savaged by Spain's Dutch foes, de-clared independence under John IV of Braganza. The growing cry for Olivares's removal succeeded in 1643, when Philip dismissed him. Don Luis de Haro took over direction of policy and sought peace. In 1648 Philip conceded Dutch independence at Münster, but war with France continued over holdings both crowns claimed. Even as Philip recovered Catalonia in 1655, England joined France against Spain. Beaten, in 1659 Philip signed the Peace of the Pyrenees, which both ceded territory and gave his eldest daughter Maria Teresa as bride to Louis XIV of France. Though she renounced all claims to Spain's throne for herself and her heirs, most jurists held that she could not bind them. When Philip IV died in 1665, his sickly four-year-old son Charles II (ruled 1665–1700) became king. Charles's sister, Margarita, married Emperor Leopold I (ruled 1658–1705).

The reign of Charles proved the nadir of Spain's fortunes, though after 1680 there was some faint hope for recovery. Always sickly, he sired no offspring. Bourbon Louis XIV and Habsburg Leopold I each sought to win Spain's throne for a candidate of his dynasty, while Louis nibbled at Charles's possessions that bordered France. In Spain Juan José de Austria (1629–1679), Philip IV's bastard, and the count of Oropesa, chief minister (1685–1691), struggled to maintain government while England and the Dutch tried to arbitrate the anticipated Spanish succession by partition of the inheritance among rival candidates. But Charles rejected partition and Spaniards supported him. Irritated by the Habsburg party at court and aware that France, not Austria, had a navy, Charles's counselors, led by Cardinal Portocarrero of Toledo, persuaded Charles to will his inheritance to Philip (1683–1746), duke of Anjou, grandson of Maria Teresa and Louis XIV, who became Philip V of Spain.

BOURBON SPAIN, 1700–1808

On Charles's death (1 November 1700), Louis accepted Charles's will and dispatched Philip V (ruled 1700–1724, 1724–1746) to Spain. Leopold declared war and claimed Spain for his younger son Charles. In 1702 England and the Dutch joined Leopold in the War of the Spanish Succession. When it ended in 1713, Philip retained only Spain and its overseas empire. Aided by Frenchman Jean Orry, dedicated ministers undertook fruitful reforms. In 1724 Philip abdicated to his son Luis, who quickly died, and Philip resumed the throne. His second wife, Elisabeth Farnese, involved Spain in wars that successfully won the Two Sicilies for her son Charles and Parma for her son Felipe. Philip and his son Ferdinand VI (ruled 1746–1759) continued to enjoy the services of ministers committed to improvements, such as Zenón de Somodevilla (1702–1781), marquis of La Ensenada. As Ferdinand was childless, Charles III (ruled 1759–1788) came to Spain from the Two Sicilies.

His enlightened reign saw Spain prosper, after the so-called Esquilache riots of 1766, spurred by the high cost of bread, prompted further reform. Modernizing ministers included the counts of Aranda, Campomanes, and Floridablanca, and Gaspar de Jovellanos (1744–1811), the most renowned. Threatened, the church and old nobility opposed many reforms, and in 1767 Charles expelled the Jesuits, but the Inquisition, an embarrassment to many, survived. Spain allied with France against Britain in the war of American Independence. With Louisiana ceded to Spain by France in 1763, and California opened to colonization, the empire reached its greatest extent.

A year after Charles IV (ruled 1788–1808) succeeded his father, revolution erupted in France. Spain joined the antirevolutionary coalition and went to war. When the regicides who guillotined Louis XVI were overthrown, Spain made peace with France. Manuel de Godoy (1767–1851), Charles's chief minister and purported lover of Queen Maria Luisa, came to dominate the Spanish government and renewed the French alliance. War as France's ally, however, proved disastrous. The battles of Cape St. Vincent (1797) and Trafalgar (1805) destroyed Spain's navy. Napoleon coerced Louisiana from Charles and sold it to the United States. Spaniards demanded peace and at Aranjuez in 1808 popular riots forced Charles IV to abdicate to his son Ferdinand VII (ruled 1808–1833). Napoleon promptly invaded Spain, imprisoned Charles and Ferdinand in France, and put his brother Joseph Bonaparte on Spain's throne. Spain's war of Independence (1808–1813) followed, leaving Spain devastated and its American empire in revolution. The restoration in 1814 of the absolutist Ferdinand quashed the effort of the 1812 Cortes of Cádiz to make Spain a constitutional monarchy, and created a state of political instability that racked Spain during the nineteenth century.

See also **Armada, Spanish; Barcelona; Bourbon Dynasty (France); Bourbon Dynasty (Spain); Cádiz; Catalonia; Cateau-Cambrésis (1559); Cervantes, Miguel de; Charles III (Spain); Charles V (Holy Roman Empire); Charles VI (Holy Roman Empire); Columbus, Christopher;** *Comuneros* **Revolt (1520–1521);** *Conversos;* **Dutch Revolt (1568–1648); Ferdinand of Aragón; Ferdinand VI (Spain); Góngora y Argote, Luis de; Goya y Lucientes, Francisco de; Habsburg Dynasty; Inquisition, Spanish; Isabella of Castile; Joanna I, "the Mad" (Spain); Juan de Austria, Don; Leopold I (Holy Roman Empire); Lepanto, Battle of; Lerma, Francisco Gómez de Sandoval y Rojas, 1st duke of; Louis XIV (France); Madrid; Mantuan Succession, War of the (1627–1631); Maria Theresa (Holy Roman Empire); Moriscos; Moriscos, Expulsion of (Spain); Netherlands, Southern; Olivares, Gaspar de Guzmán y Pimentel, Count of; Philip II (Spain); Philip III (Spain); Philip IV (Spain); Philip V (Spain); Pyrenees, Peace of the (1661); Spain, Art in; Spanish Colonies; Spanish Literature and Language; Spanish Succession, War of the (1701–1714); Thirty Years' War (1618–1648); Utrecht, Peace of (1713); Vega, Lope de; Wars of Religion, French.**

BIBLIOGRAPHY

Brown, Jonathan. *The Golden Age of Painting in Spain.* New Haven, 1991.

Callahan, William. *Church, Politics, and Society in Spain, 1750–1874.* Cambridge, Mass., 1984.

Defourneaux, Marcelin. *Daily Life in Spain in the Golden Age.* Translated by Newton Branch. Stanford, 1979.

Domínguez Ortiz, Antonio. *The Golden Age of Spain, 1516–1659.* Translated by James Casey. London, 1971.

Elliott, John H. *The Count-Duke of Olivares: The Statesman in an Age of Decline.* New Haven, 1986.

——. *Imperial Spain, 1469–1716.* London, 1963.

——. *The Revolt of the Catalans: A Study in the Decline of Spain, 1598–1640.* Cambridge, U.K., 1963.

——. *Spain and Its World, 1500–1700: Selected Essays.* New Haven, 1989.

Glendinning, Nigel. *The Eighteenth Century.* New York, 1972. (In series *The Literary History of Spain.*)

Goodman, David C. *Power and Penury: Government, Technology, and Science in Philip II's Spain.* Cambridge, U.K., 1988.

Haliczer, Stephen. *The Comuneros of Castile: The Forging of a Revolution, 1475–1521.* Madison, Wis., 1981.

Herr, Richard. *The Eighteenth-Century Revolution in Spain.* Princeton, 1958.

Hilgarth, Jocelyn. *The Spanish Kingdoms, 1250–1516.* Vol. 2. Oxford, 1978.

Hilt, Douglas. *The Troubled Trinity: Godoy and the Spanish Monarchs.* Tuscaloosa, Ala., 1987.

Jones, Royston O. *The Golden Age: Prose and Poetry: The Sixteenth and Seventeenth Centuries.* New York, 1971. (In series *The Literary History of Spain.*)

Kagan, Richard L. *Students and Society in Early Modern Spain.* Baltimore, 1974.

Kamen, Henry. *Spain, 1469–1714: A Society in Conflict.* 2nd ed. London, 1991.

———. *The Spanish Inquisition: An Historical Revision.* London, 1997.

———. *The War of Succession in Spain, 1700–15.* London, 1969.

Lynch, John. *Bourbon Spain, 1700–1808.* Oxford, 1989.

———. *Spain under the Habsburgs.* 2 vols. Oxford, 1991, 1992.

Nader, Helen. *Liberty in Absolutist Spain: The Habsburg Sale of Towns 1516–1700.* Baltimore, 1990.

Phillips, Carla Rahn. *Ciudad Real 1500–1750: Growth, Crisis, and Readjustment in the Spanish Economy.* Cambridge, Mass., 1979.

———. *Six Galleons for the King of Spain: Imperial Defense in the Early Seventeenth Century.* Baltimore, 1986.

Phillips, Carla Rahn, and William D. Phillips, Jr. *Spain's Golden Fleece: Wool Production and the Wool Trade from the Middle Ages to the Nineteenth Century.* Baltimore, 1997.

Pike, Ruth. *Aristocrats and Traders: Sevillian Society in the Sixteenth Century.* Ithaca, N.Y., 1972.

Reher, David S. *Perspectives on the Family in Spain, Past and Present.* Oxford, 1997.

Ringrose, David. *Spain, Europe, and the "Spanish Miracle," 1700–1900.* Cambridge, U.K., 1996.

Sahlins, Peter. *Boundaries: The Making of France and Spain in the Pyrenees.* Berkeley, 1989.

Thompson, I. A. A. *War and Government in Habsburg Spain, 1560–1620.* London, 1976.

PETER PIERSON

SPAIN, ART IN. In 1469 the marriage of Ferdinand of Aragón and Isabella of Castile united their respective territories, giving form to what was, even in the fifteenth century, identified as "Hispania." Their reign saw the surrender of Granada, which brought an end to a seven-century-long campaign to regain the Iberian Peninsula from the Moors who had invaded in 711; it also saw Christopher Columbus's voyage to America. The reign of these monarchs—known as the Catholic kings—has long been seen as a "golden age" in Spanish history.

As the monarchs solidified their powers, the court of the Catholic kings was continually on the move. The historian J. H. Elliot sees in this a certain cultural advantage: Isabella, who enjoyed a European reputation as a patron of learning, brought distinguished scholars to her court, whose ideas were disseminated as the court moved about the Iberian peninsula. However, a peripatetic court is not conducive to patronage of painting or collecting. Thus, the monarchs made no effort to encourage training or patronage of native artists and often turned toward Northern Europe to fulfill their needs, which included court portraiture. Such patronage continued a trend famously illustrated by Isabella's father, John II of Castile, who had founded the Carthusian monastery of Miraflores near Burgos in 1442 and donated an altarpiece by Rogier van der Weyden, described in contemporary documents as "Master Rogier, the great and famous Fleming" (Staatliche Museen, Berlin).

Yet the Catholic kings' patronage of nonnative artists, such as the Estonian Michel Sittow or the Flemish artist simply known as "Juan de Flandes" (John of Flanders), introduces a trend that is seen throughout the history of painting in early modern Spain, namely, royal patronage of non-native artists whose style then influenced the work of other painters. In the coming centuries, Philip II commissioned from Titian several mythological paintings, known as the *poesie* and illustrating stories from Ovid's *Metamorphoses,* and Philip IV would commission of Peter Paul Rubens several works, including a series of mythological subjects to decorate his hunting lodge, the Torre de la Parada. And when, in 1701, the Bourbons replaced the Habsburgs on the Spanish throne, they looked to France and Italy for artists to fill the demands at court. The history of painting in Spain is thus a history of cross-currents and international influences, and it is misleading to reduce the story to a strictly nationalist concept of "Spanish" painting.

The influence of Flemish artists is seen in the early works of Pedro Berruguete (1450s–d. by 6

January 1504) but is tempered by lessons learned during the artist's trip to Italy sometime prior to 1483. One of Berruguete's best-known works is a series of paintings for the main altarpiece of the Dominican monastery of St. Thomas in Ávila, several panels of which hang today in the Museo del Prado, Madrid. One of these is a multifigured scene, showing Saint Dominic presiding over an auto-da-fé. While the linear rendering of the figures betrays lessons gleaned from Flemish art, the complex space of the painting, with its stairs and various platforms, suggest the artist's interest in addressing issues of perspective possibly learned in Italy.

In 1519 the grandson of Ferdinand and Isabella came to the Spanish throne as duke of Burgundy and Charles I of Spain, and would ultimately become Charles V, Holy Roman emperor. His need to oversee and protect his vast dominions, which added to the Iberian territories Burgundy, the Netherlands, Austria, Naples, Sicily, and Sardinia, meant that his court was, like that of his grandparents, peripatetic. He nevertheless met Titian in 1529, and from that developed a relationship of patron and artist that would continue until Charles's death in 1558. When Titian joined the emperor in Augsburg in 1548, the result would be a key painting in monarchic iconography that also captures the militaristic nature of his reign: the equestrian portrait *Charles V at the Battle of Mühlberg* (1548; Museo del Prado, Madrid).

PAINTING UNDER PHILIP IV

In 1561 Charles's son Philip II, who had reigned for five years, made the decision to move his court from Toledo to Madrid, perhaps because the winding, narrow streets and medieval infrastructure of Toledo could no longer accommodate Philip's growing retinue. In Madrid, the court would reside in the Moorish fortress of the Alcázar, which would be continually renovated and serve as the residence of Spanish kings until it was destroyed by fire in 1734. Perhaps because the Alcázar no longer exists, Philip II has become more closely identified with the palace-monastery at the Escorial, where the court would reside during Holy Week and on other major church feasts.

The Escorial, commissioned by Philip and built during his reign, is a unique complex encompassing apartments for the royal family and court, a semi-

nary, a monastery, a royal basilica, and a royal tomb. Begun by the court architect Juan Bautista de Toledo (d. 1567), the project was taken over after his death by Juan de Herrera (c. 1530–1597). In 1576 Juan Fernández de Navarrete (c. 1526–1579) was contracted to paint forty altarpieces to decorate the basilica. These were to represent paired saints, and their iconography reconfirmed the validity of the veneration of saints as well as the use of devotional images, both tenets reconfirmed by the Council of Trent (1545–1563). Three months before his death, Navarrete received the commission for the high altar of the basilica. Padre de Siguenza, a prior of the Escorial who in 1605 provided an invaluable account of its history, wrote that had Navarrete not died, Spain might have been spared the incursion of Italian artists who subsequently took over the decoration of the complex. The main Italian contributor was Pellegrino Tibaldi (1527–1596), who after his arrival in 1588 directed a team of artists to paint the murals in the library and also painted the main altarpiece for the basilica. But the Escorial also lured a painter destined to become far more closely identified with painting in Spain, Doménikos Theotokópoulous, more commonly known as El Greco (1541–1614).

El Greco had arrived in Toledo in 1577, where he was commissioned to paint *The Disrobing of Christ* (1577–1579, Cathedral Sacristy, Toledo) and the main altarpiece of Santo Domingo el Antiguo, the central panel of which depicts the Assumption of the Virgin (1577; The Art Institute of Chicago). In both works, vibrant colors, fluid brushwork, and complex compositions of gesticulating, elongated figures attest to lessons learned during the Greek native's sojourn in Venice and Rome (1568–1577). In the case of *The Disrobing of Christ* several iconographic details met with the disapproval of El Greco's patrons, suggesting that the artist brought with him from Italy a strong sense of artistic license to which Spanish patrons were unaccustomed. The artist's creativity also may have worked against him when, in 1580, he received a commission to paint *The Martyrdom of Saint Maurice and the Theban Legion* for the chapel at the Escorial (1580–1582; the Escorial Museum). In the final painting, El Greco goes against Counter-Reformation dictates, relegating the scene of martyrdom to the distance, while placing in the foreground the consultation among the soldiers that led to the martyrdom. This order was reversed in a second version of the theme, painted by Romulo Cincinato, which was displayed in the chapel; El Greco's painting was relegated to the chapter house of the monastery.

Having failed to win his bid for royal patronage, El Greco returned to Toledo, where he would establish his reputation among a learned group of private and ecclesiastic patrons. Here he would paint what is perhaps his greatest achievement, *The Burial of the Count of Orgaz* (1586–1588, Santo Tomé, Toledo) to decorate the count's refurbished burial chapel. The subject of the painting is the 1323 funeral of this distinguished and charitable citizen of Toledo, at which Saints Stephen and Augustine miraculously appeared to lower him into his grave. El Greco includes portraits of his contemporaries attending the funeral, as the count's soul is taken to the heavens, depicted in the upper half of the painting. Here, weightless and elongated figures are perched on the clouds, likewise witnessing the miracle.

PAINTING IN SEVILLE

During the last years of the sixteenth century, the southern port city of Seville became increasingly important, enriched by trade with the New World. Art patronage often follows wealth, so it is not surprising that the first half of the seventeenth century finds in Seville the young Diego de Velázquez (1599–1661), who would soon move to the court of Madrid and will be discussed in the context of his career there; Francisco de Zurbarán (1598–1664); and Bartolomé Esteban Murillo (1617–1682). Zurbarán and Murillo worked mainly for religious patrons, although we should not overlook the masterful still-life paintings of Zurbarán, or the genre scenes of young children by Murillo, which were the first works by the artist admired widely outside of Spain.

Zurbarán's mature style is characterized by a realism and intense chiaroscuro that give his otherworldly figures a sculptural presence in the here and now. Although these traits might recall the work of Caravaggio, Zurbarán's style is far less Italianate in its absence of mathematical perspective and rendering of volumes. Examined closely, we find his figures to be linear and somewhat flat, traits

countered by the hyperrealistic shadowing. Yet, the absence of Italianate principles does not compromise the power of his figures, exemplified by the almost life-size *Christ on the Cross* painted for the Sevillian monastery of San Pablo el Real (1627; The Art Institute of Chicago). Here, the painter's precise handling and dramatic chiaroscuro demand our attention—as it forced the monastic viewer to contemplate the humanity and sacrifice of Christ. Anatomical correctness is secondary to the overall impact: Christ's arms are too long for his form, and his body, despite its surface modeling, appears without volume in space.

By the 1640s Zurbarán's dominance of painting in Seville would be challenged by the younger Murillo, who soon moved away from a Caravagesque realism to depicting more idealized figures in a softer, more painterly idiom. It has often been suggested that Murillo's more tempered style provided an aesthetic antidote to the troubles that ravaged Seville at midcentury, as New World trade moved south to the port city of Cádiz. Certainly, the beautiful Madonnas who float in the heavens in Murillo's images of the Immaculate Conception would support this theory. But even in narrative images, such as *The Return of the Prodigal Son* painted for the Hospital of Charity in Seville (1667–1670; National Gallery of Art, Washington, D.C.) realism is tempered, and the theme of love and forgiveness emphasized.

PHILIP IV AND VELÁZQUEZ

Meanwhile in Madrid, Philip III died prematurely at the age of forty-three in 1621, leaving the throne to his sixteen-year-old son, Philip IV. The young Philip did not come alone to power but was accompanied by an Andalusian aristocrat, Gaspar de Guzmán y Pimental, better known as the count-duke of Olivares. Assuming the role of the royal favorite—that is, close adviser and confidant of the king—the count-duke was also loyal to his native Seville. This connection explains the arrival at court in 1623 of the twenty-four-year-old native of that city, Velázquez.

Soon after his arrival, Velázquez established himself as a court portraitist, painting the king, his brother (Don Carlos), and the count-duke. But equally important, his presence at court led him to study the royal collection—rich in works by

Art in Spain. Still life by Francisco Zurbarán, c. 1633. ©Francis G. Mayer/Corbis

Titian—and also to meet Peter Paul Rubens (1577–1640), who visited the court in 1628. It was perhaps this encounter that led Velázquez to attempt his first mythological subject, *The Feast of Bacchus* (1628, Prado). The painting marks a breakthrough in Velázquez's work, as he creates a multifigured scene, centered on the partially nude figure of the god. Perhaps, too, it was Rubens who inspired Velázquez to undertake in 1629 his first journey to Italy, following an itinerary that would take him to Venice, Rome, and Naples.

During the 1630s Philip IV undertook the construction and decoration of a new pleasure palace in Madrid, to become known as the Buen Retiro. He would commission twelve artists—among them Velázquez and Zurbarán—to paint scenes commemorating recent military triumphs for the ceremonial hall known at the Hall of the Realms. Velázquez's contribution, *The Surrender at Breda* (1634–1635, Prado), shows the degree to which his style had matured since his arrival at court. On a canvas measuring ten feet in width, he portrays the surrender of the Dutch general Justin of Nassau to Ambrogio Spinola. Figures from both armies surround their leaders in a foreground set against a panoramic landscape that is made luminous by the liberal use of white underpainting, covered by glazes of color.

Unlike many court patrons, Philip IV apparently did not limit the range of Velázquez's work and may well have encouraged his experimentation. To be sure, Velázquez continued to paint portraits of the royal family. But he also took up other themes, including portraits of court jesters and dwarfs, mythological subjects, and complex compositions that blend mythology and contemporary genre (*The Fable of Arachne*, c. 1655, Prado). His greatest achievement, blending narrative, theater and portraiture, is *Las Meninas* or *The Maids of Honor* (c. 1656, Prado).

On one level, *Las Meninas* is a portrait of the Philip's daughter, the Infanta Margarita, attended by her retinue. But looking to the left, we find Velázquez painting at his easel and, like the infanta, looking in our direction. Although the object of his gaze is uncertain, it may well be the king and queen, who are reflected in the mirror at the center of the back wall in the painting. Some scholars have suggested that the royal couple has just entered the room, which explains why some of the figures in the painting are aware of their presence and others not. But if this is the case, what is Velázquez painting?

Velázquez marks the zenith of painting at the Habsburg court, and his capable contemporaries and successors at court are diminished by comparison. As a result, such painters as Juan Carreño de

Art in Spain. *The Surrender at Breda* by Diego Velázquez, 1635. THE ART ARCHIVE/MUSEO DEL PRADO MADRID/THE ART ARCHIVE

Miranda and Claudio Coello, who painted during the reign of Charles II (ruled 1675–1700), have not received the attention they deserve.

ART AT THE BOURBON COURT AND GOYA'S BEGINNINGS

On the death of Charles II, it was decided that the grandson of Louis XIV would accede to the Spanish throne. Although this succession was challenged by England, Austria, and the Netherlands, the death of their candidate in 1711 led to the Treaty of Utrecht, which gave the Spanish throne to the Bourbons, who reign to the present day.

This change in dynasty signaled a major change in patronage, as the Bourbon monarchs brought to Spain Italian and French painters, sculptors, and architects, such as René Carlier, who in the 1720s designed the rococo gardens of the palace at La Granja outside Segovia. Adopting French models, the Bourbons also founded establishments for the manufacture of luxury goods needed by the court, including porcelains, silks, and tapestries. Painters, like the architects and designers brought to Spain by the Bourbons, introduced a radical stylistic change, epitomized by the group portrait *The Family of Philip V* (1743; Prado) by Louis Michel van Loo (1707–1771). Here, members of the court, including Philip's second wife, Elizabeth French, pose in French costume before a draped colonnade that opens onto a park. The Bourbons also encouraged

Art in Spain. *The Family of Carlos IV* by Francisco Goya, 1801. ©ART RESOURCE

new genres, including scenes of life at court, and views of the royal palaces created by Michael-Ange Houasse during the 1720s.

The major artistic undertaking of the mid-eighteenth century was the building of the royal palace, to replace the Alcázar, destroyed by fire in 1734. The Italian Giovanni Battista Sacchetti (1690–1764) worked on the project until 1760, when the new king, Charles III (himself recently arrived from Naples) replaced him with Francisco Sabatini (1721–1797). It was during Sabatini's tenure as first court architect that Anton Raphael Mengs and Giambattista Tiepolo arrived in Madrid to paint ceiling frescoes within the palace. Mengs, in turn, trained Spanish artists, including Francisco Bayeu y Subías, who, as court painter, would proba-

bly introduce his brother-in-law, Francisco Goya y Lucientes, to court in 1774.

Although Goya is more often linked to Velázquez than to any other painter, we should not underestimate the extent to which the cosmopolitan patronage of the Bourbons informed his training. His early training in Saragossa was with a Neapolitan-trained painter, and he traveled to Parma and Rome in the early 1770s, developing a late baroque figural style seen in religious paintings done on his return to Saragossa in 1772. When he was invited to Madrid in 1774, it was to create designs, or cartoons, for tapestries to be woven by the Royal Tapestry Factory of Santa Barbara—one of the luxury goods factories established by the Bourbons. Although his first series, done under the supervision of Francisco Bayeu, were rather staid hunting scenes, he soon received permission to conceive scenes of "his own invention." The impetus for the innovative nature of these scenes of life in and around Goya's Madrid has never been explained but may be indebted in part to the work of French genre painters, such as Houasse (whose works were in the royal collection) or Jean-Antoine Watteau (whose works Goya might have known through engravings).

When Goya turned to portraiture in the 1780s, he worked in a very detailed and descriptive style inspired by Mengs, as illustrated by *The Marquesa de Pontejos* (1786; National Gallery of Art, Washington, D.C.). The marquesa stands against a pastel landscape, wearing a dress of gauze decorated with flowers and ribbons, in a work whose tones and compositions recall the portraits of Mengs.

In April 1789 Goya won the long-sought position of court painter. But with the downfall of the Bourbons in France, Goya's patrons would demand an independent identity and iconography. Goya himself would create this identity, as in his royal portraits of the late 1790s—including *The Family of Carlos IV* (1800–1801; Prado); he looked back, not to the French artists brought to Spain under the Bourbon court, but to Velázquez, whose somber palette and painterly style he now emulated. Thus the artist creates a "Spanish tradition" in his quest to define the Spanish identity of his patrons. It is at this point that we can begin to speak of Spanish painting as a willed construction rather than a historical fact.

See also **Art: Artistic Patronage; Bourbon Dynasty (Spain); El Greco; Ferdinand of Aragón; Goya y Lucientes, Francisco de; Painting; Philip IV (Spain); Velázquez, Diego; Zurbarán, Francisco de.**

BIBLIOGRAPHY

Baticle, Jeannine, et al. *Zurbarán*. Exh. cat. New York, 1987.

Brown, Jonathan. *Painting in Spain, 1500–1700*. New Haven and London, 1998.

———. *Velázquez, Painter and Courtier*. New Haven and London, 1986.

Brown, Jonathan, and J. H. Elliott. *A Palace for a King: The Buen Retiro and the Court of Philip IV*. 2nd ed. New Haven and London, 1986.

Cherry, Peter, and Xanthe Brooke. *Murillo: Scenes from Childhood*. London, 2001.

El Greco of Toledo. Exh. cat. Washington, D.C., 1982.

Elliott, J. H. *Imperial Spain, 1496–1716*. New York, 1963.

Jordan, William B., and Peter Cherry. *Spanish Still Life from Velázquez to Goya*. London, 1994.

Stratton-Pruitt, Suzanne, et al. *Bartolomé Esteban Murillo, 1617–1682: Paintings from American Collections*. Exh. cat. New York, 2002.

Tomlinson, Janis. *Francisco Goya: The Tapestry Cartoons and the Early Career at the Court of Madrid*. Cambridge, U.K., and New York, 1989.

———. *Francisco Goya y Lucientes, 1746–1828*. 2nd ed. London, 1999.

———. *From El Greco to Goya: Painting in Spain, 1561–1828*. New York, 1997.

JANIS TOMLINSON

SPANISH ARMADA. *See* **Armada, Spanish.**

SPANISH COLONIES

This entry includes six subentries:
AFRICA AND THE CANARY ISLANDS
THE CARIBBEAN
MEXICO
OTHER AMERICAN COLONIES
PERU
THE PHILIPPINES

AFRICA AND THE CANARY ISLANDS

The geographic frontier between the Iberian Peninsula and North Africa is well defined by the Strait of Gibraltar. However, the cultural and religious frontier between those geographical areas has not always been so clear. For five centuries (the eighth to the twelfth centuries) Muslim invaders from North Africa ruled more than half the territory that now defines Spain and Portugal. Thereafter the Christian kingdoms in Portugal and Spain took advantage of factional strife in Al-Andalus—as the Muslims called their Iberian lands—to make rapid territorial gains. Once the great cities of Cordoba (Cordova) and Seville fell to Christian troops in 1236 and 1248, respectively, Castilian armies pushed southward against the remnant of Muslim territories.

The final assault against the Nasrid kingdom of Granada in 1492 completed the Spanish Reconquista. Thereafter the "Catholic monarchs" Ferdinand of Aragón (ruled Castile 1474–1504; ruled Aragón 1479–1516) and Isabella of Castile (ruled Castile 1474–1504; ruled Aragón 1479–1504) established several strongholds on North African shores, forming a new frontier against the kingdom of Morocco and the Ottoman regencies set up in Algiers and Tunis. In geopolitical terms the most dynamic forces were driving from north to south instead of from south to north, as they had in medieval times. Nonetheless, despite the differences in religion and economic outlook that divided the peoples on opposite sides of the frontier, they should be considered as parts of the same complex Mediterranean civilization, as Ferdinand Braudel so eloquently argued. Scholars have traced the divergent history of the eastern Mediterranean (the Maghreb) and the western (the Iberian Peninsula), so a few centuries later Latin Catholics and Sunni Muslims living at opposite ends of the Mediterranean seemed to have little in common.

Regardless of scholarly controversies about the matter, it seems obvious to most observers that the union of the crowns of Castile and Aragón in 1479 and the overseas discoveries from 1492 on impelled Spanish naval and commercial interests to establish several strongholds along the northern coast of modern Maghreb: Melilla in 1497; Oran, Bejaïa (Bougie), and Tripoli in the first decade of the sixteenth century; and finally Ceuta, which had been in Portuguese hands since 1415, in 1580. Thereafter for the rest of the early modern period these and other forts along the Mediterranean and Atlantic coasts of North Africa formed a Christian frontier against Islam.

Exerting an attraction for kings, sailors, and adventurers from both Spain and Portugal, these strongholds also might have served as springboards for further conquests into Africa but for several historical developments. First, the development of Spain's American colonies and Portugal's Asian colonies exhausted most of the energy and resources they had available for overseas development. Second, the strong resistance of local peoples and their Muslim leaders thwarted Christian attempts to capture substantial territory in the Maghreb. The disastrous defeat of Portuguese forces at the battle of Al-Qasr (Al-Kasr Al-Kabir) in 1578 proved to be a powerful deterrent to Iberian ambitions across the Strait of Gibraltar for the rest of the early modern

period. Those ambitions were only renewed in the halcyon days of empire building in the late nineteenth century.

The military conquest and administrative inclusion of the Canary Islands within the crown of Castile took place over the course of the fifteenth century—in other words, as Iberian mariners and adventurers explored into the western Mediterranean and Atlantic Ocean with royal backing. Although such adventures became possible during the last two centuries of the Christian Reconquest of the peninsula from the Muslims, it was by no means easy due to the remoteness of the Canary Islands from mainland Europe and the strong resistance of the native Canarians (Guanches). Eventually, as Iberian colonies were settled on each of the seven islands, a new society began to evolve but largely in a random and unplanned manner. Although precise statistics do not exist, many scholars think that most of the native population succumbed to European diseases and warfare and that those remaining intermarried with their conquerors. For all practical purposes they ceased to exist as a distinct group. By the end of the sixteenth century the whole Canarian archipelago probably held about fifty thousand people.

From the late fifteenth century to 1821 the Canaries underwent a process of increasing assimilation into Spanish political and cultural norms, despite periodic attacks from North Africa and from Dutch and English privateers and pirates in the seventeenth century. By the early twenty-first century the Canary Islands still formed part of the Spanish state, included in the 1978 constitution. Ceuta and Melilla were the last remnants of Spain's colonial presence in North Africa. They were also part of the Spanish state, their position defined by the 1978 constitution and by negotiations in the 1980s.

See also **Colonialism; Exploration; Ferdinand of Aragón; Isabella of Castile; Spain.**

BIBLIOGRAPHY

Béthencourt Massieu, Antonio de, et al., eds. *Historia de Canarias.* Las Palmas de Gran Canaria, 1995.

Braudel, Ferdinand. *The Mediterranean and the Mediterranean World in the Age of Philip II.* 2 vols. Translated from the French by Siân Reynolds. New York, 1972. First French edition, Paris, 1949.

Clancy-Smith, Julia, ed. "North Africa, Islam, and the Mediterranean World." Special issue. *Journal of North African Studies* 6, no. 1 (Spring 2001).

Fernández-Armesto, Felipe. *The Canary Islands after the Conquest: The Making of a Colonial Society in the Early Sixteenth Century.* Oxford and New York, 1982.

Hess, Andrew C. *The Forgotten Frontier: A History of the Sixteenth Century Ibero-African Frontier.* Chicago, 1978.

Morales Lezcano, Víctor. *Las fronteras de la Península Ibérica en los siglos XVIII y XIX: Esbozo histórico de algunos conflictos Franco-Hispano-Magrebíes.* Madrid, 2000.

VÍCTOR MORALES LEZCANO

THE CARIBBEAN

Historiography often renders the Spanish Caribbean islands of the early modern period either as mere backwaters, the initial significance of which was rapidly overtaken by the much larger and more lucrative colonies of New Spain and Peru, or as the "Caribbean experiment," the sites where insular colonialism was first tried before being perfected on the continents. However, from the very first moment of contact the encounters and clashes between Spaniards and native peoples of the Caribbean forged the intellectual and cultural template for Spain's subsequent colonial rule in the rest of the hemisphere. Though the major colonies of Cuba, Puerto Rico, and Hispaniola became the imperial periphery after the conquest and colonization of the mainland empire, they remained strategically important as a periphery that Spain nonetheless defended fiercely. Thus Spain's Caribbean colonies must be understood as integral parts of the early modern colonial system.

CONQUEST AND COLONIZATION

When the inhabitants of the Caribbean islands first laid eyes on Christopher Columbus and his men in 1492, they could not have known that they were witnessing the creation of the modern world. Nor could Columbus himself have understood the fundamental difference of the world that lay before him, as evinced in his assertion, in his famous letter of the first voyage, that Cuba was part of mainland Asia, a continent already known to Europe. The *Capitulaciones de Santa Fe*—the contract between Columbus and the Catholic monarchs of Spain Ferdinand (ruled 1474–1516) and Isabella (ruled 1474–1504) for dividing the imagined spoils of his first voyage, which was typical in form and content to other commercial contracts of its time—also points to the extent to which the monarchs imagined a purely commercial enterprise, not the spiritual and military conquest that New World colonization would become. The necessity of this transformation quickly became apparent with Columbus's return with "Indian" slaves in tow as a gift to the queen. This act, by proving the existence not of the "human monsters" predicted by medieval lore but rather of souls thought ignorant of the word of God, immediately transformed the venture into one of colonization. It also presented a first challenge to the ways in which the world was understood, especially through the Bible, as a known, closed system. Notable among early attempts to recuperate the newly found peoples into received understandings of history include that of Hernán Pérez de Oliva. Despite having never seen the new possessions himself, he wrote a florid account of the meeting of Columbus with the Arawak *cacique*, 'chief', Guarionex in Hispaniola, in which both protagonists deliver stately speeches in the rhetorical style of classical Roman history writing, as exemplified by Cicero. Pérez de Oliva followed classical rhetorical style because it defined historical truth in late antiquity; eyewitness accounts from the New World would fundamentally alter this definition of historiographic authority.

The realities of cultural clash and adaptation on the new colonial ground were far more complex than anything Pérez de Oliva could imagine, and constructing eyewitness accounts of them was a much more compelling exercise for Europeans actually present in the Caribbean. The Caribbean gave rise to the first ethnographic treatise of the modern world, in Fray Ramón Pané's *An Account of the Antiquities of the Indians.* Pané, a friar who accompanied Columbus on his second voyage, was charged by the admiral with learning the religious practices of the inhabitants of Hispaniola. His account, in a form as garbled as Pérez de Oliva's was logical, highlights his constant struggle with cultural understanding, particularly his failed attempts to grasp the structure and function of Arawak narrative style.

These problems of cross-cultural communication were not benign; rather, they directly contributed to the enormity of violence inflicted on the

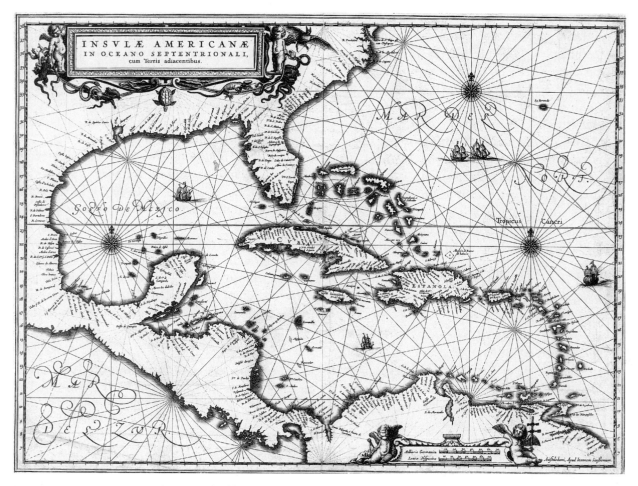

Spanish Colonies: The Caribbean. This map, which first appeared in a Dutch atlas of 1636, was based on a rare chart of the Caribbean by Hessel Gerritsz compiled several years earlier. In 1628 Gerritsz sailed to South America and the West Indies, charting many of the islands in the area. His influential map was widely copied by other mapmakers. MAP COLLECTION, STERLING MEMORIAL LIBRARY, YALE UNIVERSITY

native inhabitants of the new colonies. The link between the pretense of linguistic comprehension and violent conquest is present in the ritual, unique to Spanish colonialism, of the *requerimiento,* 'requirement'. Conquistadores were legally bound to read this document aloud, in the original Castilian, to natives to announce the act of colonization. Once the native peoples were thus conquered, native territories would be subject to the *repartimiento,* the "allocation" of a *cacique* and his people to a particular conquistador, the abuses of which were one of the key factors in the demographic collapse of the native population. In addition, the first systems of anthropological classification of Caribbean peoples, as either Caribs or Taínos (known today to ethnologists as Arawaks), also set the stage for violence. While Taínos were thought docile, Caribs—

said to be ethnologically distinct from Taínos—were considered fierce, wild, and subject to conquest. Peter Hulme's textual analysis of contemporary Spanish documents, however, shows that this distinction was highly fluid and selectively applied to meet the political and strategic needs of a particular moment. Indeed, one of the key traits meant to distinguish one group from the other was its reaction to conquest: those whose response was deemed peaceful could be designated Taíno, while those who showed signs of resistance risked being classified as Carib.

The combined effects of the *repartimiento*—forced labor, population dislocation, and epidemics (particularly of smallpox in 1518–1519)—led to the demographic collapse of the native populations of the Caribbean. Natives on Hispaniola alone, of whom Massimo Livi-Bacci estimates there were up to 300,000 before the arrival of Columbus—numbered only 60,000 by 1508; by 1520 they were well on the road to extinction. Yet while the Caribbean saw the birth of genocide and violent conquest in the Americas, it also was the source of the first colonial critiques. Bartolomé de las Casas (1474–1566), who would become the most passionate defender of Indians throughout the Americas, witnessed the conquest of Cuba firsthand as a colonizer before a religious conversion left him a fierce opponent of colonial abuse. While he later catalogued (and some say exaggerated) maltreatment from many colonies, it was his initial witness in the Antilles that served as the template for the moral outrage and rhetorical power that made his most famous work, *Short Account of the Destruction of the Indies,* so influential in its day.

OUTPOSTS OF EMPIRE

After the conquest of New Spain (1521) and Peru (1532), the importance of the Caribbean islands shifted: no longer the principal site of Spanish colonization, they became a colonial periphery. Although the islands had been "granted" to Spain by papal bull, rival imperial powers fiercely contested Spain's initial dominance in the New World. Although Columbus had in theory claimed all the islands he laid eyes on for the Spanish crown, in practice, significant settlement was limited to Cuba, Puerto Rico, and eastern Hispaniola, leaving many islands underdefended and open to being claimed by rival powers in the early modern period. Thus Jamaica, initially settled by Spaniards in 1509, was captured by the British in 1655, while in 1697 the western portion of Hispaniola, the island that had seen Spain's first settlement in the Americas, was ceded to France for what would become its most lucrative colony, Saint Domingue. The remaining major colonies—Cuba, Puerto Rico, and Santo Domingo—became the gateway to an empire and were of enormous strategic importance to Spain as it continually fought off the English, French, and Dutch. Havana and San Juan became highly fortified cities, particularly in response to the presence in the Caribbean of British corsairs (Sir Francis Drake was defeated outside San Juan in 1595).

Though now a periphery with the shift of the center of empire to New Spain, the Caribbean colonies were still a part of the colonial system. Havana, because of its role as an entrepôt in the fleet system that lay at the heart of Spanish mercantilism, became a bustling port by the end of the sixteenth century. Because the fleets departed only twice a year, and because the Caribbean colonies were not as self-sufficient as New Spain and Peru, the islands necessarily depended on illegal trade with foreigners. The Bourbon reforms of the eighteenth century, which liberalized colonial trade within Spain and reorganized the empire's bureaucratic structure, meant a political and economic restructuring for the whole of the empire. For the Caribbean islands the Bourbon reforms marked economic growth and demographic change—the latter due to peninsular immigration and the slave trade—that would not be complete until the full flowering of the plantation societies of the nineteenth century and the return of these colonies to the center of a greatly reduced empire.

See also **British Colonies: The Caribbean; Colonialism; Columbus, Christopher; Dutch Colonies: The Americas; French Colonies: The Caribbean; Las Casas, Bartolomé de; Slavery and the Slave Trade.**

BIBLIOGRAPHY

Primary Sources

"Las Capitulaciones de Santa Fé." In *1492–1992: Re/discovering Colonial Writing,* edited by René Jara and Nicholas Spadaccin. Minneapolis, Minn., 1989.

Casas, Bartolomé de las. *Short Account of the Destruction of the Indies.* Translated by Nigel Griffin. New York, 1999.

Columbus, Christopher. *The Four Voyages of Christopher Columbus.* Translated by J. M. Cohen. New York, 1969.

Pané, Fray Ramón. *An Account of the Antiquities of the Indians.* Edited by José Juan Arrom. Translated by Susan C. Griswold. Durham, N.C., and London, 1999.

Pérez de Oliva, Hernán. *Historia de la invención de las Yndias.* Edited by José Juan Arrom. Bogota, 1965.

"The Requirement." In *History of Latin American Civilization: Sources and Interpretation,* edited by Lewis Hanke, vol. 1, pp. 93–95. Boston, 1973.

Secondary Sources

Burkholder, Mark A., and Lyman L. Johnson. *Colonial Latin America.* 3rd ed. Oxford, 1998.

Dussell, Enrique. *The Invention of the Americas: Eclipse of "the Other" and the Myth of Modernity.* Translated by Michael D. Barber. New York, 1995.

Fuente, Alejandro de la, César García del Pino, and Bernardo Iglesias Delgado. "Havana and the Fleet System: Trade and Growth in the Periphery of the Spanish Empire,

1550–1610." *Colonial Latin American Review* 5, no. 1 (1996): 95–115.

Hulme, Peter. *Colonial Encounters: Europe and the Native Caribbean, 1492–1797*. London and New York, 1986.

Kicza, John E. "Patterns in Early Spanish Overseas Expansion." *The William and Mary Quarterly* 49, no. 2 (1992): 229–253.

Knight, Franklin W. *The Caribbean: The Genesis of a Fragmented Nationalism*. 2nd ed. Oxford and New York, 1990.

Livi-Bacci, Massimo. "Return to Hispaniola: Reassessing a Demographic Catastrophe." *Hispanic American Historical Review* 83, no. 1 (2003): 3–51.

Phillips, William D., Jr., and Carla Rahn Phillips. *The Worlds of Christopher Columbus*. New York, 1992.

Rabasa, José. *Inventing A-M-E-R-I-C-A: Spanish Historiography and the Formation of Eurocentrism*. Norman, Okla., and London, 1993.

Seed, Patricia. *Ceremonies of Possession in Europe's Conquest of the New World, 1492–1640*. Cambridge, U.K., 1995.

Wagenheim, Olga Jiménez de. *Puerto Rico: An Interpretive History from Pre-Columbian Times to 1900*. Princeton, 1998.

JAVIER MORILLO-ALICEA

MEXICO

The Spanish presence in Mexico began in 1519 when Hernán Cortés and his companions landed on the mainland of North America and established a permanent Spanish presence there. The Spanish called the colony the viceroyalty of New Spain. The name of the principal Aztec city—Tenochtitlán—eventually became Mexico (today Mexico City), and this was later applied to the whole territory. The viceroyalty originally covered the whole of what is now Mexico and Central America, as well as much of the Caribbean and the American Southwest. With the growth of Spanish population and the conquest and pacification of more regions, the Spanish divided New Spain, creating additional territories including Guatemala, which consisted of Central America and parts of what is now southern Mexico, and New Galicia, which included the northwestern parts of modern Mexico and the American Southwest, with its capital in Guadalajara.

A viceroy based in Mexico City oversaw the government of the region. Appointed by the Spanish crown, he exercised the administrative function and served as a physical embodiment of the monarch. Each division of the region (Mexico, New Galicia, and Guatemala) had a high court of justice or *audiencia*. Judges appointed by the king served on these courts and heard cases on appeal from lower courts throughout the colony. In the absence of the viceroy, and in the two inferior territories (Guatemala and New Galicia), the court also exercised some administrative functions. Local magistrates administered smaller internal territories. These magistrates, known as *corregidores, alcaldes mayores,* or *gobernadores,* had many duties and obligations, most importantly the collection of taxes and the maintenance of order. The crown occasionally appointed local magistrates, but normally that authority fell to the viceroy or *audiencia*. Within New Spain there were over 200 local magistrates. The towns and cities, governed by municipal councils, constituted the lowest level of government. The councils consisted of aldermen, either elected to long terms by the citizens of the city or appointed to life terms by the king, who also appointed two justices or *alcaldes ordinarios,* who served one-year terms.

Native communities occupied a complex place in Spanish colonial administration. On the one hand, they were subject to Spanish royal authority. On the other hand, the Spanish recognized their preexisting right to self-government, provided that their laws and customs did not violate Christian principles. Native communities, then, had both traditional leaders and a government imposed by the Spanish. Traditional leaders, who might be chosen from any of a number of members of a ruling family, tended to conform eventually to Spanish inheritance patterns, the eldest male heir taking precedence. Native peoples participated in elections for town council members, but these positions too came to be associated with various families and clans.

New Spain's society consisted of a complex scheme of different castes, each legally defined and occupying a specific place in society. The Spanish occupied the pinnacle of society. Internally a distinction was drawn between Spaniards native to the Iberian Peninsula, called *peninsulares,* and those born in the New World, known as *creoles.* The native peoples, at least in legal theory, consisted of an independent, self-governing republic, the *república de los indios.* Along with these groups, the Spanish brought African slaves. Free persons of color, at least initially, formed part of the Spanish caste. With the passage of time, mixed groups emerged: *mestizos* (Spanish-Indian offspring), mulattoes (Spanish-African offspring), and *zambos* (Indian-African offspring). Each came to be identified as a caste. With the emergence of other mixtures, the caste system became nearly unworkable. Eventually a middle group of *pardos* (persons of color) emerged to encompass all of the mixed groups, as well as free persons of color and natives who had abandoned native customs, dress, and other cultural attributes.

The ecclesiastical territory contained seven dioceses. Each of the major cities of the region—Mexico, Puebla, Valladolid (modern Morelia), Guadalajara, Oaxaca, Mérida, and Guatemala—had a bishop exercising episcopal control with an archbishop reigning in Mexico. But the evangelization of Mexico largely fell to the religious orders, not to the secular clergy. As the religious orders arrived, they tended to concentrate their missionary efforts in different parts of the region. The Franciscans, who arrived in 1524, just a few years after the conquest, tended to dominate the central and western region. The Dominicans, who arrived in 1528, focused their efforts on the central and southern region. In 1533 the Augustinians arrived, concentrating their efforts on the western region and filling various gaps in the central zone. Lastly, the Jesuits arrived in 1569, and while they established colleges in the major towns and cities, they focused their missionary efforts on the northern frontier.

THE ECONOMY OF COLONIAL MEXICO

The colonial economy quickly came to depend on the extraction of natural resources, principally silver and gold, and on agricultural production and commerce. Mexico has large silver and gold deposits. The climate of the region varies from dry, desert-like conditions in the northwest, to a temperate

Spanish Colonies: Mexico. Map of Mexico City and environs, engraving by Didac Cisneros c. 1618. ©CORBIS

climate in the mountain valleys of the central region, to hot, humid coastal areas. This allowed for the production of a wide range of agricultural commodities. The mining and agricultural industries were highly interdependent. The crown taxed gold and silver production at 20 percent (the royal *quinto,* or fifth). Much of the gold and silver ended up going to Spain, either as tax remittances or as payment for finished goods imported from Europe. A small part remained to circulate in the local economy, having been minted into coins in Mexico. While nearly every region had some mining, the silver mines were largely at various points along the western cordillera (mountain range). Principal mining districts included Zacatecas in the near north central region in the sixteenth and seventeenth centuries, and Taxco, in the south central region, in the seventeenth and eighteenth centuries. Pachuca, immediately north of Mexico City, was a steady producer throughout the colonial period. After the first high-quality ores had been extracted, miners had to deal with poor-quality ores that defied simple refining processes. In the sixteenth century the Spanish introduced the amalgamation process, in which ores are combined with mercury in a chemical reaction to better extract the silver. This increased production, but the cost of the mercury also increased production costs. The crown declared a monopoly on both salt and mercury, two elements essential to the process; in so doing it could easily regulate overall production of silver, since that production was based on proportions of salt and mercury consumed in the amalgamation process.

Agricultural production fulfilled two major functions. On the one hand, it provided many of the raw materials for mining and the small industrial sector. On the other hand, it produced goods destined for export. Among the agricultural products in highest demand were wool, sugarcane, and cattle. The wool went to local mills, or *obrajes,* which supplied the local economy. The cattle provided hides for export, tallow, bone, and other products for local industry and consumption. Sugarcane was processed by refineries *(ingenios)* and then exported. Niche products included cochineal (a dyestuff), pulque (a mildly intoxicating beverage made from the maguey [agave]), and silk, until that industry was destroyed by regulations and cheaper Asian imports.

Major agricultural areas developed in colonial Mexico. The lowlands became focal points for sugarcane and other tropical products. The temperate zones with sufficient water specialized in the production of cereal grains, fruits, and vegetables. The dry areas of the north central region specialized in livestock production. It was in this last area that the large landed estate, the hacienda, developed, characterized by livestock production and a moderately large fixed labor force. Nevertheless, similar large-scale ranches and farms also developed to produce cereal grains and sugar. In the case of sugar production, the operations were heavily vertically integrated, with the largest producers owning both production land and the sugar mills.

The commercial sector of colonial Mexico was of tremendous importance. Commerce linked the colony to Spain. Pedro Menéndez de Avilés (1519–1574), captain general of Spain's Indies fleet, organized the annual convoys from Spain to the New World and back in the mid-sixteenth century. Under this system, all ships sailing to New Spain departed from Seville at the same time, and sailed in a fleet to the Lesser Antilles. There the fleet divided, with some ships proceeding to Panama, others to Hispaniola, and the largest part on to the port of Veracruz, in Mexico. Similarly, ships returning to Spain would rendezvous in Havana, Cuba, and sail as a fleet back to Europe. This allowed the Spanish government both to protect the convoy from pirates and to closely monitor all goods and people sailing to or from New Spain. As a result, commercial goods from Europe all landed in Mexico at the same time. The Spanish merchants' guild or *consulado* controlled transatlantic trade. After about 1570, transpacific trade developed between Manila in the Philippines and Acapulco in southern Mexico. This became an important source of exotic goods in the Mexican market, and evolved to such a degree that the *consulado* feared Asian goods would cut into the market for European products. As a result, by the early seventeenth century all Asian goods had to be shipped to Spain before returning to Mexico, though smugglers often avoided the requirement.

MEXICO'S NATIVES IN DECLINE

One of the important features of colonial Mexico was the dramatic decline in the native population. Estimates of the population before the arrival of the Spanish vary, but modern consensus holds that about 25 million natives lived in the region encompassed by modern Mexico. Within 125 years of the conquest, the population had declined to approximately 1.5 million people. The dramatic decline was a result of several factors, most importantly warfare and diseases imported from the Old World to the New. Many natives perished either directly as a result of war or indirectly in the chaos that followed. Among diseases, smallpox, measles, plague, and malaria lead the list of probable pathogens. Added to these factors, the Spanish treatment of the natives also influenced levels of mortality, along with disruptions of social structure, of modes of production, and environmental change.

Immediately after the conquest, the Spaniards sought to control the two most important limited resources: land and labor. The use of natives for the purpose of labor service was important among the rewards provided to the conquerors. Based vaguely on a peninsular Spanish precedent, the institution known as the *encomienda* allocated the labor of a specific population of natives to a conqueror. Although legislation provided for a quasi-contractual arrangement between the natives and the Spaniards, in reality the native peoples fell under the effective control of the Spaniards. As a result of abuses in the system, and other examples of poor treatment of the natives, the crown, spurred on by the Dominican friar Bartolomé de las Casas (1474–1566), eventually placed severe limits on the *encomienda* and set forth a program for its ultimate abolition in a set of decrees known as the New Laws (1542). The crown then moved toward a policy of incorporating the native peoples into a system of free wage labor: that is, natives would contract independently for their services. The crown provided a transitional process called the *repartimiento,* wherein natives were required to perform labor services on a rotational basis, but were paid at an officially established rate. The funds would go to the native community in order to pay taxes back to the state and its designees. In this way the natives would slowly enter into the money economy. By the early seventeenth century, the *encomienda* was rapidly disappearing, and the

repartimiento reached its peak. Neither institution fully disappeared, but continued to decline into the eighteenth century. The final coercive labor institution was debt peonage, which grew consistently through the seventeenth and eighteenth centuries. Under debt peonage a Spaniard would make a small cash advance to a native in return for future labor services. Once engaged, the native could not successfully work off the debt and thus became permanently tied to the Spanish employer.

The eighteenth century saw dramatic changes in New Spain. With the change in ruling houses in Spain, administrative changes followed; the colony fell under more direct royal supervision as a result of reforms implemented by Bourbon rulers. The old system of over 200 *corregidores* was abolished in favor of a dozen or so well-trained *intendants.* The military, which had never played a significant role in the colony, was organized and greatly augmented; militias and new royal units were created. The fleet system disappeared in favor of individually licensed vessels. Control over trade passed from the Spanish merchants' guild to new guilds created in various ports. The crown authorized intercolonial trade. The church lost some of its independence and fell more under the control of the crown, especially as the crown attempted to take over lands and investment capital held by the church. In 1767 the Jesuit order was expelled from the Spanish colonies. These and other reforms served as the impetus for creole dissatisfaction with the Spanish crown, leading eventually to the wars of independence in the early nineteenth century.

See also **Colonialism; Cortés, Hernán; Las Casas, Bartolomé de; Mexico City; Missions and Missionaries: Spanish America; Shipping.**

BIBLIOGRAPHY

Lockhart, James. *The Nahuas after the Conquest.* Stanford, 1992.

MacLachlan, Colin, and Jaime E. Rodríguez. *The Forging of the Cosmic Race.* Berkeley, 1980.

JOHN F. SCHWALLER

OTHER AMERICAN COLONIES

The initial phase of Spanish imperial activity in the Americas involved finding, subjugating, and then exploiting nucleated Native American settlements. Later, Spaniards developed mechanisms for creating nucleated settlements from semi-nomadic Native American groups, gangs of enslaved Africans, and free Hispanic labor. Subjugation was followed by limited Spanish immigration. In the parts of North America that became the United States and Canada, these early purposes were soon expanded to include defensive ones as Spain tried to protect the Bahama Channel and Gulf of Mexico trade routes and, later, to create remote frontiers to protect the mines of northern Mexico from its European imperial rivals.

EXPLORATION AND SETTLEMENT

The Spanish explorers of the coasts of southeastern North America (the area that became the United States)—Francisco Alvarez de Pineda, Diego de Miruelo, Juan Ponce de León, Pedro de Salazar, Pedro de Quejo, Lucas Vázquez de Ayllón, Pánfilo de Narváez and Alvar Núñez Cabeza de Vaca—found a coastal zone lacking nucleated settlements except for the areas around Sapelo Sound (Georgia) and the Caloosahatche River (southwest Florida). Ayllón and Narváez, in Georgia and Florida, and Cabeza de Vaca, in the Rio Grande valley, picked up hints of nucleated settlements in the interior. Hernando de Soto's epic peregrination in the southeast checked on the former, while Fray Marcos de Niza and Francisco Vásquez de Coronado examined the latter, in each case reporting not only the hardships of their journeys but also the existence of towns of sedentary Indian agriculturalists. Explorations on the coasts of Baja and Alta (U.S.) California failed to find nucleated settlements.

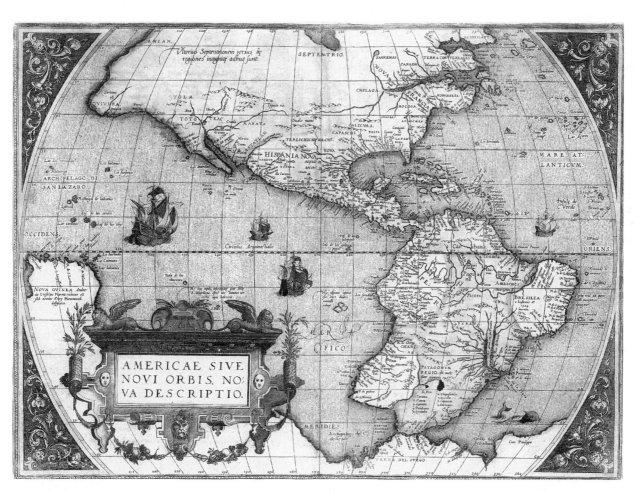

Spanish Colonies: Other American Colonies. This map of the Americas appeared in Abraham Ortelius's *Theatrum Orbis Terrarum,* the first modern atlas, published in many editions between 1570 and 1612. It was more accurate than other contemporary maps, especially in regard to the Caribbean and Central America. The odd-looking bulge in the west coast of South America was corrected in later editions after 1587, but the northwest coast remained unexplored and unknown. MAP COLLECTION, STERLING MEMORIAL LIBRARY, YALE UNIVERSITY

The Tristan de Luna expedition (1559–1562) to the Mobile-Pensacola area was intended to follow up de Soto's findings with conquest and exploitation of the interior chiefdoms of Coosa and Cofitachequi, but it failed to do so. Supply problems led to a mutiny, and Philip II (ruled 1556–1598) ordered most of the men removed to the Point of Santa Elena (Tybee Island, Ga.); this was in response to what he believed was a French plan to occupy a port on the Atlantic coast and thereby attack the vital Bahama Channel sailing route.

Thus diverted to the east coast and as a counter to French designs, Spanish imperialism in the American southeast took on the defensive posture that would characterize its later actions in North America. French colonies at Charlesfort (Parris Island, S.C., 1562–1563) and Fort Caroline (near modern Jacksonville, Fla., 1564–1565) resulted in the founding of St. Augustine in 1565. It remained the anchor of Spain's southeastern presence until the eighteenth century and the acquisition of Louisiana.

An effective sequel to Coronado's discoveries of the pueblos of the upper Rio Grande Valley was delayed until Juan de Oñate took up the task beginning in 1598. Several earlier efforts had failed.

MISSIONS AND PRESIDIOS: THE MATURE COLONIAL SYSTEM

By the time New Mexico was being subjugated, the Spaniards had worked out the mission-presidio system for inducing semi-sedentary peoples to accept life in nucleated agricultural communities. Offering food, clothing, tools, and protection from raiders (the ostensible reason for the garrison) to gather a population, the mission sometimes used coercion to retain it. Baptisms of the gathered Native Americans provided a justification for continued royal support when the crown, during the years 1600–1608, considered withdrawing the garrison at St. Augustine, the Florida missions, and Oñate's colony. Thereafter, defense against European rivals (in Florida) and Native American raiders of New Mexico again brought the defensive rationale to the fore, even as the missionary impulse continued.

For the balance of the seventeenth century and into the early eighteenth century, the mission-presidio system expanded in both Florida and the southwest whenever the Franciscan friars who manned it could persuade the crown to allow, and pay

for, new ventures. In Florida that meant missions in the nucleated settlements of coastal Georgia and northeast Florida, then inland along the central Florida Ridge, and then in the area of modern Tallahassee after 1633. The Franciscans claimed in excess of 35,000 converts at the height of the missions' population. As Old World diseases reduced Native American populations, the friars relocated the people of outlying settlements into the central mission towns. The Hispanic population numbered less than 3,000. The next extension of the Florida missions would have been into the Creek towns in the Chattahoochee River drainage had not Englishmen from Charleston offered the Creek better prices and products and no overt political or religious control, beginning in 1685. In New Mexico, the nominally converted Indian population was some 17,000 on the eve of the Pueblo Revolt of 1680; there were some 2,500 Hispanic residents there at that time. The Spanish reoccupation of 1693–1694 was followed by less energetic missionary work. Warfare against raiders such as the Comanches and Navajos began long before 1680 and continued after 1694. New Mexico lived a precarious existence but grew to have a population of 19,276 Hispanics and 9,732 Puebloans in 1800.

EIGHTEENTH-CENTURY CHALLENGES

The dawn of the eighteenth century brought new international challenges and a new focus on defensive reasons for Spanish imperial activity in North America. In 1704 a Creek–English force destroyed the Florida missions and effectively confined the Spanish presence to St. Augustine. Farther west, the development of French La Louisiane (1699) provoked the extension of Spanish missions into eastern Texas (San Antonio) and western Louisiana (1690–1693 and after 1716), supposedly to stop smuggling as well as to save souls, although they did little of either. Then in 1763 French Louisiana (population about 10,000) was divided into the British West Florida, along the Mississippi south of modern Vicksburg (and Indian territory between West Florida and the Appalachians), and Spanish Louisiana, which embraced the "Isle of Orleans" and all of the land west of the Mississippi. Viewed from the beginning as a remote defense of Mexico, much as Texas had been, Louisiana became, with Havana, the basis for the Spanish conquest of British West Florida in 1779–1781, as Spain sought to restore its control of

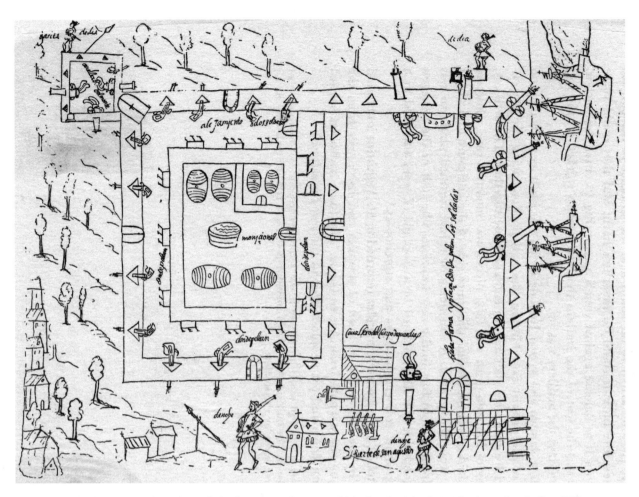

Spanish Colonies: Other American Colonies. An early pen-and-ink sketch of the fort at St. Augustine, built c. 1565.
©BETTMANN/CORBIS

the entire Gulf of Mexico as a defense for its economic interests in Mexico. The peace treaties of 1783 ratified that conquest and restored East Florida to Spain (it having been lost in 1763).

In the 1770s on the west coast of North America, rumors of Russian and British interest in sea otter pelts seemed to pose a threat to the use of harbors in California as emergency ports for Spain's Manila galleon trade. Beginning in 1769, the Spaniards built a string of mission-presidios in California as far north as San Francisco, ultimately embracing twenty missions and more than 21,000 converts. In the 1780s Spaniards began to assert their claims as far north as Nootka Sound, on Vancouver Island. The result was the Nootka Sound crisis of 1789–1790, which almost brought Spain and Great Britain to war. Spain backed down because of general naval and military weakness and because Revolu-

tionary France was unwilling to honor the Franco-Spanish alliance against Great Britain. By agreement, in 1795 both Spaniards and Englishmen abandoned permanent camps at Nootka Sound.

THE EBB OF SPANISH IMPERIALISM IN NORTH AMERICA

The Spanish retreat at Nootka Sound marked the beginning of what proved to be a general retreat of imperial activities in the Mississippi Valley and the southeast in the face of growing U.S. demands that Spain recognize the Mississippi River and 31 degrees north as the western and southern boundaries of the United States. Although supportive of the major Native American nations in the southeast in their struggles against American encroachment and instrumental in increasing Louisiana's francophone population, Spain failed to develop a large, loyal Hispanic population in Louisiana and so lacked the

Spanish Colonies: Other American Colonies. Illustration from Arnoldus Montanus's *Unknown New World,* published in Amsterdam in 1673, depicts Spanish settlers arriving in St. Augustine. ©BETTMANN/CORBIS

local means to defend the colony. In 1803, the population was about 50,000, half of them African slaves. Moreover, Louisiana and Florida rapidly became economic dependencies of the United States despite Spanish efforts to foster trade within their own empire and with France (before 1793). Pinckney's Treaty of 1795, the Treaty of San Lorenzo of 1800 (the conditional retrocession of Louisiana to France), and the transfer of Louisiana to France in November 1803 marked the steps in Spain's retreat. The Adams-Onís treaty of 1819, effective in 1821, conveyed the Floridas to the United States and set the western boundary of the Louisiana Purchase, preserving Texas (population of about 2,500) as a Spanish province. The Mexican Revolution for Independence of 1821 removed Spanish control of the southwest, ending over three centuries of imperial activity in the areas that became the United States and Canada.

See also **Colonialism; Exploration; Spain.**

BIBLIOGRAPHY

Hoffman, Paul E. *Florida's Frontiers.* Bloomington, Ind., 2001. Best recent study of Florida's Spanish periods and up to 1860.

Weber, David J., ed. *New Spain's Far Northern Frontier: Essays on Spain in the American West, 1540–1821.* Albuquerque, 1979. Useful collection of detailed studies.

———. *The Spanish Frontier in North America.* New Haven, 1992. Best overview.

PAUL E. HOFFMAN

PERU

The viceroyalty of Peru covered virtually all of Spanish-speaking South America, an area that today encompasses all or part of Colombia, Ecuador, Peru, Bolivia, Chile, Argentina, and Paraguay. Its topography and climates vary, from the deserts of coastal Peru and Chile to the rainforests of the upper Amazon basin, the Mediterranean climate of Chile's central valley, and the glaciated Andean peaks and nearby alpine meadows. The unifying element is the

Andes Mountains, which stretch down the western coast of Central and South America from Panama to Tierra del Fuego.

GEOGRAPHICAL SETTING

The Andean mountain range extends south 4,971 miles (8,000 km) from northern Colombia to Tierra del Fuego. In Chile the range is narrow; in Bolivia it is broadest. South of the Gulf of Guayaquil the mountains seem to rise abruptly out of the Pacific, and there is a deep-sea trench along the coast. The highest summits approach 22,966 feet (7,000 m). The vertical distance from the deepest part of the trench to the Andean peaks reaches 45,931 feet (14,000 m). Numerous volcanoes—active, dormant, and extinct—occur throughout the chain, and there are frequent earthquakes. Although ferrous metals and coal are absent, there is abundant mineral wealth, and for centuries deposits of gold, silver, copper, lead, and zinc have been exploited.

The cold-water counterclockwise Humboldt Current sweeps northward along South America's coast; in northern Peru it curves westward. This current, with its prevailing southwesterly winds, provides a temperate climate—even near the equator—and is responsible for the desert conditions of coastal Peru as well. During El Niño periods, the current shifts, and a warm coastal countercurrent from Ecuador filters southward. Rapid increases in humidity, heavy rainfall, and flooding along the normally desert coast occur, causing catastrophic damage. The Humboldt Current also nurtures rich marine life, providing a staple food in communities along the western coast of South America.

PRECONQUEST PERU

When the Spanish arrived in the sixteenth century, the population was spread over the region, on the coast, highlands, and upper Amazon basin. Andean peoples were settled agriculturalists, supplementing their diets by fishing and hunting. In desert coastal valleys some had developed highly sophisticated irrigation and terrace agriculture. There is debate over the number of Amerindians when the Spanish came; 14 million in the polity established by the Inca is generally accepted as a reasonable estimate. That population was composed of several dozen ethnic entities. Quechua and Aymara were the principal language groups, and there were many dialects and other discrete languages. Under Inca Pachacuti

in the mid-1400s, the Quechua-speaking Inca united many Andean ethnic groups in a period of rapid expansion from their base in and around the Cuzco Valley. This relatively recent empire was in turn quickly conquered by a small group of Europeans under Francisco Pizarro.

EUROPEAN CONQUEST AND SETTLEMENT

In contrast to Mexico, where Spanish conquest and stable political organization came quickly, Peru's first years were characterized by native resistance, rebellion, and internal strife among the conquerors. A division of authority among partners Francisco Pizarro, Diego de Almagro, and Panamanian cleric Hernando de Luque (acting for a silent investor) led to dissension. Pizarro conducted most of the exploration along South America's west coast, Almagro supplied men by sea, and Luque handled affairs in Panama.

Hardships were extreme and many explorers died. The halting second expedition (1526 to mid-1528) reached the mid-coast of Peru, where they first encountered conclusive evidence of wealthy populations. The partners agreed to return Pizarro to Spain to report and secure royal authorization for conquest and settlement. The contract with the crown (26 July 1529) provided Pizarro with the lion's share as governor and captain general, leaving Luque bishop of Tumbes, and Almagro the administration of its fortress.

The suspicions of the partners in Panama were realized—Pizarro was untrustworthy—and future interactions among the men were based on distrust and greed. Almagro's complaints to the crown ultimately led to his appointment as governor of the land south of Pizarro's jurisdiction, but the boundaries and wealth of the territory were unclear.

The third and final voyage of discovery began in December 1530. Much time was wasted in coastal Ecuador, with the result that it was not until September 1532 that San Miguel de Piura was founded as a Spanish town on Peru's north coast. At San Miguel, Pizarro left the ill and old and marched toward the Inca heartland. There were only 168 Spaniards, but they took Indian allies with them. The Inca Atahualpa was resting with a large army near Cajamarca, following victories over his half-brother Huascar. Both had contested the succession after their father Huayna Capac succumbed to

Spanish Colonies: Peru. This bird's-eye view of the Inca capital of Cuzco in Peru was published in Braun and Hogenberg's *Civitates Orbis Terrarum* not long after the Spanish conquest. Supposedly based on travelers' accounts, the plans of Cuzco and Mexico City were the only views of New World cities to appear in this famous collection of urban plans. MAP COLLECTION, STERLING MEMORIAL LIBRARY, YALE UNIVERSITY

smallpox in the mid-1520s. Atahualpa was surprised, taken captive by the Spanish, and forced to rule as a puppet until his execution (26 July 1533). The Spanish were offered a ransom—Atahualpa promised to fill two large rooms, one with gold, the other with silver—but, in spite of his compliance, he was killed on the basis of dubious charges.

The Spanish then marched southward through the Andes toward the Inca capital, and finally entered Cuzco (14 November 1533). Native resistance was modest; not all Andean ethnic groups rallied to the Inca cause. Pizarro, as the expedition's governor and captain-general, held extensive political authority. His contract with the crown empowered him to distribute treasure, provide the conquistadors with tributary grants (encomiendas, a system that gave the Spanish control over native populations and required those populations to pay tribute to them), establish cities, and distribute unclaimed lands. His power was checked only by Spanish custom and the presence of a royal legal agent and treasury official.

Spanish cities were quickly founded: Cuzco (23 March 1534), Lima (6 January 1535), with Trujillo, Puerto Viejo, and Guayaquil before year's end; Chachapoyas and La Plata in 1538, Huamanga in 1539, and Arequipa in 1540. Personal rivalries and the internecine fight for spoils, however, prevented the early creation of a stable administration. To summarize a complex series of events: Almagro set out from Cuzco to explore his supposedly rich domain to the south in July 1535. Shortly thereafter a generalized rebellion against Spanish rule in the Andes, extending from north of Lima to Lake Titicaca, erupted under the leadership of Manco Inca. Cuzco was besieged by thousands of natives and communications were cut between the Spanish camps. Almagro returned from his disastrous reconnaissance of Chile in 1537 and helped lift the siege. He now claimed that Cuzco lay within his jurisdiction and captured Hernando Pizarro. But at the Battle of Las Salinas (26 April 1538), Almagro was captured, tried, and subsequently executed by Pizarro. Three years later (26 July 1541), a group of Almagrists under Almagro's mestizo son, Diego de Almagro the Younger, surprised and assassinated Francisco Pizarro in Lima and took control of the realm. The crown already had sent a new administrator, Cristóbal Vaca de

Castro, who carried orders to investigate the problems besetting Peru and bring to justice those implicated in Pizarro's death. In the ensuing Battle of Chupas (16 September 1542), Governor Vaca de Castro defeated Almagro the Younger, who was later captured and executed.

At this juncture one might expect that royal authority had been fully established. Indeed, by the New Laws of 1542, the viceroyalty of Peru was created, and its audiencia (royal court) authorized. Both the justices (oidores) and the first viceroy, Blasco Núñez Vela, were authorized to sail to Peru and to found a government in the coastal capital of Lima, but the New Laws also included important provisions for the protection of Amerindians living under the encomienda regime. Most devastating for settlers hoping to establish American dynasties, the grant was to be only temporary. In Mexico, Viceroy Antonio de Mendoza suspended enforcement of the legislation pending review of its impact, thereby avoiding rebellion.

In Peru, Núñez Vela made clear his intent to enforce the new order no matter the consequences. Not surprisingly, the encomenderos (the Spaniards who collected tribute from the Indians) resisted. Their captain was a reluctant Gonzalo Pizarro, another Pizarro sibling. The new viceroy's arrogance and his involvement in the killing of a royal official convinced wavering colonists to join the movement. The viceroy was imprisoned and shipped to Spain, but escaped in Ecuador and collected a royalist force. The rebels under Pizarro defeated the viceroy at the Battle of Añaquito near Quito (18 January 1546), and the viceroy was killed.

Aware of the deteriorating situation in the Andes, the Council of the Indies named cleric Pedro de la Gasca president of the audiencia, gave him broad powers, and sent him to inspect the land and reestablish royal authority. Armed with blank papers signed by the king, he reached Panama in August 1546 and slowly began to collect adherents by issuing pardons and rewards. In spite of their rebellious nature, the Peruvian elite largely supported the monarchy; there was, after all, no alternative example of an independent Andean realm under European leadership.

There were two important battles. In the first, the Battle of Huarina (21 October 1547), royalists were soundly defeated by Caravajal's effective use of artillery. Pizarro, however, was unable or unwilling to complete his victory, and he moved southward toward Lake Titicaca instead. In the Battle of Xaquixahuana (9 April 1548), near Cuzco, Pizarro's supporters deserted and crossed the field to the side of La Gasca. Pizarro was taken and executed, along with Caravajal and other ringleaders, a few days later. This victory largely brought the Spanish settlers under royal authority, although there would be brief, weak uprisings in the mid-1550s.

ADMINISTRATIVE ORGANIZATION

By the early 1560s the administrative superstructure was largely complete and the viceroyalty system seemed firmly established. Lima was the capital. The viceroy, sometimes a relative of the royal family, who by birth and education could command respect, was appointed in Spain by the Council of the Indies. The viceroy's arrival in Peru with his large retinue of extended family and other officials was celebrated with festivities and civic displays. There were twenty-three Peruvian viceroys under the Habsburg dynasty; their average tenure was eight years. Frequently, they first served as viceroy of New Spain, a less prestigious post. The viceroy was the chief military and administrative officer: he sat as president of the *audiencia* when it was in session, appointed lesser officials and supervised administration, and was responsible for defense in times of emergency. His power was checked only by treasury officials with a direct link to the Council of the Indies, and individuals who were willing to communicate directly to the crown to voice their concerns. This occurred surprisingly frequently, for subjects could always directly petition the king. There could be open or secret investigations *(visitas)* of his administration, and, at the end of his term, he was subject to review *(residencia)*.

The *audiencia* in the viceregal capital took precedence over lesser courts. *Audiencias* were established in Panama (1538), Lima (1542), Santa Fe de Bogotá (1549), Charcas (1559), Quito (1563), Chile (1565, 1609), Buenos Aires (1661, reverted to Charcas in 1671), and finally Cuzco (1787). The president presided with four to a dozen *oidores* ('chief justices'), depending on the period and importance of the jurisdiction. The president was usually the oldest *oidor,* and, when a viceroy died or was

absent for some reason, the president of the *audiencia* served as chief official. In its normal activity as a court, the *audiencia* met several times weekly. Appeals of the court's decisions went directly to Spain's Council of the Indies. There were several associated officials of the court including a secretary, a recorder, a solicitor *(procurador),* a chaplain, and the crown's attorney (fiscal). Almost all the higher officials came from Spain.

The closest experience to local rule in the viceroyalty was the town councils *(cabildos).* The *cabildo* had jurisdiction over all the territory from the boundary of one Spanish city to another. Officials came from the local elite, those with land and Indian *encomiendas;* they were named by the leader when the town was founded. Pizarro, for example, founded towns such as Lima and Trujillo, and made the original land grants, both urban plots and rural agricultural lands, and named local officials. Afterward, the city, as a corporation, assumed the right to sell or rent lands, levy taxes, regulate trade and prices, oversee the markets and construct bridges, public buildings, and a water supply. The council met regularly. In the first meeting in January the body elected officials such as the two *alcaldes ordinarios* ('town magistrates'), the *regidores* ('town councilmen' or 'aldermen'), the *alguacil mayor* ('sheriff'), a jailor, and inspectors of weights and measures and other officials. The number of *regidores,* usually four to eight, depended on the importance of the place. Under the Habsburgs the crown sold many offices to relieve financial strain. The *cabildo* could act as a minor court in lesser crimes. According to Viceroy Francisco de Toledo's Ordinances, Indian towns had a similar administrative structure.

At first, control of the native population of the countryside was left to *encomenderos,* but because of their abuses of power this quickly changed. In the mid-1560s Governor Cristóbal Garcia de Castro introduced the *corregimiento* system that divided the viceroyalty into several dozen units under an Indian agent called a *corregidor.* By then the *encomenderos* were forced to reside in the nearest Spanish city rather than in their *encomienda.* The *corregimientos,* often composed of several *encomiendas,* paralleled Andean ethnic units or Inca provinces. The *corregidores* collected tribute in goods and cash, administered justice as judges in

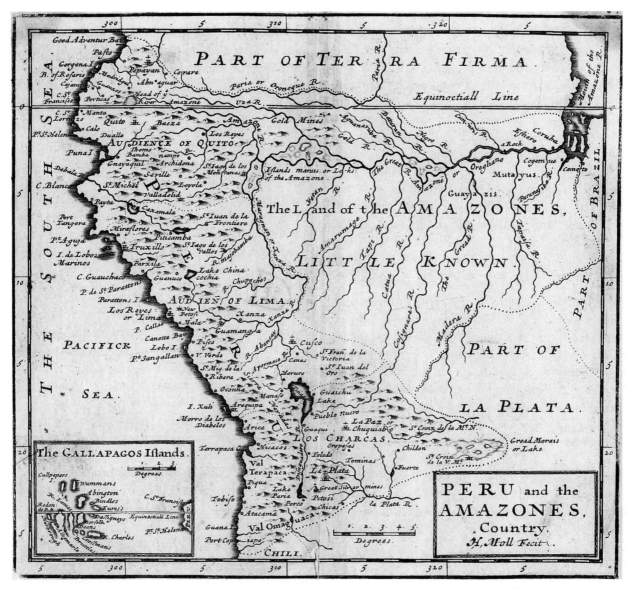

Spanish Colonies: Peru. A map of Peru and the Amazon watershed, identified as "The Land of the Amazones, Little Known," from an early-eighteenth-century edition of Herman Moll's *The Compleat Geographer*. MAP COLLECTION, STERLING MEMORIAL LIBRARY, YALE UNIVERSITY

minor cases, supervised local church activities, and provided security. They also disbursed funds to pay the salaries of local leaders and teachers of religion, and doled out to the *encomenderos* their share of the tribute. Their term of office averaged three to five years, and, in order to avoid corruption, they were to come from the outside and not have relatives in the same district. There were frequent abuses, however, because their salaries were insufficient and there were numerous ways in which an enterprising *corregidor* could supplement his income.

THE COLONIAL ECONOMY

The colonial Andean economy was based on three pillars: a largely Amerindian labor force; mining, principally silver and, concurrently, mercury, which boosted silver output; and agriculture. Several economic cycles operated. In the first months and years the economy was blatantly exploitative; the goal of most Spaniards was to extract the maximum amount of wealth as quickly as possible and return to Spain. The sacking of local leaders and despoliation of burial sites went on as long as the treasures, amassed over generations, could be easily expropriated. Incredible riches were despoiled: 168 men, for example, shared the booty of Atahualpa's ransom. The astute and fortunate quickly returned to Spain. Unfortunately, the men who arrived earliest had control of the lion's share of the treasures. One quickly sought-out source of wealth and power was the *encomienda,* which provided a cash tribute payment plus access to labor in return for bringing Christianity and "good government" to the Indians. A large *encomienda* permitted a life of leisure for the Spanish recipient, so grants were worth fighting for. The first systematic distribution of *encomiendas* by Pizarro occurred in 1538, although he had made grants earlier when the first Spanish cities were founded.

Another avenue to wealth came through land. In early colonial Peru a land grant without laborers was almost worthless. Here the Spanish attitude of *hidalguía* ('nobility') prevailed: a gentleman did not labor with his hands. As long as there was an ample native population, or, later, African slaves, there was no problem, but the number of Amerindians began to decline steadily. Around 1560, however, land became a viable source of wealth and power; by then all the available Indians had been granted in *encomienda.* Outright enslavement of Indians was prohibited by the crown, and, except for a trickle of captives taken during rebellion or in frontier regions, Indian slavery did not provide labor for the colony.

The state played little economic role in the conquest; the enterprise was largely left to individuals or family investors, who pooled resources to join in the expeditions. Spain merely authorized the actions, naming someone to be the principal leader, and then made certain that royal treasury officials were present to take the king's share. At first the most important revenue for the crown was the *quinto,* or fifth, that the government received for any mineral wealth, precious stones, and other key products. With the mines, the crown received a stable and reliable source of *quinto* revenues for many decades. The crown also administered part of Indian tribute. The sales tax, or *alcabala,* was collected on petty commerce in the Spanish cities, but not in the barter economy of the rural countryside. There were many other minor sources of revenue: government monopolies on playing cards, ice, and stamped paper;

taxes on the sale of slaves; and special taxes to assist in paying costs for transportation and defense. In the seventeenth century, the crown increasingly resorted to the sale of public offices.

Much gold was taken during the first years of the colony, with much of it being plundered. Gold was also extracted in many places in the viceroyalty; for substantial production, placer mining in riverbeds that carried alluvial gold dust and nuggets was preferred. Unfortunately, the costs of placer mining, which required a large labor force, often consisting of expensive imported slaves, were too high to warrant exploitation, save for a few very rich gold sources such as Carabaya in the upper Amazon basin or Colombia's Atrato River.

Silver ore, on the other hand, was ubiquitous, and silver mining was the key to the economy of colonial Peru, and, indeed, fueled Spanish imperial activities. There were dozens of quickly exploited mines. The most famous was Potosí; the mountain, which had been known by native miners, was "discovered" by Spaniards in April 1545. Within months there were more than a dozen significant mine operators, each vying to secure the richest veins and competing for laborers. A principal problem was extracting the silver from the crushed ore, which required substantial heat. There was no coal, or even wood for charcoal, at Potosí's elevation of 13,123 feet (4,000 m). Native technology relied on small puna-grass-fired blast furnaces located on the top of slopes where wind was strong and predictable. Such a method of combustion functioned only while the supply lasted. Fortunately, it was discovered that mercury has an affinity for silver, and under the right conditions combines with it, extracting silver from crushed ore. The amalgam can be heated at relatively low temperatures, the mercury comes off as a gas, and the molten silver remains to be poured into a mold to form an ingot. One of the world's richest sources of mercury was discovered at Huancavelica in Peru's central Andes in 1565.

With the technical problem of production solved, the labor supply once again became the primary issue. Viceroy Toledo solved that dilemma with the *mita* system. By his order, one-seventh of the tributary population of sixteen Indian provinces near Potosí was required to work in the mines one month each seven years as *mitayos*. It was paid labor, and there was a daily stipend and travel allowance, although the amount was less than the market price. Toledo partly borrowed the idea from the Incas, who used *mitayos* on great public works projects. Under Toledo, *mitayos* were also used in Spanish cities for the *mita de plaza* to help build churches, city offices, bridges, and water systems, and they were also used in other essential activities. Such labor demands could disrupt native subsistence activities, with damaging consequences. Furthermore, work in the mercury mines was unhealthy, and there were constant fatalities associated with all mining efforts: cave-ins, flooding, and dangerous gases.

Although colonial mining was the economic engine supporting Spain and her imperial demands in Europe, agriculture also played a role in the viceroyalty of Peru. Herding and the associated production of wool were a constant in the Andean highlands. The animals could be native llamas and alpacas, or imported sheep, and woolen cloth was required as part of the Indian tribute payment in wide sectors of the Andes. Production tended to be in the hands of families, with women doing most weaving, similar to "cottage production" in premodern Europe. Here, however, it was not for profit, but tribute payment. The amount varied, but was usually not more than one piece per adult male tributory each year. Quality also varied, with substantial cloth production consumed internally rather than being sold for export. In some regions small textile mills *(obrajes)* were established by European entrepreneurs, with production for export in mind. Indians worked in these—those in the *audiencia* of Quito district were famous for their blue woolens—and female and child labor caused cries of alarm by those witnessing abuses.

Wheat was introduced and proved adaptable to highland production. At first wheat production tended to be cultivated near Spanish cities, for the European populations, but by the eighteenth century much wheat produced in the viceroyalty was grown in the central valley of Chile. The native population continued to prefer native staples: corn, potatoes, quinua, or, in warm humid areas, corn and manioc. Of course there were a host of native plants that had been domesticated that continued to be preferred by the autochthonous population. Europeans introduced grape and olive cultivation, but

these products competed directly with Andalusian wine and olive oil shipped by Sevillian merchants, and regulations against American production, coupled with technical difficulties, meant that they never achieved true export status in the colonial period.

For alcoholic beverages the native populations used *chicha*, a light corn beer, or *aguardiente,* produced from sugarcane. Sugarcane was introduced into some of the irrigated valleys of north and central coastal Peru, and by the early seventeenth century was produced in quantities ample for local supply. In Paraguay, however, sugarcane was planted for export. Jesuits often participated in the direction of the plantations in both locales.

THE SOCIAL ORDER

Colonial society was hierarchical, with clear distinctions, making it possible to identify one's position in society. At the same time there was a near caste order, with the blocks of Amerindians, Europeans, and sub-Saharan Africans providing the human material for an evolving colonial society. Although the social groups were initially separate, the evolution was toward a mestizo world.

When the Europeans entered the Andean world, indigenous ethnic peoples varied; there were dozens of separate linguistic groups, with a wide range of possible cultural characteristics. The Inca empire covered much, but not all, of the territory that would be called the viceroyalty of Peru. The Inca had accepted and maintained local folkways, even as they were attempting administrative uniformity, religious acceptance of a general Inca cult, and the use of the Quechua language. The Spanish continued Inca policies, including quechuaization, with Christianity replacing the imperial cult. The common division of native society was between commoner and leader, called a *kuraka* ('chieftain'). Leadership was usually not hereditary, but based on merit, although the tendency was for leadership to be held within certain families. There was always a group of elders that commanded respect and was involved in any important community decisions. In Andean societies there was rough gender equality, with parallel inheritance. The fundamental social unit was the *ayllu*, an extended family unit that understood itself as having a common ancestor, generally not identified as a person, but as a physical place, such as a volcano, spring, or lake. The *ayllu* shared resources and production, and collaborated on various activities necessary for group survival. It was not a money economy; products were exchanged as needed among *ayllu* members on the basis of customary value equivalencies. In the central Andes there was also a moiety-like structure, with divisions into halves called *saya*. There is considerable debate about the nature of both *ayllu* and *saya* among ethnohistorians. There was competition between the *saya*, some of it ritualized, which may have contributed to community stability.

The Spanish adopted these rather complex structures as they set up the viceroyalty of Peru. They ruled in conjunction with the local *kurakas*, giving them a special status, permitting them to wear silk, bear arms, and ride horses, normally prohibited for the Indian commoners. The *kuraka* helped collect tribute for the Spanish officials, they chose the *mitayos*, and they helped maintain community solidarity. Although all Amerindians could participate in agricultural activities, there was specialization of labor.

Hierarchy also existed within the African community, and the legal condition of slave or free marked the first boundary. Africans came on the earliest expeditions, and their number increased rapidly after the Spanish began to found cities. The number of free blacks engaged in the trades was initially small, and they clustered in skills such as blacksmithing and tanning. Successful wealthy conquerors often purchased household slaves, who provided a status symbol representing conspicuous consumption, since slaves were costly in the early colony. With the collapse of the Amerindian population along the viceroyalty's coast, increasing numbers of slaves were imported to labor on coastal sugar and cotton estates. The Jesuits came to use large numbers on various plantations. Slaves were also used in placer gold extraction in the Esmeraldas district of coastal Ecuador and in rivers of the upper Amazon basin.

Labor conditions were so harsh in some of these that numerous slaves escaped and set up runaway communities of their own. Those of coastal Colombia and Ecuador are particularly well-documented. The Catholic Church viewed the soul of the African to be just as valuable as the soul of anyone else. As a

result, the question of the immorality of holding another person in bondage worried the Spaniard, and manumission was viewed positively. There were frequent manumissions of slaves by their masters at important life events, such as a marriage, birth of a child, or the approach of death. The demographic consequence within the viceroyalty was a continuously growing population of free blacks, who tended to cluster in the Spanish cities, especially along the coast. Within that free black community there was also a hierarchy, with some slaves also owning slaves.

There were two principal elements in the European group, the *peninsulares*, those who were born in Europe, and the creoles, those born in the New World. The *peninsulares* usually held the political appointments, whereas the creoles tended to be wealthier. It is no surprise that there was friction between them. The European social ladder was based on wealth; nonetheless all Europeans, no matter how poor they might be, saw themselves as superior to the other groups. Hence, Spaniards of lesser status, including miners, artisans, and craftsmen, as well as drifters in search of fortune, attempted to throw off their low-status baggage and emulated the lifestyle of the elite. Although it was difficult to convince other Spaniards of their new status, the Indians, blacks, and mestizos had little choice but to suffer their overbearing ways. Given that only the first conquerors had any real chance of success in securing an *encomienda*, the newcomer might make it through trade, perhaps first as a merchant's factor, or in mining, given technical knowledge. Any excess capital would be invested in land, which provided the foundation for social recognition.

Preferred marriage was within the group. Although families played a large role in the selection of a spouse, during the sixteenth and seventeenth centuries there was a remarkable degree of individual choice. The Spanish woman was expected to uphold all the Christian virtues and to be an emblem of the family; beyond this there was a remarkable range of possibilities. The married Spanish woman could expect to have a household servant or even a slave, which was less likely for her female relative in the peninsula. In the absence of a male in the household, either by death or prolonged absence, the woman assumed the full range of economic activities, administering the household, supervising business, even buying and selling properties. The Spanish pattern of inheritance was for equal distribution of the estate, which provided the daughters with virtually the same capital as their brothers. Only the very rich with an entailed estate *(mayorazgo)* provided the eldest son with the major property and title.

The process of mixing the three primary ethnic populations began immediately and continued throughout the colonial period. From the European standpoint the mixture was most pronounced in the first decades when there were few Spanish women. Francisco Pizarro, Diego de Almagro, and other leaders set the example. The mixed offspring foreshadowed the future population, but their access to high social standing was frustrated. In the first place

many, if not most, were illegitimate. Many conquistadores took Indian women or black slaves as concubines and produced numerous progeny, only later to discard the mother and her brood and marry a Spanish woman. In some cases elite native women, for example the Inca princesses *(ñusta),* or daughters of *kurakas,* who brought land, livestock, and other sources of wealth into the relationship, might secure legal matrimony. There are several well-known cases of such matches, perhaps the best-known being the marriage of *ñusta* doña Beatriz Coya, one of the granddaughters of Inca Huayna Capac, to Captain Martín García de Loyola, a relative of the founder of the Jesuit Order. The possibility for social advancement of the mestizos was limited, for they were between worlds. Raised by their mothers and too often rejected by their fathers, they

Spanish Colonies: Peru. *Corpus Christi Procession, Cuzco,* detail showing Inca princes, eighteenth century. THE ART ARCHIVE/MUSEO PEDRO DE OSMA LIMA/MIREILLE VAUTIER

were portrayed in the popular literature as shifty, untrustworthy, and volatile. The church might have provided an avenue of social mobility for them, but after several notorious cases of misbehavior by mestizo clergy, the church rejected the idea. The church also rejected an Indian clergy. Not all mestizos were unsuccessful, however, and many gained status and recognition as majordomos, muleteers, petty merchants, and miners.

SPIRITUAL CONQUEST

The process of effective Christianization of Andean South America was slow and required generations. Hernando de Luque, one of the three original participants in the conquest of Peru, was named "Protector of the Indians" and bishop of Tumbez in 1528, although he never reached his post. The first clergyman in Peru was friar Vicente de Valverde, who confronted the Inca Atahualpa with religious text in hand at the square of Cajamarca in 1532. The encounter boded ill for Christianization. Efforts to bring Christianity to the Indian populations were at first left to the leading figures. Pizarro invited clerics and friars, and with grants of *encomiendas* the Spanish recipients were initially required to find someone to catechize their Indian charges. By the 1540s representatives of the principal church orders were present: Dominicans, Franciscans, Mercedarians, and the Augustinians. The Jesuits arrived in 1569 and soon played a major role in educating the children of the region's elite. Much of the conversion of Indian parishes (called *doctrinas*) was left to the friars; the secular clergy preferred to work in the churches of the Spanish cities where opportunities for advancement were greatest. Soon convents were established in the major centers for daughters of the conquistadores and the native elite; Cuzco alone had the convents of Santa Clara (1558), Santa Catalina (1605), and finally Santa Teresa (1673).

The church's administrative hierarchy evolved rapidly. In 1538 Dominican friar Vicente de Valverde became first bishop of Cuzco, a diocese that extended from modern Colombia to Chile. Lima became the seat of a bishopric in 1541, under the leadership of another Dominican friar, Jerónimo de Loaysa, and by 1549 it had become an archbishopric holding spiritual jurisdiction over all Spanish South America. By the early seventeenth century, bishoprics were seated in Charcas, Paraguay, Buenos Aires, Tucumán, Santiago de Chile, and Concepción. For effective conversion it was necessary for the clerics to learn Amerindian languages, and dictionaries and grammars prepared by missionaries quickly began to circulate in manuscript form. The first book published in South America was the *Doctrina Cristiana,* a trilingual text in Spanish, Quechua, and Aymara, published in Lima in 1584.

There were several general church councils to oversee the Andean mission. One of the most important was the Third Lima Church Council of 1583, which resulted in the standard catechism, in conformity with the precepts of the Council of Trent. Purity of the faith of the Amerindians was handled by religious inspections ordered by the bishops, a principal task being to extirpate idolatries. The natives were exempt from the Inquisition, however, introduced into Peru by Viceroy Francisco de Toledo in 1570. During its active years, between 1573 and 1773, thirty people were condemned and executed for a variety of offenses, from witchcraft to Protestantism of various sorts to "converted" Jews who practiced Judaism in secret. Hundreds of others received lesser sentences, and the institution successfully checked the spread of nonconformity in the colony, as it reinforced respect for authority. Although the conversion of Andean peoples was largely successful, native traditions were deeply embedded and quickly blended into the daily practices of the colonial church.

See also **Buenos Aires; Colonialism; Lima; Missions and Missionaries: Spanish America; Pizarro Brothers; Potosí.**

BIBLIOGRAPHY

Bakewell, Peter. *Miners of the Red Mountain: Indian Labor in Potosí, 1545–1650.* Albuquerque, 1984.

Bowser, Frederick P. *The African Slave in Colonial Peru, 1524–1650.* Stanford, 1974.

Burns, Kathryn. *Colonial Habits: Convents and the Spiritual Economy of Cuzco, Peru.* Durham, N.C., 1999.

Cieza de León, Pedro de. *The Discovery and Conquest of Peru: Chronicles of the New World Encounter.* Translated and edited by Alexandra Parma Cook and Noble David Cook. Durham, N.C., 1998.

Cobo, Bernabé. *Inca Religion and Customs.* Translated and edited by Ronald Hamilton. Austin, Tex., 1990.

Cole, Jeffrey A. *The Potosí Mita, 1573–1700: Compulsory Indian Labor in the Andes.* Stanford, 1985.

Cook, Alexandra Parma, and Noble David Cook. *Good Faith and Truthful Ignorance: A Case of Transatlantic Bigamy.* Durham, N.C., 1991.

Cook, Noble David. *Demographic Collapse: Indian Peru, 1520–1620.* New York and Cambridge, U.K., 1981.

Davies, Keith A. *Landowners in Colonial Peru.* Austin, Tex., 1984.

Fraser, Valerie. *The Architecture of Conquest: Building in the Viceroyalty of Peru, 1535–1635.* New York and Cambridge, U.K., 1990.

Griffiths, Nicholas. *The Cross and the Serpent: Religious Repression and Resurgence in Colonial Peru.* Norman, Okla., 1996.

Hemming, John. *The Conquest of the Incas.* London, 1972.

Lockhart, James. *The Men of Cajamarca: A Social and Biographical Study of the First Conquerors of Peru.* Austin, Tex., 1972.

———. *Spanish Peru, 1532–1560: A Colonial Society.* Madison, 1968.

MacCormack, Sabine. *Religion in the Andes: Vision and Imagination in Early Colonial Peru.* Princeton, 1991.

Mills, Kenneth. *Idolatry and Its Enemies: Colonial Andean Religion and Extirpation, 1640–1750.* Princeton, 1997.

Salles-Reese, Verónica. *From Viracocha to the Virgin of Copacabana: Representation of the Sacred at Lake Titicaca.* Austin, Tex., 1997.

Spalding, Karen. *Huarochirí: An Andean Society under Inca and Spanish Rule.* Stanford, 1984.

Stern, Steve J. *Peru's Indian Peoples and the Challenge of Spanish Colonialism: Huamanga to 1640.* Madison, Wis., 1982.

Tibesar, Antonine, O.F.M. *Franciscan Beginnings in Colonial Peru.* Washington, D.C., 1953.

Varón Gabai, Rafael. *Francisco Pizarro and His Brothers: The Illusion of Power in Sixteenth-Century Peru.* Norman, Okla., 1997.

Wightman, Ann M. *Indigenous Migration and Social Change: The Forasteros of Cuzco, 1570–1720.* Durham, N.C., 1990.

NOBLE DAVID COOK

THE PHILIPPINES

The powerful nations of Europe undertook a global project of imperialism and colonization in the late fifteenth century. Spain and Portugal, followed by other European states, used religion as a motivating force for economic expansion. As a result of Europe's conquests and attempted conquests, the Americas and large segments of Asia were eventually subjugated and annexed as European possessions or outposts. Following Columbus's expeditions to America, Cortés's conquest of Mexico in 1519, and Magellan's "discovery" of the Philippines in 1521, a series of unsuccessful Spanish attempts to colonize the Philippine archipelago took place. It was not until 1565 that the first permanent Spanish settlement succeeded under Miguel López de Legazpi, a minor Spanish official in Mexico. It remained part of the Spanish empire until 1898.

On 13 February 1565, an expedition set out from New Spain (Mexico), reaching Gamay Bay off Samar Island, then proceeding to touch at Leyte, Camiguin, Bohol, and finally Cebu on 27 April. In May 1571 the group of settlers moved to Manila. Thereupon, Juan de Salcedo conducted an expedition of conquest around Laguna de Bay and down the Cagayan River. Martín de Goiti and one hundred soldiers penetrated the center of the island of Luzon. After 1571, Manila became the center of Spanish colonization. The original Spanish incentives to occupy the Philippines were control of the spice trade and control of Pacific trade routes. However, the Philippines were too far from the spice routes, and other European powers never acknowledged Spanish hegemony in the Pacific Ocean.

The Spanish home government set up a jurisdiction that placed the Philippines under the rule of the viceroy of Mexico. Like the Americas, the archipelago had a governor-general, an *audiencia* ('advisors and court'), and a *cabildo* ('town council') for the city of Manila. In the areas outside of Manila, *alcaldías* ('provinces') were organized, with an *alcalde mayor* ('provincial governor') as head.

What proved to be the major cultural force in the archipelago were the religious orders. Augustinians, Jesuits, Dominicans, and Franciscans were the frontline representatives of Western culture who indoctrinated and converted local peoples. They were followed by the secular clergy, who gradually took over the task of ensuring that the new converts to Christianity did not "relapse." Although the archipelago consists of almost seven thousand islands, not all were inhabited or came under Spanish rule. The southernmost parts of the archipelago were Muslim and remained so throughout Spanish occupation. As Christianity was extended throughout

Spanish Colonies: The Philippines. Perhaps the best-known and most influential early map of the Philippines, Spain's most distant colonial outpost, was that by the Jesuit Pedro Murillo Velarde, published in Manila in 1734. The reduced copy shown here, which added a small inset map of Manila, appeared in a German-language book on the Philippines published by Leopold Kaliwoda in Vienna in 1748. Map Collection, Sterling Memorial Library, Yale University

the islands, the Western value system it represented was incorporated into the native Malay society.

Local income from the tribute taxes imposed by the Spaniards was so low that it soon became clear that the maintenance of the Philippine archipelago as a colony in the Pacific was a financial drain on the Spanish Empire, and retaining the colony as the only Christian outpost in Asia became the new motivating force. The economy of the islands was in the hands of the "Manila Galleon," merchants who loaded a large ship with Asian luxury items each year and sold them in Acapulco, Mexico. On its return the Manila Galleon carried silver pesos.

In the latter part of the eighteenth century, a concentrated effort was made to develop agriculture and mining under the Bourbon dynasty. In the nineteenth century the external trade of the islands grew considerably, sparked by capital growth, large-scale imports of raw materials, and a rising population. English and American vessels unloaded wines, copper, nails, oil, and other manufactured goods, and in return carried away hemp, sugar, tobacco, and rice.

Spain's long colonial rule produced deep-rooted changes in Philippine society. Christianity, foreign commerce, and new political and economic relations, as well as new concepts of land use and land distribution, affected native society profoundly.

See also **Colonialism; Dutch Colonies: The East Indies; Magellan, Ferdinand; Manila; Pacific Ocean.**

BIBLIOGRAPHY

Cushner, Nicholas P. *Spain in the Philippines: From Conquest to Revolution.* Quezon City, Philippines, and Rutland, Vt., 1971.

Lyon, Eugene. "The Manila Galleon." *National Geographic* (January 1998).

Phelan, John Leddy. *The Hispanization of the Philippines: Spanish Aims and Filipino Responses, 1565–1700.* Madison, Wis., 1959.

Wickberg, Edgar. *The Chinese in Philippine Life, 1850–1898.* Manila, Philippines, 2000.

NICHOLAS P. CUSHNER

SPANISH LITERATURE AND LANGUAGE.

Spanish thought in the early modern period was greatly influenced by Renaissance humanism, the Counter-Reformation, the growth of the Spanish empire, and the institutionalized persecution of Jews and their descendants. The high-water mark of Spanish letters is said to have ended in 1681 with the death of the dramatist Pedro Calderón de la Barca. Spanish literature faded in the eighteenth century, and the Spanish version of the Enlightenment can properly be considered as a reflection of, or a reaction against, French influence.

LANGUAGE AND EMPIRE

In 1492—the year of the conquest of Granada, the expulsion of the Jews from Spain, and Columbus's first voyage to the New World—Elio Antonio de Nebrija published *Grammatica Castellana.* The momentous events of 1492 heralded the advent of a new world empire, and Nebrija explicitly wished his book—the first grammar of a modern European language—to be an instrument of that empire. Addressing Queen Isabella the Catholic in his prologue, Nebrija wrote:

> Most noble Queen, when I ponder upon and contemplate the antiquity of all the things that were written for our memory, I come to one certain conclusion: that language was always the companion of empire, and accompanied it in such a way that together they began, they grew and flourished, and afterwards together they fell.

Nebrija believed the codification of a nation's language was a necessary step in the development of a great power.

By Nebrija's time, Castilian had already progressed from being simply one of many Latin-derived dialects spoken on the Iberian Peninsula to the legal and administrative language of the most powerful kingdom in Spain. The language of Castile now became the administrative and literary language of her colonies. In time, the predominant language of the kingdoms of Spain became known simply as Spanish.

THE CRITIQUE OF EMPIRE

The conduct of the Spanish conquistadores in the New World has been rightly criticized over the years. One of the remarkable aspects of the whole endeavor, however, was the open and lengthy debate that took place in Spain over the proper handling of the conquest. Almost from the very beginning of the conquest, intellectual opinion in Spain had been divided over what should be the goals of the adventure and what should be the empire's policy toward the natives. Following Aristotelian precepts, some scholars argued that Indians were naturally subhuman and, by nature, were designed to be the slaves of their Spanish betters. Wars against them were therefore justified. The other argument held that the Indians were well adaptable to Christianity and ought to be won over to the faith by persuasion and gentleness. The fact that they were barbarians did not mean that they were incapable of rational thought or that they were incapable of being good Christians. Spain was the first imperial power in history to publicly agonize over the rights of the conquered.

One of the most powerful advocates for the natives was Bartolomé de Las Casas. Las Casas first traveled to the New World in 1502. There, on the island of Hispaniola, he lived as a gentleman planter. The future defender of the American natives even owned slaves. In 1515 he had a change of heart, gave up his property, and dedicated the rest of his life to working for the benefit of the Indians. During his long life, he produced voluminous writings in both Latin and Spanish decrying the treatment of the Indians by the colonists and advocating for their rights. A pivotal moment came in 1550 when he disputed with Juan Ginés de Sepúlveda, who advocated the position that the Indians ought to be exploited. Against Sepúlveda, Las Casas argued that the Indians were rational people. He went on to write some of his most important work, including the *Brevísima relación de la destrucción de las Indias* (1552). This tract caught on with Spain's enemies and was partially responsible for the Black Legend, which consisted of the often wildly exaggerated tales of Spanish perfidy embraced by anti-Spanish and anti-Catholic propagandists from the Renaissance up to the present day.

FIFTEENTH-CENTURY COURT CULTURE

The enthusiastic Renaissance culture sponsored by the court of Ferdinand and Isabella did not arise in a vacuum. Court culture during the earlier reign of John II had fostered poetic trends that embraced not only traditional Spanish poetic forms, but also was influenced by Italian humanism. Many in the nobility were themselves poets. Among these was Iñigo López de Mendoza, the Marqués de Santillana (1398–1458), an accomplished wielder of traditional verse forms, who also tried his hand at Italian-style sonnets. Jorge Manrique (c. 1440–1479), meanwhile, marshaled a host of classical tropes to lament the death of his father in "Coplas por la muerte de su padre." Santillana and Manrique were among the many poets who were anthologized in the *cancioneros* (songbooks) of the fifteenth century. As the name suggests, the *cancioneros* were devoted to lyric poetry on a wide range of subjects, from love to satire. In addition to the poetic wordplay of the *cancioneros,* reading tastes ran to sentimental romance, such as the elaborate love allegory *Carcel de amor,* and early versions of chivalric romances, the genre that Cervantes would later parody so successfully in *Don Quixote.* The fifteenth century also saw the first time that the traditional Spanish ballads, or romances, were anthologized. Often derived from medieval epics, ballads related tales of history and heroic deeds.

The University of Alcalá, founded by Cardinal Francisco Jiménez de Cisneros, confessor to Queen Isabella, archbishop of Toledo, and later grand inquisitor, made an early and lasting contribution to humanistic studies with the publication in 1522 of the Complutensian Polyglot Bible, a six-volume critical edition that placed the Hebrew, Chaldean, and Greek texts of the Bible in parallel columns with the Latin Vulgate.

JEWS, *CONVERSOS*, INQUISITION

While the court of Ferdinand and Isabella sponsored Renaissance openness and reform, their reign is also notable for increasing animosity toward the Jews. This culminated in the establishment of the Spanish Inquisition by 1480 and the expulsion of the Jews from Spain in 1492.

Relations between Jews and their Christian neighbors had begun to deteriorate rapidly in 1391 with a series of pogroms that shook the long-established Jewish communities of Spain. This was the first large-scale violence against the Jews in Spain, and its immediate effect was a massive demographic shift, as Jews from established communities in the cities began to relocate to the relative safety of the smaller towns. Another effect was the conversion of many Jews to Christianity.

The pogroms of 1391 and the mass conversions that followed added a new element to Spanish life:

the *converso,* or convert. *Conversos,* also called New Christians, soon found themselves at odds with so-called Old Christians, and as New Christians achieved positions of greater prominence, Old Christians began to doubt the sincerity of their conversions. Because *conversos* who returned to their former faith were seen as dangerous to the health of the church and the society, Ferdinand and Isabella sought and received in 1478 papal permission to establish an Inquisition in Spain. Unlike the earlier medieval inquisition, which was subordinate to the papal authority, the Spanish Inquisition became an arm of the government, with the monarchs themselves retaining the right to appoint inquisitorial officials.

Many scholars have suggested that the tensions inherent in the *converso* experience inevitably created a sort of conflicted *converso* identity, and that out of this identity crisis sprang the intellectual fervor of the early Renaissance, as well as many—if not most—of the great literary works of Spain's Golden Age. Under this thesis, almost any Spanish voice supporting church reform or any kind of upending of the social order must arise from the conflicted tensions of the *converso* writer. While it is undeniable that many of the great writers of the Golden Age had Jewish roots, and some of them explored new forms of social realism, there is no evidence to attribute their writings as a group to a specific *converso* experience.

The undisputed masterpiece of the reign of Ferdinand and Isabella, however, was indeed written by a *converso,* and it also represented an antidote to the cultural pretensions of court literature. Written by Fernando de Rojas, and first published in 1499, the *Tragicomedy of Calisto and Melibea,* also known as the *Celestina,* tells a sordid story of sexual transgression, seduction, and suicide. The work breaks new ground in both form and content. It is written in dialogue, but is clearly not a play. Instead, it seems to occupy a middle ground between drama and novel. The story concerns the efforts of a young nobleman, Calisto, to seduce a young woman, Melibea. His servant Sempronio helps him secure the services of a go-between, the old crone Celestina. Celestina is a procuress, and her task in life is to arrange liaisons between lustful young men and the often reluctant objects of their affection. The seduction succeeds, but also sets in motion a series

of events that ends in the deaths of all the principal characters of the story. The book puts an ironic twist on the conventions of courtly love and intersperses this with something new to literature: the wily and unscrupulous servant. Instead of patiently and faithfully serving their masters, the servants in this work criticize and conspire against them, motivated by a lust for money in much the same way their masters are motivated by sexual lust. Through the *Celestina,* the reader can catch a realistic glimpse of class relations during the reign of Ferdinand and Isabella. This peek from the margins can be considered a precursor to the squalid realities depicted in that most Spanish of genres, the picaresque novel.

THE PICARESQUE

While stirrings of the form appeared earlier in the century, the first great picaresque work was *Lazarillo de Tormes,* published in 1554. The book narrates in the first person the adventures of a young boy set loose on the world and the life lessons he learns from a succession of employers. Through the eyes of Lazarillo, the reader is able to see the hypocrisies of Spanish society laid bare. Lazarillo serves, in turn, a blind beggar who abuses him, a priest who allows him to starve, and a minor nobleman whose misplaced pride in his status prevents him from seeking gainful employment that might keep him from starving. The rest of Lazarillo's employers throughout the course of this very brief book are churchmen of varying degrees of venality. Lazarillo's prime motivation through all of this is hunger: hunger to improve his own position in the world, and, in the process, keep himself from ever having to go hungry again. The subversive nature of the book led to its being placed on the Inquisition's Index of Prohibited Books in 1559, and some scholars have assumed from the fierce criticism directed at church officials that this anonymous masterpiece was written by a *converso.*

Lazarillo—the young, aimless rogue—is the quintessential *pícaro,* and his story is the first good example of picaresque fiction: episodic adventures reflecting society's various social strata, related by a less-than-reliable, first-person narrator. The next important picaresque novel, *Guzmán de Alfarache,* by Mateo Alemán, was published in two parts in 1599 and 1604. Francisco de Quevedo, one of Spain's two greatest baroque poets, also wrote a very funny—and very bitter—picaresque novel known today as *El Buscón,* published in 1626.

THE ITALIANATE REVOLUTION

The political connections between Spain and Italy eventually led to the conquest of Spanish poetry by Italian literary forms. This permanent infiltration of Italian literary forms into Spanish letters largely occurred through the efforts of two poets: Juan Boscán (1493–1542) and Garcilaso de la Vega (1503–1536). Boscán wrote that he was prompted to attempt writing Spanish poetry in the Italian style through a direct challenge from the Venetian ambassador to Spain. The challenge lay in adapting Italian meter to the rhythms of Spanish. Boscán accepted the challenge and also prevailed upon his friend Garcilaso to try his hand at Italian-style poetry as well. The efforts of these two poets permanently altered the literary landscape of Spain. Boscán was a competent poet, but Garcilaso de la Vega was the true genius of the two. In many ways the quintessential Renaissance poet, Garcilaso died in battle in 1536.

THE COUNTER-REFORMATION

If the reigns of Ferdinand and Isabella, and later of Charles V, represent an early embrace of Renaissance values, the reign of Philip II proved to be very different. After the Council of Trent and the beginning of the Counter-Reformation, Philip began to transform Spain into a closed society. Philip believed Spain to be the last line of defense for the Catholic world and that it needed to be guarded from foreign influences. Students studying at foreign universities were recalled, and foreign books were banned, along with many literary works from Spain's earlier and more open Renaissance. Scientific inquiry also suffered in the Spain of the Counter-Reformation, although there was considerable interest in applied science and technology, including ballistics and navigation.

LUIS DE LEÓN

The climate created by the Inquisition and the Counter-Reformation had an impact on Spanish letters. One scholar to come under suspicion was Fray Luis de León, a professor at the University of Salamanca. Born in 1527, Fray Luis was of *converso* heritage and had a background in Hebrew scholarship. Luis de León came under suspicion partly because of his desire to use Hebrew in his commentaries. Not content with the Latin biblical tradition, Luis de León wished to resort to Hebrew to settle theological questions. He was imprisoned by the Inquisition in 1572 for publishing and commenting on the Song of Songs in Castilian and was detained by the Inquisition for five years. Once he was set free, he returned to his post at the university. Tradition holds that he began his first lecture in Salamanca after five years imprisonment with, "As we were saying yesterday, . . . " He died in 1591.

Fray Luis is known today as one of Spain's greatest Renaissance poets. His work is distinctly Neoplatonic in tone. His poetry extols the virtues of simple living, away from the tumult of society, and expresses the belief that art can lift the spirit to a higher sphere of consciousness and closer to communion with God.

MYSTICISM

While not a true mystic, Fray Luis shared with the mystics an intense desire to liberate the soul from the shackles of the world and move toward a higher plane of experience. True mystics seek a union of the soul with God. This union is the essence of the mystical experience, and arises out of the ecstatic experience of the pure love of God. Marriage and sex become useful poetic metaphors for ecstatic union.

The most well-known mystics of Golden Age Spain were Saint Teresa of Ávila (1515–1582) and St. John of the Cross (1542–1591). Born Teresa de Ahumada in Ávila in 1515, Teresa entered the Carmelite order in 1534 and later gained fame through her efforts to reform the order. Of her many prose works describing her mystical experiences, the most important is *El castillo interior* (1577). A close associate of St. Teresa was Juan de Yepes, who was later canonized as St. John of the Cross. Born in 1542 in the province of Ávila, he entered the Carmelite order in 1563. He was twice jailed for his reforming activities, and much of his writing seems to draw from the experience of having been imprisoned. St. John sought to express his mysticism through highly charged, complex poetry. He often compared the relationship of the soul to God with that of a wife and her husband. His most famous poem is the "Noche oscura del alma." Here the soul's search for union with God is figured as a young girl waiting until the house is quiet so she can sneak out and meet her lover. Their sexual rendezvous represents the moment of the soul's union with God.

CERVANTES

Golden Age Spain's most renowned writer was, without a doubt, Miguel de Cervantes Saavedra. Born in Alcalá de Henares in 1547, he was the son of an unsuccessful barber-surgeon. When young, he enlisted as a soldier and fought in the battle of Lepanto in 1571. There he received a wound that rendered his left hand useless to him. On the return trip to Spain in 1575, he was captured by pirates and taken to Algiers, where he was held captive for five years. Upon his ransom and return to Spain in 1580, he worked a series of low-paying jobs and began his writing career. He finally received a government post, but discrepancies in his accounts led to his being jailed twice in Seville. Cervantes dabbled in the major literary genres of the age. Although he tried his hand at theater and poetry, his fame rests on his prose works, principally the *Novelas ejemplares* and his masterpiece, *Don Quixote.*

Critics have been debating *Don Quixote* for close to four hundred years and will surely continue to do so. The work that many consider Western literature's greatest novel started out as a broad parody of the novels of chivalry that had been in vogue throughout the sixteenth century. Don Quixote is an impoverished gentleman from a forgotten corner of Castile who goes mad from too much reading and comes to believe he is a knight errant. Clad in rusty antique armor, he ranges the countryside—first alone, and then in the company of his trusty peasant "squire" Sancho Panza—attempting to right wrongs and live the code of chivalric honor. Even to Cervantes's readers, an armor-clad knight errant was a laughable anachronism, and the humor of the book arises from the incongruities of a daft, idealistic knight set loose on modern and more cynical society. Quixote is often said to represent idealism, and Sancho the realism of the world he butts up against.

Published in 1605, Don Quixote was a huge success, but Cervantes did not profit from it. The success of the first book led Cervantes to publish a very popular sequel in 1615, the year before he died.

BAROQUE

Spanish baroque literature is characterized by elaborate style and often by excessive metaphors. Two poetic movements in particular stand out: *culturanismo* and *conceptismo*. Both were intellectual movements that emphasized extreme use of language. *Culturanismo* sought to create a highly intellectual poetic language that looked to Latin as its model. It used neologisms, extreme metaphors, and greatly contorted syntax. The representative poet of *culturanismo* was Luis de Góngora y Argote (1561–1627). Góngora wrote poetry in traditional Spanish as well as Italian forms, with his later work tending to be highly artificial and, consequently, much harder to understand than his earlier work. His long poems "Polifemo" and the unfinished "Soledades" do not lend themselves easily to casual reading, but can nevertheless be extremely rewarding. *Conceptismo,* epitomized by Francisco de Quevedo (1580–1645), stressed the creation of audacious poetic conceits. Although poets from the two schools bickered—often writing withering satires about one another—the two are not mutually exclusive, and there was much overlap. Quevedo today is remembered as a writer of cutting satire and one of the great picaresque novels, *El Buscón.* Góngora fell into disfavor, but was rediscovered by Spain's poetic Generation of 1927.

LOPE DE VEGA AND THE COMEDIA

Cervantes's lack of success as a dramatist was more than compensated by that of Felix Lope de Vega Carpio. Cervantes himself called Lope a "freak of nature" and blamed him for altering the theatrical landscape and changing public taste to the point that his own plays could not be successful. Lope did not invent theater in Spain, but he transformed it to such a degree that he is considered the creator of the Spanish national theater. Born in 1562 in Madrid, Lope was a true literary phenomenon. He claimed to have written more than 1,800 plays, in addition to lyric poetry, epic poetry, and novels. Some five hundred of Lope's plays still survive.

If Lope's plays seem a little formulaic, it is because they are. Lope sought to make his plays appeal to a wide public, and he was not ashamed to admit that he loaded them with elements designed to make them popular. He codified his dramatic theory in *Arte nuevo de hacer comedias en este tiempo* (1609), where he specified a three-act structure. According to Lope's plan, the first act should set up the argument, the second should develop the tension, and the third should bring a swift and unpredictable conclusion after a period of heightened suspense. Lope lived a dissolute personal life, but his plays are essentially conservative reaffirmations of society's mores. For example, *Fuenteovejuna*, about a real peasant uprising in 1476, becomes an apology for the policies of Ferdinand and Isabella. The citizens of Fuenteovejuna rebel against and murder their lord and then collectively take responsibility for the action, saying that Fuenteovejuna itself committed the crime. The lord in question had fought against Ferdinand and Isabella in the recent civil war, and when the Catholic Monarchs eventually forgave the town, the action could be taken as an affirmation of royal authority.

The other great dramatists of the Golden Age were Tirso de Molina (1583–1648) and Pedro Calderón de la Barca (1600–1681). Tirso, the pen name of Gabriel Téllez, is principally remembered today as the first dramatist to treat the Don Juan theme, in *El burlador de Sevilla y convidado de piedra*. Many critics consider Calderón a greater dramatist than Lope, if not in quantity, then at least in quality. His finest achievement was *La vida es sueño*, which pulls out all the stops in its exploration of the fine line separating dreams from reality.

THE ENLIGHTENMENT

Spain's literary Golden Age ended with the death of Calderón in 1681. But while literature may have been moribund in the eighteenth century, the situation for other intellectual pursuits was not as dire. Spanish scientists had been isolated from the rest of Europe, but changes did begin to seep in. Medical thought began to drift away from strict adherence to Aristotelian precepts, with some physicians accepting William Harvey's theories of blood circulation. Renewed interest in medicine and science in Spain led in 1700 to royal recognition for the Royal Society of Medicine, one of the first of the learned academies that would spring up during the Enlightenment.

With the advent of the Bourbon dynasty in Spain in 1700, Spanish culture began to be heavily influenced by French thought. The Enlightenment emphasis on scientific categorization led to the founding of the great national academies. In addition to the Royal Society of Medicine, another important academy was the Royal Spanish Academy, founded in 1714. This academy focused on purity of the language and produced within a short time its six-volume *Diccionario de autoridades*.

In literature, the essay form dominated. The premiere essayist of the first half of the eighteenth century was Benito Jerónimo Feijoo (1676–1764). His eight-volume *Teatro crítico universal* contained learned essays on a wide variety of subjects, from science to superstition. Gaspar Melchor de Jovellanos (1744–1811) was another essayist who sought to reform Spanish society and letters. Whereas there was a new openness to science and learning, art and literature in Spain stagnated in the eighteenth century, characterized by largely imported and derivative production.

See also **Calderón de la Barca, Pedro; Cervantes, Miguel de;** *Conversos;* **Drama: Spanish and Portuguese; Exploration; Góngora y Argote, Luis de; Jews, Expulsion of (Spain; Portugal); Las Casas, Bartolomé de; Portuguese Literature and Language; Sepúlveda, Francisco de; Spanish Colonies; Teresa of Ávila; Vega, Lope de.**

BIBLIOGRAPHY

Alemán, Mateo. *Guzmán de Alfarache*. Edited by Enrique Miralles García. Barcelona, 1988.

Alonso, Alvaro, ed. *Poesía de Cancionero*. Madrid, 1995.

Boscán, Juan, and Garcilaso de la Vega. *Obras completas*. Edited by Carlos Clavería Laguarda. Madrid, 1995.

Calderón de la Barca, Pedro. *La vida es sueño*. Edited by José María García Martín. Madrid, 1983.

Casas, Bartolomé de las. *Brevísima relación de la destrucción de las Indias*. Edited by José María Reyes Cano. Barcelona, 1994.

Cervantes, Miguel de. *Don Quijote de la Mancha*. Edited by Francisco Rico, et al. Barcelona, 2001.

Chandler, Richard E., and Kessel Schwartz. *A New History of Spanish Literature*. Rev. ed. Baton Rouge, La., 1991.

McClelland, I. L. *Benito Jerónimo Feijóo*. New York, 1969.

Molina, Tirso de. *El burlador de Sevilla y convidado de piedra*. Barcelona, 2000.

Nebrija (Lebrija), Antonio de. *Grammatica Castellana*. 1492. Facsimile reprint. Menston. U.K., 1969.

Penny, Ralph. *A History of the Spanish Language*. 2nd ed. Cambridge, U.K., and New York, 2002.

Quevedo, Francisco de. *La vida del Buscón*. Edited by Fernando Cabo Aseguinolaza. Barcelona, 1993.

Rivers, Elias L., ed. *Poesía lírica del Siglo de Oro.* Madrid, 1979.

Rojas, Fernando de. *Tragicomedia de Calisto y Melibea.* Edited by María José Sánchez-Cascado. Barcelona, 1997.

Vega, Lope de. *El arte nuevo de hacer comedias en este tiempo.* Edited by Juana de José Prades. Madrid, 1971.

———. *Fuente Ovejuna.* Edited by Donald McGrady. Barcelona, 1993.

La vida de Lazarillo de Tormes y de sus fortunas y adversidades. Edited by Florencio Sevilla Arroyo. Madrid, 1998.

MICHAEL HAMMER

SPANISH SUCCESSION, WAR OF THE (1701–1714).

The succession to the extensive Spanish empire had been a live issue since the 1660s, when rumors spread that Philip IV's (ruled 1605–1665) only surviving son, crowned Charles II in 1665, was unlikely to survive childhood.

PARTITION TREATY OR INTEGRAL INHERITANCE?

The assumption that the new reign would be short motivated the first partition treaty between the head of the Austrian branch of the Habsburgs, Leopold I (ruled 1658–1705), and Louis XIV (ruled 1643–1715) of France in January 1668. This treaty remained a dead letter since Charles II, though not siring an heir, survived the next three decades and only finally weakened during the 1690s. During this time the issue of the Spanish succession had not become less contentious. After the War of the League of Augsburg (1688–1697), Louis believed that France could not afford another major conflict. But this new realism about military resources was counterbalanced by considerations of dynastic honor and future French security; Louis could not accept that the entire Spanish inheritance might pass to the Austrian Habsburgs. This, however, was precisely what Leopold I now wanted, and, thanks to his conquests in Ottoman-controlled Hungary and his successful leadership of a substantial coalition of German princes in the recent war, he was unprepared to discuss partition. Louis nonetheless found an apparent ally in his previous archenemy, William III (ruled 1689–1702), king of England and de facto ruler of the Dutch Republic. William

was equally anxious to avoid another costly war and had no wish to establish the same branch of the Habsburg family across western and central Europe. Bilateral negotiations in the summer and autumn 1698 proposed the exclusion of both Habsburg and Bourbon dynasties from the full succession, nominating instead Joseph Ferdinand, young son of the Bavarian Elector, as heir to most of Charles II's inheritance. As compensation it was proposed that Louis's son would receive the kingdoms of Naples and Sicily, and Milan would go to Leopold's second son, Archduke Charles. The sudden death of Joseph Ferdinand in 1699 annulled the plan, and Louis XIV's diplomats now proposed that France, Britain, and the Dutch Republic should sponsor a simple partition: France would receive all of Spanish Italy but would allow the rest of the empire to pass to Leopold I's son, Archduke Charles. Despite the apparent generosity of the offer, the Austrians realized that without the linchpin of Milan, the two Habsburg dominions could never function together, and the security of much of the Spanish inheritance would be jeopardized. Nevertheless Louis and William signed this new partition treaty in March 1700, hoping that Leopold would follow. Leopold had still refused to sign on 1 November when Charles II finally died. Against expectations—though rumors had been flying around the Spanish court for the previous month—Charles II's final will did not name Archduke Charles as his universal heir of choice. Giving priority to maintaining the territorial integrity of the empire, Charles II's councillors had persuaded him to make over the entire inheritance to Philip of Anjou (1683–1746), Louis's second grandson.

Historians have long debated Louis's decision to accept the will in the name of his grandson, but it is difficult to see that he could have done otherwise. Leopold had refused to ratify the partition treaty; if Louis rejected the Spanish offer, Charles II's testament then offered the entire inheritance to Archduke Charles. Louis could call on the military support of the English and the Dutch to make good his claims under the partition treaty, but there was little chance that either would act to uphold French dynastic rights. France would be left to fight the combined Habsburg powers to try to prize Italy from their grip. In contrast, by accepting Charles's will Louis would ensure that Spain and her territories would be his allies in any confrontation with the Austrian Habsburgs.

Louis's real error lay in the inability to see that consolidating the position of his grandson without provoking European war required qualities of restraint and empathy in dealing with other states. Leopold soon declared war, but so long as the Maritime Powers were reluctant to intervene, any conflict might be contained by France. Yet a succession of preemptive moves and provocations turned an ambiguous situation into one in which France was again faced by a hostile alliance of major powers. By moving French troops into the Spanish Netherlands and occupying the "barrier fortresses" garrisoned by Dutch troops since 1697, Louis undermined the key Dutch gain from the treaty of Ryswick (1697). Granting French merchants exclusive trading advantages in the Spanish New World antagonized both the Dutch and the English, while Louis's refusal to explicitly repudiate Philip's position in the French order of succession caused widespread consternation. By the time Louis formally recognized James II's son as James III of England and Scotland, the process of alienation had already led to renewal of the military alliance between the Austrian emperor, the English, and the Dutch (September 1701), and there was no turning back.

THE COURSE OF THE WAR

Louis was initially optimistic that France's situation was better than it had been in the previous conflict: France would fight beside Spain and the Spanish empire, whose subjects had acclaimed Louis's grandson as Philip V and accepted French support to preserve the integrity of the kingdoms; Portugal, Savoy, and Bavaria were initially also allies of Louis XIV. But defeating the coalition would depend on rapid French military success, and despite some striking achievements in the first two years of war, this proved elusive. In 1703 the opportunity to launch a Franco-Bavarian campaign against the Austrian lands was lost. Meanwhile, English naval success at Vigo Bay (1702) was instrumental in persuading Portugal to abandon the French alliance, while Victor Amadeus II of Savoy (1666–1732) saw the north Italian operations of the imperial general, Prince Eugène (1663–1736) of Savoy, as an opportunity to slip out of his own commitment to France. The critical reversal came in August 1704 when

allied armies under the Duke of Marlborough and Eugène annihilated the Franco-Bavarian forces at Blenheim and removed any prospect of knocking the Austrians out of the war. The subsequent four years of conflict saw a few successful French initiatives and some capacity to recover ground lost after the hammer-blows of subsequent allied victories at Ramillies (1706), Turin (1706), and Oudenarde (1708), but the balance had tipped toward the assertive, battle-seeking strategies of Marlborough and Eugène. The situation in Spain appeared even worse as allied forces acting in the name of Archduke Charles, now proclaimed Charles III of Spain, had by 1706 occupied Madrid, Barcelona, and other major cities.

The situation stabilized to some extent when French forces imposed huge casualties on the allies as the price of their victory at Malplaquet (1709); military affairs had been improving in Spain since 1707, above all because the population remained fiercely loyal to Philip V. But apparent revival was offset by domestic crisis in France, where a miserable harvest followed by the bitter winter of 1708–1709 led to catastrophic mortality, mass starvation, and tax failure. As in the 1690s, France lacked the resources to continue the war; faced with collapse at home not counterbalanced by overwhelming success in the field, Louis's diplomats began to negotiate for a settlement on allied terms.

PEACE NEGOTIATIONS AND FRENCH RECOVERY

Allied demands in the spring of 1710 were as harsh as France's worst expectations: Philip V would be ejected from the Spanish throne; France would relinquish most of her territorial gains since 1648. Yet Louis was desperate to extricate France from a war that threatened invasion and disintegration at home. Only the imputation that France should act alone in removing his grandson from Spanish territory finally led Louis to break off negotiations. The allies continued to take fortresses and breached the French frontiers in 1710, and once again managed briefly to expel Philip from Madrid. But beneath this success the allied coalition was cracking; the English, and to some extent the Dutch, recognized that they could now get everything they demanded in terms of security and economic advantage while the French military humiliation rendered France less prepared to sanction a Habsburg-dominated Europe. The fall of the Whig government in Britain signaled the end of Marlborough's political and military ascendancy. Soon after, the sudden death of Joseph I (ruled 1705–1711), ruler of the Habsburg lands and Holy Roman emperor since the death of his father Leopold in 1705, left Archduke Charles in 1711 as successor to his eldest brother in central Europe and allied claimant to the Spanish inheritance. During 1711 the English effectively withdrew from the war effort and drew up a bilateral peace with France. This winding-down of the war was abruptly halted by the sudden deaths of three of Louis XIV's direct heirs in the winter of 1711–1712, leaving the French succession to the two-year-old duke of Anjou and, after Anjou, to Philip V. But the dangerous issue of the separation of the Bourbon crowns was finally resolved through a further and explicit renunciation of the French throne by Philip. English forces once again withdrew from the conflict, and in July 1712 a French victory at Denain permitted the recapture of crucial frontier fortresses, blocking further allied incursions into France. The main settlement between France and the Maritime Powers was made at Utrecht in the first months of 1713. France escaped lightly, the peace being bought by Spanish concessions in Europe and the Americas. Britain in particular gained substantial colonial and commercial benefits from Spain's transatlantic empire. Archduke Charles, now Emperor Charles VI, held out to the end of 1713, but French successes in the empire persuaded him to settle at Rastatt in November, gaining Milan, Naples, and the Spanish Netherlands in return for accepting Philip V and the Bourbon succession to Spain. The settlements were finally ratified in 1714.

See also **Bourbon Dynasty (France); Bourbon Dynasty (Spain); Charles II (Spain); Habsburg Dynasty; League of Augsburg, War of the (1688–1697); Leopold I (Holy Roman Empire); Louis XIV (France); Philip IV (Spain); Philip V (Spain); Spain; Utrecht, Peace of (1713); William and Mary.**

BIBLIOGRAPHY

Primary Sources

Callières, François de. *The Art of Diplomacy.* Reprint. Edited by H. M. A. Keens-Soper and Karl W. Schweizer. New York, 1983.

Frey, Linda, and Marshal Frey, eds. *The Treaties of the War of the Spanish Succession.* Westport, Conn., 1995.

Symcox, Geoffrey, ed. *War, Diplomacy and Imperialism, 1618–1763.* New York, 1974. See pp. 62–74 for a translation of the final will of Carlos II.

Secondary Sources

Bély, Lucien. *Espions et ambassadeurs au temps de Louis XIV.* Paris, 1990.

Chandler, David G. *Marlborough as Military Commander.* London, 1973.

Ingrao, Charles W. *In Quest and Crisis: Emperor Joseph I and the Habsburg Monarchy.* West Lafayette, Ind., 1979.

Jones, J. R. *Marlborough.* Cambridge U.K., 1993.

Kamen, Henry. *The War of Succession in Spain, 1700–1715.* Bloomington, Ind., 1969.

Lossky, Andrew. *Louis XIV and the French Monarchy.* New Brunswick, N.J., 1994.

Lynn, John A. *The Wars of Louis XIV.* London, 1999.

McKay, Derek. *Prince Eugene of Savoy.* London, 1977.

Roosen, William J. "The Origins of the War of the Spanish Succession." In *The Origins of War in Early Modern Europe,* edited by Jeremy Black, pp. 151–171. Edinburgh, 1987.

Rule, John C. "Colbert de Torcy, an Emergent Bureaucracy and the Formulation of French Foreign Policy, 1698–1715." In *Louis XIV and Europe,* edited by Ragnhild M. Hatton, pp. 261–288. London, 1976.

Storrs, Christopher. *War, Diplomacy and the Rise of Savoy, 1690–1720,* Cambridge, U.K., 1999.

Thompson, Mark A. "Louis XIV and the Origins of the War of the Spanish Succession." In *William III and Louis XIV: Essays 1680–1720 by and for Mark A. Thompson,* edited by Ragnhild M. Hatton and John S. Bromley, pp. 140–161. Liverpool and Toronto, 1968.

Wolf, John B. *Louis XIV.* New York, 1968.

DAVID PARROTT

SPAS AND RESORTS.

Water therapy and visiting spas had a long history in Europe, especially in areas where the Roman legacy was deeply ingrained. There was growing interest in hydropathy in late medieval Italy, in some cases using bathing facilities that survived from the Roman era, and in fourteenth-century Hungary the granting of town status to a settlement frequently prompted the erection of a bathhouse.

THE PATTERN OF DEVELOPMENT

The tradition of the spa may have been less strong on the western edges of Europe. Not until the late sixteenth century did visiting spas became fashionable in France and Britain. Under the influence of royal and aristocratic patronage, and stimulated by professional promotion, a series of centers emerged in France, but only three of these—Bourbon, Vichy, and Forges—were consistently patronized by the elite. Prior to the French Revolution, most Gallic spas remained small in size and appear to have focused on their medicinal roles, eschewing the formation of sophisticated social facilities.

Events took a different course in Britain. The late Tudor and early Stuart phase of growth, which saw important investment in Bath and Buxton and the discovery of Tunbridge Wells, was curtailed by the political instability of the years surrounding the Civil Wars (1638–1660). After the Restoration, however, the discovery and formation of spas accelerated. Many served a local or regional market, such as the cluster of semirural centers—including Epsom, Islington, Hampstead, and Sadler's Wells—that sprang up on the edge of London. A few spas catered to a national clientele, and in 1700 Tunbridge and Bath were the market leaders.

Change forged ahead faster in Britain than France. A key factor was that, whereas in France the state kept a tight rein on development, a resident *intendant* ('superintendent') controlling the pace and character of new initiatives and keeping the emphasis firmly on health, in Britain no such regulatory framework existed. Competition and commercialization were given full play. Such was the level of demand in Britain that it spilled over to the Continent. Although spas in France and Italy were visited by Britons in the eighteenth century, the principal destinations were Spa and Aachen, which offered an engaging social life, including opportunities for intensive gambling. Some Britons also traveled to the many spas in central Europe (such as Baden, which capitalized on the demand from Vienna), many of which possessed several baths that catered to a range of social classes.

The rising level of demand in Britain also led it to pioneer what was to prove a critical diversification in water cures, the development—particularly in the coastal counties closest to London—of the seaside resort, a trend clearly underway by the 1750s. Serious investment in continental coastal resorts only began to occur from the 1790s. Parallel with the emergence of the seaside resort, and as a consequence of economic growth in the English Midlands and North, a second wave of spa development began, which stimulated both the expansion of Bath (to the point where, by 1800, it was among the top ten or so cities in England), and the rise of spas like Cheltenham, Malvern, Buxton, Matlock, Harrogate, and, later, Leamington.

RESORT CULTURE

Central to the character of spa and resort culture were the waters themselves. Popular interest in holy wells, sacred springs, and sea bathing was long established, but elite involvement stemmed from two factors. First, there was in the early modern period a growing fascination with and sympathy for the natural world as a whole. This expressed itself in areas such as gardening (which combined water and horticultural elements) and the picturesque and romantic movements, and led to the reconceptualization of the sea as a phenomenon to be admired and enjoyed rather than feared and avoided. Second, emphasis on the curative chemical properties of water was closely aligned with the rise of natural philosophy and science, and the shift from sacred and magical forms of health treatment to a regime based on rational "scientific" principles. In playing to the agendas of nature and science, water therapy articulated two of the principal themes of the Enlightenment, and demonstrated itself to be as much a cultural as a medical phenomenon.

One aspect of this was that spas and resorts became centers of pleasure as well as of health. In Britain the watering places were one of the key factors in an urban renaissance which, from the later seventeenth century, helped elevate the cultural status of the town. The water resorts acquired an ensemble of social facilities that included assemblies, theater, concerts, gambling, walks and pleasure gardens, sports like bowling and horse racing, and circulating libraries, together with a range of luxury shops and services. The scale and sophistication of this package would vary according to the importance of the resort, but its standardized character was striking. So also was the highly formalized daily routine that bound together the various parts of the package and propelled visitors into contact with each other. As one account of 1737 put it, "you cannot well be a free agent, where the whole turn is to do as other people do; it is a sort of fairy circle; if you do not run round in it, you cannot run at all, or are in everybody's way." This holiday camp mentality placed a huge premium on corporate behavior, and it is clear that one of the functions of the watering places was to weld together the members of the ruling order who flocked to them. In Britain the boundaries of this elite were expanding to accommodate a growing middling order of professionals and businessmen, and the resorts—particularly in their function as marriage markets—played an important role in merging old and new social groups. Such a process was tenable so long as the expansion of the middling order remained within certain limits. However, by the late eighteenth century such was the growth within this sector of society that spa life began to fragment, with social events becoming increasingly cliquish and privatized, and many among the landed elite vacating the big spas for smaller, exclusive coastal resorts.

See also **Aristocracy and Gentry; Gambling; Sports.**

BIBLIOGRAPHY

Borsay, Peter. "Health and Leisure Resorts, 1700–1840." In *The Cambridge Urban History of Britain*, Vol. 2, *1540–1840*, edited by Peter Clark, pp. 775–803. Cambridge, U.K., and New York, 2000.

Corbin, Alain. *The Lure of the Sea: The Discovery of the Seaside in the Western World, 1750–1840.* Translated by Jocelyn Phelps. Cambridge, U.K., and Berkeley, 1994.

Hembry, Phyllis. *The English Spa, 1560–1815: A Social History.* London and Rutherford, N.J., 1990.

Porter, Roy, ed. *The Medical History of Waters and Spas. Medical History,* supplement no. 10 (1990).

Walton, John K. *The English Seaside Resort: A Social History, 1750–1914.* Leicester, U.K., and New York, 1983.

PETER BORSAY

SPENSER, EDMUND

(1552 or 1553–1599), English poet and author. Born in London, perhaps at East Smithfield, Spenser was educated at the newly founded Merchant Taylors' School and at Pembroke Hall, Cambridge. His family may have been related to the Spencers of Althorp. As both politically engaged author and dutiful state servant, he first came to public notice in 1569. In that year, he translated verses by Petrarch (1304–1374) and

Joachim Du Bellay (c. 1522–1560) for *A Theatre for Worldlings,* an English version of a work by the Dutch Calvinist Jan van der Noot (c. 1540–c. 1595)—a key text for the reforming tradition of militant Protestantism to which Spenser belonged—and was paid on 16 October for bearing letters from Tours in France for Sir Henry Norris, English ambassador there, to Queen Elizabeth—the beginning of a long secretarial career.

At Cambridge he began a long-lasting friendship with fellow scholar Gabriel Harvey. He received his B.A. in 1573 and his M.A. in 1576. After a few years in which little is known of his activities or whereabouts, Spenser exploded onto the literary scene in 1579 with *The Shepheardes Calender,* a pastoral poem in the form of a collection of "eclogues," or conversations among shepherds. Much more than a publication, it was a literary event. *The Shepheardes Calender* founded the myth of Gloriana, contributing to the cult of Elizabeth at the very moment when Spenser, frustrated in his efforts to secure preference at court, was seeking his fortune abroad. Despite its panegyric to the queen in the April Eclogue, it contains a covert critique of church and state. Like his later work, it contests the very authority to which it apparently commends itself.

Published anonymously, but carefully timed to coincide with correspondence with Harvey containing clues to its authorship, *The Shepheardes Calender* came complete with the kind of editorial apparatus associated with classical texts by canonical authors, yet was illustrated with woodcuts, and contained dialogue written in the language of ordinary country folk. This mix of playfulness and purposefulness, with its inventive and often subversive borrowing from high and low culture, is characteristically Spenserian. *The Shepheardes Calender* was dedicated to Sir Philip Sidney, earning Spenser a mention in Sidney's *Apology for Poetry* (1595).

In 1580 Spenser became secretary to the new lord deputy of Ireland, Arthur, Lord Grey de Wilton. Ireland remained Spenser's home until his death. Having presented himself as the most promising poet of his generation with *The Shepheardes Calender,* Spenser failed to publish for a decade, busy both with the writing of his epic poem, *The Faerie Queene,* and with his role as secretary. From

1588, he occupied an estate of three thousand acres at Kilcolman, County Cork, one of many parcels of land seized from the late earl of Desmond as part of a government plan to settle lands in Munster with English tenants. This earned him the title of gentleman and provided a base from which to pursue his literary projects. He associated with Sir Walter Raleigh (1554–1618), who was a neighbor.

In September 1598 Spenser was appointed sheriff of Cork. Weeks later, Kilcolman was razed as part of a popular uprising. Spenser fled to Cork City, and from there to London, carrying a letter from the provincial president, Sir Thomas Norris, to the Privy Council, outlining the plight of the settlers. This last commission came thirty years after the performance of a similar duty for Norris's father. Spenser died in London on 13 January 1599.

THE FAERIE QUEEN

The first three books of *The Faerie Queene* appeared in 1590. A heady brew of Italianate romance, classical epic, and indigenous idioms inspired by Geoffrey Chaucer, John Gower, William Langland, John Lydgate, and John Skelton, its verbal density and formal difficulty marked a radical break with English poetic form, impacting later developments in poetry. Its sheer ambition coupled with an intimate attachment to landscape inspired poets from John Milton, John Dryden, and Alexander Pope, to Samuel Taylor Coleridge, William Wordsworth, John Keats, and Seamus Heaney. Its greatest innovation was the Spenserian stanza, a nine-line fusion of French "rhyme royal" and Italian "ottava rima," eight pentameters ending on an alexandrine, with a rhyme scheme of ababbcbcc. The second part of *The Faerie Queene*, books 4–6, appeared in 1596. Critics detect a darkening of purpose in the later books, as the allegory becomes more historical and political, especially in book 5, "The Legend of Justice." The "darke conceit" of *The Faerie Queene* shadows—and shares in—the dark doings of the English in Ireland, from martial law to massacres. Cowardice was not part of Spenser's makeup. Those who condemn his role in the government's violent suppression of resistance to colonization in Ireland respect a writer who had the courage of his convictions.

Spenser's work retained its critical edge right to the end, whether published in his own lifetime or in posthumous parting shots, from the anticourtly sentiments of *The Shepheardes Calender* and *Colin Clout's Come Home Againe* (1595) to the sharp criticisms of government that litter the prose dialogue *A View of the State of Ireland* (1596; published 1633), and, in *The Faerie Queene* itself, from the provocative account of the trial and execution of Mary, Queen of Scots (1542–1587), in canto 9 of book 5—which so enraged her son, James VI (ruled 1567–1625), that he asked for the poem to be destroyed and the poet punished—to the sniping from the margins in the "Mutabilitie Cantoes" that form a fragment of book 7 (unpublished until 1609).

Spenser lacked the means—perhaps even the muse—to write in England the national epic he was able to forge freely in Ireland. Born and buried in England, his career and corpus were made in Ireland. Spenser's colonial status both empowered and impaled him. His Irish experiences continue to engage and enrage critics in equal measure. For some, Spenser's astonishingly varied and vibrant literary output remains unbound by any context, historical or political. For others, the poetry, like the prose, is tainted by the world of violence from which it sprang. But where Ireland was once associated with the burden of history in Spenser studies, it has recently opened up his work to new readerships and new readings. Given his location between two cultures, as an imperial servant who became increasingly attached to his adopted country, it is no surprise that Spenser has received attention from postcolonial critics. His fusion of forms has attracted others who see him as an early postmodernist. One thing is clear: studying Spenser is, like his writing itself, an endless work.

See also **Elizabeth I (England); English Literature and Language; Ireland; Patronage; Sidney, Philip.**

BIBLIOGRAPHY

Primary Sources

Spenser, Edmund. *The Poetical Works of Edmund Spenser.* Edited by J. C. Smith and E. de Selincourt. London, 1912. Reprinted 1985.

———. *A View of the State of Ireland (1633): From the First Printed Edition.* Edited by Andrew Hatfield and Willy Maley. Oxford, 1997.

———. *The Works of Edmund Spenser: A Variorum Edition.* Edited by E. A. Greenlaw, et al. 11 vols. Baltimore, 1932–1949.

Secondary Sources

Burrow, Colin. *Edmund Spenser.* Plymouth, U.K., 1996.

Hadfield, Andrew. *Spenser's Irish Experience: Wilde Fruit and Savage Soyl.* Oxford, 1997.

Hamilton, A. C., ed. *The Spenser Encyclopedia.* Toronto, 1990.

Maley, Willy. *A Spenser Chronology.* New York, 1994.

Shire, Helena. *A Preface to Spenser.* London, 1978.

WILLY MALEY

SPINOZA, BARUCH (Benedictus de Spinoza; 1632–1677), Dutch philosopher. Baruch Spinoza's radical metaphysical, theological, moral and political ideas made him one of the most vilified thinkers of his day. Spinoza was born in Amsterdam to a Portuguese-Jewish family. He was raised and educated within the city's community of Sephardic Jews, many of whom had once been forced converts *(conversos)* to Christianity in Spain and Portugal. At the age of twenty-three, however, Spinoza, now a young businessman, was expelled from the congregation. The writ of *cherem,* or ban, the most vitriolic ever issued by the community's leaders, speaks only of his "abominable heresies and monstrous deeds," and the specific reasons for his expulsion remain vague. It is fairly certain, however, that among the offenses for which Spinoza was punished were his ideas on God, Jewish law, and immortality.

Spinoza's earliest philosophical writings, dating from the late 1650s and early 1660s, include the *Treatise on the Emendation of the Intellect* and the aborted *Short Treatise on God, Man, and His Well-Being.* He first came to public attention with the publication of a critical exposition of Descartes's *Principles of Philosophy* (1663). It was the anonymously published *Theological-Political Treatise* of 1670, however, that brought him great notoriety. The reaction to this stunningly bold work of Bible criticism and political thought was immediate and harsh; it was banned by numerous political and religious authorities, and its author was excoriated as a blaspheming atheist. As a result of the outcry, Spinoza decided not to publish his philosophical masterpiece, the *Ethics;* it did not appear in print until after his death, together with other unpublished writings, including *A Compendium of Hebrew Grammar,* some correspondence, and the never-completed *Political Treatise.*

In the *Ethics* Spinoza rejects the traditional providential God of the Jewish and Christian religions. The notion of a benevolent, wise, purposive, judging God is, he insists, an anthropomorphic fiction, one that gives rise only to superstition and irrational passions. God, according to Spinoza, is nothing but the active, generative aspects of nature. In an infamous phrase, Spinoza refers to *Deus sive Natura* (God, or Nature), and identifies it with the substance, essential attributes, and causal principles of the universe. All beings are "in" God, but only in the sense that Nature is all-encompassing, and nothing stands outside Nature's laws. Everything happens in Nature with a deterministic necessity. Even human beings, often (he alleges) regarded as autonomous creatures whose freedom puts them outside Nature's dominion, are a part of Nature and thus subject to its rigorous determinism. Some measure of freedom or "activity" is obtainable for human beings but only insofar as they can achieve an intellectual understanding of Nature and themselves and thereby exercise control over their passions. Spinoza adopts a Stoic conception of human well-being. Happiness is the result of virtue and consists in success in the pursuit of knowledge and self-mastery. Moreover, the rewards of virtue are to be found in this life. While human beings do "participate" in eternity, particularly through the knowledge they acquire, there is no personal immortality. Spinoza's metaphysics, epistemology, and moral philosophy reveal a variety of influences, especially Descartes, medieval Jewish philosophy, and ancient sources. However, there can be no denying the originality of his thought.

In the *Theological-Political Treatise* Spinoza turns to a critique of organized religion and an investigation into the status, history, and interpretation of the Bible. He begins with a deflationary account of prophecy (the prophets, he insists, were simply people with highly active imaginations) and a denial of the possibility of miracles (since Nature's laws admit of no exceptions). He insists, moreover, that Jewish ceremonial law was only of temporary validity (that is, during the Temple period) and is no longer binding on contemporary Jews. His most stunning theses, however, concern Scripture. Spinoza argues that the Bible is not literally of

Baruch Spinoza. Undated portrait engraving. ©BETTMANN/
CORBIS

divine origin and that its first five books (the Pentateuch) are not the writings of Moses. Rather, Scripture as we now have it is simply a work of literature, a compilation of human writings passed down through generations and edited in the Second Temple period. Others before Spinoza had suggested that Moses was not the author of the entire Pentateuch, but no one had taken that claim to the extreme limit that Spinoza did, arguing for it with such boldness and learning and at such length. Nor had anyone before Spinoza been willing to draw from it the conclusions about the interpretation of Scripture that Spinoza drew. The meaning of Scripture is to be sought not by appeal to theological dogma or to demonstrated truth—after all, the authors of Scripture were neither theologians nor philosophers—but by a close examination of the texts themselves and by a historical investigation into the backgrounds and intentions of its authors. If there is a universal truth conveyed by Scripture, it is a simple moral principle: love God and your neighbor.

Spinoza's discussion of Scripture takes place in the broader political context of his argument for a liberal, tolerant secular state, one in which the freedom to philosophize is defended against attempts to make it conform to so-called religious truth. For it is the "excessive authority and egotism of preachers," he tells one of his correspondents, that most threatens the freedom "to say what we think." The key to diminishing the undue influence of the clergy, who justify their abuses by appealing to the holiness of a certain book as the Word of God, is to demonstrate the true nature of Scripture and its message and eliminate the "superstitious adornments" of popular religion. By naturalizing Scripture, Spinoza hopes to redirect the authority invested in it from the words on the page to its moral message; and by formulating what he takes to be the proper method of interpreting Scripture, he seeks to encourage his readers to examine it anew and find therein the doctrines of the true religion. Only then will people be able to delimit exactly what needs to be done to show proper respect for God and obtain blessedness.

See also **Atheism; Bible: Interpretation;** *Conversos;* **Descartes, René; Stoicism.**

BIBLIOGRAPHY

Primary Source

Spinoza, Benedictus de. *The Collected Works of Spinoza.* Translated by Edwin Curley. Princeton, 1984.

Secondary Sources

Allison, Henry. *Benedict de Spinoza: An Introduction.* Rev. ed. New Haven, 1987.

Garrett, Don, ed., *The Cambridge Companion to Spinoza.* Cambridge, U.K., and New York, 1996.

Nadler, Steven. *Spinoza: A Life.* Cambridge, U.K., and New York. 1999.

STEVEN NADLER

SPORTS. Sport was an essential and socially significant pastime in the early modern world, an arena in which individual identity and ability were expressed by king and milkmaid alike. Capable sportsmanship at tennis, jousting, and even wrestling were increasingly perceived as the markings of a strong monarchy, which determined the athletic displays and rites of passage that prevailed in an aristocratic court. The sporting culture, in turn, was philosophically sanctioned by many humanists who extolled the "gentlemanlike pastimes" of swimming, archery, swordplay, and horseback riding as valuable components of any elite education.

Peasants and those of the lower orders also engaged in sport for their own purposes, reinforcing community cohesion by carving out their own particular spheres of play. Not all sport was universally embraced, however, and over the course of the period Puritans and others began to lament the "devilish" activity that joined other activities such as drinking, gambling, and dancing to produce "moral degeneracy." Nevertheless, sport prevailed against these assaults and emerged from the period more varied and popular than ever.

In the *Book of the Courtier* (1528), Baldassare Castiglione (1478–1529) set the tone through his admonitions regarding proper court behavior and etiquette, in which sport occupied—at least for males—a central and elevated position. Sport, however, was conceived by such writers in very different terms than those who came before (or perhaps since). For them, personal skill at a game such as archery was offset by the concept of *Fortuna* ('Lady luck'), a capricious goddess who determined the tides and turns of one's own personal luck. Sport was also imbued with a humanist regard for man, his body as well as his soul. According to Castiglione, the perfect man at court was "well built and shapely of limb," and displayed his physical capabilities by excelling at games of war—archery, horsemanship, and swordplay—as well as less martial physical activity, notably swimming, running, throwing, and jumping. Especially in games of mock war, such as jousting, the point was to achieve individual distinction on a physical level, as one performed on a stage that recalled traditions of military triumph. Even kings entered the game in this sense, as was the case with the famous encounter on the Field of the Cloth of Gold in 1520, when Henry VIII of England engaged Francis I of France in a wrestling match, alongside other gaming activities.

Despite its dangers and the increasing obsolescence of mounted and armored warfare on the battlefield, jousting sports continued to flourish in the form of fencing, which witnessed a shift to the long thin-bladed rapier and the use of point and the

lunge, and with it an increasing emphasis on speed, dexterity, and technique. Another sport in which actual weapons figured prominently was archery, which sustained its popularity even as the bow and arrow became increasingly archaic in war. According to Roger Ascham (1515–1568) in 1546, "How honest a pastime for the mind [is archery]; how wholesome an exercise for the body; not vile for great men to use, not costly for poor men to sustain." Finally, horses also continued in their martial importance, as they were used in the hunt, and in races such as the Italian *palio* and in England during annual competitions. Dressage, which was an extremely difficult, technical, disciplined—and time-bound—form of classical riding, was undertaken by military academies, though it, too, enjoyed a reputation as a more elevated sporting spectacle, and one that reinforced and perhaps played out social hierarchies in presenting the mounted rider—according to one Tudor writer—as a force of "majesty and dread to inferior persons." At the same time, the increasing precision of horsemanship, in the form of dressage, reflected a greater emphasis on uniformity and mathematical rules, as reflected in the writings of Descartes or by the early modern military shift to the use of drill.

Other activities enjoyed by the upper levels of society included tennis, which became the sport of kings such as Henry VIII, most notably, and was referred to in the writings of Erasmus, More, and Montaigne (with the latter's brother dying after being hit in the head with a tennis ball—no trivial accident when balls were frequently decried as too hard). After 1600, however, tennis declined in popularity, though it continued to ebb and flow in the elite consciousness alongside the new sport of golf.

Meanwhile, though football and related communal games tended to be spurned by elites and their writers, the similar game of *càlcio* ('soccer') flourished in Italy, allowing gentlemen, in the words of Cardinal Silvio Antoniano, to appear "more erect and more eager, and [enabling] them to meet sadness and depression with unruffled brow." Like other sports of the day, *càlcio* was affected by increasing bureaucratic intervention and mathematical quantification, as rules were drawn up to establish standards of play as well as objective and (increasingly) recorded scoring systems.

While sport among the elite was lauded by religious and secular leaders, sport among the lower orders was subject to greater condemnation on the part of authorities, who might have feared the disruptive and violent potential it could contain. The church and civic officials had long attempted to curtail football and other peasant games, with writers such as Sir Thomas Elyot (1490?–1546) advocating that football, in particular, be "put in perpetual silence." Urban footballers, or those who practiced their exertions near churches, were particularly odious to churchwardens, city administrators, and other leaders, who understandably feared the destruction of property. The "bloody and murdering" practice of football continued, however, in spite of Puritan hostility and denunciation, and despite the increasingly restricted fields that were fenced in after the enclosure movement in England. While games were allowed within proscribed time periods and special festival occasions such as Shrove Tuesday or May Day, the community- and identity-reinforcing benefits of sports proved too enticing for villagers and townspeople alike.

Such attachments were due in part to the fact that certain sports were so embedded in the peasant tradition, where football—usually involving two opposing teams that kicked or threw the ball against the opponents' goals—extended back centuries. In England the game had mythical origins, with claims that it had originated among Roman legionnaires in Britain, or later, among Saxons. Whatever the truth, the term *futball* first appears in records of the fourteenth century, with indications that the sport had already existed for a while. Similar to football, but more like modern-day soccer, was the game known in France as *la soule à pied,* which also extended back to the Middle Ages and involved opposing villages or specifically designated individuals competing to propel a leather ball forward by feet alone. *Shouler à la crosse*—which would evolve, with American Indian contributions, into modern lacrosse—involved similar feats using sticks, while the stick-based game of hockey—derived either from the French *hocquet,* meaning 'shepherd's staff', or the Anglo-Saxon *hoc,* meaning 'hook'—also originated in the Middle Ages.

Less physically taxing than fencing or football, though perceived as sport by upper and lower orders alike, were gambling games and related pastimes such as cockfighting. Though an ancient and universal game, dicing in early modern Europe continued its popularity and used the familiar cubed objects rather than the original knucklebones, though some dice were carved in the image of men or beasts. German mercenaries called *landsknechts* (literally, 'servants of the country') were particularly renowned dicing gamblers of the time, while knights and ladies, along with children and villagers, also continued to participate. Not surprisingly, objections were raised by Puritans, although enforcement of prohibitions was uneven. Gambling was not simply a "profane exercise" but also quite clearly a sin and banned in places such as John Calvin's Geneva. As one epigrammatic writer put it in 1636, the banning of sport and games resulted in "dull iron times" that made one long for "the Golden Age's Glories." Restrictions were subsequently eased, however, in reaction to the failed suppression of sport; partly as a result, the eighteenth century witnessed a veritable explosion of games and gambling, which continued, as they already had, to provide a sphere in which to exhibit, perform, show off, display physical prowess, and fashion one's identity through the kick of a ball, the lunge of a sword, or the roll of *Fortuna*-imbued dice.

See also **Aristocracy and Gentry; Castiglione, Baldassare; Cities and Urban Life; Court and Courtiers; Enclosure; Festivals; Gambling; Games and Play; Humanists and Humanism; Hunting; Peasantry; Popular Culture; Puritanism; Tournament.**

BIBLIOGRAPHY

Baker, William J. *Sports in the Western World.* Totowa, N.J., 1982.

Cox, R. W. *History of Sport: A Guide to the Literature and Sources of Information.* Frodsham, U.K., 1994.

Dunning, Eric. *Sport Matters: Sociological Studies of Sport, Violence, and Civilization.* London and New York, 1999.

Mason, Tony, ed. *Sport in Britain: A Social History.* Cambridge, U.K., and New York, 1989.

SARAH COVINGTON

SPRAT, THOMAS (1635–1713), author of *The History of the Royal Society of London, for the Improving of Natural Knowledge* (1667), an important document for those interested in Baconianism, the nature and program of the early Royal Society, and the development of English prose style. Educated at Wadham College, Oxford (B.A. 1654; M.A. 1657) and patronized by John Wilkins (1614–1672), the warden of Wadham College and an important figure in the founding of the Royal Society, Sprat appears to have been groomed for a clerical and literary career. His first publication was a panegyric to Oliver Cromwell (1659).

Commissioned by the Royal Society in 1663 to publicize and defend its aspirations, methods, and accomplishments, Sprat's *History of the Royal Society* was guided by a society committee and by John Wilkins. Scholars differ as to whether the sentiments expressed should be considered those of Sprat or Wilkins and the extent to which it represents the "official ideology" of the society. Sprat's *History* offers a Baconian vision of a useful, experimental, natural philosophy, although it accepts mathematics and hypothesis to a greater extent than Bacon did. Like Bacon's *Advancement of Learning* (1605), it argues that the pursuit of natural philosophy was not politically, socially, or religiously dangerous. Publication of the *History* was delayed by the plague and the fire in London. In the interim Sprat defended English science from the critique of Samuel Sorbiere (1615–1670).

The *History* is prefaced by a laudatory poem by Abraham Cowley (1618–1667) praising Bacon, the efforts of the Royal Society, and Sprat's literary style. Soon after, Sprat supervised the publication of Cowley's works and provided an account of his life and writing. Book I of the *History* is an outline of the history of learning, giving special attention to the defects of the Scholastic method and to the society's "new way of Inquiry." The accomplishments of the ancients are admired, but their authority rejected. Sprat emphasizes the detrimental effects of religious controversies and the need for peace if knowledge is to flourish.

Book II contains a description of the Royal Society's origins, its constitution, and legal structure. Although the society is characterized as open to men of all religions, nations, and professions, the role of gentlemen is particularly emphasized. Sprat notes the society's avoidance of politics, morality, oratory, and religion and describes its method of inquiry, highlighting the role of experiment, its preference for cooperative over individual investigation, and its rejection of the Cartesian method. It also includes a survey of the society's experiments and activities.

Book III, more apologia than history, defends experimental philosophy, emphasizing the society's hostility to religious fanaticism and other varieties of dogmatism. Sprat argues that experimental natural philosophy is not injurious to traditional education and its disciplines, altering only natural philosophy. Although the society did not meddle in spiritual things, its investigations supported natural religion, Christian belief, and the Church of England. The experimental approach also benefited the manual arts, the nobility and gentry, and wits and writers as well as encouraging the spread of civility and obedience to civil government. The *History* was attacked by Henry Stubbe (1632–1676), and modern scholars have questioned the accuracy of Sprat's account of the society's origins, the degree to which it represented accurately the society's methodology and goals, the extent of society supervision, and whether the *History* should be considered a latitudinarian document.

The best-known portions of the *History,* those advocating a plain, unadorned prose style devoid of metaphor and other figures of speech, have been central to discussions of scientific writing and prose style more generally. Sprat suggests that eloquence ought to be banished from civil society and that ornaments of speech are opposed to reason. The society therefore resolved "to reject all the amplifications, digressions, and swellings of style: to return back to the primitive purity, and shortness, which men delivered so many things, almost in a equal number of words." Sprat supported creation of an academy to polish the English language.

Sprat was a popular preacher and participant in high-church politics, holding a number of clerical posts before becoming bishop of Rochester in 1684. He defended the doctrine of the divine right of kings, wrote against the Whigs and the Rye House Plot, and served on James II's (ruled 1685–1688) ecclesiastical commission. Although willing to read James's *Declaration for Liberty of Conscience* from the pulpit, Sprat resigned from the commission, refusing to prosecute those unwilling to do so. Sprat accepted the Revolution of 1688.

See also **Bacon, Francis; Cartesianism; Church of England; Communication, Scientific; Descartes, René; Divine Right Kingship; Empiricism; James II (England); Johnson, Samuel; Scholasticism; Scientific Method; Wilkins, John.**

BIBLIOGRAPHY

Primary Sources

Bacon, Francis. *The Advancement of Learning.* London, 1605.

Birch, Thomas. *The History of the Royal Society of London for Improving of Natural Knowledge from Its First Rise.* 4 vols. London, 1756–1757. Reprint, New York, 1968.

Glanvill, Joseph. *Plus Ultra, or, the Progress and Advancement of Knowledge since the Days of Aristotle.* London, 1668.

Sprat, Thomas. "An Account of the Life of Mr. Abraham Cowley." In *The Works of Abraham Cowley.* London, 1669.

———. *The History of the Royal Society of London, for the Improving of Natural Knowledge.* Edited with critical apparatus by Jackson I. Cope and Harold Whitmore Jones. Saint Louis, 1958. Originally published London, 1722.

———. *A Loyal Satyr against Whiggism.* London, 1682.

———. *Observations on Monsieur de Sorbier's Voyage into England.* London, 1665.

———. *The Plague of Athens: Which Hapned in the Second Year of the Peloponnesian War.* London, 1659.

———. *Sermons Preached on Several Occasions.* London, 1722.

Secondary Sources

Hunter, Michael. "Latitudinarianism and the 'Ideology' of the Early Royal Society: Thomas Sprat's *History of the Royal Society* (1667) Reconsidered." In *Establishing the New Science: The Experience of the Early Royal Society,* pp. 45–71. Woodbridge, U.K., 1989.

Jacob, J. R. "Restoration Ideologies and the Royal Society." *History of Science* 18 (1980): 25–38.

Lynch, William T. *Solomon's Child: Method in the Early Royal Society of London.* Stanford, 2001.

Shapiro, Barbara. "Latitudinarianism and Science in Seventeenth-Century England." *Past and Present* 40 (1968): 16–41.

Wood, P. B. "Methodology and Apologetics: Thomas Sprat's History of the Royal Society." *British Journal for the History of Science* 13 (1980): 1–26.

BARBARA SHAPIRO

STAR CHAMBER. The court of Star Chamber took its name from the Camera Stellata in Westminster where its sessions were routinely held. The term does not appear to have been used before 1550 and only became popular in 1618 in Ferdinand Pulton's *Collection of Sundrie Statutes.* The court grew out of the medieval practice of the king's council hearing cases by petition, an alternative to the cumbersome process of the common law courts. Under Cardinal Wolsey's chancellorship (1515–1529), these legal functions of the council were separated from its administrative functions and the business of the court increased tenfold. Privy councillors, sometimes joined by the leading common law judges and lawyers, heard petitions and passed judgment. Most of the court's business in the early sixteenth century was civil, but by the 1560s an increasing number of criminal cases were heard. From 1566 the court also dealt with sedition, and its reputation for hearing politically sensitive cases increased. The court's business declined under the early Stuart kings, but its unsavory reputation for summary trial without jury and use of arbitrary power by the crown increased. Political show trials, such as those of the Puritans Alexander Leighton in 1630 and William Prynne, John Bastwicke, and Henry Burton in 1637, and the cruel and unusual punishments inflicted meant that Star Chamber became a prime target of opponents of Charles I in 1640–1641. On 5 July 1641, the Long Parliament abolished Star Chamber along with that other symbol of prerogative justice, the Court of High Commission.

See also **Charles I (England); Law: Courts.**

BIBLIOGRAPHY

Baldwin, J. F. *The King's Council in England during the Middle Ages.* Oxford, 1913.

Barnes, T. G. "The archives and archival problems of the Elizabethan and early Stuart Star Chamber." *Journal of the Society of Archivists* 2 (1963): 345–349.

Guy, John. *The Cardinal's Court: The Impact of Wolsey in Star Chamber.* Hassocks, U.K., 1977.

———. *The Court of Star Chamber and its Records to the Reign of Elizabeth I.* London, 1985.

Phillips, H. E. "The Last Years of the Court of Star Chamber, 1630–1641." *Transactions of the Royal Historical Society,* 4th series 21 (1939): 103–131.

DAVID GRUMMITT

STATE AND BUREAUCRACY.

The years between 1450 and 1789 were crucial in the development of the modern European state and state system. Political communities became increasingly centralized, territorialized, and bureaucratized. In much of Europe, state sovereignty displaced imperial and feudal conceptions of authority. These changes meant a reduction in the number and variety of actors participating in what we would now call "international politics." Familiar notions of statecraft, such as the importance of the "balance of power" and "reason of state," gained widespread acceptance, and by the latter part of the seventeenth century, religion was no longer a major factor in interstate relations.

Despite these trends, the states of early modern Europe were very different from our own. Dynastic notions of legitimacy contoured both domestic and interstate politics; the scope of the state's authority remained limited and fragmented by the standards of contemporary advanced industrialized countries. Nationalism and the goal of national self-determination did not emerge as significant forces in European politics until after the French Revolution. Yet many scholars believe that developments in the early modern period explain patterns of authoritarianism and democratization into the early twentieth century.

A number of factors share responsibility for the significant changes in European political institutions that took place in the early modern period. Among these, three kinds of large-scale processes were particularly important. First, frequent and increasingly expensive warfare placed great fiscal pressures upon states and their rulers. These pressures produced political bargains, administrative adaptations, and social struggles that altered the scope and nature of state power. Second, changes in the European economy associated with the rise of preindustrial capitalism and the development of direct trading connections—often through imperial expansion—with Asia, Africa, and the Americas brought about shifts in the relative influence and resources of different social actors and, at the same time, led to new sources of revenue and power for many rulers. Third, new ideas and ideologies, particularly those connected with the Protestant Reformation and the Enlightenment, played important roles in shaping and justifying new and old forms of state power.

THE CONCEPT OF THE STATE

It was not until the end of the sixteenth century that the word "state" became a common term to describe governments and their territories. Used in late medieval Europe to refer to the standing of a ruler or the state of his realm, the term gradually came to encompass the territories held by a political community and then the political community itself. The fact that "state" took on its now familiar meaning at the start of the early modern period suggests that the state—as an institution—emerged at roughly the same time.

Our contemporary understanding of the state derives directly from these conceptual innovations and the ways in which they were consolidated in the seventeenth and eighteenth centuries. The "state" may be taken, at a minimum, to refer to the combination of a government, the people it governs, and its territories. Such a thin concept of the state allows analysts to speak of a variety of different kinds of states. For example, Florence, Venice, and Genoa are often called "city-states," although each came to control subservient cities and regions. Some historians—perhaps misleadingly—have referred to the monarchies of medieval England and France as "feudal states." Many scholars now use the term "composite state," coined by H. G. Koenigsberger, to describe the patchwork quality of early modern states. States have been, and still are, organized in a variety of ways; the states of late medieval and early modern Europe had quite different characteristics from those associated with modern, particularly industrialized, nation-states.

Contemporary accounts of the development of the European state and state system rely heavily upon the work of the German social scientist Max Weber (1864–1920). According to Weber (pp. 55–56), the modern state is "an administrative and legal order subject to change by legislation, to which the organized activities of the administrative staff, which are also controlled by regulations, are oriented." A key feature of the modern state is that rule is impersonal. Political authority derives from the office, not from the person occupying that office. The consistent application of the legal code takes priority over personal relationships, and rulers may only change law through settled procedures. These features entail the rise of professional and meritocratic forms of administration at the expense of patrimonial office holding. In patrimonial systems, offices are "owned" by individuals and their families, who occupy them by right rather than by merit.

Weber also argued that the modern state "claims binding authority, not only over the members of the state, the citizens, most of whom have obtained membership by birth, but also to a very large extent over all action taking place in the area of its jurisdiction. It is thus a compulsory organization with a territorial basis." Indeed, "today, the use of force is regarded as legitimate only so far as it is either permitted by the state or prescribed by it. . . . The claim of the modern state to monopolize the use of force is as essential to it as its character of compulsory jurisdiction and of continuous operation." The modern state exercises territorial sovereignty. No other actor may claim the right to make or enforce rules within the boundaries of a state—at least without the express permission of that state. States also enjoy autonomy with respect to their external relations, exercised through the sole right to make treaties, declare war, and regulate their borders for themselves and their citizens.

Despite the influence and insightfulness of Weber's discussion of the characteristics of the modern state, we need to be careful about how we use it in analyzing historical processes. Indeed, some historians question the usefulness of Weber's definition. They argue that it promotes teleological accounts of European state formation, blinding analysts to the variety of manifestations of the state that have existed over the last few hundred years. It also, critics contend, leads scholars to overestimate the true power that expanding central bureaucracies actually wielded. The existence of an extensive bureaucratic infrastructure does not necessarily indicate a high degree of practical centralization and state power.

Such problems often plague analysis of state formation, but they should not lead us to abandon Weber or his definition of the state. Weber's discussion of the nature of the state is what he calls an "ideal-typical" construction, not a description of actual states. No political community, in any period of human history, has ever perfectly fit his definition of the state. Ideal types are the starting point of discussion and analysis, not descriptions of concrete reality. If we keep this fact in mind, Weber's understanding of the state remains a valuable tool for understanding the development of states in early modern Europe.

STATE FORMATION IN EARLY MODERN EUROPE

The most important source of variation in early modern state formation into the seventeenth century was created by the uneven expansion of princely, or dynastic, power. Trends in this direction date back into the fourteenth century, but their contours began to take shape in the late fifteenth century. In western Europe, particularly in England, France, and Castile, princes expanded their control at the expense of the autonomy of other concentrations of power, such as towns, nobles, and the church. The result, by the beginning of the sixteenth century, was the formation of what some historians call the "new monarchies" of western Europe. At the same time, territorial princes in Germany were in the process of appropriating legislative power—with mixed success—into their own hands. The trend toward princely power was not limited to kingdoms and principalities. In Italy, where city-states rather than kingdoms predominated, great families were busy establishing their own dynastic control over most formerly independent communes and republics. In all three cases, princes were able to expand their power by successfully manipulating divisions between other political actors, mostly within the nobility and the towns, while also tying the fortunes of both to princely authority.

Elsewhere, attempts to expand princely power met with rather different fates. Until the second half of the seventeenth century, the Danish nobility successfully curtailed princely authority—a situation dramatically reversed in 1660 when an alliance between the Danish King Frederick and the non-noble estates (burghers and clergy) led to the establishment of an absolutist system of government. An open succession in Hungary in 1439 allowed its national assembly to reassert the elective principle of that kingdom's monarchy. Baronial interests ultimately thwarted attempts at centralizing reforms. After the division of the kingdom between the Habsburgs and the Ottomans stabilized in 1541, the relative power of the Habsburgs remained comparatively weak. The ascendancy of the nobility was even more pronounced in Poland, where the powerful diet checked monarchial authority; Poland became a "republic of nobles" with little centralized power.

Variation in the expansion of princely and dynastic power had an impact across three directions of state formation. The first was the eclipse of the influence of nondynastic pathways of state formation. With the exception of the Dutch Republic and the Swiss Confederation, city-states and urban federations gradually ceased to be major players in international politics. The second was the loss of international influence of alternative centers of power within dynastic states, such as cities and nobles. These two trends were related: the same factors that oriented actors' struggles for influence toward the states in which they resided also undermined the viability of nondynastic states. The third trend involved the balance between agglomerative and consolidative impulses in dynasticism, and the ultimate rise of consolidation as the most effective pathway of state formation.

THE RISE OF DYNASTIC STATES

The expansion of princely authority in many regions of Europe made dynastic states the crucial players in European power politics. City-states, city-leagues, and the majority of nobles—in other words, those who were not directly implicated in dynastic politics—saw a corresponding reduction in their independent international influence. The crucial question for most of the sixteenth and seventeenth centuries was not whether dynastic states would expand their preeminence over international politics, but what kinds of dynastic states would predominate in Europe: the relatively—with an emphasis upon "relatively"—more centralized, territorially compact dynastic states represented by the English and French monarchies, or the confederal and more expansive forms of dynastic states represented by the Habsburg monarchies.

To understand the significance of this transformation, we need to consider that there were a number of different kinds of international actors contending for power from the late medieval into the beginning of the early modern period. In addition to powerful nobles and towns within kingdoms and

principalities, there were a variety of nondynastic states active in international politics. Like dynastic states, most of these were "composite states," cobbled together from heterogeneous institutions, regions, and linguistic groups.

One important type was city-states. These were composite polities dominated by a single urban community. Although the name suggests a city whose borders were coterminous with a state, in reality city-states were, at minimum, made up of a city and attached—usually dominated—regions. Most German city-states were of this type, but their Italian cousins had, by the late medieval period, come to control a number of formerly independent communes. These dominated entities retained their distinctive legal and institutional personalities and were usually accorded some degree of autonomy over certain spheres of rule. In other words, city-states were really empires run by an urban core. This is particularly apparent if we consider the great Italian city-states, such as Venice, that controlled and fought over maritime empires in the Mediterranean.

By the end of the fifteenth century, Venice was the only Italian city-state that had not become integrated into, to borrow a phrase from Richard Mackenney, dynastic micro-empires headed by powerful Italian families such as the Medici. This process was reinforced after the French invasions of Italy began in 1494 and the peninsula became the focus of dynastic competition between the French Valois, on the one hand, and first the Aragonese Trastámara and then the Habsburgs on the other. The growth of princely power in much of Europe combined with the standard operating procedures of dynasts—based upon marriage alliances and dynastic claims—to empower dynasts even in those regions where princely power was less well developed, not only in Italy but in the elective monarchies of eastern Europe. Most German city-states had the status of imperial cities, and their fate was tied up in the consequences of the Protestant Reformation.

Another alternative to dynastic states was federative polities. Federations often had strong urban components, but they also included rural regions and even, as in the case of the German Swabian League (founded in 1385), small principalities, knights, and monasteries. Federations originated as alliances motivated by the commercial and security concerns of political actors unable to fulfill those needs through their own recognizance. Although many federations originated in the Middle Ages, they enjoyed a resurgence in the face of dynastic consolidation in the early modern period. A number of federations, including the Hanseatic League and the Swiss Confederation, amounted, unlike the Italian city-leagues, to more than temporary balancing alliances.

The fate of federations was a bit more complex than that of city-states. The Swiss remained viable in this period and were joined by the Dutch in the latter part of the sixteenth century. In general, the fate of most federations was directly linked to that of princely power. The territories of many federations overlapped with those under the titular rule of princes. As princely power expanded, the relative influence of independent and quasi-independent federations, particularly urban federations, declined. In essence, they were absorbed into consolidating dynastic states. The same trends that favored princely power directly undermined the autonomy of federations. The Hanseatic League, for example, scored its last major victory when its principal city, Lübeck, helped secure Swedish independence from the kingdom of Denmark in 1522–1523. By the end of the Thirty Years' War in 1648, the league was in precipitous decline.

CONSOLIDATION AND AGGLOMERATION
The rise of dynasticism in this period still left a great deal of room for different manifestations of dynastic states. The expansion of dynastic authority occurred through two processes: consolidation and agglomeration. The former involved the integration of dynastic holding and the latter the accumulation of holdings under a single dynastic line.

The accumulative potential of dynasticism stemmed from the significance of marriage in cementing alliances and brokering relations between different families. Decades, and sometimes centuries, of strategic marriages between important European families and dynastic lines led to intricate webs of hereditary claims to kingdoms, counties, and principalities. Since there was little legal basis by which a dynast could renounce a familial claim to a particular territory, an heir could always invoke such a claim as a justification for political loyalties or outright conquest. For example, long after the English

had been routed at the end of the Hundred Years' War, Elizabeth I's royal title still referred to her as the "king of France."

The processes of integration and accumulation interacted in a variety of ways to produce different dynastic configurations. The addition of new holdings brought new institutional arrangements under the auspices of a dynastic line, and could therefore increase the heterogeneous character of a dynastic state. For instance, from 1369 to 1477 the dukes of Burgundy created a "middle kingdom" by conquering or accumulating parts of modern-day Belgium, Luxembourg, France, Germany, and the Netherlands. The majority of those territories subsequently transferred to Habsburg hands as a result of marriage and inheritance. Early modern France was itself the product of a period of reconstitution and expansion during the later stages of the Hundred Years' War. There, dynastic practices produced a complicated array of institutions and jurisdictions with different rights and exemptions vis-à-vis the monarchy.

But the most profound transformation resulting from the agglomerative possibilities of dynasticism was the sudden creation of a vast confederal empire united through the person of Charles of Habsburg (Emperor Charles V). Starting in 1517, Charles became ruler of a large swath of territories in western, central, and southern Europe. In only a few years, the Habsburg line amassed unparalleled power in sixteenth-century Europe. As Holy Roman emperor and the dynastic head of a vast and heterogeneous collection of territories, Charles's position revived the prospects for universal empire in Latin Christendom. After he abdicated his various titles between 1556 and 1557 (see below), Charles's holdings were divided between his son Philip II of Spain (ruled 1556–1598) and his brother, Ferdinand I (king of Bohemia and Hungary, 1526–1564; Holy Roman emperor, 1558–1564). The rump Habsburg lands of the Spanish monarchy still made Charles the most powerful international actor in Christendom until the dénouement of the Thirty Years' War. Ferdinand also controlled a formidable, and formidably heterogeneous, agglomeration including Austria and the remnant of the Kingdom of Hungary. In the eighteenth century, Austria would emerge as a great power in its own right.

During the sixteenth and seventeenth centuries, the crucial question of state formation was whether the Habsburg model would prove more significant and enduring than the more compact alternative represented by the French monarchy, or indeed how the balance between consolidation and agglomeration would play out in dynastic states in general. In the end, consolidation, along with a movement toward sovereign territoriality, became the preponderant pathway of state formation in most of Europe.

PROCESSES OF CHANGE

A combination of three factors influenced the rise of princely power: transformations in the conduct of warfare, developments in the art of rule, and economic changes. The first undermined the ability of towns and lesser nobles to mount effective opposition to princely authority, the second helped to transform social relations and the balance of influence among different groups within states, and the third led to new coalitional possibilities for princes. These factors varied in their configuration, orientation, and timing in different places in Europe. They also interacted with preexisting institutions to produce different results; this helps to explain why some polities saw a decline in princely authority instead of its expansion.

Developments in the nature of warfare had a profound influence on state formation in the entire period under consideration. These changes involved the increasing importance and sophistication of gunpowder artillery in conjunction with new organizational tactics—most famously associated with the Swiss pike square—and the rise of new fortification techniques designed to cope with the impact of gunpowder artillery on siege warfare. Together they are sometimes called the "military revolution," but more recent scholarship suggests that the changes in warfare in early modern Europe were more evolutionary, and hence more complicated in nature. Two key changes associated with the military-technical revolution, the rise of mercenary forces recruited by independent and quasi-independent contractors and the decline in importance of feudal levies in warfare, actually began in the medieval period, although their importance only grew over time. The development of the revenue expropri-ation apparatus needed to finance mercenary armies also predates the early modern period.

The introduction of combat-effective handheld gunpowder artillery in the fifteenth century combined with the continued shift toward mercenary armies gave important advantages to those with the power to extract and wield greater fiscal resources. Simultaneously, these changes began to undermine the kinds of armies fielded by lords and their retainers. In practice, the advantage went to princes and regional magnates, but large cities with high concentrations of wealth could also afford to hire mercenaries. Meanwhile, the castles and fortifications of the lesser nobility were obsolete in the face of new siege techniques that made use of gunpowder.

The new reality was that most cities and nobles simply could not, on their own, amass the concentration of wealth and manpower necessary to mount forces capable of challenging princes. If princes could exploit the divisions inherent in composite dynastic states—between regional interests and social classes—they were relatively insulated from successful challenges to their power.

To aid them with this task, dynasts had new ideologies and techniques of rule at their disposal. With the growth of patronage as the basis for durable political ties—itself connected to economic changes discussed below—heads of state, particularly in those kingdoms already marked by comparative centralization aided by hereditary rule, found themselves situated at the top of a complex network of patron-client relations. Their prerogatives made a great many of their subjects ultimately dependent upon them for continued financial and status perquisites. This, combined with increasingly sophisticated propaganda drawing upon theories of royal authority, gave princes ideological and material resources with which to prevent the formation of effective coalitions against them.

Finally, economic changes had a crucial impact. Growth in the European economy in the Middle Ages, particularly with respect to long-distance trade, had already contributed to the rise of towns. Where rulers had successfully pivoted between burghers and nobles—as in France, Aragon, and England—they had already done much to build a position of comparative strength. Population pressures, economic growth in the sixteenth century, the influx of silver from the newly discovered Americas, and numerous other causes of the "price revolution" that accompanied the expansion of preindustrial capitalism in early modern Europe, played a decisive role in accelerating the breakdown of what was left of feudal forms of loyalty. New sources of wealth, changing social classes, and diverging economic interests increased the distributional role of the state in the allocation of money and prestige.

Moreover, these developments generally favored entrepreneurial merchants and the higher nobility. The latter not only benefited from the increasing price of agricultural goods, but could also derive income from patronage and military activity. In western Europe this made them more dependent on the crown, not only with respect to patronage but also because monarchical brokerage became essential to the ability of large landowners to raise rents and squeeze profits from the peasantry. In contrast, lords in northeastern Germany and Poland were particularly powerful and held extensive lands, which meant they did not need to become dependent upon their titular rulers. Indeed, such nobles were able to institute a neo-serfdom far more burdensome than the older variety, and these regions became the principal exporters of grain for an urbanizing western Europe.

As this last point suggests, the conjunction of economic and military factors also exerted strong influence over the early development of bureaucratic elements in state administration. In general, significant aspects of bureaucratic administration first appeared in dynastic holdings that contained concentrations of capital resulting from urban trade, where rulers already had some relative advantage over their domestic competitors, and where rulers were engaged in intensive warfare utilizing newer, more expensive recruitment techniques and military technology. The first two factors provided the means to expand tax collection and the administration of debt, while the last provided the impetus for increasing royal control. Thus, western European kingdoms such as France and Castile developed early aspects of bureaucratic governance. These techniques were insufficient to finance the debts incurred by conflict, and periods of war making were abruptly halted by financial pressures and outright bankruptcies. But the management of debt itself provided a crucial impetus to the kinds of ad hoc administrative arrangements that laid the seeds for later bureaucratization.

Even in the new monarchies of the early sixteenth century, princes were not as strong as their propaganda and their increasingly extravagant court cultures sought to suggest. The smooth functioning of their authority depended upon the cooperation of regional magnates and urban centers, and on preventing coalitions against princely authority from forming between various regional and local actors. In the sixteenth and seventeenth centuries, resentment against the centralizing tendencies of dynasts mixed with religious dissent to plunge large swaths of western and central Europe into political conflict and civil war.

THE EMERGENCE OF A MULTISTATE, SOVEREIGN-TERRITORIAL EUROPEAN POLITICAL ORDER

The Protestant Reformation and the Peace of Westphalia of 1648, which marked the end of the Thirty Years' War, were once seen as watersheds in European history that ended the prospects for an intra-European universal empire and established a sovereign-territorial, multistate system. Although some scholars defend qualified versions of this interpretation, there is very little evidence to suggest that the Reformation and Westphalia led directly to the modern state system. In fact, even before the Reformation, the position of the church in many dynastic states was becoming subordinate to the interests of secular rulers.

A more balanced understanding of the role of the Reformation in the emergence of a multistate, sovereign-territorial European order is that it accelerated some trends already caused by military-technical and economic change, while undermining others, particularly aspects of the more confederal, dynastic agglomerative pathway of state formation. In this way, it tilted the balance toward a sovereign, multistate system but was not decisive in its development.

Thus, in the German regions of the Holy Roman Empire, the rise of Protestantism ultimately enhanced the importance of territorial princedoms. Charles V's unwillingness to engage in a long-term compromise on the issue of religious belief convinced many of the princes that they could only preserve Protestantism by relying on self-help. Their eventual victory over Charles led to his abdication and the 1555 agreement at Augsburg that specified, with some qualifications, that each prince would determine the religion of his territory. Augsburg led to a period of confessionalization, in which hardening doctrinal divisions between different sects of Christianity tended to coincide with territorial boundaries.

Some scholars argue that confessionalization, whether through processes of the Reformation or Counter-Reformation, played a major role in expanding the scope, nature, and territorial authority of the state not just in Germany, but throughout Europe. For instance, the state took on oversight of responsibilities such as social welfare concerns that had been largely local and ecclesiastical in the medieval period. Although some of these claims are exaggerated, it is clear that confessionalization forwarded existing trends in those directions.

For its part, the spread of Calvinism into France and the Netherlands temporarily worked to undermine the advantages gained by princes as a result of military-technical change and political institutional effects. Calvinism provided a basis for cooperation that transcended regional and class differences. These differences were crucial components of the divide-and-rule strategies used by dynasts and institutionalized in dynastic composite states. Moreover, the organizational abilities and transnational connections afforded by Calvinism—and by militant Catholicism in France—allowed nonstate actors to gain access to sufficient resources to mobilize competitive military forces.

The Dutch Revolt, in which religious tensions played a decisive role in escalating other grievances against Habsburg rule, led directly to Spanish strategic overextension and contributed a great deal to Spain's eventual failure to maintain European primacy. Moreover, major innovations in fiscal administration developed in Holland during Habsburg rule were expanded during the Dutch Republic's war for independence against Spain (1568–1648). The Dutch were forced to field continuous and substantial military forces on a predominately mercantile financial base.

In contrast, the French Wars of Religion (1562–1598) were, in the short term, much more devastating to France's cohesion and international position. Yet they also revealed the advantages that more compact dynastic states had in the context of religious strife—even when the Huguenots established a "state within a state," secession from the French crown was never a serious option. The experience of the wars provided added impetus for the expansion of sovereign authority in the kingdom, and, somewhat paradoxically, thus led to the growth of a more integrated, centralized state.

The religious conflicts that engulfed various parts of Europe between the promulgation of Martin Luther's Ninety-Five Theses in 1517 and the end of the English Civil War in 1648 played some role in important conceptual changes in European statecraft. Their most direct impact can be found in developing ideas about sovereignty. The experience of religious civil war led directly to Jean Bodin's (1530–1596) and Thomas Hobbes's (1588–1679) different formulations of sovereignty, as well as to new syntheses of ideas about the right of resistance to unlawful or unjust rulers. These debates, and those that followed from them, were pivotal in making questions about state sovereignty—who ultimately holds it and what its limits are—a central element of political theorizing.

Religious conflicts also made a significant contribution to the (largely implicit) adoption of Italian notions of "reason of state" in Europe. Reason of state, or, more frequently, "necessity," was the justification for reconciling temporary accommodation of confessional differences or even putting aside religious differences in the support of enemies of one's own dynastic opponents. Of course, it was generally the opponents of religious compromise who accused moderates of adopting Machiavellian attitudes or "politique" positions, but the processes of making these decisions involved formulating the antecedents of ideas about state interests.

Religious struggles were less important in the emerging notion of the "balance of power," which owed more to the propaganda campaign inspired by fears of Habsburg primacy. Since the Habsburgs were the main dynastic backers of the Catholic cause, these debates were often tinged with religious concerns, but the more important concern was the possibility of a more robust Habsburg hegemony or even a Habsburg universal empire in which the other princes of Europe would be subordinate players. The threat of Habsburg hegemony led to a critique of empire that served as a justification for defensive aggression: lesser powers could engage in proactive strategies—from alliances to warfare—to prevent one actor from accumulating an imbalance of power. These arguments were refined during the wars of Louis XIV in the later seventeenth and early eighteenth centuries. Indeed, France admitted in the 1713 Treaty of Utrecht that it was fear of French power that motivated the War of the Spanish Succession—the first mention of the balance of power in a European peace treaty.

CONSOLIDATION AND BUREAUCRATIZATION

The conflicts of the seventeenth and eighteenth centuries forced those states that had not been subject to the same opportunities and pressures that initially favored bureaucratization in western Europe to launch their own administrative reforms. In general, states such as Sweden, Brandenburg-Prussia, and Austria lacked the kind of access to domestic capital sources that played an important role in early European bureaucratization. Where princes were comparatively strong, particularly in Prussia, in some of the German principalities, and for more contingent reasons, in Sweden, they built extensive bureaucracies capable of extracting enough resources to compensate for their comparatively poor access to trade revenues. In Poland, by contrast, patrimonial administration persisted and ultimately led to the demise of the commonwealth. Indeed, some argue that the ways in which states financed warfare in the sixteenth and seventeenth centuries determined whether they became, in the nineteenth, moderately democratic or authoritarian.

In general, state formation in the second half of the seventeenth and eighteenth centuries was characterized by a decisive shift toward territorial sovereignty and greater bureaucratization of the state's financial and administrative activities. Enlightenment ideas of rationality and the obligation of rulers to subjects provided an important impetus to these developments, although financial pressures and political interests played perhaps a more decisive role.

A major impetus to additional bureaucratization came from the replacement of mercenary forces with professional militaries. Professional armies and navies were usually recruited from within the state and were always integrated into the state's institutional structure. This greatly expanded the fiscal and administrative costs of warfare, but also increased the reliability of military forces. It was this transformation that placed the means of organized violence beyond the reach of citizens and subjects.

Although these changes meant greater centralization of authority, they did not necessarily lead to particularly efficient or coherent bureaucratic structures. The sale of offices for revenues, problems with particular administrative bureaucracies, and other factors often led to duplicative governmental activity. France developed such patchwork institutions. Indeed, local revolts against royal demands for revenue and greater authority continued to plague French administration in the decades before the French Revolution. Britain, borrowing directly from Dutch innovations and with the advantage of parliamentary oversight, was more successful at creating an efficient fiscal-administrative system.

Brandenburg-Prussia is usually taken to be the most extreme case of this fusion of military and administrative centralization. Prussia's reliance on centralized, coercive fiscal-military institutions stemmed from its precarious geographical position, expansionist foreign policies, and the fact that its resource base lacked extensive trade and capital endowments. These factors meant, initially, that expansion, such as the seizure from Austria of Silesia, and foreign subsidies were crucial to Prussia's ability to sustain its great-power status. Such pressures also led to a bureaucratic framework that lacked the functional specialization found in other European states.

If Prussia represents one extreme, then Austria might be considered another divergent case. Austria remained a relatively confederal dynastic agglomeration. In fact, it had come close to collapsing in 1618–1620 under the pressure of religious contestation and local rebellion. However, after the War of the Spanish Succession (1701–1714), the Austrian dynastic empire controlled more territory in Europe than the Spanish monarchy ever had. Starting in the middle of the eighteenth century under Maria Theresa, Austria's Habsburg rulers began to make real progress in administrative reform. But these successes were often checked by assertive local actors, particularly the nobility. Austria's rulers could often squeeze more revenue from their heterogeneous domains, but they generally could not overcome their dependence on cooperation from local elites.

Throughout Europe, direct and indirect rule continued to coexist; by and large, the expansion of bureaucratic administration was often more impressive in a formal sense than a practical one. The erosion of patrimonial officeholding in many parts of Europe did not prevent bureaucratic officeholders from seeking to enrich themselves at the expense of the state. In France, and even at some points in Prussia, rent seeking emerged as an enormous problem for the new bureaucracies.

The early modern period witnessed a decisive transition to territorial sovereignty within Europe, and it saw the emergence of robust bureaucratic forms of governance and the expansion of state administration into a variety of new areas, but it did not mark the triumph of the Weberian bureaucratic state. However, such states, to the extent that they ever existed, were a result of the transformative effects of nationalism and industrial capitalism upon the institutional infrastructures and international political practices developed between 1450 and 1789.

See also **Absolutism; Aristocracy and Gentry; Authority, Concept of; City-State; Divine Right Kingship; Hansa; Military; Monarchy; National Identity; Officeholding; Provincial Government; Sovereignty, Theory of.**

BIBLIOGRAPHY

Anderson, Perry. *Lineages of the Absolutist State.* London, 1974.

Armitage, David, ed. *Theories of Empire, 1450–1800.* Aldershot, U.K., and Brookfield, Vt., 1998.

Blockmans, Wim P., and Charles Tilly, eds. 1989. *Cities and the Rise of States in Europe, A.D. 1000 to 1800.* Boulder, Colo., 1989.

Bonney, Richard. *The European Dynastic States: 1494–1660.* Oxford and New York, 1991.

Brewer, John. *The Sinews of Power: War, Money and the English State, 1688–1783.* Cambridge, Mass., 1990.

Bussman, Klaus, and Heinz Schilling. *1648: War and Peace in Europe.* Münster, 1998.

Downing, Brian M. *The Military Revolution and Political Change: Origins of Democracy and Autocracy in Early Modern Europe.* Princeton, 1992.

Elias, Norbert. *The Civilizing Process.* Translated by Edmund Jephcott. Oxford, 1994.

Elliott, J. H. *Richelieu and Olivares.* Cambridge, U.K., 1984.

Eltis, David. *The Military Revolution in Sixteenth-Century Europe.* London and New York, 1995.

Ertman, Thomas. *The Birth of Leviathan: Building States and Regimes in Medieval and Early Modern Europe.* Cambridge, U.K., and New York, 1997.

Gorski, Philip S. "Calvinism and State-Formation in Early Modern Europe." In *State/Culture: State-Formation after the Cultural Turn,* edited by George Steinmetz, pp. 147–181. Ithaca, N.Y., 1999.

Greengrass, Mark, ed. *Conflict and Coalescence: The Shaping of the State in Early Modern Europe.* London, 1991.

Gross, Leo. "The Peace of Westphalia, 1648–1948." *American Journal of International Law* 42, no. 1 (1948): 20–41.

Hall, Rodney Bruce. *National Collective Identity: Social Constructs and International Systems.* New York, 1999.

Hintze, Otto. *The Historical Essays of Otto Hintze.* Translated by Felix Gilbert with Robert M. Berdahl. New York, 1975.

Hsia, R. Po-Chia. *Social Discipline in the Reformation: Central Europe, 1550–1750.* London and New York, 1989.

Ingrao, Charles W. *The Habsburg Monarchy, 1618–1815.* 2nd ed. Cambridge, U.K., 2000.

Koenigsberger, H. G. *Estates and Revolutions: Essays in Early Modern European History.* Ithaca, N.Y., 1971.

———. "The Organization of Revolutionary Parties in France and the Netherlands During the Sixteenth Century." *Journal of Modern History* 27, no. 4 (December 1955): 335–351.

———. *Politicians and Virtuosi: Essays in Early Modern History.* London, 1986.

Krasner, Stephen D. "Westphalia and All That." In *Ideas and Foreign Policy: Beliefs, Institutions, and Political Change,* edited by Judith Goldstein and Robert O. Keohane, pp. 235–264. Ithaca, N.Y., 1993.

Lynn, John A. *The Wars of Louis XIV, 1667–1714.* London, 1999.

Mackenney, Richard. *Sixteenth Century Europe: Expansion and Conflict.* Basingstoke, U.K., 1993.

Osiander, Andreas. "Sovereignty, International Relations, and the Westphalian Myth." *International Organization* 55, no. 2 (Spring 2001): 251–288.

Parker, Geoffrey. *The Military Revolution: Military Innovation and the Rise of the West 1500–1800.* Cambridge, U.K., 1988.

Philpott, Daniel. *Revolutions in Sovereignty: How Ideas Shaped Modern International Relations.* Princeton, 2001.

Schilling, Heinz. *Religion, Political Culture and the Emergence of Early Modern Society: Essays in German and Dutch History.* Leiden and New York, 1992.

Skinner, Quentin. *The Foundations of Modern Political Thought.* Vol. 1, *The Renaissance.* Vol. 2, *The Reformation.* Cambridge, U.K., 1978.

Spruyt, Hendrik. *The Sovereign State and Its Competitors: An Analysis of Systems Change.* Princeton, 1994.

te Brake, Wayne. *Shaping History: Ordinary People in European Politics, 1500–1700.* Berkeley, 1998.

Tilly, Charles. *Coercion, Capital, and European States, A.D. 990–1990.* Oxford and Cambridge, Mass., 1990.

Tracy, James D. *Holland under Habsburg Rule, 1506–1566: The Formation of a Body Politic.* Berkeley, 1990.

Weber, Max. *Economy and Society: An Outline of Interpretative Sociology.* Translated by Ephraim Fischoff et al. Edited by Guenther Roth and Claus Wittich. Berkeley, 1978.

DANIEL NEXON

STATISTICS. The word statistics comes from the German *Statistik* and was coined by Gottfried Achenwall (1719–1772) in 1749. This term referred to a thorough, generally nonquantitative description of features of the state—its geography, peoples, customs, trade, administration, and so on. Hermann Conring (1606–1681) introduced this field of inquiry under the name *Staatenkunde* in the seventeenth century, and it became a standard part of the university curriculum in Germany and in the Netherlands. Recent histories of statistics in France, Italy, and the Netherlands have documented the strength of this descriptive approach. The descriptive sense of statistics continued throughout the eighteenth century and into the nineteenth century.

The numerical origins of statistics are found in distinct national traditions of quantification. In England, self-styled political and medical arithmeticians working outside government promoted numerical approaches to the understanding of the health and wealth of society. In Germany, the science of cameralism provided training and rationale for government administrators to count population and economic resources for local communities. In France, royal ministers, including the duke of Sully (1560–1641) and Jean-Baptiste Colbert (1619–1683), initiated statistical inquiries into state finance and population that were continued through the eighteenth century.

Alongside these quantitative studies of society, mathematicians developed probability theory, which made use of small sets of numerical data. The emergence of probability has been the subject of several recent histories and its development was largely independent of statistics. The two traditions of collecting numbers and analyzing them using the calculus of probabilities did not merge until the nineteenth century, thus creating the modern discipline of statistics.

The early modern field of inquiry that most closely resembles modern statistics was political arithmetic, created in the 1660s and 1670s by two Englishman, John Graunt (1620–1674) and William Petty (1623–1687). Graunt's *Natural and Political Observations Made upon the Bills of Mortality* (1662) launched quantitative studies of population and society, which Petty labeled political arithmetic. In their work, they showed how numerical accounts of population could be used to answer medical and political questions such as the comparative mortality of specific diseases and the number of men of fighting age. Graunt developed new methods to calculate population from the numbers of christenings and burials. He created the first life table, a numerical table that showed how many individuals out of a given population survived at each year of life. Petty created sample tables to be used in Ireland to collect vital statistics and urged that governments collect regular and accurate accounts of the numbers of christenings, burials, and total population. Such accounts, Petty argued, would put government policy on a firm foundation.

Political arithmetic was originally associated with strengthening monarchical authority, but several other streams of inquiry flowed from Graunt's and Petty's early work. One tradition was medical statistics, which developed most fully in England during the eighteenth century. Physicians such as James Jurin (1684–1750) and William Black (1749–1829) advocated the collection and evaluation of numerical information about the incidence and mortality of diseases. Jurin pioneered the use of statistics in the 1720s to evaluate medical practice in his studies of the risks associated with smallpox inoculation. William Black coined the term *medical arithmetic* to refer to the tradition of using numbers to analyze the comparative mortality of different diseases. New hospitals and dispensaries such as the London Smallpox and Inoculation Hospital, established in the eighteenth century, provided institutional support for the collection of medical statistics; some treatments were evaluated numerically.

Theology provided another context for the development of statistics. Graunt had identified a constant birth ratio between male and females (14 to 13) and had used this as an argument against polygamy. The physician John Arbuthnot (1667–1735) argued in a 1710 article that this regularity was "an Argument for Divine Providence." Later writers, including William Derham (1657–1735), author of *Physico-Theology* (1713), and Johann Peter Süssmilch (1707–1767), author of *Die Göttliche Ordnung* (1741), made the stability of this statistical ratio a part of the larger argument about the existence of God.

One final area of statistics that flowed from Graunt's work and was the most closely associated with probability theory was the development of life (or mortality) tables. Immediately following the publication of Graunt's book, several mathematicians, including Christiaan Huygens (1629–1695), Gottfried Leibniz (1646–1716), and Edmund Halley (1656–1742) refined Graunt's table. Halley, for example, based his life table on numerical data from the town of Breslau that listed ages of death. (Graunt had to estimate ages of death.) In the eighteenth century, further modifications were introduced by the Dutchmen Willem Kersseboom (1690–1771) and Nicolaas Struyck (1686–1769), the Frenchman Antoine Deparcieux (1703–1768), the German Leonard Euler (1707–1783), and the Swede Pehr Wargentin (1717–1783). A French historian has recently argued that the creation of life tables was one of the leading achievements of the scientific revolution. Life tables were used to predict life expectancy and aimed to improve the financial soundness of annuities and tontines.

The administrative demands brought about by state centralization in early modern Europe also fostered the collection and analysis of numerical information about births, deaths, marriages, trade, and so on. In France, for example, Sébastien le Prestre de Vauban (1633–1707), adviser to Louis XIV

(ruled 1643–1715), provided a model for the collection of this data in his census of Vézelay (1696), a small town in Burgundy. Although his recommendations were not adopted, a similar approach was pursued decades later by the Controller-General Joseph Marie Terray (1715–1778), who requested in 1772 that the provincial intendants collect accounts of births and deaths from parish clergy and forward them to Paris. Sweden created the most consistent system for the collection of vital statistics through parish clerks in 1749. Efforts in other countries failed. In England, two bills were put before Parliament in the 1750s to institute a census and to insure the collection of vital statistics. Both bills were defeated because of issues concerning personal liberty. While these initiatives enjoyed mixed success, they all spoke to the desire to secure numerical information about the population. Regular censuses, which would provide data for statistical analysis, were not instituted until the nineteenth century.

See also **Accounting and Bookkeeping; Census; Graunt, John; Mathematics; Petty, William.**

BIBLIOGRAPHY

Primary Sources

Arbuthnot, John. "An Argument for Divine Providence Taken from the Regularity Observ'd in the Birth of Both Sexes." *Philosophical Transactions* 27 (1710–1712): 186–190.

Black, William. *An Arithmetical and Medical Analysis of the Diseases and Mortality of the Human Species.* London, 1789. Reprinted with an introduction by D. V. Glass. Farnborough, U.K., 1973.

Jurin, James. *An Account of the Success of Inoculating the Small Pox in Great Britain with a Comparison between the Miscarriages in That Practice, and the Mortality of the Natural Small Pox.* London, 1724.

Petty, William. *The Economic Writings of Sir William Petty.* Edited by Charles Henry Hull. 2 vols. Cambridge, U.K., 1899.

Secondary Sources

Bourguet, Marie-Noëlle. *Déchiffrer la France: La statistique départementale à l'époque napoléonienne.* Paris, 1988.

Buck, Peter. "People Who Counted: Political Arithmetic in the Eighteenth Century." *Isis* 73 (1982): 28–45.

———. "Seventeenth-Century Political Arithmetic: Civil Strife and Vital Statistics." *Isis* 68 (1977): 67–84.

Daston, Lorraine. *Classical Probability in the Enlightenment.* Princeton, 1988.

Dupâquier, Jacques. *L'invention de la table de mortalité, de Graunt à Wargentin, 1622–1766.* Paris, 1996.

Dupâquier, Jacques, and Michel Dupâquier. *Histoire de la démographie*. Paris, 1985.

Hacking, Ian. *The Emergence of Probability*. Cambridge, U.K., 1975.

———. *The Taming of Chance*. Cambridge, U.K., 1990.

Hald, Anders. *A History of Probability and Statistics and Their Applications before 1750*. New York, 1990.

Klep, Paul M. M., and Ida H. Stamhuis, eds. *The Statistical Mind in a Pre-Statistical Era: The Netherlands, 1750–1850*. Amsterdam, 2002.

Patriarca, Silvana. *Numbers and Nationhood: Writing Statistics in Nineteenth-Century Italy*. Cambridge, U.K., 1996.

Pearson, Karl. *The History of Statistics in the 17th and 18th Centuries against the Changing Background of Intellectual, Scientific and Religious Thought*. Edited by E. S. Pearson. London, U.K., 1978.

Porter, Theodore M. *The Rise of Statistical Thinking, 1820–1900*. Princeton, 1986.

Rusnock, Andrea. *Vital Accounts: Quantifying Health and Population in Eighteenth-Century England and France*. Cambridge, U.K., 2002.

ANDREA RUSNOCK

STEELE, RICHARD (1672–1729), English essayist and dramatist. Steele's name is associated with that of Joseph Addison, with whom he collaborated. Born in poor circumstances in Dublin, Steele was brought up by his aunt and uncle, Lady Katherine Mildmay and Henry Gascoigne. His extended family were influential Protestant gentry, but little is known of his parents. At fourteen, Steele went to the Charterhouse School, where he met Addison.

In 1689 Steele went to Oxford University, where he did not take a degree but joined the second troop of Life Guards in 1692. His first publication was a poem on the death of Queen Mary II in 1694; it was dedicated to Lord Cutts, colonel of the Coldstream Guards, who rewarded him with the rank of captain and made him his secretary. Steele had a daughter with Elizabeth Tonson. He did not acknowledge the fact at first, but later brought the child up in his home. While stationed in Suffolk as commander of a garrison, he composed *The Christian Hero* (1701). In this reforming tract and moral manual, Steele contrasted the passion and universal heroism of Christianity with his perception of the false reasoning of Stoicism of the Roman emperors. Steele wrote his first play, *The Funeral, or Grief à la Mode*, the same year. A didactic satire on hypocritical undertakers and dishonest lawyers, it was praised by William III. Unfortunately, the king died before conferring any favors on Steele. Finding promotion in the army increasingly difficult to achieve without powerful connections, Steele left in 1705 to pursue success as a writer. In his second play, *The Lying Lover* (1702), he continued his didactic dramatic vision, portraying virtuous characters as models for audiences to emulate, as opposed to the predominantly "immoral" characters on the Restoration stage.

In 1705, Steele married Margaret Ford Stretch. Because of his theatrical success, he was well acquainted with London society and became involved in Whig politics. He was appointed gentleman waiter to Prince George of Denmark, Queen Anne's husband, in 1706. Engaging in the pamphlet war with satirical essayist Jonathan Swift, his public opponent, Steele wrote *The Crisis*, attacking the Tory ministry for its unenthusiastic support for a Protestant successor to the throne. In 1707, after his first wife's death, Steele married Mary Scurlock. At this time he was editor of the *London Gazette*, the official government periodical.

Steele's fame rests on his founding of *The Tatler* (1709–1711) and *The Spectator* (1711–1712), forerunners of modern journalism, which he wrote anonymously with Joseph Addison with the object of targeting the intellectual and political melting pots of London's coffeehouses and bookshops. *The Tatler*, a series of thrice-weekly papers in which Steele planned to educate "Politick Persons," was addressed predominantly to fashionable society, whereas *The Spectator* appealed to a wider audience. Using the idea of a club of different personalities, politics, culture, and foreign and domestic topics were explored in *The Tatler*. Steele used the figure of Isaac Bickerstaff, created by Jonathan Swift, to satirize the annual almanacs. Steele's fundamental purpose was moral didacticism: he wished to inculcate a practical morality in an accessible style. Swift, however, attacked Steele's loose use of syntax and the use of juxtaposition in his writing.

Published daily, *The Spectator* developed from *The Tatler* and included essays on relationships between the sexes, manners, London life, taste, and politics. *The Spectator* assembled a club of narrators whose personalities, eccentricities, and political viewpoints were revealed in concrete detail. Led by Mr. Spectator, the narrators included the Tory country squire Sir Roger de Coverly, and Sir Andrew Freeport, a Whig mercantilist. Steele's contribution to *The Spectator* is distinguished for his use of the letter form and the dialogue between either fictional personae or a writer and a reader (real or imagined). His essays on women such as "The Education of Girls" (no. 66, 16 May 1711) reveal both his sentimentalism and his open, sympathetic stance towards women's social and sexual status.

Steele's desire to be more politically outspoken against the Tory ministry produced two anti-Tory periodicals, *The Guardian* (with Addison's help) in 1713, and *The Englishman* (1713–1714), as well as several pamphlets and short-lived periodicals. Elected as M.P. for Stockbridge in 1713, his position in the House of Commons was disputed, and a Tory majority expelled him. Steele was granted a governorship of Drury Lane Theatre in 1714 to, as he expressed it in his pamphlet *Town Talk,* "Chastise the Vices of the Stage, and promote the Interests of Virtue and Innocence." In 1715, he was knighted by George I, and made a surveyor of the royal stables. Steele argued publicly with Addison in 1718 over the peerage bill, an incident that led to the revocation of the Drury Lane patent. He then began a biweekly paper called *The Theater* and later issued pamphlets about the South Sea Bubble. His last play, *The Conscious Lovers* (1722), was based on Terence's *Andria;* in it Steele portrayed ideals of male and female manners and began the tradition of the sentimental comedy. The play's success enabled him to settle his debts. Steele retired in ill health to his estate in Wales and died in Carmarthenshire in 1729.

See also **Addison, Joseph; English Literature and Language; Journalism, Newspapers, and Newssheets.**

BIBLIOGRAPHY

Primary Sources

Steele, Richard. *The Plays of Richard Steele.* Edited by Shirley Strum Kenny. Oxford, 1971.

———. *Selections from The Tatler and The Spectator.* Edited by Angus Ross. London, 1982. Reprint 1988.

———. *The Spectator.* Edited by Donald F. Bond. 5 vols. Oxford, 1987.

———. *The Tatler.* Edited by Donald F. Bond. 3 vols. Oxford, 1987.

Secondary Sources

Alsop, J. D. "New Light on Richard Steele." *British Library Journal* (1999): 23–33. Examines the evidence that Steele may have had a brother.

Dammers, Richard H. *Richard Steele.* Boston, 1982. An introductory overview of Steele's life and work.

Winton, Calhoun. *Captain Steele: The Early Career of Richard Steele.* Baltimore, 1964. The standard biography, which examines Steele's life up to 1714 with generous excerpts from *The Tatler* and *The Spectator.*

———. *Sir Richard Steele M.P.: The Later Career.* Baltimore, 1970. The sequel to the above volume.

MAX FINCHER

STENO, NICOLAUS (Niels Stensen; 1638–1686), Danish anatomist, paleontologist, and geologist. Born 11 January 1638 to a Copenhagen goldsmith, Steno attended the University of Copenhagen from 1656 to 1660, where he studied medicine and anatomy with Thomas and Erasmus Bartholin. Moving on to Amsterdam and Leiden from 1660 to 1664, he made several important discoveries concerning glands, which were a new field of investigation. Inspired by René Descartes's *Treatise on Man* (published posthumously in Leiden in 1662), Steno began studying the physiology of the heart, and he came to argue, against both Descartes and William Harvey, that the heart was not a specially endowed organ but merely a muscle. Failing to secure a position at the University of Copenhagen, Steno traveled to Paris, came under the patronage of Melchisedec Thevenot, and continued his anatomical studies. He gave a lecture on the brain in 1665 in which he took further issue with Descartes's theories of brain function, and he argued that ideas about brain physiology should be grounded in the results of detailed dissection. This lecture was published four years later as *Discourse on the Anatomy of the Brain* and was the most influential of his anatomical works.

Continuing his slow journey south, Steno spent some time in Montpelier in 1665, and in 1666 he arrived at Pisa and the summer court of the Medici family of Florence. He was invited to join the circle of the Accademia del Cimento, and he readied for publication a study of muscle anatomy. His career abruptly changed course when he was given the head of a giant white shark to dissect by the grand duke, Ferdinand II. Steno was indeed interested in the muscle anatomy of the shark, but he was even more fascinated by its teeth, which closely resembled the fossil objects known as *glossopetra* or tonguestones. Tonguestones, and nearly all other fossils, were commonly regarded as mineral objects that grew in the rocks where they were found and were not thought to have an organic origin. Steno considered the problem and offered compelling reasons why tonguestones must have once been sharks' teeth. When he published his *Elements of Myology* in 1667, he appended to it a short treatise, "The Dissection of the Head of a Shark." This essay marks the beginning of the science of paleontology.

Steno then addressed the more general problem of ascertaining the history of rock formations by examining the clues within them. He formulated principles by which he could determine if formations had been moved or altered after they had been laid down and which formations had been deposited first. Within eighteen months, he had completed his major geological treatise, *Prodromus to a Dissertation on Solids Naturally Contained Within Solids*. Steno argued here that rock strata are like the pages in a book of history, and that proper understanding of the principles of stratigraphy will allow that book to be read. The *Prodromus* marks the beginning of historical geology.

Steno resumed his travels in 1668, touring much of central Europe; he returned to Florence in 1670 for two years and then was invited back to Copenhagen in 1672, where he was royal anatomist until 1674. But his interest in anatomy had been waning for some time. Steno had converted to Catholicism in 1667, and he gradually turned his attention to religious and churchly matters. He returned to Florence in 1675 to be ordained a priest; in 1677 he was appointed apostolic vicar of the northern missions (Germany), and shortly thereafter became the titular bishop of Titiopolis. He spent the last nine years of his life in Hanover, Münster, and Hamburg, trying to bring the followers of Luther back into the Catholic Church. He died on 5 December 1686 in Schwerin. The grand duke of Florence, Cosimo III de' Medici, had Steno's body brought back to Flor-

ence, where he was buried in the cathedral of San Lorenzo. About three hundred years later, on 23 October 1988, Steno was beatified by Pope John Paul II.

See also **Anatomy and Physiology; Descartes, René; Florence; Geology; Harvey, William; Scientific Revolution.**

BIBLIOGRAPHY

Primary Sources

Steno, Nicolaus. *Discours sur l'anatomie du cerveau*. Paris, 1669.

——. *Elementorum Myologiae Specimen . . . cui Accedent Canis Carchariae Dissectum Caput*. Florence, 1667.

——. *De Musculis & Glandulis Observationum Specimen*. Paris, 1664.

——. *De Solido Intra Solidum Naturaliter Contento Dissertationis Prodromus*. Florence, 1669.

——. *Steno: Geological Papers*. Edited by Gustav Scherz. Translated by Alex J. Pollock. Odense, 1969.

Secondary Sources

Kardel, Troels. *Steno: Life, Science, Philosophy*. Copenhagen, 1994.

Scherz, Gustav, ed. *Dissertations on Steno as Geologist*. Odense, 1971.

——. *Nicolaus Steno and His Indice*. Copenhagen, 1958.

WILLIAM B. ASHWORTH, JR.

STEPHEN BÁTHORY (1533–1586; ruled 1576–1586), king of Poland and prince of Transylvania (from 1571). Báthory was brought up at the imperial court in Vienna, was well educated, and knew several languages. In 1559 he was appointed commander of the Wardar fortress, took part in John Sigismund Szapolyai's struggles against the Habsburgs, participated in peace negotiations with the emperor in Vienna, and was interned there for several years. As prince of Transylvania he had to acknowledge his subordination to both Turkey and the emperor; he organized a mercenary army, reformed education, and upheld the principles of religious tolerance.

After Henry of Valois's flight from Poland (1574), Báthory submitted his candidacy for the Polish throne and expressed his intention to marry Princess Anna Jagiellonka. Despite the fact that the primate, Jacob Uchański, proclaimed the emperor

Stephen Báthory. Sixteenth-century portrait engraving.
©BETTMANN/CORBIS

Maximilian II king of Poland (12 December 1575), many magnates (including Jan Zamoyski), clergymen, and a majority of the nobility supported Báthory, who was proclaimed king on 15 December 1575. On 1 May 1576 Báthory married Anna and was crowned in Cracow. The former followers of the Habsburg candidate gradually came over to his side. Báthory launched a campaign against Gdańsk, which had supported the emperor, and after a lengthy blockade and siege, a compromise agreement was reached (12 December 1577), in which Gdańsk recognized Báthory's election, agreed to pay a high contribution to the royal coffers, and preserved its extensive autonomy.

In his internal policy Báthory, backed by Chancellor Zamoyski's advice, sought to strengthen royal power and did not shrink from overcoming the opposition of magnates and noblemen by force (for instance, in the execution of Samuel Zborowski in 1584). However, when Livonia was threatened by Russia, the king, wishing to start war preparations, made some concessions to the nobility, as its consent to additional taxes was indispensable in order to pay the army. He gave up some of the royal judicial prerogatives and set up supreme courts of appeal in Poland (1578) and Lithuania (1581). He pursued a policy of religious toleration, observing the provisions of the Compact of Warsaw (1573), which guaranteed freedom of religion and equal rights to Catholics and dissidents. In 1578 he transformed the Jesuit college in Vilnius into a higher school, the Vilnius Academy.

Báthory's military reforms were of great significance: he organized (1578) an infantry composed of peasants from the crown estates (the so-called selected infantry), furnished the cavalry with lighter protective equipment and firearms, strengthened the artillery, introduced pontoon bridges, and brought over specialists in the construction of fortifications. Having assembled a nearly 30,000-strong army, he attacked Russia. In three victorious campaigns (1579–1581) he defeated the forces of Ivan IV the Terrible, took Polotsk and Velikiye Luki, and laid siege to Pskov. In the armistice concluded at Iam Zapol'skii (15 January 1582) Ivan gave up Polotsk and land and castles in Livonia, while the Poles returned Velikiye Luki to Russia. Báthory's ambitious plans to conquer Russia and launch an expedition against Turkey (supported by papal subsidies) were interrupted by his death. Báthory was one of Poland's most prominent rulers and an excellent military commander. Despite his attachment to Hungary, he was motivated in his work by Poland's *raison d'état*—but he never learned Polish. He was buried in the cathedral on Wawel Hill in Cracow.

See also **Livonian War (1558–1583); Poland-Lithuania, Commonwealth of, 1569–1795.**

BIBLIOGRAPHY

Besala, Jerzy. *Stefan Batory.* Warsaw, 1992.

Olejnik, Karol. *Stefan Batory, 1533–1586.* Warsaw, 1988.

MARCIN KAMLER

STERNE, LAURENCE (1713–1768), English novelist.

Sterne is perhaps most famous as the author of *Tristram Shandy* (1759–1767), his serially published comic novel that propelled him from his quiet life as an Anglican clergyman in Yorkshire to the heart of London's literary society. The son of an infantry ensign, Sterne grew up living in army barracks in England and Ireland before attending school in Yorkshire at the age of ten. From there, Sterne went to Jesus College, Cambridge, and in 1738 took holy orders, obtaining a living (an endowed ecclesiastical position) at a country parish church near York with the help of his uncle, an influential church lawyer. His career in the ministry was made more lucrative when, in the 1740s, he was employed by his uncle to campaign on behalf of the Whig party in local county elections. In return for this, Sterne received ecclesiastical preferment, becoming a prebendary (recipient of a stipend given to a member of the clergy) of York Minster.

Marrying Elizabeth Lumley in 1741, Sterne added the living of Stillington to his ministerial duties and lived a relatively quiet life in Yorkshire until 1759, when he published his first imaginative prose, *A Political Romance* (also known as *The History of a Good Warm Watch Coat*). This satire on local ecclesiastical courts included uncomplimentary and thinly veiled portraits of Minster clergy and was ordered by the archbishop of York to be burned.

In the same year, and with more success, Sterne also published the first two volumes of *Tristram Shandy*. This serialized novel tells the life story of its eponymous hero, beginning with the exact time of his conception, and including long, often absurd or bawdy, digressions about his family, especially his flamboyant father Walter and his soldier brother Toby. Volumes 3 and 4 were published in 1761, 7 and 8 in 1765, and the last volume, 9, in 1767. In the final volume, a conversation between Tristram's mother and the parson Yorick about Walter's bull seems to sum up the entire story inadvertently: "'L-d!' said my mother, 'what is all this story about?'—'A COCK and a BULL,' said Yorick—'And one of the best of its kind I ever heard.'" When Sterne visited London in 1759, shortly after the first two volumes had gone on sale, he discovered that his novel was an immediate success and had sold out at the booksellers. Declaring that he wrote "not [to] be fed, but to be Famous," Sterne nevertheless capitalized on his success with *Tristram Shandy* by persuading his London bookseller to publish a selection of his sermons in 1760.

With his literary reputation established and his financial position secure, in 1762 Sterne headed for France and Italy. For many years, Sterne's wife Eliz-

abeth had suffered from mental illness (at her worst, she believed herself to be the queen of Bohemia); Sterne had suffered with consumption (tuberculosis) since his days at Cambridge, and the trip to Europe was hoped to be beneficial for both. Finally returning to London in 1767, Sterne began an affair with Elizabeth Draper, the wife of an official in the East India Company. When she was forced to move to India with her husband, Sterne began his *Journal to Eliza* (also called the *Bramine's Journal*), which he kept for six months, and which was discovered in 1851. In 1768, Sterne published his next, and final, novel, *A Sentimental Journey in France and Italy*, which drew on his own experiences of touring in Europe and resurrected the impulsive parson, Yorick, from *Tristram Shandy*, as its protagonist. As with *Tristram Shandy*, which satirized the conventions of the contemporary "Life of . . ." narrative (or novel), *A Sentimental Journey* satirized the conventions of travel writing by claiming to be a journal of a grand tour (a tour of the Continent traditionally undertaken by young Englishmen) and "a quiet journey of the heart in pursuit of NATURE," with comic, and famously bawdy, encounters.

As the author of *Tristram Shandy*, Sterne is credited with being the originator of the "stream-of-consciousness" novel, influencing modern authors Virginia Woolf and James Joyce in particular. Even in its day, this book was celebrated because it brought a new level of consciousness to the developing novel by satirizing the manipulation of fact for the purpose of fiction, and by casting comic doubt on the idea of capturing a life in writing. In his own life, Sterne also trod a fine line between fact and fiction, living in "Shandy Hall" and writing to friends under the name of "Yorick." A month after the publication of *A Sentimental Journey*, Sterne died in his lodgings in London; the *Journal to Eliza* was published for the first time in 1904.

See also **Burney, Frances; Defoe, Daniel; English Literature and Language; Fielding, Henry; Richardson, Samuel; Smollett, Tobias.**

BIBLIOGRAPHY

Primary Sources

Sterne, Laurence. *Letters of Laurence Sterne.* Edited by Perry Lewis Curtis. Oxford, 1935.

———. *The Life and Opinions of Tristram Shandy, Gentleman.* Edited by Ian Campbell Ross. Oxford and New York, 1983; rev. ed., 2000.

———. *A Sentimental Journey through France and Italy* with *The Journal to Eliza* and *A Political Romance*. Edited by Ian Jack. Oxford and New York, 1968; repr. 1984.

———. *The Sermons of Laurence Sterne*. Edited by Melvyn News. 2 vols. Volumes 4 (text) and 5 (notes) of the Florida Edition of Laurence Sterne. Gainesville, Fla., 1996.

———. *Sterne's Memoirs: A Hitherto Unrecorded Holograph Now Brought to Light in Facsimile*. Edited by Kenneth Monkman. Coxwold, U.K., 1985.

Secondary Sources

Basker, James G. *Tobias Smollett: Critic and Journalist*. Newark, N.J., 1988.

Loveridge, Mark. *Laurence Sterne and the Argument about Design*. London, 1988.

New, Melvyn. *Critical Essays on Laurence Sterne*. New York and London, 1998.

Ross, Ian Campbell. *Laurence Sterne: A Life*. Oxford and New York, 2001.

ALISON STENTON

STOCK EXCHANGES.

Stock exchanges are formally organized secondary markets for financial assets that have already been issued in primary capital markets. Stock markets have become the hallmark of successful modern capitalist economies, despite the frequency of volatile price movements that lead to excessive speculation followed by panics and despite repeated scandals. They play an important role, however, for both the primary capital market and the mobilization of bank credit within any economy, basically by providing liquidity for the initial investors in government or corporate debt or in corporation stock. The assurance that a ready market exists for the sale of an investor's holdings in case of second thoughts, emergencies, or better alternatives for investment makes it easier to place debt or equity in the first place on the primary capital market. The daily pricing of all such financial products on a stock exchange also makes them ideal instruments as collateral for loans. In sum, stock exchanges are important complements to the efficient operation of the rest of an economy's financial sector.

The historical development of worldwide stock exchanges shows that three features are essential for their long-term success: a large stock of homogeneous, readily identified financial assets available to the public; a numerous and diverse customer base that is aware of the financial assets available; and a set of trustworthy intermediaries to handle trades of the various financial products among the customers.

The first feature arose with the creation of large-scale government debt, initially by Italian city-states such as Venice, Florence, and Genoa in the fourteenth and fifteenth centuries. While a secondary market of sorts existed, the city debts do not appear to have been widely held, as they took the form of forced loans from the wealthiest merchants and gentry. The second feature appeared with the creation of the joint stock of the Dutch East India Company or VOC (Vereenigde Oost-Indische Compagnie) in 1602, which was a forced amalgamation of a series of trading ventures organized within six different cities of the United Provinces. The existing shareholders were numerous and varied greatly in wealth and investment objectives; many were unhappy at the forced amalgamation and loss of voice in the management of the company. Active trading in the shares arose soon afterward, and a group of specialists in trading VOC shares appeared on the Amsterdam Beurs, which was the general wholesale market for commodities. According to de le Vega, these traders met in a corner of the exchange when it was open and continued business after hours in nearby coffeehouses. But this grouping does not appear to have had a formal organization or many other trading opportunities in other securities. Even though each city and province in the Netherlands issued large amounts of debt, each issue was closely held and seldom traded outside the city or province of origin. Not until 1795, when the Batavian Republic instituted reforms inspired by the French Revolution, did a regularly printed list of stock prices appear in Amsterdam, even though Dutch newspapers had reported prices of the leading securities since at least 1723.

In 1688, when Dutch financial techniques were grafted onto the English system of central government with parliamentary control over a constitutional monarch, the new British governments rapidly increased both their debt and the transferable stock of corporations holding government debt, such as the Bank of England, the New East India Company, and the South Sea Company. Despite the general collapse of share prices after the South

Sea Bubble of 1720, the customer base for English securities was large and increasingly diverse, comprising foreigners as well as provincial customers throughout England. Dedicated professional traders appeared who usually acted as brokers and often as dealers holding stock on their own account as well. Not until 1773, however, do we find documented evidence that they had a formal organization to assure confidence in trading with each other and on behalf of the general public.

With the substantial increases in government debt during the Napoleonic Wars, however, a formal exchange was created: the London Stock Exchange, with its self-regulated set of trading rules and information system. In response, the Paris Bourse, which had come under strict government control in 1726 after the collapse of the Mississippi Bubble in 1720, and then fell into disuse during the financial disruptions caused by the French Revolution, was revitalized by the French government and maintained under Napoleon. In the United States, the creation of federal debt in 1790 led to the appearance of the New York Stock Exchange, as well as other exchanges in Philadelphia, Boston, and elsewhere, eventually leading to over two hundred regional exchanges in the United States by World War I.

See also **Banking and Credit; Capitalism; Commerce and Markets; Interest; Trading Companies.**

BIBLIOGRAPHY

Dickson, P. G. M. *The Financial Revolution in England: A Study in the Development of Public Credit, 1688–1756.* London, 1967.

Garber, Peter. *Famous First Bubbles: The Fundamentals of Early Manias.* Cambridge, Mass., 2000.

Neal, Larry. *The Rise of Financial Capitalism: International Capital Markets in the Age of Reason.* New York, 1990.

t'Hart, Marjolein, Joost Jonker, and Jan Luiten van Zanden, eds. *A Financial History of the Netherlands.* Cambridge, U.K., and New York, 1997.

Vega, Josseph de la. *Confusion de Confusiones.* Translated by M. F. J. Smith. The Hague, 1939.

Vidal, Emmanuel. *The History and Methods of the Paris Bourse.* Washington, D.C., 1910.

LARRY D. NEAL

STOCKHOLM. The capital of Sweden, Stockholm originated as a fortress on a small island (*holme* in Swedish), part of an archipelago on the Baltic Sea at the mouth of Lake Mälaren. Tradition attributes construction of the fortress to Birger Jarl, one of Sweden's early kings, and dates it about 1250. Its strategic location helped protect against attacks by sea; it served as a lock on the entry to the navigable waters of Mälaren as well as a transit point for export of iron and copper from inland provinces. By the mid-fifteenth century, Stockholm was already referred to as Sweden's capital, although it was not yet the permanent residence of the monarch. With about six thousand inhabitants, mostly merchants and artisans, Stockholm was an important Baltic trading center. About half the population consisted of German merchants from cities such as Lübeck.

In the late fifteenth century Stockholm was besieged on several occasions, primarily during conflicts with Denmark. After a definitive split from the loose union that had governed Sweden, Denmark, and Norway, Sweden became a nation-state with a more powerful monarchy. Under Gustav I Vasa (ruled 1523–1560), Stockholm began to change from a self-governing town to *Hans Nådes stad* (the city of His Grace, the king) and became the seat of royal authority. Stockholm's development since then has always been linked to the state. Whereas the city had previously been dominated by merchants, the percentage of the population engaged in government administration increased significantly by the reign of Gustav I's son, John III (ruled 1568–1592).

Physical changes to the city came about in connection with the Reformation and Gustav I's subsequent appropriation of Catholic church property, including the tearing down of cloisters and churches. Stockholm was still, however, a city within walls, mostly confined to the area now known as Gamla Stan (the Old Town). In the seventeenth century Stockholm entered a period of expansion related to Sweden's emergence as a European military power under Gustavus II Adolphus (ruled 1611–1632). The city's population grew from about 10,000 in 1620 to more than 40,000 by 1660. City authorities drew up new street plans during the 1630s, and the Swedish nobility used for-

Stockholm. Johann Baptist Homann's detailed early-eighteenth-century plan clearly shows the expansion of the city from its original nucleus of three islands in Lake Malar. This expansion was accelerated during Sweden's Age of Greatness, from the reign of Gustavus II Adolphus (1611–1632) through that of Charles XII (1697–1717). MAP COLLECTION, STERLING MEMORIAL LIBRARY, YALE UNIVERSITY

tunes secured in foreign wars to build palatial residences. One result of these changes was the disappearance of most of the city's medieval towers and walls.

New economic policies encouraged trade through Stockholm's ports. The city also became the center of military production in support of Sweden's aggressive foreign policy. While Sweden was unable to establish a monopoly over Baltic trade, Stockholm did have a virtual monopoly on the export of tar, produced in the extensive forests of Sweden and Finland, which was still part of Sweden at this time.

During Queen Christina's reign (1644–1654) the royal court resided more or less permanently in Stockholm for the first time. Christina's diverse intellectual interests helped make Stockholm, rather than the university towns such as Uppsala, the center of literary activity. Artists began to produce paintings and engravings showing views of the city during this period. The most complete pictorial record of Stockholm at this time is Erik Dahlberg's (1625–1703) book of engravings, *Suecia Antiqua et Hodierna* (Sweden ancient and modern), first published in its entirety in 1716. In 1697 a fire ravaged the royal castle, allowing extensive renovation of the antiquated building in the classical style by the architect Nicodemus Tessin the Younger (1654–1728). These renovations were not completed, however, for almost fifty years.

Population growth stalled after 1705 as the city entered a period of stagnation, due in part to the many wars of the period; from over 55,000 in the 1680s, the population declined to about 45,000 by 1720. An outbreak of plague in 1710 also claimed a third of the population. Political changes after the death of Charles XII (ruled 1697–1718) led by the 1730s to protectionist economic policies that promoted manufacturing (especially of textiles) while restricting imports drastically. These policies tended to favor Stockholm over other parts of Sweden, which resulted in an increase in the city's population, to about 70,000 by 1760. Most of this population growth came from immigration, however, as the mortality rate in Stockholm was very high; one in three children died in the first year of life.

After 1760, political changes led to a decline in manufacturing subsidies, slowing Stockholm's development. The city lost its privileged trading status in the Baltic, and the west coast city of Göteborg began to develop as a port. Though Stockholm remained by far the country's largest city, and the only one with over 10,000 inhabitants, the percentage of Swedish citizens living in Stockholm, about 4 percent in the mid-eighteenth century, declined over the following century.

See also **Baltic and North Seas; Charles XII (Sweden); Christina (Sweden); Gustavus II Adolphus (Sweden); Sweden; Vasa Dynasty (Sweden).**

BIBLIOGRAPHY

Ahnlund, Henrik. *Historia kring Stockholm: Före 1520.* Stockholm, 1965.

Hammarström, Ingrid, ed. *Historia kring Stockholm: Vasatid och stormaktstid.* Stockholm, 1966.

Högberg, Staffan. *Stockholms historia 1.* Stockholm, 1981.

Landell, Niks-Erik. *Den växande staden: Stockholms bebyggelse- och naturhistoria.* Stockholm, 1992.

PAUL NORLÉN

STOICISM. In the century after Aristotle's death, the Greek founders of Stoicism recognized three interrelated constituents of philosophy: logic, physics, and ethics. The study of logic taught the recognition of truth and the avoidance of error, preparing the mind to understand the physical construction of the world and to engage in ethical behavior. The Stoic cosmos was an organic unity that unfolded according to the *logos* or plan of a universal mind or soul. The physical basis for the universal mind was the *pneuma*, an all-pervasive animating spirit. At the beginning of each cosmic cycle, the *pneuma* condensed, producing the terrestrial elements of earth, water, and air at the center of a spherical universe but continuing to pervade the heavens as life-giving fire. The planets were regarded as the natural creatures of this celestial region: they burned fuel provided by transporting terrestrial elements into the heavens. When this process had exhausted the finite supply of terrestrial elements, the cosmos returned to its primordial state and the entire cycle repeated. Within this cosmos individual entities, including human beings, were defined by the portion of the universal *pneuma* that animated them, and they played roles in the history of the cosmos completely controlled by the *logos*.

For the Stoics, ethical action accorded with the steadily unfolding plan of the cosmos. But the cosmos frequently unfolded in ways that were painful or frustrating to human beings. The Stoics believed that control over nature was illusory except for the contents of the human mind. Practically, they taught the cultivation of *apatheia*, a state of mind permitting the tranquil disregard of suffering, and *autarcheia*, or self-sufficiency. Equally indifferent to wealth and poverty, fame and disrepute, Stoic sages were rendered immune to the vicissitudes of human life. Drawing all three aspects of philosophy together, they were expected to carry out their ethical duty, following the physical plan of the cosmos as revealed by logic, regardless of personal cost.

THE RENAISSANCE REVIVAL OF STOIC ETHICAL AND POLITICAL DOCTRINES

Although Roman authors like Cicero and Seneca examined all aspects of Stoic doctrine, later writers, for example Epictetus (fl. 90–115 C.E.) and Marcus Aurelius (emperor of Rome, 161–180), were primarily interested in the ethical teachings. Their works were known in various forms throughout the Middle Ages but received new attention when humanist philological skills were applied to newly available Greek texts during the Renaissance, and the recovery of Diogenes Laertius provided new information on both Stoic doctrines and the biographies of the founders. Early modern interest in Stoicism developed from an initial phase, in which Stoic ideas were combined eclectically with other doctrines, until writers like Justus Lipsius (1547–1606) attempted to renovate the Stoic doctrines as a distinct school. Parallel to this later stage, Stoic physical ideas were briefly important in debates on the nature of the heavens and planetary motion.

Throughout this period Stoic doctrines entered humanist literature, although they were limited and conditioned by the authors' Christian opinions. Petrarch (1304–1374) advocated an essentially Stoic scheme for the subjugation of the passions in *De Remediis Utriusque Fortunae* (Remedies against good and ill fortune) and became the first of many Renaissance writers to borrow Stoic providential design arguments to prove the existence of God. Politian (Angelo Ambrogini; 1454–1494) translated Epictetus's *Enchiridion* (Handbook) into Latin; Politian's translation appeared in 1497, and the work was published in Greek in 1528. François Rabelais's *Pantagruel* stories appeared between 1532 and 1564. Later books in the series presented central characters who exemplified the virtues of Stoic sages and a Stoic worldview identifying God and nature as a single, all-pervasive creative principle. However, Desiderius Erasmus and later Michel de Montaigne denied that a Stoic sage could achieve happiness without divine assistance, while Philipp Melanchthon criticized the Stoic ambition to achieve by human reason what can only be achieved with God's assistance, although he freely used the same Stoic proofs of God's existence that had attracted Petrarch.

The most important reviver of Stoic doctrines was Lipsius, who taught at Louvain. In 1584 he published *De Constantia* (On constancy), the title indicating a form of *apatheia* that would help its readers cope with the religious and civil strife of their times. Lipsius attempted to collate the surviving fragments of Stoic doctrine in ancient literature in his *Manuductionis ad Stoicam Philosophiam* (1604; Guide to Stoic philosophy). In his *Physiologiae Stoicorum* (1604; Physiology of the Stoics) he attempted to reconcile Stoicism with Christian

doctrine. At about the same time, translations of Epictetus appeared in France, England, and Spain.

THE REVIVAL OF STOIC PHYSICS

Stoic physical ideas reappeared later than Stoic ethics. A renewed interest in Pliny revived the doctrine that the substance of the heavens was a fluid through which the planets moved themselves. An early endorsement came from Jacob Ziegler (1531). The Parisian mathematician Ioannes Pena (Jean de la Pène; 1528–1558) derived the same idea from Cicero. Pena explained the apparent failure to observe the bending of light rays as they entered the atmosphere from the ether above by denying that there was any sharp boundary between the earth and the heavens, which were occupied by Stoic vital air. Writing in 1586, the German astronomer Christoph Rothmann borrowed Pena's arguments to explain why comets were able to move freely in regions that should have been impenetrable ether according to Aristotle. Rothmann corresponded with the Danish astronomer Tycho Brahe (1546–1601), who saw these ideas as the solution to a central problem facing the cosmology he favored, in which the sun went round a central earth, but the planets went round the sun. In this system the spheres supporting the sun and Mars interpenetrated in ways forbidden for the Aristotelian celestial substance. Brahe adopted a fluid heavens and redefined the celestial spheres as geometrical boundaries in it (1588). Johannes Kepler (1571–1630) adopted the latter view in a sustained defense of heliocentrism (1596), although he later rejected the Stoic view that the planets moved themselves and was led thereby to introduce a force, emanating from the sun, to do the same work.

Early in the seventeenth century, the revival of atomism and the appearance of the mechanical philosophy limited the development of exclusively Stoic physical ideas, although they remained influential in alchemy and chemistry throughout Isaac Newton's lifetime. But Stoic ethical doctrines held a continuing appeal, as shown by the favorable treatment of Stoicism in Ralph Cudworth, new editions of Epictetus, and Thomas Stanley's 1655–1662 history of philosophy, which allots more space to Stoicism and its rival Epicureanism than to the philosophies of Plato and Aristotle.

See also **Astronomy; Brahe, Tycho; Cosmology; Humanists and Humanism; Kepler, Johannes; Lipsius, Justus; Philosophy; Rabelais, François; Scientific Revolution.**

BIBLIOGRAPHY

Primary Sources

Brahe, Tycho *De Mundi Aetherei Recentioribus Phaenomenis.* Uraniburg, 1588.

Cudworth, Ralph. *The True Intellectual System of the World.* Bristol, U.K., 1995. Originally published London, 1678.

Epictetus. *The Handbook of Epictetus.* Translated by Nicholas P. White. Indianapolis, 1983.

Kepler, Ioannes. *The Secret of the Universe = Mysterium Cosmographicum.* Translated by A. M. Duncan. New York, 1981. Translation of the 1621 edition, containing the complete text of the first edition (Tübingen, 1596).

Lipsius, Justus. *Manuductionis ad Stoicam Philosophiam.* Antwerp, 1604.

———. *Physiologiae Stoicorum Libri Tres.* Antwerp, 1604.

———. *Two Bookes of Constancie.* Edited by Rudolf Kirk. New Brunswick, N.J., 1939. A new version of Sir John Stradling's 1594 translation of *De Constantia.*

Marcus Aurelius. *The Emperor's Handbook: A New Translation of the Meditations.* Translated by C. Scot Hicks and David V. Hicks. New York, 2002.

Rabelais, François. *Gargantua and Pantagruel.* Translated by Burton Raffel. New York, 1991.

Stanley, Thomas. *A History of Philosophy.* 3 vols. New York, 1978. Originally published London, 1655–1662.

Ziegler, Jacob. *Iacobi Ziegleri, Landavi, Bavari, In C. Plinii De Natvrali Historia Librum Secundum Commentarius.* Basel, 1531.

Secondary Sources

Barbour, Reid. *English Epicures and Stoics: Ancient Legacies in Early Stuart Culture.* Amherst, Mass., 1998.

Barker, Peter. "Stoic contributions to early modern science." In *Atoms, Pneuma, and Tranquillity: Epicurean and Stoic Themes in European Thought.* Edited by Margaret J. Osler. Cambridge, U.K., and New York, 1991.

Chew, Audrey. *Stoicism in Renaissance English Literature: An Introduction.* New York, 1988.

Monsarrat, Giles. *Light from the Porch: Stoicism and English Renaissance Literature.* Paris, 1984.

Oestreich, Gerhard. *Neostoicism and the Early Modern State.* Edited by Brigitta Oestreich and H.G. Koenigsberger. Translated by David McLintock. Cambridge, U.K., and New York, 1982.

Shifflett, Andrew Eric. *Stoicism, Politics, and Literature in the Age of Milton: War and Peace Reconciled.* Cambridge, U.K., and New York, 1998.

Zanta, Léontine. *La renaissance du stoïcisme au XVIe siècle.* Paris, 1914.

PETER BARKER

STRASBOURG. Founded in 16 C.E., the Alsatian city of Strasbourg owed its subsequent prosperity and influence to its situation on the left (western) bank of the Upper Rhine, where it commanded the last bridge over that river before its mouth. The city's trading network extended north and south along the Rhine, as well as east deeper into the Holy Roman Empire, and west into France. Though an annual fair was held beginning in 1228 and the city became a regional banking center by 1500, it failed to develop an indigenous manufacturing sector beyond cheap woolen goods known as "Strasbourg gray." The city remained vulnerable to external pressures that threatened to disrupt its livelihood and food supply.

The most important of these pressures was the local prince-bishop, who initially controlled the city, but was ejected by its inhabitants in 1262 and took up residence in Dachstein castle, about 10 miles (16 kilometers) to the west. Though the city was now a self-governing free city, the bishop still exercised jurisdiction over its clergy, convents, and the huge cathedral that was never finished. The bishop was a prince of the empire with a voice in imperial institutions and his own territory extending across 276 square miles (715 square kilometers) of land to the west, south, and southeast and populated by around sixty thousand people by the late eighteenth century. Strasbourg itself had sixteen thousand inhabitants in 1444, rising to between twenty and twenty-five thousand by the early sixteenth century. The population thereafter remained stable, reflecting the city's declining influence and economic stagnation that set in from the 1550s. There were another ten thousand or more peasants outside the walls who lived under the city's jurisdiction.

Urban government was transformed by a series of violent protests between 1332 and 1449 that secured representation through the city's twenty guilds, but the patriciate gradually hardened into a new oligarchy of thirty to forty families who controlled the key decision making committees. This process was not yet complete by 1522 when many councillors accepted the Reformation. Strasbourg intellectual life had been stimulated by local humanist scholars, including Jacob Wimpfeling (1450–1528), Johann Geiler von Kaysersberg (1445–1510), and Sebastian Brant (1458?–1521), who helped make the city an important publishing and educational center. However, their attempt to reform local spiritual life contributed to the already strong tradition of anticlericalism left by the earlier struggles against the bishop. The Reformation was introduced with popular support but passed swiftly into the hands of the magistrates, who ensured a moderate course after 1529. The chief reformer was Martin Bucer (1491–1551), who sought a theological compromise between North German Lutheranism and Swiss Zwinglianism; in this Bucer complemented the council's strategy, guided by its leader Jacob Sturm (1489–1553), of negotiating a broad Protestant urban alliance. The city was drawn into the Schmalkaldic League and suffered from its defeat by Emperor Charles V in 1547. Conservatives controlled the council until 1562, when Calvinist influence grew and radicals again called for a more energetic external policy, culminating in armed intervention in the bishop's affairs in 1593–1594. Moderates regained control and reaffirmed orthodox Lutheranism in 1598. Though Strasbourg joined the Protestant Union in 1608, it remained neutral after 1618 and avoided further political ambitions. Johannes Sturm (1507–1589) made a lasting impact on Protestant German education and also founded a grammar school in 1538 that became the University of Strasbourg in 1621. Johann Wolfgang von Goethe was a student there and received a law degree, but the university was closed by the French revolutionaries in 1793 and not reopened until 1872.

New defenses, built 1633–1680, failed to save Strasbourg from French annexation in 1681 as the magistrates surrendered rather than face a bombardment. The bishop also acknowledged French jurisdiction over his lands west of the Rhine and was allowed to return to the city. Sébastian Le Prestre de Vauban strengthened the fortifications 1682–1690, and Strasbourg became a major French garrison, held by ten thousand mainly German-speaking soldiers. Urban self-government remained while the economy revived, and the population grew to fifty thousand by 1789. French became the second language, and half the population converted to Catholicism. Strasbourg became a symbol for early German national sentiment, but little effort was made to recover it, although in 1697 the French were obliged to surrender the small fort of Kehl, built at the eastern end of the Rhine bridge between 1683 and 1688. The empire failed to maintain Kehl, which the French periodically recaptured (1703–1714, 1733–1735), and the place was abandoned in 1754. The bishopric remained formally part of the empire, but in 1682 the emperor refused to acknowledge the election of the French candidate, Wilhelm Egon von Fürstenberg, and his successors after 1704 were appointed from Paris. Strasbourg's full incorporation within France only came after 1789, while the bishopric maintained a precarious existence in its lands east of the Rhine until these were annexed by the state of Baden in 1803.

See also **Brant, Sebastian; Free and Imperial Cities; Holy Roman Empire; Reformation, Protestant; Schmalkaldic War (1546–1547).**

BIBLIOGRAPHY

Abray, Lorna Jane. *The Peoples' Reformation: Magistrates, Clergy and Commons in Strasbourg 1500–1598.* Ithaca, N.Y., 1985.

Brady, Thomas A., Jr. *Protestant Politics: Jacob Sturm (1489–1553) and the German Reformation.* Atlantic Highlands, N.J., 1995.

———. *Ruling Class, Regime and Reformation at Strasbourg 1520–1555.* Leiden, 1978.

Chrisman, Mariam Usher. *Strasbourg and the Reform: A Study in the Process of Change.* New Haven and London, 1967.

Ford, Franklin L. *Strasbourg in Transition 1648–1789.* Cambridge, Mass., 1958.

Livet, Georges, and Francis Rapp, eds. *Histoire de Strasbourg des origines à nos jours.* Vol. 2, *Strasbourg des grandes invasions au XVe siècle.* Vol. 3, *Strasbourg de la guerre de Trente Ans à Napoléon, 1618–1815.* Strasbourg, 1981.

O'Connor, John T. *Negotiator out of Season: The Career of Wilhelm Egon von Fürstenberg, 1629 to 1704.* Athens, Ga., 1978.

Rapp, Francis. *Réformes et Réformation à Strasbourg: Église et société dans le diocèse de Strasbourg (1450–1525).* Paris, 1974.

Wunder, Gerhard. *Das Strassburger Gebiet: Ein Beitrag zur rechtlichen und politischen Geschichte des gesamten städtischen Territoriums vom 10. bis zum 20. Jahrhundert.* Berlin, 1965.

PETER H. WILSON

STRIKES. Collective work stoppages, or "strikes" (a modern term), have been part of the industrial landscape since the Middle Ages, although their frequency increased during the early modern centuries. Such stoppages occurred for many reasons stemming from conflicted relations between employers (master artisans) and employees (increasingly the trained workers who came to be called journeymen). Workers' strikes centered on such issues as hiring practices, wage rates, piece rates, the duration of the workday, and the freedom to come and go as workers pleased, but resistance always began in one way or another with journeymen's demands to work according to the rhythms of life that structured their existence and framed its meaning. This understanding entailed an assumption about freedom of movement in and out of shops and worker discretion about the pace of work.

Directly or indirectly, work practices reflected a certain relationship between labor and time. Workers often understood the relationship one way and masters another. The craft economy of the early modern centuries was increasingly dynamic, diversified, and specialized, and demand for craft products grew, at certain times and in certain places, dramatically. Masters responded to the pressure on production schedules by trying to extend the workday and by keeping workers on the job more continuously than had been customary. Moreover, more and more masters combined a new morality of industriousness with this imperative about time and production, and disparaged uncooperative workers as not only insubordinate but lazy.

PRE-EIGHTEENTH-CENTURY STRIKES

Workers defending a customary labor regimen often resisted the more disciplined scheme of their employers. Until the eighteenth century, examples of resistance in the form of work stoppages were most evident in the manufacturing sectors such as printing and, above all, textiles, where substantial demand was regularly exerted upon production practices and schedules. In the sixteenth century in the printing industry, to maintain or increase profits in an expanding and increasingly competitive market, master printers tried to reduce wages and increase working hours. An especially well documented strike in the printing industry occurred in Lyon in 1539, when the work stoppage was orchestrated by a "company" of journeymen pressmen, typesetters, correctors, and proofreaders called the Griffarins. In response to masters' attempts to eliminate the customary arrangement of monetary wage plus meals at the master's table, the Griffarins coordinated an industrywide strike throughout the city that lasted almost four months. The Griffarins physically assaulted any journeymen or apprentices who tried to work, and so solidarity within the ranks of the strikers was maintained. In the end the journeymen forced their employers to reinstate the customary food and wage arrangement for another thirty years.

In the textile industry, especially in the Low Countries, between the fifteenth and seventeenth centuries the most effective weapon for workers was the *uitgang*. In this practice, laborers collectively left town if employers did not meet worker demands. This happened in Leiden in 1478, when all the fullers left after their thirty-four demands went unsatisfied. This was certainly not the first *uitgang*, for they referred to similar walkouts "staged by our forefathers." Nor was it to be the last, for the weavers of Amsterdam staged an *uitgang* in 1523, and the shearers of Leiden in 1643. In the seventeenth century, however, the *uitgang* gave way to the strike, and a wave of the latter in the mid-seventeenth century shows that the coordination of the workers' activities spanned cities. From 1636 to 1639, for example, strikes led by shearers were staged in Haarlem, Hoorn, Gouda, and Rotterdam, and strikers held clandestine meetings to coordinate their actions and blacklist strikebreakers. Leiden, the clothmaking center of Europe and home in 1670 to 45,000 textile workers out of a total population of 70,000, was also the scene of frequent strikes during the turbulent seventeenth century, occurring in 1619, 1637, 1644, 1648, 1700, and 1701.

EIGHTEENTH-CENTURY STRIKES

Until the eighteenth century work stoppages largely occurred in industries that most felt the pressure of demand. During the eighteenth century, with the stimulus of the "consumer revolution," however, this pressure spread to many more trades than ever before and the number of strikes increased proportionally. At times the number of striking workers was enormous; twenty thousand silk workers shut down production in Lyon in 1779. In France alone between the 1720s and 1780s, work stoppages and boycotts occurred in more than sixty towns. In Paris more than fifty incidents of strikes took place, involving, for example, the stocking-cap makers in 1724, the blacksmiths in 1731, the locksmiths in 1746, the cutlers in 1748, the hatters in 1764, the bookbinders in 1776, and the masons and stonecutters in 1785.

Workers in most trades called strikes all over Great Britain as well—373 between 1717 and 1800, with 120 in London alone. Wool workers in various cities and regions struck sixty-four times, ship's carpenters thirty-seven, and tailors twenty-two. Weavers, too, were ready to protest, largely against wage reductions. In the late 1720s striking wool-weavers from Wiltshire, calling themselves "regulators," descended upon some employers' houses in the town of Frome in Somerset and presented a list of wage demands. If an employer rejected the demands, "the windows paid for it," as a local commentator put it.

Early modern laborers, mostly journeymen who were organized into brotherhoods and thus could coordinate their actions more effectively than the unorganized simple wage earners, struck over many issues—manipulation of the relationship between the length of the workday and the daily wage, depressed or stagnant wages in the face of rising prices, denser working days, or, increasingly in the eighteenth century, over payment in kind or "truck," whereby masters overvalued the goods and so effectively depressed wages. Whatever the cause, long before the industrial revolution of the nineteenth century and the "labor movement" emerging at that time, workers in Europe had discovered the power of collective action and work stoppage to redress common grievances.

See also **Guilds; Industrial Revolution; Industry; Laborers; Textile Industry; Wages.**

BIBLIOGRAPHY

Davis, Natalie Z. "A Trade Union in Sixteenth-Century France." *Economic History Review* 19 (1966): 48–70.

Dekker, Rudolph. "Labour Conflicts and Working Class Culture in Early Modern Holland." *International Review of Social History* 35 (1990): 377–420.

Farr, James R. *Artisans in Europe, 1300–1914.* Cambridge, U.K., and New York, 2000.

Rule, John. *The Experience of Labour in Eighteenth-Century English Industry.* New York, 1981.

Truant, Cynthia M. *The Rites of Labor: Brotherhoods of Compagnonnage in Old and New Regime France.* Ithaca, N.Y., 1994.

JAMES R. FARR

STUART DYNASTY (ENGLAND AND SCOTLAND). The Stuart dynasty was descended from Marjorie, daughter of Robert I (the Bruce) by her marriage to Walter Steward. Their son, Robert II, became king of Scotland in 1371, but the late fourteenth and fifteenth centuries saw a succession of weak monarchs, four minors, and a polity dominated by rebellious nobles. James IV (ruled 1488–1513) was killed fighting against the English but had, in 1503, married Margaret Tudor, daughter of Henry VII (ruled 1485–1509). Thus the Stuarts had a legitimate claim to the English throne. This became especially important during the reign of Mary, Queen of Scots (ruled 1542–1567), a feckless schemer who was deposed by her subjects in 1567. Her scheming to depose Elizabeth I of England led to her execution in 1587, but her son, James VI of Scotland, succeeded Elizabeth in 1603 as James I of England. The Stuart dual monarchy never came to terms with ruling two very different realms, and James's son, Charles I, was executed by his English subjects in 1649. The Stuarts were restored in 1660 but both Charles II (ruled 1660–1685) and his Catholic brother, James VII and II (ruled 1685–1688), proved less than effective rulers. James was deposed in 1688 and replaced by William III (ruled 1689–1702) and Mary II (ruled 1689–1694). William, the Dutch prince of Orange, was the grandson of Charles I, and Mary was the daughter of James II, but, more importantly, they were Protestants. William and Mary had no children, and the thrones of England and Scotland passed to Anne (ruled 1702–1714), younger daughter of James II. Anne also died childless, and while the English succession had been settled in 1701 on the Protestant Sophie of Hanover, granddaughter of James VI and I, many Scots continued to support the exiled Catholic descendents of James VII and II. In 1714 Sophie's son, the Hanoverian George I, became king of the United Kingdom of Great Britain, thus ending the rule of the Stuarts. The Stuarts still pressed their claim to the throne; however, any pretensions were effectively ended when the pretender Charles Edward Stuart, "Bonnie Prince Charlie," was defeated at the Battle of Culloden in 1746.

See also **Anne (England); Charles I (England); Charles II (England); England; Hanoverian Dynasty (Great Britain); Jacobitism; James I and VI (England and Scotland); James II (England); Scotland; Tudor Dynasty (England); William and Mary.**

BIBLIOGRAPHY

Kishlansky, Mark. *A Monarchy Transformed: Britain 1603–1714.* London, 1997.

Lynch, Michael. *Scotland: A New History.* London, 1992.

DAVID GRUMMITT

SUBLIME, IDEA OF THE. The sublime (from the Greek *hypsous*) entered the language of aesthetic theory from its use in the treatise *Peri hypsous* (On the sublime). The unknown author of this work has been called by tradition "Longinus," and its probable period of composition is the first half-century C.E. Longinus associates the sublime with the feeling of surpassing glory that powerful words may impart. This glory becomes for a reader the evidence of a great soul—the writer's soul, of course, but also the reader's own. The peculiarity of the sublime is that it overwhelms the ordinary distinctions of sense. Its effects come only at moments, even in the greatest writing. It "scatters everything before it like a thunderbolt."

Much of Longinus's book is devoted to analysis of some characteristic verbal traits of sublimity. The exuberance of a great soul may show itself in irregular syntax, and Dionysius of Phocaea is praised for the inversion of logical order in the phrase "Our fortunes are on the razor's edge, men of Ionia," which arrests attention by giving the metaphor before the circumstance it evokes. The sentence from Genesis, "Let there be light, and there was light," is cited as an instance of a tremendous effect that suggests a tremendous cause, the power of words here becoming indistinguishable from the power of a deed.

The modern revival of Longinus dates from the late sixteenth and early seventeenth centuries. The writings of Nicolas Boileau-Despréaux (1636–1711) and Alexander Pope (1688–1744) reflect much of the new emphasis, and Pope adapted a Longinian sentiment when he wrote in his "Essay on Criticism" (1711) that genius may "snatch a grace beyond the reach of art." The sublime now came to stand at the center of a larger riddle about art: it gives pain as well as pleasure; and yet, knowing this, we are eager for the sensations of art. Edmund Burke (1729–1797) in *A Philosophical Enquiry into the Origin of Our Ideas of the Sublime and Beautiful* (1757) explicitly links the sublime with pain. The passion that corresponds to the sublime is astonishment, or "that state of the soul, in which all its motions are suspended, with some degree of horror."

The sublime for Burke is an idea and not a property of objects themselves. Yet certain attributes are consistently associated with the sublime, among them obscurity, power, vastness, and infinitude. Like Longinus, Burke draws his literary illustrations eclectically, from Homer, the book of Job, William Shakespeare, and John Milton. Unlike Longinus, he places the natural on a par with the man-made sublime: a soulless thing may yield as vast an idea as an oration; prominent examples are the sight of the ruins of a great city after an earthquake and the spectacle of the hanging of a state criminal. Burke's *Enquiry* initiated the discussion of the moral and nonmoral foundations of taste that occupied many of the subtlest minds of the later eighteenth century. In response to Burke's sensational and nonmoral theory, Immanuel Kant (1724–1804) in the *Kritik der Urteilskraft* (1790; Critique of judgment) undertook to relate the sense of the sublime to all that finally exceeds understanding in the experience of human autonomy.

See also **Art: Art Theory, Criticism, and Historiography; Boileau-Despréaux, Nicolas; Burke, Edmund; Kant, Immanuel; Pope, Alexander.**

BIBLIOGRAPHY

Primary Sources

Burke, Edmund. *A Philosophical Enquiry into the Origin of Our Ideas of the Sublime and Beautiful.* Edited by James T. Boulton. Rev. ed. Oxford, 1987.

Longinus. *Longinus on the Sublime.* Edited by W. Rhys Roberts. New York, 1987.

Secondary Sources

Abrams, M. H. *The Mirror and the Lamp: Romantic Theory and the Critical Tradition.* New York, 1953.

Monk, Samuel H. *The Sublime: A Study of Critical Theories on Eighteenth-Century England.* Ann Arbor, Mich., 1960.

DAVID BROMWICH

SUGAR. The expansion of European involvement in the sugar industry mirrored western Europe's expansion and domination of the Atlantic basin. Sugar, which had long been considered a luxury available only to the elites of medieval and renaissance Europe, was transformed into a household staple by the colonization of the New World. The combination of conquered tropical and subtropical lands, African slave labor, and capital advanced by northern European merchants transformed the European diet. Furthermore, sugar's importance to overseas trade is reflected in contemporary observations that proclaimed the sugar industry to be at the heart of national wealth; it was often noted that the plantation trade created enormous profits for sugar planters and merchants, employment for European laborers, and significant tax revenues for the mother countries. Although it is clear that sugar did indeed dominate colonial policy of the major powers in the seventeenth and eighteenth centuries, economic historians have recently questioned the extent to which sugar generated national riches.

Muslims first introduced sugarcane to the Mediterranean region in the seventh century. While the soils of the Levant, Sicily, Cyprus, Crete, and Malta supported this early cane cultivation, the actual export of sugar to Continental markets did not take place until the Crusades, when Venetian merchants provided the capital and mercantile connections required for regular trade. The historian Noel Deerr has suggested that this coordination of European credit and trade "may be seen [as] the germ of the colonial system" that was fully developed in the Americas during the early modern period.

The center of the European sugar supply moved west with Portuguese exploration of the Atlantic basin. Iberian settlers on the island of Madeira established commercial sugar production in 1432, as well as on the African coastal island of São Tomé, where African slave labor was used exclusively to produce sugar in the early sixteenth century. During the next hundred years, Portuguese settlers in Brazil replicated this slave-based business plan after briefly experimenting with indigenous labor. With the assistance of Dutch financiers, the Portuguese planters and mill owners of northeastern Brazil developed the most productive sugar-producing region in the world. This symbiotic relationship between the two imperial powers helped generate the lion's share of sugar consumed in Europe, but in 1624 the Dutch gained tighter financial control over the industry by using military force, capturing the richest sugar-growing regions of Brazil. Although the Dutch were eventually expelled, the chaos inflicted by war disrupted Brazilian sugar production, thereby providing an opportunity for English and French West Indian sugar growers to emerge as important competitors in supplying Europe's increasing demand for sugar.

The leading sugar-producing nations expended tremendous resources protecting their colonists and their plantation trade. Laws similar to Britain's Navigation Acts or France's Colonial Pact were implemented by every colonial power as a means of ensuring that the benefits of imperialism would be maximized. Adherents to this political philosophy believed that the colonists' role in the larger economy was subordinate to the home country's drive for riches and power. Thus, each nation's set of mercantilist laws was designed to control colonial trade so that the commerce from the colonies would provide home governments with valuable tax revenues while stimulating each respective nation's merchant navy.

The major sugar-planting zones of Brazil and the Caribbean littoral had an enormous appetite for slave labor. The growing demand for sugar in Europe, combined with the negative natural population growth, fueled an unprecedented demand for labor. Throughout the early modern period, Euro-

Sugar. An engraving from Theodore de Bry's *Grand Voyages*, 1590–1597, shows a colonial sugar processing operation using native labor. THE LIBRARY OF CONGRESS

pean planters expanded total production while simultaneously ignoring the poor nutrition, disease-infested living conditions, and excessive work endured by their slaves. The relatively low cost of importing new African slaves permitted planters to maintain healthy profits despite the regular loss of life. To illustrate the human cost of supplying the European craving for sugar, over half of the 5.7 million slaves transported to the Americas during the eighteenth century were destined to work in the cane fields or in related branches of the industry.

The sheer volume of the slave trade, the capital-intensive nature of sugar planting, and the contemporary assumptions about the importance of sugar colonies have led some modern historians to conclude that sugar and slavery were essential to the economic development of the metropole. Eric Wil-

liams, an Oxford-trained West Indian historian, did the most to promote this thesis in *Capitalism and Slavery* (1944). In this monumental work, Williams argued that the demand for sugar created a highly profitable colonial trade, which enabled slavers from Bristol and Liverpool to dominate the forced migration of Africans during the peak years of the slave trade. He posited that the slave trade generated an important stream of British capital accumulation, and that these funds, combined with the profits generated from the sugar industry, fueled Britain's industrial revolution.

Scholarship since *Capitalism and Slavery* has revised Williams's estimate that the slave trade produced 30 percent returns to investors. Although there were, indeed, examples of slave traders earning significant sums of money on individual voyages, the slaving business was a very risky and competitive lottery, with many investors losing money. If, therefore, one considers the whole range of returns on slave trading, the average is calculated to have been somewhere between 5 and 10 percent during the eighteenth century. With this more realistic view of slave-trading profits, the economic historian Stanley Engerman calculated that the net national return on the British slave trade represented less than 1 percent of total British income. This deflated view of the slave trade's importance to the British economy has been matched by more moderate assessments of the effect the total sugar industry had on the home country. The most recent research describes the colonial sugar industry as an important sector that contributed to the economic growth of the major sugar-growing nations, but was not essential to the industrial transformation of England or Europe.

See also **Portuguese Colonies: Brazil; Slavery and the Slave Trade; Trading Companies; Triangular Trade Pattern.**

BIBLIOGRAPHY

Curtin, Philip D. *The Rise and Fall of the Plantation Complex: Essays in Atlantic History.* Cambridge, U.K., 1990.

Deerr, Noel. *The History of Sugar.* Vols. 1 and 2. London, 1949–1950.

Eltis, David, and Stanley L. Engerman. "The Importance of Slavery and the Slave Trade to Industrializing Britain." *Journal of Economic History* 60 (2000): 123–144.

Klein, Herbert S. *The Atlantic Slave Trade.* Cambridge, U.K., 1999.

Morgan, Kenneth. *Slavery, Atlantic Trade, and the British Economy, 1660–1800.* Cambridge, U.K., 2000.

Williams, Eric. *Capitalism and Slavery.* Chapel Hill, N.C., 1944.

DAVID RYDEN

SUICIDE. When early modern authors and intellectuals considered the topic of suicide, they started out with one salient contrast in mind: Whereas the ancient Greeks and Romans had often approved of suicide, Christians did not. For many, this contrast illustrated the superiority of Christian thinking, but throughout the Renaissance and into the seventeenth century, some who admired the ancients drew a more nuanced set of conclusions.

Thomas More's *Utopia* (1516), for example, presents voluntary euthanasia for the terminally ill in a favorable light, although More condemned suicide vigorously in other works. The bishop of Guadix, Antonio de Guevara, took inspiration from the heroic suicides of classical antiquity (for example, Cato, Diogenes, Zeno, Lucretia, Seneca) and praised the nobility of barbarians who did not overvalue life in this world. Similarly, Michel de Montaigne touched on the question of suicide repeatedly and in "A Custom of the Island of Cea" considered the topic at considerable length, thoughtfully assembling moral, religious, social, and legal views. Although he admired the deaths of the noble ancients, he was reluctant to give his blanket approval to all who sought to escape shame or pain through suicide, and in the end he thought one might kill oneself only as a last resort to avoid intense pain or torture.

Shakespeare's characters commit suicide with remarkable frequency (there are fifty-two cases in his plays), and Hamlet's soliloquy ("To be or not to be") dwells on the topic, presenting arguments both for and against (although ignoring specifically Christian objections), before concluding, famously, that the future was too murky to make self-murder a safe option. In other plays Shakespeare presents suicide as the result of tragic misunderstanding *(Romeo and Juliet)* or as grand examples of freedom or despair *(Julius Caesar, Antony and Cleopatra,* and *Othello).* In 1610 John Donne went further, arguing in *Biathanatos* that sometimes suicide was justified or at least excusable. He did not proceed, as others had, from the example of ancient worthies but specifically considered the Christian grounds for condemning suicide. In a nutshell, he concluded that suicide did not necessarily and always violate the laws of nature, reason, or God. Despite the daring independence of this view, Donne forbade the publication of his book, and it only appeared in print in 1647, sixteen years after his death. This fact illustrates the ongoing and deep anxiety early modern Christians felt about suicide as both a crime and as the result of despair, the ultimate sin. Usually Protestants and Catholics united to condemn "self-murder" and to depict the devil as the prime mover or inspiration for most cases of self-destruction. As a result, throughout early modern Europe, suicides were denied burial in hallowed ground and often suffered desecration of their corpses. The worldly goods of suicides were sometimes confiscated by the crown, as was the case in England and Scotland.

In the seventeenth and eighteenth centuries, however, this legal and moral position decayed, not so much because suicide became positively defensible but more commonly because it seemed increasingly to be the result of melancholy madness. Moralists and theologians had regularly made provision for a sort of insanity defense of suicide. They viewed both sin and crime as actions that proceeded from free and voluntary decisions; condemning actions one could not prevent or avoid did not seem to make moral sense. Indeed, Martin Luther had carried this point so far that he thought suicides were driven to their deaths by the devil, thus extinguishing human responsibility: "I have known many cases of this kind, and I have had reason to think in most of them, that the parties were killed, directly and immediately killed by the devil, in the same way that a traveler is killed by a brigand." Most theologians, however, understood the role of the devil as that of a tempter or seducer, and therefore left ample room for the harsh condemnation of suicide, as long as it seemed clear that the victim had acted deliberately, intentionally, or voluntarily.

THE SECULARIZATION OF SUICIDE

By the late seventeenth century, suicide began to seem so alien to right reason, so much the product of melancholy or delusion (what we might call acute depression), that coroners, villagers, pastors, and magistrates were prepared to grant decent (even if quiet) burials inside the churchyard. Townsmen and villagers alike might also (as in England and Scotland) unite to portray a suspicious death as the result of illness or accident in order to circumvent the crown's efforts to confiscate a victim's estate, a move that usually added to the burdens on local poor relief. Thus from about 1650 onwards, we can mark the "secularization of suicide," that is, the development of medical or other naturalizing explanations and excuses for suicide. This evolution of public sentiment was supplemented during the eighteenth century by the moral philosophizing of the Enlightenment. Montesquieu's *Persian Letters* (1721), for example, sharply criticized the condemnation of suicide. Voltaire went further and saw suicide as a question of liberty. It could not harm

God or society, in his view, to exit the world when one could no longer enjoy life or contribute to the welfare of others. David Hume also defended an individual's absolute right to suicide. Despite hesitations and equivocations, however, many philosophes were drawn to the medical conclusion that suicide was usually the result of madness or bodily disturbances.

THE SOCIAL HISTORY OF SUICIDE

Broadly speaking, this array of opinions on suicide has been well known and well described for several generations. In recent years, scholars have renewed their attention to suicide and have made several noteworthy contributions, not so much to high religious or intellectual history, but to the sociology or social distribution and cultural understandings of suicide. In this work they have often taken inspiration from the foundational work of Émile Durkheim, *Le suicide* (1897), which tried to demonstrate that social dynamics account for almost all the statistical variations in suicide found in modern countries. Roughly stated, Durkheim held that higher rates of suicide were prompted by increasing conditions of social isolation, so that tight webs of social support served to protect populations from the effects of urbanization, individualism, migration, and other conditions of modernity. It seemed to make sense, from this point of view, that Protestants (as part of a "modern," "secularizing," and "individualizing" movement) should always and everywhere have higher rates of suicide than presumably more traditional and more socially cohesive Catholics. This schema has inspired a great deal of modern sociological investigation, and recently scholars have extended these efforts to the early modern period. However, one supreme difficulty has been that neither the numbers of suicides nor early modern populations were reliably recorded, making the calculation of a suicide rate (the number of suicides per 100,000 population) doubly problematic.

Suicide in Britain and Germany. After an extraordinary and energetic attempt to count the number of suicides in early modern England, for example, Terence Murphy and Michael MacDonald abandon the task of calculating the varying suicide rate from place to place and from time to time, turning instead to an examination of the varying meanings of suicide. In an excellent study of suicide in far northern Germany, Vera Lind draws similar conclusions, heaping criticism on those who have imagined that medieval or early modern rates of self-murder could be calculated unproblematically. In a vast and complex survey, Alexander Murray draws the same conclusion with respect to medieval Europe, but then curiously hazards the guess that whatever the medieval rate may have been, suicide became far more common in the sixteenth century.

Suicide in Switzerland. The most impressive recent attempt to scrutinize all the suicides in a fairly controlled population is Jeffrey Watt's study of early modern Geneva, where suicide remained rare until the end of the seventeenth century and then increased slowly in the early eighteenth century. After 1750, however, the rate jumped up by a factor of five or more, and it went even higher after 1780. Watt has been careful to count not only those cases regarded as suicide by the Genevan authorities, but to look for "disguised" suicides as well, deaths from falls or from drowning that may well have been self-inflicted even if contemporaries declined to label them self-murder. Watt's evidence is so rich and so complete that, at least for this city, a genuine suicide rate can probably be calculated. Recognizing a dramatic escalation after 1750 seems unavoidable. Rejecting an easy equation of Calvinism with higher rates of suicide, however, Watt points out that Geneva during the Reformation had promoted just as tight an integration of society as in any Catholic city or principality. Yet by the late eighteenth century, Genevans from top to bottom had grown more secular in their attitudes, abandoning belief in the devil and often in hell as well. These processes may have developed more quickly or more profoundly for men than for women, which might explain why the disproportion of male suicides became even more pronounced after 1750. On this reading, growing secularization accomplished more than just the decriminalization or medicalization of suicide; increasingly a more secular society relaxed its supportive web as well as its sanctions against self-killing. Taking one's own life became far easier to contemplate.

This finding runs counter to the conclusion of a study of suicide in Zurich, in which Markus Schär connects the rapidly escalating numbers of self-inflicted deaths in the eighteenth century not with increasingly secular attitudes but with the growth of acute religious despair among people who doubted that they could ever gain God's mercy. Oddly enough, however, both Watt and Schär agree in emphasizing the importance of religious and cultural changes, rather than social changes (such as demography, economy, and urbanization), as crucial stimulants to suicide.

THE EIGHTEENTH CENTURY

As far as eighteenth-century Europeans were concerned, England was the classic land of melancholy and suicide. In the absence of reliable comparative studies, it is not clear that this stereotype was fully deserved. It does seem certain, however, that suicide notes and newspaper publicity about recent suicides first proliferated in England, for reasons well explored by Murphy and MacDonald. In Germany, the popularity of Goethe's *Sorrows of Young Werther* (1774) led to a wave of widely publicized suicides supposedly inspired by the romantic death of that lovelorn protagonist. By the late eighteenth century suicide had been common enough that it seemed symptomatic of the cultural and social disruptions endured by nations undergoing rapid urbanization, industrialization, or secularization.

See also **Death and Dying; Madness and Melancholy; Religious Piety.**

BIBLIOGRAPHY

Bernardini, Paolo. *Literature on Suicide, 1516–1815: A Bibliographical Essay.* Lewiston, N.Y., 1996.

Donne, John. *Biathanatos.* Edited by Ernest W. Sullivan II. Newark, Del., and London, 1984.

Jansson, Arne. *From Swords to Sorrow: Homicide and Suicide in Early Modern Stockholm.* Stockholm, 1998.

Lind, Vera. *Selbstmord in der frühen Neuzeit: Diskurs, Lebenswelt und kultureller Wandel am Beispiel der Herzogtümer Schleswig und Holstein.* Göttingen, 1999.

Minois, Georges. *The History of Suicide.* Translated by L. Cochrane. Baltimore, 1999.

Murphy, Terence R., and Michael MacDonald. *Sleepless Souls: Suicide in Early Modern England.* Oxford, 1990.

Murray, Alexander. *Suicide in the Middle Ages.* 2 vols. Oxford, 1998, 2000.

Schär, Markus. *Seelennöte der Untertanen: Selbstmord, Melancholie und Religion im Alten Zürich, 1500–1800.* Zurich, 1985.

Watt, Jeffrey R. *Choosing Death: Suicide and Calvinism in Early Modern Geneva.* Kirksville, Mo., 2001.

H. C. ERIK MIDELFORT

SULEIMAN I (1494/95–1566; ruled 1520–1566), tenth Ottoman sultan, born in Trabzon, the son of Hafsa, a Crimean Tatar princess, and the future sultan Selim I (ruled 1512–1520). Under Suleiman, the Ottoman Empire became the Islamic world's Sunni exemplar. Suleiman spent his childhood in Trabzon, where Selim was governor. As a prince, Suleiman himself received the governorship first of Kefe (Fedosiya) and then, in 1513, of Manisa. In 1514–1515 he acted as regent during his father's campaign against Iran. In 1516–1517, he oversaw the defense of Edirne while his father campaigned against the Mamluks in Syria and Egypt.

Suleiman suceeded to the throne in September 1520. In Syria, he immediately suppressed the revolt of a former Mamluk governor, Janberdi Ghazali, and then, using as a pretext the Hungarian maltreatment of his ambassador, he attacked Hungary in 1521, capturing Belgrade. In 1522, he conquered Rhodes, allowing the Knights of St. John to depart freely. In 1526 he invaded Hungary again, defeating and killing King Lajos (Louis II) at Mohács. Following Suleiman's departure, the Hungarian Diet elected János Szapolyai (John Zapolya) as king of Hungary, but later in the year, the Diet of Bratislava elected the Habsburg counter-claimant, Ferdinand of Austria. In 1529, Ferdinand occupied Buda. Suleiman, however, expelled him from Buda, re-enthroned Szapolyai, and unsuccessfully besieged Vienna, the highwater mark of Ottoman expansion efforts. In 1530, Ferdinand again besieged Buda, and Suleiman again invaded, forcing Ferdinand to an agreement that left Szapolyai as king of central and eastern Hungary and himself as king in the west and north, both ruling as Suleiman's tributaries.

The truce freed Suleiman to attack the Shi'ite Safavids of Iran, for which a series of defections on both sides of the frontier gave a pretext. In 1533, Suleiman's grand vizier Ibrahim Pasha reoccupied Bitlis, whose lord had defected to Shah Tahmasb. Next year he occupied Tabriz and, after the sultan had joined him, Baghdad. By 1536, the sultan had added Baghdad, Erzurum, and, temporarily, Van to his empire. In 1533, recognizing the need to counter the threat especially of Spanish power in the Mediterranean, Suleiman had appointed as admiral the privateer-ruler of Algiers, Hayreddin (Khayr ad-Dīn) Barbarossa, admiral of the Ottoman fleet. The Spanish threat materialized with the conquest of Tunis by Charles V—king of Spain, Holy Roman emperor, and brother of Ferdinand—in 1535. This was a factor persuading Suleiman to agree in 1536 to an anti-Habsburg alliance with France, which lasted until the Franco-Spanish treaty of 1559. A proposed Franco-Ottoman campaign in Italy in 1537 failed to materialize. Instead Suleiman unsuccessfully besieged Venetian Corfu. In 1538, by contrast, Barbarossa captured most of the Venetian islands in the Aegean and defeated a combined Spanish, Venetian, and papal fleet in the Gulf of Prevesa. The war ended in 1540, concluding the period of Suleiman's major conquests.

In Hungary, meanwhile, Szapolyai's death activated Ferdinand's claim, and in 1541 and 1542 he besieged Buda. Suleiman responded by converting central Hungary to an Ottoman province and Transylvania in the east to a kingdom under Ottoman suzerainty for Szapolyai's infant son, John Sigismund. In 1543, he led a campaign to Hungary, securing a line of fortresses along the western border. The war ended in 1547, but Ferdinand's claim to Transylvania continued. It was not until 1556, following campaigns in 1551 and 1552 and the Ottoman occupation of Temesvár, that the king and his mother could return to the kingdom. In the Mediterranean, too, the war with the Habsburgs continued. Charles V's failure to capture Algiers in 1541 encouraged Francis I to renew the Ottoman alliance, and in 1543 a Franco-Ottoman force stormed Nice. The Spanish occupation of Monastir and Mahdia on the Tunisian coast in 1550 encouraged further cooperation, but when in 1551, the French fleet failed to appear for a joint campaign, the Ottoman admiral, Sinan Pasha, instead seized Tripoli from the Knights of St. John. Ottoman expansion in North Africa continued with the capture of Wahran and Bizerta in 1556–1557 and the expulsion of the Spaniards from Jerba in 1560. However, Suleiman's last major naval campaign against the Knights on Malta, in 1565, was a failure.

Immediately after 1547, Suleiman's main concern was the eastern front and Iran. In 1548, the flight of Shah Tahmasb's brother to Istanbul gave Suleiman the opportunity to invade, but again without conquest apart from the recapture of Van. A third Iranian campaign in 1553–1554 was equally unproductive, concluding with the treaty of Amasya in 1555, fixing the borders between the two empires. After 1564, the sultan's attention turned to Hungary again. With the bulk of Ottoman forces at Malta, Ferdinand's son Maximilian pressed his claim to Transylvania: Suleiman's response was to launch a major campaign in 1566. In September 1566 he died during the siege of Szigetvár.

During his reign, Suleiman had added central Hungary, Iraq, and territories in eastern Anatolia, the Aegean, and North Africa to the Ottoman Empire, while from the 1530s his fleets dominated the eastern Mediterranean. The kings of France, Muslim rulers in India, and the sultan of Aceh (Sumatra) sought him as an ally, emphasizing his stature as ruler of a world empire. His reach into the western Mediterranean, however, depended on cooperation with the French and the semiautonomous Algerians. After 1540, Habsburg power in central Europe and the Mediterranean, and the Safavids on his eastern border, together with geographical constraints, limited the scope for further conquest and, in the age of Iberian maritime empires, the Ottoman Empire remained essentially land-based. Despite a memorandum of 1525 urging Suleiman to establish an Ottoman hegemony in the Indian Ocean, efforts to disrupt Portuguese shipping at sea and to dislodge the Portuguese from Diu in 1538 and Hormuz in 1552 were unsuccessful.

Despite incessant warfare, the reign was a period of prosperity in the Ottoman Empire. Tax censuses indicate a rising population, with an increase in the number and size of settlements. The treasury remained in surplus, and the standard of the silver currency relatively stable. There were, however, discontents, particularly in Anatolia, leading to a series of popular revolts in the 1520s. In particular, the Safavid shahs made messianic claims, and their many adherents in the Ottoman East posed a constant threat of rebellion, which the sultan controlled through a network of informers.

Suleiman I. Contemporary Venetian portrait. ©ALI MEYER/ CORBIS

Suleiman's reign brought conflict within the dynasty. The royal family reproduced through concubines: the practice of marriage, abandoned after 1450, had served political, not reproductive ends. It had also been customary to limit each concubine to one son, with civil war and fratricide deciding which one was to succeed. As an only son, Suleiman had succeeded to the throne unchallenged. However, early in his reign Suleiman became infatuated with his Slavic concubine Hurrem (known as Roxelanna in the West) who bore him more than one son and, in 1534, became his wife. In 1553, when rivalry for the succession increased, Suleiman, probably with the collusion of Hurrem and her faction, executed Mustafa, his son by the concubine Mahidevran, leaving Hurrem's sons Bayezid and Selim as sole contestants. After her death in 1558, Bayezid rebelled. Suffering defeat in 1559, he fled to Iran, where, after Shah Tahmasb had extracted a peace agreement and a payment from Suleiman, he was executed, leaving Selim as sole heir.

Suleiman was intensely conscious of his image. A number of European engravings, all deriving from a single original, give a sense of his appearance, which he clearly tended, applying make-up in his old age to hide blemishes. To his ordinary subjects, however, he would appear only occasionally as a distant figure in a magnificent cavalcade. More enduring are his titles. To Europeans, he is "the Magnificent" in reference to the extent of his empire, and to his youthful ostentation, best known to the Venetians in his commission of a bejewelled triple tiara in 1532. To Muslims he is "the Lawgiver," a title first attested in the eighteenth century, but presumably used earlier. This reflects his promulgation of a new recension of the "feudal" code compiled circa 1500, under Bayezid II, but more importantly his co-operation with the chief mufti, Ebu's-su'ud, in systematizing some areas of of Islamic law, and Ebu's-su'ud's reformulation of "feudal" land law in Islamic terms. It was under Ebu's-su'ud's influence that Suleiman became conspicuously pious in the second half of his reign. Suleiman was the first Ottoman sultan to adopt formally the title of caliph, implying leadership of the Islamic world. The impetus for the claim came from his overwhelming power, his status as guardian of the Holy Cities, and the need to counter Safavid claims and to emulate Charles V's status as Holy Roman emperor. After the Ottoman-Habsburg treaty of 1547, where Charles V no longer used the title "Emperor," Suleiman also adopted the epithet "Caesar" or "breaker of Caesars." In the same year, he began the construction of the Suleimaniye Mosque in Istanbul, a masterpiece of his chief architect Sinan, as a monument to his imperial pretensions. Its completion in 1557 coincided with Bayezid's rebellion, an event that undermined his caliphal-imperial image. Nonetheless, his death on the battlefield secured him the posthumous title of "Holy Warrior and Martyr."

See also **Levant; Mediterranean Basin; Ottoman Dynasty; Ottoman Empire; Piracy.**

BIBLIOGRAPHY

Busbecq, Ogier Ghislain de. *The Turkish Letters of Ogier de Busbecq, Imperial Ambassador at Constantinople, 1554–1562.* Oxford, 1927.

İnalcik, Halil, and Cemar Kafadar, eds. *Süleimán the Second [sic] and his Time.* Istanbul, 1993.

Kunt, Metin, and Christine Woodhead, eds. *Süleiman the Magnificent and His Age.* London and New York, 1995.

Veinstein, Gilles, ed. *Soliman le Magnifique et son temps.* Paris, 1992.

COLIN IMBER

SULTAN. Sultan, which originally meant 'power' or 'authority', evolved by the tenth century to its present meaning of the holder of that authority, such as a ruler, lord, or monarch. The most spectacular sultans of history were those of the Ottoman dynasty, who ruled most of the territory of the Middle East and North Africa, as well as large parts of eastern Europe, from 1300 to 1923.

Origins of the term are somewhat obscure. Probably Akkadian, and Syriac, the word appears in Arabic in the Koran with the meaning of empowering of someone over another, and connoting magical or moral authority such as possessed by prophets, or by Satan. In early Islamic societies, "sultan" came to convey political power, and was often applied to lesser rulers who shared power with the caliphs, who were presumed to be the religious head of the community, and, at least until around 1000 C.E., to be descended from the Prophet Muhammad. The hadith, or stories of the prophet, generally employ the word "sultan" for governmental or political power, but occasionally for the power of God. As governance became more complicated in early Islamic societies, and disputes emerged about the rightful leaders of the Muslim community, the term became an honorific, or personal title, most consistently, although not exclusively, applied to rulers of Turkic or Persian stock, and Central Asian origins. Ibn Khaldun, writing just as the Turkic dynasties began to populate and usurp power in much of the Arab and Persian lands, noted with disdain their appropriation of honorifics such as "sultan." Such was also true, by his account and others, of the Barmakids, an extremely powerful Persian family under the Abbasid caliph Harun al-Rashid (786–809). Most contemporary sources point to Mahmud of Ghazna (998–1030) as the first independent sovereign to be called a sultan by the Abbasid caliphs. Whether or not the caliph conferred the title, it appears certain that after the fall of the Abbasid dynasty in 1258, "sultan" had acquired the meaning of independent sovereign. Thus the Mamluks, a slave elite of Turkish, Circassian, and

Georgian origins, who ruled Egypt from 1250–1517, were so labeled. All such independent dynasties were champions of Sunni Islam, and it is no coincidence that a revitalized Muslim orthodoxy emerged in the eastern Mediterranean in response to the threat, first of all, of the sectarian Shi'ites, but also of the crusaders, whose ventures in the Levant began in 1096. Sunnism was reinvigorated by the Seljuk kingdoms of Turkey and Iraq, between 1051 and 1300. Muslim theorists had by that time evolved a philosophy of rule that designated the Mamluks and their rivals, including the Ottomans, as sultans, the "Shadows of God on Earth," or the "Caliphs of God on Earth," in matters of government.

OTTOMAN SULTANATE, 1453–1566

The Seljuks—after 1071 there were two centers of overlapping power, one in Baghdad, and the other in Konya and Alanya—created a courtly style and manner of governance that was Central Asian and Muslim in flavor but influenced by the Byzantines, and was adopted by the later Ottoman Empire. Of the Ottoman sultans prior to 1453, Bayezid II (1481–1512) is said to have requested the title of sultan from the titular caliph in Cairo. Mehmed II (also known as Fatih, 'conqueror', of Istanbul, 1451–1481), adopted the title sultan as his own. Nonetheless the preferred term continued to be *padishah,* Persian for supreme sovereign, and sultan generally topped an increasingly long list of titles in official documents.

By the time of the death of Suleiman the Magnificent in 1566, the Ottomans had conquered Egypt and the sacred cities of Mecca and Medina, subdued and colonized Hungary, and threatened the walls of Vienna. Ottoman sultans recast their legitimacy in canonical Islamic terms, as promoters and defenders of Islamic law *(shari'a),* and created an immense religious hierarchy run by the grand mufti (Turk., *Şeyhülislâm*), as he came to be known in Europe. In Turkish, Suleiman acquired the epithet "Law-Giver" precisely because of his consolidation of the imperial offices and law codes. By the time of the conquest of Baghdad by Murad IV (ruled 1623–1640), the Ottoman sultan styled himself "the most glorious Padishah who is the Defender of the faith, whose Majesty is a great as that of Solomon, who is the substitute of God in the world, and who has justified the maxim that 'An equitable Sultan is the shadow of God on earth' . . . the supporter of Islamism and Musulmans, the exterminator of heresies and of the polytheists, the Sovereign of the two Orients and the two Occidents, the servant of the two Holy Cities, the Treasure of Mankind and the apple of the age, who is protected by the Supreme Being whose divine assistance men implore, and favoured by the most High and propitious God" (quoted in J. C. Hurewitz, *The Middle East and North Africa in World Politics,* 2nd ed, vol. 1, p. 25).

Suleiman's long reign (1520–1566) roughly coincided with that of the Habsburg emperor Charles V (ruled 1519–1556), as well as that of Francis I (ruled 1515–1547), and Henry VIII (ruled 1509–1547), and contemporaries equated the terms sultan and emperor as imperial rivals. In this period, lasting impressions of real Ottoman Turkish (Muslim) power were embedded in the European psyche, as well as imaginative, largely fictive representations of imperial institutions such as the harem. "Sultan" thus came to represent absolute power in its most exoticized version, especially in Paul Rycaut's *Present State of the Ottoman Empire* (1660).

Suleiman's age became the idealized gold standard for subsequent eras, often referred to as the "classical age" of the empire. In later reigns, the striking change was the withdrawal of the sultan into palace precincts, with weekly highly ritualized journeys to Friday prayers. The "sultanic" presence became iconographic and theatrical, as his deputy, the grand vizier, took his place in public spaces, such as on the battlefield, and as head of the Imperial Council (Divan). While that is characteristic of the seventeenth century, in the eighteenth, another change occurred, with the reassertion of power by sultans such as Ahmed III (1703–1730) and Selim III (1789–1807), both of whom, it should be noted, were removed from their thrones by widespread resistance to their attempts at invigorated leadership and reform. Eighteenth-century Europe, especially France, made of the sultan the worst exemplar of the despotic, in the debates on the excesses of the Bourbon monarchy. Creative productions such as Mozart's *Abduction from the Seraglio,* or Montesquieu's *Persian Letters,* cemented the image and continue to exert their influence even in contemporary histories of the empire.

See also **Ottoman Empire; Vizier.**

BIBLIOGRAPHY

Inalcik, Halil. *The Ottoman Empire: The Classical Age, 1300–1600.* London, 1973.

Kinross, Patrick, Lord. *The Ottoman Centuries: The Rise and Fall of the Turkish Empire.* London, 1977. Still the best of the histories organized by reigns.

Kramers, J. H. "Sultān." In *Encyclopaedia of Islam.* CD-Rom edition. Vol. 9, pp. 849–851. Leiden, 1999.

Kunt, Metin, and Christine Woodhead, eds. *Süleyman the Magnificent and His Age: The Ottoman Empire in the Early Modern World.* London, 1995. A superb collection of studies on Suleiman's era.

Spandounes, Theodore. *On the Origin of the Ottoman Emperors.* Translated and edited by Donald M. Nicol. New York, 1997. From a 1538 text.

VIRGINIA H. AKSAN

SUMPTUARY LAWS. Sumptuary laws regulated clothing, ornamentation, food, drink, and other forms of luxury, imposing a hierarchy of consumption. These laws prohibited certain ranks of persons from wearing specified cloths, garments, or ornamentation. Typically, the rarest furs were reserved for royal families, lesser furs for nobles, and inferior furs for commoners. An English proclamation of 1559 stipulated: "None shall wear in his apparel any cloth of gold, silver, or tinsel; satin, silk, or cloth mixed with gold or silver, nor any sables; except earls and all of superior degrees."

HIERARCHICAL REGULATION OF CONSUMPTION

Sumptuary laws can be traced back to antiquity, but they proliferated rapidly during the later Middle Ages and Renaissance. These laws embodied a paradox: they distributed luxury by rank by imposing constraints on luxury. They focused on rank, specifying the apparel thought to be appropriate to each social class, at the same time moralizating about the vanity of luxury. Such laws were found throughout Europe and were, despite the repeal of all extant sumptuary legislation in England in 1603, taken by the colonists to the New World, where the critique of luxury was endorsed by Puritan sentiment and

expressed itself in dress rules and injunctions against "tippling" (idle drinking, the enemy of work), testimony to the widespread moralizing linkage of luxury with idleness.

There was a marked variation in the extent to which sumptuary laws targeted the two sexes; in some periods males were the primary target; at other times it was women's dress. In medieval sumptuary law, men's apparel was the subject, but with the rise of urban mercantile classes, the focus of sumptuary law shifted to women's dress. However, the pattern was complex. For example, the period of sharpening tension between old and new wealth in mid-sixteenth-century England was precisely the time when women were exempt from sumptuary restrictions. Both men and women, however, were subject to respectability regulation: female décolletage and male codpieces attracted the legislators' attention.

Attempts to regulate female dress employed contradictory tactics. The first played on the distinction between the respectable woman and the whore, denying fashionable dress to prostitutes to decrease the attraction of prostitution as a way of life while "rewarding" virtuous women by granting them access to fashionable attire. The second tactic reversed the first: it allowed fashion and luxury to prostitutes in the hope that respectable women would be discouraged from emulating their sinful sisters.

EARLY MODERN SUMPTUARY LAWS

There was much continuity in sumptuary regulation through the Middle Ages into the early modern period, but by the end of the eighteenth century only sparse instances of sumptuary laws remained. However, some significant developments occurred during that time. The sumptuary ethic was strongly implicated in some of the most crucial phases of the expansion of urbanization and the transition from mercantile to manufacturing capitalism. The most extensive and intensive phase of sumptuary law was to be found not only in the great Italian mercantile cities of Venice and Florence, but in the German, Dutch, and English cities as they became the key sites of capitalist development.

Sumptuary regulation came to embrace a variety of objectives in addition to hierarchical ordering, captured in the standard preamble to a number of sixteenth-century English statutes: "the commons of the said realm, as well Men as Women, have worn and daily do wear excessive and inordinate Array and Apparel to the great Displeasure of God, and impoverishing of this realm of England and to the enriching of other strange Realms and Countries to final the Destruction of Husbandry of this said Realm." This statement combines issues of luxury, economic protectionism, and a counterposing of consumption and production with a moral admonition.

A new feature of sumptuary discourses also emerged in the sixteenth century: legislators voiced anxieties and complaints about the difficulty of distinguishing the social rank of individuals. In 1530 the Augsburg Diet drew up clothing regulations "to ensure that each class should be clearly recognized apart." A Nuremberg law of 1657 bluntly stated: "It is unfortunately an established fact that both men and womenfolk have, in utterly irresponsible manner, driven extravagance in dress and new styles to such shameful and wanton extremes that the different classes are barely to be known apart."

The attempt to regulate appearance came up against the slow but inevitable increase in consumerism. As fashion became accessible to more people, the possibilities of competitive consumption increased. An English proclamation of 1575 reveals a certain desperation by prohibiting anyone from "devising any new forms of apparel." In the "world of strangers" of urban settings, not being able to "read" rank from apparel must have been perplexing. This has been described as a crisis of recognizability: in a social terrain of competition, the rising bourgeois classes sought to secure their identities in the process of distinguishing themselves from others, while those above them sought to resist their challenge. This strife resulted in still more overtly urban regulation, and new laws included dress rules for burghers (members of the urban middle class) and merchants, and imposed rules that maintained a visible separation between ladies and their maidservants by specifying the length of headdresses and the width of sleeves.

Attempts to promote the work ethic and to further the Protestant Reformation unleashed enormous legislative energy intended to restrain feasting, drinking, and other indulgences. The contemporary importance of sumptuary law is attested by the fact that the Diet of Worms in 1521, at one of the critical turning points in the political realignment of Reformation Europe, took the time to articulate the urgent need for sumptuary legislation in order to maintain the visibility of social status in attire. When bourgeois interests secured power, they used it to impose sumptuary restrictions or fiscal burdens on the patrician classes, for example, restricting expenditures on weddings, feasts, and funerals; these efforts were also linked with struggles to regulate the size of dowries. Although there is little evidence regarding the degree of enforcement, it is worth noting that a number of Italian cities had officers specifically appointed to enforce sumptuary laws.

It was in Italy that another significant form of regulation, one that had long existed in Florence, spread: it became easier to purchase a license of exemption from sumptuary rules, the harbinger of a shift toward an increasingly fiscal approach. While licensing remained important in Italy, elsewhere economic protectionist motives became increasingly mixed into sumptuary regulation. Protectionism was at the heart of the economic debates during the mercantilist period and sumptuary laws and discourses were increasingly part of these wider economic debates. Hostility to "foreign" goods was woven into sumptuary discourses with the imposition of luxury taxes or prohibitions on the import and sale of foreign goods.

Sumptuary laws did not so much "die" as undergo a process of metamorphosis such that the original is barely recognizable in the result: luxury taxes and import restrictions are the legacy of sumptuary laws. Such laws can perhaps best be regarded as inhabiting the threshold of modernity, without themselves being an active feature of modernity.

See also **Capitalism; Class, Status, and Order; Clothing; Commerce and Markets; Consumption; Equality and Inequality; Law; Mercantilism; Mobility, Social; Prostitution; Puritanism; Reformation, Protestant; Women.**

BIBLIOGRAPHY

Greenfield, Kent R. *Sumptuary Law in Nürnberg: A Study in Paternal Government.* Baltimore, 1918.

Harte, N. B. "State Control of Dress and Social Change in Pre-Industrial England." In *Trade, Government, and Society in Pre-Industrial England,* edited by D. C. Coleman and A. H. John, pp. 132–165. London, 1976.

Hunt, Alan. *Governance of the Consuming Passions: A History of Sumptuary Law.* New York, 1996.

Vincent, John M. *Costume and Conduct in the Laws of Basel, Bern, and Zurich 1370–1800.* Baltimore, 1935; reprinted New York, 1969.

ALAN HUNT

SURGEONS. The period between the Renaissance and the Enlightenment witnessed slow, then accelerating progress in surgery. Surgeons made advances in controlling hemorrhage; devised simpler and safer dressings for battle wounds; and improved methods and invented new instruments for amputating limbs, cutting for stone of the urinary bladder, operating for hernias and dilatations of arteries, combating the hazards of giving birth, and repairing certain deformities. In the 1740s, the time-honored procedure of couching for cataracts of the eye gave way to modern extraction, a rare example of radical innovation. Greater attention to cleanliness may have reduced infection, although the unsanitary conditions under which surgery was performed, especially in many hospitals, remained appalling even by standards of the time. Likewise, the pain of operations was likened to torture, even though it was masked in part by suffering due to the ailment. Skilled surgeons needed to work with great dexterity and speed to complete major procedures in just a few minutes. Only relatively few dared to undertake these high-risk interventions, and then infrequently, compared with ordinary tasks—bloodletting, incision of boils, treatment of skin and venereal diseases, reducing dislocations, setting fractures—that made up the ordinary barber-surgeon's stock-in-trade.

Progress in the social status and scientific knowledge of elite surgeons in large cities moved at a much more rapid pace than technical change. By the end of the eighteenth century, surgical guilds in Paris, London, Edinburgh, Madrid, Vienna, Copenhagen, and elsewhere had evolved into professional bodies with distinctive liberal institutions: colleges for education and academies for advancing knowledge. Major surgery in the sixteenth century remained the preserve of exceptional individuals of humble backgrounds—the renowned French barber-surgeon, Ambroise Paré, was the outstanding example of this sort—or bold itinerants, and family

dynasties like the Chamberlens, French/British Huguenots, who managed to keep the secret of their obstetrical forceps for well over a century. By the High Enlightenment, organized professionals shared a repertoire of surgical knowledge and practices. Expertise in the craft conferred exclusively by formal regulation, as well as custom, to guilds, appropriately known as "mysteries," began to be the province of new, more open institutional structures concerned with scientific progress. Academic surgical societies used publications and correspondence networks to share and propagate their work.

The centralized European state fostered the professionalization of surgery. In France, Louis XIV's surgeon used the occasion of his successful anal fistula operation on the king in 1686 to gain benefits for the guild of barber-surgeons. At the time, the status of royal surgeon was little more than that of a domestic servant. But during the Regency period (1713–1723) the office of premier surgeon to the king assumed an increasingly important professional leadership role. Georges Mareshal and François de la Peyronie, successively premier surgeons to Louis XV, consolidated centralized jurisdiction over guilds throughout the kingdom, established a central school of surgery in Paris in 1724 and a Royal Academy of Surgery in 1731, and secured legislation in 1743 requiring a university degree of surgeons and separating the company or college of surgeons from the barbers' guild. The precedent was emulated by larger provincial communities.

In Great Britain, the surgical profession developed in less centralized fashion. To be sure, kings lent their patronage to the London barber-surgeons guild, as depicted in Holbein's portrait of Henry VIII presiding over the union of the two guilds in 1540. And the London surgeons separated from barbers in 1745, just two years after their Paris counterparts. Capital cities in Prussia, Spain, and Russia followed suit. In Dutch and most German and Italian centers, barber-surgeons' guilds survived, but their members no longer did barbers' work, and they too enjoyed upward social mobility. Rembrandt's collective portrait of the Amsterdam guild in his *Anatomy Lesson* (1632) bears witness to their academic pursuits and bourgeois status.

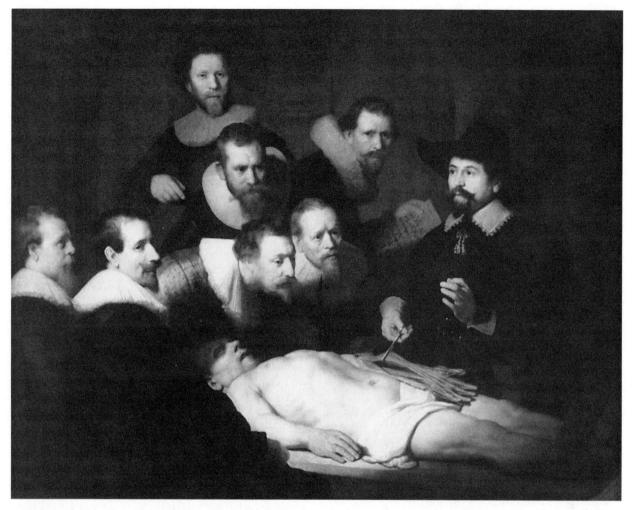

Surgeons. *The Anatomy Lecture of Dr. Nicolaes Tulp* by Rembrandt, 1632. Tulp was a prominent Amsterdam surgeon who commissioned the renowned Rembrandt to create this portrait. It was Tulp's idea that he should be depicted delivering an anatomy lecture. The Surgeons Guild at the time permitted one public dissection per year and stipulated that the cadaver must be that of an executed criminal. ©FRANCIS G. MAYER/CORBIS

During the second half of the eighteenth century, elite surgeons across Europe achieved a rank in society comparable to that of medical doctors. Since medieval times, medical superiority had derived from the educational attainment of physicians and their collective status alongside law and theology in the university. In principle, and by statute, the medical faculty had jurisdiction over surgical instruction, licensing, and practice. All this came under question and successful challenge when educated surgeons set up autonomous institutions. Surgeons gained admission to prestigious scientific academies in numbers equal to, if not surpassing, physicians. As classical humoral theory, along with the Latin language of medical discourse, declined, surgical

knowledge anchored in sensory experience and anatomical pathology took the ascendancy. Anatomy was the surgical science par excellence. Surgeons performed dissections on the cadaver for various purposes: research, training—especially in private courses where students could purchase cadavers for hands-on learning—and forensic autopsies seeking to reveal the causes of death. Surgical knowledge was associated with empirical epistemology, pathological anatomy, and a localist conception of disease, while medical knowledge, when not abstract and purely theoretical, could point only to chemistry for scientific validation. Given these contrasts, it is not surprising that the eighteenth-century philosophes extolled the practical usefulness of the surgi-

Surgeons. *A Barber Surgeon Tending a Peasant's Foot,* seventeenth-century painting by Isaack Koedijk. ©CHRISTIE'S IMAGES/CORBIS

cal side of medicine. Diderot's *Encyclopédie* reproduced illustrations of operations and instruments recently published by the Academy of Surgery, while the Academy's secretary, Antoine Louis, contributed some seventy articles on his field to the encyclopedia project.

In smaller towns, villages, and the countryside, surgeons were the only licensed medical practitioners available to serve people of modest means. Fragmentary evidence indicates that rural master surgeons, surprisingly numerous in proportion to the population, faced stiff competition from a variety of illegal healers, whose ranks included roving journeymen, empirics and "charlatans," women healers and midwives, clergy, and army and naval surgeons. Surgical guilds, in principle, but not often in practice, had licensing authority over midwives and so-called specialists: oculists, hernia experts, bonesetters, and tooth pullers, who had experience only in their particular craft skill.

At the level of country surgeon, distinctions drawn between external surgical diseases and internal medical ailments had little meaning. Surgeons

and barber-surgeons did not hesitate to dispense purges and other medical remedies. Phlebotomy (bloodletting), for prevention as well as treatment of most ailments, was a mainstay. A medical recourse common to both barbers and surgeons, bloodletting helped perpetuate the link between the two crafts in continental Europe. In Great Britain, apothecary-surgeons, rather than barber-surgeons, took care of the medical needs of common folk.

As in other craft guilds, apprenticeship, followed by a period as a journeyman, constituted the core of training for barber-surgeons. By the eighteenth century, practical experience began to be supplemented by formal courses. In France, during the second half of the century, vast numbers of aspiring young surgeons *(garçon chirurgiens)* from all over the realm attended courses at the Paris surgical school.

Hospitals increasingly became a site for practical training for surgeons as these church foundations for poor relief came under secular administration and adopted medical objectives. Surgeons worked, learned, and sometimes resided in hospitals, where they displaced clerical healers and constituted an elaborate hierarchy of responsibility for patient care. Medical students and physicians seldom took on hospital employment. A similar preponderance of surgeons characterized medical services in European armies and navies. In public health matters, notably in the organized response to plague and other epidemics, surgeons outnumbered their medical counterparts, especially at the grassroots level.

The eighteenth century saw the rise of a subcategory of surgeons, known as man-midwives, who began to preside over childbirth in well-to-do families. To some extent, fashion paved the way for obstetricians *(accoucheurs)* to displace traditional midwives. But men also legitimated their takeover of this lucrative practice by means of demonstrably superior knowledge in anatomy, displayed in magnificent atlases of the stages of pregnancy, and their use of new techniques and instruments for delivery, notably the obstetrical forceps. Because of their systematic exclusion from surgical guilds as well as university medical faculties, women healers could only practice illegally. However, guild custom permitted widows of master surgeons to lease to journeymen the practice of their deceased husbands.

The prevalence of religious and magical healing is difficult to assess. Evidently, it persisted in the eighteenth century and beyond. Among the surgical elite, such beliefs and practices clearly declined. In the sixteenth century, Ambroise Paré had described monsters and marvels, attributed birth defects to maternal impressions, acknowledged witchcraft, and naively repeated accounts of travelers' sightings of mermaids. His eighteenth-century successors adopted a more critical, often skeptical, attitude. By the Academy of Surgery's rigorous criteria, medical miracles were judged to be either errors, products of religious fanaticism, or frauds. Surgical power, based upon pathological anatomy, could explain and often cure conditions heretofore ascribed to supernatural forces. Operations repaired the congenital deformity of harelip, restored sight to those blinded by cataracts, and cured impotence resulting from anatomical lesions of the urogenital organs.

Surgical progress, and more specifically, the social ascension of surgeons in urban centers of early modern Europe, paradoxically, planted the seeds of the demise of surgery as an autonomous profession. Success narrowed the social and cultural gap with physicians and introduced a more empirical and anatomical orientation to medicine in general. Suggestive analogies likened hidden, poorly understood internal ailments to familiar external lesions. Postmortems took on instructive significance for physicians. By the eve of the French Revolution, reformers had called for the abolition of separate institutions and the unification of medicine and surgery into a single profession. Future practitioners were to be trained in a common "school of health" and to practice the healing art as a whole. Country surgeons would be replaced by a subordinate level of health officers. In 1794 the National Assembly instituted the new professional order, a pattern that was subsequently adopted in other European countries.

See also **Academies, Learned; Anatomy and Physiology; Magic; Medicine; Midwives; Obstetrics and Gynecology; Public Health; Scientific Revolution.**

BIBLIOGRAPHY

Burke, Michael E. *The Royal College of San Carlos: Surgery and Spanish Medical Reform in the Late Eighteenth Century.* Durham, N.C., 1977.

Gelfand, Toby. *Professionalizing Modern Medicine: Paris Surgeons and Medical Science and Institutions in the 18th Century.* Westport, Conn., 1980.

Gentilcore, David. *Healers and Healing in Early Modern Italy.* Manchester, U.K., and New York, 1998.

Lawrence, Susan C. *Charitable Knowledge: Hospital Pupils and Practitioners in Eighteenth-Century London.* Cambridge, U.K., 1996.

Lindemann, Mary. *Health and Healing in Eighteenth-Century Germany.* Baltimore, 1996.

Moulin, Daniel de. *A History of Surgery with Emphasis on the Netherlands.* Dordrecht and Lancaster, U.K., 1988.

Pelling, Margaret, and Charles Webster. "Medical practitioners." In *Health, Medicine, and Mortality in the Sixteenth Century,* edited by Charles Webster, pp. 165–235. Cambridge, U.K., 1979.

Ramsey, Matthew. *Professional and Popular Medicine in France, 1770–1830: The Social World of Medical Practice.* Cambridge, U.K., 1988.

TOBY GELFAND

SURVEYING.

Surveying, initially the geometrical and legal description of local lands and county seats, gained importance throughout the early modern period as legal and economic arguments came to rely on accurate descriptions and, increasingly, on measurement and "plotting." By the late seventeenth century, surveying included the mapping of larger political units; by the eighteenth, military leaders and colonial governors, as well as landed individuals, employed surveyors and cartographers. Techniques and instruments developed throughout the period produced a coherent body of theory and practice used for imperial mapping in the late eighteenth and nineteenth centuries.

At the end of the fifteenth century, surveying consisted largely of written descriptions of fields and estates based on visual inspection of an area. Although landmarks and natural division points were more crucial for determining land ownership, these methods were often accompanied by some sort of measurement. In the first half of the sixteenth century, surveying was often restricted to "viewing" or chain-measuring, and the chain often symbolized the surveyors' profession. As the century progressed, and more standardized techniques of measurement were developed and surveying moved from linear and geometrical methods to those based on angular or trigonometric measurement, surveyors began to produce maps or "plots." Although such advanced mathematical methods were developed by the end of the century, chain-measuring continued to be used into the eighteenth century.

The introduction of triangulation methods, the plane table, and the theodolite, as well as rules of acceptable practice, transformed surveying into an exact art. Leonard Digges's *Pantometria* (1571), for example, introduced these techniques and instruments into England. Throughout the seventeenth century the new surveying instruments were refined, a number of surveying manuals were published, and surveyors were increasingly trained in mathematics and astronomical techniques. Surveying, unlike mapping on a larger scale or the later colonial and country surveys, such as the Ordnance Survey of Ireland (1824–1846), did not require longitude and latitude placement, and therefore did not use astronomical observations in order to achieve accuracy.

Part of the transformation in surveying that took place during the early modern period was related to the changing awareness on the part of landowners of the desirability of surveying and mapping their lands. As surveyors gradually convinced their patrons of the utility of scale maps, this cognitive shift led to a cartographic revolution. Carefully measured and drawn maps (as opposed to earlier sketch maps) began to be used by landowners as evidence in court cases, by generals planning their military strategies, and by governors interested in inventories and tax collecting. All of this was symptomatic of the developing map culture, driven in part by the increasing study of geography at schools and universities.

By the end of the early modern period, Europeans were surveying their own lands and the other parts of the world they were conquering. They believed that, through measurement and cartographic depiction, they could control the land and the people who lived there. Only the impressive developments of surveying instruments and techniques, and the conceptual acceptance of the scale map as an objective and controllable representation of the land, made that idea plausible.

See also **Astronomy; Cartography and Geography; Colonialism; Earth, Theories of the; Engineering: Civil; Exploration; Landholding; Mathematics; Property; Scientific Instruments; Taxation.**

BIBLIOGRAPHY

Bennett, James A. *The Divided Circle: A History of Instruments for Astronomy, Navigation and Surveying.* Oxford, 1987.

Kain, Robert J. P., and Elizabeth Baigent. *The Cadastral Map in the Service of the State: A History of Property Mapping.* Chicago, 1992.

Richeson, Allie Wilson. *English Land Measuring to 1800: Instruments and Practices.* Cambridge, Mass., 1966.

LESLEY B. CORMACK

SWEDEN. The early modern period was particularly important in the formation of Sweden as a state. During this time Sweden played a central role in northern European power politics for more than a century, the country's economy grew in scale and complexity, and it became more closely integrated into the mainstreams of European cultural and intellectual development.

Early modern "Sweden" was not what one sees today on a map. In 1500, the southern provinces of Skåne, Blekinge, and Halland belonged to Denmark, and the border areas of Bohuslän, Jämtland, and Härjedalen were parts of Norway. (Norway gradually lost its status as an independent state in the fifteenth century, and from the mid-1530s was, in all but name, a territory of Denmark.) Northern Sweden was sparsely settled and loosely controlled. Finland, smaller than it is today, was an integral part of the country. The borders of current Sweden date mostly from 1658/60 and 1809. In addition, Sweden, in a broad sense, included a Baltic empire that was built and then lost in this period. In population the country numbered, without Finland, less than a million in 1500 and around two million in 1800.

POLITICAL DEVELOPMENT

In 1397, a federation of the medieval kingdoms of Denmark, Norway, and Sweden was established, called by posterity the Kalmar Union. Denmark was its most powerful member. At several times during the fifteenth century, Sweden broke with the union, and a series of rebellions and wars of reunion punctuated the years down to the early 1520s. The last of these union wars began in 1521 and was led by Gustav Eriksson Vasa. Within three years the Swedes had established their independence, aided by the Hanseatic League and a revolt in Denmark.

Gustav was elected king as Gustav I Vasa in 1523. Since then, Sweden has had an unbroken history of independent development.

Sweden's history was not, however, free of internal conflict. As elsewhere in Europe, a basic constitutional struggle ran through the entire early modern period between crown and nobility, between monarchy and aristocratic constitutionalism. Kings wanted to be kings; nobles wanted to preserve their historic rights and liberties and at least share power with the crown.

A third factor in this history was the Parliament (*Riksdag*), which began to develop in the fifteenth century. Called by kings or factions of great men, it dealt with matters of war, peace, taxation, and succession. Usually, a meeting included representatives from each of the four principal "estates": clergy, nobility, burghers, and freehold farmers. Over time the frequency of meetings increased, procedures were formalized, and its prerogatives grew. It was least important during the absolutist period (1680–1719) and most important during the Era of Liberty (1719–1772).

In a series of episodes that has been likened to a swinging pendulum, Sweden experienced times of strong monarchy, times of balance, and times of noble ascendancy. Gustav I Vasa was able to advance royal power, aided by the fact that many of his likely noble opponents had been executed on order of the Danish king, Christian II, in the so-called Stockholm Bloodbath in 1520. Gustav was a very able politician who played the Parliament to achieve his ends, exploited the Reformation, used the new church as a means of royal propaganda, and enhanced state finances by confiscating church lands. His sons Erik XIV (ruled 1560–1568), John III (ruled 1568–1592), and Charles IX (ruled 1599–1611), as well as his nephew Sigismund I (ruled 1592–1599), were less successful. Each antagonized factions of the nobility. Charles IX was the most ruthless, executing five noble opponents at Linköping in 1600. A new phase began with the succession of Gustavus II Adolphus (ruled 1611–1632). In order to secure the throne, he was compelled to promise to respect the privileges of the nobles. Until his death in 1632 a remarkably amiable cooperation developed between crown and nobility. Each needed and used the other to run the affairs of state at home and to fight wars abroad. Noble importance grew under Christina, during both her minority (1632–1644) and her active reign (1644–1654). Charles X Gustav (ruled 1654–1660) was an absolutist at heart, but he was unable to accomplish very much during his short reign (1654–1660). During the minority (1660–1675) of Charles XI (ruled 1675–1697), the high nobility recklessly ran the affairs of state. Charles was able to change the system fundamentally, however, by exploiting social discontent between commons and nobles and within the nobility. Between 1680 and 1693, Sweden was transformed into an absolutist state. Although privilege was not challenged, the crown recovered most of the domain lands donated away since the late sixteenth century and asserted the right to rule without either the nobility's advice through the council or that of the Parliament.

Absolutism lasted only until 1719. The enormous costs of war, the obsessive leadership of Charles XII (ruled 1697–1718), and an uncertain succession allowed leaders of the nobility to dictate a new constitution. The order of primacy was inverted during the so-called Era of Liberty (1719–1772). For much of this period the nobility dominated through the council and the Parliament. Toward the end the burghers and farmers played increasingly important roles. From about 1740 to 1772 a fascinating political life developed, centered on two conflicting factions, the Caps and the Hats, which resembled modern political parties. The more reform-minded Hats advocated changes that were revolutionary for the time including press freedom, laissez-faire economics, and an end to privilege. As interesting as this period was, it was fraught with problems. Some of the ideas advanced were simply too radical. More important, political strife was viewed as a way to keep Sweden weak and was encouraged through bribes and influence buying by Russia, France, and England. Gustav III (ruled 1771–1792) ended the experiment in August 1772 with a bloodless palace coup, and strong monarchy returned. Gustav was not content to play a minor role in anything and dreamed of restoring Sweden's greatness. An adventuresome foreign policy was coupled with a drift back toward royal absolutism, and irate nobles conspired to assassinate the king in 1792.

Despite these shifts in power and constitutional balance, Sweden developed as a reasonably well run state. Beginning around 1620, an administrative system was adopted under which responsibilities were assigned to five "colleges," each headed by one of the "great officers" of state (chancellor, treasurer, steward, marshal, and admiral). This was most clearly spelled out in the 1634 Form of Government and was likely the collaborative work of Gustavus II Adolphus and his chancellor, Axel Oxenstierna. The country's court system went through several reforms in the seventeenth century and a new national law code was promulgated in 1734. The beginnings of a national bank were created in 1668. Regional government was organized around counties *(län)* headed by governors. Responsibility, accountability, and reporting were standardized. Although the nobility retained its privileged claim to offices and officer appointments, ability and education were factors in selection, especially in the eighteenth century.

Sweden also went from a "domain state" to a tax and/or warfare state during this period. Before the Reformation, the crown owned only about 5 percent of the land and was expected to live from this, in theory at least. There was never enough money, however, and a system of regular taxes, primarily on the lands of freehold farmers, dates from the Middle Ages. (Noble and church lands were exempt.) The crown increased its holdings through confiscations in the Reformation, and Gustav I actually left his sons a budgetary surplus. Fiscal problems grew from the 1560s, driven by foreign policy. Concurrently, the crown's domain position worsened through donations to the nobility. By 1660, the crown held less than 10 percent of the land, while the nobility held over 60 percent. The state was forced to turn to higher taxes and more effective tax extraction from the commons, which, in turn, undercut the economic position of the freehold farmers. Sweden was spared a social-economic revolution by the radical reduction (reclaiming) of noble holdings carried through by Charles XI after 1680. During the Great Northern War (1700–1721) taxes rose again. They remained high for much of the eighteenth century, while crown holdings diminished through direct sale.

EMPIRE

The imperial phase in Swedish history lasted from about 1560 to 1721. Growth defines the first one hundred years, decline the last sixty. In the growth phase Finland was enlarged, Kexholm, Ingermanland, Estonia, Livonia, Pomerania, Wismar, and Bremen-Verden were added, and the Danish and Norwegian territories bordering the kingdom were annexed. During the 1650s, Sweden also operated a trade fort at Cape Coast (Ghana), and it maintained a colony in North America between 1638 and 1655. The high point in the empire's history was reached in 1658. Small losses were incurred in 1660. The worst came in the last decade of the Great Northern War (1700–1721), when, except for Pomerania, Wismar, and most of Finland, all the Baltic territories were lost. More of Finland was taken by Russia in the 1740s. In the closing decades of the century, Gustav III dreamed of restoring the empire and Sweden's importance. A war against Russia in 1788–1790 gained nothing. Finland became a Russian grand duchy in 1809.

The imperial chapter in Swedish history has long attracted the attention of historians. Why did the leaders of this poor and sparsely populated country choose to build and maintain an empire, and how did they manage to do so? Sweden's assets, relative to the weaknesses of the competitors, made possible its expansive policies. Once begun, the empire became a kind of imperative and for a time even paid for itself. International rivalries also encouraged the establishment of imperial outposts. For survival in a competitive state system, Sweden needed to have places and resources outside the country proper to support its security. There were also economic motives. Merchants sought to control the lucrative Baltic trade, while Sweden's acquisitive nobility found in the empire a setting for military careers and a source of spoils. In addition, the personal fortunes and careers of individual nobles, support of the Lutherans in Germany and fears of the Catholic Counter-Reformation, exploitation of the empire to enhance the status of the crown, and the competitive nature of the European state system are cited.

ECONOMIC DEVELOPMENT

For the most part Sweden was and remained a poor agricultural state throughout the early modern period. Except for the far south and the area around

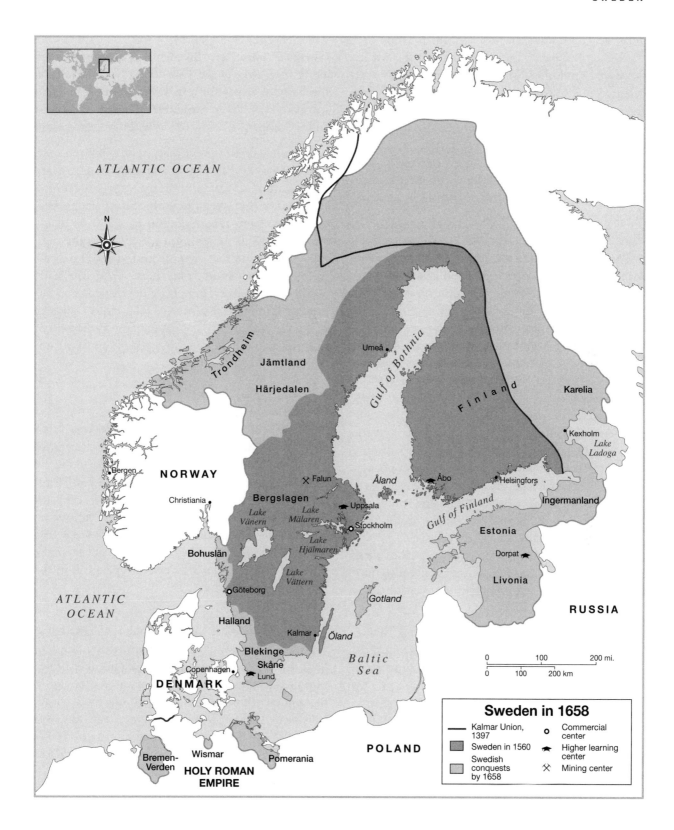

ATLANTIC OCEAN

N

ATLANTIC
OCEAN

Trondheim

Jämtland

Härjedalen

Umeå

Gulf of Bothnia

Finland

Karelia

Kexholm
Lake
Ladoga

Bergen

NORWAY

Falun

Åland

Åbo

Helsingfors

Ingermanland

Christiania

Bergslagen

Lake
Vänern

Lake
Mälaren

Uppsala

Stockholm

Estonia

Bohuslän

Lake
Hjälmaren

Dorpat

Lake
Vättern

Göteborg

Gotland

Livonia

Halland

RUSSIA

Kalmar

Öland

Blekinge

Skåne

Copenhagen

Lund

Baltic
Sea

0   100   200 mi.
0 100 200 km

DENMARK

Bremen-
Verden

Wismar

Pomerania

POLAND

HOLY ROMAN
EMPIRE

Sweden in 1658

— Kalmar Union,
1397

○ Commercial
center

▬ Sweden in 1560

🐦 Higher learning
center

▫ Swedish
conquests
by 1658

✕ Mining center

Lake Mälaren, soils were generally poor. Tools and methods were centuries old. Yields could be pitifully small. Crop failures and the ensuing famines were frequent. Grains, livestock, milk, butter, and cheese were the main products. Many farmers supplemented their incomes by working in the forests, mining, or fishing. Whether held by the crown, nobility, or commons, agricultural life was organized around villages. Land was "owned" in small strips and worked collectively. In a few areas single-owner farmsteads prevailed. Some important changes were initiated in the eighteenth century. Cultivation of the potato became increasingly common after about 1750. Its adoption had important dietary results and symbolized a growing willingness to experiment with new crops. At the same time, an effort to consolidate the small strip holdings of many farmers into fewer fields and to break up the old agricultural villages was begun. This would take nearly a century to complete.

Sweden possessed four great assets beyond its arable land: the riches of the inland lakes and rivers and the seas surrounding the country, coniferous forests (sources of timber, charcoal, and tar), iron ore from the Bergslagen region of east-central Sweden, and copper chiefly from the great mine, Stora Kopparberget, at Falun. These resources were essential to Sweden's achievements in the period. Herring, bar iron, smelted copper, masts and spars, and tar were vital products in European markets and Sweden's most important exports. For part of the seventeenth century, Sweden was Europe's leading supplier of copper. Bar iron became more important in the eighteenth century. Also, these resources attracted technology and investment and stimulated domestic shipbuilding, finished metal production, and armaments industries. The state played important roles in developing and controlling all of these activities through licensing, subsidies, granting monopolies, encouraging immigration, oversight, and direct participation.

Trade operated on four levels: internal, Baltic, European, and global. Internal was the most limited and the most restricted. Baltic and European commerce were inseparably linked, and the struggle for dominance in this sphere is one of the main themes of the period's history. To control the flow of salt, grains, timber, metals, and other products that flowed through the ports of the Baltic was to become rich. Denmark, Sweden, Russia, the Dutch Netherlands, Poland, and England were some of the players in this competition. Sweden never actually gained control of the trade, but it did control many of the ports that fed it from around 1630 to 1720. In the global economies of the early modern period, Sweden was a minor actor. Hopes of gaining a place in the Africa trade lasted only through the 1650s,

when Sweden maintained a fort at Cape Coast (Ghana). The New Sweden colony, established along the banks of the Delaware River in 1638 on the basis of hopes for a lucrative trade in furs and tobacco, was never profitable. The Swedish East India Company (1731–1813) was more successful.

Connected to the economic and political developments of the period was a gradual trend toward urbanization. Most important was Stockholm. Founded in the mid-thirteenth century, its population grew from around 6,000 in 1500 to nearly 90,000 in 1800. In addition to serving as the capital, it was a center for manufacturing and the country's most important trade port. From the early seventeenth century, Göteborg developed as an important commercial center. A conscious policy of urban development was pursued, and twenty-eight new towns were founded in Sweden (and Finland) in the seventeenth century.

CULTURE AND INTELLECTUAL DEVELOPMENT

Sweden's cultural and intellectual life was influenced by growing ties with Europe, a conservative Lutheran church, and the country's relative poverty for much of the early modern period. In 1500 Sweden was on the fringes of Europe. Except for churches and a network of medieval royal castles, architecture was at best rustic. Schools were few, and the country's one university at Uppsala, founded in 1477, virtually ceased operation in the late sixteenth century.

Although Sweden never became a leader in cultural or intellectual activity, much of this backwardness faded over the course of the early modern period, and the country produced a number of important scholars, writers, and artists, especially in the eighteenth century. Court life was modeled on European standards from Gustav I on, and was especially vibrant under Christina during the 1640s and Gustav III from 1772 to 1792. Royal palaces copied continental styles. Drottningholm was built between 1665 and 1703. Fire destroyed the centuries-old Three Crowns Castle in Stockholm in 1697, and work began almost immediately on a new rococo palace designed by Nicodemus Tessin the Younger. During the middle decades of the seventeenth century, Sweden's aristocracy built and furnished fine city and country residences in European styles. Court painters like David Klöcker (ennobled Ehrenstrahl) produced superb portraits from around 1650; and the eighteenth century saw the work of such masters as C. G. Pilo, Pehr Hilleström, and the sculptor J. H. Sergel.

From the early seventeenth century, education received greater attention. New secondary schools (*gymnasia*), an academy at Åbo; (1640), and new universities at Dorpat (1632) and Lund (1668) were established. Uppsala University received more regular support. It was home to Olof Rudbeck the Elder (1630–1702), a co-discoverer of the lymphatic system and an exponent of Gothicism, an interpretation of Sweden's history that tied it to ancient biblical tribes and linked the country's monarchs to Noah's son Magog. These ideas were first expressed in the fifteenth century and developed most fully in Johannes Magnus's *Historia de Omnibus Gothorum Sveonumque Regibus* from 1554. Placing Sweden at the center of Western cultural development and regarding it as the site of the lost city of Atlantis, Gothicism was used to legitimize both the Swedish nation and the monarchy. In the eighteenth century Sweden produced a number of distinguished scientists including the botanist Carl Linnaeus (Linnaeus; 1707–1778), the physicist and mathematician Anders Celsius (1701–1744), and the multitalented mystic Emanuel Swedenborg (1688–1772).

See also **Charles X Gustav (Sweden); Charles XII (Sweden); Christina (Sweden); Denmark; Gustavus II Adolphus (Sweden); Kalmar, Union of; Linnaeus, Carl; Lutheranism; Northern Wars; Oxenstierna, Axel; Stockholm; Swedenborgianism; Swedish Literature and Language; Thirty Years' War (1618–1648); Vasa Dynasty (Sweden).**

BIBLIOGRAPHY

Barton, H. Arnold. *Northern Arcadia: Foreign Travelers in Scandinavia. 1765–1815.* Carbondale, Ill., 1998.

Magnusson, Lars. *An Economic History of Sweden.* London and New York, 2000.

Nordstrom, Byron. *A History of Sweden.* Westport, Conn., 2002.

Oakley, Stewart. *A Short History of Sweden.* New York, 1966.

Scott, Franklin. *Sweden: The Nation's History.* Carbondale, Ill., 1988.

Important journals include *Historisk tidskrift,* 1881–current; *Scandinavian Economic History Review,* 1953–current; *Scandinavian Journal of History,* 1976–current; *Scandinavian Studies,* 1917–current.

The Internet offers many fine sites. Two good starting points are: http://www.sweden.se/ and http://www.markovits.com/nordic.

BYRON J. NORDSTROM

SWEDENBORGIANISM. A religious movement based on the revelations of Emanuel Swedenborg (1688–1772), an eighteenth-century Swedish scientist and religious visionary. The son of a Swedish Lutheran theologian and bishop, Swedenborg was educated at Uppsala, and then traveled through the Continent and England. A visionary theoretical scientist, Swedenborg anticipated many later scientific discoveries, but gradually became convinced that material nature had an essentially spiritual foundation. His religious visions, which began in 1736, climaxed with a vision of Jesus in 1744, and from then on he devoted himself to his extensive spiritual writings. The essence of his thought centered around a correspondence between the physical and spiritual worlds; life on earth is merely preparation for a heavenly existence. The New Jerusalem Church, of which he was the prophet, would be the world's ultimate religion. Swedenborg did not intend, however, to form a separate church, but a fellowship of like-minded individuals. His thought had the most influence in England, where two Anglican priests, Thomas Hartley (d. 1784) and John Clowes (1743–1831), were early disciples. In 1787, a separate New Jerusalem Church was founded in London by former Wesleyan pastors, an organization that now has branches worldwide, mainly in English-speaking countries.

Swedenborg's thought and visions affected several major artists and writers; William Blake was a follower, and Swedenborgian influences have been seen in the works of Samuel Taylor Coleridge and Honoré de Balzac, among others. Immanuel Kant was an early critic of Swedenborg and wrote his "Dreams of a Spirit-Seer" (1766) as a scathing polemic against his thought.

See also **Catholic Spirituality and Mysticism.**

BIBLIOGRAPHY

Benz, Ernst. *Emanuel Swedenborg: Visionary Savant in the Age of Reason.* Translated by Nicholas Goodrick-Clarke. West Chester, Pa., 2002. Translation of the 2nd German edition of 1969.

Lamm, Martin. *Emanuel Swedenborg: The Development of his Thought.* Translated by Tomas Spiers and Anders Hallengren. West Chester, Pa., 2000. Translation of the Swedish original of 1915.

MARK GRANQUIST

SWEDISH LITERATURE AND LANGUAGE.

In 1500 the Swedish language had relatively low standing as a vehicle for literature. Latin was the language of the church and of scholarship and would be used as an academic language until the end of the eighteenth century. The Reformation was key to the development of Swedish as a literary language; in Sweden as elsewhere in Europe, it created a need for Scriptures in the vernacular. Foreign influence on Swedish language and literature continued to be strong, with German serving as an important source of loanwords in the 1500s and 1600s, after which French became more influential, especially among the aristocracy. In the sixteenth century, Swedish literary production was centered around the Reformation. During the following century, Sweden's military campaigns and emergence as a major European power provided a focus, with most literary activity in service to the state. And in the eighteenth century, Swedish literature became imbued with Enlightenment impulses imported from France and England.

In 1523 a revolt led by Gustav I Vasa led to the dissolution of the Kalmar Union, which had linked Denmark, Norway, and Sweden since 1397. Gustav I Vasa quickly consolidated his authority, appropriating church property and establishing a state-controlled Lutheran church. Out of these drastic changes came a milestone in Swedish literary history: the translation of the New Testament into Swedish in 1526. It is not known who was responsible for the translation, but Laurentius Andrae and Olaus Petri, both important advisers to Gustav I Vasa, were involved. The translation, based on Desiderius Erasmus's Latin translation of 1516 as well as Martin Luther's German translation of 1522, proved to be crucial for the development of modern written Swedish. A translation of the entire Bible, popularly known as Gustav I Vasa's Bible, was published in 1541. Revised somewhat in 1618 and 1703, it remained the standard version in Swedish until 1917, and it is the most important Swedish literary work of the sixteenth century. The Reformation also fueled a short-lived burst of literary activity in the form of polemical writings in support of the new Lutheran church (exemplified by Olaus Petri) and hymns, often based on German models.

The brothers Johannes and Olaus Magnus wrote two significant humanistic historical works, both of which were originally written in Latin and later translated into Swedish. Both brothers lived in exile in Rome due to their continued allegiance to the Catholic Church. Johannes Magnus wrote *Historia de Omnibus Gothorum Sueonumque Regibus* (1554; History of all the Gothic and Swedish kings), while Olaus Magnus produced *Historia de Gentibus Septentrionalibus* (1555; History of the Nordic peoples). These complementary works were highly regarded in continental Europe, as well as by seventeenth-century Swedes, who sought evidence of past greatness in the legendary Goths. While most of the writing in schools and universities was in Latin, attempts were made to create dramatic works in Swedish. The most ambitious of these "school dramas" were the plays of the controversial historian Johannes Messenius (1579?–1636).

LITERATURE DURING THE "PERIOD OF GREAT POWER" (1630–1718)

The cultural climate in Sweden improved somewhat under Gustavus II Adolphus (ruled 1611–1632). The country's military successes during the Thirty Years' War (1618–1648) meant the acquisition of important manuscripts as well as renewed contact with European culture, belatedly bringing Renaissance ideas to Sweden. Gustavus II Adolphus died on the battlefield in Germany. His daughter Christina became queen in 1644 but ruled only ten years before abdicating the throne. During her reign the royal court became a center of intellectual activity.

The major literary figure of the time was Georg Stiernhielm (1598–1672), known as "the father of Swedish poetry." Stiernhielm composed works in Swedish during a relatively short period of his life;

like many others of the time, he wrote mainly in Latin and other languages. His major work is *Hercules* (1658), a long hexameter poem based on the mythological motif of the hero at a crossroads in life; it is primarily a dialogue between Fru Lusta and Fru Dygd (Madam Desire and Madam Duty), who represent opposing moral principles. Important figures of the generation after Stiernhielm include Samuel Columbus, author of *Odae Sueticae* (1674; Swedish odes), and Haquin Spegel, author of *Guds Hverk och Hwila* (1685; God's work and rest), both of which proclaim new ideals for Swedish poetry.

Most Swedish literature of the 1600s and early 1700s falls into the category of "occasional poetry"—poems produced for weddings, funerals, or other occasions. Two colorful individuals stand out among the authors of the thousands of poems printed in this genre. Lars Wivallius (1605–1669) was an adventurer and occasional author of songs, such as the well-known "Klagovisa över denna torra och kalla wåhr" (1642; Lament over this dry and cold spring); he composed many of his songs during various prison terms. Lars Johansson (pseudonym "Lucidor"; 1638–1674) was a bohemian figure, a prolific author of wedding and funeral poems, and one of the few who attempted to make a living, albeit meager, from his writing. Gunno (Eurelius) Dahlstierna's *Kunga Skald* (1697; Hymn to the king), written at the death of Charles XI, exemplifies the important genre of panegyric. A type of occasional poem cultivated at court, the panegyric could serve both as political propaganda and as homage to a royal benefactor. Dahlstierna was the foremost Swedish representative of the ornate baroque style then popular in Europe.

The first woman in Sweden to be a professional author, Sophia Elisabet Brenner, (1659–1730) also wrote Sweden's first feminist work, *Det Qwinliga Könetz rätmätige Förswar* (1693; The righteous defense of the female sex). Letter writing, diaries, and autobiographies were increasingly important as a means of expression, though they were seldom printed. A notable example of this type of writing is the autobiography of Agneta Horn, written about 1657.

Most books printed during this period were devotional, while the number of books intended solely for recreation remained small. From the early 1600s

Stockholm's printers were under the watchful eye of an inspector. Censorship of all printed materials was instituted in the 1660s, and the office of *censor librorum* was established in 1686, hampering the spread of reading material for pleasure rather than for religious or other instruction. The first official hymnbook, compiled by Jesper Swedberg (father of Emmanuel Swedenborg), appeared in 1694 but was immediately withdrawn and revised for republication in 1695. Examples of hymnbooks from religious movements outside the state church include the Pietist hymnbook *Mose och Lambses wisor* (1717; Songs of Moses and the Lamb) and the Moravian *Sions sånger* (1743–1745; Songs of Zion).

ENLIGHTENMENT AND THE GUSTAVIAN ERA (1730–1809)

The death of Charles XII in 1718 signaled the end of the Swedish "Period of Great Power." The period from 1718 to 1772, marked by the change from an absolute monarchy to a parliamentary system, is often called the "Era of Freedom," and it coincides with an influx of Enlightenment ideas, especially from France and England, leading to a cultural renaissance in Sweden by the end of the century.

The use of a simpler, conversational style in written Swedish can be seen in the work of Olof von Dalin (1708–1763). His 1740 political allegory *Sagan om hästen* (The tale of the horse) became a Swedish classic. Previously, from 1732 to 1733, Dalin had published an influential newspaper, *Then swänska Argus* (The Swedish Argus), modeled on Joseph Addison and Richard Steele's *The Tatler* and *The Spectator*. In the pages of his newspaper, Dalin criticized foreign influence on the Swedish language, as had Stiernhielm in the previous century. Most novels in Sweden at this time were foreign imports, but a notable exception was the high-spirited *Min son på galejan eller en ostindisk resa* (My son on the galley, or An East Indian journey), by a ship's chaplain named Jacob Wallenberg (1746–1778).

In the spirit of the Enlightenment, various learned societies were formed for the advancement of science and the arts. Vitterhetsakademien (Academy of Letters), founded by Lovisa Ulrika in 1753, was a precursor to the Swedish Academy established by her son, Gustav III, in 1786. Literary societies were organized on Masonic models. Tankebyggarorden (Thought Builders), established in 1753, included important poets such as Hedvig Charlotta Nordenflycht (1718–1763), Gustaf Fredrik Gyllenborg (1731–1808), and Gustav Philip Creutz (1731–1785), whose works appeared in the society's publications. The naturalist Carl Linnaeus (1707–1778) wrote his scientific works in Latin, but his accounts of exploratory journeys to various Swedish provinces were written in Swedish. His students continued his work, publishing reports of their far-flung travels, which helped establish the travel account as a popular literary genre in Sweden.

Gustav III was keenly interested in theater and served as a patron of the arts. Many of the most notable poets of the era collaborated with him on works for the theater and opera. Among these was the poet and critic Johan Henrik Kellgren (1751–1795), who also edited the newspaper *Stockholms Posten* for several years. A frequent, though anonymous, contributor to *Stockholms Posten* was Anna Maria Lenngren (1754–1817), whose poems show a keen eye and a satiric edge. Sweden's most popular poet of all time, Carl Michael Bellman (1740–1795), took the popular practice of musical parody (setting words to familiar melodies) to unparalleled heights in the collections *Fredmans epistlar* (1790; Fredman's epistles; with a famous preface by Kellgren) and *Fredmans sånger* (1791; Fredman's songs).

The era of Enlightenment came to a definitive close in 1809. In politics, its end was marked by Sweden's defeat in the Napoleonic Wars and the subsequent loss of Finland to Russia; in literature, it was heralded by the appearance of the Romantic movement.

See also **Bible: Translations and Editions; Censorship; Christina (Sweden); Enlightenment; Gustavus II Adolphus (Sweden); Journals, Literary; Linnaeus, Carl; Reformation, Protestant; Sweden; Vasa Dynasty (Sweden).**

BIBLIOGRAPHY

Algulin, Ingemar. *A History of Swedish Literature.* Translated by John Weinstock. Stockholm, 1989.

Algulin, Ingemar, and Bernt Olsson. *Litteraturens historia i Sverige.* Stockholm, 1987.

Lönnroth, Lars, and Sven Delblanc, eds. *Den svenska litteraturen.* Vol. 4, *Från forntid till frihetstid, 1800–1718.* Stockholm, 1987.

Tigerstedt, E. N. *Ny illustrerad svensk litteraturhistoria.* 4 vols. Stockholm, 1967. Part one covers ancient times through the Vasa era; part two covers through the Gustavian era.

Warme, Lars G., ed. *A History of Swedish Literature.* Lincoln, Nebr., 1996.

PAUL NORLÉN

SWIFT, JONATHAN (1667–1745), English satirist, poet, and clergyman. Swift was born in Dublin to English parents, Jonathan and Abigale Erick (or Herrick) Swift. His father had died before Swift's birth, and he was raised by his father's family from the age of three when his mother returned to Leicestershire in England. He attended Kilkenny Grammar School, where William Congreve, the future dramatist, was a fellow pupil, and went on to Trinity College, Dublin, where, because of his infractions of discipline, his degree was conferred on him only by "special grace" in 1686.

Swift went to England in 1689 and became a secretary to the retired statesman Sir William Temple at Moor Park in Surrey. It was here that he met Esther Johnson ("Stella"), who was nine at the time, and became her tutor. They were lifelong friends, and she was the "Stella" of his *Journal to Stella,* written 1710–1713. (Some believe that they were secretly married in 1716, but the evidence is inconclusive.) In 1689, Swift suffered an attack of Ménière's disease, which affects the inner ear and causes vertigo and nausea; the affliction was to plague him for the rest of his life. Swift had taken an M.A. at Oxford, which provided him with the necessary qualification for ordination, and after leaving Temple's service in 1694, he went to Ireland, where he was ordained in the Anglican division of the Irish church and received the small prebend of Kilroot, near Belfast. In 1696 he returned to Moor Park, where he edited Temple's letters and wrote his first important prose works, *The Tale of a Tub* and *The Battle of the Books,* both of which were not published until 1704. The former is an allegorical satire attacking corruption in the church and scholarly pedantry, the latter a mock-heroic satire ridiculing the controversy about the ancients and the moderns that was raging at the time.

After Temple's death in 1699 left him homeless and without a patron, Swift went to Ireland where he received a prebend in St. Patrick's, Dublin, and the living of Laracor. On frequent visits to London he met Joseph Addison, Richard Steele, and Alexander Pope and associated with various Whig writers. During this time he wrote several defenses of Christianity (such as *An Argument against Abolishing Christianity,* 1708), vicious lampoons of public figures, and satirical essays under the pseudonym of "Isaac Bickerstaff" (1708–1709). In 1710 Swift traveled to London to petition against a tax crippling the Irish clergy and remained there for three years. Disenchanted with Whig policies, especially the party's association with Dissenters and what he regarded as its animosity toward the Anglican Church, he became an advocate for Tory politics and edited the party's newspaper, *The Examiner,* in 1710–1711. He also contributed to *The Tatler, The Spectator,* and *The Intelligencer* and wrote *The Conduct of the Allies* (1711), a treatise that outlined the Tory plan for ending the War of the Spanish Succession. Swift participated in the intellectual debates and lampoons of the Scriblerus Club, formed with Alexander Pope, John Arbuthnot, John Gay, Thomas Parnell, and Robert Harley, earl of Oxford.

Swift had alienated the establishment in England, and it appears that the influence of his friends in high places was not sufficient to secure his advancement. Bitterly disappointed, he returned to Ireland. He had been awarded a Doctor of Divinity in 1701 and was appointed dean of St. Patrick's Cathedral in Dublin in 1713; except for brief absences, he remained in Ireland for the rest of his life. Biographical detail between 1715 and 1720 is sketchy. In 1708 he had met Esther Vanhomrigh ("Vanessa"), who had fallen in love with him; she followed him to Ireland, where she was disappointed by Swift's lack of response to her feelings for him. His own feelings are reflected in *Cadenus and Vanessa,* a pastoral and comic self-reflection that he wrote around 1713, though it was not published until 1726, three years after Vanessa's death.

The Whigs had returned to power in 1714, and Swift began writing attacks on their unfair policies toward Ireland. His patriotism emerged with the enormously popular *A Proposal for the Universal Use of Irish Manufacture* (1720), a lampoon that

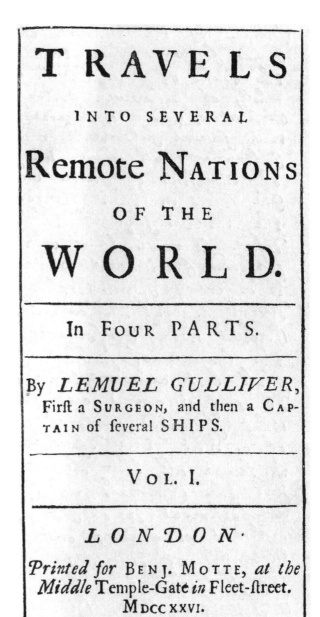

Jonathan Swift. Title page to the first edition of *Gulliver's Travels,* 1726. ©BETTMANN/CORBIS

attacked the England treatment of the Irish poor. Along with *The Drapier Letters* (1724), an exposé of a patent to introduce a new copper coin that would have devalued Ireland's currency, it established Swift as a national hero.

In 1726 Swift spent the summer with Alexander Pope at Twickenham and published his most popular work, *Gulliver's Travels.* An anti-Whig satire, a dazzling adventure story, and a narrative that perceives humanity from four different viewpoints through Gulliver's voyages to Lilliput, Brobdingnag, Laputa, and Houyhnhnmland, the work has profound political implications. Swift's financial security was assured by this time, but ill health and mental problems manifested themselves in the late 1720s, especially after the death of Stella in 1728. In 1729, his bitter and ironic *A Modest Proposal* appeared; it is a parody and an indictment of the amoral economic utilitarianism of the Whigs. The 1730s also saw Swift writing elegiac poems to Stella, and scatological poems such as "Lady's Dressing Room." Between 1730 and 1735, he published *Rhapsody of Poetry* and *Verses on His Own Death.* He also continued to correspond with friends in London. Bookseller George Faulkner published a complete edition of Swift's works, including a corrected edition of *Gulliver's Travels,* in 1735. In the late 1730s, Swift wrote *A History of the Peace of Utrecht* and *Directions to Servants,* both of which were published posthumously.

Swift's great popularity with Dublin's population was secured through his preaching and his writings on the unfair treatment of Ireland, but especially through his generous contributions to charity; at his death he left £11,000 to found a hospital for the mentally ill. His health deteriorated seriously and that, plus memory loss, affected his writing. Beginning in 1742, he suffered from dementia; he died 19 October 1745. He was buried next to Stella at St. Patrick's and was universally mourned by Dublin.

See also **Addison, Joseph; Ancients and Moderns; Dublin; English Literature and Language; Ireland; Pope, Alexander; Steele, Richard.**

BIBLIOGRAPHY

Primary Sources

Swift, Jonathan. *The Complete Poems.* Edited by Pat Rogers. Harmondsworth, U.K., 1983.

———. *Gulliver's Travels and Other Writings.* Edited by Claude Rawson. New York, 2002.

———. *Major Works.* Edited by Angus Ross and David Woolley. Oxford, 1984.

———. *A Modest Proposal and Other Satirical Works.* London, 1996.

Secondary Sources

Boyle, Frank. *Swift as Nemesis: Modernity and Its Satirist.* Stanford, 2000. Reads Swift's satirical prose as a criticism of the beginnings of a narcissistic modernity.

Hunting, Robert. *Jonathan Swift.* Rev. ed. Boston, 1989. A useful introduction and outline of Swift's important works.

Kelly, Ann Cline. *Jonathan Swift and Popular Culture: Myth, Media, and the Man.* New York, 2002. Argues for Swift's status as a popular writer manipulating his fictionalized literary persona to ensure his popularity.

Nokes, David. *Jonathan Swift, a Hypocrite Reversed: A Critical Biography.* Oxford and New York, 1985. An excellent biography which examines Swift's public and private roles.

MAX FINCHER

SWITZERLAND. The region and the state known as Switzerland took shape during the late medieval and early modern periods. Before 1300, the country north of the central Alps simply lay within the Swabian and Burgundian parts of the Holy Roman Empire. By 1789, in contrast, the Swiss Confederation possessed a distinct national identity and enjoyed sovereignty under international law. The confederation included thirteen self-governing *Orte* or cantons, several subsidiary but autonomous allies, and various subject territories. Geography played a considerable role in shaping Switzerland over these centuries. The region's central location, spanning western Europe's major language boundaries and containing mountain passes used by traders and travelers, ensured that the Swiss experienced all of Europe's major political and cultural movements. Yet the difficult terrain of the Alps and the area's relative poverty also left Switzerland marginal to Europe's great centers of power and wealth.

Modern Switzerland is known for being multilingual, democratic, neutral, and wealthy. The early modern confederation acquired these characteristics only slowly. All but one of the ruling cantons were German-speaking, although they did have French- and Italian-speaking subjects. Voting by male citizens played an important role in some cantons, but political control mostly rested with a few families, while the subject territories and many areas outside city walls had limited political rights. Especially before 1550, the confederation was also warlike, playing a major role in the Burgundian Wars of the 1470s and the Italian Wars after 1494. Finally, most early modern Swiss were poor, and even the richest had only modest fortunes by European standards.

POLITICS

Three related processes shaped the Swiss Confederation during the late Middle Ages: the growth of overlapping alliances among the cantons and their associates, the consolidation of internal regimes that controlled well-defined territories, and the development of shared responsibilities and institutions. Switzerland's development also depended on changing relations with the Holy Roman Empire, the Habsburg family of dynasts and emperors, and powerful neighbors to the west and south. The local economy rested on agriculture (including cattle and dairy products for export), transit, and mercenary services; by the eighteenth century, proto-industrial production of textiles and other goods provided further sources of wealth.

The confederation acquired its thirteen full members in two major waves, one before 1360 and the second after 1480. The first took place in an era of weak imperial authority and constant feuding among the region's nobility. This spurred communities to form alliances that could defend the public peace and increase local autonomy. The earliest known Swiss alliance linked Uri, Schwyz, and Unterwalden in 1291; though unusual in having only rural members, it resembled similar leagues across the region. Further alliances with Lucerne in the 1330s and with Zurich, Zug, Glarus, and Bern in the 1350s produced a substantial confederation of rural and urban communities that proved its significance by defeating the key regional dynasts, the Habsburgs, in the Sempach war of 1386.

Internal consolidation in each canton accompanied the growth of the Swiss system. In the rural cantons, the political base broadened as local nobles yielded power to communal assemblies after the 1360s. In Zurich and Basel, guild regimes took power; various accommodations widened political participation in other towns as well. Across the countryside during the 1400s, peasant communes became better organized and increased their economic and judicial authority. Both the urban and rural cantons sought to expand their influence,

though they used very different strategies. Towns like Zurich and Bern became lords over the countryside outside their walls through purchase, mortgage, or conquest. The rural cantons, above all Schwyz, allied themselves with regional peasant movements against lords, notably in Appenzell, thus gaining allies for further expansion. The two methods came into conflict in the 1440s, when the confederation nearly collapsed during a bitter territorial war between Zurich and Schwyz.

The growth of shared institutions helped mute such rivalries. In 1415 and 1460, the Swiss seized the Aargau and the Thurgau from the Habsburgs. Shared rule over these territories led to intensified interaction among the cantons, as did military efforts to expand south of the Alpine passes. Regular meetings of a diet, the *Tagsatzung*, began after the 1430s. Although the diet had little power to enforce its decisions, it did provide a forum for negotiation as the confederation faced new challenges. The alliance's growing power also attracted five new cantons in the late 1400s (Schaffhausen, Fribourg, Solothurn, Basel, and Appenzell) as well as a series of "associates" ranging from rural valleys to the Abbey of St. Gallen. Tensions between the urban and rural cantons led to a 1481 agreement, mediated by Switzerland's later patron saint, Niklaus von der Flüe (1417–1487), that guaranteed each canton's internal autonomy and provided for mutual support in case of social turmoil.

In the late 1400s, a national mythology of liberty and community emerged in Switzerland, centered on the figure of William Tell. In songs, chronicles, popular dramas, and stained-glass decorations the Swiss celebrated how they had expelled their corrupt lords during the 1300s. Often bitterly critical of aristocracy, the liberation sagas praised peasant liberty and virtues and expressed loyalty to the empire. No historical evidence supports Tell's existence, nor did Swiss calls for peasant liberty lead them to abolish serfdom among their own subjects. Nevertheless, this historical mythology reflected a growing awareness that the confederation differed fundamentally from the princely states taking shape around it.

Between 1460 and 1513, Swiss troops played an important role on Europe's battlefields. Unbeatable during the Burgundian Wars (1474–

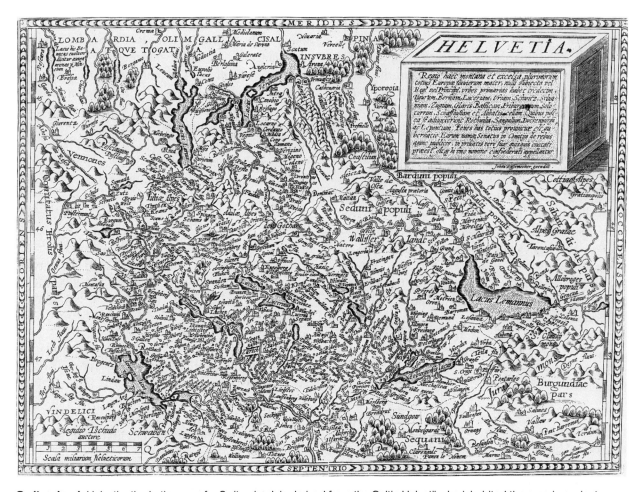

Switzerland. Helvetia, the Latin name for Switzerland, is derived from the Celtic Helvetii who inhabited the area in ancient times. This often-reproduced map by Aegidius Tschudi, originally compiled in the mid-1500s, is from the *Geographisch Handbuch* of Mathhias Quad, published in Cologne in 1600. MAP COLLECTION, STERLING MEMORIAL LIBRARY, YALE UNIVERSITY

1477), they were in high demand as mercenaries during the Italian Wars (1494–1559). In the Swabian War of 1499, a string of Swiss military victories ended Habsburg ambitions south of the Rhine and brought outlying regions such as Graubünden and the Valais closer to the confederation. The Peace of Basel in 1501 also confirmed that the Swiss were exempt from most imperial laws and courts. Military and political developments after 1500 soon reduced Switzerland's international importance, however, even as long-term treaties with France and the Habsburgs stabilized Switzerland's place in the international system. After 1530, moreover, the Swiss split into Catholic and Reformed parties that threatened to tear the confederation apart. From the 1520s until 1798, therefore, Swiss politics were dominated by internal social and religious conflict, while the confederation withdrew

from foreign entanglements. Although tempted to help coreligionists on both sides, the cantons managed to stay out of the Thirty Years' War, unlike their allies in Graubünden. The Peace of Westphalia in 1648 formally recognized the cantons' sovereignty within the Holy Roman Empire, and neutrality became their official policy during the long wars that followed—easier to maintain because of the declining importance of Swiss mercenaries. The premodern confederation was finally conquered by the French in 1798.

Switzerland became an early center of the Protestant and the Radical Reformation after Huldrych Zwingli (1484–1531) began preaching in Zurich in 1519. Zwingli's theology rested on evangelical ideas similar to Martin Luther's, but he also stressed the reform of Christian society along communal lines, in keeping with the region's values. In the confederation, he called for an end to mercenary service and rejection of the pensions that foreign rulers paid Swiss politicians. Zwingli quickly gained adherents in many Swiss and south German towns; his ideas spread to Bern, Basel, and Schaffhausen during the 1520s, and gained support in many allied towns and rural areas. Some of Zwingli's associates sought even deeper changes in church and society, laying the groundwork for the early Anabaptist movement. However, the rural cantons in central Switzerland, together with Lucerne, opposed the Reformation. The population there valued the old ceremonies and had confidence in their locally appointed clergy, while their magistrates resented Zwingli's attacks on a main source of their income, foreign pensions.

Zwingli's efforts to evangelize the subject territories provoked rising tensions within the confederation. Civil war was delayed by a 1529 religious peace, but finally broke out in 1531. Lukewarm support from its allies led to Zurich's defeat at the Battle of Kappel, where Zwingli lost his life. The Second Religious Peace of Kappel in 1531 created a lasting framework for religious coexistence. The thirteen ruling cantons and their self-governing allies could choose between Catholic and Reformed adherence; in the subject territories, existing Reformed congregations were tolerated although Catholic worship was often restored. Ultimately, four cantons and two half-cantons became Reformed, while seven and two halves remained Catholic. The close coexistence between two faiths that followed produced endless wrangling that sometimes threatened the confederation's survival. In 1656 and 1712, local conflicts led to significant religious wars. The first preserved the status quo of 1531, but a Reformed victory in the second increased Zurich and Bern's influence.

Religious struggles coincided with growing social tensions in Switzerland. In both cities and countryside, a minority of families increasingly monopolized wealth and political participation. Oligarchy was most visible in the cities, where ever fewer families qualified to sit in the city councils. City authorities also eroded the autonomy of peasant communes under their lordship, despite occasionally violent resistance. In the countryside, high citizenship fees barred many residents from voting or using communal economic resources. In 1653, peasants around Lucerne and Bern rose up against urban domination, calling for a new "peasant's league" to combat their rulers. The urban elites in Reformed Zurich and Bern and Catholic Lucerne cooperated fully in suppressing the peasant movement.

CULTURAL MOVEMENTS

Swiss thinkers absorbed the main intellectual movements of early modern Europe. Renaissance humanism appeared late in the 1400s. Authors such as Albrecht von Bonstetten (c. 1442–1504) and Felix Hemmerli (c. 1388–1458) described the confederation's political system by mixing humanist-style historiography with the region's rich chronicle tradition, while later Swiss humanists such as the two Glarus scholars Heinrich Loriti ("Glareanus," 1484–1563) and Aegidius Tschudi (1505–1572) wrote polished Latin treatises based on classical sources. Meanwhile, the confluence of Basel's thriving printing industry, its university, and the city's trade links made it the only canton where humanism really flourished, as illustrated by Erasmus of Rotterdam's choice to live there.

The Reformation disrupted the confederation politically and forced thinkers and artists to choose between the faiths. In St. Gallen, the well-known humanist and physician Joachim Watt ("Vadianus," 1484–1551) returned home to lead the local Reformation, while the painter and playwright Niklaus Manuel (c. 1484–1530) of Bern dedicated his work to the cause. In Basel, the Reformation divided the humanists after the city turned Protestant in 1528. Both Erasmus and Glareanus chose to leave, but the city's intellectual life later benefited from learned Protestant refugees such as Sebastian Castellio (1515–1563). Religious questions fully occupied Swiss intellectuals by the mid-1500s as Heinrich Bullinger in Zurich and John Calvin in Geneva struggled to define Reformed Protestant doctrine. Their efforts shaped the Second Helvetic Confession of 1566, and helped make Switzerland an important center for the Reformed church. English, Polish, and Hungarian scholars studied there, often in exile, while Italian dissidents escaped persecution by fleeing through Switzerland.

Increasingly rigid social and religious boundaries after 1600 stifled cultural innovation until the early 1700s, when Swiss thinkers began receiving Enlightenment ideas. Zurich authors such as

Albrecht Haller (1708–1777) and Johann Jakob Bodmer (1698–1783) participated actively in the literary debates of the German Enlightenment; Genevan social philosophers such as Jean-Jacques Burlamaqui (1694–1748) and, above all, Jean-Jacques Rousseau (1712–1778) made major contributions to the French Enlightenment. The presses of French Switzerland became a major source for books banned by French censors, and French intellectuals such as Voltaire found refuge in the Vaud when threatened by the French authorities. Within Switzerland, Enlightenment ideas eventually undermined the barriers between Catholic and Reformed elites through the formation of the Helvetic Society, a forum for intellectual discussion that met annually in Bad Schinznach after 1761.

SWITZERLAND AND EUROPE

Switzerland's existence puzzled many early modern Europeans. Jean Bodin condemned it as anarchic and disorderly, while Niccolò Machiavelli saw it as a model for free and armed city-states. After Swiss troops killed and despoiled Charles the Bold of Burgundy in 1477, aristocratic thinkers encouraged criticism of the "cow-Swiss" who dared to violate the natural order of lords and subjects. In the end, however, Switzerland was less important as a model, positive or negative, than as a crossroads. Neutral, divided by religion, and fragmented politically, the Swiss Confederation offered a haven to many refugees and dissidents, most notably the founders of the Reformed movement. Even if little of what passed through seemed to rub off on the Swiss, the confederation still went through changes parallel to the ones that transformed all of early modern Europe.

See also **Calvin, John; Enlightenment; Geneva; Habsburg Dynasty: Austria; Reformation, Protestant; Thirty Years' War (1618–1648); Westphalia, Peace of (1648); Zwingli, Huldrych.**

BIBLIOGRAPHY

Bergier, Jean-François. *Histoire économique de la Suisse.* Paris, 1983. Authoritative synthesis of the economic history of Switzerland by an early modern specialist.

Bonjour, Edgar, H. S. Offler, and G. R. Potter. *A Short History of Switzerland.* Oxford, 1952. Concise introduction by a major Swiss historian, although dated.

Handbuch der Schweizer Geschichte. Zurich, 1972–1977. Contains substantial articles with extensive references on the late medieval period, the Renaissance and Reformation, and the seventeenth and eighteenth centuries.

Historisches Lexikon der Schweiz. Basel, 2002–. Most recent encyclopedic guide to Swiss history and biography, replacing the 1931 edition. An online edition, with articles in German, French or Italian, is available at http://www.snl.ch/dhs/externe/index.html.

Mesmer, Beatix, ed. *Geschichte der Schweiz, und der Schweizer.* Basel, 1982–1983. Produced to fill the need for an up-to-date survey of Swiss history based on the best recent scholarship.

Schneider, Boris, and Francis Python, eds. *Geschichtsforschung in der Schweiz: Bilanz und Perspektiven—1991.* Basel, 1992. Critical review of Swiss history writing, produced in the wake of the controversial seventh centennial of 1291.

Sablonier, Roger. "The Swiss Confederation." In *The New Cambridge Medieval History,* Vol. 7, *c. 1415–c. 1500,* edited by Christopher Allmand, pp. 645–670. Cambridge, U.K., 1998. Succinct comparative discussion of the politics and society of late medieval Switzerland.

RANDOLPH C. HEAD

30°W 20°W 10°W 0° 10°E

60°N

ICELAND
(Denmark)

Faroe
Islands

Shetland
Islands

NORWAY
(Denmark)
Christiania

Lake Vänern

Orkney
Islands

Scotland

Firth of Forth
• Edinburgh

North
Sea

DENMARK
Copenhagen

Va/t

50°N

Shannon

• Dublin

**GREAT
BRITAIN**

Ireland

Isle of
Man

Bann

Trent

Severn

Wales

Thames

England
• Bristol
London •

Amsterdam •

NETHERLANDS

Hanover

Cologne

Brussels •
• Austrian
Netherlands

Rhine

• Frankfurt

Main

**HOLY ROMAN
EMPIRE**

Weser

Elbe

Saxony

Bo

Prag

Be

**ATLANTIC
OCEAN**

FRANCE

Seine

Aisne

• Paris

Loire

Meuse

Neckar

Danube

Bavaria
• Munich

40°N

PORTUGAL

Douro

Tagus

Madrid •

SPAIN

Lisbon •

• Seville

Ebro

Garonne

Pyrenees

ANDORRA

• Barcelona

Balearic Islands

Iviza
(Spain)

Minorca
(Great Britain)

Majorca
(Spain)

Rhône

Lyon •

**SWISS
CONFED.**

Turin •

Marseille •

Milan •
MILAN

SARDINIA
Genoa •
GENOA

LUCCA

VENICE
Venice •

Po

PARMA
MODENA

Arno

TUSCANY

Appennines

**PAPAL
STATES**
Rome •

Adri

Corsica
(France)

SARDINIA

Naples •

Mediterranean Sea

Sicily

A F R I C A

Malta